Jesus' Death
in New Testament Thought

Jesus' Death in New Testament Thought

VOLUME 1: BACKGROUND

DAVID A. BRONDOS

Comunidad Teológica de México Theological Community of Mexico
Ciudad de México Mexico City
2018

JESUS' DEATH IN NEW TESTAMENT THOUGHT
Volume 1: Background

© 2018 David Allen Brondos. All rights reserved. Except for brief quotations in critical articles or reviews, no part of this book may be reproduced in any manner without prior written permission from the author or publisher.

© 2018 David Allen Brondos. Todos los derechos reservados. Ninguna porción de este libro podrá ser reproducida, distribuida, o transmitida en cualquier forma o por cualquier medio, o almacenada en algún sistema de recuperación, sin la autorización previa por escrito del autor o la editorial.

Comunidad Teológica de México/Instituto Internacional de Estudios Superiores
Av. San Jerónimo 137
San Ángel
01000 México, CDMX
México

Scripture quotations, unless otherwise noted, are either the author's own or from the New Revised Standard Version Bible, copyright © 1989 National Council of the Churches of Christ in the United States of America. Used by permission. All rights reserved worldwide.

Imagen de la portada / Cover image: Georges Rouault, *Ecce Homo* (*Christ aux outrages*) (1942-43). © 2018 Artists Rights Society (ARS), New York / ADAGP, Paris. Digital Image: © bpk-Bildagentur / Staatsgalerie Stuttgart.

Primera edición/First edition: 2018

ISBN: 978-607-98034-0-7 (obra completa)
ISBN: 978-607-98034-1-4 (Vol. 1)

Design/diseño: Joel Friedlander, Marin Bookworks

Printed in the U.S.A./Impreso en los Estados Unidos de Norteamérica.

Contents

Acknowledgments ix
Presentación de la Obra xi

VOLUME 1: BACKGROUND

Introduction 1
Chapter 1. Jesus' Death in Traditional Christian Thought 15
Chapter 2. Second-Temple Jewish Soteriology 81
Chapter 3. Sacrifice and Atonement in Second-Temple Jewish Thought ... 125
Chapter 4. Vicarious Suffering and Death in Ancient Jewish Thought 203
Chapter 5. Jesus' Death in the Context of His Ministry 279
Chapter 6. The Crucified Jesus as Lord and Mediator 369
Chapter 7. Jesus, God's Will, and the Law 407
Chapter 8. Jesus' Death and the New Covenant Community 471
Chapter 9. The Fulfillment of the Scriptures and the Divine Plan 529
Chapter 10. Jesus' Death for Others: The Story and the Formulas 585

VOLUME 2: TEXTS

Introduction to Volume 2 661
Chapter 11. Justification, Salvation, and the Work of Christ in
Paul's Thought 665
Chapter 12. The Allusions to Jesus' Death in Paul's Epistles 745
Chapter 13. Jesus' Death in the Disputed Pauline Letters and 1 Peter 841
Chapter 14. Jesus' Death in the Synoptic Gospels and Acts 903
Chapter 15. Jesus' Death in the Epistle to the Hebrews 965
Chapter 16. Jesus' Death in the Gospel of John, 1 John, and Revelation ... 1043
Chapter 17. Jesus' Death in the Thought of the Apostolic Fathers and
Justin Martyr 1109
Chapter 18. The Work of Christ in the Thought of Melito of Sardis and
Irenaeus of Lyons 1191
Conclusion 1243
Abbreviations 1263
Bibliography 1267
Index of Ancient Sources 1329
Index of Authors 1349
Index of Subjects 1359

Contents by Chapter

Acknowledgments ix
Presentación de la Obra xi
Introduction 1
Chapter 1. Jesus' Death in Traditional Christian Thought 15
   The Three Types of Traditional Interpretations of Christ's Death 20
   Penal Substitution Interpretations of Christ's Work in New Testament
   Scholarship 24
     Theological Problems and Presuppositions 32
       Premise 1: God's justice must be satisfied before God can remit sins 33
       Premise 2: Christ's death was absolutely necessary for human salvation, since
         nothing else could have made it possible for God to remit the sins of human
         beings without compromising God's justice 36
       Premise 3: What Christ suffered in his passion and death was sufficient to
         satisfy God's justice 37
       Premise 4: In order for Christ to satisfy divine justice, he had to be perfectly sinless 41
       Premise 5: In order for Christ to die as the substitute for sinful humanity,
         he had to be fully divine and fully human 43
       Premise 6: Both the incarnation and the earthly life of God's Son had as their
         sole objective his substitutionary death for others 44
       Premise 7: Human beings are saved and delivered from God's wrath solely by
         Jesus' substitutionary death on their behalf, yet they must still come to faith
         in order to receive that salvation 45
   Physical Interpretations of Christ's Work in New Testament Scholarship 49
     Theological Problems and Presuppositions 65
       Premise 1: Powers such as sin and death are ontological in nature and as such
         can be dealt with in much the same way that ontological realities or
         substances are dealt with in the physical world 65
       Premise 2: It was not possible for human beings, human nature, or the nature
         of the created order to be transformed ontologically or delivered from the
         powers to which they were subject without Christ's incarnation, life, death,
         and resurrection 68
       Premise 3: Before the ontological transformation of humanity or the world
         could be brought about in its eschatological fullness, it was necessary to
         bring it about in part in the present time 70
       Premise 4: Although all human beings have been ontologically transformed
         or united to Christ, each individual must come to faith in order to be saved ... 72
       Premise 5: Although the notion of an ontological participation was clear to
         people in Paul's day, it is no longer clear to people in ours 74

Revelational Interpretations of Christ's Work in New Testament Scholarship....76
    Theological Problems and Presuppositions..79
        Premise 1: Christ's death was necessary because what it revealed to human beings could not have been revealed by God in any other way................79
        Premise 2: Christ's death was necessary because there was no other way in which God could have brought about in human beings the ethical transformation necessary for them to be saved...80

Chapter 2. Second-Temple Jewish Soteriology 81
The Election of Israel..84
Israel and the Law...87
    The Law and Human Well-Being..88
    Divine Justice and Mercy...90
Reward and Punishment..93
    The Purposes of Divine Punishment...95
    Judgment, Justice, and Righteousness...99
    God's Judgment and God's Love..102
    Grace and Merit..111
Second-Temple Jewish Eschatology...112
    Conditional and Unconditional Salvation..114
    Eschatological Hopes and Beliefs...115
    Jewish Apocalyptic..119
    The Afterlife in Second-Temple Jewish Thought................................120

Chapter 3. Sacrifice and Atonement in Second-Temple Jewish Thought 125
Sacrificial Interpretation in New Testament Scholarship:
Views and Presuppositions...128
    Assumption 1: Sacrifices made atonement for sins..............................128
    Assumption 2: Sacrifices were thought to "work" in some way to produce certain salvific "effects," such as expiation and purification.................130
    Assumption 3: Sacrifice involved propitiation......................................136
    Assumption 4: There could be no remission of sins without sacrifice....137
    Assumption 5: Sacrifice was understood as substitution.......................138
    Assumption 6: Sacrifice was understood in terms of representation and participation..139
    Assumption 7: Sacrifice reveals the mechanism of sacred violence.......140
Basic Tenets of Ancient Jewish Sacrificial Thought.................................141
    1. Sacrifices were essentially *offerings* and *gifts* presented to God........142
    2. Sacrifice was inseparable from prayers and petitions........................145
    3. What made sacrifices and prayers acceptable to God was the inner disposition and commitment to God's will of those offering them or those on whose behalf they were offered..150
The Logic of Ancient Jewish Sacrificial Practice....................................155
The Purpose of Sacrifice in Ancient Jewish Thought.............................160
Sacrifice and the Jewish View of God..162

Reconsidering the Traditional Assumptions Regarding Sacrifice 170
    Assumption 1: Did sacrifices make atonement for sins? 170
    Assumption 2: Were sacrifices thought to "work" in some way to produce certain salvific "effects," such as expiation and purification? 172
    Assumption 3: Did sacrifice involve propitiation? 185
    Assumption 4: Was the remission of sins possible without sacrifice? 189
    Assumption 5: Was sacrifice understood as substitution? 192
    Assumption 6: Was sacrifice understood in terms of representation and participation? 197
    Assumption 7: Was sacrifice thought to reveal the mechanism of sacred violence? ... 199

Chapter 4. Vicarious Suffering and Death in Ancient Jewish Thought 203

Isaiah 53 203
    The Difficulties of Interpreting Isaiah 53 208
    A Penal Substitution Reading of Isaiah 53 212
    An Alternative Reading of Isaiah 53 215
Vicarious Death and Atonement Elsewhere in the Hebrew Scriptures 223
Vicarious Death and Atonement in Ancient Greco-Roman Literature 226
Vicarious Death and Atonement in Second-Temple Jewish Literature and Rabbinic Thought 231
    Vicarious Suffering and Death in 2 Maccabees 231
    Suffering for the Law in 4 Maccabees 241
    Vicarious Death in 4 Maccabees 244
    The Story of Taxo 256
    Atonement through Suffering and Death in Rabbinic Thought 258
Merits, Prayer, and Atonement in Ancient Hebrew and Jewish Thought 264
    Atonement by Prayer 267
    The Merits of the Fathers 271

Chapter 5. Jesus' Death in the Context of His Ministry 279

The Aims of Jesus' Ministry 280
    Jesus' Proclamation of God's Reign 281
    Jesus' Teaching 288
    Jesus' Healings and Exorcisms 294
    Jesus' Preparation of Disciples 300
The Conflicts Generated by Jesus' Ministry 305
    Jesus' Authority 306
    Jesus' Fellowship with Sinners 310
    Jesus' Focus on Justice and the Conflicts over the Mosaic Law 318
Jesus' Final Days in Jerusalem 325
    Jesus' Ministry in Jerusalem 326
    Jesus' Entry into Jerusalem 328
    Jesus' Action in the Temple 332
    Jesus' Death and His Conflicts with the Jewish Authorities 338
    The Last Supper 344
    Jesus' Words over the Bread and Wine 350
    The Arrest, Condemnation, and Execution of Jesus 356
    The Redemptive Significance Jesus Ascribed to his Death 358

Chapter 6. The Crucified Jesus as Lord and Mediator ... 369
Jesus as Lord and Christ ... 371
Jesus' Lordship for Others ... 375
Justice, Jesus' Lordship, and the Reign of God ... 383
Jesus' Death in Light of His Lordship ... 388
Jesus as Mediator ... 390
Jesus' Authority as Mediator ... 391
Jesus' Death and His Role as Mediator ... 396
The Need for Jesus' Mediation ... 401

Chapter 7. Jesus, God's Will, and the Law ... 407
Faith in Jesus and the Redefinition of God's Will ... 407
The Will of God and Jesus in the Book of Acts ... 411
The Will of God and Jesus in Paul's Letters ... 414
The Will of God and Jesus in the Disputed Pauline Letters ... 419
The Will of God and Jesus in the Synoptic Gospels ... 420
The Will of God and Jesus in the Gospel and Epistles of John ... 424
The Will of God and Jesus in the Other New Testament Writings ... 427
Justification, Faith in Jesus, and the Law ... 428
The Role of the Law Among Jesus' First Followers ... 432
The Relations between Jews and Non-Jews in the Communities of Jesus' First Followers ... 438
Reinterpreting Obedience to the Law ... 444
The Arguments of Jesus' Followers regarding the Purpose of the Law ... 454
Plight and Solution ... 465

Chapter 8. Jesus' Death and the New Covenant Community ... 471
A New Covenant ... 471
The Covenant and Eschatological Hopes ... 473
Old Covenant and New ... 476
Jesus' Followers as a Distinct Community ... 480
The Incorporation of Gentiles and the Redefinition of Israel ... 485
Defining the Identity of Jesus' Followers ... 493
New Covenant, New Temple ... 500
A Holy People ... 503
The Forgiveness of Sins under the New Covenant ... 511
Jesus' Death and the New Covenant ... 517
Jesus' Death and the New Temple ... 521

Chapter 9. The Fulfillment of the Scriptures and the Divine Plan ... 529
The Fulfillment of the Scriptures in Jesus' Death and Resurrection ... 530
The Development of Beliefs regarding the Fulfillment of Scripture in Jesus ... 534
The Typological Interpretation of Scripture ... 541
The Divine Plan ... 547
The Divine Plan in the Pauline Epistles and Other New Testament Writings ... 548
Jesus' Death as Part of the Divine Plan ... 558
Election and the Divine Plan ... 564

The Divine Plan and the Development of Christology 569
   Christology and the Eternal Divine Plan 572
   Jesus' Relation to God 576
   God's Love and Jesus' Death 579
   Non-Jewish Influences on the Christology of the New Testament 582

Chapter 10. Jesus' Death for Others: The Story and the Formulas 585

Jesus' Death in the Context of the Story Told by His First Followers 585
   Jesus' Death and Resurrection as the Consequence of his Ministry 588
The Development of Beliefs Regarding the Salvific Significance of
Jesus' Death 591
   Jesus' Death as the Death of a Prophet 594
   Did Jesus' First Followers Believe He Had Undergone the Messianic Tribulation? 598
   Jesus' Death and Isaiah 53 601
   The Influence of 2 and 4 Maccabees on the Early Interpretations of Jesus' Death 608
   Jesus' Death and the Akedah, the Bronze Serpent, and the Passover Lamb 613
   The Use of Sacrificial Language to Speak of Jesus' Death 617
   Jesus' Death and the Christus Victor Idea 625
   Jesus' Death and Greco-Roman Beliefs regarding Vicarious Death 626
The Common, Shared Formulas Used to Refer to Jesus' Death 627
   Jesus' Death "For Us" 629
   Jesus' Death or Blood as the Means of Salvation 636
   Redemption and Acquisition through Jesus' Death 638
   "For Our Sins" 645
   Suffering and Dying with or for Christ 650
   Christ's Death "For Us": Some Analogies 652

Introduction to Volume 2 661

Chapter 11. Justification, Salvation, and the Work of Christ in Paul's Thought 665

Justification and the Juristic Interpretation of Jesus' Death 665
   The Traditional Forensic Reading of Paul's Teaching on Justification 666
   Problems with the Traditional Forensic Interpretation of Paul's Doctrine of Justification 668
Paul and Participation in Christ 674
   The Language of Participation 674
   Paul's "with Christ" Language 684
   Dying and Being Buried with Christ 688
   "All Have Died" (2 Cor. 5:14-15) 699
   Christ, Adam, and "All" in Romans 5 and 1 Corinthians 15 702
   Union with Christ and his Body 707
   Paul's "in Christ" Language 710
   Participation in Christ, Justification, and Inaugurated Eschatology 713
   The Origins and Development of Paul's "with Christ" and "in Christ" Language 720

Rethinking Paul's Understanding of Justification and Salvation ... 724
   Faith, Works, and Justification ... 730
   Justification, Righteousness, and Love ... 733
Jesus' Death and Justification in Paul's Thought ... 734
   The Sufferings and Death of Jesus and Paul ... 737

Chapter 12. The Allusions to Jesus' Death in Paul's Epistles ... 745

Jesus' Death in 1 Thessalonians ... 746
Jesus' Death in 1 Corinthians ... 749
   1 Corinthians 1–4 ... 749
   1 Corinthians 5-8 ... 757
   1 Corinthians 10-11 ... 760
   1 Corinthians 15 ... 765
Jesus' Death in 2 Corinthians ... 769
Jesus' Death in Galatians ... 777
   Galatians 1:4 ... 777
   Galatians 2:19—3:1 ... 780
   Galatians 3:13 ... 787
   Galatians 5-6 ... 796
Jesus' Death in Philippians ... 802
Jesus' Death in Romans ... 804
   Romans 3:21-26 ... 806
   Romans 4:24-25 ... 814
   Romans 5:6-11 ... 817
   Romans 5:15-21 ... 823
   Romans 6 ... 825
   Romans 7:4-6 ... 827
   Romans 8 ... 828
   Romans 14:1—15:12 ... 833

Chapter 13. Jesus' Death in the Disputed Pauline Letters and 1 Peter ... 841

The Allusions to Jesus' Death in Colossians ... 841
   Colossians 1 ... 843
   Colossians 2:11-16 ... 853
The Allusions to Jesus' Death in Ephesians ... 863
   Ephesians 1:7-8 ... 864
   Ephesians 2 ... 865
   Ephesians 5 ... 870
Allusions to Jesus' Death in the Pastoral Epistles ... 873
   1 Timothy 2:1-8 ... 873
   2 Timothy 2:10-13 ... 876
   Titus 2:11-14 ... 877
Allusions to Jesus' Death in 1 Peter ... 879
   1 Peter 1 ... 880
   1 Peter 2 ... 886
   1 Peter 3-4 ... 894

Chapter 14. Jesus' Death in the Synoptic Gospels and Acts 903
  The Significance of Jesus' Sufferings and Death in Mark 904
    Jesus' Sufferings and Death "for Others" in Mark's Gospel 905
    The Ironies in Mark's Passion Story 912
    Jesus' Death, the Divine Plan, and the Fulfillment of the Scriptures 914
    The Love of God and Jesus for Others 916
    Mark 10:45 and 14:23-25 919
  The Significance of Jesus' Death in Matthew's Gospel 927
    Matthew 1-2 929
    Jesus' Ministry, Passion, and Death in the Thought of Matthew 933
    Matt. 20:25-28 and 26:26-29 945
  The Significance of Jesus' Sufferings and Death in Luke and Acts 951
    Jesus' Death in the Thought of Luke 952
    Acts 20:28 963

Chapter 15. Jesus' Death in the Epistle to the Hebrews 965
  Hebrews 1 967
  Hebrews 2 978
  Hebrews 3-5 995
  Hebrews 6-8 1001
  Hebrews 9 1007
  Hebrews 10 1025
  Hebrews 11-13 1035

Chapter 16. Jesus' Death in the Gospel of John, 1 John, and Revelation 1043
  Jesus' Death in the Gospel of John 1043
    Salvation and Belief in Jesus in the Fourth Gospel 1045
    Jesus' Death in the Fourth Gospel 1052
    Jesus' Death "for Others" 1057
    Jesus' Body as a New Temple 1075
    Jesus' Death "for Others" in John's Passion Narrative 1076
    Jesus as the Lamb of God 1079
  Jesus' Death in 1 John 1089
  Jesus' Death in the Book of Revelation 1100

Chapter 17. Jesus' Death in the Thought of the Apostolic Fathers and Justin Martyr 1109
  Jesus' Death and Blood in *1 Clement* 1109
    1 Clement 1-21 1110
    1 Clement 22-55 1114
  Jesus' Death in the Epistles of Ignatius of Antioch 1117
    Ignatius and the Docetists 1117
    Flesh and Spirit 1121
    Jesus' Flesh and Blood 1124
    Jesus' Passion and Death 1128
    The Constitution of a New People through Christ's Life, Sufferings, and Death 1132
    Ignatius as Antipsuchon for Others 1137

Jesus' Death in the *Epistle of Polycarp to the Philippians* 1141
Jesus' Death in the *Martyrdom of Polycarp* 1143
Jesus' Death in the *Epistle of Barnabas* 1145
    Barnabas 1-4 1146
    Barnabas 5 1147
    Barnabas 6-10 1152
    Barnabas 11-19 1155
Jesus' Death in the *Epistle to Diognetus* 1159
    Diognetus 9 1159
The Death of Jesus in the Thought of Justin Martyr 1167
    Jesus' Death in Justin's *Apologies* 1168
    The Typological Interpretation of Jesus' Death in Justin's *Dialogue with Trypho* 1171
    Sacrificial Typology in the *Dialogue* 1175
    Jesus' Death for Others in the *Dialogue* 1179
    Christ as Accursed in the *Dialogue* 1184

Chapter 18. The Work of Christ in the Thought of Melito of Sardis and Irenaeus of Lyons 1191

The Work of Christ in the *Peri Pascha* of Melito of Sardis 1192
    Christ's Sufferings and Death in Melito's Peri Pascha 1195
    The Salvation of "Man" in the Peri Pascha 1202
    Christ's Saving Work in the Fragments of the Peri Pascha 1214
The Work of Christ in the Thought of Irenaeus 1222
    The Son of God's Assumption of "Man" 1224
    The Salvation of "Man" 1228
    The Defeat of the Devil 1230
    Irenaeus's Use of Tradition 1232
    The Argument for Necessity 1236
    Salvation as an Objective Reality 1239

Conclusion 1243
    Justification by Works or by Faith? 1249
    Rethinking God and the Cross of Christ 1255

Abbreviations 1263

Bibliography 1267

Index of Ancient Sources 1329

Index of Authors 1349

Index of Subjects 1359

Acknowledgments

It is truly an honor and a privilege for me to have the present work, which is the culmination of four decades of research and reflection, published by the educational institution that I have served with immense joy for over twenty years, the Theological Community of Mexico. I am deeply indebted to the school's Rector, Dan González Ortega, as well as other members of the administration and faculty, including especially Angela Trejo Haager, Moisés Pérez Espino, and Maritza Macín Lara, for the tremendous support they have given to me in my work throughout these years and now in the publication of these two volumes. To many biblical scholars and theologians, it will seem extremely odd to have a work of this sort—written in English—published by a theological school in Mexico. From my perspective, however, nothing could be more fitting, since it is here at what many consider the "margins" that I have come to develop the interpretation of the biblical texts and in particular the death of Jesus that is articulated in the pages that follow. While the extensive reading, studying, and research I have done and which is reflected in this work has been vital to the formulation and presentation of an understanding of Scripture and of Jesus' death on a Roman cross that constitutes a radical break with traditional Christian thought, I consider my interaction with my colleagues and students here in Mexico City and elsewhere in Latin America to have been just as vital, if not more so. They have taught me countless things that I could never have grasped or learned from the vast amount of literature published on the subjects I address in these volumes, no matter how much reading I might have done, and for that I am deeply grateful to them.

I am also extremely grateful for the support that Global Mission of the Evangelical Lutheran Church in America has given me, making it possible for me to serve, teach, and learn in this context. Special thanks are due to Rafael Malpica Padilla, Executive Director of ELCA Global Mission, and to Raquel Rodríguez, who has recently retired from her position as Director for the Latin America and Caribbean desk.

In addition, I would like to express my gratitude to Neil Elliott, now Senior Acquiring Editor at Lexington/Fortress Academic, and Mark Allan Powell, the Robert and Phyllis Leatherman Professor of New Testament at Trinity Lutheran Seminary in Columbus, Ohio, for the encouragement, orientation, and feedback they provided for me in the process of publishing this work. It has also been a pleasure working with Joel Friedlander of Marin Bookworks in this process.

Above all, however, I am thankful to my wife Alicia for the understanding, support, patience, and strength she has given me over the years, but especially during the time I have been working on this project. Words can never express all that she has meant in my life.

David A. Brondos
Mexico City, Mexico
March 2018

Presentación de la Obra

> *¿Por qué murió Jesús?*
> *Simplemente porque dedicó su vida a ser el instrumento de Dios*
> *Para dar "Shalom" y salvación a su pueblo.*
> *Su fidelidad absoluta a esa tarea le costó la vida,*
> *pero también hizo posible su glorificación a la diestra de Dios,*
> *lo cual significa que el "Shalom",*
> *el perdón y la salvación que buscó para nosotros*
> *es y será una realidad en él.*[1]
> -Dr. David Brondos

En los albores de una nueva centuria que conmemora el movimiento desencadenado en Alemania por el Dr. Martín Lutero, la Reforma Protestante del siglo XVI (1517), es una verdadera fortuna contar con personas que honran esa herencia por su filiación religiosa (el movimiento luterano) y por su compromiso con la continuidad en la producción de conocimiento.

En México tenemos una de esas luminarias que encomian la tradición luterana, por su compromiso de fe, pero sobre todo por su quehacer teológico; su persona no necesita mucha presentación en los círculos teológicos de este país a donde llegó como misionero a temprana edad: el Dr. David Allen Brondos Luecke.

Mente privilegiada, investigador disciplinado, escritor sistemático… pueden fácilmente ser adjetivos que describan la personalidad de David el teólogo luterano, estadounidense por nacimiento, pero mexicano por adopción. Sin embargo, personalmente prefiero hablar del Maestro que ha formado a generaciones enteras de estudiantes de teología con una pasión desbordante por la educación. Es el profesor afable, amigo de sus estudiantes, que logra transmitir con mucha facilidad el amor a la investigación teológica.

Yo, como estudiante que fui de él, pero ahora como amigo y compañero en la tarea de la educación teológica ecuménica, me siento honradísimo de ser invitado para presentar lo que, sin temor a equivocarme, resultará ser la obra cumbre de su pensamiento teológico, esto es, su más alto legado teológico.

En esta obra el Dr. David Brondos nos presenta fundamentalmente un ejercicio de doble vía. Por un lado, la práctica profundamente deconstructiva

---

1. David Brondos, "¿Por qué murió Jesús? Una mirada a la historia." *Oikodomein* (México, Ed. Comunidad Teológica de México), No. 5, 1998, p. 110.

de la perspectiva cristológica muy arraigada en la teología protestante. Revisar el concepto de "salvación forense" y decolonizarlo para así poder ensayar ese segundo camino donde se propone una Cristología mucho más cerca de "La Gracia". Ese otro lado del camino nos conduce por las calzadas que avanzan hacia una idea de Dios más amorosa. Un Dios realmente liberador, ese Dios que no se deja colonizar por la muerte y el dolor como medio para lograr "salvación".

De esta manera, David vuelve a una tradición por demás luterana y reformada, el retorno a la teología bíblica. Aunque Brondos se asume como un teólogo sistemático, su metodología está íntimamente comprometida con la hermenéutica bíblica. Moloc queda desenmascarado en las formas como la misma teología cristiana ha exigido "sacrificios humanos" para obrar el acto salvífico. Queda de manifiesto el verdadero Dios de Jesús, el Dios de Gracia infinita que se manifiesta a través del "Shalom". Esa paz que no puede mediarse a través de ninguna muerte. Así, Dios no pide la muerte de nadie y mucho menos la de su propio hijo. Brondos sostiene que la muerte de Jesús es una denuncia profética a los sistemas diabólicos de este mundo de todos los tiempos.

Esta posibilidad poscolonizadora de relectura en nuestras teologías resulta un tremendo aporte luterano, por demás coherente con los dos momentos existenciales del Dr. Lutero, al principio agobiado por sus sentimientos de culpa, pero que resulta sorprendido por el amor infinito y eterno del Dios de la Vida. Una tremenda posibilidad de reencontrarnos con la intención original de los Evangelios al reconstruir "La vida" de Jesús y no su muerte, el desafío constante de resignificar "La resurrección" como palabra última ante la muerte atroz. Y el "Shalom" como proyecto definitivo de la existencia humana, pero del sentido de la iglesia que deberá tener como misión: la empatía ante el dolor, la solidaridad como poder, la justicia a modo de fin irrenunciable, el amor a manera de fuerza inquebrantable y, por lo tanto, "La Paz" como condición de bien integral para el mundo en su integridad.

El Dr. David Allen Brondos Luecke nos entrega en este opúsculo mucho más que el resultado de sus investigaciones de décadas, muchísimo más que la síntesis de sus inquietudes teológicas… nos hereda una parte muy importante de su vida.

Este texto resulta, pues, un acto resurreccional.

La eternidad es el sustento profundo de esta obra. La memoria que se resiste a morir es la motivación de su autor. Una vida consagrada a pensar y repensar el amor de Dios como fuente inagotable de vida es la razón suficiente para acoger este testimonio de fe como una herencia en nuestras manos.

Estoy seguro que esta obra será un texto fundamental e imperecedero para la teología protestante mexicana. Es ya un parteaguas en la forma como se deconstruye-reconstruye la cristología liberadora desde México. Un ejemplo honesto e invaluable para honrar la tradición luterana en su intención incesante de profundizar en la Biblia, la teología y la pastoral. Una resignificación de la teología de la cruz que nos compromete a seguir buscando caminos de esperanza en la América Latina que tanto necesita hacer teología con perspectivas ecuménicas y misionales rigurosas, tanto en sus metodologías como en la producción de saberes.

No queda sino agradecer al teólogo, biblista, pastor, misionero; pero sobre todo maestro y amigo: Dr. David Allen Brondos Luecke, por su generosidad al entregarnos este don eterno de su pensamiento.

¡Salud amigo David!

Todo aquel que cree en Cristo es justo;
todavía no lo es plenamente en cuanto a los hechos,
pero sí en la esperanza.
Ha comenzado, en efecto, a ser justificado y sanado.
Pero entretanto que es justificado y sanado,
no le son imputados,
a causa de Cristo,
los pecados que todavía quedan en su carne.[2]
                        -**Dr. Martín Lutero.**

Dr. Dan González-Ortega
Rector de la Comunidad Teológica de México
Ciudad de México, Cuaresma del 2018.

---

2. *Obras de Martín Lutero*, Vol. 8. Buenos Aires: Ediciones La Aurora, 1982, p. 104.

Introduction

The aim of the present two-volume work is to change forever the way in which the New Testament allusions to the salvific significance of Jesus' death are understood. Needless to say, that is an extremely bold objective. I firmly believe, however, that those who read through this work will become convinced, not only that the interpretations of the New Testament passages that allude to Jesus' death that have prevailed since patristic times are no longer tenable, but also that those passages reflect a common understanding of the meaning and purpose of Jesus' death.

In the Introduction of my 2006 book *Paul on the Cross: Reconstructing the Apostle's Story of Redemption*, I wrote the following regarding Paul, which I believe is true for the rest of the New Testament as well:

> For Paul, Jesus' death did not save anyone or reconcile anyone to God; it did not have "redemptive effects." According to his letters, while Paul regarded Jesus' death as sacrificial, he did not teach that it expiated sins, propitiated God, or exhausted God's wrath at sin, or that human sin was judged, taken away, or atoned for on the cross. Nor did Paul maintain that Jesus' death liberated humanity from sin, death, the devil, or the power of evil. Paul did not regard Jesus as a corporate or representative figure who summed up or included others, so that what was true of him was thereby true of them as well. Nor did he believe that Jesus had died as humanity's substitute or representative, or in order to make it possible for God to forgive sins while remaining righteous. Jesus' death, for Paul, was not the basis upon which people were justified or their sins forgiven; neither was it some type of cosmic event that put an end to the world as it was and ushered in a new age. Our sinful humanity was not destroyed, put to death, renewed or transformed when Jesus was crucified. In Paul's thought, Jesus did not die for the purpose of setting an example for others to follow; revealing some truth about God, humanity, or the world; enabling people to participate in his death and resurrection; or providing them with a means of transfer from this age into the new one. Believers are not saved by trusting in the efficacy of Christ's death for their salvation.[1]

The intention of that passage from my book was to make clear my conviction that all of the traditional readings of the Pauline passages that ascribe saving significance to Jesus' death from patristic times to the present are foreign to the thought of Paul. In the present work, I will argue that those readings are foreign to the thought of the rest of the New Testament writings as well. Among the interpretations of the meaning and purpose of Jesus' death that I regard as inaccurate representations of New Testament thought are those of Irenaeus of Lyons in the late second century and the other church

---

1. David A. Brondos, *Paul on the Cross: Reconstructing the Apostle's Story of Redemption* (Minneapolis: Fortress, 2006), x.

fathers from his time forward, such as Gregory of Nyssa and Athanasius, who discussed the subject repeatedly in their writings. Equally lacking any basis in the New Testament texts are the interpretations of the salvific significance of Jesus' death that developed in the Western church out of the writings of Anselm of Canterbury (d. 1109), Peter Abelard (d. 1142), the sixteenth-century Reformers, and biblical scholars and theologians in general from the time of the Protestant Reformation to the present. Among those scholars and theologians, I include figures from the first half of the twentieth century such as Albert Schweitzer, Karl Barth, and Rudolf Bultmann, as well as those whose interpretations of the New Testament thought regarding the significance of Jesus' death have gained prominence in more recent decades, such as E. P. Sanders, James Dunn, and N. T. Wright. I will argue that the ideas and presuppositions that are central to these traditional and contemporary readings of Paul's epistles and the other New Testament texts have no basis in those writings and have mistakenly been read back into those passages that speak of Jesus' death as salvific.

Throughout most of the Christian church's history, there has been a great deal of discussion, debate, and disagreement over the precise manner in which Jesus' death leads to human salvation. At no point in that history have Christian thinkers, theologians, and biblical scholars reached any type of consensus on that question. Strong arguments have been made both for and against almost all of the interpretations of Jesus' death mentioned above. This has led most biblical scholars and theologians today to the conclusion that there are elements of truth in all of those interpretations, yet none of them can be said to capture fully the significance ascribed to Jesus' death in the New Testament.

While that question continues to be debated today in many circles, in recent years increased attention has been given to the historical circumstances surrounding Jesus' death on a Roman cross. As a result of the extensive research into the social, economical, political, and religious realities in the Palestine of Jesus' day, rather than discussing the *theological* reasons why Jesus was put to death, many scholars have come to focus on the *historical* reasons for his crucifixion. Interest in this question has been evident especially among those who emphasize Jesus' opposition to the authorities, traditions, systems, and practices that he believed were responsible for the injustice, violence, and oppression that he encountered in the society of his day.

According to virtually all biblical scholars and theologians today, however, those historical reasons for Jesus' crucifixion did not form the basis for affirmations such as those that we find in the New Testament, where Jesus is said to have died "for us" and "for our sins," and where cleansing, redemption, justification, and reconciliation with God are said to have been achieved on behalf of believers by means of his death or blood.[2] Instead, it is generally assumed that in the years following Jesus' death, those who believed in Jesus

---

2. On this point, see my article "Why was Jesus Crucified? Theology, History and the Story of Redemption," *SJT* 54 (2001): 484-503.

as the Messiah sent by God looked to a variety of ideas taken from different sources and contexts in order to interpret the significance of his death. These included passages from texts such as Isaiah 53 and the Second and Fourth books of the Maccabees, ancient beliefs and practices associated with the offering of sacrifice, common conceptions of noble and vicarious death, expectations regarding a time of great tribulation soon to occur, and a variety of other religious beliefs and practices found not only among Jews but among non-Jewish peoples as well. Supposedly, ideas taken from these sources led to the development of the interpretations of the significance of Jesus' death just mentioned above.

In recent decades, many Christian believers, theologians, and biblical scholars have come to criticize and reject the interpretations of Jesus' death that have traditionally predominated in ecclesial and theological circles. In particular, liberation theologians and feminist theologians have argued that those traditional interpretations present an oppressive view of God and God's will and have contributed to much of the violence, injustice, inequity, and oppression that have been present throughout the history of the church and Western society.[3]

One of the main arguments of this work is that the common understanding of the salvific significance of Jesus' death that we find in the New Testament began to disappear among Christians by the late second century. In its place, there arose a wide variety of interpretations of Jesus' death that are not in accordance with New Testament thought, such as those mentioned at the outset of this Introduction. These interpretations, along with the ideas and presuppositions on which they are based, were then read back into the Hebrew and Christian Scriptures in order to claim that they were rooted in biblical thought. As a result, from the patristic period up to the present, the gospel that has been proclaimed is in important respects fundamentally distinct from the gospel articulated in the New Testament.

The primary objective of this work, however, is not to offer yet another critique of the traditional interpretations of Jesus' death, but to reconstruct the beliefs of Jesus' first followers regarding the salvific significance of his death as these are articulated in the New Testament. Undoubtedly, these beliefs varied somewhat from one time and place to another and were constantly in a process of change and development. Because each of the New Testament allusions to Jesus' death is unique in some way or is found in a different context, in one sense we must use the plural so as to speak of the *interpretations* of the significance of Jesus' death found in the New Testament. Yet because these various interpretations revolve around certain basic ideas, we can also speak of a single, common interpretation of the significance of Jesus' death that lies behind all of the New Testament writings that allude to it.

---

3. See, for example, Leonardo Boff, *Passion of Christ, Passion of the World*, trans. Robert R. Barr (Maryknoll, NY: Orbis, 2011), 86-101; J. Denny Weaver, *The Nonviolent Atonement*, 2nd ed. (Grand Rapids: Eerdmans, 2011), 129-217.

From my perspective, the failure to capture and communicate accurately the gospel regarding Jesus and his death found in the New Testament has led to the proclamation of a message that has been incapable of impacting the world and transforming the lives of people in the way that the gospel proclaimed by Jesus' first followers originally did.[4] Although due to many factors the Christian church grew over time and continues to grow in many areas of the world today, in the majority of countries and regions in which Christianity has predominated for centuries, it is now in crisis and decline. Furthermore, while many admirable things have taken place in the church throughout its history, there can be no denial of the fact that Christians of every generation have practiced and promoted injustice and oppression at times, often in the name of God and on the basis of Scripture. From my perspective, this is in large part the consequence of the distortion of the gospel that has taken place due to the adoption of interpretations of Jesus' death that are foreign to New Testament thought and even run contrary to it.

These convictions explain why I consider it so important to reconstruct faithfully the salvific significance that Jesus' first followers ascribed to his death on the basis of the New Testament texts. I believe that their understanding of Jesus' death played a decisive role in the establishment of communities characterized by a strong commitment to all that Jesus and his cross stood for in the eyes of those communities. Only by returning to the interpretation of Jesus' death that we find reflected throughout the New Testament can we rediscover and recapture the transforming power of the Christian gospel as it was originally understood and proclaimed.

Because the aim of this work is that of *historical reconstruction*, I will not be addressing questions regarding the meaning and relevance of the material presented for us today or attempting to define the manner in which we should understand and articulate the ideas and beliefs examined in our modern contexts. I regard my task here as a *descriptive* rather than a *prescriptive* one. I will be seeking to reconstruct the beliefs of people in antiquity, particularly Jews of the second-temple period and the followers of Jesus in the first and second

---

4. Following scholars such as Donald H. Juel, who have argued that "Christianity," like "normative Judaism," is a "creation of the second, third, and fourth centuries C.E.," throughout the present work I will avoid using terms such as "Christian" and "Christianity" to refer to the first believers in Jesus and the faith they practiced ("The Future of a Religious Past: Qumran and the Palestinian Jesus Movement," in *The Bible and the Dead Sea Scrolls: The Second Princeton Symposium on Judaism and Christian Origins*; ed. James H. Charlesworth; Waco, TX: Baylor University Press, 2006, 1:63). As Juel affirms, "the new material made available to us through the painstaking work of a generation of scholars forces the whole academic—and nonacademic—world to acknowledge that *'Christianity'* began as a Jewish sect and that the New Testament belongs to what should be called the 'pre-Christian' era (or proto-Christian literature)" (1:64). Rather than speaking of the "first Christians," I will use designations such as "Jesus' first followers" or "the first believers in Christ." Of course, any designation one chooses to use will inevitably be problematic in some way. I am aware that these designations are rather ambiguous, since they can be understood as referring to the very first disciples of Jesus who knew him during his lifetime as well as to those who came to faith in Jesus as the Messiah in the decades immediately following his death. Yet it is precisely because of this ambiguity that I prefer to use these designations, as I wish to stress the continuity between those who identified themselves as Jesus' followers from the time of his ministry up until the end of the apostolic era.

centuries. Above all, I will be inquiring as to the salvific significance that Jesus' first followers came to ascribe to his death. The primary basis for this reconstruction will be the New Testament texts, although it will also be necessary to examine other texts from antiquity as well as the work of modern-day scholars who have studied all of these texts and the contexts in which they arose.

There are several reasons why I believe it is important to emphasize that this work is aimed at *historical reconstruction*. First of all, if we are to reconstruct faithfully the beliefs reflected in the New Testament and other texts from antiquity, we cannot read those texts as if they were written for us today. Instead, we must limit ourselves to asking either what the authors of those texts wished to communicate to those for whom they wrote or how those who read or heard those texts in antiquity would have understood them. This requires that we make a careful distinction between what those texts meant in antiquity and what they may mean for us in our own time and place.[5]

This is a point often overlooked by biblical scholars. The belief that the biblical writings were divinely inspired leads many biblical scholars to read those writings as if they were written for believers of all times and places. This often involves assuming that passages that allude to the believers to whom those writings were originally addressed allude as well to believers of later generations, including our own. The manner in which the biblical texts are applied to our present-day contexts thus interferes with the process of discerning what those texts meant in their original contexts.

This manner of interpreting the biblical texts is especially evident when passages containing prescriptions for believers are read today. For example, when Christian interpreters read imperatives such as Paul's words in 1 Thess. 5:16, "Rejoice always," they tend to apply those words directly to their lives today and even believe that, when Paul wrote them, God was inspiring him to write words intended for Christians of all times and places. However, when we remember that Paul was addressing those words only to a particular group of believers in Thessalonica, we will ask historical questions aimed at capturing his original intention for writing those words. In 1 Thess. 4:13, for example, Paul mentions those who grieve the death of a loved one as if they had no hope, and shortly thereafter he exhorts the Thessalonian believers to encourage one another (1 Thess. 4:18; 5:11). On this basis, we may conclude that Paul was exhorting the believers in Thessalonica to rejoice always, not because he was simply repeating some general exhortation he customarily made to all believers, but due to specific circumstances that he was addressing in Thessalonica. The same observations could be made regarding Paul's exhortation to the

---

5. I regard as reductionist questions such as whether or not it is possible to discern the original meaning of a text or know what an author's intentions were. From my perspective, rather than framing such questions in simple Yes and No terms, we must recognize that, while it is impossible to reconstruct fully or completely a text's original meaning or the intentions of its author, we can nevertheless do so to a considerable extent. This means that we can discuss and attempt to arrive at a certain degree of consensus regarding how well or how poorly any particular interpretation or translation of a text reproduces the meaning that its author intended to convey and the manner in which its original readers would have understood it.

Romans to "owe no one anything, except to love one another" (Rom. 13:8), or his oft-cited words regarding *agapē* love in 1 Corinthians 13: if we wish to grasp adequately the original intention or meaning of these passages, rather than reading them as if they were intended for Christians of all times and places, we must view them in the context of the particular situations that Paul was addressing in the Roman and Corinthian churches.

Of course, to speak in these terms is by no means to affirm that Christians are not to apply passages such as those just cited to their present lives and realities. On the contrary, a basic tenet of the Christian faith is that the canonical writings of the Old and New Testaments were inspired by God in a way that other texts are not in order that people might know God's will regarding what they are to believe and how they are to live. It is one thing, however, to affirm that God inspired Paul to write what he did to his contemporaries in Thessalonica, Rome, and Corinth, and another thing quite different to claim that, when Paul was composing those epistles, God was inspiring him to write words directed at believers who would live all around the world and speak countless different languages many centuries later. In addition to believing that Paul's epistles were divinely inspired, Christians generally maintain that God's Holy Spirit enables them to understand the words of Paul today and apply those words to their lives in the way that God desires. Many would also say that, when God inspired Paul to write those epistles, it was God's plan that they be transmitted from one generation of Christians to another and that they come to form part of what we now know as the New Testament.

Nevertheless, Christians must also acknowledge that it would be impossible for them to read and understand today the words of Paul and the authors of the other biblical writings without the efforts of scholars to reconstruct the original meanings of those words and subsequently to translate and interpret them for our modern-day contexts. For this to happen, of course, scholars must also work to reconstruct as precisely as possible the original content of the biblical writings on the basis of ancient manuscripts and seek to understand the historical contexts in which those writings were composed. In other words, before Christians can carry out the *prescriptive* task of interpreting those texts so as to discern what they mean and how they are to be applied today, the *descriptive* task of historical reconstruction must first be carried out.

While I am well aware that for many readers of this work none of the points just mentioned represent anything new, I believe it is important to stress them before we turn to passages such as 1 Cor. 15:3, where Paul affirms that "Christ died for our sins." It is extremely common for believers today to assume that, when Paul wrote those words, he was referring to the sins of believers of all times and places or to the sins of every person who had ever existed or would exist throughout human history. Strictly speaking, from a grammatical standpoint, all that we can infer from Paul's use of the first-person plural possessive pronoun "our" is that he was referring to himself and someone else. For biblical interpreters to apply Paul's words directly to our present-day contexts without first attempting to reconstruct what they meant in the original contexts in which they were spoken and written is to pass over the question of what Paul intended the addressees of his letters to understand when he wrote those words. This involves disregarding questions such as why Paul included those words in the passage from 1 Corinthians in which they appear and precisely which sins Paul had in mind. Although virtually all scholars would affirm that Paul was thinking of the sins of the Corinthian believers to whom he wrote as well as the sins of other believers in Christ in his day, it is possible that Paul was alluding only to the sins of particular people or groups. For example, he could have had in mind the sins of the people of Israel in the past or those of Jews like himself in his own day. It is also possible that he was referring specifically to the sins that characterized the life of the gentile peoples in general, although the fact that Paul was not himself a gentile might be regarded as making it unlikely that he would include himself among the gentiles for whose sins Christ had died. Rather than alluding to the sins of future generations, Paul may have had in mind only the sins "previously committed" that God had passed over "in his divine forbearance" (see Rom. 3:25; Acts 17:30). Of course, the possibility that Paul was referring to the sins of human beings or believers of all times and places can by no means be ruled out. In fact, because in 1 Cor. 15:3 Paul is citing a saying that had been passed on to him by others, one might even argue that Paul did not understand that saying in the same way that other believers had previously, or that he was applying that saying to a situation that was very different from that in which it first arose.

Before addressing the question of how believers should understand 1 Cor. 15:3 today, therefore, it is necessary first to address numerous questions regarding how and why Paul cited the phrase "Christ died for our sins" in the context of the argument he was developing in that part of his epistle and what he intended the Corinthian believers to understand by it. Because those words were passed on to Paul by other believers, one may also wish to reconstruct the context in which that saying first arose and the meaning it originally had in that context. If questions such as these are not addressed, Paul's words easily come to be understood as expressing a "universal truth" regarding "Christ's once-for-all atoning death on behalf of all humanity," and ideas that arose in the theological discussions of later centuries may be read back into Paul's affirmation.

A second reason why I wish to stress that my aim in this work is that of historical reconstruction is that I believe it is extremely important to distinguish the thought of the authors of the biblical texts from my own. To affirm that a certain idea is found in one or more passages from Scripture is not necessarily to agree with that idea. This is another point that many biblical scholars fail to acknowledge properly. Today, for example, in large part as a result of the holocaust during the Second World War in which over six million Jews died, many New Testament scholars are very careful to avoid interpretations of the New Testament that might be seen as fomenting hostile attitudes toward Jewish people or as encouraging the claim that Christians have replaced the Jews as God's chosen people.

This concern is reflected in debates that have taken place in recent years as to whether the Epistle to the Hebrews reflects supersessionist ideas or whether Paul was in some sense "anti-Jewish." For example, in an essay published in 2009 titled "'Here We Have No Lasting City': New Covenantalism in Hebrews," Richard Hays argues that the thought and language of Hebrews should be considered "New Covenantalist" rather than supersessionist—though he recognizes that the latter term runs the risk of being anachronistic.[6] According to Hays, "The New Covenantalism of Hebrews is certainly not supersessionist in the classic sense that it replaces one religious system with a new stable religious system that allows readers to stand in a position of secure superiority."[7] In the two essays that follow that of Hays in the same volume—all of which were presented in 2006 at the St. Andrews Conference on Hebrews and Theology—Oskar Skarsaune and Mark Nanos question whether the "New Covenantalism" that Hays finds in Hebrews is in reality something distinct from supersessionism.[8] Whether or not the critiques of Hays's work offered by Skarsaune and Nanos are justified, what is noteworthy is Hays's reluctance to label the thought of Hebrews as supersessionist in any sense. This same reluctance is reflected in the work of other New Testament scholars as well. Hays himself points to Charles P. Anderson, Gabriella Gelardini, Elke Tönges, and Pamela Eisenbaum as examples of scholars who "question the supersessionist paradigm for reading Hebrews...."[9] Similarly, in recent years, a growing number of Pauline scholars have come to insist that, while Paul opposed the notion that non-Jewish believers in Christ should adopt a Jewish lifestyle by submitting to the prescriptions of the Torah, he did not reject Judaism per se and even remained Torah-observant himself as a faithful Jew. For these and other reasons, he should not be regarded as "anti-Jewish."[10]

Throughout discussions such as these, what is often assumed is that if supersessionist or "anti-Jewish" views are present in the New Testament, Christians would be justified in regarding Judaism as an inferior religion that has now been replaced and superseded by Christianity. In reality, such a

---

6. Richard B. Hays, "'Here We Have No Lasting City': New Covenantalism in Hebrews," in *The Epistle to the Hebrews and Christian Theology* (ed. Richard Bauckham, Daniel R. Driver, Trevor A. Hart, and Nathan McDonald; Grand Rapids: Eerdmans, 2009), 151-73; see 154.

7. Ibid., 172.

8. Oskar Skarsaune, "Does the Letter to the Hebrews Articulate a Supersessionist Theology? A Response to Richard Hays," in *Epistle to the Hebrews*, ed. Bauckham et al., 174-82; Mark D. Nanos, "New or Renewed Covenantalism? A Response to Richard Hays," in *Epistle to the Hebrews*, ed. Bauckham et al., 183-88.

9. Hays, "'No Lasting City'," 152-53, n2-5.

10. On this designation, see, for example, Jeffrey S. Lamp, "Is Paul Anti-Jewish? *Testament of Levi* 6 in the Interpretation of 1 Thessalonians 2:13-16," *CBQ* 65 (2003): 408-27. Lamp concludes that, contrary to some readings of 1 Thess. 2:13-16, Paul does not regard "the Jews" in general as corporately responsible for the crimes he mentions in that passage and does not therefore "consign all Jews forever to the wrath of God" (424, 426).

conclusion is a *non sequitor* and once again involves confusing the *descriptive* with the *prescriptive*. Undoubtedly, there are very good reasons to question and even reject the traditional readings of certain New Testament passages that appear to reflect a negative view of Judaism and to condemn as being unfaithful to the God of Israel those Jews who did not accept Jesus as the awaited Messiah. However, even if hostile attitudes toward Judaism and Jews who did not believe in Jesus are present in some New Testament passages, it does not follow that Christians today are justified in assuming those same attitudes, as if to do so were to be faithful to the Scriptures. On the contrary, it can be argued that Christians who assume such attitudes are being *unfaithful* to the thought of Jesus, Paul, and the New Testament as a whole. The same can be said of those who justify any type of discrimination, sexism, racism, or injustice on the basis of passages from the New Testament by arguing that to do so runs contrary to the spirit of Jesus, Paul, and the New Testament.

Ultimately, however, such considerations should play no role in the task of attempting to discern the original meanings of biblical texts if that task is understood as a *descriptive* one, aimed purely at historical reconstruction. In principle, every historical reconstruction should be done as objectively as possible, without taking into account the implications it may have or the ways in which it may be applied to present-day contexts. All biblical scholars, of course, are heavily influenced by their particular interests and concerns, the traditions and perspectives they have inherited from others, the contexts *in* which and *for* which they carry out their work, and a strong desire to guide other Christians in discerning how they are to relate to the world around them. All of these considerations make it impossible for any historical reconstruction to be fully objective. Furthermore, virtually every historical reconstruction will inevitably tend to be interpreted as providing a basis for supporting and promoting certain beliefs and practices while rejecting others. All of this means that it is impossible for the *descriptive* task of historical reconstruction to be entirely divorced from the *prescriptive* task of biblical interpretation, which involves using those historical reconstructions as a basis for defining the ways in which the biblical texts are to be applied to reality today. It is one thing, however, to attempt to examine the evidence as objectively as possible in an effort to determine whether or not certain ideas are actually present in the biblical texts, and another thing altogether to manipulate and misrepresent the evidence available in order to offer biased historical reconstructions that provide support for ideas or actions that one wishes to promote or that call into question attitudes and practices that one wishes to condemn or reject on the basis of the biblical texts.

By emphasizing that the present work is aimed almost entirely at historical reconstruction, therefore, I hope to convince the reader that there is very strong evidence to support the affirmations that I have made above with regard to the salvific significance ascribed to Jesus' death in the New Testament and later Christian thought, and that I have examined that evidence as objectively as possible. While I am aware that the historical reconstructions proposed in this work will inevitably be interpreted as promoting certain applications of the biblical texts to our present reality, I have made every effort to lay aside my own interests, biases, beliefs, and concerns in order to come as close as possible to discerning the original meaning of the texts examined. At the same time, I have attempted to avoid reading back into those texts ideas that are foreign to them. This means that the ideas I seek to articulate throughout the present work are those of the writings under consideration rather than my own.

A third reason why I wish to stress that my aim here is that of historical reconstruction is that, in contrast to some of the other writings I have published, I will for the most part not be using gender-neutral language in speaking of God. Instead, following the practice of the biblical writings and other ancient Jewish and Christian texts, I will use masculine pronouns to refer to God. My main reason for doing so is that I believe that it is important to distinguish the question of how we should conceive and speak of God *today* (a *prescriptive* consideration) from the question of how those who wrote the texts under consideration conceived and spoke of God *in the past* (a *descriptive* consideration). While of course Christians would insist that the God in whom we believe today is the same God of whom the Hebrew Scriptures and the New Testament writings speak, in reality those texts reflect conceptions of God that to some extent differ not only among themselves but also from our conceptions of God today. Nevertheless, because in antiquity both Jews and Christians used masculine pronouns to refer to the God in whom they believed, I believe it is appropriate to do the same today when attempting to reconstruct their beliefs and conceptions regarding God.

This work can be divided into six different sections that vary greatly with regard to their length. In Chapter 1, I examine the interpretations of the salvific significance of Jesus' death that are found in the writings of Christian theologians and biblical scholars from patristic times to the present, classifying those interpretations in three groups. At the same time, I point out the theological assumptions underlying the interpretations considered. This will provide the basis necessary to explore further on in this work the question of whether those assumptions are in accordance with the beliefs we find in Jewish and Greco-Roman thought from the second-temple period. Although it will be necessary to go into some detail when analyzing certain of the ideas and assumptions associated with the traditional interpretations of the meaning of Jesus' death, such an analysis is necessary in order to consider in the following chapters whether those interpretations are grounded in New Testament thought.

In Chapters 2–4, I will look at second-temple Jewish beliefs regarding God and the salvation of Israel and the nations, as well as other beliefs and practices of antiquity that may have influenced the manner in which Jesus' first followers interpreted his death. In particular, I will consider the meaning that Jews, Greeks, and Romans in antiquity ascribed to the sacrificial practices of their day, their beliefs regarding vicarious death, suffering, and atonement, and passages from biblical and non-biblical texts of the second-temple period in order to consider the ways in which those practices, beliefs, and texts could have influenced Jesus' first followers as they reflected on the salvific significance of his death.

Chapter 5, the third part of this work, will be dedicated to the question of how Jesus himself interpreted his sufferings and death in light of the aims of his ministry. While it is of course impossible to provide any definitive answers to that question, by considering the contexts in which Jesus carried out his ministry and analyzing the words and deeds that the Gospels attribute to him, we can explore the possibility that the interpretations that Jesus' first followers ascribed to his death were shaped at least to some extent by Jesus himself.

Chapters 6–10 constitute the heart of this work. Chapter 6 develops the argument that the conviction of Jesus' first followers that he had been raised from the dead and exalted into heaven led them to see him as Lord over all. In the light of his total dedication to his ministry on behalf of others, however, they interpreted his lordship as something that he had sought, not merely for his own sake, but *for the sake of others*. Because Jesus had been put to death as a result of his refusal to put an end to his work on behalf of others, as he went to his death he must have continued to seek what he had sought throughout his ministry, namely, the salvation and well-being of others. Jesus' first followers must therefore have seen his willingness to give up his life in obedience to God as an implicit petition to God on behalf of others, as well as a petition that his work on behalf of others might achieve its goal rather than coming to an end. Consequently, they would have interpreted his resurrection as God's response to that petition: God had raised Jesus precisely so that he might continue his activity on behalf of others and serve as God's agent and instrument for bringing about in definitive fashion the salvation he had sought for all in life and death. In addition, this belief led Jesus' followers to view him as mediator between God and all who would be incorporated into the community that lived under his lordship. Therefore, Jesus must also have been seeking to be placed in that role for the good of others as he offered up his life to God.

In Chapters 7 and 8, I argue that the conviction that the crucified Jesus was Lord and that salvation depended on faith in him as the one who ultimately defined God's will led to tensions and conflicts in the first communities of Jesus' followers and in the Jewish communities where they were active. The belief that one's life and conduct were now to revolve around Jesus as Lord led to questions and debates regarding the Mosaic law: if obedience to God's will was now equated with living under Jesus' lordship and following him as the one who represented and spoke for God, what role was the Mosaic law now to play in the lives of believers? Their conviction that Jesus was God's Son seemed to make observance of the law a matter of secondary importance. That conviction also eventually led Jesus' followers to reach out to non-Jews, proclaiming that through faith in Christ one could live in accordance with God's will without submitting to all of the prescriptions of the law. Furthermore, if God's desire was that all follow Jesus in faith as the one who defined his will, then all that was necessary to be accepted by God as righteous and obtain God's forgiveness was to live in faith under Jesus' lordship as a member of the community that he had sought to establish in life and death. By giving up his life rather than seeking to save it when his activity on behalf of others had led to the threat of death, Jesus had laid the basis for a new community in which all would relate to God and to one another in new ways. Jesus' followers thus understood themselves to be living under a new covenant as God's people, and even spoke of themselves as a new temple inhabited by God's Spirit, who transformed their hearts so that they might dedicate themselves to serving God and others in the way Jesus had.

In Chapter 9, I examine the ways in which Jesus' followers applied the Scriptures to the reality they now experienced as members of God´s people. The belief that God had exalted his Son Jesus as Lord over all out of love for all led Jesus' first followers to conclude that, from even before creation, God had intended to send his Son into the world in order to bring into existence the community of which they had come to form part. This plan contemplated all that had taken place in history prior to Jesus' coming, as well as everything that had followed upon that event. Those who lived as members of the community established through Jesus would obtain the salvation God had promised from of old. When Jesus' first followers affirmed that his sufferings and death had been "necessary," they meant that these events had formed part of God's plan from the start. Jesus' death had also been necessary for the community established through him to be characterized by the same type of love that Jesus had shown by giving up his life on behalf of others. Only through Jesus' total commitment to God's will could a community of people be created that would share that same commitment; and for that to happen, it was necessary for God to give his Son over to a violent death that would be the inevitable result of the prophetic ministry on behalf of others that he would carry out once God had sent him into the world.

Chapter 10 will offer a reconstruction of the development of the beliefs of Jesus' first followers regarding the salvific significance of his death. Initially, Jesus' first followers would probably have regarded his death as comparable to the deaths of other prophetic figures. As a result of their conviction that Jesus had been raised from the dead and exalted to God's right hand as Lord and Christ, however, they would soon come to the conclusion that, in accordance with his Father's will, Jesus had given up his life so that the type of alternative community that God had intended to bring about through him might become a reality. If they applied to Jesus' death passages from texts such as Isaiah 53 and 2 and 4 Maccabees, as well as the story of the binding of Isaac in Genesis 22, they would have understood these passages as affirming that Jesus had borne the sins of others by dedicating his life to delivering them from their persistent sinfulness so that they might be purified and obtain divine forgiveness for their sins. These things would happen as they came to live as members of the community of those who had been brought into conformity with God's will through Jesus' ministry, death, and resurrection. On the basis of these and other beliefs regarding Jesus, his first followers came to affirm that he had died "for others" and "for their sins," and that they had attained redemption, justification, and reconciliation with God through his death or blood.

The fifth part of this work is the most lengthy. In Chapters 11-16, I will examine each of the New Testament passages that ascribe salvific significance to Jesus' death. Two questions will be addressed when considering these passages: first, the reason why the author alludes to Jesus' death in the context of the situation he is addressing and the argument he is developing, and second, the thought that lies behind each of these allusions. In this way, it will become evident that each of those passages reflects the basic understanding of Jesus' death developed in the preceding chapters of this work rather than any of the traditional interpretations of Jesus' death considered in Chapter 1.

Finally, in Chapters 17 and 18 I argue that throughout the writings of the Apostolic Fathers and Justin Martyr, we find language and ideas that are in continuity with New Testament thought regarding Jesus' death. However, beginning with Melito's *Peri Pascha* and Irenaeus's work *Against Heresies*, the manner in which Jesus' death is viewed as salvific undergoes important changes. There we find for the first time many of the assumptions and ideas mentioned in Chapter 1, such as the arguments regarding the necessity of Christ's coming and death for human salvation and the notion of an ontological transformation of humanity and creation as a whole by virtue of the union between the divine and the human that took place in Christ. In the Conclusion, I offer a final summary of the way in which Jesus' first followers interpreted his death and address several issues that those interpretations raise.

This work is the result of nearly forty years of research on the topic and has taken me seven years to write. To my knowledge, it is the most complete and in-depth study published to date of the passages from the New Testament and other early Christian writings that allude to the salvific significance of Jesus' death. Of course, because the interpretations that Jesus' first followers ascribed to his death were based on their convictions concerning God, God's will, and God's activity in the world from its beginning to its end, a careful examination of those convictions must form part of any attempt to reconstruct the thought behind the allusions to Jesus' death in the New Testament. This means that the question of how Jesus' first followers understood his death cannot be addressed adequately without considering their worldview and belief system as a whole, as I have done here. Furthermore, no matter how complete or thorough this or any other study on this subject may strive to be, there is no way that it can even come close to addressing all of the questions and issues related to the interpretation of the New Testament allusions to Jesus' death. To interact with anything more than a fraction of all that has been written on this topic is, of course, an equally impossible task.

Thus, although I by no means seek or wish that this work be regarded as any kind of definitive word on the subject of the meaning ascribed to Jesus' death in the New Testament, I do hope that it will help take discussion on this subject in a new and different direction. I recognize, of course, that it is extremely difficult for Christian believers, theologians, and biblical scholars to leave behind the traditional and often treasured interpretations of the significance of Jesus' death in order to embrace new ones. To fail to do so when the evidence demands it, however, is to continue to adhere to understandings of the gospel that do not represent faithfully the gospel proclaimed by Jesus, his first followers, and the authors of the New Testament writings.[11]

---

11. This is one of the central arguments of my book *Redeeming the Gospel: The Christian Faith Reconsidered* (SLHT; Minneapolis: Fortress, 2011).

CHAPTER 1

Jesus' Death in Traditional Christian Thought

Throughout the various writings of the New Testament, we repeatedly find passages in which salvific significance is ascribed to Jesus' death or blood. In virtually every case, this is done through the use of formulas that are brief and rather enigmatic:

"The Son of Man came not to be served but to serve, and to give his life as a ransom for many" (Mark 10:45; Matt. 20:28).

"This is my blood of the covenant, which is poured out for many for the forgiveness of sins" (Matt. 26:28).

"This is my body, which is given for you. Do this in remembrance of me".... "This cup that is poured out for you is the new covenant in my blood" (Luke 22:19-20).

"Here is the Lamb of God who takes away the sin of the world!" (John 1:29).

"I am the good shepherd. The good shepherd lays down his life for the sheep" (John 10:11).

"Keep watch over yourselves and over all the flock, of which the Holy Spirit has made you overseers, to shepherd the church of God that he obtained with the blood of his own Son" (Acts 20:28).

They are now justified by his grace as a gift, through the redemption that is in Christ Jesus, whom God put forward as a means of expiation by his blood (Rom. 3:24-25).

Jesus our Lord... was handed over to death for our trespasses and was raised for our justification (Rom. 4:24-25).

For while we were still weak, at the right time Christ died for the ungodly. Indeed, rarely will anyone die for a righteous person—though perhaps for a good person someone might actually dare to die. But God proves his love for us in that while we still were sinners Christ died for us. Much more surely then, now that we have been justified by his blood, will we be saved through him from the wrath of God. For if while we were enemies, we were reconciled to God through the death of his Son, much more surely, having been reconciled, will we be saved by his life (Rom. 5:6-10).

Christ died for our sins in accordance with the scriptures (1 Cor. 15:3).

For the love of Christ urges us on, because we are convinced that one has died for all; therefore all have died. And he died for all, so that those who live might live no longer for themselves, but for him who died and was raised for them (2 Cor. 5:14-15).

The Lord Jesus Christ... gave himself for our sins to set us free from the present evil age (Gal. 1:4).

Christ redeemed us from the curse of the law by becoming a curse for us—for it is written, "Cursed is everyone who hangs on a tree" (Gal. 3:13).

In him we have redemption through his blood, the forgiveness of our trespasses, according to the riches of his grace (Eph. 1:7).

But now in Christ Jesus you who once were far off have been brought near by the blood of Christ (Eph. 2:13).

Through him God was pleased to reconcile to himself all things, whether on earth or in heaven, by making peace through the blood of his cross (Col. 1:20).

For God has destined us not for wrath but for obtaining salvation through our Lord Jesus Christ, who died for us, so that whether we are awake or asleep we may live with him (1 Thess. 5:9-10).

For there is one God; there is also one mediator between God and humankind, Christ Jesus, himself human, who gave himself as a ransom for all (1 Tim. 2:5-6).

He it is who gave himself for us that he might redeem us from all iniquity and purify for himself a people of his own who are zealous for good deeds (Tit. 2:14).

When he had made purification for sins, he sat down at the right hand of the Majesty on high (Heb. 1:3).

He has appeared once for all at the end of the age to remove sin by the sacrifice of himself (Heb. 9:26).

You know that you were ransomed from the futile ways inherited from your ancestors, not with perishable things like silver or gold, but with the precious blood of Christ, like that of a lamb without defect or blemish (1 Pet. 1:18-19).

He himself bore our sins in his body on the tree, so that, free from sins, we might live for righteousness; by his wounds you have been healed (1 Pet. 2:24).

The blood of Jesus his Son cleanses us from all sin (1 John 1:7).

Jesus Christ... loves us and freed us from our sins by his blood (Rev. 1:5).

"You were slaughtered and by your blood you ransomed for God saints from every tribe and language and people and nation" (Rev. 5:9).[1]

The fact that these same kinds of formulas appear scattered throughout so many of the New Testament writings suggests not only that Jesus' death was of primary importance for believers in apostolic times, but also that among them it was extremely common to allude to Jesus' death through the use of such formulas. The authors of these writings would hardly have made such frequent use of those formulas in the way that they did unless they anticipated that their readers were well-acquainted with the thought behind them and

---

1. Many other passages could be added to these; see, for example, John 11:50-52; 12:24; Rom. 8:3-4, 32; 14:9; 1 Cor. 5:7; 8:11; 2 Cor. 5:18-21; Gal. 2:20; Eph. 2:16; 5:2, 25; Col. 1:22; 2:14; Heb. 2:9; 9:11-14, 28; 10:10, 12, 19; 13:12; 1 Pet. 1:2; 3:18; 1 John 2:2; 4:10; Rev. 7:14.

would therefore readily understand them. In many cases, the New Testament writers appear to be citing fixed formulas from an already-established tradition rather than composing such formulas on their own. There can thus be little doubt that the use of such formulas was already widespread in the earliest Christian communities.[2]

Unfortunately, however, none of the writings of the New Testament offer any clear explanation as to how the first believers understood such formulas. The most detailed accounts of Jesus' death that we possess are the passion accounts found in the four canonical Gospels; yet these accounts seem to contain little if any information that might be of help in interpreting the various formulaic allusions to Jesus' death found throughout the New Testament. Outside of Jesus' words over the bread and wine at the Last Supper, which are also formulaic in nature (Matt. 26:26-28; Mark 14:22-24; Luke 22:19-20), nowhere in those passion accounts is Jesus' death or blood said to redeem or save anyone, reconcile people to God, propitiate God's wrath, or obtain the remission of sins for others.

For the most part, the writings of the church fathers in the centuries immediately following the apostolic period are also of little help in attempting to discern the original meaning of the formulaic allusions to Jesus' death found in the New Testament. Beginning with the *Peri Pascha* of Melito of Sardis and Irenaeus's work *Against Heresies*, both of which date to the latter half of the second century, we encounter a variety of theological and philosophical ideas that are not readily evident in the New Testament texts, as we shall see in Chapter 18. These ideas were developed further by the church fathers in the following centuries. Undoubtedly, the church fathers often used biblical terms such as *redemption, reconciliation,* and *recapitulation* to allude to what had taken place through Christ, yet they tended to interpret these terms in ways that are not fully in continuity with New Testament thought. Even though the New Testament never speaks of the redemption of the human nature in which all people share and its reconciliation and union with the divine nature, this concept became central in patristic teaching. The incarnation of God's Son, the Word or Logos, came to be seen as the primary means by which human nature was joined to the divine, with the result that Jesus' death seemed to become almost of secondary importance. Some of the fathers also argued that God had offered God's Son as a ransom to the devil in order that the devil might release human beings from their bondage to him.

---

2. In this regard, Helmut Koester argues that Paul must be considered a contemporary of Jesus and that his writings must be regarded as preserving a number of traditional formulae ("The Memory of Jesus' Death and the Worship of the Risen Lord," *HTR* 91 [1998]: 343-44). Koester also affirms that those formulae were "a kind of shorthand reference to a larger context. It is inconceivable that only such formulae existed at the beginning, while larger narrative contexts were developed at a later time" (347). Nevertheless, he adds that among the earliest believers, "the story of Jesus' suffering and death remained fluid for a long time" (350).

Ideas such as these were commonly read back into the New Testament texts, including especially passages that use the type of formulas mentioned above.³

The renewed attention given to the biblical texts during the period of the Protestant Reformation led to interpretations of the New Testament allusions to Jesus' death that were very different from those of the church fathers and drew instead on ideas taken from medieval scholars such as Anselm of Canterbury and Peter Abelard. The need to understand the New Testament passages in their original contexts came to be stressed, especially following the rise of biblical scholarship in the late eighteenth and early nineteenth centuries. Yet, rather than coming to a consensus on the original meaning of the passages that ascribe salvific significance to Jesus' death, biblical scholars and Christian theologians became polarized over their interpretation. Some affirmed that behind most of these passages was the idea that Christ had saved humanity from death and divine condemnation by undergoing the penalty due to human sin on the cross in the place of guilty sinners, as most of the Reformers had taught. Others, however, argued strongly against such interpretations. Often they claimed instead that Christ's death saves human beings by revealing to them some divine truth, such as the extent of the love of God and Jesus for humanity. Intense debates among scholars over these two interpretations continued well into the twentieth century.

In 1931, the English edition of Gustav Aulén's *Christus Victor* was published. Aulén offered an alternative to these two traditional views that in essence involved a return to patristic thought. He argued that the idea that Christ had triumphed over the forces of evil in his death and resurrection was in fact behind many of the New Testament passages considered above.⁴ Subsequently, in 1977, developing the ideas of Rudolf Bultmann and other biblical scholars, E. P. Sanders proposed that the primary idea behind many of the New Testament allusions to Jesus' death was that of *participation in Christ*: one dies with Christ to the power of sin by becoming united to him as a single person.⁵ Since then, this proposal has grown considerably in popularity among both biblical scholars and Christian theologians, though the other views mentioned above continue to be maintained as well. Today it has become common to claim that all of these different views can be discerned in the New Testament, though precisely how they are to be combined or reconciled with one another is by no means clear.

---

3. See, for example, Gregory of Nyssa's interpretation of Gal. 3:13 in *Against Eunomius* 2.11; 5.5; 12.1, as well as the discussion of the thought of Gregory and Irenaeus of Lyons in David A. Brondos, *Fortress Introduction to Salvation and the Cross* (Minneapolis: Fortress, 2007), 49-75. See also Gustav Aulén, *Christus Victor: An Historical Study of the Three Main Types of the Idea of Atonement,* trans. A. G. Hebert (New York: MacMillan, 1969), 16-60.

4. See Aulén, *Christus Victor*, 4-6, 61-80.

5. E. P. Sanders, *Paul and Palestinian Judaism: A Comparison of Patterns of Religion* (Philadelphia: Fortress, 1977), 495-514, 519-23, 549, 552. For Rudolf Bultmann's thought regarding participation in Christ, see his *Theology of the New Testament*, trans. Kendrick Grobel (New York: Scribner, 1951), 1:295-96, 298-99, 302-3, 311-13.

Because of the formulaic nature of the allusions to Jesus' death in the New Testament, those allusions lend themselves to having a wide variety of different ideas read back into them. Phrases such as "Christ died for us," "he gave himself for our sins," "we have been reconciled to God through the death of his Son," "we have redemption through his blood," and "the blood of Jesus cleanses us from all sin" are so ambiguous, terse, and enigmatic that they can be understood on the basis of practically all of the traditional Christian interpretations of Jesus' death. This means that we cannot take those formulaic allusions themselves as a starting-point for asking how the authors of the New Testament understood Jesus' death to be salvific for others.

Throughout the present work, I will argue that biblical scholars and Christian theologians have wrongly read back into the New Testament texts all of the various ideas just outlined and that such ideas are grounded, not in the thought and worldview of Jesus' first followers, but in later theological and philosophical ideas that are foreign to New Testament thought. Needless to say, this argument involves questioning virtually every aspect of the interpretations given to Jesus' death from the patristic period to the present. To ascribe to the authors of the New Testament writings the views just presented involves ascribing to them as well a series of related ideas, presuppositions, and premises that serve as the basis for those views, along with a variety of problems, inconsistencies, and even contradictions that are inherent to those views.

The purpose of the present chapter is to summarize and analyze the different interpretations given to the New Testament allusions to the salvific nature of Jesus' death, along with the problems that each of these interpretations entails. Unfortunately, because of the wide variety of these interpretations, this chapter will need to be fairly lengthy and, for many readers, perhaps somewhat laborious. Nevertheless, without entering into a careful and detailed analysis of the various interpretations of the New Testament teaching regarding Jesus' death and the ideas associated with those interpretations, it is impossible to address in the following chapters the question of whether they reflect faithfully the New Testament teaching and early Christian thought.

The analysis provided here goes well beyond the type of discussion to which most New Testament scholars are accustomed in their task of interpreting the biblical texts. When considering the New Testament allusions to the salvific nature of Jesus' death, most biblical scholars and interpreters simply repeat the ideas handed down in traditional Christian teaching without ever analyzing carefully those ideas and asking whether they in fact represent the thought of the authors of the New Testament texts. This involves making a series of historical and theological assumptions that are rarely brought out into the open so that they may be scrutinized. Because those interpreters who make these assumptions claim to be presenting not their own thought but the thought of the authors of the New Testament writings, they inevitably attribute to the biblical writers the same assumptions in an uncritical manner.

It is precisely those hidden assumptions that I intend to articulate clearly and examine here.

THE THREE TYPES OF TRADITIONAL INTERPRETATIONS OF CHRIST'S DEATH

In spite of the extremely wide variety of interpretations given to passages such as those cited at the outset of this chapter, as well as the many doctrines or "theories" of atonement that have been put forward to explain the biblical teaching regarding the death of Christ, I would argue that all of the traditional understandings of Christ's work can be classified under three headings: satisfaction, physical, and revelational views or interpretations. However, because the only type of satisfaction view that is commonly attributed to the New Testament writers today is the penal substitution view, I will use this designation to refer to the first of these views. Corresponding to these three understandings of Christ's work are three types of changes that Christ's work is said to bring about in the condition of human beings: forensic, ontological, and ethical.

Satisfaction views of Christ's work became common as a result of the work of Anselm of Canterbury, who completed his influential book *Cur Deus Homo* (*Why God Became Man*) in 1098. According to Anselm, because God's justice made it impossible for God to forgive sins freely, either punishment or satisfaction for human sin was necessary in order for human beings to be saved. Through his passion and death, Christ offered God the satisfaction human beings needed in order to be spared punishment.[6]

Over the next several centuries, Anselm's interpretation of Christ's saving work was modified and eventually came to be replaced by a *penal substitution* interpretation. This was the interpretation adopted by most of the Protestant Reformers. While a penal substitution view also affirms that God's justice was satisfied by Christ's passion and death, it *equates* that satisfaction with the execution of the penalty to which human beings were subject, rather than seeing satisfaction and punishment as *alternatives* in the way that Anselm did. Perhaps the simplest way to explain the difference between the two ideas is to imagine a group of human beings who have incurred such an enormous debt that they have all been sentenced to the death penalty. According to Anselm's view, these human beings are delivered from their plight by someone who satisfies justice by paying that debt in their stead; once the debt is paid, they are no longer subject to any penalty. In contrast, according to a penal substitution view, justice is satisfied by an innocent person coming to endure in the place of those in debt the death penalty to which they were subject. Thus, whereas for Anselm Christ paid humanity's debt but did not endure humanity's penalty, for proponents of penal substitution views Christ satisfied the demands

---

6. For references and a summary of Anselm's argument in *Cur Deus Homo*, see Brondos, *Fortress Introduction*, 76-87.

of divine justice precisely by enduring the penalty to which all were liable on account of their sins.

In both cases, the result of Christ's work is a change in the *forensic* status of human beings. The plight of human beings is defined in terms of being *guilty of sin* before God or God's law. This makes them subject to divine punishment. Because Christ endured that punishment in their place, they are no longer subject to divine condemnation. Salvation is thus equated with the *remission of sins*. It is important to note that penal substitution views define the relation between sin and human condemnation as well as the relation between Christ's work and human salvation in *extrinsic* terms: in both cases, what is involved is a *divine decision or verdict*. The punishment and salvation of human beings does not follow as a *natural or intrinsic consequence* of their deeds. Rather, ultimately *God* determines personally whether each human being will be punished or saved in accordance with God's justice.

The term *physical* has been applied to the second kind of interpretation of Christ's work to be considered here because it revolves around a particular understanding of human *nature* (*physis* in Greek), as well as the nature of the created order in general. Both human nature and the world in general are viewed as having become subject to sin, which is understood as a *power* that must be overcome rather than as something that simply requires forgiveness. This power tends to be seen either as an impersonal force residing in human nature or else as a personal being such as the devil. In either case, the power may be regarded as exerting influence on human beings from *within* them or from *outside* of them. Other powers, such as corruptibility, death, and at times even God's law are also said to have established their dominion over all human beings as a result of their subjection to the power of sin. Because fallen human beings are incapable of saving themselves from these powers, Christ must save them by healing and transforming the nature in which he comes to share with them and with the created order by means of his incarnation. However, it is not only Christ's incarnation but also his life, death, and resurrection that are viewed as bringing about this healing and transformation of human nature and nature in general.

In contrast to a forensic view, here there is an *intrinsic* relation between sin and its consequences. The power of sin in human nature leads *in and of itself* to negative consequences such as corruptibility and death. These consequences are therefore due, not to any type of direct divine intervention or divine judgment, but to a natural cause-and-effect process.

According to a physical understanding of Christ's work, Christ's incarnation, death, and resurrection effect an *ontological* change in human beings, that is, a change in their *being*. Because it is God alone who effects this change by sending Christ into human nature, human beings are seen as initially playing only a *passive role* in the deliverance of their fallen nature from sin's power. Nevertheless, once that deliverance has taken place, it must still become a full reality in them by means of their faith.

The third understanding of Christ's saving work to be considered here defines it in terms of *revealing* to human beings what is necessary in order for them to be saved. This revelation may be directed at their *mind* or *understanding* as well as their *heart* or *will*. According to the first of these two ideas, Christ's life, death, and resurrection provide human beings with the *knowledge* they need to be saved. According to the second, the love of God manifested in these events *inspires* and *motivates* human beings to live differently. In both cases, as a result of the revelation they receive through Christ, they are brought to put away their sinful behavior and live in accordance with God's will. Because what God has done in Christ is salvific through the "moral influence" it exerts on human beings, that phrase is often used as a label for this type of view of Christ's work.

The change brought about in human beings according to a revelational understanding of Christ's work is therefore an *ethical* change. Whereas forensic views posit first and foremost a salvation from the *guilt* of sin and ontological views speak of a salvation from the *power* of sin, ethical views define salvation in terms of being delivered from sinful *behavior* and *actions* that are contrary to God's will. As their way of thinking is transformed by the revelation they receive through Christ and his life and death, believers are enabled to amend their conduct. In this case, human beings play an *active* role in the change that occurs in them by responding to what Christ has done. This difference sets this view apart from both the forensic and ontological views, where human beings receive passively the change in status or transformation of their being that is effected by Christ.

Both the *Christus Victor* idea and the participatory understandings of Christ's work inevitably take the form of one of the three views just mentioned. The *Christus Victor* idea can be understood in terms of Christ making *satisfaction* to the devil so that *forensically* human beings are no longer liable to sin and death, in terms of Christ defeating evil or the devil *physically* so that *ontologically* human beings are delivered from the powers of sin and death, or in terms of Christ *revealing* to human beings how they can overcome sin, death, and the devil by altering their behavior *ethically*. Similarly, participatory views of Christ's work define the notion of participation in *forensic*, *ontological*, or *ethical* terms, as we shall see below. This means that the *Christus Victor* and participatory interpretations of Christ's work are not *alternatives* to the three views already mentioned, as is often claimed, but are actually different forms or expressions of these same views.

Corresponding to the three distinct definitions of sin as guilt, as a power, and as conduct contrary to God's will are three distinct manners of understanding the nature of salvation. *Forensic* views tend to define salvation primarily in *other-worldly* terms: God's decision to remit sins enables believers to be received into God's presence in the life to come, even though to some extent they enjoy a reconciled relationship to God in this life as well. *Ontological* views speak of a process of transformation that begins in this life but is completed and perfected after death. *Ethical* views tend to see salvation as something that takes place primarily in the *present* world as people come to live and act differently, though that ethical change also constitutes the basis upon which they attain salvation in the afterlife or the world to come.

Although each understanding of Christ's work is associated with a different type of change in human beings or their situation, these different types of change may also be seen as resulting from something *other* than Christ's coming, life, death, and resurrection. In fact, virtually every Christian soteriology combines the three in some way. The *forensic standing* of human beings before God may be attributed to the ontological change that has taken place in them or to their new life of obedience rather than to what Christ did in his death: their sins are forgiven on account of the new nature they receive or the change in their conduct brought about by the revelation given to them. An *ontological* transformation may be seen as the result of something such as the work of the Holy Spirit or the reception of the sacraments rather than Christ's incarnation, life, death, and resurrection per se. The *ethical* change taking place in believers may be ascribed primarily, not to the revelation they have received, but to the change that Christ's death has brought about in their forensic standing before God or the ontological transformation that has taken place in them. It is also common to claim that those who have obtained forgiveness by means of Christ's death must nevertheless come to live a life of obedience to God in order to continue to receive the forgiveness of their sins. In this case, while initially the forensic status of believers depends on Christ's death, they can only retain that status by means of ethical behavior that is in accordance with God's will.

All of these views make any change in human beings or their condition dependent upon God's grace, yet in each view this grace is understood differently. This is true both with regard to the way Christ's work is understood and with regard to the way salvation is defined. A penal substitution view sees God's grace manifested in God's sending Christ to undergo the punishment for human sin in the stead of sinful human beings and on that basis delivering them from condemnation. According to a physical interpretation of Christ's work, God's grace takes the form of sending God's Son into the world so that the human nature in which all people share can be transformed by virtue of its union with the divine nature. A revelational view, of course, sees God's grace in terms of the revelation that God provides.

On this basis, according to a forensic view of salvation, God's grace is understood as a *favorable disposition* toward human beings. An ontological understanding of grace conceives of God's grace as a *power* transmitted to human beings in some way. This divine power, which is often identified with the Holy Spirit, transforms those who receive it. In an ethical view, grace is understood in terms of God's providing human beings with the *knowledge* or *inspiration* they need in order to amend their conduct.

In order to address the question of the extent to which these various views of Christ's work reflect faithfully New Testament thought, it is important to examine the premises, suppositions, and foundations on which each view rests. This analysis will provide us with the basis necessary to consider in Chapters 2–4 whether there is any evidence that the ideas that form the basis for each of these different views were in existence in the first century CE and therefore might have influenced the way in which Jesus' first followers came to understand the significance of his death.

PENAL SUBSTITUTION INTERPRETATIONS OF CHRIST'S WORK IN NEW TESTAMENT SCHOLARSHIP

From the time of the Protestant Reformation to the present, biblical scholars have commonly interpreted New Testament passages such as those cited at the outset of this chapter on the basis of the idea of penal substitution. In fact, this interpretation has become so firmly entrenched in biblical scholarship that even those who have expressed a strong aversion to the notion of penal substitution have felt compelled to recognize that it is indeed present in the New Testament writings, most notably those that bear Paul's name.[7]

Undoubtedly, it would be an oversimplification to affirm that biblical scholars who interpret the New Testament allusions to Christ's death on the basis of the idea of penal substitution agree fully as to precisely how penal substitution should be understood. Nevertheless, in spite of the differences among them with regard to certain details or the interpretation of particular passages, a number of basic ideas are commonly repeated by the majority of these scholars. Even when they do not mention many of these basic ideas explicitly, the reason for this seems to be that it has become so axiomatic that these ideas represent faithfully New Testament thought that those commenting on passages that allude to Christ's death generally see no need to offer any type of substantive argument in favor of the claim that these ideas are actually present in those passages.

The central tenet of penal substitution interpretations is that the penalty to which human beings were liable because of their sins was endured by Christ on the cross, with the result that human beings are no longer subject to that penalty. Thus, for example, Leon Morris, one of the most ardent defenders of this type of view, claims that in numerous passages Paul clearly teaches that "Christ has borne the penalty for our sins. And because he has borne the

---

7. The liberal Protestant theologian Hastings Rashdall, for example, strongly rejected the penal substitution view, yet felt compelled to admit: "It is impossible to get rid of this idea of substitution or vicarious punishment, from any faithful representation of Paul's doctrine" (*The Idea of Atonement in Christian Theology*; London: Macmillan, 1920, 92). Similarly, biblical scholars such as D. E. H. Whiteley and Sanders, who wish to replace a penal substitutionary interpretation of many Pauline passages with a participatory one, feel forced to acknowledge that the juristic idea is not totally absent from Paul's writings; according to Whiteley, in Paul's letters there are "passages in which the possibility of substitutionary thought cannot be excluded" (*The Theology of St. Paul*, rev. ed.; Oxford: Basil Blackwell, 1974, 130; see also Sanders, *Paul and Palestinian Judaism*, 500-503).

penalty we no longer face it. It is taken out of the way."[8] Similarly, George Eldon Ladd attributes to Paul the notion that "Christ suffered the penalty and judgment of God in the stead of the sinner by virtue of which the sinner will never experience that awful penalty.... God visited upon sin its just doom and penalty in him who is not only the sinner's representative but also his or her substitute, Jesus Christ."[9]

This same basic idea is expressed in terms of Christ having endured the *judgment* or *condemnation* that sinners deserved for their sin. For this reason, this understanding of Christ's work is often referred to as "juridical" or "juristic." New Testament scholars commonly ascribe to Paul, for example, ideas such as that "through his own death, [Christ] has taken the judgment of death and condemnation upon himself, thereby liberating humanity from this judgment," and that, "in so dying, Christ submitted to a judgment that God passed in Christ's death upon all humanity, all whom Christ represented."[10] For this reason, human beings "are no longer subject to the judgment he has borne for them."[11] At times, it is even affirmed that in Paul's thought the judgment Christ endured was the eschatological judgment: "the final judgment of God has become manifest in his death.... Christ's death was a demonstration of God's righteous judgment on the sin of the world.... In Christ's death God has sat in judgment, has judged sin, and in this way he has caused his eschatological judgment to be revealed in the present time."[12] "The crucifixion should therefore be understood as a prolepsis of the eschatological judgment of God. He delivered and condemned Christ, instead of the ungodly, instead of all."[13] While the verdict of condemnation was pronounced upon the innocent Christ, the verdict of acquittal was consequently pronounced upon human beings, who are therefore declared righteous or justified: "this acquittal, justification, which consists of the divine absolution of sin, has already been effected by the death of Christ and may be received by faith here and now."[14]

Paul's affirmation in Gal. 3:13 that "Christ redeemed us from the curse of the law by becoming a curse for us" has commonly been regarded as one of the clearest statements of the penal substitution idea in the New Testament. Ronald Fung claims that this verse "represents Christ's death as a vicarious

---

8. Leon Morris, *The Cross in the New Testament* (Grand Rapids: Eerdmans, 1965), 243.

9. George Eldon Ladd, *A Theology of the New Testament*, rev. ed. (Grand Rapids: Eerdmans, 1993), 468, 470.

10. Arland J. Hultgren, *Christ and his Benefits: Christology and Redemption in the New Testament* (Philadelphia: Fortress, 1987), 54; cf. 51; A. J. M. Wedderburn, "2 Corinthians 5:14—A Key to Paul's Soteriology?," in *Paul and the Corinthians: Studies on a Community in Conflict. Essays in Honour of Margaret Thrall* (ed. Trevor J. Burke and J. Keith Elliott; NovTSup 109; Leiden: Brill, 2003), 282.

11. Morris, *Cross*, 230.

12. Herman N. Ridderbos, *Paul: An Outline of his Theology*, trans. John Richard de Witt (Grand Rapids: Eerdmans, 1975), 167-68. Cf. Ben Witherington III, *Paul's Narrative Thought World: The Tapestry of Tragedy and Triumph* (Louisville, KY: Westminster John Knox, 1994), 259-60.

13. Cilliers Breytenbach, "The 'For Us' Phrases in Pauline Soteriology: Considering Their Background and Use," in *Salvation in the New Testament: Perspectives on Soteriology* (ed. Jan G. van der Watt; NovTSup 121; Leiden: Brill, 2005), 180.

14. Ladd, *Theology*, 484.

bearing of the curse of the law which delivers his people from the same curse."[15] According to Bradley McLean, "God transferred this curse from humanity to a substitutionary victim, Christ.... The curse borne by Christ (3.13) is the same curse previously borne by Christians before their baptism...."[16] Often this is understood in terms of a transaction between God and Christ: "Gal. 3.13 states that Christ offered his own life as payment for (in exchange for) the lives of Christians who were slaves to the law. This commercial metaphor explains how Christians are freed from the curse at the cost of Christ's life which was given in exchange."[17] The New Testament passages that speak of Christ bearing the sins of others (Heb. 9:28; 1 Pet. 2:24) have also generally been interpreted on the basis of these ideas. It is said that Christ assumed not only the *penalty* for human sin but human sin or guilt itself. This may be described either in terms of imputation, which involves the sin of others being reckoned or accounted to Christ, or in terms of some type of actual transmission or transfer of human sin from sinners onto Christ in his death, as if it constituted some type of concentrated substance.[18]

All of these ideas can be understood in two different ways. When the relationship between sin and death is regarded as *extrinsic*, death is seen as a punishment that God inflicts personally and directly on those who sin. According to a penal substitution interpretation, God elects to deliver sinful human beings from the punishment of death that their sins deserve by inflicting that punishment instead on the innocent Christ as their substitute. However, death can also be understood as an *intrinsic* consequence of sin. In this case, human sin leads to death naturally, independently of any personal and direct intervention by God. Undoubtedly, it can be argued that God originally played a role in establishing an intrinsic relationship between sin and death when God created the world in such a way that sin would lead naturally to death. However, when people now die as a result of their sin, God is not seen as intervening personally to bring about their death. The notion of *penalty* is usually understood in terms of an *extrinsic* relationship, whereas the word *consequence* is generally used to refer to an *intrinsic* relationship between a deed and its result. Human salvation can therefore be seen as resulting from Christ's substitutionary death either *extrinsically* or *intrinsically*.

This distinction becomes fundamental when Christ is said to have endured God's wrath in the place of sinful human beings. Generally, to speak of God's wrath is to refer to a personal trait of God, who responds to human sin by inflicting punishment directly on human beings or on Christ as their substitute. Among some New Testament scholars, however, it is common to see

---

15. Ronald Y. K. Fung, *The Epistle to the Galatians* (NICNT; Grand Rapids: Eerdmans, 1988), 150.

16. B. Hudson McLean, *The Cursed Christ: Mediterranean Expulsion Rituals and Pauline Soteriology* (JSNTSup 126; Sheffield: JSOT, 1996), 124-25.

17. Ibid., 131.

18. See, for example, Margaret E. Thrall, *A Critical and Exegetical Commentary on the Second Epistle to the Corinthians* (ICC; Edinburgh: T & T Clark, 1994), 1:444; J. Louis Martyn, *Galatians: A New Translation with Introduction and Commentary* (AB 33A; New York: Doubleday, 1997), 318; McLean, *Cursed Christ*, 205.

God's wrath in impersonal terms as a force that acts on its own through some type of cause-and-effect relationship. On that basis, it is commonly said that Christ's death "exhausted" God's wrath at sin. Death can also be understood as a "judgment" that is a natural consequence of sin, rather than a judgment dictated by God personally. Strictly speaking, such views do not understand Christ's death in terms of penal substitution. Rather, they must be classified as *physical* views of Christ's work, since they present Christ's death as effecting human salvation through the intrinsic and natural consequences that it has on human nature. These views will therefore be considered in the next section.

In reality, many proponents of penal substitution interpretations alternate between these two views. The reason for this is that when an *extrinsic* view between Christ's death and human salvation is maintained, God must be said to have poured out God's wrath *personally* on Christ and even to have condemned or cursed Christ. As feminist theologians have argued, such a view of Christ's death seems to portray God as a "divine child abuser" who inflicts punishment on Christ directly.[19] Many biblical scholars therefore prefer to speak of Christ enduring the punishment or curse dictated by God's *law* or God's *justice* rather than by God personally. Stephen Westerholm, for example, affirms that "Christ, in his crucifixion, was himself the object of the law's curse.... thereby he exhausted its force for those otherwise cursed who believe in him. (Indeed, the curse that the law pronounces on transgressors is hardly to be distinguished from the divine condemnation that looms over all who fall short of God's required righteousness—a condemnation that can also be said to have been absorbed by Christ's death.)."[20] According to Westerholm, Christ endured the judgment to which people of all times and places were subject, even those who lived in the centuries before Christ: "far from overlooking human wrongdoing, God had merely postponed its decisive condemnation until it could be channeled onto the crucified Christ rather than onto the wrongdoers themselves."[21] Here it is *God's law* that cursed Christ, with the result that its "force" was "exhausted" when Christ "absorbed" its condemnation in his death; the condemnation to which wrongdoers were subject was "channeled" onto Christ when he died. These terms all imply natural "cause-and-effect" processes in which God does not seem to intervene personally.

While affirmations such as these apparently make it possible for proponents of penal substitution views to avoid portraying God as a violent parent or harsh judge whose wrath at human sin is placated only when God has poured out that wrath on God's innocent Son, they raise a different problem: God's law and God's justice are conceived of as personal agents, as if they had a mind and a will of their own and acted independently of God. This

---

19. See Joanne Carlson Brown and Rebecca Parker, "For God So Loved the World?," in *Christianity, Patriarchy, and Abuse: A Feminist Critique* (ed. Carlson Brown and Carole R. Bohn; New York: Pilgrim, 1989), 23.
20. Stephen Westerholm, *Perspectives Old and New on Paul: The "Lutheran" Paul and his Critics* (Grand Rapids: Eerdmans, 2004), 376.
21. Ibid., 284.

makes the relationship between Christ's death and salvation an intrinsic one and removes God from the equation. For this reason, proponents of penal substitution views tend to jump back and forth between the extrinsic and intrinsic understandings of Christ's death, seeking to avoid presenting God as the one who personally cursed and condemned Christ while at the same time attempting to avoid the notion that God's law and God's justice law function on their own, independently of God.

Nevertheless, since the biblical writings frequently speak of God's wrath at human sin, many biblical scholars insist that one must not shy away from affirming that God poured out God's righteous wrath at sin on Christ in the place of sinners, no matter how objectionable that affirmation may sound. For these scholars, to deny this idea is to deny a clear teaching of the New Testament. Ladd, for example, insists: "In his identification with sinful humankind, [Christ] is the object of the holy wrath of God against sin, and in Gethsemane as the hour of the passion approaches the full horror of that wrath is disclosed…. We may therefore conclude, even though the Scriptures nowhere use this terminology, that Christ in his death in a real sense of the word experienced the wrath of God in the place of the guilty sinner."[22] Similarly, Ben Witherington III claims that in Paul's thought "God's anger is a righteous indignation against sin" in order to claim: "This wrath is poured out on Christ in the place of sinners."[23] In his death, Christ placated God's wrath: "the cross was the place where God expressed divine wrath against sin and was propitiated."[24] According to Witherington, this idea derives from Jesus himself: "Jesus saw his task in life to come and die, enduring God's overwhelming wrath."[25] It is also common among biblical scholars to speak of God's righteous wrath in terms of God's enmity or hostility toward sin or sinners, which is said to have come to an end when Christ endured it on the cross.[26]

According to penal substitution views, by delivering human beings from the penalty, condemnation, or curse to which they were previously subject, Christ has reconciled them to God, since God no longer holds anything against them.[27] Those who come to faith are also justified or acquitted on the basis of Christ's death in the sense that God declares them righteous.

---

22. Ladd, *Theology*, 191, 473. See also Simon J. Gathercole, who argues extensively for this idea ("Justified by Faith, Justified by his Blood: The Evidence of Romans 3:21—4:25," in *Justification and Variegated Nomism*, Vol. 2: *The Paradoxes of Paul*; ed. D. A. Carson, Peter T. O'Brien, and Mark A. Seifrid; WUNT 2/181; Tübingen: Mohr Siebeck, 2004, 169-81).

23. Witherington, *Paul's Narrative*, 161. See also Frank J. Matera, *II Corinthians: A Commentary* (NTL; Louisville, KY: Westminster John Knox, 2003), 141-44; Gathercole, "Justified," 168-81.

24. Witherington, *Paul's Narrative*, 164.

25. Ben Witherington III, *The Christology of Jesus* (Minneapolis: Fortress, 1990), 124.

26. See, for example, Morris, *Cross*, 250, 405, 415; Werner G. Kümmel, *The Theology of the New Testament according to its Major Witnesses: Jesus–Paul–John*, trans. John E. Steely (London: SCM, 1974), 204.

27. Simon Gathercole, for example, claims that in the New Testament, and particularly Paul's epistles, "there is actually very good evidence for seeing substitutionary atonement as intrinsic to the biblical presentation of how God has reconciled the world to himself in Christ" (*Defending Substitution: An Essay on Atonement in Paul*; ASBT; Grand Rapids: Baker Academic, 2015, 28).

Nevertheless, this righteousness involves a *forensic status* before God rather than any type of actual or ethical righteousness on the part of believers.

Although views of Christ's work that are based on the notion of participation are often regarded as representing an alternative to penal substitution or juridical views, in reality participation in Christ and his death can also be understood forensically. In this case, all are said to have participated in Christ's death or to have died with Christ in the sense that "all are, juridically, regarded by God as having died. This would mean that, whilst Christ alone in actuality suffered the penalty for sin, all are regarded *as though* they had suffered it themselves."[28] C. E. B. Cranfield interprets Romans 6 in the sense that believers "died with Christ in God's decision" or "in God's sight."[29] "God's decision to take our sins upon himself in the person of his dear Son was tantamount to a decision to see us as having died in Christ's death."[30] According to a purely forensic understanding of participation, believers do not die with Christ in a real, ontological sense, nor do they simply identify ethically with his death. Rather, they are merely viewed by God *as if* they had undergone the penalty of death they deserved, even though in actuality they have *not* done so.

A number of German scholars have attempted to bring the ideas of substitution and participation together by speaking of two types of *Stellvertretung*, which can roughly be translated "place-taking": an "exclusive" place-taking (*excludierende* or *ausschließende Stellvertretung*) and an "inclusive" place-taking (*inkludierende* or *einschließende Stellvertretung*).[31] According to this latter idea, Christ and sinners become one so that the death of Christ is the death of the sinner as well. The notion of penal substitution, however, corresponds more closely to the "exclusive" place-taking, since in his death Christ is said to occupy "exclusively" a place that sinful human beings do *not* occupy together with him.

The *Christus Victor* idea, which like the participatory interpretations of Christ's death is often seen as an alternative to penal substitution views, also exists in a forensic form. It is said that, when human beings sinned, the devil acquired juridical or legal *rights* over them. In this way, humanity fell under the devil's power and became subject to death. The devil lost his rights over human beings, however, when he took Christ's life. According to one version of the forensic *Christus Victor* idea, the devil acted unjustly by having the

---

28. Thrall, *Second Corinthians*, 1:410, referring to the teaching of Hans Lietzmann and F. F. Bruce. Douglas J. Moo speaks explicitly of a "forensic" union with Christ and rejects the notion that Paul understood this union ontologically (*The Epistle to the Romans*; NICNT; Grand Rapids: Eerdmans, 1996, 395). See also Ladd, *Theology*, 468-69; A. J. M. Wedderburn, *Baptism and Resurrection: Studies in Pauline Theology against its Graeco-Roman Background* (WUNT 44; Tübingen: J. C. B. Mohr, 1987), 351.

29. C. E. B. Cranfield, *A Critical and Exegetical Commentary on the Epistle to the Romans*, 6th ed. (ICC; Edinburgh: T & T Clark, 1975), 1:311.

30. Ibid., 1:316.

31. See Otfried Hofius, *Paulusstudien* (WUNT 51; Tübingen: J. C. B. Mohr, 1989), 33-49. Hofius credits Harmut Gese for this distinction. For an English summary of this distinction and references from the works of German scholars, see Daniel P. Bailey, "Concepts of *Stellvertretung* in the Interpretation of Isaiah 53," in *Jesus and the Suffering Servant: Isaiah 53 and Christian Origins* (ed. William H. Bellinger Jr. and William R. Farmer; Harrisburg, PA: Trinity Press International, 1998), 236-50.

innocent Christ put to death, and therefore God was no longer under any obligation to respect the devil's rights over human beings.[32] According to a second version, however, either God or Christ himself offered Christ's life to the devil as a ransom payment in exchange for the release of the human beings under the devil's power. When the devil accepted the ransom payment, he ceded his rights over human beings, but subsequently the devil lost all when Christ rose from the dead by virtue of his divine power.[33] In both cases, if the "penalty" to which human beings were legally subjected on account of their sin is defined in terms of coming under the power of death and the devil, then by enduring this same penalty as their substitute, Christ has freed human beings from this penalty.

Few biblical scholars today would claim that this forensic *Christus Victor* understanding of Christ's work is present in the New Testament. Nevertheless, as mentioned above, it is common for scholars to affirm that God's *law* obtained rights over human beings when they fell into sin. Often it is argued that Paul conceived of the law as a personified power. According to this idea, once the law unjustly condemned Christ to death, it lost its right to condemn sinful human beings. In this way, they are delivered from the law's condemnation. Because this law is said to have been given by God, such an understanding of Christ's work is not an *alternative* to the penal substitution view but another *expression* of it: as *Christus Victor*, Christ overcomes the power of God's law to condemn sinful human beings by taking that condemnation upon himself as their substitute, thereby making the law forfeit the rights it had over them.[34]

Proponents of penal substitution interpretations often use language that is more frequently associated with other views of Christ's work, yet they nevertheless understand that language differently. They may speak of a "new humanity," yet by this they mean not some type of ontologically-transformed human nature but a humanity that is no longer under the penalty of death. Paul's allusion to a "new creation" can also be taken to refer to the new forensic standing that belongs to believers, who are now free from the penalty of death thanks to Christ. Some scholars also attribute to Paul the idea that Christ's death brought about the "turn of the ages" or "ushered in a new age," which has now "dawned," yet this language can likewise be seen as referring simply to a new situation in which human beings are no longer under the condemnation dictated by God's law.[35]

The affirmation that those who have been freed from the punishment due to their sins on account of Christ's substitutionary death is also commonly combined with the claim that they have been freed from the *power* of

---

32. See Aulén, *Christus Victor*, 50–51.
33. See ibid., 49, 52–53.
34. See, for example, Hultgren, *Christ*, 98: "The law can no longer accuse, for trespasses brought to light by the law have been given their due in the atoning death of Jesus."
35. See, for example, Hultgren, *Christ*, 54; Witherington, *Paul's Narrative*, 143, 149; Ralph P. Martin, *Reconciliation: A Study of Paul's Theology* (NFTL; Atlanta: John Knox, 1981), 103.

sin. Ladd, for example, writes: "By the death of Christ the believer finds not only an objective atonement for sin; she or he finds also deliverance from the power of sin and the domination and bondage of the Law and of the world."[36] Similarly, Gordon Fee claims that for Paul the death of Christ "for our sins" (1 Cor. 15:3) "almost certainly includes not only forgiveness of past sins, but in a very real sense deliverance from the bondage of one's sinfulness as well."[37] In this case, however, the power of sin is understood as the burden of bearing divine condemnation for one's sins. The knowledge that one is under God's judgment supposedly drives one to despair of one's salvation and to fall more deeply into sin. However, once a person has attained assurance of forgiveness and salvation, that person no longer feels burdened by sin, fear, and guilt and becomes free to live differently.

Penal substitution views also exist in what can be labeled a "historicized" form. Since the time of Albert Schweitzer, a number of biblical scholars (including especially Dale Allison, N. T. Wright, and Brant Pitre) have affirmed that Jesus understood his death in terms of enduring the so-called messianic woes or messianic tribulation in the place of his disciples.[38] In Wright's thought, the traditional notion of divine punishment is replaced with that of *exile*. This represents a historicized understanding of the plight of sinful human beings: "Forgiveness of sins is another way of saying return from exile," which was viewed by the prophets of Israel "precisely as the result of, or the punishment for, her sins." Thus, if "Israel were to be brought back from exile, this would mean that her sins were being punished no more; in other words, forgiven."[39]

According to Wright, Jesus delivered others from the punishment coming upon them by going to Jerusalem in order to undergo that punishment himself on the cross: "Jesus was now going ahead of the nation to undergo the punishment which above all symbolized the judgment of Rome on her rebel subjects.... Jesus believed he would suffer the fate that was hanging over Jerusalem; indeed, he desired to take it upon himself so that she might avoid it."[40] This involved enduring God's wrath in the place of others in a historical sense: "Jesus therefore not only took upon himself the 'wrath' (which, as usual in Jewish thought, refers to hostile military action) which was coming upon Israel because she had compromised with paganism and was suffering exile. He also took upon himself the 'wrath' which was coming upon Israel because she had refused his way of peace."[41] Wright readily affirms his agreement with

---

36. Ladd, *Theology*, 470.

37. Gordon D. Fee, "Toward a Theology of 1 Corinthians," in *Pauline Theology*, Vol. 2: *1 and 2 Corinthians* (ed. David M. Hay; Minneapolis: Fortress, 1993), 49. See also Morris, *Cross*, 299, 301.

38. For a summary of the views of Schweitzer and other biblical scholars on this subject, see Brant Pitre, *Jesus, the Tribulation, and the End of the Exile: Restoration Eschatology and the Origin of the Atonement* (WUNT 2/204; Tübingen: Mohr Siebeck, 2005), 8-23.

39. N. T. Wright, *Jesus and the Victory of God*, Vol. 2 of *Christian Origins and the Question of God* (Minneapolis: Fortress, 1996), 268 (emphasis removed).

40. Ibid., 570-71.

41. Ibid., 596 (emphasis removed).

Schweitzer on these points: "Schweitzer was right: Jesus believed that the messianic woes were about to burst upon Israel, and that he had to take them upon himself, solo."[42]

Elsewhere, Wright argues that Paul later developed these same ideas further. According to Wright, in his letter to the Romans, Paul affirms that Christ's death had delivered not only Israel but humanity as a whole from divine punishment:

> The *katakrima* [condemnation] which hung over the head of Adamic humanity (5.16) has been meted out on the real culprit, namely, sin (7.17, 20). It is therefore true to Paul to speak of the punishment which all have deserved being enacted, instead, on the cross.... [Paul] is careful to say that on the cross God punished (not Jesus, but) sin.... [T]he death of Jesus can be interpreted in this way because he represents Israel and Israel represents humankind as a whole.[43]

For Paul, "Christ, as the representative Messiah, has achieved a specific task, that of taking on himself the curse which hung over Israel.... [T]he Messiah, as Israel's representative, allows the full weight of [sin] to fall on himself."[44]

Of course, scholars who defend the claim that the notion of penal substitution is behind much of the New Testament's language regarding Jesus' death must explain how this idea came to be characteristic of the thought of Paul and the other New Testament writers. To do this, such scholars have looked not only to passages from the Hebrew Scriptures but also to Jewish and Hellenistic writings of the second-temple period in order to argue that the basis for the notion of penal substitution is found there. Among the most important of these passages are Isaiah 53 and the accounts of the deaths of the Maccabean martyrs in 2 and 4 Maccabees, which are thought to affirm the atoning efficacy of the death of a righteous person on behalf of others. Many scholars claim that this same idea is present in the rabbinic writings as well. Proponents of penal substitution views also generally claim that in ancient Jewish thought, when those who had sinned presented animal victims as a sacrifice for their sins, those animal victims were enduring the punishment or penalty that the sinners deserved in their place, thereby liberating sinners from that punishment or penalty.

Theological Problems and Presuppositions

Penal substitution interpretations of Christ's work are based on a number of theological and philosophical premises, some of which are highly problematic

---

42. Ibid., 609.
43. N. T. Wright, *The Climax of the Covenant: Christ and the Law in Pauline Theology* (Edinburgh: T & T Clark, 1991), 213. Here Wright is commenting on Rom. 8:3. It is not entirely clear how Wright can claim that, on the cross, God was punishing sin rather than Jesus, since all of the suffering there was endured by Jesus rather than by sin independently of Jesus.
44. Wright, *Climax*, 151-52. Because the difficulties raised by this "historicized" version of the penal substitution view are of a somewhat different nature than those associated with the more traditional interpretations of Jesus' death as substitutionary, I will analyze it further in Chapter 5 rather than in the present chapter.

from a theological standpoint. For this reason, to ascribe such ideas to Paul and other authors of the New Testament writings necessarily involves ascribing to them these theological and philosophical premises as well as the theological problems associated with them. Furthermore, if Paul and the other New Testament writers interpreted Jesus' death on the basis of ideas taken from Jewish or Hellenistic sources, then some of the same basic premises must be found there as well. All of this makes it important to look closely at these premises in order to analyze the theological and historical problems each one raises.

Premise 1: God's justice must be satisfied before God can remit sins.

This is the most fundamental premise inherent to penal substitution views of Christ's work. It was central to the argument of Anselm, who claimed that it would be a mockery of God's justice for God to show mercy and freely forgive sin without demanding either punishment or satisfaction: "for this kind of divine mercy is utterly contrary to God's justice, which allows only for punishment to be requited for sin. Therefore, as it is impossible for God to be at odds with himself, so it is impossible for him to be merciful in this way."[45]

This same claim that free forgiveness of sin is impossible for God because it conflicts with God's justice and God's holy nature is found in the writings of biblical scholars who advocate penal substitution views. Cranfield, for example, argues that "for God simply to pass over sins would be altogether incompatible with his righteousness. He would not be the good and merciful God had he been content to pass over sins indefinitely; for this would have been to condone evil—a denial of his own nature and a cruel betrayal of sinners."[46] Similarly, Simon Gathercole finds in Rom. 3:21-26 the idea of "God's infallible punishment of sin.... [I]t is a Pauline presupposition that sin(s) must be punished."[47] According to I. H. Marshall, "Somehow God has to act in such a way that his justice is upheld (Rom. 3:26). This is achieved by Christ's death which enables God to pardon sinners while upholding justice."[48] Christ "has done representatively what was needed for sinful humanity so as to uphold the holiness and righteousness of God."[49] Ladd attributes to Paul the idea that "it is an ethical and religious necessity that the holiness of God manifest itself in wrath against sin."[50]

---

45. Anselm, *Cur Deus Homo* 1.24. Quotations taken from Vol. 3 of *Anselm of Canterbury* (trans. and ed. Jasper Hopkins and Herbert Richardson; Toronto: Edwin Mellen, 1976).
46. Cranfield, *Romans*, 1:211-12 (emphasis removed).
47. Gathercole, "Justified," 168-69. For similar affirmations, see Heikki Räisänen, *Paul and the Law*, 2nd ed. (WUNT 29; Tübingen: J. C. B. Mohr, 1987), 60, referring to the thought of Peter Bläser and Albrecht Oepke; Ladd, *Theology*, 472-73; Peter Stuhlmacher, *Reconciliation, Law, and Righteousness: Essays in Biblical Theology*, trans. Everett R. Kalin (Philadelphia: Fortress, 1986), 55; Westerholm, *Perspectives*, 278.
48. I. Howard Marshall, *Aspects of the Atonement: Cross and Resurrection in the Reconciling of God and Humanity* (London: Paternoster, 2007), 38.
49. Ibid., 97.
50. Ladd, *Theology*, 495.

This premise is indispensable to penal substitution views. If God *could* forgive sins freely, then it would not have been necessary for God to send God's Son into the world to die, and Christ's death would then have had no real salvific purpose. Nevertheless, the idea that God could not forgive sins without Christ's death is problematic in that it makes God subject to a certain understanding of God's law, God's nature, or God's justice, so that God is *under obligation* to act in a certain way in relation to sin. In other words, there is something that by nature is *impossible* for God to do, namely, overlook sin without punishing it. Naturally, scholars defending penal substitution views deny that any problem exists in this regard. Morris, for example, affirms that "the eternal law of righteousness cannot be allowed to suffer disrepute" and speaks of "the inflexible law which is at the very basis of the being of God,"[51] yet insists: "It is an error to think of law as something set over God and to which he is in subjection. But, since law 'is in harmony with his very being' he will act in harmony with the highest law."[52] Such an affirmation hardly resolves the problem, however. Even if this law is said to be that of God's very being, it is still something to which God must be subject and which God is obliged to obey.

Penal substitution views of Christ's work imply that God's law must remain inviolate for *God's* sake: God must punish sin to respond to an *inner need* on God's part. If God did not satisfy the "law of his very being," God would cease not only to be holy and righteous but to be God. Often, however, it is argued instead that God cannot let sins remain unpunished *for the sake of human beings*. This was Anselm's argument: if God did not punish sins, then the order and beauty of the universe would be disturbed, since human beings would commit all kinds of injustice, knowing that they would not be punished.[53] Biblical scholars make the same claim today. Commenting on Rom. 3:25-26, C. K. Barrett writes: "Because of the past God must now vindicate his righteousness, which otherwise would be impugned. Men might say, God does not care about sin; anyone may sin as much as he pleases and get away with it."[54] Similarly, commenting on the same passage, Cranfield affirms: "For God to have forgiven men's sins lightly—a cheap forgiveness which would have implied that moral evil does not matter very much—would have been altogether unrighteous, a violation of his truth and profoundly unmerciful and unloving toward men, since it would have annihilated their dignity as persons morally accountable."[55] According to Stephen Travis, "God's patient holding back of his wrath might have been interpreted to mean that he was indifferent to human sins—which would be a denial of his own nature."[56]

---

51. Leon Morris, *The Apostolic Preaching of the Cross*, 3rd ed. (Grand Rapids: Eerdmans, 1965), 279, 295-96.
52. Morris, *Cross*, 383, n48 (reacting to a quote from Albrecht Ritschl).
53. Anselm, *Cur Deus Homo* 1.12, 15.
54. C. K. Barrett, *Paul: An Introduction to his Thought* (Louisville, KY: Westminster John Knox, 1994), 101.
55. Cranfield, *Romans*, 1:213-14. For similar affirmations, see G. B. Caird, *New Testament Theology* (ed. and comp. L. D. Hurst; New York: Oxford University Press, 1994), 146; Ladd, *Theology*, 473.
56. Stephen H. Travis, "Christ as Bearer of Divine Judgment in Paul's Thought about the Atonement," in *Jesus of Nazareth: Lord and Christ. Essays on the Historical Jesus and New Testament Christology* (ed. Joel B. Green and Max Turner; Grand Rapids: Eerdmans, 1994), 339.

According to scholars such as these, God cannot let sin go unpunished *for the good of human beings themselves*, since to forgive sins freely would involve giving human beings a license to sin. This idea, however, is problematic on a couple of accounts. First, it implies that God's ultimate aim in demanding that human beings avoid sin and threatening them with punishment if they disobey is that justice and well-being may prevail among them. In this case, God must punish sin in order to dissuade or prevent human beings from practicing it. Experience would indicate, however, that under certain circumstances one may let sin or wrongdoing go unpunished and still accomplish that objective. For example, a judge may decide to suspend or revoke the sentence that has been imposed on a person guilty of a misdemeanor if the judge is convinced that the person is sufficiently remorseful of his or her action and is unlikely to violate the law again in the future. This is not considered unjust on the part of the judge, since the objective is not to satisfy the demands of the law, but to do what contributes most to the good of society, as well as the good of offenders themselves and others affected by the judge's decision.

For the same reasons, if God's true concern in punishing sin were human well-being, then there are circumstances under which God might leave sin *un*punished. By refusing to allow for this possibility, however, and instead insisting that God *must* punish sin because by nature God *cannot* forgive freely, biblical scholars who defend the notion of penal substitution in effect maintain that God's ultimate concern is not for human beings but for God's own nature. The absolute need for punishment is therefore due to the impossibility that God might act contrary to God's perfectly holy and righteous nature and not to a concern on God's part that failing to punish sin might result in human beings taking sin lightly. This means that ultimately God must punish sin and satisfy the demands of God's nature, not for the sake of human beings, but *for God's own sake*.

A second problem, however, is that if Christ is said to have endured the punishment of all human beings collectively in their place, with the result that they are no longer under threat of punishment or condemnation, then God ends up doing precisely what God wanted to avoid in the first place: sinners can sin freely and practice all the injustice they want because they know that they will not be punished now that Christ has undergone their punishment in their place. In this case, thanks to Christ's substitutionary death, they *can* now say confidently, "God no longer cares about sin; anyone may sin as much as he pleases and get away with it," to use Barrett's words.

To argue on the contrary that those who have been saved must still practice obedience to God if they want to avoid divine punishment would require denying that Christ endured in their place the punishment for *all* of their sins. This involves what is often called "double justification": whereas the initial forgiveness believers receive depends on Christ's death, any subsequent forgiveness depends on their ethical behavior. This idea is clearly implied in Morris's affirmation: "There is a divine wrath against every evil thing and when that has been put away by what Christ did we must have a due horror of arousing it again."[57] Here it is clear that, if one can "arouse" God's wrath again, it has *not* been put away definitively by Christ's death; believers must still live obediently in order to remain free of that wrath. This contradicts Morris's claim that "Christ has really put our sins out of the way, effectively and finally,"[58] since ultimately one's forgiveness and salvation depend, not on what Christ accomplished in death, but on the way in which those saved continue to live after they have initially been delivered from God's wrath.

Clearly, then, penal substitution views see God's ultimate objective in sending Christ to die not as that of reforming sinners, promoting justice in the world, or preserving "the beauty and order of the universe," but satisfying a necessity found in God's nature, which prevents God from tolerating sin. As F. F. Bruce comments with regard to Heb. 9:24: "If sinners are to appear before God, even by proxy, through the representation of a sinless high priest, they must be cleansed from sin, or else the very presence of God would be polluted."[59] The purpose of Christ's death is to safeguard God's perfect holiness and justice by keeping all sin and impurity out of God's presence while still allowing God to save human beings from the punishment they deserve for their sins.

According to penal substitution views, the type of justice to which Christ's substitutionary death responds is not *restorative* justice or *distributive* justice, which are aimed at healing and equity, but *retributive* or *punitive* justice, which demands retribution for wrongs committed in the past. In this case, God's justice is satisfied through Christ's death, not because his death brings about some desired change in the condition of human beings directly, but because it satisfies God's just demand that sin receive its proper retribution. Undoubtedly, a change in the human condition results from Christ's death, in that believers are now forgiven whereas previously they were not, but this change is *indirect* rather than *direct*: Christ's death effects a change *in God*, transforming a God who could *not* forgive sins into one who *can*. The change in the human condition is the result of this prior change in God.

Premise 2: Christ's death was absolutely necessary for human salvation, since nothing else could have made it possible for God to remit the sins of human beings without compromising God's justice.

This premise follows from the previous one. Biblical scholars defending penal substitution views must insist that, outside of sending Christ to die, there was *no other way* for God to be able to save sinners from the punishment due to them for their sins. Ladd, for example, commenting on Rom. 3:26, writes: "If there had been no death of Christ, God would have been *unable* to justify the sinner."[60] Peter Stuhlmacher finds the same idea in texts such as Mark

---

57. Leon Morris, *The Atonement: Its Meaning and Significance* (Downers Grove, IL: Inter-Varsity, 1983), 204.
58. Morris, *Cross*, 6.
59. F. F. Bruce, *The Epistle to the Hebrews*, rev. ed. (NICNT; Grand Rapids: Eerdmans, 1990), 230.
60. Ladd, *Theology*, 473 (emphasis added).

10:45 and 14:24: "The sin offering of the sinless one, desired by God—the vicarious sacrifice of Jesus' life—made it *possible* for God the judge to acquit sinners and give them life without any lessening of his no to sin."[61] To say that without Christ's death God would have been *unable* to justify sinners or that Christ's self-offering made it *possible* for God to acquit sinners is to say that it would have been *impossible* for God to do these things without Christ's death. Morris in particular stresses this point: "If God simply forgives, then nothing more is needed. The cross is not needed. The cross is no more than a piece of useless embroidery. The cross is emptied of its meaning.... If his death did nothing to bring about our forgiveness, then exactly why did Christ die?"[62]

The problem with Morris's logic here, of course, is that it involves assuming precisely what needs to be demonstrated, namely, that God would not have sent God's Son to die such a cruel and horrible death had it not been absolutely necessary for human salvation. In reality, this is the starting-point from which penal substitution views develop their arguments, rather than the previous premise that God's justice must be satisfied before God can remit sins; this latter premise is maintained only so that Christ's death can be spoken of as indispensable for human beings to be forgiven and saved. The ultimate concern, however, is to uphold the notion that Jesus' death was an act of immense love on the part of both God and Jesus himself, as Paul and the other New Testament writers repeatedly affirm. Witherington explains the idea thus: "If Jesus' death was optional, not absolutely necessary for the salvation of the world, it is hard to see how anyone could view God as a truly loving God. No parent who loved an only child would send him to die such a hideous death unless it was absolutely necessary and the situation demanded it. Yet Paul tells us that God did this as an act of love and mercy."[63]

Premise 3: What Christ suffered in his passion and death was sufficient to satisfy God's justice.

In order to maintain that it was necessary for Christ to die in order for God to remit sins justly, it must be shown that his death was sufficient to satisfy the penalty or consequences that God's law dictated upon those to be saved. This affirmation is often made explicitly by New Testament scholars. According to Eduard Schweizer, when Paul alludes to Christ's death in Colossians, he affirms the "sole and full sufficiency of Christ."[64] Similarly, George Buchanan attributes to Paul the idea that "[i]n his record system God valued Christ's death as sufficient credit to balance the books...."[65]

---

61. Stuhlmacher, *Reconciliation*, 55 (emphasis added).
62. Morris, *Cross*, 369, 371.
63. Witherington, *Paul's Narrative*, 160.
64. Eduard Schweizer, *The Letter to the Colossians: A Commentary*, trans. Andrew Chester (Minneapolis: Augsburg, 1982), 257.
65. George W. Buchanan, "The Day of Atonement and Paul's Doctrine of Redemption," *NovT* 32 (1990): 244. See also F. F. Bruce, *The Epistles of John: Introduction, Exposition, and Notes* (Grand Rapids: Eerdmans, 1979), 50; Witherington, *Paul's Narrative*, 165.

The claim that Jesus' death was sufficient to satisfy the demands of God's justice requires that one posit some type of equivalency between what Christ endured in his death and the penalty or consequences to which sinful humanity was subject. Some criterion must be established in order to distinguish what is *sufficient* from what would have been *insufficient* and then, on that basis, Christ's death must be quantified in some way so as to maintain that it fulfilled the criterion of sufficiency.[66]

It is rather rare for biblical scholars to discuss this question, primarily because it is not addressed anywhere in the New Testament. Nevertheless, like the first two premises just mentioned, this premise is indispensable in order to sustain that God's justice was satisfied by Christ's substitutionary death: if what Christ suffered was not equivalent to what human beings collectively were condemned to suffer because of their sins, then Christ's death cannot be considered sufficient for them to be saved. Those New Testament scholars who do deal with the question tend merely to assume this equivalence without presenting any type of evidence from Scripture in support of their assumption, so that once again we are dealing with a presupposition rather than a biblically-grounded argument.

Virtually all proponents of the penal substitution interpretation of the New Testament writings identify the penalty endured by Christ in the stead of others as death itself. Serious problems arise, however, when one attempts to equate what Christ endured with what human beings supposedly were condemned to endure on account of their sins. Morris, for example, states that "the death of the One took the place of the death of the many.... Christ died the death that sinners should have died."[67]

Yet what does this death involve? And how is it equivalent to the death that human beings were condemned to suffer? If the penalty is identified with physical death, Christ can hardly be said to have endured that penalty on the cross in the place of others, since all people continue to die physically. Traditionally, the penalty to which human beings are said to be subject on account of their sins is eternal death and damnation. Yet it can hardly be sustained that Christ endured this in the stead of sinners, since he did not become subject to eternal damnation. Although the suffering he endured in his passion and death was undoubtedly immense, it was not eternal, but lasted only for several hours. The New Testament does speak of Christ descending to hell after dying, yet it does not say that he suffered there. Furthermore, if the necessity were that Christ experience the torments of hell, then he would not have needed to die on a cross. Rather, the suffering that would be redemptive would be that which he endured *after* he had died and descended into hell rather than that which he endured while hanging on the cross.[68]

---

66. See, for example, Ben Witherington III, "The Death of Sin in the Death of Jesus: Atonement Theology in the NT," *WeslTJ* 50 (2015): 11, 13.

67. Morris, *Cross*, 220–21.

68. Gathercole misses entirely the point from my book on Paul when he argues that, in Paul's thought, the death from which Christ saves others by dying as their substitute is distinct from the one which all people

The problem of equivalency also arises when it is claimed that the penalty Christ endured was sufficient to deliver billions of human beings from the penalty to which they were subject. According to what understanding of justice can the death of one innocent person be regarded as equivalent to the death of countless individuals of all times and places?

In an attempt to resolve this problem, proponents of penal substitution views usually understand the penalty endured by Christ in terms of some type of *spiritual experience* of death. Morris, for example, quotes Goguel's affirmation that "the sense of being abandoned by God must have caused unfathomable pain to him" in order to claim:

> The death that Jesus died was full of horror.... It is the terrible nature of the death that he died that is significant, and not merely the fact that he did die.... [The incarnation] means among other things that it became possible for Christ to die... the most bitter of deaths, the death of God-forsakenness.... Jesus Christ, perfect man, has drunk to the very dregs the cup of our sins. He has endured their consequences to the uttermost extent. So fully did he make himself one with sinful man that he entered into the God-forsakenness that is the lot of sinners. He died their death.[69]

This kind of affirmation, however, is extremely problematic. The New Testament undoubtedly speaks of believers being "dead in trespasses and sins" (Eph. 2:1), and this may perhaps be referred to as a spiritual death. In reality, however, to speak of death in this way is to describe metaphorically the life of sinful human beings who have distanced themselves from God in *this* world, very few of whom in fact endure some type of ongoing hellish experience of God-forsakenness while on earth. Although it might be argued that this condition of separation from God becomes eternal if one dies in it, once again it cannot be said that Christ suffered this condition eternally in the place of others. Furthermore, if the necessity was that Christ endure this *spiritual* death in intense fashion, it is not clear why he also had to endure the *physical* death that

---

experience at the end of their lives (*Defending Substitution*, 80, n1; see David A. Brondos, *Paul on the Cross: Reconstructing the Apostle's Story of Redemption*; Minneapolis: Fortress, 2006, 108-9). Gathercole distinguishes between physical death, which he calls "death #1," metaphorical death, which he labels "death #2," and a third type of death ("death #3") to which Paul refers in passages such as Rom. 1:32, 6:23, 8:13, and 2 Cor. 2:16, among others. According to Gathercole, in these passages, "Paul does not mean 'die' in the everyday sense; he means something like 'suffer the divinely ordained penalty for sin'" or "perish" (*apollumi*; *Defending Substitution*, 80-82). While Gathercole—perhaps deliberately—does not state explicitly what "the divinely ordained penalty for sin" consists of, there can be no doubt that he has in mind eternal condemnation or damnation. However, because Christ did *not* undergo eternal condemnation or damnation during or after his crucifixion, Gathercole finds it impossible to affirm that Christ endured *that* death—eternal condemnation—in our place. Therefore, he is limited to stating that Christ died in our place a death that is *similar to* the eternal punishment for sins: "Christ has undergone a death *like* death #3 to save us from death #3.... Christ's substitutionary death addresses the plight not of death #1 (at least not directly) but of death #3. It is *like* 'perishing' in that it is the divinely ordained consequence of sin.... Paul's description of Christ's substitutionary death in 1 Corinthians 15:3 makes good sense *on analogy* with 'perishing' (death #3).... Christ *did* in his substitutionary death release us from the destiny of perishing...." (83; emphases added). For Christ to have truly died as humanity's substitute, however, it was not enough that he die a death that was *like* eternal condemnation or *analogous* to it, but that he actually undergo *that very same death*, that is, eternal condemnation—which, according to the New Testament, he did not.

69. Morris, *Cross*, 48-49. Cf. I. H. Marshall, *Aspects*, 3, 29, 30, 62-63, 67, 130, n34.

he did. In what sense, then, can his physical sufferings have been substitutionary and sufficient to satisfy the just demands of God or God's law?

As is evident from the quotations just cited, proponents of penal substitution views tend to address these problems by affirming that what Christ suffered was far more intense and painful than anything any other human being has ever suffered. Yet this also seems difficult to maintain. According to 2 Maccabees 6 and 7, for example, the Jewish martyr figures who refused to renounce obedience to the Mosaic law were whipped, tortured on the rack, had their tongues, hands, and feet cut off and their skin peeled off, and were scalped. Then, still conscious after all these torments, they were placed in frying pans to die there a slow, agonizing death. The physical sufferings that Jesus endured in his passion and death seem to pale in comparison. Physical tortures similar to those described in 2 Maccabees—and perhaps even worse—have continued to take place throughout human history, so that Jesus' death can hardly be said to have saved all human beings from sufferings that were at times far greater than his own.

For the same reasons, those proponents of penal substitution views who affirm that Jesus suffered the *intrinsic consequences* of human sin rather than any type of extrinsic divine punishment or penalty seem to have little basis for sustaining that what Jesus suffered was equivalent in value to what all of humanity was condemned to suffer. Therefore, there seems to be no basis for arguing that the suffering that Jesus endured during his last hours was equal to the suffering that people of all times and places throughout human history have deserved for their sins. A further problem is that the penalty supposedly dictated by God or God's law was simply *death itself* rather than a particular amount of suffering or a certain *manner* of death.

Many critics of penal substitution views have also observed that it can hardly be considered just for an innocent person to be put to death instead of the guilty. Even if the innocent substitute offers to die voluntarily, this type of substitution runs contrary to justice as well as to human laws. Morris counters such an objection by arguing that, while this kind of substitution "is not permitted in the legal systems with which we are familiar," "we are not being saved with reference to our legal systems" but "with reference to the eternal law of God," which does not run "in all points exactly like all our human laws."[70] It is not clear, however, on what basis Morris can affirm the existence of such an "eternal law of God" that on this point is different from the laws that exist among human beings and are based on what God has revealed to them. There is no biblical basis for such a claim.

For these and other reasons,[71] the notion that what Jesus suffered in his passion and death was sufficient to satisfy God's justice is extremely prob-

---

70. Morris, *Cross*, 387.

71. For further arguments against the idea that what Christ suffered was equivalent to the penalty to which human beings were subject, see David A. Brondos, *Redeeming the Gospel: The Christian Faith Reconsidered* (SLHT; Minneapolis: Fortress, 2011), 64–66.

lematic to sustain. Yet if no equivalency can be established between what Jesus endured in his death and what sinful human beings were condemned to endure for their sins, then the basis upon which penal substitution views rest is taken out from under them. At best, it can be argued that God *accepted* what Jesus endured as sufficient to compensate for human sin and to satisfy divine justice, yet this would appear to be an arbitrary decision on God's part rather than something strictly demanded by God's righteous nature. Such an argument also undermines the claim that Jesus' sufferings and death were absolutely necessary for God to remit human sins justly, since God might have accepted something less as sufficient in order to forgive.

Once again, of course, the problem is not only that penal substitution views present serious theological difficulties such as these but also that, by ascribing the notion of penal substitution to the New Testament writers, proponents of these views inevitably imply that these same difficulties were present in the thought of Jesus' first followers. In that case, when the first believers taught that Jesus' death was sufficient to meet God's just demands for the punishment of sin and was equivalent to the penalty to which human beings collectively were subject, they must also have had to address all of the problems that such a teaching raises. There is, however, no evidence that either Jesus' followers or anyone else in antiquity ever discussed such problems.

Premise 4: In order for Christ to satisfy divine justice, he had to be perfectly sinless.

According to penal substitution views, if Jesus had not been perfectly sinless, he would not have been qualified to die in the place of others, since in that case he would have had to die for *his own* sins. Ladd, for example, comments: "Of all human beings, Jesus alone knew no sin (2 Cor. 5:21), and therefore being guiltless he did not have to die. His death was not the result of his own sin or guilt; it was suffered in the stead of others who were guilty and who deserved to die. By virtue of his unmerited death, sinners are delivered from the doom of death and from the experience of God's wrath that they eminently deserve."[72] Likewise, Paul Achtemeier, commenting on 1 Pet. 3:18, affirms that "it was possible for Christ's death to be 'for sin'" because "as righteous he did not need to die for his own sin."[73]

The implication of affirmations such as these is that, if Jesus had not chosen to die for others as their substitute, he would have lived forever on earth as long as he remained sinless. This presupposes that each human being dies as a result of his or her own sins. Such a view also raises the question of why Jesus was not born naturally mortal like all other human beings. Generally, this objection is answered by appealing in some way to Jesus' divinity, which

---

72. Ladd, *Theology*, 468.
73. Paul J. Achtemeier, *1 Peter: A Commentary on1 Peter* (ed. Eldon Jay Epp; Hermeneia; Minneapolis: Fortress, 1996), 247.

supposedly prevented him from being subject to sin and death by nature as the rest of human beings are.

When the claim that Christ had to be sinless and perfect in order to be able to die as humanity's substitute is combined with the notion that Christ's death was sufficient to satisfy God's justice, then it must also be maintained that God's justice would not allow God to accept any human being who was not entirely without sin. Hans Hübner, for example, writes that for Paul, "only total obedience to the Law is obedience to the Law at all.... [E]ven if just a single prescription of the Law is transgressed against, the effect is as if the entire Torah had been disregarded, i.e., total loss of righteousness...."[74]

The claim that God demands perfect sinlessness on the part of human beings in order to accept them is often made together with the claim that Christ's perfect righteousness and his sinlessness are imputed to believers.[75] Besides the fact that it is questionable that Paul thought in these terms, as even many proponents of penal substitution views now recognize,[76] it is problematic to attempt to combine this idea with that of penal substitution, which is distinct. If Christ's imputed righteousness is the basis upon which God forgives human beings and declares them righteous, then it is no longer Christ's *death* that serves as the basis for their forgiveness and justification, but the fact that Christ was perfectly sinless and righteous throughout his life to the very end and now shares that perfect righteousness with them. According to a distinction made in traditional Protestant teaching, this involves the imputation of Christ's *active* righteousness to believers, that is, the righteousness that results from his having committed no sins during his time on earth. In penal substitution views, however, what is reckoned to believers is Christ's *passive* righteousness, that is, his having endured willingly and innocently the penalty to which all were subject. Believers are declared righteous in the sense that they are now free of sin and no longer liable to any punishment because their sin received its due punishment when it was reckoned to Christ and he died in their stead.

To affirm that both Christ's *active* righteousness *and* his *passive* righteousness are imputed to believers therefore results in confusion and redundancy. Believers are said to be free from divine punishment both because they are sinless in God's eyes through the perfect righteousness of Christ that is reckoned to them *and* because Christ endured their punishment in their stead. It is not clear why both of these things should have been necessary; one or the other would have been sufficient. If Christ's sinlessness is imputed to

---

74. Hans Hübner, *Law in Paul's Thought*, trans. James C. G. Greig (ed. John Riches; SNTW; Edinburgh: T & T Clark, 1984), 24.

75. See, for example, Herman Ridderbos, "The Earliest Confession of the Atonement in Paul," in *Reconciliation and Hope: New Testament Essays on Atonement and Eschatology Presented to L. L. Morris on his 60th Birthday* (ed. Robert Banks; Exeter: Paternoster, 1974), 84; Morris, *Apostolic Preaching*, 282-83; Matera, *II Corinthians*, 144.

76. See, for example, David E. Aune, "Recent Readings of Paul Relating to Justification by Faith," in *Rereading Paul Together: Protestant and Catholic Perspectives on Justification* (ed. Aune; Grand Rapids: Baker Academic, 2006), 231-33.

Penal Substitution Interpretations of Christ's Work in New Testament Scholarship 43

believers, then there was no need for the sins of believers and their punishment to be imputed to Christ; but if the sins of believers were imputed to Christ, they are sinless, not by virtue of Christ's sinlessness being reckoned to them, but by virtue of their sin having been reckoned to Christ. In response to this difficulty, Protestant theologians who have defended penal substitution interpretations of Christ's work have historically taught that the role that Christ's *active* obedience plays in justification is not that it is reckoned to believers in lieu of their own righteousness, but that it qualified Christ to die in their stead as their innocent substitute. Christ therefore had to live a perfectly sinless life, not so that his sinlessness could be imputed to others, but so that he might die for the sins of others rather than any sins of his own. The teaching that Christ's righteousness is imputed to believers has also commonly been criticized for implying that justification involves a "legal fiction," since God accepts believers as righteous and innocent even though they are *not* truly righteous, but instead remain sinners.

Biblical scholars commonly combine conflicting ideas such as these without recognizing the confusions and theological difficulties involved. Then, when they read those ideas back into Paul's writings, they feel obliged to conclude that Paul was "not a systematic thinker."[77] By this they mean that there are theological inconsistencies and even apparent contradictions running throughout his writings. Rarely do they acknowledge that the problem lies not with Paul, but rather with the fact that they have read back into Paul later theological ideas that are not his own.

Premise 5: In order for Christ to die as the substitute for sinful humanity, he had to be fully divine and fully human.

This claim was central to Anselm's argument. Anselm argued that, since the debt to be paid to God was owed by human beings, only one who was human could pay it. Yet, because the debt was infinitely greater than any sinful human being could pay, only one who was God could pay it. A similar claim is made in penal substitution views, although strictly speaking the argument is slightly different: in these views the problem is not that a debt of obedience must be paid to God, as Anselm taught, but rather that a sentence of death must be executed. Since it was human beings who were liable to that sentence, the one who was to die for other human beings as their substitute had to be a human being himself. Thus Witherington writes: "If Jesus had not been a human being, humans would not have had redemption, resurrection, reconciliation…. In short, for salvation to reach and to redeem humankind, it had to take the form of a human being."[78]

At the same time, as just noted under the previous premise, Jesus had to be a *sinless* human being. Yet because sinlessness is an impossibility for fallen

---

77. See, for example, Calvin J. Roetzel, *Paul: The Man and the Myth* (SPNT; Minneapolis: Fortress, 1999), 93-94; Sanders, *Paul and Palestinian Judaism*, 506; Räisänen, *Paul*, xi. For a critique of this idea, see Douglas A. Campbell, *The Quest for Paul's Gospel: A Suggested Strategy* (JSNTSup 244; London: T & T Clark, 2005), 29-34.
78. Witherington, *Paul's Narrative*, 141-42.

human beings, the one who was to die as their substitute had to be divine, since only a divine being could live a perfectly sinless life. If a doctrine of original sin is maintained, according to which all human beings are born into a sinful and thus mortal condition, then it must also be argued that God's Son was born into an *unfallen* nature that was free of original sin. Such an idea is ascribed to Paul by scholars such as Witherington: "like Adam, Jesus was born with an unfallen nature... but *unlike* Adam, Jesus remained sinless and so could be an unblemished sacrifice for sin.... Paul seems to think that Jesus as divine, or God, was not subject to, nor could he be subject to, death."[79]

Premise 6: Both the incarnation and the earthly life of God's Son had as their sole objective his substitutionary death for others.

Anselm affirmed plainly that God's Son "became human for the purpose of dying."[80] This is maintained by biblical scholars as well. As noted above, Witherington claims that "Jesus saw his task in life to come and die, enduring God's overwhelming wrath."[81] Likewise, Morris, commenting on Heb. 2:9, affirms: "The whole purpose of the incarnation is seen as death. He came to die. He came to die 'for every man.'"[82]

It is important to note, however, that when the remission of sins is attributed exclusively to Jesus' death and not to anything that human beings do, Jesus' death must be seen as the *only* objective of the incarnation as well as Jesus' earthly life. Proponents of penal substitution views rarely make such an affirmation, and many would no doubt reject it. However, if salvation and forgiveness are based *solely on what Christ did on the cross, enduring humanity's punishment*, then Christ's saving work cannot be understood in terms of transforming human hearts or enabling human beings to change their behavior so as to live in accordance with God's will, since supposedly this new life is not the basis upon which human beings are forgiven and saved. The transformation of the conduct of believers thus plays no role whatsoever in their justification. To claim that believers must now live morally upright lives in order to be saved and forgiven is to deny that the sole basis for their salvation and forgiveness is the substitutionary death of Christ, and to contradict the affirmation that human beings "no longer need to assuage the wrath of God through their actions."[83]

For the same reason, according to penal substitution views, the sole objective of Christ's earthly life must have been to preserve himself free from sin and guilt by making sure that he never transgressed the law. In effect, this reduces Jesus' teaching and ministry to an unnecessary pastime, something that kept him occupied until he would die for others. Because believers are

---
79. Ibid., 140-41.
80. Anselm, *Cur Deus Homo* 2.16.
81. Witherington, *Christology*, 124.
82. Morris, *Cross*, 278.
83. Martin Hengel, *The Atonement: The Origins of the Doctrine in the New Testament* (Philadelphia: Fortress, 1981), 31.

saved only by Christ's death and not by any works of their own, what Christ taught by word and example contributes in no way to human salvation and there is no real need for human beings to follow Christ's teaching. Obviously, such affirmations raise the question of why the four evangelists bothered to preserve in writing Jesus' teaching rather than merely announcing that he lived a sinless life and on that basis was able to endure the punishment human beings deserved in their place.

As noted above, advocates of penal substitution views often make the claim that it was necessary for God to punish human sin rather than freely forgiving it so that human beings might know that God does not look upon sin lightly or tolerate it. Witherington, for example, writes: "Christ had to die to reflect God's just and righteous character and meet God's just demands for the punishment of human sin.... Christ's death showed that God was righteous and could not pass over sin forever."[84]

This claim raises the same difficulty just mentioned: if Jesus died in order to demonstrate that God does not leave sin unpunished, then his death had one of two purposes: it was designed by God either to dissuade human beings from sinning, or else to let them know of the need they had for Christ to endure their punishment in their stead, since God cannot leave sin unpunished. In either case, Christ's death is then seen as salvific by virtue of *what it reveals* to human beings. Their forgiveness, justification, and salvation ultimately depend, not directly on Christ's death, but on their responding in faith and repentance to the revelation they have received through Christ. Furthermore, as noted above, if human beings are no longer subject to punishment for their sins because of Christ's substitutionary death, then what his death reveals is not that they must refrain from sinning because God inevitably punishes human sin, but that they now can sin freely without being concerned about divine punishment. God cannot justly punish their sins a second time, since God has already had Christ endure their punishment in their stead. This difficulty leads to the final premise to be considered.

Premise 7: Human beings are saved and delivered from God's wrath solely by Jesus' substitutionary death on their behalf, yet they must still come to faith in order to receive that salvation.

Proponents of penal substitution views have commonly made a distinction between an *objective* and a *subjective* salvation. Christ's death is said to bring about an *objective* salvation in that it saves *humanity as a whole* in some sense. Nevertheless, human beings must still receive that salvation subjectively by faith in order for it to be effective. Pauline scholars such as John Ziesler, for example, have claimed that the first Christians believed that "Christ's death was a sacrifice for *all* human sin" and "that it was of universal effect."[85] According to Rudolf Schnackenburg, Paul taught that Christ "has reconciled

---

84. Witherington, *Paul's Narrative*, 66, 259-60.
85. John A. Ziesler, *Pauline Christianity*, rev. ed. (Oxford: Oxford University Press, 1990), 92.

the whole of humanity to God."[86] Herman Ridderbos attributes to Paul the teaching that justification is "rooted in what Christ once accomplished for us and without us (*pro nobis et extra nos*)," and that this constitutes "the 'objective' significance of Christ's death and resurrection as the only and unrepeatable act of atonement...."[87] Morris finds in the New Testament the idea of a "completed work" accomplished in Christ: "he offered himself once for all on the cross.... The offering made by Jesus is perpetual in its efficacy.... Thus our forgiveness rests upon the fact that our penalty has been borne for us. And since the penalty has been borne, it cannot be imposed on us again."[88] In other words, the objective salvation of all humanity was accomplished once and for all when Christ died on the cross, bearing the penalty of all people as their substitute. Once again, Morris's words indicate that human beings are now free to sin as they desire without having to fear any punishment: "since the penalty has been borne, it cannot be imposed on us again," no matter how much sin and evil we commit. To affirm that one *can* fall under sin's penalty again by living contrary to God's will is to maintain that Christ *did not* take away definitively divine punishment for human sin in his death, since that punishment can be reimposed. Whether that happens or not depends on how we live, and therefore depends, not on what *Christ* did, but on what *we* do. This is double justification: while justified initially on the basis of Christ's death, from then on we must *justify ourselves* through our works by living as God desires in order to avoid falling back under God's wrath.

As several of these quotations demonstrate, this objective salvation is generally understood in terms of some type of "effect" produced by Jesus' death. New Testament scholars routinely speak of the "redemptive effects of Jesus' death and resurrection,"[89] "the complete and abiding efficacy of Jesus' death as an atoning sacrifice,"[90] and the "continuing effects" and "continuing power of his death."[91] When Jesus' death or blood is said to have propitiated God, this "effect" is thought to involve a change in God: God has been changed from a God who invariably punishes human beings for their sins into a God who now forgives them their sins freely. According to Morris, "God now treats the sinner differently from before. Instead of God's severity the sinner experiences God's grace, which is only another way of saying that propitiation has taken place.... God now looks on man no longer as the object of his holy and

---

86. Rudolf Schnackenburg, *Ephesians: A Commentary*, trans. Helen Heron (Edinburgh: T & T Clark, 1991), 126.

87. Ridderbos, "Earliest Confession," 84.

88. Morris, *Cross*, 283, 382. See also Morris, *Apostolic Preaching*, 225-26.

89. Larry W. Hurtado, *Lord Jesus Christ: Devotion to Jesus in Early Christianity* (Grand Rapids: Eerdmans, 2003), 127.

90. Barnabas Lindars, *The Theology of the Letter to the Hebrews* (NTT; Cambridge: Cambridge University Press, 1991), 10; cf. 14, 36, 40. See also Paul Barnett, *The Second Epistle to the Corinthians* (NICNT; Grand Rapids: Eerdmans, 1997), 314.

91. Paul Ellingworth, *The Epistle to the Hebrews: A Commentary on the Greek Text* (NIGTC; Grand Rapids: Eerdmans, 1993), 163; Schnackenburg, *Ephesians*, 249.

righteous wrath, but as the object of his love and his blessing."[92] Thanks to Christ's death, the God who looked upon and treated human beings in one way has been transformed into a God who looks upon and treats human beings in a different way.

Yet if Christ's death effects the forgiveness and salvation of all humanity universally, why should people still need to come to faith subjectively in order to be saved? Once it is said that faith is necessary for one to be forgiven and saved from God's wrath and condemnation, then it seems clear that those who *do not* come to faith are *not* forgiven nor saved from God's wrath and condemnation. If only "those who are of faith no longer need fear the wrath," as Morris claims,[93] then those who are *not* of faith *do* need to fear the wrath and were *not* actually saved from it by Christ's death. When Christ died, not all people were saved, but only those who would have faith. In this case, ultimately it is not Christ's death that obtains salvation and deliverance for people, but their faith. If people do *not* come to faith, then their sins and God's wrath at those sins have *not* been put away by Jesus' death "effectively and finally" and the penalty for their sins is indeed imposed on them again. Their sins are therefore punished twice: once when Christ died and again when they suffer divine condemnation.

In order to address this problem, it has been common to make a distinction between the *sufficiency* and the *efficiency* of Christ's death. Witherington ascribes this distinction to Paul: "Christ's death is seen as sufficient for all, but only efficient for those who respond to the offer of salvation." Even though it was sufficient for all people, "not all receive it and believe it, and for those there is the fate of facing eternal destruction."[94] Yet if faith is necessary for one to be saved instead of "facing eternal destruction," then Christ's death is *not* sufficient for this end, since something else *in addition* to Christ's death is required, namely faith. Ultimately, it is their response to the offer of salvation that saves people rather than the cross.

Another way in which New Testament scholars have addressed this problem is by making a distinction between the *ground* and the *means* of justification or forgiveness: Christ's death constitutes the *ground* upon which people obtain the remission of sins, while faith constitutes the *means* by which they receive this remission.[95] This distinction becomes meaningless, however, once faith is regarded as necessary for salvation, since those who do not come to faith are *not* ultimately justified and thus any ground for their justification is removed or nullified.

In the Reformed tradition, it has been common to respond to this problem by positing a "limited atonement." According to this idea, Christ died only for the sins of those whom God had predestined for salvation, that is,

---

92. Morris, *Apostolic Preaching*, 212-13, 247.
93. Ibid., 201.
94. Witherington, *Paul's Narrative*, 165. See also Witherington, "Death of Sin," 13.
95. See, for example, Ladd, *Theology*, 490; John A. Ziesler, *The Meaning of Righteousness in Paul: A Linguistic and Theological Enquiry* (SNTSMS 20; Cambridge: Cambridge University Press, 1972), 168.

those in whom God had previously determined to create saving faith. Christ therefore did not endure the penalty of unbelievers, who must suffer that penalty themselves. Once again, however, if faith is said to be necessary for salvation, then Christ's death is *not* sufficient for believers to be saved, since something else is required on their part, namely, that they be brought to faith. Furthermore, what ultimately saves human beings is not Christ's death, but God's decision to elect them for salvation. Christ's death is thereby reduced to a mere formality.

A related difficulty arises when it is affirmed that, even though Christ has *already* delivered believers from God's wrath, he continues to make intercession to God for them when they sin. It is not clear why it should still be necessary for Christ to implore God to put away God's wrath at sinners and forgive them if, when he died, God's wrath was taken away "effectively and finally." Biblical scholars usually attempt to combine these two ideas by affirming that Christ intercedes to God on the basis of what he did in the past. He perpetually stands before God in heaven presenting God with his blood, which continues to have atoning power.[96] Nevertheless, this ongoing intercession seems to be unnecessary and superfluous if God already granted forgiveness once and for all when Christ died.

When faith is said to be necessary for salvation, not only is Christ's death regarded as insufficient for that salvation, but the meaning of his death is changed as well. As just noted above, its purpose becomes that of bringing about faith in people through what it *reveals*. In addition to letting all people know that God does not leave human sin unpunished so that they may recognize their need to be delivered from that punishment by turning to Jesus in faith, Jesus' death supposedly reveals to them the immensity of God's love. This love consists of having sent Christ to endure the punishment due to human beings rather than punishing human beings themselves. Yet if the divine revelations given through Christ's death were necessary for people to come to faith in order to be saved by that faith, then what delivers them from divine wrath and punishment is not Christ's substitutionary death, but the faith that Christ's death has made possible through that which it reveals.

In penal substitution views, therefore, the effectiveness and sufficiency of Jesus' death come to be regarded as *the object and content of saving faith*. Human beings are saved by *believing* that Jesus' death accomplished their salvation. Johan Christiaan Beker, for example, affirms that "faith in Christ's death for us will be the decisive criterion at the future last judgment."[97] For Witherington, God acquits and accepts "only those who have faith in Christ and his atoning work.... [F]aith in Christ's death is reckoned or credited to believers as acquittal, leaving them in right-standing with God."[98] In this case, God saves them,

---

96. See, for example, Philip E. Hughes, *A Commentary on the Epistle to the Hebrews* (Grand Rapids: Eerdmans, 1977), 382-83; Morris, *Cross*, 283-84.

97. Johan Christiaan Beker, *The Triumph of God: The Essence of Paul's Thought*, trans. Loren T. Stuckenbruck (Minneapolis: Fortress, 1990), 84.

98. Witherington, *Paul's Narrative*, 260-61.

not because Christ's death was sufficient to atone for their sins, but because *they believe* that Christ's death was sufficient to atone for their sins.

Proponents of penal substitution views also regard Christ's resurrection as salvific by virtue of what it reveals. It demonstrates that God accepted Jesus' substitutionary death as atoning so that people might believe that his death was sufficient to propitiate God's wrath and attain God's forgiveness for them. In the words of Ridderbos, "Christ's resurrection is the indispensable complement of his death for our sins. Christ's death alone is for that reason insufficient.... It was in his death that he atoned for our sins and in this he was recognized and accepted by God in his resurrection. For that reason we would 'still be in our sins' had Christ not been raised. Christ's resurrection is the public recognition and acceptance by God of his (Christ's) sacrifice as the eradication and expiation of our sins."[99] In other words, Christ's resurrection is salvific because it enables people to believe that his death was effective in dealing with sins. Yet if people must *believe* that Christ's death was effective in order for it actually to *be* effective, then what makes Christ's death effective is the faith of believers rather than his death per se, which was *insufficient* for their salvation, as Ridderbos himself is forced to recognize here.

For this reason, proponents of penal substitution inevitably end up making faith the one "work" necessary for human beings to obtain forgiveness and salvation. Initially, all people are forgiven and reconciled to God by virtue of Christ's substitutionary death. However, if they do not come to faith, they forfeit this forgiveness and reconciliation and fall back under God's wrath and punishment. In Ladd's words, "until God's offer of objective reconciliation has been received, no person is in fact reconciled to God; she or he is still a sinner and in the last day will suffer the full and awful outpouring of the wrath of a holy God."[100] This makes the objective/subjective distinction meaningless.

In the end, then, most proponents of penal substitution views in reality do not maintain that Jesus' death actually attained salvation and forgiveness for all, but only that it *opened up the possibility* that human beings might now be saved by having faith in his death. What obtains forgiveness for believers and delivers them from God's wrath is their faith in Christ's death rather than Christ's death per se. This means that what has changed as a result of Christ's death is simply that previously human beings could *not* be saved by faith in his death, but now they *can*.

PHYSICAL INTERPRETATIONS OF CHRIST'S WORK IN NEW TESTAMENT SCHOLARSHIP

According to a physical understanding of Christ's work, his incarnation, life, death, and resurrection were aimed at bringing about some type of ontological change in the nature (*physis*) of human beings or the created order as a

---

99. Ridderbos, "Earliest Confession," 78.
100. Ladd, *Theology*, 496-97.

whole. This physical understanding exists in numerous forms, yet a common element is that there is some power present in nature to which human beings have become subject and from which they must be delivered.

On the basis of the New Testament allusions to Christ's defeat of evil powers and principalities,[101] it has been common to claim that Christ's work was thought to consist of conquering the devil and other demonic beings in order to liberate human beings from their bondage to those beings. This is the most common form of the *Christus Victor* idea. According to this idea, because these forces of evil are supernatural, they are stronger than human beings, making it impossible for human beings to overcome those forces on their own. For this reason, it was necessary for God to send God's Son, who delivers human beings from their slavery to these powers by virtue of the superior divine strength he possesses. At the same time, through his death and resurrection, Christ also delivers creation as a whole from its subjection to those forces.

Some scholars, such as Wright, claim that these ideas go back to Jesus himself, who saw his death in terms of a "battle" against "satan," the "real enemy" who stood behind the Jewish and Roman authorities. Jesus thought that by engaging these forces of evil and letting them do their worst to him, he would defeat evil.[102] Other scholars attribute similar ideas to Paul, who allegedly conceived of Christ engaging "hostile spiritual powers" in combat.[103] These powers included not only demonic forces but other "representatives of the old age—sin, death, the law, and the flesh," all of which "have been overthrown and caused to release their grip on those who are now in Christ."[104] Obviously, to speak in these terms involves personifying realities that we generally regard as impersonal, as if these forces had a will of their own and could hold human beings in their grip. Paul is thus said to have taught that "the rule of sin and death is finally broken" by means of "[t]he act of God whose victory over sin was accomplished in the death and resurrection of Jesus...."[105] According to Beker, Paul conceived of "major apocalyptic forces" as "ontological powers that determine the human situation within the context of God's created order and that comprise the 'field' of death, sin, the law and the flesh." The death of Christ "marks the defeat of the apocalyptic powers" as "the final judgment of the old age" and "inaugurates the cosmic triumph of God...."[106]

When the powers to which human beings are subject are instead regarded as *impersonal*, an intrinsic *cause-and-effect* relationship is posited between sin

---

101. See John 12:31; Col. 2:15; Heb. 2:14; 1 John 3:8; Rev. 17:14; 20:10; cf. Eph. 1:20-21; 1 Pet. 3:22.
102. Wright, *Jesus*, 564-65.
103. F. F. Bruce, *The Epistles to the Colossians, to Philemon, and to the Ephesians* (NICNT; Grand Rapids: Eerdmans, 1984), 75.
104. Don B. Garlington, *Faith, Obedience, and Perseverance: Aspects of Paul's Letter to the Romans* (WUNT 79; Tübingen: J. C. B. Mohr, 1994), 72.
105. Brice L. Martin, *Christ and the Law in Paul* (NovTSup 62; Leiden: Brill, 1989), 70. See also Chris Forbes, "Paul's Principalities and Powers: Demythologizing Apocalyptic?," *JSNT* 82 (2001): 61-88.
106. Johan Christiaan Beker, *Paul the Apostle: The Triumph of God in Life and Thought* (Philadelphia: Fortress, 1980), 189.

and its consequences, such as death. Christ's divinity allows him to absorb those powers into himself and thus deliver human beings from suffering the consequences they produce. In this way, the maleficent forces in human nature are neutralized or destroyed through their contact with the divine.

James Dunn, for example, claims that Paul understood sin as something analogous to a poison, virus, or malignant cancer dwelling within the flesh of human beings: according to Paul, "there is also a violent toxin within, whose poison, if allowed to spread unchecked, will slowly kill the whole organism."[107] Death is the consequence of this power in human flesh.[108] In order to overcome this malignant power, God sent God's Son in the flesh. Through his death, Christ puts an end to the "infected" flesh of human beings and then, through his resurrection, he brings a new creation into existence. Dunn explains:

> The cancer of sin had taken such a firm root on the flesh, on humankind, that the surgery had to be radical; the flesh had to be destroyed, humankind had to die. The old age had to be wound up and a new beginning made. For Paul the good news was that this was just what God had done in Christ: Christ's complete oneness with sinful flesh meant that his death effected the destruction of that sinful flesh, just as his resurrection meant a new beginning for humankind.[109]

According to Dunn, "The sting of death has been drawn by having been used on Christ, absorbed by him, its poison exhausted in the death of Christ...."[110] What took place in Christ "actually deals with the power of sin, destroying the malignant cancer in death...."[111] "His death was itself an epochal event which broke the consequence of sin's hold on the flesh...."[112] Together with his death, Christ's resurrection is "the beginning of a new humanity, no longer contaminated by sin and no longer subject to death."[113] Dunn compares this to a vaccination: "In vaccination germs are introduced into a healthy body in order that by destroying these germs the body will build up its strength. So we might say the germ of sin was introduced into Jesus, the only one healthy/whole enough to let that sin run its full course.... [H]is new humanity is 'germ resistant,' 'sin-resistant'...."[114]

Dunn is willing to speak of God's wrath in this context, yet insists on understanding that wrath in terms of a natural consequence of sin that is removed by Christ's death: "God's wrath means a process willed by God—the outworking of the destructive consequences of sin...."[115] "[T]he atoning act

---

107. James D. G. Dunn, *The Theology of Paul the Apostle* (Grand Rapids: Eerdmans, 1998), 81; cf. 214-15, 386; Dunn, *Romans 1-8* (WBC 38A; Dallas, TX: Word, 1988), 182, 439.
108. Dunn, *Theology of Paul*, 96.
109. Dunn, *Romans 1-8*, 439.
110. Ibid., 372.
111. Ibid., 182. Cf. Dunn, *Theology of Paul*, 223.
112. Dunn, *Romans 1-8*, 421; see also 422.
113. James D. G. Dunn, "Paul's Understanding of the Death of Jesus," in *Sacrifice and Redemption: Durham Essays in Theology* (ed. S. W. Sykes; Cambridge: Cambridge University Press, 1991), 52. See also Dunn, *Romans 1-8*, 372.
114. Dunn, "Paul's Understanding," 50.
115. Ibid., 49; see also 50.

thus removes the sin which provoked God's wrath, but it does so by acting on the sin rather than on God. The imagery is more of the removal of a corrosive stain or the neutralization of a life-threatening virus than of anger appeased by punishment."[116] In this case, it is not Christ's death itself that removes God's wrath. Rather, Christ's death and resurrection remove the power of sin present in human nature and, because this sin was the cause of God's wrath, that wrath is also taken away. For Dunn, however, ultimately this is valid only for believers who identify with Christ: "the wrath of God exhausted itself in the death of Jesus, and so is already exhausted for believers insofar as they identified themselves with Christ in his death."[117]

The notion that Paul conceived of God's wrath as a natural process rather than a divine disposition is commonly associated with C. H. Dodd, who made such a view popular. Dodd claimed that Paul "constantly uses 'wrath' or 'the Wrath' in a curiously impersonal way" in order "not to describe the attitude of God to man, but to describe an inevitable process of cause and effect in a moral universe."[118] However, God's wrath can also be understood in terms of not intervening to interrupt the cause-and-effect process, but instead allowing it to work itself out naturally. Dunn hints at this idea in the passage quoted above, where he describes God's wrath as "a process willed by God." Christopher Marshall claims that this idea is present in Rom. 1:18-32, where the allusion to God's wrath should be understood as "God's personal consent to the intrinsic outworking of people's estrangement from God...."[119] In this case, Christ can be said to have endured God's wrath at sin only in the sense that God had him experience the natural consequences of human sin without intervening to save him.

As noted above, like the notion of God's wrath, the idea of death as a "penalty" can be understood as involving the natural consequences of sin rather than something God imposes from above as a personal agent. This idea has been associated not only with Dodd but with a number of other biblical scholars as well.[120] Among more recent proponents of this interpretation is Travis, who argues that in passages such as Rom. 1:18-32, Paul does not speak of God's wrath in terms of "the retributive inflicting of punishment from outside, but God's allowing of people to experience the intrinsic consequences of their refusal to live in relationship to him."[121] Therefore "to speak of Christ on the cross suffering our 'punishment,' or enduring a retributive pen-

---

116. Dunn, *Theology of Paul*, 214-15.
117. Dunn, *Romans 1-8*, 268.
118. C. H. Dodd, *The Epistle of Paul to the Romans* (MNTC 6; New York: Harper and Brothers, 1932), 21, 23.
119. Christopher D. Marshall, *Beyond Retribution: A New Testament Vision for Justice, Crime, and Punishment* (Grand Rapids: Eerdmans, 2001), 64.
120. For a summary of this discussion, see Gathercole, "Justified," 169-81. In contrast to Dodd and Marshall, Gathercole rejects what he calls "the 'immanentist' view of punishment, whereby the effects of sin are bound up with, and the outworking of, the nature of sin itself" (169).
121. Travis, "Christ," 338; cf. 345. See also C. Marshall, *Beyond Retribution*, 62: "this is not a matter of a penalty being added on to an offense as an arbitrary, external retributive punishment. It is the penalty of inherent consequences, something intrinsic to the nature of the offense itself."

alty for our sins, is to go further than Paul himself goes."[122] Like other New Testament scholars, Travis prefers to use verbs that refer to natural processes, such as "absorb," "exhaust," and "neutralize." He thus speaks of "Christ's death absorbing or neutralizing the effects of sin.... Paul says that [Christ] entered into and bore on our behalf the destructive consequences of sin. Standing where we stand, he bore the consequences of our alienation from God. In so doing he absorbed and exhausted them, so that they should not fall on us."[123]

Scholars interpreting the New Testament language concerning Christ's death in this way often use the language of "judgment," yet this too is understood differently than in penal substitution views. God's judgment against sin is not a forensic pronouncement but an *actual destruction* of evil powers such as sin and death. Dunn, for example, argues that "for Paul the way in which Christ's death cancels out man's sin is by *destroying* it...."[124] On the cross "God passed judgement on sin in the flesh."[125] According to Travis, Christ "experienced divine judgment on sin in the sense that he endured the God-ordained consequences of human sinfulness"; thus this judgment "is not inflicted by God 'from outside,' but is the intrinsic outworking, under God's control, of the consequences of human choices and actions...."[126] The "apocalyptic powers" can also be said to have been judged in Christ's death in that they are stripped of their power:[127] "The death of Christ is indeed the negation of the evil powers, but even more it is their judgment."[128]

In order for salvation to follow upon this judgment of destruction, of course, there must be some type of new creation arising out of the judgment. This is usually linked with Christ's resurrection, which ushers in a new age, a new reality, and new possibilities for human beings.[129] Dunn attributes these ideas to Paul:

> It is by his death and resurrection that Christ breaks through the cul-de-sac of death and inaugurates a new humanity as last Adam.... Jesus is the only one who, having reached the end of this age of Adam, broke through the road-end barrier of death into the age beyond; who, having died Adam's death as an act of obedience, rose to a new life beyond. Christ's death and resurrection thus provide the doorway—for Paul the only doorway—through death to life, from this age under the power of sin to the new age free from sin.[130]

---

122. Travis, "Christ," 341.
123. Ibid., 337, 345. See also Timothy Gombis, "The 'Transgressor' and the 'Curse of the Law': The Logic of Paul's Argument in Galatians 2-3," *NTS* 53 (2007): 90; Westerholm, *Perspectives*, 376, 432; Fung, *Galatians*, 149.
124. Dunn, "Paul's Understanding," 49.
125. Ibid., 51.
126. Travis, "Christ," 345.
127. Beker, *Triumph*, 80, 82-83.
128. Beker, *Paul*, 191; see also 189-90.
129. See, for example, Hultgren, *Christ*, 35; Richard B. Hays, "Crucified with Christ: A Synthesis of the Theology of 1 and 2 Thessalonians, Philemon, Philippians, and Galatians," in *Pauline Theology*, Vol. 1: *Thessalonians, Philippians, Galatians, Philemon* (ed. Jouette M. Bassler; Minneapolis: Fortress, 1991), 233; Scot McKnight, *Jesus and his Death: Historiography, the Historical Jesus, and Atonement Theory* (Waco, TX: Baylor University Press, 2005), 346.
130. Dunn, *Romans 1-8*, 285, 329.

According to this type of interpretation, then, the purpose of Christ's death and resurrection was to bring into existence a "new humanity." This represents another idea commonly ascribed to Paul. Richard Hays, for example, affirms that for Paul Christ "constitutes in himself a new, faithful humanity."[131] According to Don Garlington, in Paul's mind Christ "was not simply one just man amongst many, but a man of universal significance, the 'last Adam,' patriarch of a new humanity."[132] Robin Scroggs similarly writes: "In his body of glory Christ is true humanity.... Christ by virtue of his resurrection is... changed into the true man.... Christ not only is true humanity; he also mediates this true humanity to the believer...."[133] Christ is the "reality of God's intent for humanity" and the "direct agent of this humanity," in whom "the restoration of man's humanity" has taken place.[134] As Margaret Thrall notes, Christ can also be spoken of as the "prototype of this new humanity."[135] "In Christ's death the old form of human life was brought to an end, in order that a new kind of human existence might become possible."[136] For Paul, this new humanity liberated from sin and death involves a "new creation." In Beker's words: "Just as in Christ's death the powers of sin, the law, the flesh, and death are judged, so in Christ's resurrection the 'new creation' emerges."[137]

Christ's death is thus seen as bringing about a change in the *ontological* condition of human beings rather than in their forensic status before God. Undoubtedly, God forgives the sins of those who form part of this new humanity and declares them righteous, yet God does so not by virtue of Christ's death but on account of the ontological change effected in them by Christ and his death and resurrection. If powers such as sin, death, the law, and the curse are said to be involved, what is removed is their actual *power* to bring about the death of human beings rather than their *right* to do so, as in penal substitution views of Christ's work. Instead of speaking of a change taking place *in God*, physical interpretations of Christ's work posit a change *in the natural order*: sin no longer results in death as its consequence because what has taken place in Christ has negated sin's consequences. Together with his resurrection, Christ's death is salvific either in the sense that it removes the power of sin from the flesh or nature that all human beings share, or else in the sense that it alters the relationship between sin and death so that, even though sin remains in human beings, its power to cause death in the way it did previously has been "neutralized."

In order for what took place in Christ to have an effect in others as well, some type of link between Christ and others must be posited. Pauline scholars

---

131. Richard Hays, *The Faith of Jesus Christ: The Narrative Substructure of Galatians 3:1–4:11*, 2nd ed. (BRS; Grand Rapids: Eerdmans, 2002), xxx.
132. Garlington, *Faith*, 154.
133. Robin Scroggs, *The Last Adam: A Study in Pauline Anthropology* (Philadelphia: Fortress, 1966), 92-93, 102 (emphasis removed).
134. Ibid., 108-9.
135. Thrall, *2 Corinthians*, 1:429.
136. Ibid., 1:424.
137. Beker, *Paul*, 204.

generally use the language of "participation" to speak of this link. Although this term has been understood in different ways, many scholars attribute to Paul the idea of an *ontological* or *ontic* participation. Jan Lambrecht, for example, claims that Paul understood "participation" as the "natural result or effect of his union with Christ," and adds: "However difficult it may be to specify that unity, a kind of ontological union with Christ is presupposed by Paul and referred to frequently in his writings."[138] According to Douglas Campbell, for Paul this union involves a "radical ontological transformation of the person."[139] Similarly, Scot McKnight writes: "Jesus' death for Paul is fundamentally about the eschatological transfer from one sphere to another.... [T]he transfer is ontic transformation.... [T]he believer acquires this transformed existence by inclusion in the eschatological Second Adam, in Christ, and by participation in the death and resurrection of the Representative One, that is, by *co-crucifixion* and *co-resurrection*."[140] Beker also claims that for Paul "the term 'the new creation' does not just refer to a moral change but has ontological status."[141]

This type of interpretation of Paul's soteriology goes back to Adolf Deissmann at the end of the nineteenth century.[142] Deissmann pointed to Paul's repeated use of the phrase "in Christ" and similar phrases, such as "in Christ Jesus," "in the Lord," and "into Christ," in order to describe the relation of believers to Christ. According to Deissmann, Paul intended such phrases to be understood "vividly and mystically," since for Paul Christ was "not a 'historical' personage, but a reality and power of the present, an 'energy.'"[143] Deissmann spoke of Paul's "passion mysticism," claiming that each member of the body of Christ "mystically experiences all that that Body experienced and experiences."[144] Although Deissmann used the language of mysticism to characterize Paul's thought, he also ascribed to Paul the idea of an ontological union between Christ and believers: "Just as the air of life, which we breathe, is 'in' us and fills us, and yet we at the same time live in this air and breathe it, so it is also with the Christ-intimacy of the Apostle Paul: Christ in him, he in Christ."[145]

Following Deissmann, in his book *The Mysticism of the Apostle Paul*, Schweitzer affirmed that Paul did not think of the body of Christ as "an isolated entity, but as the point from which the dying and rising again, which began with Christ, passes over to the elect who are united with him; just as,

---

138. Jan Lambrecht, "The Nekrosis of Jesus: Ministry and Suffering in 2 Corinthians 4,7-15," in *Studies on 2 Corinthians* (ed. Reimund Bieringer and J. Lambrecht; BETL 112; Leuven: Leuven University Press, 1994), 326. Joseph A. Fitzmyer similarly speaks of the presence of Christ in believers as an "ontological reality" (*To Advance the Gospel: New Testament Studies*, 2nd ed.; Grand Rapids: Eerdmans, 1998, 177).
139. Campbell, *Quest*, 60.
140. McKnight, *Jesus*, 350-51.
141. Beker, *Paul*, 227.
142. On what follows, see Brondos, *Paul*, 151-66.
143. Adolf Deissmann, *Paul: A Study in Social and Religious History*, trans. William E. Wilson, 2nd ed. (London: Hodder and Stoughton, 1926), 136, 138, 140.
144. Ibid., 182.
145. Ibid., 140.

on the other hand, the elect no longer carry on an independent existence, but are now only the body of Christ."[146] For Schweitzer, whoever is "baptized into Christ is united in one corporeity with him and the other elect who are 'in Christ' (Gal. iii.27-28), and undergoes with him his dying and rising again (Rom. vi.3-4)."[147] According to Schweitzer, "The mystical body of Christ is thus for Paul not a pictorial expression, nor a conception which has arisen out of symbolical and ethical reflections, but an actual entity," which is "founded on the fact that the existences in question are physically inter-dependent in the same corporeity, and the one can pass over into the other."[148] On the basis of 1 Cor. 6:16-17, he refers to Paul's "doctrine of the union of believers with Christ as a physical bodily union," and elsewhere sees baptism and the Lord's Supper as bringing this union about: "What happens in the 'Lord's meal' is that which is asserted in the mystical doctrine of the being-in-Christ. The eating and drinking effects union with the body of Christ in the same way that baptism does. This is, according to Paul, what Jesus meant when he spoke at the Supper of eating and drinking his body and blood."[149]

In his work *The Body: A Study in Pauline Theology*, published in 1952, the British New Testament scholar John A. T. Robinson followed Deissmann and Schweitzer in claiming that "the concept of the body forms the keystone of Paul's theology."[150] After reviewing the Pauline passages that speak of dying with Christ, Robinson affirmed that in Paul's thought

> Christians have died in, with and through the crucified body of the Lord (have a share, that is, in the actual death that he died unto sin historically, 'once for all'.... It is only by baptism into Christ, that is 'into (the) one body' (1 Cor. 12.13), only by an actual 'participation in the body of Christ' (1 Cor. 10.16, R.V.M.), that a man can be saved through his body on the Cross. The Christian, because he is in the Church and united with him in the sacraments, is part of Christ's body so literally that all that happened in and through that body in the flesh can be repeated in and through him now....[151]

Robinson concludes: "It is almost impossible to exaggerate the materialism and crudity of Paul's doctrine of the Church as literally now the resurrection *body* of Christ."[152]

Throughout the twentieth century and into the twenty-first, Pauline scholars have continued to regard the idea of union with Christ and his death as central to Paul's thought, often presenting it as an alternative to his forensic or

---

146. Albert Schweitzer, *The Mysticism of Paul the Apostle*, trans. William Montgomery (Baltimore: Johns Hopkins University Press, 1998), 118. The German original *Die Mystik des Apostels Paulus* appeared in 1930 (Tübingen: J. C. B. Mohr).
147. Ibid., 19.
148. Ibid., 127.
149. Ibid., 128, 269.
150. John A. T. Robinson, *The Body: A Study in Pauline Theology* (SBT 5; London: SCM, 1952), 9; see also 48: "the concept of the Body supplies the lynch-pin of Paul's thought."
151. Ibid., 47 (emphasis removed).
152. Ibid., 51.

juristic soteriology.[153] The thought of both Bultmann and Karl Barth was particularly influential.[154] The terminology of participation became widespread among New Testament scholars in large part due to the 1977 publication of Sanders's book *Paul and Palestinian Judaism: A Comparison of Patterns of Religion*. Drawing on the work of Bultmann and that of biblical scholars such as D. E. H. Whiteley, Robert Tannehill, and Morna Hooker, Sanders argued that, while juristic categories are undoubtedly present in Paul's thought, the notion of participation in Christ or in his death is "the heart of his soteriology and Christology," and that the "real bite of his theology lies in the participatory categories...."[155] Sanders went so far as to claim that "even the foundation stones of the substitutionary theory—Rom. 8.3f.; II Cor. 5.21; Gal. 3.16 [sic]—do not really convey the doctrine of redemption by substitution. They are primarily participationist."[156]

Although Sanders did not employ the terminology of ontological participation and transformation explicitly, such a concept is implied in his insistence that Paul spoke of a "real participation in Christ."[157] Sanders rejected the notion of a "magical transfer," yet stressed his conviction that it is "best to understand Paul as saying what he meant and meaning what he said: Christians really are one body and Spirit with Christ...."[158] Other Pauline scholars have employed similar language, claiming that Paul conceived of the relationship between Christ and believers as an "essential unity" or as a "fundamental union" that is "real" or "supernatural."[159] This relationship has even been described as a "real 'physico-hyperphysical' union."[160] Other Pauline scholars have continued to use the language of mysticism, yet understand this in an ontological sense: there is a "mystical fellowship" or a "mysterious personal union" between Christ and believers, as well as a "mystical participation in Christ."[161] In order to insist that in Paul's thought the union with Christ is "real" and should not be understood merely in terms of identifying oneself

---

153. For a review of the history of this discussion, see L. Gregory Bloomquist, *The Function of Suffering in Philippians* (JSNTSup 78; Sheffield: JSOT, 1993), 34-70.
154. See my summary of the thought of Bultmann and Karl Barth in Brondos, *Fortress Introduction*, 130-53.
155. Sanders, *Paul and Palestinian Judaism*, 453, 502.
156. Ibid., 466. Instead of "Gal. 3.16" the text should read "Gal. 3.13."
157. Ibid., 522.
158. Ibid., 522.
159. See respectively Martin Kitchen, *Ephesians* (NTR; New York: Routledge, 1994), 59; Thrall, *2 Corinthians*, 1:334; Hays, *Faith*, 213-15; Otto Semmelroth, "The Christ-Event and Our Salvation," in *Man before God: Toward a Theology of Man. Readings in Theology*, trans. Donald Becker et al. (ed. Denis Burkhard et al.; New York: P. J. Kenedy, 1966), 215.
160. Bloomquist, *Function of Suffering*, 36 (referring to the work of Wilhelm Heitmüller, *Taufe und Abendmahl im Urchristentum*; RV I, 22/23; Tübingen: J. C. B. Mohr, 1911).
161. See respectively Thrall, *2 Corinthians*, 1:108; Hays, *Faith*, 224; McLean, *Cursed Christ*, 205. E. P. Sanders has recently acknowledged that he chose to speak of "participation" rather than "mysticism" when he wrote *Paul and Palestinian Judaism*, even though for him the basic idea was the same: "I accepted the heart of Schweitzer's view; but, since the term *mysticism* was widely misperceived, I substituted *participationism* and called Paul's theology 'participationist eschatology': see *Paul and Palestinian Judaism*, 434n19, 440n49, 453-63, 549, and elsewhere" (*Comparing Judaism and Christianity: Common Judaism, Paul, and the Inner and Outer in the Study of Religion*; Minneapolis: Fortress, 2016, 263, n37).

with Christ, many scholars have stressed that what is involved is more than an *imitatio Christi*.[162]

In addition to speaking of participation in Christ, scholars have used a wide variety of other terms and phrases to characterize Paul's concept of the relationship between Christ and other human beings. It is said that Paul thought of Christ as a "corporate or inclusive person": "the inclusive unity which the Christians enter is Christ himself.... They form one person because they are included in Christ."[163] Believers participate in Christ's "inclusive humanity" and also in his body, which is an "inclusive body."[164] Paul supposedly even conceived of Christ as a "universal person."[165] For Paul, just as all human beings are related to Adam, so Christ is in "solidarity" with humankind as a whole.[166] The "incorporation into Christ" that takes place through faith, baptism, and the Lord's Supper involves "being mystically incorporated into Christ."[167] Some even speak of Christ as constituting a "power centre," a "power field," or a "field of force."[168]

According to most New Testament scholars, Paul taught that believers participate not only in Christ as a *person* but also in his death and resurrection as *events*. For Paul, those who are "in Christ" participate in Christ's sufferings,[169] in his death and resurrection,[170] and in the "Christ-event."[171] Christ's death and resurrection are therefore "inclusive events, involving a corporate entity."[172] Hooker attributes to Paul the notion of a "mutual participation" that involves an "interchange of experience" in which believers "share in Christ's experience."[173] The notion of "inclusive place-taking" (*inkludierende Stellvertretung*) is similarly understood in terms of a relationship with Christ in which "Christ has not simply come alongside the sinner in order to take away something—namely, guilt and sin; he has rather become identical with

---

162. See, for example, Rudolf K. Bultmann, *The Second Letter to the Corinthians*, trans. Roy A. Harrisville (Minneapolis: Augsburg, 1985), 24; Lambrecht, "Nekrosis," 328; Thrall, *2 Corinthians*, 1:108; Hooker, "ΠΙΣΤΙΣ ΧΡΙΣΤΟΥ," *NTS* 35 (1989): 339; Robert C. Tannehill, *Dying and Rising with Christ: A Study in Pauline Theology* (BZNW 32; Berlin: Alfred Töpelmann, 1967), 100.

163. Tannehill, *Dying*, 20, 22. See also the discussion in Thrall, *2 Corinthians*, 1:424-29.

164. Ian G. Wallis, *The Faith of Jesus Christ in Early Christian Traditions* (SNTSMS 84; Cambridge: Cambridge University Press, 1995), 125, 143, 217; Tannehill, *Dying*, 48.

165. R. Martin, *Reconciliation*, 103.

166. Morna D. Hooker, *From Adam to Christ: Essays on Paul* (Cambridge: Cambridge University Press, 1990), 27; B. Martin, *Christ*, 73; Wedderburn, *Baptism*, 352.

167. See respectively Fung, *Galatians*, 274; Hooker, "ΠΙΣΤΙΣ ΧΡΙΣΤΟΥ," 335; McLean, *Cursed Christ*, 201.

168. Ziesler, *Pauline Christianity*, 64; Tannehill, *Dying*, 19; Hays, *Faith*, xxxi; Sam K. Williams, "Again Pistis Christou," *CBQ* 49 (1987): 440-41, 443.

169. See, for example, Peter T. O'Brien, *The Epistle to the Philippians: A Commentary on the Greek Text* (NIGTC; Grand Rapids: Eerdmans, 1991), 405-6; Bultmann, *Second Corinthians*, 24.

170. See, for example, McKnight, *Jesus*, 351, 353; Ziesler, *Pauline Christianity*, 29; B. Martin, *Christ*, 156; Tannehill, *Dying*, 21-24; Thrall, *2 Corinthians*, 332-35.

171. Schnackenburg, *Ephesians*, 95.

172. Tannehill, *Dying*, 123; see also 27, 30, 40, 52, 64, 70, 71.

173. Hooker, *Adam*, 4, 15-17, 26, 34, 40-45. See also Wright, *Climax*, 51-55.

the sinner...."[174] The idea that what is "true of Christ" is "true of all" is repeatedly attributed to Paul as well.[175]

Following Sanders, it has become customary to use the term "transfer" in order to communicate a number of these ideas. Some speak of sin, its curse, or its consequences being transferred from believers to Christ.[176] Wright refers to a "transfer of attributes" between Christ and believers.[177] More commonly, however, Pauline interpreters speak of human beings themselves as being transferred from one realm or sphere into another. Believers in particular are transferred into a "new 'order of being'" or into "a new eschatological reality in Christ."[178] For many scholars, this involves the transfer of believers from one lordship, dominion, or sphere into another under Christ's rule.[179] By virtue of their union with Christ's death and resurrection, they die with Christ to the old age or aeon so as to enter into a new one.[180]

Behind the frequent use of the vocabulary of "transfer" among Pauline scholars to characterize Paul's soteriological thought seems to be a concern for the Protestant teaching that the salvation that believers receive is due, not to anything they have done or must do, but to God's activity alone. Because Protestant theology has stressed so strongly the idea that salvation is by faith alone apart from any works on behalf of believers, Protestant interpreters of Paul have generally insisted that Paul's language regarding suffering and dying with Christ and being crucified with him must be understood in a *passive* sense as involving something done *to* believers rather than something they actively do themselves. From this Protestant perspective, to claim that for Paul the salvation of believers depends on their consciously and intentionally suffering, dying, and being crucified with Christ would involve salvation by works. Because those who are "transferred" from one place to another have something done *to* them rather than actively doing something themselves, the vocabulary of "transfer" enables Protestant biblical scholars to avoid ascribing to Paul the idea that believers save themselves by bringing themselves to participate in Christ or in his death by putting away their sin or old nature

---

174. Bailey, "Concepts," 243 (translating a selection from Otfried Hofius, "Das vierte Gottesknechtslied in den Briefen des Neuen Testamentes," *NTS* 39 [1993]: 416).

175. Wright, *Climax*, 48; Dunn, "Paul's Understanding," 40; Tannehill, *Dying*, 25; Ziesler, *Pauline Christianity*, 52; Moyer V. Hubbard, *New Creation in Paul's Letters and Thought* (SNTSMS 119; Cambridge: Cambridge University Press, 2002), 125.

176. See, for example, Martyn, *Galatians*, 18; McLean, *Cursed Christ*, 124, 205.

177. Wright, *Climax*, 48.

178. Tannehill, *Dying*, 8; Corneliu Constantineanu, *The Social Significance of Reconciliation in Paul's Theology: Narrative Readings in Romans* (LNTS 421; London: T & T Clark, 2010), 143.

179. See, for example, Ziesler, *Pauline Christianity*, 96; Dunn, *Theology of Paul*, 400; Beker, *Paul*, 261; Tannehill, *Dying*, 21; Morna D. Hooker, "Paul and Covenantal Nomism," in *Paul and Paulinism: Essays in Honour of C. K. Barrett* (ed. Hooker and S. G. Wilson; London: SPCK, 1982), 53; McKnight, *Jesus*, 350; Frank J. Matera, *Galatians* (ed. Daniel J. Harrington; SP 9; Collegeville, MN: Liturgical Press, 1992), 103; Williams, "Again," 443.

180. See, for example, Raymond Pickett, *The Cross in Corinth: The Social Significance of the Death of Jesus* (JSNTSup 143; Sheffield: Sheffield Academic Press, 1997), 111; Beker, *Paul*, 272; Tannehill, *Dying*, 70; Hultgren, *Christ*, 38-39; David Seeley, *The Noble Death: Graeco-Roman Martyrology and Paul's Concept of Salvation* (JSNTSup 28; Sheffield: JSOT, 1990), 147.

through their own efforts in order to live differently. The ontological change occurring in believers is thus not the result of anything *they* have done, but only of what God has done in Christ *for* them, *to* them, and *in* them.

New Testament scholars seem to be divided on the question of whether the union between Christ and others should be understood as embracing *all people* or only *believers*. In some cases, scholars seem to affirm both ideas simultaneously, either because they are unaware of the problems involved in doing so, or because they claim that this contradiction lies beyond the scope of biblical scholarship, which does not attempt to resolve the theological problems raised in Scripture. Of course, this is to presuppose that Paul himself affirmed both of these ideas at the same time.

The notion that *all people* are united to Christ or participate in him and the events of his death and resurrection is generally based on the concept of a common human nature in which all human beings share. This idea goes back at least to the time of the church fathers, whom some scholars even cite explicitly in support of this interpretation of Paul.[181] There can be little doubt that the fathers were influenced by Platonic thought in this regard, in particular the way in which Plato related the many to the one through his doctrine of ideas or forms. When applied to human beings, this doctrine affirms that all human beings participate or share in the universal idea of "man," so that the word "man" can be used to refer not only to all human beings collectively, but also to the human nature in which all share. In this latter sense, all human beings *participate* in "man" rather than merely *constituting* "man." In Plato's thought, this universal "man" was not merely an abstract idea but an actual reality. In fact, for Plato, because the ideas were eternal and unchangeable, they were more real than the particulars that participated in them.[182] In recent years, the desire to use inclusive language has greatly complicated attempts to communicate this idea since, unlike the word "man," terms like "humanity," "human," or "human being" cannot be used to refer simultaneously to a single person, to human beings collectively, and to a common nature in which all share.

Whether this reality in which all share is referred to as "man," "humanity," or "human nature," it is regarded as existing in a fallen state under the powers of sin and death. Now that Christ has come to participate in it by virtue of his incarnation and has transformed it through his death and resurrection, however, this shared reality is delivered and liberated from the malevolent powers to which it was subject. In this way, all human beings are delivered and liberated from those powers as well, since by nature they participate in that shared reality. Rather than speaking of Christ participating in the same humanity or nature common to all human beings, some theologians regard Christ himself as the "universal man" or the human being in which all others

---

181. See, for example, Dunn, who when discussing Jesus' solidarity with all human beings attributes to Paul the "theological logic" of Gregory of Nazianzus, Irenaeus, and Athanasius (*Theology of Paul*, 203-4).

182. On Plato's theory of ideas or forms as well as his use of "participatory" language, see especially Paul Friedländer, *Plato*, Vol. 3: *The Dialogues, Second and Third Periods*, trans. Hans Meyerhoff (Princeton: Princeton University Press, 1969), 198-217; David Ross, *Plato's Theory of Ideas* (Oxford: Clarendon, 1951), 226-33.

share or participate. In this way, their old being or old person is replaced by a new being or new person, who is Christ himself. This is equivalent to identifying Christ with the Platonic form or idea of "man."

On the basis of these ideas, Paul is said to have thought that "all humanity is encapsulated in that one man," that is, Christ.[183] Because Christ is the "eschatological representative of humanity," when he died, "humanity died."[184] Similarly, it is claimed that "Christ's death and resurrection are facts which contain a comprehensive reality that affects the whole of humanity."[185] "In the death of Christ, all men did really undergo the death of their sinful selves: this 'death' was an objective reality.... Paul conceives of Christ's representative function in such strong terms that the whole of humanity was really included in his death."[186] According to this reading of Paul, in 2 Cor. 5:14 he "implies that Christ's death includes the whole of humankind."[187]

For those who interpret Paul's thought in this way, what is now necessary is not that people come to be united to Christ, since that is already the case independently of whether or not one believes it to be true. Rather, through faith in Christ, people must become conscious of what has already happened to them and to humanity as a whole by virtue of Christ's death and resurrection. Thus the rite of baptism, for example, does not actually unite people to Christ but serves as a recognition of the fact that they were *already* united to him in his death and resurrection: "their baptism signified, pointed to the fact, that they were already 'with' him in his past and resurrection."[188] "[B]aptism is the acknowledgment that Christ's death and its salvific implications encompass—and always have done—the person baptized."[189] In this case, "baptism will be understood only as proclamation, thanks, and praise of that which has already occurred in Christ and was also appropriated...."[190] The influence of Karl Barth's thought is readily evident here.

As noted above, the word *body* can be used similarly to refer to a collective entity embracing all people, now assumed and transformed through Christ. Tannehill, for example, understands the allusions to the destruction of the "body of sin" in Rom. 6:6 and the putting away of the "body of flesh" in Col. 2:11 as something that took place in the humanity shared by all people. Tannehill interprets the condemnation of "sin in the flesh" in Rom. 8:3 and the taking off of the old person and putting on of the new in Col. 3:9-10 in

---

183. Bruce, *Colossians*, 284.
184. Matera, *II Corinthians*, 134.
185. Wedderburn, *Baptism*, 67 (citing Paul Althaus, *Der Brief an die Römer*, NTD 6; Göttingen: Vandenhoeck & Ruprecht, 1949, 55).
186. Thrall, *2 Corinthians*, 1:410 (summarizing the thought of Hans Windisch, *Der zweite Korintherbrief*, ed. Georg Strecker; KKNT 6; Göttingen: Vandenhoeck & Ruprecht, 1970, 182-83, and Gerhard Delling, "Der Tod Jesu in der Verkündigung des Paulus," in *Apophoreta: Festschrift für Ernst Haenchen zu seinem 70. Geburtstag*, ed. Walther Eltester and Franz Heinrich Kettler; BZNW 30; Berlin: Töpelmann, 1964, 91, 94).
187. Breytenbach, "'For Us' Phrases," 180.
188. Wedderburn, *Baptism*, 347.
189. Wallis, *Faith*, 126.
190. Markus Barth and Helmut Blanke, *Colossians: A New Translation with Introduction and Commentary*, trans. Astrid B. Beck (AB 34B; New York: Doubleday, 1994), 369.

the same terms. For Tannehill, when Paul speaks of the "crucifixion of 'our old man' with Christ" and the "destruction of the 'body of sin'," he is not referring "to the 'old man' and 'body' of each individual, but to a collective entity which is destroyed in the death of Christ.... [T]his body is at the same time the body which died on the cross and a corporate body in which believers were included.... Thus this old man and new man are corporate figures, related to the idea of Christ as a corporate person...."[191] According to Tannehill, like Adam, for Paul Christ is "a figure who determines the existence of the many because they share in his nature, so that what is true of the one is true of the many."[192]

The idea of participation in Christ and his sufferings, death, and resurrection can alternatively be understood as involving a *personal* relationship. In this case, it is not all human beings but only *believers* who participate in Christ and in his death and resurrection.

Ziesler, for example, speaks of a "faith-participation in the saving death and resurrection of Jesus."[193] Wedderburn, citing G. Otto, writes: "What happened to Christ happened to all with him who ever are or will be Christians."[194] Here only believers participate in the Christ-event. Other Pauline scholars stress that it is not merely through faith that this participation takes place but also through baptism and the Eucharist. According to Eduard Lohse, it is "in baptism in which the Christian is taken up into the death and resurrection of Christ."[195] Cilliers Breytenbach similarly affirms: "The baptism of believers is their integration into the body of Christ.... Through the Lord's Supper believers experience participation (*koinōnia*) in the body of the crucified. Baptism and the Lord's Supper integrate those who are baptized and remember the death of the Lord into his body and end their old existence."[196] According to many scholars, this is what Paul meant when he spoke of being "in Christ": "To be 'in Christ' is to have become incorporated through baptism into the community which is the body of Christ.... Christ is, after all, seen by Paul as an 'inclusive' or 'corporate' person.... Believers are included 'within' Christ's being so that his death and resurrection become theirs...."[197]

Many scholars attempt to maintain simultaneously that in Paul's thought *all* people are in some sense joined to Christ and his death and resurrection and that only *believers* participate in such a union. Dunn, for example, writes that for Paul "Jesus' death is the death of all humanity.... The death of the one is the death of the all." Nevertheless human beings must still "in faith identify

---

191. Tannehill, *Dying*, 24-25.
192. Ibid., 25; cf. 36, 46-47.
193. Ziesler, *Pauline Christianity*, 29. See also Fung, *Galatians*, 274.
194. Wedderburn, *Baptism*, 351 (quoting G. Otto, *Die mit σύν verbundenen Formulierungen im paulinischem Schriftum*; Dissertation; Berlin: Universität Berlin, 1952, 40).
195. Eduard Lohse, *Colossians and Philemon: A Commentary on the Epistles to the Colossians and to Philemon*, trans. William R. Poehlmann and Robert J. Karris (ed. Helmut Koester; Hermeneia; Philadelphia: Fortress, 1971), 104-5.
196. Breytenbach, "'For Us' Phrases," 181.
197. Thrall, *2 Corinthians*, 1:425-26.

themselves with Christ" for Christ's death to have this significance.[198] "[F]or those who find in Christ's death the answer to sin and death, who identify with him in his death, there is the prospect of sharing with him also in his resurrection beyond death."[199]

Although physical views of Christ's work are generally seen as constituting an alternative to penal substitution interpretations, it is also common to attempt to combine the two. This involves affirming both that Christ died *in the stead* of believers and also that they die *with* Christ. Wright, for example, writes: "'Participation' does not of itself exclude 'substitution', however frequently that spurious 'either-or' is asserted."[200] The problem with affirming these two concepts simultaneously is that, according to a substitutionary understanding, believers *do not* die because Christ died in their place, while in a participatory view, sinful believers *do* in fact die *together with* Christ. One could, of course, argue that both of these things are true, yet this would involve changing the sense in which the words *participation* and *substitution* are used. Furthermore, if believers are said to be saved and forgiven on the basis of Christ's substitutionary death, it is not clear why they should also need to be united to Christ or participate in his death and resurrection. This participation would contribute nothing further to their salvation. However, if salvation is instead said to depend on their being united with Christ and his death and resurrection, then it is this participation rather than Christ's substitutionary death that constitutes the basis upon which God forgives them and declares them righteous.

Many biblical scholars claim that Paul spoke not only of *believers* being ontologically transformed through Christ and his death and resurrection but the *entire created order* as well. Beker, for example, claims that in Paul's thought Christ's death and resurrection are "cosmic-ontological events" that effected the transformation of the cosmos *as a whole*.[201] For Victor Furnish, when Paul affirmed that in Christ there is a "new creation" (2 Cor. 5:17; Gal. 6:15), he had in mind "an ontic reality which transcends the new being of individual believers."[202] Joseph Fitzmyer claims that "Paul sees reconciliation as having not merely an anthropological dimension, but also a cosmic dimension; it affects not only the relation of human beings to God, but also that of the created universe."[203] According to Raymond Pickett, central to Paul's thought is his concept of "the objective transformation of reality effected by Christ's death."[204] Lohse affirms that in Colossians Paul teaches that "[t]he universe has been reconciled in that heaven and earth have been brought back

---

198. Dunn, *Theology of Paul*, 210-11.
199. Ibid., 233. See also 223, 268, 329, 372; Dunn, *Romans 1-8*, 182, 439-40.
200. Wright, *Climax*, 153, n54.
201. Beker, *Paul*, 196.
202. Victor Paul Furnish, *II Corinthians: Translated with Introduction, Notes, and Commentary* (AB 32A; Garden City, NY: Doubleday, 1984), 332.
203. Fitzmyer, *To Advance*, 169.
204. Pickett, *Cross*, 157.

into their divinely created and determined order through the resurrection and exaltation of Christ. Now the universe is again under its head and thereby cosmic peace has returned."[205]

Often the language of apocalyptic is used in connection with these ideas. Beker, for example, claims that "Paul interprets the death and resurrection of Christ primarily in terms of a cosmic-apocalyptic judgment and renewal. Just as in Christ's death the powers of sin, the law, the flesh, and death are judged, so in Christ's resurrection the 'new creation' emerges."[206] These "ontological powers that determine the human situation within the context of God's created order" are for Paul "major apocalyptic forces."[207] Elsewhere Beker speaks of Christ's resurrection as "ontological-apocalyptic" in nature and claimed that it "has inaugurated a new ontological reality...."[208] "Because the resurrection is an apocalyptic-cosmic event that inaugurates the cosmic triumph of God, it draws the death of Christ into its apocalyptic orbit."[209]

Nevertheless, as this last quote makes clear, many scholars claim that Paul conceived of the ontological transformation of reality brought about by Christ as something that is not yet complete. According to Beker, while "the cross is God's judgment of the world," the resurrection is only "the *beginning* of the ontological renewal of creation that will come to completion in God's new age."[210] Beker uses the word "proleptic" to describe this: Christ's resurrection "is a proleptic event that inaugurates the new creation."[211] He also points to Oscar Cullmann's "analogy of D-day and V-day of World War II" to illustrate the tension between the "already" and the "not yet." Citing A. M. Hunter, he writes: "though the campaign may drag on and V-day, the day of final glory may still be out of sight, D-day is over and the powers of evil have received a blow from which they can never recover."[212]

Similar ideas are found in the writings of other scholars, who also distinguish between the "already" and the "not yet" in Paul's thought. Tannehill writes: "The decisive event has already taken place, an event which Paul understood in eschatological terms. Nevertheless, the old world continues to exist and to exercise a certain power.... The new world is already present, but it is hidden within the old...."[213] Like Beker, many use the term *proleptic* to describe this reality: "cosmic peace (*shalom*) and salvation have been *proleptically* manifested in Christ."[214] It has also become common to claim that

---

205. Lohse, *Colossians*, 59.
206. Beker, *Paul*, 204.
207. Ibid., 189.
208. Ibid., 196.
209. Ibid., 189.
210. Ibid., 211 (emphasis added).
211. Ibid., 159.
212. Ibid., 159 (the citation is from Archibald M. Hunter, *Interpreting Paul's Gospel*; London: SCM, 1954, 127).
213. Tannehill, *Dying*, 75, 78; see also 127.
214. Garlington, *Faith*, 76. See also Scott J. Hafemann, *Paul, Moses, and the History of Israel: The Letter/Spirit Contrast and the Argument from Scripture in 2 Corinthians 3* (WUNT 81; Tübingen: J. C. B. Mohr, 1995), 343.

Paul thought in terms of an "inaugurated eschatology" rather than a "realized eschatology." According to Allison, the latter phrase mistakenly "implies fulfillment without remainder.... The earliest Christian preaching contained an 'already' that by no means excluded a 'not yet.' In fact, the two went hand in hand."[215] Because believers are united to Christ and he has died and risen, however, they can have full certainty that this ontological transformation will ultimately reach its goal: "[A]ccording to Paul [Christ's] resurrection guarantees the final resurrection of Christians as well.... His resurrection not only stands to guarantee a future general resurrection, but it also marks the beginning of the age to come in advance of its final consummation."[216]

Theological Problems and Presuppositions

The physical interpretations of Christ's saving work just outlined are based on a number of premises that are not usually made explicit among those who attribute those interpretations to Paul and other authors of the New Testament writings. Here I will discuss five of the most important of these.

Premise 1: Powers such as sin and death are ontological in nature and as such can be dealt with in much the same way that ontological realities or substances are dealt with in the physical world.

Dunn's interpretation of the work of Christ provides an excellent example of this premise. By conceiving of sin as some type of malignant cancer, poison, or virus, he presupposes that the problem of sin can be addressed in the same way that medicines or vaccines are introduced into the body in order to reverse or alter certain biological, chemical, or physical processes.[217] Because of Christ's divine nature, union with Christ or participation in his death and resurrection then becomes the means by which human beings or the entire created order are delivered from the malevolent powers or substances to which they have been subjected.

These ideas are reflected in the language that proponents of physical views of Christ's work often use. For God to "absorb," "exhaust," or "neutralize" the power of sin and death in human beings involves reversing *natural consequences*, the "cause-and-effect" mechanisms that are at work in the world or in human nature. On this basis, many biblical scholars speak of salvation in Christ as involving some type of "mechanics" or "mechanism" and inquire as to how Christ's death and resurrection "work" to produce their salvific "effects."[218]

---

215. Dale C. Allison Jr., *The End of the Ages Has Come: An Early Interpretation of the Passion and Resurrection of Jesus* (Philadelphia: Fortress, 1985), 150.
216. Bruce A. Lowe, "Oh διά! How is Romans 4:25 to be Understood?," *JTS* 57 (2006): 153. See also C. E. Hill, "Paul's Understanding of Christ's Kingdom in 1 Cor. 15:20-28," *NovT* 30 (1988): 303-6.
217. See, for example, Dunn, *Theology of Paul*, 214-15: "The imagery is more of the removal of a corrosive stain or the neutralization of a life-threatening virus than of anger appeased by punishment." See also ibid., 223; Dunn, "Paul's Understanding," 50; Dunn, *Romans 1-8*, 182, 372, 439, 442; Martyn, *Galatians*, 318.
218. See, for example, Constantineanu, *Social Significance*, 110, 143; Dunn, *Theology of Paul*, 218; Campbell, *Quest*, 60; Stephen Finlan, *The Background and Content of Paul's Cultic Atonement Metaphors* (AcBib 19; Atlanta: SBL, 2004), 190; R. Martin, *Reconciliation*, 98; McKnight, *Jesus*, 346.

Other scholars use mechanistic language to describe what takes place in Christ: "God's resurrection of Jesus from the dead not only frees Jesus Christ from the powers, but it *sets in motion* the defeat of Sin and Death...."[219] Jesus' death serves to "*trigger* the general resurrection,"[220] while "the beginning of new creation... has been *triggered* by the resurrection of God's crucified Son."[221] To set something in motion or trigger something is to initiate a series of cause-and-effect reactions that follow one upon another automatically and mechanically.

According to these ideas, Christ's incarnation, death, and resurrection were necessary to alter the laws of nature in some way or to overpower or extirpate some maleficent ontological forces from the world or from the nature in which all human beings share. Salvation seems to be understood almost as some type of genetic mutation in the human makeup or the result of a change in the molecular structure of reality or the cosmos. The ontological alteration of the universe or of the human condition that supposedly took place as a consequence of humanity's fall into sin is reversed by Christ so that human nature or nature as a whole is now healed and restored to harmony and order. According to Hooker, for example, "Paul represents redemption in Christ as a radical restructuring of human nature...."[222] Similarly, Hays attributes to Paul the idea that "Jesus' death terminates the old age and ushers in a new one, in such a way that the very structure of reality is transformed."[223]

Proponents of this type of explanation often view divinity itself as some type of power or substance that is capable of transforming human nature or the nature of the world. The introduction of the divine substance or essence into human nature or the world acts like leaven introduced into bread dough to make it rise.[224] On this basis, it is argued that it was necessary for Christ to be both fully divine and fully human: only the power of the divinity was capable of bringing about the ontological transformation or healing necessary for salvation. In order for that power to be introduced into the world, it was necessary for the divine to become human in Christ.

When humanity or human nature is conceived of as some type of ontological reality that is present in all human beings or in which all share, defining precisely how each individual human being relates to this common humanity is highly problematic. How exactly does the physical interconnectedness

---

219. Beverly Roberts Gaventa, "Interpreting the Death of Jesus Apocalyptically: Reconsidering Romans 8:32," in *Jesus and Paul Reconnected: Fresh Pathways into an Old Debate* (ed. Todd D. Still; Grand Rapids: Eerdmans, 2007), 139 (emphasis added).

220. McKnight, *Jesus*, 361 (emphasis added).

221. Brigitte Kahl, *Galatians Re-Imagined: Reading with the Eyes of the Vanquished* (PCC; Minneapolis: Fortress, 2010), 222.

222. Hooker, "ΠΙΣΤΙΣ ΧΡΙΣΤΟΥ," 338.

223. Hays, "Crucified," 239. See also Jens Schröter, *Der Versöhnte Versöhner: Paulus als unentbehrlicher Mittler im Heilsvorgang zwischen Gott und Gemeinde nach 2 Kor 2,14—7,4* (TANT 10; Tübingen: Francke, 1993), 286. There Schröter argues that *kainē ktisis* should be understood in an ontological sense and claims that for Paul "mit dem Tod Christi der alte Äon untergegangen ist und eine den ganzen Kosmos betreffende Erneuerung stattgefunden hat."

224. For this interpretation of Paul's thought, see Nonna Verna Harrison, "Theosis as Salvation: An Orthodox Perspective," *ProEccl* 6 (1997): 436.

between human beings work? Did Paul, for example, think that Adam as the progenitor of all human beings had been infected with some substance or power that he then passed down to all his descendants? When Christ is compared to Adam in this regard, it is not clear how all human beings can be affected by the transformation brought about in Christ's own humanity, since human beings do not descend physically from Christ as they do from Adam. Therefore some other ontological link must be posited between Christ's humanity and that of the rest of human beings so that what takes place in him can produce some "effect" in all others as well. Christ's work is then defined in terms of bringing into existence some type of ontologically transformed humanity in which others can participate.

Similar affirmations can be made regarding the notion that Christ has delivered fallen human beings from the personal demonic powers to which they were subject. Christ's entrance into the realm in which those forces are at work effects an ontological change in the cosmos by neutralizing those forces or hindering them from affecting human beings in the ways that they did previously by virtue of the superior divine power that he possesses.

The way in which sin and death are thought to relate to one another is also problematic in physical views of redemption. If death is said to be the natural consequence of sin, once human beings are freed from the power of sin, it would seem that they are thereby automatically delivered from death as well. However, death or mortality can also be seen as an ontological substance, reality, or power present in human nature that is dealt with directly through Christ's assumption of human nature and the transformation of that nature effected through his death and resurrection. In this case, it would appear that human beings can be saved from the power of death without necessarily being delivered from the power of sin, which may remain present in human nature or the world. This is true whether sin and death are thought to be brought about by forces of evil that are impersonal or personal.

The relation between the salvation of human beings and that of the world or cosmos also raises difficulties in physical views of Christ's work. Precisely how does the ontological transformation of human beings affect the cosmos? Or, conversely, how does the ontological transformation of the cosmos affect human beings? Furthermore, when the ontological transformation occurring in Christ is said to result in the ontological transformation of the cosmos and of human beings, the question then becomes how Christ relates ontologically both to the cosmos and to human beings. How is one to understand, for example, the affirmation that in Paul's thought "[t]he redemption that is in Christ Jesus is a cosmic redemption; its healing virtue streams out to the farthest bounds of creation"?[225] How does what happened in Christ affect everything or everyone else? Clearly, some type of ontological link must be posited between Christ and the rest of reality.

---

225. Bruce, *Colossians*, 113.

Proponents of physical views of Christ's work generally claim that the ontological transformation effected by Christ brings about an ethical renewal of human beings as its consequence.[226] Once delivered from the the personal or impersonal forces of evil that exerted their malicious influence over them, human beings are now able to live differently. The evil inclination in human hearts is overcome or substantially weakened so that now human beings are able to do good. This, however, raises the question of whether their salvation from death is to be attributed directly to the ontological transformation that has taken place in them or instead to the change in their conduct to which that ontological transformation leads. In the former case, they are saved from death, not because their conduct is now acceptable to God, but because their being or nature has been ontologically transformed so as to be freed from the power of death. In the latter case, however, a forensic component is added to the equation. On the basis of the ethical transformation that takes place in those who have been transformed ontologically, God forgives them their sins, declares them righteous, and saves them from death. In this case, the ontological transformation effected by Christ does not in itself effect the salvation of human beings, but merely makes it possible for them to undergo an ethical transformation on the basis of which God then acts to save them.

Premise 2: It was not possible for human beings, human nature, or the nature of the created order to be transformed ontologically or delivered from the powers to which they were subject without Christ's incarnation, life, death, and resurrection.

Physical understandings of God's work in Christ generally posit the necessity of Christ's coming, death, and resurrection in order for humanity and the world to be saved. They can only posit this necessity, however, by claiming that it was impossible for the ontological transformation of the cosmos or human nature to take place without such a transformation taking place first in Christ.

Thus, for example, Dunn argues, "Sinful flesh could be dealt with only by killing it. The power of sin could exhaust itself only in death. Jesus' death embodied and enacted that fact."[227] Elsewhere he writes: "God *could only* deal with the problem of 'sinful flesh' by sending his Son in complete solidarity and identity with humankind in its existence under the powers of sin and death.... This evidently, so far as Paul was concerned, was *the only way* God could deal with the power of sin and death. The sentence of death on the infected portion of humanity was the means to life for the rest of humanity."[228] Here it is clear that the only way in which sin and death could be overcome in humanity as a whole was for them to be overcome or "killed" first in Christ's own

---

226. See, for example, Charles Talbert, "Paul, Judaism, and the Revisionists," *CBQ* 63 (2001): 20–22. There Talbert comments that for Paul the ontological transformation of the believer is "divine empowerment" that leads to obedience. Similarly, McKnight affirms that, in Pauline theology, "the death of Christ rescues by a co-crucifixion and co-resurrection that lead to behavioral change and to life" (*Jesus*, 353).

227. Dunn, *Theology of Paul*, 318.

228. Ibid., 202–3, 223 (emphasis added).

humanity. Similarly, Scroggs' affirmation that "Christ not only is true humanity; he also mediates this true humanity to the believer"[229] presupposes that the "true humanity" had to be brought about first in Christ. Only then could Christ mediate this same new, true humanity to others.

But why was this the case? Why God could not just bring about in humanity or the world the type of ontological transformation that was needed *independently* of Christ? Could not God have simply destroyed the malevolent powers holding humanity in bondage or have eradicated the power of sin and evil in the world or in human nature by *fiat*?[230] Why could God not do away with the consequences of human sin without those consequences being "exhausted" first by being "absorbed" by Christ in his death? There simply seems to be no basis for claiming that the curse pronounced by God's law on sinners "could only be thrown off by Christ offering himself as a substitutionary victim."[231] Why was it not possible for God simply to remove the curse present in human nature by an act of divine power, *without* Christ becoming human and dying?

Once again, biblical scholars rarely address these kinds of questions. They merely ascribe such ideas to Paul and excuse themselves from dealing with the theological problems involved by claiming that they are not theologians but biblical scholars, and therefore that such problems lie outside the realm of their discipline. In so doing, they lay the theological mess at the feet of Paul, as if he were to blame, refusing to recognize that in reality it is not Paul but they who have created the mess by reading all kinds of ideas foreign to Paul's thought back into his writings.

---

229. Scroggs, *Last Adam*, 92, 98, 99, 102.

230. Traditionally, three arguments have been used to answer the question of why God could not have delivered humanity from evil by *fiat*. The first is of an *ontological* nature. This argument may take the form of affirming that fallen human nature or the cosmos was incapable of receiving the divine power that needed to be transfused into it because the latter was so great in strength that it would overpower or overwhelm humanity or creation in some way. This argument goes back to Irenaeus of Lyons, who claimed that in Christ humanity needed to be gradually accustomed to its union with divinity, as we shall see in Chapter 18. The problem with such an argument is that salvation is essentially conceived of in terms of bringing together two different substances, the divine and human, and making the human compatible with the divine. God's work in Christ is then in effect to bring about some type of physical, biological, or chemical transformation in human nature or the world. A second argument involves claiming that the ontological transformation necessary in human beings had to be effected first in Christ because that ontological transformation had to be preceded by a proper ethical response, and Christ alone was capable of making such a response. This argument is found in the doctrine of the Council of Trent as well as in Protestant thought: in order for God to infuse the grace needed or pour out the Holy Spirit on human beings, Christ needed to *merit* such a gift on their behalf through his death. A third argument looks to forensic ideas of justice to claim that it would have been *unjust* for God to bring about the ontological transformation necessary for human salvation by *fiat*. As noted previously, some of the church fathers claimed that God had to respect the devil's rights in rescuing human beings from his power and thus had to offer the devil his Son in exchange for the release of human beings. All of these arguments are problematic and seem to provide no satisfactory or convincing answer as to why God could not simply have brought about by *fiat* the ontological transformation required in human beings in order for them to be saved without first bringing that transformation about in Christ.

231. McLean, *Cursed Christ*, 201.

Premise 3: Before the ontological transformation of humanity or the world could be brought about in its eschatological fullness, it was necessary to bring it about in part in the present time.

This idea is closely related to the previous point. The stress here, however, is on the notion that the *full and definitive* transformation of human beings and the cosmos that is generally associated with the *eschaton* must be preceded by a *partial* transformation. The argument for the *necessity* of this partial transformation prior to the final one is not generally made explicitly, but instead tends to be simply assumed.

In both ancient Judaism and early Christianity, those who envisioned an ontological transformation of human beings and the created order generally regarded it as something that would take place at the *eschaton*, when the promised new age of salvation would arrive. The early Christian proclamation also appears to have asserted that some type of ontological transformation had already taken place in Christ's own body when he was raised from the dead. Physical views of Christ's work, however, take the further step of claiming that the ontological transformation that took place in Christ when he was raised affected not only him but others as well. They therefore posit some type of partial or inaugurated transformation in human nature or the nature of the created order that must still come fully to completion and perfection, as we have noted above.[232]

One image commonly employed by Pauline scholars to characterize Paul's understanding of the new reality brought about by Christ through his death and resurrection is that of the dawn of a new age. "Through his death and resurrection, the eschatological age of salvation has begun to dawn."[233] "[T]he new covenant of the future has already been inaugurated in Christ and the final salvation and judgment have already begun.... It is the proleptic dawning of the new age itself.... What distinguishes Paul's thought is his conviction that the new age has already begun in Christ...."[234] Nevertheless, while "[t]he New Creation *has dawned*," there are "still battles to be fought...."[235] Thus more still needs to be done.

Language of the new age "breaking in" or being "ushered in" by Christ is also common: "Christ ushered in the new era at the 'turn of the ages'...."[236] "The cross, then, is the apocalyptic turning point of history. The breaking-in of the new age means the destruction and judgment of the old age."[237] "The old world has been crucified and new creation has broken in through Jesus's death and resurrection...."[238]

---

232. For other allusions to these ideas, see Tannehill, *Dying*, 75, 78; Beker, *Paul*, 149, 211; J. Louis Martyn, "Apocalyptic Antinomies in Paul's Letter to the Galatians," *NTS* 31 (1985): 411-12.

233. Terence L. Donaldson, *Paul and the Gentiles: Remapping the Apostle's Convictional World* (Minneapolis: Fortress, 1997), 187. See also Allison, *End*, 65, 80.

234. Hafemann, *Paul*, 343.

235. Martyn, "Apocalyptic Antinomies," 420.

236. R. Martin, *Reconciliation*, 103.

237. Beker, *Paul*, 205.

238. Hays, *Faith*, xxix. See also Hays, "Crucified," 233.

Closely related to this kind of affirmation is the idea that the evil powers or principalities have been defeated in principle, but this defeat must still be completed. As noted above, it is common to maintain that in his death and resurrection Christ won a "decisive victory" over the evil powers, yet the *definitive* victory still lies in the future.[239] "The apocalyptic battle between God and the powers of sin and death has been fought and won at the cross."[240] As Cullmann's analogy of D-day and V-day implies, "the decisive victory has been won but mopping up operations remain."[241]

Such language is problematic for two reasons. First of all, it contradicts our historical reality today, just as much as it contradicted the historical reality of people in the first century. Humanity is just as much subject to sin and death as it was before Christ came. Human nature, like nature in general, remains essentially the same as it has always been. There is no evidence that any type of hidden, mysterious ontological change took place in human beings or the world when Christ died and rose. Nor is there any empirical basis for affirming that human nature has undergone a "radical restructuring" or that "the very structure of reality is transformed" as a result of what has taken place in Christ. One can hardly maintain that the amount of evil in the world suddenly decreased immediately following Christ's death and resurrection. On the contrary, evil remains just as prevalent as it was before. If this is attributed to evil forces in the world, it can hardly be said that their power has been taken away by Christ and their defeat ensured, since those forces continue to win many victories and will ultimately take down a large portion of humanity with them. In that case, all that took place in Christ is that the situation of humanity and the world has been changed from one in which the defeat of the forces of evil *did not* yet exist "in principle" to one in which it now *does* exist "in principle," though not in reality. Of course, the New Testament itself speaks of the defeat of the forces of evil through Christ, yet as I shall argue later on, there is no clear basis there for interpreting this in the sense that the power of evil actually came to an end or was substantially diminished when Christ died and rose.

A second problem with such language is that it implies that the ontological transformation of humanity or the cosmos is something that takes place gradually and progressively. For example, when the initial victory of the Allied forces took place on D-day in Europe during World War II, those forces gradually established themselves over an increasingly greater territory until all of the conquered territories were finally taken back. This involved a series of progressive stages by which Europe eventually was liberated from the Nazi regime and its allies. To use this type of imagery suggests that Christ is now

---

239. See, for example, Caird, *New Testament*, 119-20; Judith L. Kovacs, "'Now Shall the Ruler of this World be Driven Out': Jesus' Death as Cosmic Battle in John 12:20-36," *JBL* 114 (1995): 229, 246; John M. G. Barclay, *Colossians and Philemon* (NTG; Sheffield: Sheffield Academic Press, 1997), 85.

240. Normand Bonneau, "The Logic of Paul's Argument on the Curse of the Law in Galatians 3:10-14," *NovT* 39 (1997): 69.

241. B. Martin, *Christ*, 108.

slowly imposing his reign over the world in the way that the Allied forces did over Europe.

Such a gradual process over time is also implied by the image of a new age "dawning." Dawn is a stage following upon the darkness of night and preceding the full brightness of daytime, which inevitably follows. To maintain that a new age has dawned implies that gradually this new age will grow in intensity and develop into its fullness over time, as if a promised utopia is to become a historical reality little by little. In fact, the way in which many interpreters speak of the new age having "dawned" implies that we have now been stuck at dawn for centuries without advancing any further, as if the earth had stopped turning. Few biblical scholars would admit openly that such an understanding of the gradual arrival of the new age is found in the New Testament in general and the Pauline writings in particular. Nevertheless, scholars continue to use such language widely and uncritically, seemingly oblivious to the theological and historical problems it involves.

The concern of many scholars in all of this is to claim that, as a result of Christ's death and resurrection, something has actually happened to the world and to humanity. The "Christ-event" must have "effected" some type of real, ontological change in reality in some way; otherwise, it would appear that Christ's coming, death, and resurrection constituted isolated events that had no major impact on human beings or the created order. For many, this would involve minimizing or denying the universal significance of what took place in Christ and call into question the idea that something new has come into existence as a result of Christ's incarnation, life, death, and resurrection.

Premise 4: Although all human beings have been ontologically transformed or united to Christ, each individual must come to faith in order to be saved.

Physical interpretations of Christ's work raise the same problem mentioned previously with regard to penal substitution views: they affirm on the one hand that *all human beings* have been saved objectively, while on the other hand they maintain that salvation depends on the subjective response of human beings to what God has done in Christ.

If it were truly the case that through Christ humanity as a whole has been liberated from its subjection to the forces that held all in bondage, so that "evil has already been judged and cast out" and "sin's power has been eradicated in Christ,"[242] then all people would automatically be saved, independently of any response on their part to what God has done in Christ. Nothing more would be required of anyone. However, once it is maintained that some human response such as faith or a transformed life is necessary in order to be saved, then the affirmation that all human beings have been

---

242. Beker, *Paul*, 215, 219; Allison, *End*, 54 (commenting on John 12:31). For other examples of these ideas, see Markus Barth, *Ephesians: Introduction, Translation, and Commentary* (AB 34; Garden City, NY: Doubleday, 1974), 1:235; Schnackenburg, *Ephesians*, 126; Martyn, *Galatians*, 326; Matera, *II Corinthians*, 133-34; Beker, *Paul*, 193.

saved through Christ must be qualified in some way. Generally, this is done by affirming that all people have been saved "potentially" or "in principle," but end up being *actually* saved only if they come to faith. What Christ has done merely makes their salvation *possible*: "when Christ who was a representative or inclusive figure was raised all were *potentially* raised with him...."[243] "The Christ event has *in principle* destroyed 'the flesh,' and engendered the *possibility* of new life for those who themselves allow 'the flesh' to be mortified in their own human life."[244] "Christ's death for their sins made *possible* their deliverance from the evil age, their freedom from the enslaving powers, and their knowledge of the true God.... Christ, in his crucifixion, was himself the object of the law's curse ('Cursed is everyone who hangs on a tree,' [Gal. 3:13, citing Deut. 21:23]); thereby he exhausted its force for those otherwise cursed *who believe in him*."[245]

As this last quote makes clear, in this way it is claimed that, even though Christ has conquered the powers that held all of humanity and the world in bondage, ultimately only believers are actually saved: "The representatives of the old age—sin, death, the law, and the flesh—have been overthrown and caused to release their grip on *those who are now in Christ*."[246] "Jesus' lifting up in John 12,20-36 has cosmic-juridical effects.... [T]his decisive judgment and destruction of the cosmic 'ruler' behind the world also amounts to *eschatological* and *soteriological* effects that benefit *those who believe*."[247]

Affirmations of this type are problematic for a couple of reasons. First, it simply makes no sense to claim that all human beings have been saved in principle or potentially, but that they must still come to faith in order for that salvation to be actual. One would have to affirm that the only thing that Christ's coming has changed is that human beings have passed from a condition of *not* being saved potentially or in principle into a new condition in which they *are* saved potentially or in principle. Conversely, if a proper response is necessary for one ultimately to be saved, those who *were already* saved by Christ from the forces of evil become *unsaved* if they do not make such a response. In that case, the ontological transformation that took place in the humanity of all is reversed, negated, or undone in those who do not respond properly to it.

The second problem with such affirmations is that, strictly speaking, they attribute human salvation, not to what God has done in Christ, but to the *human response* to what God has done in Christ. Even if through Christ God is said to have delivered all human beings from the powers that held them in

---

243. Ernest Best, *A Critical and Exegetical Commentary on Ephesians* (ICC; Edinburgh: T & T Clark, 2010), 215 (emphasis added).
244. Thrall, *2 Corinthians*, 1:337 (referring to the thought of Ehrhard Kamlah, "Wie beurteilt Paulus sein Leiden? Ein Beitrag zur Untersuchung seiner Denkstruktur," *ZNW* 54 [1963]: 230-31; emphasis added).
245. Westerholm, *Perspectives*, 369, 376 (emphasis added). See also Thrall, *2 Corinthians*, 1:424.
246. Garlington, *Faith*, 72 (emphasis added).
247. John Dennis, "The 'Lifting up of the Son of Man' and the Dethroning of the 'Ruler of this World': Jesus' Death as the Defeat of the Devil in John 12,31-32," in *The Death of Jesus in the Fourth Gospel* (ed. G. Van Belle; BETL 200; Leuven: Leuven University Press, 2007), 680 (emphasis added).

bondage, in reality God ends up delivering from bondage only those human beings who *respond properly* to God. As in a forensic view of Christ's work, if a response of faith is necessary for one to be saved, then ultimately it is not Christ's life, death, and resurrection that effect salvation but one's faith. Salvation is no longer the automatic consequence of what Christ has done but depends on a divine decision to bring about the necessary transformation in those whose faith God regards as sufficient for that purpose. If faith is instead said to effect salvation automatically or mechanically, then faith becomes a necessary cog in the mechanism of salvation or part of a magic formula that "works" only when faith is present. Similarly, when it is claimed that all human beings have been transformed and that Christian baptism is merely a recognition that one has already been saved, the question arises as to whether it is possible for one truly to be saved without ever becoming aware of it or recognizing it.

Premise 5: Although the notion of an ontological participation was clear to people in Paul's day, it is no longer clear to people in ours.

Attempting to define the way in which Paul understood believers to be united to Christ or to participate in his death and resurrection has been highly problematic for biblical scholars. As noted above, Sanders struggled with this question: on the one hand he insisted that this union was "real," yet he rejected not only the idea of a "magical transfer," but also Bultmann's claim that what was involved was merely a "revised self-understanding."[248] He concluded that we "lack a category of 'reality'—real participation in Christ, real possession of the Spirit—which lies between naive cosmological speculation and a revised self-understanding on the other. I must confess that I do not have a new category of perception to propose here. This does not mean, however, that Paul did not have one.... [W]hat Paul concretely thought cannot be directly appropriated by Christians today."[249]

In essence, this involves taking Paul's participatory language *literally* so as to interpret Paul as "saying what he meant and meaning what he said,"[250] yet then affirming that if we take it literally, it is unintelligible today. Other Pauline scholars follow suit. Hays, for example, writes: "How does union [with Christ's death] occur? Unfortunately, this is not as clear as we might wish.... [T]he matter remains mysterious."[251] According to Troels Engberg-Pedersen:

> One feature of Paul's 'theology' *cum* 'cosmology' is an idea of a kind of physical participation in Christ on the part of Christ-believers: they are 'one with' Christ in a manner that was probably understood by Paul in a very reified way. (Fortunately, however, he also understood it in other ways that are more accessible to us.) Now scholars often speak of Paul's idea here as if it made immediate sense and indeed was more or less readily acceptable to us. But it is not. On the contrary, it looks

---

248. Sanders, *Paul and Palestinian Judaism*, 522.
249. Ibid., 522–23.
250. Ibid., 522.
251. Hays, "Crucified," 242.

as if it is very far from constituting a real option for us. That also means, however, that it is very difficult to develop, even as part of doing one's existentially neutral, historical work, what it all meant to Paul. Since it appears so strange to us, one really cannot feel sure that one has got it sufficiently right for it to be possible to develop it further and combine it with other similar ideas. A shared level of discourse is lacking.[252]

Pauline scholars make similar observations regarding other concepts that they attribute to Paul. Among these are the idea of a transfer of sin or the transfer of believers from one realm or aeon to another, the understanding of Christ as constituting some sort of "power field," and the precise manner in which Christ's death and resurrection supposedly brought about an ontological change in humanity or in creation as a whole.

For people of all different times and places to be united to Christ's death and resurrection, it is necessary either to make those events omnipresent in some way or to establish some type of timeless ontological link between all people and the historical event of the cross. Bultmann chose to affirm the first of these alternatives, claiming that for Paul the "cosmic event" of the cross "may no longer be considered as just the historical event of Jesus' crucifixion on Golgotha. For God made this event the eschatological occurrence, so that, lifted out of all temporal limitation, it continues to take place in any present moment, both in the proclaiming word and the sacraments."[253] Otto Semmelroth similarly affirmed that in Paul's thought "the Christ event does not remain bound to the historic past but has been brought into a continuing state of actuality in the presence of the eternal God by Christ's resurrection and ascension...."[254] In contrast, Karl Barth opted for the second alternative, in effect placing all human beings at Golgotha on the cross together with Jesus: "For then and there, in the person of Christ taking our place, we were present, being crucified and dying with him. We died. This has to be understood quite concretely and literally.... We died: the totality of all sinful men and women.... His death was the death of all."[255] For Barth, all human beings died with Christ because they all share in the same humanity or human nature that Christ assumed in the incarnation and put to death on the cross.

One cannot help asking, however, whether it is true that these strange and mystifying concepts that are no longer comprehensible to us in our modern age were perfectly intelligible for people in Paul's day. Have we really become incapable of grasping ideas that people two thousand years ago understood clearly without any difficulties? Or does the real problem lie with modern interpreters who have mistakenly attributed to Paul and the other New

---

252. Troels Engberg-Pedersen, *Paul and the Stoics* (Louisville, KY: Westminster John Knox, 2000), 27. See also Dunn, *Romans 1-8*, 328; Dunn, *Theology of Paul*, 409-10.
253. Bultmann, *Theology*, 1:303.
254. Semmelroth, "Christ-Event," 218.
255. Karl Barth, *Church Dogmatics* (ed. and trans. G. W. Bromiley and T. F. Torrance; Edinburgh: T & T Clark, 1936-1969), 4/1:295.

Testament writers ideas and notions that would have been just as strange and mystifying to people in antiquity as they are to us today?

REVELATIONAL INTERPRETATIONS OF CHRIST'S WORK IN NEW TESTAMENT SCHOLARSHIP

When Christ's death and resurrection are regarded as salvific by virtue of what they *reveal* to human beings, a seemingly endless list of possibilities exists with regard to the manner in which the content of that revelation is defined. It can be said that for Paul "Jesus' death on the cross reveals the faithfulness, love, and paradoxical power of God,"[256] or that "the purpose of Jesus' life and death, according to John, was to unmask and undo violence.... For John, the serving, self-giving love revealed in Jesus has the *power* to *transform* the believer, and indeed the world, making it whole, completing the creation."[257] The cross can be seen as "the event that discloses the free and sovereign God [and] reveals also that God is deeply and lovingly involved with humanity and humanity's predicament.... The Christian community finds in the crucifixion the clue as to where God is present in the world, where divine grace, albeit in a hidden and mysterious way, is active."[258] Jesus' death can similarly be said to reveal countless other truths regarding God, Christ, humanity, the nature of the world, and our relations both with God and with one another.

Typical of this type of interpretation of Christ's death and resurrection is the work of Robert Hamerton-Kelly, who looked to the thought of René Girard regarding "sacred violence" to interpret Paul's language concerning the salvific nature of Christ's death. Commenting on 1 Cor. 2:6-8, which speaks of the rulers of this age crucifying Christ, he claims that for Paul the "murder of God's son sealed their doom because it revealed with vivid clarity the origin of this world in sacred violence."[259] Thus, according to Hamerton-Kelly, "for Paul the primary saving effect of the Cross is as a disclosure of religious violence, not as a sacrificial transaction that appeases the divine wrath."[260] Hamerton-Kelly can even speak of Christ enduring wrath on the cross, yet not in the sense that proponents of penal substitution views understand such an idea:

> for Paul wrath is not the active divine vengeance but the effects of sacred violence in the human world: The wrath that falls on Christ instead of on humanity is, therefore, human vengeance dissembled through the Sacred and borne with absolute vulnerability, with the result that Christ stands out as the one complete victim

---

256. Michael J. Gorman, *Apostle of the Crucified Lord: A Theological Introduction to Paul and his Letters* (Grand Rapids: Eerdmans, 2004), 135.
257. John Painter, "The Death of Jesus in John: A Discussion of the Tradition History and Theology of John," in *Death of Jesus*, ed. Van Belle, 345-46.
258. Charles B. Cousar, *A Theology of the Cross: The Death of Jesus in the Pauline Letters* (OBT; Minneapolis: Fortress, 1990), 181, 183.
259. Robert Hamerton-Kelly, *Sacred Violence: Paul's Hermeneutic of the Cross* (Minneapolis: Fortress, 1992), 85.
260. Ibid., 79; see also 76-77, 85, 87, 109.

and target of the wrath.... He alone eschews all aid from sacred violence and bears the wrath for us, to disclose and thus disarm it.[261]

According to this type of interpretation, the objective of Jesus' death was to bring about an ethical change in human beings. Larry Hurtado, for example, claims that in the New Testament "Jesus' death functions as inspiring and exemplary for Christian behaviour, as descriptive of, and criterion for, Christian existence—indeed as the crucial event by which Christian ethical effort, discipleship, and consequent suffering are defined and given their significance."[262] John Painter comments that, for John, "The cross is God's ultimate appeal and offer of his love to the world. It has the power to transform the consciousness of those who believe, to love one another as God in Jesus has loved the world."[263] This means, of course, that Christ's death does not save *all* people, but only those who respond to it in faith: "The faithfulness of God demonstrated in the faith of Jesus must be met by the human response of faith for the death to be effective."[264]

Like the notion of God's wrath, much of the language and imagery traditionally associated with penal substitution and physical understandings of Christ's work can also be interpreted according to a revelational understanding. For example, rather than understanding the *Christus Victor* idea in a forensic or ontological sense, it can be said that by re-enacting what Christ did, believers can overcome the evil forces that hold human beings in bondage:

> when believers re-enact Jesus' death in their own lives, they are freed from the rule of Sin.... In Romans 6, Paul asserts that believers die with Christ during baptism, i.e. they re-enact his death in their own lives.... By re-enacting Jesus' death in this way, they are transferred from the aeon of Sin to the aeon ruled by him.... When one 'dies with' Christ, even though one does not literally die, one gains liberation from and shares in a victory over the evil tyrant, Sin.[265]

Christ's death and resurrection can also be said to bring about a new age, a new humanity, and a new creation. In this case, however, those events do so by means of the effect they have on human minds and hearts through faith. Ziesler, for example, characterizes Paul's thought thus:

> The life in Christ is the life of faith: to believe is to be in Christ.... To be in Christ is to be in the new Adam, in a solidarity of life, and of righteousness, as against being in 'natural' humanity, the old Adam, in a solidarity of sin and death.... [T]o be in Christ, in the new humanity, is to be in the Church, the embodiment of that humanity.... Being in Christ also involves dying and rising with him. This dying may refer to a previous death *in* sin (Eph. 2.1-5) or to the death of the old self, as death *to* sin, i.e. an entering into Christ's representative action. This leads to a new

---

261. Ibid., 81.
262. Larry W. Hurtado, "Jesus' Death as Paradigmatic in the New Testament," *SJT* 57 (2004): 413-14.
263. Painter, "Death," 360.
264. Michael J. Gorman, *Cruciformity: Paul's Narrative Spirituality of the Cross* (Grand Rapids: Eerdmans, 2001), 116.
265. Seeley, *Noble Death*, 104, 147-48. See also Tannehill, *Dying*, 124-28.

life, both ethically and relationally, a risen life which is a new creation, gift as well as demand, imperative as well as indicative....[266]

Of course, according to views such as these, it is not actually Christ's death and resurrection in themselves that bring about a new age, a new humanity, or a new creation, but rather the ethical transformation that takes place in believers as a result of what Christ's death and resurrection have revealed to them.

The language of participation and transfer can also be understood in a purely ethical sense. In this case, rather than being of a forensic or ontological nature, one's union with Christ and participation in his death and resurrection involve a conscious, intentional identification with Christ and those events. According to McKnight, for example, in Matthew's Gospel, "the death of Jesus is *exemplary* and his followers become so by *participation* in his representative death."[267] Hamerton-Kelly agrees with Sanders that Paul had a "participationist soteriology," yet he understands this not ontologically but metaphorically, "in the sense of imaginative participation in the death of Christ.... Paul, therefore, metaphorically describes entering the Christian life as a co-crucifixion and that alone suggests that the metaphor is rooted in his own conversion experience."[268] According to this understanding, to participate in Christ is thus to identify with his story and follow the model he laid down in his life and death:

> God's reconciling initiative by the death of Christ on the cross as the result of his obedient life to God (Rom. 5:19), becomes not only the very act and pronouncement of reconciliation of humanity with God, but also the ground and model for reconciling relationships among people.... [T]he faithfulness and obedience of Jesus were particularly highlighted by Paul as a model to be followed. Christ's story is not only his own story but includes the story of the believers. By virtue of their participation in Christ, believers can live rightly and be active actors, as the story of Christ is being unfolded in their midst.[269]

In this case, the only sense in which believers participate in the past event of Christ's death is that they consciously identify with it.[270]

While many scholars who understand Jesus' death as salvific through what it reveals reject penal substitution or ontological interpretations of his work, others attempt instead to combine these interpretations. Virtually all of those who hold to the notion of penal substitution recognize that there is an exemplary aspect to Christ's death, although this is secondary to its primary purpose of obtaining divine forgiveness for others. Ladd, for example, writes:

---

266. Ziesler, *Meaning*, 165-66. See also P. H. Towner, "The Present Age in the Eschatology of the Pastoral Epistles," *NTS* 32 (1986): 430.
267. McKnight, *Jesus*, 360-61.
268. Robert Hamerton-Kelly, "Sacred Violence and the Curse of the Law (Galatians 3.13): The Death of Christ as a Sacrificial Travesty," *NTS* 36 (1990): 98, 101.
269. Constantineanu, *Social Significance*, 208.
270. On the idea that believers are saved by identifying with Christ's death, see also Dunn, *Theology of Paul*, 223, 233.

> The moral influence of Christ's death on the lives of people is not to be ignored because the teaching has been abused and wrongly made the central truth of the atonement.... The main significance of Christ's death is to be found in its objective character as a propitiatory, substitutionary sacrifice, the benefits of which are to be received by faith as a gracious gift; but the subjective influence of his death in arousing the response of love in the hearts of men and women can be neither denied nor ignored.[271]

As mentioned above, however, if the basis upon which one's sins are forgiven is solely the substitutionary death of Christ and not anything believers themselves do, then while the cross may arouse a response of love in human hearts, this love plays no role whatsoever in their salvation. The same problem arises when one attempts to combine a physical view of Christ's work with a revelational view. If people are saved by virtue of the ontological transformation that has taken place in them as a result of their union with Christ's death and resurrection, then while they may be renewed ethically, this is the consequence not of the cross per se, but of the ontological transformation in them that it has brought about. This is true whether their salvation is seen as a natural and intrinsic consequence following upon that transformation or as the result of a divine judgment or decision. If the divine judgment or decision is based on their ethical behavior, and the role of the cross is that of bringing about such behavior through the revelation it provides, then salvation is not attributed to any type of ontological transformation resulting directly from Jesus' death and resurrection. Ultimately, therefore, if salvation depends on an ethical change in believers and this change is attributed to the revelation communicated through Jesus, it makes no sense to claim that it is also the result of some ontological transformation produced in believers through their union with Christ's death and resurrection.

Theological Problems and Presuppositions

The idea that the purpose of Christ's death was to bring about an ethical change in human beings through what it reveals has been criticized on a variety of grounds.[272] Nevertheless, for our purposes here, there are two presuppositions that are problematic.

Premise 1: Christ's death was necessary because what it revealed to human beings could not have been revealed by God in any other way.

Whatever Christ's life, passion, death, and resurrection are said to reveal to human beings, the question arises as to whether it was possible for that revelation to have been given in some other way. Was Jesus' crucifixion really the only way in which people could come to know of the "faithfulness, love, and paradoxical power of God," or that God could "disclose and thus disarm"

---

271. Ladd, *Theology*, 474.
272. See, for example, Brown and Parker, "For God So Loved," 11–13.

sacred violence?[273] Was it absolutely necessary for Jesus to die in order for others to have something to "re-enact" or to die metaphorically to sin and rise to a new way of living? Could not God have accomplished the same purposes through other human beings or by acting in other ways in human history? The claim that what was revealed through Christ's death could have been revealed by God in no other way is not based on anything found in the New Testament, where no such arguments for necessity are found, but is instead a presupposition.

Premise 2: Christ's death was necessary because there was no other way in which God could have brought about in human beings the ethical transformation necessary for them to be saved.

Can we really say that "*only* with that event do humans—Jews as well as gentiles—have the possibility of living in a faithful relationship with God"?[274] Did not people have the possibility of living in such a relationship prior to and independently of Christ's death, as was the case with Old Testament figures such as Abraham, Moses, and Elijah? The New Testament never claims explicitly that only through Christ is it possible for people to live in accordance with God's will and be declared righteous by God on that basis. In fact, passages such as Luke 1:5-6, 2:25, Acts 10:34-35, and Rom. 2:9-16 imply that in New Testament thought it was indeed possible to live righteously in God's sight prior to and independently of any faith in Jesus' death. Thus the notion that, outside of Christ's death, there was no other way for God to bring about in people the righteousness and obedience that God desired and demanded has no clear biblical basis but once again involves a presupposition.

* * *

In the end, all of the interpretations of the salvific significance of Jesus' death that we have examined in this chapter are problematic for different reasons. Here we have noted the *theological* difficulties that these various views raise. However, the *historical* difficulties associated with these views have yet to be addressed. These difficulties revolve around the question of whether any of these understandings of Jesus' death have any basis in New Testament thought or can be traced back to Jesus' first followers. That question will be considered throughout the remainder of this work.

---

273. Gorman, *Apostle*, 135; Hamerton-Kelly, *Sacred Violence*, 81.
274. Robin Scroggs, "Salvation History," 225 (emphasis added).

CHAPTER 2

SECOND-TEMPLE JEWISH SOTERIOLOGY

When Jesus' first followers spoke of salvation, they told a story that revolved around Jesus of Nazareth and his death and resurrection. This story, however, grew out of another story that had been passed down from one generation of Jews to another in both written and oral form. Because of this, in order to understand properly the story told by Jesus' first followers, we must begin by examining the story that was told by Jews in general in the first century CE.[1]

In a sense, of course, there was no single story but a variety of stories, just as there was no unified or normative Judaism. Yet even if we insist on speaking of "Judaisms" in the plural, the fact that we use the same term to refer to all of them means that there were certain characteristics that were common to the various forms or currents of Judaism that existed under Persian, Greek, and Roman rule.[2]

The same observations must be made regarding the story of Israel that was told among those who considered themselves Jews. There were a number of core elements of that story that virtually all Jews held in common: Israel's God YHWH had created the world, chosen the descendants of Abraham, Isaac, and Jacob to be his special people, redeemed this people from slavery

---

1. I am aware that the question of whether to translate *Ioudaioi* as "Jews" or "Judeans" is an extremely complex one (see Steve Mason, "Jews, Judaeans, Judaizing, Judaism: Problems of Categorization in Ancient History," *JSNJ* 38 [2007]: 457-512; Ruth Sheridan, "Issues in the Translation of οἱ Ἰουδαῖοι in the Fourth Gospel," *JBL* 132 [2013]: 689-90, n67; Daniel R. Schwartz, *Judeans and Jews: Four Faces of Dichotomy in Ancient Jewish History*, Toronto: University of Toronto Press, 2014; Mark Nanos, "Rethinking the 'Paul and Judaism' Paradigm: Why not 'Paul's Judaism'?," May 28, 2008 online version at http://www.marknanos.com/Paul'sJudaism-5-28-08.pdf, 1, n1; accessed on 12/26/2016). Although here I have chosen to use terms such as "Jews" and "Judaism," I understand these terms, not as referring to a "religion" or those who practiced it, but as embracing all those who identified themselves as *Ioudaioi* as well as the general worldview and faith that was common among the majority, according to the evidence we have.

2. Virtually all biblical scholars today would agree with Richard A. Horsley that "[a]t the time of Jesus there was no such thing that could be labeled 'Judaism'" (*Jesus and Empire: The Kingdom of God and the New World Disorder*, Minneapolis: Fortress, 2003, 10). Yet it is important to avoid the other extreme of positing a diversity of "Judaisms" that shared nothing in common. Because of this, I believe that it makes little difference whether or not we speak of a "common Judaism," as E. P. Sanders and James Dunn do, or follow other approaches to the subject, such as that of Lester Grabbe, who argues that we should instead speak of "currents" within Judaism (see E. P. Sanders, *Judaism: Practice and Belief, 63 BCE–66 CE*; Philadelphia: Trinity Press International, 1992, 47; James D. G. Dunn, *Jesus Remembered*, Vol. 1 of *Christianity in the Making*; Grand Rapids: Eerdmans, 2003, 280-81; see 258-81 for his discussion of the question in general; Lester L. Grabbe, *An Introduction to First Century Judaism: Jewish Religion and History in the Second Temple Period*; Edinburgh: T & T Clark, 1996, 111-12). For Grabbe, to speak of "currents" reflects "diversity, interaction, and movement," yet allows us to recognize that no single current "makes up the entire stream"; rather, each current "was a constituent of the whole." Whatever terms we use, we must constantly be aware of the diversity among those who understood themselves as Jews in antiquity as well as the beliefs and practices that were common among them.

in Egypt, and given them the law through Moses.³ He had also given them a land and promised to bless them if they obeyed his commandments. Their failure to obey that law sufficiently, however, had led YHWH to chastise them in various ways, including exile from the land and other forms of suffering. However, most Jews hoped that at some point YHWH would act to restore Israel's fortunes and fulfill the promises of blessing he had made of old.

These common core elements of Israel's story are found throughout the Hebrew Scriptures, the basic content of which the vast majority of Jews accepted as normative.⁴ Of course, we can find many variations of this basic story in those Scriptures themselves as well as in other Jewish writings of antiquity. Events from Israel's history were narrated and interpreted in different ways in these writings and the same was no doubt true when those events were shared in oral form. Even the biblical narratives were altered and embellished, as is evident from numerous writings of the second-temple period, such as those of Flavius Josephus and Philo of Alexandria. Thus, while the Hebrew Scriptures shaped the way in which Israel's story was told, the reverse was also true: certain ideas were read back into those writings by those who interpreted them.

The narratives that we find in the Hebrew Scriptures were also fit into a broader, overarching framework that gave fuller meaning to them. This framework involved beliefs regarding what had taken place prior to the story of creation told in Genesis: God was thought to have created the world with a plan and certain intentions in mind. Many Jews also believed that events not narrated in the biblical account had taken place, such as the creation of angelic beings, some of whom had disobeyed God and been punished. That framework included a wide variety of beliefs concerning the future as well. Many, for example, looked forward to the coming of a messianic figure, the defeat of Israel's enemies, the resurrection of the dead, and a final judgment. Others rejected such ideas. Even those who affirmed these ideas tended to understand them differently. Once more, therefore, although in one sense we can speak of a single overarching narrative framework, in another sense we must speak of a diversity of such frameworks that nevertheless had certain ideas in common.

Curiously, however, some of the most basic questions that such frameworks were intended to answer are not addressed explicitly in the second-temple Jewish writings we possess. Did Israel's God have a purpose in creating the world or electing Abraham and his descendants as his chosen people? Was Israel's election an end in itself or was it instead a means by which YHWH

---

3. Throughout much of this work, when referring to the God of Israel of whom the Hebrew Scriptures speak, I will use the *tetragrammaton* in order to emphasize that here I am talking about a particular conception of God commonly held by a majority of Jews in antiquity.

4. As George W. E. Nickelsburg notes, "Although the Jews recognized no formal biblical canon in the Hellenistic and early Roman periods, by the turn of the era most sectors of Judaism considered almost all the books of the Tanak to be authoritative" (*Ancient Judaism and Christian Origins: Diversity, Continuity, and Transformation*; Minneapolis: Fortress, 2003, 185).

proposed to carry out some type of greater plan or project with regard to the rest of the world? For what reason had YHWH given Israel the law through Moses? Why did YHWH constantly demand that Israel obey that law and punish the people when they failed to do so? Was this punishment an end in itself or did it have some greater purpose? Why had YHWH forbidden certain foods or commanded Israel to celebrate festivals and offer up sacrifices? What was the meaning of the different ceremonies associated with the sacrificial rites, such as the sprinkling and pouring out of the blood taken from the sacrificial victims?

With a few exceptions, explicit answers to questions such as these are not found in the Hebrew Scriptures or the Jewish writings of the second-temple period that are available to us. Because of this, biblical scholars have generally been reluctant to discuss the way in which Jews in antiquity would have responded to them. While some of these questions are not entirely ignored by scholars, such as that of the meaning of certain sacrificial rites, it seems to be assumed generally either that ancient Jews did not reflect on many of these questions or else that, if they did, the ancient writings we have do not provide us with sufficient information to determine how they answered them.

In this chapter and the two that follow, I would like to challenge that assumption. I believe that, by examining closely the Jewish writings of the period on the basis of a clear understanding of certain theological ideas, we can indeed discern answers to many of the questions just raised and at the same time penetrate more deeply into the story of Israel as it was told by many Jews in antiquity. Rather than constituting an end in itself, however, this is a necessary first step to reconstructing the story told by Jesus' first followers that lies behind the writings that make up the New Testament, since this story builds upon the Jewish story and developed out of it. This will also provide a basis for beginning to address some of the questions raised in Chapter 1.

Naturally, the limitations of the present work make it impossible to explore in an exhaustive fashion the way in which the story of Israel is presented in the Hebrew Scriptures and ancient Jewish literature. For my purposes here, however, it will suffice to outline and examine from a theological perspective the general components of that story that run throughout those writings. Because the objective is to grasp more clearly how the story of Israel was understood in the New Testament period in particular, I regard as irrelevant for this task questions concerning the original meanings and contexts of the Hebrew Scriptures and will not address them here.[5] My interest in this and

---

5. This distinction has often been overlooked by New Testament scholars, many of whom discuss questions related to the original meaning of a passage from the Hebrew Scriptures before examining how it is quoted or alluded to in the New Testament. Daniel P. Bailey, for example, explores the work of scholars such as Hartmut Gese and Otto Hofius, who attempt to discern the original meaning of Isaiah 53 on the basis of the concept of *Stellvertretung* and discuss the original meaning of the imposition of hands on a sacrificial animal in the sacrificial prescriptions of Leviticus, and then on that basis examine the use of these passages in Paul's epistles and 1 Peter ("Concepts of *Stellvertregung* in the Interpretation of Isaiah 53," in *Jesus and the Suffering Servant: Isaiah 53 and Christian Origins*; ed. William H. Bellinger Jr. and William R. Farmer; Harrisburg, PA: Trinity Press International, 1998, 241-50). To proceed in this way presupposes a doctrine of the inspiration of

the following two chapters lies not in what those writings may have meant originally or the intention of those who composed them, but rather in the way in which they may have been understood by those reading them in the time of Jesus and his first followers.

THE ELECTION OF ISRAEL

Perhaps the most basic claim inherent to the story of Israel as told by Jews of old was that the creator God YHWH had elected Israel as his special people. This claim formed the basis for virtually all of the other beliefs among Jews regarding the land of Israel, the law of Moses, the course of history, and the way life was to be lived.

Although the theme of Israel's election runs throughout the foundational passages of the Pentateuch as well as the Hebrew Scriptures as a whole,[6] answers to the question of *why* God chose Israel are not so abundant or clear in the Hebrew Scriptures. This question can be understood in at least two different ways: the first is why God chose Israel rather than some other people or nation, while the second is whether God had some purpose or objective in electing Israel.

The election of Israel over against other nations could be attributed either to an act of pure grace on God's part or else to some quality or characteristic that distinguished the people of Israel from all others. Certain passages from the Hebrew Scriptures suggest the former idea: God's election of Israel took place independently of any merit on Israel's part or anything Israel had done or would do.[7] The problem with such an idea, however, is that God appears to have acted arbitrarily and thus to have shown favoritism. This problem is resolved to some extent by claiming that God chose the people of Israel, not simply to bless them in particular, but in order that they might carry out a special task among the other nations.[8] In that case, though Israel might

---

Scriptures according to which the authors of the writings that make up the New Testament had access to the original beliefs and practices reflected in the Hebrew texts, written centuries earlier, because the same Holy Spirit who had inspired those texts was at work in them as well. In using the Hebrew Scriptures in order to attempt to reconstruct second-temple Jewish thought, the question that must be addressed is how those Scriptures were read during this period. Of course, this does not mean that we can ignore entirely questions regarding the original meaning of the biblical texts, since we must also recognize that, to a certain extent, there were meanings embedded in those texts that would have been as clear to readers in antiquity as they are to those who read those texts carefully today.

6. The particularly relevant texts from the Pentateuch include Gen. 12:2; 17:6; 18:18; Exod. 6:7; 19:5; Lev. 26:12; Deut. 7:6, 14; 9:6, 29; 10:15; 14:2; 28:9. See also Ps. 33:12; 100:3; Isa. 41:8-9; 44:1; Jer. 7:23; Ezek. 20:5; Hag. 2:23, among many others. For a background to the beliefs regarding Israel's election found in the Hebrew Scriptures and the scholarly discussion on that subject, see especially Brevard S. Childs, *Biblical Theology of the Old and New Testaments: Theological Reflection on the Christian Bible* (Minneapolis: Fortress, 1993), 425-28.

7. See, for example, Deut. 4:37; 7:7; 10:15; Ezek. 16:1-63; Hosea 11:1. On this idea in rabbinic thought, see E. P. Sanders, *Paul and Palestinian Judaism: A Comparison of Patterns of Religion* (Philadelphia: Fortress, 1977), 85-87. As Martin McNamara has shown, the same idea is found throughout the Targums ("Some Targum Themes," in *Justification and Variegated Nomism*, Vol. 1: *The Complexities of Second Temple Judaism*; ed. D. A. Carson, Peter T. O'Brien, and Mark A. Seifrid; WUNT 2/140; Tübingen: Mohr Siebeck, 2001, 324-32).

8. On this idea in the Dead Sea Scrolls, see Ellen Juhl Christiansen, "The Consciousness of Belonging to God's Covenant and What it Entails according to the Damascus Document and the Community Rule," in

initially be blessed more than other nations, the ultimate objective was that other nations might be attracted to Israel's God YHWH so as to receive blessings from him after observing the many blessings he bestowed on Israel. In later rabbinic thought, some argued instead that the election of Israel was based on some type of merit on Israel's part. It was said, for example, that God had offered the law to all of the peoples of the earth but the only nation to accept it was Israel.[9] Such an idea, of course, is nowhere to be found in the Hebrew Scriptures.

These various ideas were often combined with one another. The book of Genesis begins its narrative about Abraham with YHWH promising to bless Abraham before he had apparently done anything to be deserving of that election, yet it also mentions the blessing of others through Abraham from the very outset (Gen. 12:1-3; cf. 18:18). Further on, however, YHWH promises to bless Abraham on the basis of his willingness to obey him even to the point of sacrificing Isaac his son: "*Because you have done this*, and have not withheld your son, your only son, I will indeed bless you, and I will make your offspring as numerous as the stars of heaven and as the sand that is on the seashore.... [A]nd by your offspring shall all the nations of the earth gain blessing for themselves, *because you have obeyed my voice*" (22:16-18). This passage implies some merit on the part of Abraham. On this basis, it might be argued that God elected the people of Israel, not due to anything they had done or would do, but because of what Abraham their forefather had done. Yet the idea that God chose Abraham and thus Israel in order to bless other nations as well is also evident here and elsewhere.

There seems to be evidence that, by the first century CE, some Jews had come to regard the election of Israel as something that took place *before* the creation of the world, even though such an idea is never affirmed explicitly in the Hebrew Scriptures. This belief could be tied together with similar claims about the patriarchs, the giving of the Torah, and even the coming of the Messiah.[10] Such ideas imply not only a divine plan but some type of determinism in human history, according to which God not only foresaw but foreordained what was to come and what human beings would do. Curiously, however, such claims were apparently not thought to call into question the notion that human beings have free will and are ultimately responsible for

---

Qumran between the Old and New Testaments (ed. Frederick H. Cryer and Thomas L. Thompson; JSOTSup 290; Sheffield: Sheffield Academic Press, 1998), 90-93.

9. See Sanders, *Paul and Palestinian Judaism*, 87-89. On the understanding of Israel's election in second-temple Judaism, see also N. T. Wright, *The New Testament and the People of God*, Vol. 1 of *Christian Origins and the Question of God* (Minneapolis: Fortress, 1992), 259-68.

10. This is implied in passages such as the *Assumption of Moses* 1, which affirms that God "created the world on behalf of his people." For other relevant texts of the period, see McNamara, "Some Targum Themes," 311-12; Werner Förster, *Palestinian Judaism in New Testament Times*, trans. Gordon Harris (Edinburgh: Oliver & Boyd, 1964), 183-87; Jacob Neusner, *Torah: From Scroll to Symbol in Formative Judaism* (Philadelphia: Fortress, 1985), 118-19.

their own actions, since in many second-temple Jewish writings these apparently conflicting ideas are found alongside one another.[11]

Reflected in these various views were different attitudes toward the other nations or "gentiles." If God's purpose in electing Abraham was that of blessing not only his descendants Israel but also the nations through them, then in principle the nations could be regarded as being just as much the object of God's love as Israel. Nevertheless, if the condition for Israel's blessings was obedience to the law given through Moses, then it might be expected that the nations could only attain the same blessings promised to Israel by submitting fully to that law. If the gentile nations were not expected to keep the Mosaic law fully, they might hope to be blessed to a lesser extent than Israel by obeying a series of other, more general commandments, such as those believed to have been given to Noah in Gen. 9:1-17. The failure of non-Jews to accept and obey either the Mosaic law or some general or natural law given to all people might also be seen as the basis for interpreting their present or future suffering as divine punishment and justifying their ultimate destruction, whether in this world or the next.[12] Of course, the failure of the nations to be drawn to the God of Israel might also be blamed on Israel's lack of obedience to God's law, which led the nations to condemn not only Israel for the people's sinful and unjust behavior but the God whom Israel worshiped as well.

All of these views can be found in both the Hebrew Scriptures and many Jewish writings from antiquity and could serve to maintain that God had not been impartial or unjust in electing Israel as his special people.[13] Precisely which of these views were adopted depended to a large extent on the context in which the Jewish people adhering to them found themselves. Those living in Palestine, for example, would tend to long for liberation from the nations to which they had to pay homage and tribute and thus view non-Jews in more negative terms, whereas those Jews living in the diaspora might instead long for better relations with their non-Jewish neighbors and see non-Jews in a more positive light. This diversity of views and contexts would also lead to different ways of relating to non-Jews. Some might seek to incorporate them into Israel through proselytism, though this does not appear to have

---

11. This idea is particularly prominent in the Dead Sea Scrolls. See especially Philip S. Alexander, "Predestination and Free Will in the Theology of the Dead Sea Scrolls," in *Divine and Human Agency in Paul and his Cultural Environment* (ed. John M. G. Barclay and Simon J. Gathercole; London: T & T Clark, 2006), 27-49; Eileen Schuller, "Petitionary Prayer and the Religion of Qumran," in *Religion in the Dead Sea Scrolls* (ed. John J. Collins and Robert A. Kuglar; Grand Rapids: Eerdmans, 2000), 35-38. Kyle B. Wells has particularly studied the question of the manner in which second-temple Jewish writings, including those of Paul, integrate the idea that God has foreseen and predestined what is to take place with the idea that human beings continue to have free will. Wells notes that in general those writings do not consider these two ideas to be contradictory (*Grace and Agency in Paul and Second Temple Judaism: Interpreting the Transformation of the Heart*; NovTSup 157; Leiden: Brill, 2015). On this point, see also E. P. Sanders, *Paul: The Apostle's Life, Letters, and Thought* (Minneapolis: Fortress, 2015), 682-83; Sanders, *Comparing Judaism and Christianity: Common Judaism, Paul, and the Inner and Outer in the Study of Religion* (Minneapolis: Fortress, 2016), 108-10, 186-87.

12. On these ideas in second-temple Jewish writings, see Sanders, *Judaism*, 266-70, 291-92, 295.

13. On this point, see especially Michael F. Bird, *Jesus and the Origins of the Gentile Mission* (LNTS 331; London: T & T Clark, 2006), 126-30.

been common and could easily lead to tensions with non-Jews.[14] For this reason, when the salvation of the nations was spoken of, it was often seen as an eschatological occurrence: when Israel's redemption came, many from the nations would come to recognize YHWH as the one true God and come to live obediently under him together with Israel.[15]

ISRAEL AND THE LAW

While we cannot say how many of those who identified themselves as Jews in the second-temple period considered themselves to be observant of the Mosaic law, it can hardly be questioned that most currents of Judaism in antiquity regarded such observance as central for Jewish life. Of course, precisely what constituted faithful observance of that law was a matter of constant discussion and debate among Jews.

One of the most fundamental questions regarding the Jewish law must have been why God had given it to Israel. Once again, while there are certain passages in both the Hebrew Scriptures and other second-temple Jewish writings that suggest some possible responses to this question, it is rarely addressed explicitly. Much less do we find any type of extensive discussion on the subject.

Before examining the responses that we can discern in the ancient Hebrew and Jewish literature, however, it is important to consider a response commonly given by Christian writers to the question of the law's purpose. As we have seen in the previous chapter, among Christian theologians from the time of the Reformation to the present, the law has generally been regarded as an expression of God's perfectly holy and righteous nature.[16] According to this idea, what motivated God to give the law was the need to keep human sin at a distance, since due to God's perfection, by nature God cannot tolerate sin in God's presence. Through the law, God also sought to make manifest to human beings that only those who are perfectly holy and righteous as God is are able to be received into God's presence. Thus, God gave the law out of an inner need grounded in his divine essence or nature.

On the basis of this idea, Protestant thought has claimed that fulfillment of God's law on the part of human beings is impossible, since the perfection required by that law is beyond human possibilities. Therefore, the law can only demonstrate to human beings that they are sinners and consequently are

---

14. See Scot McKnight, *A Light among the Gentiles: Jewish Missionary Activity in the Second Temple Period* (Minneapolis: Fortress, 1991); Shaye J. D. Cohen, "Crossing the Boundary and Becoming a Jew," *HTR* 82 (1989): 13-33.

15. For the background to this idea in the Hebrew Scriptures, see Donald E. Gowan, *Eschatology in the Old Testament* (Philadelphia: Fortress, 1986), 48-57.

16. Thus, for example, Ben Witherington III affirms: "Law is a necessary expression of God's holiness, but if Paul were to describe God in a short phrase, it would be as holy love" (*Paul's Narrative Thought World: The Tapestry of Tragedy and Triumph*; Louisville, KY: Westminster John Knox, 1994, 66). Similarly, Leon Morris quotes with approval the affirmation of the Scottish theologian P. T. Forsyth, "God's holy law is his own holy nature," and then speaks of "the inflexible law which is at the very basis of God's being" (*The Apostolic Preaching of the Cross*, 3rd ed.; Grand Rapids: Eerdmans, 1965, 294-96).

subject to God's wrath and punishment for their sins. Because the law thus threatens and condemns human beings, it can hardly be regarded as a blessing or an expression of divine love. On the contrary, it is an expression of God's strict justice, which cannot be violated.

In recent decades, numerous studies have demonstrated that such an understanding of the law is foreign to ancient Jewish thought. The most notable of these studies is that of E. P. Sanders, who argued that in ancient Judaism the law was seen in positive terms as a divine blessing: "Rabbinic scholars have pointed out that Judaism does not regard the obligations which God imposed upon his people as onerous. They are instead regarded as a blessing, and one should fulfill them with joy. They are accompanied by strength and peace, and they are a sign of God's mercy...."[17] While much of Sanders's argument is based on rabbinic material, it is clear that the same ideas run throughout both the Hebrew Scriptures and second-temple Jewish literature in general, which also see the law as an expression of YHWH's love and blessing.

The Law and Human Well-Being

Although it must be recognized that the reasons and logic underlying many of the commandments that make up the Mosaic law are not always clear and that, from a modern perspective, many of the biblical commandments seem not only illogical but at times even cruel,[18] it would have been as clear to Jews in antiquity as it is for anyone reading the law today that the primary purpose of the commandments was that of contributing to human well-being and social justice and equity. In fact, in virtually every human society, this is understood to be the primary purpose of laws: they are designed to protect and promote the well-being and interests of the members of the society that has established them.

In the case of many of the commandments of the Mosaic law, this purpose is obvious. Commandments against stealing, killing, adultery, false testimony, and honoring one's parents (Exod. 20:12-17; Deut. 5:16-21) serve to maintain the social fabric and preserve healthy relationships in families and communities. The commandments that prescribe certain days and periods of rest for people, animals, and the land promote the well-being of human beings and their environment. In fact, the commandments themselves speak of enabling people, animals, and the land to be "refreshed" and to "enjoy" their existence (Exod. 31:12-17; Lev. 26:34; Deut. 5:14).

Similarly, numerous commandments had the goal of protecting the needy and less fortunate, such as those that prescribed care for slaves, foreigners, the poor, the disabled, orphans, and women who had been widowed or divorced (Lev. 19:15; Deut. 1:16-17; 16:18-20; 27:19). Those that owned slaves were

---

17. Sanders, *Paul and Palestinian Judaism*, 110.

18. This would include, for example, commandments such as those that mandate stoning people for offenses such as blaspheming, worshiping gods other than YHWH, failing to honor one's parents, and committing fornication (Lev. 24:16; Deut. 17:5; 21:20; 22:23-24).

not to oppress them, but treat them well, and workers were to be paid on the same day they had labored (Deut. 24:14-15). The balances and weights of those selling were to be fair and just, and no interest was to be charged on loans (Lev. 19:35-36; 25:35-37). Fields were not to be reaped to the border nor vineyards fully stripped so that the poor might have something to eat (Lev. 19:9-10). Other commandments sought to establish a legal system that would ensure justice, avoid corruption and bribery, and guarantee that the weaker elements of society would not be trampled upon (Lev. 19:15; Deut. 1:16-17; 16:18-20; 27:19). In fact, the people were commanded not only to refrain from oppressing or mistreating one another but also to love one another, care for those in need, and avoid taking revenge or bearing grudges; even the commandment to help one's enemies is present in the Mosaic law (Lev. 19:17-18; Exod. 23:4-5). One does not need to know anything specific regarding the original contexts in which these commandments first arose to see that they have the purpose of promoting social justice and the well-being of human beings and the environment in which they live.

Implicit in this understanding of the law is the notion that there is an *intrinsic* relation between obedience to its commandments and human well-being. This means that fulfillment of the law's precepts leads to well-being as a *natural consequence*, while conversely the lack of obedience to the commandments in and of itself undermines and destroys such well-being. The Sabbath rest, for example, enables one to be refreshed and reinvigorated. In and of itself, refraining from murder, adultery, robbery, and other acts of violence helps preserve justice and equity in a society. This stands in contrast to an *extrinsic* understanding of the relation between obedience to the law and its consequences. According to this idea, human well-being results from obedience to the commandments because God intervenes from heaven to reward that obedience with blessings, while the lack of obedience has negative consequences because of the way God responds to that disobedience by imposing hardships or suffering. Even though this intrinsic/extrinsic distinction is nowhere mentioned or discussed explicitly in the ancient sources, of course, it is clearly assumed and presupposed there.

Precisely because the commandments of the law promote justice and equity for the good of all, they are repeatedly said to be "just" or "righteous" (Deut. 4:8; Ps. 19:7-9; 119:7, 62, 106, 137-38, 164). Undoubtedly, it can rightly be said that the law is a reflection of the nature of Israel's God, who is also just and righteous. However, this should not be understood in the sense that, due to his holy nature, Israel's God must isolate himself from any type of sin and impurity and therefore must punish any human action that is in conflict with that nature. Such an understanding of justice emphasizes *retribution*, as if merely inflicting punishment for sin established justice. Instead, Israel's God is regarded as just and righteous in the sense that he is committed to the well-being of the people. The law he gives is therefore also just and righteous in that it contributes to that well-being. For this reason, a number of passages from the Hebrew Scriptures relate justice and the law to *shalom*, a term that denotes not merely peace but also prosperity, happiness, and wholeness in a general sense.[19]

The justice that the Mosaic law promotes, therefore, is not first and foremost a *retributive* justice but a *distributive*, *restorative*, or *reconstructive* justice.[20] In biblical thought, that law is a means by which God seeks to ensure the well-being of all, particularly the underprivileged and those in greatest need.[21] Besides legislating fairness and equity among the people, it seeks to prevent the powerful from oppressing the weak. Undoubtedly, retributive justice is an important and vital part of the Mosaic law. Penalties are prescribed for behavior that undermines *shalom* in the community and for acts that destroy the lives of others, harm them in some way, or affect adversely the well-being of all. In biblical thought, however, retribution is *not an end in itself*, as if the goal were simply to punish wrongdoing for its own sake. Instead, *retributive* justice exists for the sake of *distributive* justice. It contributes to the well-being of all by serving as a *deterrent* to oppression and injustice and by impeding those who harm others from continuing to do so. Its objective is to prevent the mistreatment of some by others and to correct such mistreatment when it takes place.

Divine Justice and Mercy

Because in biblical thought Israel's law promotes the well-being of all, particularly those who are weakest and at a disadvantage, it is seen as an expression not only of God's *justice* but of God's *mercy*. In much traditional Christian thought, justice and mercy are viewed as *opposites*. This is due primarily to the stress on *retributive* justice that characterizes that thought: to show mercy is to leave sin unpunished. When justice is identified with the well-being of all, however, then to do justice is to show mercy, love, and compassion. For this reason, the Hebrew Scriptures frequently equate justice with mercy, compassion, grace, and love. This is particularly evident in the parallelisms found in the Psalms and elsewhere:

> He loves righteousness and justice; the earth is full of the steadfast love of YHWH (Ps. 33:5).[22]

---

19. See Lev. 26:3-6; Ps. 85:10; 119:165; Isa. 32:16-17; 54:13-14; 59:8; 60:17; Mal. 2:5-6.

20. On these distinctions and what follows, see Christopher D. Marshall, *Beyond Retribution: A New Testament Vision for Justice, Crime, and Punishment* (Grand Rapids: Eerdmans, 2001), 45-53. For a modern Jewish reading of the Mosaic law and the Hebrew Scriptures that emphasizes these points, see Jeremiah Unterman, *Justice for All: How the Jewish Bible Revolutionized Ethics* (JPSEJS; Philadelphia: Jewish Publication Society, 2017), 15-84.

21. On these ideas, see also Christofer Frey, "The Impact of the Biblical Idea of Justice on Present Discussions of Social Justice," in *Justice and Righteousness: Biblical Themes and Their Influence* (ed. Henning Graf Reventlow and Yair Hoffman; JSOTSup 137; Sheffield: JSOT, 1992), 91-104; Moshe Weinfeld, "'Justice and Righteousness'—*Mishpat Utsedeqah*—The Expression and its Meaning," in *Justice and Righteousness*, ed. Reventlow and Hoffman, 228-46.

22. In quoting passages from the Hebrew Scriptures in the NRSV, at times I have substituted "YHWH" for "the Lord" to reflect the Hebrew original more clearly.

I have not concealed your justice in my heart; I have spoken of your faithfulness and your salvation; I have not concealed your steadfast love and your faithfulness from the great congregation (Ps. 40:10).

Righteousness and justice are the foundation of your throne; steadfast love and faithfulness go before you (Ps. 89:14).

YHWH is gracious and just; our God is merciful (Ps. 116:5).

They shall celebrate the fame of your abundant goodness, and shall sing aloud of your righteousness (Ps. 145:7).

YHWH is just in all his ways and kind in all his actions (Ps. 145:17).

Therefore YHWH waits to be gracious to you; therefore he will rise up to show mercy to you. For YHWH is a God of justice; blessed are all those who wait for him (Isa. 30:18).

I act with steadfast love, justice, and righteousness in the earth, for in these things I delight, says YHWH (Jer. 9:24)

He has told you, O mortal, what is good; and what does YHWH require of you but that you do justice, love kindness, and walk humbly with your God? (Mic. 6:8).[23]

There can be little doubt that the frequent recitation of the Psalms and perhaps some of these other passages as well would have reinforced among Jews in antiquity the idea that God's justice is an expression of God's love and mercy.

For this reason, in the Hebrew Scriptures and second-temple Jewish literature, the affirmation that the law is righteous or just is a motive for rejoicing. In much traditional Christian thought, this is not the case: because the law demands that human beings conform perfectly to God's righteousness and holiness, which is impossible for them, it strikes fear into them and condemns them. However, when the law is instead seen as a divine instrument for promoting justice, *shalom*, and equity among the people, it is seen as a gracious gift from God for which all of God's people should be profoundly grateful:

The law of the Lord is perfect, reviving the soul;
the decrees of the Lord are sure, making wise the simple;
the precepts of the Lord are right, rejoicing the heart;
the commandment of the Lord is clear, enlightening the eyes;
the fear of the Lord is pure, enduring forever;
the ordinances of the Lord are true and righteous altogether.
More to be desired are they than gold, even much fine gold;
sweeter also than honey, and drippings of the honeycomb (Ps. 19:7-10).

My soul is consumed with longing for your ordinances at all times....
Your decrees are my delight, they are my counselors....
I find my delight in your commandments, because I love them....
The law of your mouth is better to me than thousands of gold and silver pieces....
I will never forget your precepts, for by them you have given me life....
Oh, how I love your law! It is my meditation all day long....
Truly I love your commandments more than gold, more than fine gold....

---

23. For further examples, see Ps. 36:5-6; 98:2-3; 103:6-8; 111:3-4; 112:4; 143:11-12; Hosea 2:19; 12:6.

Seven times a day I praise you for your righteous ordinances.
Great peace have those who love your law; nothing can make them stumble (Ps. 119:20, 24, 47, 72, 93, 97, 127, 164-65).

This understanding of the Mosaic law as a divine blessing is also reflected in the fact that the Hebrew word used to refer to the law is *Torah*, which literally means instruction or guidance. In ancient Jewish thought, the law is the primary means by which YHWH graciously shows his people how to live for their own good. Through the law he commands things that intrinsically and naturally contribute to human well-being and prohibits things that intrinsically and naturally oppose, undermine, or prevent human well-being.

Undoubtedly, at times the law was seen as a burden.[24] However, this is not because it was considered oppressive, but because it made great demands upon those who submitted to it. Just as people often make great sacrifices and willingly endure sufferings in order to attain some desired goal, so also diligence, hard work, and perseverance are required of those who submit to the law in order to enjoy the benefits that follow upon obedience to it. For this reason, as Philip Alexander points out, the Mishnah "describes the Torah, not only as a burden, but also as a 'precious instrument' and its revelation to Israel as an act of divine love."[25] The law was considered a "delightful yoke."[26]

There can be little doubt that this was precisely how most Jews viewed the law in the second-temple period. The writings of Flavius Josephus and Philo of Alexandria, for example, provide ample evidence of these ideas. Josephus repeatedly speaks of the law as a great blessing given to Israel, designed to give happiness and well-being to the people. He insists that the law given by God through Moses is more excellent than any other law precisely because it promotes the good of all those who keep it and brings justice and equity (*Ant.* 16.44; 18.266; *Ag. Ap.* 2.173-88, 277-95). Because of its divine origin, it is superior to the laws of all other nations and is therefore the source of tremendous joy for God's people (*Ant.* 3.93, 223; 4.114; 12.110-11).

Similarly, Philo claims that the law given through Moses is in accordance with nature and virtue and thus promotes peace (*Abraham* 4-6, 60-61; *Spec. Laws* 2.129; *Virtues* 132-33). Because of this, the Jewish law is a thing of beauty, admired by other nations (*Moses* 2.25; *Virtues* 113, 183). He writes that whoever examines carefully the commandments of the Mosaic law "will find that they seek to attain to the harmony of the universe and are in agreement with the principles of eternal nature" (*Moses* 2.52). For Philo, the law given by God is full of gentleness, humanity, and compassion and thus confers its benefits on all, including not only human beings but animals (*Sp. Laws* 2.79; *Virtues* 125, 132-33, 141-42). Its superiority over all other laws will eventually lead other nations to come to observe it, thereby imitating Israel,

---

24. See Sanders, *Paul and Palestinian Judaism*, 110-11.

25. Philip S. Alexander, "Torah and Salvation in Tannaitic Literature," in *Justification*, ed. Carson et al., 1:282.

26. Ed Condra, *Salvation for the Righteous Revealed: Jesus amid Covenantal and Messianic Expectations in Second Temple Judaism* (AGJU 51; Leiden: Brill, 2002), 67.

who is to serve as an example.[27] These ideas are repeated in the rabbinic writings as well.[28]

All of these passages provide evidence that the purpose of the law in ancient Hebrew and Jewish thought was that of promoting the people's wellbeing and *shalom*. This means that Israel's God was believed to desire and command that the people obey the law, not for *his own* sake, but *for the sake of the people themselves*. Because of the intrinsic relation between obedience to the law and justice, the law was regarded as a blessing for the people.

REWARD AND PUNISHMENT

Running throughout the Hebrew Scriptures and ancient Jewish literature as a whole is the idea that Israel's God rewards obedience with blessings and punishes disobedience with various types of hardship, suffering, and destruction. This idea constitutes the basis for interpreting the history of Israel as a people, as well as individuals and groups within Israel.[29] According to this interpretation, there is an *extrinsic* relation between what people do and the consequences that result from their actions. But *why* is this so? *Why* should God bless the obedient and punish the disobedient?

Once again, discussions regarding this question are extremely rare in biblical scholarship, in large part because neither the Hebrew Scriptures nor other ancient Jewish sources address it explicitly. This means that the answer to this question is simply assumed, both by biblical scholars in the present and by those who composed the various Hebrew and Jewish writings in the past. In the case of biblical scholars, however, the influence and predominance of ideas related to the Anselmian and penal substitution views of Christ's work has led to the assumption that, just as God gave the law for God's own sake, so also God rewards obedience and punishes disobedience for *God's own sake*, due to God's holy and righteous nature. As Anselm argued, God's justice makes it impossible for God to simply overlook sin, and therefore God *must* punish it.[30]

This argument runs throughout Protestant thinkers who have sustained the penal substitution idea. John Calvin wrote that because God is "a righteous Judge, he does not allow his law to be broken without punishment, but is equipped to avenge it."[31] Similarly, James Denney claimed that it is "necessary that God may be true to himself and to the moral order he has established in the world—that sin, in the very process in which it is forgiven, should also, in

---

27. On this idea in Philo, see Peder Borgen, "Philo of Alexandria," in *Jewish Writings of the Second Temple Period: Apocrypha, Pseudepigrapha, Qumran Sectarian Writings, Philo, Josephus* (ed. Michael E. Stone; CRINT 2; Philadelphia: Fortress, 1984), 234-35.

28. See especially Friedrich Avemarie, *Tora und Leben: Untersuchungen zur Heilsbedeutung der Tora in der frühen rabbinischen Literatur* (TSAJ 55; Tübingen: J. C. B. Mohr, 1996), 284-90.

29. Of course, this is the case in the New Testament as well. Nickelsburg notes: "The notion that God rewards and punishes human beings on the basis of their actions is so widespread in the New Testament as to be cliché" (*Ancient Judaism*, 51).

30. Anselm, *Cur Deus Homo* 1.12.24.

31. John Calvin, *Institutes* 2.16.1. Quotation taken from John Calvin, *Institutes of the Christian Religion*, trans. Ford Lewis Battles (ed. John T. McNeill; LCC 20; Philadelphia: Westminster, 1960).

all its reality, be borne."³² God "would not do justice to himself if he displayed his compassion for sinners in a way which made light of sin, which ignored its tragic reality, or took it for less than it is. In this case he would again be doing himself injustice."³³ According to David Hill, "The wrath of God against sin required righteous judgment upon it so that God's own righteousness might be maintained...."³⁴

According to this logic, the need for God to conform to God's own nature not only moved God to give the law to human beings but requires that God punish those who do not observe that law. Once this punishment has taken place, God's justice or righteousness is satisfied and God is once again at peace both with God's own nature and with human beings. I. Howard Marshall, for example, claims that in ancient Jewish thought, "when people fall into sin and apostasy they arouse the wrath of Yahweh. He proceeds to punish them, and on the completion of the punishment his anger is satisfied and he is reconciled to the people.... God is reconciled, i.e., abandons his anger, as a result of the prayer of the people and their endurance (in themselves or their representatives) of the punishment which he inflicts upon them."³⁵ In this case, punishment becomes an end in itself, since it satisfies a *divine need* to uphold the law, just as the giving of the law itself responds to an inner divine need for God to keep all sin and unrighteousness far away from his presence. As Christopher Marshall notes, according to such views, "God *cannot* forgive until the punishment demanded by the law is exacted. The law becomes the supreme principle, and punishment becomes a necessity imposed on God by a superior rule."³⁶ Here the starting-point is not human well-being but God's own holy and righteous nature, which by definition cannot tolerate or allow for any type of unrighteousness on the part of human beings.

Ideas such as these not only are absent from the Hebrew Scriptures and the ancient Jewish writings we possess but also *run contrary* to what we find in those writings. If the law is seen as a means by which Israel's God sought to bless Israel because of the intrinsic consequences that result from obedience to the commandments of that law, then God must be understood to bless obedience and punish disobedience to the commandments *not for God's own sake but for the sake of the people themselves*, as well as for the sake of others outside of Israel whom God seeks to bring to live in accordance with the law for their own good. When divine punishment for sins is understood in this manner, as *chastisement* or *correction*, it is regarded as a consequence of God's love, which seeks to oppose evil and injustice and bring back to obedience those who have sinned.

---

32. James Denney, *The Christian Doctrine of Reconciliation* (London: Hodder and Stoughton, 1917), 161.
33. James Denney, *The Death of Christ* (London: Tyndale, 1950), 189.
34. David Hill, *Greek Words and Hebrew Meanings: Studies in the Semantics of Soteriological Terms* (SNTSMS 5; Cambridge: Cambridge University Press, 1967), 158.
35. I. Howard Marshall, "The Meaning of Reconciliation," in *Unity and Diversity in New Testament Theology: Essays in Honor of George E. Ladd* (ed. Robert A. Guelich; Grand Rapids: Eerdmans, 1978), 121.
36. C. Marshall, *Beyond Retribution*, 66.

The Purposes of Divine Punishment

The Hebrew Scriptures use a number of different words that are often translated as "punish" or "punishment" in English, including *paqad*, *awon*, and *shafat*. In and of themselves, none of these terms implies any clear purpose.[37] More commonly associated with the notion of divine punishment, however, are the noun *musar* and its verb cognate *yasar*. These communicate the idea of correcting or disciplining. When YHWH is said to inflict suffering or hardships, his purpose is seen to be that of bringing people into conformity with his will. In biblical and ancient Jewish thought, therefore, YHWH punishes sin not for the sake of his own holy and righteous nature, but for the sake of promoting justice and well-being among the people.

Numerous passages from both the Hebrew Scriptures and ancient Jewish writings convey this understanding of divine punishment. In the Torah, the prophetic writings and other biblical passages, YHWH is repeatedly said to bring chastisements both on individuals and on the people as a whole in order to correct them.[38] In the Septuagint, the Greek terms most commonly used to translate *musar* and *yasar* are *paideia* and *paideuein*, which also communicate the idea of instructing, correcting, or disciplining others. These terms and similar ones are used throughout numerous writings of the second-temple period as well, particularly the Wisdom of Solomon and the *Psalms of Solomon*, in order to speak of the sufferings that the people endure at God's hands.[39] Philo understands God's purpose in punishing sinners in the same way. He writes that God's powers are

> both beneficial and punitive, assuming that the punitive are to be classed among the beneficial, not only on the ground that they are a part of laws and statutes, since no law can be complete unless it includes two provisions—honours for things good and punishment for things evil, but because the punishment of others often admonishes offenders and calls them to wisdom, or, certainly at any rate, their neighbours. For penalties are good for the morals of the multitude, who fear to suffer the like (*Embassy* 7; cf. *Moses* 1.110, 143; *Unchangeable* 80).[40]

In the Hebrew Scriptures and ancient Jewish literature, this inflicting of chastisements is consistently seen as an expression of God's love, especially for Israel. God is often compared to a parent who lovingly seeks to correct and discipline his or her children for their own good: "My child, do not despise

---

37. Klaus Koch even argues that there is no Hebrew word in the Old Testament for punishment ("Is There a Doctrine of Retribution in the Old Testament?," in *Theodicy in the Old Testament*; ed. James L. Crenshaw; IRT 4; Philadelphia: Fortress, 1983, 77). On the distinction between punishment and chastisement in the Hebrew Scriptures, see also Matthias Klinghardt, "Sünde und Gericht von Christen bei Paulus," *ZNW* 88 (1997): 66-69.

38. See, for example, Lev. 26:18; 26:28; Deut. 4:36; 8:5; 11:2; Job 5:17; 36:10; Ps. 50:17; 94:10-12; Isa. 26:16; Jer. 7:28; 10:24; 16:21; 30:11; 31:18; 32:33; Ezek. 5:15; 14:10; Hosea 5:2; 7:12.

39. Wis. 3:5; 11:9-16; 12:2, 10, 20; *Pss. Sol.* 3:4; 7:3, 9; 8:26, 29; 13:7-12; 14:1; 16:11; 17:5; 18:7-8; see also *2 Bar.* 1:4; 4:1.

40. All quotations from the works of Philo in this and the following chapters are taken from Philo of Alexandria, *Works*, 12 vols. (ed. F. H. Colson, G. H. Whitaker, J. W. Earp, and R. Marcus; LCL; Cambridge, MA: Harvard University Press, 1929–1953).

YHWH's discipline or be weary of his reproof, for YHWH reproves the one he loves, as a father the son in whom he delights" (Prov. 3:11-12). Josephus presents Moses as warning the Israelites when they had sinned that God "would exact punishment, not indeed in keeping with their misdeeds, but such as fathers inflict upon their children as an admonition (*epi nouthesia*)" (*Ant.* 3.311). Perhaps the clearest expression of the idea that divine punishment is an act of love and mercy is found in 2 Maccabees. After describing the torments experienced by the Jewish people under Antiochus Epiphanes, the author writes:

> Now I urge those who read this book not to be depressed by such calamities, but to recognize that these punishments were designed not to destroy but to discipline our people. In fact, it is a sign of great kindness not to let the impious alone for long, but to punish them immediately. For in the case of the other nations the Lord waits patiently to punish them until they have reached the full measure of their sins; but he does not deal in this way with us, in order that he may not take vengeance on us afterward when our sins have reached their height. Therefore he never withdraws his mercy from us. Although he disciplines us with calamities, he does not forsake his own people (2 Macc. 6:12-16; cf. 7:32-33; 10:4)

Another analogy commonly used to describe the purposes of divine punishment is that of cleansing or purging the people of their sin. The *Psalms of Solomon*, for example, affirm: "He who makes ready his back for strokes shall be cleansed, for the Lord is good to those who endure chastening (*paideia*)" (*Pss. Sol.* 10:2).[41] The language of cleansing or purification is particularly common in the *Thanksgiving Hymns* from Qumran.[42] In the Hebrew Scriptures, this process is compared to the refining of metals, winnowing, or the use of a sieve.[43] As many of these passages make clear, what is involved is not merely a removal of guilt, but a change of behavior in which those made to suffer or others who observe their suffering are moved to cease practicing sin in order to do God's will.

The idea that chastisements are an act of divine mercy aimed at purifying and correcting those who endure them is found repeatedly throughout the rabbinic writings as well.[44] Jacob Neusner summarizes rabbinic thought thus: "people are expected to accept suffering as a mark of divine favor and love, as an indication that God has special confidence in them, or that God has a particular purpose in dealing with them as he does."[45] While God's purposes are not always entirely clear, it is generally presupposed that they are always

---

41. For similar affirmations, see also Ps. 51:2; Isa. 4:4; Ezek. 24:13; 36:25-26; 37:23; Dan. 12:10; *Pss. Sol.* 3:4; 13:7, 10; 14:1-2; *Jub.* 50:5.

42. See 1QH 1:32-33; 3:21-22; 4:37-38; 6:5-6, 8; 11:8-12.

43. See Jer. 15:7; Ezek. 22:20-22; Dan. 12:10; Amos 9:9; Zech. 13:9; Mal. 3:3; cf. Matt. 3:12.

44. For relevant quotes and commentary, see Adolf Büchler, *Studies in Sin and Atonement in the Rabbinic Literature of the First Century* (JCP 11; London: Oxford University Press, 1928), 170-75, 187-89, 210-11, 337-42.

45. Jacob Neusner, *Judaism When Christianity Began: A Survey of Belief and Practice* (Louisville, KY: Westminster John Knox, 2002), 130.

loving and merciful. In rabbinic thought, therefore, when Israel's God chastises people, he does so not for *his own* sake but for *theirs*.

Divine discipline or chastisement was thought to take many different forms, yet inevitably it involved some type of suffering. This might be disease, famine, oppression, slavery, exile, destruction, or other types of hardships for the people collectively. In the case of individuals, it could involve an untimely death, a painful illness, poverty, or personal hardships both for the one being punished as well as for that person's loved ones.[46]

At times, the Hebrew Scriptures and other ancient Jewish writings see this suffering not primarily as divine punishment but as a natural, intrinsic consequence of one's actions. The book of Proverbs repeatedly stresses this idea: "The iniquities of the wicked ensnare them, and they are caught in the toils of their sin" (Prov. 5:22). "[T]hose who miss me [i.e., wisdom] injure themselves" (Prov. 8:36). "The righteousness of the blameless keeps their ways straight, but the wicked fall by their own wickedness. The righteousness of the upright saves them, but the treacherous are taken captive by their schemes" (Prov. 11:5-6; cf. 13:6). "The wicked are overthrown by their evildoing" (Prov. 14:32). "Those who mislead the upright into evil ways will fall into pits of their own making" (Prov. 28:10; cf. 17:20; 22:16).

The book of Jeremiah reflects the same ideas. To turn away from God is to go after "worthless things" that "do not profit" (Jer. 2:5, 8, 11, 13; 16:19). The prophet repeatedly tells the people that their own actions bring suffering on themselves and their own wickedness punishes them (Jer. 2:19). In the midst of their hardships, he insists: "Your ways and your doings have brought this upon you" (Jer. 4:18). "Your sins have deprived you of good" (Jer. 5:25). Similarly, the prophet Isaiah reproaches the people because they "walk in a way that is not good, following their own devices" (Isa. 65:2), while Hosea claims that "Israel has spurned the good" (Hosea 8:3).

The Jewish writings of the second-temple period repeat the same type of affirmations. According to Tobit 12:10, "those who commit sin and do wrong are their own worst enemies." The *Letter of Aristeas* 131-32 points to "the injurious effects of sin." The Wisdom of Solomon speaks of those whom God "tormented through their own abominations" and punished by means of their own gods (Wis. 12:23, 27). The author invokes Israel's God, recalling: "In return for their foolish and wicked thoughts, which led them astray to worship irrational serpents and worthless animals, you sent upon them a multitude of irrational creatures to punish them, so that they might learn that one is punished by the very things by which one sins" (Wis. 11:15-16). Elsewhere he adds that God's creation "exerts itself to punish the unrighteous" (Wis. 16:24).

Some modern interpreters have claimed that divine punishment in the Hebrew Scriptures should be understood exclusively in these terms. The most notable of these has been Klaus Koch, who argued that, throughout the

---

46. E. P. Sanders, for example, notes: "It was standard in Judaism to think that premature death was punishment for unrepented sin" (*Paul: The Apostle's Life*, 297).

Hebrew Scriptures, there is a "built-in and inherent connection between an action and its consequences."[47] Rather than actively administering punishment or exacting retribution, the creator God YHWH established an order in which human actions lead to consequences that are intrinsic to those actions.[48] Though such interpretations may be attractive from the perspective of our modern worldview, it is highly problematic to read such ideas back into the ancient texts. Instead, in those texts the notion that people suffer the intrinsic consequences of their sin stands alongside the idea that God personally punishes sin. In ancient Hebrew and Jewish thought, Israel's God does not merely stand back and allow his people to suffer the natural consequences of their actions, but also intervenes actively in order to bless or chastise them according to his purposes, which are regarded as ultimately loving and merciful.

Yet while the Hebrew Scriptures and ancient Jewish literature posit an *extrinsic* relation between the people's wrongdoing and the divine punishment that follows upon it, they regard this extrinsic relation as being dependent on the *intrinsic* relation between sin and its consequences. As noted above, in the Mosaic law, God was thought to have commanded and prohibited certain actions *for the good of the people themselves*, on account of the positive or negative consequences of those actions. In biblical thought, when Israel's God acts to punish sin, he does so precisely because of the intrinsic connection between sin and its consequences: God wants the people to avoid doing things that bring harm and suffering upon themselves and instead to do what is beneficial for them. At times, of course, God simply lets the people suffer the consequences of their sins by not intervening to save them from those consequences. Because he is omnipotent, however, God has the power to deliver human beings from the sufferings that result naturally and intrinsically from their actions. Therefore, when God chooses not to intervene, those sufferings must be seen as taking place according to his will.

The people's well-being and *shalom* are therefore regarded as depending on both the intrinsic consequences of their actions as well as God's response to those actions. When they live in the way YHWH has commanded them for their own good, they are blessed, not only because of the natural consequences of their behavior, but also because YHWH responds to that behavior by granting them even greater blessings. According to passages such as Lev. 26:3-13 and Deut. 28:1-14, YHWH rewards the people's obedience by multiplying their offspring, providing them with abundant harvests, and saving them from threats such as wild animals and enemy armies. Conversely, if they disobey YHWH's commandments, acting in ways that lead intrinsically to their harm and destruction, YHWH chastises them by sending various types of suffering upon them in an attempt to restore them to obedience for their own good (Lev. 26:14-45; Deut. 28:15-68).

---

47. Koch, "Doctrine," 59.

48. Ibid., 57-87. The original version of Koch's article, not all of which was included in the English translation, was published as "Gibt es eine Vergeltungslehre im alten Testament?," *ZTK* 52 (1955): 1-42.

These two aspects are so closely connected to one another in the biblical texts that generally no distinction is made between them. It is simply said that, depending on the people's behavior, things will go well or badly for them, without specifying whether this will be the natural consequence of their actions or the result of divine intervention. Many passages can be interpreted on the basis of either or both ideas. In Deut. 6:25, for example, Moses is presented as telling the people: "And there will be justice for us (*utsedaqah tihyeh lanu*) if we are careful to do all this commandment before YHWH our God, as he has commanded us." This can be understood both in the sense that justice will be the intrinsic consequence of their obedience and in the sense that God will intervene from heaven to establish justice among them if they obey. Similarly, when they are told that all will go well with them and that they will prosper if they obey God's commandments, the idea is not only that God will bless them if they obey, but that in itself their obedience will contribute intrinsically to their well-being.[49]

The logic behind such affirmations is not difficult to grasp. If things such as respect for parents and healthy family relations are neglected and various forms of injustice and inequality are allowed to proliferate, for example, the moral and social fiber of the society may be weakened to such an extent that the people are easily defeated by foreign powers. Thus their oppression at the hands of foreigners can be seen *intrinsically* as the natural consequence of their actions and at the same time *extrinsically* as an act of divine retribution for their sins. In contrast, if Israel obeys the commandments that promote respectful, just, and equitable human relations, the society will tend to be healthy, whole, and strong. In this case, their ability to resist their enemies can be attributed both to their obedience in and of itself and at the same time to an act of God, who protects them from those who would harm them. Nevertheless, while the people's well-being is the result of observance of the law for both *intrinsic* and *extrinsic* reasons, ultimately the *extrinsic* relationship between the people's behavior and its consequences is dependent upon the *intrinsic* relationship: God rewards behavior that contributes to their well-being and chastises behavior that is harmful and destructive to that well-being.

Judgment, Justice, and Righteousness

In biblical thought, Israel's God must constantly judge his people to see how best to respond to their actions in order to accomplish his purposes. When YHWH considers that people have been striving to obey and live in accordance with his will, he generally responds by blessing them. In certain contexts, when some are being treated unjustly by others, YHWH's judgment takes the form of saving the oppressed from their oppressors. Since the purpose of such judgment is that of promoting the people's well-being and defending what is right, it is regarded as an expression not only of YHWH's

---

49. See, for example, Deut. 5:16; 6:18; 12:28; 29:9.

justice but also of his *love and mercy*. For this reason, in the Hebrew Scriptures, to *judge* is also to *save*. By executing justice, YHWH and those who serve as his agents act to protect the weak, the needy, and the oppressed. Such judgment is thus repeatedly seen as a cause for rejoicing and celebrating throughout the Hebrew Scriptures.[50]

Although at times YHWH's judging activity serves to establish justice and well-being among the people by doing away with those who inflict harm and suffering on others, it can also bring those who suffer to repent of their deeds and change their behavior. Ultimately, in his love and mercy, what YHWH seeks through judgment is not to destroy sinners but to bring them to repentance. In ancient Hebrew and Jewish thought, repentance involves not merely a feeling of remorse over the sin and evil that one has done but above all a renewed commitment to living according to YHWH's will. The Hebrew word commonly used for repentance, *teshuvah*, expresses this idea clearly: what Israel's God seeks is that the people turn back to him in obedience and reorient their conduct so that it may be in conformity with the commandments he gave them for their own good.[51] For this reason, it is incorrect to affirm, as Sanders repeatedly does, that in biblical and Jewish thought, punishment atones for sin.[52] *Only repentance and turning back to God in obedience can atone for sin and obtain God's forgiveness.* If divine punishment does not attain that goal, it does not bring about atonement or forgiveness.

In ancient Hebrew and Jewish thought, the difference between the righteous who are *saved* through divine judgment and the sinners who are merely *punished* and subsequently destroyed is that the former repent when they are subjected to suffering, whereas the latter do not. In a sense, of course, the righteous are also sinners. For this reason, they stand in need of repentance as well as constant correction by God. As Sanders has stressed, in ancient Judaism righteousness was not equated with perfection, nor was perfect obedience to the commandments expected or required. On the contrary, it was regarded as an impossibility. This is evident from the fact that the law itself made provisions for sin, thus anticipating that even those committed to observing the commandments would fail at times.[53] What distinguishes the righteous from those classified as "sinners" is that the righteous recognize their sin, repent of it, and seek to live in conformity with God's will. As Severino Pancaro has shown, this understanding runs throughout the Hebrew Scriptures, the second-temple Jewish literature (including the Qumran writings), and the rabbinic material. What characterizes the just or righteous is their attitude

---

50. For examples of all of these ideas, see Deut. 10:17-19; Ps. 9:7-9; 10:17-18; 67:4; 71:2, 15; 76:9; 82:3-4; 89:14; 103:6, 17; 112:9; 135:14; 146:5-10; Prov. 31:9; Isa. 1:17; 11:4; 59:11; Jer. 5:28; 9:24; 21:12; 22:3, 15-16; 33:15-16. God's judging is therefore a motive for rejoicing: Ps. 33:5.

51. Neusner, *Judaism When Christianity Began*, 154-58.

52. See, for example, Sanders, *Comparing Judaism and Christianity*, 75-76, 80, 324.

53. Sanders, *Paul and Palestinian Judaism*, 137-38, 204-5. Sanders notes that the rabbis often used the language of "confessing the commandments" in order to speak of the necessary commitment to obedience (92-96, 234).

toward the law and their earnest endeavor to observe it: "The 'just' are not sinless, but are characterized by the basic acceptance of and obedience to the Torah and their prompt repentance when they have transgressed some precept of the Law."[54]

These two understandings of the purpose of divine judgment are reflected as well in the petition of the righteous that God judge them. In the Psalms, this petition is made in a context of injustice and oppression. The righteous person asks YHWH to examine his or her heart and conduct to see if it conforms to YHWH's will. If it does not, then the suffering that he or she is enduring is thought to be justified, since it is aimed at bringing him or her back to YHWH in repentance. However, if the supplicant's heart and conduct are in conformity with YHWH's will, it is expected that YHWH's justice should be manifested in putting an end to the oppression that he or she is suffering at the hands of others.[55]

This understanding of righteousness and judgment represents an additional point of conflict with much traditional Christian thought. Christian theologians and biblical scholars have often claimed that, in ancient Hebrew and Jewish thought, God expected and demanded perfect obedience to the law. As noted in Chapter 1, for example, Hans Hübner ascribes to Paul the idea that "only total obedience to the law is obedience to the law at all. This postulate of the fulfilment of the contents of the law as a whole means that even if just a single prescription of the law is transgressed against, the effect is as if the entire Torah had been disregarded, i.e. total loss of righteousness."[56] According to such an understanding of righteousness, no one would ever ask God to judge him or her as the Psalmists do, since the result of such a petition would inevitably be punishment and condemnation rather than salvation. This makes it clear that much traditional Christian thought on this subject is foreign to what we find in both the Hebrew Scriptures and other ancient Jewish writings. One does not cease to be righteous by sinning per se, but by failing to repent of one's sins and by refusing to commit oneself to living in conformity with God's will as expressed in the commandments. What God expects is not perfect obedience but a sincere commitment to doing his will.

In addition to bringing those who have sinned to repentance and putting an end to the oppression of some at the hands of others, in biblical thought divine punishment was thought to contribute to justice and well-being among the people in other ways as well. Israel's God was believed to punish those who did evil in order to set an example and dissuade others from following the same path. By punishing evildoers, YHWH not only saves the oppressed

---

54. Severino Pancaro, *The Law in the Fourth Gospel: The Torah and the Gospel, Moses and Jesus, Judaism and Christianity according to John* (NovTSup 42; Leiden: E.J. Brill, 1975), 41; see especially 30-44, where he contrasts the Jewish distinction between the righteous and the sinners. On this distinction, see also Steven M. Bryan, *Jesus and Israel's Traditions of Judgement and Restoration* (SNTSMS 117; Cambridge: Cambridge University Press, 2002), 57-72.

55. See, for example, Ps. 7:8; 18:20-24; 26:1-12; 35:24; 43:1; 119:121-22. Cf. 2 Kgs. 20:2-6; Job 31:3-40.

56. Hans Hübner, *Law in Paul's Thought*, trans. James C. G. Gerig (Edinburgh: T & T Clark, 1984), 24.

from their oppressors but also serves warning to others that if they fall into similar sins, they will suffer the same fate.[57] In this case, punishment serves as a deterrent.

To execute judgment on sinners may also be seen as having the purpose of stamping out sin or evil before it can spread further and affect even more people. Philo, for example, speaks of the flood in Noah's days not as a punishment but as a purification (*katharsis*) of the earth from evil (*Moses* 2.64). In ancient Hebrew and Jewish thought, because this type of judgment ultimately seeks to put an end to injustice and establish a basis for justice and *shalom* to prosper once more, it was also considered an act of love and mercy on God's part.

In some cases, the ancient Hebrew and Jewish writings present God as imposing suffering on those who are not guilty of any grave sin and thus undeserving of any discipline for the purpose of testing them. If they fail to pass the test and instead rebel against God, then God knows that they need to be corrected and refined further. However, if they remain faithful to God in the midst of that suffering, then God knows that they are trustworthy and are capable of being used as God's instrument in order to accomplish his purposes through them.[58] Such testing also serves to strengthen the faith and resolve of those who endure it.

God's Judgment and God's Love

Because all people sin, including the righteous, God's act of purifying people through chastisements constitutes an ongoing process. In the case of individuals, of course, that process ends when they die, since in Jewish thought no further purification or correction takes place after death. In the case of the people as a whole, however, that process is never finished in this world.

In the Hebrew Scriptures, the periods in which the people of Israel live in obedience to God's law are generally presented as being relatively short-lived. As a result, a pattern or cycle of events is repeated continuously: the people sin, God chastises them, the people repent, and God saves them. After a time, however, the people fall into sin once more and this pattern or cycle is repeated. As Joseph Klausner has shown, this cycle can be traced throughout the Hebrew Scriptures and various second-temple Jewish writings, and thus forms the basis upon which Israel's history is interpreted.[59]

---

57. See, for example, Jer. 3:8; Ezek. 5:15; 23:8-11; Wis. 16:5-6, 10-11; Philo, *Embassy* 7; Josephus, *Ant.* 1.116-17.

58. See Neusner, *Judaism When Christianity Began*, 126-30.

59. Joseph Klausner, *The Messianic Idea in Israel, from its Beginning to the Completion of the Mishnah Cycle*, trans. W. F. Stinespring (New York: MacMillan, 1955), 38-46, 58, 117-22, 237-38, 307-8, 427-28. The classic example of this cycle can be found in the book of Judges. There, after God has introduced the Israelites into the promised land, they fall into sin, provoking the anger of YHWH, who then punishes them through their enemies. However, when the people then repent and cry out to YHWH for help, he responds by raising up a judge to deliver them once more. After a time, however, they fall into sin again, and the cycle is repeated (see Judg. 2:12-20; 3:7-15; 4:1-3; 6:1-10; 10:1-16).

In these passages and others in the Hebrew Scriptures, the punishments YHWH inflicts are presented as gradually increasing in duration or intensity.[60] This occurs when the people fail to repent sufficiently after being chastised. In Lev. 26:14-39, for example, Moses describes a number of punishments that YHWH will inflict upon the people when they disobey, each of which is more severe than the previous one. The description of each form of punishment is introduced by phrases that indicate that its severity is increased when the people refuse to be corrected by the previous punishment: "if in spite of this you will not obey me" (v. 18); "if you continue hostile to me" (v. 21); "if in spite of these punishments you have not turned back to me" (v. 23); "if, despite this, you disobey me and continue hostile to me" (v. 27). The same type of progression is found in Amos 4:6-11, where YHWH lists a series of increasingly harsher punishments he has inflicted on the people and, after each one, complains to the people, "yet you still did not return to me."[61] In his treatise on *Rewards and Punishments*, Philo describes the same process. After classifying the different types of divine punishment from the most lenient to the most severe, he affirms that, "if after this they fail to learn wisdom and still go crookedly away from the straight paths which lead to truth," those punishments grow harsher (*Rewards* 148). He then insists, however, that the purpose of all these things is not the people's destruction but their admonition. The purpose is that they might be "shamed into a whole-hearted conversion" and "reproach themselves for going thus astray, and make a full confession and acknowledgement of all their sin, first within themselves with a mind so purged that their conscience is sincere and free from lurking taint, secondly with their tongues to bring their hearers to a better way" (*Rewards* 163; see 118-64).

Although at times YHWH is presented as actively punishing the people for their sins by inflicting suffering upon them, on occasion this punishment is described in terms of merely "hiding his face."[62] This involves giving them up to their own sinfulness and letting them suffer the painful consequences of their actions without intervening. Nevertheless, simply to let this go on indefinitely would be to abandon the people and give up on his efforts to bring them back into obedience to himself. YHWH's love for Israel will not permit him to do this. Therefore, while he may abandon them for a time, in the end he will turn back to them in order to continue his efforts to cleanse them of their sinfulness.[63]

At times, YHWH is presented as anxious to effect the purging and purification of the people. He becomes weary of this endless cycle that seems to lead nowhere and thus refuses to listen any more to the people's petitions for

---

60. See, for example, Neh. 9:16-31; Ps. 78:34-38; 106:40-46.

61. For similar ideas, see Jer. 5:3; Hag. 2:17.

62. Deut. 31:17-18; 32:20; Judg. 6:13; 2 Kgs. 17:18, 22-23; 2 Chron. 24:20; Job 13:24; Ps. 13:1; 44:22-24; 88:14; Isa. 57:17; 59:2; 64:7; Jer. 33:5; Mic. 3:4.

63. See, for example, Lev. 26:44-45; 1 Sam. 12:20-22; Ps. 94:14; Isa. 49:14-15; Hosea 11:8-9.

forgiveness, since they are insincere.[64] He may even desire that the people *not* repent, since their repentance will only be half-hearted and short-lived as it has repeatedly been in the past. Such repentance can be seen as an obstacle to YHWH's long-term plan of bringing about an obedient people who will no longer stray from his covenant, since when they repent divine punishment appears unjustified. In Isa. 6:9-13, for example, YHWH sends Isaiah to make the people's minds dull, stop up their ears, and shut their eyes so that they may not turn to him and be healed. This will justify his carrying out a thorough purification of the people, yet the prophet's words will also enable those who end up surviving the destruction YHWH will send to understand why he punished them as severely as he did.

As this passage from Isaiah indicates, when YHWH's efforts to bring the people back into obedience have repeatedly failed, it is thought that he must take the drastic measure of destroying a part of the people in order to leave a small remnant. Like the shoot that grows out of a stump that remains after a large tree has been felled, this remnant will constitute a "holy seed" that will form the nucleus of a people who will finally live in conformity with his will (Isa. 6:13; cf. 11:1).[65] A number of texts from the Hebrew Scriptures and second-temple Jewish writings interpret the exile in these terms: once the people have been thoroughly cleansed through the harsh experience of exile, they will finally live in the way YHWH desires.[66] As noted above, Philo interprets the flood on the basis of the same ideas: the destruction of all human beings except Noah and his family made a new start for humanity possible (*Moses* 2.64).

In the midst of the many allusions to punishment, destruction, exile, and divine wrath that we find in the Hebrew Scriptures and other ancient Jewish writings, the idea that the God of Israel continually acts out of love in relation to his people is constantly stressed. We have already examined above the passages from Prov. 3:11-12 and Josephus's *Antiquities* 3.311 that compare YHWH's punishments with those of a parent lovingly disciplining a child, as well as 2 Macc. 6:12-16, which insists that the chastisements God sends are a manifestation of God's kindness and mercy. Similarly, in the *Psalms of Solomon*, it is said that God "corrects the righteous as a beloved son, and his chastisement is as that of a firstborn. For the Lord spares his pious ones and blots out their errors by his chastening" (*Pss. Sol.* 13:9-10). In *2 Baruch* 78:6, Baruch tells the tribes in exile: "you have suffered now for your good." Thus even the destruction of exile is seen as an act of love on the part of YHWH, who seeks to cleanse his people from sin.

---

64. See, for example, Isa. 1:14; Jer. 6:11; 7:16-20; 11:14; Ezek. 14:12-20.

65. On this point, see also Ezra 9:8-15; Isa. 4:3-4; 10:20-22; Ezek. 14:10-11, 22-23; Zeph. 3:11-13; Zech. 13:8-9. In addition, see Mark Adam Elliott, *The Survivors of Israel: A Reconsideration of the Theology of Pre-Christian Judaism* (Grand Rapids: Eerdmans, 2000), 621-37; Michael E. Fuller, *The Restoration of Israel: Israel's Re-gathering and the Fate of the Nations in Early Jewish Literature and Luke-Acts* (BZNW 138; Berlin: Walter de Gruyter, 2006), 54-62, 75-84.

66. Bar. 2:29-35; *Pss. Sol.* 17:1-31; *Jub.* 1:12-16; *1 En.* 10:16-17; 83:7-9; 90:6-39.

In a number of passages from the Hebrew Bible, the people are reminded that, before ever punishing them for their sins, YHWH warns them repeatedly of the possible consequences of their disobedience. He did so not only when he gave them the law through Moses but also when he sent them his prophets. In the book of Jeremiah, YHWH repeatedly tells the people that he has spoken to them unceasingly, sending them prophets who "rose up early" to address them; in spite of this, however, they have refused to listen: "From the day that your ancestors came out of the land of Egypt until this day, I have persistently sent all my servants the prophets to them, day after day; yet they did not listen to me, or pay attention, but they stiffened their necks" (Jer. 7:25-26).[67] In a lengthy prayer presented in Nehemiah 9, Ezra the priest recalls how the Israelites of former generations refused to turn back to YHWH their God in spite of the goodness and mercy he consistently showed to them in many ways. Even though YHWH punished them, however, he never abandoned them (Neh. 9:6-37).

Another idea running throughout various books of the Hebrew Scriptures is that YHWH is "slow to wrath."[68] He is patient with his people, yet when they repeatedly refuse correction, he must act to discipline and correct them. The book of 2 Chronicles concludes its account of the destruction of Jerusalem and the deportation of its inhabitants under the Babylonian king Nebuchadnezzar in the following terms:

> The Lord, the God of their ancestors, sent persistently to them by his messengers, because he had compassion on his people and on his dwelling-place; but they kept mocking the messengers of God, despising his words, and scoffing at his prophets, until the wrath of the Lord against his people became so great that there was no remedy. Therefore he brought up against them the king of the Chaldeans, who killed their youths with the sword in the house of their sanctuary, and had no compassion on young man or young woman, the aged or the feeble; he gave them all into his hand (2 Chron. 36:15-17).

A number of passages express YHWH's pain and regret at having to chastise the people. In the book of Ezekiel, YHWH insists that he takes no pleasure in the death of anyone but seeks only that those who have sinned repent and change their ways so that they may live (Ezek. 18:23, 31-32). In the midst of the destruction of Jerusalem, the writer of Lamentations affirms: "For the Lord will not reject forever. Although he causes grief, he will have compassion according to the abundance of his steadfast love; for he does not willingly afflict or grieve anyone" (Lam. 3:31-33).[69] Similarly, YHWH tells those who have suffered exile: "'For a brief moment I abandoned you, but with great compassion I will gather you. In overflowing wrath for a moment I hid my face from you, but with everlasting love I will have compassion on you,' says the Lord, your Redeemer" (Isa. 54:7-8). "And after I have plucked them up, I will again have compassion on them, and I will bring them again to their

---

67. See also Jer. 7:13; 11:7-8; 25:3-7; 26:4-6; 32:33; 35:14-15.
68. Exod. 34:6; Num. 14:18; Neh. 9:17; Ps. 86:15; 103:8; 145:8; Joel 2:13; Jonah 4:2; Nah. 1:3.
69. On this idea, see also Isa. 1:5; 48:18-19; Jer. 8:21-22; 9:1; Ezek. 33:11.

heritage and to their land, every one of them" (Jer. 12:15; cf. 30:12-17; 31:18-20). In Ps. 106:46, YHWH is even said to have expressed his love for those in exile by causing them "to be pitied by all who held them captive."

The book of Judges presents YHWH as repeatedly delivering his people from their enemies simply because he could not bear watching them suffer: "for the Lord would be moved to pity by their groaning because of those who persecuted and oppressed them" (Judg. 2:18). In Hosea 11:6-9, YHWH is even presented as suffering intense anguish over the punishment that he has sent upon the people. After noting how they are being ravaged and devoured by the sword and affirming that he refuses to heed their cries for help because of their disobedience, YHWH laments over them: "How can I give you up, Ephraim? How can I hand you over, O Israel?.... My heart recoils within me; my compassion grows warm and tender" (v. 8).

Other passages combine these ideas. In Psalm 81, for example, we read of YHWH's grief over having had to give the people up to their own sinfulness and his wish that he might have blessed them instead:

> "But my people did not listen to my voice;
> Israel would not submit to me.
> So I gave them over to their stubborn hearts,
> to follow their own counsels.
> O that my people would listen to me,
> that Israel would walk in my ways!
> Then I would quickly subdue their enemies,
> and turn my hand against their foes....
> I would feed you with the finest of the wheat,
> and with honey from the rock I would satisfy you" (Ps. 81:11-14, 16).

The same type of lament is found in Isa. 48:17-19. After telling the people that he teaches them "for their own good" and leads them in the way they should go, YHWH exclaims:

> "O that you had paid attention to my commandments!
> Then your prosperity would have been like a river,
> and your success like the waves of the sea;
> your offspring would have been like the sand,
> and your descendants like its grains;
> their name would never be cut off
> or destroyed from before me."

Alongside these expressions of YHWH's love for Israel, of course, are countless passages in which YHWH is presented as a God who destroys his enemies, takes vengeance on those who have done wrong, and even punishes children for the sins of their parents. At times, YHWH can appear excessively violent and even cruel. Obviously, these passages present problems for the claim that YHWH was thought to act solely out of love for his people and others in all that he did. They also seem to provide support for the idea that divine retribution can be an end in itself, as if merely venting his wrath on those who do evil could satisfy YHWH's justice.

No doubt many of those who read these passages in antiquity found them to be as problematic as we tend to regard them today. While we cannot be sure how they would be read, there are numerous passages from second-temple Jewish writings that similarly present YHWH as a wrathful God who uses violent means to punish evildoers. In many places, the New Testament also speaks of divine punishment in similar terms. This seems to make it difficult to claim that God's justice was consistently believed to be an expression of God's love.

If we view these passages in the light of the ideas we have seen above, however, such an interpretation is by no means entirely out of the question. Those passages may have been read as reflecting an intense zeal on the part of Israel's God for his people and a passionate commitment to establishing *shalom* and social justice in the land, together with a deep outrage at the oppression and injustice that become widespread. If what was thought to move YHWH to great wrath and motivate him to strike out against those who persisted in evil was ultimately a concern, not for himself or his own holy nature, but for human well-being and salvation, then such expressions of violence would have been regarded as being in accordance with his intense love.

In English, for example, the language of vengeance generally implies retribution for its own sake: one inflicts suffering on those who have caused others to suffer for the sole purpose of making them pay for what they have done. A close look at the biblical material, however, reveals that, while the idea behind the language used in the original Hebrew and Greek certainly conveys the idea of retribution, this retribution is presented as having a positive purpose and thus is not regarded as an end in itself.

An excellent example of this is found in the book of Nahum. The book begins by affirming: "A jealous and avenging God is the Lord, the Lord is avenging and wrathful; the Lord takes vengeance on his adversaries and rages against his enemies.... Who can stand before his indignation? Who can endure the heat of his anger? His wrath is poured out like fire, and by him the rocks are broken in pieces" (Nah. 1:2, 6). Immediately, however, the tone changes: "The Lord is good, a stronghold in a day of trouble; he protects those who take refuge in him, even in a rushing flood. He will make a full end of his adversaries, and will pursue his enemies into darkness" (Nah. 1:7-8). YHWH then tells his people: "Though they are at full strength and many, they will be cut off and pass away. Though I have afflicted you, I will afflict you no more. And now I will break off his yoke from you and snap the bonds that bind you" (Nah. 1:12-13). The first chapter then ends with the words: "Look! On the mountains the feet of one who brings good tidings, who proclaims peace! Celebrate your festivals, O Judah, fulfill your vows, for never again shall the wicked invade you; they are utterly cut off" (Nah. 1:14-15). Here it is evident that the raging wrath and vengeance of YHWH have the purpose of purifying the people and doing away with those who afflict them. For this reason, it is at the same time "good tidings," since once those who cause oppression have been "utterly cut off," they will no longer be able to do the people harm. All of this would have been as evident to first-century readers of this passage as it is to us today.

These same ideas are found in numerous other passages from the Hebrew Scriptures, which relate God's vengeance to the salvation of the people and regard that vengeance as an expression of God's compassion, since it is aimed at doing away with evil and oppression:

> "Vengeance is mine, and recompense, for the time when their foot shall slip; because the day of their calamity is at hand, their doom comes swiftly." Indeed the Lord will vindicate his people, have compassion on his servants, when he sees that their power is gone, neither bond nor free remaining (Deut. 32:35-36).

> Therefore says the Sovereign, the Lord of hosts, the Mighty One of Israel: "Ah, I will pour out my wrath on my enemies, and avenge myself on my foes! I will turn my hand against you; I will smelt away your dross as with lye and remove all your alloy. And I will restore your judges as at the first, and your counselors as at the beginning. Afterward you shall be called the city of righteousness, the faithful city" (Isa. 1:24-26).

> Say to those who are of a fearful heart, "Be strong, do not fear! Here is your God. He will come with vengeance, with terrible recompense. He will come and save you" (Isa. 35:4).

> The spirit of the Lord God is upon me, because the Lord has anointed me; he has sent me to bring good news to the oppressed, to bind up the brokenhearted, to proclaim liberty to the captives, and release to the prisoners; to proclaim the year of the Lord's favor, and the day of vengeance of our God (Isa. 61:1-2).

In addition to these passages, many others could be cited that speak of YHWH's wrath and vengeance in the context of the salvation of his people and their deliverance from their oppressors.[70] That wrath also serves to purify the people of their sin and provide an example for others so that they do not fall into sin and injustice.[71] Such vengeance is therefore seen as a cause of rejoicing, not because of any morbid pleasure at seeing the guilty suffer, but rather on account of the liberation of those who suffered from their afflictions. It is logical to assume, therefore, that many of those in antiquity who read those passages that speak of the devastation and destruction carried out by YHWH in his wrath and indignation would interpret them on the basis of the same ideas we have seen previously. Rather than seeing them as contrary to YHWH's commitment to the well-being of his people and human beings in general, they would have seen such passages as *expressions* of that commitment.

The same can be said regarding those passages that use the Hebrew verb *padah* to speak of YHWH "visiting" the people for their iniquities. This has often been understood in the sense of effecting punishment for its own sake. However, such punishment could once more be seen as having other purposes,

---

70. See, for example, Isa. 47:3-4; 59:14-20; 63:1-9; 66:12-16; Jer. 51:6-10; Ps. 58:1-11; 94:1-23; 149:1-9; Zeph. 3:5-13.

71. See, for example, Ezek. 5:13-15; 24:13.

such as those mentioned previously. It might serve as a deterrent or as a means to purify the people from sin and injustice by bringing them to repentance, as well as fulfilling the purpose of stamping out injustice and oppression before they can spread further. Thus, for example, when the ancients read that YHWH promised to visit the sins of the parents on their children down to the third and fourth generations, there is no reason to suppose that they would have understood this merely in terms of divine vengeance, as if punishment were an end in itself. Rather, they would probably have regarded God's purpose as that of cleansing the people thoroughly from their sin over the period of several generations so that eventually they might be able to live in a way that contributed to their own well-being and that of others.

If YHWH's wrath was viewed in the context of a divine plan to bless the other nations or families of the earth through Israel, then his intention to purify Israel from its sin could also be seen as something that he did for the sake of the nations as well. The logic would be that, once the people were restored to obedience so as to become the object of YHWH's blessing, it would then be possible for other nations to be attracted to YHWH for their own good. In this way, Israel would serve God's purpose of being a "light" and "witness" to the nations, as the book of Isaiah stresses (Isa. 43:10; 44:8). A number of passages express concern about how the other nations will view YHWH on the basis of his treatment of Israel as well as Israel's behavior.[72] Implicit in these passages is therefore a concern for the salvation of the nations, who will be moved to worship YHWH by what they observe in Israel. All of these ideas are expressed in numerous passages from the Hebrew Scriptures.[73]

Of course, throughout those Scriptures, YHWH's wrath is directed just as much at the nations as it is at Israel, if not more so. Once again, however, this would not necessarily be understood as a lack of love for the nations. Rather, if the sin of the nations was seen as an obstacle to YHWH's plan for the salvation of many, their destruction would be seen as serving to put an end to that sin and prevent it from extending to Israel and elsewhere. As was the case with Israel, in some ways divine punishment or chastisement of the nations might be regarded as being motivated by YHWH's desire to ultimately bless them. The fact that YHWH was thought to send prophets to the nations would also be viewed as a sign of his love for them. Had he not wished to bring them to correct their ways, he would simply have destroyed them without bothering to speak to them through prophets as he did.

A number of passages from the Hebrew Scriptures, in fact, speak of YHWH's love for the nations, often in surprising terms. In Isaiah 19, for example, God's love for Israel's enemies is mentioned in the same context as their destruction. After describing the afflictions that YHWH will inflict on the Egyptians in the first part of the chapter (vv. 1-17), the prophet affirms:

---

72. See, for example, Exod. 32:11-2; Lev. 26:45; Num. 14:13-19; Ezek. 36:16-36.

73. See, for example, Ps. 18:49; 22:27; 67:2-5; 86:9; 96:3; 108:3; Isa. 2:2-3; 42:6; 49:6; 56:6-7; 60:3; 66:19; Jer. 16:19-21; 33:9; Mic. 4:1-3; Zech. 2:11; 8:20-23.

The Lord will make himself known to the Egyptians; and the Egyptians will know the Lord on that day, and will worship with sacrifice and burnt-offering, and they will make vows to the Lord and perform them. The Lord will strike Egypt, striking and healing; they will return to the Lord, and he will listen to their supplications and heal them. On that day there will be a highway from Egypt to Assyria, and the Assyrian will come into Egypt, and the Egyptian into Assyria, and the Egyptians will worship with the Assyrians. On that day Israel will be the third with Egypt and Assyria, a blessing in the midst of the earth, whom the Lord of hosts has blessed, saying, "Blessed be Egypt my people, and Assyria the work of my hands, and Israel my heritage" (vv. 21-25).

A similar idea is found in an interesting passage from the Babylonian Talmud. After describing the manner in which God saved the Israelites by drowning the Egyptian army in the Red Sea, the text affirms: "In that hour the ministering angels wanted to sing a song before God, but God rebuked them, saying, 'My handiwork is drowning in the sea and you want to sing to me?'" (*Sanh.* 39b). While this passage is from a later period, its affirmation of the intense love of Israel's God even for those whom he destroys suggests that there were Jews in antiquity who interpreted the biblical passages regarding YHWH's wrath toward the nations as compatible with his love for them. In fact, the book of Jonah no doubt lent itself to being interpreted as reflecting the same type of love for Israel's enemies on the part of YHWH.

On the basis of all of these passages, there is good reason to suppose that Jews in antiquity would have understood the biblical language regarding divine wrath, vengeance, and retribution on the basis of the conviction that ultimately Israel's God sought not only the well-being of Israel but that of other nations as well. YHWH was a God committed to justice, equity, and *shalom* in the world. Undoubtedly, Jews in antiquity often spoke of divine retribution and claimed that God made those who practiced sin and evil pay for their actions. What is important, however, is that there is no reason to conclude that they believed that their God acted in this way *for his own sake*, merely because he was a holy God who by nature could not tolerate evil. Contrary to what we find in later Christian theology, nowhere in the ancient Hebrew and Jewish sources do we find any type of argument that God was under some obligation to punish evil due to an inner need to be "true to himself" or safeguard his holy and perfect nature. In ancient Jewish thought, if Israel's God did not tolerate evil and wished to be known as a God of justice in the world, it was only because of his commitment to establishing a world in which all might live in a way that made it possible for them to enjoy his love and blessings.

From our modern perspective, of course, the language we find in the Hebrew Scriptures and ancient Jewish literature regarding divine punishment, wrath, retribution, and vengeance is extremely problematic. No longer do most people today consider it acceptable to claim that God employs violent means such as those mentioned in the Hebrew Scriptures in order to accomplish some loving purpose or plan, destroying entire populations or inflicting terrible suffering in order to accomplish some "higher good." Our notions of justice are very different from those of biblical times. Theirs was a cruel and violent world, and this is reflected in the way people regarded and executed justice.

What matters for our purposes here, however, is that there are good reasons for maintaining that Jews in antiquity would not have seen God's justice as being in opposition to God's love and mercy. On the contrary, there is abundant evidence to support the claim that they would consistently have read the Hebrew Scriptures and interpreted historical events on the basis of the conviction that the one God, creator of all, was ultimately committed to the well-being of people everywhere, even though, because of sin and evil in the world, he was not always able to manifest that love in the way he desired. For this reason, their ideas regarding divine punishment, wrath, retribution, and vengeance were considered not only *compatible* with their belief in God's love and mercy but as ultimately *grounded* in that love and mercy.

Grace and Merit

If Israel's God was regarded as constantly being gracious and merciful by nature, even when he executed justice as an expression of that grace and mercy, the notion that one might earn or merit God's grace was excluded from the outset. Because God's love was a given and therefore unconditional, what the actions of people or individuals were thought to merit was not God's love and grace per se but a *particular form* of that love and grace. In ancient Jewish thought, when people lived in the way God had commanded for their own good, that grace would generally take the form of various types of *blessing*, though at times it might also take the form of *testing* them to strengthen even more their reliance on God or *disciplining* them so as to continue to purify them of the sin that still remained in their heart. This was considered necessary due to the belief that not even the righteous were perfect or without sin. In the case of those whose sin was greater, God's grace would also take the form of *discipline* or *chastisement* in order to bring them to repentance and restore them to obedience for their own good and that of others. When in spite of repeated attempts to correct them, people remained unrepentant and there was no longer any hope of bringing them into conformity with God's will, their resistance to God's grace erased any possibility that it might accomplish God's purposes in them. In that case, the most that God's grace could do was to restrain and prevent those who were unrepentant and stubbornly persisted in their sin from doing harm to others or exerting a bad influence on them by acting against them in some way. In all of these cases, God was thought to be acting in grace.

Divine forgiveness was also inevitably understood on the basis of these same ideas. When those who had sinned returned to God so as to strive to live in conformity with God's will, God's grace would take the form of forgiveness. However, when those who acted sinfully remained unrepentant and instead insisted on behaving in ways that did harm to themselves and others, God's grace would take the form of *not* forgiving them but attempting to chastise and correct them for their sins. If even that did not work, there was no longer any sense or purpose in forgiving them, since that forgiveness would not accomplish any positive purpose. Instead, it would only lead to greater sin and injustice on their part, since they would be able to sin freely without any concern for divine retribution. Thus for the sake of others whom God loved and who were adversely affected by the sinful actions of the unrepentant, God's love and grace would take the form of punishment rather than forgiveness. In ancient Hebrew and Jewish thought, only in this way could God deal with sin and injustice effectively, seeking the best interest of all. Therefore, in the Hebrew Scriptures and second-temple Jewish literature, while God's *love* is consistently presented as being unconditional, God's *forgiveness* was not, since forgiveness in itself does not always lead to justice and well-being.

SECOND-TEMPLE JEWISH ESCHATOLOGY

If God had created the world and chosen Israel with a plan and purpose in mind, why had this plan and purpose not yet been accomplished? Would the justice and well-being God had intended for Israel and the world ever become a reality? Would the seemingly never-ending cycle of sin and punishment ever come to an end? These were the kinds of questions that Jewish eschatology sought to answer.

Generally, the obstacle to the fulfillment of the intentions of Israel's God was believed to be the persistent sinfulness of Israel. It might be hoped that eventually YHWH's efforts at purifying the people from their sinful ways would meet with success. Perhaps the repeated punishments, the exiles, and the establishment of a small but righteous remnant might finally result in a people who would live in conformity with YHWH's will. Nevertheless, the fact that the promises of blessing made through the patriarchs, Moses, and the prophets had apparently not yet been fulfilled led many Jews to expect that some type of radical change still needed to take place.

Among many Jews, the persistence of Israel and the other nations in sin came to be attributed in part to a sinful human nature. The idea that Israel is by nature a stubborn, rebellious people who constantly refuse to submit to God's will is found in a number of texts from the Hebrew Scriptures and second-temple Jewish writings.[74] By Jesus' day, there is evidence that some Jews believed there was some type of sinful inclination that prevented the people from obeying God as they should. The most explicit mention of this idea is found in *4 Ezra* 7:48: "For an evil heart has grown up in us, which has alienated us from God, and has brought us into corruption and the ways

---

74. See, for example, Deut. 9:27; Judg. 2:18-21; 2 Chron. 36:14-16; Ezek. 9:7; Neh. 9:16-35; Jer. 4:22; 8:5-7; 32:21-23, 30-35; Mal. 4:7; Bar. 1:15-22; *Jub.* 23:17. On the idea of a sinful inclination in the Hebrew Bible, see Frank Thielman, *From Plight to Solution: A Jewish Framework for Understanding Paul's View of the Law in Galatians and Romans* (NovTSup 61; Leiden: E.J. Brill, 1989), 29-36.

of death, and has shown us the paths of perdition and removed us far from life—and that not just a few of us but almost all who have been created!"[75] This idea came to be characteristic of much rabbinic thought, which posited an evil tendency or *yetser hara* which stood in contrast to a tendency for good or *yetser hatob* in human hearts.[76] A similar idea is found in the Dead Sea Scrolls, which speak of two spirits in human beings.[77]

Christian scholars have often understood this evil inclination in *ontological* terms, as if it involved some kind of actual power or force residing in the human heart or mind. It is important not to assume, however, that this was the ancient Jewish understanding and subsequently read this idea back into the texts. Though generally some type of divine assistance was believed to be necessary, the law itself could be seen as enabling those who study and apply it to overcome this sinful tendency.[78] This suggests that many Jews did not think that the only solution to the problem was for God to effect some type of ontological transformation of the human heart in order to eliminate this tendency or hold it in check.

Nevertheless, a number of texts from the Hebrew Scriptures and second-temple Jewish literature foresee the day when Israel's God would change the people's hearts so that they might finally become obedient. The prophet Jeremiah speaks of YHWH writing his law within the people's hearts (Jer. 31:31-34), while in Ezekiel YHWH tells the prophet: "I will give them one heart, and put a new spirit within them; I will remove the heart of stone from their flesh and give them a heart of flesh, so that they may follow my statutes and keep my ordinances and obey them. Then they shall be my people, and I will be their God" (Ezek. 11:19-20; cf. 36:26-27). Similar ideas can be found in other passages from the Hebrew Scriptures and other ancient

---

75. See also *4 Ezra* 3:20; Wis. 12:10-11. A number of passages from the Hebrew Scriptures imply the same idea: Jer. 3:17; 5:23; Ezek. 3:7; 11:19; 36:26; Ps. 51:5. For further discussion on this point and references, see Thielman, *From Plight to Solution*, 30-32. As David M. Hay has shown, Philo also affirms such an idea ("Philo of Alexandria," in *Justification*, ed. Carson et al., 1:376).

76. For references and discussion of this idea in rabbinic thought, see Friedrich Avemarie, "The Tension between God's Command and Israel's Obedience as Reflected in the Early Rabbinic Literature," in *Divine and Human Agency in Paul and His Cultural Environment* (ed. John M. G. Barclay and Simon J. Gathercole; London: T & T Clark, 2006), 65-66. See also Serge Ruzer, *Mapping the New Testament: Early Christian Writings as a Witness for Jewish Biblical Exegesis* (JCPS 13; Leiden: Brill, 2007). Ruzer claims that it is "highly possible that the term *yetser ha-ra* predates the New Testament" (154; see 151-68). A fuller treatment of this subject is found in G. H. Cohen Stuart, *The Struggle in Man between Good and Evil: An Inquiry into the Origin of the Rabbinic Concept of* Yeṣer Hara' (Kampen: J. H. Kok, 1984).

77. On the Qumran doctrine of the two spirits, see especially Stephen Hultgren, *From the Damascus Covenant to the Covenant of the Community: Literary, Historical, and Theological Studies in the Dead Sea Scrolls* (STDJ 66; Leiden: Brill, 2007), 415, 422-23, 445-46; Thielman, *From Plight to Solution*, 36-38; John R. Levison, "The Two Spirits in Qumran Theology," in *The Bible and the Dead Sea Scrolls: The Second Princeton Symposium on Judaism and Christian Origins* (ed. James H. Charlesworth; Waco, TX: Baylor University Press, 2006), 2:169-94.

78. The idea that study of the Torah itself overcomes the evil inclination, without any type of ontological change being effected in human beings, is characteristic of rabbinic teaching; see Bruce Chilton and Jacob Neusner, *Classical Christianity and Rabbinic Judaism: Comparing Theologies* (Grand Rapids: Baker Academic, 2004), 189-95.

Jewish writings.[79] The common idea is that in the end YHWH will solve the problem of the people's sinfulness and disobedience by doing something that will enable the people to live in the way he desires for their own good, thus making it possible for them to enjoy his blessings fully.[80]

Conditional and Unconditional Salvation

On the basis of these ideas, in the ancient Hebrew and Jewish writings salvation can be understood as both *conditional* and *unconditional*. It is conditional in the sense that the people must become obedient to God's will in order to be saved. As we have seen, because of the intrinsic relation between their behavior and the consequences of that behavior, it was thought that the people could not experience the well-being God desired for them if they did not practice justice and righteousness, caring for those in need and rooting out oppression and injustice from their midst. For this reason, their salvation was considered to be *conditional* upon their obedience to the law. God would act to save them when they lived as he had commanded for their own good.

At the same time, many passages see Israel's salvation as *unconditional*. Although YHWH may punish Israel, destroy a portion of the people, send them into exile, and abandon them for a time, ultimately he will redeem them.[81] Undoubtedly, YHWH's forgiveness depends on the people returning to him in obedience.[82] However, because YHWH will act to bring that obedience about in them, they can be assured that in the end he will forgive and save them. To give up on his people definitively or allow their total destruction would be to abandon not only his beloved people Israel but his plan of bringing salvation, justice, and well-being to the nations as well. Thus while God's *love* for his people is always *unconditional*, his *saving activity* is at times presented as *conditional* and at other times as *unconditional*.

Scholars have at times seen this unconditional promise of salvation as an unconditional commitment to *Israel*. The idea of God's righteousness as "covenant faithfulness" is often understood in this way.[83] In reality, however,

---

79. On this idea, see also Deut. 30:6; 1 Kgs. 8:58; 1 Chron. 29:18; Ps. 51:10; Jer. 24:7; Mal. 4:5-6; 2 Macc. 1:3; Bar. 2:31.

80. For the idea that God alone is capable of overcoming the sinful tendency in human beings, see Thielman, *From Plight to Solution*, 28-45. David Lambert has shown that the idea that God will overcome the power of sin in his people and transform their hearts is found in *Jub.* 1:15-25, as well as other passages from *Jubilees* and the writings from Qumran, yet he also demonstrates that this idea stands alongside the idea that the people must repent in order to be saved ("Did Israel Believe That Redemption Awaited Its Repentance? The Case of *Jubilees* 1," *CBQ* 68 [2006]: 631-50). Hultgren also points to passages from the Qumran writings that communicate the idea that God will ultimately give his people the obedience they need in order to be redeemed (*Damascus Covenant*, 454-49). Perhaps the most thorough consideration of these ideas is found in Wells, *Grace*, 25-206.

81. Among the many passages that speak of such unconditional salvation, see Lev. 26:44-45; Neh. 9:17, 19, 31; Ps. 89:31-33; Isa. 11:1-9; 35:1-10; 40:1-11; 49:7-26; 60:1-22; 62:1-12; 65:17-25; Jer. 23:3-8; 24:4-7; 29:4-14; 30:10-11, 18-22; 31:2-37; 32:36-44; 46:27-28; Ezek. 11:14-20; 20:40-44; 28:25-26; 34:11-16, 22-31; 36:22-38; 39:17-29; Hosea 14:4-7; Joel 2:18-29; Mic. 7:18-20; Tob. 13:1-18; 14:5-7; Bar. 4:18-37.

82. See, for example, Isa. 1:16-19; 27:9; 55:7; Jer. 36:3; Ezek. 33:14-16.

83. On this idea, see N. T. Wright, "On Becoming the Righteousness of God, 2 Cor 5:21," in *Pauline Theology*, Vol. 2: *1 & 2 Corinthians* (ed. David M. Hay; Minneapolis: Fortress, 1993), 206-7. On the problems

YHWH's commitment is to *justice* within Israel: what YHWH promises is not to save Israel no matter what the people do, but to bring about within Israel a righteous people who will do YHWH's will so that he may accomplish his purposes through them, including the salvation of the nations. In other words, God's commitment is not *to bless and save Israel* no matter what the people do but to *transform them into a people who will do his will*. For this reason, even when YHWH punishes his people and sends them into exile, he is seen to be acting out of faithfulness to his covenant promises.

The idea that YHWH would eventually redeem his people no matter how disobedient they had been did not lead to the conclusion that it was no longer necessary for them to strive to be obedient to his commandments. On the contrary, even though Israel as a people would be saved, the question of precisely who formed part of Israel still had to be answered. Furthermore, while it might be expected that YHWH would graciously give his people the new heart and new spirit they needed in order to become obedient, it was nevertheless possible to maintain that only those who were deserving of salvation would receive that new heart and new spirit. The fact that Israel had not experienced any type of full, definitive salvation in Jesus' day thus led many Jews to inquire as to what was still lacking in order for YHWH to bring about Israel's redemption. The obvious answer was that Israel had not yet become sufficiently obedient to the law or perhaps that not enough Israelites had done so. In this case, it was necessary to work to bring more people into conformity with YHWH's will as expressed in the commandments.

The lack of redemption might also be attributed to an inadequate interpretation of the commandments. Those commandments could hardly be properly obeyed if they were not properly interpreted. Because of this, debates over the way in which the commandments were to be put into practice became extremely common and led to divisions among the people. The various teachers of the law might even blame one another for misleading people through their erroneous interpretations of what the law commanded, and thereby impeding or delaying the redemption of Israel.

Eschatological Hopes and Beliefs

Existing alongside the diversity of interpretations of the law was a wide diversity of eschatological beliefs.[84] Most Jews seem to have continued to affirm the basic ideas associated with the biblical eschatology, according to which those who kept God's commandments would enjoy blessings such as long life,

---

of understanding God's righteousness as covenant faithfulness, see Mark Seifrid, "Paul's Use of Righteousness Language against its Hellenistic Background," in *Justification and Variegated Nomism*, Vol. 2: *The Paradoxes of Paul* (ed. D. A. Carson, Peter T. O'Brien, and Mark A. Seifrid; WUNT 2/181; Tübingen: Mohr Siebeck, 2004), 40-44.

84. On this type of view and the wide variety of eschatological beliefs in second-temple Judaism, see especially Albert L. A. Hogeterp, *Expectations of the End: A Comparative Traditio-Historical Study of Eschatological, Apocalyptic, and Messianic Ideas in the Dead Sea Scrolls and the New Testament* (STDJ 83; Leiden: Brill, 2009), 31-114.

material prosperity, and well-being in this world. For many, this was sufficient. They expected history to continue its course indefinitely and merely hoped that their situation as individuals and as a people would remain the same or perhaps improve to some degree. There is evidence that some Jews, especially in the diaspora, were fairly content to live under Roman rule and did not ascribe much importance to questions of eschatology and the fulfillment of biblical prophecy.[85]

Other Jews longed for a salvation that would involve the end of Roman rule over Israel and the political independence of the Jewish people. Many hoped that conditions such as those associated with Solomon's reign would come to prevail once more: Jerusalem and the kingdom of Israel would be restored to their former glory and splendor and the nation would enjoy great prosperity, free from the oppressive rule of gentile powers. Jews in the diaspora would be able to return to the land of their forefathers and live in peace, worshiping YHWH in the temple and living faithfully according to the precepts of the Torah in order to enjoy the blessings it promised to all who obeyed it.[86]

Those Jews who hoped for political independence from Rome held different ideas regarding what was necessary for Israel's liberation. Some thought the people should simply wait patiently for God to intervene. In this case, the most they could do was to strive to be as obedient as possible in order to be deserving of God's intervention. Others, in contrast, considered that faithfulness to God meant actively struggling against Roman domination, taking up arms as they had in the days of the Maccabeans. In their minds, the people could not expect God to intervene on their behalf if they did not show concretely their trust in God by taking the initiative to rid themselves of Roman domination. Still others believed that clandestine tactics or passive resistance were called for in order to subvert Rome's power until the time for Israel's liberation came.[87] In spite of the differences over the form that obedience to God was to take, however, there was widespread agreement that Israel's redemption depended on the people repenting of their sins and living in greater obedience to God's will.[88]

Among many Jews, it became common to speak of a new world or new age that God would bring. For some, this simply involved political and national hopes such as those just mentioned and did not necessarily imply some type

---

85. See, for example, Fuller, *Restoration*, 84-101, 184-86.

86. Sanders offers a summary of the hopes common to both Palestinian and Diaspora Jews, though he cautions that there "was nothing like uniformity of expectation" (*Judaism*, 289-98).

87. On the different attitudes and approaches to Roman rule among Jews in this period, see especially Sanders, *Judaism*, 279-89; Fuller, *Restoration*, 148-62.

88. This idea runs consistently throughout the Jewish literature of the second-temple period as well as the rabbinic writings. On this point, see Dale C. Allison Jr., *The End of the Ages Has Come: An Early Interpretation of the Passion and Resurrection of Jesus* (Philadelphia: Fortress, 1985), 155-57; Klausner, *Messianic Idea*, 427-31; Jacob Neusner, *Rabbinic Judaism: Structure and System* (SFSHJ 211; Atlanta: Scholars Press, 1999), 149-62. As Bryan notes, however, the delay in the coming of the new age might be attributed, not to Israel's lack of repentance or obedience, but simply to "God's inscrutable decree" or to "God's patience in allowing others to join in the repentance" (*Jesus*, 19-20).

of dramatic divine intervention.⁸⁹ Others, however, conceived of the new age in terms of a radical break with the present age and a transformation of the present world into a very different one. God would act to bring suffering, injustice, and even death to an end. The world would become a place of peace and harmony, and Israel would attain a position of power and glory in the world.⁹⁰

Once again, there were many variations on these ideas, most of which are found in the Hebrew Scriptures themselves. However, the language of apocalyptic also came to be common to describe the end of the present age and the beginning of the new one in spectacular terms: following a period of intense conflict and tribulation, Israel's God would come in power and glory to destroy evil and evildoers forever and establish his glorious reign definitively.

A number of ideas were closely associated with this apocalyptic eschatology. Many believed that the dead would be raised in order to live once more on earth, enjoying the blessings of this new age. Although some maintained that only the righteous would be raised, others claimed that God would also raise the unrighteous and the evildoers in order to judge them.⁹¹

Many Jews believed that God would bring about this new age by means of a messianic figure.⁹² Some conceived of this figure as a king who would reign as David had, vanquishing and subduing Israel's enemies and establishing a glorious kingdom centered on Jerusalem and its temple. The writings from Qumran speak of a priestly Messiah in addition to a royal one.⁹³ Other texts

---

89. See Fuller, *Restoration*, 125; Philip S. Alexander, "Torah and Salvation," 1:275.

90. On the hopes concerning the regathering of Israel, see especially Fuller, *Restoration*, 25-84.

91. On the various Jewish beliefs regarding the resurrection of the dead in the second-temple period, see especially Hogeterp, *Expectations*, 326-31; N. T. Wright, *The Resurrection of the Son of God*, Vol. 3 of *Christian Origins and the Question of God* (Minneapolis: Fortress, 2003), 129-206. As Condra notes, for some Jews, including Jews at Qumran, the belief in the resurrection was relatively unimportant (*Salvation*, 86).

92. For a survey of beliefs regarding the Messiah in second-temple Jewish literature, see especially Condra, *Salvation*, 198-271; Sanders, *Judaism*, 295-98; Richard N. Longenecker, *The Christology of Early Jewish Christianity* (SBT 2/17; London: SCM, 1970), 63-119; John J. Collins, "Pre-Christian Jewish Messianism: An Overview," in *The Messiah in Early Judaism and Christianity* (ed. Magnus Zetterholm; Minneapolis: Fortress, 2007), 1-20. Today the scholarly consensus seems to be that no clear and distinct beliefs existed regarding a Messiah in second-temple Judaism and that expectations regarding a Messiah were not widespread. See, for example, James H. Charlesworth, "From Messianology to Christology," in *The Messiah: Developments in Earliest Judaism and Christianity. The First Princeton Symposium on Judaism and Christian Origins* (ed. Charlesworth; Minneapolis: Fortress, 1992), 19-20, 35, along with other essays in the same volume. Some scholars, however, have questioned that consensus. See, for example, William Horbury, *Jewish Messianism and the Cult of Christ* (London: SCM, 1998), 5-63. Several scholars have argued that the idea that the Messiah would suffer or die was present in a couple of passages from the Dead Sea Scrolls, but such a view has found no significant support among scholars; see John J. Collins, "Jesus and the Messiahs of Israel," in *Geschichte–Tradition–Reflexion: Festschrift für Martin Hengel zum 70. Geburtstag*, Band 3: *Frühes Christentum* (ed. Hubert Cancik, Hermann Lichtenberger, and Peter Schäfer; Tübingen: J. C. B. Mohr, 1996), 290-92. On the subject of beliefs regarding a messianic figure in the rabbinic literature, see Jacob Neusner, *Messiah in Context: Israel's History and Destiny in Formative Judaism* (Philadelphia: Fortress, 1984), 11-87.

93. On messianic beliefs in Qumran, see especially Hogeterp, *Expectations*, 423-58; John J. Collins, "What was Distinctive about Messianic Expectation at Qumran?," in *The Bible and the Dead Sea Scrolls*, ed. Charlesworth, 2:71-92; Craig A. Evans, "Qumran's Messiah: How Important Is He?," in *Religion in the Dead Sea Scrolls*, ed. Collins and Kuglar, 135-49.

conceive of God establishing this kingdom through other heavenly or human agents.[94]

Different views existed regarding the fate that awaited non-Jews.[95] Some Jews believed that all the nations would be destroyed, while others believed that those non-Jews who were righteous would in some way participate in the coming salvation together with those faithful Jews. Many thought that the nations would be subjected to Israel, perhaps becoming slaves to God's people, or be converted to the worship of YHWH so as to come to form part of God's people.[96]

All of these ideas had important political implications. Naturally, to affirm that the nations would be destroyed or subjected to Israel and that the rulers of this world would be dethroned involved seeing their power as illegitimate and contrary to God's will, at least in the long term. Even belief in the resurrection could be interpreted as an expression of protest against Greco-Roman society, since it involved claims regarding the sovereignty of God over all people as the only one who could give and take life.[97] Those Jews who believed that the righteous dead would be raised to life would be willing to put their life at risk in order to struggle against foreign powers that they considered idolatrous and oppressive. In contrast, to submit passively to those powers or collaborate with them in some way might be taken as a sign of unfaithfulness to Israel's God. However, if one believed that God was using the foreign powers as instruments to fulfill some divine purpose, such as the purification of Israel, then submission to them in the present age might be regarded not only as acceptable but necessary.

Different attitudes toward Roman rule were reflected as well in the way in which Jews viewed the Jewish authorities and institutions. Many regarded those authorities as legitimate, in spite of whatever moral shortcomings they were thought to have. Large throngs participated in the worship centered on the temple that Herod had gloriously renovated, where the high priests chosen by Rome presided. This involved a tacit acceptance of the rule of the Herods and the priesthood of figures such as Annas and Caiaphas and, by implication, of the Roman authorities who had placed them in the positions of authority they occupied. Others, such as the members of the community in Qumran, regarded the high priests, the temple, and the worship carried out there as corrupt and illegitimate and looked forward to the day when God would come to establish the proper authorities over a reconstituted Israel. In

---

94. See Nickelsburg, *Ancient Judaism*, 90-108; Fuller, *Restoration*, 170-84.

95. For a survey of views from the second-temple period regarding what would happen to Israel's enemies and the other nations, see especially Fuller, *Restoration*, 102-48. On Jewish beliefs on the subject in general, see Robert Goldenberg, *The Nations that Know Thee Not: Ancient Jewish Attitudes towards Other Religions* (BibSem 52; Sheffield: Sheffield Academic Press, 1997).

96. McKnight lists a number of Jewish texts from this period that foresee "a massive conversion of Gentiles at the Last Day" (*Light*, 47).

97. On the political and social implications of the Jewish beliefs regarding resurrection in the second-temple period, see especially Claudia Setzer, *Resurrection of the Body in Early Judaism and Early Christianity: Doctrine, Community, and Self-Definition* (Boston: Brill Academic, 2004), 21-52.

this way, God would also restore or replace the temple so that the proper worship might take place there.

Jewish Apocalyptic

The rise of apocalypticism was closely related to the social and political system in which the Jewish people lived. Apocalyptic ideas enabled faithful Jews to maintain their belief in a God who was all-powerful and opposed to evil and injustice in spite of the difficult conditions in which they lived. According to apocalyptic thought, contrary to appearances, Israel's God was indeed in control of history, but was allowing foreign nations and rulers to oppress the righteous at present in order to test his people and purify for himself a righteous remnant. Soon, however, the awaited redemption would arrive and all of God's enemies, both human and supernatural, would be defeated and destroyed definitively. For this reason, it was necessary to remain faithful and obedient.

A number of Jewish writings from the second-temple period convey the view that, before the new age would become a reality, there would be a period of intense conflict and suffering. Scholars have used a number of designations to refer to this period, such as the "great tribulation," the "messianic woes," and the "birth pangs of the Messiah." The latter two designations come from rabbinic writings.[98] While a diversity of beliefs existed concerning this period of tribulation, many saw it as a time in which there would be violent conflict that would involve not only human beings but celestial and demonic forces, as well as a series of signs in the heavens and on earth, such as earthquakes, famine, wars, and other cosmic disturbances. Among human beings, there would be mass apostasy and godlessness as well as intense suffering. Some thought Jerusalem would be the focus of the conflict and might even suffer destruction. The temple cult might also be affected, becoming contaminated or ceasing altogether. Often some type of evil tyrant or antichrist figure was expected to be at the head of this conflict. At the end of this period, there might be some type of final conflagration or destruction before the salvation promised by God finally became a reality. The righteous would be gathered into God's reign and the wicked would be destroyed forever. For many, the role of a Messiah in all of these events would be central.

Some Jews looked for these events to take place in the near future, while others believed that the period of tribulation had already arrived. After all, in the eyes of many Jews, Israel was already enduring a harsh existence under Roman rule. In either case, much of the apocalyptic language regarding visible signs in nature, cataclysmic events, and the activity of celestial and demonic

---

98. For a survey of the allusions to this idea in second-temple Jewish literature and the rabbinic writings, see Brant Pitre, *Jesus, the Tribulation, and the End of the Exile: Restoration Eschatology and the Origin of the Atonement* (WUNT 2/204; Tübingen: Mohr Siebeck, 2005), 41–129; John J. Collins, "The Expectation of the End in the Dead Sea Scrolls," in *Eschatology, Messianism, and the Dead Sea Scrolls* (ed. Craig A. Evans and Peter W. Flint; Grand Rapids: Eerdmans, 1997), 80–87; Klausner, *Messianic Idea*, 282, 440–50; Allison, *End of the Ages*, 5–25.

powers could be taken symbolically or figuratively rather than literally. There were also different views about who would suffer during this tribulation. Some believed that the righteous would be spared the intense suffering associated with the tribulation, while others believed that the tribulation would embrace righteous and unrighteous alike.

When considering these beliefs, it is important to grasp the logic behind them. If it was maintained that the righteous would be spared from enduring the tribulation, the purpose of that tribulation would be understood in terms of eradicating evil, injustice, and oppression on the earth. Once this had taken place, the righteous could return to life in order to inhabit a purified land. The stress on the magnitude of the tribulations would simply reflect the belief that evil had reached such widespread proportions on earth that nothing short of a cosmic cataclysm could do away with it definitively. If, however, the righteous were expected to endure the tribulation alongside the unrighteous, its purpose would also be understood as enabling Israel's God to determine which persons were truly committed to doing his will and to purify them of any sin that they still had. Those who remained faithful could be considered worthy to participate in the new age of salvation. God could also be certain that they would continue to live in accordance with his will once the new age had arrived. This would make it possible for the righteous to dwell in the new world God would bring about, free from suffering and injustice.[99]

Jewish beliefs regarding the coming tribulation thus provided a basis for exhorting people to remain faithful and obedient to God in the midst of suffering and hardships. Only those who endured would participate in the redemption of Israel, which was soon to come. The idea of the great tribulation or messianic woes, therefore, should not be understood simply in terms of some type of divinely-determined fate or destiny that had to come upon the world. Rather, the tribulation fulfilled a definite purpose: that of enabling the good to be separated out from the evil so that the latter might be destroyed definitively and the righteous might live in perpetual peace on the earth.

The Afterlife in Second-Temple Jewish Thought

Jewish views regarding the afterlife also developed a great deal during this period. This was the result of interaction with other belief systems in antiquity.[100] The Hebrew Scriptures speak of the dead descending into Sheol and remaining there indefinitely, independently of whether or not they had lived

---

99. In addition to bringing people to repentance and assuring God's people that, contrary to appearances, their redemption was near, Christopher Rowland argues that the tribulations were also believed to be aimed at "overwhelming all which sets itself against God and his will," and also had a "didactic purpose" (*The Open Heaven: A Study of Apocalyptic in Judaism and Early Christianity*; New York: Crossroads, 1982, 157-60). Similarly, Elliott notes that the hymns from Qumran see the final time of distress as functioning "as a kind of 'discipline' for the elect, or even as a kind of validation of their election" (*Survivors*, 589).

100. On the persistence of ancient Near Eastern ideas in Jewish thought as well as the Hellenistic influence in Jewish beliefs regarding the world and the afterlife, see especially J. Edward Wright, *The Early History of Heaven* (Oxford: Oxford University Press, 2000), 98-202; Jaime Clark-Soles, *Death and the Afterlife in the New Testament* (New York: T & T Clark, 2006), 9-59.

righteously. By the second-temple period, it had become common to make distinctions between the post-mortem fate of the righteous and that of the unrighteous. Alongside the idea that there would be a final judgment that would serve to separate the righteous from the unrighteous, there arose among many Jews the belief that this separation already took place at death. The righteous descended to a place of rest, tranquility, and bliss while the unrighteous went to a place of suffering and torment. Because those Jews who believed in the coming of a new age expected it to involve life on a renewed earth rather than in some heavenly sphere,[101] they viewed the place to which the righteous descended as a temporary abode from which they would some day be raised. The unrighteous might remain permanently in the place of sufferings to which they descended or would be raised as well only in order to be annihilated definitively or transferred anew to a place of torment.[102] Of course, the idea that people were judged at the time of their death made somewhat superfluous the need for a second and final judgment, unless it was claimed that the final fate of some of those who died was as yet undetermined.[103] In that case, they might be thought to dwell among the dead in other regions of the underworld at present, separated from both the righteous and the unrighteous, awaiting a divine decision regarding their definitive abode.

By the first century, the belief in the immortality of the soul seems to have been common among Jews as well.[104] Even though such a belief is generally regarded as Hellenistic and is often contrasted with the Jewish belief in the resurrection of the body, these two ideas can be considered complementary rather than mutually exclusive. The difference between Hellenistic and Jewish thought would be that, according to the latter, the souls of those who had died might be reunited with their bodies at the resurrection in order to live upon the earth once more rather than remaining forever in another world. In this case, what many Jews accepted and many Greeks denied was not that the soul was immortal but that one's body might become immortal as well.

These ideas remained highly fluid and were not always worked out in consistent fashion during the second-temple period. What is important, however, is to understand the logic behind them. If God's purpose was to establish a world free from evil and suffering and if, for intrinsic reasons, it was necessary for people to live in conformity to God's will in order for such a world to exist, then God would have to judge all people to determine whether they were fit to live in that world. Only those who had manifested a commitment to living

---

101. This point has rightly been stressed by a number of scholars. See, for example, Sanders, *Judaism*, 303; N. T. Wright, *New Testament*, 286, 298-302; Klausner, *Messianic Idea*, 283-84.

102. On these possibilities, see Alan E. Bernstein, *The Formation of Hell: Death and Retribution in the Ancient and Early Christian Worlds* (Ithaca, NY: Cornell University Press, 1993), 178-99.

103. As Émile Puech notes with regard to the idea in the *Book of Watchers* of *1 Enoch* that the dead descend to different places in the underworld, "the separation of souls in compartments also implies some kind of individual judgment after death" ("Messianism, Resurrection, and Eschatology in Qumran and in the New Testament," in *The Community of the Renewed Covenant: The Notre Dame Symposium on the Dead Sea Scrolls*, ed. Eugene Ulrich and James VanderKam; Notre Dame, IN: University of Notre Dame Press, 1994, 249).

104. See Sanders, *Judaism*, 298-301.

according to God's will in this lifetime could be admitted into the world to come. All others had to be excluded, since their resistance to God's will and their persistent sinful behavior would make them an obstacle to the justice, peace, and harmony that would characterize that world.

The belief that those who had done evil would be destroyed or condemned in definitive fashion should be understood on the basis of these ideas. While undoubtedly the wicked would suffer divine retribution for their sins, once more this retribution was not an end in itself but served a larger purpose, namely, making it impossible for them to continue to cause harm and suffering to others, in particular the righteous.

Of course, there are also numerous texts from this period that speak of those condemned being forced to endure torment and suffering indefinitely or even eternally. This idea is problematic in that, once evildoers have been banished from the earth, there seems to be no reason why they should continue to be tormented indefinitely. In this case, retribution would indeed appear to be an end in itself: God's objective was not to correct or purify them or prevent them from harming others but simply to make them suffer for the evil they had done. A number of the texts that speak in these terms even present God or the righteous rejoicing over the torments of those condemned.[105]

Undoubtedly, these texts are problematic for a number of reasons. Above all, they seem to contradict the notion that Israel's God was thought to have a loving purpose in all that he did. It is possible, however, that it was precisely the belief in the immortality of the soul that led to the idea that the sinners and unrighteous would suffer forever rather than being annihilated definitively. If souls were by nature immortal, then they could not be destroyed. These beliefs would preclude the possibility of the unrighteous simply ceasing to exist. In that case, they needed to be imprisoned somewhere.

Of course, this would not explain why the souls of the unrighteous should still be made to suffer in the afterlife. In spite of these problems, however, the purpose of the doctrine that evildoers would be condemned to post-mortem suffering or destruction is quite clear: such a doctrine served as a deterrent in the present world. By threatening people with punishment in the afterlife, they might be led to put an end to their practice of sin and injustice and be moved instead to live as God desired and commanded. Ultimately, therefore, the purpose of this doctrine was a positive one: that of promoting the practice of justice in the present world.

The idea that God and the righteous who would attain redemption might rejoice at the torments of those condemned is even more problematic. The only possible motive for such rejoicing would seem to be cruelty or a thirst for vengeance. However, as Richard Bauckham notes, the cause of the rejoicing might be understood to be not the sufferings of the condemned per se, but the fact that justice could now reign freely and that those condemned would

---

105. See especially Richard Bauckham, *The Fate of the Dead: Studies on the Jewish and Christian Apocalypses* (NovTSup 93; Leiden: Brill, 1998), 134-36.

no longer be able to do harm to the righteous.¹⁰⁶ In any case, it is significant that the idea that God or the righteous take pleasure at the torments of those condemned does not appear in any of the writings that were accepted into the Jewish or Christian canon. This indicates that the majority of Jews together with others who became followers of Jesus found such an idea unacceptable.

In spite of the problems raised by the idea of eternal condemnation, it is important to stress that there is nothing in the passages in which that idea is found that provides support for the claim that Jews in antiquity believed that Israel's God had to punish sin in order to remain true to his nature or satisfy an inner need to remain perfectly holy and righteous. Undoubtedly, the texts that speak of some type of ongoing torment for the condemned can in principle be interpreted in that way: God's inflexible justice demands that all sins committed receive proper retribution. However, there are several reasons for rejecting the notion that ancient Jews thought in such terms.

First, some type of equivalency between the suffering that the unrighteous had inflicted on others and the torments they endured after death would need to be established in order to claim that these torments were required by divine justice. There is no evidence in the ancient Jewish literature for considerations of any such kind. In fact, if the torments suffered by the condemned were eternal, they far exceeded any pain or harm they had caused others during their life. There is thus no basis for claiming that in ancient Jewish thought God's justice demanded a certain amount of suffering in retribution for the sins one had committed.

Second and more importantly, however, the belief that many people would be judged righteous and granted eternal salvation by God can hardly be attributed to some type of inner need for God to reward righteousness with eternal salvation. Because those who would be judged righteous had not lived perfect lives, God's justice did not place God under any kind of obligation to save them. Instead, in ancient Jewish thought, the salvation of the righteous was regarded as an act of divine mercy and not merely divine justice: God redeemed them in spite of the fact that they were not entirely deserving of such redemption.

The idea that the unrighteous would suffer eternal torment, therefore, should not be regarded as providing any support for the claim that in ancient Judaism Israel's God was thought to reward obedience and punish sin for his own sake, in order to remain true to his nature. Rather, God's justice led God to act against evil for the sake of human beings, in order to establish a world in which justice, equity, and *shalom* might prevail for the good of all who would inhabit that world.

As a final observation, it should be noted that physical death was not necessarily understood as divine punishment for one's sins.¹⁰⁷ Death could be

---

106. Bauckham, *Fate*, 136. Bauckham also notes that many texts present the righteous as interceding on behalf of the damned out of compassion for them rather than rejoicing over their condition (136-48).

107. See Ernest Best, *Essays on Ephesians* (Edinburgh: T & T Clark, 1997), 78-81.

viewed as part of a natural process and even as part of the human makeup as God had created it. What was unnatural was not that people die but that they die before their time or suffer some type of death that was particularly painful or violent. Even when this occurred, however, it was not always thought that those who died in such fashion were being punished by God for their sins. Instead, such a death could also be attributed to the sins of others or to some type of injustice committed against the person who died.

Today, of course, many of us would regard many of the ideas associated with Jewish eschatology extremely problematic. This is particularly true with regard to the notion of divine punishment, whether in a world to come or the present world. It is important to stress, however, that these beliefs were an attempt to address the question of theodicy: why a good, loving, and all-powerful God could allow evil to exist and prosper in the present world and at the same time allow the righteous and the innocent to suffer. Thus when people suffered in the present, the conviction that God was good and merciful made it necessary for them to reconcile that suffering with their belief in God's goodness by claiming that it had some positive purpose. Otherwise, they would need to deny the idea that God was good and always acted out of that goodness and love. Likewise, the belief that in the end justice would prevail and the righteous would be vindicated, while sinners would be destroyed, made it possible to maintain belief in such a God and also insist that one must live in conformity with the will of that God in order to be able to look forward to a future characterized by happiness and well-being in both body and soul.

* * *

The ideas we have discussed in this chapter will prove vital for understanding properly the beliefs regarding sin, sacrifice, suffering, death, and atonement reflected in second-temple Jewish literature that we will examine in the next two chapters. Those ideas will also enable us to address in the following chapters the question of how Jesus may have understood his death as he saw it approaching as well as the salvific significance his first followers ascribed to his death. For this reason, it is important to grasp clearly and correctly not only the soteriological beliefs that were common among Jews in Jesus' day but the logic underlying those beliefs. Only in this way will it become evident that the traditional interpretations of the New Testament allusions to Jesus' death considered in the previous chapter are based on ideas that are foreign to ancient Jewish and early Christian thought. What we have seen in the present chapter will also provide the foundation necessary to offer an alternative reading of the New Testament texts and a constructive proposal regarding the way in which Jesus and his first followers came to understand the significance of his death on the cross.

CHAPTER 3

Sacrifice and Atonement in Second-Temple Jewish Thought

Many of the brief formulas that appear throughout the New Testament to refer to the salvific nature of Jesus' death use sacrificial language. A number of these formulas explicitly relate Jesus' death to expiation and the remission of sins. On this basis, it is generally argued that the first Christians regarded Jesus' death as an atonement for sin.

Obviously, in order to understand the sacrificial language found in the New Testament, we must attempt some reconstruction of first-century beliefs regarding the nature, meaning, and purpose of sacrifice. Since the rise of biblical scholarship, countless proposals have been offered as to how sacrifice was understood in antiquity, particularly in Israel and ancient Judaism. These have often been referred to as "theories" of sacrifice. Today such terminology is used much less frequently. In part, this is because most scholars are convinced that there can be no general "theory" of sacrifice that applies to the wide variety of sacrificial practices in the different contexts and cultures of antiquity. In addition, however, well over a century of attempts to resolve the question of how sacrifice functioned or "worked," especially in ancient Hebrew and Jewish thought, has not led to any consensus on the question.[1] Today, the majority of New Testament scholars either reproduce uncritically the same basic views regarding sacrifice that have been held for over a century or simply refrain from addressing the subject at all. Because of this, in-depth discussion of the meaning and purpose of sacrifice in ancient Judaism has become relatively uncommon among New Testament scholars. If any consensus can be said to exist, it is that sacrifice in antiquity was a complex phenomenon and that any attempt to capture its "essence" will therefore inevitably fail.

Despite this lack of a clear consensus on the question of how sacrifice was understood in ancient Judaism, certain ideas on the subject are commonly found throughout the writings of New Testament scholars, especially among those who look to the ideas of penal substitution and participation to interpret the allusions to sacrifice in the Hebrew Scriptures, second-temple Jewish literature, and the New Testament. Among the most important of these ideas are the following, not all of which, of course, are held by all biblical scholars:

---

1. On some of the problems of speaking of "theories" of sacrifice, see Jonathan Klawans, *Purity, Sacrifice, and the Temple: Symbolism and Supersessionism in the Study of Ancient Judaism* (Oxford: Oxford University Press, 2006), 47-48.

1. In ancient Hebrew and Jewish thought, sacrifices properly offered were believed to make atonement for sin. Thus the reason that Jesus' first followers came to use sacrificial terminology to refer to his death was that they believed that his death had made atonement for human sin.

2. In antiquity, sacrifice was viewed as producing certain "effects" and "working" in some way to take away sin and its consequences and to make expiation or purification for sins. This led Jesus' first followers to affirm that his death had also had some such salvific "effect" and "worked" in order to take away human sin and its consequences.

3. Sacrifice was commonly understood in terms of *propitiation*: God's anger at the people's sin was appeased by the death of a sacrificial victim or by the shedding or presentation of its blood. In the same way, Jesus' first followers claimed that God's anger at human sin had been appeased or exhausted by Jesus' death or blood, with the result that human beings were no longer subject to God's wrath or condemnation.

4. According to Scripture and ancient Hebrew and Jewish thought, there could be no remission of sin without sacrifices. On the basis of this claim, it is maintained that Jesus' first followers were convinced that it was not possible for human sin to be forgiven without Jesus' sacrificial death. His death was thus *necessary* for human salvation, just as in Old Testament times, sacrificial deaths were necessary in order for God's people to obtain God's forgiveness.

5. The idea of substitution was central to the biblical and ancient Jewish understanding of sacrifice. The life of sacrificial victims was thought to substitute for the life of sinful human beings, so that the sacrificial victims endured in the stead of sinners the punishment or consequence of their sins, thereby freeing them from that punishment or those consequences. This belief therefore led Jesus' first followers to regard Jesus' death as substitutionary: he endured the punishment or consequences to which human beings were subject on account of their sins.

6. According to many scholars who reject the notion of penal substitution, in ancient times the sacrificial victims were thought to *represent* those who offered them. In this way, those presenting sacrifices were believed to die in some sense *together with* the sacrificial victim. This idea provided the basis for the first believers in Jesus to claim that, in his death, Jesus had represented human beings so that they died together with him. They therefore claimed that human beings are saved by sharing or participating in Jesus' death, just as those in ancient times shared or participated in the death of the sacrificial victims they presented at the altar.

7. According to René Girard, the idea of scapegoating was central to the ancient understanding of sacrifice among peoples such as the Hebrews. The killing of a sacrificial victim exposed the scapegoat mechanism and in this way enabled people to escape from its vicious circle of violence. In the same way, for the first Christians, Jesus' death was salvific in that it revealed the scapegoat mechanism that is common to most cultures and societies.

In this chapter, I will argue that *all* of the ideas regarding sacrifice and atonement just outlined were foreign to ancient Judaism and are nowhere to be found in the relevant texts. Obviously, if this is true, then there can be no basis for claiming that the understandings of Jesus' death just described are grounded in ancient Jewish thought regarding sacrifice. Because some scholars claim that the sacrificial language we find in the New Testament is also derived from certain Hellenistic and Roman sacrificial beliefs and practices, I will also address material from non-Jewish sources where it is pertinent.

In the first part of the present chapter, I will examine briefly the ideas associated with each of the seven affirmations regarding sacrifice just listed on the basis of scholarly reconstructions of ancient Hebrew and Jewish sacrificial beliefs and practices. In the second part, I will summarize some of the basic beliefs regarding sacrifice that run throughout the written sources we have from the second-temple period and the early rabbinic literature. Then, in the third part, I will re-examine the ideas associated with the seven affirmations just expounded in order to demonstrate that those interpretations of sacrifice are indeed foreign to the thought world of first-century Judaism. While I agree with the scholarly consensus that it would be a mistake to claim that there was a single understanding of sacrifice among Jews in antiquity and that we must therefore reject any attempt to affirm an all-embracing "theory of sacrifice," I will nevertheless argue that, on the basis of the evidence at our disposal, there were certain fundamental conceptions regarding sacrifice that were commonly held by most Jews.

Because my subject of interest here is sacrificial beliefs and practices in the time of Jesus, for the most part I regard the ancient Hebrew beliefs and practices that lie behind the texts describing sacrifice in the Hebrew Scriptures to be irrelevant in the following discussion. As I mentioned at the outset of Chapter 2, no one in Jesus' day had the means and resources necessary to reconstruct historically the original contexts and meanings of the writings making up the Hebrew Bible in the way that we attempt to do today. All that they had were the texts themselves and the interpretations of those texts handed down to them by their ancestors.

This is a point overlooked by many scholars, who enter into debates regarding the original or essential meanings of certain sacrificial practices among the ancient Hebrews on the basis of the Hebrew Scriptures and then proceed as if these same meanings can serve to explain the sacrificial language found in the New Testament. Thus, for example, what the ancient Hebrews and Israelites who lived centuries before Jesus believed they were doing when they laid hands on an animal or manipulated its blood and its remains after slaughtering it has little if any relevance for the question of how the Jews in Jesus' day understood such rites. The same must be said regarding the etymology and origin of Hebrew sacrificial terms such as *kipper* and *kofer* or the original meaning or logic behind the prescriptions regarding Hebrew sacrifice that appear in the biblical texts, most notably the book of Leviticus. Such discussions are of no value for our purposes here. Nevertheless, because one of the main purposes of this chapter is to examine scholarly reconstructions of the ancient beliefs regarding sacrifice that biblical interpreters use as a basis for understanding the New Testament allusions to the salvific significance of Jesus' death, it will be necessary to refer to the works of many scholars who ignore or overlook the important distinction between the ways in which sacrifice was understood in ancient Israel at the time in which the Hebrew Scriptures took form and the ways in which Jews in the first century CE interpreted the sacrificial rites carried out in their own day.

Of course, this does not mean that we can ignore what the Hebrew Scriptures say on the subject of sacrifice, since the Jewish sacrificial beliefs and practices of the second-temple period continued to be based primarily on those texts. For that reason, the general content of those texts unquestionably remains relevant. The same must be said regarding the material from rabbinic sources and other Jewish writings that were written after Jesus' death: while this material must be used with great caution, it can also be helpful in reconstructing ancient Jewish thought on the subject.[2]

SACRIFICIAL INTERPRETATION IN NEW TESTAMENT SCHOLARSHIP: VIEWS AND PRESUPPOSITIONS

Assumption 1: Sacrifices made atonement for sins.

Perhaps the most basic affirmation commonly made regarding ancient Jewish sacrifices is that they were believed to make atonement for sin. While there are a number of ways in which this affirmation can be understood, the point in question is that the act of sacrifice *in itself* is said to have made atonement, procuring divine forgiveness or purifying people from their sin.

It is widely accepted that such an understanding of sacrifice is found explicitly in the ancient sources. Many, for example, cite Lev. 17:11 as a basis for claiming that blood atones: "For the life of the flesh is in the blood; and I have given it to you for making atonement for your lives on the altar; for, as life, it is the blood that makes atonement." As Jay Sklar indicates, the last phrase of this verse can be translated from the Hebrew original in three different ways:

---

2. On this point, see George W. E. Nickelsburg, *Ancient Judaism and Christian Origins: Diversity, Continuity, and Transformation* (Minneapolis: Fortress, 2003), 25-26.

"it is the blood that makes atonement for one's life"; "it is the blood, as life, that effects expiation"; or "it is the blood that makes atonement, by reason of/ means of the life."³ The fact that discussions of this last phrase are rare in the ancient Jewish literature at our disposal makes it difficult to determine how it might have been understood in the second-temple period.

Even more difficult is the question of the logic that was thought to lie behind affirmations such as Lev. 17:11. While scholars commonly insist that sacrificial blood was believed to make atonement, disagreement exists regarding *how* and *why* it was thought to do so. For some, it was the destruction or killing of the victim that atoned for sins. Leon Morris, for example, looks to a number of passages from the Hebrew Scriptures to claim: "In each case, it is the termination of life, the infliction of death that atones."⁴ This claim is almost invariably understood in a substitutionary sense: the animal victim was believed to make atonement for the worshiper's sin by dying in his or her stead.⁵ According to this understanding of sacrifice, once the animal had been put to death, its blood was then presented before God as a type of ransom price.⁶ The blood itself atoned because it contained the life of the sacrificial victim and that life was presented to God in the place of the life of the offerers.⁷

Most scholars seem to agree that the belief that sacrificial offerings made atonement for sins remained widespread among Jews in New Testament times and even persisted long after the destruction of the Jerusalem temple. The Mishnah, for example, affirms regarding the sacrifices offered on the Day of Atonement: "As the blood of the goat that is sprinkled within (the Holy of Holies) makes atonement for the Israelites, so does the blood of the bullock make atonement for the priests" (*Shevu'ot* 1:7). On the basis of passages such as this, Jacob Neusner claims that the ancient rabbinical writings ascribed atoning efficacy to Israelite sacrifices: "The public offerings—the daily whole offerings—atone for Israel's sin; public offerings appease and effect atonement between Israel and its father in heaven, just as stated in the Written Torah."⁸ Adolf Büchler even claims that in rabbinic thought atonement was the automatic result of the sacrificial rites: "the mere oblation of the atoning sacrifice and the sprinkling of its blood upon the four corners or against the

---

3. Jay Sklar, *Sin, Impurity, Sacrifice, Atonement: The Priestly Conceptions* (HBM 2; Sheffield: Sheffield Phoenix, 2005), 169-74. See also N. Kiuchi, *The Purification Offering in the Priestly Literature: Its Meaning and Function* (JSOTSup 56; Sheffield: JSOT, 1987), 105-6. The choice scholars make with regard to which of these three translations is to be affirmed seems inevitably to be based primarily on theological considerations, as is evident from the work of both Sklar and Kiuchi.
4. Leon Morris, *The Apostolic Preaching of the Cross*, 3rd ed. (Grand Rapids: Eerdmans, 1965), 119. Among the passages Morris cites are Exod. 32:30-32, Num. 25:13, Deut. 21:1-9, and 2 Sam. 21:3-4.
5. See, for example, ibid., 25-26; Gordon J. Wenham, "The Theology of Old Testament Sacrifice," in *Sacrifice in the Bible* (ed. Roger T. Beckwith and Martin J. Selman; Grand Rapids: Baker, 1995), 79-85; Kiuchi, *Purification Offering*, 107-9, 155, 162.
6. See, for example, Sklar, *Sin*, 44-80.
7. See ibid., 173.
8. Jacob Neusner, *Judaism When Christianity Began: A Survey of Belief and Practice* (Louisville, KY: Westminster John Knox, 2002), 150.

wall of the altar brought atonement automatically to the people of Israel or to the individual...."[9]

Of course, sacrifice was not thought to be the only means of making atonement for one's sins in ancient Judaism. Suffering, death, prayer, almsgiving, and fasting could also atone for sins. Because the present chapter is dedicated to the subject of sacrifice, however, I will reserve discussion regarding these other means of atonement for Chapter 4.

Whatever logic is ascribed to the sacrificial rites, it is therefore widely accepted that in ancient Judaism the performance of those rites was thought to make atonement for sins and obtain divine forgiveness. This assumption seems to be so deeply entrenched in scholarly thought and in the ancient sources that, for many, even to question it would be unthinkable.

Assumption 2: Sacrifices were thought to "work" in some way to produce certain salvific "effects," such as expiation and purification.

Biblical scholars repeatedly speak in such terms. The ideas of expiation and purification can be understood in either a forensic or an ontological sense. According to a forensic understanding, sacrifices effected some change either in the way God regarded those on whose behalf they were offered or in the status of the offerers in relation to God's law or God's justice. In this case, the "effect" of sacrifice was that those who were guilty of sin were acquitted and delivered from the punishment due to them for their sins. Usually, a forensic understanding of sacrifice is based on the notion of penal substitution. This forensic interpretation of sacrifice will be examined under the next three headings rather than in the present section.

In contrast to a forensic interpretation, an ontological understanding of sacrifice posits some type of actual and even physical or material change in the people, places, or objects involved in the sacrificial rites. Usually this is seen as involving a cause-and-effect relationship between the performance of those rites and the salvific consequences resulting from them.

Thus, for example, sin and impurity can be seen as ontological realities that come to be present in human beings as a result of their actions. According to Baruch Levine, "Impurity was viewed as an external force which entered the person or attached itself to him. The primary purpose of expiation was, therefore, to rid one's self of this external force."[10] This involves attributing apotropaic power to the sacrificial rites or to certain elements, such as the sacrificial blood.[11] Similarly, Jonathan Klawans claims that, in ancient Judaism,

---

9. Adolf Büchler, *Studies in Sin and Atonement in the Rabbinic Literature of the First Century* (JCP 11; London: Oxford University Press, 1928), 441.

10. Baruch A. Levine, *In the Presence of the Lord: A Study of Cult and Some Cultic Terms in Ancient Israel* (SJLA 5; Leiden: Brill, 1974), 77.

11. See Levine, *In the Presence*, 71; Robert J. Daly, *Christian Sacrifice: The Judaeo-Christian Background before Origen* (Washington, DC: Catholic University of America Press, 1978), 111; Robert J. Daly, *The Origins of the Christian Doctrine of Sacrifice* (Philadelphia: Fortress, 1978), 30; Jacob Milgrom, "Atonement in the OT," *IDBS*, 80; Stephen Finlan, *The Background and Content of Paul's Cultic Atonement Metaphors* (AcBib 19; Atlanta: SBL, 2004), 74.

both moral and ritual impurity were believed to involve some type of invisible power or force:

> Moral impurity is best understood as a potent force unleashed by certain sinful human actions. The force unleashed defiles the sinner, the sanctuary, and the land.... In the case of ritual impurity, a real, physical process or event (e.g., death or menstruation) has a perceived effect: impermanent contagion that affects people and certain objects within their reach.... In both cases, the impurity is conveyed by contact: ritual impurity is conveyed by direct and indirect human contact, and moral impurity is conveyed to the land by sins that take place upon it.[12]

According to this type of interpretation, the impure power or force involved was believed to produce negative consequences for those who entered into contact with it. N. Kiuchi, for example, affirms that in ancient Hebrew and Jewish thought "sins have consequences," which consist of "physical or spiritual suffering" and even death.[13] Similarly, Sklar maintains that "even inadvertent sins may be followed by punitive consequences, and will ultimately result in death if not properly addressed."[14] Naturally, this impurity also affects negatively one's relationship with Israel's holy God, making communion with him impossible. This was thought to be true both for individuals and for entire communities.

In this case, the purpose of sacrifice was to rid the person or community of the pernicious substance that had negative consequences. Supposedly, this was thought to take place through some type of physical transfer. The sin might be passed from a sinful person to an animal victim, thereby enabling that sin to be absorbed, neutralized, or eliminated. As a result, the sinner was freed from his or her sin.[15] According to some interpreters, the next step was to destroy the animal by putting it to death. In this way, the sin that it had absorbed was eliminated or destroyed as well. Reflecting ideas we have seen in Chapter 1, James Dunn compares this to the way an infection or virus may be passed from one person to another. For Dunn, sin was viewed as something akin to a "malignant cancer," an infection, or a "malignant, poisonous organism" that needed to be destroyed in the same way that germs are destroyed through vaccination.[16] Sacrifice dealt with this organism or infection by putting to death the victim to which that sin had been transferred:

---

12. Jonathan Klawans, *Impurity and Sin in Ancient Judaism* (Oxford: Oxford University Press, 2000), 29, 34. Klawans distinguishes ritual impurity from moral impurity, which he claims is the result of having sinned.

13. Kiuchi, *Purification Offering*, 34, 162.

14. Sklar, *Sin*, 183.

15. See Finlan, *Background*, 73-93; J. Louis Martyn, *Galatians: A New Translation with Introduction and Commentary* (AB 33A; New York: Doubleday, 1997), 318; James D. G. Dunn, "Paul's Understanding of the Death of Jesus," in *Sacrifice and Redemption: Durham Essays in Theology* (ed. S.W. Sykes; Cambridge: Cambridge University Press, 1991), 43-47.

16. James D. G. Dunn, *Romans 1-8* (WBC 38A; Dallas, TX: Word, 1988), 182, 439; Dunn, *The Theology of Paul the Apostle* (Grand Rapids: Eerdmans, 1998), 223; Dunn, "Paul's Understanding," 50. Cf. A. J. M. Wedderburn, "2 Corinthians 5:14—A Key to Paul's Soteriology?," in *Paul and the Corinthians: Studies on a Community in Conflict. Essays in Honour of Margaret Thrall* (ed. Trevor J. Burke and J. Keith Elliott; NovTSup 109; Leiden: Brill, 2003), 273.

In some sense or other, the ritual of killing the sacrifice removed the sin from the unclean offerer.... The manner in which the sin-offering dealt with sin was by its death. The sacrificial animal, identified with the offerer in his sin, had to be destroyed in order to destroy the sin which it embodied. The sprinkling, smearing and pouring away of the sacrificial blood in the sight of God indicated that the life was wholly destroyed, and with it the sin of the sinner.[17]

According to many scholars, this transfer of sin was believed to take place when the hand of the offerer was placed upon the victim before it was sacrificed. Noam Zohar, for example, claims that in the sin-offering ritual,

> the laying of the hand should be taken to have basically the same meaning as in the Day of Atonement ritual: it marks the adherence of the sin contamination from the person to the animal.... [W]hen the impurity is conveyed to the animal, it would contaminate it as the sinner himself was contaminated. That is, it would enter into and contaminate the whole animal, but especially its *nephesh*, which in the biblical context means its blood (Gen 9:4, etc.). So this is why, when the animal is thereupon slaughtered, the main force of the contamination attached to the emerging blood, though some remains in the flesh as well.... The sinner procures an animal and transfers his sin-contamination to it. The animal is then slain, whereupon attention is focused on its essence of animation, its blood, to which the sin-contamination is now attached.[18]

Other scholars, however, reject this understanding of the laying-on of hands. Instead they regard it as symbolizing the self-identification of the offerer with the animal victim, as indicating that the animal victim belonged to the one offering it, or else as the means by which the offerer transferred his or her guilt to the victim, rather than transferring sin itself.[19]

Some scholars also speak of holiness or purity as some type of substance or power that was thought to be communicated between persons or objects.[20] At times this substance or power might even be considered divine. In this case, sacrificial rites involved transferring this pure substance or power to human beings in order to render them pure and holy as well. According to Menahem Haran, for example, the Old Testament speaks of a "contagious holiness" that "is conceived of as being virtually tangible, a physical entity, the existence and activity of which can be sensorially perceived. Any person or object coming

---

17. Dunn, "Paul's Understanding," 44, 47. Cf. Levine, *In the Presence*, 68-69, n37, who speaks of "the impurity and sins of the worshippers" being transferred to the animal victim. Jacob Milgrom also finds precedent in ancient Near Eastern thought for the practice of "the burning of the *hattat* [or sin-offering] because it absorbs the malefic impurity of the object which it has purged" (*Studies in Cultic Theology and Terminology*, SJLA 36; Leiden: Brill, 1983, 74).

18. Noam Zohar, "Repentance and Purification: The Significance and Semantics of *Hattath* in the Pentateuch," *JBL* 107 (1988): 613-14.

19. On these ideas, see respectively Dunn, "Paul's Understanding," 44-45; Bruce Chilton, *The Temple of Jesus: His Sacrificial Program within a Cultural History of Sacrifice* (University Park, PA: Pennsylvania State University, 1992), 101-2; Roy Gane, *Cult and Character: Purification Offerings, Day of Atonement, and Theodicy* (Winona Lake, IN: Eisenbrauns, 2005), 245-46.

20. B. Hudson McLean, *The Cursed Christ: Mediterranean Expulsion Rituals and Pauline Soteriology* (JSNTSup 126; Sheffield: JSOT, 1996), 39-41. Tom Holmén disagrees with this idea, claiming: "*Uncleanness* was transferable, cleanness not, and mere touching sufficed to defile" (*Jesus and Jewish Covenant Thinking*; BibInt 55; Leiden: Brill, 2001, 226).

into contact with the altar (Exod. 29:37) or any of the articles of the tabernacle furniture (30:29) becomes 'holy', that is, contracts holiness and, like the tabernacle appurtenances themselves, becomes consecrated."[21]

Jacob Milgrom also speaks of sin as a kind of impure power, substance, or force. However, instead of seeing this impurity as something that adheres to people or animals, he claims that, both in the book of Leviticus and the Mishnah, it was believed to adhere to the inner part of the sanctuary, thereby polluting it. According to Milgrom, "brazen sins possess the power not only to pollute the outer altar but to penetrate into the shrine, reaching even the holy ark."[22] "[I]mpurity is a dynamic (but not demonic) force that attacks the sanctuary.... [Man] alone can pollute the sanctuary by his physical and moral impurity and thereby drive out God from his midst."[23] Milgrom claimed that "for both Israel and her neighbors impurity was a physical substance, an aerial miasma which possessed magnetic attraction for the realm of the sacred" and had "dynamic and malefic power."[24] Milgrom even speaks of this impurity as "dangerously contagious," making it necessary for the priests to act with great caution as they performed the sacrificial rites.[25]

According to Milgrom, if this impurity was left to accumulate in the sanctuary so as to pollute it, eventually God would no longer dwell there: "the God of Israel will not abide in a polluted sanctuary. The merciful God will tolerate a modicum of pollution. But there is a point of no return."[26] Milgrom understands the Day of Atonement ritual prescribed in Leviticus 16 on the basis of these ideas. According to Milgrom, sacrificial blood functioned as a "ritual detergent": "The *hattat* blood, then, is the purging element, the ritual detergent.... By daubing the altar with the *hattat* blood or by bringing it inside the sanctuary (e.g., *Lev.*, XVI, 14-19), the priest purges the most sacred objects and areas of the sanctuary on behalf of the person who caused their contamination by his physical impurity or inadvertent offense."[27] For Milgrom, this idea is found in the Mishnah as well: "This rabbinic tradition has preserved

---

21. Menahem Haran, *Temples and Temple-Service in Ancient Israel: An Inquiry into the Character of Cult Phenomena and the Historical Setting of the Priestly School* (Oxford: Clarendon, 1978), 176. Sklar also writes that "consecration can result simply from contact with holy items" (*Sin*, 120); W. O. E. Oesterley, *Sacrifices in Ancient Israel: Their Origin, Purposes and Development* (London: Hodder and Stoughton, 1937), 225-26.

22. Jacob Milgrom, "Day of Atonement," *IDBS*, 83. Similar to Neusner, Richard D. Nelson writes that "human sin defiled holy space and holy things and, unless cleaned off or covered over, threatened to generate the 'holy-unclean fusion reaction' and bring on Yahweh's wrath" (*Raising Up a Faithful Priest: Community and Priesthood in Biblical Theology*, Louisville, KY: Westminster John Knox, 1993, 75).

23. Milgrom, "Sacrifice in the OT," *IDBS*, 766. Milgrom's rejection of the idea that this force is demonic is a response to Levine, *In the Presence*, 75-78.

24. Milgrom, *Studies*, 76.

25. Ibid., 73. Stressing that in ancient Hebrew and Jewish thought sacrificial blood was associated with *life* rather than *death*, Jane Lancaster Patterson similarly comments with regard to the sacrificial blood mentioned in Leviticus and Genesis: "The intensity of life poured out is *dangerously* alive and needs to be handled only by priests specially chosen and prepared to do so" (*Keeping the Feast: Metaphors of Sacrifice in 1 Corinthians and Philippians*; ECL; Atlanta: SBL, 2015, 71).

26. Milgrom, "Atonement in the OT," 81-82.

27. Milgrom, *Studies*, 76. See also Milgrom, "Day of Atonement," 82-83; "Sacrifices and Offerings, OT," 766-67. In this latter article, Milgrom also claims that once the blood has removed impurities, "it contaminates any object it is spilled on or touches" as well as "those who handle it" (767).

the postulate that the *hattat* blood is the ritual detergent employed by the priest to purge the sanctuary of the impurities inflicted upon it by the offerer of the sacrifice."[28] Thus when the priests sprinkled the blood on the sacred places and objects to which sin and impurity had adhered, they became pure.

While many scholars disagree with Milgrom's views regarding sacrifice, they often share similar ideas regarding the power of blood.[29] Kiuchi, for example, agrees with Milgrom that "the *hattat* purifies sancta" but, contrary to Milgrom, claims that it also purifies persons.[30] W. O. E. Oesterley also spoke of the "purificatory effect of blood" in post-exilic thought but claimed that, since the life is in the blood, when it was "sprinkled on and around the altar" it was thought to be "appropriated by the Deity, who absorbs the life."[31] S. C. Gayford claimed that not only the blood but also the flesh of the sin offering was extremely holy and thus "'hallowed' everything which it touched."[32] Bradley McLean also argues that blood not only consecrated what it touched but also absorbed its impurity.[33]

Other interpreters see the role of sacrificial blood primarily in terms of uniting the offerer to God. Robert Daly, for example, has argued that "the basic meaning of the blood rite is not so much atonement in the sense of expiation or propitiation, as it is communion or at-one-ment (the English etymological sense of the word)."[34] Godfrey Ashby claims that, when two parties make a pact, sacrificial blood joins or unites them to one another so as to produce a single life and bring about a "psychic community" between them.[35] David deSilva sees sacrificial blood in terms of a "reparative sealant" or "ritual mortar" rather than a detergent, since it unites the participants to one another.[36]

Those who focus on these different ways in which the blood was used generally see the sacrificial slaughter of the animal, not in terms of effecting its destruction or executing some type of substitutionary punishment, but of making it possible for the blood to be extracted from the animal so that it could be used in the sacrificial rites. According to Stephen Finlan, for

---

28. Milgrom, *Studies*, 77. See also Sklar, *Sin*, 106-11; Finlan, *Background and Content*, 40-41, 93. Luigi Moraldi attributes the power of blood as a ritual detergent to its containing the life-force of the animal victim (*Espiazione Sacrificale e Riti Espiatori nell'Ambiente Biblico e nell'Antico Testamento*; AnBib 5; Rome: Pontificio Istituto Biblico, 1956, 243-51).

29. For a discussion of the scholarly reaction to Milgrom's ideas, see especially Gane, *Cult*, 267-84.

30. Kiuchi, *Purification Offering*, 59. Moraldi also agrees on this point (*Espiazione*, 251).

31. Oesterley, *Sacrifices*, 234.

32. S. C. Gayford, *Sacrifice and Priesthood: Jewish and Christian*, 2nd ed. (London: Methuen, 1953), 49; cf. 70-74.

33. McLean, *Cursed Christ*, 40-41.

34. Daly, *Christian Sacrifice*, 134.

35. Godfrey Ashby, *Sacrifice: Its Nature and Purpose* (London: SCM, 1988), 40-41, citing works by Stanislas Lyonnet and Léopold Sabourin as well as Paul van Imschoot. For the same basic idea, see E. O. James, *Sacrifice and Sacrament* (New York: Barnes & Noble, 1962), 60-62; Levine, *In the Presence*, 78.

36. David A. deSilva, *Perseverance in Gratitude: A Socio-Rhetorical Commentary on the Epistle "to the Hebrews"* (Grand Rapids: Eerdmans, 2000), 312.

example, the sacrifice was "a means for obtaining a sin-cleansing substance": "the animal is not killed in order to punish it but to get access to its blood."[37]

The idea of transferring sin to an animal victim is especially associated with the scapegoat ritual prescribed for the Day of Atonement in Lev. 16:20-22. The high priest was to lay both of his hands on the goat and confess the sins of Israel over it before it was led out to the desert to be abandoned there. Many scholars understand this rite as involving the transfer of an actual substance or power to the goat. Roy Gane, for example, affirms that the rite is "the means by which the sins of the entire nation are transformed from abstraction, as if out of the air, into a concentrated, quasi-spatially containable form, gathered to the high priest, and channeled through his hands to the goat. Although he is immune to this evil, no wonder he leans his hands *before* commencing the confession, so that the toxic flow will immediately pass from him!"[38]

The biblical texts speak not only of animal victims bearing sin but also priests and the people themselves. This is often understood in terms of bearing the negative consequences of sin or its punishment.[39] Many scholars claim that these negative consequences were thought to be transferred from the sinner to the animal victim by means of the priests.[40]

Because this ontological understanding of sacrifice posits the transfer and manipulation of impersonal powers, substances, or other entities, scholars often claim that the sacrificial rites were thought to work in magical or mechanical fashion. According to Levine, for example, "biblical expiation conveyed by kippur involved acts of a magical character, specifically the magical utilization of sacrificial blood."[41] Bernd Janowski speaks of "the magical motive of elimination of impurity" in the scapegoat ritual and claims that a "magical transfer" was thought to take place.[42] Similarly, Finlan views the scapegoat rite in terms of a "magical" ritual that reflected "primitive ideas about the literal manipulation of metaphysical reality" such as "forces or spiritual conditions."[43] He also conceives of this in mechanical terms, referring to the scapegoat as "merely a sin-bearing mechanism."[44] According to Finlan, other sacrificial rites were thought to involve "an impersonal atoning mechanism" that worked independently of any divine intervention: "Just as natural

---

37. Stephen Finlan, *Problems with Atonement: The Origins of, and Controversy about, the Atonement Doctrine* (Collegeville, MN: Liturgical Press, 2005), 15, 38. For further discussion and references on this idea, see also David M. Moffitt, *Atonement and the Logic of Resurrection in the Epistle to the Hebrews* (NovTSup 141; Leiden: Brill, 2011), 257-77.

38. Gane, *Cult*, 245-46.

39. Sklar, *Sin*, 22-23.

40. On this discussion, see Finlan, *Background*, 84-86; see also Kiuchi, *Purification Offering*, 148, 156, 163.

41. Levine, *In the Presence*, 60; see also 77. Cf. Gane, who speaks of the magical protection of the sanctuary and the need to protect it from demonic incursions of evil (*Cult*, 268). Finlan similarly refers to a "magical transfer" involving the "the physical manipulation of metaphysical forces or spiritual conditions" (*Problems*, 34-35).

42. Bernd Janowski, *Sühne als Heilsgeschehen: Studien zur Sühnetheologie der Priesterschrift und zur Wurzel KPR im Alten Orient und im Alten Testament* (WMANT 55; Düsseldorf: Neukirchener, 1982), 88.

43. Finlan, *Problems*, 7, 34.

44. Finlan, *Background*, 81.

forces can, within limits, be manipulated, so spirit-forces can be manipulated with ritual."[45] Using electricity as an analogy, Finlan claims: "The positive life-charge in the blood *neutralizes* the negative death-charge in the pollution, wherever it has penetrated into the temple. Another analogy would be the Midas touch: the blood transforms and purifies the defiled symbols."[46] On this basis, he speaks of "the magical power of blood."[47]

One other interpretation of sacrifice that ascribes to it an automatic effect involves the claim that YHWH had bound himself to forgiving sins or granting petitions when sacrifice was offered to him. According to Andrea Spatafora, for example, "Sacrifices in the OT were offered as a petition to God.... God bound himself to grant what man requested."[48] In this case, once YHWH had promised in his law to grant whatever those offering sacrifices sought, he could not go back on his promise. Such an understanding of sacrificial offerings implies that they "work" automatically.

Assumption 3: Sacrifice involved propitiation.

A third common affirmation among biblical scholars is that sacrifice *propitiated* God, that is, it turned away God's wrath. Proponents of both forensic and ontological views have spoken in these terms, though they understand the idea somewhat differently. In a forensic view, it is the guilt of sinners that arouses God's wrath and must be dealt with, either by covering it up so that God no longer sees it or by transferring it to an animal victim, which is then slaughtered. In this way, the divine wrath is rechanneled away from the guilty party onto the innocent victim.

Morris, for example, defends a forensic view based on the notion of substitution, arguing in length that the sacrificial rites were understood as propitiatory, since they served to avert and appease God's wrath.[49] Gordon Wenham agrees, proposing that the "main function" of the burnt offerings "was to atone for man's sin by propitiating God's wrath. In the immolation of the animal, most commonly a lamb, God's judgment against human sin was symbolized and the animals suffered in man's place."[50] Jarvis Williams argues that behind the sacrificial rites prescribed in Leviticus is the idea that "bloody sacrifice actually satisfied God's wrath."[51] According to this conception, propitiation

---

45. Ibid., 42. Cf. Milgrom: "It is the very mechanism of the purgation that helps clarify the paradox. In effect, the *hattat* absorbs the impurity it has purged and for that reason, it must be eliminated by incineration. However, this means anyone involved in the incineration of the *hattat* is infected by it and must undergo purification" (*Studies*, 87).

46. Finlan, *Background*, 42; see also Finlan, *Problems*, 13, 37.

47. Finlan, *Background*, 95.

48. Andrea Spatafora, *From the "Temple of God" to God as the Temple: A Biblical Theological Study of the Temple in the Book of Revelation* (Rome: Editrice Pontificia Università Gregoriana, 1997), 269.

49. Morris, *Apostolic Preaching*, 144-213.

50. Gordon J. Wenham, *The Book of Leviticus* (NICOT; Grand Rapids: Eerdmans, 1979), 63.

51. Jarvis J. Williams, *Maccabean Martyr Traditions in Paul's Theology of Atonement: Did Martyr Theology Shape Paul's Conception of Jesus' Death?* (Eugene, OR: Wipf & Stock, 2010), 39-40.

involved being spared punishment for one's sins: "sacrifice appeases the anger of God against the sinner and averts punishment."[52]

In contrast, according to ontological views such as those we have considered in the previous section, the way in which sacrifice delivers sinners from God's wrath is by removing or destroying the sinful or impure substance or force that arouses that wrath.[53] This is usually understood in terms of *expiation*, which then becomes the basis for propitiation. Sam Williams explains the idea thus: "in the OT God is not a temperamental deity who must be placated at every arbitrary whim; rather, his wrath is aroused because of sin or defilement. The averting of that wrath therefore demands purification and forgiveness of sin. Thus it is precisely the expiation of sin which effects propitiation: one 'makes glad the face of God' by removing the sin which caused him to be angry with his people."[54] Milgrom and others similarly see the expiatory blood rites as fulfilling this "function of averting God's wrath...."[55] Milgrom also claims that the scapegoat was regarded as "the substance to which the evil is transferred and thereupon eliminated"; this served "to siphon off the wrath of God from the entire community."[56]

Assumption 4: There could be no remission of sins without sacrifice.

Biblical scholars commonly assert that sacrificial offerings were *necessary* in order for sin to be forgiven or taken away. The implication is that, without sacrifice, no remission of sins or purification from sin and impurity was possible. Thus, for example, Gane writes: "In pentateuchal ritual law, sacrifice is the only mechanism through which forgiveness can be obtained; there is no indication that repentance alone can result in forgiveness."[57]

This necessity is almost invariably grounded in God's perfectly holy, righteous nature, which cannot tolerate sin. According to John Oswalt, "This is what the entire sacrificial system is about: making it possible for sinful human beings to have fellowship with a holy God."[58] This is essentially the same argument of Anselm: it would be contrary to God's nature for God to forgive sins freely without some type of payment, retribution, or punishment.[59]

Those who understand sacrifice in the sense of penal substitution define the necessity of sacrifice in terms of the need for sin to be punished. David Wenham, for example, writes: "But why the need for the drastic measure of sacrifice at all? The OT picture is of an intensely pure and holy God, whose intolerance of evil is expressed in the punishment of evil. Sin is thus utterly

---

52. Roland de Vaux, *Studies in Old Testament Sacrifice* (Cardiff: University of Wales Press, 1964), 91.
53. See Levine, *In the Presence*, 78.
54. Sam K. Williams, *Jesus' Death as Saving Event: The Background and Origin of a Concept* (HDR 2; Missoula, MT: Scholars Press, 1975), 39.
55. Milgrom, "Atonement in the OT," 80; see also Levine, *In the Presence*, 78.
56. Milgrom "Atonement in the OT," 80.
57. Gane, *Cult*, 274. See also Milgrom, *Studies*, 63-64; G. Wenham, *Leviticus*, 26.
58. John Oswalt, *The Book of Isaiah: Chapters 40–66* (NICOT; Grand Rapids: Eerdmans, 1998), 385.
59. So Finlan, *Problems*, 44.

serious, and must be dealt with."⁶⁰ In contrast, those who see sacrifice in terms of the elimination or destruction of sin as an ontological reality ground this necessity in the inability of a holy God to abide in the presence of a sinful people. Gane, for example, affirms that due to the "inherent antagonism between divine holiness and human imperfection," in order for Israel's God to maintain his presence among his people, "he requires the purification of his sanctuary because the people's moral and physical imperfection, which affect his dwelling place, are incompatible with his nature."⁶¹

Assumption 5: Sacrifice was understood as substitution.

The idea that sacrifice involved substitution is most commonly associated with a penal substitution view, according to which sinners are subject to divine punishment on account of their sin. They are delivered from this punishment when it is executed on an animal victim put to death in a sacrificial rite after the sin or guilt is transferred to the victim. In this way, the animal victim endures the penalty to which the sinner was subject in the sinner's stead. Sklar, for example, finds this idea in Lev. 17:11: "the blood (= life) of the animal is given *in exchange for/in place* of the life of the person. In this regard, the animal's life-blood becomes a substitute for that of the offerer."⁶² Kiuchi interprets this same verse as affirming that "the death caused by sin and uncleanness is annulled by substitutionary death."⁶³ Similarly, Peter Stuhlmacher claims that "the essence of cultic atonement is the substitutionary sacrifice of a life for the life of others...."⁶⁴

Proponents of this type of view often claim that the rite of laying hands on the animal to be sacrificed served as the means by which the sin or guilt of the offerer was transferred to the animal victim. Angel Rodriguez, for example, argues that "through the laying on of hands sin and guilt is transferred to the animal which dies as the offerer's substitute.... [S]in but also its penalty was transferred to the sacrificial victim."⁶⁵ Some scholars also apply the idea of substitution to the ransom of the firstborn: "The Old Testament also established the practice of redeeming the firstborn (who were supposed to be given to God) by the making of a substitute offering (Exod. 13:11-16; 34:19-20). The price is a substitute for the person redeemed.... Hence the concept of substitution is present and the cost may be regarded as a penalty in the broad sense."⁶⁶

---

60. David Wenham, *Paul: Follower of Jesus or Founder of Christianity?* (Grand Rapids: Eerdmans, 1995), 151.
61. Gane, *Cult*, 327. See also Milgrom, "Atonement in the OT," 79-81; James, *Sacrifice*, 104.
62. Sklar, *Sin*, 170; cf. 47; Kiuchi, *Purification Offering*, 162.
63. Kiuchi, *Purification Offering*, 162.
64. Peter Stuhlmacher, *Reconciliation, Law, and Righteousness: Essays in Biblical Theology*, trans. Everett R. Kalin (Philadelphia: Fortress, 1986), 60.
65. Angel M. Rodriguez, *Substitution in the Hebrew Cultus* (AUSDDS 3; Berrien Springs, MI: Andrews University Press, 1979), 201, 232. See also Morris, *Apostolic Preaching*, 25-26, 33-38, 63, 166; G. Wenham, *Leviticus*, 28, 61-63.
66. I. Howard Marshall, *Aspects of the Atonement: Cross and Resurrection in the Reconciling of God and Humanity* (London: Paternoster, 2007), 47. See also S. Williams, *Jesus' Death*, 107.

Ontological understandings of sacrifice can also be seen as involving the principle of substitution. In this case, it is not the *punishment* of guilt that is borne by the substitute, but the *natural or inherent consequences* of the impurity that one has come to possess through one's sin. This impurity is transferred to the animal substitute so that the animal suffers its consequences in the place of the individual. Milgrom, for example, relates the idea of ransom with substitution: the sacrificial act involves a "substance to which the evil is transferred and thereupon eliminated" and "an action which eliminates dangerous impurity by absorbing it through direct contact (rubbing off) or indirectly (as a ransom/substitute)...."[67]

Assumption 6: Sacrifice was understood in terms of representation and participation.

Many scholars prefer to avoid the notion of substitution and instead understand sacrifice as involving the principles of participation or representation. In this case, rather than the animal victim dying or being offered to God in the place of the sinner, the sinner becomes one with the victim so as to die or be offered up to God together with the victim. Gayford, for example, claimed that "the laying on of hands in sacrifice signifies the sacrificer's bestowing upon the victim the power to represent himself.... What the victim does and suffers is then representatively the action and suffering of the sacrificer.... The 'killing,' in this light, appears as a symbol of self-immolation, the voluntary laying down of one's own life.... So the sacrificer in symbol dies to himself."[68] Similarly, Janowski maintains that the practice by which the offerer laid a hand on the animal to be sacrificed involved a real participation in its death and symbolized the offerer's identification with the dying animal. The death of the victim thus represented the surrender of the life of the sinner.[69]

At times, scholars attempt to combine representation or participation with substitution rather than regarding them as alternatives. This involves affirming an apparent contradiction: when the animal victim dies or is offered up to God, in one sense the sinner does *not* die, since the victim serves as his or her substitute, yet in another sense the sinner *does* die, since he or she dies together with the animal who represents him or her. Dunn, for example, proposes that when the offerer laid his hand on the head of the beast to be sacrificed, "the sinner identified himself with the beast, or at least indicated that the beast in some sense represented him..., that is, represented him *as sinner*, so that his sin was somehow identified with it."[70] When the sacrificial victim was then put to death, the sinner was thought to die together with it, along with his sin. This involved seeing "the death of the sacrificial animal as the death of the sinner *qua* sinner. The manner in which the sin-offering dealt with sin was by its death. The sacrificial animal, identified with the offerer in

---

67. Milgrom, "Atonement in the OT," 80; see also Zohar, "Repentance," 616-17.
68. Gayford, *Sacrifice*, 63, 65, 116; cf. 111.
69. Janowski, *Sühne*, 220-21.
70. Dunn, "Paul's Understanding," 44.

his sin, had to be destroyed in order to destroy the sin which it embodied. The sprinkling, smearing and pouring away of the sacrificial blood in the sight of God indicated that the life was wholly destroyed, and with it the sin of the sinner."[71]

As noted in Chapter 1, German scholars such as Janowski and Hartmut Gese have applied the German word *Stellvertretung* to sacrifice, yet distinguish between an "inclusive" type of representation (*einschließender* or *inkludiender Stellvertretung*) and an "exclusive" one (*ausschließender* or *exkludiender Stellvertretung*). The latter of these corresponds roughly to the idea of substitution, in which the offerers are excluded from the sacrificial death of the animal victim, since they do not share in that death. According to the former idea, however, the offerers identified with the victim so as to die together with it as their representative.[72] Gese, for example, writes: "Through the shedding of the animal's blood the life of the person who brings the sacrifice is symbolically offered up.... This sacrifice of life [is] ... an incorporation into the holy."[73] This therefore involves "the total involvement of the person in the essence of sacrifice."[74]

Assumption 7: Sacrifice reveals the mechanism of sacred violence.

One other interpretation of sacrifice that has been quite influential in biblical scholarship in recent decades is that of the French literary critic René Girard. Girard looks not only to the biblical texts but to the classics of the Western literary tradition as well, including especially Greek mythology, to seek to identify the fundamental idea underlying sacrificial rituals. According to Girard, this consists of "mimetic violence" in which a community channels blame and violence onto a victim that serves as a scapegoat. This violence becomes ritualized as religious sacrifice and involves a "scapegoat mechanism" which, once revealed for what it is, frees human beings from the endless cycle of violence to which they have fallen prone.[75]

* * *

All of the seven assumptions just presented have played an important role in the interpretations given to the passages from the New Testament that make use of sacrificial language and imagery to give meaning to Jesus' death. While there is of course much debate and disagreement among biblical scholars

---

71. Ibid., 46.
72. See especially Hartmut Gese, *Essays on Biblical Theology*, trans. Keith Crim (Minneapolis: Augsburg, 1981), 93-116; Otfried Hofius, *Paulusstudien* (WUNT 51; Tübingen: J. C. B. Mohr, 1989), 33-49; Janowski, *Sühne*, 220-21.
73. Gese, *Essays*, 107.
74. Ibid., 132.
75. For Girard's summary of his own ideas, see his "Generative Scapegoating," in René Girard et al., *Violent Origins: Walter Burkert, René Girard, and Jonathan Z. Smith on Ritual Killing and Cultural Formation*, trans. Robert G. Hamerton-Kelly (Stanford, CA: Stanford University Press, 1987), 73-105; René Girard, *The Girard Reader* (ed. James G. Williams; New York: Crossroad, 1996). Girard's most complete discussion of these ideas is found in his book *Violence and the Sacred*, trans. Patrick Gregory (Baltimore: Johns Hopkins University Press, 1977).

regarding these ideas, most New Testament interpreters have looked to one or more of them to explain how Jesus' first followers came to view his death as atoning or salvific. Therefore, it is important to analyze each of these assumptions in order to attempt to discern whether it reflects faithfully the beliefs that existed regarding sacrifice in Jesus' day, especially among those who practiced the Jewish faith. Before doing this, however, it is necessary to reconstruct in broad terms what the ancient Hebrew and Jewish literature says regarding sacrifice.

BASIC TENETS OF ANCIENT JEWISH SACRIFICIAL THOUGHT

Undoubtedly, among Jews in antiquity there was a wide variety of beliefs regarding sacrifice, as well as a great diversity of attitudes to the practice of sacrifice. I would argue, however, that there are several basic ideas and beliefs regarding sacrifice that are found repeatedly in the literary sources from antiquity that we have at our disposal. While it would be impossible to prove that all Jews were in agreement with these ideas and beliefs, the fact that they are so well-attested in those sources means that, if we wish to reconstruct in broad terms the most common ancient Jewish views on the subject, we should take them as a starting-point. On that basis, we can then return to the assumptions just mentioned to examine whether it is likely that they reflect ideas that were commonly held in Jesus' day.

It is, of course, impossible to determine the sources from which most first-century Jews derived their beliefs regarding sacrifice and its meaning and purpose. It is highly doubtful that they looked solely or even primarily to the biblical texts, since access to those texts was not readily available for most. Whether or not they participated in some way in the sacrificial rites carried out in the temple in Jerusalem, many Jews probably received some type of formal or informal instruction regarding the significance of those rites that was based on oral tradition. Non-Jewish beliefs and practices concerning sacrifice also must have influenced many Jews to some extent, not merely because some Jews may have incorporated ideas from those beliefs and practices into their own understanding of sacrifice, but also because they intentionally formulated their own views in response to the beliefs and practices of their neighbors. Unfortunately, we have access only to literary sources and cannot be sure how faithfully those sources reflect the thought of second-temple Jews regarding the meaning and purpose of sacrifice. The best we can do is to assume that the same ideas that are common in the written sources were also common in popular Jewish belief.

According to the literary sources we possess, in spite of the fact that direct access to the Hebrew Scriptures was limited, certain passages from those Scriptures were nevertheless highly influential in Jewish sacrificial beliefs and practices. The most important texts in this regard were not only the prescriptions regarding how sacrifice was to be offered to YHWH found in the books of Exodus, Leviticus, Numbers, and Deuteronomy, but also the narratives from Genesis that speak of figures such as Abel, Cain, Noah, and the patriarchs offering sacrifice. The story of Abraham's willingness to sacrifice Isaac his son, known as the *Akedah* or "binding" (Gen. 22:1-19), seems to have been the subject of a great deal of reflection in ancient Judaism and to have exercised considerable influence on the way in which sacrifice in Israel was understood. Outside of the Pentateuch, accounts such as Solomon's dedication of the temple and Elijah's confrontation with the prophets of Baal also played a significant role in shaping Jewish thought on the subject (1 Kings 8; 18:17-40; 2 Chronicles 6-7). Even those who were illiterate would be familiar with many of these stories. The allusions to sacrifice in the Psalms and the prophetic writings must also have influenced the thought of many. No doubt many Jews heard these texts read or recited repeatedly over the course of their lifetime.

When one looks at the many passages from the Hebrew Scriptures that allude to sacrifice, initially they seem to provide little if any information that would enable us to reconstruct the most basic beliefs regarding sacrifice that existed in ancient Israel and Judaism. For the most part, they merely prescribe or describe the performance of certain rituals, apparently offering no clear explanations regarding the meaning and purpose of those rituals. Nowhere, for example, are we told explicitly what acts such as laying one's hand on an animal to be sacrificed or pouring out or sprinkling an animal's blood were thought to signify. This makes it very easy to read back into those texts virtually any ideas we wish, including the ideas associated with the assumptions discussed above.

I believe, however, that in this case appearances are deceiving. The problem is that, because of the assumptions they make and the way they frame the questions, scholars have looked in the texts for ideas that are foreign to those texts and thus absent from them. Thus if we begin by asking how sacrifices "worked," as scholars repeatedly do, we are assuming that, in and of themselves, the sacrificial rituals were thought to produce some salvific "effect." Such ideas are then erroneously used as a starting-poing or basis to interpret the relevant texts from antiquity. If instead, however, we stop looking for what we wish to find in the texts and instead pay close attention to what we actually encounter there, I believe those texts provide us with a wealth of information about ancient beliefs concerning sacrifice that can help to understand fairly clearly the meaning and purpose that Jews in antiquity ascribed to sacrifice. If we proceed in this manner, I would argue that we repeatedly encounter three ideas that are particularly central.

1. Sacrifices were essentially *offerings* and *gifts* presented to God.

Throughout the Pentateuch, the words used to refer in general terms to sacrifices are primarily *qorban*, *minchah*, and *mathanah*, all of which mean "gift," "present," or "offering."[76] In order to translate these terms, the Septuagint regularly used *dōron* and *prosphora*, which convey the same meaning. The most common Hebrew verb used in these texts is *qarab* (usually in the hiphil), which is also used throughout the Pentateuch to speak of "presenting" or "bringing near" a sacrificial offering. At times, the hiphil of *ba'* is used with the same basic meaning. The Septuagint consistently translated these verbs with *prosagein*, *pherein*, and *prospherein*, which communicate the same basic ideas. In Hebrew, the word for a burnt offering is *'olah*, which refers to something that rises up, obviously to God. All of this clearly suggests that the primary meaning of the sacrificial rites was to present an offering or gift to God. The fact that the offerings included not only animal victims but things such as grain, flour, harvested fruits, spices, oil, and libations also indicates that the central idea was not that of *sacrificing* in the sense of *putting to death*, but the offering of gifts up to God.[77]

It is important to note that, in both Hebrew and Greek, the same terms just mentioned are used with regard to the *hattat* and *asham* offerings prescribed in chapters 5 and 6 of Leviticus, which had the purpose of making atonement for sin. Both of these sacrifices for sin were therefore also regarded as *gifts* or *offerings* presented to God. The fact that flour could be given as a sin offering (Lev. 5:11-13) stresses the point that it was the act of offering up of gifts to God that was thought to be the means by which people made atonement for sins rather than the act of slaughtering of animals.

The idea that sacrifice involved presenting offerings to God is not only present in virtually all of the ancient Hebrew and Jewish sources that discuss sacrifice but also plays a central role in those sources. What is consistently stressed is the aspect of the *gift*. Besides animal offerings, the Israelites presented as gifts many things that were not properly "sacrificed" but merely brought before YHWH into his presence, including not only tithes and firstfruits but things such as precious metals and stones, wood, spices, linen, and other objects of value—the same type of gifts one might offer to an earthly ruler.[78] Even the hair of the Nazirites was seen as a sacrificial gift to God.[79] Worship itself is defined in terms of giving presents to YHWH.[80] There can be no doubt that for the Jews in antiquity, as for people of other cultures, it was not the destruction of life or the mere forfeiting of something valuable that lay at the heart and center of sacrificial beliefs and practices, but the presenting of gifts and offerings to God.[81]

---

76. Other terms found in the Hebrew Scriptures include *nedabah*, which refers to a free will offering, and *zabach* and *shachat*, both of which have to do with the act of slaughtering.
77. See Exod. 35:22; Num. 31:50; Deut. 12:11; Philo, *Spec. Laws* 1.276.
78. See, for example, Exod. 35:20-35; Mal. 1:14.
79. See Josephus, *Ant.* 4.72.
80. See 1 Chron. 16:29; Jth. 16:18.
81. See, among others, Roland de Vaux, *Ancient Israel: Its Life and Institutions*, Vol. 2: *Religious Institutions*, trans. John McHugh (New York: McGraw-Hill, 1965), 451-53; Daly, *Origins*, 2-5.

This understanding of sacrifice is also evident from a number of related ideas. YHWH was thought to dwell in the Holy of holies above the mercy-seat and thus was said to meet with the high priest when he entered there (Exod. 25:22; 29:43; Lev. 16:2; Num. 7:89). Obviously, this made it possible to approach YHWH with offerings. Numerous biblical and extra-canonical texts also speak of YHWH being present, often in the form of a cloud, when the people came to offer him their gifts.[82] Those texts consistently define the ultimate desire of those making sacrificial offerings in terms of YHWH accepting what they offered to him.[83] This acceptance was often portrayed in terms of a fire descending from heaven to consume the offering. This idea is found repeatedly not only in the Hebrew Scriptures but also in non-canonical sources such as the writings of Josephus and Philo.[84]

The fact that incense tended to be mixed with the offerings and that these were spoken of as being of a "pleasing odor" to the Lord also underscores the idea that sacrifices were primarily gifts. The *minchah* included the corn, flour, bread, cakes, oil, and incense added to the sacrifice to make it pleasant to God.[85] The objective was not simply to forfeit possession of something or destroy it, but to remove it from human or profane use so that it might come into YHWH's possession. Placing something on the altar was understood in terms of presenting it as an offering before God, while burning what was offered made it ascend to God. High places were commonly sought as locations in which to offer up sacrifices to God, since this brought the offering closer to heaven, where God resided. Those who made offerings often used their hands to *elevate* their gift before God.[86] The most perfect offering was thought to be a holocaust, since the gift in its entirety ascended to God when it was burnt and nothing remained for human consumption or use.[87] According to Josephus, Abraham understood the sacrificing of his son Isaac in terms of sending him up to God (*Ant.* 1.230-31). Of course, because all things belonged to God, to give a gift to God was merely to give back to God what one had received from him.

Much more evidence of these beliefs could be offered, not only from the Hebrew Scriptures, but from various other strands of Jewish literature dating from the second-temple period, as well as the rabbinic writings in the centuries immediately following that period. The belief that in its essence sacrifice consisted in giving gifts to God is so strongly attested and stressed throughout all

---

82. 1 Kgs. 8:10-12; 2 Chron. 5:13-14; Josephus, *Ant.* 3.214-15; 8.106, 126; cf. Ezek. 43:5.

83. Gen. 4:4-5; Amos 5:22; Jth. 13:23; Josephus, *Ant.* 7.327-39; Philo, *Spec. Laws* 1.221. See also Daly, *Origins*, 21-24.

84. 1 Kgs. 18:38; 1 Chron. 21:26-28; 2 Chron. 5:13-14; 7:1-3; 2 Macc. 2:10; Josephus, *Ant.* 3.8.6; 4.33, 54-56; 8.118, 342; Philo, *Heir* 251; *Moses* 2.154-55. On the importance of the sacred fire on the altar as a sign of YHWH's presence in Israel, see Lev. 10:1-2; Num. 3:4; 26:21; Daly, *Origins*, 17-19.

85. Moshe Weinfeld, *Normative and Sectarian Judaism in the Second Temple Period* (LSTS 54; New York: T & T Clark, 2005), 122-25.

86. See, for example, Exod. 29:24; Josephus, *Ant.* 4.35-40.

87. See Stanislas Lyonnet, "The Terminology of Redemption," in *Sin, Redemption and Sacrifice: A Biblical and Patristic Study* (Lyonnet and Léopold Sabourin; AnBib 48; Rome: Biblical Institute, 1970), 169.

of the texts that allude to sacrificial practices in both the Hebrew Scriptures and ancient Jewish literature as a whole that there can be no doubt that this was the central and controlling idea in ancient Jewish sacrificial practice.

2. Sacrifice was inseparable from prayers and petitions.

This idea also runs throughout not only the Hebrew Scriptures but the literature of second-temple Judaism as well. Both the priests and the people presented themselves before YHWH in the temple, where YHWH or his name was said to dwell, primarily in order to meet with him there for the purpose of offering up to him different types of prayers. This was what the high priest was believed to do when he entered into the Holy of holies. The idea that to offer up sacrifices was in essence to offer up prayers is repeatedly assumed in the ancient texts, as passages such as 2 Sam. 24:25 demonstrate: "David built there an altar to the Lord, and offered burnt offerings and offerings of well-being. So the Lord answered his supplication for the land." The antithetical parallelism in Prov. 15:8 regards sacrifice and prayer as virtually synonymous: "The sacrifice of the wicked is an abomination to the Lord, but the prayer of the upright is his delight." The temple was regarded primarily not as a house of *sacrifice* but a house of *prayer* (Isa. 56:7; 1 Macc. 7:37). The lengthy prayer attributed to Solomon at the temple's dedication stresses this point repeatedly: in both of the biblical accounts of this event (1 Kings 8; 2 Chronicles 6–7), rather than asking God to accept the sacrifices offered there, Solomon's petition is that YHWH might *hear the prayers* offered to him by those invoking him at the temple or facing toward the temple as they prayed from afar. The same idea appears repeatedly throughout the Hebrew Scriptures: sacrifice is repeatedly tied to prayer, and prayer to sacrifice.[88]

In the periods of both the first and second temple, when the morning and evening sacrifices were offered up to God, they were accompanied by the prayers of those present at the temple as well as those who were far away; the practice of offering up prayers at those times continued even after the temple was destroyed.[89] The prayers were said to rise up to God together with the incense and the smoke of the offering being burnt on the altar: "Let my prayer be counted as incense before you, and the lifting up of my hands as an evening sacrifice" (Ps. 141:2; cf. Jth. 9:1). Even the altars were seen as places where people offered up to God not only their gifts but their prayers and petitions as well (2 Kgs.16:15). There is abundant evidence that when the sacrificial offerings were made, they were accompanied by singing directed to God, including psalms and doxologies, which in effect constituted prayers.

---

88. See, for example, 1 Kgs. 18:24-26, 36-37; 2 Chron. 20:9; Ps. 4:1, 5; 20:3-6; 27:6; 69:30; 116:17; Isa. 1:15; 19:21-22; Dan. 9:20; Amos 5:22-23; Zech. 8:22; Mal. 1:8-9; 2 Macc. 1:8, 23; 10:3-4; 14:34-35. For further references and discussion, see de Vaux, *Ancient Israel*, 2:457-59; Everett Ferguson, "Spiritual Sacrifice in Early Christianity and its Environment," in *Aufstieg und Niedergang der Romischen Welt*, Vol. II/23.1 (ed. H. Temporini and W. Haase; Berlin: De Gruyter, 1980), 1156-57.

89. Weinfeld, *Normative and Sectarian Judaism*, 124-25.

Both the communities that gathered there as well as individual worshipers might raise their songs to God.[90]

The writings of Josephus also consistently situate sacrifice in the context of prayers offered to God. Josephus repeatedly interprets the sacrificial texts in the Hebrew Scriptures in this regard, even when they do not mention prayer. For Josephus, Cain's sacrifice was a supplication that God not be extreme in his wrath, while Noah's burnt-offerings were petitions to God both for the future of the human race and for God to accept his sacrifice (*Ant.* 1.58, 96). Josephus understands Abraham's offering of Isaac in terms of a prayer, and has Moses state the purpose of the tabernacle in terms of allowing God to be present to hear the prayers of the priests and people (*Ant.* 1.58, 96). For Josephus, this is the purpose of the Jerusalem temple as well. When Solomon dedicates the temple he has built, Josephus attributes to him the following prayer:

> "I, however, have constructed this dedicated sanctuary for you, so that from it we may send up our prayers into the air, sacrificing and singing hymns and we may constantly be convinced that you are present and not far distant. For just as you look down upon everything and hear everything, you do not, even as you dwell here—as is possible for you to do—cease to be near to everyone. Rather, to each one who consults you, you are present night and day as a helper" (*Ant.* 8.108).[91]

In one passage after another, Josephus couples sacrifices with prayers, presents priests and others offering up prayers with their sacrifices, and affirms that God heeds their prayers by accepting their sacrifices.[92] Josephus understood the sacrifices offered up in the Jerusalem temple as prayers for the well-being of the people at large and even for the King of Persia, Caesar, and the Roman people.[93] All of this clearly demonstrates that for Josephus, sacrifices were in essence gifts offered to God together with prayers and petitions.

Philo clearly understood sacrifice in the same way. Like Josephus, he repeatedly uses the phrase "prayers and sacrifices," thus regarding these two as inseparable.[94] He also speaks of "sacrifices as a medium of prayer and thanksgiving" (*Sp. Laws* 1.195).[95] According to Philo, a soul seeking healing is to

---

90. See Alan F. Segal, "Covenant in Rabbinic Writings," *SR* 14 (1985): 58-59.

91. All quotations from the works of Josephus are taken from *Flavius Josephus, Translation and Commentary* (ed. Steve Mason; Leiden: Brill, 2000–).

92. See, for example, Josephus, *Ant.* 3.100; 4.243; 5.256; 6.19, 25, 102; 7.331-34; 11.17; 14.260-61; 18.15.

93. See Josephus, *Ant.* 7.331; 11.17; *J.W.* 2.197, 409; *Ag. Ap.* 2.77. E. P. Sanders also notes that "Josephus wrote that at the sacrifices prayers were offered 'for the welfare (*soteria*) of the community' (*Apion* 2.196) and that at the festivals people prayed 'for future mercies' (*Antiq.* 4.203)" (*Judaism: Practice and Belief, 63 BCE–66 CE*; Philadelphia: Trinity Press International, 1992, 255).

94. See especially Philo, *Drunkenness* 66; *Moses* 1.219; 2.133, 147, 153-54; *Spec. Laws* 1.97, 113, 224; *Unchangeable* 8. On the relation of sacrifice to prayer in Philo's work, see also Sanders, *Judaism*, 255-56; Ferguson, "Spiritual Sacrifice," 1159-60.

95. This idea is particularly stressed by William K. Gilders, who claims that Philo "offers general observations about the origin and meaning of sacrifice as a religious practice" as well as "an explicit 'theory' of sacrifice as a system of symbolic actions" ("Jewish Sacrifice: Its Nature and Function [According to Philo]," in *Ancient Mediterranean Sacrifice*; ed. Jennifer Wright Knust and Zsuzsanna Várhelyi; Oxford: Oxford University Press, 2011, 95). Gilders observes that for Philo, "Sacrifice was created as a medium of prayer and thanksgiving through which two goals could be achieved: rendering honor *to* God and seeking benefits *from* God" (96).

"come to the altar as a suppliant, beseeching grace with prayers and vows and sacrifices, by which alone it can obtain forgiveness" (*Dreams* 2.299). Like other Jews in antiquity, Philo conceives of the fire said to consume the sacrificial offerings as God's acceptance of the prayers presented and regards the daily sacrifices offered at the temple as prayers on behalf of the nation and humankind in general.[96] The offerings of individuals are supplications for their own health and well-being (*Spec. Laws* 1.167-68). Like the incense offerings, the blood offerings are for Philo prayers of thanksgiving (*Spec. Laws* 1.171).[97]

Numerous other scholars have shown that the same intimate relationship between sacrifice and prayer can be traced throughout other Jewish writings of antiquity. E. P. Sanders, for example, observes how the author of Ben Sirach relates the sacrifices offered in the temple to prayers and songs of praise and appears to have "regarded the sacrificial service as being an occasion to request God's blessings in general."[98] Klawans finds in the rabbinic tradition the notion of "the eternity of both prayer and sacrifice" and affirms that "we have no reason to doubt that the amoraic sages themselves believed fully that regular prayer was a part of the temple service...."[99] Alan Segal mentions that the rabbinic sources offer ample evidence of petitionary and supplicatory prayers offered during the temple service, not only in the form of litanies, but also in the form of individual supplications made together with the offerings.[100] Similarly, Daniel Falk notes the parallels between the *Amidah* or Eighteen Benedictions and the prayer of the Jewish priests in 2 Macc. 1:24-29 with regard to the way that these texts combine the sacrificial rites with petitions for God's favor.[101]

Particularly significant is the fact that petitionary prayer is repeatedly linked not only to sacrifices in general but also to the sacrifices of atonement aimed at procuring God's forgiveness. The Mishnah describes the prayer of confession offered up to God by the Jewish high priests while they carried out the sin-offering on the Day of Atonement (*Yoma* 6:2) and mentions the duty of all Jews to confess their sins before God in connection with

---

However, Gilders sees a gap between the symbolic significance that Philo ascribes to the different types of sacrificial actions and the way in which the actions to which he ascribes meaning were actually carried out. As a result, even though Philo seeks to affirm universal truths regarding the significance of sacrificial rites and their symbolism, his interpretation of sacrifice is in reality highly contextual and is influenced by cultural and historical factors (97-103).

96. See, for example, Philo, *Moses* 2.5, 154-55, 159. On this point, see also Klawans, *Purity*, 119.

97. On Philo's view of the temple and the sacrificial system associated with it, see especially Kåre Fuglseth, *Johannine Sectarianism in Perspective: A Sociological, Historical, and Comparative Analysis of Temple and Social Relationships in the Gospel of John, Philo, and Qumran* (NovTSup 119; Leiden: Brill, 2005), 189-219. Fuglseth particularly questions the idea that Philo viewed the Jerusalem temple and sacrifices in negative terms.

98. Sanders, *Judaism*, 254-55 (referring to Sir. 50:5, 18-19, 22-24).

99. Klawans, *Purity*, 200, 207.

100. Segal, "Covenant," 59. See also Weinfeld, *Normative and Sectarian Judaism*, 124.

101. Daniel Falk, "Prayers and Psalms," in *Justification and Variegated Nomism*, Vol. 1: *The Complexities of Second Temple Judaism* (ed. D. A. Carson, Peter T. O'Brien, and Mark A. Seifrid; WUNT 2/140; Tübingen: Mohr Siebeck, 2001), 18-20.

the sacrificial rites on that day.[102] These confessions of sin, of course, were in essence prayers for forgiveness. Every time a sin-offering or *hattat* was offered up, it was expected that the person making the offering pronounce a prayer of confession, as prescribed in the Mosaic Law (Lev. 4:5; 5:1-5; Num. 5:7).[103] Milgrom points to texts from various parts of the Hebrew Scriptures that also demonstrate that "a confessional recited by the penitent himself was an integral part of the Temple ritual" and observes: "The sanctuary prayers connected with the first-fruits and the tithes (Deut. 26:3-10, 13-15), though not strictly penitential, still may serve as evidence that the laymen did offer prayers in the Temple (cf. also Isa. 1:15)."[104]

Other sources also speak of the need for those presenting offerings at the temple to offer up prayers with their sacrifices, whether these prayers were confessions of sin, expressions of thanksgiving, or petitions for health and well-being.[105] The penitential fasting that accompanied the sacrificial rites for atonement was understood as a form of prayer as well.[106] The book of *Jubilees* presents Abraham's burnt sacrifice as a prayer for God's favor and presents God's commandment to Noah regarding the use of sacrificial blood by his descendants in the following terms: "They shall keep it for their generations so that they might make supplication on your behalf with blood before the altar on every day. And at the hour of daybreak and evening they will seek atonement on their own behalf continually before the Lord...."(*Jub.* 6:14; cf. 13:9; 16:20-31). This appears to have been the rabbinic understanding of the blood rites as well.[107] The Septuagint attests to the same connection through its use of the verb *exilaskesthai* to refer to the expiatory rites. As Royden Yerkes observes, the use of this verb "makes plain that, when men performed these rites, they were praying to God to purify themselves and his sanctuary in order that they might render him the worship which alone insured and mediated his protection."[108]

Because sacrifice was viewed as a form of prayer, numerous ancient sources attest that prayer alone could suffice when for some reason it was not possible to present God with sacrifices. This can be seen to be true with respect to those in exile after the destruction of the first temple, such as Daniel, who is presented as praying at the hours appointed for sacrifice (Dan. 6:10; 9:21). In the Septuagint additions to Daniel, the three young men in the furnace compare their contrite heart, humble spirit, and willingness to die to burnt offerings and sacrifice:

---

102. See Sanders, *Judaism*, 142; Jacob Neusner, *Messiah in Context: Israel's History and Destiny in Formative Judaism* (Philadelphia: Fortress, 1984), 125; Büchler, *Studies*, 353-54.

103. On this point, see Sanders, *Judaism*, 108-10; Milgrom, *Studies*, 55-58.

104. Jacob Milgrom, *Cult and Conscience: The Asham and the Priestly Doctrine of Repentance* (SJLA 18; Leiden: E. J. Brill, 1976), 108.

105. See E. P. Sanders, *Jesus and Judaism* (Philadelphia: Fortress, 1985), 194; Büchler, *Studies*, 441-43.

106. Büchler, *Studies*, 446-47.

107. Ibid., 430-31.

108. Royden Keith Yerkes, *Sacrifice in Greek and Roman Religions and Early Judaism* (New York: Charles Scribner's Sons, 1952), 181.

"In our day we have no ruler, or prophet, or leader, no burnt offering, or sacrifice, or oblation, or incense, no place to make an offering before you and to find mercy. Yet with a contrite heart and a humble spirit may we be accepted, as though it were with burnt offerings of rams and bulls, or with tens of thousands of fat lambs; such may our sacrifice be in your sight today...." (Dan. 3:38-40 LXX [3:15-17]).

The members of the community at Qumran similarly regarded their prayers as a replacement for sacrifice when they came to reject as corrupt the worship offered at the Jerusalem temple under the Hasmoneans.[109] The idea that prayer can replace sacrificial offerings is stated most explicitly in the Community Rule: "They shall atone for guilty rebellion and for sins of unfaithfulness that they may obtain loving-kindness for the land without the flesh of holocausts and the fat of sacrifice. And prayer rightly offered shall be an acceptable fragrance of righteousness, and perfection of way a delectable free-will offering" (1QS 9:4-5).[110] The Damascus Document also cites Prov. 15:8 as "an ideal proof for the doctrine that offerings on the altar can be adequately replaced by righteousness and prayer...."[111] The practices of the Qumranites regarding prayer also continued to revolve around the sacrificial feasts.[112] In addition, numerous texts from the rabbinic writings point to the fact that, following the destruction of the second temple, prayer was thought to take the place of sacrifice.[113]

Of course, the idea that prayer lay at the heart of sacrifice was in no way unique to Judaism. Numerous sources attest to the fact that sacrifice was seen as a form of prayer among the Greeks, Romans, and other peoples of antiquity as well.[114] Pliny the Elder, for example, wrote that "a sacrifice without prayer is thought to be useless and not a proper consultation with the gods."[115] Three centuries later, the pagan philosopher Sallustius would express the same idea: "Prayers divorced from sacrifices are only words, prayers with sacrifices are animated words, the word giving power to the life and the life animation to the word."[116] According to John Scheid, the various rites carried out in Roman sacrifice

> were accompanied by prayers which specified, without ambiguity, who was offering, who receiving, and who could expect to benefit from the ritual. In public sacrifices, the prayers always contained the formula "for the Roman people".... Praying was closely linked to ritual. It was an indispensable element in ritual

---

109. On the attitudes toward the temple reflected in the Qumran writings, see especially Fuglseth, *Johannine Sectarianism*, 219-40.
110. On this point, see especially Eileen Schuller, "Petitionary Prayer and the Religion of Qumran," in *Religion in the Dead Sea Scrolls* (ed. John J. Collins and Robert A. Kuglar; Grand Rapids: Eerdmans, 2000), 90.
111. Philip Davies, "The Ideology of the Temple in the Damascus Document," *JJS* 33 (1982): 293-94.
112. See Schuler, "Petitionary Prayer," 44-45.
113. See Ferguson, "Spiritual Sacrifice," 1161; Klawans, *Purity*, 203-7.
114. Yerkes contains ample references to this idea throughout his book (*Sacrifice*). See also de Vaux, *Ancient Israel*, 2:457-58.
115. Pliny the Elder, *Natural History* 28.10. Quoted in Kathy Ehrensperger, *Paul at the Crossroads of Cultures: Theologizing in the Space-Between* (LNTS 456; London: Bloomsbury T & T Clark, 2013), 183.
116. Sallustius, Concerning the Gods and the Universe 15:16. Quoted in Ferguson, "Spiritual Sacrifice," 1156.

and—vice versa—there was no praying without ritual. Prayers were recited while a celebrant performed the prescribed actions: like the instruments of sacrifice, prayer served as a means of celebrating the rite.[117]

The same type of observations could be made regarding the sacrificial practices of virtually every other culture known from antiquity.

There is no question, then, that in Jesus' day, when the Jewish people offered up sacrifices, they understood their actions as a form of prayer. This idea is so strongly attested throughout all of the ancient Hebrew and Jewish literature that there can be no doubt that most Jews believed that sacrifice was not primarily about carrying out rites and rituals, but offering up to God gifts together with prayers.

3. What made sacrifices and prayers acceptable to God was the inner disposition and commitment to God's will of those offering them or those on whose behalf they were offered.

According to the sources at our disposal, in ancient Hebrew and Jewish thought, no sacrifice or prayer could be acceptable to Israel's God if it was not offered with a pure heart in a spirit of sincere commitment to God's will for *shalom* and justice for all. While of course those who offered God their sacrifices or prayers often did so because they had sinned, in order for them to obtain forgiveness through sacrificial means, it was consistently expected that they repent, make restitution, and commit themselves once more to a life of obedience to God's commandments.

Although the legal prescriptions in the Pentateuch focus almost exclusively on the way in which the rites involved in the different types of sacrifice were to be carried out, those prescriptions also allude implicitly to the disposition of the offerers. The various "communion sacrifices" (*zebach, shelamim, todah, nedabah*) expressed a desire to praise and give thanks to God.[118] The holocausts were acts of homage and tribute to YHWH that recognized his sovereignty.[119] Sacrifices for sin required that one confess what one had done and, if necessary, make restitution (Lev. 5:5, 16; 6:1-7; 16:21; 26:40; Num. 5:6-8).[120] Even when one's sin was inadvertent or the need to confess and repent was not explicitly mandated, the fact that one presented a sacrifice for sin served as an implicit confession that one had sinned (Lev. 4:1-35). On the Day of Atonement in particular, it was necessary for both the priests and the people to confess their sins and fast, which involved humbling, afflicting, and denying themselves as an expression of their heartfelt repentance (Lev. 16:29, 31; 23:27, 29, 32; Num. 29:7; 30:13).

For many ancient Jews, the most perfect sacrifice—a sacrifice which, of course, was not consummated—was that of Isaac by Abraham. Abraham's

---

117. John Scheid, *An Introduction to Roman Religion*, trans. Janet Lloyd (Bloomington, IN: Indiana University Press, 2003), 84, 97.
118. See de Vaux, *Ancient Israel*, 2:417-18.
119. Ibid., 2:415-17.
120. See ibid., 2:419-21.

willingness to offer up his only son was pleasing to YHWH beyond measure precisely because it manifested concretely his full commitment to doing YHWH's will without questioning, no matter what the cost. It is this that both the Hebrew text and the ancient Jewish writings stress.[121] Josephus, for example, affirms that Abraham "put the doing of God's good pleasure even above the life of his child" (*Ant.* 1.224).

The historical books of the Hebrew Scriptures emphasize the same points with regard to sacrifice.[122] In 1 Sam. 15:22-23, after Saul has presented sacrifices to YHWH contrary to YHWH's command, Samuel insists to Saul that YHWH delights not in burnt offerings and sacrifices but in obedience to his words. The fact that this account exerted a strong influence on Jewish thought in the first century CE is evident from the manner in which Josephus expands upon it in his *Antiquities*:

> But the prophet said that the Deity was not pleased by sacrifices, but by those who are good and just. Such were those who followed his will and commands, and who thought nothing to have been done well by themselves other than what they did at God's direction. For it is not by sacrifice to him that one despises [God], but by seeming to disobey him. For those who do not obey or offer the true worship that alone is pleasing to God—even if they sacrifice many fat victims, or present magnificent dedicatory offerings made from silver and gold—he does not receive these things benevolently, but rejects them and regards them as proofs of vileness rather than of piety. Rather, it is those who keep in mind only what God has uttered and directed and who choose to die rather than transgress any of these things in whom he takes pleasure. From them he seeks no sacrifice, and, if they do sacrifice anything, however humble, he will more readily accept the honor [given him] by poverty than by the wealthiest (*Ant.* 6.147-48).

The prayers of David and Solomon related to the dedication of the temple also stress that obedience is essential for divine acceptance of sacrifices. In 1 Kgs. 8:12-61, Solomon repeatedly ties God's acceptance of the prayers and sacrifices God's people would offer up at the temple to the people's repentance and obedience. He stresses that God's decision whether to accept the prayers and sacrifices presented at the temple would depend on what God would see in the hearts of the people: "forgive, act, and render to all whose hearts you know—according to all their ways, for only you know what is in every human heart" (1 Kgs. 8:39). In his prayer of dedication for all that he had provided for the construction of the temple in 1 Chron. 29:17, David also emphasizes that God searches the heart of those making offerings and takes pleasure in uprightness. The fact that it was the disposition of the offerers that ultimately mattered rather than strict adherence to the legal prescriptions regarding the manner in which the sacrificial rites were to be performed is evident from 2 Chron. 30:18-19. There, when the people eating the Passover meal had not been able to follow ahead of time the procedures prescribed by the law for

---

121. See Géza Vermès, *Scripture and Tradition in Judaism: Haggadic Studies*, 2nd rev. ed. (SPB 4; Leiden: Brill, 1973), 209-12. See also Philo, *Abraham* 196-99.

122. On the points that follow, see especially Jeremiah Unterman, *Justice for All: How the Jewish Bible Revolutionized Ethics* (JPSEJS; Philadelphia: Jewish Publication Society, 2017), 91-108.

purifying themselves, Hezekiah prays: "The good Lord pardon all who set their hearts to seek God, the Lord the God of their ancestors, even though not in accordance with the sanctuary's rule of cleanness."

In the Psalms, it is repeated that what God desires is not sacrifices and offerings but obedience and the love of doing God's will as defined in the law (Ps. 40:6-8). Psalm 51 declares: "For you have no delight in sacrifice; if I were to give a burnt offering, you would not be pleased. The sacrifice acceptable to God is a broken spirit; a broken and contrite heart, O God, you will not despise" (vv. 16-17). According to Ps. 50:7-18, 23, God does not accept the sacrifices of those who do not offer their gifts with thanksgiving and obedience, walking in the right way. As already noted above, Prov. 15:8 affirms that "The sacrifice of the wicked is an abomination to the Lord, but the prayer of the upright is his delight." Similar ideas appear in Prov. 21:3, 27: "To do righteousness and justice is more acceptable to the Lord than sacrifice," while "the sacrifice of the wicked is an abomination."

Multiple passages from the prophetic writings can also be cited in favor of the same idea. In Isa. 1:11-17, YHWH tells the people that he detests their sacrificial worship and considers it an abomination because of the evil they do; only when they learn to do good, seek justice, rescue the oppressed, and help those in need can their offerings and worship be acceptable. The sacrificial fast that God desires is to loose the bonds of injustice and liberate the oppressed (Isa. 58:6). The prophet Jeremiah insists that YHWH will not dwell in the temple to receive the people's worship, sacrifices, and prayers if they practice oppression, shed innocent blood, and commit other abominations; when they persist in sin, YHWH rejects their offerings and fasts (Jer. 7:3-10; 11:15; 14:10-12). The prophet Hosea presents YHWH affirming, "For I desire steadfast love and not sacrifice, the knowledge of God rather than burnt offerings" (Hosea 6:6). There God also rejects their offerings when they sin, even when those offerings are of great monetary value (Hosea 8:11-13). In Amos 5:21-25, God tells the people: "I hate, I despise your festivals, and I take no delight in your solemn assemblies. Even though you offer me your burnt offerings and grain offerings, I will not accept them; and the offerings of well-being of your fatted animals I will not look upon. Take away from me the noise of your songs; I will not listen to the melody of your harps. But let justice roll down like waters, and righteousness like an ever-flowing stream." The prophet Micah stresses the same point: "'With what shall I come before the Lord, and bow myself before God on high? Shall I come before him with burnt offerings, with calves a year old? Will the Lord be pleased with thousands of rams, with ten thousands of rivers of oil? Shall I give my firstborn for my transgression, the fruit of my body for the sin of my soul?' He has told you, O mortal, what is good; and what does the Lord require of you but to do justice, and to love kindness, and to walk humbly with your God?" (Mic. 6:6-8). In the book of Malachi, God reproaches the people for offering to him what has been taken by violence as well as animals that are blemished and therefore are not an expression of sincere worship (Mal. 1:7-14; cf. 2:13-15).

Other Jewish writings tie God's acceptance of sacrificial offerings to repentance and obedience in the same ways. The book of Judith states: "For every sacrifice as a fragrant offering is a small thing, and the fat of all whole burnt offerings to you is a very little thing; but whoever fears the Lord is great forever" (Jth. 16:16). The book of Sirach insists that one should not think that God will consider the great number of one's gifts or accept an offering if one repeatedly sins or fails to pray and give alms (Sir. 7:9-10). Further on in Sirach we read:

> The Most High is not pleased with the offerings of the ungodly, nor for a multitude of sacrifices does he forgive sins. Like one who kills a son before his father's eyes is the person who offers a sacrifice from the property of the poor.... The one who keeps the law makes many offerings; one who heeds the commandments makes an offering of well-being. The one who returns a kindness offers choice flour, and one who gives alms sacrifices a thank offering. To keep from wickedness is pleasing to the Lord, and to forsake unrighteousness is an atonement. Do not appear before the Lord empty-handed, for all that you offer is in fulfillment of the commandment. The offering of the righteous enriches the altar, and its pleasing odor rises before the Most High. The sacrifice of the righteous is acceptable, and it will never be forgotten.... Do not offer him a bribe, for he will not accept it; and do not rely on a dishonest sacrifice; for the Lord is the judge, and with him there is no partiality...." (Sir. 34:23-24; 35:1-9, 14-15; cf. 38:9-11).

Similarly, according to *2 Enoch*, whoever makes offerings but does not practice judgment and righteousness is not acceptable: "Does the Lord demand bread or lambs or sheep or oxen or any kind of sacrifices at all? That is nothing, but he [God] demands pure hearts, and by means of all those things he tests people's hearts" (*2 En.* 45:3). God therefore spurns the gifts of those who offer him gifts with an impure heart; such gifts cannot obtain his favor (*2 En.* 46:1).[123]

These same ideas are particularly prominent in Philo's writings.[124] According to Philo, the altar at the temple prefigured, not the flesh and limbs of the animals to be sacrificed there, but

> the intention of the offerer. For, if the worshipper is without kindly feeling or justice, the sacrifices are no sacrifices, the consecrated oblation is desecrated, the prayers are words of ill omen with utter destruction waiting upon them. For, when to outward appearance they are offered, it is not a remission but a reminder of past sins which they effect. But, if he is pure of heart and just, the sacrifice stands firm, though the flesh is consumed, or rather, even if no victim at all is brought to the altar. For the true oblation, what else can it be but the devotion

---

123. Quotations from the Old Testament Pseudepigrapha in this and the following chapters are taken from *The Old Testament Pseudepigrapha*, Vol. 1: *Apocalyptic Literature and Testaments* (ed. James H. Charlesworth; New York: Doubleday, 1983).

124. On what follows, see especially Valentin Nikiprowetzky, "Le Spiritualisation des Sacrifices et le Culte Sacrificial au Temple de Jérusalem chez Philon d'Alexandrie," *Sem* 17 (1967): 97-116. Nikiprowetzky notes the close parallels between Philo and Plato on these matters.

of a soul which is dear to God?" (*Moses* 2.106-8; cf. *Spec. Laws* 1.171, 203; 2.35, 42; *QG* 2.52; *Names* 240).

Elsewhere, Philo stresses that Scripture "says not that God saw the offerings but that he first saw those who were offering gifts before the gifts themselves" (*QG* 1.61). He claims that the God of Israel established only one temple on the earth so that he might test those who wish to worship him by seeing whether they are willing to travel lengthy distances in order to offer him sacrifice in a pure and holy spirit (*Spec. Laws* 1.67-70). Philo also insists that there must be no taint of selfishness or self-interest in the sacrificial offerings (*Spec. Laws* 1.196). What pleases God is not offerings of great monetary value but persons who practice holiness and justice:

> God does not rejoice in sacrifices even if one offer hecatombs, for all things are his possessions, yet though he possesses he needs none of them, but he rejoices in the will to love him and in men that practise holiness, and from these he accepts plain meal or barley, and things of least price, holding them most precious rather than those of highest cost. And indeed though the worshippers bring nothing else, in bringing themselves they offer the best of sacrifices, the full and truly perfect oblation of noble living, as they honour with hymns and thanksgiving their Benefactor and Saviour, God, sometimes with the organs of speech, sometimes without tongue or lips, when within the soul alone their minds recite the tale or utter the cry of praise (*Spec. Laws* 1.271-72; cf. 1.269-70, 275-85).

According to Philo, the reason that the law prescribes purity in regard to both the offerer and the animals to be sacrificed is to symbolize figuratively the disposition, conduct, and spirit of repentance of the one making the offering (*Spec. Laws* 1.257-60). Therefore, those who sacrifice must examine themselves before presenting their offering to ensure that they are acting out of a pure spirit: "So he who intends to sacrifice must consider not whether the victim is unblemished but whether his own mind stands free from defect and imperfection. Further, let him examine the motives which determine him to make the offering" (*Spec. Laws* 1.283-84). Philo insists that "God does not delight in the fleshiness or fatness of animals, but in the blameless intention of the votary" (*Spec. Laws* 2.35). Because God sees into the heart, no one should approach him through sacrificial means without repenting and being pure in thought and action:

> For it is absurd that a man should be forbidden to enter the temples save after bathing and cleansing his body, and yet should attempt to pray and sacrifice with a heart still soiled and spotted.... He who is resolved not only to commit no further sin, but also to wash away the past, may approach with gladness; let him who lacks this resolve keep far away, since hardly shall he be purified. For he shall never escape the eye of him who sees into the recesses of the mind and treads its inmost shrine (*Unchangeable* 8-9; cf. *Spec. Laws* 1.293).

The need for a proper disposition among those who present sacrifices to God was also stressed at Qumran. In his analysis of the Qumran writings, Bertil Gärtner notes: "It is striking how many of the Qumran texts hark back to passages in the Old Testament which criticize sharply any form of temple service which fails to take account of justice and righteousness according to the demands of the Law. This is important for the understanding of the Qumran background, with its frequent stress laid upon truth and righteousness according to the Law as the only sacrifices of value in the eyes of God."[125] He and others also point to the same ideas in the rabbinic writings, where it is said that the only acceptable sacrifice is that which truly expresses repentance and obedience.[126]

The Logic of Ancient Jewish Sacrificial Practice

The three points just examined provide the basis necessary for reconstructing in general terms the meaning and purpose that Jews commonly ascribed to sacrificial practices in Jesus' day. Above all, sacrifice was understood as *worship*.[127] Like virtually all other peoples in antiquity, the Jews regarded the worship of their deity as inseparable from sacrifice. This idea is found from the very beginning of the foundational story of Israel in the book of Exodus, where the purpose of Israel's liberation from the Pharoah is stated in terms of enabling the people to "worship" or "serve" (*'abad*) YHWH; as the Hebrew original and the Septuagint translation make clear, this was understood as being synonymous with offering sacrifices to God.[128] Numerous other passages in the Hebrew Scriptures and other ancient Jewish writings equate sacrifice with worship as well.[129]

This, of course, leads to the question of what worship is. While there is no simple answer to this question, several ideas are undoubtedly central to any understanding of worship. One is that of recognizing a certain god as one's own. In the case of Israel, this involved confessing YHWH the God of Israel as the only true God, who was sovereign over all people and all things as creator of all that existed. According to this view of God, all people and all things belonged to YHWH. Sacrifice was a way of expressing this truth concretely. People gave to YHWH what was his own, including not only their possessions but their very selves. This idea is stressed repeatedly throughout the Hebrew Scriptures and the Jewish writings of the second-temple period.[130] In one sense, nothing that the people had was their own; yet in another

---

125. Bertil Gärtner, *The Temple and the Community in Qumran and the New Testament: A Comparative Study in the Temple Symbolism of the Qumran Texts and the New Testament* (SNTSMS 1; Cambridge: Cambridge University Press, 1965), 46.

126. Sanders comments that the rabbis taught "that it is all one whether one offers much or little, if only the person making the offering directs his mind towards Heaven" (*Comparing Judaism and Christianity: Common Judaism, Paul, and the Inner and Outer in the Study of Religion*; Minneapolis: Fortress, 2016, 372). See also Gärtner, *Temple*, 45; Milgrom, *Studies*, 165.

127. On the relation between sacrifice and worship in ancient thought, see especially Steven J. Friesen, *Imperial Cults and the Apocalypse of John: Reading Revelation in the Ruins* (Oxford: Oxford University Press, 2001), 195-96.

128. See especially Exod. 3:12; 7:26 (LXX 8:1); 8:25-28; 9:1, 13; 10:3, 24-26; 12:31; see also Philo, *Moses* 1.87.

129. Lev. 2:1; 18:21; Deut. 12:4-6; 2 Kgs. 17:32-33; Isa. 14:21; Jer. 26:2; Jth. 16:18; Sir. 35:9-11; Philo, *Agriculture* 127-28; *Rewards* 56; Josephus, *Ant.* 6.21-22; 7.78; 15.248; *J.W.* 1.150; 7.434-35.

130. 1 Chron. 29:14; Ps. 24:1; 50:10-12; Ezek. 18:4; Wis. 10:26; Sir. 35:12; Philo, *Spec. Laws* 1.221, 271; *Unchangeable* 6-7; Josephus, *J.W.* 5.218.

sense, what they had was theirs because God had given it to them. Through sacrificial offerings, they expressed these truths symbolically. This involved an ongoing sharing or communion between God and his people: the people gave back to God what God had given to them, while God in turn gave back to the people what he received from them. According to Philo, those offering sacrifices acted merely as stewards (*Spec. Laws* 1.221). Yet at the same time, in this giving and receiving, God and the people were not equals; rather, through their sacrificial worship the people expressed their submission to God and recognized God's sovereignty over them.

The distinction between giving of one's *self* and giving *gifts and offerings* is an important one. In a sense, these are not two separate things but one and the same; yet they must nevertheless be distinguished from one another. What was believed to be most important was that one *give of oneself* to God. This could be done in numerous ways. Obedience to God's will as it was manifested in God's law was first and foremost. The fundamental demand of that law was that the people love God: "You shall love the Lord your God with all your heart, and with all your soul, and with all your might" (Deut. 6:5). This love was understood not merely as a sentiment but as a commitment to doing God's will. However, because God's law commanded that his people do what was right, loving, and compassionate in relation to others, it was considered impossible to give of oneself to God without also giving of oneself to others, seeking their well-being. This love for God and others was a response to the love that God had first shown Israel.

One might also give oneself to God by serving God in vocations related to the worship of God, especially at the temple, or by making certain vows. In most cases, however, participation in the vocations related to worship at the temple was limited to those of priestly or Levitical lineage. Of course, one also participated in the worship of YHWH by going to the temple area physically to participate in the sacrifices and prayers offered there. This involved being present when sacrifices and prayers were offered up for the people and the world as a whole as well as offering up sacrifices and prayers of one's own at times. Those who participated in sacrificial worship therefore paid a price that included not only the cost of the victims and the goods they offered up but also the time, energy, and expenses involved in traveling to the temple. All who paid the half-shekel mandated in the Mosaic law were also regarded as taking part in the sacrificial worship offered at the temple through their financial support.[131] This gave them ownership in that worship and made the sacrifices offered in Jerusalem their own. The passage that mandates the payment of the half-shekel also affirms that those who contributed were purchasing their lives back from God (Exod. 30:11-16). By paying the half-shekel, they acknowledged that their lives belonged to God and that they were therefore obligated to dedicate themselves fully to God's service in body and soul. Nevertheless, through the payment of the half-shekel, God allowed them to

---

131. See Neusner, *Judaism when Christianity Began*, 148-51.

"purchase" themselves back from him in a sense so that they might live their own life, even though in another sense they continued to belong to God.

In these ways, then, through sacrificial worship one *offered oneself* to God; yet one did so *in concrete ways by offering up to God one's time, one's energies, one's body, and one's possessions and resources*. These two ideas complemented each other and were both regarded as essential. People could hardly claim that they offered *themselves* up to God if they were not willing to offer up some gift to God as a concrete and palpable expression of their self-offering to God. This logic is behind the commandment that no one was to come to the temple empty-handed, without presenting any offering (Exod. 23:15; Deut. 16:16; Sir. 35:6). The reason for this commandment was not that YHWH was seen as a selfish or greedy deity who desired gifts for his own sake, but rather that to worship God without presenting anything to him was thought to involve a lack of sincerity. To offer up prayers of thanksgiving to God for what he had given, express to God one's remorse over the sins one had committed, or request some blessing from God without at the same time offering up to God something material and concrete was viewed as a contradiction in terms. Under normal circumstances, such prayers were thought to consist merely of empty words, since there was nothing to back them up.[132] Where there was no material offering, there was no cost involved, no real sacrifice made by the one pronouncing the words, and therefore no apparent sincerity in one's prayer before God. It was believed that if one was truly sincere in whatever words one addressed to God, one would accompany those words with concrete gifts; and the more sincere and profound the sentiments one expressed through one's sacrifice, the more costly and precious would be the gifts one chose to present to God.[133]

Conversely, however, to offer God one's possessions and resources without offering one's own self to God was regarded as equally unacceptable. In biblical and Jewish thought, God's favor could not be purchased by sacrifice, nor could God be bribed or manipulated.[134] For this reason, the ancient Jewish texts often stress that Israel's God needs nothing from human beings.[135] If one participated in sacrificial worship in a selfish way, without submissively

---

132. Klawans notes that, even after the destruction of the temple, the rabbis continued to believe that prayer without sacrifice was inferior to that which might be presented to God with sacrificial offerings (*Purity*, 205-6). Klawans also cites the fourth-century work *On the Gods and the World* by Platonius Sallustius: "Prayer without sacrifice is only words," and paraphrases the idea thus: "talk is cheap. Sacrifice, however, costs" (*Purity*, 10).

133. The clearest example of this in the Hebrew Scriptures is David's refusal to offer to God something that had cost him nothing (2 Sam. 24:24; cf. Josephus, *Ant.* 7.331-32). Some passages stress the notion that one should offer the greatest and most costly gifts possible to God, while others denounce the giving of offerings that have cost one nothing (e.g., Mal. 1:8, 13; Sir. 35:10). On this point, see also John Dunnill, "Communicative Bodies and Economics of Grace: The Role of Sacrifice in the Christian Understanding of the Body," *JR* 83 (2003): 88-89. Dunnill stresses that the prophetic critique of sacrifice was "aimed at correcting, not rejecting, the practice of sacrifice" (88). While a proper inner disposition was necessary, this needed to be expressed in concrete forms: "a religion that has an outward form is precisely what God demands—a religion whose form extends beyond the bounds of the rite, a religion that is in solidarity with social life" (89).

134. See Philo, *Spec. Laws* 1.277; Sir. 35:14.

135. See, for example, 2 Macc. 14:35; Josephus, *J.W.* 5.218; Philo, *Posterity* 4; *Spec. Laws* 1.271, 277; *Unchangeable* 7, 107; *Virtues* 9.

acknowledging God's sovereignty over one's life and creation in general and without a sincere commitment to doing God's will, placing oneself and all that one had at God's disposal, one's sacrifices and prayers were not acceptable to God. One's gift had to be *voluntary* and represent a true expression of what was in one's heart; and this submission to God had to be manifested not only in serving God concretely with what one had received from God, but also in obeying God by seeking justice and *shalom* for all concretely with what one had received from God.[136] The giving of oneself and the giving of one's resources and possessions were therefore on the one hand *one and the same thing*, since one could not do the former without doing the latter; yet they must nevertheless be *distinguished* from one another, since to do one is not automatically to do the other.

On this basis, it should be clear that sacrifice in ancient Judaism was not primarily about killing animals, making atonement, or even performing sacred rites. Rather, it was about giving and receiving: God gave and the people received, while at the same time the people gave and God received. In general, sacrifice was characterized by joyful celebration. Naturally, where there had been sin, disobedience, and injustice, this had to be dealt with before there could be joyful celebration. Those who had sinned dealt with their sin by confessing it in a spirit of repentance, recommitting themselves to obeying God, making restitution for any damage they had done, and presenting sacrifices for sin, as we shall see in further detail below. But the expiation of sins was not an end in itself and was not regarded as the heart of sacrifice. Sacrifice revolved instead around the sharing that was expressed in concrete ways. The expiatory rites and sacrifices that took place constituted a prelude to the real objective, which involved celebrating and sharing. Even the Day of Atonement had the purpose of putting the past behind so as to rejoice in the future, as is evident from the fact that it occurs toward the beginning of the Jewish year rather than at its end.

When the Jewish people made sacrifices to YHWH, therefore, they were acknowledging God's sovereignty over all people and things. What they offered to God expressed visibly the truth that everything belongs to God. Through their sacrifices, however, they were also acknowledging God's goodness, mercy, and love, expressing their thanks and praise and their devotion to God, and giving their very selves to God as they manifested concretely their commitment to do God's will in their life. The wide variety of gifts they gave to God, including money, jewelry, libations, and foodstuffs, expressed the enormous variety of things that they had received from God.

Of course, they also presented animals to God. This generally involved putting the animal victims to death. Yet the killing was done, not as an end in itself, but in order to give and receive. They wished to offer the animal up to God and did so by sending all or part of it up to God by burning it. At

---

136. See Josephus, *Ag. Ap.* 2.196-97. Almsgiving was therefore a sign of submission to God in that it involved practicing justice and solidarity; see Sir. 3:30; 7:10; 35:1-5; Tob. 4:7-11; 12:8-10.

the same time, they sought to make their sacrifices pleasant to God by adding incense, libations, spices, and other things to the offering. Out of love for God, they wanted to adorn and embellish their gift and make it something beautiful, sweet-smelling, and precious in order to express to God what was in their heart.

Those who offered sacrifices also ate of those sacrifices. The meal was an important part of many sacrificial rites. In those sacrifices that involved eating meat, part of the animal victim was given to God and to the priests, while the worshipers ate other parts, including especially the flesh. This was essentially an act of communion in which the participants enjoyed what God had given them and shared in what they had offered to God, while at the same time expressing their communion with one another.[137] This mutual love among the members of God's people was also thought to be important and pleasing to God, who rejoiced when his people lived in harmony and solidarity.

The reason that prayer was essential to all of these rites is that it served to express verbally the meaning behind the various actions involved. One could hardly present a sacrifice of atonement without confessing one's sins and manifesting verbally one's repentance, just as one could hardly offer a sacrifice of thanksgiving without mentioning the motives for which one was giving thanks. Similarly, when sacrifices were offered together with petitions for healing and well-being for oneself and for others, it was important to verbalize those petitions before the God who heard prayer at the temple. Of course, it was thought that, like the sacrifices themselves, prayers were only acceptable to God when those offering them were committed to living in submission to God's will, both in the active sense of striving constantly to do that will and in the passive sense of accepting unquestioningly whatever God ordained in one's life. The sacrificial offerings *symbolized* and *expressed concretely* this submission to God's will.

This does not mean that prayers without sacrificial offerings were of no value before God, since under certain conditions it might not be possible to present an offering. God might still answer such prayers favorably, since God might look into the heart of those offering up the prayer and see a sincere commitment to his will that would be expressed in their lives in ways other than by sacrificial offerings. But when one had the opportunity to accompany one's petitions with a sacrificial offering, it would normally be expected that one do so, since in that way one would manifest concretely the proper spirit with which one made one's petitions. Ultimately, then, God's response both to one's prayers and to one's sacrifices depended upon what God saw in one's heart. At the same time, what was in one's heart would normally express itself concretely by means of gifts and offerings presented to God together with one's prayers of confession, thanksgiving, and praise, as well as one's petitions for oneself and others.

---

137. On the practice and significance of the sacrificial meal in ancient Judaism, see Dunnill, "Communicative Bodies," 86-89.

The Purpose of Sacrifice in Ancient Jewish Thought

These considerations enable us to grasp what Jews in antiquity understood the *purpose* of sacrificial worship to be. This purpose was multiple. Sacrifice served to remind them of who they were—the particular people of the god YHWH (Exod. 19:5). It reinforced the idea that they were his possession and thus owed themselves and all they had to him as their Lord and sovereign. The animals, fruits, and assorted food items that they offered up to YHWH reminded them that YHWH had created all that exists and that he continued to act through his creation to provide for their needs and those of all other creatures. When they poured or sprinkled the blood of animal victims before YHWH, they recalled that all life belonged to him alone. The offering of the first-fruits and the sacrifices to redeem the first-born reinforced the same truth. The sacrifices led the Jewish people to recall not only YHWH's sovereignty and activity in nature but also specific moments from Israel's history when he had acted on their behalf. In particular, the sacrificial feasts brought to the remembrance of the people the way in which YHWH had delivered them from Egypt, given them his law, and established them as a people in a land of their own.[138]

The idea that sacrifical worship was a *reminder* or a *memorial* of things such as these appears constantly in the ancient texts.[139] In Num. 10:10, Moses tells the people: "on your days of rejoicing, at your appointed festivals, and at the beginnings of your months, you shall blow the trumpets over your burnt offerings and over your sacrifices of well-being; they shall serve as a *reminder* on your behalf before the Lord your God." Not only did the sacrifices themselves serve this purpose, but other practices related to the sacrifices as well. For example, the payment of the half-shekel for the worship at the sanctuary is explicitly called a "reminder" of their redemption: their lives belonged to God not only because all created things are his, but also because he had redeemed them from Egypt to make them his own (Exod. 30:11-16). Similarly, both Josephus and Philo describe the way in which the decorations on the temple curtain, the various ornaments in the sanctuary, the high-priestly vestments, and other rites served to remind the worshipers of God's sovereignty as creator of the universe.[140]

For this reason, sacrificial worship was also seen as having a *didactic* purpose. God had ordered the people to practice sacrifice in order to instruct them and reinforce basic truths such as those just mentioned. Sacrifices also served as means to teach the people the need to be truly grateful to God and to submit obediently to the law he had given them for their own benefit.

---

138. On the variety and meaning of memorial formulas used in ancient Jewish sacrificial practice, see Joachim Jeremias, *The Eucharistic Words of Jesus*, trans. Norman Perrin (Philadelphia: Fortress, 1977), 244-47.

139. Multiple texts from the Hebrew Scriptures and second-temple Jewish writings speak of sacrifice as a reminder of various truths; see, for example, Exod. 13:3-16; 20:24; Num. 5:15; Deut. 16:3, 12, 16; Josephus, *Ant.* 8.108; *J.W.* 5.212-13, 218; *Let. Aris.* 157-59; Philo, *Heir* 113-16; *Spec. Laws* 1:261-66; 2.145-46, 150-52, 156-60, 197-203. On this idea in Philo's writings, see Klawans, *Purity*, 118-20.

140. See Josephus, *J.W.* 5.212-14; Philo, *Moses* 2.93-108, 117-35, 150-51; *Heir* 221-29.

Philo, for example, affirms that God's commandment regarding the offering of first fruits "teaches us a high truth," like the other sacrificial practices prescribed in the Mosaic law.[141]

The purpose of sacrifice, however, was not only to offer the people instruction as to how they were to think and live but also to *bring about* in them that same way of thinking and living. By performing the rites prescribed and participating in them, they were actually *putting into practice* the behavior God wanted them to acquire and reinforcing and strengthening that behavior. They not only learned that they *should* be grateful to God and obey him, but were given concrete means of *expressing* that gratitude and *manifesting* that obedience. The command to present offerings for their sins reinforced to them the importance of avoiding sin and led them to reflect constantly on their behavior to see if they were living as God desired.

Thus Philo, for example, claimed that God had commanded the sacrifice of first-fruits in order "that speech, sense perception and apprehension may be judged soundly and blamelessly according to God's standard" (*Prelim. Studies* 101). The offering of sacrifice leads one to reflect on one's actions and produces a spirit of gratitude in the worshipers (*Spec. Laws* 1.283-95). In particular, for Philo the sacrifices for sin, including those prescribed for the Day of Atonement, were aimed at bringing the people to repentance and a renewed obedience: "For those who have acknowledged their sin are changing their way for the better, and while they reproach themselves for their errors are seeking a blameless life as their new goal" (*Spec. Laws* 1.227). The rites involved in the sacrifices for sin reminded the people to refrain from sinning and allowed them to "make themselves pure by curbing the appetites for pleasure" so that they might become "enamoured of continence and piety" (*Spec. Laws* 1.193). Thus sacrificial worship was intended to induce in those who participated in it a life dedicated to practicing justice and righteousness in accordance with God's will. According to Philo, this is the ultimate purpose of all of the sacrificial worship prescribed by Israel's God.

The *Letter of Aristeas* stresses these same points with regard to the purity laws given through Moses, which were intimately related to sacrificial practices:

> In his wisdom the legislator, in a comprehensive survey of each particular part, and being endowed by God for the knowledge of universal truths, surrounded us with unbroken palisades and iron walls to prevent our mixing with any of the other people in any matter, being thus kept pure in body and soul, preserved from false beliefs, and worshiping the only God omnipotent over all creation.... So, to prevent our being perverted by contact with others or by mixing with bad influences, he hedged us in on all sides with strict observances connected with meat and drink and touch and hearing and sight, after the manner of the Law. In general everything is similarly constituted in regard to natural reasoning, being

---

141. Philo, *Heir* 114. Throughout most of *Spec. Laws* 1.168-302, Philo elaborates on the purpose for which God instituted the diverse sacrificial rites, constantly stressing the truths those rites were designed to convey and the type of life they were intended to produce; see also *Spec. Laws* 2.204-9; 4.123-24.

governed by one supreme power, and in each particular everything has a profound reason for it, both the things from which we abstain in use and those of which we partake.... The fact is that everything has been solemnly set in order for unblemished investigation and amendment of life for the sake of righteousness.... [God] has thereby indicated that it is the solemn binding duty of those for whom the legislation has been established to practice righteousness and not to lord it over anyone in reliance upon their own strength, nor to deprive him of anything, but to govern their lives righteously.... The symbolism conveyed by these things compels us to make a distinction in the performance of all our acts, with righteousness as our aim.... I have therefore given a brief résumé of these matters, indicating further to you that all the regulations have been made with righteousness in mind, and that no ordinances have been made in Scripture without purpose or fancifully, but to the intent that through the whole of our lives we may also practice justice to all mankind in all our acts, remembering the all-sovereign God (*Let. Aris.* 139, 143-44, 147, 151, 168).

The sacrificial system was therefore thought to help hold sin in check and promote greater obedience, love, and gratitude toward God among the people. These same ideas appear in other Jewish texts of the time, as well as in the rabbinic writings.[142]

Finally, in ancient Hebrew and Jewish thought, one other purpose of sacrifice was to enable people to *live* and *experience palpably* their communion with God and one another. As numerous texts affirm, the sacrificial feasts were seen as occasions to celebrate their identity and rejoice over what God had done and would continue to do for them, not only as individuals but as a people.[143] They also served as means for the people to express concretely other experiences and sentiments, such as that of remorse for their sins or the sincerity of their petitions to God. As noted above, words and actions were combined and complemented each other. Neither was sufficient without the other. Sacrificial worship therefore fulfilled the purpose of allowing the people to manifest their innermost sentiments, beliefs, and desires in concrete, palpable, and visible ways that went well beyond what words alone could ever articulate.

Sacrifice and the Jewish View of God

On the basis of what we have just seen regarding the logic and purpose of sacrifice in ancient Jewish thought, it should be clear that Jews in antiquity believed that their God had ordained sacrifice, *not for his own sake, but for theirs*. Undoubtedly, the God of Israel wanted to receive expressions of love and gratitude from his people and desired to live in communion with them. However, he was thought to desire these things not merely for his own sake. Rather, as the ancient texts constantly stress, Israel's God YHWH loved his

---

142. See, for example, Jacob Milgrom, *Leviticus 1-16: A New Translation with Introduction and Commentary* (AB 3; New York: Doubleday, 1991), 440.

143. See Deut. 12:5-18; 14:22-26; 16:9-15; Neh. 12:43; Josephus, *Ant.* 4.203-4. For a survey of the Jewish attitudes toward the Levitical sacrifices reflected in second-temple Jewish literature, see especially Lloyd Kim, *Polemic in the Book of Hebrews: Anti-Semitism, Anti-Judaism, Supersessionism?* (PTMS 64; Eugene, OR: Pickwick, 2006), 147-72.

people deeply and therefore wanted only what was best for them. In ancient Jewish thought, because YHWH is the sovereign creator and the one to whom all belongs, by definition and for intrinsic reasons, only those who love, serve, and obey him can enjoy the good he desires for all. This good is precisely what the practice of sacrifice was believed to express and promote.

This manner of understanding God stands in stark contrast to the concepts of God reflected in much traditional Christian thought. Influenced by ideas such as those mentioned previously in connection with the common assumptions made regarding sacrifice, Christian scholars have often intimated that God commanded sacrifice *for God's own sake* rather than for the sake of God's people. Undoubtedly, this does not mean that God requires or needs sacrifice in the sense that God is dependent on it in some way. Rather, according to this way of thinking, God's strict justice requires sacrifice for sins in order that God's love can accomplish its saving purposes. Because God's holiness and perfection prevent God from manifesting God's love for human beings by forgiving them freely, the death of sacrificial victims allows for the demands of that holiness and perfection to be satisfied so that God's love may prevail. The necessity of sacrifice, therefore, is rooted in the same dichotomy between God's love and God's justice that we have considered in Chapter 1: God's love wants to forgive, save, and bless God's people, yet until God's justice is satisfied, God cannot do these things.

In this way, God's commandments regarding sacrifice are seen as having the purpose of enabling God's justice to be satisfied and thus serve to meet a *divine* need rather than a *human* one. According to this manner of thinking, the fundamental problem is not that human beings are sinful; if that were the case, then the solution required would be that God enable them to stop sinning. Rather, the fundamental problem is that, because of God's perfect holiness and righteousness, God cannot accept human sin and thus save sinful people until the demands of that holiness and righteousness are met. Therefore, God requires sacrifice, not so that human beings can stop being sinful, but so that God can overlook their sins in order to save them.

As has often been noted, such an understanding of God's justice and love ascribes to sacrificial practice a *juridical* or *forensic* purpose that is alien to biblical and ancient Jewish thought regarding sacrifice. The legislation regarding sacrifice was not a penal code. While certain sacrifices were offered for sins, those who presented offerings for sin were not paying penalties or purchasing God's pardon. Rather, they were *worshiping* God, recognizing their sinfulness, and reconsecrating themselves to him. In addition, for the most part, sacrifice was offered for reasons other than that of seeking forgiveness for sin. Certainly, many sacrifices that were not strictly-speaking offerings for sin, such as the communion offerings or holocausts, were thought to be expiatory in some sense. Yet this was only because, in Jewish thought, whenever people approach God seeking that their prayers be answered, they must always be aware that they are unworthy of what they ask and are therefore in constant need of God's grace, mercy, and forgiveness in their relationship with him. In general, however, the practice of sacrifice revolved primarily around other concepts and purposes, such as celebration, thanksgiving, and petitionary prayer.

This understanding of God and God's purpose in commanding sacrifice also distinguishes Israel's God from other gods in antiquity. YHWH was different from the gods of the nations primarily in three ways. First, YHWH was viewed as the one sovereign creator to whom all things belonged and to whom all were subject. In contrast, even the most powerful gods of other nations existed alongside other gods who limited them in various ways and prevented them from being all-powerful. Creation might be ascribed to a god who was superior to the lesser gods, as in Plato's thought, but no such god was believed to have the same sovereignty as YHWH or to be omnipotent in the way that YHWH was. Second, the God of Israel was believed to be a *gracious God* who *loved those who worshiped and served him, seeking their well-being at all times while seeking nothing for himself.* He did not depend on human beings in any way and had no needs that human beings had to satisfy. At the same time, that same love for the people led YHWH to seek not only that the people love him in return for the sake of their own well-being and happiness, which could only be found in him as the sovereign creator of all, but that they love one another as well. If YHWH loved all people, those who worshiped him were also to love all people. And third, precisely because he desired the people's well-being and commanded that they love one another, what really mattered to YHWH was not the gifts that people brought to him in sacrifice but their commitment to practicing justice, helping the needy, and living a pure life for their own good and that of others.[144]

In ancient thought, it is difficult if not impossible to find gods who were said to "love" people in the same way YHWH did, or gods who were believed to be dedicated above all else to the well-being of human beings, as YHWH was. While other gods wanted human beings to *serve* and *worship* them, they rarely demanded that human beings *love* them with all their heart, soul, and strength, as YHWH did (Deut. 6:5; Josh. 22:5). Such affirmations could hardly be made of other gods mentioned in the Hebrew Scriptures, like the Baals or the god Moloch, who demanded human sacrifice.[145] These

---

144. As Sanders notes, Philo criticized the way sacrifice was offered among people of other nations to their gods, comparing it negatively to the Jewish worship of Israel's God. In his stinging critique of the other nations' practices, Philo affirms that they purify their bodies in preparation for sacrificial rites and don spotless white robes, but they do not wash off from their souls their impure passions or cleanse their spotted heart before unashamedly entering their sanctuaries. According to Philo, their wickedness leads to unholy sacrifices, unfulfilled vows, and rites that are "a mockery"; their impurity, falsehood, and worship are "a sacrilege" (*Comparing Judaism and Christianity*, 356, commenting on *Cherubim* 94-96; see also 343). For Philo, all of these things contrasted sharply with the purity of the soul that characterized Jewish sacrificial practice (357). Of course, it must be recognized that Philo's depiction of the sacrificial worship of both the other nations and the Jewish people is undoubtedly biased and involves sweeping generalizations. What is significant, however, is that he saw the sacrifices of other peoples in this way.

145. On the contrasts between ancient Hebrew thought on the following points as it is reflected in the Hebrew Scriptures and that found in ancient Babylonian thought, see Unterman, *Justice*, 1-14.

gods were not understood to be selflessly seeking the well-being of those who worshiped them. While of course one must be careful when making generalizations, for the most part the Greek and Roman gods were not said to love their worshipers in the way that YHWH loved his people or to have expected their sincere and heartfelt love in return. If love was spoken of in these relations, it was generally understood, not in terms of a disinterested commitment to the well-being of the people, but as a *do ut des* relationship involving the mutual satisfaction of the desires of both the gods and the worshipers: each gave to the other what the other wanted in order to obtain something from the other.

In general terms, the gods of other nations are rarely presented as making ethical demands on human beings intended to promote justice and mercy for all, especially those in greatest need. At times, the gods of the nations even approved of behavior that was widely regarded as immoral, such as thievery, promiscuity, deception, or even murder. In fact, many of the gods themselves were said to practice such behavior. Undoubtedly, the idea that the gods demanded moral purity from their worshipers and were pleased only with the sacrifices of those who lived pious lives was also taught in many non-Jewish circles.[146] Nevertheless, the Jewish conception of God remained fundamentally distinct. The fact that YHWH was viewed as the only true God, the sovereign creator of all people and things, made him unlike any other deity. Because in Jewish thought there were no other gods besides YHWH, he alone could be omnipotent and fully independent. He did not compete with other gods for worshipers, power, or prestige. There were no other deities, powers, or forces that could challenge him or impose their will on him. He did not depend on other gods, on human beings, or on nature in any way.

For the most part, none of these things could be said of the other gods in the polytheistic belief systems of antiquity. The fact that gods were born of other gods and goddesses or procreated other divine beings made them fundamentally different from YHWH. Like other ancient deities, the Greek and Roman gods were generally male or female and had siblings, companions, and lovers. If they had sexual relations, then they also must have had sexual desires that had to be satisfied. If they ate, drank, and slept, then they had other physical needs and desires as well. In Jewish thought, none of these things could be said of YHWH, who could not be represented in human or animal form like the other gods. This gave him a transcendence and sovereignty that other deities did not possess and made it impossible for him to be manipulated by human beings or limited in any way. Because YHWH did not have physical desires and needs like other gods or like human beings, those offering sacrifice

---

146. See for example Ferguson, "Spiritual Sacrifice," 1152-56; Nikiprowetzky, "Spiritualisation," 98-99. Of course, many of the Greek philosophers considered sacrifice itself as immoral and insisted that the practice of sacrifice was to be rejected on that ground; see James W. Thompson, "Hebrews 9 and Hellenistic Concepts of Sacrifice," *JBL* 98 (1979): 573-76.

could not appeal to any such desires and needs in order to obtain what they wanted from him.[147]

While other gods might control certain forces of nature, they were not omnipotent like YHWH. Because YHWH was not personally identified like other gods with the different elements and forces of nature, such as the sun, the wind, thunder, or the sea, nor thought to actually dwell in sacred places such as shrines, groves, or temples, he was not subject to nature in any way. YHWH *transcended* nature in its entirety rather than depending on it or being a manifestation of it. Even though certain human and supernatural forces were thought to struggle against YHWH, in Jewish thought YHWH did not have to exert himself to resist them or engage in combat with them in order to defeat them; nor could he ever be harmed or overpowered by them in any way. He might allow the angelic beings he had created to exist and act in ways that were contrary to his ultimate will, yet this was not because he was somehow powerless to control and subject them fully to himself at any moment if he so desired. While undoubtedly YHWH had his temple in Jerusalem, both the Hebrew and the Jewish literature stress that he was in no way confined spatially to the temple building. On the contrary, he transcended it from his throne far up in heaven and was present throughout the earth. The temple was merely the place YHWH had established for people to approach him. For this reason, it was generally claimed that it was YHWH's "name" rather than YHWH himself that dwelt in the temple.

Unlike the other ancient deities, YHWH was also believed to be in control of history. This was not only because no other gods or natural or supernatural forces could exert any power or influence over YHWH but also because, as sovereign creator, he was not subject to fate, destiny, or history in any sense. YHWH was subject to nothing and to no one and therefore was entirely free from any type of need or compulsion.

YHWH's character was also thought to be fundamentally distinct from that of other gods. In Jewish thought, he was not a capricious deity whose mood might change at any moment for no particular reason. He was not believed to be amused or entertained by what human beings did, and therefore no athletic games or raucous, lustful celebrations were to be celebrated in his honor. Besides the fact that he could not get inebriated and had no sexual desires that needed to be satisfied, YHWH did not have vices or moral flaws like other gods. He did not practice deception, nor did he manipulate people or other supernatural beings in order to obtain something from them. It was also not possible for others to deceive, flatter, or manipulate him. Because all things were already his, even though he had no need for anything that he had created, he could never be regarded as selfish or possessive, wanting

---

147. As Thompson notes, the idea that the deity was in need of nothing that human beings might offer was not unique to Judaism, since it is also "a frequent theme in the history of Greek thought" and "is repeated in all of the schools of Greek philosophy until the Neopythagoreans and the Neoplatonists...." ("Hebrews 9," 574).

to reserve certain things only for himself. Due to the way YHWH was conceived, even positive qualities such as courage, virility, fertility, temperance, chastity, modesty, and pride could not be attributed to him as they might be to other deities, since such qualities can only exist in relation to others who are in some sense one's equals or possess some type of power over one. The fact that the fundamental quality associated with YHWH was love for human beings meant not only that attributes such as power, justice, sovereignty, generosity, anger, wisdom, and forbearance were inextricably linked to the notion of YHWH's love, but also that YHWH was intimately involved in all that took place in the world. This was true not only on the level of nations, societies, and communities, but on the level of individuals as well. Rather than being cold, distant, disinterested, or unaffected by human beings as other gods might at times be, YHWH cared passionately about events and about people themselves, including especially the needy, the oppressed, and the marginalized.

This understanding of Israel's God necessarily led to a view of sacrifice that was very different from the views of sacrifice that were common among other peoples in antiquity. Because in Jewish thought it was not the offerings themselves that pleased YHWH or obtained his favor but a commitment to obeying his commandments, which had the goal of promoting justice, equity, and love for others, Jewish sacrifice was not a matter of *do ut des*. Other gods might be manipulated, appeased, or persuaded to grant what the offerers desired by the sacrifices they brought because those gods desired those sacrifices in and of themselves, yet with YHWH this was not the case.[148] While the idea that the divine acceptance of sacrifice depended upon the spirit of repentance and commitment to the divine will of those presenting it was not exclusive to Judaism, it certainly found greater stress there.[149] Furthermore, the fact that Israel's God not only wanted people to avoid doing harm to others but also

---

148. Patterson comments that "Ovid's entertaining description of the festivals of the Roman calendar in poetic form, the *Fasti*, satirizes the relational quality of ancient sacrifices, the very human ways in which gods and humans were seen to relate to one another through the medium of sacrifice. For example, he has Flora say, with more than a hint of mockery, 'We [gods], too, are touched by honor; we delight in festivals and altars; we heavenly beings are a greedy gang. Often when by sinning a man has disposed the gods against him, a sacrificial victim has been a sop for crimes. Often have I seen Jupiter, when he was just about to launch his thunderbolts, hold his hand on the receipt of incense. But if we are neglected, we avenge the wrong by heavy penalties, and our wrath exceeds just bounds.' (Ovid, *Fast.* 5.297-302 [Frazer])" (*Keeping the Feast*, 44). Patterson also adds, however, that there is much evidence that many of those who participated in Greco-Roman sacrifices did not view the presenting of sacrificial offerings in those terms (44).

149. E. P. Sanders points to Plato's presentation of Adimantos in the *Republic* as exemplifying the idea that, without a correct disposition and a dedication to virtue, one's sacrifices were not acceptable to the Greek gods (*Comparing Judaism and Christianity*, 328-30). Plato has Adimantos observe, however, that many people believe that, even though they willfully practice evil and deception, they may obtain the favor and pardon of the gods with their sacrifices. Sanders notes that "the Hebrews thought that this effort to evade punishment would not work. One cannot buy God's forgiveness or mercy with sacrifices" (332). He then adds: "The God of Israel, unlike the gods of Homer, to whom Adimantos refers, could not be fooled or bought by sacrifice.... [T]he sort of completely successful deception imagined by Adimantos could not be imagined by a Hebrew prophet, since they believed that God saw the heart of every person...." (332, n5). Sanders also adds that, according to Adimantos, some Greeks believed they could offer sacrifices in the present life to obtain the acceptance and blessing of the gods in the afterlife: "In the Republic, Adimantos thinks that the gods get in on the act only when a person enters the next world. The unrighteous can prepare for this by offering sacrifices in advance.

commanded that all actively reach out to those in need, practicing mercy and kindness to them, meant that the ethical demands associated with the worship of YHWH were generally greater than those associated with other deities. Because YHWH was above all a God of love, he expected and demanded sincere and heartfelt love for others from those who approached him with their offerings. Just as the notion of love was at the core of the Jewish concept of God, so also was it central to the Jewish concept of sacrificial worship.

Thus while Jews in antiquity used much of the same language and shared many of the same practices related to sacrifice that were found among those who worshiped other deities, they understood this language and these practices very differently. For example, while like other peoples the Jews held celebrations in honor of YHWH and feasted before him, their understanding of YHWH's nature and character made them believe that it was necessary to do these things in healthy, wholesome ways that did not involve drunkenness, gluttony, or lascivious behavior. Likewise, while they affirmed that YHWH desired sacrifice and sought to please him by offering costly sacrifices that were pleasant to smell and taste, in general they stressed that what really pleased YHWH was not the offering itself but the disposition of the heart of which such sacrifices were a sincere expression. For the same reason, even though sacrifice might obtain YHWH's favor and blessing and turn away his anger, in Jewish thought it was maintained that what pleased YHWH and appeased his wrath was *not the offering itself* but the spirit of repentance, obedience, and love in which it was presented.

Similarly, while like other deities YHWH was often portrayed as a monarch or ruler before whom people approached with gifts in order to seek favor and blessings, most Jews tended to see YHWH as very different from other monarchs and rulers. In the minds of virtually all people in antiquity, it was obvious that kings, emperors, and others in positions of power wanted tribute *in and of itself*, not just in order to promote the well-being of their subjects, but to satisfy their own personal desires. In fact, in most cases, their only interest in promoting the well-being of their subjects was that of keeping them as content as possible and maintaining their support so that the rulers might remain in power. Undoubtedly, those in power invariably affirmed that their subjects benefited from their rule and claimed that their rule brought peace, salvation, and well-being to their subjects. Such was the discourse of the Greeks and Romans who justified their conquests and dominion in the name of the common good. Ultimately, however, it was apparent to all that their real interest lay in satisfying their own desires for power and wealth; even when rulers served others, everyone believed that ultimately they were really serving their own interests.

For the reasons we have just seen, this was not believed to be the case with YHWH. What motivated him to command the presentation of tribute and

---

The Hebrew prophets had a simple way of dismissing this use of sacrifice: it will not work. God does not want sacrifices from dishonest people. Not only does he not want them, he despises them" (333, n5).

sacrifice was not any type of lust for wealth or power, since all things were already his. Because he had no needs, desires, or interests that had to be satisfied by human beings, he was thought to gain nothing from his rule except the satisfaction of seeing his gracious purposes for the people fulfilled. Rather than wanting something *from* his people, he wanted something *for* them; it was this that led him to prescribe sacrificial worship for the people. Sacrifice was thus regarded as a means that contributed to YHWH's objective of establishing justice and *shalom* among those who acknowledged him as Lord and sovereign. In fact, because he wanted these things not only for Israel but for all people, he was believed to desire that others come to worship him as well.[150] His desire to be worshiped by other peoples is presented as being motivated by love and concern for them rather than any type of selfish interest.

In conclusion, ancient Jewish sacrificial practices must be seen in the context of what Jews believed about their God on the basis of their Scriptures and traditions. Sacrifice was about giving oneself to this God to do his will, recognizing no other sovereign, and acknowledging that all that one was and all that one had was God's. It was considered important for people constantly to recognize and be reminded that *everything belonged to God* and thus *everything was to be used in the way that God commanded, for the good of all rather than for the interests of a few*. What Israel's God wanted was a people committed not only to loving him but loving others by doing what he commanded—most importantly, practicing justice and righteousness and seeking *shalom* for all. As those who worshiped YHWH expressed their love for him both by means of the sacrificial system and through their commitment to doing his will in relation not only to him but to others as well, they would enjoy well-being and prosperity. This well-being and prosperity would be the intrinsic consequence of their love for God and for others, yet would also result extrinsically from God's response to their commitment to doing his will. As they obeyed YHWH, suffering and injustice would no longer prevail among the people and the needy would be cared for. This was what God ultimately desired as Israel's king. The offering of sacrifice was therefore considered vital to achieving this goal, since it served to *express* and *reinforce* the total commitment of the people to serving God as their loving sovereign by doing his loving will—not for *his* sake, but for *theirs*.

Did all or even most of the Jews who participated in the sacrificial worship of YHWH in antiquity share all of the beliefs concerning YHWH just discussed and conceive of sacrifice in the way described? It is, of course, impossible to answer that question. What we *can* say with confidence, however, is that these beliefs and concepts *constantly and consistently appear throughout the ancient Hebrew and Jewish writings that we possess*. Those texts provide ample evidence that among Jews in antiquity YHWH was conceived of as being *fundamentally different* from other deities in important ways that set Judaism

---

150. See Ps. 86:9; Isa. 2:2-4; 55:5; 56:6-7; Zech. 2:11; 8:23; Josephus, *Ant.* 8.116-17; Philo, *Spec. Laws* 1.96.

apart from other belief systems and led to an understanding of sacrifice that was in many ways unique.

RECONSIDERING THE TRADITIONAL ASSUMPTIONS REGARDING SACRIFICE

On the basis of the points we have just seen regarding the meaning and purpose of sacrifice, we may now return to the seven assumptions discussed at the beginning of this chapter. To what extent are these assumptions accurate?

Like the allusions to Jesus' death in the New Testament, the passages from the Hebrew Scriptures and second-temple Jewish writings in which sacrificial practices are mentioned easily lend themselves to having a wide variety of ideas read back into them. This is due to the fact that, for the most part, they simply allude to the sacrificial rites performed without offering any explanation as to the meaning of those rites and the various rituals they involved. However, rather than reading back into those texts ideas based on speculation or assumptions for which there is no explicit evidence in the written sources we have, I would argue that we need to read these texts on the basis of the three basic ideas discussed above: to offer God a sacrifice was to offer up a gift to God; those gifts were accompanied by prayers and expressed visibly and palpably what those prayers expressed verbally; and God's acceptance of those sacrifices and prayers depended on what God saw in the hearts and lives of those who offered them up.

Assumption 1: Did sacrifices make atonement for sins?

At first glance, the fact that both the Hebrew Scriptures and the Jewish writings of the second-temple period speak of sacrifices and sacrificial blood making atonement or expiation for sin would seem to leave no alternative but to answer this question affirmatively. Most of those same texts, however, repeatedly state that there is no atonement or expiation of sins without repentance. As noted above, those participating in the rites of atonement prescribed in the Mosaic law were expected to confess their sins in sincere fashion. Yet even this was not enough. If one had harmed someone or done them an injustice, there could be no atonement unless one made proper restitution (Lev. 6:2-6). Furthermore, while repentance was necessary, it was seen as involving more than an expression of remorse for the sins one had committed. Those offering sacrifices for sins also had to commit themselves anew to doing God's will by obeying the commandments God had given. It was expected that this repentance and recommitment to obedience be manifested in concrete fashion, not only through the offering of a sacrificial victim whenever this was possible, but especially through one's actions in one's everyday life.

Curiously, these points are recognized by scholars who claim that sacrifices in themselves made atonement. Nevertheless, they generally attempt to combine that claim with the idea that repentance and obedience were necessary for atonement, thereby failing to see the contradictions involved in affirming both of these things simultaneously. Jacob Milgrom, for example, notes that in the Levitical prescriptions regarding sacrifices for sins, forgiveness "is not the automatic consequence of the priestly rite." Just as "the nonritual texts of the Bible demand repentance as the proper atonement for moral wrongdoing..., the indispensability of repentance is stipulated by the ritual texts as well.... [T]he priestly system prohibits sacrificial atonement to the unrepentant sinner, to the one who 'acts defiantly' (RSV 'with a high hand')...."[151]

As we have noted above, these points are stressed repeatedly in other second-temple Jewish writings as well. Hermann Lichtenberger identifies the same ideas in the writings of Qumran. Citing 1 QS 2:25—3:13, he notes that "he who refuses to follow God's commands as they are understood by the community obtains neither atonement nor purification. Atoning rites do not function *ex opere operato*, for they demand total submission to God's will...."[152] As Everett Ferguson notes, the rabbinical writings affirm these same ideas: "The rabbis frequently reiterated that nothing expiates without repentance. Yom Kippur atoned only for those who repented."[153] Bruce Chilton and Jacob Neusner also observe with regard to rabbinic thought: "The Day of Atonement itself does not work *ex opere operato* but only within the framework of qualifying (or at least not disqualifying) intentionality. And that fact generates another. If one rebels against God's rule and does not repent, no atonement is possible."[154]

It is common for scholars to recognize, then, that in ancient Hebrew and Jewish thought, no sacrificial offerings could atone for the sins of those who were unrepentant and refused to commit themselves to living according to God's will. Yet, precisely because repentance and a commitment to God's will were indispensable in order for those making sacrifices to receive divine forgiveness for their sins through their sacrifices, it must be affirmed that, strictly speaking, *sacrifices did not make atonement for sins*. Rather, *people made atonement for sins by expressing their repentance and their commitment to doing God's will in the future by means of sacrificial offerings*. The difference between these two affirmations is by no means insignificant, as it might initially seem. No sacrifice in and of itself could make atonement for sins. No amount of blood or offerings could purify people from their sins or obtain divine forgiveness for them. Even when the texts affirm that blood rites make atonement or

---

151. Milgrom, "Atonement in the OT," 79-81.
152. Hermann Lichtenberger, "Atonement and Sacrifice in the Qumran Community," in *Approaches to Ancient Judaism: Theory and Practice* (ed. William Scott Green; Chico, CA: Scholars Press, 1980), 2:162-63. See also Paul Garnet, *Salvation and Atonement in the Qumran Scrolls* (WUNT 2/3; Tübingen: J. C. B. Mohr, 1977), 59: "Ablutions and rituals of atonement are effective only when the attitude is right" (referring to 1QS 3:8-11).
153. Ferguson, "Spiritual Sacrifice," 1161; Ferguson lists numerous references to the rabbinic literature in support of this affirmation there.
154. Bruce Chilton and Jacob Neusner, *Classical Christianity and Rabbinic Judaism: Comparing Theologies* (Grand Rapids: Baker Academic, 2004), 199. Neusner summarizes rabbinic thought thus: "Repentance is the precondition of atonement; there is no atonement without the statement of remorse and appropriate, confirming action. If one rebels against God's rule and does not repent, no atonement is possible. But if he does repent, then the Day of Atonement effects atonement for him" (*Judaism when Christianity Began*, 156).

expiate sins, *they do not mean this in the sense that simply performing the prescribed sacrificial rites with blood makes atonement for sins.* Where there was no true repentance and no sincere commitment to doing God's will, there was no atonement or expiation, even if the rite of atonement was carried out properly down to the last detail and the person had recited a confession of sins.

In ancient Hebrew and Jewish thought, then, what actually made atonement was the repentance and commitment to God's will that was manifested in the offering of sacrifices of atonement rather than the sacrifices themselves. It was expected, however, that whenever it was feasible and possible, this repentance and commitment to God's will would be made manifest in the presenting of sacrifices of atonement in the way that God had commanded. As noted above, the logic behind this expectation was that words themselves were of little value if there was not something to back them up. It was believed that God had established those rites so that his people might express their repentance and renewed obedience in concrete ways when they had sinned and also be reminded of certain basic truths about their relationship to him and one another. It was therefore the duty and privilege of all faithful Israelites to make use of the means that God had graciously provided in order to make atonement for their sins.

Strictly speaking, therefore, it is incorrect to affirm that in ancient Jewish thought sacrificial rites made atonement for sin. Putting sacrificial animals to death or carrying out rites with their blood did not effect atonement for sins or obtain divine forgiveness. Rather, these actions formed part of a ritual that people performed in obedience and submission to God in order to make atonement for their sins. When such obedience and submission were sincerely present, God was thought to forgive their sins and accept them as pure.

For this reason, it would be inaccurate even to say that killing animals or performing blood rites atoned for sin when these actions were accompanied by repentance and submission to God's will. The killing and manipulation of blood did not have any value in itself but merely formed part of the sacrificial rite prescribed by God. It was the rite *as a whole* that served as an expression of repentance and commitment to God's will. Therefore, even when the ancient sources affirm that death or blood atone for sins, what is meant is that those who had sinned could seek and obtain divine forgiveness by carrying out with a sincere heart the atonement rites prescribed by God, including those that involved putting an animal to death and making use of its blood.

Assumption 2: Were sacrifices thought to "work" in some way to produce certain salvific "effects," such as expiation and purification?

As noted above, biblical scholars regularly claim that in ancient Judaism sacrificial rites were thought to have certain "effects" or to be "efficacious." Scholars also inquire as to how sacrifices were believed to "work" in order to take away sins. In many cases, sin is viewed in ontological terms as some type of substance capable of being transferred to an animal or object or eliminated by blood rites. According to many, sacrificial blood was a "ritual detergent" or an apotropaic agent that functioned by virtue of the life-force or substance that it was thought to contain. To claim that YHWH had bound himself to granting whatever those who offered sacrifice sought from him also involves the idea that sacrifices invariably and automatically "worked," since by virtue of his promise, YHWH was under obligation to respond favorably to any petition that accompanied a sacrifice.

Such claims raise numerous problems. The first of these has to do with the manner in which Jews in antiquity supposedly conceived of entities such as sin and purity. Did they understand sin to be some type of "malignant cancer," "poisonous organism," "toxic flow," "aerial miasma," or "dynamic and malefic power" that actually existed as a physical substance or entity, as numerous scholars have claimed? If so, should we speak in terms of "forces," "substances," or "powers," or instead use some other type of language to characterize the manner in which first-century Jews thought of sin and purity? To attribute such ideas to the Jews of antiquity inevitably involves claiming that they held mechanical and even magical views of sacrifice and believed that, by manipulating invisible and mysterious elements, forces, or substances in the sacrificial rites, they could expiate their sins.[155]

The conceptual difficulties involved in such interpretations of Jewish sacrificial practice become evident when the ideas associated with those interpretations are scrutinized closely. To demonstrate this, we may take as an example Milgrom's claim that sacrifices for sin were believed to purify the sacred places and objects to which Israel's sin had adhered. In Milgrom's words, "sin is a miasma attracted magnetic-like to the sanctuary; there it adheres and amasses until God will no longer abide in the sanctuary."[156] According to Milgrom, it was therefore necessary to remove sin from the sanctuary through the use of sacrificial blood as a ritual detergent.

To attribute such beliefs to the ancient Israelites and the Jews of antiquity raises a series of difficult questions. If one person deceived another in a financial transaction, for example, was this act believed to produce some kind of mysterious substance or force that then adhered to some person, place, or object? How and when did it end up far away in Jerusalem inside the temple sanctuary? Could it float through the air? If this impurity was believed to be washed off through the application of blood, how exactly was this thought to work? In what way did the blood neutralize or absorb the impurity? Given that the blood needed to be from an animal that was ritually pure, what happened if blood from an impure animal was used? Was there an inherent difference between the blood of a pure animal and that of an impure one so that the blood of the latter was devoid of any cleansing power or detergent

---

155. I use the word "mechanical" to refer to those views that maintained that sacrifice worked through some type of "cause-and-effect" mechanism, analogous to the way medications work in the body by means of various chemical, biological, and physical processes.

156. Milgrom, "Atonement in the OT," 79.

properties? What if the blood of a pure animal was used but for some reason the high priest who applied it was not ritually pure? Would the blood still function as a ritual detergent, or would the high priest's impurity rob the blood of its cleansing effect?

As noted above, Milgrom also claims that the scapegoat ritual described in Leviticus 16 served to eliminate sin and impurity. The scapegoat served as "the substance to which the evil is transferred and thereupon eliminated."[157] If the people's sins came to adhere to the sanctuary, how did some of those sins get from the sanctuary to the high priest in order to be transferred to the goat through his hands? And if the blood ritual performed in the Holy of holies washed away the people's sins, why was the scapegoat ritual also necessary? Were part of the people's sins transferred to the Holy of holies and another part of those sins transferred to the priest who would lay hands on the scapegoat? Or if the same sins had to be dealt with twice in different ways, why were both rites necessary?[158]

Undoubtedly, questions such as these may sound facetious and even flippant. However, they demonstrate the serious conceptual problems raised by ontological understandings of sacrifice. If ancient Jews held such beliefs, they must have had to address questions such as these. There is no clear evidence from the Hebrew Scriptures or second-temple Jewish writings that they did so, however.[159]

A second problem with ontological interpretations of sacrifice arises when qualities such as faith, repentance, and a commitment to obey God's will are said to have been necessary for the rite to "work" or have the desired "effect." Most scholars agree that the sacrificial rites were not thought to work automatically or magically, not only because of the problematic nature of such an idea, but also because the notion that there could be no atonement or expiation without repentance was firmly established in the ancient Jewish tradition. As noted above, alongside his claims that sacrificial rites were believed to eliminate the substance or "miasma" of sin, Milgrom insists that in ancient belief God's forgiveness "is not the automatic consequence of the priestly rite," since repentance was indispensable.[160]

---

157. Ibid., 80.

158. The same type of questions arise with regard to N. T. Wright's affirmations that, in Paul's thought, the "divine purpose" is "that sin be drawn onto this one place, onto Israel, so that it can be dealt with conclusively by the covenant God himself in the person, in the flesh, of Israel's Messiah...," and that "Torah was designed to draw sin onto that one place so that it could be successfully condemned right there" (*Paul and the Faithfulness of God*, Vol. 4 of *Christian Origins and the Question of God*; Minneapolis: Fortress, 2013, 1015; cf. 1017). Elsewhere Wright speaks of "the work of Torah in drawing 'sin' onto one place, in order that it might be condemned there" (1034), and affirms that "for evil finally to be eradicated from God's world it must be brought to full height, must be concentrated at one point and must be dealt with there" (1290).

159. The rabbinic writings dealt with questions similar to these when addressing the distinctions between purity and impurity and the way that these might be transmitted, yet those questions are different from the ones just raised. The latter have to do with the way in which sacrificial rites were thought to remove sin rather than the manner in which purity and impurity could be transmitted. It is important not to confuse impurity with sin in Jewish thought.

160. Milgrom, "Atonement in the OT," 79–80.

To claim that the sacrificial rites effected atonement only when those offering them were truly repentant raises the same type of difficult questions just considered. If the offender was not repentant, was the sinful entity that was generated by the offender's transgression thought to continue to adhere to him or her rather than being transported into the temple sanctuary in Jerusalem? Or if in spite of the lack of repentance the sinful entity or "miasma" came to adhere to the sacred places and objects in Jerusalem, would it be impossible to remove it from those places or objects through sacrificial blood due to the offender's failure to repent? In that case, did the blood rites effected in the sanctuary wash off only the sins for which the offerers had repented, leaving untouched those sins for which no repentance had been made? In brief, if repentance was indispensable for the sacrificial rites to produce the desired effects but the one offering the sacrifice was not sufficiently repentant, what happened when the rites were performed? Did they simply not work or work only partially? Precisely how did the lack of repentance affect the mechanics involved?

The attempt to combine mechanical views of the way sin was removed with the claim that repentance was necessary raises other problems as well. How repentant did an individual need to be for the rite to work? And who but God could determine if sufficient repentance was present by looking into the individual's heart? Milgrom claims that, "though the priest performs the rituals, it is only due to the grace of God that the ritual is efficacious."[161] But if repentance was necessary, were there not circumstances under which Israel's God might withdraw his grace so that the rite would no longer be efficacious? If so, how could one ever know whether or not the "mechanics" of the rite had really worked?

These questions become even more complicated when one considers the sacrifices for sin that were offered for the people of Israel as a whole. In the case of the Day of Atonement rites that Milgrom examines, what percentage of Israel had to be repentant in order for the rite to work and for God to continue to dwell there? Was a simple majority sufficient or was a higher percentage required? If only a portion of the people were truly repentant and committed to reforming their lives on the Day of Atonement, was *all* of the sin that adhered to the Holy of holies washed off by the blood as ritual detergent or only an amount proportional to the people that were truly repentant? Did the sins of those who were unrepentant continue to adhere to the sanctuary after the rite was performed? Similar questions can be asked of the scapegoat ritual. Did the sins of those who were not sufficiently repentant stay on the priest or his hands so that they were not transferred to the goat? If those sins were not laid on the goat, what became of them? And how profound did the people's repentance need to be in order for these rites to work?

Conversely, what if there was sufficient repentance on the part of the people but the priest did not carry out the atonement rites properly? Did the

---

161. Ibid., 81.

sinful substance or "miasma" then continue to adhere to the holy spaces so as to impede YHWH's presence there and thus prevent him from forgiving the people's sins? Or might YHWH instead overlook the fact that the rite was not carried out properly so as to continue to abide in the sanctuary, even though it remained polluted by the people's sins? If YHWH could do this, then why was the rite necessary at all? And if the efficacy of the rite depended on the people's repentance, how could the people ever know if they had been sufficiently repentant in God's eyes for the rite to be effective?

The same type of questions can be raised with regard to any of the other views considered previously that understand sacrifice in terms of the transmission, elimination, or manipulation of some type of ontological reality by means of the sacrificial rites. Once again, although such questions may sound facetious, they demonstrate the problems and contradictions involved in any attempt to combine mechanical or magical interpretations of sacrifice with the claim that repentance was necessary for the rites to "work" properly. The "efficacy" of the rite must be ascribed either to the proper performance of the rite or to the repentance of those involved, but it *cannot be ascribed to both simultaneously*. If the rites function without repentance, then obviously repentance is irrelevant. However, if the rites *do not* function without repentance, then forgiveness and atonement ultimately depend on the repentance and not on the rite. That leads to the question of whether repentance alone is sufficient to make atonement and obtain divine forgiveness. If so, then the rite becomes superfluous and unnecessary. If not, then the improper performance of the rite makes it impossible for God to forgive the people in spite of their repentance. This makes YHWH subject to the rite he has established so that he is no longer free to remit the sins of the repentant without the rite being performed properly. In effect, he must tell the people, "I am sorry, but even though you are truly repentant, I cannot forgive you your sins because the rite was not carried out correctly."

This leads to a third problem associated with ontological interpretations of Jewish sacrifice: they are based on a concept of God that is fundamentally distinct from that which we find in the Hebrew Scriptures and other ancient Jewish writings. There Israel's God is viewed as sovereign creator, subject to no other power, be it human or demonic, heavenly or earthly. He is not subject to forces of nature or the laws and rites he has established, nor does he subject himself voluntarily to such forces, laws, or rites. This means that he cannot be manipulated by rites involving sacrifices, blood, and scapegoats, and that his grace, mercy, and forgiveness cannot be obtained by magical or mechanical rituals. YHWH's presence in Israel's sanctuary was not thought to be "endangered" by the presence of some type of contagious, demonic, or destructive force that offended or threatened him there; nor did he need to be "protected" from such forces, as Levine claims.[162] Nor is there any basis in ancient Hebrew and Jewish literature for attributing to Jews in the second-temple period the

---

162. Levine, *In the Presence*, 73–78.

idea that "the strange, dangerous presence of Israel's God would dwell in their midst, first in the tabernacle and then in the Temple in Jerusalem," as N. T. Wright does.[163] Such views are not only unfounded on the basis of the evidence we possess, but also contradict the view of God that runs throughout the ancient Hebrew and Jewish writings.

In addition, throughout the Hebrew Scriptures and second-temple Jewish literature, the manner in which Israel's God is presented as relating to people is consistently said to depend on their ethical conduct. There is no evidence for the claim that Israel's God had set up some mechanical or magical way of effecting atonement or obtaining forgiveness of sins that worked by itself through some type of intrinsic "cause-and-effect" relation, independently of any consideration on his part. On the contrary, the sources speak of Israel's God as one who forgives sins and accepts people on the basis of their behavior and what he sees in their heart.

A fourth problem with ontological interpretations of sacrifice is that there is no clear evidence in the Hebrew Scriptures and second-temple Jewish writings that such interpretations existed in antiquity. We simply do not find any texts that explicitly speak of holiness and sin as contagious forces that can be transferred by means of contact between people, places, and objects. While the ancient texts describe sacrificial procedures, they do not explicitly ascribe any magical power or mechanical effects to the rites or the animals and objects involved nor suggest that the rites were understood in such a way. Undoubtedly, such ideas can be read back into the texts, which are sufficiently vague and ambiguous to lend themselves to a variety of interpretations, yet this involves mere speculation and requires that we ascribe to the Jews of antiquity problematic ideas that raise questions such as those just mentioned.

Rather than interpreting the texts in a literal, ontological sense and then attributing the conceptual problems involved in such interpretations to the ancient people who wrote and read those texts, as many scholars have done, we must question those interpretations themselves. Generally, such interpretations are based on a literal reading of the texts and take as their starting-point certain ontological conceptions that are assumed rather than demonstrated.

To be sure, there are passages from the Hebrew Scriptures that can be read as suggesting that holiness and sin were conceived of as mysterious forces or substances that acted in magical or mechanical fashion. A number of passages, for example, appear to ascribe mysterious or even magical powers to the ark of the covenant. Its presence among the Philistines causes many to become ill and die and topples the image of their god Dagon (1 Sam. 5:1-12). The Israelites who do not rejoice at the ark's return or look inside of it also die (1 Sam. 6:19-20). A close look at the text, however, reveals that in these cases it is not some type of mysterious divine force emanating from the ark that is presented as bringing these things about but the "hand of YHWH" himself (1 Sam. 5:6-7, 9, 12; 6:9, 19-20). Similarly, when Uzzah touches the

---

163. N. T. Wright, *Paul and the Faithfulness of God*, 1052.

ark improperly and is struck dead, this is said to be an act of YHWH rather than something caused by the ark itself or its contents (1 Chron. 13:9-10; cf. 15:13). In his recounting of these stories, Josephus attributes these deaths to the anger of YHWH himself and says with regard to Uzzah: "God caused his death" (*Ant.* 6.16; 7:81-82). Texts such as these, therefore, provide no basis for the claim that in antiquity God's holiness was thought to be some impersonal force that might adhere to holy spaces or objects or lead to tragic consequences for any who drew near to it improperly.

The biblical texts also speak of the consecration of Aaron and the other priests as well as objects such as the priestly vestments, the altar, the ark, and the utensils to be used in the sacrificial ceremonies (Exod. 29:1-46; 30:22-33; 40:9-15; Lev. 8:1-30; Num. 8:5-25). Those texts, however, do not provide any support for the claim that this consecration was thought to involve the infusion of some type of mysterious divine force or substance into those persons or objects, as if they acquired some quasi-magical power through the rites performed. Rather, they can be said to have been consecrated merely in the sense that they were set apart for the service of YHWH at his sanctuary. Even if those who touch consecrated objects or look at them improperly are threatened with death in the Mosaic law (Num. 4:15, 19-20), this can be understood in the sense that YHWH himself will cause them to die, rather than their death being the intrinsic consequence of their having come into contact with some mysterious or contagious power those objects possessed and transmitted.

Conversely, when holy people, places, or objects are said to become contaminated by sin in the Hebrew Scriptures, there is no reason to believe that Jews in antiquity understood this as involving some type of "toxic flow" or the transmission of a "dynamic and malefic power" or substance. While physical impurities are said to defile or contaminate YHWH's sanctuary (Lev. 15:31; Num. 19:13, 20), the same affirmation is made with regard to moral offenses, such as sacrificing human beings to Moloch (Lev. 20:2-5). There is no evidence that these moral offenses were understood as generating some type of invisible toxic substance or malefic force that entered into the sanctuary to adhere there. In fact, many of those offenses would be committed by people who were at a great distance from the sanctuary. Therefore, if the pollution of the sanctuary that resulted from moral offenses was not thought to involve any type of literal or physical contamination, there is no reason to interpret the pollution from physical impurities in that way either. Rather, the pollution of the sanctuary through both types of sin should be understood in a symbolic or metaphorical sense: any type of disobedience to God's will contaminated the sanctuary in the sense that it made the worship offered to YHWH there less pleasing in his sight.

In similar fashion, the people's sins are said to contaminate the land, especially when they worship other gods and shed blood (Lev. 18:24-30; Num. 35:33-34). There is no reason to understand this contamination literally, however, as if such deeds produced some toxic substance that then penetrated into the ground. Conversely, what purified the land from contamination was not some type of sacrificial rite that involved introducing something into the ground that would counteract or neutralize some corrosive substance that had adhered there, but the repentance of the people and their return to YHWH, together with the destruction or expulsion from the land of those who had carried out such defiling acts without repenting of them. Just as the claim that the land would "vomit up" the people was clearly to be understood metaphorically (Lev. 18:25-28; 20:22), so also the affirmation that the land was polluted by those sins was to be taken in a metaphorical sense. As the Qumran writings attest, what made atonement for the land that had become polluted by Israel's sins was not the performance of magical or mechanical sacrificial rites, but the recommitment of God's people to living in accordance with his will. The Qumranites atoned for the land by seeking to live in obedience to the law in preparation for the day when YHWH would cleanse the land from all wickedness so that only the righteous would inhabit it.[164] This cleansing was thus metaphorical and symbolic rather than literal or ontological.

This is not to deny that purity and impurity were often understood by Jews in terms of invisible forces or substances that might be transmitted through the air or by contact with people, places, and objects. When one came into contact with a corpse or human blood, for example, it was necessary that one wash or bathe oneself (see Num. 19:13, 20). However, it was not sinful to contract such impurity; at times, in fact, it was inevitable and necessary.[165] Those who became impure by burying a corpse were not committing any sin but on the contrary doing something good and right in accordance with God's will. In most cases, impurities contracted by contact with corpses and impure persons, objects, or bodily fluids were taken away, not by sacrificial rites, but merely by washing with water or by letting a certain amount of time pass in order to allow a natural process to run its course.[166] According to the laws concerning childbirth and leprosy, one had to be physically pure *before* carrying out the purification rite; if physical impurities remained, no sacrificial rite alone could remove them (Lev. 12:1-8; 14:3-8; cf. 15:25-29). The sacrificial rites that were carried out after one had been cleansed or purified would then be understood as a public declaration or recognition that one was once again in a state of purity. Such offerings may have also been understood as expressions of thanksgiving or as acts by which those persons were reconsecrated to God so that they might be reincorporated into the worshiping community.

The prescriptions prohibiting those in a state of physical impurity from entering into the temple area and participating in the sacrifices may simply

---

164. On this point, see Michael Newton, *The Concept of Purity at Qumran and in the Letters of Paul* (SNTSMS 53; Cambridge: Cambridge University Press, 1985), 48.

165. Sanders, in fact, comments: "All Jews, including Pharisees, were impure more or less all the time. Impurity was removed to enter the temple, to eat Passover, and to eat second tithe. Otherwise it was the rule" (*Comparing Judaism and Christianity*, 293).

166. See, for example, Lev. 6:27; 11:29-39; 12:1-7; 15:2-28; 22:3-7; Num. 19:11-22.

have been seen as a way of preventing those with infirmities that were possibly contagious from infecting others. This was no doubt a danger when large groups of people came together in a relatively small area. In this case, the danger was not that those who were impure might infect YHWH or the sanctuary in some way, but rather that they might infect one another. The requirement that those entering the temple precincts first bathe themselves was most likely regarded at least in part as a preventative measure, though of course it also symbolized the cleansing of one's inner being before entering into the presence of Israel's God.

There were also instances in which contact with impurity that was not exclusively physical required purification. Those who disposed of the remains of the sin-offering and released the goat for Azazel on the Day of Atonement, for example, were required to wash both their garments and themselves before being reincorporated into the community (Lev. 16:23-28). Yet there is no reason to interpret this to mean that the sins of Israel that had been dealt with through these rites were thought to have constituted some type of actual toxic substance or mysterious force that had come to rub off on those who had carried out those rites as well as the clothes they had worn. Instead, such cleansing was probably symbolic, though it may also have been regarded as necessary because those involved in the rites might have contracted some type of impurity while fulfilling their duties.

The purification of the altar, the sanctuary, and the people themselves on the Day of Atonement must also have been understood in a metaphorical and symbolic sense (Lev. 16:15-19). There is simply no textual evidence for the claim that the blood that was sprinkled or smeared on the holy places and the altar was thought to contain some mysterious life-force that washed away an impure substance that had adhered to the surfaces of those places or the altar. In fact, the people themselves were said to be purified from their sins by these rites (Lev. 16:30), even though they did not come into contact with the blood. Just as the purification of the people was not thought to be brought about by any type of physical contact with the blood, there is no reason to suppose that the blood introduced into the sanctuary or applied to the altar was thought to effect some type of literal or physical purification by contact.

If it is claimed that blood was understood as some type of "ritual detergent," this also should be understood in a symbolic rather than a literal sense. In essence, the blood was understood as something offered or returned to YHWH, to whom it belonged as the sovereign creator and Lord of life. This is explicitly stated in Ezek. 44:15, where YHWH affirms regarding the priests: "they shall stand before me to offer me the fat and the blood."[167] Philo also speaks of the sacrificial blood as a libation (*Moses* 2.150; *Spec. Laws* 1.205;

---

167. As de Vaux notes on the basis of Lev. 3:16-17, "the fat, like the blood, belongs to Yahweh" (*Studies*, 32). On this point, see also Friedhelm Hartenstein, "Zur symbolischen Bedeutung des Blutes im Alten Testament," in *Deutungen des Todes Jesu im Neuen Testament* (ed. Jörg Frey and Jens Schröter; WUNT 181; Tübingen: Mohr Siebeck, 2005), 119-37. Hartenstein concludes his analysis of the sacrificial rites involved with the affirmation: "Wenn das Blut Sitz des Lebens ist bzw. mit der Lebenskraft identifiziert wird, könnte

4.125). This indicates that the way in which blood was thought to purify was not by reason of its physical contact with impure substances in the sanctuary but by being offered to YHWH. What was believed to remove Israel's sin and make atonement was not the blood itself, but the offering and consecration of the lives of those who presented it before YHWH, which was symbolized and expressed in concrete ways through the blood rites.

The words of Lev. 17:11 should be understood on the basis of these same ideas: "For the life (*nephesh*) of the flesh is in the blood, and I have given it to you on the altar to make atonement for your souls; for it is the blood by reason of the life (*nephesh*) that makes atonement." This passage does not affirm that blood contains some mysterious life-force or substance that enables it to effect atonement in some natural, mechanical, or magical way. Rather, it conveys the idea that the blood of living beings is special and constitutes the essence of life. For this reason, human beings are to regard blood as sacred and respect it as something of supreme value. Because it is the essence of life, the blood belongs to YHWH alone as the creator and giver of life and must be used only as he commands. The presentation of sacrificial blood to YHWH may have been understood not only as giving back to YHWH what belonged to him, but also as symbolizing one's acknowledgment of his sovereignty over all life. To present the blood to YHWH was to offer to him what was most precious, sacred, and costly. What made atonement, therefore, was not the blood itself but what it expressed symbolically, namely, one's submission to YHWH as Lord of all, one's acknowledgment that all life belonged to God, and one's commitment to offering up to him continually one's own life and possessions in order to serve him in all that one did.

The affirmation that YHWH had given his people the blood to make atonement with it on the altar appears in the context of the prohibition against the consumption of blood (Lev. 17:10-14). The idea behind this passage is simply that YHWH allowed human beings to use blood only in order to carry out the atonement rites prescribed in the law. Any blood shed that was not to be used in those rites was to be poured out on the ground. In addition, any use of blood for any other purpose outside of the sacrificial rites was strictly prohibited. This commandment served to emphasize YHWH's absolute sovereignty over all life. There is therefore no reason to interpret Lev. 17:11 in the sense that sacrificial blood made atonement because it contained some inherent mysterious power to expiate and cleanse. Instead, this verse merely communicates the idea that YHWH had prescribed the use of blood in the sacrificial rites through which the people were to approach him to ask him to forgive them and declare them pure in his sight.

All of this is certainly not to deny that many Jews in antiquity believed that mysterious and demonic forces and powers existed or that some even practiced magic. On the contrary, there is evidence that the Essenes practiced various

---

mit seiner Ausschüttung an den Fuß des Altars und mit der Applikation an Altar und Heiligtum die *Rückgabe des Lebens an seinen Geber verbunden sein*" (136).

types of rites that can be understood as magical in character. The Qumran writings also contain some allusions to magical practices.[168] Although there is no evidence that the Essenes and Qumranites understood the sacrificial rites ordered in the Mosaic law to involve magical procedures and nothing in other second-Jewish temple literature to support such a claim, this possibility cannot be dismissed out of hand.

It is one thing, however, to believe in the existence of mysterious powers, forces, and substances that can be controlled through magic and another to believe that one's relation with God depends on dealing with such powers, forces, and substances through sacrificial means. If there were some Jews who thought that one could find favor with God and obtain God's forgiveness and blessings through the practice of magic or simply by carrying out rites that functioned mechanically and automatically, such beliefs could not claim to be grounded in Israel's Scriptures or whatever other sources of authority were commonly accepted.[169] Even today, we believe in invisible forces that are mysterious to most of us, such as bacteria and viruses. Yet that does not mean that we conceive of our relation with God as depending in any way on the manipulation of such forces through some type of ritual. If anything, we may believe that God can mysteriously make use of such forces or deliver us from them without maintaining that such forces can have some effect on God or can be harnessed in order to obtain God's favor, acceptance, and blessings. In the same way, even if Jews in antiquity believed that invisible forces or substances existed, there is no clear evidence in the writings available to us that they thought they could manipulate such forces through the sacrificial rites God had prescribed in order to obtain divine blessings or avert divine punishment.

Rather than assuming that ancient Jews thought sacrifices "worked" in some way to effect atonement, therefore, and then reading that assumption back into the ancient texts, we should interpret the silence of the texts on the question of how sacrifices "worked" as indicating that the rites were not believed to effect atonement through any type of cause-and-effect mechanism or through the manipulation of mysterious invisible forces and substances. Not only is there no clear and convincing evidence to support the claim that Jews understood sacrifices to effect atonement and forgiveness in ways such as these, but the evidence we do have speaks against the existence of such beliefs.

Whether or not each of the many sacrificial rites and rituals outlined in the Mosaic law was thought originally to have a clear purpose and meaning, by the first century CE many Jews themselves felt forced to acknowledge that the logic behind each of those rites and rituals was not entirely clear.

---

168. On this point, see Hartmut Stegemann, *The Library of Qumran: On the Essenes, Qumran, John the Baptist, and Jesus* (Grand Rapids: Eerdmans, 1998), 237; Florentino García Martínez, *Qumranica Minora II: Thematic Studies on the Dead Sea Scrolls* (ed. Eibert J. C. Tigchelaar; STDJ 64; Leiden: Brill, 2007), 109-30. On the subject of magic in popular Greco-Roman belief, see Hans-Josef Klauck, *The Religious Context of Early Christianity: A Guide to Greco-Roman Religions* (Minneapolis: Fortress, 2003), 209-31.

169. In fact, Deut. 18:9-11 explicitly prohibits the practice of certain forms of magic.

The rabbis themselves admitted their ignorance with regard to the meaning of many of the sacrificial rites and ultimately could only conclude that those rites should be performed as Israel's God had commanded them simply out of obedience, as an expression of submission to his will.[170] This view of sacrifice may have already been common among many Jews in Jesus' time.

This does not mean, of course, that ancient Jews found no purpose or meaning to the sacrificial rites and rituals and simply performed them out of blind obedience to YHWH's command. On the contrary, in their minds, if YHWH had given the law not for his own sake but for the sake of the people, then he must have had some didactic or constructive purpose in prescribing each of the various sacrificial rites and rituals contained in that law. When Jews in antiquity did reflect on the meaning of those rites and rituals, rather than asking how those rites and rituals "worked" or what "mechanics" were involved, as modern scholars have done, the evidence we have suggests that their questions had to do instead with the deeper, symbolic truths conveyed by each of these rites. This would have been similar to the way in which Philo, Josephus, and the author of the *Letter to Aristeas* sought to interpret the spiritual significance of the purity laws, the high priest's vestments, and the imagery on the temple curtain. In this case, God's purpose in prescribing each of the various acts and rites to be carried out when offering sacrifices would be understood in terms of conveying some symbolic meaning, reinforcing some truth to the people for their benefit, or fomenting purity of heart. God had prescribed each action or rite in order to remind them of some aspect of their relation to God, to one another, and to the world around them.[171]

While there is no way of knowing what explanations were given for all of the sacrificial rites performed, the general purpose of making offerings for sin must have been quite clear. The offerings for sin reminded those who presented them that they had acted in ways contrary to God's will and needed to repent and change their ways. They also served as a means for them to express in concrete, palpable ways their repentance and their commitment to change their ways. In the case of individuals, an important factor was the *cost* involved in offering a sacrifice for sin; the fact that they were willing to pay that cost served as an expression of the sincerity of their repentance. Other aspects of the sacrifices for sin reflected the same ideas. No part of the sacrificial offering was returned to the offerer, in contrast to other sacrifices. This meant that

---

170. See E. P. Sanders, *Paul and Palestinian Judaism: A Comparison of Patterns of Religion* (Philadelphia: Fortress, 1977), 120.

171. Sanders stresses that, although ancient Jewish sacrificial thought ascribes great importance to purity of heart, Jews in antiquity were also reminded not to disdain the external rites commanded in the Mosaic law: "ritual actions, such as purification and sacrifice, may promote spirituality. All kinds of external acts may influence our hearts or souls.... [I]nternal and external commandments go together, since God cares about all of life.... [E]xternal practice encourages internal reflection and may even produce the right feelings...." (*Comparing Judaism and Christianity*, 373-76). Patterson also notes, "The prophetic discussion of behavior incongruent with sacrifice (e.g., Mic 6:6-8; Ps 50) became the foundation for metaphorical reinterpretation of sacrifice in the Hellenistic period by various Jewish writers who did not see themselves as mitigating the importance of the cult" (*Keeping the Feast*, 4).

there would be no self-interest behind the sacrifice, since the offerer would obtain no material benefit through the sacrifice. The sprinkling of sacrificial blood may have symbolized the reconsecration to YHWH of the life of those who offered the sacrifice. If the disposal of the blood poured out at the base of the altar represented the return of the life of the sacrificial victim to YHWH, this may have reminded the worshipers that their own life, like that of the sacrificial victim, belonged to YHWH as sovereign and therefore must be presented to him. It may also have underscored the gravity of sin, symbolizing the way in which one's disobedience to God's commandments had as its consequence the destruction and loss of life.

The Day of Atonement rites were undoubtedly seen as symbolizing similar ideas. The purification of the sanctuary and sacred objects with sacrificial blood could be understood in terms similar to those mentioned in Isa. 1:18: "though your sins are like scarlet, they shall be like snow; though they are red like crimson, they shall become like wool." This is the language of simile and is clearly not intended to be taken in a literal sense. The ritual with the goat for Azazel could be understood as symbolizing the same idea stated in Ps. 103:12: "as far as the east is from the west, so far [YHWH] removes our transgressions from us." This passage is undoubtedly metaphorical. Obviously, sins are neither red nor white and transgressions are not physical entities that can be picked up and removed to another location. In the same way, the language of Leviticus 16 regarding the purification of the sanctuary, the altar, and the people, and the placing of their sins on the goat for Azazel could be understood as metaphors that were *visual* rather than *verbal*. Through these rites certain ideas were acted out in ways that symbolized divine forgiveness and God's renewed acceptance of the people.

At the same time, however, to apply the words *metaphorical* and *symbolic* to the sacrificial rites is not to limit the deeper significance that the performance of these rites possessed. There was undoubtedly a *power* to these rites. The concrete actions with sacrificial blood and the scapegoat enabled those who participated in them to experience God's forgiveness and their purification as *real*, as something *tangible* and *concrete*, rather than simply constituting an abstract idea: God *really did* forgive their sins and *really did* purify them when they carried out these rites with the proper disposition. This does not mean that something mechanical or magical was "effected." Rather, it is similar to one purifying one's soul, renouncing one's past, ridding oneself of feelings of guilt, and seeking to feel pure on the inside so as in essence to make a new beginning. Many people today, both Christian and non-Christian, perform certain rites that involve physical activities and objects primarily because of the power such rites may possess and the strong impact they may have on those participating in them. The same was true in antiquity. Milgrom, for example, notes how the presentation of a sacrifice for sin could be "therapeutic," allowing one who had sinned to express concretely his or her remorse and sense of guilt by means of ritual actions.[172] At the same time, the rites would serve as visible signs of God's forgiveness and give the participants assurance of that forgiveness due to the promises that God had attached to the rite, as long as it was performed with a sincere heart. Similarly, when those desiring to be purified in their inner being took a ritual bath, that bath would not merely symbolize metaphorically what was taking place in their heart and mind but would enable them to *express* and *experience* in a concrete, tangible, and deeply meaningful way the spiritual purification of their soul.

If one insists on speaking of the sacrificial rites "functioning" or "working" in some sense, it should be understood in this manner: those rites afforded spiritual experiences that went beyond anything that mere words or thoughts could convey. For this reason, although these concrete, physical actions were symbolical, they communicated in profound and powerful ways things such as the people's experience of God's presence in their lives and world, God's forgiveness of their sins, the purification of their hearts from sin, and their commitment to offering God their hearts and lives. If it was asked why God had instituted these rites, the answer would have been that God had done so for *the sake of the people's well-being*: God had intended that those performing them might be able to feel at peace with themselves, with God, and with one another, and experience a sense of renewed wholeness in both soul and body.

While we cannot be certain that the sacrificial rites and rituals carried out at the Jerusalem temple were understood in these ways, we must nevertheless conclude that there is no basis in the Hebrew Scriptures and the other ancient Jewish writings we possess for the claim that those rites and rituals were believed to effect atonement by mechanical or magical means. People did not obtain divine forgiveness and expiate their sins by carrying out rites that mysteriously made sin and impurity disappear or transmitted holiness by contact, but by expressing their repentance and recommitment to God's will through the rites God had graciously prescribed for them. For ancient Jews, sacrifice was not about the manipulation of invisible substances or powers, but a means of expressing symbolically and in concrete, visible, and palpable ways the various aspects of the people's relationship with their God YHWH.

Assumption 3: Did sacrifice involve propitiation?

The idea of propitiating God's wrath appears frequently throughout both the Hebrew Scriptures and the second-temple Jewish literature. At times, but not always, this is said to be accomplished by means of sacrificial offerings.

The notion that it was necessary to propitiate the wrath of the gods through sacrificial offerings was extremely common in antiquity and in fact can be found in almost all ancient cultures. Like people from other nations, Jews interpreted events such as natural disasters, illnesses, death, defeat at the hands of enemies, exile, and other forms of suffering as expressions of divine

---

172. Milgrom, *Leviticus 1-16*, 339-45, 378.

wrath. In the face of such events, it was necessary to do something in order to placate the anger of God or the gods.

Nevertheless, as I have argued above, there was a fundamental difference between YHWH the God of Israel and the gods of the nations. In the Hebrew Scriptures and other ancient Jewish literature, the wrath of Israel's God is consistently said to be provoked primarily by two things: injustice and idolatry. As we saw in Chapter 2, this wrath was believed to arise out of his concern for the well-being of his people and his commitment to justice and *shalom* for all. YHWH refused to tolerate sin and oppression and took action against those who harmed others and destroyed their lives, not for *his own* sake, but for the sake of *the people*, especially those in greatest need.

In contrast, as noted above, Jews in antiquity generally saw the gods of other nations as being *fundamentally distinct* in nature from YHWH. Whereas the ultimate concern of YHWH was the well-being of his people, the other gods were primarily concerned about having their own needs and desires satisfied. What provoked these other gods to anger, therefore, was the failure of human beings to offer them what they needed or desired. Conversely, the only way to appease the anger of these other gods was to give them what they demanded or else give them assurance that in the future they would receive what they demanded. Sacrifice was one of the primary means of doing this.

The strong rejection of the worship of other gods that we find throughout the Hebrew Scriptures and other ancient Jewish writings must be understood on the basis of this difference between YHWH and the gods of the nations. Josephus, for example, criticizes the Greeks for worshiping gods that quarrel among themselves and are "subject to all sorts of passions" (*Ag. Ap.* 2.36). According to Josephus, while those who worshiped those gods believed them to be capable of giving good things and averting evil, the worshipers needed to offer those gods sacrifices as payment in exchange for their favors: "They also endeavor to move them, as they would the vilest of men, by gifts and presents, as looking for nothing else than to receive some great mischief from them, unless they pay them such wages" (*Ag. Ap.* 2.35). Such gods would therefore bless, protect, and save those who satisfied their selfish desires and passions. The logic was that of *do ut des*. Furthermore, as noted above, for the most part gods such as the Baals and Moloch or Bacchus and Venus were not believed to make ethical demands on those who served them or to command that their worshipers love one another and practice justice, caring for the poor and needy, as YHWH did. Rather, those gods wanted sacrificial offerings for their own sake.

For this reason, throughout the ancient Jewish literature, idolatry is seen as inseparable from injustice and oppression. In the Hebrew Scriptures, idolatry is consistently associated with sacred prostitution (Exod. 34:15-17), the sacrifice of one's children and the shedding of innocent blood (Lev. 18:21; Ps. 106:36-38; Jer. 19:4-5; 32:35; Ezek. 20:31; 23:37-39), and the practice of many other types of evil and injustice that destroyed people's lives (Deut. 20:18;

32:15-17; 1 Kgs.21:25-26; 2 Kgs.21:6-9; 2 Chron. 33:4-6, 9; Isa. 57:1-10). The worship of other gods is considered to lead inevitably to a disregard for the good law given by Israel's God to ensure justice and equity (1 Kgs.18:18; 2 Kgs.17:9-17, 29-41; Jer. 9:13-15; 16:11-12; 22:9; 44:8-10, 22-23; Ezek. 20:24-26). In the book of Isaiah, those who serve idols are accused of writing oppressive statutes of their own instead of following the statutes of YHWH (Isa. 10:1-2). The worship of idols is said to promote things such as stealing, murder, adultery, and false oaths, as well as a lack of compassion for those in need (Jer. 7:9-10; Ezek. 18:6-17; 22:3-12; 33:25-26).

This is the logic behind the affirmation in the Hebrew Scriptures that YHWH is a "jealous God" who prohibits his people from worshiping other gods: the problem is not merely the worship of idols in itself, but *the unjust and oppressive conduct to which such worship leads*. This includes not only the practice of injustice but also the abandonment of the vision of justice, equity, and *shalom* associated with the worship of YHWH and with the law he had given. Israel's God was therefore thought to be jealous and prohibit idolatry, not *for his own sake, but for the sake of the people themselves*. To serve other gods undermined and destroyed their well-being rather than contributing to it.

The same kinds of criticism of idolatry as leading to injustice and evil are common in Jewish writings of the second-temple period. Worship of other gods is said to lead people to abandon the law, commit unspeakable evils, practice fornication, forget mercy and truth, and even put their own children to death.[173] The most explicit passage in this regard is found in the book known as the Wisdom of Solomon, written in the first or second century BCE:

> And this became a hidden trap for humankind, because people, in bondage to misfortune or to royal authority, bestowed on objects of stone or wood the name that ought not to be shared. Then it was not enough for them to err about the knowledge of God, but though living in great strife due to ignorance, they call such great evils peace. For whether they kill children in their initiations, or celebrate secret mysteries, or hold frenzied revels with strange customs, they no longer keep either their lives or their marriages pure, but they either treacherously kill one another, or grieve one another by adultery, and all is a raging riot of blood and murder, theft and deceit, corruption, faithlessness, tumult, perjury, confusion over what is good, forgetfulness of favors, defiling of souls, sexual perversion, disorder in marriages, adultery, and debauchery. For the worship of idols not to be named is the beginning and cause and end of every evil. For their worshipers either rave in exultation, or prophesy lies, or live unrighteously, or readily commit perjury; for because they trust in lifeless idols they swear wicked oaths and expect to suffer no harm. But just penalties will overtake them on two counts: because they thought wrongly about God in devoting themselves to idols, and because in deceit they swore unrighteously through contempt for holiness. For it is not the power of the things by which people swear, but the just penalty for those who sin, that always pursues the transgression of the unrighteous (Wis. 14:21-31; cf. 12:5-6; 14:1-20).

---

173. See, for example, *Jub.* 1:8; 11:3; *T. of Reu.* 1:4; *Pss. Sol.* 17:16; Josephus, *Ant.* 5.107-8; Philo, *Spec. Laws* 1.312; Tob. 14:6-7.

Passages such as these make it clear that the idea of propitiation was understood very differently among Jews than it was among most of those who worshiped other deities. While the anger of other gods could be appeased by offering them gifts and the blood or flesh of sacrificial victims, this was not true in the case of Israel's God. Because what angered YHWH was the sin and injustice that impeded and destroyed the well-being of the people, his wrath was regarded as an expression of his love.

For this reason, in ancient Jewish thought, there was only one way in which those who had provoked YHWH's wrath by practicing sin and injustice could propitiate that wrath: by repenting and changing their ways so as to strive to live once more according to his good commandments. This means that *it was not the offering of sacrificial victims in itself that put away God's wrath*, but the return of the people to him in trust, obedience, and a renewed commitment to doing his will. The sacrificial offerings only served as means by which people might express in concrete, palpable ways their repentance and recommitment to YHWH. It was therefore not the death of sacrificial victims or sacrificial blood in itself that was thought to appease the wrath of YHWH, but the proper disposition in those who presented him with offerings. As the prophetic books and other ancient Jewish writings stress, what Israel's God wanted from his people was not the flesh and blood of animals, but justice, righteousness, love, and compassion for those in need.[174]

Throughout the Hebrew Scriptures, therefore, it is repentance, obedience, and prayers of confession that are repeatedly said to take away the wrath of YHWH.[175] Only a few passages speak of YHWH being propitiated through sacrifice, yet even in these passages prayer is usually mentioned together with the sacrifice.[176] The idea of propitiation is virtually absent from the texts prescribing sacrificial worship in the Mosaic law. The same observations hold true with regard to the Jewish writings of the second-temple period. Both Josephus and Philo, for example, generally speak of God's wrath being appeased through repentance and prayers (Josephus, *Ant.* 1.209-10; 6.143; 7.327-29; Philo, *Abraham* 6; *Dreams* 2.292; *Moses* 1.105; 2.166, 201). Even when they mention sacrifice as a means by which God is propitiated, it is tied to the offering of prayers of repentance either explicitly or implicitly

---

174. With regard to sacrifice among non-Jewish people in antiquity, E. P. Sanders observes: "Ancient religion was, basically, the way societies organized the slaughter of quadrupeds and the distribution of red meat, and all societies had rules about the rituals that accompanied slaughter, butchery, and distribution. And so Judaism included this as well. But the Jews were also different: they thought that their God cared as much about treatment of aliens and the poor as about correct behavior in the temple. This was either rare or unique in the ancient world" (*Comparing Judaism and Christianity*, 369).

175. See, for example, Exod. 32:9-14, 30-34; Num. 11:1-2; Deut. 9:8-21; 13:17-18; 1 Kgs. 8:46-52; 2 Chron. 6:36-39; 12:12; 30:8-9; 32:24-26; Ps. 7:11-12; Jonah 3:8-10; cf. Sir. 48:10; Bar. 2:7-14; 4 Macc. 4:11; *Sib. Or.* 4.210-20). The execution of sinners can also be said to appease God's wrath in some of these writings, yet this is because it does away with disobedience before it spreads further and serves to restore the rest of the people to obedience (Num. 25:6-13; Josh. 7:10-26).

176. Both 2 Sam. 24:1-25 and Job 42:7-9 mention prayer together with sacrifice appeasing YHWH's wrath. The only passage in the Hebrew Scriptures in which sacrifice alone is said to appease YHWH's wrath is Num. 16:41-48, yet even here prayer is implied.

(Josephus, *Ant.* 1.58; 5.256; 7.331-33; 11.143-44; 13.230; Philo, *Moses* 2.147; *Names* 235-36; *Dreams* 2.299; *Spec. Laws* 1.97, 242). The fact that for Josephus it is the prayers of which sacrifices are an expression that propitiate God rather than those sacrifices themselves is evident from the words he attributes to Solomon in the prayer Solomon offered to God at the temple's dedication: "For with what else is it more appropriate for us to propitiate you when you are angry and displeased, and to render you well-disposed, than by the voice that we have from the air and that we know ascends through this [element] again?" (*Ant.* 8.112).

Scholars have often debated over the question of whether all the different kinds of sacrifice made atonement or expiation, including holocausts and communion-offerings, or only those that were specifically designated as being for sin (the *hattat* and *asham*, Leviticus 5–6).[177] However, as mentioned briefly above, once it is recognized that sacrifices were in essence forms of prayer and that all people were regarded as sinful in some sense—as is evident from the fact that all Israelites were expected to participate in the Day of Atonement rites—then any attempt to approach Israel's God in worship had to include an implicit petition for him to overlook the sinfulness of those drawing near to him in order to accept and heed their prayer favorably.

All of this means that there is no literary evidence to support the claim that Jews in antiquity believed that sacrifices appeased the wrath of YHWH. What made propitiation was not the offering of sacrifices in itself but the repentance and recommitment to YHWH's will that the offerings expressed and symbolized. For reasons we have seen in the previous section, the idea that sacrifice was thought to take away YHWH's wrath by mechanically removing or eliminating some sinful substance or force that had aroused that wrath must also be rejected.[178] What provoked YHWH to wrath was not the existence of some impure substance in the sanctuary or on the altar that had been generated by the people's sins, but the acts of disobedience to his will that destroyed the lives and well-being of the people he loved. For this reason, the only thing that could appease YHWH's wrath was that the disobedience come to an end and that his people commit themselves once more to obeying him for their own good.

Assumption 4: Was the remission of sins possible without sacrifice?

It should hardly be necessary to argue against the notion that, in ancient Hebrew and Jewish thought, it was impossible for sins to be taken away without sacrificial offerings. Yet, as noted above, biblical scholars continue to make this claim. Often Heb. 9:22 is cited as a proof text for this idea: "according to

---

177. On this point, see Jean Laporte, "Sacrifice and Forgiveness in Philo of Alexandria," *SPhA* 1 (1989): 41.
178. Particularly problematic in this regard is the claim of Levine that "Yahweh demanded that the forces of impurity, unleashed by the offenses committed, be kept away from his immediate environment. There is a reason for Yahweh's wrath. It was not mere displeasure at being disobeyed. His wrath was a reaction based on a vital concern, as it were for his own protection. The sacrificial blood is offered to the demonic forces who accept it in lieu of God's 'life', so to speak...." (*In the Presence*, 78).

the law, almost all things are purified with blood, and without the shedding of blood there is no forgiveness." The same principle is supposedly affirmed in the Talmud in *Yoma* 5a: "there is no expiation without the [shedding of] blood."[179] These words are commonly understood in a forensic sense as affirming that, due to God's strict justice and perfect holiness, sacrificial blood or death is necessary for God to forgive sins, since it would be a perversion of justice for God to forgive freely without punishing sin by death. This argument is therefore grounded in a certain understanding of God's *nature*. Scholars who defend ontological conceptions of sacrifice at times also argue for the necessity of sacrifice in order to deal with sin.

Both the biblical texts and ancient Jewish literature repeatedly mention instances of sin being forgiven or taken away by God independently of the offering of sacrifice.[180] As we have seen previously, intercession, repentance, and a renewed commitment to obedience are often said to be sufficient to obtain divine forgiveness and put away YHWH's wrath. Even when atonement was made through sacrificial offerings, these did not necessarily have to involve the death of an animal victim or the shedding of blood. According to the Mosaic law, a sacrifice of flour could atone for sins, as could incense and other types of gifts, including the offering of jewelry (Lev. 5:11-13; Num. 31:50). In passages already cited above, both Philo and Josephus also affirm explicitly that, as long as one is devoted to God and strives to obey him, sacrifice is not absolutely necessary (Philo, *Moses* 2.107-8; Josephus, *Ant.* 6.149). Because what really atoned for sins was not sacrifice itself but the repentance and commitment to God's will that sacrifice embodied and symbolized, bloody sacrifice was not indispensable. It was, however, a means designated in the Mosaic law for seeking YHWH's forgiveness, and thus it was expected that, when one had the opportunity to present such a sacrifice, one would do so in obedience to YHWH. If it was preferable to participate in sacrificial rites when seeking forgiveness, this was because those rites would enable one to express one's repentance and experience God's forgiveness in concrete ways.

The claim that YHWH could not forgive sins without the blood or death of a sacrificial animal also runs contrary to the view of YHWH that we find throughout the Hebrew Scriptures and ancient Jewish literature. There YHWH is sovereign and free to do whatever he pleases, including forgiving sins under any circumstances. His holy nature does not demand absolute perfection from human beings, nor is it subject to any laws he has established. Discussions regarding God's nature are rare in ancient Judaism. The only

---

179. See Vermès, *Scripture*, 205.

180. Gane, for example, notes that in the Hebrew Scriptures, "YHWH was able to forgive people apart from the sanctuary cult before it began to function (e.g. Exod 34:6, 7) and while it was in operation (e.g., 2 Sam 12:13; 2 Chr 33:12-13; cf. 30:18-19)" (*Cult*, 316). For other examples in the Hebrew Scriptures and second-temple Jewish literature in which God is said to forgive sins without exacting punishment or people are said to make atonement without offering sacrifice, see Num. 11:1-2; 2 Chron. 32:24-26; Prov. 16:6; Isa. 27:9; Dan. 4:27; Jonah 3:8-10; Sir. 3:3; 35:1-10; 48:10; Tob. 12:9; Bar. 2:7-14; *Pss. Sol.* 3:9; *Sib. Or.* 4.215; 1QS 3:7-10; 9:4-6.

ancient Jewish writings that touch on that subject in any detail are those of Philo. While Philo does speak of God's nature as perfect, never does he imply that this poses any hindrance to God to forgive sins freely. Rather, what Philo means when he refers to God's perfection is that God is not subject to suffering or change (*Abraham* 202; *Cherubim* 86). God is also "perfect" in the sense that he is not the cause of evil (*Confusion* 161, 180-82). Curiously, in fact, Philo even argues that God himself *never* punishes human beings because to punish is *contrary* to God's nature, since God does only what is good; God consigns the task of punishment to those who are inferior to him (*Confusion* 180; *Flight* 65-66; *Providence* 2.52-53; cf. *Planting* 85-92; *Providence* 2.2-6). Philo also claims that God is incapable of anger (*QG* 1.93-95; *Unchangeable* 51-52). There is thus no basis in Philo or elsewhere in ancient Hebrew and Jewish writings for the claim that YHWH's justice requires him to punish sin without sacrifices being presented to him.[181]

Such an idea is foreign to ancient Hebrew and Jewish thought also for the reason that sacrifice was not considered a form of executing justice on sinners or inflicting punishment on animal victims as their substitutes. As noted previously, the sacrificial prescriptions did not constitute a penal code, though at times they required restitution with payments in order to right certain wrongs committed. Contrary to what many scholars have claimed, Israel's God was not thought to have ordained sacrifice because his perfect righteousness demanded that all sins be punished by death. Rather, atoning sacrifices were means by which those who recognized their sin might draw near to YHWH again and seek his forgiveness. In fact, when the sacrificial animals were slaughtered, steps had to be taken to ensure that they suffered as little as possible.[182] The idea was therefore not to make the animals suffer what the sinners for whom they were being offered deserved on account of their sins.

The rabbinic discussions regarding the use of blood in sacrificial worship also provide no basis for the claim that it was impossible for Israel's God to forgive sins without sacrifices. The passage cited from *Yoma* 5a in the Talmud occurs in the context of a discussion regarding the proper execution of the sacrificial rites and the parts of the rites that were indispensable. Viewed in this context, the meaning of the phrase, "there is no expiation without the [shedding of] blood" is not that it is impossible for God to forgive sins without blood being shed, but that the use of blood in the expiatory rites prescribed in the law is mandatory and constitutes a necessary component of the rite in order for it to be properly carried out. Even the rabbis, of course, recognized

---

181. On the subject of arguments from necessity in ancient thought, including especially that of Philo, see James W. Thompson, "The Appropriate, the Necessary, and the Impossible: Faith and Reason in Hebrews," in *The Early Church in Context: Essays in Honor of Everett Ferguson* (ed. Abraham J. Malherbe, Frederick W. Norris, and James W. Thompson; NovTSup 90; Leiden: Brill, 1998), 306-14. Thompson notes that Philo in particular considered all forms of punishment inappropriate for God and repeatedly insisted that God is in need of nothing (310, 312).

182. On the swift, painless way in which sacrificial animals were put to death at the Jerusalem temple, see E. P. Sanders, *Judaism: Practice and Belief, 63 BCE–66 CE* (Philadelphia: Trinity Press International, 1992), 107.

that God could forgive sins freely without sacrificial offerings or blood and posited other means for making atonement in addition to sacrifice.[183]

On the basis of all of this, it is clear that sacrificial death or blood was not believed to be necessary for God to forgive sins. There was nothing in the nature of Israel's God that prevented him from forgiving freely, without receiving sacrificial offerings for sin. Certainly, God was believed to be perfectly just and committed to justice. Yet this justice was not satisfied by punishment itself, but by correcting people who had sinned and bringing them into conformity with his will, as well as taking measures against all those who insisted on practicing injustice and persistently oppressed others, in spite of his repeated calls for them to put aside their sinful behavior.

Assumption 5: Was sacrifice understood as substitution?

Both the lack of evidence for the claim that in ancient Hebrew and Jewish thought sacrifice was understood in terms of substitution and the evidence *against* that claim are so overwhelming that it is surprising that biblical scholars can continue to argue that the notion of substitution was not only present in ancient Hebrew and Jewish sacrificial thought but central to it.[184] The notion of substitution can be found in the Hebrew Scriptures and ancient Jewish writings only by reading it back into those writings.

In the prescriptions regarding sacrifice in the Pentateuch, no one who had committed an offense deserving of the death penalty could avert that penalty by offering a sacrificial animal in his or her place. In fact, the law states explicitly that the innocent are not to be put to death in the place of the guilty.[185] Any type of judicial substitutionary death was therefore simply unknown in the history of ancient Israel and Judaism. The sins for which sacrifices *were* offered were those of less gravity, rather than those intentional transgressions committed with a "high hand," for which no atonement could be made.[186] The fact that those who did not offer the prescribed sacrifices for their sins were not threatened with death but at most were excluded from the community also demonstrates clearly that offering a sacrifice and suffering a death penalty were not mutual alternatives. As already stressed above, sacrifice was not thought to revolve primarily around the killing of animals. When killing was done, it was not an end in itself but served other purposes, such as burning all or part of the victim as an offering to God, consuming its flesh, and making use of its remains in other ways. Atonement could also be made

---

183. See Ferguson, "Spiritual Sacrifice," 1161-62. Cf. Jacob Neusner, *Torah: From Scroll to Symbol in Formative Judaism* (Philadelphia: Fortress, 1985), 87. As we shall see further on, this is the idea behind Heb. 9:22 as well.

184. It is particularly surprising to see a scholar such as E. P. Sanders supporting "the ancient belief in the efficacy of substituting one death for another. Ordinarily, an animal substituted for a human, as in the story of the binding of Isaac (Gen. 22). In the sacrificial laws of Leviticus, the sacrifice of an animal atones for human wrongdoing, thus sparing the human divine punishment (e.g., Lev. 6:1-7)" (*Paul: The Apostle's Life, Letters, and Thought*; Minneapolis: Fortress, 2015, 527).

185. Deut. 24:16; see also 2 Kgs. 14:6; 2 Chron. 25:4; Ezek. 18:19-20.

186. Num. 15:28-31.

by presenting grain offerings, incense, and libations in which no killing was involved. Conversely, many of the sacrifices that *did* involve killing animals were *not* for sins, such as the communion sacrifices. All of this demonstrates convincingly that the ancient Hebrews and Jews did not believe that atonement was made by inflicting the penalty of death on animals that died as substitutes for those who had sinned.

Proponents of the idea that sacrifice involved penal substitution have generally pointed to several sacrificial rituals in particular in support of their claims. Among the most important of these is the practice of laying hands on the animal to be sacrificed. This has been understood in terms of transferring one's sin or guilt to an animal so that it might then be put to death in one's place or else in terms of designating the animal as one's substitute. Gordon Wenham, for example, writes: "The laying on of hands may indicate that the animal is taking the place of the worshipper.... One may regard the animal either as dying in the worshipper's place as his substitute, or as receiving the death penalty because of the sin transferred to it by the laying on of hands."[187]

The only passage that speaks of putting sins on an animal is Lev. 16:21, which describes the rite to be carried out with the goat for Azazel on the Day of Atonement. This is the only rite mentioned in the prescriptions regarding sacrifice in which *two* hands rather than one are placed on the animal's head, which suggests that the meaning of the laying-on of hands here is distinct from that of other rites. In reality, this rite did not involve any type of sacrifice, since the goat was not put to death or placed on an altar but merely led out to the desert and left there. The central idea was therefore that of sending the goat far away rather than killing it. Furthermore, as I have argued above, the rite with the goat for Azazel was not seen as magically or literally removing the sins and transgressions of God's people, but was understood as symbolizing the way in which those sins and transgressions would be put away definitively out of the sight of YHWH and his people. There is simply no reason, then, to interpret the rite in terms of substitutionary death.

The notion of "bearing sin" has also been interpreted as implying substitution. This is due primarily to the use of the phrase not only in Lev. 16:20-22, where the rite with the goat for Azazel is described, but also in Isa. 53:10-12, which speaks of the servant of YHWH bearing the sin and iniquities of others in the context of an apparent allusion to YHWH making the servant's life an offering for sin. Throughout the rest of the Hebrew Scriptures, however, the idea of one person bearing the sins of another is rare. In his analysis of the phrase "to bear sin" or "guilt," Sklar has shown that it is used in three different ways in the Hebrew Bible. First, according to Sklar, when the sinner is the subject, it generally refers to being guilty and liable to some type of

---

187. G. Wenham, *Leviticus*, 62. See also Kiuchi, *Purification Offering*, 111-19. Zohar understands this in an ontological sense, which must also be rejected: the laying on of hands "marks the transference of the sin-contamination from the person to the animal," which is then slain so as to do away with that sin ("Repentance," 613-14).

punishment.[188] In some cases, all that was required in order to be rid of the guilt was that one offer up a sacrifice. In other cases, one was to be banished from the community or even put to death. In neither case, however, was any type of substitution involved. When one atoned for one's guilt through the offering of an animal or a measure of flour, for example, neither the animal nor the flour were being punished for one's wrongdoing.[189] Rather, they constituted an offering made to YHWH out of a desire to restore one's relationship with him. When one committed an act for which the punishment was to be "cut off" from the community or put to death, no one else was allowed to endure this punishment in the place of that person; nor was that person given the option of offering a sacrifice in order to avert the punishment prescribed.[190]

According to Sklar, the second usage of the phrase "to bear sin" had to do with a person forgiving the wrongdoing of one who had offended him or her.[191] This usage is unrelated to the offering of sacrifice and does not appear in any of the passages that prescribe sacrificial rites for sin. Often YHWH himself is said to have borne the guilt of those who had sinned in the sense that he forgave their sins. Once again, as Sklar recognizes, no idea of substitution is present in any of the passages that speak of bearing sin in this sense, since no penalty or punishment is suffered either by the offender or by the one who forgives the offender.

According to the third usage mentioned by Sklar, the one bearing sin was neither the offender nor the offended person, but a third party. Sklar finds only three occurrences of this usage in the Hebrew Scriptures, all of which appear in the prescriptions regarding sacrifice: Exod. 28:38, Lev. 10:17, and 16:22.[192] The last of these, of course, describes the rite with the goat for Azazel on the Day of Atonement. In the other two passages, the ones bearing the sin or guilt of the Israelites are Aaron and his sons as priests. The idea, however, is simply that God had designated them to present sacrifices for sin on behalf of the people. Once more, no idea of substitution is present in these passages. The priests were not enduring some type of vicarious punishment by offering up sacrifices for others, but performing a service for them. Any cost

---

188. Sklar, *Sin*, 20-23, 88.

189. See Lev. 5:1-13, 17-18. I would question Sklar's claim that the offering of sacrifices of atonement was viewed as a means by which a sinner could "escape death" (*Sin*, 43). In Leviticus 5, those who fail to present a sacrifice of atonement for sins they have committed inadvertently are not threatened with death. Furthermore, as already mentioned, the practice of offering sacrifices was not a form of inflicting or averting punishment for wrongdoings committed.

190. See Exod. 28:42-43; Lev. 17:15-16; 19:5-8; 20:17, 19-20; 22:8-9; 24:14-15; Num. 9:13; 15:30-31; 18:22.

191. Sklar, *Sin*, 89-92. Sklar finds this usage in the following texts: Gen. 50:17 (2x); Exod. 10:17; 32:32; 34:7; Num. 14:18; 1 Sam. 15:25; 25:28; Job 7:21; Ps. 25:18; 32:1, 5; 85:3 (2x); Isa. 33:24; Hosea 14:3 (2x); Mic. 7:18. Here again, Sklar mistakenly attempts to relate this usage with the remission of punishment, as if forgiveness involved merely being spared retribution rather than restoring a broken relationship.

192. Sklar, *Sin*, 92-99. Once more, the purpose of atoning sacrifice was not to make it possible for people to be delivered from the punishment or consequences of their sins, as Sklar claims here, but to express their repentance and recommitment to God's will. This, rather than the sacrifice per se, was the basis upon which God forgave and accepted them anew.

involved for the sacrifice was borne by the offenders rather than the priests, who received payment for their services, including the flesh of the animal offered for sin, which they were allowed to consume (Lev. 6:24-27).

There is therefore no basis in any of the passages that speak of bearing sin for the claim that a priest, some other person, or a sacrificial animal served as a substitute for one who had sinned and endured that person's punishment in his or her stead. In no case did sacrifice involve any type of substitutionary death. Even though animals were slaughtered, this was not because they were enduring some penalty in the place of another but because they were being offered, consecrated, or given to God. In the case of the goat for Azazel, no sacrifice was involved, since the goat was not offered to YHWH or even slaughtered. While it would inevitably die when it was left out in the desert, the purpose of the rite was not to impose a death penalty on the goat because of the people's sins. The main idea expressed through the rite was that the sins of Israel were symbolically removed far away from the people in order to disappear forever together with the goat that perished in the desert.

Several passages from the Mosaic law that speak of one redeeming one's own life or the life of others, such as a first-born child, have also been cited as involving the principle of substitution. For example, under certain circumstances, such as when one's ox had gored another person to death (Exod. 21:28-31), one might save oneself from a death penalty by paying the redemption price or *kofer*. Although in a sense this can be said to involve substitution in that the amount paid was given by the guilty party in exchange for his or her life, neither the requirement to pay the amount nor the penalty of death were removed by being imposed on someone else. It was only the guilty party who had to pay in one way or another. In addition, because in these cases no sacrifice was prescribed, no substitution by sacrificial offering was involved. This passage therefore has nothing to do with sacrificial practice.

In Lev. 6:1-7, the requirement to make retribution for having wrongly taken something from another person is combined with the command to present a sacrifice of atonement. The offender was to restore the original amount plus an additional one-fifth. Here, however, it is important not to confuse the payment made to another human being with an offering made to God. The amount paid was not an offering, but a fine or penalty aimed at making restitution to those who had been wronged. In this way, the injustice committed was corrected. While no doubt an animal was put to death when the prescribed sacrifice for sin was offered after the required amount had been paid, this was not understood in terms of inflicting some punishment on the animal, but making an offering to YHWH aimed at restoring the relationship with him. It was the *offering* of the animal rather than its death per se that accomplished this, since such an act served as a means by which the offender could reconsecrate himself or herself to YHWH and seek his forgiveness. Here again, no principle of substitution was involved, since even if a person who had stolen something did not make retribution or present the necessary sacrifice, according to the law that person was not liable to a penalty of death. Therefore, when one paid the required amount to the person that one had wronged and presented the sacrifice to YHWH prescribed by the law, one was not thought to be making any payment in exchange for one's life.

The redemption of the first-born has also been interpreted in terms of the substitution of one life for another. A number of passages in the Mosaic law affirm that the first-born of both animals and human beings belong to YHWH and must be given to him (Exod. 13:2, 13-15; 22:29-30; 34:19-20; Lev. 27:26; Num. 3:13; 8:14-18; 18:15-17; Deut. 15:19). Leon Morris looks to the notion of substitution to interpret these passages: "The first-born belong to the Lord, they should be sacrificed to him upon the altar. But in certain cases it is permitted, or required, to offer a substitute in lieu of the forfeited life...."[193] Morris's affirmation fails to take into account the distinction between the first-born of an animal and that of a human being. In the case of animals, the idea is that, since the first-born belongs to YHWH, it must be *given* or *consecrated* to him, that is, presented to him as an *offering*, as Exod. 13:2, 22:29-30, and Num. 18:17 explicitly state. Here there is no substitution involved; by sacrificing the animal, one is merely giving to YHWH what is his own. Animals with blemishes or defects also belonged to YHWH, yet since they were unfit for sacrifice, they had to be purchased back from YHWH. A blemished donkey was to be redeemed by a sheep or lamb; otherwise, its neck was to be broken (Exod. 13:13; 34:20). This did not involve any type of punishment of the animal or its owner. Rather, the animal was either to be bought back from YHWH by offering him a sheep or lamb or to be killed so that the owner would not keep for his own use what rightfully belonged to YHWH. At times, a first-born animal with a defect that made it unfit to be sacrificed was to be redeemed with money (Num. 3:16; 18:15-16). Neither the sheep or lamb given in exchange for the donkey nor the money paid in exchange for the defective animal involved any type of penalty or fine, however.[194] Furthermore, none of this had anything to do with sin or guilt. The idea was either to offer up to YHWH what belonged to him, namely, the first-born animal, or to purchase it back from him if it was not fit for sacrifice.

Because the first-born of a human mother also belonged to YHWH, all newborns had to be redeemed. This principle is stated in Exod. 13:15, 34:20, and Num. 18:15, though no redemption price is stated. If this redemption involved the payment of an amount of money or the offering of a sacrifice, this would be understood once more in terms of buying back from YHWH what belonged to him. Again, this redemption was not regarded as a penalty or punishment, since no sin had been committed and thus no guilt was involved.

---

193. Morris, *Apostolic Preaching*, 22-23.

194. I. Howard Marshall, for example, is mistaken when he writes: "The OT also establishes the practice of redeeming the firstborn (who were supposed to be given to God) by the making of a substitute offering (Exod. 13:11-16; 34:19-20). The price is a substitute for the person redeemed, and in that the price is costly it is, we might way, painful. Hence the concept of substitution is present and the cost may be regarded as a penalty in the broad sense" (*Aspects*, 47). The law does not penalize animals or human beings for having babies!

Although an exchange was thought to take place, strictly speaking, this was not substitution but simply a purchase. Even if an animal was slaughtered in order to redeem a first-born child, this was not substitutionary killing but the presentation of an offering, which YHWH accepted in return for giving the child back to his or her family, rather than retaining the child for himself.

Morris's affirmation that, since the first-born belong to the Lord, "they should be sacrificed to him upon the altar" is obviously not true of human first-borns, since human sacrifice was strictly forbidden by the Mosaic law. While human first-borns were to be consecrated or given to YHWH, this did not involve putting them to death but dedicating them to YHWH's service, similar to the way in which Hannah gave her son Samuel to YHWH in order that he might serve YHWH at the temple (1 Sam. 1:1-28). Those that redeemed their first-born from YHWH, therefore, were simply buying the child back so that the child might live as a member of the household rather than being consecrated to the service of YHWH at the temple. They were not saving the child from death, since the child was not subject to a death penalty. This is clear from the fact that, if parents failed to redeem their first-born child as they should, the child was not taken from them in order to be sacrificed or put to death. Once again, it is important not to confuse the presentation of an offering out of joyful gratitude for the new life given by God with the payment of a penalty or fine or the inflicting of a punishment.

This understanding of what it meant for a first-born child to belong to YHWH is evident in Num. 3:12-13 and 8:14-18, where YHWH is said to take the Levites in the place of the first-born of the people of Israel. Obviously, this did not involve putting the Levites to death instead of the first-born children of the Israelites but consecrating them to YHWH so that they might serve him at the sanctuary. While in a sense this can be regarded as involving substitution, strictly speaking, it was more of an exchange: rather than taking for himself all of the first-born children of Israel so that they might be dedicated to his service, YHWH took all of the Levites instead. Furthermore, to be dedicated to the service of YHWH was not a punishment but an honor and a privilege.

Assumption 6: Was sacrifice understood in terms of representation and participation?

In a general sense, there is no question that the notions of representation and participation were basic to the understanding of sacrifice in antiquity. The sacrificial offerings of various types were means by which those who presented them offered themselves, their lives, and their possessions to God. Thus it can rightly be said that those offerings represented the worshipers. Those who offered sacrifice also participated in the rites in various ways, not only by paying for the sacrifice and carrying out certain prescribed rituals in relation to the offering, but at times consuming all or part of the animals, grains, fruits, oils, and libations that they had presented.

Because the central idea in sacrificial worship was not that of putting animals to death but rather making offerings to God, however, there is no reason to think that those who presented sacrificial victims to Israel's God believed that in some sense they were participating in the death of the animal or that they regarded "the death of the sacrificial animal as the death of the sinner qua sinner," as Dunn has claimed.[195] Nor is it clear that they saw the victim's death as "a symbol of self-immolation" in which what it "does and suffers is then representatively the action and suffering of the sacrificer."[196] While we cannot of course rule out entirely the possibility that those who presented animal sacrifices saw the animal's death as symbolizing their own death in some sense, no evidence of such a belief exists in the ancient Jewish sources at our disposal. Even if such a belief existed, it cannot be regarded as the dominant idea behind the rite. What those who offered sacrificial victims sought was not to undergo some type of death together with the animal as punishment for their sins, but to approach YHWH to receive his forgiveness and blessings. If they saw themselves as dying with the animal in symbolic fashion, they would have understood this more in the sense of putting the sin they had committed behind them and perhaps ascending to God through the offering they presented, as Josephus interprets the sacrifice of Isaac by Abraham. They were not enduring the death penalty for their sins together with the animal that represented them.

Equally absent from the ancient Jewish sources we have is the idea that those who offered sacrificial victims believed that they participated in some mystical or mysterious fashion in the death of those victims. Although many have claimed to find this idea in the so-called mystery religions of antiquity, there is no clear evidence for such beliefs among Jews in Jesus' time. Nor is there evidence that those Jews who ate of what had been offered to YHWH believed that such eating effected some mystical communion with him or enabled them to participate in his divinity in some sense. While undoubtedly eating of the sacrificial offerings was understood in terms of enjoying some type of communion or fellowship with YHWH and with others who participated in the same meal, the texts speak only of eating "before" YHWH or in his presence (Deut. 12:7, 18; 14:23-26; 27:7). This implies that YHWH was thought to be present in some way when they gathered to feast and celebrate. However, this evidently was not thought to involve the transmission of any kind of mysterious divine substance or power to those who partook of the food offered. There is no basis, then, for claiming that in ancient Judaism the "communion of food" was thought to bring about "not only a mere external proximity, but a mingling of the two substances [sacred and profane] which become absorbed in each other to the point of becoming indistinguishable."[197]

---

195. Dunn, "Paul's Understanding," 46.
196. Gayford, *Sacrifice*, 63, 65.
197. Henri Hubert and Marcel Mauss, *Sacrifice: Its Nature and Function*, trans. W. D. Halls (Chicago: University of Chicago Press, 1964), 43-44; for this concept of the sacrificial meal, see 28-45.

Such ideas may have existed in antiquity among those who worshiped other gods, but this was because those gods were viewed as being fundamentally different from YHWH, as we have noted above.

Assumption 7: Was sacrifice thought to reveal the mechanism of sacred violence?

René Girard's proposals regarding the meaning of sacrificial rites are clearly not an attempt to offer an overarching "theory" regarding how sacrifice was understood in antiquity. Girard does not work extensively with the texts from the Hebrew Scriptures that prescribe sacrificial rites, nor does he seek to interpret the meaning of those rites among ancient Jews. Nevertheless, it is important to point out several ideas reflected in Girard's thought that are foreign to the ancient Jewish understanding of sacrifice due to the influence those ideas have exerted on New Testament scholars.

The first of these ideas is that Jews in antiquity understood sacrifice primarily in terms of "sacred violence." When Jews presented sacrificial offerings, they did not consider themselves to be carrying out acts of violence. In fact, most of the sacrifices presented, such as grains, fruits, flour, oil, and wine, were offered in ways in which any kind of violence was lacking entirely. Even when the blood, fat, flesh, and other parts of animals were offered, this took place after the animal was put to death. While undoubtedly in the case of animal sacrifice, violence was involved, as we have stressed above, this was not the primary idea related to sacrifice.

A second point that should be stressed is that, in ancient Jewish thought, sacrifice was not thought to involve any type of scapegoating. The ritual with the goat for Azazel on the Day of Atonement was not viewed as a sacrificial offering. When animal victims were killed, the intention was not to inflict some type of pain or suffering on them. On the contrary, as noted above, provisions were made to make their deaths as quick and painless as possible. It is important, therefore, to distinguish sacrifice from scapegoating.

These two observations lead to a third: Jews in antiquity did not have a negative view of sacrifice nor regard sacrifice as something from which they needed to be saved, as Girard's interpretation of sacrifice implies. On the contrary, sacrifice was viewed in very positive terms. Those Jews who for various reasons were not able to participate in the sacrificial worship generally lamented the fact. Even those who rejected the sacrificial worship being carried out under Hasmonean and Roman rule did so, not because they thought sacrifice was wrong or that Israel's God was not to be worshiped by means of sacrifice at the temple, but because they believed that those presenting sacrifices at the Jewish temple were sinful, corrupt, or in error regarding how and when the rites were to be performed according to the law. When the temple was destroyed in 70 CE, Jews throughout the Roman Empire almost without exception were deeply saddened and distraught. While some who identified themselves as Jesus' followers saw the destruction of Herod's temple as a sign of God's wrath, what they believed had occasioned that wrath was not the practice of sacrifice itself, as if this had displeased God, but the sin, corruption, injustice, and oppression into which they believed many Jews had fallen, particularly those in positions of leadership.

Undoubtedly, Girard himself does not claim that the Jews understood sacrifice primarily in terms of sacred violence or scapegoating or in purely negative terms. These ideas are commonly reflected, however, in the writings of many scholars who write on the subject of sacrifice in ancient Israel and second-temple Judaism. Among Jews in antiquity, sacrificial worship was generally something to be valued greatly rather than condemned, destroyed, or replaced by some type of non-violent, "spiritual" worship. As Jonathan Klawans and other scholars have stressed, in ancient Judaism, sacrifice was not primarily a response to transgression, but an act characterized by joy and thanksgiving.[198] Sacrifice was therefore essentially spiritual in nature rather than something that needed to be "spiritualized" or superseded in some way.[199]

* * *

In light of what we have seen in the present chapter, it should be clear that there was nothing in ancient Jewish sacrificial practice and belief that could have led Jesus' first followers to interpret Jesus' death on the basis of the ideas of penal substitution or ontological participation. Neither the death of sacrificial animals, the shedding of their blood, nor the rites carried out with that blood were thought to obtain divine forgiveness or make atonement for sin. Nor were the sacrificial rites believed to "work" in some way to take away the sins of the people or restore them to a condition of purity before God. For this reason, we may safely conclude that Jesus' first followers could not have come to regard Jesus' death or blood as having atoning efficacy or as possessing some power to redeem human beings, reconcile them to God, cleanse them literally from their sins, or make them righteous in God's sight on the basis of ideas derived from Jewish sacrificial practices and beliefs. The same must be said with regard to the sacrificial practices and beliefs of other cultures in antiquity, such as the Greeks and Romans.

This does not mean, of course, that the practices and beliefs regarding sacrifice that existed in the first century CE did not influence Jesus' first followers and lead them to interpret his sufferings and death in sacrificial terms. On the contrary, as we shall see further on in our study, the beliefs of Jesus' first followers regarding sacrifice played an important role in the development

---

198. Klawans, *Purity*, 71-72; on the previous points, see also 3, 161-68, 208-10. Patterson similarly stresses that the most common type of sacrifice among the Jewish people was the *shelamim*, the offering of thanksgiving that involved feasting, communion, and joyful celebration (*Keeping the Feast*, 46-47, 51-53, 81). As she notes there, this same type of sacrifice was also the most common in Greco-Roman sacrificial practice.

199. Klawans, *Purity*, 220. See also Jonathan Klawans, "Interpreting the Last Supper: Sacrifice, Spiritualization, and Anti-Sacrifice," *NTS* 48 (2002): 12-13. For a summary of the scholarly discussion regarding the notion of spiritualization, see Albert L. A. Hogeterp, *Expectations of the End: A Comparative Traditio-Historical Study of Eschatological, Apocalyptic, and Messianic Ideas in the Dead Sea Scrolls and the New Testament* (STDJ 83; Leiden: Brill, 2009), 2-8.

of their understanding of the salvific significance of his death. The ideas that became central in their interpretations of Jesus' death, however, were the same ideas that were central in Jewish sacrificial thought. Jesus had offered up his life to God on behalf of others asking that God forgive, accept, and save those who would identify with him and his sacrificial death. Like the sacrifices presented at the Jewish temple, Jesus' death had in essence constituted an offering to God accompanied by petitions on behalf of those who would be committed to living in conformity with God's will, as he had been.

CHAPTER 4

Vicarious Suffering and Death in Ancient Jewish Thought

Virtually all New Testament scholars would agree that, when Jesus' first followers began to ascribe redemptive significance to Jesus' death, they did so on the basis of beliefs regarding vicarious suffering and death that are found in ancient sources, including not only the Hebrew Scriptures and second-temple Jewish literature, but Greek and Roman writings as well.[1] While several passages of the Hebrew Scriptures imply that the death of certain persons could benefit others or the people as a whole, the passage that is considered to have exerted the greatest influence on the earliest interpretations of Jesus' death is Isaiah 53, which speaks of the suffering and death of God's chosen servant. A number of passages from other Jewish writings of antiquity, including the rabbinic literature, are also said to affirm the idea that the death of a righteous individual could atone for the sins of others. Because these sources are thought to provide the ideas and background necessary to understand the interpretations given to Jesus' death in the New Testament and in some cases to have influenced Jesus or his first followers directly, it is important that we examine them here.

In what follows, I will not enter into discussions regarding the dating of the sources examined or consider whether the various passages analyzed may have influenced the way Jesus or his first followers interpreted his death. Besides the fact that we can have no certainty regarding these questions, I do not consider them relevant for my purposes here. Instead, my goal is to explore the logic underlying these passages and demonstrate that in reality they provide no support for the idea that, in ancient Hebrew and Jewish thought, the suffering and death of a righteous person could atone for the sins of others or appease God's wrath on their behalf.

ISAIAH 53

The New Testament provides ample evidence of the widespread use of Isa. 52:13—53:12 (hereafter simply Isaiah 53) in the first century to interpret the significance of Jesus' ministry, passion, death, and resurrection. However, since the 1959 publication of Morna Hooker's book *Jesus and the Servant*, scholars

---

1. The term "vicarious," as used here, simply refers to something that benefits others and is not to be confused with the idea of substitution. While suffering or dying in the place of others is no doubt vicarious, not all forms of vicarious suffering and death involve substitution.

have debated how soon after Jesus' death Isaiah 53 came to be regarded as a prophecy of those events. Hooker argued not only that it is unlikely that Jesus identified with the figure of Isaiah 53, but also that there is "little evidence that the identification of Jesus with the Servant played any great part in the thinking of St Paul, St John, or the author of the Epistle to the Hebrews, and no *proof* that it was known to them at all."[2] While many scholars have agreed with Hooker's arguments, others have questioned her claims.[3] Most of the allusions to Isaiah 53 in the New Testament writings view it as foretelling Jesus' ministry and sufferings, yet make no explicit reference to the verses that speak of the servant's death being "for sins." This makes it difficult to determine what role Isaiah 53 played in the development of the belief that in his death Jesus had redeemed others from their sins.[4]

For centuries, it has been common to regard Isaiah 53 as the passage that, more than any other, led Jesus' first followers to interpret his death in terms of penal substitution. This presupposes that the idea of penal substitution is present in the passage. Although some scholars have questioned this supposition, it still remains so thoroughly entrenched in New Testament scholarship that for many it is unthinkable that the passage might be interpreted in some other way.[5] In fact, I would argue that it is precisely that presupposition that has led Hooker and others who find the idea of penal substitution problematic to argue that Isaiah 53 had little influence on the way in which Jesus' first followers interpreted his death. Ultimately, what these scholars wish to reject is not so much that Isaiah 53 played a role in the earliest interpretations of Jesus' death, but that almost from the start Jesus' followers interpreted his death on the basis of the notion of penal substitution. I intend to show here, however, that it is highly unlikely that those who read Isaiah 53 in the second-temple period would have interpreted it on the basis of the notion of penal substitution.

As I have already mentioned with regard to other passages from the Hebrew Scriptures used in the New Testament writings, for my purposes here

---

2. Morna D. Hooker, *Jesus and the Servant: The Influence of the Servant Concept of Deutero-Isaiah in the New Testament* (London: SPCK, 1959), 127, 154-55. Hooker has since changed her position somewhat. In 1998, she wrote that she was "far more ready than I was forty years ago" to suggest that the use of Isaiah 53 to interpret the significance of Jesus' death may have begun with Paul ("Did the Use of Isaiah 53 to Interpret His Mission Begin with Jesus?," in *Jesus and the Suffering Servant: Isaiah 53 and Christian Origins*; ed. William H. Bellinger Jr. and William R. Farmer; Harrisburg, PA: Trinity Press International, 1998, 103; see 101-3).

3. Martin Hengel, for example, claims that "it should no longer be doubted that *Isa. 53 had an influence on the origin and shaping of the earliest kerygma*" (*The Atonement: The Origins of the Doctrine in the New Testament*; Philadelphia: Fortress, 1981, 59-60). See also Otto Betz, "Jesus and Isaiah 53," in *Jesus*, ed. Bellinger and Farmer, 71-82.

4. A related question is the importance of Isaiah 53 in pre-Christian Jewish thought. Hengel, for example, argues that the influence of Isaiah 53 can be found in numerous writings from the Hebrew Scriptures and second-temple Judaism ("The Effective History of Isaiah 53 in the Pre-Christian Period," in *The Suffering Servant: Isaiah 53 in Jewish and Christian Sources*, trans. Daniel P. Bailey; ed. Bernd Janowski and Peter Stuhlmacher; Grand Rapids: Eerdmans, 2004, 75-146). I would question, however, many of Hengel's claims and conclusions.

5. Stephen Finlan's observations regarding the passage, for example, are typical of many biblical scholars. He claims that the notion of penal substitution is clearly present in vv. 5, 6, 10, 11, and 12 of Isaiah 53, and possibly vv. 8-9 as well (*The Background and Content of Paul's Cultic Atonement Metaphors*; AcBib 19; Atlanta: SBL, 2004, 176).

there is no sense in attempting to reconstruct the "original meaning" of Isaiah 53 (as if this were even possible), exploring its original historical context or its significance in the context of Deutero-Isaiah. All of this is irrelevant to this study, since my interest lies in examining how Isaiah 53 might have been read by Jesus' first followers and other Jews with whom they were in dialogue in order to address the question of the significance of Jesus' sufferings and death. Jews in antiquity knew nothing of any "Deutero-Isaiah." In addition, a number of scholars have pointed out that interpreters of Isaiah in antiquity would not have viewed Isaiah 53 as one of several "servant songs" in the book, as if these passages formed together a unity.[6] Therefore, in analyzing Isaiah 53, there is no reason to look at the other passages often considered as "servant songs" in Deutero-Isaiah.

Discussion of Isaiah 53 is complicated by the problems associated with the text. There are significant differences between the Masoretic text (MT) and the Septuagint (LXX), and each of these presents its own textual variants. The Isaiah scroll found at Qumran also reflects differences with both the MT and the LXX. In addition, certain Hebrew phrases allow for different translations, while at times the Greek is rather awkward. All of this makes it difficult to determine precisely not only how Jesus' first followers would have read Isaiah 53 but what text they would have used. The various New Testament writings seem to show evidence of the use of both the LXX and Hebrew versions of Isaiah 53.[7] For this reason, we will take both texts into account here.[8]

In order to facilitate analysis of the passage, I will cite the NRSV translation from the Hebrew text and subsequently present a comparison between the MT and the LXX on the basis of a more literal translation of the Hebrew and Greek. This comparison includes only the verses that speak of the servant's suffering and death as redemptive or "for our sins," since the discussion below will focus primarily on these verses.

> 52:13 See, my servant shall prosper;
> he shall be exalted and lifted up,
> and shall be very high.

---

6. This argument is particularly attributed to Joachim Jeremias, "Παῖς Θεοῦ," *TDNT* 5: 682–83. On both of these points, see Lidija Novakovic, "Matthew's Atomistic Use of Scripture: Messianic Interpretation of Isaiah 53:4 in Matthew 8:17," in *Biblical Interpretation in Early Christian Gospels*, Vol. 2: *The Gospel of Matthew* (ed. Thomas R. Hatina; London: T & T Clark, 2008), 147-54; Donald Juel, *Messianic Exegesis: Christological Interpretation of the Old Testament in Early Christianity* (Philadelphia: Fortress, 1988), 125, 128.

7. As Hans-Ruedi Weber notes, there is evidence of the use of both the Hebrew text and the Septuagint translation of Isaiah 53 in the New Testament (*The Cross: Tradition and Interpretation of the Crucifixion of Jesus in the World of the New Testament*, trans. Elke Jessett; Grand Rapids: Eerdmans, 1978, 53-54).

8. On the primary differences between the MT and the Qumran text, as well as a comparison of both texts to the LXX version of Isaiah 53, see David A. Sapp, "The LXX, 1QIsa, and MT versions of Isaiah 53 and the Christian Doctrine of Atonement," in *Jesus*, ed. Bellinger and Farmer, 170-92. For the most part, the textual variants between the MT and the Qumran text are not significant for the phrases that will be discussed here. On the different emphases found in the MT and the LXX, see Jesper Tang Nielsen, "The Lamb of God: The Cognitive Structure of a Johannine Metaphor," in *Imagery in the Gospel of John: Terms, Forms, Themes, and Theology of Johannine Figurative Language* (ed. Jörg Frey, Jan G. van der Watt, and Ruben Zimmermann; WUNT 200; Tübingen: Mohr Siebeck, 2006), 228-33.

14 Just as there were many who were astonished at him—
   so marred was his appearance, beyond human semblance,
   and his form beyond that of mortals—
15 so he shall startle many nations;
   kings shall shut their mouths because of him;
  for that which had not been told them they shall see
   and that which they had not heard they shall contemplate.
53:1 Who has believed what we have heard?
   And to whom has the arm of the Lord been revealed?
2 For he grew up before him like a young plant,
   and like a root out of dry ground;
  he had no form or majesty that we should look at him,
   nothing in his appearance that we should desire him.
3 He was despised and rejected by others;
   a man of suffering and acquainted with infirmity;
  and as one from whom others hide their faces
   he was despised, and we held him of no account.
4 Surely he has borne our infirmities
   and carried our diseases;
  yet we accounted him stricken,
   struck down by God, and afflicted.
5 But he was wounded for our transgressions,
   crushed for our iniquities;
  upon him was the punishment that made us whole,
   and by his bruises we are healed.
6 All we like sheep have gone astray;
   we have all turned to our own way,
  and the Lord has laid on him
   the iniquity of us all.
7 He was oppressed, and he was afflicted,
   yet he did not open his mouth;
  like a lamb that is led to the slaughter,
   and like a sheep that before its shearers is silent,
   so he did not open his mouth.
8 By a perversion of justice he was taken away.
   Who could have imagined his future?
  For he was cut off from the land of the living,
   stricken for the transgression of my people.
9 They made his grave with the wicked
   and his tomb with the rich,
  although he had done no violence,
   and there was no deceit in his mouth.
10 Yet it was the will of the Lord to crush him with pain.
When you make his life an offering for sin,
   he shall see his offspring, and shall prolong his days;
   through him the will of the Lord shall prosper.
11 Out of his anguish he shall see light;
he shall find satisfaction through his knowledge.
   The righteous one, my servant, shall make many righteous,
   and he shall bear their iniquities.
12 Therefore I will allot him a portion with the great,
   and he shall divide the spoil with the strong;

because he poured out himself to death,
    and was numbered with the transgressors;
yet he bore the sin of many,
    and made intercession for the transgressors.

HEBREW MT	LXX
4 Surely he has carried our diseases and has borne our blows/wounds. And we considered him stricken, smitten/beaten by God and afflicted.	4 This one bears our sins and suffers for us (*peri hēmōn*), and we considered him to be in pain/distress (*en ponō*) and under a blow [of misfortune] and in affliction/oppression.
5 But he was pierced/wounded because of our transgressions (*mippesha'enu*); he was crushed/bruised because of our iniquities (*me'eonothenu*); the chastisement (*musar*) of/for our peace was upon him and by means of his blow/bruises we are healed (*nirpa'*).	5 And he was wounded because of our lawless deeds (*dia tas anomias hēmōn*) and he was made to suffer/became sick because of our sins (*dia tas hamartias hēmōn*); the instruction/discipline (*paideia*) of our peace [was] upon him; with his bruises/wounds we were healed (*hiathēmen*).
6 All of us like sheep have wandered off; we turned each one to his/her own way, but the Lord has laid upon him the iniquity of us all.	6 We have all gone astray like sheep; each one has gone astray to his/her way, and the Lord has delivered him up/handed him over (*paredōken auton*) for our sins (*tais hamartiais hēmōn*).
8 By oppression and by judgment he was taken away; and as for his generation, who considered that he was cut off from the land of the living? For the transgression (*mippesha'*) of my people the affliction/stroke [was] upon him.	8 In [his] humiliation his judgment/trial was taken away. Who will tell of his generation? For his life is taken from the earth; because of the lawless deeds (*apo tōn anomiōn*) of my people he was led to death.
10 And YHWH desired to bruise/crush him, making him suffer. If his soul makes a guilt offering (*'asham*)/If you make a guilt-offering of his soul, he will see offspring; and he will prolong [his] days. And the good pleasure of YHWH will prosper in his hand.	10 And the Lord desires to purge him from his blow [of misfortune]. If you present [an offering] for sin (*peri hamartias*), your soul will see long-lived offspring.
11 As the result of the suffering of his soul, he will see it [light]; he will be satisfied through his knowledge. [OR: Through his knowledge…] [T]he righteous one my servant will justify the many; he will bear their sins.	And the Lord desires to take away 11 from the trouble of his soul, to show to him light and to form him with understanding, to justify the righteous one who serves the many well, and he will bear their sins.
12 Therefore I will give him a portion with the great, and he will divide the spoil with the strong; because he poured out his soul to death and was numbered with the transgressors. And he bore the sin of many, and interceded for the transgressors.	12 On account of this he will inherit many and he will divide the spoils of the mighty, because his soul was delivered over to death, and he was reckoned among the lawless; and he bore [the] sins of many and was delivered up on account of their sins.

The Difficulties of Interpreting Isaiah 53

Although Christians have of course regarded Isaiah 53 as a prophecy regarding Jesus since the early days of the church, it is not clear whether prior to this time those who read or heard the passage would have understood it as speaking of a particular figure such as a prophet, the people of Israel or Judah collectively, or some particular group within Israel, such as the prophets of YHWH. Because the passage as it stands allows for multiple interpretations, we cannot rule out the possibility that it was read in any of these ways in antiquity.

The primary difficulty with understanding Isaiah 53 as an allusion to an individual is that it seems to speak of the servant being exalted and prospering after his death (52:15; 53:10-12). Prior to the Christian belief in Jesus' resurrection, it seems unlikely that anyone would expect an individual such as a prophet actually to die and then rise from the dead in order to be exalted, prosper, and continue serving others. This could have led those who read or heard the passage to understand it as referring to something such as Israel's exile and return, which might be understood metaphorically as a death and resurrection. The idea would be similar to that which we find in Ezekiel 37, where the dry bones representing Israel are brought back to life. It is also possible that the "prosperous future" announced for the servant after his death would be understood in terms of his being "integrated again into the community from which he was separated by his illness and suffering," as Henning Graf Reventlow proposes, thus taking the allusions to the servant's death solely in a metaphorical sense.[9]

The problem with interpreting the servant as referring to Israel or Judah collectively is that it leaves unanswered the question of who the narrators ("we") are, since they are the ones who describe as observers what happened to the servant. If the narrators are identified with the people of Israel or Judah, then the servant must be taken as referring to someone else. Undoubtedly, at certain points of the passage it is YHWH himself who is speaking, yet in spite of this the narrators seem to be distinct from the servant. It is of course possible to see the narrators as Israel's neighbors from other nations in order to identify Israel or Judah with the servant, yet this raises other difficulties.[10] In v. 8, for example, the servant is distinguished from "my people," which seems to be an allusion to Israel. Furthermore, when the people of Israel or Judah were punished, they were not thought to have been righteous or innocent as the servant is said to be.[11]

---

9. Henning Graf Reventlow, "Basic Issues in the Interpretation of Isaiah 53," in *Jesus*, ed. Bellinger and Farmer, 26.

10. The idea that the "we" passages would be understood as referring to "humanity as a whole," as George A. F. Knight claims, is extremely unlikely (*Deutero-Isaiah: A Theological Commentary on Isaiah 40-55*; New York: Abingdon, 1965, 234). This represents a later theologizing that, from my perspective, is foreign not only to Isaiah 53, but to the New Testament in general.

11. As James D. Smart observes, a collective interpretation is particularly problematic with regard to vv. 7-9 (*History and Theology in Second Isaiah: A Commentary on Isaiah 35, 40-66*; Philadelphia: Westminster, 1965,

One further possibility would be to associate the servant with some particular group within Israel, such as the prophets of YHWH.[12] This would require understanding the servant's being "exalted" and "prospering" in the future as referring metaphorically to this group. Such an interpretation, however, would raise the question of why the passage speaks of the servant as an individual, since one would instead expect the use of the plural "servants." Of course, it is possible to posit a change in the identity of the narrators at one or more points in the passage, as Jesper Tang Nielsen has suggested, yet this only seems to complicate things further.[13]

The basic ideas in the passage are relatively clear. It emphasizes the servant's unseemly appearance as a result of severe mistreatment by others, as well as perhaps some type of illness or infirmity sent by YHWH: he was "marred beyond human semblance" (52:14), "despised and rejected" (53:3), "stricken, struck down by YHWH, and afflicted" (53:4, 8), "wounded," "crushed," "bruised" (53:5, 10), "oppressed" (53:7), and "cut off from the land of the living." The last two verses of chapter 52, in which YHWH is the one speaking, mention nations and kings being astonished by the appearance of the servant (52:14-15). Those presented as narrators beginning at 53:1 also contemplate the servant. The passage mentions not only the servant's suffering but his death (53:9, 12), yet also speaks of him being exalted and prospering after mentioning his death (52:13; 53:10, 12).

The passage underscores the servant's innocence, since he does not suffer and die for any sins of his own but rather for the sins of the people. His suffering and death are also attributed not only to the actions of sinners but to an act of YHWH, who "afflicted" or "crushed" the servant and laid on him the iniquities of others. The allusion to YHWH chastising the servant raises the question of *how* he does so. The passage speaks of injustices committed against the servant; he was "led to the slaughter" and "taken away," evidently by others. The LXX affirms twice that YHWH "handed him over," presumably to those responsible for the servant's suffering and death. The images of physical bodily suffering involving bruises and wounds as a result of being beaten also point to some type of severe mistreatment at the hands of others. Yet once the servant's suffering is said to be inflicted by sinful human beings, it becomes problematic to see how that suffering can also be attributed to YHWH's activity. One possibility is to see those inflicting suffering on the servant as YHWH's instruments to chastise the servant. Undoubtedly, such an idea is common throughout the Hebrew Scriptures, where Israel's God

---

207). On the idea that the servant represents a "collective entity" that is "described in personal terms," see George W. E. Nickelsburg, *Ancient Judaism and Christian Origins: Diversity, Continuity, and Transformation* (Minneapolis: Fortress, 2003), 18.

12. Nickelsburg, for example, mentions: "According to one major line of early Jewish interpretation, the Servant figure is realized in the wise teachers of the Torah in the Hellenistic period" (*Ancient Judaism*, 18). Hengel notes that the servant might be identified with the remnant, though he insists: "Collective and individual interpretations need not be mutually exclusive. They are two aspects of the same thing" ("Effective History," 121).

13. Nielsen, "Lamb of God," 229-30.

uses foreign nations as instruments to chastise Israel for its sins. Paradoxically, often these other nations and their leaders are presented as sinful and spoken of as objects of divine wrath and punishment at the same time that they are said to serve as God's agents to inflict suffering on Israel.

The difference here in Isaiah 53, however, is that the servant is not considered sinful, as Israel was when it was chastised by God, but instead is viewed as righteous and innocent. This makes it somewhat more problematic to affirm that the people mistreating the servant are acting as YHWH's agents, though such an interpretation cannot be ruled out entirely. It is also possible to view at least some of the servant's sufferings as inflicted on him by YHWH himself if the sufferings of the servant involve illnesses or bodily afflictions that are not the direct result of mistreatment at the hands of others. Yet while some of the servant's sufferings might be attributed to YHWH's action alone, the passage seems clearly to attribute those sufferings to others who act unjustly toward the servant.

Another way to understand YHWH's "striking," "crushing," and "afflicting" the servant could be to affirm that YHWH sent the servant into a situation where sinful people would treat him badly and even kill him. In that case, YHWH also willed that the servant persevere in that situation even to the point of death. In this way, the servant's suffering could be attributed to YHWH in an *indirect* sense: YHWH struck, crushed, and afflicted the servant in the sense that he placed the servant in a context in which others would strike, crush, and afflict him, and then had him remain there. If the passage is interpreted in this sense, then it might be said that YHWH's primary will was not that the servant suffer, as if this were an end in itself, but that the servant accomplish some other task that required that he remain in a situation in which he was being abused by others and would eventually be killed by them. This interpretation could be combined with the idea that some of the servant's sufferings involved bodily afflictions or illnesses that were not inflicted on him directly by others but instead later followed upon the mistreatment he endured as a natural consequence. Obviously, when one is beaten and mistreated, one can become physically ill with other ailments. The servant might also be said to have come to suffer the same illnesses and afflictions that others were suffering in the context in which he became immersed if the illnesses and afflictions of others came to affect him as well.

What is not fully clear is how the relation between the servant's suffering and the sins of others is to be understood. Verses 4-6, 8, and 10-12 relate the servant's suffering to the sins of the people through the use of the same type of short, formulaic assertions that appear throughout the New Testament to speak of Jesus' suffering and death as redemptive. The servant "bears our sins and suffers for us" (v. 4 LXX) and was wounded and crushed because of "our" sins and iniquities (v. 5). The "chastisement of our peace" was on him, and "by means of his wounds we are healed" (v. 5). YHWH "laid upon him our iniquity" (v. 6 MT) or "handed him over for our sins" (v. 6 LXX). Because of the lawless deeds of the people he was struck (v. 8 MT) or led to death (v. 8 LXX). Either the servant or the people must make a guilt offering in order to see offspring (v. 10). The servant justifies many (v. 11 MT) or is himself justified by the Lord (v. 11 LXX), and will bear the sins of others (v. 11). In v. 12, the past tense is used: he "bore the sin(s) of many" and either "interceded for the transgressors" (v. 12 MT) or "was delivered up on account of their sins" (v. 12 LXX).

All of these formulaic phrases use prepositions or constructions that can be interpreted in a variety of ways. Clearly, the people's sins were the cause of the servant's suffering and in some sense the servant bore their sins, yet neither of these ideas is explained in detail. Furthermore, both the affirmation that the people were healed and obtained peace through the servant's suffering (v. 5) and the statement that the servant justifies many (v. 11 MT) can be understood either in a forensic sense—the people are now forgiven—or in terms of a restoration to wholeness and well-being in a broader sense. The Hebrew verb *tsadaq* used in the hiphil (*yatsdiq*) in v. 11 of the MT can mean "to give someone justice," "bring justice," "acknowledge that someone is just and righteous," "make someone just and righteous," or "help someone gain her or his rights." Because nothing in the passage or context suggests that any of these readings should be given preference over the others, in theory any of them are possible here.[14]

The phrase "the chastisement of our peace" in v. 5 is particularly terse and awkward. Both the Hebrew *musar* and the Greek *paideia*, usually translated as "chastisement," actually mean "correction," "discipline," or "education," as we noted in Chapter 2. Because the servant is regarded as righteous, the sufferings must be aimed at correcting or bringing about a change, not in the servant himself, but in the sinful people. Yet how this takes place is not specified. Nor is it specified how the people's peace results from what happened to the servant or how the servant's being struck and wounded leads to the people being healed.

Due to the enigmatic nature of all of these affirmations, it is possible to make sense of them only if they are viewed in the context of some larger narrative. For the most part, however, this narrative is not provided by the text and therefore must be provided by the readers. Here I would like to present two narratives that can provide the framework necessary for the passage to be understood in order to evaluate each one. The first is based on the notion of penal substitution. This represents the reading of the passage that has been predominant at least since the time of the Protestant Reformation. The second reading represents an alternative interpretation of the passage that excludes the notion of penal substitution.

---

14. Edward J. Young interprets this justification in a forensic sense (*The Book of Isaiah: The English Text, with Introduction, Exposition, and Notes*, NICOT; Grand Rapids: Eerdmans, 1972, 3:357-58). In contrast, Smart argues against such a rendering of the Hebrew: "The words 'to be accounted' in the RSV introduce a judicial idea that is alien to Second Isaiah and is nowhere present in the text. It may be translated 'he made many righteous' or 'he turned many to righteousness' or simply 'he saved many' but not 'he made many to be accounted righteous'" (*History and Theology*, 213). On the various possible interpretations of the allusions to justification here, see especially Sapp, "The LXX," 173-76.

A Penal Substitution Reading of Isaiah 53

Undoubtedly, because of the complexities associated with the idea of penal substitution, it would be a mistake to claim that all who read Isaiah 53 on the basis of that idea would interpret the passage in exactly the same way. Nevertheless, the basic elements of a penal substitution reading of Isaiah 53 would be the following:

A) The people had sinned and God's justice demanded that they be punished by being made to suffer afflictions, hardships, and a painful death. In the words of Edward Young, "Because of our sins, so the thought may be paraphrased, God was not at peace with us. If he was to be at peace with us, there must be chastisement."[15]

B) God wished to deliver the sinful people from this punishment, yet God's strict justice made it impossible for God to forgive them freely without inflicting that justly-deserved punishment on someone.[16] John Oswalt, for example, affirms that the passage speaks of "a God who wants a whole relationship with his people, but is prevented from having it until incomplete [sic] justice is satisfied. In the Servant he has found a way to gratify his love and satisfy his justice."[17]

C) God sent his servant to endure that punishment in the place of the guilty as their substitute. The servant was qualified to do so because he was sinless and thus was not liable to any type of punishment himself: he was righteous and had done no wrong (vv. 9, 11), and his suffering and death were a perversion of justice (v. 8).

D) The punishment that the servant suffered in the place of the sinful people involved being smitten, afflicted, pierced, crushed, and stricken on account of the people's transgressions and iniquities (vv. 4-5, 8, 10).[18] He was numbered with the transgressors (v. 12). In this case, it was his *suffering itself* which satisfied God's wrath. In the words of Martin Hengel, "The Servant's vicarious suffering cancels the guilt of sin...."[19] Claus Westermann similarly explains:

> two things are involved in what the Servant bears, what he has loaded upon him—the sins of the others and the punishment which results upon them.

---

15. Young, *Isaiah*, 3:349.
16. See ibid., 3:348.
17. John Oswalt, *The Book of Isaiah: Chapters 40-66* (NICOT; Grand Rapids: Eerdmans, 1998), 388.
18. Thus Smart claims that "the central theme of ch. 53 is forgiveness, God's forgiveness of the sins of men whereby he cleanses them and transforms them, delivering them from the death to which they were doomed by their sins and creating for them a new life and a new future" (*History and Theology*, 195). Janowski writes that *asham* in v. 10a refers to "a means of 'wiping out guilt,'" and stresses that the entire passage focuses on the question of how the people's guilt can justly be removed: "their own guilt has been wiped out by the Servant's suffering" ("He Bore our Sins," 67, 70). According to Oswalt, the servant "does not suffer merely as a result of the sins of the people, but in the place of the people. He suffers *for* them, and because of that, they do not need to experience the results of their sins" (*Isaiah*, 385).
19. Hengel, "Effective History," 124.

Thus, the healing gained for the others (v. 5) by his stripes includes as well the forgiveness of their sins and the removal of their punishment, that is to say, the suffering.... [W]ith his life, his suffering and his death, [the servant] took their place and underwent their punishment in their stead.[20]

All of this was God's will in the sense that God laid upon the servant the iniquities of the people (v. 6); that is, he had the servant endure the punishment their iniquities deserved and willed to make the servant suffer (v. 10 MT). According to this reading, the affirmations that the servant bore the sins of others (vv. 4 LXX, 11, 12 MT) and offered up a guilt offering on their behalf (v. 11 MT) are also to be understood in the sense that the servant bore in the place of the guilty the punishment they deserved and offered up his life in substitution for theirs: "this Servant has actually suffered the condemnation of all the sins ever committed...."[21] The idea that the servant made intercession for the transgressors (v. 12 MT) can also be interpreted in the sense that he asked God to accept his own sufferings and death in the place of those which the sinners deserved.[22]

Several of these affirmations can also be understood as implying that the servant not only bore the *punishment* that the people's sins deserved, but also that those sins themselves were actually transferred to the servant in some sense. This would involve seeing sins as some type of substance or entity that can be taken from one person and placed upon another. Some interpreters compare this to the way in which sins were supposedly transferred to the scapegoat or a sacrificial victim, which was then put to death.[23] The allusion to a "guilt offering" in v. 11 would then be understood in this sense as well. It is also common to look to the idea of an exchange in order to understand these ideas: the people's sins are transferred to the servant, who bears those sins and their punishment, while the servant's innocence is in turn reckoned to the people so that they are now considered righteous by God. This latter affirmation does not appear explicitly in the text, yet it is possible to claim that it is present by implication.

Similarly, according to a penal substitution interpretation, the affirmation that the servant suffered "because of our transgressions" (vv. 5, 8) would be understood in the sense that "our" transgressions made it necessary for God to inflict punishment on someone for those transgressions.

---

20. Claus Westermann, *Isaiah 40-66: A Commentary*, trans. David M. G. Stalker (OTL; Philadelphia: Westminster, 1969), 263, 269. For other penal substitution readings of this passage, see Otfried Hofius, "The Fourth Servant Song in the New Testament Letters," in *The Suffering Servant*, ed. Janowski and Stuhlmacher, 166-68; Young, *Isaiah*, 3:348-50.

21. Oswalt, *Isaiah*, 405.

22. Young, for example, affirms that the servant "pleads before God the merit and value of his atoning work as the only ground of acceptance of the transgressors for whom he dies. The basis of the intercession is the substitutionary expiation of the servant" (*Isaiah*, 3:359).

23. See, for example, Bernd Janowski, "He Bore Our Sins: Isaiah 53 and the Drama of Taking Another's Place," in *The Suffering Servant*, ed. Janowski and Stuhlmacher, 68.

This was because God's righteous nature does not allow God to leave sin unpunished. The same phrase can also be read as affirming that the servant suffered, not for any transgressions of his own, but due to the transgressions of others whose punishment he endured.[24]

E) The sinners are now saved in the sense that they are no longer under the punishment they deserved for their sins. The "peace" and "healing" mentioned in v. 5 should in this case be understood primarily in a forensic sense: the sinful people have "peace with God" and are "healed" in that that they now know themselves to be forgiven, although this peace and forgiveness also result in the people experiencing wholeness in a broader sense. The servant "justified" them (v. 11) in that God has declared them righteous by virtue of the fact that the servant took their sin and punishment upon himself so that they no longer stand guilty before God.[25]

Analysis

While it is possible that first-century Jews and Jesus' first followers read Isaiah 53 on the basis of the ideas just mentioned, I would argue that, for several reasons, this is extremely unlikely. The most important of these reasons is that there is no clear evidence in ancient Jewish thought for the idea that YHWH's strict justice made it impossible for him to forgive sins without punishing them (point B). Such an idea is never affirmed or even suggested anywhere in the biblical and second-temple Jewish writings. In fact, those writings conceive of YHWH as a sovereign God who is free to act as he desires, forgiving when he wishes to forgive and chastising when he chooses to chastise: "I will be gracious to whom I will be gracious, and will show mercy on whom I will show mercy" (Exod. 33:19).

This observation is crucial. The penal substitution interpretation of Isaiah 53 depends in its entirety on the claim that it was impossible for God to forgive the people's sins without inflicting punishment for those sins on a sinless substitute. If God could have simply forgiven the people freely, there would have been no need to send the servant and have him suffer and die. Point B, therefore, constitutes the lynchpin of the penal substitution interpretation of Isaiah 53, since everything else depends on it.

In addition, according to this interpretation, the problem to which the passage responds is that of how God can save the people from punishment without compromising God's justice. This is simply not a concern in the Hebrew Scriptures nor in ancient Judaism as we know it. What is consistently seen as satisfying God's justice in ancient Jewish thought is not punishment or chastisement in itself but the return of the people to God in repentance

---

24. On this point, see Hermann Spieckermann, "The Conception and Prehistory of the Idea of Vicarious Suffering in the Old Testament," in *The Suffering Servant*, ed. Janowski and Stuhlmacher, 5-6.

25. On this idea, see Young, *Isaiah*, 3:348-50. Young also finds in Isaiah 53 the idea that the servant's righteousness is reckoned to the people, though nothing in the text explicitly affirms this (3:357-58).

and obedience. If this return does not take place, God's justice is *not* satisfied nor is God's anger appeased.

The use of the Hebrew *musar* and the Greek *paideia* in v. 5 makes it clear that the sufferings God allowed to be inflicted on the servant were aimed, not at appeasing God's own wrath or demand for justice, but bringing about the correction and repentance God wanted to see in the sinful people. The novel idea in this passage is that God brought about that correction and repentance by inflicting suffering, not on the sinful people themselves, but on the servant. The idea is that of chastising an innocent person for the wrongdoings of others, not as an end in itself, but in order to bring those others to repentance for what they have done.

The two verbs used in v. 5 to represent in positive terms the results of the servant's suffering and death point in the same direction: the people have "peace" and are "healed." A penal substitution requires understanding both of these terms in a forensic sense, as if they merely involved God forgiving the people. While such a reading is certainly possible, both verbs seem to imply something more than forgiveness alone.

As I have argued in the last chapter, in ancient Hebrew and Jewish thought, the presentation of offerings for sin (*asham*, v. 10 MT) had nothing to do with the idea of penal substitution. Rather, like other sacrifices, an offering for sin was considered a form of *intercession*. The idea of intercession appears explicitly in v. 12 MT, where the servant is said to have offered up a prayer on behalf of the guilty. As we have seen previously, according to the doctrine of penal substitution, there is no need for further intercession once a sacrifice for sin has been presented and accepted by God, since once God has accepted the sacrifice, forgiveness is ensured. To make forgiveness depend on the intercession as well means that the substitutionary sacrifice in itself does not obtain that forgiveness. If those presenting the guilt-offering in v. 10 are the people rather than the servant or YHWH himself, as the LXX affirms, this would also tell against a penal substitution interpretation of the passage. There would be no sense in the people themselves making an offering for sin if the servant's death has already obtained their forgiveness.

For all of these reasons, it is extremely problematic to claim that in antiquity Isaiah 53 was read on the basis of the notion of penal substitution. A penal substitution reading not only presents serious theological difficulties but runs against many of the most basic beliefs that Jews in antiquity held regarding Israel's God.

An Alternative Reading of Isaiah 53

A second narrative can also make sense of the affirmations regarding the servant's suffering and death independently of the notion of penal substitution:

> A) The people had fallen into sin and God wished to chastise them in order to correct them and bring them back to obedience. For this

purpose, God sent the servant. Although the text does not say explicitly how the servant's presence among the people would accomplish this, it hints at the idea that the servant would reveal God's will among them, making that will prosper among them (v. 10), and perhaps lead them to practice righteousness by giving knowledge to them (v. 11). The fact that he is called a servant also implies that in some way he was dedicated to serving them (v. 11 LXX). If the servant is understood as a prophet, perhaps his task would be that of calling others to repentance, although this is not stated in the text.

B) The servant was beaten, mistreated, and abused, probably by a person or group from among the people themselves, though not all of the people may have been involved. The servant apparently also suffered other hardships that were not necessarily inflicted upon him by his abusers, such as some type of sickness, plague, or infirmity. As observers, the narrators initially thought that it was God who was inflicting this suffering on the servant, whether directly or indirectly through those who mistreated him. In accordance with the view of suffering commonly found in the Hebrew Scriptures, they thought that his suffering was sent from God in order to chastise the servant: "we accounted him stricken, struck down by God, and afflicted" (v. 4).

C) At some point, however, the people realized that the servant was innocent of any sin: "he did no wrong and no deceit was in his mouth" (v. 9). They then understood that the servant was suffering not on account of his own sins but on account of theirs, and that it was they rather than the servant who deserved to suffer the same kind of things that the servant was suffering. They also saw the servant's suffering as God's will, since God was allowing the servant to suffer as he did, and perhaps had even sent some type of illness or bodily deformity upon the servant. The passage also implies that God had sent the servant into the situation in which he was being afflicted and crushed, and willed that he remain there in spite of the sufferings this involved. Thus the narrators who observe the servant affirm that he was "smitten by God," "afflicted," "pierced because of our transgressions," and "crushed because of our iniquities" (vv. 4-5). God "laid upon him the iniquity of us all" (v. 6) and "delighted to bruise him, making him suffer" (v. 10). He was stricken "for the transgression of my people" (v. 8) and "bore their sins" (vv. 11-12).

According to this narrative, the affirmation that the servant bore the sins of others can be understood in three different senses, each of which complements the others rather than excluding them:

1) The servant bore the sins of the people in the sense that he took upon himself the task of turning the people away from their sins

and was willing to suffer whatever might be necessary in order for this to happen. He assumed responsibility for bringing the people back to God in order to reconcile them to God and also interceded to God on their behalf. It might also be said that the servant "bore the sins of the people on his heart" in the sense that, in the midst of his suffering on account of his efforts to turn the people away from their sins, he remained committed to bringing them to repentance, no matter what the personal cost to himself.

2) The servant also bore the sins of the people in that he bore the *effects* of their sinful acts. This can be understood in the sense that he entered into a situation in which the people were practicing injustice and violence toward one another and, as a consequence, he came to be affected by this injustice and violence as well. However, the servant himself can also be seen as the one against whom the aggression and violence of all or some of the people was directed.

3) In addition, the servant bore the sins of the people by enduring the suffering inflicted by God as chastisement for their sins. In ancient Hebrew and Jewish thought, God responded to sin by allowing sinners to endure the consequences of their sinful actions without intervening to save them, as well as by sending different types of hardships and afflictions on them, such as illnesses, misfortunes, violence, and oppression at the hands of enemies. However, instead of the sinful people suffering these things, it was the servant who endured them. Either the people did not suffer at all or else their suffering was not as severe or as visible as that of the servant.

In this case, however, God's purpose in inflicting suffering on the righteous servant was to bring about a change in the conduct of the people rather than the servant. Perhaps God hoped that seeing the innocent servant suffer as he carried out the task given him would convict the people of their own sins and wrongdoing, particularly if all or some of the people were themselves responsible for inflicting suffering on the servant. By seeing how much the righteous servant was suffering because of the way in which they had treated him or as a result of his efforts to bring them back to God in repentance, they would be made aware of the depths into which they had fallen and the full extent of their sinfulness and injustice. Even though repentance is not mentioned explicitly in the passage, as Nielsen notes, it is implied in the people's recognition that the suffering of the servant was due to their sins rather than his: "In the confession that the servant is slain for their sins they confess that they are sinners."[26] The servant's faithfulness to his task and his intercession

---

26. Nielsen, "Lamb of God," 231.

on their behalf in spite of the afflictions he endured might also be seen as making a strong impression on the people and bringing them to change their ways.

Similarly, the affirmation that the servant suffered "because of our transgressions" can be understood according to any of the various senses just mentioned:

1) The people's transgressions made it necessary for God to send the servant to call them back to repentance. This required that the servant enter into a context in which suffering was inevitable.

2) The innocent servant suffered due to the sin being committed by some against others in that context, and also because of the sinful deeds directed against him by some or all of the sinful people. The servant endured this out of faithfulness to his task and God willed that he continue to carry out his task, in spite of the suffering it entailed.

3) In order to bring the people to repentance, God had the servant suffer the same afflictions that he was imposing on the people to chastise them for their sins—though perhaps to a greater degree—, or else made the servant suffer afflictions that the people themselves did not suffer. Thus their transgressions led to the servant's suffering the chastisement sent by God.

D) After enduring great suffering as the result of his commitment to the task God had given him, the servant was put to death: "he was cut off from the land of the living" (v. 8); "he makes his grave with the wicked" (v. 9); "he poured himself out to death" (v. 12). Even though he was righteous (v. 11), and what was done to him was a "perversion of justice" (v. 8), he faced death willingly and passively and, instead of rebelling or lashing out against others, he offered up his life to God making intercession for the sinful people. If the "sacrifice for sin" or "guilt offering" (*asham*) mentioned in v. 10 MT is taken as referring to what the servant did, then his death might be seen as analogous to a sacrifice for sin in the sense that, as he faced death, he offered himself up to God seeking God's forgiveness for the sins of others.[27]

E) The result of the servant's suffering and death is that the people are restored to health and *shalom*: "the chastisement of our peace was upon

---

[27]. I would reject the argument of Janowski that the *asham* in v. 10 refers not to a guilt-offering but a reparation or compensation paid ("He Bore our Sins," 67-70). This involves reading back into the text the Anselmian idea that the people owe some debt on account of their sin that must be paid; the servant supposedly does this by suffering in their place. Undoubtedly, according to the Mosaic law, when one had taken something unjustly from another or caused someone else some type of loss, restitution was necessary along with the sacrifice. However, there is no hint in Isaiah 53 that the servant is making restitution to someone for some loss or damage that the people's sins have caused, either by suffering or by some other means.

him, and by his bruises we are healed" (v. 5). This can be understood in the sense that the people were led to repent by the servant's faithfulness to the task God had given him in spite of the suffering it involved for him and also by observing what happened to the servant. Both of these things made their sin evident to them and led them to repent and change their ways so they might have peace and be healed. "His sufferings bring them back to their senses, for his sufferings convict them of their sins."[28] This repentance also led to their being justified or accepted as righteous by God. In this sense, he "will justify the many" (v. 11 MT), having borne their sins.[29]

Analysis

This interpretation of Isaiah 53 accounts for all of the affirmations found in both the Hebrew and Greek versions of the text and makes perfect sense of each of them. While in principle the same can be said of the penal substitution interpretation, there are good reasons for claiming that it is much more likely that those who read Isaiah 53 in Jesus' day would have understood it in accordance with ideas such as those just outlined.

Above all, as we have seen in Chapters 2 and 3, in both the Hebrew Scriptures and second-temple Jewish literature, the condition for being forgiven was always said to be repentance and a renewed commitment to obeying God's will. What was thought to bring forgiveness was not divine chastisement in itself, but only the proper reaction to that chastisement on the part of the people.

A second factor is that, rather than focusing on the question of how YHWH can forgive sins without compromising his justice, the passage stresses the impact that the servant's suffering had on the people. The first verses of the passage repeatedly speak of those who observe the servant: as they look at him, they are astonished and startled because they see something they had never seen or heard about before (52:13-15). They proclaim what they have heard and what has been revealed to them (53:1). They see nothing desirable in his appearance (53:2) and hide their faces from him, holding him of no account (53:2). As they look at his infirm, diseased figure they consider him to be rejected and afflicted by God (53:4). While the subsequent verses do not explicitly mention the people observing the servant, they use graphic imagery that suggests that the people were touched deeply by what they saw: the way the servant was crushed, wounded, oppressed, and afflicted, as well as the fact that he was silent as he was led away like a lamb led to slaughter, created quite an impact on them (53:7-8). The images and language running throughout

---

28. Sapp, "The LXX," 186 (referring to the MT).

29. Terence E. Fretheim notes the parallels between Isaiah 53 and Ezek. 4:4-6, in which the prophet is said to bear the guilt or punishment of Israel while lying on his side (*The Suffering of God: An Old Testament Perspective*; OBT; Philadelphia: Fortress, 1984, 163). Whether or not the idea is actually the same, in both passages it would be a question of God's servant willingly enduring suffering in order to make the people aware of their sins rather than suffering in their place.

these verses therefore also focuses attention on the extraordinary and even shocking things that happened to the servant, as well as the admirable things God has done and will do through him in order to accomplish his objectives among the people.[30]

All of this strongly supports the idea, therefore, that what leads to the people having peace and being healed and justified is *their reaction to what they observed and heard*. If the offering for sin mentioned in v. 10 is understood as something presented by the people, as the LXX affirms, this would support the same conclusion: having been convicted of their guilt by what the servant endured, they respond by presenting a sin-offering up to God, either in a literal or metaphorical sense.[31]

In addition, as noted above, the use of *musar* and *paideia* communicates the idea of the *chastisement* and the *correction* of the people rather than their punishment per se. Although it is the servant who suffers rather than the people, the effect is the same: the chastisement that the servant endures moves the people to repentance and obedience. In fact, if we understand the word "punishment" in these terms, there is even a sense in which we could speak of the servant's enduring the punishment for the people's sins in their place. However, while the language would be the same, the idea would be different from that which we saw above with regard to the penal substitution interpretation of Isaiah 53: the reason that the people are restored to peace, healed, and justified is *not that the servant endured the suffering that they deserved for their sins in their place*, but rather that *the servant's suffering what they deserved for their sins, together with the ministry that led to that suffering, brought about a change in them*.

This constitutes the fundamental difference between the two readings. According to a penal substitution reading, it is the servant's suffering divine chastisement for the people's sins *in and of itself* that brings about their healing, forgiveness, and reconciliation to God and one another. According to this alternative reading, however, that healing, forgiveness, and reconciliation are the result, *not of the servant's suffering per se* but of *the manner in which the people react to the servant's unjust suffering*. For this reason, even though the innocent servant endures in the people's place a chastisement or discipline similar to that which they deserved for their sins, strictly speaking, the servant is not their *substitute*. God's objective was not to satisfy his justice by punishing the servant rather than the people for the people's sins, as if suffering itself satisfied God's justice, but to bring about a change in the people by having the servant endure the kind of punishment or chastisement that their sins deserved as a result of his ministry among them.

---

30. As Ben Witherington III notes, the LXX stresses even more than the Hebrew the speaker's having observed the distress and suffering of the servant ("Isaiah 53:1-12 [Septuagint]," in *The Historical Jesus in Context*, ed. Amy-Jill Levine, Dale C. Allison Jr., and John Dominic Crossan; Princeton, NJ: Princeton University Press, 2006, 402).

31. Hengel, for example, suggests that the "spiritual 'sin-offering'" alluded to in v. 10 of the LXX should be understood as the people of Israel's repentance, "acknowledging and confessing their sins" ("Effective History," 129).

While it is entirely plausible that Isaiah 53 would have been read in this way in the first century CE, many other readings were of course possible. It is quite likely that the servant was at times understood as representing Israel in general, in which case the passage would probably be seen as referring to Israel's exile. Even if it was read in this way, however, the idea would be, not that the suffering that Israel endured at the hands of other nations was an end in itself and satisfied God's justice, but rather that other nations would become convicted of their own injustice by contemplating Israel's suffering.[32] The same observation would hold true if the servant was understood as a particular group within Israel: in itself, the suffering that the members of this group endured as a result of their serving others who were guilty of grave sins did not lead to peace and healing for the people as a whole. Rather, what restored peace and resulted in healing was the way the people as a whole reacted to the unjust suffering of the group identified with the servant.

A number of biblical scholars have argued for a reading of Isaiah 53 based on the notion of participation or inclusive place-taking. The most notable of these is Otfried Hofius, who considers the idea of penal substitution, which he identifies with "exclusive place-taking," as "simply outrageous."[33] Hooker has claimed that in Isaiah 53, "we do not have someone who suffers *instead of* his guilty compatriots, but rather someone who *shares* in their sufferings, even though he himself, unlike them, is innocent."[34] She interprets vv. 4 and 12 against this idea: "if we remember that the Servant was not the only person to be suffering, these statements read rather differently from the way in which they are normally interpreted.... [T]he Servant suffers *as a result of the sins of others*."[35] She speaks of this as "representative suffering" or "inclusive place-taking" rather than "exclusive place-taking."[36]

Clearly, behind such interpretations of Isaiah 53 is a desire to replace the notion of penal substitution with a participatory soteriology. Knight, for example, insists that Isa 53:7 is to be interpreted in the sense that the "vicarious suffering on the part of the volunteer is therefore participative; it is neither substitutionary, nor yet is it penal."[37] However, while the passage can certainly be interpreted in the sense that the servant suffers God's chastisement *together with* the people rather than doing so *in their place*, the latter idea can also be affirmed while still rejecting the idea of penal substitution. According to the proposal I have just outlined, the servant can be said not only to suffer

---

32. For this interpretation of Isaiah 53, see Kenneth Grayston, *Dying We Live: A New Enquiry into the Death of Christ in the New Testament* (New York: Oxford University Press, 1990), 192-93.

33. See Hofius, "Fourth Servant Song," 168. In this article (164-88), Hofius does not offer a detailed exegesis of Isaiah 53 on the basis of the idea of inclusive place-taking, but simply claims that it is present in the New Testament. A more complete discussion of this idea is found in the two articles by Daniel P. Bailey, "Concepts of *Stellvertretung* in the Interpretation of Isaiah 53," and "The Suffering Servant: Recent Tübingen Scholarship on Isaiah 53," in *Jesus*, ed. Bellinger and Farmer, 223-50, 251-59.

34. Hooker, "Use of Isaiah 53," 97.

35. Ibid., 97.

36. Ibid., 98.

37. Knight, *Deutero-Isaiah*, 237.

the same things that the people suffered for their sins, but also to endure sufferings that the people themselves did *not* endure, even though they deserved to suffer similar things for their sins. In this case, the servant can be said to have suffered in their stead. Yet, as I have argued above, this should not be taken in the sense that the punishment the servant endures in itself leads to the people's healing and forgiveness, as a penal substitution interpretation affirms. Rather, what leads to the people's healing and forgiveness is *the manner in which they react to the servant's sufferings.*

It should also be noted that most proponents of a penal substitution reading would also agree that, once the servant had endured the punishment deserved by the people for their sins, a change in the people's behavior would take place as a result.[38] In fact, advocates of penal substitution interpretations often claim that, once God has had the servant punished for the people's sins, the people know that God does not overlook sin but invariably punishes it. This leads them to avoid falling back into sin, since they now know that God does not leave sin unpunished.

Such a view, however, ultimately results in a denial of the claim that the people's forgiveness depends entirely on what the servant did. If God has already punished the people's sins by inflicting the suffering they deserved on the servant, then they are no longer subject to punishment, no matter what further sins they commit. Thus it does not matter whether or not they fall back into sin, since they will still be forgiven by virtue of what the servant suffered. However, if they now know that God does not leave sin unpunished and therefore must refrain from sinning in order to be spared punishment, then any further forgiveness ends up depending on their repentance and obedience rather than on what the servant did for them in the past.

In the end, then, there are strong reasons for affirming that, when people in Jesus' day read Isaiah 53, they would have understood the basic idea of the passage in terms of the sinful people being healed, justified, and restored to peace, not by the servant's suffering itself, but as a result of their contemplation of the servant's suffering, since what they saw led to a change in their manner of thinking and behaving. Although they may have understood in different ways the affirmations that the servant bore the people's sins, along with other ideas that are found in the passage, there is no basis either in the passage itself nor in ancient Hebrew and Jewish thought for the notion that God's justice was satisfied when the servant suffered what the people deserved for their sins. Rather, as the Hebrew Scriptures and second-temple Jewish writings consistently maintain, God's justice is satisfied only when the people return to God in repentance and obedience, committing themselves to living according to God's will. This is what the servant's suffering and death would have been understood as accomplishing.

---

38. See, for example, Westermann, *Isaiah 40-66*, 263-64.

VICARIOUS DEATH AND ATONEMENT ELSEWHERE IN THE HEBREW SCRIPTURES

In important ways, Isaiah 53 is unique in the Hebrew Scriptures. No other passage speaks of people being restored to peace and healing as a result of a particular figure suffering on account of their sins. In this sense, this passage may be considered an "erratic block" in the Hebrew Scripture, as Klaus Koch has affirmed.[39] Nevertheless, Isaiah 53 does not relate the servant's death to the appeasement of YHWH's anger at sin, an idea which is never mentioned in the passage, nor does it explicitly affirm that the servant's death atones for sin. The idea that the death of certain individuals or groups of people may lead YHWH to put aside his anger at sin is found in only a couple of passages from the Hebrew Scriptures.

One of these is the story of Phinehas found in Num. 25:1-15. There YHWH commands that the Israelites who had abandoned him and had instead joined themselves to the Madianites by adopting Baal-Peor as their god be put to death. In response, Phinehas takes a spear and slays Zimri, one of the Israelites who had joined himself to Baal-Peor, together with his Madianite companion. YHWH then tells Moses: "Phinehas son of Eleazar, son of Aaron the priest, has turned back my wrath from the Israelites by manifesting such zeal among them on my behalf that in my jealousy I did not consume the Israelites. Therefore say, 'I hereby grant him my covenant of peace. It shall be for him and for his descendants after him a covenant of perpetual priesthood, because he was zealous for his God, and made atonement for the Israelites'" (25:11-13). The high regard in which Phinehas and his act of zeal were held in antiquity is evident from the fact that this account is recalled elsewhere in the Hebrew Scriptures and other second-temple writings.[40]

Proponents of penal substitution views have often pointed to this story as evidence for the idea that death was thought to make atonement for sins. Supposedly, in this case God's strict justice and God's anger at sin demanded that the people's sins be punished with death. Phinehas satisfied God's justice and appeased God's anger by slaying the guilty. Leon Morris, for example, even interprets this narrative in sacrificial terms: "Here the zealous priest by offering up the lives of the evil-doers is thought of as rendering the *kopher* which averts the divine wrath. There can hardly be serious doubt that here we have propitiation in the fullest sense, or that this propitiation is the turning away of wrath by the offering of a *kopher*."[41] According to this interpretation, the death of the guilty Israelites is a payment to God's justice and in itself averts God's wrath.

In reality, there is no basis in the Hebrew text for this type of interpretation. The noun *kopher*, "redemption payment," appears nowhere in the passage.

---

39. Klaus Koch, "Sühne und Sündenvergebung um die Wende von der exilischen zur nachexilischen Zeit," *EvTh* 26 (1996): 217-39.
40. See Ps. 106:30; 1 Macc. 2:54; 4 Macc. 18:12; Sir. 45:23; Josephus, *Ant.* 4.152-54, 159.
41. Leon Morris, *The Apostolic Preaching of the Cross*, 3rd ed. (Grand Rapids: Eerdmans, 1965), 165.

While the verb *kapar* is used, the idea is that of making atonement or expiation. Strictly speaking, however, it is not the death of the guilty idolater that is regarded as making atonement but the zealous act of Phinehas, which was an expression of his firm commitment to YHWH. In order to understand the passage, it must be read in the context of the overarching narrative of which it forms part. YHWH had brought the Israelites out of Egypt in order to make them his own people. He had given them his law so that there might be justice and equity among them. The Pentateuch and other parts of the Hebrew Scriptures see these events as ultimately having the goal of blessing other nations through Israel; they would be attracted to the worship of YHWH and be able to attain the same justice and *shalom* that Israel was to possess as a result of the Israelite's obedience to God's law.

The people's abandonment of YHWH and attachment to Baal-Peor, however, would make the realization of this plan impossible. According to the logic of the passage, it was necessary to put a stop to what was happening. The actions of Moses as well as the zeal of Phinehas were viewed as fulfilling this objective.

What was thought to have pleased YHWH and appeased his wrath, therefore, was not the death of those who had fallen into idolatry. What YHWH desired was that the people return to him in order to commit themselves to living in accordance with his will. Phinehas's act was meritorious because it served to bring back the remainder of the Israelites to the service of YHWH so that they might once more submit to his law, which was aimed at ensuring justice, equity, and *shalom* for the people. As noted in Chapter 3, the worship of other gods such as Baal-Peor was viewed as resulting in unjust and oppressive practices that undermined and destroyed the people's well-being.

Strictly speaking, therefore, in this passage it is *not the death of the guilty* that makes atonement and appeases God's wrath but *the return of the people to YHWH and his law*. This is what Phinehas's act of zeal helped accomplish. If atonement and the propitiation of God's anger were believed to be brought about merely by the death of the guilty, as if this alone effected justice, then Phinehas's act would have been unnecessary, since YHWH himself could have struck the guilty dead. There are numerous accounts in the Pentateuch in which YHWH does precisely that. For example, when in Genesis 7-9 YHWH uses the flood to destroy the vast majority of sinful human beings, this is not presented as an act aimed at satisfying his justice or appeasing his wrath, as if he simply desired to make sinners pay for their sins. Rather, his goal is that of cleansing the earth of sin so that a fresh start might be made through Noah and his family.[42] The objective of YHWH in that story, as in Numbers 25, is that of establishing a people who will practice justice and righteousness. In ancient Hebrew thought, YHWH was not some type of god like Moloch, whose wrath was appeased by the death of human beings, but rather a God committed to the well-being of the people. Yet because

---

42. As noted in Chapter 2, this is precisely how Philo interpreted the story of the flood (*Moses* 2.64).

that well-being was seen as depending on obedience to him, in the Hebrew Scriptures YHWH is presented as one who will not tolerate the people abandoning the path of justice he has laid out for them in order to follow other paths by serving other gods.

Josephus, in fact, provides concrete evidence that the story of Phinehas was understood precisely in this fashion in the second-temple period. He writes that Phinehas became "very indignant" when he saw what Zimri the Israelite had done and "determined, before his insolence should become stronger through impunity, to exact the judgment upon him by action, and to prevent the lawlessness from going further if those who started it were not punished" (*Ant.* 4.152). According to Josephus, then, what pleased God and atoned for Israel's sins was that Phinehas's act put a stop to the spread of lawlessness related to the worship of the god Baal-Peor so that the people might instead return to YHWH.

These same ideas must be kept in mind when considering the only other passage from the Hebrew Scriptures in which the possibility of atoning for sin is related to the death of a human being, namely, the story of the golden calf in Exodus 32.[43] As in Numbers 25, here the people abandon YHWH for a false god and as a consequence arouse YHWH's wrath. After relating how Moses came down from the mountain to confront the people, the narrative continues:

> On the next day Moses said to the people, "You have sinned a great sin. But now I will go up to the Lord; perhaps I can make atonement for your sin." So Moses returned to the Lord and said, "Alas, this people has sinned a great sin; they have made for themselves gods of gold. But now, if you will only forgive their sin—but if not, blot me out of the book that you have written." But the Lord said to Moses, "Whoever has sinned against me I will blot out of my book. But now go, lead the people to the place about which I have spoken to you; see, my angel shall go in front of you. Nevertheless, when the day comes for chastisement, I will chastise them for their sin" (Exod. 32:30-34).

Interestingly, in this passage, the idea that one might die for the sins of others is rejected, as is the idea that such a death might make atonement for sins. As elsewhere in the Hebrew Scriptures, YHWH refuses to accept the

---

43. In addition to the passages examined in this section, some scholars have pointed to others in the Hebrew Scriptures in which one person or group is said to suffer in the place of another or atone for the sins of others, but a careful examination of these passages indicates that they do not speak of the righteous bearing the sin of others or God's wrath at that sin in the place of the guilty. Dieter Vieweger and Annette Böckler, for example, note that Isa. 43:3b-4 speaks of God taking Egypt as a ransom price for Israel, and claim that this passage influenced the *lutron* saying of Mark 10:45 ("»Ich gebe Ägypten als Lösegeld für dich«: Mk 10,45 und die jüdische Tradition zu Jes 43,3b.4," *ZAW* 108 [1996]: 594-607). Nothing in that passage, however, suggests the innocent being put to death in place of the guilty or making atonement for their sins. Rather, the idea is that God will give up other nations in order to redeem his beloved Israel. Axel von Dobbeler points to the story of Aaron's rod putting away God's wrath at the murmuring of some of the Israelites against Moses and Aaron in Num. 17:6-15 as an example of an act of atonement on behalf of others (*Glaube als Teilhabe: Historische und semantische Grundlagen der paulinischen Theologie und Ekklesiologie des Glaubens*; WUNT 2/22; Tübingen: J. C. B. Mohr, 1987, 77). In this case, however, God puts away his wrath, not because of Moses or Aaron, but because the blossoming of Aaron's rod puts an end to the murmuring of the Israelites involved.

death of the innocent in the place of the guilty.[44] The act of atonement that Moses sought to make consisted, not of offering to give up his life in the place of the life of the many, as if this would have calmed YHWH's wrath, but of *interceding* on behalf of the people, asking God to forgive them. As we noted in Chapter 3, the idea of atonement through intercession is common throughout the Hebrew Scriptures. The implicit basis for this intercession is Moses' intention to bring the people back to YHWH in obedience. Only this could satisfy YHWH's justice and appease his wrath. As the people's leader, Moses was thought to have both the responsibility and the moral authority to make this return to YHWH happen.

As Hofius notes, therefore, Moses' offer to give up his life must be seen as an act of solidarity and has nothing to do with the notion of penal substitution: "These words are not to be understood as Moses' offer to surrender his life vicariously in exchange for the life of the people. They are rather his declaration of the deepest solidarity with them: if Yahweh refuses to forgive the guilty, then the innocent one is prepared to suffer the same fate as they."[45] The fact that YHWH offers to leave the people unpunished for the time being—although he says that, at some point later on, they must still be disciplined for what they have done—is due to his hope that under Moses' leadership the Israelites eventually will indeed become the obedient people he desires to see for their own good and the good of others. This is the logic behind the passage. As Sam Williams notes, Moses is not offering himself in the place of the people but laying before God the alternative: "forgive these people and let us live *or* if you will not forgive these people, destroy me with them. By his request to be blotted out of the book of life if the people are not forgiven, Moses expresses his desire to stand with them and to share their fate."[46]

VICARIOUS DEATH AND ATONEMENT IN ANCIENT GRECO-ROMAN LITERATURE

The idea that one person's death could benefit others in some way seems to have been more common among Jews in the period of Greco-Roman rule. Many scholars attribute this to the influence of ideas from the Hellenistic and the Roman literature of the time, where certain figures are said to have given up their lives nobly and heroically in order to save others. Hengel notes that "in ancient Israel there are hardly any examples of dying for Israel, the Law or the sanctuary, which are stressed as heroic actions."[47] Both Hengel and other

---

44. Discussing this passage and others from the Hebrew Scriptures, Henk S. Versnel rightly notes that the idea of substitution "stands in stark contradiction to other OT texts such as 'a person may die only for his own sins' (Deut 24,16; 2 Kgs 14,6; 2 Chron 25,4), and 'I blot out from my book only those who have sinned against me' (Ex 32,30-33)...." ("Making Sense of Jesus' Death: The Pagan Contribution," in *Deutungen des Todes Jesu im Neuen Testament*; ed. Jörg Frey and Jens Schröter; WUNT 181; Tübingen: Mohr Siebeck, 2005, 215, n10).

45. Hofius, "Fourth Servant Song," 169.

46. Sam K. Williams, *Jesus' Death as Saving Event: The Background and Origin of a Concept* (HDR 2; Missoula, MT: Scholars Press, 1975), 103.

47. Hengel, *Atonement*, 7.

scholars who have explored the subject of vicarious death in antiquity cite a number of passages from ancient Greek and Roman literature that speak of a person offering up his or her life to save others in order to consider whether ideas from these passages might have influenced the interpretations that Jesus' first followers gave to his death.[48] It is not necessary to examine these passages in detail here in order to address the basic logic behind them. Following Hengel's categorization, these passages can be divided into three types.

According to the first of these, one is said to die for one's family, friends, city, or nation in the context of some type of conflict.[49] In this case, the people in need of deliverance or salvation are under attack from some enemy that is seeking to subject or destroy them. By giving up his or her life in the midst of the conflict, the heroic figure secures protection for the other members of his or her family, friends, or fellow citizens, or else gains victory over those who seek them harm.[50] An excellent biblical example of this type of death for others is found in the story of Eleazar, also called Avaran, in 1 Macc. 6:43-46. In the midst of a battle with the forces of King Antiochus, who are attacking the Maccabeans, Eleazar courageously fights his way through the enemy lines, places himself beneath an armored elephant and kills it by stabbing it from below. As a result, however, the dead elephant falls upon him and he is crushed to death. In this context, it is said that "he gave his life to save his people" (v. 44).

Although at times sacrificial language can be used to refer to the way in which one voluntarily gives up one's life in battle for others, strictly speaking, this type of dying for others does not involve any type of atonement for sins. The one who dies is not undergoing any kind of divine punishment for sin or enduring divinely-inflicted suffering and death for others as their substitute. Nor is the heroic figure said to offer up his or her life to God in order to appease God's wrath or obtain divine forgiveness for the people's sins. Undoubtedly, at times the enemy forces may be seen as having been sent by God or the gods to punish the people for some disobedient act they have committed. However, the heroic figure obtains salvation or victory, not by moving God or the gods to cease afflicting the people by means of the hostile forces, but simply by carrying out some action that leads intrinsically to the defeat of those forces.

---

48. Ibid., 6-31. See also S. Williams, *Jesus' Death*, 194-95; Jan Willem van Henten, *The Maccabean Martyrs as Saviours of the Jewish People: A Study of 2 and 4 Maccabees* (JSJSup 57; Leiden: Brill, 1997), 145-51, 157-59, 213-28; Versnel, "Making Sense," 213-25, 245-50; Finlan, *Background*, 194-97.

49. See Hengel, *Atonement*, 6-15. The concept of the *devotio pro principe* mentioned by Versnel, which involved dying on behalf of the emperor, can be considered a variation of this type of vicarious death ("Making Sense," 245-48). For other examples of this idea, see van Henten, *Maccabean Martyrs*, 145-46, 157-59, 213-25.

50. It is significant, as Jeffrey B. Gibson notes, that in the Greco-Roman literature, "*never* does the one to whom the dying formula is applied die for an adversary or enemy. The death for others, especially the 'noble death,' is always undertaken in an attempt to rescue or defend *one's own*" ("Paul's 'Dying Formula': Prolegomena to an Understanding of its Import and Significance," in *Celebrating Romans: Template for Pauline Theology. Essays in Honor of Robert Jewett*; ed. Sheila E. McGinn; Grand Rapids: Eerdmans, 2004, 25).

In a second type of "dying for" formula, a person is said to die for some type of ideal, such as the laws of a city or nation, a creed, certain moral tenets, or some philosophical truth.[51] The classic example of this is the story of Socrates's death as told by Plato, particularly in his *Phaedo*. This story seems to have been widely known and highly influential in antiquity. While the authorities who accuse Socrates of perverting the youth through his teaching and on that basis sentence him to death are officially the representatives of justice, Socrates and others see them as acting *unjustly* in condemning him. Nevertheless, Socrates willingly drinks the mortal poison instead of inciting others to resist those authorities by violent means or attempting to save his life by fleeing or hiding. He can therefore be said to have died "for others" in the sense that his acceptance of death benefited others in various ways. He maintained his convictions rather than compromising them or renouncing them in the face of injustice, thus moving others to adhere to those convictions more firmly. Because those convictions are considered good and just and even worth dying for, his death thus benefits society and encourages others to defend what is right in spite of the cost involved. Also, by accepting death rather than calling on others to rise up to defend him and his cause, he avoided violence and bloodshed and thus acted in favor of others. Hengel also cites the example of Apollonius, the hero of Philostratus's *Vita Apollonii*, who tells his student Damis: "it is an obligation of the law that we should die for freedom and an injunction of nature that we should die for kinsfolk or friends or loved ones.... [I]t is the duty of the wise in a still higher degree to lay down their lives for the tenets they have embraced."[52]

Here again, there is no idea of penal substitution or atonement for the sins of others. The penalty inflicted on Socrates, for example, was unjust. It was not thought that Socrates was dying in the place of others, as if others would have been sentenced to death and executed had not Socrates willingly forfeited his life. Nor was Socrates's death believed to have atoned for the sins of others. To die for some principle or ideal simply involves being faithful to that principle or ideal at the cost of one's life and perhaps seeking to inspire and motivate others to be faithful to the principle or ideal involved as well.

A third type of vicarious, noble death found in ancient Greek and Roman writings involves the offering of life in order to put an end to some type of plague or disaster.[53] In this case, the threat of death is due, not to the aggression of other human beings, but to the gods or divine forces in nature, who have been provoked to wrath due to something human beings have done or failed to do. While the people involved have acted contrary to the will of the gods, it is not necessarily accurate to say that they have "sinned," since in many cases what the gods demand is not related to what is right and just. Instead, the gods may have some type of need or selfish desire that the people have

---

51. See Hengel, *Atonement*, 15-18.
52. Philostratus the Athenian, *Vita Apollonii* 7.14 (cited in Hengel, *Atonement*, 18).
53. See Hengel, *Atonement*, 19-28. For similar examples, see van Henten, *Maccabean Martyrs*, 245-50.

refused to satisfy. When the people do not give the gods what they need or want or act in ways that provoke the gods' wrath, the gods respond by inflicting some type of harm on the people through something such as a famine or plague or by sending some enemy against them.

Hengel, for example, cites examples such as that of the king Erechtheus, who sacrifices his daughters to assuage the wrath of Poseidon in Lycurgus's *Oratio in Leoctratem*, as well as the story of the three daughters of Leo, who "were sacrificed during a plague of a famine" in the *Varia Historia* of Aelian.[54] He also mentions the ideas of the *pharmakos*, which constitutes a type of human "scapegoat" offered to the gods to appease them, and the *sphagion* or blood sacrifice that "is offered to the powers of the underworld before great undertakings, battle, taking an oath or sacrificing to the dead."[55] A further example is that of the *devotio*, which was also a kind of "self-sacrifice" in which "a Roman general consigned himself along with the enemy army to the gods of the underworld or to other anonymous deities in order to gain victory for his own army."[56]

In a sense, such deaths can be regarded as sacrificial acts that make atonement by placating the wrath of the gods. As Hengel notes, a "fixed ingredient of almost all these traditions" is that of a "divine demand of an atoning sacrifice to deliver the people, the land or a family...."[57] In many cases, such deaths involve an act of substitution in which the gods spare the lives of the many in exchange for the human life or lives offered to them. The idea of propitiation is also present in that the gods' anger is appeased.

This third type of death for others, however, must be regarded as foreign to the concepts of God, sacrifice, and atonement that we find in the Hebrew Scriptures and other Jewish writings in antiquity. There, human sacrifice is strictly forbidden and is regarded as a great cruelty. As we have noted previously, unlike other gods in antiquity, Israel's God was not thought to have any needs that human beings had to help satisfy. In ancient Hebrew and Jewish thought, what provokes the wrath of YHWH is not some selfish desire or passion but the practice of injustice. Conversely, what appeases that wrath is repentance and a return to him in obedience. If it is not the blood of animals that pleases YHWH and placates his anger at the sins of his people but the practice of justice, compassion, and love, much less could the sacrifices of human blood or human lives please him or put away his wrath. On the contrary, such sacrifices would *provoke* his wrath. Therefore, while in other ancient worldviews this third type of death might be seen as atoning or propitiatory, in the Jewish worldview of Jesus' day this was not the case. In fact, there is nothing in the second-temple Jewish literature that can provide any evidence for the existence of such an understanding of dying for others among Jews of the period.

---

54. Hengel, *Atonement*, 19-20, 22.
55. Ibid., 19-20, 24-25.
56. Ibid., 23-24. For a fuller discussion of this idea, see van Henten, *Maccabean Martyrs*, 146-49, 159.
57. Hengel, *Atonement*, 23.

Simon Gathercole cites as an example of a substitutionary death the story of Alcestis, who endures death in the place of her husband, king Admetus, in Euripides's play *Alcestis*, written around 438 BCE.[58] Gathercole even suggests that Paul may have had this story in mind when he speaks of Christ dying for a good or righteous person in Rom. 5:6-8. According to this play, in response to kindnesses received from Admetus, the god Apollo makes a deal with the Fates, who had power over life and death, so that if Admetus ever fell ill and was at the point of death, the Fates might restore him to health in order to save his life. In exchange for this favor, however, Admetus would have to find someone who was willing to die in his place. When Admetus later becomes ill and the doctors tell him that he will not live much longer, he looks for someone who will volunteer to die for him. When he can find no one to volunteer, Alcestis offers her life in exchange for his, and as a result her soul is led down by death to the underworld. Gathercole notes that the story of Alcestis continued to be popular among people even in the first and second centuries CE, as is evident from a number of inscriptions from that period in which certain women claim to have given up their life to save the life of their husbands. Gathercole also cites other examples of individuals dying in the place of others and on that basis claims that it was stories such as these that Paul had in mind in Rom. 5:6-8.

Like the examples of substitutionary death cited by Hengel, however, in the story of Alcestis, the ones who take her life in exchange for that of Admetus are gods who are demanding that either Admetus or Alcestis die, not because Admetus has sinned and they insist that he suffer death as the consequence of his sin, but simply because they decide that it is time for them to take Admetus's soul to Hades. His death was to be the natural death that all human beings eventually experience. In this story, there is nothing to suggest the idea of Alcestis making atonement for something Admetus has done or propitiating the wrath of the gods at Admetus. Furthermore, in Greek thought, death was generally not regarded as a punishment for human sin. A person who had done something to offend the gods might die a premature or painful death, and such a death perhaps could be viewed as divine punishment for sin. Even if one wishes to argue that Alcestis endured the penalty of death in Admetus's place, she only saved Admetus from dying temporarily, since eventually Admetus would also die, undergoing the punishment to which all human beings are subject. Thus her death for Admetus only delayed his own death, but did not actually save him from death. The same is true of the other examples cited by Gathercole: the one who dies in the place of another is not atoning for the sins of that other person or paying a penalty in that person's place for that person's moral failure or sin.

While the idea of vicarious death is undoubtedly fairly common in ancient Greek and Roman literature, therefore, nowhere do we find the idea that

---

58. See Simon Gathercole, *Defending Substitution: An Essay on Atonement in Paul* (ASBT; Grand Rapids: Baker Academic, 2015), 91-97.

a righteous person could atone for the sins of others by enduring the just punishment that they deserve for their sins in their place. Even in the cases in which a god or the gods wish to punish some human beings in order to placate their anger at something that those human beings have done, their concern is for themselves rather than for the good of human beings. Those who die to save others from death by dying in their stead do so to deliver them from something or someone that cannot be compared or associated with YHWH, the God of Israel who is both loving and just, and thus constantly seeks the good of the human beings he has created by demanding that they live as he has commanded.

VICARIOUS DEATH AND ATONEMENT IN SECOND-TEMPLE JEWISH LITERATURE AND RABBINIC THOUGHT

Only a few passages from second-temple Jewish literature relate the death of human beings to atonement and reconciliation with God. The most important of these appear in the books of 2 and 4 Maccabees. Both of these books relate the manner in which the Jewish people of Palestine were delivered from the oppressive rule of the Seleucid king Antiochus Epiphanes, who sought to replace Jewish beliefs and practices with Hellenistic culture and religion in the second century BCE.

Vicarious Suffering and Death in 2 Maccabees

The Book of 2 Maccabees, composed some time in the mid- to late second century BCE, interprets the oppression and persecution that the Jews were experiencing under Antiochus as divine chastisement for their sins.[59] Chapters 6 and 7 of the book describe the sufferings of the priest Eleazar and seven brothers with their mother, all of whom are imprisoned, tortured, and put to death for refusing to submit to the measures imposed by Antiochus.[60] In the midst of his account of these sufferings, the author ascribes the following words to Eleazar, who is advanced in years:

---

59. On the main themes, purpose, and date of 2 Maccabees, as well as the development of the text, see especially Daniel R. Schwartz, *2 Maccabees* (CEJL; Berlin: Walter de Gruyter, 2008), 3-37, 518-29; Jonathan A. Goldstein, *II Maccabees: A New Translation with Introduction and Commentary* (AB 41A; Garden City, NY: Doubleday, 1983), 71-83; M. B. Dagut, "II Maccabees and the Death of Antiochus Epiphanes," *JBL* 72 (1953): 149-57.

60. I will refrain from the use of the term *martyr* to refer to Eleazar, the seven brothers, and their mother in 2 and 4 Maccabees, despite arguments in favor of its use by scholars such as van Henten (*Maccabean Martyrs*, 6). Although, as van Henten argues, the term can be defined in ways that may seem to make its use appropriate to speak of those tortured and put to death by Antiochus in 2 and 4 Maccabees, it is nevertheless not a term found in the texts themselves and carries with it certain connotations today that may reflect ideas that are foreign to those texts. In particular, despite its etymology, in modern usage the term *martyr* tends to focus attention on the death of those involved rather than their resistance to the authorities persecuting them and the strong convictions behind that resistance that result in their choosing death over submission. It is common today, for example, to speak of children or innocent civilians in areas of armed conflict being "martyred" merely in the sense of being killed as victims of violence or warfare.

"These punishments were designed not to destroy but to discipline our people. In fact, it is a sign of great kindness not to let the impious alone for long, but to punish them immediately. For in the case of the other nations the Lord waits patiently to punish them until they have reached the full measure of their sins; but he does not deal in this way with us, in order that he may not take vengeance on us afterward when our sins have reached their height. Therefore he never withdraws his mercy from us. Although he disciplines us with calamities, he does not forsake his own people" (2 Macc. 6:12-16; cf. 6:26).

The author of 2 Maccabees also attributes to two of the seven brothers the same type of affirmation. They tell Antiochus: "But do not think that God has forsaken our people.... For we are suffering these things on our own account, because of our sins against our own God" (7:16, 18). "For we are suffering because of our own sins. And if our living Lord is angry for a little while, to rebuke and discipline us, he will again be reconciled with his own servants" (7:32-33; cf. 5:17).

From other passages in the book, it is evident that the "sins" mentioned here consist of abandoning God's law in order to follow the Greek customs and practices being imposed by Antiochus (2 Macc. 4:10-17; 6:1-11; 12:42). When the narrator and the main characters of this section of the book speak of those sins as "ours" (6:15; 7:18, 32), they are referring to the wrongdoing of the people as a whole and not merely to their own personal wrongdoing. However, they also recognize their own sin and therefore are not regarded as sinless or as undeserving of God's attempts to chastise and correct them together with the rest of the people.[61]

In their efforts to break the commitment of Eleazar, the seven brothers, and the mother to observe strictly the Jewish law, Antiochus's soldiers taunt and torment them and threaten them with a cruel death. In spite of this, Eleazar, the brothers, and the mother remain faithful to the law, preferring to die rather than to violate God's commandments. Eleazar in particular notes the impact of his decision on others: if he succumbs to the pressure to violate God's commandments, he will lead others—particularly the youth—to do so as well. If on the contrary, however, he remains faithful in the midst of his torments, he will inspire others to hold fast to the Jewish laws and resist Antiochus's efforts to impose Greek customs. When the soldiers suggest that Eleazar merely pretend to eat forbidden meat while actually eating meat that is kosher so that they can affirm that he gave in to their demands, he refuses to do so because of the example this would give to others:

> "Such pretense is not worthy of our time of life," he said, "for many of the young might suppose that Eleazar in his ninetieth year had gone over to an alien religion, and through my pretense, for the sake of living a brief moment longer, they would be led astray because of me, while I defile and disgrace my old age. Even if

---

61. This point is recognized by most interpreters of the passage; see, for example, Marinus de Jonge, "Jesus' Death for Others and the Death of the Maccabean Martyrs," in *Text and Testimony: Essays on New Testament and Apocryphal Literature in Honour of A. F. J. Klijn* (ed. T. Baarda et al.; Kampen: Kok, 1988), 148; van Henten, *Maccabean Martyrs*, 138.

for the present I would avoid the punishment of mortals, yet whether I live or die I will not escape the hands of the Almighty. Therefore, by bravely giving up my life now, I will show myself worthy of my old age and leave to the young a noble example of how to die a good death willingly and nobly for the revered and holy laws" (2 Macc. 6:24-28).

The narration then continues:

When he had said this, he went at once to the rack. Those who a little before had acted toward him with goodwill now changed to ill will, because the words he had uttered were in their opinion sheer madness. When he was about to die under the blows, he groaned aloud and said: "It is clear to the Lord in his holy knowledge that, though I might have been saved from death, I am enduring terrible sufferings in my body under this beating, but in my soul I am glad to suffer these things because I fear him." So in this way he died, leaving in his death an example of nobility and a memorial of courage, not only to the young but to the great body of his nation (2 Macc. 6:28-31).

As the seven brothers and their mother in turn are tortured and put to death, they stress two things. First, they speak of dying for the *law* or *laws* (2 Macc. 6:28; 7:2, 9, 11, 23, 37; cf. 13:14). The meaning of this phrase is obvious: they willingly give up their lives so that others will remain faithful to the Jewish law, recognizing that it is of such great value that nothing should be regarded as more important than observing it—not even one's own life. As the narrative makes clear, the fact that they hold the laws in such high regard that they are willing to suffer torments and die a cruel death rather than abandon those laws inspires others to do the same and follow their example.

A second idea that the dying brothers stress is their hope in the resurrection life. They express confidence that God will raise them some day if they remain faithful to God and God's law. The second brother affirms, for example, "the King of the universe will raise us up to an everlasting renewal of life, because we have died for his laws" (2 Macc. 7:9). The third brother says with regard to his hands: "I got these from heaven, and because of his laws I disdain them, and from him I hope to get them back again" (7:11). Finally, the last brother to be killed tells Antiochus:

"For our brothers after enduring a brief suffering have drunk of ever-flowing life, under God's covenant; but you, by the judgment of God, will receive just punishment for your arrogance. I, like my brothers, give up body and life for the laws of our ancestors, appealing to God to show mercy soon to our nation and by trials and plagues to make you confess that he alone is God, and through me and my brothers to bring to an end the wrath of the Almighty that has justly fallen on our whole nation" (7:36-38; cf. 7:14, 23, 29).

These allusions to the resurrection serve to stress that, in spite of appearances to the contrary, Israel's God is just. While he is temporarily allowing Antiochus to commit acts of extreme cruelty toward God's people, in the end he will restore justice by rewarding the faithful and doing away with the evildoers and the disobedient.

However, the author of 2 Maccabees also sees God as restoring justice in the present world. Immediately after these events, Judas Maccabeus is presented as organizing his army to fight Antiochus. The narration then continues:

> They implored the Lord to look upon the people who were oppressed by all; and to have pity on the temple that had been profaned by the godless; to have mercy on the city that was being destroyed and about to be leveled to the ground; to hearken to the blood that cried out to him; to remember also the lawless destruction of the innocent babies and the blasphemies committed against his name; and to show his hatred of evil. As soon as Maccabeus got his army organized, the Gentiles could not withstand him, for the wrath of the Lord had turned to mercy (8:2-5).

The logic underlying this interpretation of the events narrated is not at all difficult to grasp. The fact that many of the Jewish people had abandoned that law had initially provoked Israel's God to wrath. By allowing Antiochus to inflict suffering and death on the people, Israel's God had been attempting to bring his people back to himself and strengthen their commitment to obeying his law (2 Macc. 5:17-18, 20; 7:33, 38; 8:5). Now that this had happened, Israel's God had put away his wrath at his people's sins.

If we recall that in ancient Jewish thought the law or Torah was consistently seen as a blessing given by Israel's God to his people for their own good, then the reasons for his wrath are understandable: because he wants the people to obey the law for their own well-being and happiness, he insists that they observe that law and is moved to wrath when they do not. This implies that the concern of Israel's God is not for *himself* or his own holiness and justice but for *the good of the people*. In fact, this idea is stated explicitly with regard to the temple: the author of 2 Maccabees affirms that "the Lord did not choose the nation for the sake of the holy place, but the place for the sake of the nation" (5:19). In other words, God's concern was not to save the holy place and punish the people for their sins for his own sake but rather to restore the people to obedience for their own good. Once God had accomplished this objective by chastising the people, he would once again shower them with his blessings. Since it was the Mosaic law that was regarded as having mandated the establishment of the holy place, it would not be unfaithful to the thought of the author of 2 Maccabees to affirm regarding the law the same thing that is said of the temple: "the Lord did not choose the nation for the sake of the law, but the law for the sake of the nation." For the author, behind God's disciplining of Israel was a concern, not for the law itself, but for the people's well-being, which could be brought about only by their obedience to the law.

This claim is also borne out by the fact that 2 Maccabees sees God's wrath against Israel and his punishment of the people's sins as a sign of *love and compassion*. This is particularly stressed in 6:12-16, already cited above, which affirms that the punishments God had inflicted on the people were a sign of his kindness and mercy. Similarly, in the midst of cruel tortures, the brothers and mothers insist that God "is watching over us and in truth has compassion on us" (7:6). While elsewhere it is said that God's wrath is turned to mercy by the endurance of those suffering (8:5), in these passages God's wrath is seen as an *expression* of God's mercy and compassion and therefore of his love as well.

According to the author of 2 Maccabees, therefore, God's objective in allowing Antiochus to persecute Israel was to establish a people in the land who would be fully committed to observing the law. The willingness of Eleazar and the brothers and mother to suffer cruel torments and death rather than renounce obedience to the law thus enabled Israel's God to accomplish his objective (see 8:27-29, 36; 10:3-8; 11:24-26, 31; 13:12; 15:7-9). As a result, God is said to have become "reconciled" to the people (5:20; 7:33; 8:29; cf. 1:5; 2:22). In the end, he acts to save the people from their sufferings at the hands of Antiochus (1:11-12; 2:17-22; 10:38; 11:13; 12:11; 13:17; 15:7-8, 21). This reconciliation and salvation, however, are clearly dependent on the people's renewed obedience to the law (2:22; 8:21-29).

Interpreters of 2 Maccabees have often claimed to find in chapters 6, 7, and 8 of the book the idea that the deaths of Eleazar and the seven brothers atone for Israel's sins and turn away God's wrath. At times this is spoken of as the "effect" of their deaths, as if suffering, death, or the shedding of blood in itself made atonement or propitiated God. Jan Willem van Henten, for example, refers to the "effective deaths" of the martyrs in 2 Maccabees and the "redemptive function of suffering," while also claiming that "purification of the fatherland and atonement for the people's sins are two related effects of the martyrs' sacrificial deaths."[62] James Dunn affirms that 2 Macc. 7:37-38 reflects "the belief that the death of one would atone for the sins of others and remove the cause of divine wrath."[63] According to Marinus de Jonge, "the views on martyrdom in 2 and 4 Macccabees are the same. The violent death of exemplary servants of God restores the right relationship between God and his people...."[64] In the same vein, Nickelsburg writes: "According to 2 Macc. 7:37-38 (cf. 8:5) the deaths of the brothers turn God's wrath to forgiveness."[65] Jarvis Williams points especially to the blood of the martyrs as propitiatory, contending that God "received the martyrs' blood as a sufficient payment to end his wrath."[66]

Other interpreters even use the language of penal substitution, claiming that the "martyrs" put away God's wrath at the sins of the people by suffering and dying in their place. After citing several passages from 2 Maccabees 7, for example, N. T. Wright affirms that those passages reflect "the belief that the significance of the martyrs' sufferings has to do with their efficacy in bearing

---

62. Van Henten, *Maccabean Martyrs*, 140, 153.
63. James D. G. Dunn, *Romans 1-8* (WBC 38A; Dallas, TX: Word, 1988), 266.
64. De Jonge, "Jesus' Death," 150.
65. Nickelsburg, *Ancient Judaism*, 20.
66. Jarvis J. Williams, *Maccabean Martyr Traditions in Paul's Theology of Atonement: Did Martyr Theology Shape Paul's Conception of Jesus' Death?* (Eugene, OR: Wipf & Stock, 2010), 52.

the wrath of Israel's god against his sinful people."⁶⁷ Scot McKnight understands "the atoning value of these martyrdoms" in terms of "exhausting God's wrath against disobedience...."⁶⁸ According to I. Howard Marshall, the logic of 2 Maccabees is that "when people fall into sin and apostasy they arouse the wrath of Yahweh; he proceeds to punish them, and on the completion of the punishment his anger is satisfied and he is reconciled to the people."⁶⁹

In light of what we have just seen, however, affirmations such as these must be rejected categorically. For the author of 2 Maccabees, *it is not the sufferings and deaths of Eleazar, the brothers, and their mother* that make atonement for Israel's sins, effect reconciliation with God, and propitiate God's wrath. Rather, what brings these things about is the manner in which their sufferings and death lead to a renewed obedience among the people. This obedience makes it possible for the conditions necessary for justice and well-being in the land to be fulfilled. As noted above, in the narration of Eleazar's death in 2 Macc. 6:24-31, it is clear that his endurance of the torments imposed on him for his unbending adherence to the law inspires others to remain faithful to Israel's God and his law in the face of persecution. What leads him to refuse to pretend to eat impure food is the effect that this might have on the youth, who would think that he had abandoned his loyalty to the law. The implication is that others are led to turn back to God in repentance and obedience through Eleazar's perseverance and, as we have seen repeatedly elsewhere, *it is this that leads God to put away his wrath at the people's sins*. Undoubtedly, at the time of Eleazar's death, such a return to God had not yet taken place among the people in general. However, Eleazar's faithfulness in the midst of torture demonstrated to God that the change he desired to see in the people was occurring and would continue to occur as a result of the exemplary behavior of Eleazar, together with that of the seven brothers and their mother.⁷⁰

The fact that for the author it was the obedience of the people that led God to put away his wrath rather than the sufferings and death of Eleazar, the brothers, and the mother per se is evident as well from the author's affirmation that the sufferings that they and the rest of the people were enduring had the purpose of disciplining or correcting the people. Because that wrath is a sign of God's mercy and compassion for Israel, what God had sought was not to "exhaust" his wrath by pouring it out on someone, but to accomplish

---

67. N. T. Wright, *The New Testament and the People of God*, Vol. 1 of *Christian Origins and the Question of God* (Minneapolis: Fortress, 1992), 323.

68. Scot McKnight, *Jesus and his Death: Historiography, the Historical Jesus, and Atonement Theory* (Waco, TX: Baylor University Press, 2005), 179.

69. I. Howard Marshall, "The Meaning of 'Reconciliation'," in *Unity and Diversity in New Testament Theology: Essays in Honor of George E. Ladd* (ed. Robert A. Guelich; Grand Rapids: Eerdmans, 1978), 121. See also Eduard Lohse, *Märtyrer und Gottesknecht: Untersuchungen zur urchristlichen Verkündigen vom Sühnetod Jesu Christi* (FRLANT 64; Göttingen: Vandenhoeck & Ruprecht, 1955), 67: "Sie nehmen die Schuld des Volkes als die ihre auf sich und tragen die verdiente Strafe."

70. Van Henten rightly notes that those put to death save others by virtue of the fact that they offer an example to be followed (*Maccabean Martyrs*, 210-12, 222-43; see 2 Macc. 6:28, 31). I would add, however, that for the author of 2 Maccabees, rather than being merely *exemplary*, the courage of those put to death for the law is *contagious* in that it moves others to defend the law at all costs and not give in to the enemy.

his loving purposes through that wrath. Therefore, in the author's mind, God's wrath is not taken away by sufferings and death but rather by the renewed obedience of the people to the law, which God desired for their own good.

The author's allusions to the resurrection of the righteous and the punishment of the wicked serve the same purpose of encouraging greater obedience to God and God's law among the people. The fact that in the midst of horrific sufferings and a violent death, Eleazar, the brothers, and the mother manifest firmly the conviction that God will raise them from the dead and punish their oppressors leads others to be equally convinced of these truths. Thus Eleazar, the brothers, and the mother inspire others to remain faithful to God and the law not only by their example but also by their conviction that God will reward those who persevere in obedience to the law, but will punish those who abandon it.

The deaths of Eleazar, the brothers, and the mother can also be seen as providing assurance to God that there was indeed a faithful remnant that was worth preserving and saving, since it would form the basis for the renewal of God's people as a whole. The logic would be similar to that found in the story of Abraham's intercession for the people of Sodom and Gomorrah in Gen. 18:16-33. Because the existence of even a small number of righteous people provides hope that they may lead others to come to live righteously as well, God will not utterly destroy the many for the sake of a few. While of course Eleazar, the brothers, and the mother would not live to form part of this righteous remnant themselves, their faithfulness unto death led to the establishment of such a remnant.

The sufferings and deaths of Eleazar, the seven brothers, and their mother are also viewed as bringing Israel's God to intervene to save Israel for another reason. If he is truly committed to establishing justice and well-being for the people in the land, God cannot continue to let the righteous be persecuted and slaughtered while at the same time overlooking the evils committed by Antiochus. Curiously, 2 Maccabees presents Antiochus both as an *instrument* of God, in that God uses him to discipline and chastise the people, and at the same time as one who is fighting *against* God as his *adversary*, committing evils that God will some day punish (7:19, 34-36; 9:18, 28). This means that Antiochus is the *agent* of God's wrath in chastising Israel for its own good as well as the *object* of God's wrath.

Therefore, according to the logic of the author of 2 Maccabees, God's concern for justice in the land moved God initially to afflict Israel when many were responding positively to Antiochus's attempt to extinguish the worship of Israel's God in the land by prohibiting the people from practicing the law. By means of these afflictions, God brought the people to repent of their sins and become obedient to the law once more. However, God's concern for justice also brought God to take action against Antiochus to put an end to the terrible injustices and acts of cruelty that he was committing against those who sought to be faithful to God's law.[71] This is stressed not only in the words of Eleazar and the brothers but also in 2 Macc. 8:2-4, where the Maccabeans implore God to listen to the spilled blood that cries out and to consider how Antiochus has oppressed the people, profaned the temple, blasphemed against God, and destroyed the innocent, including infants. The sufferings and death imposed on Eleazar, the seven brothers, and their mother also form part of the same injustices perpetrated by Antiochus. In the thought of the author, God's commitment to justice would not let him simply overlook those injustices without acting against Antiochus to deliver the people from his tyranny.[72]

This does not mean, however, that for the author of 2 Maccabees God's justice obliged God to punish sin and evil for its own sake, as if a merely retributive justice were involved.[73] Rather, for all of the reasons already noted, it is clear that God's objective was to establish peace, justice, and well-being in the land. This means that God's punishment of Antiochus had the same purpose: what God sought was not to make Antiochus pay for his crimes but to rid the land of his oppression. The logic behind the author's thought is therefore not that the suffering and deaths of Eleazar, the brothers, and the mother oblige God to act because otherwise God would be proven to be unjust, as if inflicting punishment on Antiochus for his sins would restore justice in itself or satisfy some divine need or demand that sin receive retribution. Rather, the fact that Antiochus's injustices were generating such great suffering made it necessary for God to act against Antiochus in order to establish justice in the land and put an end to the suffering he was inflicting.[74] What makes Israel's God just is not that he *punishes* but that he *saves*.

All of these ideas form the basis for the petitions to God that are presented repeatedly throughout the book (2 Macc. 1:8; 7:37-38; 8:2-4, 14-15,

---

71. As Sam Williams observes with regard to 2 Macc. 8:2-4, "God is requested to remember various other acts on the enemy's part which demand vengeance: desecration of the Temple, destruction of the holy city, the murder of infants, the blasphemies against his name. He is beseeched to show his hatred of evil by requiting those who represent and perpetrate that evil" (*Jesus' Death*, 88).

72. Commenting on this passage, David Seeley notes: "Martyrological phenomena like blood which cries out (8.3) and the murder of babies are listed alongside non-martyrological events like oppression, profanation, destruction of property, and blasphemy. This makes it all the less likely that an expiatory effect is attached to the shedding of innocent blood in *2 Macc.* 7. Rather, the totality of evils wrought by Antiochus—of whatever kind—is being held up to God as evidence that his people have suffered enough.... The brothers' deaths are not, therefore, vicarious, expiatory ones. The brothers do not regard their deaths as special, but as of a piece with the sufferings of the whole people.... They ask only that with their deaths, the suffering end. No one will benefit because of their deaths *per se*, but simply because God will have ceased his wrath with the latter. He will consider that the overall punishment and discipline have reached a point of sufficiency" (*The Noble Death: Graeco-Roman Martyrology and Paul's Concept of Salvation*; JSNTSup 28; Sheffield: JSOT, 1990, 88-89).

73. As Sam Williams stresses with regard to Judas Maccabeus's prayer, "There is no suggestion in this prayer that God's wrath has been averted through the death of Eleazar and the seven brothers" (*Jesus' Death*, 88).

74. As Stephen Cummins has observed, the idea behind 2 Macc. 8:2-4 may also be that the suffering of Eleazar, the brothers, and the mother not only bring Israel to repentance, but also increase the sins of the tormenters to a point where God must act. The steadfast obedience of those tortured makes it necessary for Antiochus to take even more extreme measures against them. In this way, his atrocities increase to such a point that God can simply no longer stand by idly without intervening (*Paul and the Crucified Christ in Antioch: Maccabean Martyrdom and Galatians 1 and 2*; SNTSMS 114; Cambridge: Cambridge University Press, 2001, 34).

29; 10:25-26; 12:42; 13:10-12; 14:15, 46; 15:21-27). The intercession of the various figures mentioned plays an important role in turning away God's wrath and reconciling him to the people in order that he may save them. Nevertheless, it is not the intercession itself that has this effect or makes atonement, but rather the desires, sentiments, and commitment to God's will of which that intercession is an expression. God saves Israel not simply because the people pray to him but because the renewal brought about by Antiochus's persecution and the resistance of those who suffered has now made it possible for God's purposes to be accomplished among the people. Just as Eleazar and the brothers and mother have been willing to die for the law, so also Judas Maccabeus and those with him are now willing to give their lives in battle to preserve the law (8:21). Their commitment to living as God's people under his law is the implicit basis upon which they make their petitions for deliverance and also constitute the basis upon which God grants those petitions.

To be sure, in some of these passages, those who ask God for deliverance appeal to their sufferings and the injustices being committed against them as a basis for their petition. In 2 Macc. 8:2-4 in particular, the blood of Eleazar, the brothers, and the mother is said to cry out to God. Yet what their blood cries out for is not simply vengeance against Antiochus and his forces, as if this were in itself their objective. Rather, the blood of those executed and those who have fallen in the fight against Antiochus cries out for God to put an end to all of the injustices being cruelly committed by Antiochus and his forces so that God's people may once more live in peace and enjoy God's blessings as they live under the law (8:16-18; 12:5-6; cf. 15:24). The Maccabeans seek a restoration of the temple so that the people may serve God there once more for their own well-being and happiness (8:2; 13:10; 14:35-36). In other words, what the blood of the dead and the intercessions of the living cry out for is not *punishment* or *vengeance* per se but *deliverance*. While those who cry out to God want him to destroy those who have practiced evil and oppression, this destruction is not an end in itself but is rather a means to another end, namely, the liberation of God's people from their oppressors and the freedom necessary to live in the land in conformity with God's will for their own well-being and happiness.

Therefore, although in their intercession the Maccabeans recall the blasphemies committed by Antiochus and his army, the profanation of the temple, and the destruction of innocent babies, the idea is not that God will correct these wrongs simply by punishing those who have perpetrated them. Rather, the basis for the petitions for deliverance is that Israel's God is a God who seeks what is right and just and does not tolerate evil and oppression due to his love for those he has created. For this reason, in spite of his efforts to purify the people through suffering, Israel's God must no longer stand by idly and let the perpetrators of such cruelties continue to practice them. While Israel's God has been attempting to establish justice by chastising and disciplining the people for their sins through Antiochus, now that his corrective purposes have been accomplished, he must now establish justice by destroying Antiochus and his army. In this way, he will "show his hatred of evil" (8:4) and uphold his law.

In light of all of this, it is clear that it is not the deaths of Eleazar, the brothers, and the mother that atone for the people's sins, but their submission to God's will in the midst of sufferings and the fact that they bring others to be equally committed to God's will. God puts away his wrath, not because the people have suffered the punishment they deserve, but because the people's response to the chastisement inflicted through Antiochus has made it possible for God to accomplish the loving purposes that led him to inflict that chastisement in the first place.[75] For the same reasons, it is incorrect to affirm that the sufferings and deaths of Eleazar, the brothers, and the mother have some salvific "effect." Their deaths do not satisfy God's justice or put God under any type of obligation to forgive sins. God's salvation of Israel is an act of God's free will made in accordance with his sovereign purposes, not the result of the fulfillment of some intrinsic requirement of divine justice that could only be satisfied through the imposition of sufferings and death on those who had sinned or someone serving as their substitute.

Similarly, contrary to what de Jonge affirms, in 2 Maccabees it is not violent death that restores the right relationship between God and his people, but the firm commitment to God's will of which that violent death is the consequence, together with the renewed obedience in others which that commitment brings about. If sufferings and death in general effected atonement or appeased God's wrath, then even unrepentant evildoers like Antiochus would atone for their sins and propitiate God's wrath simply by suffering and dying. However, if one must turn back to God in obedience by repenting in order to be forgiven, then it is repentance that atones for sins and puts an end to God's wrath rather than divine acts of violence. While it might be said that Eleazar, the brothers, and the mother bore God's wrath, this is true only in the sense that they endured the same divine wrath that was directed at the people as a whole: "the wrath of the Almighty which has justly fallen on our whole nation" (7:38). They did not bear this divine wrath *in the stead* of the people but *together* with them. Undoubtedly, they suffered more than the rest of the people and thus can be said to have experienced that wrath to a greater degree. Yet for the author of 2 Maccabees, all the people collectively experienced that wrath, as 8:2-4 makes clear, and all collectively were later saved from it. Therefore, Israel's God ultimately intervened to save his people from Antiochus, not because he had exhausted his wrath, as if this were the objective of the punishment he inflicted, but because his purposes of establishing a people firmly committed to obeying him had been accomplished.

---

75. Versnel notes regarding 2 Maccabees: "Nowhere—not even in the *en emoi* phrase [in 7:38]—do we find a trace of an explicitly *intended* causal connection between the martyr's death and the return of God's mercy.... Nor is there any explicit indication of an *effective* causal relationship in that God's mercy indeed has returned *as a result of the death of the martyr*" ("Making Sense," 260).

Suffering for the Law in 4 Maccabees

It seems likely that the author of the book of 4 Maccabees, written probably toward the end of the first century CE,[76] made use of parts of 2 Maccabees in composing his work. In this regard, van Henten comments: "The description of the martyrdoms and their prehistory is probably based upon the information in 2 Maccabees 3:1—10:9. The author of 4 Maccabees has compressed the description of the historical setting of the Maccabean martyrs' deaths and amplified the description of the martyrdoms and the praise of the martyrs."[77] Because of this, many of the basic ideas of 4 Maccabees appear to be essentially the same as those of 2 Maccabees.

Nevertheless, there are also some significant differences between the two works. Above all, the author of 4 Maccabees focuses primarily on the story of Eleazar, the seven brothers, and their mother. In contrast to 2 Maccabees, which dedicates only three chapters (6–8) to these figures, the narrative of their sufferings and death occupies the major part of 4 Maccabees (4 Macc. 5:4—17:18). The author not only presents in greater detail the tortures inflicted on Eleazar, the brothers, and the mother but also expands considerably the dialogue between them and Antiochus and adds commentaries that interpret these occurrences.

Although both works clearly hope to inspire greater obedience to the Jewish law among their readers, the argument of 4 Maccabees centers around the claim that "divine reason is sovereign over the emotions" (1:1; 6:31; 13:1). In dialogue with Hellenistic thought, the book equates reason with the observance of the Jewish law. The story of the faithfulness of Eleazar, the seven brothers, and their mother in the time of persecution under Antiochus is regarded as illustrating the truth that reason can check and overcome the emotions and passions. As Francis Watson notes, the author's purpose is to demonstrate that the law can be observed even in the most adverse of circumstances.[78]

Following a long introduction in which the author extols reason over the emotions and cites biblical figures such as Joseph, Moses, Jacob, and David as examples of this principle, he then turns to the story of the persecution under Antiochus. Antiochus is presented as attempting to impose Greek

---

76. On the question of the date of 4 Maccabees, see Jan Willem van Henten, "Datierung und Herkunft des Vierten Makkabäerbuches," in *Tradition and Re-Interpretation in Jewish and Early Christian Literature: Essays in Honour of Jürgen C. H. Lebram* (ed. van Henten et al.; SPB 36; Leiden: Brill, 1986), 136-49; Versnel, "Making Sense," 218; Cummins, *Paul*, 77-78. Of course, if 4 Maccabees was written after most of the New Testament texts, in particular Paul's letters, it could not have influenced them directly. If in fact the author of 4 Maccabees based his work in part on 2 Maccabees, however, it could provide evidence of how some Jews, including perhaps some of Jesus' first followers, were interpreting 2 Maccabees. In any case, even if most of the New Testament allusions to Jesus' death predate 4 Maccabees, we cannot rule out the possibility that the ideas found in 4 Maccabees were already common in some Jewish circles earlier in the first century.

77. Van Henten, *Maccabean Martyrs*, 296.

78. Francis Watson, "Constructing an Antithesis: Pauline and Other Jewish Perspectives on Divine and Human Agency," in *Divine and Human Agency in Paul and His Cultural Environment* (ed. John M. G. Barclay and Simon J. Gathercole; London: T & T Clark, 2006), 109. On the purpose of 4 Maccabees, its adaptations of 2 Maccabees, and its argument as a whole, see 108-15.

customs and eradicate observance of the Jewish law among the Jewish people through the use of violent means (4:19—5:3; cf. 18:5). In 4 Maccabees, however, it is not the people at large who abandon the law but only the high priest Jason and the leaders. In fact, the common people are presented as remaining law-observant and despising Antiochus's decrees in spite of his threats and punishments (4:24-26). This is true of Eleazar, the brothers, and the mother as well, who are never presented as committing or confessing any sins. This would seem to pose problems for the idea that the suffering that they and others endure is due to their sins or those of the people as a whole.[79]

According to the author of 4 Maccabees, Antiochus's aggression against the people was an act of Israel's God in response to the manner in which Jason "changed the nation's way of life and altered its form of government in complete violation of the law" (4:19). The author states: "The divine justice was angered by these acts and caused Antiochus himself to make war on them" (4:21). The purpose of the sufferings that God inflicts on the people through Antiochus is not stated. This would seem to bear out Van Henten's observation: "The author of 4 Maccabees hardly pays attention to the disciplinary aspect of the people's suffering, which is emphasized in 2 Maccabees."[80]

While this disciplinary aspect of suffering is not mentioned explicitly in 4 Maccabees, however, several passages indicate that it is unquestionably assumed. Above all, if it is remembered that, according to a disciplinary understanding of punishment, the objective is to strengthen the people in their obedience to God, then it is clear that this is what the deaths of Eleazar, the brothers, and the mother are said to accomplish. After narrating Eleazar's death, the author eulogizes him, saying: "You, father, strengthened our loyalty to the law through your glorious endurance, and you did not abandon the holiness which you praised, but by your deeds you made your words of divine philosophy credible" (7:9). When the oldest brother is being tortured by Antiochus, after indicating that he is suffering because he is defending God's law (9:15), he calls on his brothers to imitate him in fighting on behalf of their faith and customs so that, in that way, "the just Providence of our ancestors may become merciful to our nation and take vengeance on the accursed tyrant" (9:23-24). At the end of the book, referring to those who gave their lives for their faith, the author concludes: "Because of them the nation gained peace, and by reviving observance of the law in the homeland they ravaged the enemy" (18:4). Therefore, if the sufferings and death of those who remained faithful to the law are said to have inspired others to greater obedience to the

---

79. Although, as Gert J. Steyn notes, the author of 4 Maccabees does not attribute any sin or confession of sin to Eleazar, the seven brothers, and their mother, this does not necessarily lead to her conclusion that these figures die "without any sin or guilt" ("Soteriological Perspectives in Luke's Gospel," in *Salvation in the New Testament: Perspectives on Soteriology*; ed. Jan G. van der Watt; NovTSup 121; Leiden: Brill, 2005, 87). Rather, just as the idea that the people in general had sinned is implied rather than stated explicitly in the book, so also the book clearly seems to imply that those who are put to death share in the sin of Israel rather than dying as innocent victims (see 4 Macc. 17:21).

80. Van Henten, *Maccabean Martyrs*, 185.

law and God is presented as the one who sent Antiochus to make war on Israel, the obvious implication is that God sought to discipline and correct the people in order to bring them into greater conformity with his will.

Another indication that these ideas are present in the text is the view of the law's intrinsic goodness that appears there. In chapter 5, referring to the law as a "philosophy," Eleazar tells Antiochus:

> "You scoff at our philosophy as though living by it were irrational, but it teaches us self-control, so that we master all pleasures and desires, and it also trains us in courage, so that we endure any suffering willingly; it instructs us in justice, so that in all our dealings we act impartially, and it teaches us piety, so that with proper reverence we worship the only real God. Therefore we do not eat defiling food; for since we believe that the law was established by God, we know that in the nature of things the Creator of the world in giving us the law has shown sympathy toward us. He has permitted us to eat what will be most suitable for our lives, but he has forbidden us to eat meats that would be contrary to this" (5:22-26).

Here the Jewish law is unquestionably seen as an expression of God's love for Israel, since it promotes justice and well-being and commands things that lead intrinsically to the people's health and happiness. The clear implication is that God's wrath and the punishment he inflicts on Israel are thus an expression of his concern for Israel's welfare. The idea is that God wants the people to obey the law *for their own sake* and by means of the persecution under Antiochus is seeking to accomplish that objective.

The author of 4 Maccabees repeatedly presents the resistance of Eleazar, the seven brothers, and their mother in terms of a battle or struggle (6:21; 9:15-18, 24; 13:15-16;17:10-12; 18:4; cf. 1:11). Eleazar, the brothers and the mother fight on behalf of the law and virtue by refusing to give in to Antiochus. They consecrate themselves entirely to God and offer up their bodies and souls to shield and protect the law (13:13; 17:19-20; 18:3). As Sam Williams observes, the book's conclusion implies that others did the same. Commenting on 18:5, which affirms that Antiochus was not able "to compel the Israelites to become pagans and to abandon their ancestral customs," Williams notes that the allusion to the people here "indicates the author's full awareness that the nine martyrs of his story were not the only Jews who stood fast when confronted by persecution."[81] God responds to their steadfastness by driving out Antiochus and delivering the people from their oppression at his hands.

In this way, those who gave their lives in faithfulness to the law can be said to have "conquered" Antiochus and his forces (1:11; 7:4; 9:30; 11:20, 27; 16:14). This is to be understood both in the sense that Antiochus was unable to make them renounce their faith and disobey the law, as well as in the sense that, in response to their steadfastness under persecution, God intervened to deliver them from Antiochus's tyranny. The author understands this in terms of God becoming "merciful" to the people once more (6:28; 9:24; 12:17). Of course, those who die under Antiochus's persecution are also viewed as

---

81. S. Williams, *Jesus' Death*, 172.

conquering or becoming victorious in the sense that they receive the prize of immortality (7:3; 9:22; 14:5; 16:13; 17:11-18;18:3, 23).

The author of 4 Maccabees follows 2 Maccabees in presenting Antiochus both as the *instrument* of God's wrath and as the *object* of God's wrath. Initially, it is said that God sent Antiochus to make war on Israel because in his justice God had become angry at the sins being committed (4 Macc. 4:21). However, when Antiochus then goes to the extreme of attempting to eradicate the people's obedience to the law altogether and begins to persecute the faithful, such as Eleazar, the brothers, and their mother, he is no longer seen as one who is executing God's will but instead is condemned as an "enemy of heavenly justice" (9:15) and a cruel, accursed tyrant (5:37-38; 6:21-23; 8:1-3; 9:24; 17:17, 21). Instead of being God's instrument to execute his righteous wrath on Israel, Antiochus himself becomes the object of God's wrath (9:24, 11:3; 18:5). For the author, then, the one ultimately causing the death of Eleazar, the brothers, and the mother is not God but Antiochus: they die, not because God has punished them but "because of the violence of the tyrant who wished to destroy the way of life of the Hebrews" (17:9). For the author, what Antiochus did was not God's will but something worthy of divine punishment: "For these crimes divine justice pursued and will pursue the accursed tyrant" (18:22).[82]

In 4 Maccabees as in 2 Maccabees, therefore, the faithfulness and endurance of Eleazar, the brothers, and the mother moves God to act to save Israel for two reasons. First, as mentioned above, through their faithfulness and endurance they inspire others to remain obedient to the law. In this way, God's justice can be said to have been satisfied, since what God's justice seeks is not to *punish* but to *save* by bringing the people to live in accordance with his will for their own good. Second, precisely because of the justice of Israel's God and his love for the people, he cannot stand by idly when those who are committed to his will suffer unspeakable cruelties at the hands of the wicked. Therefore, the tortures endured by Eleazar, the brothers, and the mother move God to act against Antiochus and his forces. For this reason, the oldest brother tells his siblings that if they continue to fight on behalf of their faith, God will "take vengeance on the accursed tyrant" (9:24). Conversely, the fifth brother tells Antiochus: "by murdering me you will incur punishment from the heavenly justice for even more crimes" (11:3). Nevertheless, this vengeance and punishment do not constitute an end in themselves but have the purpose of delivering Israel from its oppression.

Vicarious Death in 4 Maccabees

The ideas just considered provide the background necessary to understand the two passages from 4 Maccabees that present the sufferings and death of Eleazar, the brothers, and the mother as vicarious in nature: 4 Macc. 6:27-30

---

82. In this case, as Sam Williams observes, similar to what we find in 2 Maccabees, the idea in 4 Maccabees is that of God "withdrawing his protective arm from his people" (*Jesus' Death*, 80).

and 17:20-22. Both of them present problems for translation. The most difficult word to translate is *antipsuchon*, which in general refers to something given in exchange for one's life or soul. This word appears in both of the passages just mentioned. The translation "ransom" is problematic in that it carries certain connotations that are not necessarily to be associated with the notion of an *antipsuchon*, including that of a commercial exchange or a payment made to release a hostage or free a slave. The second passage uses the term *hilastērion*, which has been translated in different ways, including "propitiation," "expiation," "propitiatory," "mercy seat" (of the ark of the covenant), and even "atoning sacrifice."[83] Due to the difficulties involved in translation, therefore, I will simply transliterate both of these terms.

In 4 Macc. 6:27-29, immediately before Eleazar is said to have died "by virtue of reason, for the sake of the law," he is presented as praying: "You know, O God, that though I might have saved myself, I am dying in burning torments for the sake of the law. Become merciful to your people, letting our punishment on their behalf suffice. Make my blood their purification and receive my soul (*psuchē*) as their *antipsuchon*." The second passage, 4 Macc. 17:20-22, occurs at the conclusion of the book, where the author writes:

> These, then, who have been consecrated for the sake of God, are honored, not only with this honor, but also by the fact that because of them our enemies did not rule over our nation, the tyrant was punished, and the homeland purified—they having become something like an *antipsuchon* for the sin of our nation. And through the blood of those devout ones and the *hilastērion* of their death, divine Providence preserved Israel that previously had been mistreated.[84]

These two passages have been seen as offering the strongest support for the idea that in second-temple Judaism, suffering and death in themselves were believed to make atonement, appease God's wrath, and satisfy God's justice. Eleazar's petition that his punishment "suffice" (6:28) is often taken to infer that the people deserved to endure a certain amount of punishment for their sins and that this was borne by Eleazar, the brothers, and the mother in the place of the rest. Wright, for example, attributes to the author of 4 Maccabees the idea that "their sufferings will have the effect of drawing on to themselves the sufferings of the nation as a whole, so that the nation may somehow escape."[85] The allusions to their blood making purification and the affirmation that their death constitutes a *hilastērion* are understood in the sense that God declares the people forgiven and puts away his wrath at their sins because the innocent deaths of Eleazar, the brothers, and the mother have satisfied the demands of his justice. Above all, the use of the word *antipsuchon*

---

83. On the use of *hilastērion* in Greco-Roman literature and the Hebrew Scriptures, see especially Stanislas Lyonnet, "The Terminology of Redemption," in *Sin, Redemption and Sacrifice: A Biblical and Patristic Study* (Lyonnet and Léopold Sabourin; AnBib 48; Rome: Biblical Institute, 1970), 155-63.

84. For our purposes here, it does not matter whether *hilastērion* is understood as an adjective or noun; on this discussion, see S. Williams, *Jesus' Death*, 38-41.

85. N. T. Wright, *Jesus and the Victory of God*, Vol. 2 of *Christian Origins and the Question of God* (Minneapolis: Fortress, 1996), 583.

in both of these passages is thought to exemplify the principle that the life of one individual can be offered up as a substitute in the place of (*anti-*) the lives of others.[86]

A close examination of these passages on the basis of what we have seen above, however, makes it clear that such interpretations involve reading back into the text ideas that are foreign to them. When Eleazar prays to God, "Become merciful to your people, letting our punishment on their behalf suffice" (*hileos genou tō ethnei sou arkestheis tē hēmetera huper autōn dikē*; 6:28), the "punishment" (*dikē*) he is referring to is clearly the suffering that he and others have endured at the hands of Antiochus. As noted above, the text claims that, by torturing Eleazar, Antiochus is no longer acting as God's instrument to chastise the people but has come to behave as a cruel tyrant (5:27; 6:21-23; 7:2). Therefore, when asking for the punishment to end, Eleazar is referring not to *divine* punishment but to the punishment being inflicted by Antiochus, who has become an "enemy of divine justice" (9:15) rather than its instrument. Of course, even if God is merely allowing Antiochus to inflict torture on Eleazar and others in passive fashion, in some sense this can be seen as being in accordance with God's will, since God does not intervene to put an end to Antiochus's actions.

In whatever manner the punishment of Eleazar and others is understood, it is said to be borne on behalf of others (*huper autōn*) and not in their stead. This should be interpreted in the sense that Eleazar and others were enduring torments in order to defend the law and preserve Israel as a people, strengthening their loyalty to the law (7:8-9). Immediately before Eleazar's petition in 6:28-29, he is presented as stating this concern explicitly:

> "May we, the children of Abraham, never think so basely that out of cowardice we feign a role unbecoming to us! For it would be irrational if we, who have lived in accordance with truth to old age and have maintained in accordance with law the reputation of such a life, should now change our course and become a pattern of impiety to the young, in becoming an example of the eating of defiling food. It would be shameful if we should survive for a little while and during that time be a laughing stock to all for our cowardice, and if we should be despised by the tyrant as unmanly, and not protect our divine law even to death. Therefore, O children of Abraham, die nobly for your faith!" (6:17-22).

The punishments that Eleazar is bearing are therefore "for others" in the sense that he is seeking to remain faithful to God in the midst of persecution so as to influence others to remain faithful and obedient to God's law as well. In that way, they will attain their deliverance. Any idea of substitutionary suffering is therefore absent.

At the same time, of course, Eleazar calls on God to be merciful to the people and to let what he and others are suffering on their behalf "suffice." The idea here is not difficult to grasp: Eleazar is simply asking God to intervene

---

86. See, for example, Grayston, *Dying We Live*, 257: "The martyr offered himself as an *antipsuchos*, dying not only for the benefit of sinners but in their stead."

so that other faithful Jews are not forced to suffer in the same way that he and others have. There is no hint of any idea that God's justice requires that a certain amount of suffering be inflicted on the sinful people to compensate for their sins.[87] Rather, the sufferings of Eleazar and others can be said to suffice in two senses. First, they are sufficient to demonstrate to God that his purpose of establishing a people that is obedient to him is in fact being accomplished. Eleazar's own steadfastness in the face of persecution is evidence of this and will also inspire others to obedience, thus giving God assurance that the objective he sought will become a reality. Second, Eleazar asks that what he and others have suffered be sufficient in the sense that, because God is just and loving, he can no longer tolerate and overlook the cruel injustices being perpetrated by Antiochus. The tyrant has gone too far and must now be stopped. For that reason, both God's justice and God's mercy should be manifested in putting an end to the suffering that Eleazar and others are enduring.

Eleazar's petition here, therefore, is that God show mercy to the people in the midst of their sufferings by bringing those sufferings to an end. This idea is paralleled in other passages from 4 Maccabees. In 9:24, one of the brothers encourages his siblings to continue resisting so that "the just Providence of our ancestors may become merciful to our nation and take vengeance on the accursed tyrant." Later, when he is about to be put to death, the youngest brother exclaims, "I do not desert the excellent example of my brothers, and I call on the God of our fathers to be merciful to our nation" (12:16-17).[88] What brings God to show mercy by intervening to save the people is not suffering per se, but the suffering of those who have shown themselves to be committed to his will, since his purpose in allowing the suffering to take place is precisely to strengthen that commitment.[89] Once the people manifest that commitment, there is no reason for God to continue allowing them to suffer.

There is nothing in the text, therefore, to support the idea that God's justice required that a certain amount of suffering be inflicted on the people as punishment for their sins and that therefore Eleazar was asking that this punishment be inflicted on him instead. To punish Eleazar as a substitute would have defeated entirely the purpose of the afflictions, since in that case they would not serve to bring the people back to God in repentance and obedience

---

87. Such an idea is affirmed, for example, by Jarvis Williams, who claims that "Eleazar prayed that God would accept his death and the death of the other martyrs as sufficient payment for the nation's sin...." (*Maccabean Martyr Traditions*, 49).

88. While this is mercy, the idea is not that "divine pity on Israel might be provoked by the sight of innocent suffering" (Philip R. Davies, "Didactic Stories," in *Justification and Variegated Nomism*, Vol. 1: *The Complexities of Second Temple Judaism*, ed. D. A. Carson, Peter T. O'Brien, and Mark A. Seifrid; WUNT 2/140; Tübingen: Mohr Siebeck, 2001, 130). Mercy must not be confused with pity.

89. See S. Williams, *Jesus' Death*, 183: "When God punishes his people, his purpose is their repentance (cf. e.g., Lev. 26). Evidence of repentance, not degree of suffering, is what propitiates an angry Yahweh. Even when it is said (e.g., Is. 40:2) that Israel has received double punishment for her sins, the prophet does not intimate that he has been 'satisfied.' Nor when he exacts vengeance upon his enemies is there any hint of his being 'filled' or 'satisfied' by their suffering (cf. e.g., Deut. 32)."

to the law. On the contrary, they could continue to sin freely since Eleazar had put away God's wrath at their sin.

The second part of Eleazar's dying petition in 6:28-29, "Make my blood their purification," reflects sacrificial imagery. Eleazar is presented as offering his life up to God sacrificially as a result of his unbroken commitment to obeying God's law. As we have just noted, however, he is doing this not merely for his own sake but for the sake of *others*: he refuses to disobey the law because he would no longer provide a good example for others, inspiring them to obey the law and to resist Antiochus's godless intentions. On the contrary, Eleazar's disobedience and disregard for the law would lead others to disobey. Therefore, just as he has been enduring torments on behalf of others, he now offers up his life sacrificially on behalf of others as well.[90] In essence, he is asking that his sufferings and death not be in vain but that they instead serve to bring about in others the same firm commitment to God's will that he is manifesting so that God might mercifully save the people.

The allusion to "blood" here should not be understood merely in the sense of violent death. It is not Eleazar's death or the spilling of his blood per se that will purify others. Rather, it is his steadfastness and endurance to the point of death. This is what 4 Maccabees repeatedly stresses.[91] In 1:11, the author points to the "courage and endurance" of Eleazar and others as the decisive factor that led to Antiochus's downfall and the purification of the people: "By their endurance they conquered the tyrant, and thus their native land was purified through them." Here it is clear that purification results, not from death itself, but from the perseverance to the point of death of Eleazar and others who shared his same commitment to God's will.

In principle, Eleazar's petition to God that his blood might serve to purify others can be understood in three different ways. First, his request may be that God permit his faithfulness and endurance and the example he has provided to purify others in the sense of inspiring and enabling them to turn away from sin and instead embrace the same type of obedience to the law that he has displayed. Second, because Eleazar's faithfulness to the end also serves as evidence that there is a faithful remnant among God's people composed of those who have recommitted themselves to living according to the law, that faithfulness provides a basis for God to forgive his people and regard them as pure once more. That purified remnant will form the foundation for a renewed Israel, which is what God ultimately desires.

There is also a third sense in which Eleazar's blood may be seen as purifying Israel. His petition is that his endurance to the end will move God to drive Antiochus out of the land so that the impure, impious enemies of God will no longer occupy it. This will make it possible for the Jewish people who

---

90. Sam Williams rightly stresses that "Eleazar prays that God will *make* his blood their purification, that is, that he will accept it as such" (*Jesus' Death*, 41).

91. See 4 Macc. 5:23; 6:9, 13; 7:9, 22; 9:6-8, 22, 28-30; 11:12; 13:27; 15:30-32; 16:17-21; 17:7-10, 12, 17, 23.

are left there to live righteous, pure lives in accordance with God's law unimpeded.[92] The conclusion of the book uses the imagery of purification in this sense: it is the "homeland" that is "purified" (17:20-21).[93] Once Eleazar has demonstrated that there is indeed a righteous remnant dedicated to serving God obediently, God is moved to rid the land of Antiochus's oppression so that this obedient people may live in peace and purity there. In effect, what Eleazar asks is that God avenge his blood by purifying the land of Antiochus's cruel tyranny. As noted previously, however, this is a cry not for retributive punishment or revenge but for salvation from an oppressor.

Of course, because these three understandings of the people's purification are not mutually exclusive, it is possible that more than one is present in the text. What is *not* present, however, is the idea of penal substitution. Nowhere does the text imply that "Eleazar is imploring God to receive his faithfulness until death as a vicarious atonement on behalf of the sins of the Jewish people."[94] Even if Eleazar's words are understood in the sense that the people are purified of their sin and guilt before God, this is not because God accepts the blood of the innocent in the place of the guilty, but because the repentance and renewed obedience brought about in others by Eleazar's endurance to the point of death leads God to overlook the past sins of the people.[95] If any type of atonement for sins is involved, it is made not by Eleazar but by the people themselves, who are inspired to return to God and his law as a result of Eleazar's faithfulness.[96] As Sam Williams notes, there is thus no basis here for claiming that, in ancient Jewish thought, "*human* blood, especially innocent human blood, could make expiation for the sins of others."

The third part of Eleazar's petition in 6:28-29, "receive my soul (*psuchē*) as their *antipsuchon*," reflects the same logic. To translate this passage, "take my life in exchange for theirs," as the NRSV does, can be misleading. In English, to take someone's life tends to be understood as synonymous with killing someone. The Greek text in no way suggests that God is the one killing Eleazar or threatening to put him to death. It is not as if Eleazar were saying, "Put me to death instead of putting them to death," as a penal substitution interpretation would imply. Eleazar's death is not regarded as a punishment inflicted by God but as a voluntary offering up of his life.

Similarly, the language of "exchange" should not be understood in the sense that Eleazar is negotiating or bartering with God, as if he were offering God his life in exchange for God not taking the lives of the rest of the

---

92. This purification of the land is twofold in that it involves the removal of the defilement of "the army of Antiochus on the one hand, the apostasy of the Jews on the other" (S. Williams, *Jesus' Death*, 179).

93. As Sam Williams notes, "The Lord 'purifies the land'—not from sins but from Israel's enemies!" (*Jesus' Death*, 84). The land is also purified from sins, however, in the sense that the people ultimately turn away from their sinful ways as a result of what has taken place.

94. Cummins, *Paul*, 81 (commenting on 4 Macc. 6:28-29).

95. Sam Williams rightly notes, "The 'removal' of the nation's sin is not described as the forgiveness of personal wrongs or as the assuaging of guilt—we hear nothing about the Hellenizers being 'forgiven'—but as the reversal of an overt situation: the *land* was purified" (*Jesus' Death*, 178).

96. S. Williams, *Jesus' Death*, 186.

people. This would suggest that what God desires or demands is simply that someone die, as if this in itself would satisfy God's justice or atone for the people's sins. Nor is Eleazar offering God his life as a ransom payment, asking God to take his soul in exchange for liberating others. In addition to being extremely problematic theologically, since God would in effect be the one holding the people captive and demanding a ransom payment to set them free, such an interpretation runs contrary to the thought of 4 Maccabees and ancient Jewish beliefs in general.

What Eleazar asks God to take or receive is his *psuchē* or soul. This word appears frequently throughout 4 Maccabees and should often be translated as "mind," "will," or "spirit."[97] This means that Eleazar is not merely offering to die but offering up his own self or being, not only to God but for the sake of the law as well. This is what he affirms at the beginning of his petition: "You know, O God, that though I might have saved myself, I am dying in burning torments *for the sake of the law*" (6:27). Throughout his torments, he has committed his life fully to God; and now that he is about to die, he continues to do so, commending his soul to God. All of these ideas are behind his prayer that God take or receive his *psuchē*.

Once again, however, Eleazar's concern is primarily *for others* rather than for himself. As his words reflect, in enduring torments for the sake of the law, he has not tried to save himself, but has instead considered first and foremost the consequences that his actions will have for other Jews, whose loyalty to the law he seeks to confirm and strengthen (7:9). Obviously, if he wants others to remain faithful to the law—particularly those who are young—, it is because he wants them to *live* and *prosper* in the land God has given them. For this to happen, the persecution and destruction that they are enduring under Antiochus must come to an end. If it does not, the nation will be further weakened and decimated and the cause for which he is giving his life will not be accomplished.

The petition "receive my soul as their *antipsuchon*" must therefore be understood on the basis of these ideas. Eleazar is willing to give up his life for the cause of the law and the people, yet at the same time he wants the sacrifice of his life to bear fruit. While he is not attempting to bargain with God, manipulate him, or compel him to act, in effect he is telling God: "I am willing to die, but what I beg and implore of you in return is that you save the people from Antiochus so that they may live free from tyranny in peace, justice, and obedience in the land." In essence, his death is a petition to God that he not die in vain, but that God respond to his death by bringing salvation for those on whose behalf he is enduring tortures and dying.

If understood according to these ideas, there is a sense in which the words attributed to Eleazar in Greek can properly be translated, "Take my life in exchange for theirs," as the NRSV does. According to the thought of 4 Maccabees, God responds to Eleazar's petition by receiving his soul and

---

97. See, for example, 4 Macc. 3:3; 8:29; 13:15; 14:6; 15:4.

granting what he requested in return, namely, the deliverance of the people from persecution and death at the hands of Antiochus, that is, "their life." However, the life that Eleazar attains for others through his death has to do with existence in the Jewish homeland rather than in a heavenly realm. At the same time, in a sense Eleazar does not forfeit his soul but obtains its immortality. This is the reward or "prize" that he attains together with the brothers and mother (17:11-12). Eleazar's words to God in 6:29, then, could be paraphrased: "Make the blood I am shedding out of faithfulness to your law a means by which your people may be purified from their sinful ways so as to be acceptable to you, and receive favorably the life that I am offering up to you with the petition that in return you allow them to live obediently in peace in their homeland by delivering them from the suffering they are enduring." Obviously, the basis upon which God would grant favorably such a petition would be the renewed obedience to the law that would result from the faithfulness of Eleazar and others to that law in the midst of their suffering.

The word *antipsuchon* is used in a slightly different manner in 17:21, where those who died for the law under Antiochus's persecution are said to have become "something like an *antipsuchon* for the sin of the nation." Here again, it is extremely difficult to translate the author's words into English. The meaning is not that the people's sins demanded some type of punishment or atoning sacrifice in order to enable God to forgive them, as if this requirement had been fulfilled by the deaths of Eleazar, the mother, and her seven sons. Nor do their deaths function as some type of ransom payment made to God in order for God to liberate them.

From the context of the book, the "sin of the nation" clearly refers to the adoption of Greek customs and the abandonment of the Jewish law under Antiochus. In the thought of the author, God had responded to this sin by sending Antiochus upon the people to chastise and correct them so as to bring them back to himself in obedience. For God to inflict this chastisement on a substitute would defeat its purpose entirely, since the objective was not to punish but to discipline and correct the people. If Eleazar's endurance unto death is said to have strengthened the people's loyalty to the law (7:9), then obviously that loyalty was previously not strong enough and needed to be increased. The same idea is present in 18:3-4: "Therefore those who gave over their bodies in suffering for the sake of religion were not only admired by men, but also were deemed worthy to share in a divine inheritance. Because of them the nation gained peace, and by reviving observance of the law in the homeland they ravaged the enemy." According to this passage, observance of the law needed to be revived. This is what those who gave their lives accomplished: in response to this renewed observance of the law, God drove Israel's enemies out and established peace in the land.

Yet while the sin in 17:21 is said to be that of the nation as a whole, those who endured the greatest suffering and torments were a very small group: Eleazar, the mother, and her seven sons (17:13). For this reason, it can be said that the chastisement aimed at bringing back to obedience the people as a whole fell on this small group. Their courage and endurance moved others to return to God and consequently led God to deliver the people from the oppression of Antiochus. As 4 Maccabees repeatedly stresses, Eleazar, the brothers, and the mother endured these torments willingly, nobly, and courageously. This means that they were not merely killed by Antiochus, but *offered up their lives* to God of their own accord. They "consecrated" themselves for the sake of God and the law (17:20). They did so, however, seeking not merely something for themselves, such as the reward of immortality, but the salvation of their fellow Jews in the present world.

For this reason, the author refers to Eleazar, the brothers, and the mother as "something like an *antipsuchon* for the sin of the nation." The term *antipsuchon* communicates the idea that they gave up their lives or souls for others so that those others might be saved from the sin they were committing as well as divine chastisement for that sin. In a sense, they can be said to have died in the place of others, in that they endured torments and sufferings that others did not and even suffered the chastisement that the people as a whole deserved. Nevertheless, this is not penal substitution, since it was not their sufferings and death per se that led God to save Israel, but the impact that their endurance and commitment to God in suffering and death had on others.

To affirm that Eleazar prays that God might "consider his sufferings as an *antipsuchos*, satisfying divine justice and purifying the nation," as Brian J. Tabb does, implies that God's justice and purification are accomplished merely by inflicting suffering on people, that is, by a purely retributive justice.[98] Once the deserved punishment is inflicted, then justice is satisfied. That this is not the thought of 4 Maccabees is clear from the fact the author affirms that Antiochus is "both punished on earth and is being chastised after his death" for the evils he committed against Israel (18:5; cf. 9:8-9; 11:3; 12:12; 17:20-21; 18:22). If the author believed that punishment itself satisfied divine justice and purified people, then even Antiochus would have atoned for his sins and been purified in God's sight merely by suffering the punishment corresponding to those sins. Obviously, this is contrary to the author's thought. Eleazar is not an *antipsuchon* for Antiochus, since Antiochus is unrepentant and does not seek to live in conformity with God's will. For the same reason, however, Eleazar cannot be an *antipsuchon* on behalf of any of God's people who do not themselves repent and seek to live in conformity with God's will. What satisfies divine justice and purifies the nation is thus not the *punishment* inflicted on the righteous, but *their faithfulness and commitment to God and his law* under such harsh circumstances. Eleazar can be an *antipsuchon* and means of purification only for those who are committed to obeying God's law, yet in that case *it is their own commitment to the law rather than what Eleazar did*

---

98. Brian J. Tabb, *Suffering in Ancient Worldview: Luke, Seneca, and 4 Maccabees in Dialogue* (LNTS 569; London: Bloomsbury T & T Clark, 2017), 86; cf. 102, 111.

that ultimately obtains for them divine acceptance and forgiveness. The affirmation that Eleazar is an *antipsuchon* for the sins of others must therefore be understood in the sense that his faithful obedience unto death serves as a type of pledge, guarantee, or demonstration that the obedience of others will follow upon his own, thus providing God the basis necessary to put an end to his activity of chastising and disciplining the people through Antiochus. Neither Eleazar's obedience nor the punishment he endures are substitutionary, since the people themselves must become obedient, and those who do not do so will eventually face punishment again, whether in this world or the next.

For the author of 4 Maccabees, however, in his death Eleazar is an *antipsuchon* for others in another sense as well. When Eleazar prays to God, "receive (and accept) my soul (*psuchē*) as their *antipsuchon*" (6:28-29), in effect he is asking God to receive favorably the soul he offers up as if it were the soul of the people themselves, offered up to God by them. In this sense he is indeed offering up his soul in their place. This is not because he is suffering the punishment they deserve for their sins as their substitute, however. Rather, the idea is that the rest of the people of God who are faithful to the law as Eleazar is and are even willing to die for the law like him and together with him are not in the same position in which Eleazar finds himself, threatened with death by execution. Furthermore, Eleazar does not want them to die. On the contrary, he wants the people to enjoy peace and wholeness in the land God has given them, experiencing God's blessings as they obey faithfully God's law. His petition, therefore, is that God accept his death, life, or soul in the place of theirs so as not to require that they demonstrate their own faithfulness to God and the law by being asked to die in the way that Eleazar is dying. Instead, at Eleazar's request, God will look upon Eleazar's offering up of his life to God out of faithfulness to the law as if it were the offering up of the lives of the people themselves, who share Eleazar's commitment to the law. On this basis, God will take only the life of Eleazar and deliver the people from Antiochus's tyranny, so that they may continue to offer up their lives to God spiritually and materially without having to forfeit their lives physically, as Eleazar will. None of this has anything whatsoever to do with penal substitution.

The same logic must be understood to lie behind the author's affirmation that Eleazar, the brothers, and their mother became "something like an *antipsuchon* for the sin of our nation" (17:21). In order to put away his wrath at the people's sins and deliver them from the chastisement or disciplining that he had sent upon them in the person of Antiochus, what God demanded was that they return to him in sincere repentance and obedience. In essence, he demanded that his people offer themselves or their lives up to him in order to be committed to doing his will in their everyday life. This was equivalent to presenting themselves to God as a sacrifice for their sins. In the case of Eleazar, the brothers, and their mother, this offering up of one's life to God had taken the form of an extremely painful physical death at the hands of Antiochus. However, because their deaths had demonstrated to God the strength of the obedience to his law that had now come to exist among his people, he ended the persecution under Antiochus so that the self-offering of the rest of his people did not have to take the form of a cruel and violent death. In this sense, Eleazar, the mother, and her sons died *in the place* of the rest of the people, since they were put to death while the others were not. Strictly speaking, it can be said that the *death* of Eleazar, the mother, and her sons was substitutionary, but *not the offering up of their life*, since in order to be delivered from the chastisement for their sins, the people still had to offer up their own life to God. They no longer had to do so by *dying*, however, thanks to the faithfulness of Eleazar, the mother, and her sons.

When these ideas are understood properly, it becomes evident that it is extremely difficult to translate into English the word *antipsuchon* as it is used in this verse. "Ransom" is inadequate, since Eleazar, the brothers, and their mother are not seen as having made some type of payment with their lives or having given God something in exchange for the liberation of the Jewish people. Their lives can be considered an offering made to God on behalf of others, yet *not in their stead*, since it was not their offering itself that led God to save the people but the renewed obedience that their faithfulness to the law brought about in others. In a sense, it can be said that Eleazar, the brothers, and their mother obtained Israel's salvation in exchange for giving up their lives, that is, at the price of their life. However, it was not the giving of their lives in itself that brought God to save Israel, but the consequences of their act. The final phrase in 17:20-21 could therefore be paraphrased: "because of them our enemies did not rule over our nation, the tyrant was punished, and the homeland purified—all of which was the result of them having given up their lives as a kind of offering to God, seeking and obtaining in return God's forgiveness of the nation's sin."

The same basic logic is behind the affirmation that "through the blood of those devout ones and the *hilastērion* of their death, divine Providence preserved Israel that previously had been mistreated" (17:22). Once again, the term "blood" must be seen as an allusion, not merely to their death, but to their endurance and faithfulness unto death for the sake of the law and to their offering up of their lives to God. In the author's own words, their blood represents "the courage of their virtue and their endurance under the tortures" (17:22-23). What pleased God was therefore their courage and endurance: "They vindicated their nation, looking to God and enduring torture even to death" on behalf of the law (17:10).[99]

A great deal of scholarly discussion has centered upon the term *hilastērion* here, particularly because of its use in Rom. 3:25. Much of this discussion is motivated by a desire to argue either in favor of or against ideas related to

---

99. As Sam Williams notes, the purification of the land in 4 Macc. 17:21a "cannot be understood except as a reference to Antiochus's departure, which IV Maccabees insists is a result of the martyrs' *endurance* (not their spilled blood)" (*Jesus' Death*, 76).

penal substitution, in particular the notion that God's wrath must be appeased through death. The author of 4 Maccabees clearly sees the sufferings that the Jewish people endured as an expression of God's anger (4 Macc. 4:21). For the author, however, what appeases that anger is not the suffering and death of Eleazar, the brothers, and the mother, but the renewed commitment of the people to God's will.

Nevertheless, according to the argument of 4 Maccabees, it can rightly be said that the deaths of Eleazar, the brothers, and the mother led Israel's God to put away his wrath at the people's sins in several senses. First, the way in which Eleazar, the brothers, and the mother gave themselves up to death for the law and for others was pleasing to God in that this type of commitment to his will is what Israel's God always desires from his people as a whole. Second, their deaths not only demonstrated the extent to which at least some of the people were committed to God's will but also laid the basis for others to be strengthened in their obedience to the law. While this did not necessarily take place immediately, God could reasonably expect that their deaths would have such an effect on others. Since it had been the lack of obedience to his law that had provoked God's wrath in the first place, once God could expect that such obedience would be restored and could see that it was indeed becoming a reality, his wrath would come to an end. And third, upon seeing such firm obedience in those who gave their lives and on that basis anticipating that such obedience would continue and increase among his people, God's justice and mercy would no longer allow him to stand by passively in the face of the cruelties being committed by Antiochus. Instead, he was compelled to put an end to those cruelties and deliver the people from Antiochus's tyranny. For all of these reasons, the deaths of Eleazar, the brothers, and the mother are said to have brought God's wrath to an end. The term *hilastērion* here might therefore be translated as "propitiation" in the sense that their faithfulness to the law to the point of death put away God's wrath, since it demonstrated to God that at least a part of his people were fully committed to obeying the law and led others to observe that law once again. *Hilastērion* might also be translated "expiation" in the sense that the faithfulness to the law of those who died moved others to become faithful as well and therefore to live purified lives; this constituted the basis upon which God declared them pure and was led to purify the land from Antiochus's tyranny.

This does not mean, however, that their deaths should be viewed as an "atoning sacrifice," as translations such as the NRSV affirm.[100] Undoubtedly, the deaths of Eleazar, the brothers, and the mother were sacrificial in the sense that they willingly offered their lives up to God, and in so doing sought God's forgiveness and favor both for themselves and others. As we saw in Chapter 3, these ideas are central to ancient Jewish sacrificial thought. The author of 4 Maccabees does not intend to convey the idea that their deaths in themselves made atonement for Israel's sins. While Eleazar, the brothers,

---

100. On the problem of translating *hilastērion* here, see Finlan, *Background*, 200-205.

and their mother may be described as a *hilastērion* in that they led God to put away his wrath at those sins, strictly speaking, they did not *atone* for those sins. In fact, the language of forgiveness is absent from 4 Maccabees, although the idea of divine forgiveness seems to be present at times in the author's mind. The reason why the author does not relate directly the deaths of Eleazar, the brothers, and their mother to forgiveness is that the idea that sufferings and death in themselves atone for sin is foreign to ancient Jewish thought. What atones for sins is repentance and a renewed commitment to obeying God. The sufferings and death of Eleazar, the brothers, and the mother would be seen as atoning only in the sense that they were an expression of this commitment and served to strengthen others in the same commitment.

The Story of Taxo

One further passage from the second-temple period that speaks of a vicarious death is found in the *Assumption of Moses*, also known as the *Testament of Moses*, a book probably written in the first century CE.[101] After describing the sins of Israel's leaders, the book presents Israel's God as being moved to wrath and stirring up a powerful king who begins to crucify, torture, imprison, and oppress those Jews who seek to remain faithful to the law and practice circumcision (*Ass. Mos.* 7-8). Many Jews are said to succumb to these measures and to be forced into idolatry and blasphemy (*Ass. Mos.* 8).

In the midst of this persecution, a man from the tribe of Levi named Taxo laments the punishment Israel is enduring in the presence of his seven sons and then tells them:

> "Now, therefore, my sons, hear me: for observe and know that neither did the fathers nor their forefathers tempt God, so as to transgress his commands. And you know that this is our strength, and thus we will do. Let us fast for the space of three days and on the fourth let us go into a cave which is in the field, and let us die rather than transgress the commands of the Lord of Lords, the God of our fathers. For if we do this and die, our blood shall be avenged before the Lord" (*Ass. Mos.* 9).

Immediately following this, the book affirms that God's kingdom will appear throughout creation. Satan will be overthrown together with Israel's enemies and Israel will enjoy peace and happiness (*Ass. Mos.* 10).

Although this passage does not speak explicitly of God's wrath being put away following the death of Taxo and his sons, this is clearly implied. On this basis, some scholars have claimed that Taxo's death makes atonement for Israel's sins and has the effect of causing God to intervene to save Israel from its oppression. Michael E. Fuller, for example, claims that "the death of Taxo and his family is presented as an atoning death" that has "redemptive value" in that it moves God to intervene on Israel's behalf; "the death of the righteous

---

101. On the date and background of the *Assumption of Moses*, see especially Kenneth Atkinson, "Taxo's Martyrdom and the Role of the *Nuntius* in the *Testament of Moses*: Implications for Understanding the Role of Other Intermediary Figures," *JBL* 125 (2006): 453-76; Cummins, *Paul*, 73.

ones may motivate God's intervention."[102] Others speak of the death of Taxo and his sons "triggering" God's intervention, as if there were a mechanical cause-and-effect relation between the two events. Marc Turnage even affirms that their deaths forced God to act: "Taxo, like the widow and her seven sons, anticipated that his death and the death of his sons would be efficacious by forcing God to bring about the day of redemption in order to avenge their blood.... The murder of Taxo and his sons because of their devoted piety to the commandments, like the deaths of the widow's sons recorded in 2 and 4 Maccabees, was expected to have a universal effect, bringing forth God's redemption and vengeance."[103]

Interpretations such as these fail to capture the logic behind the passage. Because of their firm commitment to the law, Taxo and his sons refuse to disobey it in the face of persecution. However, due to the fierce nature of the persecution, they withdraw to a secluded cave after fasting for three days so that they will not be enticed or forced by the enemy to "transgress the commands of the Lord of Lords." They thus choose death over disobedience to the law. Their objective is not to force God to act to save Israel, as if God could be manipulated or put under obligation by their deaths. Rather, Taxo trusts that God will respond to their full commitment to observing the law even to the point of death by redeeming Israel.

According to the logic of the book, then, the reason that God responds to the deaths of Taxo and his sons by bringing about the promised redemption is not that those deaths in themselves satisfy his wrath or justice. This would imply that God merely wished to see someone die as punishment for the sins Israel had committed. Rather, what must be seen as satisfying God is the faithfulness of Taxo and his sons and the total commitment to the law that they demonstrated to the point of death.

Unlike 2 and 4 Maccabees, the *Assumption of Moses* does not affirm explicitly that others were brought into obedience through the willingness of Taxo and his sons to die rather than transgress the law. This seems to be assumed, however. The simple fact that the story appears in the book implies that its purpose is to present Taxo and his sons as examples and thereby bring about greater obedience to the law. The conclusion of the book also indicates that this constituted the author's purpose: "Those, therefore, who do and fulfill the commandments of God shall increase and be prospered; but those who sin and set at naught the commandments shall be without the blessings before mentioned, and they shall be punished with many torments by the nations. But wholly to root out and destroy them is not permitted" (*Ass. Mos.* 12).

---

102. Michael E. Fuller, *The Restoration of Israel: Israel's Re-gathering and the Fate of the Nations in Early Jewish Literature and Luke-Acts* (BZNW 138; Berlin: Walter de Gruyter, 2006), 156-58. In part Fuller is drawing on an idea reflected in the views of J. Licht, "Taxo, or the Apocalyptic Doctrine of Vengeance," *JJS* 12 (1961): 98.

103. Marc Turnage, "Jesus and Caiaphas: An Intertextual-Literary Evaluation," in *Jesus' Last Week*, Vol. 1 of *Jerusalem Studies in the Synoptic Gospels* (ed. R. Steven Notley, Marc Turnage, and Brian Becker; JCPS 11; Leiden: Brill, 2006), 160-61.

However, the salvation described in chapter 10 of the book is described in apocalyptic terms and seems to refer to an eschatological redemption similar to what we find in the New Testament and other Jewish writings of the period. This salvation involves the transformation of creation together with the ultimate destruction of evil and of the enemies of God and his people. Although the resurrection of the dead is not mentioned in the book, the redeemed are apparently presented as looking from on high to see their enemies in Gehenna. The implication is thus that the faithful have been saved and are experiencing the life of the new age.

For this reason, the logic behind the account of Taxo and his sons seems to be that their faithfulness to death led God to bring about the eschatological redemption of Israel. In this case, rather than granting Taxo and his sons immortality in the way that 4 Maccabees describes, God establishes definitively the new age of salvation in order that the faithful, such as Taxo and his sons, may participate in it, evidently by being raised from the dead. God's motivation for doing so may be that, because of his justice and mercy, he can no longer permit the righteous to suffer tortures, prison, and death without intervening to save them. While the English translation speaks of God "avenging" the blood of Taxo and his sons, in the thought of the author, God's objective is not to take vengeance on wrongdoers, but to save those who obey the law from their persecutors. The notion that God desires obedience to the law for the sake of the people themselves, rather than for God's own sake, is implied by Taxo's affirmation that the people's "strength" consists precisely in not transgressing the law. This conveys the idea that obedience to the law results intrinsically in the people's well-being and fortitude.

In any case, here as in 2 and 4 Maccabees, the condition upon which God puts away his wrath at the people's sins and intervenes to save Israel is not the death of the righteous per se but their faithfulness and obedience to the law under the most adverse of circumstances. The *Assumption of Moses* never affirms explicitly that Taxo and his sons atoned for Israel's sins or obtained forgiveness for Israel through their death. However, even if this idea is thought to be implicit, what makes atonement and brings forgiveness is not their death per se, but their obedience to God's law, as expressed in their willingness to die rather than to transgress that law. It is therefore misleading to affirm that their death "triggered" God's intervention, forced God to act, or had a "universal effect." The relation between the deaths of Taxo and his sons and the eschatological redemption resulting from those deaths is seen as an *extrinsic* rather than an *intrinsic* one.

Atonement through Suffering and Death in Rabbinic Thought

Outside of the passages from 2 and 4 Maccabees and the *Assumption of Moses* just discussed, there are no other texts from second-temple Jewish literature that might be interpreted as providing support for the idea that sufferings and death could make atonement for sins. This includes the writings of Josephus,

Philo, and the scrolls of Qumran.[104] The idea of atoning for sins through suffering and death does come to prominence, however, in the rabbinic writings. Among the most significant studies discussing this question in detail are those of Adolf Büchler and Eduard Lohse dating from 1928 and 1955 respectively.[105] Although it is unclear to what extent the ideas found in the rabbinic writings date back to New Testament times, many scholars nevertheless consider these writings to be relevant to discussion of the passages in the New Testament that ascribe redemptive value to Jesus' suffering and death. In particular, it is often thought that the rabbinic writings provide evidence that either the righteousness or the punishment of one might substitute for the righteousness or the punishment of others.

Running throughout the rabbinic writings is the idea that faithful Jews can atone for their sins through suffering. Generally, suffering is seen as a means to atone for one's own sins rather than the sins of others. The belief that one can make atonement through suffering is closely tied to the view that God inflicts sufferings in order to chastise and correct sinners and thereby bring them back to him in repentance and obedience. This idea is found frequently in the rabbinic texts. Büchler summarizes the rabbinic teaching thus:

> [A]ll afflictions of man come from God and... not only the sinner but also the righteous is chastised by him. In visiting the latter God's object is to turn him aside from the path of evil into which he has exceptionally strayed, and to prevent him from departing further from his usual right course, and, at the same time, to cleanse him from the sins which he has so far committed. In thus chastising the righteous, God is not harsh, but deals with him gently, as a loving father punishes his son, or his firstborn whom he loves specially and whom he only corrects to lead him back into the right path. As he knows God's purpose in afflicting the righteous, the good man, even when stumbling under the weight of the visitation, should neither say nor think that it was undeserved, as he was free from sin, but he should acknowledge the justice of God in inflicting upon him such chastisements. And even when these are so severe as to bring him down to the ground, he should give further consideration to God's purpose and his possible intentions in his case. Not only should he not murmur against God, but he should also regard

---

104. Both Lohse (*Märtyrer*, 10-12) and Serge Ruzer (*Mapping the New Testament: Early Christian Writings as a Witness for Jewish Biblical Exegesis*; JCPS 13; Leiden: Brill, 2007, 200), who discuss the subject in detail, recognize that the idea of vicarious death is nowhere to be found in the Hebrew Scriptures or second-temple Jewish literature outside of the passages already considered. Some scholars, however, have claimed to find this idea in other passages. One of these is the story of Razis in 2 Macc. 14:37-46 (see van Henten, *Maccabean Martyrs*, 210-13). However, while Razis dies for the law by committing suicide rather than allowing himself to be captured and his death may be seen as exemplary, there is nothing in the passage that implies that his death appeased God's wrath or made atonement for his own sins or those of others. Van Henten also finds the idea of noble death in two passages from Philo (*Good Person* 88-91) and Josephus (*J.W.* 7.389-406), yet these passages have nothing to do with atonement for sins or the appeasement of God's wrath. Craig A. Evans also points to Job 42:9, *LAE* 3:1, and *T. Benj.* 3:8 as examples of the death or suffering of one "providing either atonement or benefit for others" (*Mark 8:27—16:20*; WBC 34B; Nashville: Thomas Nelson, 2001, 122), yet these passages speak only of Job's intercession for others, Eve's request to die for the sin she had committed, and the willingness of those without sin to die for the benefit of others who are guilty, but not in their place. There is no reason to read back into these passages the idea that the suffering or death of one person could atone for the sins of others in God's eyes.

105. See Adolf Büchler, *Studies in Sin and Atonement in the Rabbinic Literature of the First Century* (JCP 11; London: Oxford University Press, 1928); Lohse, *Märtyrer*.

himself happy that he visits him, and bear his sufferings patiently, as such attitude is an expression of man's love of God in truth. He must, moreover, heed the warning given by the afflictions and must not despise them, but evince readiness to repent.[106]

The logic behind the affirmation that in rabbinic thought suffering enables one to atone for one's sins thus coincides with what we have found in the writings of the second-temple period: God does not inflict suffering for its own sake, as if this satisfied divine justice, but in order to bring about a change in the conduct of his people.

According to the rabbis, however, only those who are truly repentant for their sins and are committed to a life of righteousness can atone for their sins through suffering. Because even the righteous sin, they constantly stand in need of repentance, discipline, and correction like everyone else. Consistent throughout the rabbinic writings is the claim that there can be no atonement for those who do not repent. As Büchler notes, "even chastisements inflicted by God do not purge away the sin without repentance."[107] Because suffering in this life is viewed as having a corrective purpose, those who have no intention of turning to God and living in obedience to the law cannot atone for their sins through suffering. For the rabbis, their only fate can be their destruction or perdition. Even if their punishment is thought to be ongoing after their death, those enduring post-mortem punishment in the realm of the dead are not thought to be atoning for their sins, since atonement is no longer possible for them.

In rabbinic thought, when one was suffering, rather than murmuring, protesting to God, or rebelling against him, it was expected that one recognize and confess one's sins and admit that God was just in inflicting the suffering. This reflects conformity to God's will in the passive sense of accepting whatever afflictions God may send, trusting that in his infinite wisdom God is acting for good. Naturally, this conformity with God's will was also to express itself actively in the form of obedience to God's law. In this way, suffering served to strengthen one's commitment to God's will.

Even when one protested or rebelled against God, however, one still might make atonement through one's suffering. Like a person who attempts to domesticate a stubborn and recalcitrant animal such as a donkey or horse, God might use suffering to break the will of one who resists him. Such suffering would only serve to make atonement, however, if in the end one was brought into conformity to God's will.

The notion that faithful Jews make atonement for their sins through death is also found frequently in the rabbinic writings. For the most part, however, those

---

106. Büchler, *Studies*, 171. On these points, see also N. Clayton Croy, *Endurance in Suffering: Hebrews 12:1-13 in its Rhetorical, Religious, and Philosophical Context* (SNTSMS 98; Cambridge: Cambridge University Press, 1998), 124-29. In a separate section, Croy compares and contrasts ancient Jewish beliefs regarding suffering and sin with Greek and Roman perspectives on this subject, which are in many ways similar (133-57).

107. See Büchler, *Studies*, 347, who stresses quite strongly the idea that in rabbinic thought, there is no atonement without repentance (see also 344-51).

who die atone only for their own sins, and not for the sins of others.[108] Because those who have died are no longer capable of receiving correction, it might seem that death would be regarded as a retributive punishment for the sins that those who die have committed rather than a means of atonement. In reality, however, the logic behind the idea that one atones for one's sins through death must be understood differently. This idea was closely tied to beliefs regarding the resurrection, the final judgment, and the life to come.[109] In order to participate in the resurrection life, of course, it was necessary to have lived righteously. Once again, this life of righteousness did not involve perfection but rather a sincere desire and intention to act in conformity with God's will and a passive acceptance of anything that God in his sovereignty might ordain. Thus, in accepting one's death from God's hand, one was acting righteously and could hope to be treated by God as righteous at the final judgment.

In the rabbinic writings, those Jews facing death are commended to pray to God, "Make my death an atonement for my sins."[110] By embracing death rather than murmuring or rebelling against God's decree, it was evident that one was submitting to God's will. This petition also represented a confession that one had sinned and stood in need of forgiveness. At the same time, because one was about to die, there was nothing of greater value that one could offer to God than one's life. By subjecting oneself to God's will and placing one's life in God's hands, casting oneself upon God's mercy rather than attempting to manipulate God or convince him to revoke his decree of death, one was behaving in the way God desired. As elsewhere, this is the condition upon which God was thought to grant forgiveness and salvation, whether in this life or the life to come.

From God's perspective, since death marked the end of life, when a person was nearing death there was nothing more that God could do in order to bring that person into greater conformity with his will. No further correction was possible, simply because the time for such correction had passed. Therefore, according to this logic, the only thing left for God to do was to decide whether or not the dying person should be forgiven. All that God could expect from those who were dying was that they confess their sins and ask for forgiveness. As long as they did this with a sincere heart, God would forgive them and declare them fit to enter into the world to come at the final judgment.

Some of the rabbis claimed that even those who were executed for crimes they had committed or were not fully repentant could atone for their sins

---

108. See especially Lohse, *Märtyrer*, 38-50; E. P. Sanders, *Paul and Palestinian Judaism: A Comparison of Patterns of Religion* (Philadelphia: Fortress, 1977), 172-75; Friedrich Avemarie, "Lebenshingabe und heilschaffender Tod in der rabbinischen Literatur," in *Deutungen des Todes Jesu*, ed. Frey and Schröter, 171-74, who also notes that this idea is in the oldest strands of the rabbinic literature (210).

109. See Bruce Chilton and Jacob Neusner, *Classical Christianity and Rabbinic Judaism: Comparing Theologies* (Grand Rapids: Baker Academic, 2004), 238-39; Lohse, *Märtyrer*, 42-44.

110. Lohse, *Märtyrer*, 39; C. G. Montefiore and H. Loewe, *A Rabbinic Anthology, Selected and Arranged with Comments and Introductions* (New York: Schocken, 1974), 241.

through death. This was possible only for those who formed part of Israel and applied particularly to those who had sinned inadvertently or had died a sudden death without having had an opportunity to repent.[111] The logic behind this seems to be that, even though they had not repented before their death, when God looked into their hearts, he saw that they would have repented if they had had the chance. God could also expect that even those who had been able to repent before their death but had not done so might be brought to repentance as a result of what they suffered in their death, and thereby be made fit to participate in the age to come once God had raised them from the dead.

Those who could not make atonement for their sins through suffering and death were those who consciously and deliberately chose to reject God and God's will in life and death. As Bruce Chilton and Jacob Neusner comment, in rabbinic thought, while all Israel has a share in the life to come, those who "willfully defy God in matters of eternity" and reject the Torah are not considered true members of Israel, even if they were born Jews.[112] The belief that in the age to come the evil inclination or *yetser hara* would be taken away may also have led some to conclude that, through their death, even those who are executed or die unrepentant can atone for their sins. In this case, it may have been thought that those who had lived in sin could still be reformed and renewed after their death so as to become righteous in the next world.[113]

A few passages from the rabbinic texts convey the idea that, under certain conditions, through his or her death a righteous person might atone not only for his or her own sins, but also for the sins of others.[114] This was said especially of the great biblical figures and in some cases the great rabbis as well.[115] These passages usually do not specify, however, which persons receive the forgiveness of their sins by means of the death of the righteous person. While the great figures of Israel's history might be said to have made atonement for all of Israel through their death, other righteous figures such as rabbis might be seen as having made atonement only for a particular group of people, such as those whom they instructed in the law or the members of their own generation in general.[116]

As Friedrich Avemarie notes, it is not possible to integrate into a well-defined system the rabbinic teaching regarding the manner in which righteous Israelites might atone for the sins of others through their death nor

---

111. See Lohse, *Märtyrer*, 49; Sanders, *Paul and Palestinian Judaism*, 174.
112. Chilton and Neusner, *Classical Christianity*, 239-40.
113. See Levi A. Olan, *Judaism and Immortality* (New York: Union of American Hebrew Congregations, 1971). Olan notes the rabbinic view that "[a]ll Jews go to heaven because God ever accepts the repentant sinner, and surely every man repents at the time of his death. Even at the gates of hell one may confess and return to God, and God accepts him in loving mercy" (46).
114. The most extensive treatment of this idea is found in Lohse, *Märtyrer*, 78-87.
115. See Lohse, *Märtyrer*, 87; Avemarie, "Lebenshingabe," 191-92; Jacob Neusner, *Messiah in Context: Israel's History and Destiny in Formative Judaism* (Philadelphia: Fortress, 1984), 128.
116. See Avemarie, "Lebenshingabe," 190; Hengel, *Atonement*, 63.

grasp fully the reasoning behind this idea.[117] What we can affirm confidently, however, is that a righteous person who passed away was not thought to have died as a substitute for others. In fact, all individuals would obviously die their own death at some point, and thus were not thought to have been saved from death by the death of another. Rather, the logic of rabbinic thought on this subject seems to have been that God was pleased that the person dying had remained righteous and committed to his will until the very end. That person therefore served as a model for others, particularly those who identified with that person by commemorating and reflecting on his or her life and death or being influenced by his or her teaching and example. What mattered, therefore, was the legacy left behind by the righteous person, since this legacy served to bring others into conformity with God's will.

Thus to say that a righteous person atoned for the sins of others through his or her death involved affirming that, on the basis of the righteousness which that person had demonstrated in life and death, God looked favorably upon those who continued to hold that person and his or her words and deeds in esteem and identified themselves with that person. Those who did so were forgiven and accepted by God because the respect, honor, and reverence they showed for the righteous one who had died would lead them to attempt to live in the same way. Once again, however, through their death the righteous atoned only for those who were repentant and remained committed to living in conformity with God's will. No atonement was possible for the unrepentant.

In the same context, at times the rabbis spoke of God receiving the soul of a righteous person as a pledge or guarantee for others.[118] In this case, the idea seems to have been that God would forego or postpone the chastisements that people deserved for their sins in the present on account of that person. He did so, however, with the expectation that they would seek to follow the example of the righteous person who had died. Of course, if they did not, then they could not expect forgiveness. In a sense, it might be said that God reckoned to others the righteousness of the person who had died, yet he did so only provisionally, expecting that others would come to practice the same type of righteousness as a result of the influence which that person's life had on them. Once again, therefore, what mattered was the influence that the righteous person's life and death had on those who remained in this world.

Lohse points to a number of texts that speak of innocent children atoning for the sins of others through their death, in particular the sins of their parents.[119] This belief seems to derive from the passages in the Hebrew Scriptures that speak of God chastising the sins of the parents in their children. If this was so, then when the children suffered and died, God was in fact chastising their parents, who atoned for their sins not through their own sufferings but

---

117. Avemarie, "Lebenshingabe," 193.
118. See Lohse, *Märtyrer*, 82-85.
119. Ibid., 92-94.

through those of their children. Not all found this idea acceptable, as even the Hebrew Scriptures show (Ezek. 18:19-20). It must be remembered, however, that God's purpose in punishing was not understood in terms of retribution but correction. According to this logic, therefore, by inflicting suffering or death on children, God sought to move the parents to repentance and obedience and also warned others of the possible consequences of their own sins. Strictly speaking, it was not the death of the children that atoned for the sins of others, but the repentance and correction that was expected to follow as a consequence of those deaths.

In all of these instances, then, strictly speaking, it is not suffering and death that atone for sins, but the repentance and renewed commitment to obedience that suffering and death serve to bring about.[120] In ancient Jewish thought, no amount of suffering and no death could atone for the sins of those who refused to repent sincerely of their sins and recommit themselves to living in accordance with God's will. Furthermore, nothing in the Jewish texts ever suggests that God might accept the righteousness of one person in the place of another or spare those who were guilty of sins from the punishment they deserved by inflicting that punishment on a righteous substitute. Such ideas would imply that God did not care *who* practiced righteousness or endured the punishment deserved by sins, but only that *someone* do so. Conversely, the implication would be that God did not care *who* suffered the punishment for people's sins, but only that *someone* do so. In rewarding righteousness and punishing disobedience, the God of Israel was not responding to *his own* needs or desires but seeking the well-being of his people. Therefore, to impute the righteousness of one to others or inflict punishment on an innocent party in place of the guilty would be seen as counter-productive, since it would promote sin and disobedience rather than the just and righteous behavior God desired to see in all for their own good.

MERITS, PRAYER, AND ATONEMENT IN ANCIENT HEBREW AND JEWISH THOUGHT

The idea that one can make atonement for one's sins through one's own actions is well-attested in ancient Hebrew and Jewish thought. Among these actions, of course, was the offering of sacrifices to God during the time when the Jerusalem temple existed. However, one could also make atonement through other actions in relation to both God and others. In fact, as noted in Chapter 3, offering a sacrifice was not always sufficient to make atonement for what one had done or failed to do. Certain offenses required some type of payment

---

120. This observation must also be made with regard to several other passages from the rabbinic literature cited by Craig Evans in support of the idea that death can make atonement (*y. Sanh.* 11.5; *Sipre Deut.* §333 on Deut. 32:43, and *Mek.* on Exod. 12:1 [*Pisha* §1]); see Evans, *Mark 8:27—16:20*, 387. A close examination of these passages indicates that what actually atones or makes expiation is not sufferings and death in themselves, but the way in which those sufferings and deaths are manifestations of obedience or help bring about obedience in others.

or retribution to be made to the temple or to an injured party. One could also atone for one's sins by helping out those in need or performing some type of action that would benefit others. Everett Ferguson, for example, finds in the rabbinic literature seven ways in which one might atone for one's sins: the reading and studying of the law, repentance, prayer, works of charity, fasting, suffering, and attitudes of the heart such as humility, justice, and righteousness.[121] Because such deeds could be regarded as meritorious, it could be said that one's merits might atone for one's own sin or that of others.

The Jewish belief that one could atone for one's sins by one's deeds has traditionally been regarded as extremely problematic by Protestant theologians and biblical scholars. In large part, of course, this is because in Protestant teaching, no one but Christ is able to make atonement for sins. From a Protestant perspective, the claim that one can make atonement and merit divine forgiveness through one's conduct is also unacceptable because it is seen as affirming a doctrine of works-righteousness.

In his 1977 book *Paul and Palestinian Judaism: A Comparison of Patterns of Religion*, E. P. Sanders demonstrated convincingly that Protestant biblical scholars had wrongly attributed to Jews in antiquity the belief that one could *earn* salvation through one's works.[122] Most biblical scholars today would agree with Sanders on this point. However, as I have argued elsewhere, *earning* forgiveness or salvation is not the same thing as *meriting* forgiveness or salvation.[123] The language of *earning* implies that some type of claim can be laid upon God, as if God had set up a system by which certain works could automatically obtain God's favor and acceptance. In contrast, to affirm that certain actions *merit* a certain response from God conveys a different idea. As we saw in Chapter 2, in Jewish thought, what one merited through one's actions was not God's grace or love, since that was always a given, but a certain *form* which that grace or love might take. In the case of obedience, God's grace and love generally took the form of blessing and acceptance, while in the case of disobedience, the same grace and love took the form of discipline, correction, and chastisement. In both cases, what God ultimately desired was *conformity to his will*, which one manifested by being committed to keeping God's commandments and by accepting whatever might come from God's hand in a spirit of trust and confidence in God. This was what God consistently sought to bring about in his people for their own good and the good of others.

The ancient Jewish belief that one could atone for one's sins and merit divine forgiveness through one's deeds, therefore, did not represent a denial of

---

121. Everett Ferguson, "Spiritual Sacrifice in Early Christianity and its Environment," in *Aufstieg und Niedergang der Romischen Welt*, Vol. II/23.1 (ed. H. Temporini and W. Haase; Berlin: De Gruyter, 1980), 1161-62. Joachim Jeremias also lists other means of atonement mentioned in the rabbinic literature, including indemnification and the high priestly robes (*The Eucharistic Words of Jesus*, trans. Norman Perrin; Philadelphia: Fortress, 1977, 230).

122. See Sanders, *Paul and Palestinian Judaism*, 126, 141, 179-82, 205, 320, 420-22.

123. David A. Brondos, *Paul on the Cross: Reconstructing the Apostle's Story of Redemption* (Minneapolis: Fortress, 2006), 15-16.

God's grace or involve affirming a doctrine of works-righteousness as this doctrine has traditionally been understood in Protestant thought. Whether God responded to obedience with blessing or conversely punished sin in order to correct wrongdoers, God was thought to be acting out of grace, seeking that his people obey his commandments for their own good. In fact, even when God tested the righteous by sending hardships into their life, he was regarded as acting graciously, since such hardships had the objective of strengthening the faith, trust, and obedience of those who endured them. Furthermore, in Jewish thought, it was God alone who brought about a life of righteousness in his people through the covenant relationship he had established with them, the law he had given to instruct them in the way they should live for their own good, and the rewards and punishments he handed out in order to promote obedience to his commandments. Therefore, whatever righteousness one possessed was ultimately a gift from God and the product, not of one's own efforts, but of God's gracious activity.

As we have seen in this chapter and the previous one, in Jewish thought only one thing could truly make atonement for the sins one had committed: a sincere recommitment to living in accordance with God's will. Those who made such a recommitment were able to do so only by virtue of the grace God had shown to Israel as a whole as well as to each individual member of Israel. Of course, if the commitment to doing God's will was sincere, that commitment would inevitably be manifested concretely in acts of kindness and justice toward others. Nevertheless, because perfect obedience was impossible, it was constantly necessary for all to make atonement by recommitting themselves to doing God's will. And because doing God's will was synonymous with keeping the commandments he had given through Moses, those who had sinned would recommit themselves to doing God's will by confessing their sins and, when possible, offering the sacrifices for sin that God had prescribed. However, they would also manifest their recommitment to doing God's will and make atonement for their sins through activities such as those mentioned by the rabbis: repenting, fasting, performing works of charity, and dedicating themselves to prayer and the study of the law. Because these acts served to *renew*, *strengthen*, and *express* their commitment to doing God's will, they served as means through which God's people could atone for their sins. Furthermore, because God was able to look into the hearts of his people, the proper attitude toward God and others could atone for sins. This was because that attitude would inevitably lead one to live in the way God desired and commanded.

Through one's attitudes and actions, therefore, one could make atonement for one's sins and merit divine forgiveness, as long as those attitudes and actions were expressions of a sincere commitment to living in conformity with God's will. Yet because not only those attitudes and actions but also that commitment to God's will were something that God graciously brought about in his people, no one could be said to merit God's grace, which was always a free gift. This means that divine grace must be distinguished from divine forgiveness. As we saw in Chapter 2, in biblical and Jewish thought, while God's grace was *unconditional,* God's forgiveness was *conditional.* God's grace was thought to take the form of forgiveness only when the sinner's commitment to doing God's will had been restored, renewed, and strengthened. When that did not happen, God's grace took the form of acting to chastise and correct the sinner so as to bring him or her back into conformity with God's will.

This understanding of God's grace also meant that one could not purchase God's favor and forgiveness through gifts or manipulate God in order to obtain what one wanted. Nor could one make claims upon God on the basis of one's behavior. The reason for this was not that one's behavior was always imperfect, since God did not demand perfection. In fact, even if it were possible for one to attain perfection, that perfection would be the result of God's grace, which could never be earned. Rather, to make claims upon God on the basis of one's behavior inevitably involved attempting to impose one's will upon God by demanding that God treat one in a certain way. By definition, such an attitude was contrary to God's will: rather than submitting obediently to God, one would be attempting to subject God to one's own desires and demands. For these reasons, while one could merit salvation or forgiveness through one's attitudes and actions, no one could put God under obligation to grant salvation or forgiveness or earn God's favor through obedience. Even those who outwardly observed the commandments were not really obeying them if they did so in an attempt to manipulate God or earn his favor, since they were not acting out of a pure heart and therefore were not in conformity with God's will.

Because the requirement for forgiveness was a sincere commitment to living according to God's will, at times God might even deny forgiveness to those who expressed remorse for their sins and asked to be forgiven. The reason for this was that one might be motivated to seek forgiveness, not because one was sincerely repentant, but simply because one wished to escape punishment. The story of the death of Antiochus Epiphanes in 2 Macc. 9:5-28 illustrates this idea well. Even though at the end of his life he implored God for forgiveness, he was not forgiven because he sought merely to escape divine punishment rather than to commit himself to doing God's will. To forgive those who sought forgiveness solely out of fear of punishment would not lead them to live in accordance with God's will since, once they had been forgiven, they would turn back to their life of sin and disobedience.

Atonement by Prayer

The notion that one could atone for one's sins through prayer must be understood on the basis of the same ideas. In ancient Jewish thought, not all prayer was atoning. If prayer involved an attempt to manipulate or coerce God or make demands upon him, it was not pleasing to God. If one begged God for forgiveness but was not truly committed to God's will or acted solely out of fear of punishment, one's prayer did not make atonement for one's sins. Prayer was therefore atoning only when those praying submitted both passively and actively to God's will, confessing their sins and resolving to receive from God's hand whatever God might ordain. If those who prayed with a pure and sincere heart at times reminded God of their obedience to his will and their acts of righteousness and justice as they asked for God's blessings and forgiveness, this was not because they were attempting to manipulate God or make demands upon him on the basis of their behavior. Rather, they were merely pointing to their obedience and actions as evidence of their commitment to doing God's will, since that commitment—which, as we have seen, was itself a gift of God—constituted the basis upon which God might grant them the blessings and forgiveness they sought.

Of course, those who prayed to God might seek forgiveness and blessings not only for themselves but for others as well. This means that those who were righteous might make atonement for the sins of others through their intercession. This idea is found often in the biblical texts and other second-temple Jewish writings.[124] Often this intercession is said to be accompanied by sacrifice, although, as we have seen in the previous chapter, sacrifice itself was understood primarily as a form of intercession and prayer. While the language of atonement is not always used, in the Hebrew Scriptures there are a number of examples of a righteous person interceding on behalf of others and in this way obtaining God's forgiveness for them. Among the most notable of these is the prayer of the high priest on the Day of Atonement and the intercession of Moses in Exodus 32 that we have considered above. There are also instances in the Hebrew Scriptures in which righteous persons intercede for others but do not obtain God's forgiveness for them. Of these, the most well-known is the story of Abraham interceding on behalf of the inhabitants of Sodom and Gomorrah in Gen. 18:16-33. Similarly, even though the high priests interceded on behalf of God's people and accompanied that intercession with a sacrificial offering on the Day of Atonement, if God was convinced that the people were not truly repentant of their sins and were not committed to living according to his will, God would not respond favorably to the high priest's intercession.

In order to grasp the logic behind the idea that the prayer of the righteous individual could make atonement for others, it is important to understand the role of mediators in Jewish thought. The high priests, for example, had the responsibility not only of overseeing the presentation of sacrifices on behalf of the people and interceding for them, but also that of making sure that the people received instruction and reinforcing their obedience to the law. Similarly, Moses had the task of delivering the law to the people

---

124. For biblical examples of atonement through intercession, see S. Williams, *Jesus' Death*, 85-86, n35; Jacob Milgrom, *Studies in Cultic Theology and Terminology* (SJLA 36; Leiden: Brill, 1983), 62; de Jonge, "Jesus' Death," 149.

and providing guidance for them under God's direction, not only so that they might reach the land promised to them, but also so that they might live according to his will.

While mediatorial figures with divine authority such as the high priest and Moses might intercede before God on behalf of those who had sinned and obtain a favorable response from God, the same was not true of any Israelite. A member of God's people who was not in a position of leadership could not expect to obtain divine forgiveness for the guilty people as a whole, even if that person was righteous. The reason for this is that such a person had no authority over God's people. This made it impossible for that person to bring others into conformity with God's will in the way that figures of authority such as Moses and the high priest could. And since the basis upon which God forgave the people's sins was their commitment to living in conformity with his will, those who were not in a position to bring others to assume such a commitment could not obtain divine forgiveness for them through their prayer.

In the case of Moses, for example, God accepted his prayer on behalf of the Israelites because Moses was not only fully committed to obeying God personally but was also committed to bringing the people as a whole into conformity with God's will, in faithfulness to the task God had given him. Therefore, the reason why God heeded Moses' prayer for forgiveness on behalf of the people was that God expected that through Moses his objective of bringing the people into conformity with his will would still be accomplished, in spite of the people's sinfulness. As we have noted above, in the narrative that appears in Exodus 32, even though God forgives the people their sin, he says that they must nevertheless be chastised at a later time. This was because, from God's perspective, they still needed to be disciplined so that they might learn to obey him. Merely overlooking what they had done would be counter-productive, since the people had not yet become truly repentant. What had motivated them to ask Moses to intercede for them was not a true commitment to God's will, but fear of divine punishment. In spite of this, God decided to grant Moses' petition and did not destroy the people. However, the fact that in this instance God had refrained from punishing them did not guarantee that he would continue to act in the same way in the future. When they fell back into sin, God punished them again, as the story of the bronze serpent illustrates (Num. 21:4-9). Similar ideas lie behind the account of Korah's rebellion in Numbers 16. Because God was attempting to bring about an obedient people through Moses and Aaron as his chosen instruments, he punished those who resisted Moses and Aaron, especially because what motivated that resistance was not a sincere desire to serve others in the ways that Moses and Aaron did, but a selfish lust for power over others.

The idea that the high priests atoned for the sins of the people through the sacrifices and prayers they offered up to God on the Day of Atonement reflects the same logic. When the high priest interceded on behalf of the people on that day, it was expected that both he and the people be sincere in their repentance and their intention to recommit themselves to doing God's will. If God considered that both the high priest and the people were truly repentant, God would grant forgiveness. No matter how repentant and righteous the priest might be, however, those among the people who were not committed to living according to God's will were not believed to obtain divine forgiveness, in spite of the priest's prayer. If the priest was an impious person who was not truly committed to God's will and did not seek to bring others into conformity with that will, God might nevertheless forgive the people if he saw in them a commitment to his will. However, God might also chastise the priest and the people alike, as he is said to do in 4 Macc. 4:15-21. The reason for this was that, even if the people themselves were committed to the law, as long as the impious priest was over them, it was likely that he would use his authority to lead the people into sin rather than into righteousness. Thus God's punishment of the priest would serve the purpose of either correcting him or removing him from power, while God's chastisement of the people would either move them to seek the removal of the sinful high priest or serve as a preventative measure. In the latter case, by punishing the people as a whole, God would bring back to himself those who had strayed under the high priest's influence and at the same time attempt to prevent others from falling away.

In the story of Abraham's prayer for the inhabitants of Sodom and Gomorrah in Gen. 18:16-33, the reason why God rejects Abraham's petition was that God had no basis upon which to expect that the people of these cities would eventually turn to him in repentance and obedience. Even though Abraham was righteous, because he had no influence over the sinful inhabitants of the two cities and because not even five righteous persons could be found there, it was obvious that the inhabitants would continue in their perverse ways. The lack of even five righteous persons meant that there was no reason for God to expect that anything would change there, since four righteous persons or less could not exert sufficient influence on the majority in order for them to repent and mend their ways. Had God heeded Abraham's petition to spare the inhabitants, their wickedness would probably not only have continued and increased, but it would also have spread further so as to affect the surrounding places as well. Therefore, in spite of Abraham's righteousness, God did not respond favorably to his intercession for others.

Of course, under certain circumstances, righteous persons who were not in leadership roles over God's people might also make intercession to God on behalf of other individuals who had sinned and obtain divine forgiveness and acceptance for them. The reason for this was not that God showed favoritism to the righteous. Rather, it had to do with God's purposes. The fact that a righteous person was interceding for someone else implied that the righteous person was in a certain relationship with the person on whose behalf he or she interceded and could thus seek to bring that person back into conformity with

God's will. At the same time, those who had sinned and asked a righteous person to intercede for them were in effect placing themselves in a certain relationship with that person. Implicit in their request was that they would change their ways and commit themselves to following that person's example. This would provide a basis for God to expect that the one who had sinned would be brought back into conformity with his will. Once again, however, if the sinner did not truly repent but was simply seeking to escape divine punishment, the prayer of the righteous would not attain God's forgiveness for her or him.

The Merits of the Fathers

Closely related to the idea that the prayer of a righteous person could atone for the sin of others or obtain divine forgiveness on their behalf is the rabbinic teaching regarding the *zekut 'abot*, often translated as "merits of the fathers."[125] While this idea is particularly associated with rabbinic thought, as Jacqueline de Roo notes, it is already found in a number of writings from the second-temple period as well.[126] According to this idea, the righteousness of Israel's forefathers could benefit their descendants in some way. The translation of the noun *zekut* into English is problematic, since no exact English equivalent exists. As Sanders notes, *zakah*, of which *zekut* is the plural form, may simply refer to virtue or correct behavior rather than merit: "the consistent translation of *zakah* and its cognates as 'merit' obscures the terminology and seems to imply a thoroughgoing 'doctrine'."[127] As Sanders has argued, it is doubtful that this was understood in terms of some type of "treasure of merits" that could be transferred to those who had insufficient merits of their own. Nevertheless, the righteous deeds of Abraham and the other forefathers were thought to be the basis upon which God had redeemed Israel from Egypt, provided help to his people Israel in various moments, and suspended his punishment of the world. While the *zekut 'abot* might lead God to overlook the sins of his people in the present world, the "merits of the fathers" were not believed to benefit others at the final judgment.[128] The reason for this is clear: in the present world, those who sinned might still be brought into conformity with God's will as a result of their identification with the patriarchs and the obedience to God that had characterized their life. In contrast, once the final judgment arrived, this was no longer possible.

Of all the righteous deeds attributed to Israel's forefathers, none was held in higher regard in antiquity than Abraham's willingness to sacrifice his son Isaac. Allusions to this story from Gen. 22:1-19, known as the binding of Isaac or the *Akedah*, appear repeatedly in ancient Jewish literature. As Lohse notes,

---

125. On this idea, see Lohse, *Märtyrer*, 102-4; Sanders, *Paul and Palestinian Judaism*, 183-98.
126. Jacqueline C. R. de Roo, "God's Covenant with the Forefathers," in *The Concept of the Covenant in the Second Temple Period* (ed. Stanley E. Porter and de Roo; JSJSup 71; Leiden: Brill, 2003), 192-97.
127. Sanders, *Paul and Palestinian Judaism*, 188; see also 90.
128. Ibid., 90-91, 196-97.

the biblical text does not speak of the act of Abraham or Isaac as atoning for others. Nevertheless, many scholars believe that the idea that Abraham or Isaac made atonement for their descendants through their obedience to God's command may go back to Jesus' time and have influenced the way in which his first followers interpreted his death. Florentino García Martínez, for example, argues that "some of the basic elements of the Christian interpretation of the Aqedah were already present in pre-Christian Judaism," and points to passages from the book of *Jubilees* and the Qumran literature in support of his claim.[129] Géza Vermès similarly argues that, while this story was told in many different ways and with different emphases in antiquity, the notion that Isaac's willingness to offer up his life was atoning can be traced back at least to the first century CE.[130] In contrast, J. C. O'Neill writes: "the Jewish teaching that the offering of Isaac was an expiatory and redemptive act for all Israel was not earlier than the 2nd century and arose in response to an Isaac-Jesus typology and the Christian doctrine of atonement."[131] While to some extent the Jewish understandings of the story of the binding of Isaac may have been influenced by the interpretations given to Jesus' death by his first followers, it would appear that we cannot rule out the possibility that they may also have drawn on ideas that already existed in Jewish thought.

Many Christian scholars have drawn parallels between Abraham's willingness to offer up his "only beloved son" Isaac and God's handing over of his only beloved son Jesus to death. Some have even claimed to find the notion of penal substitution in the biblical account. Gordon Wenham, for example, argues that Gen. 22:13 "states that Abraham offered up the lamb 'as a burnt offering *instead of his son*'" and thus "shows an animal suffering vicariously in a man's place." For Wenham, the passage is "paradigmatic and elucidates the OT understanding of sacrifice in general."[132] Here again we find the claim that what makes atonement is death itself.

A close look at both the passage itself and the later Jewish interpretations of that passage, however, demonstrates that there is no basis for such a claim. As Lohse notes, in the Genesis account, no atoning value is ascribed to the act of Abraham or Isaac.[133] The story has nothing to do with sin, guilt, expiation, propitiation, or punishment. The only actual sacrifice that takes place is that of the ram, since Isaac himself is never sacrificed. Furthermore, as Sam Williams observes, in ancient Jewish thought and the original narrative itself, "God commanded Abraham to offer Isaac not in order to expiate his sins but

---

129. Florentino García Martínez, *Qumranica Minora II: Thematic Studies on the Dead Sea Scrolls* (ed. Eibert J. C. Tigchelaar; STDJ 64; Leiden: Brill 2007), 143; see 131-43.

130. Géza Vermès, *Scripture and Tradition in Judaism: Haggadic Studies*, 2nd rev. ed. (SPB 4; Leiden: Brill, 1973), 196-98, 204, 217.

131. J. C. O'Neill, "Did Jesus Teach That His Death Would Be Vicarious As Well As Typical?," in *Suffering and Martyrdom in the New Testament: Studies Presented to G.M. Styler by the Cambridge New Testament Seminar* (ed. William Horbury and Brian McNeil; Cambridge: Cambridge University Press, 1981), 13.

132. Gordon J. Wenham, "The Theology of Old Testament Sacrifice," in *Sacrifice in the Bible* (ed. Roger T. Beckwith and Martin J. Selman; Grand Rapids: Baker, 1995), 80.

133. Lohse, *Märtyrer*, 91.

to manifest his devotion and obedience."[134] Both the Genesis account and the later Jewish interpretations of the passage emphasize the absolute trust in God displayed by Abraham through his willingness to offer up to God that which was most precious to him, namely, the life of Isaac his son.[135] Over time, Jewish interpreters also came to stress the willingness of Isaac to give up his own life, although this idea is absent from the biblical account.[136]

In either case, what came to be seen as atoning was not the near-death of Isaac, and much less the death of the ram, but the commitment to God's will manifested by both Abraham and Isaac. The purpose of God's command that Abraham offer up Isaac was understood to be that of testing Abraham's faith.[137] Given Sarah's advanced age, Abraham could hardly hope that she might give him another son through whom the promises of blessing that God had made to him and his descendants might be fulfilled. God's command to sacrifice Isaac thus forced Abraham to choose whether or not he would trust God fully, even to the point of apparently making it virtually impossible for God to fulfill the promises he had made to Abraham by putting Isaac to death. Most of those who heard or read the story would also have agreed that it was much more difficult to offer up one's only son than to offer up one's own life. Abraham's willingness to obey God's command to sacrifice his son was therefore considered the most perfect expression possible of trust in God and obedience to God's will.

To anyone who read or listened carefully to the story of the binding of Isaac, therefore, it was evident that it was not so much a story about sacrifice as it was a story about absolute obedience to God's will. As a result of Abraham's obedience, God tells Abraham: "Because you have done this, and have not withheld your son, your only son, I will indeed bless you, and I will make your offspring as numerous as the stars of heaven and as the sand that is on the seashore. And your offspring shall possess the gate of their enemies, and by your offspring shall all the nations of the earth gain blessing for themselves, because you have obeyed my voice" (Gen. 22:16-19). Here, in contrast to Gen. 12:1-9, where God's promises to Abraham are unconditional, God's election of Abraham's descendants is said to be a reaction to Abraham's obedience. In other words, according to the story of the binding of Isaac, while God initially had promised to bless Abraham's descendants out of pure grace and not because of anything Abraham had done previously, God reiterated that promise after Abraham had been willing to sacrifice Isaac in obedience to God's command. Israel's election was therefore due, not only to an act of grace on God's part, but also to Abraham's merit.

While some might regard these two ideas as mutually contradictory, according to the logic of the Genesis account, this is not the case. From the

---

134. S. Williams, *Jesus' Death*, 105.
135. See Vermès, *Scripture*, 195-97, 212; Lohse, *Märtyrer*, 90-91; de Roo, "God's Covenant," 194-99.
136. See Vermès, *Scripture*, 197-206.
137. Lohse, *Märtyrer*, 90; García Martínez, "Sacrifice," 136-37; Josephus, *Ant.* 1.230-32.

time that God elected Abraham, his intention had been to create an obedient people. Even though the Genesis account does not affirm that before God elected Abraham he looked into his heart and saw that he would be obedient, this seems to be implied. In any case, the logic behind the story of the binding of Isaac is that, if Abraham trusted God fully and was committed to obeying God under any circumstance without questioning him, then God could hope and expect that those who would be born of Abraham's seed and identify with Abraham would be committed to doing the same. On that basis, God is presented as reiterating to Abraham his promise to bless him and his descendants, since through his willingness to offer up Isaac, Abraham had confirmed that he did indeed trust fully in God and had provided a basis for God to expect that all who would later look to him as their father would trust in God in the same way.

According to the logic of the Genesis account, while the blessing and salvation promised to Abraham's descendants can be regarded as something God gave to Abraham personally, it can also be seen as something given to those descendants themselves on account of Abraham. In this sense, those descendants owe their blessings as God's chosen people to their father Abraham and his merits rather than to anything they had done personally. This idea, however, seems to create difficulties when we consider the question of whether or not Abraham's descendants had to *continue* to be obedient to God in order to retain their status as God's chosen people. To affirm that they could sin freely without being concerned about losing that status is obviously problematic in that it goes against the idea that God blesses obedience and punishes disobedience, an idea which is central to the belief system reflected in the Hebrew Scriptures and ancient Jewish writings. Yet to affirm that they needed to remain obedient to God's will in order for God's promises to Abraham to be fulfilled implies that God might at some point revoke those promises and reject Abraham's descendants. Neither alternative would seem to be in accordance with biblical and Jewish thought.

To some extent, this difficulty could be resolved by claiming that, even though Abraham's descendants would be chastised by God for their sins, God would never completely forsake or destroy them, but would ultimately act to bring about the obedience he desired to see in them in order to fulfill his promises. This would mean that, on account of what Abraham had done, in the end God would forgive their sins, though he would still inflict suffering on them in this world in order to chastise and discipline them for those sins. On this basis, they could trust that eventually their sins would be forgiven on account of Abraham and his merits, including especially his willingness to sacrifice his son Isaac in obedience to God. This would make Abraham's merits the basis for their forgiveness.

At the same time, those descendants of Abraham who had no desire or intention to obey God's commandments and live according to his will would forfeit their status as members of God's chosen people as long as they continued in that mindset. Commitment to God's will was therefore also a necessary condition for participation in the blessings God had promised to Abraham's descendants. Such a commitment, however, would by definition mark the lives of all faithful Jews who identified with Abraham and saw him, not only as their forefather, but as the prototype and model of who they were to be and sought to become. Undoubtedly, in their minds, no member of God's people Israel could ever expect to attain the same degree of commitment and obedience to God's will that Abraham had displayed. Nevertheless, by identifying with Abraham, they committed themselves to following his example and living righteously in the way that he had.

These ideas form the background necessary to understand the way in which the merits not only of Abraham but also of the other patriarchs and great figures from Israel's history could be said to atone for the sins of others.[138] To affirm that the merits of the forefathers atoned for the sins of later generations did not mean that one's own obedience was unnecessary and that one could sin freely, trusting in God's forgiveness on account of the promises made to the forefathers. Because one still needed to repent and commit to God's will in order to be forgiven, atonement for sin still depended on one's own actions.

However, one was forgiven not only because of one's own actions but also because of what Abraham and the other forefathers had done. Their total commitment to God's will had led God to establish the covenant with those who identified themselves as Abraham's descendants, including not only those who descended physically from Abraham but also those who looked to him as their forefather only in a spiritual sense. By establishing that covenant on account of the forefathers, God had provided their descendants with a means by which they could attain life, both in this age and the age to come. Through their example and their obedience to the commandments God had given them, the forefathers had also defined what God expected from his people and thereby had made it possible for them to live in accordance with his will so as to obtain his blessings. Chief among the commandments that God had given was the commandment to be circumcised, which dated back to Abraham's day. That commandment, however, stood alongside all of the other commandments of the law that God had given through Moses. By observing these commandments faithfully with a pure heart and making atonement through the prescribed rites whenever they sinned, the people could obtain God's blessings and forgiveness. All of this was the result of the way in which God in his grace had responded to what Abraham and the other forefathers had done; yet what Abraham and the other forefathers had done had itself been a response to God's grace.

Therefore, what made it possible for the members of God's people Israel to attain forgiveness was not only the fact that God had promised to bless them through the patriarchs and other figures from Israel's history but that,

---

138. On this idea, see de Roo, "Covenant Sacrifice," 198-99; Lohse, *Märtyrer*, 90-91.

through those same figures, God had revealed his will to them and had provided them with examples and commandments to follow. *All* of these things were necessary for the people to be able to make atonement for their sins. When they sinned, they could be confident that God would forgive them. This was not merely because of what the forefathers had done, however, as if God accepted the righteousness of the forefathers in the place of that of his people. Rather, the people could be confident of God's forgiveness because, on account of the righteousness and merits of the forefathers, out of love for his people God had established with them a covenant that made it possible for them to live according to his will and to make atonement for their sins when they fell astray. If God had gone to such great lengths to establish such a covenant with them, when they sinned he could scarcely be expected simply to destroy or abandon them without doing everything in his power to bring them back to him in obedience as his beloved people and receive them with open arms when they returned to him with a repentant heart.

Although the primary emphasis in the story of the binding of Isaac was Abraham's obedience rather than the act of sacrifice per se, the sacrificial ideas found in the story led later Jewish interpreters to relate it to Israel's sacrificial worship. All other sacrifices came to be seen as dependent upon the *Akedah* or binding of Isaac. The logic of this belief was that the *Akedah* served as the ideal model and prototype of what a sacrifice should be. In that way, it not only indicated to the people of Israel how they were to present their own sacrifices, but also provided them with assurance that, when they offered up their sacrifices with the same spirit seen in Abraham and Isaac, God would receive those sacrifices favorably. The story of the *Akedah* thus not only *taught* them how to sacrifice to God but *motivated* them to do so. Therefore, when Jews in the second-temple period offered sacrifices at the temple, they often pleaded that their sacrifice be acceptable to God as that of Abraham and Isaac had been. Of course, as they presented their sacrifices, they were aware that they could never match the purity of soul and conformity with God's will that Abraham and Isaac had displayed. However, by invoking the *Akedah*, they communicated to God their sincere wish that they might attain a level of purity and conformity that would at least come close to that of Abraham and Isaac.[139] In essence, they were identifying themselves with the obedience and total commitment to God's will that Abraham and Isaac had manifested in the story of the binding of Isaac and expressing solidarity with their forefathers. After the temple's destruction, this understanding of sacrifice as the offering of oneself to God in order to conform to God's will grew in importance, since the people could no longer present actual sacrifices at the temple. Therefore, the most they could do was to identify with the way in which Abraham and Isaac had offered up to God what was dearest to them, namely, their own life or the life of the one they most loved.

---

139. On these points, see especially Vermès, *Scripture*, 206-17; Robert Hayward, "Appendix: The Aqedah," in *Sacrifice* (ed. M. F. C. Bourdillon and Meyer Fortes; London: Academic Press, 1980), 84-87.

Once again, this meant that, while Abraham's descendants were forgiven their sins on account of their own repentance and the sacrificial offerings they presented to God, they were also forgiven on account of what Abraham and Isaac had done. The merits of Abraham and Isaac, however, were not thought to be reckoned or imputed to their descendants or accepted by God in lieu of their own righteousness. The merits of the forefathers atoned for their descendants only in the sense that they provided the basis upon which their descendants might atone for their own sins. They did this by asking God to forgive and accept them on the basis of their identification with what Abraham and Isaac had done and their profound desire and intention to be conformed to the same faith and obedience that Abraham and Isaac had displayed.

* * *

According to what we have seen in this chapter, the literary sources from antiquity that we have at our disposal provide no basis whatsoever for the claim that, in second-temple Jewish thought, suffering and death were thought to atone for sins. Rather, what consistently atoned for sins was repentance and a commitment to living in the way God desired and commanded for the good of all. The suffering and death of the righteous could only contribute to the salvation of others by helping in some way to bring them into conformity with God's will. Nothing could take away the sins of those who were unrepentant or repented solely out of fear of divine punishment: neither sacrifices, suffering, death, prayers, good works, nor the intercessions and meritorious deeds of others.

This means that there is nothing in the Hebrew Scriptures or ancient Jewish and Greco-Roman thought that would have led Jesus' first followers to conclude that, in themselves, his sufferings and death had atoned for the sins of others, much less humanity as a whole. Rather, like other Jews of their day, they would have believed that, in order for them and others to receive the forgiveness of their sins and salvation, it was necessary for them to renounce their sinful ways and commit themselves to living in accordance with God's will. Jesus' sufferings and death would therefore be seen as the consequence of his dedication to the task of bringing about that new way of life in others, yet also would be thought to have played a vital role in his accomplishing that task. Above all, by remaining faithful unto death out of dedication to bringing others into conformity with God's will out of love for them, he had redefined how God's will was to be understood.

CHAPTER 5

JESUS' DEATH IN THE CONTEXT OF HIS MINISTRY

For over two centuries, biblical scholars and historians have vigorously debated the question of the meaning that Jesus ascribed to his death without reaching any type of consensus on the subject. Disagreements exist with regard not only to the extent to which Jesus foresaw and foretold the circumstances surrounding his death but also the way in which he believed that it would benefit others, if at all.[1] As in other areas of historical Jesus research, answers to these questions inevitably depend on the presuppositions that those who address them take as their starting-point. This makes it extremely unlikely that any consensus regarding how Jesus understood his death can ever be attained.

Even if it were possible to ascertain how Jesus interpreted his death, this would not necessarily be relevant to the main question being addressed in this work, namely, the manner in which the New Testament writings understand the salvific significance of Jesus' death. Jesus' first followers may have understood and interpreted his death in ways that he never did or may have forgotten, misunderstood, or altered what Jesus shared with them in this regard. Yet it is much more likely that Jesus' own views on the significance of his death did play at least some role in the interpretations his followers later gave to what had taken place. This makes it important to explore the question of how Jesus understood his death.

Yet because Jesus' first followers and perhaps Jesus himself almost certainly viewed his death in the context of the life and ministry that preceded it, any inquiry into the meaning they gave to his death must not ignore the question of the meaning they gave to his life and ministry as well. It is possible, of course, that Jesus' first followers viewed his death as having a meaning or purpose that was fundamentally different from the meaning or purpose they ascribed to his life and ministry. Many interpretations of Jesus' death, most notably those based on the notion of penal substitution, in effect see Jesus' death as having a very different objective from his ministry. According to those interpretations, it was not in his life and ministry but in his death

---

1. For a survey of views regarding the way in which Jesus understood his impending death, see Scot McKnight, *Jesus and his Death: Historiography, the Historical Jesus, and Atonement Theory* (Waco, TX: Baylor University Press, 2005), 50-56, 155-56; Rudolf Hoppe, "How Did Jesus Understand His Death? The Parables in Eschatological Prospect," in *Jesus Research: An International Perspective. The First Princeton-Prague Symposium on Jesus Research, Prague 2005* (ed. James H. Charlesworth and Peter Pokorný; Grand Rapids: Eerdmans, 2009), 154-69.

that Jesus bore and took away the sins of the world, exhausted God's wrath at human sin, or conquered the forces of sin, death, and evil. Although what Jesus did and taught prior to his death provides believers with guidance and instruction in the way they should live, strictly speaking, one does not obtain salvation by striving to follow what Jesus taught and exemplified in his ministry, but by trusting in the efficacy of his atoning death. Such views therefore tend to isolate Jesus' death from the ministry that preceded it rather than seeing the two as a unified whole.

For the purposes of this work, it is not necessary to attempt an extensive reconstruction of the historical details surrounding Jesus' life and death. It will be sufficient to look at certain aspects of his ministry and his final days that are widely attested in the sources we have, and thus are broadly accepted today as having a historical basis.[2] This will enable us to draw some general conclusions regarding how Jesus viewed his own death and provide the background necessary for considering in the next five chapters the question of how Jesus' first followers came to interpret his death after it had taken place.

THE AIMS OF JESUS' MINISTRY

Biblical scholars and historians have offered a wide variety of answers to the question of what Jesus was attempting to accomplish in his ministry. Those who stress Jesus' apocalyptic and eschatological views tend to see him as a preacher of repentance who understood his task as announcing the imminent arrival of God's reign and preparing and gathering others to participate in that reign.[3] Others see Jesus as a social prophet whose aim was to denounce injustice and call people to repentance and obedience to God in order to promote a more just and egalitarian society.[4] Those who view Jesus primarily as a

---

2. For this reason, I will not enter here into any discussion regarding the criteria of authenticity addressed by many scholars who have written on the subject of the historical Jesus. In reality, however, I am giving priority to the criterion of multiple attestation, since I will be discussing ideas that are well-attested in more than one source. I would also add that, as Dale C. Allison Jr. has noted, "even stories that do not reproduce historical events may tell us indirectly about Jesus because they incorporate features which his followers knew to be congruent with what he was all about" ("Behind the Temptations of Jesus: Q 4:1-13 and Mark 1:12-13," in *Authenticating the Activities of Jesus*, ed. Bruce Chilton and Craig A. Evans; NTTS 28/2; Leiden: Brill, 1999, 208).

3. For summaries of the diverse views among scholars regarding Jesus' aims, see especially Mark Allan Powell, *Jesus as a Figure in History: How Modern Historians View the Man from Galilee* (Louisville, KY: Westminster John Knox, 1998); Ben F. Meyer, "Jesus' Ministry and Self-Understanding," in *Studying the Historical Jesus: Evaluation of the State of Current Research* (ed. Bruce Chilton and Craig A. Evans; NTTS 19; Leiden: Brill, 1994), 337-52; Bruce Chilton, "Jesus within Judaism," in *Jesus in Context: Temple, Purity, and Restoration* (Chilton and Craig A. Evans; AGJU 39; Leiden: Brill, 1997), 179-201; David S. du Toit, "Redefining Jesus: Current Trends in Jesus Research," in *Jesus, Mark, and Q: The Teaching of Jesus in its Earliest Records* (ed. Michael Labahn and Andreas Schmidt; JSNTSup 214; Sheffield: Sheffield Academic Press, 2001), 82-124.

4. According to Richard A. Horsley, for example, Jesus defined his mission in terms of "catalyzing the renewal of the people" and bringing about "a historical transformation," rather than serving primarily as a "'teacher' of timeless truths or a preacher of cosmic catastrophe...." (*Jesus and the Spiral of Violence: Popular Jewish Resistance in Roman Palestine*; Minneapolis: Fortress, 1993, 207-8). According to Sean Freyne, Jesus sought to bring others to adopt an alternative way of life based on a set of values distinct from those that predominated in the society of his day ("The Geography, Politics, and Economics of Galilee and the Quest for the Historical Jesus," in *Studying the Historical Jesus*, ed. Chilton and Evans, 120-21).

teacher define his objectives in terms of instructing his followers how to live and relate to others.⁵ Others have interpreted Jesus' aims in social and political terms, seeing him as a social organizer or even a revolutionary. While few scholars today believe Jesus sought to lead an armed rebellion against Rome, as S. G. F. Brandon argued, many claim that Jesus' goal was to form some type of non-violent resistance movement in response to the Roman occupation of Palestine.⁶ Naturally, these diverse interpretations of Jesus' aims exist in many variations and are not mutually exclusive, but can be combined in various ways.

Rather than evaluating each of these views of Jesus' aims and arguing in favor of one or the other, I will begin by examining several fairly broad and uncontested claims regarding Jesus' ministry in order then to draw some general conclusions that will enable us to consider the questions of what led to Jesus' death and how he may have understood his death. To address these questions, it is sufficient to consider merely in general terms the possible aims or objectives behind the primary activities to which Jesus dedicated himself in his ministry.

Jesus' Proclamation of God's Reign

Most scholars today would agree that the coming of God's reign or kingdom was "*the* central and governing image in Jesus' proclamation."⁷ Without entering into the complex question of how Jesus or the evangelists intended *hē basileia tou theou* to be understood, the use of the phrase itself tells us a great deal. Whether it is interpreted primarily as a realm to be established on earth or in heaven, as a symbol for some transcendent reality, or as referring to God's act of reigning,⁸ the fact that in Jesus' proclamation that reign is something that is yet to come is highly significant. If God's reign had not yet

---

5. John H. Elliott, for example, questions the idea that Jesus sought to form a "community of equals," yet nevertheless argues that his goal was to promote "the communal identity, unity, intimacy, and loyalty of the believers in relation to God, Jesus Christ, and one another" ("The Jesus Movement Was Not Egalitarian but Family-Oriented," *BibInt* 11 [2003]: 205; see 173-210). See also Powell, *Jesus*, 181.

6. See S. G. F. Brandon, *Jesus and the Zealots: A Study of the Political Factor in Primitive Christianity* (Manchester: Manchester University Press, 1967). Most scholars today would agree with Horsley that, if Jesus was in some sense a "revolutionary," he was "not a violent political revolutionary" (*Spiral*, 326). However, it is common to see Jesus as a "subversive" who presented a "challenge to the structures of society" (Andrew Chester, "The Jews of Judaea and Galilee," in *Early Christian Thought in its Jewish Context*, ed. John Barclay and John Sweet; Cambridge: Cambridge University Press, 1996, 23), or as a proponent of "active nonviolent resistance" to Rome (Walter Wink, "Neither Passivity nor Violence: Jesus' Third Way [Matt 5:38-42 par.]," in *The Love of Enemy and Nonretaliation in the New Testament*, ed. Willard M. Swartley; Louisville, KY: Westminster John Knox, 1992, 103).

7. John P. Meier, *A Marginal Jew: Rethinking the Historical Jesus*, Vol. 2: *Mentor, Message, and Miracles* (New York: Doubleday, 1994), 177.

8. On these diverse interpretations of Jesus' proclamation of the reign of God, see E. P. Sanders, *Jesus and Judaism* (Philadelphia: Fortress, 1985), 123-56; Bruce Chilton, "The Kingdom of God in Recent Discussion," in *Studying the Historical Jesus*, ed. Chilton and Evans, 255-80; Mary Ann Beavis, *Jesus and Utopia: Looking for the Kingdom of God in the Roman World* (Minneapolis: Fortress, 2006), 71-83; Norman Perrin, "Jesus and the Language of the Kingdom," in *The Kingdom of God in the Teaching of Jesus* (ed. Bruce Chilton; Philadelphia: Fortress, 1984), 92-106. Reflecting the observations of scholars such as Alexander J. M. Wedderburn, who stresses that the kingdom of God in Jesus' teaching refers not only to a thing to be received or a place to be entered but "God's activity," here I will speak of "the reign of God" rather than "the kingdom of God," since the

arrived, then whatever realities existed could not be identified with that reign, and in some sense even had to be seen as contrary to it.[9]

On the basis of several Gospel passages, some have argued that Jesus understood the reign of God primarily as something already present in his own day, rather than something to be expected in the future.[10] The most important of these passages is Luke 17:20-21, where Jesus tells the Pharisees who inquire as to the coming of God's reign, "The kingdom of God is not coming with things that can be observed; nor will they say, 'Look, here it is!' or 'There it is!' For, in fact, the kingdom of God is among you." Even here, however, Jesus speaks of the reign as something yet to come in some sense, an idea repeated in the following verses, where he speaks of the coming of the Son of Man (17:22-37). Furthermore, because it is hidden to the Pharisees, it clearly cannot be identified with any of the kingdoms or reigns of the time or the political, social, and economic realities that existed in Jesus' day. In Luke 11:20 and its parallel Matt. 12:28, a Q saying, Jesus affirms, "if it is by the finger/spirit of God that I cast out the demons, then the kingdom of God has come to you." Here, while God's reign is said to be present, it is associated with Jesus' activity. It is clear, therefore, that in some sense Jesus seems to have regarded God's reign as a present reality, yet at the same time he repeatedly spoke of that reign as something that would be established in the future.[11]

Precisely what Jesus thought God's reign would look like when it arrived in its fullness is difficult to determine. Numerous Jewish ideas were associated with the notion of God's reign, including a variety of eschatological expectations as well as apocalyptic visions that found acceptance in certain Jewish circles.[12] The Gospels attribute many of these ideas to Jesus as well, though they also present him as rejecting certain hopes that existed among other Jews.[13] Today New Testament scholars recognize that Jesus' proclamation of

---

word *reign* can be understood as a verbal noun ("Paul and Jesus: The Problem of Continuity," *SJT* 38 [1985]: 195-96; see 189-203).

9. See Meier, *Marginal Jew*, 2:299: "If, then, Jesus makes a major object of his prayer the petition that God come to rule as king, this naturally means that in some sense, according to Jesus, God is not yet fully ruling as king." Warren Carter similarly notes that to use the word *basileia* and pray for God's Empire in the midst of the empire of Rome is to express profound dissatisfaction with Roman rule (*Matthew and Empire: Initial Explorations*; Harrisburg, PA: Trinity Press International, 2006, 5).

10. This view has especially been associated with C. H. Dodd, who is generally recognized as having coined the phrase "realized echatology" (see *Parables of the Kingdom*; New York: Scribner, 1961, 159).

11. Most scholars today would agree that, when Jesus spoke of God's reign, he had in mind both a present and a future reality. Thus, for example, Hartmut Stegemann argues that, for Jesus, "the Reign of God was not a static force that is either already present in its fullness or is still to come as a whole. It was a dynamic force, whose operation begins at a given point and reaches its completion only at a later time" (*The Library of Qumran on the Essenes, Qumran, John the Baptist, and Jesus*; Grand Rapids: Eerdmans, 1998, 241).

12. On the Jewish background to the idea of the reign of God, see Bruce Chilton, *Pure Kingdom: Jesus' Vision of God* (Grand Rapids: Eerdmans, 1996), 10-12, 19, 23-34, 141; Michael Lattke, "On the Jewish Background of the Synoptic Concept, The Kingdom of God," in *Kingdom of God*, ed. Chilton, 72-91; Géza Vermès, *Jesus and the World of Judaism* (Philadelphia: Fortress, 1983), 32-35. Vermès notes that "the kingdom of God relates to God's sovereignty itself rather than to the realm over which he governs" (33)

13. Beavis rightly notes: "If, as some interpreters assert, Jesus used the language of kingdom to subvert Roman imperialism, he may have wished to disavow Jewish dreams of *basiliea* as well" (*Jesus*, 96; see also 98-99).

God's reign must be viewed in the context of the social and political realities of the Galilee in which he worked, rather than being understood in some abstract, idealized form, as was common among many liberal scholars in the nineteenth and early twentieth centuries.[14] For Jesus, the coming of God's reign no doubt had to do with an end to the suffering and hardships experienced by many, especially in rural areas such as those of Galilee. Although it seems unlikely that Jesus and his closest disciples came from a background of extreme poverty, according to the Synoptics, the people to whom he reached out and directed his message were primarily those in greatest need.[15]

Numerous scholars have described the harsh realities that existed in Galilee in Jesus' day, stressing the poverty, inequity, and injustices that the majority of the population had to endure under Roman governance.[16] Our modern modes of thinking tend to divide reality up into spheres that are considered to be somewhat independent of one another, such as the political, social, economic, and religious. In antiquity, however, these different aspects of reality all formed part of a unified whole. In his description of Galilean social life, Sean Freyne stresses "how interconnected the political, social, economic and cultural aspects really were."[17] The reign of God as proclaimed by Jesus therefore embraced all of these aspects. This means that we cannot isolate the social, political, and economic realities that existed in Galilee from their theological underpinning. As scholars such as Warren Carter have argued, Rome justified its rule over the nations it subjected on the basis of an imperial theology that proclaimed that the system in place was divinely-ordained:

> Basic to imperial theology was the claim that Rome rules its empire because the gods have willed Rome to rule the world.... Imperial theology creates and reinforces in words and rituals an understanding of a relationship between the emperor and the gods. The emperor as ruler of the Roman Empire is the chosen

---

14. On the understanding of God's reign in liberal Protestant thought in the late nineteenth and early twentieth century, see Helmut Koester, *From Jesus to the Gospels: Interpreting the New Testament in Context* (Minneapolis: Fortress, 2007), 199-203.

15. On this point, see Jens Schröter, "Jesus of Galilee: The Role of Location in Understanding Jesus," in *Jesus Research*, ed. Charlesworth and Pokorný, 36-55; John P. Meier, *A Marginal Jew: Rethinking the Historical Jesus*, Vol. 3: *Companions and Competitors* (New York: Doubleday, 2001), 522, 620.

16. See especially Richard A. Horsley, *Galilee: History, Politics, People* (Valley Forge, PA: Trinity Press International, 1995); Sean Freyne, *Galilee and Gospel: Collected Essays* (WUNT 125; Tübingen: Mohr Siebeck, 2000), 195-96; James G. Crossley, *Why Christianity Happened: A Sociohistorical Account of Christian Origins (26-50 CE)* (Louisville, KY: Westminster John Knox, 2006), 43-56. Some scholars have questioned the claim that the economic and political conditions in Galilee during Jesus' time were particularly difficult. Ekkehard W. Stegemann and Wolfgang Stegemann claim that the economic situation in first-century Galilee was basically the same as that which existed in other Mediterranean societies of the time (*The Jesus Movement: A Social History of its First Century*, trans. O. C. Dean Jr.; Minneapolis: Fortress, 1999, 15-95). Schröter argues that Galilee was relatively stable during Jesus' lifetime ("Jesus," 46-48). Sanders also questions the reconstructions of Horsley and others, yet nevertheless acknowledges that the general populace was "hard pressed" and endured various types of oppression (*Judaism: Practice and Belief, 63 BCE-66 BC*; Philadelphia: Trinity Press International, 1992, 157-69). Mark A. Chancey rightly insists on the need to exercise caution when describing the reality of first-century Galilee due to the uncertainties that exist regarding social and economic conditions ("Disputed Issues in the Study of Cities, Villages, and the Economy in Jesus' Galilee," in *The World of Jesus and the Early Church: Identity and Interpretation in the Early Communities of Faith*; ed. Craig A. Evans; Peabody, MA: Hendrickson, 2011, 53-67).

17. Sean Freyne, *Galilee, Jesus, and the Gospels* (Minneapolis: Fortress, 1988), 175.

agent of the gods.... If he represents the divine rule and will, the imperial system over which he rules... is presented as being sanctioned by the gods.[18]

In Galilee, as in other parts of the empire, there were a number of shrines dedicated to Caesar. Although most Jews did not frequent these shrines, they promoted among both Jews and non-Jews the idea that God or the gods had placed Caesar as ruler over the region and thus served to perpetuate Rome's power there.[19]

Many scholars have used the term "restoration" to characterize the hopes related to Jesus' proclamation of God's reign.[20] This word is employed to bring together a number of concepts, including the liberation of Israel from its oppressors, its political independence, and a state of social justice. Yet it also implies the notion of returning to a situation that existed previously. In this sense, its use seems inappropriate, since Jesus does not seem to have envisioned a return to the supposed "glory days" of Israel under King David or King Solomon, which were marked by a great deal of social inequality, corruption, and injustice. Nor does Jesus appear to have conceived of God's reign as involving the re-establishment of conditions that existed during some other period of Israel's history. Instead, Jesus' vision seems to have transcended anything from Israel's past. Precisely how Jesus thought that God's reign would be established definitively is also not clear. Some argue that he expected some type of spectacular, cataclysmic divine intervention in history, while others characterize his hopes more in terms of the establishment of a new society. If Jesus spoke of a final judgment, he must have regarded its purpose as that of ridding the world of evil so that righteousness and peace might prevail.[21]

What is clear, however, is that Jesus' proclamation of the coming reign of God implied that the rule of Rome and its allies, such as the Herodian kings who served Roman interests in Galilee, were to be overcome and replaced

---

18. Carter, *Matthew and Empire*, 20, 33-34. Koester also contrasts the realized eschatology of Augustus, who claimed to have brought a new order of peace and prosperity as Roman emperor, with the alternative eschatology of Jesus and his followers (*From Jesus to the Gospels*, 205-10).

19. On this subject, see Monika Bernett, "Roman Imperial Cult in the Galilee: Structures, Functions, and Dynamics," in *Religion, Ethnicity, and Identity in Ancient Galilee: A Region in Transition* (ed. Jürgen Zangenberg, Harold W. Attridge, and Dale B. Martin; WUNT 210; Tübingen: Mohr Siebeck, 2007), 337-56. Bernett rightly stresses that the Roman imperial cult in Galilee was both a political *and* a religious phenomenon. See also Sean Freyne, *Jesus, a Jewish Galilean: A New Reading of the Jesus Story* (London: T & T Clark, 2004), 133-34; Richard A. Horsley, "Introduction. Jesus, Paul, and the 'Arts of Resistance': Leaves from the Notebook of James C. Scott," in *Hidden Transcripts and the Arts of Resistance: Applying the Work of James C. Scott to Jesus and Paul* (ed. Horsley; Semeia 48; Atlanta: SBL, 2004), 1-7.

20. For a summary of hopes regarding Israel's restoration, see Craig A. Evans, "Aspects of Exile and Restoration in the Proclamation of Jesus and the Gospels," in *Exile: Old Testament, Jewish and Christian Conceptions* (ed. James M. Scott; JSJSup 56; Leiden: Brill, 1997), 276-81. Evans also argues elsewhere that "Jesus envisioned the full restoration of Israel in every sense, political, economical, and cultic" ("The Twelve Thrones of Israel: Scripture and Politics in Luke 22:24-30," in *Jesus in Context*, Chilton and Evans, 479). For other understandings of "restoration eschatology," see Horsley, *Spiral*, 205-7; Sean Freyne, "Jesus and the Servant Community in Zion," in *Jesus from Judaism to Christianity: Continuum Approaches to the Historical Jesus* (ed. Tom Holmén; London: T & T Clark, 2007), 110-13.

21. For this interpretation of Jesus' proclamation of a coming judgment, see Marius Reiser, *Jesus and Judgment: The Eschatological Proclamation in its Jewish Context* (Minneapolis: Fortress, 1997). See especially his conclusions on 316.

by God's reign. Even if Jesus' message is interpreted as having to do primarily with coming eschatological realities rather than social reform, it was politically-charged.[22] Since the political reality was inseparable from the social and economic realities, the reign of God spoken of by Jesus must be seen as involving an entire *system* rather than only isolated aspects of human existence. Jesus was proclaiming the coming of a radically different system in which God alone would rule as sovereign, while at the same time articulating his rejection of the system that was then in place.

Because Jesus' proclamation of God's reign embraced religious aspects as well, it also implied a rejection of the Jewish leadership, particularly the high priestly families who were at the cusp of power in Jerusalem. Their control of the income generated by the temple, which included the temple tax and tithes that the Jewish population of Galilee was expected to pay, meant that in the minds of some Galileans they were also in large part responsible for the difficult conditions of many in Galilee.[23] It was common knowledge that the Jewish high priests were appointed by Rome and therefore had to be obedient to Rome and serve Roman interests to remain in power.[24] Caiaphas could never have lasted from 18 to 36 CE in the high priesthood had he not worked in close collaboration with Rome. Many Jews must have seen the high priests as servants of Rome who would do whatever was necessary to please Caesar in order to remain in power. The corruption that was commonly associated with the chief priests, evidence of which can be found in multiple sources, also must have led many to question whether they were truly the representatives of the God of Israel.[25]

---

22. As Joan E. Taylor argues, in the context of first-century Galilee, not only Jesus' proclamation of the kingdom but also his call to repentance would have been seen as highly political and anti-imperial, as the message of John the Baptist had been (*The Immerser: John the Baptist within Second Temple Judaism*; SHJ; Grand Rapids: Eerdmans, 1997, 213-22).

23. Marcus J. Borg rightly notes: "The high priest and the traditional high priestly families were not only the religious elite, but the political and economic elites. During the time of Roman governors, the high priesthood was primarily responsible for domestic political rule" (*Conflict, Holiness, and Politics in the Teachings of Jesus*; Harrisburg, PA: Trinity Press International, 1998, 13-14). Borg also stresses the role of the temple as "the center of an economically exploitative system legitimated in the name of God" (15). On this point, see also Horsley, *Spiral*, 323-25. It is important to note, however, that many Galileans remained attached and loyal to Jerusalem and its temple, as Freyne has argued (*Galilee and Gospel*, 73-85).

24. In this regard, Edwin K. Broadhead notes that, when the Romans conquered Palestine, they originally named the high priests directly. However, "[w]hen the power of appointment was restored to the Herodian dynasty, priests were appointed from wealthy, influential families who formed a Sadducaean oligarchy. The Talmud (b. Yom. 18a; b. Yeb. 61a) says the high priests bought the office and were changed each year…. In the time of Jesus the office of high priest was a limited appointment subject to the whims of the Herodians or to the transactions of the Sadducaean oligarchy. As such, the leading priests would be largely viewed as wealthy collaborators. In the eyes of the people, their status could hardly compare with the ideals of Aaron and Eli and Zadok" ("Jesus and the Priests of Israel," in *Jesus from Judaism to Christianity*, ed. Holmén, 127).

25. For the evidence of widespread criticism of the high-priestly families in Jesus' day, see especially Jonathan Klawans, *Purity, Sacrifice, and the Temple: Symbolism and Supersessionism in the Study of Ancient Judaism* (Oxford: Oxford University Press, 2006), 147-50; Richard A. Horsley, "The Dead Sea Scrolls and the Historical Jesus," in *The Bible and the Dead Sea Scrolls: The Second Princeton Symposium on Judaism and Christian Origins* (ed. James H. Charlesworth; Waco, TX: Baylor University Press, 2006), 1:45-50; Craig A. Evans, "Jesus' Action in the Temple: Cleansing or Portent of Destruction?," in *Jesus in Context*, Chilton and Evans, 408-28, 433-34. On the criticisms of the high-priestly hierarchy in the rabbinic literature, see Evans, "Early Rabbinic Sources

The same conclusions could be drawn with regard to those who represented the high priests or were loyal to them. This group would have included the Pharisees, if they did in fact have close ties to the high priests, as some scholars have maintained.[26] While it might be argued that Israel's God had used the Romans to put the current high priesthood in place according to his will, the only way the high priesthood could be dissociated from the system imposed by Rome would be for the high priests to proclaim a message similar to that of Jesus: that the current system was not ultimately the one desired by God but had to be replaced by a different system. There is no evidence that they did so; if they had, they would almost certainly have faced reprisals from Rome.

In this context, Jesus' proclamation of the coming of God's reign was by nature polarizing. One could either accept his proclamation or reject it. To ignore it was in essence to reject it. If one rejected it, one was rejecting not only Jesus himself but the God proclaimed by Jesus, who had sent Jesus to announce the coming of his reign. If one accepted Jesus' proclamation, then one would subsequently submit as well to Jesus' teaching on other points, seeing him as God's representative. Those who viewed and followed Jesus in that way would inevitably have come to be regarded as constituting a group or community that was defined over and against those who rejected or disregarded Jesus' message of God's reign. As Jesus is reported to have said, one was either with him and the God he proclaimed or against him and that God (Matt. 12:30; Mark 9:40; Luke 9:50; 11:23). To be with Jesus was to follow him in rejecting the political, religious, and economic system of the time as a system over which God was not reigning.

Polarization between those who opposed Roman rule and those who did not must certainly have been widespread in Palestine, including Galilee. Undoubtedly, there was a wide spectrum of opinions with regard to the prevalent system, ranging from strong support to strong rejection. Many Jews in Palestine benefited from the system imposed by the Roman emperor and his appointed representatives, such as the Herodians and the high priests, and therefore would have supported this system. This would have included not only a middle or retainer class but even laborers or peasants who found employment within the system or received some other type of benefit or advantage from it. There must have been sharp divisions among those living in poverty and especially in rural areas, as is evident from the fact that, according to the Gospels, Jesus' message concerning God's reign was rejected by many,

---

and Jesus Research," in *Jesus in Context*, Chilton and Evans, 31-44. Of course, as Andreas J. Köstenberger notes, there is also ample evidence for widespread Jewish support for the Jerusalem temple during this period, as is demonstrated by the pilgrimages made to the temple and the monetary offerings presented there ("The Destruction of the Second Temple and the Composition of the Fourth Gospel," in *Challenging Perspectives on the Gospel of John*; ed. John Lierman; WUNT 2/219; Tübingen: Mohr Siebeck, 2006, 83).

26. Anthony J. Saldarini in particular has argued that the Pharisees were in direct contact with the Jerusalem leadership and acted in their service in places such as Galilee (*Pharisees, Scribes and Sadducees in Palestinian Society: A Sociological Approach*; Wilmington, DE: Michael Glazier, 1988, 157-73).

including entire villages whose inhabitants perhaps benefited from the system in place (Matt. 11:20-24; Mark 6:1-6; Luke 10:13-15; John 12:37).[27]

In Jesus' mind, the God he proclaimed as coming to reign was also the God of Israel and of the Hebrew Scriptures. To reject his message regarding God's reign was therefore to reject the God of Israel and the Scriptures as well. This means that Jesus' proclamation must have led him and his followers to redefine Israel in the way that other groups whose proclamation was similar did. According to Jesus, to believe in the God of Israel was to accept what Jesus taught about him; and to form part of the true Israel was to accept as the true God of Israel the God proclaimed by Jesus. In this regard, Jesus' proclamation was similar to that of John the Baptist and those who wrote the Dead Sea scrolls, who appear to have maintained that not all those claiming to be Israel actually belonged to Israel, but only those who lived in conformity with their teaching.[28] This aspect of Jesus' proclamation of God's reign would also have led to tension and polarization. Those who consciously rejected Jesus' message could be regarded as having excluded themselves from membership in the faithful Israel that would share in God's reign as proclaimed by Jesus. This does not mean, however, that Jesus would have regarded his followers alone as the true Israel. Rather, he seems to have thought that all who were committed to the values of the reign he proclaimed and conceived of God in the way he did could be regarded as belonging to Israel, whether or not they identified themselves with Jesus.

In spite of the difficulties involved in defining precisely how Jesus understood the reign of God he proclaimed, on the basis of what we have seen in this section, there are a couple of conclusions that we can draw with a considerable degree of certainty. First, Jesus desired that a new social, political, and economic order be established and therefore hoped that the existing order be brought to an end or transformed into something radically different. He must also have believed that if this was to happen, it would need to be a work of God rather than of human beings alone. When and how Jesus thought God would act to bring this new order about is not entirely clear, yet there can be little doubt that he trusted that at some point God would indeed establish his reign in definitive fashion.

Second, the nature of Jesus' ministry demonstrates that, even if he thought that ultimately God alone would bring about the reign that he awaited and proclaimed, he did not believe that God had called him and others merely to await passively and idly the coming of that reign or simply to announce that all must be prepared for its arrival at any moment. Rather, through his teaching and healing activity, Jesus dedicated himself to seeking the well-being

---

27. As Freyne has stressed, reality could vary a great deal from one village to another in Galilee (*Galilee, Jesus, and the Gospels*, 145-50).

28. On these points, see Markus Bockmuehl, "1QS and Salvation at Qumran," in *Justification and Variegated Nomism*, Vol. 1: *The Complexities of Second Temple Judaism* (ed. D. A. Carson, Peter T. O'Brien, and Mark A. Seifrid; WUNT 2/140; Tübingen: Mohr Siebeck, 2001), 390-94; Robert L. Webb, *John the Baptizer and Prophet: A Socio-Historical Study* (JSNTSup 62; Sheffield: JSOT, 1991), 197-202.

of others in the present world. He sought to transform the way in which his listeners related to one another and to form a community committed to living according to the ideals and values of the reign he proclaimed. He also constantly showed a deep concern for the physical, emotional, spiritual, and social needs of those to whom he reached out.

Even if Jesus expected that God would come soon to establish his reign, therefore, he believed that in the meantime he was to dedicate his attention to the immediate needs of others. This involved leaving up to God the question of when God would act to inaugurate his reign. Jesus' logic appears to have been that, if God desired justice, healing, wholeness, and well-being for all people in the future, God must also desire these same things for all in the present. In what way Jesus thought that the future well-being of others depended on their attaining well-being in the present age is not clear. However, it is likely that he was convinced that his work on behalf of others in the present age would contribute in some way to their well-being and wholeness in the age to come as well, when God's reign would come in its fullness.

Jesus' Teaching

In addition to proclaiming God's reign, Jesus devoted a large portion of his ministry to teaching. Although some of this teaching was directed exclusively or primarily at his closest disciples, the Gospels give many indications that at times he also taught publicly and openly to any who wished to listen.

In principle, Jesus' teaching activity could have been motivated by a variety of aims. A teacher in antiquity might seek to gain wealth, fame, or power through his or her teaching. It seems highly unlikely that Jesus taught in order to become wealthy, since all the evidence points in the opposite direction: Jesus gave up a great deal and endured many hardships in order to carry out his ministry. Whether intentionally or not, he did attain a certain amount of fame through his teaching and came to be recognized as a powerful teacher who possessed considerable moral authority. There is no evidence, however, that he used this fame and power for personal gain or political ends. Instead, whatever fame and moral authority he attained enabled his teaching to spread to others.

In considering the aims of Jesus' teaching ministry, then, the important question is whether Jesus taught *for his own sake*, motivated primarily by some sort of self-interest, or whether he taught *for the sake of others*. While of course these two alternatives are not mutually exclusive, it seems that Jesus' primary concern in his teaching ministry was the well-being *of others*. Whether Jesus' objective in his teaching ministry was that of making it possible for others to attain some type of eschatological salvation or instead that of improving their life in the present age, in either case he taught others because he cared for them and desired that they obtain some kind of blessing or benefit through his teaching. The fact that he apparently dedicated a great deal of time and energy to his teaching ministry, making considerable sacrifices and taking certain risks in order to carry it out, must be seen as indicating that the good that he sought for others through his teaching was of great importance to him.

The *content* of Jesus' teaching also indicates that he taught out of a concern for others rather than out of a desire for personal gain or to pursue his own interests. A central theme running throughout his teaching in the Gospels is precisely the importance of loving others and seeking their well-being together with one's own. There seems to be no reason to doubt that this emphasis in Jesus' teaching is grounded in historical fact. Not only Jesus' words but his actions drove home time and again the importance of caring for the needs of others and seeking their good. He expected and demanded from his followers the same loving commitment to the well-being of others manifested in his own activity and made that commitment the condition for being considered his disciple and forming part of his community of followers.

Yet it is important once more to view Jesus' teaching about loving others in its original context. In Western society today, love tends to be understood in individualistic terms having to do primarily with being kind, affectionate, generous, and forgiving in relation to other persons. In a context of injustice, oppression, systemic violence, suffering, and social inequity such as that which existed in first-century Palestine, however, love for others must also be seen in terms of *standing in opposition to the system that is generating those harsh realities* in order to reform or replace that system. This opposition can take the form of resistance, prophetic denunciation, and attempts to form an alternative community or society. The objective is to alleviate the suffering of others by identifying and confronting the political, social, economic, and religious beliefs and practices that uphold the system or status quo that is the root cause of that suffering.[29]

It is clear that Jesus' ministry involved all of these things. He called on his followers to resist many of the values, practices, and traditions of his day in order to adopt other values and practices that often put them in conflict or tension with others, including at times their own families.[30] He also denounced prophetically the injustices and oppressive policies of many of the leaders of the people as well as the predominant system in general. Through his teaching he attempted to lay the basis for communities that would practice solidarity and overcome divisions resulting from greed, selfish interests, and a lust for power and recognition. These communities would be based on bonds that went beyond loyalties to family and friends and at times even replaced those loyalties. While Jesus insisted that his followers were to love all

---

29. Warren Carter rightly notes that "Jesus' teachings and actions... promote societal structures, practices, and visions that are alternatives to those of the Rome-allied, Jerusalem-centered, elite" ("Love as Societal Vision and Counter-Imperial Practice in Matthew 22:34-40," in *Biblical Interpretation in Early Christian Gospels*, Vol. 2: *The Gospel of Matthew*, ed. Thomas R. Hatina; LNTS 304; London: T & T Clark, 2008, 40). According to Carter, seen in the context of an oppressive system, Jesus' teaching regarding love must be regarded as "subversive" and "socially transformative," aimed at challenging the status quo (31-33, 37-44).

30. Freyne has particularly stressed the notion that Jesus sought to transform the value system of his day, including that of the market economy; see *Galilee and Gospel*, 111-13, 203-6.

others, including their enemies, this love involved seeking the common good by demanding that those who practiced injustice, oppression, and different forms of violence change their ways for the good of all, as well as calling on all who heard him to seek the well-being of others in concrete ways.[31]

When this understanding of love for others is seen in the context of Jesus' proclamation of God's reign, it is clear that, from his perspective, those in power were not practicing love by seeking the common good, as they undoubtedly claimed to be doing. Instead, they were acting contrary to love and God's will by promoting and sustaining a system that exploited and abused others and led to widespread poverty, inequity, and suffering.[32] In spite of this, however, those in power justified their rule by affirming that it brought peace, security, justice, and abundance for all. Jesus' proclamation of the reign of God represented a rejection of those claims and called on people to identify instead with the God who had sent him to lay the foundation for a different, alternative order.[33]

Jesus, of course, stressed not only love for others but love for God as well (Matt. 22:37-40; Mark 12:28-34; Luke 10:25-28; 16:13). Yet once more, in Jesus' thought this love for God did not merely involve personal sentiments of affection and appreciation toward God, as love for God is often understood in Western culture. Rather, for Jesus, loving God involves assuming a firm commitment to doing God's will. As Jesus repeatedly teaches in the Gospels, God's will is that all people seek the well-being of others together with their own. To love the God proclaimed by Jesus is to follow God in loving others in the way that Jesus did and therefore to love and follow Jesus as well. To love the God proclaimed by Jesus is also to submit to that God as sovereign Lord and king, doing what that God commands in the way defined by Jesus. Once again, according to Jesus' teaching regarding what it means to love God, those in power were *not* loving and serving God. This was especially true of the Jerusalem elite, who claimed to be God's representatives, chosen by God to promote and defend his will on earth.

In addition to love for God and others, Jesus' teaching stressed the need to have faith in the God he proclaimed and to accept Jesus' words as coming from that God. Throughout the Gospels, such faith is commonly contrasted with fear, which involves a lack of trust in God (Matt. 8:26; 14:28-31; 21:21;

---

31. Horsley argues that Jesus' teaching regarding loving one's enemies had the purpose of promoting cooperation and solidarity among those experiencing hardships in the communities where he worked in Galilee and overcoming divisions in that context (*Spiral*, 255-73). For a similar understanding of Jesus' teaching, see Marius Reiser, "Love of Enemies in the Context of Antiquity," *NTS* 47 (2001): 411-27.

32. As Bruce Longenecker observes, Jesus' concern for the poor went hand-in-hand with his criticism of those in power in Jerusalem and Rome, and ultimately even led to his death ("Good News to the Poor: Jesus, Paul, and Jerusalem," in *Jesus and Paul Reconnected: Fresh Pathways into an Old Debate*; ed. Todd D. Still; Grand Rapids: Eerdmans, 2007, 64).

33. These ideas are reflected in many of Jesus' parables, some of which bore "a clearly political message," questioning the legitimacy of the ruling classes and their "unjust forms of administering the law" (Annette Merz, "How a Woman Who Fought Back and Demanded Her Rights Became an Importunate Widow: The Transformation of a Parable of Jesus," in *Jesus from Judaism to Christianity*, ed. Holmén, 79).

Mark 4:40; 5:36; Luke 8:25, 50; 12:4-7). Jesus insists that his followers are to trust God for their daily needs, and especially to hold fast to their faith in God in the midst of hardships and persecution (Matt. 6:26-34; 10:24-30; Luke 12:4-7, 22-32). The need not only to love God but to trust fully in God therefore seems to have been a central and dominant theme in Jesus' teaching.

These two ideas are intimately related to each other. When people are fearful of suffering, dying, or losing the persons and things that are most important to them, that fear tends to absorb and paralyze them. As a result, they are unable to act out of love and show concern for others. In Jesus' words, their primary concern is to "save their life" rather than losing it (Matt. 10:39; 16:25; Mark 8:35; Luke 9:24; 17:33; John 12:25). Jesus' stress on faith overcoming fear must be seen in the context of the oppressive system that existed in Palestine and elsewhere under Roman rule. Then as now, such systems remain in place by instilling fear in their subjects, thereby enslaving them in a sense.[34] Those systems demand that one dedicate one's time, energy, and resources to serving the interests of those in power rather than serving others who are in need and attending properly to one's own needs and desires. Rather than speaking out against the injustice and the oppressive ways of the system, those enslaved in this way remain silent out of fear. People are therefore constantly forced to make a choice between submitting obediently to the system and seeking justice and well-being for themselves and others.

If we look at these various aspects of Jesus' teaching against the background of his proclamation of God's reign, it appears that for Jesus the problem was that, rather than submitting to God's reign, out of fear the populace was submitting to oppressive political and religious leaders and authorities that held them in bondage through their ambition and their desire to control and dominate others. This led Jesus to stress the two basic ideas we have just seen in his teaching. First, he constantly insisted that, rather than seeking power, wealth, and privilege, his disciples were to seek the well-being of others in love through humble service, as he did. Second, he taught that it was necessary to have faith and trust in the God he proclaimed rather than living out of fear. From Jesus' perspective, what was needed was a different kind of community characterized by mutual love and solidarity as well as faith and trust in the God he proclaimed. These seem to have been the core values of Jesus' teaching. For Jesus, love for God and others and trust in God were inseparable from one another, since one could not love and trust God without dedicating one's life to doing what God desired and commanded, namely, seeking wholeness and well-being for all, including oneself.

The itinerant life-style Jesus led and demanded of his closest followers must be seen against this background. In Jesus' thought, true love for God and

---

34. In this regard, Richard Horsley observes: "Roman leaders understood that the two basic motives for conformity to the dominant order were fear and consent. Fear, particularly important among the masses, was evoked by force or coercion. Consent, on the other hand, was evoked by persuasion" ("Rhetoric and Empire—and 1 Corinthians," in *Paul and Politics: Ekklesia, Israel, Imperium, Interpretation. Essays in Honor of Krister Stendahl*; ed. Horsley; Harrisburg, PA: Trinity Press International, 2000, 77).

others required that one reach out to others actively. This stands in contrast to the ascetic lifestyle promoted by groups such as the Essenes and those at Qumran, who withdrew from society. Jesus' itinerant ministry also contrasted with the form of ministry carried out by John the Baptist.[35] While John directed his call to repentance to all Jews and thereby can be said to have sought their salvation out of love for them, he nevertheless required that people come to him. Jesus, however, manifested his love for others and his desire for the salvation of all by going out to encounter people with his message where they were at, in the villages of Galilee and elsewhere in the region.

The itinerant lifestyle adopted by Jesus also required that he and his disciples depend on God and others to provide for their needs. One of Jesus' objectives in requiring that his disciples join him in following an itinerant lifestyle must have been to teach them to learn to place their faith and trust in God and overcome their fears.[36] This may have been the reason why, when Jesus sent his disciples out in pairs to carry out a ministry modeled on his own, he prohibited them from taking with them some of the basic necessities (Matt. 12:5-10; Mark 6:7-9; Luke 9:1-3; 10:3-8). That lifestyle also required that Jesus' disciples learn to depend not only on God but also on the solidarity and generosity of others. In this way, both Jesus' disciples and those who provided support for their ministry learned to give generously as well as to receive with a spirit of gratitude. Jesus therefore must have also wished to teach and promote solidarity by means of the itinerant ministry he carried out with his closest disciples.

The same understanding of the relation between love for others and trust in God mentioned above seems to be behind a number of Jesus' sayings about following him. If Jesus' call to deny oneself and take up one's cross is regarded as authentic in some form (Matt. 10:38; 16:24; Mark 8:34; Luke 9:23; 14:27), then he would have been calling on his followers to be willing to stand up to the oppressive structures and systems that crucify those who oppose them in order to seek the well-being of others.[37] They would do so only if they were committed to living in love in the way Jesus had taught and if they trusted fully in God. Such love and trust would also lead them to abandon the common way of seeking security, which involved submitting obediently to those who possessed the power, resources, and control necessary to make the populace dependent on them, in order to seek that security instead in God and the practice of solidarity with others.

---

35. Michael F. Bird speaks of Jesus' ministry as "centrifugal" in comparison to that of John (*Jesus and the Origins of the Gentile Mission*; LNTS 331; London: T & T Clark, 2006, 165-68). See also Meier, *Marginal Jew*, 2:169-70. On the parallels and contrasts between John's ministry and teaching with the ministry and teaching of Jesus, see especially Taylor, *Immerser*, 149-53.

36. See Freyne, *Jewish Galilean*, 118; Allison, "Behind the Temptations," 210.

37. On the authenticy of Jesus' call to his followers to take up their cross to follow him and the meaning of this idea in its original context, see Brad H. Young, "A Fresh Examination of the Cross, Jesus and the Jewish People," in *Jesus' Last Week*, Vol. 1 of *Jerusalem Studies in the Synoptic Gospels* (ed. R. Steven Notley, Marc Turnage, and Brian Becker; JCPS 11; Leiden: Brill, 2006), 191-209; Meier, *Marginal Jew*, 3:64-67; John Dominic Crossan, *The Historical Jesus: The Life of a Mediterranean Jewish Peasant* (San Francisco: HarperSanFrancisco, 1991), 353.

The strong criticisms of wealth and the wealthy attributed to Jesus in the Gospels must also be seen in the context of Jesus' emphasis on love and trust in God. Often Jesus' teaching has been interpreted as implying that poverty is something inherently good, to be valued, as if being poor were a virtue to be sought as an end in itself. While Jesus is said to have declared the poor to be blessed (Matt. 5:3; Luke 6:20), when he called on his disciples to leave behind their family and possessions in order to follow him, his concern was not that they adopt poverty as a lifestyle but that they dedicate themselves to serving others together with him. Jesus' stress on solidarity also led him to pronounce a blessing on those who rely on God and one another for their needs, in contrast to the wealthy who trust in their own riches rather than God and refuse to share what they have with others (Matt. 19:23-24; Mark 4:19; 10:25; Luke 8:14; 12:16-21; 18:25). What Jesus taught, therefore, was not that wealth was bad and poverty was good, but rather that, for one's own good and the good of others, it was necessary to practice generosity and solidarity, expressing one's trust in God by sharing with others rather than clinging to one's possessions out of fear or selfishness.[38]

Jesus may also have chosen to carry out an itinerant ministry in order to remain out of the grasp of authorities who might seek to silence him.[39] At various times, such as after the arrest of John the Baptist, Jesus is presented as traveling to isolated places and attempting to avoid the crowds (Matt. 4:12; 14:13; Mark 6:32; 7:24; Luke 9:10). However, rather than being motivated by fear, Jesus seems to have been acting out of concern for his ministry. Had he fallen into the hands of the authorities, he would not have been able to continue proclaiming God's reign, teaching, healing, and training his disciples.

Jesus' itinerancy should thus be seen as an indication that he sought that his message regarding God's reign reach as many people as possible. The fact that he spoke enigmatically through parables and elected only a relatively small group of disciples to accompany him wherever he traveled should not be interpreted as an indication that he intended his teaching to be only for a select few. Had that been the case, Jesus would simply have withdrawn with his group of disciples to an isolated location in order to remain there indefinitely and would not have taught openly and publicly.

All of this brings us back to the question of why Jesus dedicated himself to a ministry of teaching. Clearly, his concern was not for himself or his own interests. Rather, what moved Jesus to make tremendous sacrifices and even put his life at risk by carrying out a ministry of teaching in the way that he

---

38. For an analysis of the possible reasons why Jesus chose the lifestyle he did during his ministry and required that same lifestyle of his closest disciples, see David A. Fiensy, *Jesus the Galilean: Soundings in a First Century Life* (Piscataway, NJ: Gorgias Press, 2007), 135-45.

39. On this point, see Douglas Edwards, "The Socio-Economic and Cultural Ethos of the Lower Galilee in the First Century: Implications for the Nascent Jesus Movement," in *The Galilee in Late Antiquity* (ed. Lee I. Levine; New York: Jewish Theological Seminary of America; Cambridge, MA: Harvard University Press, 1992), 72-73. Gerd Theissen notes that Jesus' journeys outside of Galilee could have been motivated by the same concern ("Jesus as an Itinerant Teacher: Reflections from Social History on Jesus' Roles," in *Jesus Research*, ed. Charleston and Pokorný, 110).

did must have been a profound love for others—a love that sought to bring others to love in the same way for their own good and the good of those around them.

Jesus' Healings and Exorcisms

Virtually all historical Jesus scholars today acknowledge that Jesus had a reputation as one who healed and performed exorcisms. Most also recognize that, at least to some extent, this reputation was probably grounded in historical reality. This does not necessarily involve ascribing to Jesus supernatural powers, but rather seeing him as one who had a gift for healing, as many persons were thought to possess in antiquity.[40]

If Jesus did in fact perform healings and exorcisms, we may ask once more about his possible motives and objectives. According to Matthew and Luke, Jesus' adversaries claimed that his work of casting out demons was carried out in collusion with "Beelzebub, the ruler of the demons" (Matt. 12:24-29; Mark 3:22-27; Luke 11:17-20). The implication of this accusation was that Jesus was seeking to deceive people into thinking he was ultimately seeking their well-being, when in reality his objective was to serve his own interests or those of Beelzebub.[41] The Synoptics present Jesus as dismissing this accusation as absurd and even blasphemous. They also provide evidence that he was not moved by selfish motives. We have no reports of Jesus seeking or receiving any type of personal gain from healing others and casting out demons. On the contrary, he seems instead to have been willing to endure the criticism and opposition of the leaders of the people and even to have faced rejection from some of those he sought to help. While he did gain fame and moral authority in the eyes of others as a result of his healings and exorcisms, there is nothing in the Gospels to suggest that he used that fame or moral authority for any personal ends of his own.

Seen in the context of Jesus' teaching and his itinerant lifestyle, which stressed and exemplified the need to love and serve others in spite of the sacrifices involved, we are left to conclude that what motivated Jesus to heal

---

40. Barry L. Blackburn observes that "scholars almost unanimously agree that this Galilean performed both cures and exorcisms, the success of which led both to a devoted following and opponents who charged him with sorcery" ("The Miracles of Jesus," in *Studying the Historical Jesus*, ed. Chilton and Evans, 392). On the historicity of Jesus' healing activity, see also Meier, *Marginal Jew*, 2:679-727, 969-70; Craig A. Evans also compares Jesus with other ancient figures who had reputations as healers, such as Honi the Circle Drawer (*Fabricating Jesus: How Modern Scholars Distort the Gospels*; Downers Grove, IL: InterVarsity, 2008, 139-57). Nevertheless, as H. Stegemann notes, Jesus' exorcisms and acts of healing were different from those performed by other figures in antiquity in that Jesus did not make use of magical prayers, rites, or objects (*Library of Qumran*, 237-38).

41. As Graham Stanton argued, the accusation that Jesus was working in collusion with Beelzebub was undoubtedly due in large part to the fact that his healings and exorcisms led many to see him as "a disruptive threat to social and religious order. His claims to act and speak on the basis of a special relationship to God were rightly perceived to be radical. For some they were so radical that they had to be undermined by an alternative explanation of their source" ("Jesus of Nazareth: A Magician and False Prophet Who Deceived God's People?," in *Jesus of Nazareth: Lord and Christ. Essays on the Historical Jesus and New Testament Christology*, ed. Joel B. Green and Max Turner; Grand Rapids: Eerdmans, 1994, 180; see 164-80).

others and exorcize demons was once again a deep concern for the well-being of others. To recognize this is not necessarily to affirm that his only motivation was to rid those he healed of their illnesses or the demons that tormented them. It is possible, for example, that he desired to communicate some deeper truth by means of his healings and exorcisms, making manifest to all the nature of God's reign, or allowing others to experience the blessings of that reign in the present. Such a desire would also be rooted in his concern for the salvation and well-being of others rather than arising out of some type of self-interest on his part.

Jesus' dedication to the task of delivering others from illnesses, physical disabilities, and demon possession inevitably raised the question of why these things existed and were so widespread. It was common to see them as punishments sent by God to chastise the people for their sins. Even if the purpose of this chastisement was believed to be that of disciplining and correcting those who had sinned in order to bring them back to God, such a belief nevertheless implied that those who were ill or disabled were themselves to blame for their condition, since they were suffering due to the sins they had committed.[42] Had they not sinned, it would not have been necessary for God to discipline and correct them. Demon possession could also be interpreted in the same way: while God was not believed to be the one who sent demons to torment those who sinned, he evidently allowed demons to possess certain people by not intervening to protect them from those demons.

Rather than seeing illnesses, physical disabilities, and demon possession as punishments sent by God, however, Jesus may have considered them to be the consequences of the oppressive rule of Rome and the Jewish authorities and leaders, as Carter has argued: "disease results in part from the imperial economic (taxation) system that removes adequate nutrition and food supplies from much of the population."[43] Seen in the context of the social realities that existed, those various ailments would be interpreted as signs that the society in general was in a state of crisis and deterioration. According to this way of thinking, the problem was not that God was making sinful individuals pay for their personal sins by inflicting suffering on them, but that countless individuals were experiencing the consequences of the sinful and unjust system that was in place.[44]

While some have argued that Jesus accepted the idea that sufferings were divine punishment for sins, there are good reasons for questioning such a view. A couple of passages from the Gospels seem to suggest that Jesus rejected the idea that those who suffered were being punished for their own sins or those of their parents (Luke 13:1-5; John 9:1-3). More important is the fact that,

---

42. See H. Stegemann, *Library of Qumran*, 243; Jonathan Klawans, *Impurity and Sin in Ancient Judaism* (Oxford: Oxford University Press, 2000), 98-99.

43. Carter, *Matthew and Empire*, 5; see also 70-73.

44. According to Horsley, the "rulers' intensified exploitation of their productivity" left people in Galilean villages "poor, hungry, despairing, divided against themselves, and even 'possessed' by demonic forces" ("The Dead Sea Scrolls and the Historical Jesus," in *The Bible and the Dead Sea Scrolls*, ed. Charlesworth, 1:51).

according to the evidence we have in the Gospels, Jesus never asked those who came to him for healing to acknowledge their sin or repent of it before he healed them. Had he thought that God was chastising them for their sins, he would have wanted to make sure that the chastisement sent by God had produced its desired effect before reversing what God had done.[45] In one significant passage, Jesus is presented as simply declaring the sins of a paralytic forgiven before the paralytic had said or done anything (Matt. 9:1-8; Mark 2:1-12; Luke 5:17-26). This suggests that Jesus saw the suffering of those he healed as something that was not *in conformity* with God's will, but *contrary* to it. Precisely for this reason, he sought to alleviate their suffering. His healing activity was therefore also closely tied to the forgiveness of sins, since those healed could no longer be said to be enduring any type of divine punishment for their sins.

It is often claimed that Jesus intended his healings and exorcisms to serve as proof that he was truly God's Son or the divine Savior God had promised to send.[46] This claim is then used as a basis to affirm that, when Jesus healed others, his objective was to bring people to faith in him in order that they might attain the salvation that truly mattered, namely, that of the age to come. Such an interpretation, however, implies that Jesus was in effect using those he healed for ends that he considered of greater importance than their physical well-being itself. Often this interpretation of Jesus' activity is related to the soul/body dualism that has been predominant in Christian theology since patristic times. According to this dualistic manner of thinking, what ultimately concerned Jesus was the salvation of souls rather than the healing of bodies.

There is good reason, however, to reject such ideas and instead affirm that Jesus saw the healings and exorcisms he performed as *ends in themselves* rather than as a means toward some greater end. In this case, if Jesus wanted others to believe in him, it was *for their sake*: his desire was that they might continue to find healing and wholeness through him, both in the present and the future. A number of passages from the Gospels provide evidence that Jesus did indeed think in these terms. First, he is often reported to have told those he healed, "Your faith has saved you" (Matt. 9:22; Mark 5:34; 10:52; Luke 7:50;

---

45. As H. Stegemann notes, Jesus' healing activity would have been seen as subversive in that it challenged the notion that the existing reality was in conformity with God's will: "The healing of the sick was basically regarded as impermissible interference with God's punishment" (*Library of Qumran*, 243). Freyne similarly notes that Jesus' healing activity would be considered subversive not only from a religious perspective but from a social perspective as well, since it questioned prevalent norms by restoring people to the social world from which they had been excluded, supposedly in accordance with God's will (*Jewish Galilean*, 148-49). On this point, see also Maureen W. Yeung, *Faith in Jesus and Paul: A Comparison with Special Reference to 'Faith that Can Move Mountains' and 'Your Faith Has Healed/Saved You'* (WUNT 2/147; Tübingen: Mohr Siebeck, 2002), 100.

46. E. P. Sanders, for example, regards the notion that Jesus was motivated by compassion "amusing," claiming instead that Jesus wished to authenticate his status as spokesman for God (*Jesus and Judaism*, 160-63, 170-73, 338-39). In that case, what Jesus sought was not primarily to help others but to gain recognition for himself; in effect, he was using those whom he helped for his own personal ends rather than acting out of love. Such a view is entirely at odds with the view of Jesus that we find throughout all four Gospels.

8:48; 17:19; 18:42).[47] This indicates that he understood salvation in terms of being restored to physical well-being, though no doubt he also considered it important to restore others to spiritual and emotional health. Second, just as the Gospels do not present Jesus laying down any conditions for granting healing to those who came to him, they do not provide any evidence that he asked anything of those he healed or freed from demon possession *after* they had been made well. Rather than demanding that they believe in him and follow him, in most cases, Jesus is presented as sending them back to their families and communities.[48] While on occasion those restored to health are said to have praised God through Jesus or to have become his followers, they are presented as doing this spontaneously. Even when Jesus expected those healed to be grateful to God for being restored to health, as the story of the healing of the ten lepers in Luke 17:11-19 illustrates, he seems not to have *demanded* any expression of gratitude from those he healed.

This means that Jesus was not using those he healed for other ends that he considered more important than their physical well-being itself. He was not trying to gain supporters or manipulate people through his healings and exorcisms. Rather, he saw other people as ends in themselves and sought simply that they be restored to health. Of course, he probably hoped that through his healing activity both those healed as well as others who had observed the healing or heard about it would come to believe in him as one who brought wholeness, not only in the present age, but the age to come as well.

Jesus' commitment to restoring others to wholeness in body and soul must be viewed in connection with his proclamation of God's reign. The God he proclaimed as coming to reign was one who sought wholeness for all and thus wanted to reign for *their* sake rather than *his own*. The fact that Jesus desired that those he had healed be restored to life in communities and a society from which they had become isolated, marginalized, or excluded because of their illness also indicates that Jesus understood salvation in terms of the restoration of community and the reconciliation of people to one another within the communities of which they formed part.

However, the reconciliation that Jesus intended to bring about through his healings and exorcisms was not merely a reconciliation among those who had become alienated from one another due to illness, physical ailments, or demon possession, but also a reconciliation with God. In traditional Christian thought, divine forgiveness of sins has generally been regarded as an end in itself and as synonymous with salvation. In Jesus' practice, however, forgiveness itself was not the end, as if his ultimate objective were to enable others to be acquitted by God at the final judgment. Rather, for Jesus forgiveness was a *means* to the goal of restoring people's relationships with God and with one

---

47. On Jesus' use of this phrase, see Craig L. Blomberg, "'Your Faith Has Made You Whole': The Evangelical Liberation Theology of Jesus," in *Jesus of Nazareth*, ed. Green and Turner, 76-82; Yeung, *Faith*, 59-62.

48. As Horsley notes, Jesus sought to restore people "to regular social interaction in their own communities" rather than drawing them away from those communities (*Spiral*, 228).

another so that they might experience wholeness not only on an individual level but on the level of communities as well. By declaring those whom he healed forgiven and accepted by God, whether explicitly or implicitly—that is, by freeing them from ailments that were commonly seen as divine punishment for their sins—, Jesus sought to remove any barriers to their full inclusion in the communities to which they belonged. If through Jesus God had declared his forgiveness and acceptance of a person who had been ill or possessed by demons by restoring that person to wholeness, no one else had a right to continue to condemn, marginalize, or exclude that person from the community on the basis of the idea that God was punishing that person for his or her sins.

When we look closely at Jesus' teaching and practice, it becomes clear that the criterion for forgiveness is not that one repent in the traditional sense, but simply that one desire to be made whole and approach God or Jesus himself with a sincere heart seeking that wholeness. Only if the people to whom Jesus ministered drew near confidently to God or Jesus in that way could they receive that wholeness. Therefore, Jesus' priority was not calling others to repentance so that they might be forgiven, but enabling them to be restored to health and subsequently live in ways that promoted their own well-being, together with that of others. While he undoubtedly wanted to see repentance in others, this was because, in Jesus' thought, for intrinsic reasons people cannot be whole if they are not committed to living in accordance with God's will. When he did call on others to repent or rejoiced that people had repented, he did so out of a concern that others experience not only divine forgiveness but also the well-being and wholeness that he and the God he proclaimed desired for them. Even when Jesus forgave sins, he sought to convey to others that the God in whose name he was acting desired above all else that people approach that God confidently, without fear, in order to experience his full acceptance together with his healing power in all aspects of their life as individuals and communities.

Jesus' teaching and practice thus stand in stark contrast to the teaching and practice of those who oppose Jesus in the Gospels. Whereas his opponents claim that God forgives people on the condition that they submit to his commandments and his sovereignty, according to Jesus, God uses forgiveness as a means to make people whole. Undoubtedly, this includes attempting to bring about in them a life of obedience to God's will, since only by living as God commands for their own good can people attain the wholeness God desires for them. But whereas Jesus' opponents proclaim a God who is ultimately concerned about obedience to his commandments for his own sake and for the sake of the law he had given, Jesus proclaims a different God whose ultimate concern is that all come to experience wholeness and well-being.

For the reasons we have seen, Jesus' healing activity must be regarded as a critique of the theology that viewed suffering as divine punishment for sins. On this basis, Jesus rejects the God of those who oppose him, a God whose primary concern is to safeguard his holiness and uphold his law and therefore constantly acts to punish those who disobey him. In the proclamation of Jesus' opponents, to call sinners to repentance involves threatening them with divine punishment. In contrast, the God Jesus proclaims is one who wants sinners to repent and change their ways, not for *his* sake but *their own*. While Jesus' God undoubtedly allows illness and suffering to exist among his people, through Jesus he seeks to draw people to himself in love by forgiving and accepting them so that they may experience healing and wholeness and come to live in ways that contribute to their well-being and that of others. Therefore, the God of Jesus does not inflict suffering on people in this life to punish them for their sins, as if retribution were his concern, but rather reaches out to them in love and solidarity to save them from living in ways that bring suffering on themselves and others.

When viewed in the context of other aspects of his teaching and ministry, Jesus' practice of healing and casting out demons must have been considered subversive. His healings and exorcisms served to authenticate his message of the coming of God's reign, which was a critique of the prevalent reigns and systems of his day, and reinforced the notion that he was a savior-figure serving as God's instrument to bring a salvation that transcended what Rome and the political and religious powers in Jerusalem offered. As his healings and exorcisms attracted people to himself, they also served to create a community of followers who pledged their allegiance to Jesus and the God he represented, rather than to Rome or Jerusalem.[49]

Jesus was therefore seen as proclaiming a different God, a God who was distinct not only from the divinities in whose name the Romans ruled, but also from the God represented by the Jewish elites. The God proclaimed by Jesus was a God who was not in favor of the systems and structures of the day. Nor was he a God who was using the Romans to punish the Jews for their sins. Jesus' God was also radically distinct from the God of the religious leaders who opposed Jesus and claimed that he was acting on behalf of Beelzebul. When he lashes out at them verbally, this is because for Jesus it is they who are serving a false God and therefore doing the work of Beelzebul by preventing others from coming to Jesus to be made whole.

Undoubtedly, like those who opposed him, Jesus claimed that one day the God he proclaimed would judge all people, condemning those who had refused to live according to his will, but saving and forgiving those who had lived in the way he desired and commanded. While Jesus was concerned for the well-being of others in the present world, this did not mean that he ascribed no importance to the life to come. On the contrary, he apparently

---

49. Some scholars have argued that, by restoring physical well-being to those who suffered from various ailments, Jesus in effect fulfilled one of the primary roles of the Jerusalem temple, where many Jews went in order to ask God for healing and health. On that basis, they claim that this is one more reason why Jesus' acts of healing and his exorcisms would be seen as subversive and as a challenge to the religious and social order. See, for example, R. David Kaylor, *Jesus the Prophet: His Vision of the Kingdom on Earth* (Louisville, KY: Westminster John Knox, 1994), 185-87; Freyne, *Galilee, Jesus, and the Gospels*, 238-39.

spoke a great deal of the coming judgment and the world to come. His focus, however, was fundamentally different from that of his opponents. For Jesus, God's purpose in establishing a new world and judging all people was that of destroying evil and injustice, together with all who aligned themselves with evil and injustice, so that those who desired to be made whole might finally experience that wholeness in its fullness. According to Jesus' teaching as Matthew presents it, God's angels will come to "collect out of his kingdom all causes of sin and all evildoers" and "throw them into the furnace of fire," thereby enabling the righteous to "shine like the sun in the kingdom of their Father," free from all oppression, injustice, and suffering (Matt. 13:41-43). In contrast, for those who opposed Jesus, it seems that the purpose of the final judgment and the establishment of the world to come was that of rewarding all who had been faithful to the system that the God they proclaimed had established in the present world, while at the same time punishing and excluding from the blessings of the new age those who had refused to submit obediently to that system and the authorities God had placed over it.

To whatever extent Jesus' eschatology is regarded as apocalyptic, what really matters is that the future he announced through his teaching and his healings and exorcisms was one in which God would put an end to the present, oppressive system in order to replace it with a radically different system over which God alone would reign. This new system or new age would be characterized by the wholeness and well-being that results from love, justice, and solidarity. Through both his message and his acts of power, Jesus communicated to all that it was necessary for them to identify with one or the other of these two systems. If they identified with the dominant, oppressive system through their way of life and their complicity with its unjust and corrupt practices, they would not inherit God's reign. His hope was that all would instead identify with the coming system that God would establish in which all would enjoy God's blessings of wholeness. To identify with that system, however, meant adopting the values and ways of relating to God and others inherent to that system.

Jesus' Preparation of Disciples

There seems to be no reason to doubt that Jesus formed a group of disciples around himself.[50] In addition to the group of the twelve, the Gospels speak of others who followed Jesus during his ministry, some of whom had a close relationship with him. Among these followers were women.[51] The Gospels also affirm that during his own lifetime Jesus sent these disciples out into the Galilean villages to heal people, cast out demons, and proclaim the coming of

---

50. See Meier, *Marginal Jew*, 3:41-47.
51. On the question of the women who identified themselves as Jesus' followers during his ministry, see especially Freyne, *Galilee and Gospel*, 282-86; Meier, *Marginal Jew*, 3:630-31. Kathleen Corley agrees that Jesus probably ate and traveled with women, but claims that this was not entirely novel or special in his context ("The Egalitarian Jesus: A Christian Myth of Origins," *Forum* 1-2 [1998]: 314).

God's reign. The book of Acts, the letters of Paul, and other early Christian writings offer evidence that after Jesus' death many of these same disciples formed the core of Jesus' group of followers and that at least some of them played an important role in the expansion of that group.

For what purpose did Jesus choose a group of disciples and prepare them to carry out a ministry that was essentially the same as his own? The four Gospels and Acts imply that Jesus anticipated that his ministry would be relatively short-lived, since he would die an early death. If he wanted his followers to continue to minister to others in the same way he had, reaching out even further to more people to proclaim the coming of God's reign, teach them how to live in that reign, and alleviate the suffering of those afflicted in body and soul, he needed to prepare disciples who would be capable of doing these things well and could assume a leadership role within the community of those who would continue to identify themselves as his followers. Many scholars, however, would question the notion that Jesus believed that his ministry would be cut short by an early death and doubt that he intended to establish an *ekklēsia*, that is, a "church" or community of followers that would carry on his work after his death.[52]

Jesus' election of the twelve has usually been regarded as a symbolic act related in some way to the twelve tribes of Israel. For many, the symbol is that of Israel's restoration.[53] A couple of passages from the Gospels anticipate a day when the twelve disciples will judge or govern Israel (Matt. 19:28; Luke 22:30). As Richard Horsley notes, this would be understood in terms of liberating, redeeming, or establishing justice for the tribes of Israel.[54] While this implies that Jesus was preparing his disciples for some eschatological role, it seems doubtful that this was his only plan for them, since there is ample evidence that the instruction he gave them included much more than guidelines for some future task of judging Israel; in fact, the tradition never speaks of Jesus providing them with any such guidelines. Instead, the Gospels in general present Jesus as preparing the disciples for a future role as leaders, teachers, and proclaimers of the message of God's reign in the present age. To recognize this does not necessarily require postulating that Jesus foresaw his

---

52. For the most part, in the present work I will avoid the term *church* due to the connotations that it has come to have and instead speak of the community of Jesus' followers. I would agree with the affirmation of Craig Evans, who writes: "I don't think that Jesus originally envisioned the 'church,' at least as it eventually came to be. Jesus spoke of a community and expected his followers to live and think in certain ways. But the church itself was a more or less ad hoc development of this community idea. The church took on the characteristics that it did in order to deal with the new challenges it faced in the years and decades following Jesus' death and resurrection" ("The Jesus of History and the Christ of Faith: Toward Jewish-Christian Dialogue," in *Who Was Jesus? A Jewish-Christian Dialogue*, ed. Paul Copan and Evans; Louisville, KY: Westminster John Knox, 2001), 70. N. T. Wright similarly notes that, rather than seeking to establish a "church," Jesus "intended his people, those who were loyal to him in the villages and towns, to form cells, groups or gatherings...." (*Jesus and the Victory of God*, Vol. 2 of *Christian Origins and the Question of God*; Minneapolis: Fortress, 1996, 295; see also 275).

53. See, for example, Sanders, *Jesus and Judaism*, 98-106. On the significance of Jesus' election of twelve disciples, see also Evans, "Aspects," 281-83; Borg, *Conflict*, 85; Bird, *Jesus*, 132-34; Meier, *Marginal Jew*, 3:148-63.

54. Horsley, *Spiral*, 204-5.

own untimely death, since he may have expected that he would still be alive when the disciples carried out the tasks for which he was preparing them.

Jesus' formation of a group of disciples has led many scholars to speak of a "movement" founded and directed by Jesus.[55] Because this term is not found in the New Testament writings, however, caution must be used in employing it. Any answer to the question of whether Jesus intended to establish a movement depends on how that term is understood. Today we tend to define a movement as a group of people united in a common cause, usually guided by certain shared principles and objectives. It is not clear, however, that the followers of Jesus understood themselves in this way. The Gospels imply that, when his disciples began to follow Jesus at his petition (rather than at their own initiative), they were somewhat uncertain about what they would be doing, where they would be going, or what Jesus' objectives and purposes for them were. Instead, they seem to have set their hopes on him personally as someone who was to carry out some important task or achievement in which they would be involved.

Similarly, it is not clear that what brought the disciples together was merely a common commitment to certain shared principles. According to the Gospels, whatever principles Jesus' disciples came to adopt were taught to them by Jesus *after* they decided to follow him. The evidence indicates that from the start their commitment was thus not to some common cause, task, or principle but to *Jesus himself and the God he proclaimed*. In a sense, *Jesus* was the cause rather than anything he taught or represented. They were following *him* rather than merely following his ideas or example.

Yet because Jesus' life was one of service, in another sense it was *his ministry* that was the real cause. They saw him not merely as a figure to be served and obeyed, but one who wanted them to follow and obey him because he was dedicated to serving others and wished for them to do so as well, together with him and under his guidance. Their task was not to promote Jesus personally, as if that were an end in itself, but to promote his work on behalf of the well-being of others. During his ministry, the disciples appear to have played both a support role for Jesus as well as the role of learners.

According to the Gospels, however, Jesus was seen as more than an instructor or leader. He was also a savior figure. The Gospels repeatedly speak of Jesus as one who gave authority to his disciples. As Dale Allison Jr. has noted, "Jesus himself stood outside the symbolic group. He was not one of the twelve. He was instead the one who chose the twelve."[56] Since the nineteenth century, it has been common to affirm that Jesus did not proclaim *himself*, but rather God's reign. However, while that reign was undoubtedly central for Jesus, throughout the Gospels it is intimately and inextricably tied to Jesus himself. The Gospels consistently stress Jesus' divine authority and see him

---

55. On the use of the term "movement" by scholars and the problems of speaking of a "Jesus movement," see especially Douglas E. Oakman, *The Political Aims of Jesus* (Minneapolis: Fortress, 2012), 143-47.

56. Dale Allison Jr., "Jesus and the Covenant: A Response to E. P. Sanders," *JSNT* 29 (1987): 67.

playing a unique role in the redemption of Israel, however that redemption is understood. He is presented, not merely as a teacher of divine truths or principles, but as a figure in whom others deposited their hopes of salvation. His teaching is viewed as authoritative in a way that distinguishes him from other teachers or prophets. For the evangelists, Jesus represented God in a way that no one else did.

Of course, many would argue that Jesus came to be seen as a savior figure with unique divine authority only after his death, when his disciples became convinced that he had risen from the dead, and that all four Gospels are unreliable on this point. Such an argument, however, is problematic. As Nils Dahl has insisted, in itself, belief in Jesus' resurrection would not necessarily have led to the conclusion that he was a savior figure. Elijah, for example, was thought to have been exalted to heaven rather than suffering death, yet he was not on that account viewed as the same type of savior figure that Jesus was. According to Dahl, "If he was crucified as an alleged Messiah, then—but only then—does faith in his resurrection necessarily become faith in the resurrection of the crucified Messiah."[57] This suggests that Jesus was seen as a savior figure *prior* to his death. As noted above, he called on others, not merely to follow his teaching, but to follow *him*.

For all of these reasons, if we are to speak of Jesus as one who led a *movement*, we must exercise caution. The book of Acts uses the word *sect* (*hairesis*) to refer to the group of Jesus' followers after his death, although this designation is also problematic, especially due to the connotations it has acquired in modern English.[58] In the New Testament, the term *hairesis* is not found on the lips of Jesus' followers themselves as a self-designation. It thus seems to represent a designation formulated by people outside of their group. The advantage of using this term, however, is that it can be understood as implying commitment and allegiance to a particular *person* rather than a *cause*. Of course, this may reflect modern usage of the term rather than ancient usage of the Greek *hairesis*, where allegiance was not always to a particular leader or figure. For my purposes here, I will merely speak of Jesus' *community* or *group* of followers, though I am conscious that both of these words are also absent from the Gospel accounts and may carry certain connotations that are foreign to the self-understanding of those who originally followed Jesus. The use of these terms in the singular also implies that there was only one community or group, which may be misleading. During his ministry, Jesus may have had various groups of followers, at least at a local level, and his community of followers should probably be seen as a community of smaller communities.

---

57. Nils A. Dahl, *Jesus the Christ: The Historical Origins of Christological Doctrine* (Minneapolis: Fortress, 1991), 38.

58. On the use of the word *sect* in biblical scholarship, see especially Robin Scroggs, "The Earliest Christian Communities as Sectarian Movement," in *Christianity, Judaism, and Other Greco-Roman Cults: Studies for Morton Smith at 60* (ed. Jacob Neusner; SJLA 12; Leiden: Brill, 1975), 2:1-23; Albert I. Baumgarten, *The Flourishing of Jewish Sects in the Maccabean Era: An Interpretation* (JSJSup 55; Leiden: Brill, 1997), 5-15.

These considerations bring us back to the question of why Jesus chose and prepared a group of disciples. While we cannot offer any definitive answers to this question, we can at least affirm from Jesus' ministry that he had in mind the expansion of the work he was doing, both in a spatial and a temporal sense. He prepared his disciples to go out to other places and, on at least one occasion, he actually sent them out for a short time to carry out the things he had taught them to do on their own. The fact that, according to Luke, Jesus had them then return to share their experiences and continue to receive further instruction from him suggests that he intended that they continue in the future the work for which he had sent them out (Luke 9:10; 10:17-20). Whether or not Jesus foresaw his death in Jerusalem, whatever he was preparing his disciples to do, he had them remain attached to himself throughout his ministry until his crucifixion, rather than sending them out to work independently of himself. Jesus did not have them set up any bases of operations in other places. If Jesus anticipated that he might be put to death when he went up to Jerusalem with his closest disciples, he must have desired to continue instructing and preparing them there until the time in which his death would come.

In addition to those who accompanied Jesus throughout his journeys, Jesus had many followers whom he did not ask or expect to follow him from one place to another.[59] In many of the sayings attributed to him, Jesus also calls these other followers his disciples. In a sense, they formed part of his community of disciples or followers as well, even when they remained in their villages and homes.

If Jesus did intend to found a community that would continue to exist in the future even after his death and would also extend to other places, his election and training of a core group of disciples should be seen as an attempt to prepare some type of leadership for this community that would also allow it to extend elsewhere. Naturally, because this preparation required time, Jesus would have sought to avoid conflict with the authorities when possible, as well as anything else that might cut that time short. This may have been one of the reasons he stayed away from urban centers such as Sepphoris and Tiberias. Because these cities were centers of power and thus were controlled more closely by the authorities, there was a greater risk that he might be arrested there. This would have prevented him from accomplishing fully his objective of preparing his disciples for the tasks he wanted them to carry out.[60]

---

59. Scholars today generally recognize that Jesus had different groups or circles of followers or disciples, not all of whom accompanied him in his itinerant ministry. Adriana Destro and Mauro Pesce distinguish between Jesus' "itinerant disciples" and his "sedentary disciples," who "remain within their own households and attend their usual activities" (*From Jesus to his First Followers: Continuity and Discontinuity. Anthropological and Historical Perspectives*, BIS 152; Leiden: Brill, 2017, 14-16). On this point, see also Meier, *Marginal Jew*, 3:626-32. As Freyne has noted, Jesus' band of followers was probably always a fairly small, limited group (*Galilee, Jesus, and the Gospels*, 263).

60. Of course, Jesus may have stayed away from centers such as Sepphoris for other reasons as well, such as his opposition to the system those centers represented. On this point, see Sean Freyne, "Archaeology and the Historical Jesus," in *Jesus and Archaeology* (ed. James H. Charlesworth; Grand Rapids: Eerdmans, 2006), 81-82.

Jesus' purpose in establishing this community and planning for its expansion, of course, must be seen in relation to his proclamation of God's reign. What mattered to Jesus was not simply that a community of his followers continue to exist, but that those followers be fully committed to what Jesus had taught in word and example. They were to identify not only with Jesus but with the God he had proclaimed, submitting to the reign of that God rather than the human reigns that demanded their subjection and loyalty over and against the God of Jesus.

THE CONFLICTS GENERATED BY JESUS' MINISTRY

According to the Gospels, conflict characterized Jesus' ministry from the start and eventually resulted in his death. Nevertheless, we cannot assume that the reasons why Jesus was put to death in Jerusalem were related to the reasons for the opposition to his ministry in Galilee. Therefore, it is important to consider separately the conflicts that are said to have arisen during his time in Galilee.

Precisely what was behind these conflicts is a complex question. Most of the conflicts are reported to have been with the Jewish scribes and Pharisees. However, many scholars have questioned the portrayal of these groups in the Gospels and have argued that the Gospel accounts instead address conflicts that arose after Jesus' death between the followers of Jesus and others in the Jewish communities in which Jesus' followers were active. There are also diverse views regarding who the Pharisees were and what they represented. Some have seen them purely as religious leaders, while others have instead stressed their ties to the political system in which the rulers and Jewish authorities collaborated with Rome.[61]

For our purposes here, however, it is not necessary to address these questions. The evidence seems strong that Jesus had strong critics during the time of his ministry, whether or not they were scribes and Pharisees and whether or not those critics represented the scribes and Pharisees as a whole. For that reason, I will generally refer to those who entered into conflict with Jesus simply as his critics, adversaries, or opponents. What is important is not whether someone actually held the positions attributed to the scribes and Pharisees in the Gospels or who those persons were, but what the passages that relate conflict tell us about Jesus' message, beliefs, and practices. If there was conflict, it was because some disagreed strongly with what Jesus said and did. As I have argued above, at the heart of these accounts of conflict are different understandings of God and God's will. The question that interests us here, therefore, is how the narratives of conflict found in the Gospels enable us to reconstruct the manner in which Jesus conceived of God and defined God's will.

---

61. On this discussion, see especially N. T. Wright, *The New Testament and the People of God*, Vol. 1 of *Christian Origins and the Question of God* (Minneapolis: Fortress, 1992), 181-203; Roland Deines, "The Pharisees Between 'Judaisms' and 'Common Judaism'," in *Justification*, ed. Carson et al., 1:443-504; Meier, *Marginal Jew*, 3:289-340, 549-60.

If we look at the Gospel accounts as a whole, the stories that mention conflict during Jesus' ministry revolve around three particular themes: Jesus' authority, his relation to those regarded as sinners, and the priority he gives to concerns regarding human well-being over against other competing concerns, including primarily the proper observance of the Mosaic law. Because these three themes appear so frequently throughout the Gospel accounts, we can assume with a fair degree of certainty that they did indeed constitute sources of conflict during Jesus' Galilean ministry, even though the identity of those who disagreed with Jesus over these matters is unclear.

Jesus' Authority

Although Jesus undoubtedly believed he had authority from God to say and do the things he did, precisely how he understood his relationship to God is an extremely difficult question to answer. Inevitably, the presuppositions with which one approaches that question will determine to what extent one accepts the claims regarding Jesus' divine sonship found in the New Testament as well as the way in which one understands that sonship.

The question of whether Jesus regarded himself as the Messiah that many Jews expected is also extremely difficult to answer. As we observed in Chapter 2, most scholars now agree that there was no universally-accepted set of beliefs concerning the Messiah among the Jews of Jesus' day. Some Jews, in fact, apparently had few if any expectations regarding a Messiah. If Jesus did allow others to regard him as the Messiah, he appears to have done so somewhat reluctantly and must have defined the title in terms that were different from those that were common among other Jews.[62]

Similar difficulties must be noted with regard to other titles attributed to Jesus in the Gospels, such as Son of Man, Son of God, and Son of David. Evidence suggests that Jesus may have attributed to himself only the first of these three titles,[63] yet scholars remain divided over what Jesus may have meant when he spoke of the Son of Man. Many have even doubted that Jesus identified himself with the Son of Man.[64] Because of the uncertainties involved, it seems problematic to approach the question of who Jesus understood himself to be by taking as a starting-point the common beliefs

---

62. See James D. G. Dunn, "Messianic Ideas and Their Influence on the Jesus of History," in *The Messiah: Developments in Earliest Judaism and Christianity. The First Princeton Symposium on Judaism and Christian Origins* (ed. James H. Charlesworth et al.; Minneapolis: Fortress, 1992), 372-74.

63. As Aquila H. I. Lee has shown, most scholars agree that Jesus did not see himself as the Son of God (*From Messiah to Preexistent Son: Jesus' Self-Consciousness and Early Christian Exegesis of Messianic Psalms*; WUNT 2/192; Tübingen: Mohr Siebeck, 2005, 25-30). If Jesus accepted the title of Messiah, of course, he may also have accepted the title "Son of David."

64. For a summary of the scholarly discussion on this subject, see especially Delbert Burkett, *The Son of Man Debate: A History and Evaluation* (SNTSMS 107; Cambridge: Cambridge University Press, 1999). Burkett notes that many scholars now consider "unsolvable" the question of whether Jesus referred to himself as the Son of Man and, if so, how he understood that title (2). Burkett also concludes that most scholars now agree that "no unified 'Son of Man' title or concept existed in pre-Christian Judaism," that "the titular use of 'Son of Man' originated in a christological interpretation of Daniel 7.13," and that there is an increasing tendency "to dissociate the Son of Man sayings from Jesus and attribute them to the early church" (121-22, 124).

concerning these figures in order then to ask which if any of these titles Jesus applied to himself or allowed others to apply to him.

What does seem fairly certain, however, is that Jesus believed that the authority he had from God was in some way unique and set him apart from other authority figures.[65] According to all four Gospels, conflicts over Jesus' authority arose repeatedly during his ministry. Although these conflicts are especially emphasized in the Fourth Gospel, they are also central to the plot of all three of the Synoptics, as Jack Kingsbury in particular has argued.[66] During his ministry, the scribes and Pharisees take offense when Jesus pronounces the sins of a paralytic forgiven and question Jesus' authority to speak and act in other ways (Matt. 9:28, 32-34; 12:22-24; Mark 2:1-12; 3:22; Luke 5:17-26; 11:14-15; John 5:1-18; 9:1-41). Once Jesus has arrived in Jerusalem, they approach Jesus with the express purpose of asking him regarding his authority (Matt. 21:23-27; Mark 11:27-33; Luke 20:1-8). Similarly, throughout the Synoptic passion narratives, the question constantly addressed is whether Jesus is truly the Messiah and God's Son. The fact that heated discussions over the question of Jesus' identity and authority are so prominent in the Fourth Gospel as well means that there can be little doubt that this question was indeed a cause of considerable conflict during Jesus' ministry.

Even though the Synoptics do not present Jesus repeatedly making explicit claims regarding his unique relationship to God as God's Son in the way that the Fourth Gospel does, many of the narratives they contain suggest that he did believe that he had divine authority to say and do things that other human beings did not. According to the story of the healing of the paralytic, Jesus believed he had divine authority to forgive sins and declare who was acceptable before God (Matt. 9:2-8; Mark 2:1-12; Luke 5:17-26; cf. 7:48). Even if Jesus' declaration to the paralytic that his sins were forgiven is not seen as implying that he believed he was divine in some sense, the Gospels nowhere affirm that Jesus thought that others could forgive sins in the same way that he did, unless they did so with the authority he gave them (Matt. 16:18-19; 18:18; cf. John 20:23). It is not clear whether Jesus taught that when God's reign arrived he would have the task of judging others, as a number of passages from the Gospels affirm, yet at the least he appears to have claimed to know who would be allowed entrance into that reign.[67] Whether or not he expressed openly and explicitly in the presence of others his beliefs regarding his unique relationship with God, those beliefs inevitably came across in the things he said and did. The healings and exorcisms he performed also seemed to authenticate whatever claims he made regarding himself. Others would not

---

65. On this point, see especially Lee, *From Messiah*, 122-201. Dunn notes that, for the evangelists, the category of prophet was "certainly not of sufficient weight to embody the significance of Jesus" ("Messianic Ideas," 377). See also Ben F. Meyer, *The Aims of Jesus* (London: SCM, 1979), 147-53.

66. See Jack Dean Kingsbury, *Conflict in Mark: Jesus, Authorities, Disciples* (Minneapolis: Fortress, 1989), 65-69, 86-88; Kingsbury, *Conflict in Luke: Jesus, Authorities, Disciples* (Minneapolis: Fortress, 1991), 81, 105-7; Kingsbury, *Matthew as Story*, 2nd ed. (Philadelphia: Fortress, 1988), 125-26.

67. On this point, see especially Sanders, *Jesus and Judaism*, 208, 240, 273-74.

have been offended and angered by Jesus' teaching and practice unless what he did and said communicated at least implicitly that he was acting with divine authority as one who related to God in ways that no one else did.

Jesus' customary practice of referring to God as his "Father" should also be seen as an expression of his belief that his relation to God was unique. Scholars have debated to what extent it was common for Jews in antiquity to refer to Israel's God as their Father, yet even if Jesus' use of this designation did not distinguish him entirely from other Jews, the *way* in which he used it certainly did. While at times he apparently taught others to call God Father as well, his words and actions seem clearly to reflect the conviction that he represented and spoke for God in a way that others did not. Although most scholars now agree that Joachim Jeremias overstated his case when he claimed that Jesus' use of the term *Abba* was equivalent to calling God "Daddy," there can be little doubt that Jesus did see his relationship with God as being extremely close and intimate.[68] Of course, Jesus apparently also desired that others see God in the same way, though this need not be understood as an indication that he believed that others shared the same relationship to God that he did. The fact that *Abba* was the term Jesus preferred to refer to the God he proclaimed underscores once more that his understanding of God was distinct from that of other Jewish teachers and leaders, especially those who claimed to represent Israel's God as his mediators and spokespersons.

Jesus' teaching as the Gospels present it also reflects a certain presumption to know God's will. According to the Gospels, Jesus did not customarily base his teaching on the sources of authority recognized by other Jews in his day, most notably the Hebrew Scriptures and the Jewish tradition as a whole. Instead, he is often presented as claiming to have immediate knowledge of God's will independently of the traditional sources of authority.[69] Once again, this claim would have generated conflict due to the widespread belief among the Jewish people that any authority a teacher or leader had needed to be grounded in the authorities recognized as being of divine origin, such as the written and oral law, the Hebrew Scriptures as a whole, and the institutions God had established, including especially the high priesthood.

For Jesus to claim to have an authority from God that was distinct and independent from these traditional sources of authority involved questioning implicitly the absolute authority not only of those sources themselves, but also of those who opposed him on the basis of those sources. Furthermore,

---

68. See James Barr, "*Abba* Isn't Daddy," *JTS* 39 (1988): 28-47. For different perspectives on Jesus' understanding of God as his Father and his use of the term *Abba*, see also Lee, *From Messiah*, 122-80; Mary Rose D'Angelo, "Abba and Father: Imperial Theology in the Contexts of Jesus and the Gospels," in *The Historical Jesus in Context* (ed. Amy-Jill Levine, Dale C. Allison Jr., and John Dominic Crossan; PRR; Princeton, NJ: Princeton University Press, 2006), 64-78.

69. As Freyne observes, rather than being based on tradition or the Scriptures, in the Gospels Jesus' words "are deemed authoritative in their own right" (*Galilee, Jesus, and the Gospels*, 259). Irving M. Zeitlin also notes that Jesus' idea that "he had an especially intimate relationship with God" would have led him to claim a certain authority over the Hebrew Scriptures (*Jesus and the Judaism of His Time*; New York: Basil Blackwell, 1988, 101).

by rejecting the authority that others claimed to have received from God, Jesus also rejected their view of God. The God whom Jesus proclaimed and whom his critics rejected was a God who had given Jesus a special and unique authority. The God whom Jesus rejected and others affirmed was a God who called on all to submit obediently to the dictates of the political and religious authorities he had established as his representatives on earth. Just as Jesus rejected the God that others proclaimed, others rejected the God whom Jesus proclaimed and therefore rejected Jesus' claims to authority as well. While both Jesus and those who criticized him believed their God was the true God of Israel, at stake were two conflicting views of God and God's will.[70] Furthermore, because each view of God was identified with a different order or system, Jesus was in effect challenging the system in place by proclaiming a God who was distinct from the one who had supposedly established the status quo.[71] The system to which Jesus' God had aligned himself was not the one that was in place in Palestine and the Roman Empire, but the coming reign of which Jesus spoke.

This understanding of Jesus' authority and the God he proclaimed provided the basis for the claims regarding Jesus that his first followers began to make after his crucifixion, once they became convinced that the God he had proclaimed and called *Abba* had raised him from the dead. Jesus' resurrection would be interpreted as demonstrating the truth of everything that he had conveyed concerning his unique authority and relation to God. What Jesus had taught about himself, both explicitly and implicitly, would explain in large part why, shortly after his death, his first followers began to proclaim him as Christ, Lord, and especially Son of God. It was not only the use of these terms by Jesus' followers but the *way* in which they used them that set Jesus apart from other authority figures, including not only the political and religious authorities of his day and prophetic figures such as John, but the authorities from Israel's past, such as the patriarchs, Moses, David, and the prophets. It is difficult to explain how Jesus' first followers could have come to view Jesus in such terms *after* his death if Jesus' words and deeds *before* his death had not laid some basis for those interpretations of Jesus and his relation to the God of Israel.

---

70. While it would be inaccurate to affirm that what distinguished the God proclaimed by Jesus from that of those who opposed him was that Jesus' God was one of love and mercy, I believe there is a certain degree of truth in the claim of William A. Simmons that "Jesus' deeds and words reveal a very distinctive understanding of God" and that, even though "such elements [i.e., love and mercy] have always been a part of the faith of Israel, the degree to which Jesus pushed these concepts to the forefront was extraordinary for the context in which he lived" (*A Theology of Inclusion in Jesus and Paul: The God of Outcasts and Sinners*; MBPS 39; Lewiston, NY: Mellen Biblical Press, 1996, 36).

71. In this regard, Carter comments that at the root of Jesus' conflicts with the Jewish leaders as reported in Matthew's Gospel is the fact that those leaders are "part of the ruling elite committed to defending the current social order from which they benefit. Jesus and the religious leaders occupy very different places in the imperial world. The religious leaders are part of its power structure. They represent its interests.... No conflict is 'just' or 'simply' a religious one. The conflicts have social, political, and economic dimensions also.... Jesus conflicts with representatives of the ruling class, people who want to preserve the current social structure" (*Matthew and Empire*, 35).

Jesus' Fellowship with Sinners

Numerous passages in the Gospels present the scribes and Pharisees taking offense at the way in which Jesus enjoyed fellowship with certain people whom they considered sinners (Matt. 9:10-13; 11:19; Mark 2:15-17; Luke 5:30-32; 7:34-50; 15:1-32). Once again, scholars have debated extensively precisely why Jesus' practice in this regard was offensive to many, yet there can be little doubt that the primary reason was that it called into question the social and religious norms of the society of that day.[72] As in most societies, it was expected that a moral and upright person manifest one's disapproval of those who do not live according to those norms, especially if that person is viewed as a leader or authority figure.[73] Jesus apparently refused to do this. Instead, he entered into various degrees of fellowship with those who violated those norms.

Of course, it is possible to regard Jesus' acceptance of those whom others labeled "sinners" as a strategy on Jesus' part to bring those who did not live in accordance with those norms into compliance with them. By initially showing them acceptance, he might gain their trust and then attempt to convince them to change their lifestyle so as to live in the way that the predominant social norms dictated. Yet Jesus' practice can also be seen as a rejection of many of those norms. It involved questioning the way in which the majority had come to define good and bad, right and wrong, righteous and sinner. Jesus' fellowship with those considered sinners is an indication that he did not agree with many of those norms, particularly those that demanded that one manifest outwardly one's rejection of those who behaved in ways that were deemed unacceptable. Once again, because the norms that were prevalent in the society of Jesus' day were believed to have been established by Israel's God himself, through his actions Jesus would have been seen as rejecting the God that was associated with the system in place in order to proclaim a different God—a God who related as Jesus did to those considered sinners and thus rejected the social norms that Jesus himself questioned.[74]

To make this claim is not to affirm the traditional Protestant view that Jesus proclaimed a God of grace in contrast to other Jews who rejected the

---

72. On these conflicts, see especially David Neale, *None but the Sinners: Religious Categories in the Gospel of Luke* (JSNTSup 58; Sheffield: JSOT, 1991), 68-95; Crossley, *Why Christianity Happened*, 75-96. On the historicity of Jesus' fellowship with those labeled "sinners," see especially Craig L. Blomberg, "The Authenticity and Significance of Jesus' Table Fellowship with Sinners," in *Key Events in the Life of the Historical Jesus: A Collaborative Exploration of Context and Coherence* (ed. Darrell L. Bock and Robert L. Webb; WUNT 247; Tübingen: Mohr Siebeck, 2009), 215-44.

73. On the predominance of the idea that sinners must be treated as outcasts in ancient Jewish thought and second-temple Jewish literature, see Tom Holmén, *Jesus and Jewish Covenant Thinking* (BibInt 55; Leiden: Brill, 2001), 200-205; James D. G. Dunn, "Jesus, Table-Fellowship, and Qumran," in *Jesus and the Dead Sea Scrolls* (ed. James H. Charlesworth; ABRL; New York: Doubleday, 1992), 267-68.

74. Jesus' practice of admitting those considered sinners into the intimacy of his table fellowship, of course, also seemed to represent a lack of respect for the Jewish law, since it communicated the idea that it was acceptable for people to disregard the commandments God had given. On this point, see William R. Farmer, "Reflections upon the 'Historical Perimeters for Understanding the Aims of Jesus'," in *Authenticating*, ed. Chilton and Evans, 74.

idea of a gracious God and instead taught a doctrine of works-righteousness. E. P. Sanders rightly insisted that divine grace was a central concept in first-century Judaism, contrary to many Christian caricatures of ancient Jewish beliefs, and demonstrated convincingly that the idea that it was necessary to earn God's grace and favor was foreign to Jewish thought.[75] Nevertheless, Sanders seems to have overlooked the fact that God's grace could be defined and understood in many different ways. Clearly, Jesus' understanding of God's grace differed in important ways from that of his critics. For Jesus, God's grace demanded that he enter into fellowship with those others condemned as sinners, while for Jesus' critics God's grace precluded such fellowship. Thus Jesus was not only proclaiming a God who was different from the God in whom many other Jews of his time believed, including those who opposed him, but a distinct understanding of God's grace and God's will as well.[76]

In his book *Jesus and Judaism*, Sanders argued that, if Jesus had called on sinners to repent, religious leaders such as the Pharisees would have welcomed his efforts to bring others to repentance rather than objecting to those efforts or being offended by them.[77] This observation, together with other considerations, led Sanders to the conclusion that Jesus did not call on the sinners with whom he had fellowship to repent and that repentance was not an important element of Jesus' teaching.[78]

Numerous scholars have questioned Sanders's claim that the call to repentance was not a central aspect of Jesus' message.[79] One of the main problems, however, is that Sanders simply inquires as to whether Jesus proclaimed the need to repent without considering the possibility that Jesus and his critics understood repentance in two very different ways. In addition to defining repentance differently, it appears that Jesus disagreed with his critics over two other issues as well: how sinners should be brought to repentance and who was in need of repentance.

Most Jews in first-century Palestine seem to have understood repentance in terms of recognizing that one had failed to keep God's commandments as they had traditionally been interpreted and turning back to those commandments in order to be committed to obeying them to the best of one's abilities.[80] One particularly important way of expressing repentance was participation in

---

75. Sanders, *Judaism*, 275-78.

76. Greg Forbes has argued that several of the parables attributed to Jesus in Luke's Gospel portray God in a way that is in continuity with the understanding of God that appears in the Hebrew Scriptures, yet stands in contrast with the view of God found in certain circles of Judaism in Jesus' day (*The God of Old: The Role of the Lukan Parables in the Purpose of Luke's Gospel*; JSNTSup 198; Sheffield: Sheffield Academic Press, 2000, 261-306).

77. Sanders, *Jesus and Judaism*, 200-204.

78. According to Sanders, "Jesus did not call sinners to repent as normally understood, which involved restitution and/or sacrifice, but rather to accept his message, which promised them the kingdom" (*Jesus and Judaism*, 210).

79. See, for example, Bruce D. Chilton, "Jesus and the Repentance of E.P. Sanders," *TynB* 39 (1988): 1-18; Allison, "Jesus and the Covenant," 57-78.

80. As Daniel Falk notes, knowledge and observance of the Torah were thought to be a prerequisite for repentance, though both of these things were regarded as a gift graciously given by God ("Prayers and Psalms," in *Justification*, ed. Carson et al., 1:22).

the activities carried out at the temple in Jerusalem, in particular the offering of sacrifices for sin and the Day of Atonement rites.

Many scholars suppose that Jesus must have understood repentance in the same way as other Jews,[81] yet there are good reasons for rejecting such a supposition. Consideration of this question is complicated both by the difficulties involved in defining what the Mosaic law was thought to command regarding repentance and how obedience to that law was understood. Undoubtedly, Jesus desired that sinners return to a life in conformity with the general moral principles of the Mosaic law. According to the Gospels, however, rather than simply insisting on the need to obey the commandments given by Moses, he called on people to believe in the gospel he proclaimed and to follow him. As we shall see in the next section, Jesus' understanding of obedience to the law seems to have been different from that of his critics.

On this basis, there seems to be some truth to Sanders's claim that Jesus did not generally call to repentance those regarded as sinners. The main reason for this, however, seems to have been that most would have understood such a call in terms of turning back to a God who was distinct from the God proclaimed by Jesus. When Jesus' critics condemned as sinners many of those with whom he entered into table fellowship, they did so in the name of the God of the system and the status quo that they defended and proclaimed.[82] Both Jesus and those "sinners" with whom he enjoyed fellowship would therefore have regarded not only the God of Jesus' critics as oppressive but those who proclaimed that God as well. To accept their call to repentance would by definition involve accepting at the same time not only their view of God but also their definition of who was a sinner and who was righteous.

For this reason, while Jesus seems to have preached the need to repent, he apparently did not call others to repent in the sense in which other Jewish leaders understood repentance. In fact, he may have avoided to some extent the language of repentance precisely because he thought that those hearing him would associate that language with the understanding of repentance that he questioned. Undoubtedly, Jesus wanted *all people* to repent in the sense of recommitting themselves to living in accordance with God's will as he understood it whenever they had behaved in ways that ran contrary to that will. This would have been true as well for those whom others labeled "sinners." The Gospels do, of course, present Jesus calling others to repent and teaching on the subject of repentance. Luke also mentions two individuals whose actions in response to Jesus' ministry can be understood as an expression of repentance: the sinful woman who washed his feet and Zacchaeus (Luke 7:36-50; 19:1-10). However, because Jesus proclaimed a God who was

---

81. I would question, for example, the claim of Crossley that, for Jesus, repentance involved bringing people back to observance of the commandments, at least as they were commonly interpreted at the time (*Why Christianity Happened*, 91-92).

82. On this understanding of Jesus' practice of table fellowship with those labeled "sinners," see especially Borg, *Conflict*, 92-134. Borg comments that Jesus' practices in this regard represented a protest against the oppressive structures in place (134).

distinct from the oppressive God of his critics, when he called on others to repent, he sought that they turn to the God he proclaimed and represented rather than the God whom his critics proclaimed and represented.[83]

According to Jesus' practice as it is presented in the Gospels, Jesus also disagreed with other Jewish groups regarding the way in which sinners were to be brought back to God in repentance. From what we know of groups such as the Essenes and the Qumran community, it seems that a common practice in Jesus' day was for those who considered themselves righteous to avoid contact with those who failed to conform to their understanding of the norms of conduct dictated by God. This involved shunning and ostracizing those whom they regarded as sinners. Jesus' critics expected him to do the same and on that basis rejected his practice of openly receiving those deemed sinners into fellowship with himself.[84]

Jesus' practice of seeking out fellowship with those whom others labeled "sinners" seems to have been something he engaged in intentionally and deliberately. Just as he rejected the path of asceticism and chose to reach out to the general populace through his itinerant ministry rather than waiting for others to come to him, so also he appears to have taken pains to seek out actively those whom the society and its leaders had rejected as sinners. This must be seen as an expression of love and concern for others on his part. If Jesus wanted those considered sinners to change, he believed that the way to make this happen was not to condemn or ostracize them as others did, but to accept and befriend them.

If the words attributed to Jesus in Mark 2:17 (Matt. 9:12-13; Luke 5:31-32) are accepted as authentic, this would explain in large part Jesus' attitude toward those whom others considered sinners. There Jesus says that he came "not to call the righteous but sinners," since "it is not those who are well who need a physician but those who are ill." To speak of sinners as "those who are ill" would be to conceive of them as persons who need help and support rather than requiring censure and condemnation. When Jesus showed acceptance toward those ostracized by others as sinners, he was not condoning any sinful behavior on their part, but viewing them in the same way that a physician views those who need to be restored to health. He sought to establish relations of solidarity with them so that he might help bring them to live in ways that contributed to their own well-being as well as that of others.

A second way in which Jesus appears to have differed from his critics on the subject of repentance is that he insisted that all without exception were

---

83. In principle, I would therefore agree with Tobias Hägerland that Jesus did preach repentance, but did not uphold the customary rites of repentance ("Jesus and the Rites of Repentance," *NTS* 52 [2006]: 166-87). Nevertheless, from my perspective, what Jesus questioned was not so much the customary rites, but the concept of God that had come to be associated with those rites among many Jews under the influence of the religious leaders.

84. Jesus seems to have believed that, in order for people to turn to God, it was necessary first to show them God's love and acceptance, rather than insisting that they first turn back to God as a condition for accepting them. Meyer summarizes Jesus' "revolutionary contact and communion with sinners" in terms of "communion first, conversion second" (*Aims*, 160-61). On this point, see also Meier, *Marginal Jew*, 2:148-49.

equally in need of repentance as he had come to redefine it. This included especially those who considered themselves more righteous than others. Whether or not Jesus actually told the parable of the Pharisee and the tax or toll collector (Luke 18:9-14), there can be little doubt that it reflects his thought: the real sinners were those who looked down on others and rejected them in God's name, claiming to be superior to them, as the Pharisee of the parable did. In contrast, those who acknowledged their sinfulness and their need for God's grace, mercy, and assistance as the tax collector did were in reality righteous. This was because their attitude made it possible for them to receive the help necessary to be brought into conformity with God's will. In contrast, the attitude of those who presumed to be already living fully in accordance with God's will, such as the Pharisee of the parable, made it impossible for them to recognize that they too needed to change their conduct. From the perspective of the parable, it was not only the Pharisee who was unjust and oppressive, but also the God in whom he believed and to whom he prayed. His was a very different God than the God of the tax collector, who was also the God whom Jesus proclaimed.[85]

Many New Testament interpreters have claimed that Jesus' saying about having come to call not the righteous but sinners should be understood in the sense that he believed that leaders such as the scribes and Pharisees were not sinful or unrighteous, and therefore were not in need of repentance or a "physician."[86] The simple fact that those who believed Jesus was sinning by entering into fellowship with persons whom they considered sinners while Jesus believed he was doing what God desired and commanded is sufficient evidence that such a claim is untenable. If Jesus believed that it was God's will that one enter into fellowship with sinners, and his critics not only refused to do so themselves, but condemned him for doing so, then they were sinning by rejecting Jesus and refusing to do God's will as Jesus understood it. Their behavior was contrary to God's will, not only because of the way they condemned and ostracized others as sinners, but also because they opposed Jesus for doing what according to him was God's will. This means that, from Jesus' perspective, his critics were also to be included among those who were ill and in need of a physician.[87] As the parable of the Pharisee and the tax collector

---

85. As William R. Herzog II notes, a central element of the parable is that, by depersonalizing and dehumanizing the toll collector, the Pharisee "participates in the systematic, institutionalized violence originating from the Temple" (*Parables as Subversive Speech: Jesus as Pedagogue of the Oppressed*; Louisville, KY: Westminster John Knox, 1994, 191).

86. Craig Evans, for example, interprets Mark 2:17 in the sense that "Jesus understands his ministry in terms of a call to those who are truly sick and those who are truly sinners. Scribes and Pharisees who faithfully observe the Torah are among the righteous...." ("Who Touched Me? Jesus and the Ritually Impure," in *Jesus in Context*, Chilton and Evans, 354). Likewise, Taylor affirms that, for Jesus, "Pharisees are among those who have not gotten lost or strayed from home" (*Immerser*, 202). From my perspective, it is astonishing that anyone who reads through the canonical Gospels, including especially passages such as Matthew 23, could conclude that Jesus did not regard the Jewish religious leaders and teachers as sinners. It is they who consistently bear the brunt of his criticisms and accusations of sinful behavior.

87. Borg rightly notes regarding those who claimed to be righteous as God's representatives, but in reality practiced oppression and injustice: "the healthy were not healthy after all. Therefore, one cannot claim that the

shows, for Jesus those who claimed to be righteous were in reality sinners, whereas those who acknowledged their need for help and were willing to draw near to Jesus to receive that help were in reality righteous in God's eyes.[88]

Numerous other passages in the Gospels present Jesus condemning the scribes and Pharisees for oppressing others and committing injustices through their hypocrisy and interpretations of the law.[89] This idea is so widespread throughout the Jesus tradition that it seems fairly certain that there were at least some scribes and Pharisees whom Jesus condemned as oppressive. Even if those Jesus condemned were not representative of these groups taken as a whole, Jesus would have expected that other members of these groups concur openly with his views and join him in condemning and denouncing the hypocrisy and oppression committed by some within their ranks. It appears to be doubtful that this happened, and if it did not, Jesus would probably have considered the behavior of those who refused to speak out as being oppressive and unjust as well. The failure of most of the scribes and Pharisees to join Jesus in rejecting openly the teaching and behavior of certain members of their groups would therefore also have led Jesus and his first followers to condemn the scribes and Pharisees as a whole, even though not all scribes and Pharisees acted in the ways that Jesus criticized.

Because Jesus regarded those who opposed him as sinners in need of repentance, he treated them differently than other sinners, condemning them harshly. This was not only because, unlike many of the other sinners with whom he entered into fellowship, Jesus' critics believed themselves to be righteous instead of acknowledging their sin. They also served as obstacles to the repentance of the sinners with whom Jesus entered into fellowship, since in the eyes of the God proclaimed by Jesus' critics, it was they who were righteous and those they condemned who were sinners. This prevented those labeled "sinners" from repenting, since to repent in the ways that Jesus' critics defined repentance was to acknowledge them as righteous and as representatives of the true God. Such repentance would also require those considered sinners to accept the label that had been placed on them, and to acknowledge as well the view of God and God's will that constituted the basis upon which they were condemned as sinners.[90] Their failure to acknowledge the God proclaimed by the religious authorities would be seen as merely confirming further the fact

---

sick were to be made like them" (*Conflict*, 109). On the idea that Jesus had in mind the Jewish leaders when he spoke of those who were ill, see also Ed Condra, *Salvation for the Righteous Revealed: Jesus amid Covenantal and Messianic Expectations in Second Temple Judaism* (AGJU 51; Leiden: Brill, 2002), 319-20.

88. Crossley's argument that, in ancient Jewish sources, the term *sinners* generally refers to the rich and powerful who exploited others would also mean that Jesus saw the Jewish leaders as those who were "ill" and needed to heed his call to repentance (*Why Christianity Happened*, 75-96, 119-21). Conversely, as Falk observes, in the Hebrew Scriptures, "The righteous are not those who by their effort have avoided sin, but those who confess their sins and seek God's mercy" ("Psalms," 42).

89. On this point, see especially Moshe Weinfeld, *Normative and Sectarian Judaism in the Second Temple Period* (LSTS 54; London: T & T Clark, 2005), 279-85. Weinfeld notes there that, in the rabbinic sources, passages that criticize the Pharisees for their hypocrisy are fairly common.

90. Jon Sobrino captures these ideas well when he writes that, in the Gospels, what Jesus requires from the oppressed is "acceptance of the fact that God is not like the image they have introjected from their oppressors

that they were sinful and godless. According to the Gospels, all of this aroused Jesus' anger not only against his critics, but also against those who refused to join with him in condemning their teaching and behavior.

Reflected in Jesus' way of relating to both the "sinners" and his critics is Jesus' teaching on love and forgiveness. According to the Gospels, Jesus taught that love for others was to be *unconditional*. Just as the God Jesus proclaimed loves all without exception, whether righteous or unrighteous, so also in Jesus' teaching it is necessary for his followers to love others unconditionally (Matt. 5:44-48; Luke 6:32-36; cf. Matt. 22:10). This principle is manifested not only in Jesus' teaching but also in his practice.

At the same time, however, Jesus is presented as teaching that, while *love for others* must be unconditional, *forgiveness* is to be *conditional*. In this regard, his teaching follows ideas regarding love and forgiveness that we have seen in Chapter 2. Undoubtedly, he tells Peter that one is to forgive others seventy times seven (Matt. 18:22; cf. Luke 17:4). This seems to imply an unconditional forgiveness. When Jesus speaks of forgiveness in this sense, he seems to have in mind the idea of not harboring hatred or ill feelings toward those who have done one harm and refraining from any attempt to take retaliation or seek revenge. According to Jesus' teaching, one is always to forgive one's enemies in the sense of continuing to love them by seeking their well-being.

Yet while in that sense one is always to forgive, in another sense one is only to forgive those who have harmed others if and when they repent and commit themselves to changing their ways. In the same immediate context in which Matthew cites Jesus' command to forgive an offender seventy times seven (Matt. 18:21-22), he presents Jesus' teaching regarding one who sins against one's brother or sister (Matt. 18:15-17). There Jesus affirms that, if an offender refuses to acknowledge his or her sin after being confronted first in private, then in the company of two or three witnesses, and finally in the presence of the entire congregation, he or she should be regarded by the members of the community "as a Gentile and a tax collector." Here forgiveness is clearly *conditional*. Jesus' words in Luke 17:3 also reflect this idea: "If another disciple sins, you must rebuke the offender, and if there is repentance, you must forgive."

The parable of the unforgiving servant that Jesus tells immediately after telling Peter that one must forgive an offender seventy times seven illustrates the same ideas (Matt. 18:23-35). On the one hand, like the king in the parable, God forgives freely those who cannot pay their debts. On the other hand, however, God expects those forgiven to forgive others freely as well; when they refuse to do so, God revokes the forgiveness he had granted them. The parable thus teaches that one is *always* to forgive in the way God forgives, yet also presents a God who does *not* forgive those who refuse to forgive others: after the king of the parable has the servant who refused to forgive his co-servant cast into prison and tells him that he will not be released until he

---

and the ruling class culture...." (*Jesus the Liberator: A Historical-Theological Reading of Jesus of Nazareth*, trans. Paul Burns and Francis McDonagh; Maryknoll, NY: Orbis, 1993, 97).

has paid his entire debt, the parable concludes with Jesus affirming: "So my heavenly Father will also do to every one of you, if you do not forgive your brother or sister from your heart."

In other contexts, Jesus repeats the same idea: God forgives those who forgive others but does not forgive those who refuse to forgive others (Matt. 6:12, 14-15; Mark 11:25-26; Luke 6:37; 11:4).[91] Therefore, in Jesus' teaching, while God's *love* is *unconditional*, God's *forgiveness* is *conditional* upon one treating others in the way God desires and commands.

The logic of Jesus' teaching is not difficult to grasp. To love others unconditionally is to seek at all times their well-being, together with the well-being of others and oneself. Out of love, one is always to forgive offenders in the sense of remaining committed to seeking their well-being, rather than desiring or attempting to do them harm in response to the offenses they have committed. However, for their own good and the good of others, one is also to demand that they stop doing others harm and change their ways in order to practice instead love toward all. If they do not do so, steps must be taken either to continue to insist that they repent and change or, when necessary, to attempt to impede them in some way from continuing to treat others unjustly and do them harm. To treat offenders in this way is not to act contrary to love, since one remains committed to their well-being, as well as to the well-being of others affected by their behavior.

For this reason, when Jesus angrily criticizes and condemns the scribes and Pharisees in passages such as Matthew 23, reproaching them for their oppressive behavior and for committing tremendous injustices while pretending to be acting as God's servants, in reality he is acting out of love (cf. Mark 12:38-40; Luke 11:37-54; 20:45-47). His purpose is not only to defend those affected negatively by the behavior of the scribes and Pharisees, but to provoke a change of behavior in the scribes and Pharisees themselves for their own good (Matt. 23:26). In spite of the harshness of Jesus' words, therefore, they are an expression of love and concern both for those whom he castigates, as well as others who learn from Jesus' words not to act as the scribes and

---

91. E. P. Sanders is entirely mistaken when he affirms that Matt. 6:14-15 ("For if you forgive others their trespasses, your heavenly Father will also forgive you; but if you do not forgive others, neither will your Father forgive your trespasses") "is the clearest single expression... of the view that forgiveness can be bought by a good deed" (*Comparing Judaism and Christianity: Common Judaism, Paul, and the Inner and Outer in the Study of Religion*; Minneapolis: Fortress, 2016, 76). What obtains God's forgiveness is repentance and a recommitment to living in accordance with his will. One aspect of this will is that believers are always to forgive in the sense of not seeking to harm those who have harmed them. Those who forgive others are not "buying" God's forgiveness, but manifesting their commitment to doing God's will, and this makes them acceptable to God, who wants all people to live according to his will, not for *his* sake, but for *their own*. However, because God cannot be manipulated by human beings and always looks into their hearts to see if they are truly acting out of love for him and others, any who attempt to put God under obligation to forgive them by forgiving others are not acting in conformity with God's will. Their act of forgiveness is not acceptable to God because, in God's eyes, forgiveness must arise out of love for others; otherwise it is not truly forgiveness. If the "forgiveness" they offer another is an attempt to "buy" God's forgiveness, it is unpleasing to God not only because such "forgiveness" does not arise out of true love for God and others but also because it is motivated by a desire to manipulate God in order to obtain his forgiveness.

Pharisees do, and not to submit passively to those who mistreat them. Instead, they are to raise their voice to defend themselves and others. This does not involve desiring the wrongdoers ill or attempting to harm them, but demanding that they put an end to their oppressive and unjust ways.[92]

Jesus' Focus on Justice and the Conflicts over the Mosaic Law

Like the word "salvation," "justice" can be understood in many different ways. As we have noted in Chapter 2, in the Hebrew Scriptures the stress is generally on *distributive* justice: justice exists when the needs of all are met and all are able to live full lives instead of suffering. *Retributive* justice has the goal of promoting *distributive* justice. This understanding of justice is thus intimately tied to the concept of *shalom* or wholeness, which involves human well-being in a general sense. Justice therefore can be said to exist when all enjoy *shalom* individually and collectively.

This same understanding of justice must be seen as running throughout Jesus' teaching and practice. As I have argued above, Jesus' ministry was aimed primarily at seeking the wholeness and well-being of others. According to the Gospels, however, this emphasis led to conflicts with other Jewish teachers in that it led Jesus to interpret God's will in ways that ran contrary to their own understanding of God's will. In general terms, from their perspective, God's will was to be identified with a strict adherence to the commandments given by Moses both in their written form and in the form of the oral tradition that had been passed down to them.

In recent decades, scholars have dedicated a great deal of attention to the subject of Jesus' views regarding the Mosaic law. They have discussed extensively how Jesus interpreted the law, the extent to which his interpretations were in continuity or discontinuity with other interpretations of his day, whether Jesus himself was obedient to the Jewish law, and whether he declared the law to be abrogated or superseded in some sense.[93] For our purposes here, it is not necessary to enter into discussions regarding these questions. From my perspective, many of those discussions are not only irrelevant and anachronistic, but also misguided in that they assume certain definitions of what it meant to observe the Jewish law and on that basis then debate whether Jesus was law-observant.[94] The question is not whether Jesus considered the

---

92. In general terms, I would agree with Wink that, when Jesus teaches his disciples to respond to aggression by "turning the other cheek," he has in mind not the passive acceptance of injustice, but seeking to preserve one's dignity and neutralize the power of the oppressor ("Neither Passivity Nor Violence," 102-25).

93. On these discussions, see especially John P. Meier, *A Marginal Jew: Rethinking the Historical Jesus*, Vol. 4, *Law and Love* (AYBRL; New Haven, CT: Yale University Press, 2009), 40-47; Klawans, *Impurity*, 144-46; Roger P. Booth, *Jesus and the Laws of Purity: Tradition History and Legal History in Mark 7* (JSNTSup 13; Sheffield: JSOT, 1986), 109-12.

94. On the problem of speaking about observance of the Mosaic law in Jesus' day, see Karin Hedner Zetterholm, "The Question of Assumptions: Torah Observance in the First Century," in *Paul within Judaism: Restoring the First-Century Context to the Apostle* (ed. Mark D. Nanos and Magnus Zetterholm; Minneapolis: Fortress, 2015), 79-90. Zetterholm rightly notes that "Torah observance means different things to different groups and people, and, accordingly, different people define a violation of Torah observance differently" (80).

Mosaic law a valid expression of God's will and taught that it was necessary to observe it, but *how* he understood the law and its proper observance. In addition, behind many of the contemporary scholarly discussions on this subject are concerns and interests regarding how Jews and Christians today should relate to one another.[95] It is important to set these aside if we are to attempt to understand Jesus' own views regarding the law and God's will.

In addressing the question of Jesus' teaching regarding the Mosaic law, from the outset it is important to stress that what we today call the Jewish law or Torah did not yet exist in a fixed form in Jesus' day.[96] While this is true with regard to its written form, since the biblical texts were still in a fluid state, it is especially true with regard to the oral traditions that served as a basis for defining and interpreting the law. Simply stated, this means that what the different parties and groups in Palestine and the diaspora understood as "the law" or Torah varied considerably. For this reason, it is anachronistic to ask whether Jesus observed, upheld, or abrogated the law, since no uniform definition of the law existed. In a sense, there was no Jewish law or Torah, but only different interpretations of the commandments found in the Pentateuch and different understandings of what constituted God's will.[97]

Once this is clear, we can grasp the fact that the debates between Jesus and the religious leaders of his day over what was "lawful" were simply *debates over how God's will was to be understood*. In this case, it matters little whether or not activities such as healing and plucking grain on the Sabbath were understood by Jews in antiquity as forms of work that were prohibited by the law, or whether or not Jesus' teaching regarding purity ran contrary to other interpretations of the Mosaic commandments that were prevalent in his day. Ultimately, what matters is not whether Jesus practiced obedience to the commandments as interpreted by others in antiquity and taught others to follow his same approach to those commandments, but how he interpreted God's will. Thus, for example, rather than debating the question of whether Jesus' practice of healing on the Sabbath was considered a violation of the Sabbath commandment, we must ask how and why his understanding of God's will in that context differed from those who criticized him.

---

95. On this point, see John P. Meier, "The Historical Jesus and the Historical Law: Some Problems within the Problem," *CBQ* 65 (2003): 52-79; see especially 53.

96. In this regard, Meier comments that "the very concept of Torah, even the written Torah of Moses, was still in flux at the time of Jesus," and that "the Hebrew text of the Mosaic Law circulating in Palestine around the turn of the era contained variant readings...." ("The Historical Jesus," 55-56). Those groups that held the law in esteem even felt free to rewrite certain laws to coincide with their practices, considered their own traditions normative, and claimed that "the written Law of Moses contained important commandments that, from our historical perspective, simply are not there in the text" (57-58).

97. Richard Horsley notes that different views and practices regarding the law existed not only in Judaism in general or Palestine, but in Galilee itself: "no standardized Jewish Torah or Law would have been known in Galilean villages at the time of Jesus' mission and the development of early Jesus movements" (*Hearing the Whole Story: The Politics of Plot in Mark's Gospel*; Louisville, KY: Westminster John Knox, 2001, 156-60). Evans also observes that in Jesus' day "differing interpretations of the purity laws of Torah set one faction, or one individual, apart from another" ("Who Touched Me?," 356).

This brings us back to the question of Jesus' authority and the concern for the well-being of others that lay at the heart of all of the different aspects of his ministry. Whatever view Jesus had of the Mosaic commandments, and whatever authority and validity he ascribed to them, ultimately what mattered to him was justice in the sense just defined above. For Jesus, to do God's will was to seek the wholeness and well-being of all. It was this definition of God's will that placed Jesus in conflict with those who defined God's will differently on the basis of their understanding of the Mosaic commandments.

Throughout the Gospels, what constantly occupies Jesus' attention is not discussions regarding the law, but his proclamation and teaching with regard to God's reign as well as his concern for the well-being of others, which derives from his understanding of God's reign. In fact, outside of the sermons attributed to Jesus in Matthew 5–7 and Luke 6:20-49, Jesus rarely brings up the subject of the law at his own initiative. Instead, it is his opponents who direct questions to Jesus related to the interpretation of the law and accuse Jesus of acting in ways that represent a violation of the Mosaic commandments.

When Jesus discusses obedience to God and the commandments God has given and responds to the objections and criticisms of his adversaries, the Gospels consistently present him as emphasizing above all else the need to be concerned for human well-being. This principle lies at the heart of his interpretation of the law and overrides all other concerns.[98] What matters for Jesus is practicing justice, mercy, love, truth, compassion, and solidarity. Fulfillment of the commandments that prohibit murder and adultery involves not only obeying those commandments in a literal sense but refraining from harming and offending others or seeing them as objects to be used for one's own selfish desires (Matt. 5:21-30). Love for others involves speaking the truth without having to swear oaths and not pronouncing judgment on others (Matt. 5:33-37; 7:1-5; Luke 6:37-38, 41-42).[99] At the heart of the law are the commandments to love God with all of one's being and to love others as one loves oneself (Matt. 22:37-40; Mark 12:28-34; Luke 10:25-28). Those who claim to adhere strictly to the law but fail to practice justice, mercy, faith, and love of God are in fact disobeying the law (Matt. 23:23; Luke 11:42).

According to the Gospels, for Jesus the Sabbath is properly observed when it serves to meet human needs and one seeks to do good and to save life rather than to do harm or to kill (Mark 2:23—3:6).[100] Human beings were not

---

98. Numerous scholars have stressed this point. See, for example, Borg, *Conflict*, 6-8; Steven M. Bryan, *Jesus and Israel's Traditions of Judgement and Restoration* (SNTSMS 117; Cambridge: Cambridge University Press, 2002), 177; Richard Bauckham, "The Scrupulous Priest and the Good Samaritan: Jesus' Parabolic Interpretation of the Law of Moses," *NTS* 44 (1998): 475-89; see especially 484-85; Robert J. Banks, *Jesus and the Law in the Synoptic Tradition* (SNTSMS 28; Cambridge: Cambridge University Press, 1975), 99, 242-44.

99. On Jesus' teaching regarding oaths and its relation to Jewish practice in antiquity, see especially Holmén, *Jesus*, 170-87; Meier, *Marginal Jew*, 4:188-206.

100. As numerous scholars have stressed, in Jesus' mind, he was not violating the Sabbath or setting aside Sabbath observance, but interpreting differently what proper observance of the Sabbath consisted of; see Zeitlin, *Jesus*, 73-77; Dale Allison Jr., *Resurrecting Jesus: The Earliest Christian Tradition and its Interpreters* (New York: T & T Clark, 2005), 160-61, 183-84, 195; Horsley, *Hearing*, 166; Thomas Kazen, *Scripture, Interpretation*,

created for the sake of the Sabbath, but the Sabbath for the sake of human beings, since the purpose of the Sabbath is to promote human well-being (Mark 2:27). According to Jesus, what makes one truly impure is not what one eats or drinks, but the evil intentions that proceed from one's heart and lead to violence, falsehood, injustice, and the mistreatment and abuse of others (Matt. 15:10-20; Mark 7:14-23).[101] Here as elsewhere, Jesus does not reject the distinction between pure and impure, but merely insists that any concern for purity must have at its root a concern for human well-being, which is what ultimately matters.[102] Similarly, for Jesus it is acceptable to enter into physical contact with those who according to the law are impure when one is seeking to restore them to health and wholeness (Matt. 8:1-4; 9:20-22; Mark 1:40-45; 5:25-34; Luke 5:12-16; 8:43-48).[103] While it is right and proper to tithe and present offerings to God, those who do so must first concern themselves with being at peace with others and not use their observance of those commandments as a pretext to justify the failure to fulfill their responsibilities in relation to their parents and others (Matt. 5:23-24; 15:3-6; Mark 7:9-13).[104] Marriage is to be held in respect as something God has ordained for human well-being, and men are not to mistreat their wives by dismissing them unjustly (Matt. 5:31-32; 19:1-12; Mark 10:1-12; Luke 16:18).[105]

---

or Authority? Motives and Arguments in Jesus' Halakic Conflicts (WUNT 320; Tübingen: Mohr Siebeck, 2013), 105-9. Jesus' claim to be "Lord of the sabbath" (Matt. 12:8; Mark 2:27; Luke 6:5) also communicates the idea that he was in some sense above the Sabbath commandment and had authority over it, yet it is not clear to what extent such an idea actually goes back to Jesus.

101. Many scholars have pointed out that Mark 7:15, 19 provides no evidence that Jesus himself abrogated the Mosaic commandments regarding food. Rather, he simply interpreted these commandments against the background of his overall understanding of what proper observance of the law consisted of; see Klawans, *Impurity*, 147; Holmén, *Jesus*, 221-51; Peter J. Tomson, "Halakhah in the New Testament: A Research Overview," in *The New Testament and Rabbinic Literature* (ed. Reimund Bieringer et al.; JSJSup 136; Leiden: Brill, 2010), 264-68. Most scholars would agree with Fiensy that the notion that "Jesus is discarding ritual purity altogether" in Mark 7 is "Mark's conclusion as he interprets these words for his community years later. Jesus, himself, did not ever say that all food was clean or kosher" (*Jesus*, 184; see 181-86).

102. Fiensy has argued that Jesus must have kept ritual purity as commonly understood in his time, especially if he entered the temple, since all those entering there had to purify themselves by bathing (*Jesus*, 177-78).

103. In this regard, Jesus' practice once again stresses that concerns for human well-being override or even fulfill concerns for purity; see Holmén, *Jesus*, 232-35; Evans, "Who Touched Me?," 365-70.

104. While on the one hand Jesus does not appear to have been greatly concerned about tithing, as Holmén has argued (*Jesus*, 127-28), he may also have opposed the practice among those he served in Galilee because it impoverished them and instead contributed to the enrichment of the Jerusalem elites; see Horsley, *Hearing*, 170; Herzog, *Parables*, 181-82.

105. I would argue that the use of the term *divorce* to discuss Jesus' teaching in passages such as those indicated from the Synoptics is anachronistic. The Greek speaks of dismissing one's spouse or putting one's spouse away. This is quite different from divorce practices and laws today. For a background on Jewish beliefs and practices in this regard and Jesus' teaching on the subject, see especially Meier, *Marginal Jew*, 4:102-28; Peter J. Tomson, "Divorce Halakhah in Paul and the Jesus Tradition," in *The New Testament and Rabbinic Literature*, ed. Bieringer, 289-332. Some scholars have argued that Jesus' prohibition of dismissing one's wife was based on a concern for the abusive practices of men in relation to their wives (see, for example, Phillip Sigal, *The Halakhah of Jesus of Nazareth according to the Gospel of Matthew*; SBLSBL 18; Atlanta: SBL, 2007, 105-43). Many scholars reject such an idea, however. Others such as Horsley have argued that the "divorce question" was really political, since the peasantry was affected adversely by the maneuvering for position and power that took place among the elite through marriage and remarriage (see *Hearing*, 173).

Once again, for our purposes, there is no point in discussing in detail here to what extent the Gospel accounts of Jesus' teaching on these points and the conflicts that arose between Jesus and his critics are historically accurate. What matters is that, taken as a whole, these passages provide abundant evidence that Jesus was remembered as one who was in disagreement and often in conflict with the Jewish leaders of his day over questions pertaining to the law. Furthermore, in all of the passages just mentioned, Jesus' understanding of God's will is consistently seen as being based on a *concern for justice* as defined above, that is, the well-being of all, and particularly those in greatest need. When seen against the background of the social, political, and economic system of the time, Jesus' words must also be understood as expressing a concern not only for just and loving relationships between individuals, but also for an alternative order or community based on the notions of love, justice, and solidarity.

Many of the ethical demands that Jesus made on others were not derived from the Mosaic law. The most important of these was the demand to follow him. This demand implies that those who obey Jesus' command to follow him are doing God's will, while those who consciously reject Jesus are at the same time rejecting God's will.[106] As Sanders has argued, Jesus even seems to have regarded the command to follow him as overriding other obligations that were considered sacred, such as obeying one's parents under every circumstance and burying a parent who had passed away.[107] It should be remembered, however, that because Jesus was committed to serving others and seeking their wholeness and well-being, when he commanded others to lay aside other concerns and obligations in order to follow him, he was demanding from them his same commitment to the wholeness and well-being of others. Therefore, in calling others to follow him, his concern once more was not for himself, but for others, and particularly for justice and human well-being, which took precedence over everything else.

---

106. Banks, for example, has argued that Jesus' command to follow him is unparalleled in the Judaism of his day. He contrasts the reverence displayed for the "teacher of righteousness" reflected in some of the writings from Qumran with the way in which Jesus defined the relationship of his followers to himself: "there is no parallel to the type of ministry exercised by Jesus or the kind of allegiance demanded by him.... Most significant is the culmination of Jesus' instruction in the command to follow him, a call to a life of discipleship for which no real parallel can be found in the rabbinic writings" (*Jesus*, 261-62). Bruce Chilton and Jacob Neusner have similarly stressed that discipleship to Jesus was not to be equated with discipleship to the Torah (*Judaism in the New Testament: Practices and Beliefs*; London: Routledge, 1995, 159). Some scholars have argued that Jesus placed following him above all else, not because of his views regarding his own identity, but primarily out of a concern for the urgency of the mission in which he was involved with his followers; see Markus Bockmuehl, "Halakhah and Ethics in the Jesus Tradition," in *Early Christian Thought*, ed. Barclay and Sweet, 273.

107. For Sanders, Jesus' command to "let the dead bury the dead" was based on the idea that following him was more important than observing the law. Jesus thereby challenged "the adequacy of the Mosaic dispensation" (*Jesus and Judaism*, 255). Other scholars, however, have claimed that Jesus' words to the man who wished to bury his father before following Jesus were not intended in a general sense as applying to all people, but were merely a response to a particular situation in which the man was attempting to justify a lack of full commitment to following Jesus; see Géza Vermès, *The Religion of Jesus the Jew* (Minneapolis: Fortress, 1993), 27-29; Allison, *Resurrecting Jesus*, 169-70.

Of course, Jesus was in no way unique in giving emphasis to the principles underlying the commandments, including especially the commandment to love others. The same emphasis ran throughout Jewish teaching regarding the law. As we saw in Chapter 2, it was generally acknowledged that the commandments themselves were an expression of God's love for the people, designed to promote their well-being, and that they needed to be interpreted on the basis of that concern.[108] This means that those who insisted on a strict literal observance of the commandments as they understood them could also appeal to the same principle.[109] If God had commanded that people rest on the Sabbath for their own well-being, then it was important to obey that law strictly, rather than to make the type of exceptions that Jesus was making and justify them on the basis of the same principle that lay behind the law.[110]

Therefore, whether Jesus called into question some of the interpretations of the Mosaic law of the Jewish leaders with whom he came into conflict or merely refused to accept the validity of their oral tradition, clearly Jesus defined God's will in a way that distinguished him from them.[111] This becomes particularly clear when we compare other Jewish writings of the time with the way in which the Gospels present Jesus. Many of the writings from Qumran, for example, contain extensive rules and regulations regarding all sorts of legal questions, including especially those having to do with purity. While it is not clear how much of the material in the Mishnah goes back in some form to Jesus' day, the tone of the discussions is entirely different from what we find in Jesus' teaching as it is presented in the Gospels.[112] One can hardly imagine Jesus propounding anything such as the Community Rule of Qumran or the detailed regulations found in the Mishnah. The later rabbinic idea that one should obey

---

108. See, for example, Scot McKnight, "Jesus' New Vision within Judaism," in *Who Was Jesus?*, ed. Copan and Evans, 90: "Jesus' teaching on love is fundamentally and thoroughly Jewish. He may have given love a centrality not otherwise attested in Judaism, but what he says about love is from Judaism." Although Jesus can be said to appeal to "higher principles" in his disputes with others regarding law-observance, Bockmuehl rightly stresses that these were "'higher principles' *within the Torah*...." ("Halakhah," 267). Nevertheless, Serge Ruzer has argued that, while there are points of agreement between Jesus' teaching and other Jewish sources that also stress love as fulfillment of law, there are also significant differences ("The Double Love Precept in the New Testament and the *Community Rule*," in *Jesus' Last Week*, ed. Notley, Turnage, and Becker, 81-104).

109. Weinfeld rightly points out that the insistence that the letter of the law needed to be observed strictly and meticulously was also derived from the notion that love for God and neighbor was at the heart of the law (*Normative and Sectarian Judaism*, 293). The point in question, therefore, was not whether love constituted the fulfillment of the law, but what forms that love was to take.

110. As James Dunn observes, the debate between Jesus and his critics was not about *whether* the Sabbath should be observed but only *how* (*The Parting of the Ways Between Christianity and Judaism and Their Significance for the Character of Christianity*, London: SCM, 1991, 114).

111. Scholars have expressed the difference between Jesus' understanding of the law and that of other Jews in various ways. Meyer speaks of Jesus' "scandalous view that the Torah as it stands does not suffice" and his "radicalization of Torah prescriptions" (*Aims*, 144). Sanders alludes to Jesus' "sovereign freedom" over the law, which he did not consider "final or absolutely binding" (*Jesus and Judaism*, 267). Banks claims that Jesus' view of the law "moves in a different realm" and that his teaching "transcends the Law" (*Jesus*, 141, 233). Meier characterizes Jesus' approach to the law as "ad-hoc" and "freewheeling" (*Marginal Jew*, 3:525; 4:655).

112. Meier outlines the significant differences between Jesus' interpretation of the law and the interpretations found in the writings of Qumran, noting, for example, Jesus' lack of interest in details of halakah, the minutiae of the law, and questions related to the Jewish calendar (*Marginal Jew*, 3:522-32).

each commandment of the law faithfully even if one does not understand its purpose would have also been entirely foreign to Jesus' thought.[113]

Many scholars have argued that during his lifetime and ministry Jesus was careful to observe the law as it was commonly understood, including the commandments regarding purity, and expected his disciples to be fully law-observant as well. According to these scholars, if certain passages from the Gospels present Jesus as disregarding the law or even abrogating certain commandments, this is because those passages represent the practices of some of the communities of his followers several decades after Jesus' death, rather than those of Jesus himself. However, if we look at the rest of the writings collected in the New Testament, we find essentially the same approach to the law that we find in the teaching and practice attributed to Jesus in the Gospels. This approach to the law seems to be rooted in the Jesus-tradition, where we repeatedly encounter not only a certain flexibility with regard to the literal observance of certain commandments, but also an almost total lack of interest in entering into debates and discussions regarding legal questions, as noted above.[114] There is good reason, therefore, to suppose that these general tendencies found throughout the early Christian tradition derive from the teaching and practice of Jesus himself.[115]

At the heart of the conflicts between Jesus and other Jewish leaders over questions related to the Jewish law are once again two very different visions of God and God's will. The God proclaimed by Jesus approved of Jesus' actions that were rejected by Jesus' critics, while their God rejected Jesus' actions as unacceptable and as a violation of the commandments he had given through Moses.[116] These conflicting visions of God also represented different visions for what society should look like and how people should relate to one another. If the Jewish leaders who were critical of Jesus' actions were recognized as authorities in the society of that time, then they would probably have maintained that God had determined that Jewish society should look as it did. This would involve supporting and maintaining the status quo. Even if they were critical of the social reality as it existed under Roman rule and rejected it as

---

113. On this idea in rabbinic thought, see Sanders, *Paul and Palestinian Judaism: A Comparison of Patterns of Religion* (Philadelphia: Fortress, 1977), 120.

114. On the relative indifference that Jesus shows with regard to matters of the law in the Gospels, see Holmén, *Jesus*, 102-5, 249-51. Crossan has also written that Jesus "did not care enough about such ritual laws either to attack or to acknowledge them. He ignored them, but that, of course, was to subvert them at a most fundamental level" (*Historical Jesus*, 263).

115. It has been common for scholars to point to Matt. 5:17-19, where Jesus says that he has come not to abolish the law but to fulfill it and claims that not a jot or tittle of the law will pass away in the present age, to argue that Jesus taught that the whole law must be observed carefully. Nevertheless, as a number of scholars have shown, the words attributed there to Jesus can be interpreted in other senses that do not imply that Jesus was insisting on a strict, literal observance of each of the commandments of the law. See, for example, Sigal, *Halakhah*, 24-27; Serge Ruzer, *Mapping the New Testament: Early Christian Writings as a Witness for Jewish Biblical Exegesis* (JCPS 13; Leiden: Brill, 2007), 17.

116. As Evans notes, Jesus' failure to observe the rules of purity as these were commonly interpreted in the Judaism of his day would have been seen as implying that he had "little regard for God" and even was failing to respect God ("Who Touched Me?," 357). The same could be said regarding other aspects of Jesus' practice and teaching regarding the law.

divinely ordained, the basis for their criticism of that reality and their proposal for a different reality nevertheless represented a vision that was distinct from that of Jesus. Jesus would also have regarded their interpretations of the law, not only as mistaken, but as oppressive.[117]

JESUS' FINAL DAYS IN JERUSALEM

Why did Jesus go up to Jerusalem at the end of his ministry? Albert Schweitzer posited two possible answers to that question: to work or to die. Schweitzer himself argued in favor of the latter alternative.[118] In reality, however, a wide variety of answers are possible. Jesus may simply have desired to visit the city or the temple, perhaps to celebrate Passover there.[119] While it is highly doubtful that he planned to lead an armed uprising, his motivation may have been to carry out an act of prophetic protest in the temple, confront the Jerusalem leadership in some way, or carry out a mission related to his work for justice and equity. Some have thought that his intention was to renew or reform the sacrificial cult as practiced in the Jerusalem temple, or even to establish there a system of worship that would constitute an alternative to that practiced at the temple.[120] It is possible that he wanted to continue his ministry of preaching and teaching and even healing there, particularly since Jerusalem was regarded as the spiritual and symbolic center of Israel. Jesus may have considered his work in Galilee as completed, either because he had accomplished what he desired there or because he felt it would not advance any further.[121] In that case, he wanted to move on elsewhere. He could have gone up to Jerusalem hoping to gain more followers or to be acclaimed king or savior. It is even possible that he felt drawn by God to Jerusalem without knowing why. In theory, any of these or other motivations are possible.

All four of the Gospels affirm that Jesus knew that he would be put to death in Jerusalem and even saw this as part of a plan preordained by God. Many scholars and historians question this possibility, yet it seems likely that Jesus was at least aware that his life would be in danger there, especially in light of what he intended to do at the temple.[122] Some have thought that

---

117. If, as Brigitte Kahl claims, "the dominant interpretation of Torah was linked to temple and high-priesthood, both tightly controlled by Rome," then of course Jesus' interpretations of the law would have been regarded as opposed to both the Jerusalem temple and its hierarchy (*Galatians Re-Imagined: Reading with the Eyes of the Vanquished*; PCC; Minneapolis: Fortress, 2010, 217, echoing the ideas of Seth Schwartz).

118. Albert Schweitzer, *The Quest of the Historical Jesus: A Critical Study of its Progress from Reimarus to Wrede*, trans. William Montgomery (New York: MacMillan, 1950), 388-92. For a survey of views regarding the reason why Jesus traveled to Jerusalem with his disciples shortly before his death there, see Kim Huat Tan, *The Zion Traditions and the Aims of Jesus* (SNTSMS 91; Cambridge: Cambridge University Press, 1996), 4-22.

119. On this idea, see McKnight, *Jesus and his Death*, 89-93. McKnight also considers there other possibilities regarding Jesus' purpose in going up to Jerusalem.

120. On these ideas, see Freyne, *Jesus, a Jewish Galilean*, 152-63; Chilton, *Pure Kingdom*, 124-25. Klawans, in turn, argues against the notion that Jesus rejected the Jerusalem temple and intended the eucharistic meal he instituted as a replacement for the temple (*Purity*, 213-45).

121. For Jesus to believe that his work in Galilee was done does not necessarily mean that he regarded his work there as for the most part unsuccessful, as Reiser claims (*Jesus*, 229).

122. As Tan mentions, Jesus may have expected to be stoned to death rather than to be crucified (*Zion Traditions*, 108).

Jesus actually *wished* to die in Jerusalem for some reason, primarily because he thought his death would bring about salvation for others.[123] The Gospels also claim that Jesus expected to be raised from among the dead shortly after his death, yet although some scholars argue in favor of the historicity of this claim, most historians find it highly problematic.[124]

Ultimately, all of these possibilities involve speculation. We simply cannot know what Jesus thought or why he decided to go to Jerusalem. The presuppositions with which one approaches that question will also define what one considers possible or not. Because those possibilities are so numerous and difficult to evaluate from a historical perspective, I will not enter into a detailed discussion of them here. However, similar to what I have done in the previous sections of this chapter, I would like to look at certain of the occurrences related to Jesus' last days in Jerusalem that are widely accepted as historical in order to draw some general conclusions that will be important for the remainder of this study.

Jesus' Ministry in Jerusalem

The Synoptic Gospels all report that Jesus was active teaching on the temple precincts in the days preceding his arrest. Matthew also speaks of Jesus effecting healings (Matt. 21:14). This suggests that Jesus' purpose in going to Jerusalem was to continue to carry out there the same ministry he had been carrying out in Galilee. Since Jews from all over the world came to the temple, especially during the festivals, Jesus could expect that those who became acquainted with him and what he represented and proclaimed would share what they had seen and heard with others when they returned to their places of origin. Thus it is likely that the trip to Jerusalem was part of a strategy to extend his message and ministry further, and perhaps expand his circle of followers as well.

---

123. Ben Witherington III, for example, affirms, "There is some justice in the assessment that Jesus saw his task in life to come and die, enduring God's overwhelming wrath.... Jesus saw it as God's will that he die in Jerusalem to provide a ransom for many" (*The Christology of Jesus*; Minneapolis: Fortress, 1990, 259, 262). See also Wright, *Jesus*, 608-10. In contrast, C. F. D. Moule argued: "Such evidence as we have suggests that Jesus... did not seek death; he did not go up to Jerusalem *in order* to die; but he did pursue, with inflexible devotion, a way of truth that inevitably led him to death, and he did not seek to escape" (*The Origin of Christology*; Cambridge: Cambridge University Press, 1977, 109).

124. It has been common for scholars to repeat the affirmation made by C. K. Barrett that, if Jesus did "predict and interpret his passion, the interpretation must have included the prediction of some kind of vindication beyond the passion. It is inconceivable that Jesus simply predicted the complete and final failure of his mission" (*Jesus and the Gospel Tradition*; London: SPCK, 1967, 76). See, for example, Marinus de Jonge, *God's Final Envoy: Early Christology and Jesus' Own View of his Mission* (Grand Rapids: Eerdmans, 1998), 19. McKnight argues that for Jesus to predict his death but not his resurrection would have involved "predicting the dissolution of his movement" (*Jesus and his Death*, 229-30). Such claims, however, are unconvincing. Many figures in history who have been involved in a struggle for a cause they consider just have foreseen and predicted their own violent death, yet have nevertheless hoped and expected that the cause or movement for which they would die would continue and even grow and be strengthened in spite of their death. The same could have been true of Jesus as well: for him to predict only his death and not his resurrection would therefore by no means have involved predicting "the complete and final failure of his mission" or "the dissolution of his movement."

However, given the content of his proclamation and teaching regarding God's reign, Jesus must have been aware that his life would be in danger if he went to Jerusalem and taught publicly on the temple precincts. Whatever objective he had in going into the area where commercial activities related to the sacrifices were carried out in order to turn over tables there and drive out those selling and buying, he could hardly have believed that this action would not put his life even more at risk. Neither the Roman nor the Jewish authorities would view such an action lightly, especially at the time of the Passover. It is possible that Jesus was willing to put his life at risk through these activities because he was convinced that they would further his cause by expressing more clearly and emphatically the convictions he wished to communicate to others. He may have believed that, even if something bad did happen to him, his disciples had received sufficient preparation and would therefore be able to continue on in the work for which he had prepared them. Jesus may even have regarded the trip to Jerusalem as necessary to solidify or complete the preparation of his disciples. It seems likely, therefore, that Jesus' trip to Jerusalem had the purpose of furthering his ministry in some way.[125]

It also seems likely, however, that Jesus expected that he would be put to death in Jerusalem, especially given the actions and activity he intended to carry out there. If this is the case, then his decision to go up to Jerusalem must also be seen as a decision to embrace the death that awaited him there. Those who adhere to the traditional interpretations of Jesus' work tend to argue that Jesus wanted to die because he believed that his death would save others by atoning for their sins, propitiating God's wrath, delivering others from Satan's power, revealing the enormity of his love and that of his Father for human beings, or triggering the arrival of God's reign. For reasons we have seen and will also see further on, I believe we must rule out all of these possibilities. One of the things such proposals fail to explain is why Jesus initially dedicated his time in Jerusalem to teaching on the temple precincts and perhaps healing others there as well. It seems doubtful that his purpose in teaching and healing was merely to provoke the authorities to have him arrested and put him to death. In fact, for the most part, it is not Jesus who provokes the polemical discussions in which he engages with the Jewish leaders at the temple, but those who approach Jesus in an attempt to entrap or discredit him or provide them with some basis upon which they may accuse him before the authorities. In his responses to their questions, however, Jesus seems to take great care to avoid saying explicitly anything that might give his opponents grounds for bringing charges against him.

There is one other possibility that may be considered, however. Rather than seeing his death as having an objective that was distinct from his ministry in the way that traditional views of his work maintain, Jesus may have embraced

---

125. Tan, for example, notes that that "it is reasonable to suppose that Jesus' aims during his last days in Jerusalem were in continuity with his aims in his ministry prior to that fateful event...." (*Zion Traditions*, 4).

the death that awaited him in Jerusalem precisely because he believed that it was the best or only way for the objectives he had pursued in his ministry to be fulfilled completely. In this case, Jesus' desire was not to die, but to carry on his ministry on behalf of others, and see it strengthen and expand further. At the same time, however, he realized that the only way in which his ministry could continue and expand in the way he desired was for him to go up to Jerusalem and carry out that ministry even more boldly and openly there, knowing full well that the consequence of doing so would eventually be his arrest and in all likelihood his death as well. This is the possibility I would like to explore here: Jesus saw his suffering and probable death in Jerusalem as necessary for the objectives he had sought from the very start of his ministry to be accomplished.

Jesus' Entry into Jerusalem

All four Gospels affirm that Jesus entered Jerusalem riding on a donkey or colt while crowds of people received him enthusiastically. According to Luke and John, they explicitly acclaimed Jesus "king" or "king of Israel" (Luke 19:38; John 12:13). Matthew and Mark also associate messianic expectations with the crowd's acclamations (Matt. 21:1-11; Mark 11:1-10). Although Matthew and John see Jesus as the one who takes the initiative to enter Jerusalem in this fashion in fulfillment of the prophecy of Zech. 9:9 (Matt. 21:5; John 12:15), all four Gospels present the acclamation of the crowds as a spontaneous reaction on their part.

A number of problems exist regarding the historicity of these diverse accounts of what is presumed to be the same event. This makes it difficult to evaluate to what extent they are historically accurate. Jesus is presented not only as being conscious of his identity as the Messiah whose coming was prophesied by prophets such as Zechariah, but also as acting in a way that encouraged the multitudes to acclaim him as such.[126] This presents a stark contrast with Jesus' behavior elsewhere in the Gospels, since at no other time before or after this event does Jesus publicly encourage others to view him as a messianic or kingly figure. The crowds also are presented as grasping immediately the messianic implications of Jesus' act of riding on a donkey by acclaiming him king and son of David, even though the Gospel accounts do not affirm that Jesus or his disciples told the crowds to interpret Jesus' actions in that sense. Yet while there are reasons for doubting the historicity of the Gospel accounts, the fact that the event is so strongly attested makes it difficult to see those accounts merely as later fabrications.[127]

---

126. According to Tan, for example, Jesus deliberately managed his "triumphal entry" in order to communicate the idea that he was the divinely-appointed agent and king sent by God to bring about the promised restoration (*Zion Traditions*, 137-57).

127. On the historicity of the account of Jesus' entry into Jerusalem, see especially Brent Kinman, "Jesus' Royal Entry into Jerusalem," in *Key Events*, ed. Bock and Webb, 383-421; Tan, *Zion Traditions*, 138-43.

If the event is historical at least in general terms, it raises the question of whether Jesus saw himself as Messiah or king.[128] All of the Synoptics present Jesus as being reluctant for the most part to accept any messianic or kingly title. A number of explanations for this are possible. Jesus may simply have rejected outright the idea that he was Israel's Messiah or king. In that case, however, it is difficult to see how he could have come to be considered as such, not only *before* his death but *after* it. If the *titulus* placed on his cross is accepted as historically authentic, it provides support for the notion that Jesus was crucified as one who was regarded as a kingly pretender.[129] It also suggests that, if the Jewish and Roman authorities asked him if he was a king or Messiah during the process against him, he did not deny such a claim. Otherwise, the authorities would have had to convict Jesus of such an accusation solely on the testimony of witnesses. While the Gospels mention a number of persons testifying against Jesus, they never present those witnesses affirming that Jesus claimed to be a king or Messiah.

One reason why Jesus may have been reluctant to accept any messianic or kingly claims regarding himself may have been that he rejected many of the common conceptions associated with such figures.[130] This does not necessarily mean that Jesus was apolitical, as if he were indifferent to Roman domination

---

128. To ask whether Jesus saw himself as Messiah, of course, raises the question of how he would have understood the title. As we have noted in Chapter 2, in second-temple Judaism a wide diversity of beliefs and expectations regarding the Messiah existed.

129. David R. Catchpole comments: "If Jesus was crucified as a messianic claimant with the Roman definition of his offence defined by the *titulus* on the cross, then some earlier encouragement of the view that he was messiah must have occurred" ("The 'Triumphal' Entry," in *Jesus and the Politics of His Day*, ed. Ernst Bammel and C. F. D. Moule; Cambridge: Cambridge University Press, 1984, 328). Similarly, Martin Hengel argues that "Jesus conducted himself with 'messianic' authority, and was executed as a messianic pretender. Only thus are the development of post-Easter Christology, the accounts of his Passion, and his efficacy, historically comprehensible" ("Jesus, the Messiah of Israel: The Debate about the 'Messianic Mission' of Jesus," in *Authenticating*, ed. Chilton and Evans, 348).

130. There has been a great deal of discussion among scholars on this question. Craig Evans argues that there is "evidence that Jesus held to messianic ideas, even if he did not assert his messiahship explicitly (which would have been inappropriate, according to Jewish expectations)" ("The Jesus of History and the Christ of Faith: Toward Jewish-Christian Dialogue," in *Who Was Jesus?*, ed. Copan and Evans, 69; see 64-69). According to Dunn, Jesus reacted against some messianic conceptions, yet drew on and adapted others: "Jesus was as much shaping the messianic ideas of the time as being shaped by them... redefining the categories either by deliberate teaching or simply by the very shape of his ministry...." ("Messianic Ideas," 380-81). Ernst Bammel writes that the "messianic question must have posed itself to Jesus," yet for various reasons he would have probably responded ambivalently ("The Feeding of the Multitude," in *Jesus and the Politics of His Day*, ed. Bammel and Moule, 231-40). After considering different possible interpretations of the title "Messiah," John J. Collins concludes: "Jesus appears reticent about his own claims, but unwilling to contradict claims made in his behalf" ("Jesus and the Messiahs of Israel," in *Geschichte–Tradition–Reflexion: Festschrift für Martin Hengel zum 70. Geburtstag*, Band 3: *Frühes Christentum*; ed. Hermann Lichtenberger; Tübingen: J. C. B. Mohr, 1996, 299; see 287-302). Elsewhere Collins observes that there was "little correspondence between Jesus' career and the kind of role that the Davidic messiah was expected to play" ("What Was Distinctive about Messianic Expectation at Qumran?," in *The Bible and the Dead Sea Scrolls*, ed. Charlesworth, 2:85). Condra affirms that the diversity of messianic expectations in Jesus' day "would make it necessary for Jesus to *define* his messianic role in the light of messianic conceptions similar to or different in varying degrees from his own messiahship" (*Salvation*, 200). If Jesus accepted the title of Messiah, the question would be what *kind* of Messiah he was (227). For Condra, it was "not so much that Jesus had to radically reinterpret the messianic role, but that he had to avoid a strict identification with any role and redefine the role by stretching his audience's understanding" (279).

in Palestine and elsewhere and had no vision for a new political and social order. The words that the Fourth Gospel attributes to Jesus before Pilate, "My kingdom is not from this world" (John 18:36), should not be understood in the sense that Jesus was concerned only with an other-worldly salvation in a heavenly sphere. Rather, these words reflect his conviction that God was to transform the present world into a different one, at which time Jesus would be installed as king or ruler. When that happened, a new political, social, and economic order would be established as well. The Synoptics also suggest that this was how Jesus understood his future role in God's reign.

At first glance, the notion that Jesus desired to be established as a king or ruler would seem to run contrary to certain aspects of the teaching the Gospels attribute to Jesus. Particularly in the Synoptics, Jesus continually insists to his disciples that they are to avoid seeking positions of power or privilege for themselves. At the same time, Jesus is remembered as one who often claimed that those who are little or humble themselves in order to serve others will be exalted, and that those who are truly great are those who dedicate themselves to serving others. In Luke's Gospel, at the beginning of his ministry Jesus associates himself, not with the Davidic king or the Messiah figure mentioned in a variety of passages from Isaiah, but with the servant figure described in Isa. 61:1-2 (Luke 4:16-21). The itinerant ministry to which Jesus dedicated himself in Galilee also seems to indicate that he was not seeking glory or power as a messianic figure, but simply wished to dedicate himself to proclaiming a message of justice and hope and laying a foundation so that the work he had begun there might continue and flourish in the future. In fact, the Gospels are consistent in presenting Jesus as one who dedicated himself to serving others humbly throughout his ministry, rather than seeking any position of power or authority for himself.

It would seem, then, that Jesus did *not* actively seek to be acclaimed as king or attain a position of power over others. In fact, on the one occasion in the Gospels in which the crowds intend to make him king by force, Jesus immediately goes off into seclusion to prevent them from doing so (John 6:15). Yet this makes it difficult to explain why Jesus decided to enter into Jerusalem mounted on a donkey in royal fashion and seems to have accepted, though somewhat reluctantly, the claims of others that he was a king or messianic figure. This problem seems to disappear only if we affirm that Jesus *wanted to attain a position of power, not for his own sake, but for the sake of others*. For this reason, he refused to let others make him an earthly king and instead awaited the time when he hoped that God would establish him as king or Messiah.

Power and authority, of course, can be used to seek the well-being of others rather than to pursue one's own self-interests. If this is what one seeks, then in principle, the greater the power that one attains, the greater the ability one will have to promote the well-being of others. The fact that Jesus had a deep and ardent desire to serve others is evident from the great sacrifices he made and the hardships he endured during his ministry, in which he left everything behind to reach out to those in need and called others to join him in doing the same. On this basis, then, it is perfectly logical that Jesus would seek greater power in order to be able to use that power to serve others even more than he had in the past.

This understanding of Jesus' actions and aims would explain his apparently contradictory or conflicting attitudes toward kingship. In fact, both his commitment to serve others humbly and his desire to be placed in a position of power are reflected in his decision to enter Jerusalem in kingly fashion, receiving the acclamations of others while nevertheless riding on a lowly, humble donkey: Jesus saw himself as a king or Messiah who was fundamentally opposed to the common conceptions and models of kingship. He truly sought the well-being of others, contrary to other rulers and powerful figures, who were accustomed to claiming that their only interest was that of serving the people, when their actions made it evident to all that in reality they were pursuing instead their own selfish ends. Jesus' conflicting attitudes toward kingship would therefore explain his hesitancy to accept the kingly and messianic claims others made regarding himself, since he did not want to be the type of king others expected. Those conflicting attitudes are also reflected in his paradoxical statements about the need for those who desire to be first, greatest, or most important to make themselves last and lowliest by serving others and becoming like slaves or children (Matt. 18:1-4; 20:16; 23:11-12; Mark 9:34-35; 10:31; Luke 9:46-58; 13:30; 22:26-27; John 13:13-15). It is worth noting that Jesus does not tell his disciples that it is wrong to want to be first or great, but that in order to be first or great, one must dedicate oneself to humbly serving all.

Such a self-understanding on Jesus' part is also in accordance with his critique of the rich and powerful of his time, including the Roman and Jewish authorities and those who benefited from the system over which they ruled. It would also explain why Jesus did not reject wealth and power outright, but only the pursuit of wealth and power as ends in themselves. While he is presented as denouncing wealth, he also enters into fellowship with those who are wealthy and accepts their support under certain conditions. For Jesus, wealth, like power, is to be used for seeking justice and the good of all.

Jesus' enigmatic use of the title "Son of Man" may also be seen as an expression of this same self-understanding. As several studies have shown, this phrase is used in the Gospels to stress Jesus' suffering, humiliation, and violent death, as well as his future role as a glorious savior figure and judge.[131] If Jesus used the title in both of these ways, it was because he saw himself as one imbued uniquely with divine authority in relation to others, yet at the same time as one who would endure many hardships and humiliations due to his commitment to serving others with the power and authority given him. In

---

[131] Meier indicates that scholars generally divide the Son of Man sayings in the Gospels into three main categories: those that refer to his public ministry, those that predict his sufferings and death, and those that look forward to his future role as eschatological witness, judge, and savior (*Marginal Jew*, 4:285).

fact, I would propose that the reason that Jesus spoke of the Son of Man in the third person and at times seemed to be referring to someone other than himself is that he believed that he first had to show himself worthy of that designation by being faithful to the end in carrying out the task that he believed God had given him to accomplish.[132] In Jesus' mind, until he had completed that task, it would have been presumptuous on his part to declare himself Son of Man. No one but God could establish him as the Son of Man who would come on the clouds to establish God's reign, and for that to happen, Jesus had to prove himself deserving of such a position of power and authority. The only way for him to do this was to dedicate himself fully to serving others in obedience to God's will, even if that meant facing a violent end.

If the general outline of the account of Jesus' entry into Jerusalem is regarded as historical, therefore, it appears that Jesus saw himself as some type of alternative ruler figure who stood in contrast to the other rulers of his day and wanted others to see him in this way as well. If this was the case, however, then he must have been aware that his actions would be seen by the authorities as provocative and potentially subversive.

Jesus' Action in the Temple

Biblical historians widely accept as historical the general details of the account of Jesus' action in the temple (Matt. 21:12-13; Mark 11:15-19; Luke 19:45-46; John 2:13-22).[133] They have differed greatly among themselves, however, on the question of what Jesus intended to accomplish through that action. Most scholars today agree that Jesus' intention was not to effect some type of actual purification of the temple area, since what he did would have had a very limited and temporary effect on the trade there.[134] Thus it is much more common to see Jesus' action as a protest against what was taking place at the temple, or some other type of symbolic or prophetic act pointing to something such as the future destruction of the temple, and perhaps its replacement by a new temple as well.[135]

---

132. This idea is suggested by Marc Turnage, "Jesus and Caiaphas: An Intertextual-Literary Evaluation," in *Jesus' Last Week*, ed. Notley, Turnage, and Becker, 165. Contrary to Turnage, however, I would insist that the idea was not simply that Jesus had to die in order to be exalted as Son of Man, as if his violent death were merely some fate he had to endure, but that he had to fulfill faithfully the work on behalf of others that his Father had given him. Only in this way would he be exalted as the Son of Man so as to bring about the salvation of others.

133. Klawans, for example, notes that among scholars "it is generally accepted that *something* happened in the Jerusalem temple shortly before Jesus' death" (*Purity*, 224). Similarly, Timothy C. Gray writes: "Very few scholars doubt the authenticity of Jesus' actions in the temple" (*The Temple in the Gospel of Mark: A Study in its Narrative Role*, WUNT 2/44; Tübingen: Mohr Siebeck, 2008, 31). On this point, see also Klyne R. Snodgrass, "The Temple Incident," in *Key Events*, ed. Bock and Webb, 429-75.

134. See Sanders, *Jesus and Judaism*, 90. David Bivin even argues on the basis of Luke's account that the act that Jesus carried out at the temple was not a violent one ("Evidence of an Editor's Hand in Two Instances of Mark's Account of Jesus' Last Week?," in *Jesus' Last Week*, ed. Notley, Turnage, and Becker, 213-19).

135. For a summary of the scholarly opinions on this subject, see Fiensy, *Jesus*, 208-27; Alexander J. M. Wedderburn, "Jesus' Action in the Temple: A Key or a Puzzle?," *ZNW* 97 (2006): 1-22; Alan R. Kerr, *The Temple of Jesus' Body: The Temple Theme in the Gospel of John* (JSNTSup 220; London: Sheffield Academic Press, 2002), 68-69, n1; Jostein Ådna, *Jesu Stellung zum Tempel: Die Tempelaktion und das Tempelwort als Ausdruck*

Scholars have also debated over the question of precisely what Jesus found objectionable about what was taking place at the temple. Some have argued that Jesus was opposed to commercial activity being carried out at a certain place within the temple precincts,[136] while others have related Jesus' action to a concern for the participation of gentiles in the temple worship on the basis of the passage he quotes from Isa. 56:7, "My house shall be called a house of prayer for all peoples."[137] While some scholars maintain that Jesus rejected any type of sacrificial worship as contrary to God's will,[138] others have claimed that it was not the sacrificial worship itself that he found objectionable but the way it was being carried out.[139] Disagreements exist among scholars as to whether Jesus looked forward to a time when the temple would be purified of the errors and abuses that he associated with it or instead foretold the temple's destruction, perhaps so that it might be replaced with a new and better temple. These proposals exist in a wide variety of forms and any type of consensus on these questions is far from being achieved.

As noted above, however, there is a great deal of evidence that many Jews regarded the temple establishment as corrupt and oppressive.[140] The high priestly families who exercised control over what went on at the temple profited enormously from the wealth generated by the sacrificial worship that took place there, which was immense.[141] Their control over the temple also gave

---

seiner messianischen Sendung (WUNT 2/119; Tübingen: Mohr Siebeck, 2000), 332-87. Bivin is undoubtedly correct in stressing that the evangelists themselves differed among themselves in various ways in the meaning they ascribed to Jesus' action in the temple area ("Evidence," 213-24).

136. Klawans, however, argues against the claim that this was the motivation behind Jesus' action at the temple (*Purity*, 232-33).

137. For this interpretation, see Bird, *Jesus*, 143-55. Horsley, in contrast, insists that "Jesus' concern was almost certainly not simply to defend Gentiles' right to access to the Temple or to open the Temple eschatologically to worship by the Gentiles" (*Spiral*, 297).

138. H. Stegemann, for example, ascribes to Jesus the idea that "sacrificial worship, so important until then, had now lost every purpose and function, since God had begun to impose his rule fully independently of it" (*Library of Qumran*, 245). Similarly, Steven Bryan claims that Jesus was "against the operation of the Temple as a whole" (*Jesus*, 217). According to Holmén, Jesus saw the temple cult as promoting the idea that people could sin freely and still obtain forgiveness, thereby securing their "criminal way of life" (*Jesus*, 324).

139. Bruce Chilton, for example, has argued that Jesus was protesting the practice of allowing people to offer up animals and goods that were not genuinely their own but had instead been purchased (*Pure Kingdom*, 118-23). For arguments against Chilton's view, see Klawans, *Purity*, 234-36.

140. See above, note 25. The writings from Qumran, of course, object to the worship at the Jerusalem temple not only on the ground that the high-priestly families who controlled the sacrificial worship there were corrupt, but also because those authorities were supposedly not following correctly the prescriptions regarding sacrifice found in the Mosaic law and adhered to a calendar that was mistaken. On these points, see Bertil E. Gärtner, *The Temple and the Community in Qumran and the New Testament: A Comparative Study in the Temple Symbolism of the Qumran Texts and the New Testament* (SNTSMS 1; Cambridge: Cambridge University Press, 1965), 4-46; Robert A. Kugler, "Rewriting Rubrics: Sacrifice and the Religion of Qumran," in *Religion in the Dead Sea Scrolls* (ed. John J. Collins and Kugler; Grand Rapids: Eerdmans, 2000), 90, n1. Other Jewish writings reject the legitimacy of the sacrificial cult carried out at the Jerusalem temple for similar reasons; see Michael Knibb, "Temple and Cult in the Apocrypha and Pseudepigrapha: Future Perspectives," in *Flores Florentino: Dead Sea Scrolls and Other Early Jewish Studies in Honour of Florentino García Martínez* (ed. Anthony Hilhorst, Émile Puech, and Eibert Tigchelaar; JSJSup 122; Leiden: Brill, 2007), 509-27.

141. As Bruce Chilton stresses, it is important to distinguish between the "high priests" or "elite priests," who had control of the temple, and the priests in general, who did not ordinarily even participate in the

them control over much of the economic life of the entire region.[142] Much of the income they obtained through the temple system was also thought to be the result of their corrupt practices. Many Jews thought that the high priestly families took unfair advantage of their privileged position in order to charge excessive prices in the sale of animals and the exchange of money at the temple. On occasion it was claimed that they were taking a larger portion of the tithes and offerings than what was due to them, thus not only depriving the priests of lower status of what was rightfully theirs, but also contributing to the further impoverishment of the general populace. Some Jews also regarded the annual payment of the temple tax enforced by the chief priests as unjust and illicit.[143] This economic oppression on the part of the high priestly families seems to have been an important motivating factor in Jesus' temple action. For this reason, Jesus is presented as calling the temple "a den of thieves."

Some scholars have questioned the notion that Jesus' intention was to denounce the oppressive and corrupt practices of the high priestly leadership who had control over the temple. According to these scholars, if there was any corruption, it was on a small scale. Several have also argued that, if Jesus had wanted to express opposition to the high priestly leadership, he would have carried out some action against them directly rather than going after those who were buying and selling and exchanging money.[144] However, the reason that Jesus may not have directed his actions against the leaders themselves may simply have been that it was impossible for him to have access to those leaders, who were not generally out and about on the temple precincts. Furthermore, it is naïve to think that the buyers and money changers were simply acting on their own. Any buying and selling being done in the temple area would have been done under the supervision of the high priests, who had tight control over the temple. Those involved in selling and changing money would therefore either have been employed by the high priestly families or have been expected to give them a considerable portion of what they earned. If Jesus considered this commercial activity unjust and oppressive, it is not unreasonable that Jesus would have gone after not only those selling but those buying as well, since the latter were participating in the unjust temple system and contributing to its support through their purchases.

Thus it seems fairly certain that the high priestly families who had control over the temple area were in some sense the object of Jesus' criticism. However,

---

sacrificial worship at the temple. In fact, according to Chilton, many of the latter even had nationalist or revolutionary tendencies ("John the Purifier," in *Jesus in Context*, Chilton and Evans, 216-17).

142. On the economic impact of the Jerusalem temple in Galilee, see Freyne, *Galilee, Jesus, and the Gospels*, 178-90; Borg, *Conflict*, 12-15; Horsley, *Galilee*, 128-57.

143. On the opposition of many Jews to the temple tax in Jesus' day, see E. Stegemann and W. Stegemann, *The Jesus Movement*, 119-23; Horsley, *Spiral*, 279-84. Horsley claims that the refusal to pay the temple tax constituted a "declaration of independence from the Temple and the attendant political-economical-religious establishment" (282).

144. For these arguments, see Crossan, *Historical Jesus*, 357; Catchpole, "Triumphant Entry," 332-34. Klawans argues that at most there would have been isolated instances of corruption by those selling and exchanging money (*Purity*, 236-37, 244). Gray in particular asks why not only the sellers, but also the buyers would be the object of Jesus' demonstration if he were simply protesting unjust business practices (*Temple*, 26).

Jesus' actions must be seen as a critique not only of the chief priests and those who were in their service, but of the entire system of which they formed part. As mentioned previously, this system had to do not only with religious realities but social, political, and economic realities as well. All Jews, including Jesus, must have been well aware that the high priests were appointed by Rome and thus had to be subservient to the Romans. The daily sacrifices offered up with prayers on behalf of the Roman emperor would have been a constant reminder to all Jews of Israel's servile acquiescence to Roman rule. The cost for those sacrifices was borne by Israelites not only from Palestine but from throughout the Empire through the temple tax they paid. The daily sacrifice invoking God's blessing for the emperor was not a voluntary offering presented by the Jewish people out of gratitude for the emperor's benevolence, as both the Romans and the Jewish leadership undoubtedly affirmed publicly, but an obligation imposed forcibly by Rome. This is evident from the fact that, when the people ceased to offer this sacrifice in the year 66, that action in particular was viewed as the definitive declaration of their rebellion against Rome.[145]

Although it was clear to everyone that the temple system bowed to Rome's imperial interests, this does not necessarily mean that all Jews were opposed to the sacrificial worship that took place at the temple. Undoubtedly, among many sectors of the Jewish population there was strong opposition to both Roman rule and the power of the high priestly elites. Yet much of the Jewish population in Judea, Galilee, and elsewhere must have supported the system imposed by Rome, feeling that it benefited them, or at least that it was better than the possible alternatives. No doubt many Jews accepted favorably the Roman propaganda that touted the *pax et securitas* and well-being that Roman rule had supposedly brought to the region. There must also have been large numbers of Jews who believed that the Jewish high priests were fulfilling faithfully their divinely-appointed role as mediators between God and his people and as defenders of the Mosaic law. Even those who acknowledged that there was corruption in the system may nevertheless have supported that system in general terms; no system in antiquity was free of corruption. Many other Jews were no doubt afraid of the consequences of any type of resistance to Rome, and thus thought that it was in the best interests of all simply to submit obediently to those in power and the system they represented. Prior to his Damascus experience, Paul seems to have supported the Jewish high priesthood, like many other Pharisees and other large sections of the

---

145. Bruce Chilton notes that "the Temple in Jerusalem had come to symbolize Roman power, as well as the devotion of Israel. Rome guarded jealously the sacrifices which the Emperor financed in Jerusalem; when they were spurned in the year 66, the act was a declaration of war (see Josephus, *J.W.* 2.17.2 §409)" ("The Trial of Jesus Reconsidered," in *Jesus in Context*, Chilton and Evans, 495). For the same reasons, Horsley claims that Jesus' act in the temple constituted "a direct, blatant challenge not only to the sacred power base of the rulers of Jerusalem but also to the Roman imperial order...." ("The Politics of Disguise and Public Declaration of the Hidden Transcript: Broadening our Approach to the Historical Jesus with Scott's 'Arts of Resistance' Theory," in *Hidden Transcripts*, ed. Horsley, 76).

population. Undoubtedly, many Jews benefited from the system personally and financially, either because they found employment within the system or because they occupied themselves in activities that were profitable as a result of the opportunities that the system created or the protection it offered.

According to Matt. 17:24-27, Jesus seems to have had reservations about paying the temple tax. When he finally consents to paying it, he does not take the money out of his own pocket or from the funds that belonged to his group of followers, but sends Peter to get from the mouth of a fish the coin necessary to pay the tax.[146] On the one hand, Jesus was no doubt aware that this tax would be used to support the temple system and thereby benefit in some way the chief priests and help cover the cost of the daily sacrifices, at which prayers were offered up on behalf of the Roman emperor. This may have made him reluctant to pay it. On the other hand, however, Jesus apparently did consent to its payment, either because it was stipulated in the Mosaic law or because he felt that, for the sake of the work in which he was involved and the plan he intended to carry out, it was preferable simply to comply so as to avoid problems with the authorities. It seems doubtful that what motivated Jesus was a desire not to give offense to others, since this never appears to have been a cause of concern for Jesus during his ministry.

Jesus' rejection of the dominant system seems to be much more evident in his response to the question of whether it was licit to pay tribute to Caesar (Matt. 22:15-22; Mark 12:13-17; Luke 20:20-26). Jesus' response to that question has been interpreted in a variety of ways, yet the fact that he himself did not apparently have or use a coin bearing the image of Caesar and contrasted giving to Caesar with giving to God clearly implies that, for Jesus, living under God's rule was to be distinguished from living under Caesar's rule. Even though Jesus speaks of giving to Caesar what belongs to him, Jesus must have believed that all things ultimately belonged to God alone. While Jesus does not seem to have advocated rebellion against Rome or active opposition to Rome's rule, he does seem to have viewed faithfulness to God and commitment to God's reign as constituting an alternative way of life in which one refused to acknowledge Caesar's lordship, but instead acknowledged no one but Israel's God as Lord. For Jesus, this alternative way of life must have involved living according to the values of God's reign, rather than the values of the system imposed by Rome and supported by a large part of the population. Even if Jesus' rejection of the legitimacy of Rome's rule was implicit rather than explicit, it is not difficult to see how his teaching and practice could come to be seen as subversive, and therefore have led to his being crucified as an agitator and a threat to the system.

---

146. Among the scholars who regard it as likely that Jesus objected to the temple tax are William Horbury ("The Temple Tax," in *Jesus and the Politics of His Day*, ed. Bammel and Moule, 282-86); Craig Evans ("Opposition to the Temple: Jesus and the Dead Sea Scrolls," in *Jesus and the Dead Sea Scrolls*, ed. Charlesworth, 242), and Chilton ("Trial of Jesus," 487). Klawans notes that, if Jesus opposed the tax, his stance in this regard was not radical, since opposition was common among many Jews (*Purity*, 229-31, 237).

Jesus' negative attitude toward the Roman system upheld by the Jewish authorities and the Herodian rulers must once again be seen as derived from a distinct understanding of God. Jesus' God was not the God associated with the system. While Jesus may have believed that God was allowing Rome and the high priests to be in the position they were in, he apparently did not see them as instruments of God's will nor call on people to submit to them, because for him this would have involved submitting to the injustices they perpetrated. His action in the temple illustrates clearly his belief that God was being used to promote the interests of certain people and groups. That action, therefore, represented an implicit affirmation that the God who was being served at the temple was not the true God, but the God of those in power who held in place the oppressive system.[147]

The parable of the wicked tenants attributed to Jesus also lends support to the idea that Jesus' temple action was intended as a criticism of the ruling high priestly elites (Matt. 21:33-46; Mark 12:1-12; Luke 20:9-19).[148] The parable is problematic on a number of accounts. Scholars have debated over which form of the parable, including that of the *Gospel of Thomas* (65-66), is closest to the original.[149] While many accept that in some form it goes back to Jesus, it is difficult to reconstruct the original parable, if indeed it was originally told in only one way. The versions we have in the three Synoptics and the *Gospel of Thomas* all present a number of differences. Many scholars have doubted the authenticity of the parable for a variety of reasons.[150] Certain ideas from

---

147. In general terms, therefore, I would agree with Horsley, who regards Jesus' action in the temple as "a demonstration symbolizing destruction and directed against the high-priestly establishment.... Jesus attacks the activities in which the exploitation of God's people by their priestly rulers was most visible" (*Spiral*, 299-300). This would have involved an opposition not only to the temple but also to the entire socio-political system that it represented. In this case, as Borg argues, Jesus' act was also "an indictment of the Temple as the center of an economically exploitative system legitimated in the name of God," as well as "an indictment of city and temple as the center of the domination system" (*Conflict*, 14-15). For similar understandings of Jesus' act, see Crossan, *Historical Jesus*, 360; Evans, "Opposition," 243.

148. Matthew and Mark explicitly affirm that Jesus told this parable against the high priests (Matt. 21:45; Mark 12:12), while Luke implies the same (Luke 20:19). Randall Buth and Brian Kvasnica argue that the parable is a "stinging criticism against the temple authorities" and a critique of "bribery and fraud that led to 'legalized' violence and murder" ("Temple Authorities and Tithe Evasion: The Linguistic Background and Impact of the Parable of the Vineyard, the Tenants and the Son," in *Jesus' Last Week*, ed. Notley, Turnage, and Becker, 53, 72; see 53-80). See also Evans, *Fabricating Jesus*, 127-28.

149. On this discussion, see Klyne Snodgrass, *The Parable of the Wicked Tenants: An Inquiry into Parable Interpretation* (WUNT 27; Tübingen: J. C. B. Mohr, 1983), 52-71. Snodgrass lists elements of the parable that many regard as questionable, yet then responds to each of these in order to argue for the historicity of the parable. Many scholars, however, would disagree with Snodgrass's argument that Matthew's version of the parable is closest to the original.

150. For a summary of views on the historicity of the parable and its interpretation, see Adela Yarbro Collins, *Mark: A Commentary* (ed. Harold W. Attridge; Hermeneia; Minneapolis: Fortress, 2007), 542-44. In two different treatments of the subject, Craig Evans points to parallels to the ideas of the parable in the Targums, the Qumran writings, and the rabbinic literature, and also notes that most scholars regard the parable as authentic in some form (*Fabricating Jesus*, 127-38; "Jesus and the Dead Sea Scrolls from Qumran Cave 4," in *Eschatology, Messianism, and the Dead Sea Scrolls*; ed. Evans and Peter W. Flint; SDSSRL 1; Grand Rapids: Eerdmans, 1997, 97-99). John S. Kloppenborg, however, claims that certain theological assertions of the parable "cannot reasonably be attributed to Jesus," and thus that there are "good reasons to suppose that an originally realistic narrative was secondarily allegorized" (*Tenants in the Vineyard: Ideology, Economics, and Agrarian Conflict in Jewish Palestine*; WUNT 195; Mohr Siebeck, 2006, 70). George J. Brooke similarly notes

the parable seem improbable and unrealistic, such as the owner's decision to send his son to the vineyard after learning that the servants he had previously sent had been mistreated and killed there, as well as the tenants' belief that by killing the son they could keep the vineyard as an inheritance. As William Herzog has observed, given that absentee landowners such as the owner of the vineyard in the parable were viewed by many as unjust and oppressive, some of the poor with whom Jesus associated would perhaps have sympathized more with the tenants than the landowner.[151] The parable is also allegorical in a way that is uncharacteristic of Jesus' other parables. If Jesus told the parable as it stands about himself, which is not entirely certain,[152] he must have believed that he was in some sense God's Son and thus distinct from the prophets who had come before him. Many scholars, however, would consider it unlikely that Jesus viewed himself in that way. Questions also exist as to the identity of the groups with whom the listeners would have been expected to associate the tenants of the parable and those to whom the vineyard is subsequently given.[153]

However these questions are settled, for our purposes it is sufficient to note that the Synoptics concur that the parable was spoken against the chief priests. Even if the parable is not regarded as authentic in its present form, or the original parable was distinct or intended differently, the Synoptics seem to be preserving a tradition according to which Jesus spoke out openly yet somewhat enigmatically against the Jewish leaders in some way. If Jesus' action in the temple is viewed in light of the parable of the wicked tenants, it supports the idea that he intended that action as an expression of opposition to the high priestly elites.

Jesus' Death and His Conflicts with the Jewish Authorities

The conclusion of the parable of the wicked tenants presents Jesus as anticipating his own death at the hands of the chief priests. This idea appears throughout the Synoptics, particularly in the passion predictions attributed to Jesus. Once again, while the historicity of these predictions can be questioned, it is significant that the tradition as the Synoptics knew it claimed that Jesus expected conflict with the chief priests. If Jesus' action in the temple was premeditated, as the Synoptics imply, rather than a sudden, impulsive response to what he observed happening there, then he must have realized ahead of time that his action would contribute in some way to the decision of the chief priests to have him arrested and perhaps put to death as well.

---

that, while many scholars think the parable could go back to Jesus, only a minority hold the view that its allegorical features and the use of Psalm 118 would have been part of the original parable (*The Dead Sea Scrolls and the New Testament*; Minneapolis: Fortress, 2005, 257).

151. Herzog, *Parables*, 98-113.

152. Both Kloppenborg (*Tenants*, 86-88) and Snodgrass (*Parable*, 80-82) note that some scholars believe that the son in the parable originally referred to John, though both regard this proposal as doubtful.

153. In this regard, Steven Bryan even argues that the referent of the vineyard shifts from the Jewish leaders at the beginning of the parable to Israel as a whole at its end (*Jesus*, 55).

At the end of the parable of the wicked tenants, Jesus is presented as citing Ps. 118:22, which speaks of the stone rejected by the builders becoming head of the corner. Once again, many question the possibility that Jesus ended the parable with this quotation, in large part because some see it as an allusion to Jesus himself being constituted as the new cornerstone for a new temple after he had been raised.[154] However, the allusion need not be understood as anticipating Jesus' resurrection. If Jesus did cite the words from Psalm 118, his idea might simply have been that the consequence of his being put to death by the authorities would be that a new community, movement, or reality would spring up and grow as a result of his violent death. Both in antiquity and in our own day, the slaying of controversial leaders has at times led to the strengthening and expansion of the cause or movement to which they were dedicated, rather than its weakening or disappearance. The effect such deaths produce is thus the opposite of that which those carrying out the killing anticipated and desired. It is therefore possible that Jesus merely had this idea in mind: not Jesus himself, but his violent death at the hands of the chief priests would lay the basis for a new reality to be constructed that would in some way replace or supersede the temple. In this case, the "cornerstone rejected" might even refer to Jesus' message or his ministry rather than Jesus personally.

Scholars have commonly affirmed that the parable of the wicked tenants does not view Jesus' death as salvific. Such an affirmation derives from the traditional assumption that a death must be atoning in order to be salvific. While the death of the owner's son is certainly not seen as atoning, it does result in the salvation of others in two ways. First, it leads the owner to destroy the wicked tenants and give the vineyard to others. If the parable is understood as referring allegorically to God, Jesus, and the chief priests, it implies that Jesus anticipated a confrontation with the chief priests in which he would be put to death, but also expected that God would respond to their unjust act by destroying the chief priests. In that case, Jesus may have thought that, by confronting the chief priests in Jerusalem and calling on them to give to God the "fruits of the vineyard" that belonged to God—however these fruits are understood—he would bring about their downfall, since they would refuse to do so, and would consequently be destroyed by God. In that case, Jesus saw his rejection at their hands as having an objective. It would make their oppressive, violent, and unjust ways evident to all and bring down God's wrath upon them so that the "vineyard"—whatever it may have represented—might pass into the possession of others. Obviously, this would deliver many from the oppression of the authorities and make it possible for an alternative system to be established. Ironically, by allowing the Jewish high priestly elites to put him to death, Jesus would bring about their demise along with that of the corrupt system they held in place at the temple.

---

154. For the argument that Ps. 118:22 did not originally form part of the parable, see Kloppenborg, *Tenants*, 75-77. Other scholars, however, have questioned this view; see, for example, Buth and Kvasnica, who argue that Ps. 118:22 is integral to the original parable ("Temple Authorities," 76).

According to the parable as it appears in the Synoptics, the second consequence of Jesus' death is that it would lead to the laying of a cornerstone for a new construction. Whether this new construction is understood as a new community or a new temple in either a literal or metaphorical sense, Jesus' violent death would become the basis for some type of new reality. In that sense, it would also be salvific.

Similar ideas can be identified in the predictions attributed to Jesus concerning the destruction of the temple in Matt. 24:1-2, Mark 13:1-2, and Luke 21:5-6. While all of the Synoptics claim that Jesus predicted the temple's destruction, they do not present him giving any reason for this destruction explicitly. Because it is the temple itself that is to be destroyed rather than the leaders, the cause of its destruction would appear not to be the injustice and corruption being practiced there. If Jesus actually predicted that the temple would be destroyed, he was no doubt referring to the temple as it had been expanded and embellished by Herod. It is significant that the Synoptics present Jesus' prediction as a response to his disciples, who express their awe at the grandeur and splendor of the temple. Jesus may have seen the magnificence of Herod's temple as the result not only of a massive and unjust exploitation of the people and their resources, but as an attempt on the part of Herod and his successors to consolidate and expand their power over the region. The purpose for which rulers in antiquity constructed and embellished magnificent monuments such as the Jerusalem temple was to command the respect and admiration of the populace and perpetuate the idea that those responsible for building them were also great and powerful. In the case of the Jerusalem temple, Herod and his successors would also communicate the idea that they were dedicated to serving the God of Israel and that their rule enjoyed his favor. They were gratefully honoring the God who had put them in power.

Such enormous and sightly constructions would also lead the populace to hold in higher regard the high priestly families who controlled the temple area, and lead to a greater admiration and respect among the people for the offerings presented to God there. In other words, the magnificence and splendor of the temple edifice would convey the idea that those responsible for building and administering it, those presiding over the sacrifices offered there, as well as the sacrifices themselves, were also worthy of great admiration and brought honor, not only to the God worshiped there, but to all who participated in that worship. These beliefs would have generated even more resources for the temple and strengthened further the power and influence of the high priests. Therefore, even though Jesus speaks of the destruction of the temple itself rather than that of the Jewish authorities, it is very likely that he saw Herod's temple as symbolizing and furthering the oppression of the ruling elites.

As in the conclusion of the parable of the wicked tenants, in their accounts of the process against Jesus before the Jewish authorities as well as his crucifixion, Matthew and Mark also relate the destruction of the temple to the construction of a new reality. Jesus is said to have claimed, not only that he would destroy the temple, but also that he would raise up another one after three days (Matt. 26:61; 27:40; Mark 15:29). In Mark 14:58, the temple to be raised by Jesus is said to be "not made with hands." The Fourth Gospel also preserves this tradition and relates it to Jesus' action in the temple (John 2:13-22). The criterion of multiple attestation would suggest that there is some historical basis to Jesus' words about the raising of a new temple, even though he may not have anticipated being raised from among the dead after three days.[155] While there may be good reasons to question the historicity of the prediction attributed to Jesus regarding the temple, if he did prophesy its destruction, it is quite possible that he also prophesied the establishment of some type of new temple or reality as well.

Due to the conflicts with the Jewish religious leaders that Jesus' teaching in the temple is said to have generated, as well as his action in the temple, it would have been natural for Jesus to expect that the authorities in Jerusalem would seek to silence or eliminate him in some way. If so, he would undoubtedly have hoped that the cause to which he had dedicated himself with such great fervor during his ministry would continue after his death. Whether or not he expected to be raised from the dead, he might reasonably have expected that his violent death would serve to strengthen the resolve of his disciples and therefore lead to an expansion of his community of followers. Even though in reality his crucifixion seems initially to have had the opposite effect on his disciples, driving them into seclusion and fear, if Jesus expected that his death would further the cause to which he had dedicated himself, then he would have viewed his death as ultimately being salvific or beneficial for others by virtue of the new reality to which it would lead. From Jesus' perspective, that new reality might be the result of the way in which others would react to his death, perhaps by being outraged or inspired by it, or the result of God responding to the injustices committed there by bringing about the downfall of those responsible for those injustices, as the parable of the wicked tenants affirms.

This latter idea, in fact, appears both in Matt. 23:29-32 and in the second-century *Epistle of Barnabas*. In the first of these passages, Jesus affirms, "Woe to you, scribes and Pharisees, hypocrites! For you build the tombs of the prophets and decorate the graves of the righteous, and you say, 'If we had lived in the days of our ancestors, we would not have taken part with them in shedding the blood of the prophets.' Thus you testify against yourselves that you are descendants of those who murdered the prophets. Fill up, then, the measure of your ancestors." A similar idea is reflected in the *Epistle of Barnabas*, which seems to draw on the passage from Matthew. There it is said that God's Son came in the flesh so that he "might bring to a head the sum of the sins

---

155. Scholars such as Fiensy have observed that, even if Jesus prophesied the destruction of the Jerusalem temple, his words do not necessarily imply that Jesus himself would be the one to bring about that destruction (*Jesus*, 202-8).

of those who had persecuted his prophets to the point of death" (*Barn.* 5:11). Behind these affirmations is the idea found in the Hebrew Scriptures that the repeated rejection of God's prophets leads to God's judgment, which serves to cleanse and purge the sins and evil of the people and thus bring about a new reality. Jesus may therefore have believed that his death would benefit others in the same way.

Some have interpreted Jesus' action in the temple as having the intention of establishing some type of worship or cult that would constitute an alternative to the temple.[156] This possibility must certainly be given serious consideration, especially when it is recalled that the reason for which most people went to the temple was to seek God's favor, forgiveness, healings, and blessings. If Jesus saw these things as something that God was now offering through him and perhaps the community of disciples he was forming as well, it is possible that he intended to establish some type of alternative to the temple system. Nevertheless, the evidence we have does not seem to be strong enough to affirm this with any certainty.

In any case, it is important to stress that what must have motivated Jesus to teach at the temple and take action against the sellers, buyers, and money changers there was *a concern for others*. As was the case throughout his ministry, Jesus' objective was to benefit others in various ways, particularly those whom he regarded as the object of oppression and injustice. This understanding of Jesus' objective stands in contrast to a number of the interpretations of Jesus' action at the temple mentioned at the outset of this section. According to some interpreters, Jesus' primary concern was to defend the sanctity of the temple precincts, question the manner in which the sacrificial worship was being carried out, or even insist that the sacrificial worship commanded in the law needed to be replaced with some type of purely spiritual worship.[157]

The problem with views such as these is that they present Jesus as being concerned primarily with the proper worship of God or God's holiness rather than the well-being of human beings. Undoubtedly, these two aspects can be combined if it is maintained that Jesus believed that the well-being of others depended on the sacrificial offerings being properly presented or the holiness of God being safeguarded in the temple area. Nevertheless, such views seem to conflict with what the Gospels affirm regarding Jesus' ministry and the God he proclaimed. As noted above, according to the Gospels, throughout his ministry Jesus put the wholeness and well-being of others above any supposed concern for the sanctity of God or God's law. In fact, the conflicts associated

---

156. Chilton, for example, claims that, by instituting the Eucharist, Jesus intended the "creation of an alternative *cultus*" (*Pure Kingdom*, 123-26). Similarly, Wright affirms that "all that the Temple had stood for was now available through Jesus and his movement" (*Jesus*, 436); see also Gray, *Temple*, 91-92, 161-62. According to Dunn, by forgiving sins, Jesus was not so much usurping the role of God but rather assuming the role that God had assigned to priest and cult, thus undermining the authority of those whose power rested on the system (*Partings of the Ways*, 46). For both Horsley (*Spiral*, 296) and Bird (*Jesus*, 155-61), the new temple of which Jesus spoke was the renewed people of Israel or his group of followers.

157. For views such as these, see Fiensy, *Jesus*, 221-27; Peter Richardson, "Why Turn the Tables? Jesus' Protest in the Temple Precincts," *SBLSP* 31 (1992): 521.

with his ministry are presented as revolving precisely around the question of which of these two concerns should be primary. Jesus is consistently presented as giving priority to the well-being of others.

Just as Jesus appears to have been relatively uninterested in discussions regarding the proper interpretation of the commandments of the Mosaic law, so also he seems to have ascribed little importance to the offering of sacrifices. Scholars have debated whether or not Jesus had a favorable view of sacrifice or participated in the sacrificial offerings himself. Undoubtedly, the Gospels present Jesus at times sending those whom he healed to the priests and ordering them to present the sacrifices prescribed by the law (Matt. 8:4; Mark 7:44; Luke 5:14; 17:14). In Matthew, Jesus also teaches that one must be reconciled to one's brother or sister before offering one's gift at the altar (5:23-24), while in the Fourth Gospel Jesus participates regularly in the festivals at the temple.[158] Other scholars have argued, however, that these things do not necessarily suggest that Jesus had a positive view of the sacrificial worship offered at the temple.[159] The same must be said with regard to Luke's portrayal of Jesus' first followers as gathering regularly at the temple in Acts (Acts 2:46—3:1; 5:21, 42). Their presence at the temple does not necessarily imply that, in accordance with what Jesus had taught them, they considered it important to continue to offer sacrifices there. As Horsley has argued, they may have gone to the temple for other reasons.[160] At times the arguments in favor of the claim that Jesus viewed the sacrificial worship at the temple favorably seem to be circular: since Jesus was a faithful Jew, he must have participated in temple worship like all faithful Jews.

Whatever Jesus thought about the sacrificial worship at the temple, what the Gospel accounts repeatedly stress is his commitment to serving others. For this reason, his action in the temple must be regarded as having been motivated in some way by that commitment. If Jesus believed that the authorities would arrest him, imprison him, or sentence him to death as a result of that action, he must have been convinced either that the benefits that would result from his action for others were worth the cost or risks involved, or that the consequences he would endure would contribute to the cause to which he had dedicated himself on behalf of others. In either case, just as his ministry had been entirely "for others," his death would also be "for others," either because it would be the result of the activity he had carried out on behalf of others, or because it would bring about some new reality or situation that would be beneficial for others.

---

158. On the basis of passages such as these, as well as Jesus' participation in the Passover celebration, Klawans insists that Jesus was by no means "antitemple" (*Purity*, 217-19).

159. Freyne, for example, argues that there is no clear evidence that Jesus or his followers participated in the temple rituals during his lifetime (*Galilee, Jesus, and the Gospels*, 239-40).

160. Horsley, *Spiral*, 291-92.

The Last Supper

From a historical perspective, the Gospel accounts of Jesus' Last Supper with his disciples are problematic on a number of accounts. In addition to the fact that we can have no certainty as to what actually took place,[161] it is not clear whether the Supper as the Gospels present it was some form of Passover meal or celebration. John's account of the meal is almost completely different from the Synoptic accounts, which also reflect important differences in relation to one another.[162] In addition, the Gospels present Jesus as having foreknowledge regarding certain details of what was to take place, including Judas's betrayal and Peter's denial. The narratives of Jesus' words and action over the bread and wine also raise many questions. If Jesus' words are accepted as authentic, it is not clear precisely what his words originally were, precisely how those words are to be understood, and to what extent Jesus foresaw not only his impending death, but the continuation of such a meal among his disciples after his death.[163]

Obviously, it is not possible to address all of these questions here. Nor is it necessary, however. To address the question of the manner in which Jesus interpreted his death, it will be sufficient to consider the words over the bread and wine attributed to Jesus at the Supper. In particular, it is important to focus on the phrases "for you," "for many," and "for the remission of sins," as well as the idea of the establishment of a covenant or new covenant. While we cannot be sure to what extent these phrases actually go back to Jesus, their significance for the question of the meaning that Jesus ascribed to his death cannot be ignored. Even if Jesus never pronounced them or originally did so at another moment in a different context, they clearly seem to form part of an

---

161. For various perspectives on the historicity of the Gospel accounts of the Last Supper, see James D. G. Dunn, *Jesus Remembered*, Vol. 1 of *Christianity in the Making* (Grand Rapids: Eerdmans, 2003), 771-73; McKnight, *Jesus and his Death*, 262-64; Tan, *Zion Traditions*, 198-200; Klawans, *Purity*, 3-5; Joel B. Green, *The Death of Jesus: Tradition and Interpretation in the Passion Narrative* (WUNT 2/33; Tübingen: J. C. B. Mohr, 1988), 192-217.

162. For a summary of the arguments against and in favor of the Last Supper being a Passover meal, see Bradley S. Billings, *Do This in Remembrance of Me: The Disputed Words in the Lukan Institution Narrative (Luke 22:19b-20). An Historico-Exegetical, Theological, and Sociological Analysis* (LNTS 314; London: T & T Clark, 2006), 62-72; McKnight, *Jesus and his Death*, 264-73; Gerd Theissen and Annette Merz, *The Historical Jesus: A Comprehensive Guide* (Minneapolis: Fortress, 1998), 423-27. On this point, Klawans notes: "While few scholars today would endorse without qualification Joachim Jeremias's identification of the Last Supper as a Passover Seder, practically all scholars currently working on these materials consider the Seder ritual to be one of a small number of Jewish rites that are viewed as possible backgrounds for the Last Supper" (*Purity*, 214-15). David Stacey also observes that, "whether it was a Passover or not, the meal would have taken place in the Passover atmosphere" ("Appendix: The Lord's Supper as Prophetic Drama," in *The Signs of a Prophet: The Prophetic Actions of Jesus*; ed. Morna D. Hooker; London: SCM, 1997, 90).

163. On these questions, see especially Joachim Jeremias, *The Eucharistic Words of Jesus*, trans. Norman Perrin (Philadelphia: Fortress, 1977), 173-86; McKnight, *Jesus and his Death*, 275-92; Green, *Death of Jesus*, 192-210; Theissen and Merz, *Historical Jesus*, 405-28; Barry D. Smith, "The More Original Form of the Words of Institution," *ZNW* 83 (1992): 166-86; Bruce Chilton, "Ideological Diets in a Feast of Meanings," in *Jesus in Context*, Chilton and Evans, 60-67. Peter Stuhlmacher concludes that "it remains undecided until today whether the oldest form of the words of institution is preserved by Mark (and Matthew), or by Paul (and Luke)" ("Jesus' Readiness to Suffer and his Understanding of his Death," in *The Historical Jesus in Recent Research*; ed. James D. G. Dunn and Scot McKnight; SBTS; Winona Lake, IN: Eisenbrauns, 2005, 399).

early tradition, as 1 Cor. 11:23-25 attests. In that case, the followers of Jesus who attributed them to Jesus must at least have thought that they expressed faithfully ideas that reflected Jesus' own understanding of his death.

In the tradition as it appears in 1 Cor. 11:23-25 and Luke 22:19-20, Jesus is presented as telling the disciples as he gives the bread to them, "This is my body for you" (1 Cor. 11:24), or "This is my body, given for you" (Luke 22:19). In the Lukan version, Jesus also speaks of the cup as "poured out for you." In contrast, the version found in Matthew and Mark does not include the words "for you" in relation to the bread, and refers to the cup as Jesus' "blood of the covenant, poured out for many" (Matt. 26:26-28; Mark 14:22-24). The preposition used in all of these phrases is *huper*, with the exception of Matt. 26:28, where the phrase *peri pollōn* appears. Matthew also adds the words "for the remission of sins" to Jesus' saying over the cup. In all of these passages, the allusion is clearly to Jesus' death in some sense.

In the Lukan and Pauline versions of Jesus' words, the phrase "for you" is ambiguous and can therefore be interpreted as referring either to the disciples alone or to others as well. In contrast, the versions of Matthew and Mark explicitly refer to a larger group of people, the "many." In 1 Cor. 11:23-25, Paul appears to understand the phrase "for you" as including the believers in Corinth to whom he writes. It is therefore important not to assume that the Synoptic evangelists and Paul were all in agreement as to whom Jesus had in mind when he spoke of "you" or the "many."

Precisely because the phrases "for you" and "for many" are so ambiguous, it is possible to read back into them virtually any understanding of Jesus' death. Advocates of a penal substitution interpretation of Jesus' death read ideas associated with that interpretation back into these phrases. This often involves arguing that *huper humōn* can be translated "in your place" and not just "on your behalf." The phrases can also be understood on the basis of a revelational view of Jesus' work: Jesus' death is for others in the sense that it reveals the extent of his love for them, thus providing them with the knowledge and inspiration they need in order to live according to God's will and attain salvation. If the *Christus Victor* idea is read back into those phrases, they can be understood in the sense that Jesus will overcome the forces of evil for others, thereby liberating human beings from their bondage to those forces. For reasons seen in the first four chapters of this work, however, we can simply dismiss such interpretations here, since they are the product of later theological reflection, and are based on ideas that are foreign to ancient Jewish thought and to the New Testament. A similar observation must be made regarding the notion that, when Jesus spoke of the bread as his body and the wine or cup as his blood, he intended for his disciples to understand that he was referring to the actual substance of his body and his blood. There is no reason to suppose that Jesus believed that his actual body and blood would be multiplied repeatedly in the centuries following his death whenever his words over the bread and the cup would be recited, thereby making it possible for believers to partake of those substances in some mysterious or ontological manner. Rather, as Jonathan Klawans has insisted, Jesus' words should be taken primarily in a metaphorical sense.[164]

Due to the influence of penal substitution views, Jesus' words over the bread and wine are commonly read as conveying the idea that Jesus' death would obtain God's favor and forgiveness for others and turn away God's wrath at their sins. The fact that Matthew mentions the remission of sins seems to have reinforced this idea even further among interpreters, especially because Matthew's addition is commonly recited in the versions of Jesus' words used in liturgical settings in many churches. Once again, however, there is no clear evidence that ancient Jews, Jesus, or his later followers believed that it was not possible for God to forgive sins without exacting punishment for them, or that suffering and death were necessary to atone for sins. Furthermore, as we have seen in Chapters 2, 3, and 4 of this study, the condition for forgiveness in ancient Jewish thought was always repentance and a commitment to doing God's will. For these and other reasons, Jesus' words "for you" and "for many" should not be understood in the sense that the giving up of Jesus' life, symbolized by the breaking of the bread and the pouring out of the cup of wine, would in itself render God favorable to believers, put away God's wrath at their sins, or obtain forgiveness on their behalf.

This means that we should interpret Jesus' words in some other way. In order to do this, we may begin by noting that, seen in the context of his command for the disciples to eat of the bread and drink of the cup, Jesus words over the bread and wine would be understood not only in the sense of giving his life up *for* others but also giving himself *to* others—in this case, the disciples.[165] It is possible, of course, that Jesus anticipated that he would rise from the dead and therefore believed he would continue to give himself to his disciples and others in some way after his resurrection. However, even if this giving of Jesus' life to others is understood metaphorically rather in a literal or ontological sense, perhaps as referring to his ongoing presence in the community of believers, many scholars would regard as problematic the notion that Jesus foresaw his impending resurrection and intended that all who would subsequently become his followers throughout the world celebrate regularly the meal he was instituting, repeating the words he had pronounced over the bread and wine each time they did so. Here again, one's presuppositions will inevitably determine one's conclusions in this respect.

Whether or not Jesus anticipated being raised from among the dead shortly after his death, there can be little doubt that he had a strong desire

---

164. Jonathan Klawans, "Interpreting the Last Supper: Sacrifice, Spiritualization, and Anti-Sacrifice," *NTS* 48 (2002): 6-7, 15-17.

165. Stacey argues, for example, that the breaking of bread symbolized not violence but pluralization, that is, Jesus' giving of himself to many ("Appendix," 93). Stacey also claims that "the breaking of the bread was not primarily concerned to interpret Jesus' death. It is concerned with the whole of his teaching and mission.... The bread was broken in order that the body of Christ might be represented, not in the person of the Lord himself, but in the persons of those who believed in him and followed him" (92-93).

to remain among his disciples and continue serving them and others. John's Gospel particularly emphasizes Jesus' love for the disciples in its account of the Last Supper, though the same emphasis is implicit in the Synoptics. Jesus' apparent wish to have a final supper with his disciples also stresses his affection and concern for them. In addition, it seems logical to suppose that Jesus did not want to die. Even if one questions the historicity of his prayer in the Garden of Gethsemane, in which he asks God to be spared the cup that he was to drink (Matt. 26:39, 42; Mark 14:36; Luke 22:42), it is highly probable that his early followers who attributed the prayer to him believed it expressed faithfully the way in which he viewed his death.[166]

However, if Jesus knew that he was in danger of being arrested and put to death by the authorities because of the things he had said and done in defiance of those authorities, as well as the impact his work was having on many of the people, then he essentially had two options. He could either stand firm and embrace whatever consequences his words and actions might have, or else try to avoid arrest and death. If he chose the second alternative, he might go into hiding, flee to a more secure place, or put an end to what he had been doing and saying, perhaps admitting openly that he had been wrong or misguided. If in spite of this he was arrested, he could then try to convince the authorities not to act against him in a number of ways: by defending himself, promising to put an end to his activities, publicly recognizing his errors, telling his followers to disband, insisting that he and his followers posed no threat to the authorities, or simply begging for mercy. There is no evidence that Jesus did any of these things. On the contrary, according to the Gospels, up until his arrest he continued to teach openly in the temple after boldly carrying out his prophetic act there. To back down from the consequences of his actions would have been regarded both by Jesus and by others as a denial of everything he had stood for in his ministry.

For Jesus to back down would also have had drastic consequences for the community that he sought to establish. Jesus had repeatedly spoken of being committed to loving others and giving oneself for them. Throughout his ministry he had embodied that love. How could Jesus expect total dedication and absolute commitment to that type of love for others if, when confronted with the possibility of arrest and death, he had turned in on himself, attempting to save his own life and putting an end to his work for others? Similarly, Jesus had constantly stressed the need to trust fully in God under all circumstances. How could he expect others to do so if, when in danger, he had sought to run or hide or backed down from his ministry? If Jesus really believed what he had proclaimed, taught, and lived, he had no choice but to embrace the consequences of what he had been doing, whatever those might be. This was

---

166. On the question of the historicity of the Synoptic accounts of Jesus' prayer in Gethsemane, see especially Raymond E. Brown, *The Death of the Messiah: From Gethsemane to the Grave. A Commentary on the Passion Narratives in the Four Gospels* (ABRL; New York: Doubleday, 1994), 1:216-34. On the content of Jesus' prayer, see 1:165-78.

the only way he could hope to establish a community of people fully committed to God and to solidarity with others, a community willing to stand up to injustice and oppression and resist the powers in place.

In fact, this may have been the reason why Jesus had decided to go up to Jerusalem. If Jesus had been preparing his disciples to serve others and had been seeking to establish an alternative community that would practice solidarity and resistance in relation to the system in place and its authorities, he must have realized as he did so that that the greatest obstacle his disciples would face was *fear*. As had been evident from Jesus' own ministry, truly to serve those in need and stand up for them in love generated conflict with those in power. Such service and love required that one denounce the injustice and violence that was inherent to the system that those in power propagated and defended. Then as now, it is not possible to be fully committed to seeking the well-being of others if one remains silent and passive in the face of the systemic oppression that is the greatest hindrance to that well-being. Similarly, a community of the type envisioned by Jesus cannot live in fear and seclusion, hoping to evade confrontation and conflict. It must live openly, boldly, and defiantly in the way that he did, committed to the well-being of all no matter what the consequences.

Given this reality, if Jesus wished to inspire absolute trust in God and overcome fear in others so that they might live as members of a community characterized by total commitment to the well-being of all, he had no choice but to live in that way himself. Yet, in Jesus' context, to live in that way inevitably meant conflict, opposition, and in many cases a violent death. The powers that ultimately prevented people from living in that way in the context of such a community were the Roman imperial authority and the Jerusalem hierarchy. Rome threatened those it regarded as subversives with violence of various types, particularly physical violence such as crucifixion. For their part, the Jerusalem hierarchy and those in their service maintained power and inspired fear through their theology—or ideology—and their interpretation of the law and of the Scriptures. They claimed to be the unique divinely-appointed representatives of God, the mediators between God and God's people. According to this ideology, those who desired to enjoy God's favor had to approach God through the high priests and the priests in general. This meant presenting their sacrifices through the priests and participating in the divinely-ordained system of worship the priesthood represented by offering their sacrifices and tithes and paying the temple tax. In this and other ways, the high priestly elites propagated the claim that whoever refused to submit to their authority refused to submit to God as well, and thus was under divine condemnation. Jesus' action in the temple was inevitably seen as a rejection of ideas such as these.

If Jesus truly wished to challenge these beliefs and inspire others to follow him, as well as to create the type of community he desired, he may have realized that he had no choice but to go up to Jerusalem. He could not accomplish his purposes in the same way by merely continuing to minister in the Galilean villages. Nor could he accomplish those purposes by taking a stand against lesser authorities, such as those in leadership roles in the villages or the representatives of Rome in the cities of Tiberias and Sepphoris. As noted above, this may have been the reason why he had evaded the Galilean cities and had sought to avoid danger previously; the right time and place to stand up to the authorities had not yet presented itself.[167] If Jesus were to be imprisoned or executed by a lesser authority, his death would not have the same impact as if he died at the hands of the Jerusalem authorities such as the high priest, the Sanhedrin, and perhaps the Roman procurator himself. He may have realized this after seeing the manner in which John's death at the hands of Herod Antipas had impacted the populace, as well as John's disciples.

This is not to say that Jesus went to Jerusalem because he *wanted* to die there. Rather, what he wanted to do was to bring his disciples and others to trust fully in God as they stood firm in all that he had taught and proclaimed. Only in this way could he establish the type of community he desired to see. For that reason, he had to go up to Jerusalem and take a public stand against the system, embodying undauntedly everything he stood for. Though Jesus may have had other reasons for going to Jerusalem as well, it is likely that he saw his presence and activity there as vital and indispensable to attaining his ends. If Jesus affirmed that it was not possible for a prophet to die outside of Jerusalem, as Luke 13:32-33 reports, he may have had in mind the idea that only by dying in Jerusalem could one be remembered as a prophet and make a powerful prophetic statement through one's death. In other words, if sooner or later he was going to be put to death for his work, he would choose the time and place according to his own purposes and objectives, rather than leaving it up to others or to chance.

Jesus must also have truly trusted in God in order to take such a step. While he may not have believed that he would be raised after three days, he must at least have been confident that God would raise him some day in the future. He may also have believed that God would intervene to prevent him from dying. His cry of dereliction from the cross may be an indication of that belief: he felt God had abandoned him (Matt. 27:46; Mark 15:34). Nevertheless, the evangelists Matthew and Mark may have reported Jesus' cry because they saw it, not as a cry of despair, but as a cry of faith.[168] Writing for others who were experiencing the same persecutions Jesus had endured, both evangelists may have wanted their readers to know that God had not actually abandoned Jesus, even though he felt that way, since in the end God would

---

167. As Richard Beaton notes, this idea is found in Matthew's Gospel, where "Jesus sidesteps potential threats to his life until the time is right for him to advance to Jerusalem to die (16.21)" ("Messiah and Justice: A Key to Matthew's Use of Isaiah 42:1-4?," *JSNT* 75 [1999]: 18).

168. So argues Dan Cohn-Sherbok: "Jesus' words should not be understood as a cry of despair and desolation in the face of death, but rather as a prayer for the dawning of the reign of God" (*Rabbinic Perspectives on the New Testament*; SBEC 28; Lewiston, NY: Edwin Mellen, 1990, 52-53). On the different interpretations of Jesus' cry, see Brown, *Death of the Messiah*, 2:1043-51.

raise him from among the dead. In the same way, when the readers felt abandoned by God, they should know that such was not actually the case.

Jesus' Words over the Bread and Wine

All of the ideas just considered provide the background necessary to address the question of what Jesus meant when he told the disciples, "This is my body," after breaking bread and giving it to the disciples to eat. Even if he did not add the words "for you" or "given for you," as Luke and Paul report, the context would have indicated that this was what he intended his disciples to understand. By breaking and distributing the bread, Jesus was communicating to the disciples that, for their sake, he was accepting the consequences of the ministry he had carried out for others in Galilee and in Jerusalem by embracing the suffering and death that awaited him, rather than running away from it. While in a sense Jesus' actions and words over the bread expressed the idea of giving himself or his life *to* his disciples, they also implied that he would not resist those who sought to harm and kill him, but would hand himself over to them, placing his life and work in God's hands. Yet he was doing this, *not for his own sake*, but *for the sake of his disciples and others*. Only in this way, by remaining faithful to all that he had lived for, could he continue to be committed to their well-being and that of others.

While Jesus may also have intended the words he spoke over the bread in the sense that his handing himself over to death would in some way result in the salvation of his disciples and others in the future at the *eschaton*, it is important to keep in mind that Jesus had constantly exhorted them to be willing to give of themselves by serving others as well. Jesus desired this not only for the sake of those whom the disciples would serve, but also because he firmly believed that one's own well-being depended on one living out of love for others by giving of oneself to and for them in one's daily life. In this case, even if Jesus was addressing his words only to the disciples when he told them that the bread was his body "for them," he must have been concerned for the wholeness and salvation, not only of his disciples, but of others as well, who would be transformed by the ministry that his disciples would continue to carry out in Jesus' name. Only as they dedicated themselves to serving others as Jesus had done could they experience true wholeness.[169] Thus, while Jesus' primary concern at that moment may have been his disciples, in the context of everything else he had done, he must also have been thinking of others, including especially those who would come to form part of his community of followers after his death.

---

169. While Jesus' role as servant is particularly stressed in the Last Supper account in the Fourth Gospel, where Jesus washes the feet of his disciples (John 13:3-17, 34-35), the same idea can be seen in the Synoptic accounts. Crossan notes that the act of breaking and distributing the bread was the work of a servant; therefore Jesus assumes the role of servant, in addition to that of being master and host. Crossan even argues that Jesus took on the role of female as well (*Historical Jesus*, 404).

In this context, for Jesus to tell the disciples to eat of his body and drink of his blood would be to invite them to commune, not with *elements* or *substances*, but with the *way of being* that Jesus had manifested throughout his ministry and would continue to manifest up to the moment of his death. To eat of his body would involve not only receiving Jesus' gift of his own person to them and recalling how he had given himself up in love for them, but also assuming the same commitment to give of oneself to and for others together with Jesus.[170] Similarly, to drink his blood would be to identify oneself as a member of the community for which he had poured out his life, as well as to share in the same spirit of being willing to give one's own life to and for others, as Jesus had done. This means that Jesus would have intended his words regarding eating his body and drinking his blood to be understood in terms of recalling the depth of his love for all and being committed to sharing that same love with others.

Jesus must also have desired that the alternative community he had worked to establish continue to exist, not only for the sake of the disciples themselves, but for the good of others as well. As we have seen above, the only way in which this community would continue to exist and take the form Jesus desired it to take was for Jesus to be willing to give up his life. By doing so, he would not only make the continued existence of this community possible, but also place his stamp definitively on that community. Thanks to Jesus' faithfulness to death in seeking the well-being of others, by definition, that community would be one in which all were willing to give themselves to and for one another in the way that Jesus had given up his life for the community. Jesus could only expect that community to be characterized by a full commitment to the well-being of all if he embodied in himself that commitment by being willing to die so that such a community might continue to exist after his death.

Jesus' words regarding a covenant or new covenant should be interpreted on the basis of these same ideas. In ancient Jewish thought, a covenant involved a divinely-instituted system of relating to God.[171] It contained promises of salvation for those forming part of the covenant people, but also expectations regarding their conduct. Whether or not Jesus saw the covenant of which he spoke as replacing the covenant with Israel,[172] he must have interpreted it in terms of the establishment of relationships characterized by the same commitment to the well-being of all that he had embodied in life and was now embodying by giving up his life. He also must have conceived of those committed to living in those relationships in obedience to him as constituting a community that would be identified with the covenant of which he spoke.

---

170. McKnight stresses this idea: "the consumption of that bread and wine entails a similar commitment to give one's life for Jesus and his followers" (*Jesus and his Death*, 328).

171. On the notion of covenant in second-temple Jewish thought, see especially Holmén, *Jesus*, 39-50. See also Alan F. Segal, "Covenant in Rabbinic Writings," *SR* 14 (1985): 53-62.

172. Scholars have debated whether or not Jesus spoke of a "new covenant," and if so, in what sense he would have understood this designation. For this discussion, see McKnight, *Jesus and his Death*, 304-20; Tan, *Zion Traditions*, 200-220.

Jesus therefore must have intended his giving himself up for others as a *foundational act*: it would define forever how his followers would relate to God and one another, and thus form the very heart and nucleus of the covenant he was establishing or ratifying.

If Jesus intended that his followers continue to break bread and drink a cup of wine together periodically after his death, he would have understood the act of partaking of the bread and especially the wine or cup as defining one as a member of the community living under that covenant. Participation would therefore be a means by which one manifested one's commitment to Jesus and the ideals associated with his life and death.[173] On the basis of Jesus' words, the cup would remind those who drank of it that Jesus had poured out his life or blood so that they might form part of his community of followers by living in the covenant established through his self-giving unto death. It would also remind them that the same kind of love that Jesus had manifested in life and death was expected and required of them. Nevertheless, to live in that same love would be seen not as an onerous burden, but as a motive of great joy and hope. For that reason, to share in the bread and cup together would serve not only to recall Jesus' death, but to celebrate his love, which thanks to his death had come to be the same love of all who ate and drank together.

If Jesus' allusion to the forgiveness of sins in the Matthean version is regarded as historical, that forgiveness must be seen as constituting one of the primary promises associated with the covenant Jesus was establishing. Jesus would not have intended his words to be understood in the sense that he was pouring out his blood or life in order to make it possible for God to do something that he previously could not do, namely, forgive sins without compromising his perfection, holiness, and righteousness. Such an idea must be regarded as entirely foreign to Jesus' thought. Instead, Jesus would have meant that those who would form part of the covenant community he was establishing by offering up his life could have assurance that, as long as they remained in that community and lived under that covenant, God would accept them and forgive them their sins. In that sense the cup represented the blood of his covenant, "poured out for many for the forgiveness of sins." In life and in death, Jesus had sought to form a community that might live in love according to God's will as defined through him, and had taught that those who would live as members of that community would enjoy God's forgiveness and blessings. It is this to which he must have been referring. In other words, in Jesus' mind, the relation between the pouring out of his blood or life and the forgiveness of those who would live under the covenant established through him is not that his blood or death in itself would obtain the remission of sins, but that the giving up of his life would lead to a new, divinely-established

---

173. According to Alexander J. M. Wedderburn, "the act of distributing and the shared eating can be seen as an action that means fellowship, friendship and solidarity and would have been seen as such in the society of that time" (*The Death of Jesus: Some Reflections on Jesus-Traditions and Paul*; WUNT 299; Tübingen: Mohr Siebeck, 2013, 83).

community in which all would enjoy the forgiveness of sins. The *basis* for their forgiveness would not be Jesus' death per se, but their living as members of the community of his followers for which he had offered up his life or poured out his blood.

A number of scholars have argued that Jesus' words over the bread and wine should be understood in the sense that he was attempting to set up an alternative to the Jerusalem temple cultus.[174] According to this argument, whereas previously it had been maintained that forgiveness was obtained by participation in the sacrificial rites associated with the temple, Jesus was now instituting a new means by which those participating might obtain assurance of divine forgiveness. There may be some truth to this idea, although once again it must be stressed that in Jewish thought, God's forgiveness was not always tied to participation in the sacrificial worship carried out at the temple. However, there seems to be no question that Jesus sought to establish an alternative community and, if some form of the words Jesus is said to have spoken over the cup is authentic, he related the idea of a covenant or new covenant with the community of those who would identify themselves as his followers.

Whether Jesus regarded those who would belong to this community as forming *part* of Israel or as constituting the true Israel is unclear. In either case, however, he must have believed that outside of his community of followers there were others who could obtain God's acceptance and forgiveness merely by living in accordance with God's commandments, independently of any faith in him or relation to him. He might even have believed that this was true not only for Jews, but for non-Jews as well. Nevertheless, on the basis of Jesus' interpretation of the law, he would have understood true obedience to the law in terms of living in love and practicing justice in the way that he had taught. Jesus would therefore see himself and his death as redefining the *basis* upon which people would be forgiven and saved by God. From that point on, what would define one as a member of God's people would no longer simply be a literal observance of the Mosaic law, but a life of love and solidarity that fulfilled the true purpose of the law in the way Jesus had taught and embodied. It is possible that Jesus even saw himself, not only as the one who defined what the proper interpretation of the law consisted of, but also as the one to whom the law pointed as its fulfillment.

Jesus' words over the bread and wine reflect sacrificial ideas as well. Although Jesus does not explicitly speak of his death as a sacrifice offered to God on behalf of others, this is undoubtedly implied in Jesus' affirmations that his body would be "given" and his blood would be "poured out" for

---

174. See, for example, Chilton, *Pure Kingdom*, 124-26; Theissen and Merz, *Historical Jesus*, 431-36; Jostein Ådna, "Jesus' Symbolic Act in the Temple, Mark 11:15-17: The Replacement of the Sacrificial Cult by his Atoning Death," in *Gemeinde ohne Tempel=Community without Temple: zur Substituierung und Transformation des Jerusalemer Tempels und seines Kults im Alten Testament, antiken Judentum und frühen Christentum* (ed. Beate Ego, Armin Lange, Peter Pilhofer, and Kathrin Ehlers; WUNT 118; Tübingen: Mohr Siebeck, 1999), 461-75. For arguments against the idea that Jesus intended the Eucharist as a replacement for the temple cult, see Klawans, *Purity*, 213-17; Dunn, *Jesus Remembered*, 795-96.

others.[175] If Jesus believed that he would be put to death, it is very likely that he saw his death as being comparable to a sacrifice offered for others. In fact, given what we have seen, it would have been strange for him *not* to think in these terms. This does not mean, of course, that Jesus applied to himself all of the sacrificial ideas and motifs that later developed among his followers. It is probable that Jesus' followers came to speak of Jesus as paschal lamb and high priest and to draw other comparisons between Jesus' death and the sacrificial worship carried out at the temple only later, some time after his crucifixion. Nevertheless, it is possible that Jesus saw some correlation between what was taking place in his last hours and certain ideas, symbolisms, stories, and figures that appeared in Israel's Scriptures and traditions.

The allusion to the forgiveness of sins may appear to be somewhat out of place in Matthew's account of the Last Supper and his version of Jesus' words over the cup. It seems rather unlikely that in his last moments with the disciples, Jesus was preoccupied with the question of the basis upon which God might forgive his followers their sins. However, if he did believe that he was establishing a covenant with his disciples and others who would come to form part of his community of followers, he must also have thought that this covenant would be valid and acceptable in the sight of God. For Jesus, this would mean that those who would live in the covenant of which he spoke would also be acceptable before God. By definition, such acceptance would involve the forgiveness of their sins. Furthermore, even if Jesus did not anticipate that he would be raised shortly after his death, his words over the cup indicated that he believed that the basis upon which his followers would be deemed acceptable to God would be their commitment to following in his footsteps by dedicating themselves to serving others in love, as Jesus had done. In that case, Jesus saw his death as being for his disciples and the "many" in the sense that God would accept and forgive all who would come to identify with his self-offering on their behalf, responding to what he had done by offering themselves up to God's service as he had and together with him.

Such an idea also implies that Jesus saw himself in the role of a mediator between God and his disciples. Once again, even if he did not expect to be raised from the dead in the days following his death, he would have gone to his death asking God to accept all who would come to identify with him and with the way of thinking and living that he had sought to instill in others in obedience to his Father. From Jesus' perspective, his death would be "for others" in the sense that his intercession on behalf of those who would live as his followers would constitute a new foundation on the basis of which they might approach God confidently to obtain God's acceptance and forgiveness. In other words, by offering his life up to God asking that God accept and forgive all who would come to follow him by living in the way that he had taught

---

175. Klawans notes that "the symbolic value of Jesus' act of giving (present in all the narrative traditions) may well draw its meaning from the presence of the notion of giving in sacrificial traditions," even though the implications of Jesus' words and act "may not be exclusively sacrificial" ("Interpreting the Last Supper," 15).

and embodied, Jesus would attain that acceptance and forgiveness for others. Because in Jewish thought sacrifices involved the presentation of offerings and prayers to God, Jesus would not only have viewed his death as sacrificial, but would have seen himself playing a role similar to that of a priest, who served as a mediator on behalf of others by offering up sacrifices and prayers on their behalf.

Ultimately, of course, what Jesus must have been seeking as he went to his death was not only that God accept, forgive, strengthen, and accompany his community of followers in the present world, but also that they might some day attain the eschatological salvation he associated with God's reign. According to the Synoptics, in his last moments with his disciples, Jesus told them that he would not drink of the fruit of the vine again until he did so with them in God's reign (Matt. 26:29; Mark 14:25; Luke 22:18). While this involved contemplating his own future following his death, it also involved contemplating the future of the disciples, whom he loved deeply. As he ate and drank with them for the last time, his hope and prayer was that they might all be together again when the reign of God he had proclaimed became a reality. By remaining faithful all the way to the end to the task he believed had been given to him by God—namely, that of forming a community of followers who would live according to God's will as God had defined that will through Jesus—Jesus would attain not only his own entrance into God's reign, but that of all who would live as his disciples as well. Their conviction that, in spite of the scandalous and shameful way he had been put to death, Jesus had indeed been sent by God and had dedicated himself to bringing about in others a life of conformity to God's will throughout his ministry up until his very last breath would lead them to live as his followers, dedicating themselves to doing God's will by loving others as Jesus had done. In that way, thanks to Jesus' faithfulness unto death to the task given him and his love for them, they would attain the salvation Jesus had sought for them and others. Once again, Jesus almost certainly had this idea in mind as well when he affirmed that his body would be given or broken and his blood poured out on behalf of the "many."

All of the Gospels also claim that Jesus expected that, after his arrest, at least some of his disciples would fail to remain faithful to him and to the mission in which they had come to be involved as a result of his having called them to follow him as his disciples. If this was indeed the case, Jesus may have mentioned the forgiveness of sins at the Last Supper in order to assure them that, even if they did fall away, they could find forgiveness and acceptance before God by identifying themselves once again with Jesus and the love for others he would manifest in his death. Of course, this would also involve identifying themselves with the covenant he was establishing with them in the presence of God. Jesus would therefore have understood himself to be offering up his life on behalf of his followers in the sense that he would go to his death asking that God always receive his followers favorably whenever they would approach God with a sincere heart, asking him to forgive their sins and accept them anew. Once again, this would involve seeing himself as acting in the role of mediator on behalf of his disciples in his death and seeing his death as sacrificial.

In the end, while it is impossible to know precisely what Jesus said and did when he dined with his disciples for the last time, there can be little doubt that he understood his death as an act of love for others and prayed that, by giving up his life rather than seeking to save it, the community of followers that he had worked to establish would be strengthened in their commitment to live in the way he had taught so as to attain salvation when God came to reign. Just as throughout his ministry he had consecrated himself to the salvation of others out of his deep love for all, so also he must have consecrated himself to that same end as he approached his death.

The Arrest, Condemnation, and Execution of Jesus

The interpretations that Jesus' first followers gave to his death after his crucifixion undoubtedly were influenced greatly not only by what Jesus himself communicated to them and others through his words and deeds in the last days and hours of his life, but also by what they believed had happened in the time between his arrest and his crucifixion. Here again it is virtually impossible to determine to what extent the Gospel accounts are historically reliable. There are significant differences among the Gospels with regard to what took place in Jesus' last hours. If Jesus' followers were not present when he appeared before the Jewish and Roman authorities, some answer must be given to the question of how they later learned what had taken place.[176] Scholars continue to debate the reasons why Jesus was condemned to die on a cross and to what extent the Jewish authorities were involved. Obviously, Jesus was seen as a threat, yet why this was so is not entirely clear.[177]

Most of these questions can be left unaddressed here. Only a few of them are relevant for reconstructing how Jesus viewed his death and what

---

176. Crossan has argued that "Jesus' closest followers knew nothing more about the passion than the fact of the crucifixion, that they had fled and later had no available witnesses for its details" (*Historical Jesus*, 375-76). Others, however, have questioned such a view, claiming that there are various ways in which Jesus' followers may have been able to discover what happened to Jesus between the time of his arrest and his crucifixion. See, for example, Darrell Bock, "The Son of Man Seated at God's Right Hand and the Debate over Jesus' Blasphemy," in *Jesus of Nazareth*, ed. Green and Turner, 181-84; K. Schubert, "Biblical Criticism Criticized: With Reference to the Markan Report of Jesus's Examination before the Sanhedrin," in *Jesus and the Politics of his Day*, ed. Bammel, 385-402.

177. For different views on these questions, see Ingo Broer, "The Death of Jesus from a Historical Perspective," in *Jesus from Judaism to Christianity*, ed. Holmén, 145-68; Theissen and Merz, *Historical Jesus*, 444-69; Nils A. Dahl, "Messianic Ideas and the Crucifixion of Jesus," in *The Messiah*, ed. Charlesworth et al., 382-403; Gerard S. Sloyan, *Jesus on Trial: A Study of the Gospels*, 2nd ed. (Minneapolis: Fortress, 2006), 1-28, 97-103; Richard A. Horsley, "The Death of Jesus," in *Studying the Historical Jesus*, ed. Chilton and Evans, 395-422; Dunn, *Jesus Remembered*, 784-90; D. R. Catchpole, "The Problem of the Historicity of the Sanhedrin Trial," in *The Trial of Jesus: Cambridge Studies in Honour of C. F. D. Moule* (ed. Ernst Bammel; SBT 2/13; London: SCM, 1970), 47-71; Ernst Bammel, "The Trial before Pilate," in *Jesus and the Politics of his Day*, ed. Bammel, 415-51. Other essays in both of the last two volumes edited by E. Bammel also address many of the historical questions surrounding Jesus' death.

he communicated to his followers through his words and actions after his arrest. As noted above, there is no evidence that Jesus sought to avoid his death either before or after his arrest. If he knew or expected that he would be betrayed by Judas and arrested in Gethsemane, that did not dissuade him from going there. Once he had been arrested, he apparently did not attempt to convince the authorities that he was innocent, insult them, struggle against them, or attempt to defend himself. According to the Gospels, at times Jesus simply kept silent, refusing to answer the questions asked of him. If this was indeed the case, Jesus may simply have been refusing to participate in a judicial process that he deemed illegitimate or to recognize that those judging him had any right or authority to do so.[178] He also may have been hesitant to answer their questions about whether he claimed to be a king or the awaited Jewish Messiah figure because he did not see himself as fulfilling these roles in the way that his interrogators defined them. In that case, he did not want to affirm plainly that he was the Messiah, since that word carried connotations that were foreign to Jesus' own understanding of his messiahship. At the same time, he did not want to deny that he was the Messiah, since that might give the impression that he was acting out of fear or attempting to save himself rather than boldly proclaiming who he believed himself to be. For that reason, he may have responded in a way that was intentionally vague, as the Synoptics report: "So you say," or, "You might say so" (Matt. 26:64; 27:11; Mark 15:2; Luke 22:70; 23:3).

In one sense, however, Jesus does appear to have defended himself when interrogated about his activities. According to the Fourth Gospel, when the high priest asked him about his teaching, Jesus claimed that he had always spoken openly and in public, thereby stressing his integrity as well as the fact that he had done nothing secretly or surreptitiously (John 18:19-23; cf. Luke 22:53). Jesus may also have responded in this way in order to contrast his own behavior with that of the authorities, who were judging him in an irregular process in secret, out of fear of the reaction of the population (Matt. 21:26, 46; Mark 11:18, 32; 12:12; Luke 20:19; 22:2). [179]

These points would all be significant for Jesus' followers, since they demonstrated that he was one who always acted with integrity and was willing to stand up firmly and boldly for what he believed to be right and true. Had Jesus resisted the authorities or attempted to save his life, his followers would have had no basis for later affirming that he had given up his life or offered it up to God on their behalf.

The spirit of love and forgiveness that had characterized Jesus' behavior from the time that he went to Gethsemane to the moment that he died would also have been significant for Jesus' first followers. If Jesus had been

---

178. Following Christopher Bryan, I will avoid the use of the word "trial" to refer to the process against Jesus, since it is "not clear exactly how those who conducted such a process would have regarded it" (*Render to Caesar: Jesus, the Early Church, and the Roman Superpower*; Oxford: Oxford University Press, 2005, 57).

179. On the question of the legality of the Jewish process against Jesus, see Donald Juel, *Messiah and Temple: The Trial of Jesus in the Gospel of Mark* (SBLDS 31; Missoula, MT: SBL, 1977), 59-64.

remembered as having cursed or insulted those who acted against him or having asked God to take vengeance on them, it is likely that his death would not have been seen as an act of love. If he was in any way resisting death, he was not offering his life up to God seeking salvation for others. The Gospels instead present Jesus as expressing love and concern for others in his last moments, however. In Luke's account of the Last Supper, Jesus mentions that he has been praying for Simon Peter and his "brothers" (Luke 22:31-32). When he is arrested, he asks that his disciples be left alone and allowed to leave (John 18:8). He does not rebuke Judas for having betrayed him nor act aggressively toward those who arrest, judge, flog, mock, and mistreat him (Matt. 26:47-55, 67-68; 27:27-31; Mark 14:43-50, 65; 15:16-20; Luke 22:47-53, 63-64; John 18:4-11; 19:2-38). According to Luke's Gospel, when some of his women followers cried out in lament as they observed him walking to his death, he told them to weep for themselves rather than for him (Luke 23:27-31). Luke also presents Jesus as asking God to forgive those who were crucifying him and telling one of those being crucified alongside of him that he would be with Jesus that same day in paradise (Luke 24:34, 43). The Fourth Gospel presents Jesus expressing concern for his mother and his beloved disciple while on the cross (John 19:26-27). Even though many scholars would question the historicity of some of these passages, they provide evidence that Jesus' followers remembered him as one who had shown love and concern for others in the midst of his sufferings and death.

Finally, to whatever extent the Jewish authorities were involved in having Jesus put to death, the fact that they were considered by many to be in collusion with the Romans, who kept them in power, means that Jesus' death would inevitably have been seen as the result of his opposition to the social, political, religious, and economical system of his day. The *titulus* placed on Jesus' cross, according to which he was being executed for his claim to be "king of the Jews," would have reinforced this idea. Jesus was ultimately put to death by the system for opposing that system through his proclamation of God's reign, the ways in which he had taught others to reject that system, and his efforts to form a community that represented an alternative to the system. The fact that he was put to death on a Roman cross rather than being stoned or put to death in some other way would also serve as a perpetual reminder that Jesus had died for standing up against the oppressive system associated with Rome, and against the Jewish authorities who remained in power by being subservient to Rome as well. Furthermore, because Jesus had taken that stand *not for his own sake* but *for the sake of others*, from the time of his crucifixion onward, Jesus' followers would see the cross as symbolizing their conviction that Jesus had *given up his life on their behalf and on behalf of others*.

The Redemptive Significance Jesus Ascribed to his Death

In numerous passages from the Gospels, Jesus is said to have foreseen and foretold not only his sufferings and death in Jerusalem but also a number of other details regarding what would take place there. Although it would have been natural for Jesus to expect to die in Jerusalem, especially if he intended to carry out a provocative act at the temple, from a purely historical perspective, it seems difficult to sustain that Jesus had foreknowledge of many of the events he is said to have foretold.

If Jesus did foresee in general terms what would take place in Jerusalem, however, it does seem quite possible that he believed that his sufferings and death would not only take place in accordance with God's will, but also formed part of a divine plan. In that case, although it is not clear precisely what Jesus thought that plan would involve, it is likely that he viewed it as including things that would happen, not only before his death, but after it as well. Among these things would have been the establishment of God's reign at some point, and perhaps the growth and extension of his community of followers as well. Whether or not Jesus expected to be raised prior to the general resurrection, he may also have thought that he would play an important or even central role in the events to take place. If Jesus thought that Israel's Scriptures foretold those events and saw them as part of a divine plan, he may have believed that those Scriptures spoke of himself as well.[180] Nevertheless, it is simply impossible to know what Jesus believed would happen in Jerusalem and whether he thought that the Scriptures foretold what would take place through him.

Once again, the presuppositions with which one approaches these questions will determine to a great extent the manner in which one responds to them. If it is claimed that Jesus had foreknowledge of his death or believed that it had been foretold in the Scriptures, however, this should not be understood in the sense that Jesus believed that there was some type of "blind fate" that he had to endure for no particular reason. At the very least, Jesus would have thought that his death would benefit others in some way and serve some divine purpose, even if he was not fully aware of what that purpose might be. Otherwise, he could not have conceived of his death as an expression of love for others.

If Jesus thought others would be benefited by his death, however, it is doubtful that he had no concept of precisely how his death would be beneficial for them. In the Synoptics, outside of the words attributed to Jesus at the Last Supper, the passage in which Jesus most clearly ascribes saving significance to his death is Mark 10:35-45 (Matt. 20:20-28; cf. Luke 22:25-27). There, in response to the petition that James and John be allowed to sit at Jesus' right hand when he is enthroned in glory, Jesus affirms that he will

---

180. On the possibility that Jesus saw his death as the fulfillment of certain passages from the Hebrew Scriptures, see especially Ben F. Meyer, "Appointed Deed, Appointed Doer: Jesus and the Scriptures," in *Authenticating*, ed. Chilton and Evans, 155-76. Richard Horsley's claim that Jesus was a person who almost certainly "did not read texts" would seem to argue against the notion that Jesus saw his death as fulfilling passages from the Hebrew Scriptures, although even if Horsley is correct, few scholars would doubt that Jesus knew the Scriptures well in oral form ("The Dead Sea Scrolls and the Historical Jesus," in *The Bible and the Dead Sea Scrolls*, ed. Charlesworth, 1:37).

undergo a "baptism" and then tells his disciples: "You know that among the Gentiles those whom they recognize as their rulers lord it over them, and their great ones are tyrants over them. But it is not so among you; but whoever wishes to become great among you must be your servant, and whoever wishes to be first among you must be slave of all. For the Son of Man came not to be served but to serve, and to give his life as a price of redemption for many" (*dounai tēn psuchēn autou lutron anti pollōn*; Mark 10:42-45).

Like the words over the bread and the wine ascribed to Jesus in the New Testament accounts of the Last Supper, this saying has generally been interpreted on the basis of ideas associated with the various understandings of atonement found in Western Christian theology. Scholars who debate the authenticity of Jesus' words then raise the question of whether Jesus could have believed that he would atone for the sins of others by dying as their substitute or whether he understood his death as a ransom paid to either God or Satan.[181] This means that the question of the historicity of Jesus' saying is answered on the basis of certain presuppositions regarding what that saying means.

On the basis of what we have seen previously, we can dismiss the possibility that Jesus understood his death in terms of penal substitution. Nowhere in the Gospels do we find any hints of such an idea. Jesus is never presented as alluding to any "problem of forgiveness" on God's part or implying that God's justice had to be satisfied before God could grant forgiveness. Nor does Jesus ever speak of dying in the place of anyone else or enduring any type of penalty or punishment on the part of God.

The Greek word *lutron* has commonly been translated into English as "ransom." Such a translation implies a price paid to free a person or group of people from a situation of bondage or slavery. The one holding the person or people is therefore seen as acting oppressively, either by enslaving the person or persons involved or by holding them for ransom in the way that a kidnapper would do. To translate *lutron* as "ransom," therefore, raises the question of to whom the ransom is paid. Traditionally, only two possibilities are considered: Jesus offered his life either to God or God's justice in order to deliver sinful human beings from the penalty to which they were subject, or else to the devil, who held human beings under his power and subjected them to death.

Both of these alternatives are extremely problematic. There is no basis in the New Testament for claiming that either Jesus or his first followers believed that God was holding human beings in captivity, demanding the death of some righteous person who could serve as their substitute in order to release them from the penalty of death to which they were liable. Such a view

---

181. On these discussions, see Peter Stuhlmacher, *Reconciliation, Law, and Righteousness: Essays in Biblical Theology*, trans. E. Kalin (Philadelphia: Fortress, 1986), 16-29; McKnight, *Jesus and his Death*, 159-75; Craig A. Evans, *Mark 8:27—16:20* (WBC 34B; Nashville: Thomas Nelson, 2001), 120-25. Hengel accepts the authenticity of Jesus' saying, yet considers it likely that it was pronounced at the Last Supper (*The Atonement: The Origins of the Doctrine in the New Testament*; Philadelphia: Fortress, 1981, 34-36, 73).

also runs contrary to the concept of God that is attributed to Jesus throughout the Gospels. While Jesus did believe that at least some human beings were influenced by Satan and perhaps even fully subject to his power, it is not clear from the Gospels that he believed that this was true of humanity as a whole. Furthermore, when Jesus is presented as casting out demons or saving others from Satan or the forces of evil, he does not offer the devil or demons some type of ransom payment in exchange for the liberation of those under their power, but simply casts them out through his word and the power of the Holy Spirit. It cannot seriously be maintained, therefore, that Jesus saw his death as a ransom payment made to God or Satan.

In contrast, to speak of Jesus' death as a price paid to redeem others does not necessarily imply that it was paid *to* someone. Just as today it is common to speak of someone paying a price to be successful or to accomplish a certain objective without implying that some type of transaction between parties is involved, so the original saying attributed to Jesus could have meant merely that, by paying the ultimate price—namely, that of his life—, Jesus would bring about the redemption of others. It is also important to stress that the saying does not speak of Jesus' *death* as the *lutron* but rather the *giving up of his life*. In reality, the saying only affirms some relation between Jesus' surrender of his life and the redemption of others from some situation or condition from which they needed to be freed. Furthermore, there is no reason to believe that this redemption merely involved the forgiveness of sins, as if the problem was one of divine punishment. Rather, the saying should be seen as referring to deliverance from some other type of bondage or slavery.

It is possible that behind the saying is a concept of redemption comparable to that which was associated with the deliverance of the Israelites from their bondage to the Egyptians in the time of Moses. If so, on the basis of Jesus' proclamation of God's reign and the age to come, Jesus would have believed that, if he remained faithful unto death to the task God had given him, God would act to make his reign and that new age a reality. However, because Jesus understood his task in terms of bringing others into conformity with God's will rather than simply dying, the reason God would act to fulfill his promises would not merely be that Jesus would die, but that his faithfulness unto death would lay the basis necessary for others to live in the way God desired so that they might participate in God's reign and the new age.

If Jesus also expected God to raise him from the dead so that he might be God's instrument to bring to fulfillment the promises God had made, then he must have believed that his faithfulness unto death to the task God had given him would make it possible for him to bring about the awaited redemption once he had been raised. It is important to stress, however, that Jesus would not expect God to raise him from the dead simply because he had *died*, as if his death itself were the necessary condition for his resurrection and exaltation. In the thought of Jesus, if God was to raise him from the dead, it would be because, by being faithful unto death, he had shown himself to be the servant on behalf of others that God had wanted him to be. Furthermore, God's purpose in raising him from the dead before bringing about the general resurrection of the dead would be that Jesus might continue to be active as God's servant until the salvation he had sought for others in life and death might be consummated through him.

Whether or not Jesus expected to be raised from the dead shortly after his death, then, he would have seen his death, not as effecting in itself the redemption of others, but as the means by which others would be redeemed from the situation of bondage or slavery in which they found themselves. While many scholars have argued that the preposition *anti* used in the phrase *lutron anti pollōn* implies some type of substitution, it should instead be understood in the sense of an *exchange*. This exchange would not involve some type of commercial transaction or exchange of goods or property. Rather, the idea is that by giving up his life, Jesus would obtain in exchange the redemption of many. This was because his faithfulness unto death would lead to the existence of a community of people who would follow all that he had taught and embodied and acknowledge him as their leader and Lord so as to be brought to live in accordance with God's will. On that basis, God would redeem them from their plight in the present age.

This understanding of the phrase *lutron anti pollōn* is consistent with the context in which it appears. Among the problems with the penal substitution and *Christus Victor* interpretations of the phrase is that those interpretations view that phrase in isolation from its context. Jesus' emphasis in Mark 10:35-45 is not on *death* but on *serving others*. The request that James and John be allowed sit at Jesus' right and left hands in his glory reflects an attitude like that of those who dominate and rule over the nations, who seek power for their own benefit in order to lord it over others and tyrannize them. In contrast, Jesus insists that his disciples are to be servants and slaves of one another, and then points to himself as an example of one who came "to serve rather than be served," and to give up his life for others. This means that the main subject Jesus is addressing in the passage is not how his death will save others, but how his disciples should be willing to serve others even at the cost of their lives, following the example of Jesus himself, rather than seeking positions of power and glory for their own benefit.

Undoubtedly, when Jesus speaks of laying down his life as a price of redemption in exchange for others, he would not seem to be suggesting that if his disciples laid down their life out of love for others, they too would bring about the redemption of others. It is not out of the question, however, that Jesus believed such an idea to be true to some extent. Earlier in the passage, Jesus speaks of his death as a "cup" that he must drink and as a "baptism" that he must suffer; yet he also affirms that James and John will some day drink the same cup and be baptized with the same baptism (Mark 10:38-39). This involves seeing their deaths as analogous to his.

If Jesus regarded the giving up of his life as a price to redeem the "many," he may have believed that the deaths of his disciples could also contribute to the redemption of others. In this case, Jesus thought that, by remaining faithful to his task of establishing a community in which all were committed to a life of love and service in conformity with God's will, such a community would indeed become a reality. In that way, he would attain the redemption of all those who would form part of that community. In the same way, as his followers would dedicate their lives to building up, strengthening, and expanding that community, and at times even surrender their lives for that objective, they would also contribute to the redemption of all who would belong to that community. Their faithfulness unto death in loving and serving others would also serve to bring others to live and even be willing to die in the same way so that they too might participate in God's reign when it arrived. Nevertheless, Jesus' disciples would be able to live and die in that way and contribute to the redemption of others only because Jesus himself had first offered up his life for that purpose. Any impact that the life and death of the disciples would have on others would be the result of the impact that Jesus' life and death had had on the disciples themselves. Their life and death would contribute to the redemption of others only because they sought to conform themselves to Jesus' life and death. Thus, while in one sense Mark 10:35-45 views Jesus' death as unique, at the same time it serves as an example and pattern for the disciples to follow in seeking the redemption of others by dedicating their lives to the service of others, even to the point of being willing to lay down their lives for them.[182]

In order to understand this idea, a modern analogy may be helpful. Both Martin Luther King Jr. and Archbishop Oscar Arnulfo Romero of El Salvador dedicated their lives to fighting in peaceful ways against oppressive systems. In both cases, they were well aware that they were putting their lives at risk and would probably be killed as a result of their activity. Yet, rather than backing down from that activity, they endured steadfastly and as a result were indeed killed. Although those who killed them hoped to strike a serious blow against the cause for which they were struggling, their violent deaths actually led to the opposite effect: they produced such outrage and indignation among others that those who were being oppressed lost all fear and began to dedicate themselves even more intensely to the objective of changing the dominant system and bringing the oppression to an end. The faithfulness unto death of Rev. King and Archbishop Romero to the objectives for which they had lived and died thus moved others to be willing to give up their lives in the struggle for liberation. Thus, while in one sense their deaths were unique due to the impact they had on others, at the same time they were *not* unique in

---

182. As Paul Garnet notes, "the aim of Jesus' statement in Mark 10:45 was not so much to indicate the precise benefits of the forthcoming ransom, as to point to the attitude of humble service on the part of the Son of Man, which motivated it, as an example for the disciples to follow" ("Atonement: Qumran and the New Testament," in *The Bible and the Dead Sea Scrolls*, ed. Charlesworth, 1:372).

that others became willing to give up their lives in the same way and for the same cause.

While Jesus' death can be regarded as similar to the deaths of Rev. King and Archbishop Romero, in some respects it was also different from theirs. Neither Rev. King nor Archbishop Romero claimed to possess the same type of divine authority that Jesus is said to have claimed for himself as God's chosen instrument to proclaim and bring in God's reign. Furthermore, only Jesus formed around himself a community of followers and prepared a well-defined group of disciples to serve as leaders of that community.

However, Jesus' allusion to the tyranny of those who ruled over the nations in the saying attributed to him may indicate that he had another idea in mind as well. That allusion would almost certainly be taken as referring to the Roman emperor and those who ruled throughout the empire under his authority. If Jesus did anticipate conflict in Jerusalem with the Roman or Jewish authorities due to his opposition to the dominant system maintained by Rome, then the idea behind his words may have been that, by surrendering his life to those authorities, many would be freed from their dominance and power. In other words, Jesus knew that the Roman and Jewish authorities would want to kill him because they would see his teaching and actions in Jerusalem as fomenting resistance to Rome or even rebellion against the system Rome had established in Palestine in collusion with the Jerusalem hierarchy it had appointed.

Therefore, Jesus may have believed that, if he let the Roman authorities take his life, the result would be that the "many" would be redeemed from their bondage and slavery to Rome. This redemption would either be the result of God's responding to Jesus' unjust death by removing the authorities from power and establishing his own reign as an alternative system, as the conclusion of the parable of the wicked tenants implies, or because Jesus' death would embolden the "many" to cease to submit slavishly to the Roman and Jewish authorities.[183] By seeing how Jesus had trusted fully in God and thus had not been afraid to stand against the system in spite of its violence toward him, many would cease to cower in fear to Rome. Instead, they would come to trust in God as Jesus had done so as no longer to live in bondage and submission. This response to Rome's power would not involve any type of armed revolt, but simply the type of resistance to Rome's demand for absolute loyalty that we see among Jesus' first followers in the decades and centuries following his death. It would also include their living in alternative communities as

---

183. I would therefore tend to agree with Max Wilcox that "the so-called 'ransom'-saying in Mark 10:45c and Matt 20:28c should be interpreted primarily historically, rather than as though it were some kind of theological statement," yet I would nevertheless question his claim that Jesus saw himself as "the 'ransom' paid to the Roman authorities" to spare Jerusalem by allowing himself to be taken and executed ("On the Ransom-Saying in Mark 10:45c, Matt 20:28c," in *Geschichte–Tradition–Reflexion*, ed. Lichtenberger, 3:173-86). Jesus' concern was not to save Jerusalem or Israel from destruction by the Romans, but to help liberate others from Roman oppression by allowing them to overcome the fear that enslaved them and to grow in their boldness to resist the system imposed by Rome.

followers of Jesus rather than of Caesar. In this case, Jesus' followers would also reject the notion that the rule of Rome and the Jerusalem hierarchy it had appointed was in conformity with God's will and that therefore the Roman and Jewish leaders were God's representatives.

Jesus may even have considered his death as a type of ransom or payment in an ironic sense: Jesus would give the rulers what they wanted, yet the result would be the opposite of what they expected. Instead of Jesus' death serving to extend and consolidate further their domination of others, it would help bring that domination to an end. It is not difficult to see how the church fathers in later centuries may have come to develop the same basic idea by claiming that Jesus had offered his life to the devil and the devil had unwittingly accepted it, thinking that he would thereby establish his dominion over all. According to these ideas, the devil did not realize that the effect of taking Jesus' life would be the opposite of what he desired: rather than gaining control over all, he would instead lose the control he possessed. A couple of passages from the Gospels, in fact, imply that the rule of Rome is the rule of the devil (Mark 5:1-9; Luke 4:5-6).[184] Furthermore, as noted above, the ailments and sufferings of the population were often attributed not only to the activity of Satan and the demons, but also to the dominant system imposed by Rome.

If Jesus expected to be raised from the dead, he would probably have also intended his affirmation that he would obtain the redemption of many in exchange for giving up his life in the sense that his heavenly Father would raise him as a result of his faithfulness unto death. In that way, Jesus himself would be able to bring about the redemption associated with God's reign and the age to come. This idea would not preclude the other ideas just mentioned, but instead would stand alongside them and complement them. When people had learned that God had raised Jesus from the dead in order to give him the power and authority necessary to establish God's reign, they would be liberated from Rome's dominance by losing their fear of Rome and instead coming to trust fully in the God who had raised Jesus. As a result, they would live in solidarity as members of the alternative community that Jesus had given up his life to establish.

This interpretation of Jesus' *lutron* saying precludes not only the penal substitution interpretations traditionally read back into Jesus' words but also the type of interpretation proposed by scholars such as Albert Schweitzer, Dale Allison Jr., N. T. Wright, and Brant Pitre, all of whom have claimed that Jesus believed that in his death he would undergo the messianic tribulation in the place of his followers, thereby saving them from that tribulation.[185]

---

184. In his discussion of the notion of authority in Mark's Gospel, Tat-Siong Benny Liew notes that there are a number of passages in Mark in which "Mark may be subtly associating Jewish authorities with the dominion of the devil" (*Politics of Parousia: Reading Mark Inter[con]textually*; BibInt 42; Leiden: Brill, 1999, 74-75).

185. For the views of these scholars, see especially Albert Schweitzer, *Quest*, 387-89; Dale Allison Jr., *The End of the Ages Has Come: An Early Interpretation of the Passion and Resurrection of Jesus* (Philadelphia: Fortress, 1985), 115-41; Wright, *Jesus*, 565, 570-72, 593-96, 608-10; Brant Pitre, *Jesus, the Tribulation, and the End of the*

Two major problems exist with regard to that interpretation. The first of these is that, in spite of the arguments to the contrary made by these scholars, a careful analysis of the New Testament texts reveals that there is nothing in them to suggest that Jesus understood his death in that way. Undoubtedly, the Synoptic Gospels present Jesus speaking of a time of great tribulation and suffering before the end and expressing his hope that his disciples and others might be spared that suffering. Jesus also is presented as anticipating that he would suffer a great deal before being put to death in Jerusalem, and believing that his sufferings and death would contribute in some way to the salvation of others. At no point, however, do Jesus, his disciples, or the evangelists combine these two distinct ideas to affirm that Jesus thought that the suffering he would endure would be that of an expected great tribulation. Much less do the texts imply that he thought that his sufferings would deliver others from that tribulation. On the contrary, even after Jesus' death, his followers expected that the tribulations of which Jesus had spoken would come to pass as he had predicted. If the Gospels mention the possibility of his disciples and others being saved from that time of tribulation, it is not because Jesus would endure that tribulation in their place, but because God would show mercy to them, because they would flee to the hills, or because Jesus or the Son of Man would return to save them (Matt. 24:1-51; Mark 13:1-37; Luke 21:5-24).

The historicized version of this idea presented by Wright is problematic for the same reason. There is no reason to suppose that Jesus thought that, through his death, he would "create a breathing space for his followers and any who would join them, by drawing on to himself for a moment the wrath of Rome and letting them escape."[186] If the Romans viewed Jesus as a threat to their order, they were going to crucify Jesus independently of what they would or would not do to the disciples. Jesus was therefore enduring Rome's wrath at his own actions rather than at the actions of his disciples. Outside of possibly asking the Jewish or Roman authorities to leave his disciples untouched, nothing that Jesus did, said, or suffered led the Romans to refrain from persecuting his disciples. If they were spared persecution, it was not because Jesus got the Romans to channel onto himself a wrath that would otherwise have fallen on the disciples but because, for whatever reason, the Romans did not regard the disciples as a threat. In the decades following Jesus' death, the Romans did indeed act against Jesus' disciples, arresting and even killing many of them. They also acted against Jerusalem and the Jewish population in Palestine when the Jewish revolt broke out. There is therefore no reason to suppose that Jesus believed that his death would in any way change the reality that Rome would continue to seek to extinguish and quell with violence any type of movement or activity that they saw as a threat to Roman domination, just as the Romans always had done.

Exile: Restoration Eschatology and the Origin of the Atonement (WUNT 2/24; Tübingen: Mohr Siebeck, 2005), 451-55, 477-78, 505-7, 513-15.

186. Wright, *Jesus*, 610.

A further problem with the claim that Jesus believed that he would endure the messianic tribulations in the place of his disciples and others is that it presupposes a view of God and the way that God works that runs contrary to the beliefs of ancient Jews in general, and Jesus himself in particular. If Jesus thought that God would channel the expected tribulation onto Jesus himself rather than bringing that tribulation onto the people as a whole, then apparently he believed that God did not care *who* suffered the tribulation, but only that *someone* suffer it. God would also accept that Jesus, as one who was righteous and innocent, suffer the tribulation in the place of those who were sinful. Besides the fact that this would be unjust on God's part, it would defeat the entire purpose of the tribulation, which was to test and purify God's people so that a righteous remnant would be left who would be deserving of the life of the new age. The tribulation was not intended to punish sinners and exact retribution for their sins—that would take place in Hades or the place of the dead *after* the end had come. Rather, it would play a vital role in purging the earth and its population from evil and injustice, and enable God to determine who was truly faithful and righteous and who was not. God would not be able to do this, however, if that tribulation was channeled onto Jesus alone.

On this basis, we must reject the claims of the scholars who argue that Jesus believed that, in his death, he would endure the great tribulation so that others would be spared that tribulation and God's reign might come immediately. According to the Gospels, in fact, Jesus did not think that his death would deliver others from suffering. On the contrary, he claimed that it would be followed by even greater suffering. In his own words, he had come not to bring peace but a sword and to set fire to the earth (Matt. 10:34; Luke 12:49). Just as the authorities and others had hated and persecuted Jesus and sought his death, so also would they treat his followers in the same way, and perhaps even worse (Matt. 5:11-12; 10:16-23; 23:34-39; Luke 11:49-52; 21:10-12; John 15:18-25). His followers would therefore endure great tribulations of their own.

We must also reject the possibility that any of the other traditional Christian interpretations of Jesus' death examined in Chapter 1 of this study reflect faithfully his beliefs. This means that Jesus did not believe that he was dying for the sins of the entire world or that, on the basis of his death, God would forgive the sins of human beings of all times and places, including those who had lived many centuries before him. Nor did Jesus believe that his death would bring about some type of ontological change in human nature as a whole or in the created order. Although Jesus undoubtedly believed that his death would serve to reveal to others certain truths and exhorted others to follow him in giving up their lives for others as he would do, there is no evidence that he thought that his purpose in life was to die in order to provide some divine revelation to human beings or lay down an example for them to follow. All of these views of Jesus' death see it as having a purpose distinct from that of his ministry, and therefore imply that Jesus *died* for something different than what he *lived* for.

From Jesus' perspective, God had not designed or staged Jesus' death for some such purpose or any of the others just described. Rather, in Jesus' mind, God had sent him, not to die, as if that were the objective, but to establish a community of followers who would be committed to living in love, justice, and solidarity. The result of his commitment to that task would be his death, due to the opposition and conflicts his activity would generate. At the same time, his faithfulness unto death would be the definitive and final act on his part that would make such a community possible.

* * *

In summary, Jesus must have seen his death as the only means by which the type of alternative community that he had dedicated his ministry to establishing might be brought into existence, a community in which all would be fully committed to the same type of love and solidarity that had been the driving force behind all that Jesus had done. While he did not seek death or wish to die, he recognized that he could not continue to consecrate himself to serving as God's instrument for bringing salvation to others without actively embracing the suffering that inevitably awaited him in Jerusalem. Once there, he proclaimed his subversive message regarding God's reign boldly and openly, and even carried out an act of angry prophetic denunciation at the temple, knowing full well that the consequence of his actions would almost certainly be his arrest and probably a violent death as well. Rather than seeking to escape such a fate, however, he offered his life up to God, trusting that God would act in some way and at some time to bring to pass all that he had sought for others throughout his ministry. At the same time, as he faced his death, his deep love for others must also have led him to ask God to allow him to complete the work he had begun in obedience to God's will and to bring that work to its fullness by enabling people throughout the world to come to experience the joy of living under God's reign. Whether or not he knew precisely how he would die or had any idea what might happen after his death, Jesus simply placed his life and his work on behalf of others in the hands of the Father he loved, confident that his Father would not let his life and death be in vain.

CHAPTER 6

THE CRUCIFIED JESUS AS LORD AND MEDIATOR

On the basis of the historical reconstruction of Jesus' ministry, passion, and death presented in the previous chapter, we may now turn to the question of the theological and salvific significance that Jesus' first followers came to ascribe to those events. This is the question that we will examine in this and the following four chapters.

Precisely where in the New Testament we should look first in order to begin to reconstruct the ways in which Jesus' first followers interpreted his death is an extremely difficult question. The letters of Paul are the oldest of the New Testament writings, and thus take us back closer in time to the years immediately following Jesus' death. As we noted in Chapter 1, however, when he alludes to Jesus' death, Paul uses brief formulas that are open to a wide variety of interpretations. This is true of the other New Testament letters as well, including especially the letter to the Hebrews, where allusions to Jesus' death are particularly frequent. Because these formulas lend themselves to having all sorts of ideas read back into them, including the various interpretations considered in Chapter 1, it is extremely problematic to take them as a starting-point for understanding how Jesus' first followers interpreted his death.[1]

The four Gospels, which include a great deal of material that predates Paul's letters, provide by far the most information of all the New Testament writings regarding what took place in Jesus' last days and hours. They also include many other allusions to Jesus' sufferings and death in the narratives that precede their accounts of Jesus' passion. Nevertheless, they seem to contain relatively little theological reflection on the salvific significance of Jesus'

---

1. Albert L. A. Hogeterp, for example, questions taking Paul's letters as a starting-point for considering the earliest eschatological beliefs among Jesus' followers due to the historical distance between Paul and Jesus, and the fact that the missionary contexts in which Paul worked and wrote were distinct from those of the earliest believers (*Expectations of the End: A Comparative Traditio-Historical Study of Eschatological, Apocalyptic, and Messianic Ideas in the Dead Sea Scrolls and the New Testament*; STDJ 83; Leiden: Brill, 2009, 115-16). On this same basis, it could be argued that Paul's interpretations of the cross arose to some extent independently from those that developed among Jesus' first followers immediately following his crucifixion. In contrast, Martin Hengel sees Paul's writings as the preferred starting-point for understanding the earliest interpretations of Jesus' death among his followers due to their earlier date (*The Atonement: The Origins of the Doctrine in the New Testament*; Philadelphia: Fortress, 1981, 70-71). Hengel's approach is criticized by Joel B. Green, who asks whether texts outside the Pauline corpus might represent better the thought of the earliest Christians. Green chooses to begin with the Gospels in order to attempt to reconstruct "a pre-canonical passion narrative" (*The Death of Jesus: Tradition and Interpretation in the Passion Narrative*; WUNT 2/33; Tübingen: J. C. B. Mohr, 1988, 3-6).

death. Instead, they focus primarily on the conflicts between Jesus and the Jewish authorities, as well as the circumstances surrounding his passion and crucifixion. Furthermore, because of their later date, to take the Gospels as a starting-point would require some type of historical reconstruction in order to determine the content of the earliest traditions preserved by Jesus' followers in the years immediately following his crucifixion, prior to the composition of Paul's letters. Because of the complexities involved in such a task, reaching a consensus on which material dates back to the earliest years is virtually impossible. The book of Acts contains a number of passages that supposedly present the earliest preaching of Jesus' followers following his death, commonly referred to as the *kerygma*, yet Acts was probably written relatively late in the first century and, like the Synoptics, seems to contain little theological reflection on Jesus' death.[2]

The best approach, and the one that I will follow here, seems to be that of examining these writings together as a whole. Because they proceed from different circles and a variety of places and times, any elements that appear in more than one source have a high probability of being older. In essence, such an approach involves applying to the New Testament as a whole the criterion of multiple attestation used by historical Jesus scholars.[3] The assumption is that there is a greater probability that the ideas that appear repeatedly throughout the various strands of the New Testament writings date back to an earlier tradition than it is that those ideas arose and developed independently of one another in different contexts, although of course this latter possibility cannot always be ruled out. To be sure, this approach is not without its own possible pitfalls, including especially that of reading back from one writing into another ideas that are foreign to it. The fact that the books of Matthew, Ephesians, Hebrews, and 1 John, for example, all relate Jesus' blood to the forgiveness of sins does not necessarily mean that the authors of these writings understood that relation in the same way (Matt. 26:28; Eph. 1:7; Heb. 9:6—10:14; 1 John 1:7). To complicate matters further, the manner in which each of these writings relates Jesus' blood to forgiveness may have been different from the way in which that relation was viewed by Jesus' first followers in the years immediately following his death.

In spite of these difficulties, I believe that the approach I have chosen offers us the best possibility of reconstructing faithfully in broad terms the beliefs of Jesus' first followers regarding the salvific significance of his

---

2. On the problems of attempting to use Acts or Paul's epistles to reconstruct the earliest kerygma, see especially Brevard S. Childs, *Biblical Theology of the Old and New Testaments: Theological Reflection on the Christian Bible* (Minneapolis: Fortress, 1993), 219-25. For arguments in favor and against the historicity of the speeches in Acts, see especially Colin J. Hemer, *The Book of Acts in the Setting of Hellenistic History* (WUNT 49; Tübingen: J. C. B. Mohr, 1989), 415-27; Osvaldo Padilla, *The Speeches of Outsiders in Acts: Poetics, Theology, and Historiography* (SNTSMS 144; Cambridge: Cambridge University Press, 2008), 16-41.

3. On the criterion of multiple attestation as it has been applied to studies of the historical Jesus, see especially John P. Meier, *A Marginal Jew: Rethinking the Historical Jesus*, Vol. 1: *The Roots of the Problem and the Person* (New York: Doubleday, 1991), 174-75; Gerd Theissen and Annette Merz, *The Historical Jesus: A Comprehensive Guide* (Minneapolis: Fortress, 1998), 116-17.

death. However, because Jesus' followers interpreted his death on the basis of their beliefs regarding who Jesus was, how he related to God, and what he had done prior to his death, it is important to examine these beliefs before beginning to address the ways in which they came to interpret Jesus' sufferings and death.

JESUS AS LORD AND CHRIST

Of all the claims made regarding Jesus by his first followers, the one that is by far the most well-attested is the affirmation that he is Lord and Christ or Messiah. Although these titles may have been applied to Jesus prior to his death, their widespread use does not seem to have taken place until after the first believers began to proclaim that he had risen from the dead. Even if these two titles had been applied to Jesus during his lifetime, the way in which they were understood undoubtedly changed following his crucifixion.

Of course, it is impossible to know precisely what happened early on the Sunday after Jesus was crucified and in the days immediately following his crucifixion and burial. Whether or not one is convinced by arguments in favor of the historicity of Jesus' resurrection such as those put forward by N. T. Wright and other scholars ultimately depends on one's presuppositions regarding what is and is not possible from a historical perspective.[4] Due to the complexities involved in any attempt to answer this question, I will not address it here. In fact, I do not regard the resolution of this question as vital to the task of reconstructing the belief system of Jesus' first followers. For our purposes here, what really matters is not whether Jesus actually rose from the dead or in what sense he did so, but what his first followers *believed* had taken place. In this regard, there can be no doubt that most of those followers were firmly convinced that he had risen from among the dead (*ek tōn nekrōn*). The evidence that the New Testament provides in support of the existence of this conviction among Jesus' first followers is so strong that its historicity can scarcely be doubted.

The belief that God had raised Jesus from among the dead undoubtedly transformed the way that Jesus' first followers saw him and understood his life and death. That belief was also tied together closely with the claim that Jesus had ascended into heaven and was at God's right hand. Perhaps the most important consequence of these beliefs was that the first believers continued to regard Jesus as a living person who in some sense remained active among them and would eventually return from heaven to bring in God's reign. On the basis of the experiences of Jesus that they had had prior to his death, their

---

4. See N. T. Wright, *The Resurrection of the Son of God*, Vol. 3 of *Christian Origins and the Question of God* (Minneapolis: Fortress, 2003). For other scholarly considerations of this question, see Petr Pokorný, *The Genesis of Christology: Foundations for a Theology of the New Testament*, trans. Marcus Lefébvre (Edinburgh: T & T Clark, 1987), 142-56; Dale Allison Jr., *Resurrecting Jesus: The Earliest Christian Tradition and its Interpreters* (New York: T & T Clark, 2005), 198-375; John Dominic Crossan, *The Historical Jesus: The Life of a Mediterranean Jewish Peasant* (San Francisco: HarperSanFrancisco, 1991), 391-416.

conviction that he had been raised from among the dead led them to proclaim and confess him as Lord and Messiah or Christ.[5]

There can be no question that this confession lay at the heart of the belief system of Jesus' first followers. Throughout the New Testament, the content of their faith is frequently summarized in these terms.[6] Jesus is continually referred to simply as "the Lord," and this designation appears repeatedly in conjunction with both Jesus' name and the title "Christ," which by Paul's day had already been virtually transformed into a second or proper name for Jesus.[7]

Due primarily to the wide variety of beliefs regarding the Messiah that existed in the first century CE, Jesus' first followers may have understood the designation *Christ* in a number of different ways. Had they rejected outright the ideas that many Jews associated with this title in either its Hebrew or Greek form, they would not have accepted its use to refer to Jesus. At the same time, most scholars would agree with Nils Dahl that when Jesus' first followers spoke of Jesus as the Messiah, they understood this title differently than many other Jews of their day. For Jesus' followers, it was primarily Jesus who defined the title, rather than the title defining him.[8]

It seems clear that Christ was considered primarily a *royal* title.[9] The designation "son of David" is repeatedly applied to Jesus throughout the New Testament writings, often in conjunction with "Christ."[10] As the Messiah or Christ, it was expected that some day Jesus would reign and exercise power and dominion over others in the way that monarchs do. For this reason, Jesus

---

5. On the development and use of the title of "Lord" as applied to Jesus in the years immediately following his death, see especially Larry W. Hurtado, *Lord Jesus Christ: Devotion to Jesus in Earliest Christianity* (Grand Rapids: Eerdmans, 2003), 179-84.

6. See especially Matt. 16:16; Mark 8:29; Luke 2:10-11; 9:20; John 9:22; 11:27; 20:31; Acts 2:36; 5:42; 10:36; 11:20; 17:3; 18:5, 28; 1 Cor. 8:6; 12:3; 2 Cor. 4:5; Phil. 2:11; 1 Pet. 3:15; 1 John 5:1.

7. On this point, see David E. Aune, "Christian Prophecy and the Messianic Status of Jesus," in *The Messiah: Developments in Earliest Judaism and Christianity. The First Princeton Symposium on Judaism and Christian Origins* (ed. James H. Charlesworth et al.; Minneapolis: Fortress, 1992), 404-6. Aune argues that "the messiahship of Jesus is simply assumed in the NT epistolary literature," in contrast to the Gospels and Acts, where it is "a matter of central concern" (405). This is to be expected if the Gospels and Acts reflect the thought of an earlier period.

8. Nils A. Dahl, *Jesus the Christ: The Historical Origins of Christological Doctrine* (Minneapolis: Fortress, 1991), 17-20. Elsewhere in the same work, Dahl argues that what led to the transference of the title "Messiah" to Jesus was the *titulus* on the cross, rather than Jewish concepts of the Messiah or the belief that Jesus had been raised (58). For a summary of scholarly discussion on the subject of how the title of Christ came to be applied to Jesus and what was meant by it, see especially Paul van Buren, *According to the Scriptures: The Origins of the Gospel and of the Church's Old Testament* (Grand Rapids: Eerdmans, 1998), 13-18. According to van Buren, "the claim that Jesus was the Messiah was not a part of the early gospel, but its presupposition" (24).

9. According to Donald Juel, "The little evidence that Jewish tradition knew of a non-Davidic Messiah is relatively late" (*Messianic Exegesis: Christological Interpretation of the Old Testament in Early Christianity*; Philadelphia: Fortress, 1988, 142). In principle, of course, the term *meshiach* could refer to any anointed leader. The Dead Sea Scrolls seem to mention what might be called a priestly or Aaronic Messiah, yet this idea is not attested elsewhere. Even if the Scrolls do contemplate an Aaronic Messiah, the allusions to a Davidic Messiah are more numerous. See James VanderKam, "Messianism in the Scrolls," in *The Community of the Renewed Covenant: The Notre Dame Symposium on the Dead Sea Scrolls* (ed. Eugene Ulrich and VanderKam; Notre Dame, IN: University of Notre Dame Press, 1994), 211-34.

10. See especially Matt. 1:1; 15:22; 20:30-31; 22:41-45; Mark 12:35-37; Luke 1:32, 69; 2:11; 20:41-44; John 7:42; Acts 13:33-37; Rom. 1:3-4; 2 Tim. 2:8; Rev. 5:5; 22:16.

is also called "king" in many New Testament passages, although Jesus' first followers appear not to have been entirely comfortable with the application of this latter title to Jesus.[11]

The designation of Jesus as *kurios* also seems to have carried royal connotations. In principle, *kurios* could refer to any type of authority figure.[12] The common usage of this title in antiquity as a designation for the God of Israel raises the question of how those who called Jesus *kurios* understood his relation to Israel's God. In a number of passages in the New Testament, it is not entirely clear whether the term should be taken as alluding to God or to Jesus.[13] Generally, however, Jesus' status as Lord is seen as placing him above all powers and authorities in heaven and on earth except that of the one God.[14] The use of the title *Lord* to refer to Jesus implies that he stands in a unique position in relation both to God and to other human beings. The same is true of the title *Son of God*, which is applied to Jesus throughout the New Testament writings.

Recent scholarship has stressed that the use of all of these titles to designate Jesus represented an implicit critique and rejection of the rulers of the time, including particularly the Roman emperor.[15] The Roman imperial ideology and propaganda touted Caesar, not only as the supreme lord over all on earth, but as one who enjoyed a special and unique relation to the divinity. In a limited sense, he was even regarded as divine.[16] To some extent, the manner in which Jesus' first followers used the titles of Lord, king, and Son of God

---

11. See Dahl, *Jesus*, 36-37.

12. On Paul's use of the title *kurios*, see James D. G. Dunn, *The Theology of Paul the Apostle* (Grand Rapids: Eerdmans, 1998), 244-52. Dunn notes that "the most significant way of speaking about Christ for Paul is indicated by the title *kyrios*, 'Lord'" (244). On the use of *kurios* to refer to Jesus in the Synoptics, see Simon J. Gathercole, *The Preexistent Son: Recovering the Christologies of Matthew, Mark, and Luke* (Grand Rapids: Eerdmans, 1998), 243-49.

13. See, for example, 1 Cor. 2:16; 3:5; 5:5; Eph. 2:21; 5:17; 2 Thess. 3:16; 1 Tim. 1:14; 2 Tim. 1:18; 2:22; Heb. 12:14; James 5:7-15. On this point, E. P. Sanders observes: "It is sometimes difficult to know when by 'the Lord' Paul means God and when he means Christ" (*Paul: The Apostle's Life, Letters, and Thought*; Minneapolis: Fortess, 2015, 713). On the problems resulting from the use of *kurios* in the New Testament, and especially Paul's letters, to refer both to the God of Israel and to Jesus, see J. A. Ziesler, *Pauline Christianity*, rev. ed. (Oxford: Oxford University Press, 1990), 35-41.

14. See especially 1 Cor. 8:6; Phil. 2:9-11; 1 Tim. 6:15; Rev. 17:14; 19:16. On this point, see Dahl, *Jesus*, 20.

15. Some of this critique was no doubt also aimed at other rulers, such as the Herodian kings. Craig Evans, for example, suggests that the parable of the wicked tenants in its original form may have constituted a critique of the Herodian dynasty and presented Jesus as one who exercises a style of kingship that contrasts with the "oppression and ruthlessness" of the Herodian rulers ("Reconstructing Jesus' Teaching: Problems and Possibilities," in *Jesus in Context: Temple, Purity, and Restoration*; Bruce Chilton and Evans; AGJU 39; Leiden: Brill, 1997, 174-75). On this point, see also Tat-Siong Benny Liew, *Politics of Parousia: Reading Mark Inter(con)textually* (BibInt 42; Leiden: Brill, 1999), 81-94.

16. On the idea of divinity as applied to Caesar and Augustus, see especially George Heyman, *The Power of Sacrifice: Roman and Christian Discourses in Conflict* (Washington, DC: Catholic University of America Press, 2007), 45-93. Heyman notes that, in Latin, the Roman emperor was referred to as "a *divus* and not a *deus*" (xviii). For more on what has been called the "imperial cult," see also Neil Elliott, "Paul and the Politics of Empire: Problems and Prospects," in *Paul and Politics: Ekklesia, Israel, Imperium, Interpretation. Essays in Honor of Krister Stendahl* (ed. Richard A. Horsley; Harrisburg, PA: Trinity Press International, 2000), 17-39; Justin K. Hardin, *Galatians and the Imperial Cult: A Critical Analysis of the First-Century Social Context of Paul's Letter* (WUNT 2/237; Tübingen: Mohr Siebeck, 2008), 23-81.

to refer to Jesus thus set both him and them in opposition to Rome and its emperor.[17] Warren Carter, for example, has shown how Matthew's Gospel repeatedly contrasts Jesus' lordship with that of Caesar. Matthew "presents a *social* challenge in offering a different vision and experience of human interaction and community," as well as a *"theological* challenge" in that it contests the imperial propaganda regarding the sovereignty of Caesar. For Matthew, Jesus is the one who "forms a community by calling people to follow him as the one who manifests God's empire."[18]

Numerous passages from the other New Testament writings also implicitly contrast Jesus with the Roman emperor and can even be interpreted as proclaiming Jesus as "the true Lord or 'emperor' of the world."[19] Jesus is presented as the king of kings and Lord of lords who, unlike earthly rulers, will reign forever (1 Tim. 6:15; Heb. 1:8; Rev. 1:5; 11:15; 17:14; 19:16). Paul regards Jesus' name as being above every other name (Phil. 2:9). The letter to the Ephesians affirms that God put his power to work "in Christ when he raised him from the dead and seated him at his right hand in the heavenly places, far above all rule and authority and power and dominion, and above every name that is named, not only in this age but also in the age to come" (Eph. 1:20-21). In Colossians, it is in Christ rather than in the emperor that the fullness of the divinity dwells (Col. 1:19; 2:9). There Jesus is also proclaimed the head of all other rulers and authorities (Col. 2:10; cf. 1:16). Similar claims regarding Jesus' supreme authority are repeated in passages such as Matt. 28:18 and 1 Pet. 3:22. In addition, certain terms related to Jesus' lordship, such as *euaggelion* and *parousia*, seem to have been taken from imperial contexts.[20] In Acts, Paul and Silas are accused of "acting contrary to the decrees of the emperor, saying that there is another king named Jesus" (Acts 17:7).[21] Numerous passages from the Gospel of John also seem to stress the superiority of Jesus in relation to the Roman emperor.[22]

---

17. See Robert Jewett, "Response: Exegetical Support from Romans and Other Letters," in *Paul and Politics*, ed. Horsley, 66-71; Richard A. Horsley, "Rhetoric and Empire and 1 Corinthians," in *Paul and Politics*, ed. Horsley, 90-93; N. T. Wright, "Paul's Gospel and Caesar's Empire," in *Paul and Politics*, ed. Horsley, 166-70; Warren Carter, *Matthew and Empire: Initial Explorations* (Harrisburg, PA: Trinity Press International, 2006), 57-74; Demetrius K. Williams, "Paul's Anti-Imperial Discourse of the Cross: The Cross and Power in 1 Corinthians 1–4," *SBLSP* 39 (2000): 811-17. For a perspective on this question that is somewhat different, see Michael J. Thate, "Paul and the Anxieties of (Imperial?) Succession: Galatians and the Politics of Neglect," in *"In Christ" in Paul: Explorations in Paul's Theology of Union and Participation* (ed. Thate, Kevin J. Vanhoozer, and Constantine R. Campbell; WUNT 2/384; Tübingen: Mohr Siebeck, 2014), 209-41.

18. Carter, *Matthew and Empire*, 52-53; see also 62-89, 169-70.

19. Horsley, "Rhetoric," 92. See, for example, Rom. 1:2-4; 1 Cor. 15:24-28.

20. Dieter Georgi, for example, writes: "By using such loaded terms as *evangelion, pistis, dikaiosyne*, and *eirene* as central concepts in Romans, [Paul] evokes their associations to Roman political theology" (*Theocracy in Paul's Practice and Theology*, trans. David E. Green; Minneapolis: Fortress, 1991, 83).

21. As Max Turner has shown, the idea of Jesus' kingship is stressed not only in Acts 17:7, but throughout the book of Acts as a whole (*Power from on High: The Spirit in Israel's Restoration and Witness in Luke-Acts*; JPTSS 9; Sheffield: Sheffield Academic Press, 1996, 290-97).

22. See especially the works by Warren Carter, *John and Empire: Initial Explorations* (New York: T & T Clark, 2008) and Lance Byron Richey, *Roman Imperial Ideology and the Gospel of John* (CBPMS 43; Washington, DC: Catholic Biblical Association of America, 2007).

Nevertheless, to speak of Jesus in these terms involved more than merely positing him as an alternative or competing emperor or ruler. Jesus was regarded as exercising his lordship in a way that contrasted sharply with that of authorities such as Caesar. The imperial ideology proclaimed Caesar as supreme benefactor of all, and claimed that the peoples subjugated by Rome were better off under Roman rule, which brought peace, security, prosperity, justice, and salvation for all.[23] Such claims seem clearly to have been rejected by Jesus and his first followers, along with many other Jews and subjugated peoples. Among Jesus' followers, Jesus was confessed as the one who was to bring true justice and salvation to the world.[24]

Jesus' Lordship for Others

The New Testament texts repeatedly stress that Jesus defined his role in terms of *serving others*. In this regard, he is seen as distinct from other lords and rulers, who presented themselves as servants of others when in reality they were serving themselves and their own interests. In Luke 22:25-27, for example, Jesus tells the disciples:

> "The kings of the Gentiles lord it over them; and those in authority over them are called benefactors. But not so with you; rather the greatest among you must become like the youngest, and the leader like one who serves. For who is greater, the one who is at the table or the one who serves? Is it not the one at the table? But I am among you as one who serves."

Yong-Sung Ahn, reacting to the work of David Lull and Paul Walaskay, finds in this passage the idea of Jesus as the "servant-benefactor" for whom the rulers in the Roman world serve as an anti-type.[25] According to Ahn, this passage and others from the same Gospel constitute a critique of the Roman patron-client system, and present Jesus as promoting a "religious/political system" that stands as an alternative to the Roman imperial system.[26] Similarly, in the Last Supper scene in John 13:3-16, after Jesus washes his disciples' feet and affirms that he has done so as their "Lord and teacher," he commands them to serve one another in the same way. The same emphasis is found in Paul, who affirms in Phil. 2:1-11 and other texts that "Jesus, not Caesar, has been a servant and is now to be hailed as *kyrios*."[27]

Perhaps the most notable passage in this regard is Mark 10:42-45, which probably served as the basis for the quote from Luke's Gospel just cited above. There Jesus tells his disciples:

---

23. On these ideas, see Carter, *Matthew and Empire*, 20-34; Brigitte Kahl, *Galatians Re-Imagined: Reading with the Eyes of the Vanquished* (PCC; Minneapolis: Fortress, 2010), 192-99.
24. On this point, see especially Neil Elliott, *The Arrogance of Nations: Reading Romans in the Shadow of Empire* (PCC; Minneapolis: Fortress, 2008), 59-85.
25. Yong-Sung Ahn, *The Reign of God and Rome in Luke's Passion Narrative: An East Asian Global Perspective* (BibInt 80; Leiden: Brill, 2006), 162-67.
26. See ibid., 147-97.
27. Wright, "Paul's Gospel," 174. Cf. Rom. 15:8.

"You know that among the Gentiles those whom they recognize as their rulers lord it over them, and their great ones are tyrants over them. But it is not so among you; but whoever wishes to become great among you must be your servant, and whoever wishes to be first among you must be slave of all. For the Son of Man came not to be served but to serve, and to give his life a ransom for many."

As this last passage stresses, more than anything else, it was Jesus' death that demonstrated his willingness and commitment to seeking the well-being of others. In New Testament thought, while other lords and rulers may claim to be seeking the well-being of others, none compares to Jesus in being willing to endure hardships, abuse, and humiliation, and to sacrifice everything, even his own life, to attain that end.[28] It was this love for others that was believed to set Jesus not only *apart* from other lords and authorities, but *above* them, making him far superior to them.[29]

This irony is reflected in numerous New Testament texts. In the eyes of the world, the mere fact that Jesus was crucified makes him "like the rubbish of the world, the dregs of all things," to use a phrase from Paul's writings (1 Cor. 4:13). The proclamation that a crucified man had been exalted to God's side as Lord of all was regarded as scandalous and foolish by non-believers (1 Cor. 1:23). As many scholars have stressed, crucifixion was the most humiliating and agonizing form of execution, generally reserved for slaves and rebels.[30] Ironically, however, in the eyes of the first believers, this was what made Jesus far greater than any other human authority figure. According to Paul, Jesus is now enthroned as Lord, before whom all knees will some day bow, because he sought the interests of others rather than his own, emptying himself, taking the form of a slave, and humbling himself even to the point of death on a cross (Phil. 2:1-11). Jesus' passion and death demonstrate more than anything else his boundless love for others and his full commitment to their salvation. No matter how strongly the "rulers of this age"—both human and demonic—attempted to dissuade him from his commitment to serve others, even to the point of crucifying him, they were unable to do so (Acts 4:26-27; 1 Cor. 2:8). In his passion and death, therefore, Jesus showed himself to be stronger than the forces of evil and injustice. In that sense, he defeated them.

---

28. Undoubtedly, as Oda Wischmeyer has shown, the idea that kings and rulers are to serve their subjects is not unique to the New Testament, but is found in other Jewish, Roman, and Hellenistic sources in antiquity ("Herrschen als Dienen—Mark 10,41-45," *ZNW* 90 [1999]: 34-43). In Jesus' day, however, it was evident to virtually all that those rulers who claimed to be seeking only the interests of their subjects were in fact motivated primarily by personal interests, since this is what their actions demonstrated and how power worked.

29. The accounts of Jesus' temptations in Matt. 4:1-11 and Luke 4:1-13 also stress the idea that Jesus rejected the possibility of attaining a position of power and authority over all without enduring the suffering and death that would result from the giving of himself to and for others. On this point, see Jeffrey B. Gibson, *The Temptations of Jesus in Early Christianity* (JSNTSup 112; Sheffield: Sheffield Academic Press, 1996), 105-18. Gibson notes that passages such as Jesus' refusal to give the Pharisees a sign in Mark 8:11 and his lack of response to the mockers who tell him to come down from the cross in Mark 15:2 also reflect the idea that Jesus refrains from engaging "in the sort of triumphalistic, despotic and imperious activities that throughout Mark's Gospel he condemns and sets himself against" (194-95).

30. On this point, see especially Martin Hengel, *Crucifixion in the Ancient World and the Folly of the Message of the Cross* (Philadelphia: Fortress, 1977); David W. Chapman and Eckhard J. Schnabel, *The Trial and Crucifixion of Jesus: Texts and Commentary* (WUNT 344; Tübingen: Mohr Siebeck, 2015), 451-754.

These ideas are particularly prominent in the Gospel passion narratives, which stress Jesus' total commitment to God's will, his refusal to give in to the unjust authorities, and his dignity and majesty as king in the midst of the humiliations he endured. His silence demonstrates his refusal to dignify the proceedings against him by participating in them, since to attempt to defend himself before them would be to recognize their right to judge him (Matt. 26:63; 27:14; Mark 14:61; 15:5; Luke 23:9; John 19:9). During those proceedings, Jesus is mocked as a king, dressed in royal garb, crowned with thorns, and given a reed as a scepter (Matt. 27:27-30; Mark 15:16-20; John 19:1-3). In both the process against him and his crucifixion he is derided and acclaimed "King of the Jews" (Matt. 27:29, 37, 42; Mark 15:18, 26; Luke 23:38; John 18:36-39; 19:14-15, 19-21). In contrast to James and John, who wish to sit at Jesus' right and left hand when he comes in his kingdom, those who "sit" at his right and left hand are two criminals who join others in taunting him (Matt. 20:21-23; 27:38; Mark 10:37-40; 15:27, 32).[31] To those who make fun of him, it seems absurd that Jesus might carry out the act of powerful kings such as Nebuchadnezzar and Caesar in tearing down the temple, or follow Solomon and Herod in raising up a new one (Matt. 27:40; Mark 15:29-32). John even has the crowd state explicitly, "Everyone who claims to be a king sets himself against the emperor" (John 19:12).

Both Donald Juel and Frank Matera have shown how royal imagery pervades the Markan passion account. Through his repeated use of irony, Mark has Jesus' adversaries proclaim him as king and enthrone him.[32] Matthew also stresses the "fundamental contrast and conflict" between Jesus and Pilate, presenting Jesus as the ruler who "proclaims and embodies God's empire."[33] John Carroll and Joel Green observe that, in John's Gospel, "the trial before Pilate and the crucifixion scene constitute the enthronement of a king," and that the "majestic figure of Jesus dominates the Johannine passion account, as it has the whole Gospel."[34] According to Jerome Neyrey, in their portrayal of Jesus' passion, the Gospel narratives must be seen in the context of the "honor culture" of that time, where "stoic endurance of physical pain denotes courage and honor"; thus "the gospel inculcates an ironic point of view that death and

---

31. On this contrast, see Adela Yarbro Collins, *Mark: A Commentary* (ed. Harold W. Attridge; Hermeneia; Minneapolis: Fortress, 2007), 748.

32. Juel, *Messianic Exegesis*, 94-95; Frank J. Matera, *The Kingship of Jesus: Composition and Theology in Mark 15* (SBLDS 66; Chico, CA: Scholars Press, 1982). This idea is also stressed by T. E. Schmidt, who argues that Mark's crucifixion narrative as a whole is designed to parallel the elements of a Roman triumphal procession ("Mark 15:16-32: The Crucifixion Narrative and the Roman Triumphal Procession," *NTS* 41 [1995]: 1-18). On this point, see also Allan T. Georgia, "Translating the Triumph: Reading Mark's Crucifixion Narrative against a Roman Ritual of Power," *JSNT* 36 (2013): 17-36.

33. Carter, *Matthew and Empire*, 159; see also 162-63. On these ideas in the passion accounts of all three Synoptics, see Frank J. Matera, *Passion Narratives and Gospel Theologies: Interpreting the Synoptics through their Passion Stories* (TI; New York: Paulist, 1986), 34-59, 121-35, 213-19; Timothy Luckritz Marquis, "Crucifixion, State of Emergency, and the Proximate Marginality of Jesus' Kingship," in *Portraits of Jesus: Studies in Christology* (ed. Susan E. Myers; WUNT 2/321; Tübingen: Mohr Siebeck, 2012), 99-123.

34. John T. Carroll and Joel B. Green, *The Death of Jesus in Early Christianity* (Peabody, MA: Hendrickson, 1995), 91-92, 99-100.

shame mean glory and honor."[35] According to this idea, the greatness of Jesus as king lies precisely in his willingness to endure humiliation, shame, torture, and mocking, since this shows him to be stronger than those who heap insults on him.

The same themes appear elsewhere in the Synoptic Gospels. Jesus appears as king and as an authority figure precisely when he is most humble. Nevertheless, as Carter notes, this meekness and humility involve "compassion and service" that contrast with the rulers who "prefer rule and domination."[36] In Jesus' "royal procession" into Jerusalem, he chooses to ride on a lowly donkey (Matt. 21:1-9; Mark 11:1-10; Luke 19:29-40; John 12:12-15). The irony of this supposedly "triumphal entry" is striking. Elsewhere, when Peter proclaims Jesus Messiah or Christ, Jesus immediately affirms that he will endure suffering and a humiliating death, much to Peter's dismay (Matt. 16:21-23; Mark 8:31-33). In the Lukan birth narrative, Jesus is born as savior, Lord, and Messiah in the most humble of circumstances and in the lowly village of Bethlehem, where poor shepherds come to pay homage to him (Luke 2:1-20).[37]

The proclamation of Jesus as crucified elsewhere in the New Testament reflects the same ironies. The sermons in Acts in which Jesus is proclaimed Lord and Christ make no attempt to play down Jesus' crucifixion at the hands of the oppressive authorities, but on the contrary announce it boldly (Acts 2:23, 36; 4:10; 5:30; 10:39; 13:27-29). Paul not only stresses the "folly" of the cross, but proclaims as Lord one who was "crucified in weakness" by the rulers of this world (1 Cor. 1:18—2:9; 2 Cor. 13:4).[38] The letter to the Colossians claims that through the cross, Jesus "disrobed the rulers and authorities and made a public example of them, triumphing over them" (Col. 2:15). The book of Revelation presents the one who reigns as "Lord of lords" and "King of kings" in the form of a lowly lamb who has been slaughtered (Rev. 5:9-14; 17:14).

In the thought of the first believers as it is reflected in the New Testament, God raised Jesus and exalted him to his right hand, not only *after* he had given up his life for others, but *because* he had done so. There is thus a *causal relationship* between his willingness to suffer death on a cross and his exaltation, which was God's response to Jesus' faithfulness unto death. While this relationship is implied in a number of passages, especially in the speeches of Acts, two passages in particular stress this connection explicitly. In Phil. 2:5-11, after describing how Jesus "emptied" and "humbled" himself to take the form of a slave on the cross, Paul continues: *"For that reason (dio)* God also

---

35. Jerome Neyrey, "'Despising the Shame of the Cross': Honor and Shame in the Johannine Passion Narrative," in *Social-Scientific Approaches to New Testament Interpretation* (ed. David G. Horrell; Edinburgh: T & T Clark, 1999), 166-67; for Neyrey's entire argument, see 153-67.

36. Carter, *Matthew and Empire*, 128-29.

37. On Luke's presentation of Jesus as king in his passion account and the other parts of his Gospel, see Matera, *Passion Narratives*, 213-19.

38. See Williams, "Paul's Anti-Imperial Discourse," 811-16.

highly exalted him and gave him the name that is above every name" (v. 9).³⁹ Similarly, the author of Hebrews affirms that Jesus is "now crowned with glory and honor *because of* the suffering of death" (Heb. 2:9; cf. 5:7).⁴⁰ The same idea seems to be behind the repeated claim that the lamb who was slaughtered is "worthy" to receive acclamation, power, wealth, and glory (Rev. 5:9-14). Jesus does not exalt himself, but rather is exalted by God *as a consequence* of his obedience unto death to God's will and his total commitment to the salvation of others (Heb. 5:4-10). Richard Longenecker in particular has shown the intimate connection between the application of various Christological titles to Jesus in the New Testament and the idea that Jesus was willing to give up his life on the cross in love for others. Those titles "are founded ultimately on the early Christians' conviction regarding the full obedience and entire faithfulness of Jesus of Nazareth...."⁴¹ Jesus is acclaimed Christ, Lord, and king *precisely because he dedicated himself to serving God and others.*

For this same reason, numerous New Testament texts see not only Jesus' *resurrection* as his coronation as king and his enthronement as Messiah and Savior, but his *passion and crucifixion* as well. This idea is particularly stressed in the Fourth Gospel, where Jesus' being lifted up on the cross is at the same time his glorification and his lifting up into heaven (John 12:32-33; cf. 3:13-14; 8:28; 13:31-32; 17:1-5).⁴² Donald Senior, for example, notes that in the Johannine passion narrative, "each of the deadly details of the execution ritual are transformed and receive a new meaning: the crucifixion is the ascent of a throne; those crucified with Jesus are his retinue; the placing of the inscription becomes the proclamation of Jesus' royal status," and "the multiple languages of the inscription and the public site of the execution insure the universal transmission of Jesus' message...." This gives the entire crucifixion scene a "sense of triumph."⁴³

One can find the same idea in the Synoptics as well, though it is presented in more subtle fashion. During Jesus' appearance before the Sanhedrin, as he is about to be condemned as deserving of death, he tells the high priest

---

39. It is common to claim, as Larry W. Hurtado does, that in Phil. 2:9 "the 'therefore' makes Jesus' humiliation in some way *a basis or grounds* for God's extraordinary exaltation of him" (*How on Earth did Jesus Become a God?: Historical Questions about Earliest Devotion to Jesus*; Grand Rapids: Eerdmans, 2005, 90). As I shall argue further on, however, strictly speaking, for Paul it is not Jesus' *humiliation itself* that leads to his exaltation, but the love he showed in giving up his life for others in the way he did. The point Paul is stressing in the immediate context is that believers must show love to one another (Phil. 2:1-5). For Paul, what pleased God was not Jesus' humiliation per se, but his willingness to endure all things on behalf of others in love.

40. Once again, it is misleading to affirm that Heb. 2:9 communicates the idea that "Christ's 'suffering of death' is the ground, basis, or reason for God's action in exalting him...." (Paul Ellingworth, *The Epistle to the Hebrews: A Commentary on the Greek Text*; NIGCT; Grand Rapids: Eerdmans, 1993, 155). For the author of Hebrews, God exalted Jesus, not simply because he suffered and died, but because he gave his life seeking the salvation of others in order to bring them to glory out of love for them (Heb. 2:9-10).

41. Richard N. Longenecker, "The Foundational Conviction of New Testament Christology: The Obedience/Faithfulness/Sonship of Christ," in *Jesus of Nazareth: Lord and Christ: Essays on the Historical Jesus and New Testament Christology* (ed. Joel B. Green and Max Turner; Grand Rapids: Eerdmans, 1994), 488; see 475-88.

42. On this point, see Neyrey, "Despising," 151-59, 166-67.

43. Donald Senior, *The Passion of Jesus in the Gospel of John* (Pass 4; Collegeville, MN: Liturgical Press, 1991), 104-5.

that "immediately" or "from now on" he will be at God's right hand of power (Matt. 26:64; Luke 22:69). The centurion at the foot of the cross recognizes and confesses Jesus as God's Son precisely at the moment he breathes his last (Matt. 27:54; Mark 15:39).[44] Thus it is Jesus' death that reveals his divine sonship. In Luke's Gospel, the rebel hanging on the cross next to that of Jesus recognizes that Jesus is to "come in his kingdom" (Luke 23:42). Earlier in the same Gospel, Jesus is said to set out for Jerusalem not so much to *die* there as to be "received up" (Luke 9:51) and accomplish his "exodus" (Luke 9:31). In Matthew and Mark, Jesus' enthronement in glory is said to depend on his drinking the "cup," a clear allusion to the cross (Matt. 20:21-23; Mark 10:37-40). According to passages such as these, it is in and through his passion and death that Jesus attains his exalted position as Lord and Son of God.

Nevertheless, it is important to note that the *purpose* of Jesus' exaltation to a position of power and authority through his death and resurrection is presented in terms of making it possible for him to bring about the salvation promised to Israel and the nations. This salvation is consistently seen as lying *in the future* rather than something already accomplished by Jesus in death. Numerous New Testament passages allude to Ps. 110:1 to affirm that, now that he has sat down at God's right hand, Jesus is in the process of subjecting all things under himself (Matt. 22:44; Mark 12:36; Luke 20:42-43; Acts 2:34-36; 1 Cor. 15:24-28; Heb. 1:13). Other passages from the New Testament speak of his ongoing activity on behalf of believers from his exalted position in heaven. He intercedes to God for them, while at the same time accompanying them with his presence to strengthen, comfort, and shepherd them.[45] Therefore, through his death Jesus is raised and exalted as Lord, *not for his own sake*, but *for the sake of others*. Like his death and *because* of his death, Jesus' lordship is "for others," whom he can now serve from his exalted position at God's side in heaven.

Not only does the manner in which Jesus attains his lordship contrast with that of other lords, rulers, and authorities, but the way in which he exercises that lordship also sets him apart from all others. While other lords operate through intimidation, striking fear into others so as to impose their dominion over them by force, Jesus establishes his reign by serving others humbly and calling them to serve him by serving God and others as he has done. This leads to the creation of a community characterized by the same traits that we find in Jesus. As Robert Jewett notes, for example, in stressing that "its Lord is the crucified one, not the emperor," Paul "wishes the new community to be

---

44. Collins notes that the centurion's affirmation is not only "ironic in the dramatic sense," but anti-imperial, due to the common use of *theou huios* to refer to the Roman emperors (*Mark*, 767-69).
45. See especially Matt. 18:20; 28:19-20; Rom. 8:34; Heb. 2:18; 4:14-16; 7:25; 1 John 2:1-2. The idea that the exalted Jesus remains active from heaven is particularly prominent in Acts; see Robert F. O'Toole, *The Unity of Luke's Theology: An Analysis of Luke-Acts* (GNS 9; Wilmington, DE: Michael Glazier, 1984), 38-61. On the idea of the ongoing presence and activity of the risen Jesus in Paul's letters, see Chris Tilling, *Paul's Divine Christology* (WUNT 2/323; Tübingen: Mohr Siebeck, 2012), 147-54. The Fourth Gospel also stresses the glorified Jesus' ongoing activity among his followers, especially in the Last Supper account (John 13–17).

marked by persuasion rather than coercion."[46] Numerous passages in the New Testament present Jesus as a "meek" and "gentle" Lord, yet as Carter rightly insists, "to be meek is not to be passive," but to act "compassionately in service" to others.[47]

Curiously, among Jesus' followers the noble title "Lord" became a term of endearment.[48] This was contrary to the common use of the term in antiquity, where monarchs and rulers were imposing figures to be feared rather than loved. Undoubtedly, they were often acclaimed, idolized, and revered for their power and achievements and generally presented as benefactors of the people under them. Public expressions of support, recognition, gratitude, and even affection for such leaders was also common. Nevertheless, it would have been rare to speak of such authorities "loving" their subjects in the same way and to the same degree that Jesus as Lord was said to love the members of his community of followers and human beings generally. Even among those who believed he had been exalted to God's side with full power and authority, Jesus continued to be seen as a warm, caring, and intimate figure rather than a cold, distant, imposing monarch. One can hardly imagine anyone speaking of an emperor or king, for example, in the way that Paul does when he refers to Jesus as the one "who loved me and gave himself for me" (Gal. 2:20), and recalls the "tender affection" (*splagchnois*) of Christ (Phil. 1:8). In Ephesians, Jesus is presented not only as the one who loves believers and gave up his life for them, but also as the one who "nourishes and tenderly cares" for them, like a husband for a wife (Eph. 5:2, 29). Thus, even when the first believers spoke of submitting to Jesus, obeying him, and worshiping him as sovereign Lord, they continued to understand their relationship to him as one of intimacy and mutual affection.

Undoubtedly, there are passages in the New Testament that claim that Jesus will some day come to impose his dominion by force, removing other rulers from their thrones and destroying their power.[49] Yet it is precisely the opposition between Jesus and the "rulers of this age" that make it necessary for this to take place. Because those other rulers were corrupt and oppressive, lording it over others and practicing injustice, their reign was seen as an obstacle to the alternative reign of true justice and *shalom* that Jesus sought to bring for the good of all. Therefore, Jesus' destruction of the rival powers was thought to be aimed at the liberation of those oppressed. What would lead Jesus eventually to impose his rule was not any type of self-interest or lust for power and domination, but the same absolute commitment and dedication

---

46. Jewett, "Response," 71.
47. Carter, *Matthew and Empire*, 128.
48. One can observe a certain intimacy and affection in the use of the word "Lord" for Jesus in passages such as the following: Luke 5:12; 7:6, 13; 10:39-41; 19:31; 22:33; 24:34; John 6:28; 11:2-3, 21; 13:25, 36-37; 20:2, 13, 18, 20, 25; 21:7-8, 12, 15-17; Acts 10:33; 11:20-24; 14:3; 1 Cor. 16:19-23; 2 Cor. 12:8; Gal. 1:19; Phil. 3:8; 1 Thess. 3:12; 1 Tim. 1:12-14; 2 Tim. 4:17.
49. See, for example, Matt. 13:41-43; 18:29-31; Luke 1:68-75; 13:23-30; 1 Cor. 15:24-25; 2 Thess. 1:7-10; 2:8; Rev. 1:7.

to the well-being of others that had led both to his ministry and to his death on the cross.

Because that commitment and dedication to others was the characteristic that defined Jesus' lordship more than anything else, no one could rightly call Jesus "Lord" without assuming that same commitment and dedication to the well-being of all. If Jesus had lived and died seeking nothing but the wholeness of others, by definition, to submit to him obediently as one's Lord meant dedicating one's life to that same objective. Even if one questions Rudolf Bultmann's understanding of salvation as involving primarily a new self-understanding on the part of believers, one must recognize the truth of his affirmation that "[t]o understand another person as Lord correspondingly means *to have a new understanding of oneself*, as standing in the service of that Lord and attaining one's own identity in such service."[50] This involved becoming a "slave" or "servant" of Christ and of God together with Christ.[51]

Yet once again, contrary to the slavery practiced in the ancient world, this "slavery" was not something imposed on believers by force and violence, but something they embraced freely and joyfully. Because Jesus himself had been a "slave" of God and others, and in a sense remained so even after his glorification as Lord, those who became his "slaves" obeyed him as Lord by dedicating themselves to serving God and others in the same way. They became "slaves of justice" (Rom. 6:12-13, 16-22). If Jesus their Lord had come, not to be served, but to serve others, then they too were to serve others. Paradoxically, like other lords in his world, in a sense Jesus as Lord demanded that others submit to him and serve him, yet the service he required of his "slaves" was precisely that they become slaves to others, as he had been. This slavery toward others did not, however, involve obeying the selfish or despotic dictates of those whom they served, but seeking the well-being of all in the way defined by Jesus, even when this meant speaking out prophetically against injustices. Jesus' followers thus believed they were to obey *God* and *Jesus* rather than those whom they served. Ironically, at the same time, those who became "slaves" in reality were made truly free, adopted as God's children so as no longer to be in slavery, and accepted by Jesus as friends rather than slaves.[52] Like Jesus, they were paradoxically slaves and free or slaves and lords at the same time, yet in different senses. While all things belonged to God, all things were theirs as well (1 Cor. 3:22-23).

The result of this counterimperial and countercultural way of understanding lordship and slavery was an alternative community that was also conceived of in ways that ran counter to the predominant concepts of the time. If by definition it was impossible to call Jesus "Lord" without submitting obediently to his same way of being in relation to others as his "slave," then of necessity the community of all of those who confessed Jesus as Lord assumed the

---

50. Rudolf Bultmann, *Faith and Understanding*, trans. Louise Pettibone Smith (ed. Robert W. Funk; New York: Harper & Row, 1969), 236.

51. See Matt. 10:24-25; 20:24-28; 23:11; Mark 9:35; 10:41-45; Luke 22:26; Rom. 1:1; 6:22; 1 Cor. 9:19; 2 Cor. 4:5; 6:4; Gal. 1:10; 5:13; Phil. 1:1; Col. 4:12; 2 Tim. 2:24; Tit. 1:1; James 1:1; 1 Pet. 2:16; 2 Pet. 1:1; Jude 1.

52. See, for example, John 8:31-36; 15:15; Rom. 6:20; 1 Cor. 9:1, 19; 2 Cor. 3:17; Gal. 4:6-7; 5:1, 13.

same commitment to one another's well-being that their Lord had embodied. According to Carter, this idea is present in Matthew's Gospel, where "claims about the emperor as the agent of the gods' sovereignty, presence, and blessings collide with claims about Jesus as God's agent.... [T]he collision of these claims about Jesus with claims about the Roman imperial system and the emperor functions to contest Roman imperial claims, to challenge and subvert their legitimacy, and to point to an alternative understanding, community, and set of practices for followers of Jesus."[53] As Neil Elliott has argued, the same manner of thinking is found in the letters of Paul, which speak of the establishment of communities of discernment, resistance, and solidarity that challenged the ideologies of privilege and power that were characteristic of Rome's empire.[54]

Justice, Jesus' Lordship, and the Reign of God

Today, of course, many would regard as problematic the idea that believers are to submit obediently to Jesus as Lord. Richard Horsley, for example, writes regarding Paul's proclamation regarding Jesus:

> In offering his assembly an alternative to Caesar, Paul in effect presented Jesus Christ as the true emperor, the true Lord and Savior who was in the process of subjugating all things to himself. Such imperial language could only reinforce relations of subordination within the assembly. It would not have been difficult for the emergent monarchic polity of the Christian movement to appeal to and build on Paul's imperial counterimperial language. Already in the deutero-Pauline letters the implications of such language for relations within the movement and its adjustment to the dominant social order are abundantly evident. In its imagery of Christ as the true emperor, the Christian church was already well prepared for its own establishment under Constantine.[55]

Carter has raised some of the same concerns with regard to Matthew's presentation of Jesus' message of God's reign. According to Carter, the idea that God would defeat Rome and establish a new empire under his own sovereignty

> co-opts and imitates the very imperial worldview that it resists! For Rome and God, the goal is the supreme sovereignty of the most powerful. For both, the scope or extent of their sovereignty is the cosmos. Both appeal to the divine will for legitimation. Both understand the establishment of their sovereignty to be through a chosen agent and by means of the violent overthrow of all resistance. Both offer totalizing perspectives. Both demand compliance. Both destroy enemies without room for the different or noncompliant. Both recognize that those who welcome its sovereignty benefit from it.... Imperial rule typically presents itself as benign, especially for its immediate beneficiaries.... Ironically, and regrettably, the Gospel ultimately envisages the replacement of one imperial ideology with another.[56]

---

53. Carter, *Matthew and Empire*, 59; cf. 106-7, 159.
54. Neil Elliott, *Liberating Paul: The Justice of God and the Politics of the Apostle* (Minneapolis: Fortress, 2006), 189-226.
55. Horsley, "Rhetoric," 93.
56. Carter, *Matthew and Empire*, 89-90, 107; see also 129.

Further on in the same work, Carter adds: "Imperialism—the effort to exert control over others, whether their land, resources, or lives, whether national, ethnic, political, militaristic, economic, social, cultural, religious, personal—has not disappeared from the human community."[57] Carter also criticizes the idea that, at Jesus' return, "God will destroy all those not committed to Jesus." This turns the God of mercy into "an oppressive tyrant, like Herod and Pilate, ready to smash to pieces all who do not comply."[58] He asks: "But is violence to be the final word in imposing God's empire? That would make God nothing other than a copy of any emperor."[59] For Carter, we must instead "reconceive God's future action in a way that the Gospel does not do, not in terms of violence and imposed and dominant power but in terms of life-giving service and merciful action."[60] This would involve an understanding of God that leads people and nations to turn away from their violent militaristic ways, cancel debts, redistribute wealth, care for the needy, and "abandon the way of domination" in order to instead "embrace that of service."[61]

Similarly, in his analysis of Mark's Gospel, Tat-Siong Benny Liew writes that, "from Mark's presentation of Jesus as God's son and heir, and thus the authoritative interpreter of God's will, 'Satan' becomes anyone who does not share the mind, or obey the thoughts of Mark's Jesus. Not only do these crude methods of polarization further fuel the absolute authority of Mark's Jesus, they also lead to a duplication of the insider-outsider binarian."[62] Elsewhere Liew affirms:

> Presenting an all-authoritative Jesus who will eventually annihilate all opponents and all other authorities, Mark's utopian, or dystopian, vision, in effect, duplicates the colonial (non)choice of "serve-or-be-destroyed".... Despite the Gospel's invocation of the Deity and its rhetoric that polarizes things divine and human (8:33; 11:30), it, like most human power systems, promotes "a hierarchical, punitive, and tyrannical concept of ruler and ruled, while claiming that it was all for the best" (Sinfield, *Faultlines*, 167).[63]

Liew then continues:

> Authority is (over)power(ing); and it demands the submission of everybody, and thus also the annihilation of those who do not submit. In other words, vindication must become vindictive. The problem is that by defeating power with more power, Mark is, in the final analysis, no different from the "might-is-right" ideology that has led to colonialism, imperialism, and various forms of suffering and oppression.

---

57. Ibid., 172.
58. Ibid., 176.
59. Ibid., 178.
60. Ibid., 178.
61. Ibid., 178. Carter recognizes, of course, that in Matthew's Gospel, the imposition of God's will by violent means has as its goal the destruction of evil and the establishment of a world of justice: "Salvation comprises membership in a people that embodies and anticipates and celebrates the establishment of God's loving sovereignty, God's empire, over all, including the destruction of oppressive governing powers like imperial Rome" (178).
62. Liew, *Politics*, 102.
63. Ibid., 104. The reference is to Alan Sinfield, *Faultlines: Cultural Materialism and the Politics of Dissident Reading* (Oxford: Clarendon, 1992).

Mark's Jesus may have replaced the "wicked" Jewish-Roman power, but the tyrannical, exclusionary, and coercive politics goes on.[64]

Undoubtedly, there is much truth in these criticisms. Throughout the history of Christendom, the proclamation of God's sovereignty or reign and Jesus' lordship, as well as the call for all to submit obediently to God and to Jesus, have without question frequently led to oppression, violence, exclusion, and the domination of some human beings by others. Countless injustices and atrocities have been committed and even justified in the name of Jesus and the God he is said to have called "Father." In many contexts, the doctrine of the sovereignty of God and the lordship of Jesus has occasioned untold suffering for women, children, the weak, the poor, the marginalized, and people from countless communities, groups, societies, and nations.

What must be asked, however, is whether the problem lies with the notions of God's sovereignty and Jesus' lordship in themselves, or with the way that these notions have been interpreted. I would argue that the difficulties raised by scholars such as Horsley, Carter, and Liew can be addressed by affirming two basic ideas. First, both Jesus and the God he proclaimed must be seen as being truly and fully committed to wholeness, justice, and well-being for *all people equally and without exception*. As we have seen in the previous chapters, there is a firm biblical basis for such a conception of God and Jesus. If God and Jesus are viewed in this way, then under no circumstances can God or Jesus be regarded as oppressive or tyrannical, as if God or Jesus sought to exert power and authority in the world for their own sake. Rather, all that God and Jesus have done and continue to do is for the sake of human beings collectively and the world in which they live. Such a view of God and Jesus does not promote the idea that "might is right." Instead, what is right is that all people live in solidarity in the way God desires and commands for their own well-being.

If Jesus and the God he called "Father" are conceived of as always acting purely out of love for humanity as a whole, then all that Jesus and his God have done and will do must be seen as aimed at establishing their reign of justice, equity, and *shalom* for the good of all. To submit to Jesus as Lord, therefore, is to be committed to justice and *shalom* for all, as Jesus and his God are. All those who share that commitment are in effect doing God's will, sharing in God's reign, and following Jesus, even if they do not actually confess Jesus as Lord or call the God he proclaimed their Father. To affirm this is not to make "anonymous Christians" of people of different faiths and cultures who are committed to practicing what is truly loving, right, just, and equitable, but merely to maintain that all who live in that way are doing God's will in the way that Jesus taught and embodied.

According to such an understanding of God's reign and Jesus' lordship, what ultimately concerns God and Jesus is not that human beings believe

---

64. Liew, *Politics*, 107.

in Jesus and in God as his Father, but that they be committed to the way of life and the type of community, society, and world that Jesus sought to bring about. When Jesus calls others to believe in and follow him, he does so, not for *his* sake, but for *theirs*, since his desire is that all may come to live in relations characterized by the same type of love and solidarity that Jesus himself embodied in life and death. As Horsley, Carter, and Liew affirm, no human ruler or authority can rightly be said to act purely out of love and concern for the good of others. The same is true of any human being in general. In New Testament thought, however, Jesus and the God he proclaimed are fundamentally different from any human ruler or authority in that regard.

The second idea that must be stressed when considering the New Testament teaching regarding the sovereignty of God and the lordship of Jesus is that *no human being or human group represents or speaks for God or Jesus exclusively*. The oppression and injustices to which Horsley, Carter, and Liew allude are the result of the claim that certain people represent or speak for God in a way that others do not. For example, Horsley's affirmation that "imperial language could only reinforce relations of subordination within the assembly" is true only if certain members of the assembly are told to be subordinated to others in the same way that they are to be subordinated to God and Jesus. Undoubtedly, there are New Testament passages that reflect such an idea.[65] In principle, however, if it is maintained that *all people equally* are to be subject to God and Jesus, including all those who form part of an assembly, then there is no reason why the proclamation of God's sovereignty or Jesus' lordship should lead to "relations of subordination within the assembly."

Nor is there any reason why the "imagery of Christ as the true emperor" should lead to the type of church established under Constantine. On the contrary, the claim that Christ is the true emperor would preclude anyone such as Constantine claiming the same authority over others that Christ possesses as God's Son. To proclaim any other human being to be "the true emperor" to whom all are to be subject would be blasphemous; such a person would be usurping a position that belongs to Christ alone. It is therefore inaccurate to claim that the ideas of God's sovereignty and Jesus' lordship in themselves inevitably lead to hierarchical structures in which some human beings must submit obediently to others.

Furthermore, because all human beings and the systems, institutions, and empires they construct are inevitably sinful and corrupt, no human reign can truly be considered to be entirely just or to promote the well-being of all. For the same reason, no human being or group has the right to demand absolute obedience from others, or to seek to dominate and subjugate others through the use of coercion and violence in the name of God or the common good.

---

65. The clearest examples of this idea are found in passages such as Eph. 5:21—6:9 and Col. 3:18-22, where women, children, and slaves are exhorted to be subject to their husbands, parents, and masters respectively (cf. 1 Tim. 2:11-14). The words of Paul in Rom. 13:1-8 and 1 Cor. 11:3-16 also seem to convey the notion that certain human beings are to be subject to others in the same way that they are subject to Jesus or God, though many have proposed alternative readings of these passages aimed at questioning such a notion.

Nor do any have the right to identify themselves fully with God and justice, and on that basis demonize others or deem them enemies of God who need to be destroyed or subdued. While violence is often necessary to constrain and counter evil in the world, any use of violence among human beings will itself always be sinful and unjust, at least to some degree, and must be acknowledged as such. Things such as militarism and social inequity can never be justified in the name of Jesus and the God he called "Father."

If Jesus and the God he proclaimed, however, are fully identified with wholeness, justice, and well-being for all people equally without exception, then Jesus and God are not acting oppressively when they demand that human beings also act in justice and love, seeking the well-being of all. In that case, the obedience that God and Jesus demand is not simply obedience to *themselves*, but obedience to the practice of justice and solidarity. If God and Jesus are to establish a world in which justice and *shalom* for all will some day prevail fully, they must also act against evil and seek to bring all human beings into conformity with God's will. By definition, this cannot be done by force, violence, or imposition, but only by giving human beings freedom, while at the same time insisting that they use that freedom for the good of all and attempting to convince and enable them to do so. It is also important to stress that, in New Testament thought, no person or group can claim to know, represent, or embody God's will fully, since that would involve occupying a place that belongs solely to God and God's Son Jesus. None have the right to define God's will for others unilaterally, since only God can define God's will. All that human beings can do is to seek to discern that will together through dialogue and a common commitment to the well-being of all.

To affirm all of this is not to say that the New Testament proclamation of God's reign and sovereignty and of Jesus' lordship is not problematic. I would argue, however, that as long as God and Jesus are fully identified with the principle of justice and *shalom* for all people equally without exception, the notions of God's sovereignty and Jesus' lordship do not in themselves promote unjust, tyrannical, or polarizing relations among human beings. In fact, when rightly understood, those notions *cannot* promote or justify injustice, since by definition an all-powerful and all-loving God who is fully committed to justice and *shalom* for all cannot practice or promote injustice or oppression. For that reason, anything that is unjust or oppressive will by definition be contrary to the sovereignty of God and lordship of Jesus, and any who practice or justify injustice and oppression in the name of Jesus and the God he proclaimed cannot rightly claim to be living under Jesus' lordship or submitting obediently to God.

Strictly speaking, therefore, the problem is not with the concepts of God's sovereignty and Jesus' lordship per se, but with the way that those concepts can be and have been used to promote injustice, inequity, and the oppression of some human beings by others. To use those concepts in that way runs contrary to all that Jesus and the reign of God he proclaimed stood for. However, because human beings—including all who call themselves Jesus' followers—are by nature sinful, unjust, and oppressive, those who proclaim God's sovereignty and Jesus' lordship will inevitably at times do so in ways that are also sinful, unjust, and oppressive, even when they seek only to do good. In fact, any theological concept or idea that contributes to justice and human well-being in some contexts can have the opposite effect in other contexts, or be misused to oppress others. In order to be faithful to Jesus and the God he called "Father," therefore, what is necessary is that his followers constantly strive to proclaim God's reign and Jesus' lordship in ways that promote wholeness for all, even though they will never be entirely successful in that endeavor.

Jesus' Death in Light of His Lordship

The understanding of Jesus' lordship just presented provides the basis necessary to begin to consider the manner in which Jesus' first followers came to understand the salvific significance of his death. From their perspective, what Jesus had lived for was precisely to bring into existence the kind of alternative community described above. Due to his dedication to this objective, Jesus had come into conflict with the authorities and powers of this age. Out of self-interest, these authorities and powers had come to oppose what Jesus proclaimed, sought, and represented, and therefore looked to silence him by putting him to death. In the face of this threat, however, Jesus remained committed to that objective, in obedience to the will of his Father. As a result, he was put to death and accepted that death *for the sake of others*. These "others" included those whose lives would be transformed as they came to form part of the community he had lived and died to establish, as well as all who would be served by that community.

According to Jesus' first followers, Jesus' objective had been not only to bring this community into existence, but also to define it forever as a community in which all would follow Jesus as Lord and be fully committed to doing God's will as he had, living for God and others. At the same time, as he went to his death, Jesus had sought to be raised from the dead so that he might continue to live as Lord on behalf of others and thereby bring about their salvation. All of this was what Jesus had not only *died* for, but also what he had *lived* for. And precisely *because* he had been willing to die for what he had lived for, through death he had attained his objective of establishing that community of followers committed to doing God's will. At the same time, he had attained their salvation. That salvation was now certain to come through him, thanks to God's response to Jesus' faithfulness and dedication—a response that took the form of raising him from among the dead and exalting him as Lord over all out of love for all. Now that the crucified Jesus had been enthroned at God's right hand of power, there could be no doubt that the promises of salvation God had made of old would be fulfilled through him.

The conviction that God had raised Jesus and exalted him to his right hand, therefore, played a vital role in leading Jesus' first followers to see his death as salvific. From their perspective, it was clear that Jesus had died as a consequence of his commitment to seeking the salvation and well-being of others in accordance with God's will. They believed that this was the reason why he had desired to be established as Lord over all. As he had gone to his death, he had sought that God raise him to a position of power, not primarily for *his own sake*, but *for the sake of others*. Only by receiving "all power and authority" from God could he bring about fully the salvation of others (Matt. 28:18). As Paul states in Rom. 14:9: "For to this end Christ died and lived again, so that he might be Lord of both the dead and the living." This lordship, however, was thought to depend on an act of God, since God alone could raise the dead and confer such an honor on Jesus.

Of course, from the perspective of Jesus' first followers, God had not only raised and exalted Jesus following his death, but from the very beginning had sent him to carry out a ministry of service to others. God had also guided and accompanied Jesus throughout his ministry. When that ministry had led those in power to oppose Jesus and threaten to put him to death, God had willed that Jesus give up his life rather than seeking to save it. The reason for this was self-evident: had Jesus sought to be delivered from death or attempted to escape the cross in some way, he would have been acting solely out of a concern for himself and his own life, rather than out of concern for others. How could Jesus expect others to stand firm in the face of opposition and persecution had he not been willing to do so himself? How could he expect his followers to be fully committed to seeking the well-being of others if he himself had not been willing to do so to the very end, no matter what the consequences? How could Jesus ask God to bring about the salvation of others if, when faced with the threat of death, Jesus himself had sought his own salvation rather than that of others?

Jesus' first followers would have made similar observations when viewing Jesus' death from the perspective of God. If God had sent Jesus to bring about in others a total commitment to his will so that they might attain salvation through such a commitment, then it was necessary not only for Jesus to be willing to give up his life in order to accomplish that task, but for God himself to let his Son be put to death. Had God intervened to rescue Jesus from death, then God would have shown himself to be more concerned for his own Son than for the salvation of others. If God's objective was to form a worldwide community of people fully dedicated to the well-being of one another and others in love through Jesus, then God himself had to be fully dedicated to that objective, no matter what the cost. In Paul's words, God "did not withhold his own Son, but delivered him up for all of us" (Rom. 8:32).[66]

Because Jesus had dedicated himself fully to carrying out the task given him by God, and had even been willing to give up his life in faithfulness and

---

66. Alexander Weihs has argued that the idea that God gave Jesus up to death also appears implicitly in other New Testament passages that speak of Jesus being "handed over" or "delivered up" (*Die Deutung des Todes Jesu im Markusevangelium: Eine exegetische Studie zu den Leidens- und Auferstehungsagen*; FB 99; Würzburg: Echter, 2003, 308-31).

obedience to God's will, it could also be said that Jesus "merited" becoming Lord in order to save others. Had Jesus not been willing to *die* for others, he would not have shown himself to be worthy of being raised to God's right hand as Lord for others. How could he be worthy of reigning as Lord on behalf of others if, when faced with death, he had instead turned in on himself and sought to save his own life? How could he now intercede to God for others from God's side in heaven and expect God to respond favorably to that intercession if, at the moment of truth, he had ceased to be concerned for others and instead cared only about himself?[67]

Of course, most of these ideas are not stated explicitly in the New Testament writings. Nevertheless, they are the logical consequence of the basic beliefs we find affirmed throughout those writings. As we shall see in the following chapters, including especially Chapter 10, they also provide the background necessary to make sense of the brief formulas used to speak of Jesus' death running throughout the New Testament.

JESUS AS MEDIATOR

As we saw in Chapter 4, both the Hebrew Scriptures and the second-temple Jewish writings we possess speak of mediator figures designated by Israel's God to act on his behalf in relation to his people, and to act on behalf of his people in relation to him. In particular, this was the task assigned to the priests, who carried out their role as mediators by offering up to God the prayers and sacrifices God had ordained in the Mosaic law, and by communicating God's will to the people. Although all of the priests took part in this mediating activity, they did so under the leadership and supervision of the high priest, who was the most important of the mediators designated by God through the law.[68] In ancient Israel, monarchs were also seen as mediating figures, though their task consisted primarily of implementing God's will among the people, rather than interceding before God on behalf of the people. Of course, it was also thought that God might speak and act through other human agents, such as prophets or healers who received their authority from God directly. Among Jews in the first century, a number of individuals came to be viewed in this way, including not only Jesus and John the Baptist, but also other prophetic-charismatic figures and the Teacher of Righteousness mentioned in the Dead Sea Scrolls.[69] In addition, a variety of heavenly mediators are mentioned in

---

67. Rom. 8:34; Heb. 7:25; 1 John 2:1.

68. On the concept of *mediator* (*mesitēs*) in ancient thought, the Hebrew Scriptures, and the New Testament, see Albrecht Oepke's entry, "Μεσίτης, μεσιτεύω," in *TDNT* 4: 598-624. For a summary of the state of the Jewish priesthood in Jesus' day, see especially Edwin K. Broadhead, "Jesus and the Priests of Israel," in *Jesus from Judaism to Christianity: Continuum Approaches to the Historical Jesus* (ed. Tom Holmén; LNTS 312; London: T & T Clark, 2007), 127-30. Broadhead notes that "the priestly leadership of Israel in the time of Jesus was never monolithic, and it was never exclusive" (130).

69. On these figures, see Ekkehard W. Stegemann and Wolfgang Stegemann, *The Jesus Movement: A Social History of its First Century*, trans. O. C. Dean Jr. (Minneapolis: Fortress, 1999), 162-67; E. P. Sanders, *Judaism: Practice and Belief, 63 BCE–66 CE* (Philadelphia: Trinity Press International, 1992), 342-43; Craig A. Evans,

second-temple Jewish writings, most of whom are angels or archangels.[70] Moses in particular was considered to have been the mediator *par excellence* between God and God's people Israel.[71]

Whether or not some of his followers saw Jesus as fulfilling uniquely or definitively the role of mediator between God and human beings prior to his death in Jerusalem,[72] the New Testament leaves no doubt that his first followers came to view him in that way shortly after the events surrounding his death. More than anything else, the manner in which the title "Son of God" is applied to Jesus throughout the New Testament indicates that Jesus was believed to be in a unique relation to God, and thus to represent God in a way that no other human being did or could.[73]

Jesus' Authority as Mediator

Almost all of the New Testament writings provide evidence for the existence of the belief in Jesus' unique role and authority as mediator between God and human beings. In the Synoptic Gospels, Jesus is presented as acting on God's behalf in relation to others in a number of ways. While all of the Gospels see Jesus' work of healing as empowered by God, Luke in particular stresses this point. Luke's account of Jesus' ministry begins with Jesus reading Isa. 61:1-2 in a synagogue at Nazareth (Luke 4:16-21). In this way, Luke presents Jesus as the one anointed by God's Spirit to bring good news to the poor, release those in bondage, give sight to the blind, and set the oppressed free. The idea that God is behind all that Jesus does is stressed in several of Luke's healing accounts, where the crowds respond to Jesus' acts of power by praising God and proclaiming what *God* has done, rather than what *Jesus* has done (Luke 8:39; 9:42-43; 17:12-15; 19:37). In the sermons of Acts, Luke repeats the idea

---

"Aspects of Exile and Restoration in the Proclamation of Jesus and the Gospels," in *Exile: Old Testament, Jewish and Christian Conceptions* (ed. James M. Scott; SJSJ 56; Leiden: Brill, 1997), 300-305.

70. On ancient Jewish beliefs regarding agent figures, both human and transcendent, see George W. E. Nickelsburg, *Ancient Judaism and Christian Origins: Diversity, Continuity and Transformation* (Minneapolis: Fortress, 2003), 89-108; Andrew Chester, "Jewish Messianic Expectations and Mediatorial Figures and Pauline Christology," in *Paulus und antike Judentum* (ed. Martin Hengel and Ulrich Heckel; WUNT 58; Tübingen: J. C. B. Mohr, 1991), 17-89.

71. This is particularly emphasized in the *Testament of Moses*; see Robert A. Kugler, "Testaments," in *Justification and Variegated Nomism*, Vol. 1: *The Complexities of Second Temple Judaism* (ed. D. A. Carson, Peter T. O'Brien, and Mark A. Seifrid; WUNT 2/140; Tübingen: Mohr Siebeck, 2001), 195-96.

72. R. David Kaylor, for example, argues that Jesus did not teach his disciples "to consider him an intermediary, but rather to imitate him in approaching God without intermediary" (*Jesus the Prophet: His Vision of the Kingdom on Earth*; Louisville, KY: Westminster John Knox, 1994, 197). Although in the Synoptics Jesus does not speak of himself as mediator between others and God, the notion that Jesus fulfilled a mediatorial role would seem to follow naturally from Jesus' ministry of teaching and healing, which reflected the idea that he had a unique relationship with God and was able to mediate God's blessings to others.

73. The use of the title "Son of God" varies from one author to another in the New Testament. On these differences, see Richard N. Longenecker, *The Christology of Early Jewish Christianity* (SBT 2/17; London: SCM, 1970), 98-99. There Longenecker concludes that, "while Son of God very soon came to signify divine nature, it was probably used in a more functional manner by the earliest Jewish believers to denote Jesus' unique relationship with God the Father and his obedience to the Father's will." Longenecker also notes that Paul uses "'Son of God' only three times and 'the Son' twelve" (98). Of course, Jesus' divine sonship is stressed particularly in the Fourth Gospel. On the use of the "Son of God" title in the Synoptics, see Gathercole, *Preexistent Son*, 272-83.

that God was at work through Jesus in his ministry (Acts 2:22; 10:36-38). The Fourth Gospel also stresses not only that Jesus was *sent* by God, but also that all of Jesus' work is at the same time the work of God (John 5:19-23, 36; 7:28-29; 9:3-4; 10:37-38; 14:10-11; 17:3-4). The same Gospel continually affirms that Jesus' words and teachings are not his alone, but those of his Father, in whose name and on whose behalf Jesus speaks (John 6:45; 7:16; 8:26, 40; 12:49; 14:24; 15:15). The idea that Jesus' activity is at the same time the activity of God himself is assumed in many other passages from the Gospels, even when that idea is not mentioned explicitly.

All of the Gospels also emphasize the notion that God bestowed Jesus with a unique authority during his ministry. This authority allowed him to speak and act in God's name, to subdue evil spirits, and to equate following and obeying him with following and obeying God himself. In Matt. 11:27, Jesus proclaims that "all things" were handed to him by his Father and therefore that "no one knows the Son except the Father, and no one knows the Father except the Son and anyone to whom the Son chooses to reveal him." The claim that to know Jesus is at the same time to know God is especially prominent in the Fourth Gospel (John 8:19; 14:7-11; 16:3).

Closely related to this authority to speak and act as God's representative and reveal God's will is the authority to judge others and enable access to God for others. Several passages in the Synoptics affirm the idea that one's relation to God depends on one's relation to Jesus. In Matt. 7:21-23, Jesus states, "Not everyone who says to me, 'Lord, Lord,' will enter the kingdom of heaven, but only the one who does the will of my Father in heaven. On that day many will say to me, 'Lord, Lord, did we not prophesy in your name, and cast out demons in your name, and do many deeds of power in your name?' Then I will declare to them, 'I never knew you; go away from me, you evildoers.'" Here one's entrance into God's reign is dependent on Jesus' approval. A similar idea appears in Matt. 10:32-33, where Jesus tells the disciples, "Everyone therefore who acknowledges me before others, I also will acknowledge before my Father in heaven; but whoever denies me before others, I also will deny before my Father in heaven." Luke presents a slightly different version of both of these sayings, which suggests they are both from the common source Q (Luke 12:8; 13:25-27). Following Peter's confession of Jesus' messiahship in Mark and Luke, Jesus affirms, "Those who are ashamed of me and of my words, of them the Son of Man will be ashamed when he comes in his glory and the glory of the Father and of the holy angels" (Luke 9:26; cf. Mark 8:38). All three Synoptics include the account of the paralytic healed by Jesus in which Jesus declares the man's sins forgiven (Matt. 9:1-8; Mark 2:1-12; Luke 5:17-26). To whatever extent this account is historical, and in whatever way Jesus' words there are interpreted, it reflects the same idea that Jesus has the authority to declare who is and is not forgiven and accepted by God.[74]

---

74. On this discussion, see Gathercole, *Preexistent Son*, 57-58; E. P. Sanders, *Jesus and Judaism* (Philadelphia: Fortress, 1985), 38-40, 200-202, 273-74.

While these passages imply that the judgment God will pronounce regarding each person depends on Jesus' approval or disapproval of that person, other passages take the further step of presenting Jesus himself as judge. In Matt. 25:31-46, Jesus is portrayed as the Son of Man who will judge people from all the nations on the basis of how they treated those in greatest need, who are identified with Jesus himself. Similar ideas appear elsewhere in Matthew and the other Synoptics as well (Matt. 7:21-23; 13:41-43; 24:30-31; 26:64; 28:18; Mark 13:26-27; Luke 12:8-9; 21:27-28).[75] In Acts 17:31, Luke has Paul proclaim that God "has fixed a day on which he will have the world judged in righteousness by a man whom he has appointed, and of this he has given assurance to all by raising him from the dead."

The Fourth Gospel also speaks of judgment as a task of both God and Jesus and claims that God has given Jesus the authority to judge all people (John 5:19-30; cf. 8:16). Elsewhere in the Fourth Gospel, Jesus tells his disciples that God will respond favorably to the petitions they make to God in Jesus' name (John 14:13; 16:23-24; cf. 11:22; 15:7; Matt. 18:19). At the same time, the risen Jesus himself may also grant petitions addressed to him (John 14:14). In the book of Acts, the apostles pray both to God and to Jesus and perform many mighty acts "in Jesus' name" (Acts 3:6, 16; 4:10, 30).[76] The idea behind these and other passages in the New Testament is that Jesus' name has authority because of his unique relation to God, who responds favorably to those who invoke him through Jesus.

In the Gospels, the strongest affirmation of Jesus' authority as mediator is found in John 14:6, where Jesus tells Thomas: "I am the way, and the truth, and the life. No one comes to the Father except through me." Here access to God is limited to those who approach God through Jesus, though this does not necessarily mean that those who have not known Jesus or have rejected him can have no access to God. Rather, it can be understood merely in the sense that Jesus is the one whom God has designated as mediator so that all may now have access to him. In Acts 4:12, Luke presents essentially the same claim in the words of Peter before the Jewish authorities: "There is salvation in no one else, for there is no other name under heaven given among mortals by which we must be saved." The clear implication is that Jesus is the only mediator through whom one may obtain fully God's blessings of salvation. Once again, however, this does not necessarily mean that any who do not confess Jesus will not be saved, but only that all those who will be saved will attain that salvation through Jesus, rather than through some other savior or mediator.

In a couple of passages from his letters, Paul also claims that some day Jesus will judge all people (1 Cor. 4:4-5; 2 Cor. 5:10). While for the most part Paul follows Jewish tradition in seeing judgment as a task that ultimately

---

75. On this idea in the Synoptics, see Sanders, *Jesus and Judaism*, 142-46.
76. On the allusions to Jesus' "name" in Acts and other New Testament writings, see especially Hurtado, *Lord Jesus Christ*, 197-206.

belongs to God, at times Paul implies that the mediation of Jesus plays a role in enabling believers to be judged favorably by God. In Rom. 8:34, after stating that no one can make any charge against those chosen by God, Paul writes: "It is Christ Jesus, who died, yes, who was raised, who is at the right hand of God, who indeed intercedes for us." Paul also mentions "the confidence that we have through Christ towards God" (2 Cor. 3:4; cf. 1 Pet. 1:21), and presents Christ as the one who will save believers from God's wrath (Rom. 5:9). In Rom. 2:16, Paul even attributes to God and Jesus simultaneously the act of judging all people by affirming that God will judge the secret thoughts of all "*through* Jesus Christ."

Similarly, the letter to the Ephesians points to Christ as the one through whom believers "have access in one Spirit to the Father" (Eph. 2:17-18). Those who are in Christ "have access to God in boldness and confidence through faith in him" (Eph. 3:11-12). The author of Hebrews presents the exalted Christ as a heavenly high priest who "is able for all time to save those who approach God through him, since he always lives to make intercession for them" (Heb. 7:25). Other passages from Hebrews also present the risen Jesus as a high priest through whom believers are able to approach God confidently (Heb. 4:14-16; 10:19-22).[77]

Although the Gospels do not explicitly present Jesus as fulfilling the mediatorial role traditionally associated with Israel's high priests, a number of scholars have pointed to passages in which this idea seems to be implicit.[78] The heavenly intercession of Jesus is explicitly mentioned in 1 John 2:1-2: "if anyone does sin, we have an advocate with the Father, Jesus Christ the righteous; and he is the propiatiation (*hilasmos*) for our sins, and not for ours only but also for the sins of the whole world." Several of the New Testament epistles also speak of believers offering up prayers and spiritual sacrifices to God *through* Jesus (Eph. 5:20; Col. 3:17; Heb. 13:15; 1 Pet. 2:5). Of course, the most explicit affirmation of Jesus' role as mediator in the New Testament is found in 1 Tim. 2:5: "For there is one God, and one mediator between God and human beings, the human being Jesus Christ."

Behind all of these claims regarding Jesus' unique role as mediator before God is a certain logic that has often been overlooked. If in New Testament thought it is necessary to approach God through Jesus, this is because Jesus is

---

77. As David M. Hay observes, in developing the idea that Jesus was exalted to be high priest, it is likely that the author of Hebrews was drawing on Psalm 110, which speaks of the one exalted as "Lord" to God's right hand as a priest of the order of Melchizedek (*Glory at the Right Hand: Psalm 110 in Early Christianity*, SBLMS 18; Nashville: Abingdon, 1973, 149-50).

78. Donald Senior sees a possible allusion to the idea of Jesus as high priest in John 19:23, where Jesus' robe is said to have been "seamless," noting that Josephus speaks of the high priest's vesture in the same terms (*Passion of Jesus in John*, 106). Alan R. Kerr also points to a number of Johannine passages that possibly represent Jesus as fulfilling the role of the high priest (*The Temple of Jesus' Body: The Temple Theme in the Gospel of John*; JSNTSup 220; London: Sheffield Academic Press, 2002, 314-70). Timothy C. Gray argues that the Davidic king could also be seen as a high priest and claims that this idea is present in Mark's Gospel (*The Temple in the Gospel of Mark: A Study in its Narrative Role*, WUNT 2/44; Tübingen: Mohr Siebeck, 2008, 88-89). Many have seen an allusion to the idea that Jesus becomes high priest at his death in the accounts of the tearing of the temple veil in Matt. 27:51, Mark 15:38, and Luke 23:45.

regarded as the one who reveals and defines God's will fully and completely as God's Son. According to passages such as Matt. 7:21-23 and Luke 13:25-27, only those who do God's will are acceptable to God. Yet because it is through Jesus that God makes his will known in unique fashion, it is those who submit to Jesus' teaching and lordship who approach God properly.

There is thus a *reason* why access to God is said to be through Jesus alone. In ancient Jewish thought, the reason why Moses was able to function as mediator before God on behalf of the Israelites was that he was God's chosen instrument to bring about a people who would live according to God's will. In the same way, the unique mediatorial role Jesus' first followers ascribed to him had as its basis the belief that Jesus had been chosen by God to reveal God's will and bring people into conformity with that will. As we saw in Chapter 4 with regard to the role of mediators in ancient Jewish thought, these two aspects were thought to be interdependent and inseparable from one another.

In other words, for the authors of the New Testament writings, the basis upon which Jesus acts as mediator in relation to God on behalf of others is the activity that he carries out on behalf of God in relation to those to whom God has sent him. If God heeds Jesus' intercession on behalf of others, it is because those on whose behalf Jesus intercedes are those who have acknowledged him as the one who represents and speaks for God. By definition, such acknowledgment involves a commitment to do God's will as God has defined that will through Jesus. If one must confess Jesus as Lord and receive his approval in order to be acceptable before God, it is because, as God's Son, Jesus has received from God the task of establishing a community of people committed to living as God desires. The claim that God has given Jesus the authority to judge others is derived from and dependent on the idea that Jesus communicates and embodies God's will. Therefore, to submit to God is to submit to Jesus as Lord and obey him.

Many scholars would argue, of course, that the sayings attributed to Jesus in the Gospels regarding his future role in the judgment of humanity do not go back to Jesus himself, but instead originated in the communities formed by his first followers. While Jesus may have believed that he represented and spoke for God in some unique or special way, he would have had to have a very exalted view of his own person or to have conceived of himself as superior to all other human beings in some sense in order to claim that he would some day judge all people, and that one's relation to God depended on one's relation to Jesus himself. Once again, the presuppositions with which one approaches the Gospel accounts will determine whether or not one believes that Jesus viewed himself in that way. Even if he did not, however, once his disciples came to believe that he had been raised and exalted to God's right hand as God's Son, it was logical for them to come to the conclusion that he had been constituted as the mediator through whom it was necessary to approach God, and that he had received from God the authority to judge all people.

These beliefs regarding Jesus, then, placed him not only above other prophetic figures such as John and political figures such as the Roman emperor,[79] but also above the Jewish religious hierarchy, including particularly the Jewish high priest. Because the priests were thought to mediate God's forgiveness to the people and mediate as well the access of the people to God, once Jesus' followers came to see him as the one whom God had seated at his right hand to serve as the mediator who was far above any other mediator, it was natural for them to claim that Jesus now fulfilled the role that the law had previously assigned to Israel's priests and the high priest in particular. God was now to be approached *through Jesus* rather than through other priestly mediators.

Obviously, however, Jesus had not been a priest or of priestly lineage. As the letter to the Hebrews notes, he was of the the tribe of Judah rather than of the priestly lineage associated with the tribe of Levi (Heb. 7:14). During his lifetime, Jesus had also not performed any of the priestly tasks at the temple at Jerusalem. However, once his followers came to believe that Jesus had been installed in heaven as one who had immediate access to God in a way that no earthly high priest ever did, it was inevitable that they would also ascribe to him the tasks traditionally assigned to the high priest—not only that of offering up prayers and sacrifices on behalf of the people God had placed under him, but also that of serving as the one through whom those people offered up to God their own prayers and sacrifices. Furthermore, the idea that Jesus was superior to the high priest would also lead to the belief that the prayers and sacrifices offered up by Jesus and through him were superior to those offered up by the high priest.

Jesus' Death and His Role as Mediator

At some point, the beliefs of Jesus' first followers regarding his mediating activity from God's side at heaven came to influence the way in which they interpreted his death. As we have noted above, because Jesus was thought to have offered up his life to God seeking forgiveness and salvation for others, it was natural for his followers to see his death as sacrificial. The fact that Jesus had been put to death by others, who had shed his blood, also meant that his death could be seen as comparable to the way in which sacrificial animals were slaughtered at the temple. If Jesus actually spoke the words Paul attributes to him at the Last Supper over the bread and wine in 1 Cor. 11:24-25, his allusions to the giving of his body and the pouring out of his blood on behalf of others would also have led his first followers to interpret his crucifixion in sacrificial terms. In any case, because Jesus had offered up his own life rather than that of a sacrificial animal, he could be understood as having fulfilled not only the role of high priest, but that of sacrificial victim as well.

---

79. As Scott D. Mackie notes, the idea that access to God is through Jesus could also be seen as anti-imperial, since it involved the implicit claim that Jesus had replaced the Roman emperor as *pontifex maximus* of the empire (*Eschatology and Exhortation in the Epistle to the Hebrews*; WUNT 2/223; Tübingen: Mohr Siebeck, 2007, 148-49, commenting on passages from the epistle to the Hebrews).

As the letter to the Hebrews demonstrates, these beliefs would lead to the claim that the sacrifice Jesus had presented to God was far greater than the sacrifices presented by the priests, who did not offer up to God their own lives, but only the lives of animal victims. At the same time, Jesus' resurrection and exaltation to God's side would then be understood as God's acceptance of Jesus' sacrifice on behalf of others. Such a belief would lead Jesus' followers to regard his offering of himself as far superior to the offering of the animal victims presented at the Jerusalem temple, since those animals did not enter into God's presence in heaven in the way that Jesus had.

What is absent from the early tradition recorded in the New Testament writings, however, is the idea that in his last hours Jesus had offered up the type of prayer that the high priest offered to God when he presented sacrifices to God. In addition, Jesus' execution on the cross did not seem to provide any basis for the notion that in his death he had fulfilled some type of mediating activity on behalf of others. Undoubtedly, the Gospel passion narratives include a number of prayers attributed to Jesus. The most important of these is Jesus' prayer in Gethsemane shortly before his arrest (Matt. 26:36-44; Mark 14:32-41; Luke 22:39-46). Yet this prayer is presented in terms of a petition for God to spare him from the "cup" or death he was to endure, and does not involve any type of intercession on behalf of others. In the context of the Last Supper in the Gospels of Luke and John, Jesus prays that Peter be strengthened so as to resist Satan (Luke 22:31-32), and asks God to be with his disciples and others who would come to believe in him after his death (John 17:6-25); yet no petition for divine forgiveness on behalf of others is mentioned in those passages. The only such petition attributed to Jesus in his last hours occurs in Luke 23:34, where Jesus prays from the cross, "Father, forgive them, for they do not know what they are doing." There are doubts as to whether these words originally formed part of Luke's Gospel.[80] In any case, this petition embraces only those involved in the act of crucifying Jesus. Nowhere in the tradition do we find attributed to Jesus anything like the petition ascribed to Eleazar in 4 Macc. 6:30: "Make my blood their purification, and receive my soul as an offering on their behalf (*antipsuchon autōn*)."

It is possible, of course, that the saying attributed to Jesus in which he speaks of giving his life as a "*lutron* for many" (Mark 10:45; Matt. 20:28) and the words he was remembered to have pronounced over the bread and wine at the Last Supper led his first followers to see his death as an act of mediation on the part of others. Even if this is the case, however, what must have played an even more significant role in the development of the belief in Jesus' mediating activity on behalf of others in his death was the interpretation his followers gave to the ministry he had carried out, and the way in which they believed Jesus had faced his death. Whatever Jesus may have said regarding

---

80. On this question, see especially Raymond E. Brown, *The Death of the Messiah: From Gethsemane to the Grave. A Commentary on the Passion Narratives in the Four Gospels* (ABRL; New York: Doubleday, 1994), 2:975-81.

the significance of his death would have been understood against the background of the way in which he had lived and died.

When they looked back at Jesus' ministry, it must have been obvious to his first followers that Jesus had dedicated himself to seeking the salvation of others, as we saw in Chapter 5. They would have regarded this salvation as embracing a number of different aspects, including things such as physical well-being, social justice and equity, the deliverance of people from powers, practices, and persons that oppressed them, and the establishment of healthy and just relationships in people's daily lives. The salvation that Jesus was thought to have sought for others, however, was also understood in eschatological terms as the attainment of the blessings that God had promised to bestow on Israel and other nations. Obviously, what impeded this salvation was human sin and evil. People needed to be saved from their own sinful acts, the sins of others, the sinful structures that existed, and the powers of evil present in individuals, society, and the spirit world. For salvation to become a reality, it was necessary for people to repent and change their ways and for God to intervene from heaven to deliver people from the powers to which they were thought to be subject. When his disciples looked back on the ministry Jesus had carried out, they recalled the manner in which he had dedicated himself to bringing people to live, behave, and think differently, while at the same time seeking that God act to fulfill the promises of salvation that he had made of old.

It would have been logical for Jesus' first followers to come to the conclusion that, if Jesus had *lived* for these things, he must also have *died* for them. In fact, it was his commitment to seeking the salvation of others that had ultimately led him to go up to Jerusalem, teach in the temple, take action against the commercial activities being carried out there, and stand firm against those who opposed his work on behalf of others. When faced with the possibility that the authorities might take action against him and perhaps even have him put to death, Jesus had not backed down from the work he was doing, but had carried on in that work boldly and undauntedly. His followers would therefore have interpreted his death as the consequence of his dedication to the objective of making it possible for others to attain the salvation he desired for them, in obedience to God.

Upon reflection, Jesus' first followers must have come to the conclusion that, if Jesus had faced death in this way, then during his last hours and minutes he must have commended to God not only his own life, but also the salvation of others to which he had tirelessly dedicated himself. If this was the case, then they would have understood Jesus as in effect presenting a petition to God as he went to his death in which he asked God that the salvation he had sought for others throughout his life might become a reality fully some day through him. In essence, this is the activity of a mediator, who intercedes to God on behalf of others. They may also have thought that Jesus sought, not only that God act to bring about the salvation of others to which Jesus had dedicated himself, but that God enable Jesus himself to accomplish that salvation by raising him from the dead, thereby making it possible for him to complete the task he had begun. Furthermore, because it was human sin that constituted the obstacle to that salvation, Jesus' death would also be understood as a petition that God forgive the sins of those whose salvation Jesus sought, and also bring about in them the change of life necessary for them to be saved. In other words, *Jesus had died, as he had lived, seeking that God save others from their sins.*

Whether or not the *lutron*-saying in Mark 10:45 and the words over the bread and wine ascribed to Jesus at the Last Supper are regarded as authentic in some form, it seems beyond doubt that they formed part of a very early tradition. While these sayings can be interpreted in the sense that Jesus' death would benefit others by virtue of some intrinsic consequence that would result from it, they can also be understood in the sense that Jesus was offering up his life seeking that God act to bring about the salvation of others to which Jesus had been dedicating himself. In order that he might bring that salvation to pass, Jesus had also sought to be exalted to God's side. For Jesus to seek these things from God for others was in effect to intercede to God on their behalf. Once again, this would be seen as comparable to the type of mediation carried out by the priests, who also offered up to God sacrifices together with prayers asking for forgiveness, blessings, and salvation for the people.

On the basis of these ideas, it seems clear that Jesus' first followers would have come to see his death as an implicit petition to God for the salvation of others. This petition would have been viewed as a supplication, not only that God forgive and save others through Jesus, but also that God bring about in others through Jesus the life of conformity to his will necessary for their salvation. This new life would be the result of the instruction, revelation, and example Jesus had given in the past, his continuing activity through the Holy Spirit once he had been raised, and the hope that his future coming inspired in believers. Jesus' petition would be that all of this activity in relation to others would contribute to their transformation. As is evident from the New Testament, this mediating activity would be seen as something Jesus had carried out both in his death and as something he continued to carry out following his exaltation into heaven. In fact, almost all of the New Testament passages cited above that present Jesus as a heavenly mediator also contain an allusion to his death in the immediate context (Rom. 8:32-34; Eph. 2:13-18; 1 Tim. 2:5-6; Heb. 7:25-27; 10:19-21; 1 John 1:6—2:2).[81]

If the first believers viewed Jesus and his death in these terms, the question arises as to how they came to regard others considered mediators in the Judaism of the day. It is evident from the Gospels that they viewed Jesus as greater than John the Baptist and, from what we have seen above, superior

---

81. The same connection between Jesus' death and his ongoing heavenly mediation may be present in Heb. 5:7-10, which speaks of Jesus offering up prayers and supplications in his death in the context of the argument that God constituted Jesus as high priest to offer sacrifices for others.

to the Roman emperor and the Jewish priests and high priest as well.[82] For this reason, his mediation in relation to God would probably have been seen, not only as superior to that of other mediator figures, but also as annulling or replacing their mediating activity. Otherwise, Jesus' followers would have had to believe that they attained God's blessings and forgiveness in part through *Jesus'* mediation and in part through that of *others*.

To underscore this point, we may consider the question of whether Jesus' first followers would have participated in the annual Day of Atonement rites carried out at the temple at Jerusalem. For those believers who resided in Jerusalem or could travel there, this would probably have involved attending those rites at the temple. For those unable to be present in Jerusalem, such participation would have involved observing the prescriptions mandated for the observance of that day for all Jews, such as confessing their sins and turning toward Jerusalem to pray at the same time that the sacrificial rites were being performed there. Because Caiaphas occupied the high priesthood until the year 36 CE, the same high priest whom Jesus' first followers regarded as largely responsible for Jesus' unjust condemnation would have been the one carrying out the Day of Atonement rites and entering into the Holy of holies in the years immediately following Jesus' death. After Caiaphas, the high priesthood was occupied by other sons of Annas, who was also believed to have played an important role in the process against Jesus.

Would Jesus' first followers, then, have believed that they obtained the forgiveness of sins and God's favor by means of their participation in the Day of Atonement rites carried out under Caiaphas in the Jerusalem temple? Would they have thought that God looked with favor on the prayer and sacrifice of Caiaphas as high priest on behalf of Jews such as themselves? This seems extremely unlikely. It also seems unlikely that they would have believed that their sins were forgiven in part on account of Jesus' past and present mediating activity, and in part on account of the mediating activity of high priests such as Caiaphas and Annas's sons. Furthermore, if they no longer ascribed the same value to the Day of Atonement rites performed by those high priests, they would most likely have also had to rethink the value of other sacrificial rites carried out in the temple, not only by the high priest but by other priests. If in their mind they now obtained divine forgiveness by means of Jesus, who had offered himself up to God on their behalf and now interceded for them from God's side in heaven, of what use could the sacrifices and prayers offered up by the priests in the Jerusalem temple be to them? As we shall see in

---

82. The idea that God offered the forgiveness of sins through the risen Jesus would not only imply that Jesus had replaced the Roman emperor as *pontifex maximus* of the empire, as noted above, but would also contrast Jesus with the Roman emperor in that the emperor alone enjoyed the privilege of granting *clementia* to those who had committed some wrong against Rome. Susanna Morton Braund has pointed out that, from a Jewish perspective, such *clementia* could be seen as being roughly equivalent to the forgiveness of sins ("The Anger of Tyrants and the Forgiveness of Kings," in *Ancient Forgiveness: Classical, Judaic, and Christian*; ed. Charles L. Griswold and David Konstan; New York: Cambridge University Press, 2012, 88-92).

Chapter 8 of this work, at most they would have seen those rites as anticipating what would take place in Jesus and pointing to him as their fulfillment.

Jesus' first followers would have considered Jesus' mediation as superior to that of the Jewish high priests such as Caiaphas for a couple of reasons. First, throughout his life and in his death, Jesus had shown himself to be morally superior to the leaders of Israel. In contrast to those leaders, many of whom were regarded as corrupt and power-hungry, Jesus had embodied virtues such as truth, justice, purity, and a concern for the well-being of others. The love for others he had shown in life and death contrasted sharply with the greed and ambition of the Jewish authorities. Second, by virtue of his exaltation to God's right hand as well as his divine sonship, Jesus enjoyed a proximity to God that no other mediator possessed. A number of passages from the New Testament writings speak of God being "pleased" with Jesus as his Son (Matt. 3:17; 12:18; 17:5; Mark 1:11; Luke 3:22; Col. 1:19; 2 Pet. 1:17). In fact, God had raised and exalted Jesus precisely because God had been so pleased with the love for others that Jesus had manifested in life and death.

Jesus' death, therefore, would have been understood as being "for others" in the sense that he had gone to his death asking that God allow and enable him to continue carrying out his mediatorial role on behalf of others, and perhaps even carry that role out in a greater way. Believers would also affirm that Jesus had given himself up for the sins of others, both in the sense that he had gone to his death seeking God's forgiveness and acceptance of others in spite of their sins, and in the sense that he had desired to be exalted to a position at God's side from where he might continue to carry out his mediating activity on behalf of others and enable them to leave behind their sinful ways. Jesus' resurrection and exaltation would be understood as a favorable divine response to the intercession he had made on behalf of the salvation of others. In this sense, when God raised and exalted Jesus, God could be said to have granted salvation in definitive and irreversible fashion to all who would follow Jesus, since nothing could now prevent Jesus from returning in power to deliver his followers from the present evil age and inaugurate God's reign.

The Need for Jesus' Mediation

One of the questions that this understanding of Jesus' role as mediator raises is why any mediating activity on his part would have been considered necessary. Why could God not simply save people and forgive them their sins, independently of Jesus? Why had it been necessary for God to hand Jesus over to death and for Jesus to offer up his life? Questions such as these would have been answered in a way that is very different from the way in which Christian theologians have traditionally responded to them. As we saw in Chapter 1 of this study, in penal substitution views, the argument for the necessity of Jesus' death has traditionally been rooted in a certain understanding of God's nature: because God is perfectly just, it was impossible for God to forgive sins freely. For this reason, it was necessary for Jesus to intervene, undergoing the punishment due to human sin and exhausting God's wrath at that sin. In this case, Jesus' work as mediator was ultimately necessary *for God's sake*, in order that God might save human beings without contradicting God's nature or compromising God's justice.

The logic of the first Christians would have been quite different. The argument for the necessity for Jesus' work as mediator would have been grounded, not in the need for God's perfectly righteous nature to be satisfied, but in the need for human beings to put away the sinful conduct that destroys their well-being, as well as the need for them to come to practice the justice, righteousness, and love that God desired and commanded of them for their own good. God's love for human beings would not allow God simply to tolerate sin without acting to deliver them from their sinfulness.

In Jewish thought, throughout history, God's first and primary reaction to sin had always been to call people to repentance and obedience through his prophets so that they might return to the way of life that would enable them to enjoy the blessings God desired for them. When the people failed to respond properly, God continued to send prophets and chastise or discipline the people in various ways in order to move them to return to him. Only after God's repeated efforts had failed to accomplish his purposes did God become wrathful and act against those who persisted in practicing evil, seeking to restore justice for the good of all.

According to Jesus' first followers, after centuries of sending prophets and showing patience with Israel and the nations, God had finally sent his own Son to make it possible for people to live according to his will. In New Testament thought, *this was Jesus' primary task: to bring about in others the kind of life God desired and commanded for the good of all*. Jesus was to accomplish this task, not only by means of his teaching and example, but also by actively opposing sin and evil and enabling others to do the same. Although he had died as a result of his dedication to this task, he had redefined for others what it meant to be committed to doing God's will in order to bring about that same commitment in them.

Of course, it was not only Jesus' activity in the past, present, and future that was thought to enable others to live as God desired, but also God's response to Jesus' activity, which consisted of raising and exalting him so that he might continue to be active bringing others into conformity with God's will, in large part through the Holy Spirit. This response gave assurance to all people that, if they were committed to living according to God's will as Jesus had been, they too would be raised from the dead so as to participate in the life of the new age. Furthermore, since all of Jesus' activity had also been the activity of God *through* Jesus as his obedient Son, ultimately it was not only Jesus who had made it possible for people to be brought into conformity with God's will, but God himself. The result of all that Jesus had done and all that God had done through Jesus was the new, alternative community that God had intended to bring about through Jesus his Son. By consecrating himself fully in life and death to the creation of that community, Jesus had not only made it possible for it to exist, but had also stamped and defined it forever as a community in which all would live in the same love seen in Jesus, guided by God's Spirit.

Nevertheless, in the minds of Jesus' followers, it was not yet possible for them to live in perfect conformity with God's will as God desired. In a sense, whenever they sinned, they found themselves subject to God's disapproval again, since God's love would not allow God simply to overlook their sinfulness due to the harm which that sinfulness caused them and others. As had been the case in ancient Israel, the people's persistence in sin made the work of a mediator such as Moses or the high priest necessary. In Jesus, God had provided both Israel and the nations with the ultimate and definitive mediator who had full divine power and authority to bring about in others the way of life God had always desired to see in all. Jesus' mediating activity in relation to God on behalf of others, however, had as its basis his past, present, and future activity aimed at bringing about in them the way of life God desired and commanded. It was thought that God had responded favorably to Jesus' petition for forgiveness on behalf of his followers due to God's expectation that, as a result of Jesus' past, present, and future activity, they would continue to be empowered to leave behind their sinful behavior and become new people.

This, then, is the logic behind the claim that Jesus' activity as mediator was necessary. While it can rightly be said that, in the minds of the first believers, God's strict justice required that Jesus serve as mediator on their behalf due to their sin, this was because in principle God refused to accept them in their sinful condition, not *for his own sake*, but *for theirs*. Both his demand that they live according to his will and his gift of Jesus to them as mediator would thus be seen as an act of love on God's part. Through his Son, God had provided a way for them to be brought into conformity with his will for their own good, and had also graciously given them a mediator who might render them acceptable to him in spite of their ongoing sinfulness.

These ideas provide the background necessary for understanding properly the New Testament passages considered above that present Jesus as mediator on behalf of others. God had sent Jesus to carry out the ministry that he did in order to establish the new, obedient people God desired to see, composed not only of persons belonging to Israel, but persons from the gentile nations as well. The reason Jesus had lived and died was not because *God* needed Jesus' life and death to save human beings, but because those sinful human beings needed to be brought into conformity with God's loving will for their own well-being and that of others. The consequence of Jesus' work on behalf of others had been his death, yet his death had also been the *means* by which the community of believers had been established. Once people had been brought into that community and had begun to have their lives transformed there, Jesus interceded to God on their behalf, asking God to forgive and accept them in spite of the fact that they had not yet come to live fully in accordance with God's will. Besides asking God's forgiveness for them, Jesus was also thought to ask God to strengthen, guide, and protect them, just as he had prayed for his disciples during his ministry and in his last hours. In addition, of course, Jesus would be thought to intercede, not only on behalf of believers, but also on behalf of all those who had not yet come to form part of the community under him. Nevertheless, in both cases, the basis for Jesus' petition would be essentially the same: that God accept and forgive all those who would be committed to living according to God's will as defined through Jesus, in spite of the fact that they were still far from achieving the kind of obedience God sought to see in them out of love for them and others.

In New Testament thought, then, the reason why no other person or "name" could serve as a means to approach God was that, as God's Son, Jesus alone was capable of bringing about in others conformity to God's will as the one who understood, embodied, and revealed that will fully. Because even believers remain sinful, rather than approaching God directly, they must do so through Jesus. If there is only "one mediator between God and human beings, the human being Jesus Christ" (1 Tim. 2:5), this is because there is no other human being more capable of bringing about in others the life God desires and commands for their own good.

For the same reasons, in the New Testament, the prayers and "spiritual sacrifices" that are most pleasing to God are those offered to him through Jesus (Heb. 13:15; 1 Pet. 2:5). While God may graciously and mercifully accept the prayers and expressions of love of any who approach him with a sincere heart, including both those who acknowledge Jesus as Lord and those who do not, those prayers and expressions of love are never in perfect conformity with God's will because those who offer themselves up to God remain sinful. For their own sake and the sake of others who are harmed by their sin, God desires that those who offer up themselves and their prayers to him be free of sin. However, because this is beyond their possibilities, God grants them Jesus to bring about in them the life he desires, and then, on the basis of that new life, he accepts their prayers and offerings when they approach him through Jesus. When believers pray in Jesus' name, they identify themselves as his followers, and this makes them and their prayers pleasing to God.

In his role as mediator, then, Jesus provides assurance to God that those on whose behalf he intercedes are being brought to live in accordance with God's will. As 1 John 2:1-2 states, even when they fall into sin, believers can have certainty that God will forgive them and put away his wrath at their sins, since their Lord, "Jesus Christ the righteous one," serves as their advocate before God, assuring God that as they live under his lordship, they will be transformed into the obedient people God desires. The same logic is behind Rom. 8:34 and the passages from Hebrews that speak of Jesus interceding on behalf of believers so as to enable them to approach God confidently and without fear (Heb. 4:14-16; 7:25; 10:19-22). In New Testament thought, while believers know themselves to be loved unconditionally by God, the fact that they still fall into sin might prevent them from drawing near to God with confidence and trust. However, because Jesus intercedes to God on the basis of the new life he is bringing about in them through all of his past, present, and future activity, those who adhere to Christ can be sure that, in spite of their sinfulness, God accepts them.

Paul's affirmation in Rom. 5:9 that Jesus will save believers from God's wrath must be understood on the basis of the same ideas. As Paul states at the outset of Romans, God's wrath is directed against all who practice injustice and suppress the truth regarding his loving will for all (Rom. 1:18). In a sense, all without exception are sinners devoid of righteousness (Rom. 3:9-19). According to the teaching of Paul and the first believers, God intends to destroy sin and evil some day, along with all those who insist on practicing that sin and evil, so that justice and *shalom* can prevail on earth. Because those who submit to Christ as their Lord are being enabled to live as God desires and commands, when that day of wrath comes, Christ will deliver them from that wrath.

A proper understanding of these ideas also makes it possible to understand why Jesus' ongoing intercession on behalf of believers was thought to be necessary, in addition to the offering of himself that he had made on their behalf in his death. As the letter to the Hebrews maintains, both Jesus' offering of himself on behalf of others and God's acceptance of that offering were one-time events that could not and need not be repeated (Heb. 7:27; 9:12, 26-28; 10:9). By raising and exalting Jesus, God had granted forgiveness, acceptance, and salvation *once and for all* to all those who would live under Jesus' lordship so as to be brought into conformity with God's loving will.

According to the thought of Jesus' first followers, however, although their adhesion to Jesus as Lord provided them with certainty regarding their ultimate salvation, they continued to need God to guide and correct them in their daily life on account of their ongoing sin. The letter to the Hebrews, for example, speaks of God chastising or disciplining believers in the present for their own good (Heb. 12:3-13). Because they were unable to live without sin, they still needed Jesus to continue to intercede for them, not only so that God might forgive them the sins they still committed, but also so that they might be enabled to progress in their perfection, rather than falling away or succumbing to temptation (Heb. 4:14-16; 6:1-12). It was necessary for them to depend on God's grace at all times by continually drawing near to God through Christ. Jesus' ongoing intercession on their behalf from God's right hand gave them assurance that God would continue to forgive and accept them and accomplish his will in them so that they might obtain his blessings, both in the present world and the age to come.

CHAPTER 7

JESUS, GOD'S WILL, AND THE LAW

The claim that, through his life and death, Jesus had redefined God's will and had been established as Lord over all had far-reaching consequences for the manner in which Jesus' first followers related to their fellow Jews. Whereas previously the Mosaic law had been at the center of their life, it was now their adherence to Jesus and all that he represented that defined above all else who they were and how they were to live. For them, it was no longer simply obedience to the commandments of the law that determined who was righteous and acceptable before God, but a commitment to living in the way that Jesus had taught and embodied as God's Son. This affirmation, however, runs contrary to traditional Western Christian teaching, where the basis upon which believers are justified and saved is said to be Jesus' life, suffering, and death, rather than the life of believers themselves.

In order to grasp clearly the role that Jesus' first followers ascribed to his death in their justification and salvation, it is necessary first to examine their beliefs regarding the will of God and the Mosaic law. As we shall see in the present chapter, those beliefs led Jesus' followers to understand God's will in a way that was fundamentally distinct from that of other Jews in antiquity. Eventually, this new understanding of God's will had as its result the incorporation of non-Jews into the communities of Jesus' followers, and also generated tensions and conflicts that became almost impossible to resolve.[1]

FAITH IN JESUS AND THE REDEFINITION OF GOD'S WILL

Although almost all Jewish teachers stressed the need for a literal observance of the commandments, which were interpreted not only on the basis of the written text but oral tradition as well, the vast majority of teachers also focused on the principles underlying the Mosaic commandments, as Jesus and the Hebrew prophets had done. Of course, these two emphases were not regarded as mutually exclusive. Even those who called for a strict literal observance of the commandments recognized that it was necessary to understand and fulfill the fundamental principles on which the law was based, such as love

---

1. The Greek term *ethnē* as used in the New Testament is notoriously difficult to translate. In general, throughout the present work, I prefer to speak of *non-Jews* or the "nations," yet I use the term *gentile* in a theological sense to refer to the way in which non-Jews were viewed in the communities of Jesus' first followers and among most Jews.

of neighbor and care for the needy. It was also commonly acknowledged that at times obedience to the law required setting aside or even breaking a commandment in its literal sense in order to fulfill the spirit of the law or observe some other commandment that was of greater importance.[2] As many scholars have stressed, Jesus' teaching in this regard was not entirely unique in his day.

In recent years, many scholars have argued in favor of the view that not only Jesus himself but also his first Jewish followers remained committed to observing literally the precepts of the Jewish law as commonly interpreted in second-temple Judaism.[3] In this regard, Jesus' followers were in basic agreement with other Jews regarding the centrality and importance of the Mosaic law. Supposedly, the differences of opinion and conflicts over questions of law-observance that arose among Jesus' first followers, as well as between them and other Jews, were the result of the incorporation of uncircumcised non-Jews into the communities of believers in Jesus. While it was agreed that believers of Jewish origin should continue to observe the law in the way they had done before, the debates centered primarily on the extent to which believers of non-Jewish origin should submit to the Mosaic law.

While I would not question the idea that Jesus' first followers continued to observe the Mosaic law much as they had previously, from my perspective the reconstruction just outlined is problematic in that it suggests that disputes over the role that the Mosaic law was to play in the lives of Jesus' followers arose as a result of their work among non-Jews, rather than in the earliest stages of the apostolic proclamation. The book of Acts, for example, mentions conflicts between Jesus' first followers and other Jews occurring almost immediately after Jesus began to be proclaimed as Messiah and risen Lord (Acts 4:1-30; 5:17-41). Both Acts and Paul's letters also mention Paul and other Jews persecuting the first believers in Jesus shortly after Jesus' death, apparently prior to the incorporation of non-Jews into the community of believers.

---

2. Undoubtedly, a wide variety of views regarding the literal observance of the commandments existed even in Jesus' day. As John P. Meier notes, Philo knew of "some extreme allegorizers in Diaspora Judaism (probably in Alexandria) who felt that they were not held to the literal observance of the Law as long as they understood and followed its symbolic sense" (*A Marginal Jew: Rethinking the Historical Jesus*, Vol. 4: *Law and Love*; AYBRL; New Haven, CT: Yale University Press, 2009, 72, n82; see also 43-46). Jonathan Klawans also notes that "we do know of groups of Jews who, at various times in antiquity, rejected purity laws or even all Jewish law, without necessarily rejecting their Jewish identity" (*Impurity and Sin in Ancient Judaism*; Oxford: Oxford University Press, 2000, 145).

3. I am aware, of course, that in a sense it is improper to speak of the Mosaic law as it was "commonly" or "traditionally interpreted" among Jews in the first century. As Calvin J. Roetzel notes, the "multiple revisions" of the law that were taking place in Paul's day "should serve as a cautionary tale against referring to the 'law' or Torah as if that signifier pointed to a uniform, static reality" ("Paul and *Nomos* in the Messianic Age," in *Reading Paul in Context: Explorations in Identity Formation. Essays in Honour of William Campbell*; ed. Kathy Ehrensperger and J. Brian Tucker; London: T & T Clark, 2010, 118). According to Roetzel, the interpretation of the Torah varied according to changing historical crises and ongoing challenges to Jewish identity: "all either in belief or practice hold an understanding of *nomos* that is flexible, or at times even unstable or contradictory" (119). We have already noted in Chapter 5 the wide varieties of interpretations of the law that existed in Jesus' day and the fact that both the text of the Mosaic law as well as the law itself were in a state of constant flux. In spite of this, I would argue that we may still speak of a common or traditional understanding of the law, since there were certain general interpretations of the law and its commandments that were held by the vast majority of Jews.

This Jewish opposition to Jesus' first followers must not be seen merely as a rejection of the claims they were making regarding his resurrection and divine authority as Lord and Messiah. Rather, at the heart of the tensions and conflicts were questions regarding the Mosaic law as well. In Acts, even before the message about Jesus is proclaimed to non-Jews, Stephen is accused of speaking "blasphemous words against Moses and God," repeatedly saying things against the temple and the law, and claiming that Jesus would change the customs handed down from Moses (Acts 6:11-14). While we cannot be entirely certain about the motives that led Paul to persecute the first believers, there are good reasons to believe that they were grounded in the zeal for the law that he mentions in Gal. 1:13-14 and Phil. 3:4-6, passages in which he recalls explicitly his persecution of the church.[4] Paul, or Saul, therefore, seems to have been persecuting believers *before* the work among non-Jews had begun.

The reason that the early proclamation concerning Jesus as Lord inevitably led to conflicts over the Mosaic law becomes clear when we examine closely the implications of that proclamation. Once it began to be maintained that God had established Jesus as Lord and had given him full authority to represent him as ruler and judge, then submission *to God* became inexorably linked to submission *to Jesus*. Among Jesus' followers, refusal to submit to Jesus and acknowledge him as Lord could only be understood as disobedience to the God of Israel, who had sent Jesus. The proclamation regarding Jesus thus involved *a fundamental redefinition of God's will*. Once Jesus was proclaimed as the one sent by God with full divine authority, no matter how obedience to the Mosaic law was defined and how earnest an effort people made to live according to that law, from the perspective of Jesus' followers, ultimately only those who believed in and followed Jesus as Lord could be said to be living fully in accordance with God's will. This is the position that we find repeatedly throughout the New Testament writings.

Furthermore, these beliefs regarding Jesus led not only to the conclusion that obedience to God's will is inseparable from submission to Jesus as Lord, but also to the claim that *it is not the Mosaic law that ultimately defines God's will, but Jesus*. As George Nickelsburg stresses, the New Testament presents

---

4. For a survey of views on the reasons why Saul or Paul persecuted the first believers, see Claudia Setzer, *Jewish Responses to Early Christians: History and Polemics, 30-150 C.E.* (Minneapolis: Fortress, 1994), 10-16. There Setzer affirms the probability that the persecution was rooted in "Paul's passion for the law" and "what he regarded as an assault on Torah-observance" (10-11). I would question Justin Taylor's argument that Paul persecuted the first believers because they refused to be involved in the struggle for liberation from Rome ("Why Did Paul Persecute the Church?," in *Tolerance and Intolerance in Early Judaism and Christianity*, ed. Graham N. Stanton and Guy G. Stroumsa; Cambridge: Cambridge University Press, 1998, 99-120). I also regard as problematic Arland J. Hultgren's claim that it was solely the proclamation of Jesus as Messiah that led Paul to persecute the church, rather than any questions having to do with law-observance ("Paul's Pre-Christian Persecutions of the Church: Their Purpose, Locale and Nature," *JBL* 95 [1976]: 97-111; see especially 99-103). Instead, as Larry W. Hurtado has argued, even if it was their devotion to Jesus and the exalted christological claims they made that led Paul to persecute the first Jewish believers, these questions were closely tied to disagreements regarding the interpretation of the Torah (*How on Earth Did Jesus Become a God?: Historical Questions about Earliest Devotion to Jesus*; Grand Rapids: Eerdmans, 2005, 168-71).

the early church "defining its identity around Jesus of Nazareth rather than the Torah.... That is, christology rather than Torah was determinative of one's status as a true Israelite."⁵ While obedience to God's will was still thought to determine one's status as a member of God's people, for Jesus' first followers God's will became indistinguishable and inseparable from *Jesus himself*. From their perspective, rather than simply asking what *God* commands, it was necessary to ask what God commands *through Jesus* or *what Jesus* commands, since Jesus was viewed as the one who possessed full divine authority as God's spokesperson and Son.

No matter what significance one ascribed to the Mosaic law, these beliefs regarding Jesus ultimately led to a posture regarding that law that diminished its importance, removing it from the central position it had occupied in Jewish thought and relegating it to secondary status. If what truly mattered was obedience to Jesus rather than to the Mosaic law alone, then strictly speaking, to obey Jesus was to obey the law, of which he was the fulfillment, and to obey the law was to obey Jesus, to whom the law pointed. And because obedience to Jesus could not simply be equated with obedience to the Mosaic law, conflict became inevitable. Such conflict only intensified further when those Jews who rejected Jesus' lordship claimed that they were in fact obeying God and doing God's will by observing the law faithfully, in spite of their refusal to believe in and submit to Jesus. At some point they even came to insist that, in order to obey God and the law, it was necessary to reject the messianic claims made concerning Jesus. These positions would have been rejected by Jesus' first followers, who would in turn have been accused by their opponents of placing allegiance to Jesus above allegiance to the law.

Of course, there were undoubtedly many followers of Jesus who maintained a strict adherence to the law as it had been traditionally understood, such as James the Just. Yet there are good reasons to think that their motives for doing so changed after they became followers of Jesus. They may have obeyed the law carefully in order to win over other Jews who would be scandalized if they observed Jesus' followers disregarding the law, and on that basis would want nothing to do with them. It is also possible that many of Jesus' followers observed the law in order to preserve their Jewish identity, because they wished to continue to be fully accepted in the Jewish community, or because they saw Jesus as the law's true fulfillment. In this case, their careful observance of the law constantly led them to reflect more deeply regarding Jesus and the way in which God had defined his will through him. Perhaps many of Jesus' first followers obeyed the law simply because they believed such obedience still constituted the will of God or of Jesus for them. It can hardly be doubted, however, that their faith in Jesus affected the way in which

---

5. George W. E. Nickelsburg, *Ancient Judaism and Christian Origins: Diversity, Continuity and Transformation* (Minneapolis: Fortress, 2003), 183. On the contrast between beliefs regarding Jesus and beliefs regarding the Torah, see also Bruce Chilton and Jacob Neusner, *Judaism in the New Testament: Practices and Beliefs* (London: Routledge, 1995), 156-59.

they viewed the law and their reasons for continuing to observe that law. All Jews who heard the message about Jesus had to determine whether to place Jesus or the law at the center of their life. Either Jesus was one who ultimately defined what proper observance of the law consisted of, or he did not.

The inevitable result of these discussions regarding Jesus and the law was a hardening of two positions that would eventually be regarded as mutually exclusive: one had to choose between declaring one's allegiance to Jesus and declaring one's allegiance to the law *independently* of Jesus. This choice would be imposed on Jesus' first followers particularly by their Jewish opponents, who would condemn them for placing Jesus in a position of authority that rightly belonged only to the law. Jesus' followers would respond by insisting that they continued to respect the law and observe it. Even they would be forced to acknowledge, however, that, while in their minds they were not rejecting the law but affirming it, they were indeed rejecting the law *in many of the ways it had traditionally been understood by their fellow Jews*. It would not be long before the alternative would be understood as *either Jesus or the law*. While Jesus' followers in general would refuse to pit obedience to Jesus against obedience to the law, ultimately they would adopt the position that what *really* mattered in God's eyes was one's position in relation to Jesus, rather than one's observance of the law as interpreted by other Jewish authorities who rejected Jesus as the one through whom God defined his will. The claim that Jesus had a unique relationship to God as God's Son, the risen Lord and Christ, made it impossible for him to be viewed merely as one authority on the law among others.

The Will of God and Jesus in the Book of Acts

Throughout the New Testament, we repeatedly find the idea that God's will is defined through Jesus rather than through the Mosaic law alone. In Acts, the early apostolic proclamation or kerygma does not assume any distinctive type of stance in regard to the law, but merely calls on Jewish audiences to believe in Jesus as Lord and Messiah.[6] The first discussions over the law occur in the account regarding Stephen. In response to the accusation that he spoke against the law of Moses and the temple (Acts 6:11-14), Stephen insists that it is the Jewish authorities who actually stand in opposition to Moses and the law (7:35, 39, 53). Although Stephen seems to criticize the central role that the temple had come to occupy in Jewish thought and practice,[7] what ultimately leads the authorities to stone him is his denunciation of their role in murdering Jesus as their ancestors had murdered the prophets, as well as

---

6. It is significant, for example, that in his summary of the contents of the kerygma as it appears in the speeches of Acts, James D. G. Dunn makes no mention whatsoever of the Mosaic law (*Unity and Diversity in the New Testament: An Inquiry into the Character of Earliest Christianity*, 2nd ed.; London: SCM, 1990, 16-21).

7. Serge Ruzer rightly notes that Stephen does not proclaim the destruction of the temple by Jesus, as his accusers claim in 6:11-14, but rather that its construction was neither needed nor desired by God from the very beginning (*Mapping the New Testament: Early Christian Writings as a Witness for Jewish Biblical Exegesis*; JCPS 13; Leiden: Brill, 2007, 193-94).

his accusation that they had not kept the law (7:48-53). Stephen's affirmations that God "does not dwell in houses made with human hands" and that the people of Israel received "the law as ordained by angels" are evidently an attempt to set God at a certain distance from both the temple and the Mosaic law. These aspects are all intimately linked to one another: according to Stephen's speech, the reason the Jewish leaders had murdered Jesus was that they had made of the law, including the commandments prescribing sacrificial worship at the sanctuary, something contrary to that which God had intended it to be. In this way, they had misinterpreted and disobeyed not only the law, but the will of God himself.[8]

The next passage in which the subject of the law comes up in Acts is the account of Peter's visit to the house of Cornelius (Acts 10:1—11:18). There the risen Jesus reveals to Peter and subsequently to all those present that the commandments regarding purity are no longer binding in the case of Cornelius and, by implication, other uncircumcised gentiles upon whom God has chosen to pour out the Holy Spirit as well. The risen Jesus tells Peter three times: "What God has made clean, you must not call profane" (10:15). Here the idea that Jesus is above the law and can even alter or invalidate it as the one who speaks on behalf of God is clear: it is no longer the law that ultimately defines what is pure or impure, but Jesus.

When the apostles and elders gather at Jerusalem in Acts 15, the Holy Spirit leads James, Peter, and the group as a whole to declare that gentile believers need not submit to circumcision and the law. Significantly, Peter himself refers to the law there as "a yoke that neither our ancestors nor we have been able to bear," and then claims that both Jews and gentiles "will be saved through the grace of the Lord Jesus" (15:10-11, 19-29). Here a negative attitude toward the law as a yoke too heavy to bear is combined with the claim that its observance ultimately plays no role in salvation, since for both Jewish and non-Jewish believers, salvation comes through the grace of Jesus as Lord.[9] In both of these accounts, it is explicitly stated that, within the community of believers, distinctions between those who observe the Jewish law

---

8. The idea that Jesus is superior to the law also seems to be present in Acts 7:37, where Stephen quotes Deut. 18:15 concerning the prophet God promised to raise up. As Alan Watson observes, when this text is viewed in the context of Deut. 18:18-20, the "clear meaning of the Deuteronomic passage is that this prophet will have the power to change the law" (*The Trial of Stephen: The First Christian Martyr*, Athens, GA: University of Georgia Press, 1996, 44-45).

9. Undoubtedly, as Bruce Chilton has noted, the stipulation in Acts 15 that believing gentiles observe basic requirements concerning fornication, blood, and idolatry can be interpreted in the sense that, in that way, they acknowledge the law and show their respect for it ("Paul and the Pharisees," in *In Quest of the Historical Pharisees*, ed. Jacob Neusner and Bruce Chilton; Waco, TX: Baylor University Press, 2007, 151-53). Even if that was the original intention, however, the stipulation regarding food sacrificed to idols in Acts 15:19-20, 28-29 may also be seen in terms of asking gentile believers in Christ who were in principle free to eat of meat sacrificed to idols to make concessions on behalf of those Jewish believers whose conscience regarding food sacrificed to idols would impede them from having table fellowship with the gentile believers. This interpretation might be supported by both vv. 19 and 28 of Acts 15, which speak of not wishing to "trouble" the gentile believers or "impose further burdens" on them. In this case, rather than being viewed as an acknowledgment of the validity of the law or a sign of respect for it, that stipulation could instead be seen as reflecting a negative view of the law as a yoke from which one must be freed, as Peter affirms (Acts 15:10).

and those who do not are to disappear. Peter reports to the Jewish believers in Jerusalem that the Holy Spirit told him "not to make a distinction between them and us" (11:12). Then, when the apostles and elders gather in Jerusalem, Peter affirms: "in cleansing their hearts by faith [God] has made no distinction between them and us" (15:9). "No distinction" can only mean that, where there is faith in Christ, in God's eyes observance or non-observance of the law as traditionally interpreted no longer defines one's status within the community of believers.

In the most extensive sermon attributed to Paul in Acts, he affirms that all who believe his message are set free by Jesus from all of the sins from which they could not be freed by the law (Acts 13:39). In other words, Paul declares that the law is incapable of bringing salvation; only Jesus can do this. In the following chapters, Paul is presented as facing constant opposition and even violence as a result of the message he proclaims. In particular, he is accused of teaching against the Jewish law (18:12-15). The conflicts between Paul and other Jews over the question of the law reach their head in Jerusalem. There James and the elders ask Paul to participate in a purification rite with four men at the temple to demonstrate that there is no truth to the accusations that he teaches others to forsake the law and the traditional Jewish customs, and to leave their children uncircumcised (21:18-21). Despite his participation in the rite and his presence at the temple to worship, some Jews who had heard Paul in Asia angrily accuse him of having taught "everyone everywhere against our people, our law, and this place" (21:28). After his arrest, Paul is presented as repeatedly defending himself against the accusation that he preaches against the law, while at the same time he focuses his proclamation on Jesus as risen Lord and Son of God (24:10-21; 25:8; 28:17-20).

Throughout Acts, the apostles repeatedly proclaim the need for repentance. Significantly, however, this repentance does not involve turning back in obedience to the Mosaic law, as was usually the case in Judaism, but instead consists of accepting Christ as Lord (Acts 2:36-38; 3:19-21, 26; 5:31; 11:17-18; 17:30; 20:21; 26:20-23; cf. Luke 24:46-47).[10] The "repentance that leads to life" that God gives to the uncircumcised gentiles is not explicitly connected in any way to the literal observance of the commandments (11:18). Instead, "repentance toward God" is equated merely with "faith toward our Lord Jesus" (20:21). Similarly, when Jesus is proclaimed as the one by whom God will judge the living and the dead and the world itself (10:42; 17:31), any allusion to the law as the basis upon which people will be judged is absent. This implies that all will be judged, not on the basis of their observance of the commandments given through Moses, but rather on the basis of their relation to Jesus and their conformity to God's will as defined by him.

Even if the historicity of many of these accounts from Acts is questioned, taken together they provide evidence of a common set of beliefs regarding

---

10. This understanding of repentance as coming to faith in Jesus is particularly stressed by Guy D. Nave Jr., *The Role and Function of Repentance in Luke-Acts* (AcBib 4; Atlanta: SBL, 2002); see especially 222-24.

Jesus and the law among Jesus' first followers. According to these beliefs, now that Jesus has been exalted as Lord and Messiah, observance of the Mosaic law as traditionally interpreted is no longer a primary concern. What really matters is believing in Jesus and following him. As we have seen, Acts not only places Jesus at an exalted position as Lord at God's side, but even tends to disparage to some extent the law and the sacrificial worship at the temple. The law is a heavy burden impossible to bear, given by angels, and incapable of saving anyone or being kept.

Undoubtedly, these passages stand alongside others in Acts that present the apostles continuing to observe the law, visit the temple, and even offer sacrifices there (Acts 20:6; 21:21-26; 22:12). Nevertheless, the reader is left wondering about the purpose of this observance. It contributes in no way to salvation, since that salvation is repeatedly tied to Jesus, who offers what the law cannot. Ultimately, for Luke, literal observance of the law makes no difference before God, since those who live under Christ as Lord without observing the law as traditionally interpreted are just as pleasing to God as those who remain law-observant. It also seems to make no difference within the community of believers, where God has abolished any type of distinction between those who observe the law as traditionally understood and those who do not. In spite of the apostles' protests to the contrary, in the eyes of those Jews who did not come to faith in Jesus, in a sense Jesus' followers had in fact rejected the law and sacrificial worship at the temple because, according to their proclamation, these no longer affected one's status before God or one's salvation in any way. In Acts, the law seems to have been reduced merely to a question of customs handed down by tradition that those of Jewish origin such as Paul should keep so as not to offend other Jews, though those customs may remain meaningful for Jesus' followers as well.

The Will of God and Jesus in Paul's Letters

When we turn to Paul's letters, we find that, even though he often refers to the Jewish law, he rarely uses it as a basis upon which to make moral exhortations. Rather than deriving his ethical teaching directly from the law, Paul consistently looks to Jesus to define the way believers are to live. In spite of the fact that, with a couple of exceptions, Paul does not allude explicitly to Jesus' teaching, he repeatedly mentions certain attitudes and ways of dealing with others that Jesus emphasized and presents Jesus as a pattern or model to be followed.[11] When Paul exhorts believers to remain humble, show generosity,

---

11. The two passages in which Paul seems to cite explicitly commands of Jesus are 1 Cor. 7:10 and 9:14. There is undoubtedly much truth in Jens Schröter's comment that, in his epistles, Paul's intention is "not to hand on, word for word, what was spoken by the earthly Jesus but to connect to a tradition grounded in the authority of the Lord as the basis of early Christian teaching. In instances involving words that originated with the earthly Jesus, Paul is interested in the fact they are Jesus' words only insofar as the earthly Jesus is also the one raised and exalted by God" ("Jesus and the Canon: The Early Jesus Traditions in the Context of the Origins of the New Testament Canon," in *Performing the Gospel: Orality, Memory, and Mark*; ed. Richard A. Horsley, Jonathan A. Draper, and John Miles Foley; Minneapolis: Fortress, 2006, 109). On the idea that

avoid repaying evil for evil, and refrain from boasting and judging others, his teaching clearly seems to be derived from the Jesus tradition rather than the law (Rom. 12:3, 13-21; 14:1-13; 1 Cor. 3:18-21; 5:6; 13:4; 16:1-2; 2 Cor. 8:7-17; 9:7-14; 1 Thess. 5:15).[12] Paul instructs believers to reflect the same type of love and commitment to the well-being of others that was found in Jesus, caring for the needs of their sisters and brothers and seeking to build them up (Rom. 12:9-13; 13:8-10; 14:15; 15:1-2; 1 Cor. 8:9-13; 10:24-33; 13:1-8; 14:1, 26; 2 Cor. 5:14-15; Gal. 6:10-14; 1 Thess. 4:9; 5:11).[13] For Paul, love is not merely an ethical principle derived from the law, but a willingness to live and even die for others as Jesus did and to be generous in the way that Christ was when he became poor to enrich others (Rom. 14:7-8; 2 Cor. 8:8-9). Rather than being guided by the law per se, believers are to be guided by the "mind of Christ" that they have received, together with the Spirit of God and of Christ (Rom. 8:5, 9, 13-14; 12:2; Gal. 5:16-25; 1 Cor. 2:16; Phil. 2:1-8). Instead of telling believers to present sacrifices at the Jerusalem temple, Paul calls on them to offer up their bodies as a living sacrifice to God (Rom. 12:1) and thanks the Philippians for having sent to him "a fragrant offering, a sacrifice acceptable and pleasing to God" (Phil. 4:18). Paul even presents himself as a priest who offers sacrifices that are distinct from those offered by the Jewish priests at the temple (Rom. 15:15-16). The ethical exhortations Paul makes tend to be of a general type, rather than being grounded in particular commandments of the Mosaic law: believers are to live honorably in a way worthy of God, abstain from evil, and do what is right, just, pure, and commendable (Rom. 13:13; Gal. 6:9; Phil. 4:8; 1 Thess. 2:12; 5:21-22).

While these values are undoubtedly *in accordance with* the Mosaic law, Paul does not seem to have *derived* them from that law.[14] Even when he does cite the Mosaic law to argue that one who serves the gospel should be paid, he derives a general principle from the prohibition against muzzling an ox while it is treading grain, and ultimately bases his argument on a commandment of Christ as Lord (1 Cor. 9:8-14). The obedience to which Paul repeatedly calls believers is not obedience to the law, but to Christ and the gospel (Rom. 10:16; 2 Cor. 9:13; 10:5; Phil. 1:27; cf. Rom. 1:5; 6:17; 15:18; 16:26; 2 Thess. 1:8). At times Paul even points to himself as an example to imitate, yet this is not because he keeps the law, but because in his own life and ministry he is imitating Christ (1 Cor. 4:16; 11:1; Gal. 4:12; Phil. 2:17; 4:9; 1 Thess. 1:6; cf. 2 Thess. 3:9).

Christ's life serves as a pattern or model in Paul's thought, see especially Alexander J. M. Wedderburn, "Paul and the Story of Jesus," in *Paul and Jesus: Collected Essays* (ed. Wedderburn; JSNTSup 137; Sheffield: Sheffield Academic Press, 1989), 171-83.

12. There is good reason to think that these emphases in Paul's thought are derived from the Jesus tradition; see Christian Wolff, "Humility and Self-Denial in Jesus' Life and Message and in the Apostolic Existence of Paul," in *Paul and Jesus*, ed. Wedderburn, 145-60.

13. On the influence of the Jesus tradition in these passages from Paul, see David Wenham, *Paul: Follower of Jesus or Founder of Christianity?* (Grand Rapids: Eerdmans, 1995), 255-71.

14. On this point, see Martin Meiser, "The Torah in the Ethics of Paul," in *The Torah in the Ethics of Paul* (ed. Meiser; LNTS 473; London: T & T Clark, 2012), 120, 131-35.

To be sure, in several passages Paul affirms that believers fulfill the law. Even then, however, he does not regard the law as the primary basis for determining how believers are to live. In Rom. 13:8-10, echoing Christ's teaching, Paul affirms that "the one who loves another has fulfilled the law." After citing several of the commandments of the decalogue, Paul then says that these, "and any other commandment, are summed up in this word, 'Love your neighbor as yourself.' Love does no wrong to a neighbor; therefore, love is the fulfilling of the law."[15] The Jesus tradition also seems to be reflected in Paul's affirmation that "the whole law is summed up in a single commandment, 'You shall love your neighbor as yourself'" (Gal. 5:14). When Paul writes that "the just requirement of the law" is fulfilled in those who "walk according to the Spirit" (Rom. 8:3-4), he seems to be referring to the basic demands of the law or the principles underlying it. In passages such as these, however, his logic is not that believers must strive to obey the Mosaic law because it reflects the will of God, but rather that, if they live according to Christ and the Spirit, they will inevitably practice the love that the law commands.[16] Thus, as long as they live out of faith and walk in love, their lives will conform to the law's demands for righteousness and they do not depend on the Mosaic law to regulate their conduct. Similarly, when in Gal. 5:22-25 Paul describes the fruit of the Spirit as love, joy, peace, patience, kindness, generosity, and faithfulness, he observes simply that "there is no law against such things." Here again, rather than telling his readers to concern themselves with the law in the ways that most Jews did, Paul tells them that they need not be concerned about fulfilling the law as long as they live under the Spirit's guidance.

In several passages, Paul even speaks of obeying the law while at the same time disregarding the literal commandment. In Rom. 2:14-15, he speaks of gentiles "who do not possess the law," yet "do instinctively what the law requires," since this is "written on their hearts." Here even one who is ignorant of the law may do what it requires. A few verses later, he mentions the "physically uncircumcised" who "keep the requirements of the law" and thus "keep the law" itself (Rom. 2:26-27). Given that circumcision was one of the commandments of the Mosaic law, Paul regards it as possible to disobey willfully a literal commandment of the law, and yet observe the law and do what it requires.

The same logic is behind Paul's affirmation in 1 Cor. 7:19: "Circumcision is nothing, and uncircumcision is nothing; but obeying the commandments of God is everything." In Jewish thought, this would be a contradiction in terms: one cannot be said to be obeying the commandments of God if one disobeys

---

15. As Michael B. Thompson has argued, in Rom. 13:8-10, Paul clearly seems to be drawing on the Jesus tradition (*Clothed with Christ: The Example and Teaching of Jesus in Romans 12.1–15.13*; JSNTSup 59; Sheffield: Sheffield Academic Press, 1991, 121-40).

16. In his study on Galatians, Todd A. Wilson notes that "Paul nowhere appeals simply and directly to the Law itself to sanction his ethical injunctions, something one might have expected him to do from time to time if the Law was for him really an abiding standard of behaviour. Even his comments about the fulfilment of the Law in 5.14 and 6.2 are not prescriptive, but descriptive" (*The Curse of the Law and the Crisis in Galatia: Reassessing the Purpose of Galatians*; WUNT 2/225; Tübingen: Mohr Siebeck, 2007, 7).

what God commanded regarding circumcision. This makes it clear that, for Paul, true obedience to the law goes beyond observing its literal commandments in order to fulfill the fundamental principles underlying those commandments. If "true circumcision" is not "something external and physical," but rather "a matter of the heart—it is spiritual and not literal" (Rom. 2:28-29), the same can be said of the other commandments of the law. Undoubtedly, this does not mean that one can arbitrarily set aside the literal observance of many of the commandments. Yet, as Stephen Westerholm has observed, in Paul's teaching, the commandments that are still to be kept literally are almost exclusively those having to do with ethical rather than ritual matters.[17]

Paul's affirmations that believers are not under the law must be understood on the basis of these same ideas. In Rom. 6:14-15, he teaches that believers are "not under law but under grace." Similarly, Paul tells the Galatians, "if you are led by the Spirit, you are not subject to the law" (Gal. 5:18). In 1 Corinthians, he claims that he is "not under the law" (1 Cor. 9:20) and repeats twice the idea that "all things are lawful" (6:12; 10:23). The latter idea is reflected as well in Romans 14: "nothing is unclean in itself" (v. 14) and "everything is indeed clean" (v. 20). In Rom. 7:4-6, Paul affirms that believers have "died to the law" and are "discharged" from it, since they now serve under the "newness of the spirit" rather than the "'oldness' of the letter." Paul also claims to have "died to the law" in Gal. 2:19 and affirms many of these same basic ideas in Gal. 3:19—6:2. The logic behind all of these passages is basically the same: as long as believers practice the love and justice which that law demands in obedience to Christ and the gospel, they do not need to concern themselves with the Mosaic law. While at times Paul speaks of believers observing commandments regarding things such as food and festival days, he affirms that they have freedom in this regard, as long as they do not harm the conscience of others (Rom. 14:1-23; 1 Cor. 8:1-13; 10:23-33). Even in these cases, then, what truly matters is love for others rather than the literal observance of such commandments.

In two passages from his letters, Paul alludes to "the law of Christ." He writes to the Corinthians that, even though he is himself "not under the law," he is nevertheless "not free from God's law" but "under the law of Christ" (1 Cor. 9:20-21). Similarly, in Gal. 6:2 he exhorts believers to bear one another's burdens and thereby "fulfill the law of Christ." Scholars have debated over the precise meaning of this phrase.[18] It is not clear whether the idea is that of

---

17. Stephen Westerholm rightly recognizes that the distinction between the ritual or ceremonial demands of the law and its moral demands appears nowhere in the Gospels or the Pauline epistles and argues that, in the Jesus tradition, the ritual or ceremonial demands "pertain to the peripheral rather than the central concerns of the law" ("Law and Gospel in Jesus and Paul," in *Jesus and Paul Reconnected: Fresh Pathways into an Old Debate*; ed. Todd D. Still; Grand Rapids: Eerdmans, 2007, 32-34). I would question, however, Westerholm's affirmation that the difference between Jesus' ethic and that of Paul is that Paul constructs "a Christian ethic independent of the law," in contrast to Jesus' ethic, which is still based on the law (34). While Paul's ethic is not *derived* from the law, it is by no means *independent* of the law, since it constitutes the law's fulfillment.

18. For a summary of the different interpretations of Paul's allusions to the "law of Christ," see Martinus C. de Boer, *Galatians: A Commentary* (NTL; Louisville, KY: Westminster John Knox, 2011), 378-81; Graham N. Stanton, "The Law of Moses and the Law of Christ," in *Paul and the Mosaic Law* (ed. James D. G. Dunn;

a law that *replaces* the Mosaic law or simply Jesus' own interpretation of that law, in which case Jesus was not understood to have abrogated the Mosaic law but simply to have reinterpreted it. Paul may instead have had in mind Jesus' own teaching and example. In any case, however, it is clear that what matters for Paul is living in accordance with what Jesus taught rather than adherence to the Mosaic law as it had commonly been interpreted. If believers submit to the "law of Christ," they will fulfill the principles behind the Mosaic law and thus fulfill that law, even though they may disregard many of the literal commandments of that law, such as those having to do with circumcision and purity regulations.[19]

In his paraenesis, Paul points repeatedly not only to Christ himself as the *basis* for the ethical conduct of believers, but also to his understanding of their relationship to Christ. They are to conduct themselves in the ways Paul prescribes, not because they are subject to Moses, but rather because they are joined to Christ through faith and belong to him as their Lord. As slaves of God and of Christ, they are not only to obey Christ as their master, but seek to please him by devoting themselves to serving God and others as he did as a slave or servant of God (Rom. 6:13-22; 7:4, 22; 12:11; 14:9-10, 18; 15:7-8; 16:18; 2 Cor. 13:5; Phil. 2:3-8). As members of Christ's body, they are to follow him as their head and to base their way of thinking on his (Rom. 7:4; 12:4-8; 1 Cor. 11:3; 12:12-27). The basis upon which Paul exhorts believers to chastity of life is not the law, but the fact that they are temples of Christ and God's Spirit, and that Christ lives in them (Rom. 8:9-10; 1 Cor. 3:16-17; 6:19-20; 2 Cor. 6:16; 13:5). Believers are to live as Christ did because they have put him on as a garment (Rom. 13:14; Gal. 3:27). Because through faith and baptism they have died with Jesus and become crucified with him, they are to crucify their flesh, consider themselves dead to sin, and die to the world as he did (Rom. 6:1-23; 2 Cor. 5:14; Gal. 2:19-20; 5:24; 6:14). Throughout Paul's writings, therefore, it is Christ rather than the law that defines not only *how* believers are to live, but also *why* they are to live in that way.

In his moral exhortation, Paul also points to the belief that some day Christ will return as judge and that all will need to answer to him and to

---

WUNT 89; Tübingen: J. C. B. Mohr, 1996), 99-116; John M. G. Barclay, *Obeying the Truth: A Study of Paul's Ethics in Galatians* (SNTW; Edinburgh: T &T Clark, 1988), 125-45; Michael Winger, "The Law of Christ," *NTS* 46 (2000): 537-46.

19. Paul certainly may have expected believers of Jewish origin to continue to observe the Mosaic law in the way they had previously, in contrast to non-Jewish believers, who were not under the law, as numerous scholars have argued. Mark D. Nanos, for example, claims that "there is evidence throughout Paul's letters that he held that Jews who were followers of Jesus, such as himself, were still members of Israel and thus were beholden to be faithful to the covenant; that is, they were to observe Torah as a matter of covenant fidelity, which would include circumcising their sons and observing Jewish diets and days" ("The Question of Conceptualization: Qualifying Paul's Position on Circumcision in Dialogue with Josephus's Advisors to King Izates," in *Paul within Judaism: Restoring the First-Century Context to the Apostle*; ed. Nanos and Magnus Zetterholm; Minneapolis: Fortress, 2015, 141). It is significant, however, that in Paul's letters, he never states explicitly that Jewish believers are to remain law-observant. At most, it can be said that he assumes such observance on their part. Of course, it must be taken into account that Paul's letters seem to have been addressed primarily to non-Jewish believers rather than those of Jewish origin.

his Father for what they have done (Rom. 2:5-16; 1 Cor. 4:5; 2 Cor. 5:10). The basis upon which Christ will judge all is not obedience to the precepts of the Mosaic law, but the good and evil people have done in general terms. Undoubtedly, in Rom. 2:13, Paul affirms that it is those who obey the law who will be declared righteous before God at the final judgment. Yet throughout Romans 2 he understands obedience to the law merely in terms of "doing good" and not practicing evil (Rom. 2:7-8). For this reason, as just noted above, he can speak of uncircumcised gentiles doing instinctively what the law requires, even though they do not possess the Mosaic law. What will matter are the "secret thoughts" that Christ will see when he looks into the hearts of all (Rom. 2:14-16; cf. 1 Cor. 4:5).

The Will of God and Jesus in the Disputed Pauline Letters

Most of the same ideas just outlined are also reflected in the disputed Pauline letters. Although a few passages seem to allude to teachings of Christ that have been passed down to believers (Eph. 4:20; Col. 2:8; 3:16; 1 Tim. 6:3; 2 Tim. 3:14-15), as in the undisputed Pauline letters, the allusions to Jesus' teaching and example tend to be implicit rather than explicit. As Jesus taught, believers are not to judge others but to be humble, patient, and kind (Eph. 4:2, 32; Col. 3:12; 2 Tim. 2:24; Tit. 2:5). Above all, believers are repeatedly exhorted to love others (Eph. 1:4; 3:17; 4:2-3, 14-15; 5:2, 21-33; Col. 2:2; 3:14; 2 Thess. 3:5; 1 Tim. 1:5; 4:12; 6:11; 2 Tim. 1:13; 2:22; Tit. 2:2-5). In this regard, they are to follow Jesus as their model, forgiving and giving their life for others as he did and treating others as he has treated them (Eph. 4:32; 5:2, 25-29; Col. 3:13). Rather than being told to obey the Mosaic law or seek to live a life based on its commandments, they are instructed to obey Christ, live their lives rooted in him, and do all things in his name (Eph. 5:10; 6:5; Col. 2:6-7; 3:17). Similarly, the works they are to perform are not those of the law, but good works in general that are worthy of Christ and pleasing to him and to God (Eph. 2:10; Col. 1:10; 2 Thess. 2:16-17; 1 Tim. 2:10; 6:18; 2 Tim. 2:21; 3:17; Tit. 2:17; 3:1, 8, 14). When the will of God is mentioned, it is understood independently of any reference to the Mosaic law (Eph. 5:17; 6:6, Col. 1:1, 9; 4:12; 2 Tim. 1:1).

While Ephesians bases the exhortation to obey one's parents on the commandment found in the Mosaic law (Eph. 6:2-3), curiously the letter also claims that Christ "has abolished the law with its commandments and ordinances" (Eph. 2:15). In 1 Tim. 5:18, the commandments not to muzzle an ox and to pay laborers for their work are cited from the Mosaic law, yet there, as in 1 Cor. 9:8-14, these commandments are used as a basis for maintaining the need to support those who work on behalf of the gospel. When the same letter alludes to the "commandment" believers are to keep, it is unrelated to anything found in the Mosaic law (1 Tim. 6:14). The author of 1 Timothy also implicitly rejects the purity distinctions by claiming that "everything created by God is good, and nothing is to be rejected, provided it is received with thanksgiving" (1 Tim. 4:4). The author of Titus similarly insists that "to the pure all things are pure, but to the corrupt and unbelieving nothing is pure" (Tit. 1:15). The letter to the Colossians affirms that believers are free with regard to Jewish customs having to do with food, drink, and festival days (Col. 2:16-22), while 1 Tim. 1:8-11 appeals not only to the law to define conduct that is to be condemned, but also to "the sound teaching that conforms to the glorious gospel." Throughout the disputed Pauline letters, then, once again God's will is defined by Christ and the gospel rather than the Mosaic law. Undoubtedly, what is commanded is *in conformity* with the principles underlying the Mosaic law, but it is not *directly derived* from the law. Instead, it is subject to what has been given and communicated through Christ.

Like the undisputed Pauline letters, these writings look not only to Christ himself but to the relationship of believers to him in order to ground their paraenesis. They are to live in love as God commands because they are joined to Christ as members of his body and because God dwells in them as his temple (Eph. 1:22-23; 2:19-22; 3:6, 17; 4:12-16; 5:29-32; Col. 1:18, 27). Their conduct is to reflect the reality that they have died and been crucified with Christ and have also risen with him (Eph. 2:4-10; Col. 2:20; 3:1-8). By virtue of their relation to him, they have put off their old self and are clothed with a new self (Eph. 4:20-24; Col. 3:5-14). Both slaves and slave owners are exhorted to obedience on the ground that they belong to Christ, their master (Eph. 6:6-9; Col. 3:22—4:1). The affirmation that they will some day be judged by Christ is also used as a basis for insisting on the need for obedience to him (Eph. 6:7-8; 2 Tim. 4:1-8).

The Will of God and Jesus in the Synoptic Gospels

Although each of the Synoptic Gospels views Jesus, God's will, and the law somewhat differently, we find in them the same basic ideas that we have just noted in Acts and the letters attributed to Paul. All three Synoptics describe tensions and conflicts arising repeatedly between Jesus and the Jewish leaders over matters of law observance. Even if one questions the historicity of many of these accounts and regards much of this material as the creation of the early church or the evangelists themselves, there can be no question that they provide abundant evidence that Jesus' first-century followers believed Jesus to be in serious disagreement with other Jewish teachers on the question of the authority and interpretation of the Mosaic law. In addition, they clearly place Jesus *above* the law. The most categorical expression of this belief is found in Matt. 12:8, Mark 2:27-28, and Luke 6:5, where Jesus as the Son of Man claims to be "Lord of the sabbath." While this can be understood in different ways, at the very least it implies that Jesus has divine authority to set aside Sabbath observance as traditionally understood among many Jews in antiquity and perform actions that some Jews considered a violation of the Sabbath.[20] At the same time, the words attributed to Jesus in all three Synoptics point to the fulfillment of the Sabbath commandment as involving general principles related to human well-being: because it was given for the sake of human beings, what it really prescribes is that those observing it concern themselves with the needs of others, do good, and act in ways that contribute to life and healing (Matt. 12:1-13; Mark 2:23—3:6; Luke 6:1-11; 13:10-17). The conflicts arise not only because Jesus' opponents fail to understand and fulfill the principles underlying the Sabbath commandment, but because they refuse to recognize his authority over the Sabbath as well as the law in general.

As in the rest of the New Testament, throughout the Synoptics the law also tends to be relegated to a position of secondary importance in relation to Jesus. As Robert Banks pointed out several decades ago, the teaching ascribed to Jesus in the Synoptics stands in stark contrast to that of the rabbinic tradition that was developing in the first century, in which the Mosaic law "not only moves to central position, it becomes almost the sole object of concentration."[21] Noting the strong christological emphasis in Matthew's Gospel, for example, Banks observes that "at almost every point a moving into the foreground of the personal authority of Christ is discernible.... As a result it is not so much his relation to the law that he is concerned to depict (and not at all that to Moses), as how the law now stands in relationship to Jesus as the one whose teaching and practice transcend it and fulfill it."[22]

Similar observations can be made with regard to the other Synoptics. Unlike the rabbis of later centuries, in his teaching Jesus does not refer constantly to the Mosaic law in order to offer his own interpretation or commentary on that law and derive specific halakic prescriptions from it. As mentioned in Chapter 5, with the exception of a few passages in which Jesus points to the need to obey the decalogue or fulfill basic principles underlying the commandments, at no point in the Synoptics does Jesus himself ever bring up questions related to observing or interpreting the law.[23] Unlike the teaching of the scribes and Pharisees, the authority of Jesus' teaching is derived not from Moses or the law given through him, but from Jesus' personal and direct relation to God his Father (Matt. 7:28-29; 21:23-27; Mark 1:22, 27; 11:27-33; Luke 4:32; 20:1-7).

---

20. After affirming that Matthew's version of this account highlights Jesus' absolute sovereignty and authority, Ulrich Luz rightly notes that, in Matthew's version of this account, "Jesus does not contradict the Torah in its depth, but it is by virtue of his absolute authority that he does not contradict it" (*Matthew: A Commentary*, Vol. 2: *8-20*, trans. Wilhelm C. Linss; Hermeneia; Minneapolis: Fortress, 2001, 158).

21. Robert J. Banks, *Jesus and the Law in the Synoptic Tradition* (SNTSMS 28; Cambridge: Cambridge University Press, 1975), 58.

22. Ibid., 251-52; cf. 245. E. P. Sanders is probably justified in criticizing Banks for proposing that Jesus "adopted a position which was not in conscious relation to the law one way or another, although opposition to the law was *latent* in his position" (*Jesus and Judaism*; Philadelphia: Fortress, 1985, 254). The Synoptics see Jesus, not as opposing or merely ignoring the law, but transcending and fulfilling it, as Banks himself affirms in the passage just cited.

23. The passages in the Synoptics in which Jesus himself brings up the subject of the law are Matt. 5:17-32; 19:16-21; 23:23; Mark 10:17-22; Luke 11:42; 18:18-23.

According to the Synoptics, the imperative that appears by far most frequently on Jesus' lips is simply, "Follow me." As E. P. Sanders pointed out, this imperative seems to override all other sacred duties and obligations, including that of burying one's father (Matt. 8:21-22; Luke 9:59-62).[24] Jesus tells the rich young man that, even if he has kept all of the commandments since youth, that is not sufficient; if he wishes to enter into life, he must sell all he has, give it to the poor, and follow Jesus (Matt. 19:16-21; Mark 10:17-21; Luke 18:18-22). Only those who are willing to leave all, take up their cross, and commit themselves to following him will be judged worthy of the life to come (Matt. 10:37-39; 16:24-25; Mark 8:34-35; 10:28-30; Luke 9:23; 14:25-33). This involves serving others in the same fashion as Jesus, and even being willing to give up one's life like him (Matt. 20:25-28; Mark 10:41-45; Luke 22:24-27). Jesus is presented as calling on others to hear and do, not the words of the Mosaic law, but his own words (Matt. 7:24-27; Luke 6:46-49). It is Jesus' words, rather than the words of the law, that will never pass away (Matt. 24:35; Mark 13:31; Luke 21:33). He is the one who defines God's will and determines who is truly obeying that will (Matt. 7:21-23). When Jesus tells his followers to be "perfect" and insists that they must do God's will, he is not alluding merely to observance of the Mosaic commandments, but to things such as loving one's enemies and leaving all behind in order to follow him (Matt. 5:43-48; 19:21). While it is not clear if in Jesus' day it was already said that, wherever several gather to study the law, God's glory is in their midst, according to Matthew's Gospel, it is Jesus who is present where two or three gather in his name (Matt. 18:20).[25] Jesus' last words to his disciples in Matthew express the same idea that what truly matters is Jesus' word and teaching on the basis of the authority he has received from God: his disciples are to make others disciples of Jesus himself, rather than the law, and teach them to obey, not the Mosaic commandments, but what Jesus has commanded (Matt. 28:18-20). This can be understood as implying that Jesus himself constitutes a new Torah in some sense.

Ultimately, then, in all of the Synoptics, while believers are undoubtedly not called to reject or disobey the law, the basic command is to follow Jesus as their Lord and master. This involves conduct that goes beyond what the law commands. Important elements of Jesus' ethical teaching, such as the commands to love one's enemies, forgive others, remain humble, serve others, and refrain from judging are certainly in accordance with the Mosaic law, yet they are not directly derived from it (Matt. 5:43-48; 6:12, 14-15; 7:1-5; 18:21-35; 20:26-28; 23:12; Luke 6:27-46; 11:4; 17:3-4).

As we have noted in Chapter 5, the idea that true fulfillment of the law consists of observing the principles behind it runs throughout Jesus' teaching and practice in the Synoptics. It is repeatedly stated that what the law

---

24. Sanders, *Jesus and Judaism*, 252-55.
25. See Martin McNamara, *Targum and New Testament: Collected Essays* (WUNT 279; Tübingen: Mohr Siebeck, 2011), 529-30.

ultimately commands is the practice of justice, compassion, and love (Matt. 9:13; 12:7; 22:34-40; 23:23; Mark 12:28-34; Luke 10:25-38; 11:42). Those regarded by Jesus as "blessed" are not those who simply keep the commandments, but those committed to justice, mercy, and making peace, as well as those who are willing to suffer for doing what is right (Matt. 5:6-10). The righteousness or justice of Jesus' disciples is to surpass that of the scribes and Pharisees in the sense that it goes beyond merely observing the commandments in the manner that the members of these groups do (Matt. 5:20-30). In the thought of the Synoptics, the purity that matters most is not that which relates to what one eats or drinks, but that which consists of treating others properly (Matt. 15:10-20; Mark 7:1-23). While the law cannot be *reduced* to loving God and one's neighbor and doing to others as one would have others do to oneself, it does appear that, as Paul teaches, as long as one truly acts out of love for God and others, one is fulfilling the law (Matt. 7:12; 22:34-40; Mark 12:28-34; Luke 10:25-28).

In Matt. 5:17-18, Jesus is presented as affirming that he has come not to abolish the law but to fulfill it, and that not even the smallest stroke of a letter will pass from the law until all is fulfilled. These verses should be understood on the basis of the ideas just considered. For Matthew, the "fulfillment" mentioned here seems to refer, not so much to the literal observance of each and every commandment, but to the deeper meaning underlying them all.[26] For this reason, such a fulfillment is spoken of as something that will be accomplished some day in the future, rather than a reality belonging to the present.[27] It should also be remembered that, by the time Matthew was written, the destruction of the temple at Jerusalem had made it impossible to fulfill each and every prescription of the Mosaic law literally, since many of those commandments had to do with sacrificial offerings. In fact, as Ivor Jones notes, the authority Jesus gives to Peter and the other disciples to bind and loose in Matt. 16:19 and 18:18 may have alluded "to the right of church leaders not merely to interpret but actually to annul parts of the law."[28] Although in Matt. 5:17-18 and 23:23 Matthew presents Jesus as teaching that a literal observance of all the commandments is important, these verses must be seen in the context of the Gospel as a whole. While Matthew no doubt values the

---

26. Roger Mohrlang proposes four different senses in which the verb *plērosai* in Matt. 5:17 can be understood: "(1) to obey or carry out the demands of the law; (2) to affirm or validate the law; (3) to explicate or live out the deeper meaning and intent of the law; (4) to complete or bring to pass the ultimate goal of the law—an interpretation that is sometimes taken to imply that some or all of the precepts of the law are now set aside as no longer applicable" (*Matthew and Paul: A Comparison of Ethical Perspectives*; SNTSMS 48; Cambridge: Cambridge University Press, 1984, 8).

27. As Phillip Sigal notes, in the context of Matthew 5, Jesus' saying in Matt. 5:17-19 seems to imply that in the following verses he will expound on the teaching already implicit in the law as a whole (*The Halakhah of Jesus of Nazareth according to the Gospel of Matthew*; SBLSBL 18; Atlanta: SBL, 2007, 24-26). I would argue that the phrase "until all that is commanded is fulfilled" alludes to the fulfillment of the law's deeper meaning, or what the law prophesied or foresaw, rather than the literal fulfillment of each and every precept, which for many Jews was simply not possible, especially after the destruction of the Jerusalem temple.

28. Ivor Jones, "Matthew," in *Early Christian Thought in its Jewish Context* (ed. John Barclay and John Sweet; Cambridge: Cambridge University Press, 1996), 63.

law highly and maintains that its commandments should for the most part be kept literally, like Mark and Luke he emphasizes much more strongly the call to follow Jesus and the fulfillment of the principles underlying the law; that is what one's status before God ultimately depends on.

Like the other New Testament writings considered above, Matthew and Luke both maintain that the basis upon which all will be judged is precisely their conformity to what Jesus himself taught and practiced (Matt. 5:22; 12:36-37; 13:40-42, 50; 18:21-35; 23:1-36; 25:31-46; Luke 6:37; 20:46-47). Those who will be condemned, among whom are many teachers of the law, are those who have failed to conform to the principles of justice, mercy, and love and instead have oppressed others with their practices and teaching. When Jesus is presented as affirming that not all who call him Lord will enter the kingdom, but only those who do his Father's will (Matt. 7:21-23), the fact that he speaks not merely of *God's* will but the will of *his Father* implies that God's will is defined, not merely by God himself, but by God *through Jesus as his Son*. Because he is Lord, it is Jesus who must be obeyed rather than the law itself: "Why do you call me 'Lord, Lord,' and do not do what I tell you?" (Luke 6:46).

The most striking passage in this regard is Matt. 25:31-46, in which Jesus is presented as eschatological judge. Here all people are to be judged for the way they have treated Jesus himself, who is in some way present among those who suffer and are in need. Rather than understanding this passage in the sense that Jesus is somehow incarnated or mysteriously present in those who experience the hardships he mentions, the idea seems to be that, because of Jesus' love for all, when he sees people suffering, he suffers as well. Therefore, whenever someone alleviates the suffering of the "little ones," Jesus' own suffering is alleviated together with theirs. In any case, as Robin Scroggs notes, this passage is remarkable given that Matthew is generally seen as the evangelist who insists most strongly on the need to continue to observe literally the commandments of the Mosaic law: "the most startling feature of the parable is what is *not* included. Any reference to Torah is completely absent; whether one acts to care for persons in distress is all that matters."[29]

The Will of God and Jesus in the Gospel and Epistles of John

Many of these same themes are repeated in the Fourth Gospel. Almost from the start, the author draws a contrast between Jesus and the law: "The law indeed was given through Moses; grace and truth came through Jesus Christ" (John 1:17). This is said in the context of the claim that Jesus is God's word who was with God from the beginning (1:1-18). To speak in these terms is to

---

29. Robin Scroggs, "Eschatological Existence in Matthew and Paul: Coincidentia Oppositorum," in *Apocalyptic in the New Testament: Essays in Honor of Louis J. Martyn* (ed. Joel Marcus and Marion L Soards; JSNTSup 24; Sheffield: Sheffield Academic Press, 1989), 140.

ascribe to Jesus a place often ascribed to the law in ancient Jewish thought.[30] The light and life that the Hebrew Scriptures associate with the law is now associated with Jesus (John 1:4-9; cf. Exod. 24:29-35; Deut. 30:15, 19; Ps. 119:105; Isa. 51:4).[31] Behind the account of Jesus' turning water into wine seems to be the idea that what Jesus gives is greater than the law, represented in the jars for purification that hold water and then wine (John 2:1-11).[32] He brings a new form of worship in "spirit and in truth" that is greater than that practiced on Mount Gerizim or the temple at Jerusalem, where sacrifices were offered according to the law (4:20-24). The fact that Jesus is the one about whom Moses wrote puts him above the law as the one to whom the law points and leads (1:45; 5:37-39, 46). As William Loader affirms in his summary of the Fourth Gospel's understanding of the law, "John's Jesus sees the chief role of the law as that of bearing testimony to himself."[33]

The accounts of conflict in the Fourth Gospel center not only upon questions related to the law, but also the identity of Jesus as God's Son. When he heals a man with paralysis on the Sabbath, the Jewish leaders begin to persecute him (John 5:1-18). Jesus responds that, like his Father, he works on the Sabbath, an affirmation that is understood as "making himself equal to God" (5:17-18). Here Jesus is not merely "Lord of the sabbath," but the one who like God can break the Sabbath by doing work on that day. The passage continues by having Jesus claim that to honor God and do God's will requires believing in Jesus as the one God has sent (5:19-47). To reject Jesus, in fact, is to reject both God and the law. For this reason, it is not Jesus but Moses himself who will accuse before God those who reject Jesus (5:45-46). Similar ideas are repeated in John 9:1-41, where the Pharisees condemn Jesus for breaking the Sabbath law (9:16) and tell the blind man: "You are his disciple, but we are disciples of Moses. We know that God has spoken to Moses, but as for this man, we do not know where he comes from" (9:28-29).

In all of these passages, the evangelist not only places Jesus above the Mosaic law, but also insists that those who do not believe in Jesus are not truly

---

30. James F. McGrath notes that "John's use of Wisdom categories to interpret the significance of Christ in comparison/contrast to that of Moses/Torah is closely related to similar approaches taken by earlier New Testament authors. John presents Jesus as the embodiment, as the appearance in human history, of that which 'the Jews' claimed to be found in Torah, namely Wisdom and light" (*John's Apologetic Christology: Legitimation and Development in Johannine Christology*, SNTSMS 111; Cambridge: Cambridge University Press, 2001, 153-54).

31. On the relation between the Mosaic law and light in rabbinic thought, see Oskar Skarsaune, *The Proof from Prophecy. A Study in Justin Martyr's Proof-Text Tradition: Text-Type, Provenance, Theological Profile* (NovTSup 56; Leiden: Brill, 1987), 354.

32. Commenting on John 2:6, Urban C. von Wahlde writes: "The mention of the number of jars present has led some to think a symbolism is intended (i.e., the number six indicating imperfection, the contrast of the Jewish water with the eschatological wine).... Thus, the imperfect Jewish laws (e.g., of purification) are now being superseded by the fulfillment that is Jesus who brings wine, not water. This may be possible. If so, then, in a general way, it can be said that Jesus is portrayed as the one who is superior to the old order and is himself bringing about the new" (*The Gospel and Letters of John*; ECC; Grand Rapids: Eerdmans, 2010, 2:83, 85-86).

33. William Loader, *Jesus' Attitude towards the Law: A Study of the Gospels* (Grand Rapids: Eerdmans, 2002), 483; for further discussion regarding the role that the law plays in John's thought and his Christology, see 432-91.

observing the law. Furthermore, while in these passages and others in the Gospel it is not Jesus himself but those who reject him who repeatedly place Jesus in opposition to the law, these passages suggest that a choice was being imposed on Jesus' followers in the communities to which they belonged: they were being told by some Jews who did not believe in Jesus that they must either follow the law of Moses or follow Jesus, but that they could not do both. Tensions over this alternative reach their head in the Johannine passion account, where the authorities tell Pilate: "We have a law, and according to that law he ought to die because he has claimed to be the Son of God" (John 19:7). According to this affirmation, if one is faithful to the Mosaic law, one must reject Jesus and even give approval to his crucifixion.

Questions concerning the law of Moses appear in John 7:14-24 as well. There Jesus insists that his teaching is not his own but that of his Father and equates that teaching with the will of God. He also tells the Jews opposing him, "Did not Moses give you the law? Yet none of you keeps the law." He then argues that, if the law allows circumcision on the Sabbath, he has not broken the law by healing a man's entire body on the Sabbath (7:22-23). In this passage and others, Jesus speaks of the law as something given to "the Jews" through Moses and refers to it as "your law" (7:19; 8:17; 10:34; cf. 15:25; 18:31). This is further indication that the believers in the community to whom the Fourth Gospel was addressed had been pressured to concede that the Mosaic law no longer belonged to them, but only to those who observed it as it had traditionally been understood by most Jews. Passages such as these make it clear that at least some of Jesus' followers did not consider themselves subject to the Mosaic law as commonly interpreted in second-temple Judaism, even though they still claimed that true submission to the law involved believing in Jesus, to whom that law had pointed from the start.

The fourth evangelist stresses Jesus' superiority over the law in other ways as well. While Moses was thought to have spoken with God personally and to have received the law from him directly, Jesus' relation to God as God's Son is described as being even more intimate, making his word of greater authority than the law (John 1:18; cf. 7:17; 12:50; 14:10). Thus only those who know Jesus truly know the Father (7:28-29; 8:19; 10:15, 17; 14:7-10; 16:3). Because God's word is inseparable from that of Jesus, whom God sent, and because Jesus has received the words he speaks from God himself, it is the word or words of Jesus that purify people, make them free, and give them eternal life, rather than the word or words of the law (3:34; 5:24; 6:63, 68; 8:31, 42-55; 12:47-50; 14:10, 24; 15:3; 17:6-8, 14). For the fourth evangelist, the only one truly worthy of the title "rabbi" or "teacher" is Jesus (1:38, 49; 3:2, 26; 4:31; 6:25; 9:2; 11:8; 20:16).[34]

---

34. The only exception is John 3:10, where Jesus marvels at the ignorance of Nicodemus as a "teacher of Israel." In the Synoptics, the only passage in which anyone other than Jesus is called teacher is Luke 2:46, where the young Jesus enters into discussion with the teachers of the law at the temple.

In the Fourth Gospel, therefore, what all are called to obey is Jesus' word and teaching rather than the word of the law and the teaching of Jewish leaders. It is Jesus' commandments rather than the commandments of the law that are to be observed, since Jesus' commandments are also God's commandments (John 12:47-50; 14:15, 21; 15:9-17). His divine authority is evident from the fact that he gives his followers a "new commandment" (13:34). In essence, this consists of following Jesus' example as their Lord and teacher (13:12-15). They are told to hear and follow, not the Mosaic law, but the voice of Jesus their shepherd (5:24; 8:12; 10:3-4, 27; 12:26). Similarly, the work that they must do is not that which is prescribed in the law, but simply that of believing in him whom God has sent (6:28-29). As in the Synoptics, Jesus is the one appointed by God to judge the world (5:22-23; cf. 8:16). The basis upon which all will be judged is not their obedience to the Mosaic commandments, but their adherence to Jesus and his word (5:24; 12:48).

The Johannine epistles echo many of the same themes. Rather than being instructed to obey the commandments of the Mosaic law, the readers are told to obey the commandments of Jesus and God, as well as Jesus' word and teaching (1 John 2:3-5; 3:21-24; 4:7-21; 5:2-4; 2 John 4). Nevertheless, the "new commandment" given by Jesus is actually the same commandment they received of old, although it is new in him (1 John 2:7-8; 2 John 5-6). This new commandment that believers are to obey involves walking in the way Jesus walked and giving up their life for others as he did, thus taking him as their example (1 John 2:6; 3:16). What God commands is not only to love others, but to believe in Jesus as his Son (1 John 3:23). Instead of appealing to the Mosaic law to define God's will, these epistles look to the love of God and Jesus and view God's will in broad terms as loving in the way God and Jesus have loved, abiding in God, living in the light, and doing what is right and good (1 John 2:9-11, 15-17, 29; 3:7-18; 4:7-21; 3 John 11).

The Will of God and Jesus in the Other New Testament Writings

An analysis of the other New Testament writings reveals the same basic understanding of Jesus, the law, and God's will. Hebrews points to the teaching concerning Christ (Heb. 6:1), stresses the need to live in love and do what is good and just (5:14; 6:10; 10:24; 13:1, 16, 21), and points to Jesus as a model to be imitated (12:2-3; 13:12-14). The Mosaic law is said to have "only a shadow of the good things to come and not the true form of these realities" (10:1). Believers are specifically told not to concern themselves about "regulations about food, which have not benefited those who observe them" (13:9).

The letter of James reflects much of the same ethical teaching found in Matthew's Gospel and points to the "law of liberty" as the "perfect law" (James 1:25).[35] While it looks to the commandments regarding adultery and murder to argue that anyone who breaks the law in one point has broken the

---

35. On the relation between the ethical teaching found in James and that of Matthew, see especially Donald Guthrie, *New Testament Introduction*, 3rd ed. (Downers Grove, IL: Inter-Varsity, 1970), 743-46.

whole law, in the same immediate context it speaks of love as the fulfillment of the "royal law" and affirms that believers are to be judged on the basis of the "law of liberty" (2:8-12). James also defines obedience to the law in terms of not practicing evil toward others and understands sin as failing to do what one knows is right (4:11-12, 17).

The emphasis on love and doing what is good and right in general terms runs throughout 1 and 2 Peter as well, where the law is not mentioned explicitly (1 Pet. 1:22; 3:6-14; 4:9; 2 Pet. 1:6-7). In 1 Peter, the readers are called to imitate Christ, forgiving those who do them wrong and practicing love and humility (1 Pet. 2:19-23; 4:1-2; 5:5-6). Rather than being told to obey the Mosaic law, they are instructed simply to obey Christ, the truth, and the gospel (1 Pet. 1:2, 22; 4:17).

This survey of the New Testament writings, of course, can no doubt give the false impression that they all view in the same way the relation of the Mosaic law to Christ and the role which that law is to play in the life of believers. It must be remembered that there were many differences of opinion on these questions among Jesus' first followers, and also that some of the writings just considered were written at least half a century after Jesus' death and the early proclamation of the gospel. Roger Booth rightly stresses "the very fluid state of early Christianity in all quarters," noting that within a single community there would inevitably be different viewpoints on questions such as these.[36] As Nickelsburg observes, the New Testament texts themselves give evidence of a wide range of attitudes reflecting "ongoing discussion in the first-century church over the issue of Torah."[37] Nevertheless, a recognition of the diversity that existed does not prevent us from concluding in general terms that the New Testament writings provide abundant evidence for the claim that, among Jesus' first followers, it was no longer the Mosaic law that was thought to define God's will fully and definitively, but Jesus. In order to discern that will, rather than looking primarily to the Mosaic law, they looked to Jesus' teaching, the love and humble service that he had embodied in life and especially in his death, and the relationship that they had with him and with God through him in the context of his community of followers, where they were guided by God's Spirit.

JUSTIFICATION, FAITH IN JESUS, AND THE LAW

The redefinition of God's will that took place among Jesus' first followers inevitably led to a redefinition of who the righteous were thought to be. Among believers in Christ, the criterion for inclusion within the community of those regarded as righteous before God was no longer simply obedience to the Mosaic law. Rather, the righteous were those who believed in Jesus as God's Son and Messiah and submitted to him as their Lord in order to do God's will as it had come to be defined through Jesus.

---

36. Roger P. Booth, *Jesus and the Laws of Purity: Tradition History and Legal History in Mark 7* (JSNTSup 13; Sheffield: JSOT, 1986), 78-79.

37. Nickelsburg, *Ancient Judaism*, 54-57.

Undoubtedly, the various New Testament writings use different language to describe this relationship to Jesus. The Synoptics prefer to speak in terms of "following" Jesus, though they also use the language of having faith and believing in Jesus and the God he called "Father." In Acts, Luke no longer speaks of following Jesus and instead defines the relationship of believers to Jesus primarily in terms of having faith in him or his name. Both the undisputed and disputed Pauline letters follow the same pattern as Acts, but also speak repeatedly of believers being "in Christ." As noted previously, those letters also make use of a number of other concepts, such as being slaves of God, belonging to Christ, being clothed with Christ, living as members of his body, and constituting a temple in which Christ dwells. The Fourth Gospel and the Johannine epistles repeatedly speak of believing in God and in Jesus as God's Son and Messiah. They also speak of being in Christ and Christ being in believers, though the language is somewhat different than that of Paul. A number of other metaphors are used in the Fourth Gospel as well. Believers "know" Jesus, follow him as their shepherd, eat his flesh and drink his blood, cling to him as branches to a vine, and receive from him living water.

Despite these differences, however, all of these ways of referring to the relationship of believers to Christ boil down to the same basic idea: what is involved is a relationship with Jesus in which one acknowledges him as Lord, Messiah, and Son of God, living in love for the God Jesus proclaimed and seeking to do God's will as it has been defined through Jesus by loving others. When the authors of the New Testament writings speak of believing in Christ or having faith in him, they invariably have in mind *both* the acknowledgment of his lordship *and* the submission to that lordship that results from that acknowledgment. These are conceived of as *inseparable from one another*. Faith in New Testament thought does not simply involve an intellectual assent to the claim that Jesus was sent by God and has now been raised and exalted by God as Lord and Messiah. Rather, by definition, to believe that Jesus is Lord and to trust in him is to live in the way he taught and embodied, obeying and following him. Those who refuse to live in this way are no longer truly believing in Jesus as Lord or in the God he called "Father," because they are no longer truly trusting in his word and putting their life and their being in his hands. Commenting on Paul's language of the "obedience of faith" in Rom. 1:5 and 16:26, as well as his allusions to the faith of Abraham in Romans 4, James Dunn affirms that for Paul, "faith means total and unconditional reliance on God..., complete trust in God, total reliance on God's enabling. *That* is the root of obedience for Paul: unless obedience springs from that, it is misdirected. The 'obedience of faith' is that obedience which lives out the sort of trust and reliance on God which Abraham demonstrated."[38] Those justified are those who live "out of faith" (*ek pisteōs*), basing their lives on that trust

---

38. James D. G. Dunn, "'The Law of Faith,' 'the Law of the Spirit' and 'the Law of Christ,'" in *Theology and Ethics in Paul and His Interpreters: Essays in Honor of Victor Paul Furnish* (ed. Eugene H. Lovering Jr. and Jerry L. Sumney; Nashville: Abingdon, 1996), 68.

and reliance on God and his Son Jesus. Furthermore, they trust in God *not only for forgiveness but for the new life of obedience that God desires to see in all for their own good.* Truly to believe in and trust another person is to do what that person says. For this reason, in the thought of Paul and the rest of the New Testament, faith and obedience to the God of Jesus are inseparable, since only those who are committed to obeying God are truly trusting in God and having faith in God as he has now made himself known through Jesus his Son.

In New Testament thought, therefore, it is faith understood in the sense just stated that defines who are considered to be righteous before God as members of God's people or community. When Paul speaks of justification by faith rather than works of the law, *this is what he has in mind.* While many scholars have seen justification by faith as primarily or exclusively a Pauline doctrine and have questioned its centrality, not only in Paul's thought, but in the New Testament as a whole, on the basis of what we have seen here, there can be no question that this idea lies at the very heart of the New Testament. Undoubtedly, the language of justification by faith appears in only a few of Paul's letters, although it is also attributed to Paul by Luke in Acts 13:38-39. However, other New Testament writers express the same idea with different words. In the Synoptics and Acts, as we have seen, the righteous are those who believe in and follow Jesus as their Lord and do God's will *as defined through Jesus.* It is they who are regarded as acceptable to God and who will be judged worthy of God's reign. Likewise, in John's Gospel and the Johannine letters, it is those who believe in and follow Jesus as Christ and Son of God who receive God's approval and will attain the promised salvation.

The same basic ideas appear throughout the other New Testament writings: as we have just seen, God's will is consistently defined in terms of acknowledging Jesus as Lord and submitting to him in love and obedience. What defines membership among God's people and the community of those who are accepted as righteous by God is their conviction that Jesus is Lord and Messiah and the way of life that results from that conviction. This contrasts with other currents of Judaism of the time, in which membership in Israel and inclusion among those considered righteous before God was defined on the basis of one's commitment to obeying certain interpretations of the Mosaic law.[39] While Jesus' first followers undoubtedly claimed that they were living in conformity with the Mosaic law, they also maintained that full conformity with that law involved living under Jesus' lordship. In their mind, therefore, those who consciously refused to believe in and follow Jesus were not living fully in accordance with God's will and were not truly fulfilling the law, since that law pointed to Christ and ultimately was fulfilled only through faith in him.

---

39. On the predominance of the idea that, in second-temple Jewish thought, righteousness was based on works of the law, see Craig A. Evans, "Paul and Works of the Law Language in Late Antiquity," in *Paul and his Opponents* (ed. Stanley E. Porter; PS 2; Leiden: Brill, 2005), 201-26.

Once all of this is understood, it becomes clear that *the traditional controversies over the doctrine of justification dating from the time of the Protestant Reformation are based on a profound misunderstanding of what the first-century debates and tensions were all about.* These debates and tensions had nothing to do with whether obedience to God and good works done in accordance with justice, love, and mercy were necessary in order to be declared righteous and accepted by God. On that point, *all were in full agreement.* Never in the New Testament is it said or implied that people will be judged solely on the basis of what they believe in an intellectual sense. Rather, judgment is consistently seen as depending on how people live and act in relation to God and others. Jesus' followers were undoubtedly in full agreement with the Jewish understanding of judgment by works, as explained by Kent Yinger in his commentary on Romans 2: "It is the standard Jewish expectation that one's outward behavior (one's *works* or *way*) will correspond to, and be a visible manifestation of, inward reality. Thus, neither in Judaism nor here in Paul does one obey *in order to become* righteous. Nor is such obedience understood as sinless perfection, but as a consistent and wholehearted conformity to God's will."[40] This is just as true for Paul as it is for the authors of the rest of the New Testament writings. Furthermore, the New Testament writings agree with the Hebrew Scriptures and second-temple Jewish literature in maintaining that obedience to God's will on the part of those who constitute God's people is entirely a gracious gift of God, rather than something that human beings bring about in themselves.

The question that was at the heart of the debates and conflicts among Jesus' first followers, as well as other Jews with whom they were in dialogue, had to do with *precisely how obedience to God's will was to be understood.* The traditional Jewish view equated obedience to God's will with a commitment to living in conformity with the Mosaic law. While there were seemingly endless discussions and disagreements over the question of how that law was to be correctly interpreted and applied, virtually all were agreed on the need to obey faithfully its commandments. This included observing the commandments in their literal sense, as well as striving to obey the basic principles underlying those commandments and doing so gladly and willingly, from the heart.

However, once Jesus' first followers began to define God's will in terms of submitting to Jesus as Lord and placed him *above* the law, so that full obedience to God and God's law was inseparable from obeying and following *Jesus,* tensions and conflicts arose and intensified. Such a view inevitably led Jesus' first followers to the conclusion that those who consciously *rejected* Jesus in order to define righteousness exclusively in terms of obedience to the Mosaic

---

40. Kent L. Yinger, *Paul, Judaism, and Judgment according to Deeds* (SNTSMS 105; Cambridge: Cambridge University Press, 1999), 181. Chris VanLandingham has also presented abundant evidence that, throughout second-temple Jewish writings that speak of a final judgment, this judgment is said to be made on the basis of one's *works*: "Early post-biblical Jewish texts consistently and thematically state that the criterion for survival or approbation at the Last Judgment is deeds" (*Judgment and Justification in Early Judaism and the Apostle Paul*; Peabody, MA: Hendrickson, 2006, 171; see 66-174).

law as traditionally interpreted were not truly practicing the righteousness desired and commanded by God.

The discussion between those Jews who believed in Jesus as God's Son and those who rejected him, therefore, was *never* about whether a commitment to living a life in conformity with God's will was necessary in order to be accepted by God and saved.[41] No one, including Paul, was claiming that a simple affirmation of faith in Jesus, understood solely in an intellectual sense, was sufficient in order to be counted among those whom God regarded as righteous. If "justification by faith *alone*" is understood in that way, it is *entirely foreign to the thought of Paul and the rest of the New Testament*. Faith and works were never put in opposition to one another in the way that this has occurred in discussions among Christians since the time of the Protestant Reformation.

Instead, at the center of the debate among Jesus' first followers and other Jews was the question of *how God's will was to be defined*. Was one to look primarily or exclusively to the *Mosaic law* to define that will, or to *Jesus as the one God had designated Messiah, Lord, and eschatological judge of all*? Clearly, Jesus' first followers were strongly convinced of the truth of the latter affirmation. When contrasting "faith in Christ" to "the works of the law," they were not affirming that a commitment to living in accordance with God's will was no longer necessary, since faith in Christ alone was now sufficient. Rather, they were claiming that what truly mattered in God's eyes was that one live according to God's will in the way that it had been defined *through Jesus*. The distinction was not between *faith and works*, but rather between following and obeying *Jesus* and following and obeying the Mosaic law alone, independently of faith in Jesus as Lord. And the tensions that arose within the community of Jesus' first followers had to do with the question of what role the law was to play in the life of believers now that God's will had come to be defined by Jesus, rather than by the law as understood and interpreted independently of faith in Jesus.

THE ROLE OF THE LAW AMONG JESUS' FIRST FOLLOWERS

The most difficult questions that the redefinition of God's will through Jesus raised for Jesus' first followers had to do with what should be done regarding the Mosaic law. It was precisely the law that had defined Judaism and had distinguished Jews from non-Jews. Among faithful Jews, virtually everything in life and the world itself was believed to revolve around the law. Now, however, according to Jesus' followers, everything in life and the world revolved around

---

41. E. P. Sanders is therefore both right and wrong when he writes: "The issue between 'Paul' and 'Judaism' was not whether or not people should behave correctly, fulfill 'the law,' and do good deeds. Everyone agreed they should. The issue was whether or not people should be members of the body of Christ. Here they parted company" (*Comparing Judaism and Christianity: Common Judaism, Paul, and the Inner and Outer in the Study of Religion*; Minneapolis: Fortress, 2016, 83). While the first two sentences of Sanders's affirmation are accurate, the following one is not: the issue that made them "part company" was whether or not God's will was ultimately defined through Jesus as God's Son and spokesperson.

Jesus, who had been established by God as Lord and eschatological judge over all. The law had been displaced from its position at the center of life and faith and relegated to secondary status.[42]

Obviously, such a view represented a tremendous upheaval and made it necessary to rethink everything, including especially that which had always been most sacred within Judaism: the law itself. If it was not the law but Jesus who constituted the ultimate and definitive expression of God's will, to what extent was God's will still to be associated with that law? Why had God even given the law if from the beginning he had always intended to define his will fully through Jesus rather than through the law? Why had God attached promises of salvation to observance of the commandments of Moses if he had intended the promised salvation to come through Jesus? If people were now to approach God through Jesus, what need was there for them to approach God through the priests and the sacrificial worship offered at the Jerusalem temple?

The belief that it was Jesus who ultimately defined God's will also raised questions about the ongoing validity of the Mosaic law, particularly given the fact that many Jews remembered Jesus as one who had been accused of failing to observe that law faithfully and had also taught others to disregard proper observance of the law. Of what use was the law now that God's will had been fully defined instead through Jesus? Why should one strive to obey the Mosaic law if what truly mattered was living under Jesus as Lord? Might one even dispense with that law altogether in order to follow Jesus alone? It was extremely difficult questions such as these that lay at the heart of the debates, controversies, and conflicts in the Jewish communities of which Jesus' first followers formed part.[43]

Responses to these questions are found throughout the New Testament and other early Christian writings. Given the central position that the Mosaic law had occupied among Jews and the deep-seated belief they shared in its divine origin, Jesus' first followers could hardly declare that the law was now of no use or value, and much less accept such a claim themselves. Nor was it plausible or even conceivable initially to affirm that the Mosaic law had now been abolished or could simply be disregarded. Even if the law did not constitute the *supreme* expression of God's will, which was now associated with Jesus, among Jesus' first followers it undoubtedly continued to be seen as an *extremely important* expression of that will. To say that the law was no longer at the center but had become secondary was not to say that it was now

---

42. As David J. Bolton notes with regard to Paul's thought in Romans, what was involved was "not a *re*placement for (parts of) the *nomos*, but a *dis*placement of it, in terms of the *nomos* acting as an exclusive salvific source.... Paul, in line with his aim throughout the letter, is trying to move the community forward to a different understanding of righteousness than one that is *exclusively* Mosaic-based...." ("Who Are You Calling 'Weak'?: A Short Critique on James Dunn's Reading of Rom. 14,1—15,6," in *The Letter to the Romans*, ed. Udo Schnelle; BETL 226; Leuven: Peeters, 2009, 626).

43. For a history of the scholarly discussion regarding the ongoing significance of the law among believers in Christ and the problems raised by this question, see especially Heikki Räisänen, *Paul and the Law*, 2nd ed. (WUNT 29; Tübingen: J. C. B. Mohr, 1987), 140-61.

unimportant and could simply be done away with entirely. One could hardly argue that God's will had changed to such an extent that what he had willed previously was now no longer his will at all.

Furthermore, while Jesus' teaching seemed to provide a basis for questioning the importance of observing literally all of the commandments in the way that many Jews had traditionally done, Jesus had never gone so far as to consider that the law itself was no longer valid or could simply be laid aside among his followers. On the contrary, for the most part, Jesus himself had faithfully observed the Mosaic commandments and had expected his followers to do the same. As Friedrich Avemarie has argued, it seems beyond doubt that Jesus' first Jewish followers continued to observe the law, including the regulations regarding purity: "for Jesus and his early Jewish followers, the validity of the Mosaic purity laws was beyond question."[44]

The emphasis on the need to fulfill the deeper principles underlying the law found throughout Jesus' teaching, however, easily lent itself to the view that literal observance of the commandments could be set aside in order to concern oneself merely with fulfilling those principles. Even if for Jesus this had been the exception to the rule, when taken to its logical conclusion, it would eventually *become the rule itself*. The fact that Jesus' own views on the law had reflected many subtleties and seemed to be more occasional and situational rather than constituting a clearly-defined body of teaching made it difficult even for those who were well-acquainted with the Jesus tradition to summarize those views. As Tom Holmén observes, "If we weigh early Christian statements about the law, we may reason that there had to have been something in Jesus' assessment of the issue that was not always so clear even to his closest followers.... Jesus' attitude towards the law was apparently so unusual that it was difficult to categorize him on grounds the conventional forms of apprehending the law even though these also exhibited considerable variety."[45] In urban centers such as Antioch, as well as other diaspora communities in which they shared their faith, Jesus' first followers also found themselves facing new contexts and situations and came into contact with a diversity of people that Jesus' original disciples had never encountered during their time with Jesus in rural Galilee and Jerusalem. The question of how to maintain continuity with Jesus' teaching in these new contexts was therefore not clear. Because of this, Jesus' followers could easily come to adopt a variety

---

44. Friedrich Avemarie, "Jesus and Purity," in *The New Testament and Rabbinic Literature* (ed. Reimund Bieringer et al.; JSJSup 136; Leiden: Brill, 2010), 279; see 255-79. James G. Crossley has also argued that "the Q traditions show no indication of rejecting the law and the observance of major commandments was accepted or assumed" (*Why Christianity Happened: A Sociohistorical Account of Christian Origins [26-50 CE]*; Louisville, KY: Westminster John Knox, 2006, 102). According to Crossley, "the Jesus movement began with a particular stress on the law that maintained the full validity of biblical law" (142). In "earliest Christianity... we have an initially law-observant Jewish movement...." (153). It was only later that there occurred "a shift from a law-observant movement to a movement that included increasing numbers of friends of friends of friends who did not feel obliged to observe major commandments, such as food laws and the Sabbath, or to be circumcised" (171).

45. Tom Holmén, *Jesus and Jewish Covenant Thinking* (BibInt 55; Leiden: Brill, 2001), 340-41.

of different positions regarding the observance of the law, each of which could be viewed as being in continuity with what Jesus had taught.

Eventually, therefore, those who desired to set aside the observance of commandments regarding questions related to circumcision, food, purity, the observance of the Sabbath, and other practices that were not customary for non-Jews could also claim to be acting in accordance with what Jesus had taught. This is precisely what we find in Mark 7:14-23, for example. There the author of the Gospel concludes that Jesus "declared all foods clean" (v. 19) in the context of his teaching that it is not what goes into a person that makes him or her unclean, but the evil intentions that come out of the heart and lead one to commit sinful actions. Of course, as Jonathan Klawans notes, there is near unanimity today among scholars that Jesus never explicitly declared all foods to be clean.[46] David Fiensy also rightly observes that even Mark probably did not intend his words here to be taken in the radical sense that all foods whatsoever were now clean.[47] Rather than claiming that Jesus himself had explicitly abolished the purity laws concerning food, however, Mark may simply have meant that the logical conclusion of Jesus' teaching regarding what makes people clean or unclean is that, as long as one acts out of purity of heart and avoids actions that are evil or impure in an ethical sense, one is free not to follow strictly the Jewish purity laws regarding foods. In any case, what is clear from this passage in Mark's Gospel is that the *exception* has now become the *rule*: it is not just that the purity laws can be set aside under certain extraordinary circumstances. Rather, they can be set aside *regularly* or even *all the time* on a daily basis, at least as they had traditionally been understood.

Jesus' teaching regarding the Sabbath could be applied in the same way so as to maintain that it was acceptable to disregard the observance of the Sabbath, not only when basic human needs demanded it, but on a consistent basis, as long as one continued to put into practice the principles underlying the Sabbath commandment. While Jesus had apparently taught nothing on the subject of circumcision, the law itself could be used to argue that the circumcision that truly mattered was not the physical one, but that of the heart (Lev. 26:41; Deut. 10:16; 30:6; Rom. 2:25-29). Following the same logic, it could then be concluded that, as long as one's heart was circumcised, physical circumcision did not really matter.

Of course, these beliefs and practices regarding the Jewish law probably did not develop significantly until after uncircumcised non-Jews began to be incorporated into the communities of Jesus' followers. Precisely how this process began to take place is not entirely clear. The book of Acts speaks of "God-fearers" and "pious" gentiles who already worshiped the God of Israel as the first non-Jews to come to faith in Jesus, yet it is not clear exactly who

---

46. See Klawans, *Impurity*, 147. Géza Vermès was among the first to argue that we are "bound to conclude *a priori* that in a Palestinian environment the abolition of all distinction between pure and impure food is almost inconceivable" (*Jesus and the World of Judaism*; Philadelphia: Fortress, 1983, 46)

47. David A. Fiensy, *Jesus the Galilean: Soundings in a First Century Life* (Piscataway, NJ: Gorgias Press, 2007), 183-84.

these persons were or if they constituted a well-defined group.⁴⁸ Even if the integration of non-Jewish believers in Christ took place in the way described in certain passages of Acts, we cannot be sure that the process of inclusion was the same everywhere. Furthermore, Acts describes the incorporation of gentiles into the community as something that was not originally the result of a conscious effort by Jesus' original followers, virtually all of whom were Jewish. Instead, the apostles proclaim the gospel primarily to Jews, yet among those who respond favorably to their proclamation are increasing numbers of non-Jews. Scholars have debated whether or not Jesus intended an outreach to non-Jews either during his lifetime or after it.⁴⁹ At the very least, however, it seems that the inclusion of non-Jews was a logical conclusion of certain aspects of Jesus' teaching and ministry, such as his redefinition of what constituted observance of the law, his emphasis on following him, and his openness to those considered sinners.⁵⁰ Many have argued that Jewish beliefs regarding the eschatological ingathering of the nations also played a role, though those beliefs were quite varied.⁵¹

While non-Jews had almost always been allowed to participate in Jewish communities in a variety of ways, in general they seem not to have been accepted on equal terms as full members of those communities unless they were circumcised and became fully law-observant. Even those who did become law-observant proselytes often did not find full acceptance among those Jews who belonged to Israel by birth.⁵² Initially, this seems to have been

---

48. Among others, John J. Collins has argued that the identity of these non-Jewish worshipers of Israel's God is uncertain, since there were various levels of attachment of non-Jews to Judaism, and the terms "God-fearers" and "pious" were not technical terms ("A Symbol of Otherness: Circumcision and Salvation in the First Century," in *"To See Ourselves as Others See Us": Christians, Jews, "Others" in Late Antiquity*, ed. Jacob Neusner and Ernest S. Frerichs; SPSH 9; Chico, CA: Scholars Press, 1985, 179-85). On the variety of ways in which non-Jews could identify with Judaism in antiquity, see Shaye J. D. Cohen, "Crossing the Boundary and Becoming a Jew," *HTR* 82 (1989): 13-33, and Scot McKnight, *A Light among the Gentiles: Jewish Missionary Activity in the Second Temple Period* (Minneapolis: Fortress, 1991), 90-101. McKnight also discusses in detail the subject of Jewish missionary activity among non-Jews in antiquity (102-17).

49. For a survey of views on the question of whether Jesus intended a mission to non-Jews, see Eckhard Schnabel, "Jesus and the Beginning of the Mission to the Gentiles," in *Jesus of Nazareth: Lord and Christ. Essays on the Historical Jesus and New Testament Christology* (ed. Joel B. Green and Max Turner; Grand Rapids: Eerdmans, 1994), 37-58. Michael F. Bird offers a more extensive treatment of the question in *Jesus and the Origins of the Gentile Mission* (LNTS 331; London: T & T Clark, 2006). Both Schnabel and Bird argue that the "gentile mission" grew out of the teaching and practice of Jesus himself. For a review of scholarly opinions concerning the reasons why Jesus' followers began reaching out to non-Jews, see Philip Finny, *The Origins of Pauline Pneumatology: The Eschatological Bestowal of the Spirit upon Gentiles in Judaism and in the Early Development of Paul's Theology* (WUNT 2/194; Tübingen: Mohr Siebeck, 2005), 217-21.

50. See, for example, Crossley, *Why Christianity Happened*, 101-2.

51. On the variety of different views among Jews regarding the eschatological salvation of non-Jews in the second-temple period and rabbinic thought, see Robert Goldenberg, *The Nations that Know Thee Not: Ancient Jewish Attitudes towards Other Religions* (BibSem 52; Sheffield: Sheffield Academic Press, 1997), 29-107.

52. Matthew Thiessen notes that among Jews there was a wide variety of attitudes toward gentiles and that some Jews rejected gentile proselytism, claiming that gentiles should not be circumcised and submit to the law of Moses; while it was good and proper for gentiles to worship the God of Israel, they were to do so as gentiles and not as Jewish proselytes (*Paul and the Gentile Problem*; Oxford: Oxford University Press, 2016, 14-42). In fact, together with many other Pauline scholars today, Thiessen claims that Paul himself did not believe that gentiles could actually become Jews by being circumcised and observing the Mosaic law, although through Christ and the Holy Spirit gentiles could become children of Abraham (44, 70-71, 100-101, 160-63).

the case among many of Jesus' Jewish followers as well, who insisted that non-Jewish believers were not fully part of their community unless they became circumcised and came to observe the entire law. Even non-Jewish believers who did not come to observe fully the Mosaic law probably did not consider themselves to have become Jews. Nevertheless, they did adopt a Jewish way of life, coming to "live according to Jewish *ethos* ('custom' or 'habit'), *nomos* ('law,' 'convention,' or 'principle'), or *patrios* ('ancestral [tradition]')," as Mark Nanos has argued.[53]

While those non-Jews who became followers of Jesus did not come to see themselves fully as Jews, their refusal to take part in the worship of pagan gods or the cultic practices revolving around the Roman emperor, as well as the new lifestyle they adopted as believers in Christ, set them apart from other non-Jews.[54] This means that they were caught in a type of "social and religious no-man's land."[55] In Caroline Johnson Hodge's words, believers in Christ were "not Jews" and "not really gentiles any longer either," but came to "occupy an in-between space, hovering around the borders of identities that they were not quite."[56] In fact, there appears to have been no specific designation or category for such believers in the decades immediately following Jesus' death.

At what point the non-Jewish members came to outnumber those of Jewish origin is not clear. Paul's letters, however, give indication that, by the time they were written in the early 50s, at least in some places the communities of believers in Christ were composed primarily or perhaps even exclusively of persons of non-Jewish origin. The New Testament also gives evidence that the relationships between Jewish non-believers, Jewish believers, and non-Jewish believers in Christ were different from one place and time to another.[57]

Even though there was undoubtedly a significant amount of diversity among Jesus' first Jewish followers regarding the observance of the Mosaic law almost from the start, as James Crossley notes, the incorporation of non-Jews into the communities of believers in Christ inevitably led to a growing relaxation of law-observance in those communities.[58] This complicated

---

On the question of the association of Jews with non-Jews in antiquity, see also Sanders, *Comparing Judaism and Christianity*, 290-305.

53. Nanos, "Question of Conceptualization," 111. Nanos also speaks of non-Jewish believers in Christ "*behaving like* Jews (or 'jewishly,' practicing Judaism)" without actually "*becoming* Jews" (110), and mentions King Izates as an example of a non-Jew "*observing a Jewish way of life* as prescribed in the Torah *apart from circumcision*, apart from becoming a Jew, and thus, apart from becoming under Torah on the same terms as a Jew...." (119).

54. On this point, see Paula Fredriksen, "The Question of Worship: Gods, Pagans, and the Redemption of Israel," in *Paul within Judaism*, ed. Nanos and Zetterholm, 175-89.

55. Ibid., 187.

56. Caroline Johnson Hodge, "The Question of Identity: Gentiles as Gentiles—but also Not—in Pauline Communities," in *Paul within Judaism*, ed. Nanos and Zetterholm, 153-54.

57. See the essays by Wayne A. Meeks, "Breaking Away: Three New Testament Interpretations of Christianity's Separation from the Jewish Communities," in *"To See Ourselves,"* ed. Neusner and Frerichs, 93-115, and Collins, "Symbol of Otherness," 163-86.

58. Crossley, *Why Christianity Happened*, 174.

the relationships among Jesus' followers even more, since not only Jewish believers in Christ but non-Jewish believers as well had to determine to what extent members of both groups were expected to live in conformity with the Mosaic commandments as they had traditionally been interpreted.

The Relations between Jews and Non-Jews in the Communities of Jesus' First Followers

Once non-Jews who did not observe the Mosaic law in the way that most Jews did were accepted into the communities of Jesus' followers, another serious problem would arise: if non-Jewish believers could be viewed as living in accordance with God's will simply by following Jesus, without submitting literally to all of the commandments of the Jewish law, why could not Jewish believers do the same if they wished? In order to maintain the need for Jewish believers to continue to observe the Mosaic law as traditionally understood, it would be necessary to make some type of distinction between them and those who were not Jewish or did not live strictly according to the Jewish law. One possible way of doing this was to regard the latter group as being of inferior status in some way. This was the approach generally taken in ancient Judaism with regard to non-Jews who renounced idolatry, attended the synagogue, and adhered to many Jewish beliefs and practices without becoming circumcised or fully law-observant. Such non-Jews could be considered righteous before God to some extent, but could never be as fully righteous as those who lived in full compliance with the Mosaic commandments, since those commandments represented the most complete expression of God's will.

However, because the Jews who constituted Jesus' first followers were now claiming that the ultimate expression of God's will was to be identified with Jesus rather than the Mosaic law alone, it was difficult for many of them to regard non-Jewish believers in Jesus in that way. To some extent, such a practice would involve putting the Mosaic law back on the same level as Jesus in order to claim that what defined the righteous was submission *both* to Jesus *and* to the Mosaic law simultaneously. This view would also be problematic in that, under certain circumstances, one would inevitably still have to give priority *either* to Jesus *or* to the Mosaic law as traditionally interpreted, deciding which of these should define the other. Furthermore, to adopt the traditional Jewish stance would create a divided community in which some would in essence be "full citizens" of God's reign, while others would be relegated to the status of "second-class citizens." By definition, this would involve marginalizing some in the community. In his own teaching and practice, however, Jesus had strongly opposed any type of marginalization within his community of followers. On the contrary, he had consistently stressed the need to accept fully the outcasts, the needy, the meek, the children, and others who had generally been neglected, ignored, or considered of lower status. This, together with other considerations, no doubt led many within the community of Jesus' first followers to rule out the possibility of establishing and maintaining such distinctions among themselves.

Nevertheless, there was another way in which Jewish and non-Jewish believers in Christ might be distinguished from one another on the basis of the Mosaic law. It could be maintained that God had given the Mosaic law only to those who belonged to God's people Israel "according to the flesh," and therefore that only they were under obligation to observe the law. In principle, this would not make the law-observant group *superior* to the group that was non-observant, but only *different*.[59]

Such a position, however, would raise other problems and leave certain questions unanswered. If there were two distinct groups in the community, it would be almost inevitable for discussions to arise as to which of the two groups was superior or was in greater conformity with God's will. The stereotypes that Jews and non-Jews had regarding each other would not disappear easily. This position would also create difficulties when put into practice. When gathering for common meals, for example, those who had lived their entire lives observing the Jewish dietary laws would not find it easy to sit at a table at which others were eating food they considered impure and perhaps even repulsive, in part because it may have been dedicated to idols.[60] It would be even more difficult for observant Jews to attempt to eat such food themselves.[61]

In this regard, Markus Bockmuehl has proposed that there were basically four options for observant Jews within the communities of believers: to "(1) refuse all table fellowship with Gentiles and refuse to enter a Gentile house, (2) invite Gentiles to their house and prepare a Jewish meal, (3) take their own food to a Gentile's house, or indeed (4) dine with Gentiles on the explicit or implicit understanding that food they would eat was neither prohibited in the Torah nor tainted with idolatry."[62] Obviously, the first of these options would not allow for fellowship between Jews and non-Jews. The second and

---

59. In essence, this is the position of most of the contributors to the book *Paul with Judaism: Restoring the First-Century Context to the Apostle* already referenced above. See also Ellen Juhl Christiansen, *The Covenant in Judaism and Paul: A Study of Ritual Boundaries as Identity Markers* (AGJU 27; Leiden: Brill, 1995), 279-91.

60. On the development and diversity of practices regarding the eating of meals in the early communities of Jesus' followers and the impact that the incorporation of non-Jews had on those practices, see especially Hermut Löhr, "Speisenfrage und Tora im Judentum des Zweiten Tempels und im entstehenden Christentum," *ZNW* 94 (2003): 17-37. Löhr rightly stresses that, like Jesus, the first believers did not simply break with Jewish tradition in their observation of purity law regarding food, yet neither were they in full continuity with that tradition.

61. As Michelle Slee has pointed out, Jewish concerns about sharing meals with non-Jews may have had to do more with the possibility of partaking of food offered to idols than the purity of the food eaten (*The Church in Antioch in the First Century CE: Communion and Conflict*; JSNTSup 244; London: Sheffield Academic Press, 2003, 17-23). Even in that case, however, when the Jewish believers refrained from food eaten by gentile believers when the two groups ate together, the gentile believers might see this as an implicit criticism of their actions, either because according to the Jewish believers the gentiles were eating food that was impure or because the Jewish believers were giving the impression that, by eating of the food they did, the gentile believers were possibly participating in idol worship.

62. Markus Bockmuehl, *Jewish Law in Gentile Churches: Halakhah and the Beginning of Christian Public Ethics* (Edinburgh: T & T Clark, 2000), 58.

third alternatives would also be problematic and lead to tensions. If the non-Jewish believers adapted themselves to the Jewish customs and ate only food considered pure when they gathered for meals, eventually some would ask, "Why must we eat only *their* food? Why can we not eat the food *we* usually prepare and enjoy?" Conversely, if Jews took their own food to gentile houses to eat it there while refusing to eat of what the gentiles were eating, the gentile believers would feel that they were being looked down on or viewed as inferior: it was acceptable for them to eat Jewish food, but not for Jews to eat theirs. The fourth alternative was equally problematic in that many Jews might fear eating of food that had been sacrificed to idols without their knowledge, and this ran against the deep-seated convictions with which they had been raised. Yet to refuse to eat the food served by their hosts out of fear of idolatrous practices would be interpreted as a slight against their hosts and as an act of distrust toward them.

There were no easy solutions to these problems.[63] One way or another, one group would need to make concessions to the other. While the group making the concessions might be seen as inferior, it might also be seen as superior in that it showed greater love by adapting itself to the other group. In time, however, even this might prove problematic, with some even boasting or claiming to be superior in love because they were the ones making concessions to the others.

To preserve harmony in such a context, it would be necessary to constantly repeat that to make such concessions was an act of *love*, as Paul did. In Romans 14, Paul stresses that what really matters is "not so much the consumption of foodstuffs... but rather fellowship," which revolves around justice, peace, and joy.[64] Once again, questions of law observance would have to become secondary to mutual love and solidarity within the community. Nevertheless, maintaining unity in the face of traditional practices would by no means be easy due to the diversity of such practices and the great importance those practices had in the lives of many.

Similar problems would occur with regard to other commandments of the Jewish law, such as the observance of the Sabbath. What if a non-Jewish member of the community wished to invite believers of Jewish origin to some type of gathering or activity on the Jewish Sabbath that involved participating in practices that were normally not acceptable for Jews on a Sabbath, or even simply involved being in the presence of non-Jewish believers participating in those practices? If it was a social occasion, some of the non-Jews invited might not even be believers in Jesus. Even if Jewish believers simply attended such gatherings without fully taking part in those practices themselves, their lack of full participation would inevitably be interpreted as a tacit rejection of

---

63. On the problems related to common meals in the community of Jesus' followers, see especially Ekkehard W. Stegemann and Wolfgang Stegemann, *The Jesus Movement: A Social History of its First Century*, trans. O. C. Dean Jr. (Minneapolis: Fortress, 1999), 267-71.

64. Peter-Ben Smit, "A Symposium in Rom. 14:17? A Note on Paul's Terminology," *NovT* 49 (2007): 52.

those practices, and they would be seen as isolating themselves from the rest of those present.[65] If they simply did not attend the gathering or activity, their actions would be interpreted in the same way, as if they were being stand-offish. Even if they did decide to attend and participate fully, they would no doubt feel somewhat out of place. Many of them would be in a context in which they were not fully at ease, speaking to people they were not used to associating with socially and participating in activities that put them out of their "comfort zone." Both their non-Jewish hosts as well as other non-Jews might also feel awkward, not entirely sure how to treat these people who were "different," what to offer them to eat and drink, and even what subjects to discuss with them. There would also be discussions within the Jewish communities and even Jewish families over the extent to which it was permissible to participate in such activities with non-Jews, not only on a Sabbath, but on any day of the week.

One can also ask what would happen when a male child was born into a Jewish family that belonged to the community of believers, and the family wished to have the child circumcised on the eighth day, according to the Jewish tradition they had inherited from their parents and ancestors. Inevitably, the members of the family would have to decide whether to invite non-Jewish members of the community of believers in Christ to celebrate with them. If they chose not to invite non-Jewish believers to their celebration, those believers could easily feel slighted and discriminated against. The Jewish believers could also be seen as hypocritical, since in some contexts they had fellowship with non-Jewish believers in Christ, but in other contexts they excluded them. Most probably, some of the family and relatives of the child's parents would not be followers of Jesus. Would the Jewish parents of the child invite non-Jews to participate in a Jewish celebration of this type? If so, how would they fit in with the Jews who were present, including especially those who were not followers of Jesus? Whatever option they chose, inevitably problems and tensions would arise.

The Jewish parents might also consider the option of not inviting their family members who were not believers to the ceremony of circumcision, so as instead to invite only their "brothers and sisters in Christ," yet this would generate tremendous tensions within their family. The Jewish family members and relatives that were left uninvited would feel slighted and rejected, and the failure to invite them would be interpreted by the Jewish community at large as a grave offense against their community. Of course, if only one of the parents was a member of the community of Jesus' followers and the other was not, tensions and conflicts would most likely arise between the two of them as well, and the problems would be further compounded.

---

65. These same problems would arise when believers would meet in homes, as they seem to have done originally, since the home would have to be either Jewish or non-Jewish (see E. Stegemann and W. Stegemann, *Jesus Movement*, 276-77).

The same kinds of problems would arise with regard to other Jewish practices, such as the celebration of Jewish holidays, pilgrimages to Jerusalem, and participation in the sacrificial worship offered at the Jerusalem temple. One did not need to travel to Jerusalem to take part in that sacrificial worship, since one could do so through monetary contributions from afar. This was true not only for Jews but non-Jews as well, who could also participate in that worship to some extent both in Jerusalem or from a distance. The Jewish festivals and holy days would pose problems for non-Jewish believers in Christ. Should they celebrate Jewish holidays and make contributions to the temple or even pilgrimages to Jerusalem?[66] Were those non-Jewish believers who did these things in some way being more pious or godly than those who did not? And were those non-Jews who either could not participate in those aspects of Jewish life or elected not to do so showing disrespect and contempt for their Jewish sisters and brothers in the faith, or being *less* godly than those non-Jews who *did* participate? Would there not be discussions and perhaps even intense debates among non-Jewish believers over the question of whether or not they should participate in Jewish practices such as these?

As just noted above, Jewish believers would need to face different questions. Should they invite non-Jewish believers into their home to share in their traditional celebrations of holy days and acts of worship?[67] Would such invitations be viewed with approval by their Jewish friends and relatives, including both those who believed in Christ and those who did not? If they did invite non-Jews, would the non-Jews feel pressured to accept, even if they did not really wish to participate, since to decline the invitation might be seen as a slight against those who had invited them? Once there, would they not feel uncomfortable and out-of-place? Even if their hosts went out of their way to make them feel welcome, this would still involve giving them special treatment, and thus make them feel as if they were not fully part of the group. And if the Jewish believers chose *not* to invite non-Jewish believers to their gatherings, would they not be seen as discriminating against their sisters and brothers in the faith, or failing to show them the proper considerations and hospitality because they were different? All of these questions and others would create tensions, conflicts, and even divisions, not only between the Jewish and non-Jewish believers, but also among members of each of the two groups respectively. One can scarcely imagine the enormity and complexity of the problems raised by taking the position that Jews and non-Jews could form

---

66. On the participation of non-Jews in the worship at the Jerusalem temple through gifts and sacrifices, see James S. McLaren, "The Temple and Gentiles," in *Attitudes to Gentiles in Ancient Judaism and Early Christianity* (ed. David C. Sim and James S. McLaren; LNTS 499; London: T & T Clark, 2013), 105-8; Daniel R. Schwartz, *Studies in the Jewish Background of Christianity* (WUNT 60; Tübingen: J. C. B. Mohr, 1992), 102-16.

67. Crossley rightly observes that, in general, Jews did not have any problem having non-Jews present at their gatherings, as long as the non-Jews obeyed the Jewish customs while there: "inclusion of Gentiles does not automatically mean that the law must be rejected in any significant way.... Gentiles could be present at a gathering of law-observant Jews or Jewish Christians and, naturally, keep the law at least whilst present" (*Why Christianity Happened*, 124).

part of the same community of believers irrespectively of their observance of the Jewish law as it had traditionally been interpreted and put into practice.[68]

There is abundant evidence of these problems in the New Testament. The most obvious examples are Paul's discussions regarding the weak and the strong in Romans 14–15 and 1 Corinthians 8 and 10 as well as his account of the conflict with Peter and others over table fellowship in Antioch in Gal. 2:11-21. The discussions regarding circumcision and other Jewish practices reflected particularly in Acts, Romans, and Galatians were also the result of this attempt to bring Jews and non-Jews together on an equal basis. As the Antioch incident illustrates, answers to these questions were just starting to be offered in the early communities of Jesus' followers and, on the basis of what we have just seen, experience would eventually demonstrate that there was simply no satisfactory solution to many of those questions. Conflict was inevitable.

Against this background, one can also understand the predominance of the "family" language that pervades virtually all of the New Testament writings.[69] Because of the tensions that the questions just considered would create among believers and non-believers, eventually both the Jewish and non-Jewish members of each community of believers would need to make an extremely difficult decision: should they remain faithful to their family "according to the flesh," or should they remain faithful instead to the other members of their "family of faith"? Unless their whole family joined the community, this question would eventually be forced upon believers in Christ, not only by their family, but by the other members of the community of believers: "Are you with *them* or with *us*?" Many believers would have to make such a choice not only on special occasions but on a daily basis.

Therefore, when they chose the community of believers over their family, in many cases their family would spurn and even shun them. This would be true not only for those of Jewish origin, but for those of non-Jewish origin as well, who might be ostracized by their families and friends for abandoning their traditional beliefs and customs in order to adopt beliefs and customs that were considered Jewish.[70] Left without a traditional family, the only "family" they had was the community. Other believers became their sisters and brothers. Older believers might be seen as their "new parents," while younger believers could be seen as the "children" of the older believers, who gave them the affec-

---

68. Nanos notes, for example, that "the larger Jewish communities would have responded negatively" to Paul's reception of non-Jews as "full members of the family of Abraham, as more than guests and yet not candidates for becoming Jews." At the same time, their non-Jewish family members would have found "incomprehensible and scandalous" their lack of respect for the family and civic cult ("Question of Conceptualization," 150).

69. On the predominance of the "family" language throughout the New Testament, see N. T. Wright, *Paul and the Faithfulness of God*, Vol. 4 of *Christian Origins and the Question of God* (Minneapolis: Fortress, 2013), 400-402; Wayne A. Meeks, *The First Urban Christians: The Social World of the Apostle Paul* (New Haven, CT: Yale University Press, 1983), 85-88.

70. On this point, see Hurtado, *How on Earth*, 60-62, who mentions the tensions that would have arisen in the families of believers of both Jewish and non-Jewish origin as a result of their participation in the communities of Jesus' followers.

tion and support that they no longer received from their natural family. An understanding of this reality enables us to capture not only the extensive use of kinship language throughout the New Testament, but also the logic behind the Gospel passages in which Jesus says that one must not choose one's family over him, and in some instances must even come to "hate" one's family (Matt. 10:37; Luke 14:26). Naturally, this did not mean that believers were not to continue to love their parents, siblings, and other relatives; after all, Jesus had taught his followers that they were to love even their enemies. What Jesus had meant was rather that, when their parents, siblings, and relatives forced them to make a choice between the community and their natural family, they were to choose the community, no matter what the consequences with their family might be. Only in such a way would they be faithful to all that Jesus had taught and embodied.

The decision that observance of the Jewish law was optional in the community of believers, as well as the practice of full inclusion and openness toward those who chose not to observe the Jewish law in the traditional ways, would result in other problems as well. If among some believers the commandments of the Jewish law as traditionally interpreted were no longer practiced, this would seem to lead to the conclusion that the law was no longer relevant and had lost its meaning, purpose, and validity. This would be regarded as true, not only for non-Jews, but for those of Jewish origin as well. Sooner or later, such a position regarding the Jewish law in the community of believers would lead faithful Jews outside of that community to make precisely the accusation that was directed at Stephen and Paul in Acts 6:11-14 and 21:28: they were teaching against the Jewish law, the temple, and the Jewish people.

Reinterpreting Obedience to the Law

Naturally, those Jewish believers in Christ who advocated full inclusion and equal status in the community of believers for those who did not live according to the Jewish law as traditionally interpreted would have rejected the accusation that they were not respecting and upholding the law as they should. They might strive to show themselves to be fully law-compliant in order to ward off criticism by participating in traditional Jewish rites and practices, as Paul was asked to do in Acts 21:17-26. This would not counter fully the criticism, however, since the way they were thought to be disregarding the law was not by failing to observe it themselves, but by affirming that both Jews and non-Jews who chose not to live according to the law were just as acceptable to God as those Jews who did, as long as they lived out of faith in Jesus. The accusations and criticisms leveled against Jesus' first Jewish followers, therefore, forced them to develop arguments to convince their critics that, in spite of their openness to those who did not observe the law, they did indeed value and respect it.

One of the ways they might attempt to do this was by following the approach mentioned above: they might redefine what true observance of the

Jewish law consisted of by claiming that it involved fulfilling the fundamental principles underlying the law. In making such a claim, they could appeal not only to the Jesus tradition, but to the Hebrew Scriptures and Jewish tradition itself, which also stressed the importance of fulfilling those principles.

While such an argument might be well-received within the community of believers in Christ, when it was used to justify the non-observance of many of the commandments as they had traditionally been understood, Jews who were not part of that community would find it unconvincing, and ultimately would reject it. They would claim that, if God cared only about the observance of general principles, he would not have given concrete and specific commandments, and would not have commanded literal obedience to them, as he clearly had. In fact, the idea that one who was intentionally disregarding and disobeying specific commandments given by God could be said to be living in full conformity with the law just because he or she was practicing principles such as love, mercy, and justice would have even sounded absurd to many faithful Jews. While to a certain point they might be willing to concede that argument somewhat hesitatingly when non-Jewish outsiders were involved, most of those within the Jewish community expected that their own members follow the commandments, customs, and norms in the ways that faithful Jews were believed to have done for centuries. In most Jewish contexts, any person within the Jewish community who taught that one could set all of this aside and nevertheless live a life in full conformity with the law simply by adhering to the law's general ethical principles would probably be censured and even seen as a threat to the rest of the community.

A second way in which believers might claim to continue to be faithful to the Mosaic law and hold it in esteem was by re-signifying it on the basis of the idea that the law found its fulfillment in Jesus. This could lead to what has been called the "spiritualization" of the law. Undoubtedly, as Klawans has insisted, the use of this term can be problematic if it is contrasted with the claim that in Jewish thought the law and the rituals it prescribed were simply to be performed literally, without ascribing any spiritual significance to them.[71] As we have seen in Chapter 3 of this work, this was in no way the case. On the contrary, the idea that many or even all of the commandments of the Mosaic law pointed to deeper spiritual realities seems to have already been

---

71. See Jonathan Klawans, "Interpreting the Last Supper: Sacrifice, Spiritualization, and Anti-Sacrifice," *NTS* 48 (2002): 12-13. I would reject Klawans's affirmation that "in order to speak of a spiritualization of sacrifice (or of any ritual for that matter) one must assume that that particular ritual lacks all spirit (or meaning) to begin with" (12). As Stephen Finlan has shown, the language of spiritualization can be used in many different ways (*The Background and Content of Paul's Cultic Atonement Metaphors*; AcBib 19; Atlanta: SBL, 2004, 60-68). Nevertheless, in the context under discussion here, the language of spiritualization involves the claim that one can fulfill a commandment spiritually while not obeying it literally. Contrary to Klawans, therefore, a spiritualized understanding of sacrifice such as that which we find in Rom. 12:1 does not necessarily lead to the conclusion that the literal observance of sacrificial rites was devoid of any spirit or meaning. Instead, the idea is that the commandment to present sacrifices can be fulfilled by offering up one's own self spiritually, rather than presenting a material sacrifice to God. Such an idea was common in ancient Judaism, especially after the destruction of the Jerusalem temple.

well-established in Jewish circles long before the mid first-century CE. The approach of Jesus' followers, however, was somewhat different in that, rather than merely arguing that some deeper spiritual truth lay behind each commandment, they also claimed that the commandments pointed to Jesus and the new reality that had been brought about by God through him.

The idea that one can obey a commandment spiritually without obeying it literally is found in a number of passages from the New Testament. In Rom. 2:29, Paul distinguishes circumcision "of the heart" and "in spirit" from that which is done according to the letter of the law. Similarly, the author of Colossians tells his readers that they have been "circumcised with a circumcision not done with hands," namely, "the circumcision of Christ" (Col. 2:11). In Rom. 12:1, Paul exhorts the Romans to "present your bodies as a living sacrifice, holy and acceptable to God, which is your spiritual worship." Although the Greek word used there is *logikos* rather than *pneumatikos*, the latter term does appear in 1 Pet. 2:5, where believers are told "to offer spiritual sacrifices acceptable to God through Jesus Christ."

While in Jewish thought a literal observance of a commandment was to be accompanied by its spiritual observance as well, the idea that what truly mattered was fulfilling the commandments in a spiritual sense could easily lead to the conclusion that it was no longer necessary to fulfill them in a literal sense. This seems to be Paul's argument with regard to circumcision in Rom. 2:25-29, where he contrasts "those who are physically uncircumcised but keep the law" with those who "have the written code and circumcision but break the law." He then continues: "For a person is not a Jew who is one outwardly, nor is true circumcision something external and physical. Rather, a person is a Jew who is one inwardly, and real circumcision is a matter of the heart—it is spiritual and not literal." Here it seems that one can fulfill the commandment to be circumcised *without* observing that commandment literally.[72] Similarly, Rom. 12:1 and 1 Pet. 2:5 imply that even those who did not participate in the sacrificial system prescribed by the Mosaic law could be said to present spiritual sacrifices that were just as pleasing to God as those offered at the temple in Jerusalem.[73] These spiritual sacrifices seem to be understood in terms of offering up one's life to God and practicing the love, mercy, and justice that God demands. Just as Paul claims that those spiritually circumcised are more pleasing to God than those physically circumcised who do not do God's will,

---

72. Nanos questions the notion that Paul is affirming in Rom. 2:25-29 that uncircumcised non-Jews become true Jews if their heart is circumcised. According to Nanos, "Paul argues that (male) non-Jews who are not circumcised implicitly endorse God's judgment of Jews who are but who do not live up to the set-apart lifestyle that being circumcised marks them to pursue, that circumcision of the flesh of such Jews is undermined if not accompanied by circumcision of their heart. That is not the same thing as attributing circumcision or Jewish ethnic identity to non-Jews; it only shows that they can be equals or even superior to ethnic Jews in terms of God's acceptance of them, although remaining non-Jews" ("Question of Conceptualization," 115, n17).

73. As Bertil E. Gärtner has pointed out, 1 Pet. 2:5 not only "'spiritualizes' the concepts of the priests and the sacrifices," but also speaks of believers as a new, spiritual temple (*oikos pneumatikos*) (*The Temple and the Community in Qumran and the New Testament: A Comparative Study in the Temple Symbolism of the Qumran Texts and the New Testament*; SNTSMS 1; Cambridge: Cambridge University Press, 1965, 72-75).

so it might be said that God looked with greater favor on the spiritual sacrifices of believers in Christ than he did on the physical sacrifices offered at the temple by those who rejected Christ.

The purity laws could be interpreted in the same way. In 1 Cor. 5:8, for example, Paul contrasts "the old yeast, the yeast of malice and evil" with "the unleavened bread of sincerity and truth." In this case, those who cleaned out the "old yeast" from their heart were more pleasing to God than those who followed the Passover ritual literally by removing the yeast from their homes, if the latter did so without purifying their heart through faith in Christ. Observance of the Sabbath could be spiritualized in the same way.

To some extent, the Hebrew Scriptures themselves could be cited in support of the idea that God is more pleased with a spiritual observance of the law than a literal observance that does not also involve a spiritual observance. As noted above, Moses had commanded the people to circumcise their heart (Deut. 10:16; 30:6).[74] In Matthew, Jesus repeats twice that the prophet Hosea had taught that God demands mercy rather than sacrifice (Matt. 9:13; 12:7; Hos. 6:6). Micah had proclaimed that what pleases God is not sacrifices but the practice of justice and kindness (Mic. 6:6-8). The same idea is repeated in Isa. 1:11-18, which mentions celebrations of the Sabbath and the new moon as well, criticizing those who observe these festivals while acting oppressively in relation to others. The book of Isaiah also claims that the fast God truly desires is that one practice justice, oppose oppression, and share with the needy (Isa. 58:3-7). Originally, of course, these passages were not intended or understood in the sense that the literal observance of the commandments regarding sacrifice was not necessary, yet they could be read this way, as second-century Christian writings such as the *Epistle of Barnabas* and Justin's *Dialogue with Trypho* demonstrate.[75]

Jewish thought, of course, also stressed that the commandments had been given precisely to bring those who practiced them to reflect on the deeper spiritual truths that the ritual practices symbolized. Rather than being opposed to each other, these two aspects complemented one another. From a Jewish perspective, therefore, if the literal observance of many of the commandments was set aside, the spiritual aspects associated with them would also be lost, and those commandments could no longer fulfill their purpose of strengthening the faith and obedience of those who practiced them.

It is important not to assume, however, that this stress on the spiritual fulfillment of many of the commandments led Jesus' first followers to disregard or abolish their literal observance. On the contrary, there is evidence that Jesus' first disciples and even Paul continued to observe the Jewish commandments

---

74. James D. G. Dunn cites 1QpHab 11:13, 1QS 5:5, *Jub.* 1:23, and Philo, *Spec. Laws* 1.305, as examples of "the distinctively Jewish recognition that the distinctively Jewish rite, circumcision in the flesh, was not in itself sufficient, but needed to be matched by circumcision of the heart" ("The Colossian Philosophy: A Confident Jewish Apologia," *Biblica* 76 [1995]: 160).

75. *Barn.* 2:5; 3:1-4; 9:3-5; 15:8; Justin, *Dial.* 15:1—16:1; 19:1-3; 22:1-10; 28:4-5; 41:2-4; 117:1-2.

faithfully, at least under certain circumstances.⁷⁶ In 1 Cor. 9:20, Paul himself indicates that, when he sought to reach Jews, he lived as a Jew under the law. In his *Dialogue with Trypho*, Justin also mentions the existence of believers of both Jewish and non-Jewish origin who continued to observe the commandments literally in his own day.⁷⁷ Even when the first believers did follow the traditional Jewish commandments, rites, and customs, however, they undoubtedly *re-signified* them. If, as we have seen above, they believed that the key figures and offices of Israel's history as well as the temple and the sacrificial activity carried out there had found their fulfillment in Jesus and the new reality brought about through him, they would also have found new meaning in many of the commandments associated with the Mosaic law. In the same way that God had established certain offices, places, and rites to point forward to Jesus as their fulfillment, God could be thought to have established many of the commandments given to Israel for the purpose of foreshadowing the new realities that he intended to bring about some day by means of his Son.

This reinterpretation of the meaning of many commandments could lead to two very different views regarding the role that the law should play in the life of Jesus' followers, even when it was agreed that law-observance as traditionally understood made no difference with regard to one's standing before God or in the community. Some might reject the ongoing observance of the Mosaic commandments as meaningless or even contrary to God's will, since now that Jesus had come, those commandments had been superseded and were no longer of any real importance. Others, however, might come to the opposite conclusion: continuing to observe the commandments of the Mosaic law could be profoundly meaningful in that it would serve as an ongoing reminder of the significance of Jesus, to whom the entire law pointed. In this case, it could be argued that one should continue to observe the commandments literally because, through Jesus, they had been filled with new meaning and constantly pointed believers to the new and fuller reality that had now come about in Christ.⁷⁸

Circumcision, for example, might be rejected by some believers as no longer necessary once it was maintained that they had received the spiritual circumcision associated with Christ. Paul's affirmations that circumcision and uncircumcision are unimportant or "nothing" in 1 Cor. 7:19 and Gal. 5:6 and 6:15 could be read in this way: there is no point in being circumcised, because

---

76. Among Jesus' first followers, the figure most closely associated with careful law-observance is James the brother of Jesus; see Acts 21:17-25; Gal. 2:9-12; Josephus, *Ant.* 18.197-203.

77. See Eric Francis Osborn, *Justin Martyr* (BHT 47; Tübingen: J. C. B. Mohr, 1973), 159-60. As Osborn observes, while Justin considered those believers who continued to practice the Jewish laws and customs weak or ignorant, he did not condemn them, as long as they did not attempt to pressure others into practicing the law as they did.

78. Thomas Kazen, for example, comments: "While certain practices, such as circumcision, were soon abandoned, at least by Gentile Christians, other customs and rules were held on to much longer and a number of ritual rules were spiritualized, rather than discarded" (*Scripture, Interpretation, or Authority? Motives and Arguments in Jesus' Halakic Conflicts*; WUNT 320; Tübingen: Mohr Siebeck, 2013, 7).

it is meaningless. The idea that literal circumcision was to be rejected on this ground was common at least by the second century.[79]

Alternatively, however, one could argue just as strongly in favor of the continuing practice of circumcision among Jewish believers in Christ if they saw it as a visible sign and symbol of the new reality that had come through Jesus.[80] Even Paul may not have been opposed to the circumcision of non-Jews when it was done in that spirit. According to Acts 16:3, in fact, Paul himself took Timothy to be circumcised, though of course Timothy was Jewish by birth. If one decided to be circumcised, not from any sense of obligation or belief that it would change one's status in relation to God, but simply to have on one's body a visible reminder of the spiritual circumcision one had received through faith in Christ, Paul and others who thought like him may not have had any serious issues with such a decision.[81] In that case, circumcision could be seen, not as an act necessary for salvation, but as a symbol, sign, and reminder of the "righteousness of faith" present in Abraham that both Jewish and gentile believers now possessed.

Once this is clear, one might even argue that the Pauline passages just cited above regarding spiritual circumcision do not necessarily imply any type of opposition to literal circumcision as something that has been superseded in Christ. Rather, those passages can also be interpreted in the sense that it does not matter whether or not one is physically circumcised, because both physical *circumcision* as well as physical *uncircumcision* could serve to remind believers that they had received the true circumcision that really mattered, namely, that of Christ. In the case of uncircumcision, it could be seen as a sign or symbol of the fact that in Christ there is no Jew and Greek, as Paul says in Gal. 3:28, and therefore that such differences were now abolished within the community of believers. This is also how 1 Cor. 7:19 and Gal. 5:6 and 6:15 can be read: not that both circumcision and uncircumcision are meaningless, but rather that both can be meaningful in different ways.[82] However, when efforts

---

79. Paul van Buren observes that the positions among the anti-Jewish polemecists in antiquity ranged from seeing circumcision as being simply useless to regarding it as a "mark of infamy" (*According to the Scriptures: The Origins of the Gospel and of the Church's Old Testament*; Grand Rapids: Eerdmans, 1998, 165).

80. I would agree with William S. Campbell that Paul "does not think that to be circumcised or uncircumcised is a matter of indifference.... Far from being indifferent to these things, these forms of living, in circumcision or in the foreskin, are still significant factors for Paul...." ("Covenantal Theology and Participation in Christ: Pauline Perspectives on Transformation," in *Paul and Judaism: Crosscurrents in Pauline Exegesis and the Study of Jewish-Christian Relations*; ed. Reimund Bieringer and Didier Pollefeyt; LNTS 463; London: T & T Clark, 2012, 46).

81. For this reason, it would be improper to speak of "Paul's rejection of circumcision," as Collins does ("Symbol of Otherness," 185-86). Collins rightly notes, however, that even among Jews there were different beliefs and practices regarding circumcision and disagreements over the question of whether it was necessary for salvation (170-79).

82. The notion that both circumcision and uncircumcision can be meaningful in different ways supports the conclusion expressed by James Dunn, according to which Paul has an overall positive evaluation of the law rather than a negative one ("Two Covenants or One? The Interdependence of Jewish and Christian Identity," in *Geschichte–Tradition–Reflexion: Festschrift für Martin Hengel zum 70. Geburtstag*, Band III: *Frühes Christentum*; ed. Hermann Lichtenberger; Tübingen: J. C. B. Mohr, 1996, 116). From 1 Cor. 9:20-21 and other passages from his epistles, it is evident that Paul did value a literal observance of the law under certain conditions. For

were made to convince gentile believers to be circumcised on the basis of a reasoning that was very different, claiming that their salvation or status before God and in the community depended on their converting fully to Judaism—understood as an "old reality" pre-dating the "new creation" in Christ—, then Paul would have been strenuously opposed. This is what we see in his letter to the Galatians.

For years, scholars have debated precisely *why* Paul was opposed to the circumcision of non-Jewish believers in Christ. Previously, it was common to argue that Paul simply had a negative view of the law or saw the circumcision of non-Jewish believers as an expression of works-righteousness. Today, however, many scholars have come to question such claims. Recently, a number of scholars have argued that Paul's opposition to the circumcision of non-Jewish believers was based on his beliefs regarding the eschatological inclusion of gentiles as members of God's people. According to this idea, "in Paul's view, God's larger plan requires gentiles to worship the God of Israel *as gentiles*, not as proselytes or something else.... [T]his eschatological pilgrimage tradition—both in Paul and in earlier Jewish literature—envisions gentiles turning to God as non-Jews, not as proselytes."[83]

Together with Terence Donaldson, I would question such a characterization of Paul's thought. As Donaldson notes, there is virtually no evidence in second-temple Jewish thought for the idea that the gentile "end-time pilgrims" were "necessarily expected to be categorically differentiated from Jews as far as Torah observance is concerned."[84] Donaldson concludes his discussion of the subject by affirming that "the argument in these interpretations—that Paul's distinctive approach to the *ethnē* can be accounted for on the basis of an eschatological model that requires the distinction between non-Jews and Jews to be maintained—faces significant obstacles."[85] From my perspective, the interpretations of Paul that Donaldson questions are also problematic in that they assume that Paul believed that the awaited new age had dawned or been ushered in as a result of Christ's death and resurrection. As we shall see further on in this work, such an idea is foreign both to Paul and the rest of the New Testament writings, at least as it has commonly been understood.

---

the same reason, I would question Friedrich Avemarie's affirmation that, even though Paul "firmly clung to the *scriptural basis* of Jewish observance," his "attitude to the traditional *observance* of Jewish law was negative" ("Paul and the Claim of the Law according to the Scripture: Leviticus 18:5 in Galatians 3:12 and Romans 10:5," in *The Beginnings of Christianity: A Collection of Articles*; ed. Jack Pastor and Menachem Mor; Jerusalem: Yad Ben-Zvi, 2005, 126).

83. Johnson Hodge, "Question of Identity," 168. Here she is referring also to the thought of Paula Fredriksen. Similar arguments are put forward by other contributors to the volume *Paul within Judaism: Restoring the First-Century Context to the Apostle*, and are summarized by Terence L. Donaldson in his contribution to the same volume, titled "Paul within Judaism: A Critical Evaluation from a 'New Perspective' Perspective," 285-87. Nanos in particular speaks of the "chronometrical claim of the gospel" to claim that, in Paul's thought, for gentiles to become Jews would "subvert the chronometrical claim that they represent the children from the rest of the nations promised to Abraham as a blessing (the argument through Rom. 3-4 and Gal. 3-5)" ("Question of Conceptualization," 130).

84. See Donaldson, "Paul within Judaism," 286-93.

85. Ibid., 298.

I would argue instead that Paul's opposition to the circumcision of non-Jewish believers in Christ had to do with *practical* concerns. If *some* of the non-Jewish believers decided to become circumcised and submit to the Jewish law, the result would inevitably be confusion, tensions, and divisions within the community of believers. The decision of some non-Jews to become circumcised would set them apart from other non-Jewish believers and suggest that those circumcised became superior in some way to those who remained uncircumcised. Those circumcised might be seen as more faithful or dedicated to God and Jesus, or as possessing a superior status or greater righteousness in God's sight than those who did not become circumcised. Inevitably, the circumcision of some non-Jewish believers would place pressure on the uncircumcised to follow in their footsteps and undergo the same rite. For this reason, Paul insisted that both the circumcised and the uncircumcised should remain in the condition in which they found themselves at the time of their "calling" (1 Cor. 7:18-19). While his concern is no doubt theological in some sense, it is above all *practical*: for some non-Jewish believers to become circumcised would destroy harmony and create divisions in the community, since such a step implied that, for some reason, it was better or more acceptable to be circumcised than uncircumcised and that, both within the community of believers and in the eyes of God, the distinctions between Jew and gentile, circumcised and uncircumcised, still mattered.

Like circumcision, other practices ordained in the law, such as Sabbath observance, fasting, offering sacrifices, and eating unleavened bread, could be seen as symbolizing deeper, spiritual truths that had now become clear in Christ, and as reminding believers of the significance of Christ and what had taken place through him. In this case, rather than abolishing or abandoning such practices, the first believers might continue to adhere to them, understanding them in new ways that enriched their faith. This would be true with regard to both Jewish and non-Jewish believers.

Paul's words in 1 Cor. 5:7-8, already mentioned above, can serve to illustrate this: "Clean out the old yeast so that you may be a new batch, as you really are unleavened. For our paschal lamb, Christ, has been sacrificed. Therefore, let us celebrate the festival, not with the old yeast, the yeast of malice and evil, but with the unleavened bread of sincerity and truth." One could interpret this passage in the sense that there is no longer any sense in celebrating the rites associated with Passover, such as the removing of yeast from one's home and the celebration of a ritual meal revolving around a lamb, since these old realities had now been fulfilled in Christ. In that case, all that was necessary was to reflect spiritually on the new reality of Christ, who supersedes all of the ancient Jewish customs.

However, one could just as easily conclude from this passage that Paul and the first believers—including non-Jews such as those in Corinth—continued to celebrate the traditional Jewish Passover rites in some way. The book of Acts, in fact, presents Paul observing both Passover and Pentecost in Jerusalem

(Acts 20:6, 16), while Paul himself writes of waiting to spend Pentecost in Ephesus (1 Cor. 16:8). If he did keep these festivals with other believers in Christ, including non-Jews, they no doubt recalled together not only what God had done in Moses' day, but also what God had now done in Christ. The various rites involved served as types and symbols that pointed to the deeper realities that they now associated with their faith in Christ, and therefore served to enrich and strengthen that faith.

In this case, one can even imagine Paul and other Jews teaching non-Jewish believers in Christ to celebrate the Jewish Passover rite, while ascribing to the various ritual actions involved new meanings derived from their faith in Christ. Perhaps Paul taught the believers in Corinth who were mostly of non-Jewish origin how to carry out the ritual removal of the yeast from their homes, for example. If so, it would not be surprising if Paul and others made up new recitations to accompany those ritual actions, altering whatever Jewish recitations existed so as to include allusions to Christ and the redemption attained through him. It must be remembered that, when Paul wrote 1 Corinthians as well as his other letters, the Jerusalem temple was still standing and functioning. There would therefore be no reason to believe that either Israel's God or Jesus had abolished the rites associated with the Passover celebration. If Jesus' Last Supper with the disciples was thought to have been a Passover meal, the words attributed to him over the bread and wine could be seen as complementing the traditional words spoken over the food to be eaten in the Jewish rite rather than replacing them. Nothing in the Synoptic accounts of the Last Supper implies that the Passover meal was no longer to be celebrated every year because it had now been superseded by Jesus' own sacrificial death.[86]

The temple in Jerusalem might be viewed in the same way. Besides the fact that Jesus' first followers may have been critical of the temple establishment, as we have seen in Chapter 6, the idea that Jesus' death was sacrificial and that he was the true high priest appointed by God may have led his followers to distance themselves from the sacrificial worship at Jerusalem. In this case, if they continued to gather in the temple precincts, it was not to participate in sacrificial rites, but because the temple was a public space that could be used for other purposes, as a number of scholars have argued.[87]

The same beliefs regarding Jesus and his death, however, may instead have led his first Jewish followers to continue to participate in certain sacrificial rites at the temple, in spite of any criticisms they may have had of the sacrificial worship or the authorities there.[88] Rather than rejecting the temple and

---

86. According to Bolton, for example, Paul's letter to the Romans provides evidence that Paul took it for granted that his readers in Rome continued to observe purity laws and the Sabbath commandment ("Who Are You Calling 'Weak'?," 618-24).

87. On the different reasons why Jesus' first followers may have continued to frequent the temple, see especially Joshua J. Schwartz, "Temple and Temple Mount in the Book of Acts: Early Christian Activity, Topography, and Halakhah," in *Beginnings of Christianity*, ed. Pastor and Mor, 279-80.

88. Sean Freyne, for example, argues that the Jerusalem Jesus community led by James remained Torah-observant and active at the Jerusalem temple, since in this way they hoped "to bring the light of Torah to the nations, not by abandoning the distinction between Israel and the nations, but by replacing the dividing

the sacrificial activity associated with it, they may have felt they were its rightful heirs, since it pointed to Jesus as its fulfillment.[89] They may have seen in some of the rites carried out by the priests a reminder of Jesus' own priesthood and sacrificial death. In fact, if some of the Jewish priests became followers of Jesus, as Acts 6:7 affirms, both they and the believers in Christ whom they served may have expressed their faith in some way during the performance of the traditional rites. Believers might also ascribe new meanings to those rites, just as Paul ascribed a deeper meaning to the removal of the yeast in the Passover preparations. The fact that they believed that in Jesus they possessed "something greater than the temple" (Matt. 12:6), and that through him they attained a salvation superior to that which participation in the temple worship could offer, need not have led to the conclusion that those rites had been superseded and were now meaningless. Instead, they could be seen as filled with even greater meaning.

Paul's language about the freedom of believers should be understood against this background (Rom. 7:3-4; 1 Cor. 8:9; 9:17-21; 10:29; 2 Cor. 3:17; Gal. 2:4; 4:31; 5:1, 13). What is involved is not merely a freedom from a literal observance of the Mosaic law, but a freedom to follow such an observance as well. While at times Paul opposed attempts to impose the practice of commandments such as circumcision on non-Jewish believers, in a number of passages he also insists on the freedom of believers to *obey* the Mosaic commandments literally if they so choose. In Romans 14, for example, Paul speaks not merely about respecting the conscience of others who think differently rather than judging them, but also about doing what is *edifying* and *meaningful* both for oneself and others. Paul's exhortation is therefore not just about avoiding what might harm the conscience of another, but also about following whatever practice enables one to honor Christ and give thanks to God in one's heart (Rom. 14:5-6, 19; cf. 1 Cor. 10:23-33). Thus, if a literal observance of certain commandments fulfilled this purpose, it was to be considered as something good. For the same reason, from his perspective, Paul was not being fickle or hypocritical when he lived as a Jew among the Jews and when he lived as a non-Jew among non-Jews (1 Cor. 9:20-23). Rather, he was making himself a "slave of all" so that both groups might be built up in their faith in the gospel (1 Cor. 9:19).[90]

Nevertheless, while the practice of observing the law literally under some circumstances and not observing it under others may have been well-received

---

wall of hostility by one of mutual respect"; they would "live out their Torah-centred calling in the midst of the Gentiles" ("Jesus and the Servant Community in Zion," in *Jesus from Judaism to Christianity: Continuum Approaches to the Historical Jesus*; ed. Tom Holmén; London: T & T Clark, 2007, 121-23).

89. Steve Walton has shown that Acts presents both positive and critical views of the temple simultaneously ("A Tale of Two Perspectives?: The Place of the Temple in Acts," in *Heaven on Earth: The Temple in Biblical Theology*; ed. T. Desmond Alexander and Simon Gathercole; Carlisle: Paternoster, 2004, 135-49).

90. According to Mark Nanos, Paul's words in 1 Cor. 9:19-23 should be read, not in the sense that Paul was acting hypocritically, but rather that he was "adapting rhetorically" to his readers ("Paul's Relationship to Torah in Light of his Strategy 'to Become Everything to Everyone' [1 Corinthians 9.19-23]," in *Paul and Judaism*, ed. Bieringer and Pollefeyt, 139; see 106-40).

within the community of believers in Christ, particularly because it contributed to harmony and communion there, Jews who were not members of the community would find such a practice problematic. It would appear to many Jews that someone such as Paul was indeed acting hypocritically, pretending to be one person when with Jews and another when with non-Jews, even if he was fully open with all as to the reasons why he followed different practices in each context. In fact, as Crossley has noted, tensions could also arise among both Jewish and non-Jewish members of the community when non-Jewish believers would be observant of the Jewish law at a common gathering, but then be seen outside of the gathering exhibiting non-kosher behavior in a pagan setting.[91] Ultimately, therefore, neither the argument that true obedience to the law consisted in fulfilling the principles behind it, nor the claim that in Christ the true meaning of the law had been revealed, would convince Jews who were not followers of Jesus of the claim that one could observe the law faithfully without obeying the commandments literally, as they had traditionally been taught and understood in Judaism.

The Arguments of Jesus' Followers regarding the Purpose of the Law

If unable to argue in ways that convinced other Jews that they practiced and promoted obedience to the Mosaic law, even though under certain conditions they made its literal observance optional, Jesus' first followers could at least respond to those who accused them of failing to observe and respect the law in another way: by making the counter-accusation that it was those *opposing* them who did not observe the law. This could be argued on the basis of the ideas already mentioned above. Since the law pointed to Christ as its fulfillment, those who rejected Christ were rejecting the law as well. It might also be argued that those Jews who claimed to be law-observant in reality violated the law in the sense that they did not fulfill the principles underlying the law. This would be a difficult claim to maintain in a general sense, however, since many of the Jews who did not accept Jesus as the Messiah undoubtedly lived in ways that reflected those principles faithfully.

As we see in Stephen's speech in Acts 7, when Jesus' followers accused their Jewish opponents of acting contrary to God's will, they could point not only to the way in which Jesus had been rejected, but also to the Hebrew Scriptures themselves. The idea that Israel had constantly been a disobedient, hard-hearted people was well-established in both the Hebrew Scriptures and ancient Jewish thought. In Rom. 10:16-21, for example, after arguing that Isaiah foretold the proclamation of the gospel among the nations, Paul continues: "But of Israel he says, 'All day long I have held out my hands to a disobedient and contrary people'" (v. 21). All four of the Gospels present Jesus as leveling this same accusation against those who opposed him (Matt. 5:12; 19:8; 23:29-37; Mark 10:5; Luke 11:49-51; John 12:37-41). Whether or not Jesus himself stressed this

---

91. Crossley, *Why Christianity Happened*, 174.

idea, the fact that it also appears in other New Testament writings is evidence that it played a prominent role in the discussions that took place between his followers and those Jews who rejected their message.[92]

This idea could also be used to explain why God had given the law to Israel, as well as to argue that it no longer applied to believers in Christ. In response to the Jewish question of why God had given Israel the commandments if he did not desire that they be obeyed literally, at least some of Jesus' followers came to respond that God *did* desire that they be obeyed literally, yet *only for a certain period of time*, until the promised Messiah would come. Furthermore, because even in Jewish thought God had given the Mosaic law only to Israel, if the idea that Israel was a hard-hearted people who constantly disobeyed God was stressed, it could be argued that the Mosaic law itself had been given in response to Israel's persistent sinfulness.

The notion that laws have the purpose of restraining human beings from practicing evil and injustice, of course, is common to all cultures. Therefore, for Jesus' followers to make this claim regarding the Mosaic law would be neither innovative nor controversial. This idea appears explicitly in 1 Tim. 1:8-10: "Now we know that the law is good, if one uses it legitimately. This means understanding that the law is laid down not for the innocent but for the lawless and disobedient, for the godless and sinful, for the unholy and profane, for those who kill their father or mother, for murderers, fornicators, sodomites, slave traders, liars, perjurers," and those engaged in other practices contrary to God's will. This passage may in fact be referring not to the Mosaic law specifically, but to laws in a general sense. In either case, the affirmation that the purpose of establishing and enforcing laws is to keep evil and injustice in check focuses more on the negative purpose of laws than on the positive purpose of promoting human well-being, equity, and social justice. In insisting that the law is "good," the author of 1 Timothy also seems to be reacting to the possible objection that either he or the community of believers teaches that the law is *not* good. As we have seen, this type of accusation was probably leveled against Jesus' followers by Jews who considered the beliefs and practices of Jesus' followers to constitute a rejection of the law.

As H. W. Hollander and J. Hollemann have argued, such a negative view of the law was common in certain Hellenistic circles. The popular Hellenistic philosophers "regard law(s) as part of the deplorable state of humanity, i.e. of its wretchedness and wickedness (*kakia*), or to use a more Jewish-Christian word, sin (*hamartia*)."[93] Both the Sophists and the Cynics claimed that, "because laws were the result of men's wickedness, the laws themselves were not good either. Men should return to the time when there were no laws, the

---

92. See, for example, Acts 28:25-27; 2 Cor. 3:14; Heb. 3:7-19. For a list of passages from the Hebrew Scriptures that allude to Israel's persistent sinfulness, see Frank Thielman, *From Plight to Solution: A Jewish Framework for Understanding Paul's View of the Law in Galatians and Romans* (NovTSup 61; Leiden: Brill, 1989), 30-32.

93. H. W. Hollander and J. Hollemann, "The Relationship of Death, Sin, and Law in 1 Cor. 15:56," *NovT* 35 (1993): 280.

golden time of their ancestors when people lived according to nature (*kata physin*).... The laws were introduced because of man's wickedness, and were of no help in repelling this wickedness."⁹⁴ Laws worked by instilling fear of punishment in people and constraining them to act against nature. This made laws and nature directly opposed to one another. True righteousness is not to be found in laws, "because they are mere human convention."⁹⁵ For that reason, it was necessary for good and wise people to become free and independent of human laws, since such laws suppressed and enslaved people and ran contrary to nature: "laws are composed because of the degeneration of humanity, they are the proof of man's wickedness," and "are made by wicked people."⁹⁶

When applied to the Mosaic law, therefore, these ways of viewing the purpose of laws would easily lead to the claim that God had given Israel the law to restrain sinfulness and injustice among the people. In this case, however, the fact that the Mosaic law had been given *only to Israel* would lead to the idea that it had been designed by God specifically to check *Israel's* sinfulness.

In making this claim, Jesus' followers could once more point to the Hebrew Scriptures themselves and, even more importantly, to the biblical account of the giving of the law to Israel at Sinai. According to Exodus 32, immediately after God had redeemed Israel from its slavery in Egypt and had taken the people to Sinai in order to give them the law there through Moses, the people had turned away from him by building the golden calf under Aaron's leadership. This had taken place precisely while Moses was receiving the law from God on the mountain. Upon seeing what the people were doing, YHWH had become consumed with anger and had told Moses, "They have quickly turned aside from the way which I commanded them. They have made for themselves a molten calf, and have worshiped it and have sacrificed to it and said, 'This is your god, O Israel, who brought you up from the land of Egypt'.... I have seen this people, and behold, they are a stiff-necked people. Now then let me alone, that my anger may burn against them and that I may destroy them" (Exod. 32:8-10). According to the biblical narrative, when Moses came down from the mountain with the tablets, upon seeing the calf and the people dancing, he threw the tablets down and shattered them (Exod. 32:19). After the incident, even though YHWH first tells Moses that he himself will rewrite the same commandments on another pair of tablets, ultimately it is Moses who is said to inscribe them there (Exod. 34:1, 27). This could be interpreted in the sense that the second pair of tablets was somehow inferior to the first pair, which had been "written by the finger of God" (Exod. 31:18). Even in the Jewish tradition, this story was often viewed as the clearest and most paradigmatic

---

94. Ibid., 286-87.
95. Ibid., 281-82.
96. Ibid., 289. On this point, see also F. Gerald Downing, *Order and (Dis)order in the First Christian Century: A General Survey of Attitudes* (NovTSup 151; Leiden: Brill, 2013), 211-30.

expression of Israel's persistently sinful tendency and as the fountainhead of all of the sins that the people would eventually come to commit.[97]

This passage, therefore, which constituted an important part of Israel's foundational story, lent itself to the idea that God had given Israel the law due to its hardness of heart. Because the people tended so strongly toward disobedience and idolatry, God needed to check this tendency by imposing strict regulations on them. Only in this way could they be controlled. The idea that Israel is "stiff-necked" or hard of heart is repeated four times in the immediate context of the Exodus account, and appears in other passages from the Torah and the prophets as well (Exod. 32:9; 33:3, 5; 34:9; Deut. 9:6, 13; 31:27; Isa. 48:4; Ezek. 2:4; 3:7).

This is precisely the accusation that Stephen levels against his accusers and the Jewish authorities in Acts 7, where he uses the adjective *sklērotrachēlos*, the same word used in the Septuagint in the Exodus narrative: "You stiff-necked people, uncircumcised in heart and ears, you are forever opposing the Holy Spirit, just as your ancestors used to do. Which of the prophets did your ancestors not persecute? They killed those who foretold the coming of the Righteous One, and now you have become his betrayers and murderers. You are the ones that received the law as ordained by angels, and yet you have not kept it" (Acts 7:51-54). The allusion to the people being "uncircumcised in heart and ears" points back to Deut. 10:16, where Moses tells the people: "So circumcise your heart and stiffen your neck no longer," as well as the Septuagint version of Jer. 4:4: "Be circumcised to your God and circumcise your hardness of heart (*sklērokardia*).[98] In addition to pointing to the obstinacy of the Jewish leaders, Stephen alludes to the giving of the law "as ordained by angels" and claims that his opponents "have not kept it" (Acts 7:54). Shortly before this, he also alludes to the golden calf incident (7:39-41), and then claims that God turned away from the people and handed them over to idolatrous practices (7:42). Here Stephen cites the Septuagint version of Amos 5:25-27, where the prophet tells the house of Israel that they had not offered sacrifice during their time in the desert and reminds them how they had served the gods Moloch and Rephan. While Stephen does not explicitly say that God had given the law and commanded Israel to offer him sacrifices in order to check their sinful and idolatrous ways, the basic ideas are all present.

We find these ideas expressed and developed explicitly in Justin Martyr's *Dialogue with Trypho* in the second century. Justin repeatedly points to the golden calf incident and associates it with Israel's persistent sinfulness so as

---

97. Later Jewish tradition linked the Day of Atonement with the giving of the second tablets of the law; see Philip Goodman, *The Yom Kippur Anthology* (Philadelphia: Jewish Publication Society of America, 1971), 22-23. There Goodman cites *Lamentations Rabbah* 33: "It is quite right that the Day of Atonement [should be an occasion for dancing] since it was a day of forgiveness and expiation for Israel, and the day upon which the second tablets [of the Law] were given." Frédéric Manns also notes that the rabbis "admitted that the sin of the Golden Calf had been the sin *par excellence*, from which Israel had never been completely absolved" ("Justin's Dialogue with Trypho," in *Beginnings of Christianity*, ed. Pastor and Mor, 377).

98. The "uncircumcision of the ears" alludes to Jer. 6:10, while the idea of the uncircumcision of the heart appears in Lev. 26:41 and Jer. 9:26.

to argue that God gave Israel the law on that account.[99] According to Justin, commandments having to do with circumcision, fasting, abstention from certain foods, and the observance of the Sabbath and other holy days had the purpose of constantly keeping God before the people's eyes so that they might not turn away from him, as they were prone to do.[100] For Justin, the commandments regarding sacrificial offerings were aimed at checking the people's desire to serve other gods due to their idolatrous heart.[101] Justin repeatedly tells Trypho the Jew that God gave the Jews these commandments "because of your hardness of heart" (*sklērokardia*) and "because of your sins" (*dia tas hamartias/adikias humōn*).[102] By the latter phrase, Justin clearly means that God's intention was to restrain Israel's persistent sinfulness. Many of these ideas also appear in other Christian writings from the second century onward. According to Marcel Simon, throughout these writings we find the view that "[t]he law was intended only for the Jews. The law alone, by restraining their evil propensities, was capable of keeping them in the right way."[103]

Some of these ideas can be found in the New Testament writings as well. While we must of course be careful not to assume that these ideas had developed to the same extent that they had by the second century, they clearly existed at least in an incipient form by the middle of the first century. Allusions to the sin of Israel in the desert and the people's persistent hardness of heart appear in Hebrews 3:7—4:9 as well as in 1 Cor. 10:5-10. In the latter passage, Paul also alludes briefly to the story of the golden calf, citing Exod. 32:6: "Do not become idolaters as some of them did; as it is written, 'The people sat down to eat and drink, and they rose up to play'" (1 Cor. 10:7).[104] Although the idea that God commanded Israel to present him sacrifices in order to hold in check their strong inclination toward idolatry is not found in the New Testament, the epistle to the Hebrews does affirm that the purpose of the sacrifices for sin was to serve to remind the people of their sins (Heb. 10:3).[105]

Stephen's affirmation that God gave the law through angels is repeated by Paul in Gal. 3:19. There Paul responds explicitly to the question of why God had given the law: "Why then the law? It was added because of transgressions, until the offspring would come to whom the promise had been

---

99. *Dial.* 19:5-6; 20:4; 73:6; 102:6; 132:1; cf. *Barn.* 4:6-8; 14:1-5. On what follows, see especially Judith M. Lieu, *Image and Reality: The Jews in the World of the Christians in the Second Century* (Edinburgh: T & T Clark, 1996), 113-24.

100. Justin, *Dial.* 19:5—21:4; 23:1-2; 27:2-5; 30:1; 43:1; 45:3; 46:5-7; 47:2; 67:4-8; 92:4-5.

101. Justin, *Dial.* 19:6; 22:1-11; 67:8; 92:4-5.

102. The former phrase, generally *dia tēn sklērokardian*, appears in *Dial.* 27:2; 43:1; 46:5, 7; 47:2; 67:4, 8 (cf. 45:3), while the latter is in 21:1; 22:1, 11 (cf. 23:2).

103. Marcel Simon, *Verus Israel: A Study of the Relations between Christians and Jews in the Roman Empire (135-425)*, trans. H. McKeating (Oxford: Oxford University Press, 1986), 169. For references and a discussion of these ideas in Christian writings from the second to the fifth century, see 86-91, 163-69.

104. On Paul's allusions to the golden calf incident in 1 Cor. 10:7, see B. J. Oropeza, *Paul and Apostasy: Eschatology, Perseverance, and Falling Away in the Corinthian Congregation* (WUNT 2/115; Tübingen: Mohr Siebeck, 2000), 139-43.

105. For references from second- and third-century Jewish and Christian writings to the idea that the law was given on account of Israel's sinfulness, see Skarsaune, *Proof from Prophecy*, 314-20.

made; and it was ordained through angels by a mediator." The phrase "because of transgressions" (*tōn parabaseōn charin*) should be understood in the sense that God gave the law to hold Israel's sin in check.[106] The idea would be the same as we have noted in Justin's *Dialogue with Trypho*, though the Greek phrase is different. Paul develops this idea further when he speaks of the law as a "custodian" or "disciplinarian" until Christ came (Gal. 3:24—4:7). While scholars have disagreed over precisely how to understand the word *paidagōgos* used here by Paul, the image seems to be that of a person who has the task of keeping a child or young person under control until he or she becomes an adult, even though the idea of instructing that child or young person may also be involved. Paul seems to view the law in similar terms in Rom. 7:6, where he refers to the law as "that which held us captive." The Greek *kateixometha* in this verse can also be translated in terms of being held back or restrained.

It is not entirely clear where the notion that angels gave the law originated, since it is not present in the Exodus account or elsewhere in the Hebrew Scriptures.[107] If this idea had not at least become part of a Jewish oral tradition, however, it seems questionable that Paul and Luke would have cited it, since otherwise most Jews would have rejected that claim outright. To say that the law was given through angels as mediators, of course, is not to deny that it came from God.[108] It does imply, however, that the Mosaic law is not to be equated with God's ultimate and primary will, since it puts the law at a certain distance from God.

In later Christian thought, it was maintained that the law that Jews observe was not the original law that God had written on the tablets that Moses first received and subsequently shattered, but rather a second law that God had given in anger in response to the golden calf incident. The third-century *Didaskalia Apostolorum* refers to the second set of tablets given to Moses as the *deuterosis* or "second legislation": "This is the primarily ritual code that Moses received during his second sojourn on the mountain. It is this code which the rest of the Old Testament, and especially the Deuteronomic and Levitical codes, is concerned to develop and fill out, and which was imposed

---

106. De Boer argues that *tōn parabaseōn charin* in Gal. 3:19 can be understood either in the sense of "because of the transgressions" or "in order to produce the transgressions," that is, in order to bring the reality of sin into the open. He argues for the latter interpretation, since he wishes to reject the notion that the law had a "saving, life-giving function or purpose." Instead, by revealing sin, it pointed to the need for Christ to come and die and the need for all to depend on Christ for salvation rather than depending on observance of the law (*Galatians*, 230-31). Contrary to de Boer's interpretation of this verse, however, I would argue that Paul's idea is that God gave Israel the law in order to limit Israel's transgressions or hold them in check until Christ would come in the "fullness of time" (Gal. 4:4).

107. On the Jewish background to the idea that the law was given by means of angels, see de Boer, *Galatians*, 228-30. Stefan Nordgaard argues that Paul believed that "God was 'behind' the law, but at the same time neither attached to nor responsible for it"; according to Paul, "the law had been ordained by a group of angels whom God had commissioned for this task so that he himself could both have the law and also remain unblemished by its fundamental imperfection" ("Paul and the Provenance of the Law: The Case of Galatians 3.19-20," *ZNW* 105 [2014]: 79; see 64-79).

108. The extreme position that God had not given the law at all does not appear in Christian writings until the second century; see Simon, *Verus Israel*, 86-87.

on the Jews because of their idolatry. It was meant for the Jews alone and was the instrument of divine punishment. The Lord himself promulgated it only with reluctance, in the heat of anger."[109] While of course this idea is never mentioned in the New Testament, like Gal. 3:19-20, it does reflect a view of the law according to which it does not represent God's original will but was instead a response to Israel's transgressions.

Paul's claim in Gal. 3:24—4:7 and possibly the idea that God gave the law as a *temporary measure* runs contrary to ideas we find regarding the law in other ancient Jewish sources. Scholars have looked extensively in those sources for the idea that God intended the law only for the present age and that in the age to come the Mosaic law would either disappear altogether or be replaced by a different law. As W. D. Davies demonstrated, however, there is little if any evidence for this idea there.[110] The law itself, of course, affirms that the commandments are to be kept perpetually.[111] The passages from Jeremiah and Ezekiel that affirm that in the future the law will be internalized do not necessarily mean that it is to be replaced by another law (Jer. 31:31-34; Ezek. 11:19-20; 36:26-27); rather, what is to be inscribed may be the Mosaic law itself.[112] The claim that God gave the law only as a temporary stopgap measure also represents a rejection of the ancient Jewish view that the Mosaic law existed before creation and had served as a type of blueprint for the created order, constituting the perfect embodiment or expression of God's wisdom. At least to some extent, then, both the speech attributed to Stephen and Paul's words in Gal. 3:24—4:7 affirm ideas that seem to be foreign to ancient Jewish thought regarding the law.

If the idea that God had given Israel the law as a temporary measure to check Israel's persistent sinfulness was not derived from the Jewish tradition,

---

109. Ibid., 88. As Graham Stanton notes, the author of the *Epistle of Barnabas* also argues that the covenant was canceled immediately because of the people's idolatry when Moses shattered the tables of the law, yet he does not mention the making of the second tablets ("Other Early Christian Writings: 'Didache', Ignatius, 'Barnabas', Justin Martyr," in *Early Christian Thought in its Jewish Context*, ed. Barclay and Sweet, 183). Pieter Willem van der Horst also observes that, according to the *Didaskalia*, believers in Christ were no longer under this "Second Legislation," not only because it had been given only to the Jews, but also because they had been set free from idolatry by baptism and therefore had no need for that legislation. Therefore, those who submitted to the law implicitly recognized their idolatrous tendency ("I Gave Them Laws that Were Not Good: Ezekiel 20:25 in Ancient Judaism and Early Christianity," in *Sacred History and Sacred Texts in Early Judaism: A Symposium in Honour of A. S. van der Woude*; ed. J. N. Bremmer and F. García Martínez; CBET 5; Kampen: Kok Pharos, 1992, 109-10).

110. See W. D. Davies, *Torah in the Messianic Age and/or the Age to Come* (JBLMS 7; Philadelphia: SBL, 1952). In the conclusions to his study, Davies comments that the evidence in favor of the belief in antiquity that a "new Messianic Torah" would be given "cannot be regarded as very impressive" (90). Instead, the common Jewish expectation was that "the Torah in its existing form would persist into the Messianic Age when its obscurities would be made plain...." (84). Joseph Klausner, however, points to passages from the rabbinic sources that suggest that, when the age to come arrived, the Torah would no longer be in force (*The Messianic Idea in Israel, from its Beginning to the Completion of the Mishnah Cycle*, trans. W. F. Stinespring; New York: MacMillan, 1955, 449).

111. The affirmation that certain commandments are to be kept perpetually or "for all generations" appears frequently in the Pentateuch; see especially Num. 15:22-23; 35:29; Deut. 4:40; 7:9-11; 28:45-46; 29:29.

112. As Davies observed, "the reference in Jeremiah 31:31ff to a law written 'in the heart' or 'in the inward parts' does not necessarily imply any rejection of the written law as such" (*Torah*, 23).

it may have had its origin instead in the Jesus tradition. The Gospels of Matthew and Mark include the account in which the Pharisees approach Jesus to ask whether it is lawful for a man to dismiss his wife (Matt. 19:3-12; Mark 10:2-12). There, Jesus responds, "What did Moses command you?" After the Pharisees answer, Jesus says, "Because of your hardness of heart he wrote this commandment for you. But from the beginning of creation, 'God made them male and female'" (Mark 10:5-6). Jesus' words here imply that the commandment in question came from Moses rather than God himself. They also reflect the idea that the law was given, not to Jesus and his followers, but only to other Jews, since the phrase used is "to/for you" rather than " to/for us."

Many scholars consider this passage to have a strong historical basis.[113] Whether or not that is the case, however, here we find the ideas we have just considered: the commandment given by Moses concerning dismissing one's wife did not represent God's original will, but was given on account of Israel's hardness of heart (*sklērokardian*). In other words, it was a concession to the people's inherent sinfulness and their inability to live up to what God had originally desired when he created the world and human beings. Here Jesus is presented as questioning the idea that the Mosaic commandments represented God's ultimate will on the basis of the Torah itself: God's original intention was that expressed in Genesis, yet since many Israelites were unable to fulfill that intention due to their sinful heart, Moses allowed them to dismiss their wives in a way that preserved order in the society and to some extent protected the parties affected by such a practice. In addition, of course, this narrative underscored the notion that Jesus was above the law and thus above Moses as well, not merely because he invalidated the Mosaic commandment, but also because he knew what God's original intentions were and did not consider himself and his disciples to be under the Mosaic commandment.

For reasons we have seen, it is not clear how convincing or effective the argument that God had given Israel the law in response to Israel's hardness of heart would have been in the context of the discussions and conflicts concerning the law that arose among Jesus' first followers and other Jews. As we shall see in Chapter 9 of this study, this argument may have led those Jews that were not followers of Jesus to emphasize even more strongly the ideas that the law had its origin in God even before the creation of the world, and that God had intended it to be observed perpetually, not only in this world, but also in the world to come. Whether or not this argument was well-received, however, it did provide a strong basis to justify the practices regarding the law that were being implemented in many of the communities of Jesus' first followers. As Paul claims in Gal. 3:21—4:7, because the law was given only as a temporary measure due to Israel's sin, now that Christ had come to bring a new situation

---

113. Holmén notes that "despite many controversial points, the authenticity of Jesus' total rejection of divorce and remarriage is unanimously acknowledged" (*Jesus*, 162), while Meier comments that "Jesus' prohibition of divorce is perhaps the single best-attested teaching in what we call his *halākā*" (*Marginal Jew*, 4:118).

into existence, it was no longer necessary for believers to observe it in the way Jews had traditionally done.

At the same time, this argument could be made without implying that the law was in some sense defective or did not represent God's will. On the contrary, as Paul insists in Romans 7 after affirming that believers are "discharged from the law, dead to that which held us captive," and that the law is not "sin" (vv. 6-7), believers could still maintain that "the law is holy, and the commandment is holy and just and good" (v. 12). This stands in contrast to the claim later found in Justin and other Christian polemicists who argued that the law was *not* good, partially on the basis of Ezek. 20:25: "I gave them statutes that were not good and ordinances by which they could not live."[114] By arguing that the real problem was not the law but human sin (Rom. 7:7-25), Paul could uphold the goodness of the law and therefore defend himself against the accusation that, because he taught that it was no longer necessary to observe the law literally, he rejected the law as an expression of God's will.

On the basis of these ideas, Paul also points to another purpose of the law: it was given not only to restrain sin, but also to reveal to human beings their sinfulness. Without the commandment, one would not know what sin is or be aware of one's sin: "If it had not been for the law, I would not have known sin. I would not have known what it is to covet if the law had not said, 'You shall not covet'" (Rom. 7:7). The same idea appears earlier in the same letter, where Paul affirms that "through the law comes the knowledge of sin" (Rom. 3:20). In Romans 3, Paul combines the idea that the law reveals sin with two other ideas considered above: no one can keep the law (vv. 9-20), and the law was given to point to Christ as its fulfillment (vv. 21-22). According to this argument, God had given Israel the law not only to hold sin in check, but also to bring Israel to repentance by revealing to the people their sins. This would lead them to ask God, not only for forgiveness, but for the obedience he demanded of them for their own good (Rom. 2:4-5). As Judith Lieu notes, such a notion is echoed in Justin's *Dialogue with Trypho*: "the law had its purpose, a negative one as a response to their unbelief and hard-heartedness (18.2; 23.2; 46.5), but one which at the same time had a positive side in leading them to penitence and obedience (30.1)."[115]

Nevertheless, the claim that the Mosaic law was designed to hold sin in check until Israel's Messiah would come also runs contrary to ancient Jewish thought on the law in that it denies the law any salvific role other than preparing the way for what was later to come. In contrast with much traditional Protestant thought, where it is claimed that human beings could have been saved if they had kept the law, Paul teaches that from the start it was never God's intention to save Israel or others by means of the law. In Galatians, he writes: "Is the law then opposed to the promises of God? Certainly not!

---

114. On the idea that the law was not good in early Christian thought, see van der Horst, "I Gave Them Laws," 94-118.

115. Lieu, *Image*, 118.

For if a law had been given that could make alive, then righteousness would indeed come through the law. But the scripture has imprisoned all things under sin, so that what was promised through faith in Jesus Christ might be given to those who believe" (Gal. 3:21-22). Here Paul defends himself against the accusation that he taught that the law played no role in salvation. Yet his argument is not that the law could have brought salvation if human beings had only obeyed it, but rather that it was never designed as the means by which God would give human beings the life he intended for them. This is because the law itself could not resolve the problem of human sinfulness. It could only hold that sinfulness in check for a time until Christ would come to bring about in human beings the righteousness God desired to see in them.

This argument could also be used to respond convincingly to the question of why God had apparently attached promises of salvation to obedience to the commandments in the Mosaic law. Undoubtedly, in passages such as Leviticus 26 and Deuteronomy 28, God had told the people that, if they obeyed his precepts, he would bless them with well-being and prosperity, but if they disobeyed, he would chastise them in many different ways. Rather than identifying the blessings promised to obedience with Israel's eschatological salvation, however, Paul and others could argue that those blessings merely constituted temporal rewards in the present world that also served as a means to hold Israel's sin in check. In other words, the promises contained in the law were not to be associated with the definitive redemption of Israel that many Jews were expecting; for Paul, that was only to come through Christ. Instead, those promises were equivalent to the custodian or disciplinarian (*paidagōgos*) keeping a child in line, not only by punishing the child's bad behavior, but also by offering the child rewards for good behavior.[116] Yet just as those temporary rewards were not to be confused with the full inheritance that the child would obtain some day as an adult, so also the rewards for obedience promised to Israel in the Mosaic law were not to be confused with the eschatological salvation that God had promised to bring about. This would come, not through the law, but through Christ.

To many Jews, the claim that God had given the Mosaic law to Israel only as a temporary measure on account of Israel's sinfulness and that God had never intended it as a means to salvation would sound not only strange, but offensive as well. In spite of the insistence of Jesus' followers that they valued and respected the law, their arguments seemed to denigrate the law and minimize its importance, as well as to take away any motivation for observing it. Why should one bother to live according to the law if it was merely a stopgap disciplinary measure God had taken in response to Israel's sin and God had not attached any promises of eschatological salvation to its observance? The notion that God had given the Mosaic law to Israel alone on account of the

---

116. Wilson points out that "one should be careful to note that Paul does not describe the *Law itself* as a 'pedagogue', but only the particular historical *function* of the Law before the 'coming of faith' (3.23), when it was itself enclosed 'under sin' (3.22)" (*Curse*, 39).

people's sinfulness also seemed to imply that Israel was even more sinful than other nations, to whom God had *not* given the law. Therefore, though their arguments depended on the claim that Israel was a sinful people, if Jesus' followers wanted not only to counter Jewish objections to their teaching, but also to attract other Jews into their communities, they needed to present their ideas in ways that were less aggressive and would not alienate their hearers.

One of the ways in which they might accomplish this objective was by affirming that those Jews who rejected their message were acting out of ignorance rather than ill will. We find this idea in Acts in the speeches of Peter and Paul, who claim that those who killed Jesus did so, not out of malice, but out of ignorance regarding God's plan (Acts 3:17; 13:27; cf. 1 Cor. 2:8).[117] Paul uses this argument as well in Rom. 9:30—10:4, where he says that those from Israel who have zealously strived to attain righteousness on the basis of the law have not fulfilled the law. In a conciliatory tone, however, he attributes this to the fact that they have been "ignorant of the righteousness that comes from God." In this same context and elsewhere, he also attributes Israel's sinfulness and rejection of Jesus to the people's lack of enlightenment regarding God's plan, as well as the hardening of their hearts and minds that God himself has brought about temporarily in order to accomplish his salvific purposes among the nations (Rom. 9:6-24; 11:7-10; 2 Cor. 3:14-16). This type of argument enabled Jesus' followers to claim that their hearers were not entirely to blame for their failure to obey God's will in the way that they should.

Another way in which Jesus' followers could attempt to appeal to a Jewish audience without alienating their hearers, while at the same time responding to the criticism that they failed to respect and observe the law as they should, was to argue that in reality *no one* keeps the law. *All* are sinners and fail to live as God desires and commands. While of course this still involved claiming that faithful Jews were sinful and failed to observe the law, such a claim tended to be much less aggressive in that it involved pointing, not only to the sins of others, but also to the sins of believers themselves. In this way, Jesus' followers could acknowledge their agreement with the accusation that they did not observe the law fully, rather than denying that accusation, yet at the same time accuse those opposed to them of failing to observe the law in a way that avoided offending them. This strategy would tend to be more effective than simply pointing to the sins of those who had not accepted Jesus as Messiah, since it would involve communicating a conciliatory message to the effect that, "We are in need of God's grace, just as you are, because we share the same problem that you do."

The clearest example of this argument is found in Rom. 3:9-24. There, after pointing out the sinfulness of both non-Jews and Jews in Rom. 1:18—3:8,

---

117. The same argument regarding ignorance could be used with regard to gentiles as well. We find this in Acts 17:30, where Paul tells his hearers at the Areopagus that God was willing to overlook the "times of human ignorance" that had prevailed up until then, but now commanded all to repent. The idea of gentile ignorance is also present in passages such as Eph. 4:18 and 1 Pet. 1:14.

Paul concludes that all people, both Jews and Greeks, are under sin (v. 9). Then, in 3:10-18, Paul cites a catena of passages from the Psalms and Isaiah in support of the claim that no one is righteous or fears God, before affirming that there is no distinction before God, since all are equally accountable before him; "all have sinned and fall short of the glory of God" (Rom. 3:19, 23). Here, while the law reveals sin and shows all to be guilty, it also points to Christ and the righteousness that is given through him (3:19-21). As we can see in this passage, the argument that all are sinners and no one keeps the law could also be grounded in the Hebrew Scriptures. While neither Paul nor any of the authors of the other New Testament writings develop this argument as fully as Paul does here in Rom. 3:9-24, the basic idea does appear elsewhere. The claim that human sinfulness makes it impossible even for those who desire to observe the law is at the heart of Paul's argument in Rom. 7:7-25. In the same context, Paul affirms that the law was incapable of dealing with sin in order to bring about the righteousness it demands, and that those in the flesh cannot submit fully to God's law (Rom. 8:3-4, 7). In Gal. 6:13, Paul tells the Galatians, "Even the circumcised do not themselves obey the law." In general, the claim that no one can be justified on the basis of the law is derived from the idea that ultimately all are sinners, and thus no one can be fully obedient to the law (Acts 13:38-39; Rom. 3:20, 27; Gal. 2:15).

Plight and Solution

When Jesus' followers affirmed that *no one* kept the law, it is important to note that they did so in response to the accusation that they were living and acting in disobedience to God's will as Jews had traditionally defined that will on the basis of the law. By claiming that all inevitably sin and that no one can live in full conformity to the law, they were able not only to justify their teaching that one could be acceptable before God without observing the Mosaic law as traditionally understood, but also to argue that what God really commanded was that all submit to Jesus as Lord. It was this, rather than observance of the law, that made one righteous.

It must be stressed, however, that the idea that it was faith in Christ rather than submission to the law that led to the righteousness God desired had its origin, not in the experience of Jesus' first followers or their observation of reality, but their conviction regarding Jesus' lordship. In other words, while they certainly could have concluded that all people are sinful merely by looking around themselves at the injustice that existed in the world, it was not this that led them to argue that all are sinners and that no one can keep the law. Similarly, while they undoubtedly observed within their communities a strong commitment to loving others both inside and outside of the community and saw that the lives of many who had come to faith had been transformed, it was not this that led them to conclude that true righteousness was the result of faith in Christ rather than efforts to observe the Jewish law. Instead, it was their convictions regarding Jesus and his lordship that led them to claim that the righteousness God desired came through faith in Christ, and that what God really desired and commanded was that all follow Jesus. This in turn led them to make the claims that righteousness did not come through the law and that in reality no one could keep the law.

To some extent, this involves affirming the position put forward by E. P. Sanders in his book *Paul and Palestinian Judaism*, according to which Paul went from solution to plight: he first became convinced that salvation came through faith in Christ, and only then defined the plight in terms of the belief that "all the world—both Jew and Greek—equally stands in need of a saviour...."[118] Yet while there is certainly some truth in Sanders's view, it overlooks the fact that in Judaism the plight had *always* been defined in terms of the failure of God's people to live in conformity with his will in the way he desired. This continued to be the teaching of Jesus' followers as well. Thus, when Jesus' followers came to identify God's will with Jesus as the one who defined and embodied that will most perfectly, they could only conclude that the promises of salvation God had made were to come, not through observance of the law, but through Jesus. It was this, rather than any opposition to the law per se, that led to their views regarding the Mosaic law and human sinfulness.

Nevertheless, as we have seen, these views inevitably led to problems, tensions, and conflicts because they clashed with traditional Jewish thought on the law. Undoubtedly, it was their experience of Jesus that led Jesus' followers to the conviction that salvation was through him, rather than some preconceived notion or experience of a plight from which they needed to be saved. In this respect, like Krister Stendahl before him, Sanders was correct in maintaining that the experience of Paul was not that of Luther, who desperately sought a salvation he could not find until he looked to God's grace in Christ, rather than to his own efforts to obey God's law.[119] Where Sanders errs, however, is in affirming that Paul redefined not only the solution on the basis of his faith in Christ, but the plight as well. Contrary to what Sanders affirms, for Paul the plight was not that, because God saved through Christ, human beings must have needed a savior. Rather, Jesus' followers understood the plight in the same way that it had always been understood in Judaism: the failure of people to live in conformity with God's will. What distinguished Jesus' first followers from other Jews was that Jesus' followers identified God's will with Jesus, while other Jews identified God's will with the Mosaic law.[120]

---

118. E. P. Sanders, *Paul and Palestinian Judaism: A Comparison of Patterns of Religion* (Philadelphia: Fortress, 1977), 443.

119. See Krister Stendahl, *Paul among Jews and Gentiles and Other Essays* (Philadelphia: Fortress, 1976), 78-96.

120. While I would question Sanders's claims that Paul believed that Christ's death was "necessary for man's salvation," and that "all other possible ways of salvation are wrong" (*Paul and Palestinian Judaism*, 443), I would agree with him that Paul "did not come to his understanding of man's plight by analysing man's transgressions, and consequently he did not offer as the solution to man's plight the obvious solution for transgression: repentance and forgiveness" (499). For Paul and his fellow believers in Christ, the problem was

A proper understanding of all of these ideas also leads to the conclusion that, contrary to what we find in traditional Protestant teaching, the claim that all human beings are sinners subject to God's wrath and that none are fully righteous was not the starting-point and foundation of the argument of Jesus' first followers regarding the need for faith in him as Lord. They did not begin their proclamation by arguing that all people are under divine condemnation eternally because they have not kept God's law, and that therefore their only hope is to look to Christ for forgiveness and salvation. On the contrary, the argument that all sinned and no one kept the law fully was originally a *contextual* argument designed to counter the accusations that Jesus' followers did not keep the law themselves. For this reason, that argument appears primarily in Roman and Galatians, where Paul is responding to the criticism that he teaches others to disregard and disobey the law. Because those making this criticism must have claimed that they themselves kept the law and that other believers in Christ, including non-Jews, had to do so as well, Paul was led to insist that no one can truly keep the law.

Outside of the context of this argument, however, the idea that people *can* live righteously and even be blameless according to the law appears throughout the New Testament. Luke, for example, affirms that Zechariah and Elizabeth "were righteous before God, living blamelessly according to all the commandments and regulations of the Lord" (Luke 1:6). In Acts, Luke speaks of Cornelius as "righteous" even before he meets Peter or knows anything of Jesus (Acts 10:22). Paul considered that his conduct prior to becoming a believer had been "blameless" according to the law (Phil. 3:6). Even from the perspective of believers, then, there was a sense in which one could live righteously, observe the law, and even be blameless, with or without faith in Christ (Acts 22:12; 1 Cor. 1:8; Phil. 1:10; 2:15; 1 Thess. 2:10; 1 Tim. 3:10; Tit. 1:6-7).

The traditional Protestant argument that, because human beings of every time and place are sinners, all without exception are condemned to eternal damnation unless they come to faith in Christ is also foreign to New Testament thought. While in certain contexts Jesus' first followers claimed that no one can keep the law, this did not constitute the fundamental doctrine on the basis of which they understood Christ's work, nor was it the kind of categorical affirmation that it later became in Protestant thought. Undoubtedly, those who persistently practiced injustice and oppression were believed to be under God's wrath and condemnation, which would become fully manifest at the end of the present age. However, just as among Jews it was maintained that many righteous gentiles would be saved, so also among Jesus' first followers it was believed that there were many righteous people outside of their community and around the world whom God regarded as righteous, and who therefore might participate in some way in the salvation to come.

---

not merely that human beings needed to obtain divine *forgiveness*, but that they needed to be changed into the obedient people God desired them to be for their own good. Only then would they obtain God's forgiveness.

In Rom. 2:9-16, Paul speaks of gentiles doing what the law prescribes, even though they do not know the law, and affirms that many will be excused by their conscience and pronounced righteous at the judgment. The gentiles Paul has in mind here are not only those who become followers of Christ. This is clear from the fact that any non-Jew who became a member of the community of believers would inevitably become acquainted with the Jewish law and what it commands. Thus Paul cannot be referring to non-Jewish believers when he speaks of gentiles who do not know the law.[121] His affirmation there that "God shows no partiality" (Rom. 2:11), made in the context of the distinction between those who do evil and those who do good, points to the same conclusion. The idea that God is impartial appears repeatedly elsewhere in the New Testament in order to make the same point (Luke 20:21; Gal. 2:6; Eph. 6:9; Col. 3:25; James 2:1, 9; 1 Pet. 1:17). In Acts, Peter states this explicitly before Cornelius and his household have even heard of Jesus: "God shows no partiality, but in every nation anyone who fears him and does what is right is acceptable to him" (Acts 10:34-35). This is true, not only within the community of believers, but with regard to human beings as a whole, independently of Jesus. When Peter proclaims in Acts 4:12 that "there is no other name by which one can be saved," the idea is not that it is impossible to be saved without a conscious faith in Jesus but that, because Christ is Lord and will ultimately be the one to judge all people, everyone who will be saved will be saved through him. The idea is similar to Phil. 2:10, where Paul says that every knee will some day bend before Jesus and every tongue will confess his name.

In New Testament thought, then, the plight or problem is not that all human beings are under divine condemnation and need to be saved through Christ, but rather that neither Jews nor gentiles have been able to live in the way God commands for their own good, practicing justice and righteousness to the extent he desires. Furthermore, in continuity with their Jewish roots, Jesus' first followers would have seen this problem from a *collective* rather than an *individualistic* perspective. God's intention was not that of bringing into existence isolated individuals who would do his will on a personal level, but that of forming a *people* who would practice the justice and righteousness he desired. It was thought that the establishment of this people, who would in essence constitute a "community of communities" throughout the world, was not only God's *objective*, but also the *means* by which God would accomplish his purposes of bringing greater numbers of people to live in conformity with his will. What Paul and others who proclaimed the gospel taught was that these communities were to be built, not through the Mosaic law, but through

---

121. For a review of the discussion regarding who the gentiles who "do instinctively what the law requires" and "keep the law" in Rom. 2:14, 27 are, see Robert Jewett, *Romans: A Commentary* (Hermeneia; Minneapolis: Fortress, 2007), 212-17. I would disagree, however, with Jewett's affirmation that "Paul is here describing the status of converted Gentiles" (213). Instead, I would concur with Sanders that the gentiles mentioned "are not Gentile Christians" and that Paul is not "speaking hypothetically" in these verses (*Paul, the Law, and the Jewish People*; Philadelphia: Fortress, 1983, 125-26).

Christ. For this reason, it was important that no distinctions exist among those who formed part of them.

To Protestant ears, of course, the affirmations that all who do good will be justified (Rom. 2:9-16) and that anyone who does what is right is acceptable to God (Acts 10:35) seem to reflect the idea of salvation by works.[122] Those affirmations also raise the question of why it was necessary for God's Son to become a human being and die in order for human beings to be saved. These concerns, however, are those of later Christian theologians and not those of Paul or Jesus' first followers. For the latter, as for Jews in general, perfect obedience was never expected or required of people in order for them to be considered righteous before God. Rather, what was expected and required was that people be committed to living according to God's will. While no one could do this perfectly, such a commitment would inevitably manifest itself concretely in one's words and deeds. This was true as well for gentiles who did not know the Mosaic law, yet were committed to obeying the law written in their heart and in some sense already knew God, who had revealed himself to them (Rom. 1:19-21, 32; 2:14-15). Thus, in their case as well, if they practiced righteousness, it was due only to God's grace.

Judgment by works, therefore, was about God looking into a person's heart to see what was concealed there (*ta krupta*, Rom. 2:15); this is what one's works would reveal. As noted above, the idea that was new among Jesus' followers was not that a commitment to living in conformity with God's will was necessary to be saved, but that this will was now defined, not primarily by the law, but by Jesus as Son of God and Lord. According to New Testament thought, the reason that Jesus had come was not to make it possible for God to forgive and save sinful human beings, but to define God's will in a new and more complete way through him and to constitute a new kind of community. This community would be committed to living according to God's will and to bringing others into conformity with it as well. To believe and proclaim this did not lead to the conclusion that no one outside of that community could do God's will or be judged righteous by God. Following Paul's logic in Rom. 2:9-16, for example, it might be said that, just as gentiles could keep the law and practice the righteousness it commanded without even knowing the law, so also could those who did not know of Christ practice righteousness in the way he had taught and live according to his teaching without consciously knowing of Christ. This could be regarded as true not only of gentiles, but of Jews as well. Nevertheless, the hope was that many more people throughout

---

122. Due to their view that the basis upon which people are justified is their faith in Christ rather than the new life that results from that faith, New Testament scholars have struggled with Paul's affirmation in Rom. 2:13 that "it is not the hearers of the law who are righteous in God's sight, but the doers of the law who will be justified" (see, for example, the discussion in Richard N. Longenecker, *The Epistle to the Romans: A Commentary on the Greek Text*; NIGTC; Grand Rapids: Eerdmans, 2016, 260-70). In reality, however, there is no contradiction in affirming that one is justified by faith and that one will be justified on the basis of one's observance of the law, since the reason why "faith alone" leads to justification is that it inevitably results in a life in conformity with God's will. Of course, in Paul's thought, it is those who live under Christ's lordship who truly observe the law (Rom. 2:26; 13:8-10; Gal. 5:14).

the world might come to form part of the community of Jesus' followers so as to be brought into conformity with God's will as it had now been defined through Jesus.

* * *

As Judith Lieu has noted, it would be misleading to speak of a "parting of the ways" between Christianity and Judaism, since "Second Temple Judaism was pluralistic" and Judaism and Christianity did not exist as "discrete and enclosed systems" in New Testament times.[123] Nevertheless, on the basis of what we have seen here, it seems clear that the idea that Jesus represented the most complete and definitive expression of God's will ultimately could not co-exist with the belief that it was the Mosaic law alone that defined God's will most fully. For both Jews and non-Jews, in the end it was extremely difficult to hold Jesus and the law together due to the claims Jesus' followers were making about Jesus and the ways in which the law had come to be interpreted in second-temple Judaism. Sooner or later, those claims made most Jews feel that it was necessary to choose between following Jesus and following the law alone, independently of Jesus.

While it may not be immediately clear how the material considered in this chapter relates to the question of how Jesus' first followers came to interpret his death, in reality what we have seen has a great deal to do with that question. In the thought of Jesus' first followers, God had sent Jesus to carry out a task that in Judaism had traditionally been ascribed to the law: that of defining God's will and establishing a people who would live in conformity with that will. The consequence of Jesus' dedication to that task had been his death, yet at the same time the way in which he had given up his life for others came to be seen as the ultimate and definitive expression of everything that God's will for human beings entailed. The convictions of Jesus' first followers regarding the significance of Jesus' death were therefore intricately intertwined with the beliefs they adopted with regard to the Jewish law. On the one hand, their beliefs regarding the law exerted an important influence on the meaning they ascribed to Jesus' death, while on the other, their understanding of the significance of Jesus' death forced them to rethink their beliefs regarding the purpose of the Jewish law and the role God had intended it to play in human salvation. Furthermore, it was not only their convictions regarding Jesus the crucified Messiah that led to tensions and conflicts with their fellow Jews, but the views on the law to which those convictions had led. For these reasons, it is impossible to comprehend fully the significance Jesus' first followers ascribed to his death without understanding the ways in which they came to regard the Jewish law as well.

---

123. Judith M. Lieu, "Self-Definition vis-a-vis the Jewish Matrix," in *The Cambridge History of Christianity*, Vol. 1: *Origins to Constantine* (ed. Frances M. Young and Margaret M. Mitchell; Cambridge: Cambridge University Press, 2006), 215.

CHAPTER 8

JESUS' DEATH AND THE NEW COVENANT COMMUNITY

One of the primary arguments of the present work is that, among Jesus' first followers, Jesus' death was regarded as salvific because of the new historical reality to which it led. Those who reflected on the significance of Jesus' death did so in the context of the community of believers. The new reality they experienced there and would subsequently experience in the world to come was thought to be the result and objective of all that Jesus had done in life and death, as well as all that God had done through Jesus. From their perspective, therefore, Jesus had given up his life precisely so that this new reality in which they found themselves might come to exist.

For this reason, if we are to understand the way in which Jesus' first followers came to interpret his death, we must take a close look at the type of community that Jesus was thought to have sought to establish in life and death. This will enable us to grasp even more clearly the salvific significance they ascribed to his death, building on ideas we have seen in the previous chapters.

A NEW COVENANT

In recent years, scholars have debated the question of how important the concept of a new covenant was for Jesus' first followers. For centuries, the centrality of this concept was simply assumed and unquestioned, as is evident from the fact that "new covenant" or "new testament" was the name given to the collection of writings that the church accepted into its canon. Outside of the epistle to the Hebrews, however, the phrase *new covenant* appears in the New Testament only in the Lukan and Pauline versions of Jesus' words over the cup at the Last Supper and in 2 Cor. 3:6. Several other passages speak of a covenant in which believers participate that seems to be distinct from the covenant God was said to have made with Israel of old, yet the adjective "new" does not appear in these passages (Matt. 26:28; Mark 14:24; Gal. 4:24). While Hebrews uses the phrase *new covenant* several times (Heb. 8:6, 13; 9:15; 10:24), in each instance it derives its usage from Jer. 31:31-34, which is the only passage in the Hebrew Scriptures where that phrase appears. There, after promising to make "a new covenant with the house of Israel and the house of Judah," YHWH says it will be distinct from the covenant originally made with Israel following the Exodus, which the people broke: "I will put my law within them, and I will write it on their hearts; and I will be their God, and they shall be my people. No longer shall they teach one another, or say to each other, 'Know the Lord,' for they shall all know me, from the least of them to the greatest, says the Lord; for I will forgive their iniquity, and remember their sin no more."

Elsewhere in ancient Hebrew and Jewish literature, the only other known occurrence of *new covenant* is in the Damascus scroll of the Qumran writings, which speaks of the "new covenant in the land of Damascus" (*CD* 6:19; 8:21). The idea there seems to be quite different from that of the New Testament writings, however, and does not seem to have been derived from Jer. 31:31-34.[1] It also appears that, throughout the Scrolls, the covenant mentioned is generally "considered to be the same covenant made and reaffirmed in the Old Testament."[2]

The fact that the language of a covenant or new covenant is not prominent in the New Testament writings has led a number of scholars to argue that the concept was not as central to the thought of Jesus' first followers as has often been assumed.[3] Attempts to define clearly how this covenant was thought to relate to the previous covenant God was said to have made with Israel as well as other covenants mentioned in the Hebrew Scriptures and Jewish writings have also proven problematic.

As Richard Bautch has noted, in reality the Hebrew Scriptures speak of a variety of covenants.[4] Some of these are made between human beings themselves (Gen. 21:22-32; 26:26-31; 31:44-55; Judg. 2:1-3; 1 Sam. 18:1-5; 2 Sam. 3:6-21). Israel's God is said to have made a number of covenants with human beings collectively, as well as with particular individuals and at times their offspring as well. Obviously, the covenant considered by far the most important is that which YHWH made with Abraham, Isaac, and Jacob

---

1. See Petrus J. Gräbe, *New Covenant, New Community: The Significance of Biblical and Patristic Covenant Theology for Contemporary Understanding* (Milton Keynes: Paternoster, 2006), 58-61.

2. Ed Condra, *Salvation for the Righteous Revealed: Jesus amid Covenantal and Messianic Expectations in Second Temple Judaism* (AGJU 51; Leiden: Brill, 2002), 93. Ellen Juhl Christiansen also notes that, in the Damascus Document, "the term 'new covenant' is never opposed to an 'old covenant.' Consequently, 'new covenant' cannot be understood simply as replacement of an old covenant. Rather, 'new covenant' is used as distinct from a broken covenant" (*The Covenant in Judaism and Paul: A Study of Ritual Boundaries as Identity Markers*; AGJU 27; Leiden: Brill, 1995, 129).

3. Scot McKnight, for example, affirms that the concept of covenant was not central in Paul's thought, but remained "on the periphery of his theology," that "Jesus probably did not use the term covenant to explain his death at the last supper," and that "it is unlikely that Jesus used covenant or new covenant as hermeneutical tools to sort out the realities of God's saving work in his mission...." (*Jesus and his Death: Historiography, the Historical Jesus, and Atonement Theory*; Waco, TX: Baylor University Press, 2005, 304, 308, 312; see 293-321). James D. G. Dunn agrees with McKnight's assessment, claiming that "'covenant' was not a primary category for Paul," and that "the link between his gospel and the idea of the 'new covenant' lay somewhat on the periphery of his thought" ("Did Paul Have a Covenant Theology? Reflections on Romans 9.4 and 11.27," in *The Concept of the Covenant in the Second Temple Period*; ed. Stanley E. Porter and Jacqueline C. R. de Roo; JSJSup 71; Leiden: Brill, 2003, 297; see 287-307). According to Dunn, "talk of covenant is not central to Paul's theologizing...." (301). Stanley Porter also argues that *diathēkē* cannot always be equated with the concept of covenant in Paul's letters ("The Concept of Covenant in Paul," in *Concept of Covenant*, ed. Porter and de Roo, 269-85).

4. Richard J. Bautch, *Glory and Power, Ritual and Relationship: The Sinai Covenant in the Postexilic Period* (LHBOTS 471; London: T & T Clark, 2009), 10-11.

together with their descendants. Several passages from the Pentateuch speak of God establishing the covenant with Israel at Sinai (Exod. 24:7-8; 34:10, 27-28; Deut. 5:3; 9:9; 29:12-15), yet this was generally understood to be the same covenant made with Abraham.

The Covenant and Eschatological Hopes

Although the Hebrew Scriptures nowhere offer a precise definition of what a covenant is, several ideas are consistently associated with God's covenant with Israel. Above all, this covenant consists of a series of promises having to do primarily with the multiplication of Abraham's descendants in the land God would give them, blessings of peace and prosperity both for them and for other nations through them, and God's ongoing presence in their midst.[5] Usually, these promises are said to depend on Israel's obedience to the commandments God has given them.[6] At times, the words "covenant" and "law" or "commandments" are even used interchangeably: to keep or violate the covenant is synonymous with keeping or violating the commandments of the law.[7] These same ideas are also predominant in the second-temple Jewish literature and the rabbinic writings.[8]

As we saw in Chapter 2 of this work, in the Hebrew Scriptures, when the people break the covenant, YHWH is said to chastise them, although he is also merciful toward them, often overlooking their sins in the hope that they will repent and mend their ways (Lev. 26:25; Deut. 4:23-31; 31:16-30; Judg. 2:20-23; Jer. 11:2-11; 34:14-18). Even when YHWH chastises them, he shows them mercy, not only by alleviating their suffering, but by eventually forgiving them and restoring their fortunes (1 Chron. 16:19-21; Ps. 78:36-39; 106:43-46; Ezek. 16:60-63). It is important to stress that when Israel's God chastises the people for their sins by sending suffering and exile on them, he is not acting *contrary* to the covenant, but in *accordance* with it. Yet while in one sense the covenant is conditional upon Israel's obedience, in another sense it

---

5. See especially Gen. 12:2-3; 15:18-21; 17:2-6; Exod. 6:4-5; 19:5-6; Lev. 26:9; 1 Chron. 16:14-18; Ps. 105:8-11; Ezek. 37:25-27; Sir. 44:21-23; 2 Macc. 1:2-5.

6. See Exod. 19:5-6; 24:7-8; 34:27-28; Lev. 26:9, 25; Deut. 4:13, 23; 7:9-11; 29:1-29; Ps. 25:10-14; 103:17-18; 105:45; Jer. 11:2-11; Sir. 17:11-15; 24:23-26; 45:5; 1 Macc. 1:57, 63; 2:20-21, 27, 50.

7. See Josh. 7:11-15; Judg. 2:20-23; 1 Kgs. 19:10; 2 Kgs. 17:15, 35-40; 18:12; Ps. 78:10-11, 36-38; Isa. 24:5; Jer. 11:2-11; 22:8; 34:14-18; Ezek. 16:59; Hosea 8:1; Mal. 2:10; 1 Macc. 1:57, 63.

8. On the Jewish concept of covenant in this period in general, see Mark Adam Elliott, *The Survivors of Israel: A Reconsideration of the Theology of Pre-Christian Judaism* (Grand Rapids: Eerdmans, 2000), 245-307; Lester Grabbe, "Did All Jews Look Alike? 'Covenant' in Philo and Josephus in the Context of Second Temple Judaic Religion," in *Concept of Covenant*, ed. Porter and de Roo, 251-66. Grabbe lists a number of Jewish texts from the second-temple period that demonstrate that "[s]ometimes 'covenant' is simply another term to be used alongside and interchangeably with divine law and statutes, and the various elements of Jewish belief and practice" (254). Grabbe concludes his examination of the subject by observing, "One can only conclude that the covenant concept was not very important to some significant writers in Second Temple Judaism.... Both Philo and Josephus appear to have had the same opinion as some other writers of the period: covenant was not that significant to them as a means of conceptualizing or expressing their religious beliefs" (264, 266). For a summary of the idea of covenant reflected in the Qumran writings, see Craig A. Evans, "Covenant in the Qumran Literature," in *Concept of Covenant*, ed. Porter and de Roo, 55-80. On the understanding of covenant in rabbinic thought, see Alan F. Segal, "Covenant in Rabbinic Writings," *SR* 14 (1985): 53-62.

is *unconditional*: even when YHWH punishes Israel and destroys a portion of the people, ultimately he intends to put an end to that punishment and bless them.[9] For this to happen, however, the condition of obedience must still be met. What the Hebrew Scriptures promise is that YHWH himself will bring about in his people the obedience he demands by giving them his Spirit, creating a new heart in them, and writing his law in their interior (Isa. 59:19-21; Jer. 31:31-34; 32:40; Ezek. 11:19-20; 36:26-27; 2 Macc. 1:2-5).

For the most part, the New Testament writings speak of this same covenant with Israel being fulfilled through Jesus. In Luke 1, Mary and Zechariah rejoice that God has remembered the covenant and the promises he made to Abraham and his children (vv. 46-55, 68-79). These promises have to do with bringing down Israel's oppressors and enemies and exalting the lowly so that God's people may serve him in holiness and justice. Though it is not said there that this takes place through Jesus, such an idea clearly seems to be implied. The most important promise mentioned, of course, is that of a savior in Jesus (Luke 1:69; cf. 2:11). The claim that Jesus is the Messiah promised of old runs throughout the New Testament and is associated not only with the covenant God was said to have made with David, but the covenant made with all of Israel as well. Paul even argues that Jesus himself was the "seed" promised to Abraham (Gal. 3:16). At the same time, of course, all believers are the seed or children of Abraham (Gal. 3:7-9, 29; Rom. 4:1-21; 9:4-7). The inclusion of people from all nations in the community of God's people thus represents the fulfillment of God's promise to Abraham that all nations and families of the earth would be blessed through him.

While the New Testament writings regard the promises associated with the covenant God made with Israel as finding fulfillment through Christ, they also reinterpret those promises in ways that represent a vision that is somewhat distinct from that of the Hebrew Scriptures. Above all, the "life" that God originally promised through the covenant made with Israel came to be understood in terms of a new age to come, which would follow upon the resurrection of the dead and the final judgment. The Pentateuch, of course, never speaks of the dead being raised and judged individually. Instead, it presents God's promises in terms of God's people enjoying peace and prosperity in the present world. As scholars such as N. T. Wright have stressed, the hope of Jesus' first followers and that of many other Jews in antiquity was not that of an eternal life in an ethereal heavenly realm, but rather the transformation of the present world into a new condition, together with all those who would

---

9. On the conditional/unconditional distinction, see Bautch, *Glory and Power*, 26-32. Mark Elliott distinguishes between an "*unconditional*" view of covenant, which emphasizes the aspect of gift or givenness," according to which it was "*inviolable* or undefilable, inasmuch as no sin could break it," and the *conditional* nature of the covenant, since it depended on "the performance of certain basic duties or requirements" (*Survivors*, 247-48). Jákob Jocz argues that the "conditionless covenant" was a prophetic innovation, and that the rabbis recognized both the conditional and unconditional aspects of the covenant (*The Covenant: A Theology of Human Destiny*; Grand Rapids: Eerdmans, 1968, 27, 39). As we saw in Chapter 2, numerous biblical texts make it clear that being in the covenant was not a guarantee of salvation, since the covenant stipulated that those who disobeyed could be subject to suffering, hardships, and even destruction when they sinned.

live in that new world for the ages to come.[10] A few New Testament passages speak in terms of the redeemed inhabiting the promised land and a new Jerusalem (Heb. 11:10-16; 12:22-23; 13:14; Rev. 3:12; 21:1—22:5; cf. Gal. 4:21-31), yet these are viewed as realities that are not to be identified fully with the land and the Jerusalem of the present age.[11] Although this new land and new Jerusalem are to exist on earth, they are viewed as already existing in heaven, from where they will descend when God brings about the promised redemption through Christ. Other New Testament writings also speak of a salvation that already exists in heaven, but will one day be manifested on earth (Col. 1:5; 3:2-4; 1 Pet. 1:4; cf. Matt. 25:34; 2 Cor. 5:1-5; Phil. 3:20-21).

For the most part, however, the promises that Jesus' first followers hoped to see fulfilled are described only in very general and broad terms. The primary hope is described simply in terms of *zoē*, "life," or *zoē aiōnion*, which is probably best translated as "life of the age to come" rather than "eternal life."[12] Nowhere in the New Testament do we find a description of what this life was thought to entail. Paul and others speak of the glory to come or an inheritance to be received.[13] Hebrews looks forward to the eschatological "rest" (Heb. 4:1-11), while Peter in Acts speaks of the "times of refreshing" to come (Acts 3:20). Paul compares the resurrection body of believers to that of Christ (Phil. 3:20-21), yet in his most detailed discussion of the subject, he simply says that the resurrected body of believers will be heavenly, glorious, spiritual, imperishable, and immortal (1 Cor. 15:35-58). Other passages also speak in terms of immortality (Rom. 2:7; 1 Cor. 15:53-54; 2 Tim. 1:10; cf. Luke 20:36; John 4:26; 6:50; 1 Pet. 1:23).

---

10. N. T. Wright, *The New Testament and the People of God*, Vol. 1 of *Christian Origins and the Question of God* (Minneapolis: Fortress, 1992), 285, 299-301.

11. On this idea in Paul's thought, see William Horbury, "Land, Sanctuary and Worship," in *Early Christian Thought in its Jewish Context* (ed. John Barclay and John Sweet; Cambridge: Cambridge University Press, 1996), 219-22. Lois K. Fuller Dow notes that, in most of the New Testament writings, the "Zion theology" found in the Hebrew Scriptures and second-temple Jewish literature "remains an intact body of ideas, but these ideas become detached from physical, earthly Jerusalem and adhere to something else instead.... The New Testament writers do not see themselves as contradicting the older form of the tradition. To them, the earthly Land, Temple and city were valued but temporary pictures foreshadowing the reality that had now arrived in Jesus Christ.... Without exception, the New Testament documents depict a shift in the application of Zion theology from earthly Jerusalem to Jesus, the church and the heavenly Jerusalem" (*Images of Zion: Biblical Antecedents for the New Jerusalem*; NTM 26; Sheffield: Sheffield Academic Press, 2010, 139-40, 178; see 139-79). Fuller Dow notes that Philo also allegorized or spiritualized the promises regarding the land (96). For a comparison with the writings of Qumran on these ideas, see Adela Yarbro Collins, "The Dream of a New Jerusalem at Qumran," in *The Bible and the Dead Sea Scrolls: The Second Princeton Symposium on Judaism and Christian Origins* (ed. James H. Charlesworth; Waco, TX: Baylor University Press, 2006), 1:231-54.

12. See, for example, Matt. 18:8-9; 19:16-17, 29; John 3:15-16, 36; 5:21; 10:28; Acts 11:18; 13:46; Rom. 2:7; 6:22-23; 1 Tim. 1:16; 2 Tim. 1:10; 1 John 2:25; Jude 21. On this point, see also Don Garlington, *Faith, Obedience and Perseverance: Aspects of Paul's Letter to the Romans* (WUNT 79; Tübingen: J. C. B. Mohr, 1994), 57.

13. See, for example, Matt. 19:29; Acts 20:32; Rom. 2:7-10; 8:18-21; 2 Cor. 4:17; Eph. 1:11, 18; Col. 1:12, 27; 3:24; 2 Tim. 2:10; Heb. 9:15; 1 Pet. 1:3-4; 5:1. Mark Forman has argued convincingly that the language of inheritance in Paul's writings is "counter-imperial" in that it challenges the Roman ideology that "there would be peace, stability and abundance through the actions and guidance of the emperor" (*The Politics of Inheritance in Romans*; SNTSMS 148; Cambridge: Cambridge University Press, 2011, 231-32). Forman also stresses that Paul's affirmation in Rom. 4:13 that, as children of Abraham, believers will "inherit the world" should not be "read in spiritualized and individualized terms," as has been common in the past (105).

Paul anticipates the day when the creation as a whole will be set free from its bondage (Rom. 8:20-23) and claims that Christ will hand the kingdom over to God, who will be "all in all" (1 Cor. 15:24-28; cf. Matt. 19:28), yet precisely what he expects this new world to look like is not clear. The author of 2 Peter looks forward to the "new heavens and new earth" described in Isa. 65:17 and 66:22, yet this imagery is also vague (2 Pet. 3:10-13). The only detailed description the New Testament offers regarding existence in the life to come is that found in Rev. 21:1—22:5, which describes the heavenly Jerusalem that is to descend to earth. Nevertheless, due to the symbolic language employed throughout Revelation, it is not clear to what extent the author intended this imagery to be taken literally.

For the most part, then, it appears that Jesus first' followers continued to look forward to the fulfillment of the same promises that many Jews of their day associated with the covenant God had made with Israel. What distinguished their beliefs from other Jews was that they seem to have disassociated the promises of a return to the land and a restoration of Jerusalem from the holy land and the Jerusalem of their own day, regarding these instead as heavenly realities that would be established on earth. They also seem to present a more universal perspective that embraces creation as a whole and emphasizes the inclusion of people from all different backgrounds and nationalities. In addition, Jesus' first followers envisaged Jesus as being at the center of the fulfillment of these promises and the new reality that would come to exist. Jesus would be the eschatological judge as well as the king who would reign over all, and his followers would sit at table to feast not only with Abraham and the patriarchs, but also with Jesus (Matt. 8:11; 26:29; Luke 22:28-30). In spite of these differences, however, it would be difficult to argue that the promises that Jesus' followers hoped to see fulfilled were not those of the covenant made with Israel of old, but entirely new promises associated with a new covenant made through Jesus. In this regard, Scot McKnight rightly notes that the expectation "is for a new start with a new people shaped by a new covenant—but it should be noted that this newness, because it is in fundamental continuity with the old, is a renewed covenant (cf. Lam. 5:21). It is development, not evolution; it is both continuity and discontinuity."[14]

Old Covenant and New

As in the Hebrew Scriptures and Jewish thought, the New Testament regards obedience to God's will as constituting the condition for attaining the covenant promises. One must remain faithful and steadfast, practicing justice, love, and mercy in order to attain the life, glory, and immortality that God will grant to all who obey him (Matt. 7:21; 25:31-46; Luke 12:35-48; Eph. 5:1-20; 2 Tim. 2:12; 1 Pet. 5:8-10; Rev. 2:10). As we have seen in detail in Chapter 7 of this study, however, this obedience is redefined in terms of following

---

14. McKnight, *Jesus and his Death*, 313-14.

Jesus and doing God's will as it has been revealed through him, rather than living in strict accordance with all of the prescriptions found in the Mosaic law. Because such obedience involves practicing the principles underlying the Mosaic law in accordance with Jesus' teaching, the commandment that believers observe is not a new commandment, but the same one given of old according to the covenant made with Israel (1 John 2:7; 2 John 5).

Nevertheless, the fact that Jesus' first followers came to view obedience to God's will as inseparable from submission to Jesus as Lord and Son of God meant that eventually they would no longer be seen by other Jews as simply living according to the same covenant that God had ratified at Mount Sinai under Moses. The acceptance of uncircumcised non-Jews into the community of those who regarded themselves as God's people would also appear to constitute a departure from the covenant made with Israel, since physical circumcision was the visible sign of that covenant. It was probably not long, therefore, before Jesus' followers came to see themselves as living under a *new* covenant centered upon Jesus rather than under the same covenant God had made with Abraham. This idea would be reinforced by the attitudes of Jews outside of the community who inevitably came to accuse Jesus' followers of abandoning the covenant with Israel as most Jews had traditionally understood it. Again, of course, Jesus' followers would probably have rejected such an accusation, at least initially, claiming to be the rightful heirs of that covenant. Yet their focus on Jesus rather than the Mosaic law would have made it necessary for even them to acknowledge that, even if they continued to live under the covenant made with Israel, that covenant had been redefined so radically that it might also be considered a new covenant. And once language of a *new* covenant began, it inevitably made it necessary to speak of an *old* covenant as well.[15]

From the start, of course, these ideas would be relatively unclear and undefined, resulting in ambiguities and even confusion. If Jesus represented the fulfillment of the covenant made with Israel as the promised Messiah through whom all of God's other promises made to Israel would be fulfilled as well, it would seem inappropriate to speak of a new covenant established through Jesus, since the promises involved were not new or different. Yet the fact that neither Jesus' followers nor other Jews considered that those who belonged to the community of believers in Jesus—particularly those of non-Jewish origin—were simply living according to the covenant made with Abraham and ratified under Moses would also require that they be regarded as living under a *new* covenant. Furthermore, when obedience to God's will was redefined around Jesus and the promises originally made to Israel came to be seen as centered

---

15. Christiansen rightly notes that, in modern usage, the adjective "old" is generally seen as something "out-of-fashion that needs a replacement," whereas in antiquity the same adjective "can have a positive value of antique, venerable.... 'New' can be either fresh, modern, or untried, inmature.... The values of 'new' and 'old' in the New Testament need to be seen in the perspective that *'new' is not necessarily better than 'old'*" (*Covenant*, 255-56). Therefore, according to Christiansen, when Paul speaks of the new covenant in 2 Cor. 3:4-6, he simply has in mind that "*a new dimension* to the Sinai covenant has been added" (258).

upon Jesus and the future role that he would play in the fulfillment of those promises, God might be said to have made new promises through Jesus that were in some ways distinct from the promises associated with the covenant with Israel.

This ambiguity is evident in Paul's writings. In the context of his comparison between the children of the slave Hagar and those of the free woman Sarah, Paul speaks of two covenants (Gal. 4:24; see 4:21-31). He associates the first of these with Mount Sinai and the earthly Jerusalem, and the second with the heavenly Jerusalem. Yet, earlier in the same letter, he speaks of Christ as the fulfillment of the promises made to Abraham and claims that the law, which was given 430 years after the covenant made with Abraham, does not annul that covenant (Gal. 3:15-18). Nevertheless, in Gal. 4:21-31 he does not speak of a second covenant made at Sinai, nor does he seem to associate the law with a second covenant in this passage or elsewhere in his letters. For Paul, the new covenant is that which Christ instituted at the Last Supper (1 Cor. 11:25), of which Paul also serves as minister (2 Cor. 3:6). Shortly after speaking of the new covenant in this latter passage, Paul alludes to the "old covenant," which he identifies with Moses (2 Cor. 3:14-15). In Rom. 9:4, Paul speaks of the "covenants"—in the plural—that belong to Israel. Then, later on in the same letter, he combines Isa. 59:20-21 with Isa. 27:9 to present God as promising, "This will be my covenant with them, when I take away their sins" (Rom. 11:27). In this last passage, there seems to be only one covenant, which will be fulfilled at the end, when "all Israel will be saved" (Rom. 11:26).

Needless to say, it is difficult to reconcile these different passages with one another. James Dunn notes that the hope of Jer. 31:31-34 "is for the law to be written in the heart, in other words, not for a different covenant, but for a more effective version of the old one," and finds this idea present in both the Damascus document (*CD*) of Qumran and the thought of Paul, for whom "the new covenant was all about a more effective way of fulfilling the old covenant."[16] Dunn also argues that for Paul there are "not two covenants, two religions, two different peoples (Jews and Christians) but one covenant, one religion, one people, Israel."[17] Ellen Juhl Christiansen similarly rejects the notion that, in Paul's thought, "the 'new covenant' replaces the 'old covenant.'" Instead, for Paul, the new covenant "is the same 'old' covenant but given a new dimension."[18]

This same ambiguity is reflected in the different versions of Jesus' words over the cup at the Last Supper that appear in the Synoptics and 1 Corinthians.

---

16. James D. G. Dunn, "Two Covenants or One? The Interdependence of Jewish and Christian Identity," in *Geschichte–Tradition–Reflexion: Festschrift für Martin Hengel zum 70. Geburtstag* (ed. Hubert Cancik, Hermann Lichtenberger, and Peter Schäfer; Tübingen: J. C. B. Mohr, 1996), 116.

17. Ibid., 118.

18. Christiansen, *Covenant*, 324, 269. William S. Campbell similarly writes with regard to Paul's thought, "It is more appropriate in my opinion to speak of a renewed rather than of a new covenant" ("Covenantal Theology and Participation in Christ: Pauline Perspectives on Transformation," in *Paul and Judaism: Crosscurrents in Pauline Exegesis and the Study of Jewish-Christian Relations*; ed. Reimund Bieringer and Didier Pollefeyt; LNTS 463; London: T & T Clark, 2012, 49).

Whereas Luke and Paul present Jesus as speaking of "the new covenant in my blood" (Luke 22:20; 1 Cor. 11:25), in Matthew and Mark, Jesus refers only to "my blood of the covenant" (Matt. 26:28; Mark 14:24). This latter phrase may be regarded as a Hebraism that should be translated: "the blood of my covenant," which would imply that Jesus' covenant is distinct from the covenant made with Israel. No matter which of these translations is preferred, even in the accounts of Matthew and Mark, Jesus seems to be presented as establishing a new and distinct covenant with his disciples rather than ratifying the covenant made with Israel. In that case, the idea of a new covenant is implied even if it is not stated explicitly, as Luke and Paul do. There is no passage in the New Testament that argues, as the second-century *Epistle of Barnabas* does, that there is only one covenant, and that it never belonged to the Jews, but only to the Christians.[19]

Most scholars would agree that Jer. 31:31-34 influenced the tradition Luke and Paul cite regarding Jesus' words over the cup at the Last Supper. As noted above, in Hebrews the passage from Jeremiah is cited several times so as to place the idea of a new covenant at the heart of the author's argument (Heb. 7:22; 8:6—9:4; 10:15-17). Both the Fourth Gospel and Paul's letter to the Romans seem to allude to Jer. 31:31-34 as well (John 6:45; Rom. 11:27). The metaphor Paul uses in 2 Cor. 3:1-6 is slightly different from that of Jer. 31:31-34, since for Paul it is not the law that is written as a letter on tablets of human hearts rather than tablets of stone, but the Corinthians themselves. Nevertheless, he may have had this passage in mind there, particularly since he alludes to the new covenant explicitly. In 2 Cor. 3:1-6, Paul also seems to be alluding to Ezek. 11:19-20 and 36:26-27, where God says that he will put a new spirit in his people, removing their heart of stone and giving them a heart of flesh so that they may keep his statutes and ordinances. The second of these passages also mentions God putting *his own* spirit within his people.[20] These passages became particularly important for the author of the *Epistle of Barnabas* and Justin Martyr in the second century.[21]

If Jesus' followers looked to Jer. 31:31-34 to develop their beliefs regarding a new covenant, the idea that God would bring about in his people the obedience he desired by transforming their hearts would no doubt be identified as one of the characteristics of this new covenant, particularly if Jer. 31:31-34 was seen in connection with passages such as Ezek. 11:19-20 and 36:26-27.

---

19. See Andrew Chester, "Messianism, Torah and Early Christian Tradition," in *Tolerance and Intolerance in Early Judaism and Christianity* (ed. Graham N. Stanton and Guy G. Stroumsa; New York: Cambridge University Press, 1998), 327; Graham N. Stanton, "Other Early Christian Writings: 'Didache', Ignatius, 'Barnabas', Justin Martyr," in *Early Christian Thought*, ed. Barclay and Sweet, 183.

20. See Frank Matera, *II Corinthians: A Commentary* (NTL; Louisville, KY: Westminster John Knox, 2003), 79-80. Hebrews 10:16-22 also seems to relate the passage from Ezekiel 36 to Jer. 31:31-34, though the allusion in Heb. 10:22 seems to be to Ezek. 36:25, which appears immediately before the ideas just mentioned: "I will sprinkle clean water upon you, and you shall be clean from all your uncleannesses, and from all your idols I will cleanse you."

21. On the idea of a new covenant in the thought of *Barnabas*, Justin Martyr, Irenaeus of Lyons, Clement of Alexandria, and Mileto of Sardis, see Gräbe, *New Covenant*, 151-74.

In fact, as we have noted previously, one of the promises that many Jews associated with the covenant was that some day Israel's God would act to bring about in his people the obedience commanded for their own good. By observing the law, they would finally be able to enjoy the blessings God promised for obedience to the commandments. The notion that those who follow Jesus attain a greater obedience and righteousness than those who merely observe literally the Mosaic commandments also seems to have been part of the Jesus tradition, as we saw in Chapter 7. Whether or not Jesus' first followers thought primarily in terms of the fulfillment of the covenant made with Israel through Abraham and Moses or the establishment of a new covenant, therefore, they undoubtedly associated both of these ideas with that of a new obedience.[22]

JESUS' FOLLOWERS AS A DISTINCT COMMUNITY

The fact that Jesus' first Jewish followers formed their own communities that transcended family relationships and were to some extent distinct from the communities to which they had belonged previously would inevitably have led them to see themselves as following an ethic that set them apart from other Jews. From the start of Jesus' Galilean ministry, the emphases in Jesus' teaching as well as the redefinition of relationships around him would have led his first followers to understand themselves as members of a distinct community practicing a more demanding obedience to God, particularly in the case of those who had left their homes to follow him. In rural areas such as Galilee, tensions and divisions between families, clans, and villages tended to be deep-seated and long-lasting. Jesus' teaching sought to overcome this, as his extensive use of family language demonstrates. Jesus' followers were to cross traditional boundaries and reach out to those with whom they would normally not associate, including the marginalized and the social pariahs, working to bring about reconciliation so as to redefine traditional relationships and gather people together in new communities that would be different from others.

These ideas seem to be stressed in Q, which may constitute the oldest components of the Jesus tradition to which we have access. John Kloppenborg, for example, notes the distinctions between the ethos of Jesus and his followers and that of his opponents in Q, as well as Q's inversion of social roles and its counter-ethic that "calls into question the integrity of the most basic social bonds of family, clan, and village."[23] Similarly, Richard Horsley argues that the "Q people" understood themselves over against other Jewish groups and aimed at "restoration of more cooperative local social-economic relations."[24]

---

22. On the new obedience associated with the new covenant in the Hebrew Scriptures, see Bautch, *Glory and Power*, 31-32.

23. John Kloppenborg, "The Sayings Gospel Q and the Quest of the Historical Jesus," *HTR* 89 (1996): 337-38, 342.

24. Richard A. Horsley, "The Q People: Renovation, not Radicalism," *Cont* 1 (1991): 57-63.

While their movement sought to revitalize local social relationships and did not seek to form any type of "sectarian enclave" that would be separate from Israel, nevertheless their message and activity distinguished them from others in the areas where they worked, attracting opposition and generating tensions and conflicts within the local communities.[25] According to Horsley, another distinguishing characteristic of the Q people was their itinerancy. Like Jesus, they seem to have gone from village to village to pursue actively their social program. To the extent that the Q people are identified with Jesus' first followers, it seems that their efforts to bring families, clans, and communities together also resulted in their being regarded as a separate group that followed an alternative ethic. Even though they claimed that this ethic was rooted in Israel's ancient traditions, others saw it as promoting division rather than unity.

While the ethic ascribed to Jesus in Q undoubtedly stresses the ways in which Jesus' followers were to relate to one another in their community life, curiously neither Q nor the Gospels in general present Jesus as attempting to establish and organize separate communities of followers during his ministry.[26] Rather, as Horsley notes, Jesus and his followers simply reach out to all Israel and proclaim the need to put into practice the values and principles of the reign of God as defined by Jesus. In the Gospels and throughout the New Testament, the basis upon which people are to be judged is not their membership in the community of Jesus' followers, but their adherence to those values and principles in their life and conduct. This observation is significant in that the values and principles proclaimed and embodied by Jesus were seen as taking priority over traditional loyalties within the families, villages, and other communities in which they were active. Jesus' followers were to resist any calls to place loyalty to certain people, institutions, or authorities above loyalty to those values and principles. It might be said that loyalty to any particular persons, whether or not they were members of the community of Jesus' followers, was to take the form of submitting unconditionally, not to those persons themselves, but to the values and principles associated with the reign of God proclaimed by Jesus. Any relation that was not based on those values and principles was not in accordance with God's will as defined through Jesus.

When Jesus' followers came to establish themselves in Jerusalem and other urban centers, their communities would tend to take on a slightly different character.[27] In those urban contexts, individuals were often less attached

---

25. David Seeley finds in Q 6:22-23 and 7:31-35 evidence for the idea that, among the Q people, "the only boundary operative is that which separates the addressees from conventional, boundary-making society. Since the Q people stand on the far side of that boundary, they are a threat to the boundary-making procedures that constitute '*norm*alcy,' and are thus a threat to society" ("Blessings and Boundaries: Interpretations of Jesus' Death in Q," *NTS* 38 [1992]: 139).

26. Christopher M. Tuckett observes that Q does not pay much attention to the incorporation of non-Jews into the community of Jesus' followers or to the idea of a gentile mission ("Q and the Gentiles," in *Attitudes to Gentiles in Ancient Judaism and Early Christianity*, ed. David C. Sim and James S. McLaren; London: T & T Clark, 2013, 126-37).

27. For a background to the urban milieu of the first Christ-confessing communities and the social interactions that characterized them, see Ekkehard W. Stegemann and Wolfgang Stegemann, *The Jesus*

to family, particularly when they had left their families behind to migrate from rural areas. This detachment from their family and home led them to look to integrate themselves into communities that might serve as their new or alternative "family." Even in the case of entire families, in an urban context these families would have the alternative of forming relationships with other families and groups in ways that were not possible in rural villages, where the options for forming new relationships were much more limited. Those who came to associate themselves with a community of Jesus' followers, therefore, would also see themselves as distinct from other Jews and regard the community of believers as a second or alternative family.

In the urban centers of the diaspora, of course, family and community ties among Jews tended to be quite strong. Nevertheless, in these contexts there would also be tensions and rivalries between different families and groups within the larger Jewish community. While certainly not all Jews who came to identify themselves as Jesus' followers would encounter opposition from their families, friends, and acquaintances, their participation in the community of believers would to some extent set them apart from Jews who were not Jesus' followers. At times entire families would join the community of Jesus' followers. Once more, however, the defining characteristic of these communities would be their commitment to living in the way Jesus had taught: they were to practice inclusion and solidarity and seek to live in harmony with all, including those outside of the community. The core value that Jesus had constantly preached was love for all, even for one's enemies, and this concern for the well-being of others would therefore be the criterion upon which everything in the community would be judged. When conflicts with family members and other social groups arose, Jesus' followers would also be expected to consider their first allegiance to be to their sisters and brothers in Christ. As Jesus had taught, when forced to choose between their family and Jesus, his followers were to choose him, which also meant choosing the community of believers over their family. Once again, allegiance to the values and principles embodied by Jesus took priority, yet at the same time that allegiance involved seeking the well-being of all, including one's family, by obeying those principles rather than obeying particular persons.

These same emphases would also make the communities of Jesus' followers different from other Jewish groups that defined themselves on the basis of their distinct beliefs and practices, such as the Pharisees, Sadducees, and Essenes. While these groups stressed the need to obey the law according to the interpretations that were particular to each, the fact that for Jesus' followers everything revolved around Jesus rather than the law would lead the community of his followers to define itself differently. The strict rules regarding membership, purity, and community life found in the writings

---

Movement: A Social History of its First Century, trans. O. C. Dean Jr. (Minneapolis: Fortress, 1999), 264-66; Wayne A. Meeks, *The First Urban Christians: The Social World of the Apostle Paul* (New Haven, CT: Yale University Press, 1983), 9-50.

from Qumran, for example, would have given the communities associated with those writings a very different feel than that which we can imagine in the communities of Jesus' followers. Just as Jesus had often set aside the literal observance of the law in order to care for human needs and seek the well-being of others, his followers would tend to focus less on the observance of purity regulations and more on the principles Jesus was thought to have taught and embodied. Even if the kind of fraternal love they preached did not always become a reality in their communities, at least it represented the ideal and the core value for them in a way that distinguished them from other Jewish communities.

We can see this not only in the Synoptic Gospels, which repeatedly stress the importance of things such as love, forgiveness, and solidarity among Jesus' disciples, but in the other New Testament writings that offer us insights into the relations between Jesus' first Jewish followers, before the incorporation of non-Jews into the community. The commands to love one's enemies, refrain from judging others, forgive one another, share one's possessions, practice solidarity, and put following Jesus ahead of everything else, including one's family, all appear in Q.[28] Q also gives evidence of active opposition to the communities of Jesus' followers on the part of other Jewish groups and communities (Luke 10:13-15; 11:29-32, 37-54).[29]

In the first chapters of Acts, Luke particularly stresses the solidarity among Jesus' first followers. Twice he offers summary descriptions of the way they lived in community with one another: they gathered to pray, worship, eat, and have fellowship with one another, and shared their possessions, especially with the needy (Acts 2:42-47; 4:32-35). Undoubtedly, this is an idealized picture of the life of the first believers, yet what matters is precisely that it is presented as the ideal and the norm to which they were to conform. While Luke's accounts regarding Ananias and Sapphira and the tensions between the "Hellenists" and "Hebrews" over the distribution of food provide evidence that the unity and solidarity that Luke describes in Acts did not always exist, those accounts also serve to demonstrate that the failure to practice such unity and solidarity was seen as unacceptable (Acts 5:1-10; 6:1-6). The fact that Paul's letters and other New Testament writings repeatedly stress the same need to be in solidarity with others in the community of believers, not only on a local level but also within the empire as a whole, leaves no doubt that this was an emphasis found in the first communities of Jesus' followers from the start. They were to share their goods with those in their midst and far away, and care for those in need.

To whatever extent such unity and solidarity actually became a reality in those communities, the constant stress upon those core values inevitably must have been reflected in practice to a considerable extent. Although the idea

---

28. See Luke 6:27-42; 9:1-6, 57-62; 11:4; 12:33-34; 14:26-27, 33; 17:3-4.

29. On these emphases in Q, see especially Richard A. Horsley, "Q and Jesus: Assumptions, Approaches and Analyses," *Semeia* 55 (1991): 184-205.

of sharing one's possessions with others in a community was by no means unique to Jesus' followers, there seem to have been certain differences between their communities and those of other Jewish groups. Those who joined the communities described in the Qumran writings, for example, were expected to donate all of their goods to the community. In fact, in at least some of those communities, the surrender of one's possessions was obligatory.[30] In this way, those communities accumulated a great deal of wealth.

In contrast, the ideal in the New Testament is seen in terms of distributing the resources to the needy and not storing those resources or accumulating wealth (Matt. 6:19-21, 24; Luke 12:15-21; 19:1-10; Acts 2:44-45; 4:34-35; 1 Tim. 6:17-19; James 5:1-8). The evidence we have regarding Jesus' first followers also indicates that, when they became members of the community of believers, the sharing of their possessions was voluntary. One was not required or pressured to give, but rather all were *exhorted* to do so generously on the basis of Jesus' teaching and example. One was also free to give as much or as little as one wished. In Acts 5, for example, Ananias was reproached, not because he had given the community only part of the proceeds of the land he had sold—Peter stresses that it was entirely acceptable for him to do so if he wished—, but for deceiving the community into believing that he had given all when he had only given part (Acts 5:1-10). When Paul exhorts the Corinthians to be generous in contributing for the needs of the community of believers in Jerusalem, he stresses that they are not to act "reluctantly or under compulsion." Rather, they are to be motivated by a spirit of solidarity and gratitude to God for all that they have graciously received through Christ, who became poor for their sakes. In that way, they will show the genuineness of their love (2 Cor. 8:8-9; 9:7-15; cf. 1 Cor. 16:1-3; Rom. 15:25-27).

Among Jesus' followers, then, the sharing of one's possessions with the community was seen as an act of love, rather than a requirement imposed on those who wished to form part of the community. Whereas in the Qumran communities the donation of one's possessions emphasized the need for each member to place himself and all he had in subjection to the community as a whole—including particularly the leaders who administered the community's resources, a task in which those individuals who became full members apparently had little say[31]—, in the communities of Jesus' followers the focus was instead on reflecting concretely their solidarity and love for others in

---

30. See especially 1QS 6:19-24. On this point and the community of goods reflected in the Qumran writings, see especially John P. Meier, *A Marginal Jew: Rethinking the Historical Jesus*, Vol. 3: *Companions and Competitors* (New York: Doubleday, 2001), 512-13, 521; Catherine M. Murphy, *Wealth in the Dead Sea Scrolls and in the Qumran Community* (STDJ 40; Leiden: Brill, 2002), 117-61; Hartmut Stegemann, *The Library of Qumran on the Essenes, Qumran, John the Baptist, and Jesus* (Grand Rapids: Eerdmans, 1998), 176-90.

31. In the conclusions to her work, Murphy notes that in the Damascus Document, "The author's community is to separate from society.... Their own alternative community provides remedies to the ills of the broader society. The Examiner will scrutinize and loosen the 'chains that bind' those who enter... and all of one's finances come under the purview of the Examiner, who oversees especially those transactions where sectarian and non-sectarian economies mingle, such as marriage, divorce, and kinship obligations" (*Wealth*, 448).

voluntary fashion, with each member deciding what, when, and how to contribute.[32] This also means that what mattered most was the well-being of each individual member. Rather than merely expecting each individual to make sacrifices for the good of the community, the community was also expected to make sacrifices for the good of each individual. In this way, the priority was not the community itself, but the needs of the members who made it up.

The stress on the acceptance of the marginalized, care for the sick, and the inclusion of women that we find throughout the Gospel accounts and other New Testament writings must also have reflected itself in the community life of Jesus' first Jewish followers. While it is unlikely that the same kind of gender equity that is valued today was characteristic of their communities, it is noteworthy that from the start, the entrance rite for women was apparently the same as it was for men. Several passages from Luke, John, and Acts also point to an openness to Samaritans that was uncharacteristic of other Jewish groups of the day (Luke 10:25-38; 17:11-19; John 4:1-42; Acts 1:8; 8:1-14, 25; 9:31; 15:3). Whether or not Jesus actually responded favorably to non-Jews, such as the Syro-Phoenician woman and the Roman centurion, the Gospel accounts of those encounters provide evidence that his first followers saw such openness to outsiders and non-Jews as a practice that they were to follow in obedience to Jesus (Matt. 8:5-13; 15:21-28; Mark 7:24-30; Luke 7:2-9; cf. Acts 10:1). It is noteworthy that, on the basis of the evidence we have, many of these characteristics do not seem to have been particularly common among other Jewish communities in Jerusalem, Judea, and Galilee.

There is therefore good reason to believe that Jesus' first Jewish followers would have understood themselves as a distinct community that practiced love, forgiveness, inclusion, and solidarity in ways that distinguished them from other Jewish groups. This would include believers not only in Jerusalem but also in Galilee and other diaspora communities around the empire in which they established themselves. To the extent that they saw themselves as living under a new covenant or as fulfilling the original covenant with Israel in ways that other Jews did not, they would have associated the concept of covenant with a new and distinct type of obedience that went beyond the Mosaic law and distinguished them from other Jews, even though they no doubt often failed to live up to their ideals and at times were even further from those ideals than other Jews.

The Incorporation of Gentiles and the Redefinition of Israel

When the communities of Jesus' followers began to incorporate non-Jews into their membership, the claim that those communities were characterized

---

32. Undoubtedly, in Qumran, the surrendering of one's possessions to the community was seen as act of love, and the goods received served to support those in need within the community (see Murphy, *Wealth*, 449, 453, 455). However, the manner in which each member was to manifest his love for others was defined for him, rather than being something that each member determined for himself or herself, as in the communities of Jesus' followers.

by a new obedience that distinguished them from other groups could become even stronger. The reason for this is that the comparisons made would no longer involve contrasting one group of Jews with another, but rather contrasting the lives of gentile believers in Christ with their former lives and the lives of gentile non-believers. It was already extremely common for Jews to sharply condemn the behavior of non-Jews in broad terms as corrupt, godless, and immoral, due especially to their idolatrous practices and sexual licentiousness.

The lists of vices appearing in passages such as Romans 1:18-31, 1 Cor. 6:9-10, Gal. 5:19-21, Col. 3:5-8, 1 Tim. 1:9-10, 2 Tim. 3:2-5, Tit. 3:3, and 1 Pet. 4:3 reflect the typical Jewish stereotypes of gentile conduct. In several of these passages, the author of the letter reminds gentile believers that they had previously lived in the way described. In 1 Cor. 6:11, after offering a list of those who practice the vices associated with gentile life, Paul writes: "And this is what some of you used to be. But you were washed, you were sanctified, you were justified in the name of the Lord Jesus Christ and in the Spirit of our God." After exhorting his readers to avoid evil and quarreling and to be gentle and show consideration to all, the author of Titus adds: "For we ourselves were once foolish, disobedient, led astray, slaves to various passions and pleasures, passing our days in malice and envy, despicable, hating one another" (Tit. 3:3). Similarly, the author of 1 Peter tells his readers: "You have already spent enough time in doing what the Gentiles like to do, living in licentiousness, passions, drunkenness, revels, carousing, and lawless idolatry. They are surprised that you no longer join them in the same excesses of dissipation, and so they blaspheme" (4:3-4). In 1 Cor. 12:2, Paul tells the Corinthians: "You know that when you were Gentiles, you were enticed and led astray to idols that could not speak." He also exhorts the Thessalonians to control their bodies "in holiness and honor, not with lustful passion, like the Gentiles who do not know God" (1 Thess. 4:4-5). As Richard Hays notes with regard to this last passage, "Paul writes as if this Gentile Christian community is 'Gentile' no longer; though they remain uncircumcised, he has transferred to them the communal ascriptions appropriate to Israel.... Paul is addressing his readers as non-Gentiles."[33] These passages, then, not only contrast the present life of gentile believers with their previous life and that of other non-Jews, but even imply that they are no longer gentiles.

Even though the gentiles who joined Jesus' communities of followers did not submit fully to the Mosaic law, they were expected to put aside entirely their idolatrous beliefs and practices and to follow in general terms the Jewish norms regarding sexual and moral conduct. Thus, the behavior and lifestyle of those non-Jews who became members of the community of Jesus' followers

---

33. Richard B. Hays, "Crucified with Christ: A Synthesis of the Theology of 1 and 2 Thessalonians, Philemon, Philippians, and Galatians," in *Pauline Theology*, Vol. 1: *Thessalonians, Philippians, Galatians, Philemon* (ed. Jouette M. Bassler; Minneapolis: Fortress, 1991), 235-36.

would contrast noticeably with the conduct of other non-Jews and draw the attention of Jews and non-Jews alike.[34]

Virtually all of the New Testament letters that are addressed to non-Jewish audiences stress these points. In 1 Thessalonians, probably the earliest of the New Testament writings, we already find Paul praising the Thessalonian believers for their "work of faith and labor of love," their exemplary conduct, and the life "worthy of God" that they lead (1 Thess. 1:3, 7-8; 2:12-14). Paul reminds them how they "turned to God from idols, to serve a living and true God" (1 Thess. 1:9), and contrasts the holiness of their way of life with the sexual immortality of other gentiles (1 Thess. 4:3-12). In fact, the theme that Jesus' followers live differently from others constitutes a central theme of the letter as a whole.

In Galatians, Paul contrasts the "slavery" of his gentile readers with their new freedom in Christ: "Formerly, when you did not know God, you were enslaved to beings that by nature are not gods. Now, however, that you have come to know God, or rather to be known by God, how can you turn back again to the weak and beggarly elemental spirits? How can you want to be enslaved to them again?" (Gal. 4:8-9). Paul also feels the need to warn them that those who practice the vices typical of gentiles will not inherit God's reign (Gal. 5:19-21). The idea that believers previously lived as slaves is also stressed in Romans. There Paul tells his readers:

> But thanks be to God that you, having once been slaves of sin, have become obedient from the heart to the form of teaching to which you were entrusted, and that you, having been set free from sin, have become slaves of righteousness.... For just as you once presented your members as slaves to impurity and to greater and greater iniquity, so now present your members as slaves to righteousness for sanctification. When you were slaves of sin, you were free in regard to righteousness. So what advantage did you then get from the things of which you now are ashamed? The end of those things is death. But now that you have been freed from sin and enslaved to God, the advantage you get is sanctification (Rom. 6:17-22).

In the same letter, Paul contrasts "those who live according to the flesh" with "those who live according to the Spirit," telling the Roman believers that they are now adopted daughters and sons rather than slaves (Rom. 8:1-17). He also reminds them that they "were once disobedient to God" and exhorts them to "lay aside the works of darkness and put on the armor of light; let us live honorably as in the day, not in reveling and drunkenness, not in debauchery and licentiousness, not in quarreling and jealousy. Instead, put on the Lord

---

34. Magnus Zetterholm mentions that for many of the non-Jews who became followers of Jesus, it may not have been possible "to break away from their Graeco-Roman religious context, socially, religiously and politically.... Was it for instance, possible for non-Jews from the upper classes, who may have had cultic obligations due to their position in society, to refrain from actions that from a Jewish perspective would be defined as 'idolatry'? We may be forced to accept the idea that not all non-Jews who were connected to the Jesus movement were wholeheartedly committed to worship only the God of Israel through Christ" ("Jews, Christians, and Gentiles: Rethinking the Categorization within the Early Jesus Movement," in *Reading Paul in Context: Explorations in Identity Formation. Essays in Honour of William Campbell*; ed. Kathy Ehrensperger and J. Brian Tucker; London: T & T Clark, 2010, 252).

Jesus Christ, and make no provision for the flesh, to gratify its desires" (Rom. 11:30; 13:12-14). These words clearly seem to be directed at believers of gentile rather than Jewish origin. The same must be said of his instructions to the Philippian believers: "Do all things without murmuring and arguing, so that you may be blameless and innocent, children of God without blemish in the midst of a crooked and perverse generation, in which you shine like stars in the world" (Phil. 2:14-15).

The contrast between the former and present life of gentile believers is particularly notable in the disputed Pauline letters. The author of Colossians tells the faithful that God "has rescued us from the power of darkness and transferred us into the kingdom of his beloved Son," and reminds them that they "were once estranged and hostile in mind, doing evil deeds" (Col. 1:13, 21). Later on he refers to the time when they were "dead in trespasses" (Col. 2:13) and, after exhorting them to put to death things such as sexual impurity, evil desires, and greed, all of which he identifies with idolatry, he continues: "These are the ways you also once followed, when you were living that life. But now you must get rid of all such—anger, wrath, malice, slander, and abusive language from your mouth. Do not lie to one another, seeing that you have stripped off the old self with its practices and have clothed yourselves with the new self" (Col. 3:5-10).

Similarly, the author of Ephesians tells his gentile readers: "You were dead through the trespasses and sins in which you once lived, following the course of this world, following the ruler of the power of the air, the spirit that is now at work among those who are disobedient. All of us once lived among them in the passions of our flesh, following the desires of flesh and senses, and we were by nature children of wrath, like everyone else" (Eph. 2:1-3). Further on in the letter, the author contrasts once more the former life of the Ephesian believers with their new life in Christ: "you must no longer live as the Gentiles live, in the futility of their minds. They are darkened in their understanding, alienated from the life of God because of their ignorance and hardness of heart. They have lost all sensitivity and have abandoned themselves to licentiousness, greedy to practice every kind of impurity" (Eph. 4:17-19). Like the Colossians, the Ephesians are told to put away their "former way of life" and their "old self, corrupt and deluded by its lusts" in order to be renewed and clothed with a new self (Eph. 4:22-24). This involves putting away the vices considered typical of gentiles, such as falsehood, anger, stealing, evil talk, slander, malice, sexual impurity, greed, vulgar talk, foolishness, and drunkenness (Eph. 4:25—5:18). The contrast between light and darkness found in other New Testament writings is also used to exhort the Ephesian believers to live differently from the gentiles who disobey God's will: "Therefore do not be associated with them. For once you were darkness, but now in the Lord you are light. Live as children of light—for the fruit of the light is found in all that is good and right and true.... Take no part in the unfruitful works of darkness, but instead expose them. For it is shameful even to mention what such people do secretly; but everything exposed by the light becomes visible, for everything that becomes visible is light" (Eph. 5:7-9, 11-14). The book of Acts also affirms that it was at Ephesus that those who had become believers abandoned certain unacceptable activities in which they had previously been involved, including especially the practice of magic (Acts 19:18-19).

Of all of the writings of the New Testament, the one that stresses most the difference between the new life of gentile believers and their previous life as unbelieving gentiles is 1 Peter. As in the passage from 1 Pet. 4:3-5 already quoted above, the author repeatedly reminds the readers of the radical changes that have taken place in their lives: "Like obedient children, do not be conformed to the desires that you formerly had in ignorance.... You know that you were ransomed from the futile ways inherited from your ancestors, not with perishable things like silver or gold, but with the precious blood of Christ" (1 Pet. 1:14, 18-19). He compares them to "newborn infants" who are now rid of malice, guile, insincerity, envy, and slander and tells them: "I urge you as aliens and exiles to abstain from the desires of the flesh that wage war against the soul. Conduct yourselves honorably among the Gentiles, so that, though they malign you as evildoers, they may see your honorable deeds and glorify God when he comes to judge" (2:1-2, 11-12). Believing slaves are exhorted to live in ways that set them apart from other slaves (2:18-25), while married women and men are to practice conduct that distinguishes them from non-believing married couples (3:1-7). The author repeatedly stresses that those who live as Christ's followers will be maligned by others and suffer for doing right but, as they respond in love, they will silence their adversaries and be rewarded by God (2:15-23; 3:9-18; 4:1-4, 13-19). From the context, it appears that the suffering described in the letter was being inflicted on the readers by non-Jews from outside of the community of believers who were upset by the fact that the readers no longer associated with them in the ways that they did previously. Evidently, those angered by the new life of believers interpret the changes in them as a rejection of their own values and way of life.[35]

Many non-Jews who were *not* followers of Jesus seem also to have been highly critical of the way in which gender, class, and ethnic distinctions were redefined in the communities of believers in which their fellow non-Jews participated. While the patterns of relations between males and females and the roles assigned to women in society varied greatly from one region of the

---

35. As Larry W. Hurtado notes, "one of the reasons that the spread of Christian faith probably angered people and also brought the hostile attention of Roman authorities was that it could have an impact upon those economic activities associated with the deities whose worship Christians shunned completely out of exclusive devotion to the one God and his Christ" (*How on Earth did Jesus Become a God?: Historical Questions about Earliest Devotion to Jesus*; Grand Rapids: Eerdmans, 2005, 81). Brigitte Kahl also points out that those non-Jewish believers in Christ who refused to participate in the public festivals and ceremonies in honor of the emperor would have faced opposition both from other non-Jews and Jews as well, since the Jewish community did not want to give the impression that it was disturbing the social order by encouraging people to abandon their customs or to cease to participate in the activities associated with the Roman imperial cult (*Galatians Re-Imagined: Reading with the Eyes of the Vanquished*; PCC; Minneapolis: Fortress, 2010, 224).

empire to another,[36] the fact that the New Testament writings addressed to non-Jewish believers frequently discuss gender relations and the role of women in both private and public settings provides evidence that these questions were a source of disagreements and tensions (1 Cor. 11:2-16; Eph. 5:22—6:9; Col. 3:18—4:1; 1 Pet. 3:1-7).[37] While to some extent this can be attributed to cultural differences between Jews and non-Jews in the communities, believers of non-Jewish origin clearly saw themselves as having broken with the patterns and norms that had characterized their previous social contexts. Today, of course, the New Testament passages that discuss the relation of males to females within the household and the community of believers hardly seem revolutionary. Instead, we tend to regard them as promoting inequities and injustices toward women. In their original contexts, however, these passages seem to have been a response to cultural norms and social practices that believers found problematic due to the ways in which they were thought to lead to the disintegration of solid and healthy relationships in both private and public spheres.

The New Testament also provides ample evidence that people of very different social classes were brought together in the communities of Jesus' followers. Although slaves are addressed in a number of the New Testament letters, Paul's letter to Philemon as well as several of the disputed Pauline epistles provide evidence that slaves and slave owners related to each other as brothers and sisters within the communities of believers (Col. 3:22—4:1; Eph. 6:5-9; 1 Tim. 6:1-2).[38] Several of the New Testament letters also point to the existence of communities in which some members were much more affluent than others. As one would expect, this seems to have led to tensions and even divisions within those communities. The problems Paul describes in 1 Cor. 11:19-34 when discussing the manner in which the Corinthian believers celebrated the Lord's Supper, as well as the favoritism toward the rich criticized in James 2:1-9, illustrate the difficulties involved in bringing together in a single community people from highly disparate social classes.

The critiques of wealth that run throughout the New Testament can also be interpreted as indicating that social inequities were a source of tension within many communities. One can scarcely imagine how complex these relationships would be. The inequalities, prejudices, stereotypes, and even hostility between those of different social classes would not be easily overcome, even

---

36. On the differences in the role and status of women in the Mediterranean region in the first century CE, see Timothy J. M. Ling, *The Judaean Poor and the Fourth Gospel* (SNTSMS 136; Cambridge: Cambridge University Press, 2006), 35-44; E. Stegemann and W. Stegemann, *Jesus Movement*, 364-77.

37. On the function of the type of household codes that appear in these texts and their background, see Margaret Y. McDonald, "Beyond Identification of the Topos of Household Management: Reading the Household Codes in Light of Recent Methodologies and Theoretical Perspectives in the Study of the New Testament," *NTS* 57 (2011): 65-90; Angela Standhartinger, "The Origin and Intention of the Household Code in the Letter to the Colossians," *JSNT* 79 (2000): 117-30; E. Stegemann and W. Stegemann, *Jesus Movement*, 403-7.

38. On the problems involved in bringing together slaves and their owners as "brothers and sisters" in a single community, see especially Hurtado, *How on Earth*, 65-67.

when the obligation to love and accept those who were different was repeatedly emphasized. Just as it would not be easy for men and women to have fellowship together in the ways that this took place in the communities of believers, so also both masters and slaves as well as rich and poor would find it extremely uncomfortable and disconcerting to sit down at the same table to eat of the same food together and treat one another as sisters and brothers in the faith in the context of the community. Nevertheless, the repeated exhortations to overcome class distinctions and live together in harmony demonstrate that this was understood to be the ideal to which all believers were expected to conform.[39]

The New Testament writings also stress the overcoming of enmities and divisions due to questions of race and ethnicity. Chief among these enmities, of course, is that which existed between Jews and non-Jews. While it is important to avoid generalizations and stereotypes, since in many contexts throughout the Roman Empire Jews and non-Jews lived together in harmony and mutual respect, there is also a great deal of evidence in antiquity of mutual contempt between the two groups.[40] Many non-Jews considered Jews to be anti-social and even accused them of being "haters of humankind" due to the fact that they remained in their own communities and often isolated themselves from public life and certain social realities. Conversely, many Jews regarded non-Jews as immoral and even impure in some sense. Even where enmity was minimal or non-existent, however, Jews and non-Jews tended to be seen as separate groups that did not mix readily with one another. This seems to have changed noticeably in the communities of Jesus' followers where Jews and non-Jews intermingled, ate together, and followed a discourse according to which the distinctions between Jews and non-Jews no longer mattered. These expressions of fellowship must have been considered surprising to all who observed them, whether they were Jews or non-Jews and whether they belonged to the community of Jesus' followers or not. That community would be seen as a place of reconciliation in which people who were profoundly different could live as one. Again, even if this principle was not always lived out, what is significant is that it represented a core value and was central to the way in which the community of Jesus' followers defined itself.

It must be remembered as well that in each of the areas in which Jesus' followers established communities, there was considerable diversity among

---

39. On the complexity of the relationships between people of different social groups and classes and the conflicts to which they would lead, see especially Meeks, *First Urban Christians*, 51-73. John S. Kloppenborg has rightly noted that the earliest churches, including especially those associated with Paul, "were 'egalitarian' in the sense that they admitted members of varying social ranks, women alongside men, and both slaves and free. Some, including Pauline groups, had women as patrons and perhaps even as leaders.... But this did not mean that social difference was effaced merely because persons of a variety of positions ate together, nor, more importantly, did it create a presumption that all members were on the same plane of moral achievement" ("Egalitarianism in the Myth and Rhetoric of Pauline Churches," in *Reimagining Christian Origins: A Colloquium Honoring Burton L. Mack*; ed. Elizabeth A. Castelli and Hal Taussig; Valley Forge, PA: Trinity Press International, 1996, 258-59).

40. On the animosity between Jews and non-Jews in the Roman empire and its causes, see especially Ling, *Judaean Poor*, 26-31.

people who came from different cultures and backgrounds and spoke different languages in addition to the *lingua franca*. The letter to the Colossians, for example, affirms not only that there is no longer Jew and Greek or circumcision and uncircumcision, but that the distinctions between barbarian and Scythian have disappeared for believers as well (Col. 3:11). These differences would be particularly evident in urban contexts, to which people from a variety of different backgrounds emigrated. The story of the pouring out of the Holy Spirit on the Day of Pentecost in Acts 2 is comprehensible only when we grasp the wide diversity of languages and cultures of people gathered together in Jerusalem for the Jewish festival. According to this account, many of those gathered in Jerusalem identified themselves not only as Jewish, but as members of other ethnic minorities whose native language (*dialektos*) was something other than Greek (Acts 2:6-11). Even if much of the historicity of Luke's account is called into question, once again it stresses the ideal that, in the communities of Jesus' followers, people from different ethnic backgrounds were expected to live together as one; and if this ideal was stressed as an important core value, it must have been realized at least to some extent in the actual communities of Jesus' followers around the empire. Once again, therefore, those communities would be seen as places of reconciliation that brought together in unity and solidarity people from very different backgrounds who normally kept their distance from one another and often were at enmity with one another due to ethnic conflicts and prejudices inherited from the past.

All of this indicates that the communities of Jesus' followers were seen both by their own members and by outsiders as truly alternative communities that were in important ways different from other communities that existed among other Jews and non-Jews. While the most notable differences would be those that existed between the non-Jews who became members of the community of believers and those who continued to practice idolatry and live according to their own traditions and customs, even those followers of Jesus who were of Jewish origin would see themselves as somewhat distinct from other Jews, as we have seen. The places in which the communities of believers met would also play an important role in their self-understanding. As long as those communities were composed primarily of Jews, they could probably meet in Jewish synagogues and places of prayer. Once the number of non-Jews grew, however, the communities of believers may not have been as well-received in those Jewish contexts. Precisely how they would enjoy table fellowship in those contexts or participate there in worship activities that revolved around the figure of Jesus is not clear. Sooner or later, conflicts would arise and lead Jesus' followers to meet in other spaces devoted to their own worship and fellowship activities. Unless they chose to meet in more than one place, they would need to choose between Jewish and non-Jewish settings.

Defining the Identity of Jesus' Followers

The fact that those believers who came from non-Jewish backgrounds gathered with Jews, especially when this took place in spaces that were regarded as Jewish, would have led both those within the community and those on the outside to wonder precisely how to define the new identity that non-Jewish believers had acquired.[41] Were they members of Israel or even Jews, even though they remained uncircumcised? Were they still to be regarded as gentiles, even though they were now very different from other non-Jews? To what extent did they still conserve their previous ethnic identities, even though they now formed part of a community in which there was "no distinction among persons" (Acts 10:34; 11:12; 15:9; Rom. 2:11; 10:12), and there was supposedly no longer Jew nor Greek, circumcision or uncircumcision, slave or free, male or female, barbarian or Scythian (Gal. 3:28; Col. 3:11)? Although there is no evidence of Christians regarding themselves as a "third race" until the second century, one cannot help but wonder how long it would have taken for Jesus' followers to begin to think in those terms.[42] In fact, Paul's affirmation that there is no longer circumcision or uncircumcision but only a "new creation" certainly lends itself to being read in the sense that believers constitute something new that is *distinct* from the previous identities of Jews and non-Jews (Gal. 6:15; cf. 1 Cor. 7:19; 2 Cor. 5:17).

It is not surprising, therefore, that in the New Testament writings we find the same problems and ambiguities with regard to allusions to Israel and Judaism that we noted above in connection with Paul's use of the term *covenant*. When Paul speaks of Jews and Israel, for example, he is usually referring to those who are Jewish by birth and who are either physically descended from the patriarchs or have been fully incorporated into the Jewish community through circumcision and full submission to the Mosaic law. At the same time, however, he also claims that "a person is not a Jew who is one outwardly, nor is true circumcision something external and physical. Rather, a person is a Jew who is one inwardly, and real circumcision is a matter of the heart" (Rom. 2:28-29). Later on in the same letter, he affirms that "not all Israelites truly

---

41. On this problem, see especially Caroline Johnson Hodge, "The Question of Identity: Gentiles as Gentiles—but also Not—in Pauline Communities," in *Paul within Judaism: Restoring the First-Century Context to the Apostle* (ed. Mark D. Nanos and Magnus Zetterholm; Minneapolis: Fortress, 2015), 153-73.

42. Many scholars would agree with Judith Lieu that the idea that believers in Christ constituted a third race "emerges at the end of the second century, and was, perhaps, adopted from the taunts of outsiders" ("Self-Definition vis-a-vis the Jewish Matrix," in *The Cambridge History of Christianity*, Vol. 1: *Origins to Constantine*, ed. Frances M. Young and Margaret M. Mitchell; Cambridge: Cambridge University Press, 2006, 214). For a more detailed analysis of this idea, see Lieu, *Image and Reality: The Jews in the World of the Christians in the Second Century* (Edinburgh: T & T Clark, 1996), 164-69, 177-78. Some scholars, however, such as Bradley S. Billings, argue that the concept of believers in Christ as a third race can be traced back to the first century and even to Paul, even though that terminology is not used explicitly in the New Testament writings (*Do This in Remembrance of Me. The Disputed Words in the Lukan Institution Narrative [Luke 22.19b-29]: An Historico-Exegetical, Theological and Sociological Analysis*; LNTS 314; London: T & T Clark, 2006, 138-40). David G. Horrell also notes that the use of the word *genos* in 1 Pet. 2:9, as well as Paul's distinction between Jews, Greeks, and the church of God in 1 Cor. 10:32, may also suggest that the first believers saw themselves as a distinct race ("'Race', 'Nation', 'People': Ethnic Identity Construction in 1 Peter 2.9," *NTS* 58 [2011]: 130-33).

belong to Israel" (Rom. 9:5). In both Romans and Galatians, he argues that the true children of Abraham are not those Jews who are merely circumcised physically and live according to the precepts of the Mosaic law, but all those who have faith, including uncircumcised gentiles who do not observe the law literally (Rom. 4:16-18; 9:6-8; Gal. 3:6-9, 29).

In 1 Corinthians, a letter written primarily or exclusively to non-Jewish believers, Paul refers to the Israelites who left Egypt under Moses as "our ancestors" (*hoi pateres hēmōn*), as if gentile believers were fully included in that group (1 Cor. 10:1; cf. Rom. 4:11-12, 16). At the end of his letter to the Galatians, Paul seems to include believing non-Jews as members of "the Israel of God" (Gal. 6:16).[43] Elsewhere he tells the Philippian believers, who seem to be primarily non-Jews: "it is we who are the circumcision, who worship in the Spirit of God and boast in Christ Jesus and have no confidence in the flesh" (Phil. 3:3). The context makes it clear that here Paul is questioning the notion that Israel is defined on the basis of physical descendancy. Paul's metaphor of the olive tree in Rom. 11:16-24 is also problematic. If the branches broken off represent unbelieving Jews and the wild shoots grafted into the tree represent believing non-Jews, what does the tree itself symbolize? And what does Paul mean when he says that "even those of Israel, if they do not persist in unbelief, will be grafted in," and that in the end "all Israel will be saved" (Rom. 11:23, 26)? The fact that these questions continue to be debated among New Testament scholars demonstrates that Paul's thought on the subject is not at all clear.[44]

Although the other New Testament writings do not use terms such as *Jew*, *Israel*, and *circumcision* in the ambiguous manner that Paul does at times, they also reflect the same lack of clarity regarding the relationship between Israel or Judaism as traditionally understood in antiquity and the community composed of believers of both Jewish and non-Jewish backgrounds. Numerous

---

43. On the different scholarly proposals regarding the interpretation of the phrase "Israel of God" in Gal. 6:16, see especially Martinus C. de Boer, *Galatians: A Commentary* (NTL; Louisville, KY: Westminster John Knox, 2011), 405-8. Michael F. Bird reduces the possibilities regarding the meaning of Paul's phrase to three: "The benediction could refer to a blessing for Jewish and Gentile Christ-believers, to Jewish Christ-believers who abide by Paul's teaching, or to ethnic Israel," and presents strong arguments in favor of the first of these possibilities (*An Anomolous Jew: Paul Among Jews, Greeks, and Romans*; Grand Rapids: Eerdmans, 2016, 163-66).

44. On the diverse interpretations of Rom. 11:16-26, see especially Robert Jewett, *Romans: A Commentary* (Hermeneia; Minneapolis: Fortress, 2007), 694-711. Campbell, for example, commenting on Rom. 11:16-26, argues that "gentile Christ-followers share in the covenant with Jews, but despite this they are not designated as Israel—they remain as a community of gentiles in Christ, a satellite gathering or congregation alongside of Israel.... The arguments that gentiles do not become Israel are exegetically very strong despite much concentrated effort to dismiss these.... Israel and the church remain two distinct entities" ("Covenantal Theology," 50-51). In contrast, as already noted above, James Dunn insists that for Paul there are not "two different peoples (Jews and Christians)," but only "one people, Israel" ("Two Covenants," 118). Bruce Chilton and Jacob Neusner attempt to resolve the difficulties involved by attributing to Paul the idea that "Israel forms an ethnic group, a family after the flesh," yet at the same time "there is another Israel, an Israel of the spirit, and to this other Israel, the other-than-ethnic one, Gentiles could adhere, and, indeed by their faith in Christ, they joined that Israel after the spirit that found its definition in faith" (*Judaism in the New Testament: Practices and Beliefs*; London: Routledge, 1995, 71).

passages in the New Testament allude to the acceptance of believing gentiles as members of God's people, but precisely how is this to be understood? Do they become members of Israel or of a new people that is distinct from Israel as traditionally understood? How should Jews or Israelites who do not form part of the community of Jesus' followers be considered? Are they still members of God's people? Do they still belong to or constitute Israel?[45]

The idea that not all those who consider themselves members of Israel or children of Abraham actually form part of God's chosen people is found for the first time in the Synoptics in the teaching of John the Baptist, who is said to have told those who pointed to their physical descendancy from Abraham that God could raise up children of Abraham from the stones. His teaching implies that only those who repent and bear fruit are truly children of Abraham (Matt. 3:9-10; Luke 3:8-9).[46] Other passages indicate that Jesus was remembered to have affirmed that the faith of a foreign woman and a Roman centurion was superior to anything found in Israel (Matt. 8:10; 15:28; Luke 7:9). In Matthew, immediately after Jesus marvels at the centurion's faith, he adds: "I tell you, many will come from east and west and will eat with Abraham and Isaac and Jacob in the kingdom of heaven, while the heirs of the kingdom will be thrown into the outer darkness, where there will be weeping and gnashing of teeth" (Matt. 8:11-12; cf. Luke 13:28-29). Jesus also tells the chief priests and elders, "the tax collectors and the prostitutes are going into the kingdom of God ahead of you" (Matt. 21:31).

In Luke, at the outset of his ministry, Jesus reminds those gathered at the synagogue in Nazareth that God sent Elijah to the gentile widow in Sidon at the time of famine, rather to any Israelite widow, while Elisha cleansed no lepers from Israel, but only Naaman the Syrian (Luke 4:25-27). Jesus also refers to a crippled woman whom he heals as a "daughter of Abraham," and calls Zacchaeus the tax collector a "son of Abraham" (Luke 13:16; 19:9). By having Jesus do so explicitly, Luke seems to be reacting to the position of some

---

45. On the ideas of a new law, a new people, and a new covenant in the Christian writings of the second century and the argument that the Christians represented the true and ancient Israel, see Marcel Simon, *Verus Israel: A Study of the Relations between Christians and Jews in the Roman Empire (135-425)*, trans. H. McKeating (Oxford: Oxford University Press, 1986), 76-91.

46. According to Robert L. Webb, "John was calling his audience to gather into some form of group... [and] denies that simply being a member of ethnic Israel is sufficient.... [I]t is only those who have undergone repentance-baptism who have become the true 'children of Abraham'" ("John the Baptist and his Relationship to Jesus," in *Studying the Historical Jesus: Evaluation of the State of Current Research*; ed. Bruce Chilton and Craig A. Evans; NTTS 19; Leiden: Brill, 1994, 196). Wolfgang Kraus sees John's baptism as relativizing circumcision and ascribes the same idea to Paul (*Zwischen Jerusalem und Antiochia: die 'Hellenisten', Paulus und die Aufnahme der Heiden in das endzeitliche Gottesvolk*; SB 179; Stuttgart: Katholisches Bibelwerk, 1999, 122-30). Nevertheless, as Christiansen observes, John's baptism was a rite of *purification* rather than *initiation* (*Covenant*, 203-4). Craig A. Evans, however, combines the ideas of purification and (re)initiation by affirming that John's baptism "was an act of eschatological purification, signifying repentance and re-entry into God's covenant with Israel" ("The Baptism of John in a Typological Context," in *Dimensions of Baptism: Biblical and Theological Studies*; ed. Stanley E. Porter and Anthony R. Cross; JSNTSup 234; London: Sheffield Academic Press, 2002, 70). To say that "re-entry" is necessary implies that the covenant relationship has been abandoned and must be reestablished. John's baptism might also be seen as a symbolic re-entry of God's people into the promised land by means of the Jordan River.

who would *not* consider such a woman or Zacchaeus children of Abraham. In the Fourth Gospel, those opposing Jesus insist that they are Abraham's children, while Jesus questions that claim on the basis that they do not do what Abraham did (John 8:33-40). To whatever extent these accounts go back to actual events in Jesus' ministry, the fact that they appear in the Jesus tradition as we find it in the Gospels seems to indicate that the process of redefining who belonged and did not belong to Israel began either during Jesus' own lifetime or shortly thereafter. This redefinition seems to have involved not only including Jewish "sinners" and at times even non-Jews as members of Israel, but also censuring as unfaithful Jews those who actively opposed Jesus and used the law to exclude and mistreat other Jews (Matt. 11:16-24; 12:34-42; 23:13-35; Mark 2:15-17; Luke 7:36-50; 15:1-2; 18:9-14).

The affirmation that believing gentiles form part of God's people appears throughout the New Testament. In Acts, the inclusion of gentiles into the community of God's people is a central theme. Peter tells those assembled in Jerusalem to discuss the question of whether gentile believers are to be circumcised that God has "looked favorably on the Gentiles, to take from among them a people for his name" (Acts 15:14; cf. 10:1—11:18). Later, when Paul is in Corinth proclaiming God's word not only to Jews but to Greeks or gentiles as well, the risen Jesus tells Paul, "there are many in this city who are my people" (Acts 18:9-10). In Acts 26:16-18, when retelling the story of his experience on the road to Damascus, Paul claims to have been told by Jesus, "I will rescue you from your people and from the Gentiles—to whom I am sending you to open their eyes so that they may turn from darkness to light and from the power of Satan to God, so that they may receive forgiveness of sins and a place among those who are sanctified by faith in me."

These passages can be interpreted either in the sense that gentile believers have come to form part of God's people Israel or in the sense that God has constituted a new people in which gentiles are included. This ambiguity is reflected in Jer. 31:33, where God says of those Israelites on whose hearts and minds he will write his law, "I will be their God, and they shall be my people." Here, while this new people is seen as being in continuity with the old, it includes only those who will become obedient. In Rom. 9:25-26, Paul also seems to speak of the formation of a new people that includes gentiles: "As indeed [God] says in Hosea, 'Those who were not my people I will call "my people," and her who was not beloved I will call "beloved".' And in the very place where it was said to them, 'You are not my people,' there they shall be called children of the living God." Paul makes the same type of affirmation in 2 Cor. 6:16-18, where, after exhorting believers not to be mismatched with unbelievers and drawing a contrast between light and darkness, he cites a catena of passages from the Hebrew Scriptures: "I will live in them and walk among them, and I will be their God, and they shall be my people. Therefore come out from them, and be separate from them, says the Lord, and touch nothing unclean; then I will welcome you, and I will be your father, and you shall be my sons and daughters, says the Lord Almighty." The idea that those gentiles incorporated into God's people become sanctified and pure mentioned in this latter passage and Acts 26:18 is repeated in Tit. 2:14, where Christ is said to have given himself to "redeem us from all iniquity and purify for himself a people of his own who are zealous for good deeds."

Numerous passages from the New Testament refer to believers as "chosen" or "elect." This is the same claim made throughout the Hebrew Scriptures regarding Israel. While at times the New Testament writings continue to refer to Israel as the elect, at times this designation is also applied to gentile believers. Paul tells the Thessalonian believers, "we know, brothers and sisters beloved by God, that he has chosen you" (1 Thess. 1:4). In Rom. 8:28-29, where he addresses an audience that is probably composed mostly of non-Jews, Paul refers to believers as those whom God "called according to his purpose," "foreknew," and "predestined to be conformed to the image of his Son, in order that he might be the firstborn among many brothers and sisters." This latter phrase reflects the notion that from of old God intended to form a family composed of Jews and gentiles. In the same context, Paul also speaks of believers as "God's elect" (Rom. 8:33). This language appears throughout the disputed Pauline epistles as well. The author of Colossians refers to his readers as "God's chosen ones, holy and beloved" (Col. 3:12).[47] In 2 Thess. 2:13, believers are called "brothers and sisters beloved by the Lord," and are told: "God chose you as the first fruits for salvation through sanctification by the Spirit and through belief in the truth." Both 2 Tim. 2:10 and Tit. 1:1 refer simply to the "elect" and relate this idea to the salvation that has been promised to believers; for the author of Titus, this is "the hope of eternal life that God, who never lies, promised before the ages began" (Tit. 1:2). The author of 2 Pet. 1:10 also uses the family language of "brothers and sisters" to exhort his readers to confirm their "call and election." All of these writings seem to be addressed primarily to non-Jewish audiences.

The same ideas are particularly stressed in Ephesians and 1 Peter, both written for a non-Jewish audience. In Eph. 1:4-5, the author writes that God "chose us in Christ before the foundation of the world to be holy and blameless before him in love" and "destined us for adoption as his children through Jesus Christ." Here, as in several of the other passages just considered, the idea that believers are holy and sanctified is closely tied to the language of election. A few verses later, the author stresses once more that his readers have been chosen by God: "In Christ we have also obtained an inheritance, having been destined according to the purpose of him who accomplishes all

---

47. James Dunn rightly notes with regard to the phrase "elect of God, holy and beloved" in Col. 3:12 that "the language of Jewish self-identity would be unmistakable for anyone familiar with the Jewish scriptures, and not least to the Jews of Colossae. The term *eklektos* is familiar enough in Greek, but the idea of a people 'chosen of God' is wholly and exclusively Jewish, a fundamental feature of Israel's self-participation.... More clearly than anywhere else in Colossians it is evident that the Gentile recipients of the letter were being invited to consider themselves as full participants in the people and heritage of Israel" ("The Colossian Philosophy: A Confident Jewish Apologia," *Biblica* 76 [1995]: 159).

things according to his counsel and will.... This is the pledge of our inheritance toward redemption as God's own people" (Eph. 1:11, 14). The language of inheritance, so common elsewhere throughout the New Testament, stresses that believers share in the same promises made to Israel of old as members of God's children or family, and also calls to mind the idea of a will or testament, which in Greek was also a covenant (*diathēkē*).

Further on in the letter, in a passage worth quoting at length, the author particularly stresses the way in which gentiles have now come to form part of God's people together with Jewish believers:

> So then, remember that at one time you Gentiles by birth, called "the uncircumcision" by those who are called "the circumcision"—a physical circumcision made in the flesh by human hands—remember that you were at that time without Christ, being aliens from the commonwealth of Israel, and strangers to the covenants of promise, having no hope and without God in the world. But now in Christ Jesus you who once were far off have been brought near by the blood of Christ. For he is our peace; in his flesh he has made both groups into one and has broken down the dividing wall, that is, the hostility between us. He has abolished the law with its commandments and ordinances, that he might create in himself one new humanity in place of the two, thus making peace, and might reconcile both groups to God in one body through the cross, thus putting to death that hostility through it. So he came and proclaimed peace to you who were far off and peace to those who were near; for through him both of us have access in one Spirit to the Father. So then you are no longer strangers and aliens, but you are citizens with the saints and also members of the household of God, built upon the foundation of the apostles and prophets, with Christ Jesus himself as the cornerstone. In him the whole structure is joined together and grows into a holy temple in the Lord; in whom you also are built together spiritually into a dwelling place for God (Eph. 2:11-22).

While we will later examine the significance ascribed to Jesus' death or blood here, several points from the passage should be noted. First, it speaks of gentiles who previously did not form part of Israel and were not contemplated in the promises of the covenant now being brought together with Jews in a single group by Christ.[48] This means that the hostility and estrangement have come to an end. Second, however, the passage speaks of God creating one new human being (*kainon anthrōpon*). The language of creation implies something totally new and brings to mind once again Paul's affirmation in Gal. 6:15 that "neither circumcision nor uncircumcision is anything; but a new creation." The claim that in Christ the two kinds of human beings are now one raises the question of whether the two have now been *combined* into a single entity or have instead been *replaced* by a third entity, the single *anthrōpos*. The fact that this single *anthrōpos* is said to be "created" seems to favor the second

---

48. In particular, Tet-Lim N. Yee has argued on the basis of Eph. 2:11-22 that the author of Ephesians redefines Israel so as to present it as "an *inclusive* community in which the Gentiles who previously had no place among the people of God could be located within the same domain" (*Jews, Gentiles and Ethnic Reconciliation: Paul's Jewish Identity and Ephesians*, SNTSMS 130; Cambridge: Cambridge University Press, 2004, 190; see especially 190-219).

interpretation, though the idea is not entirely clear.[49] If that is the case, the author seems to be affirming that, rather than gentiles being incorporated into Israel, they have come to be joined to Jewish believers in a community that is *distinct* from Israel, at least as Israel was previously understood, as well as being distinct from gentile humanity as a whole. Third, it is significant that this creation of a new human being is said to take place as a result of the abolition of the law. This implies that not even believers of Jewish origin in the community need live according to the law, and that the new entity is distinct, not only from Israel, but also from the covenant God made with Israel, which promised blessings to those who would keep the law.[50] Fourth, we find here once more the language of family, together with that of citizenship, which involves membership in a particular nation, race, or people. And fifth, the imagery of a "holy temple" stresses again the notion that previously impure gentile believers have now become holy and pure before God.

Several of these ideas are repeated in Eph. 3:6: "the Gentiles have become fellow heirs, members of the same body, and sharers in the promise in Christ Jesus through the gospel." While this implies that the inheritance that believing gentiles share is the same one that belongs to Jewish believers, here the promise seems to be distinct from that found in the covenant with Israel. The Greek, however, can also be read in the sense that it is "in Christ Jesus through the gospel" that the readers share in the promise, in which case that promise might be regarded as the same one made to Israel of old.

The author of 1 Peter begins his letter by addressing believers as "exiles of the diaspora... who have been chosen and destined by God the Father and sanctified by the Spirit to be obedient to Jesus Christ and to be sprinkled with his blood" (1 Pet. 1:1-2). He then says that God has given them "a new birth into a living hope through the resurrection of Jesus Christ from the dead, and into an inheritance that is imperishable, undefiled, and unfading, kept in heaven for you, who are being protected by the power of God through faith for a salvation ready to be revealed in the last time" (1:3-5). The contents of the letter make it clear that it is addressed to gentile believers. Therefore, the affirmation that the readers are "exiles of the diaspora" should be taken in the sense that, like the Jewish people who await the day of Israel's redemption, when all Israelites will be able to return to the promised land, so also gentile believers scattered throughout the earth are in a type of exile in that they await their redemption as well. Nevertheless, this "living hope" and inheritance "kept in heaven" seem to be seen as something distinct from the traditional hope of Israel. As we have noted above, there appears to be some type of salvific reality already existing in heaven that must be revealed by being brought down to earth. In these opening verses of the letter, the idea that the

---

49. See Andrew T. Lincoln, *Ephesians* (WBC 42; Dallas, TX: Word, 1990), 132-34.

50. As Ernest Best notes, the use of the plural "covenants" in Eph. 2:12 is strange and seems not to refer to the "new covenant" made through Christ. Best suggests the author may have in mind the renewal of the original covenant made with Abraham under Isaac and Jacob (*Essays on Ephesians*, Edinburgh: T & T Clark, 1997, 96-97).

readers have been chosen and destined by God is once again closely linked to their being holy.

These ideas are developed further in 1 Pet. 2:4-10:

> Come to him, a living stone, though rejected by mortals yet chosen and precious in God's sight, and like living stones, let yourselves be built into a spiritual house, to be a holy priesthood, to offer spiritual sacrifices acceptable to God through Jesus Christ. For it stands in scripture: "See, I am laying in Zion a stone, a cornerstone chosen and precious; and whoever believes in him will not be put to shame." To you then who believe, he is precious; but for those who do not believe, "The stone that the builders rejected has become the very head of the corner," and "A stone that makes them stumble, and a rock that makes them fall." They stumble because they disobey the word, as they were destined to do. But you are a chosen race, a royal priesthood, a holy nation, God's own people, in order that you may proclaim the mighty acts of him who called you out of darkness into his marvelous light. Once you were not a people, but now you are God's people; once you had not received mercy, but now you have received mercy.

Here the author applies language used of Israel in biblical texts to which most Jews ascribed great importance to speak of the community of believers as "a chosen race, a royal priesthood, a holy nation," and "God's people" (cf. Exod. 19:5-6; LXX 23:22). Affirmations such as these would raise the question of whether Israel as traditionally understood *continues* to be God's special, chosen, and holy people who serve him as a kingdom of priests. If these epithets continue to apply to Israel "according to the flesh," does God now have two different chosen peoples? If so, is there now a spiritual Israel distinct from the previous Israel, just as there is now a spiritual house or temple in which spiritual sacrifices are offered to God that is distinct from the temple in Jerusalem in which material sacrifices were presented? Or has that Israel instead been replaced by the community of those who follow Jesus, so that those who *were* God's people are now so no longer? A third possibility is that the author thought along the lines of Paul's metaphor of an olive tree in Rom. 11:16-24, in which case those Jews who do not believe in Jesus as Israel's Messiah are replaced by believing gentiles as members of the Israel of old. The passage itself seems to offer no clues as to how the author would have answered these questions.

The author of 1 Peter also refers to believers as the "house of God" in 4:17 and speaks of them as "elect" once more in 5:13. In a unique passage in the New Testament, he speaks of women believers as "daughters of Sarah" (1 Pet. 3:6). This is conditional on their doing what is right and living free from fear. In Pauline language, that involves living out of faith.

New Covenant, New Temple

In the passages just cited from Eph. 2:11-12 and 1 Pet. 2:4-10, the community of believers is compared to a temple that is holy and spiritual. The Ephesians passage stresses more the idea that God dwells with believers, while the passage from 1 Peter focuses on the priestly activity of believers who present spiritual sacrifices to God. Because of the uncertainties regarding the dating of these two writings, we cannot be sure if the Jerusalem temple was still standing when they were written.

The idea that believers constitute God's temple or a new temple is found in numerous other passages in the New Testament.[51] It is particularly prominent in the Corinthian letters, where it appears in three different contexts. In 1 Cor. 3:16-17, Paul writes to the Corinthians, "Do you not know that you are God's temple and that God's Spirit dwells in you? If anyone destroys God's temple, God will destroy that person. For God's temple is holy, and you are that temple." The idea is similar in 2 Cor. 6:16, a passage already considered briefly above, where Paul affirms: "For we are the temple of the living God; as God said, 'I will live in them and walk among them, and I will be their God, and they shall be my people.'" Both of these passages point to the idea of the community of believers as God's dwelling place and make no explicit allusions to the offering of sacrifices or priestly activity.[52] In 1 Cor. 6:19-20, Paul affirms that the body of each believer is God's temple: "Do you not know that your body is a temple of the Holy Spirit within you, which you have from God, and that you are not your own? For you were bought with a price; therefore glorify God in your body." Obviously, the idea in this passage is somewhat different from that of the previous passages, which speak of believers collectively constituting God's temple. The exhortation to glorify God in one's body seems to allude to the worship of God, though explicit sacrificial imagery is absent.

As we shall see below, several passages from the New Testament associate the new temple with Jesus himself rather than with believers. Nevertheless, these two ideas can be brought together by affirming that Jesus constitutes the cornerstone or foundation of a new temple that is composed of believers. This idea appears in passages such as Matt. 21:42, Mark 12:10, Luke 20:17, Acts 4:11, Eph. 2:20, 1 Pet. 2:4-8, and perhaps Rom. 9:32-33. Most of these

---

51. For an extensive survey of temple symbolism in the New Testament, see Bertil E. Gärtner, *The Temple and the Community in Qumran and the New Testament: A Comparative Study in the Temple Symbolism of the Qumran Texts and the New Testament* (SNTSMS 1; Cambridge: Cambridge University Press, 1965), 47-122. Gärtner finds evidence of the idea that believers in Christ constitute a new temple in numerous New Testament texts, including the undisputed and disputed Pauline epistles, Hebrews, 1 Peter, and the four Gospels. On the tabernacle imagery in the New Testament, which is closely related to that of the temple, see Craig R. Koester, *The Dwelling of God: The Tabernacle in the Old Testament, Intertestamental Jewish Literature, and the New Testament* (CBQMS 22; Washington, DC: Catholic Biblical Association of America, 1989), 77-183. Scholars such as George W. E. Nickelsburg have argued that the Gospel of Mark also sees Jesus' death and resurrection as "the end of the old order and the Messiah's building of a new, spiritual temple—the church, in which God's ancient promises to the nations will be fulfilled" ("The Genre and Function of the Markan Passion Narrative," *HTR* 73 [1980]: 177). Due to their use of Mark, it is possible to attribute this idea to Matthew and Luke as well.

52. On the parallels between Paul's concept of the community of believers as a temple and the notion that the Qumran community constitutes a new temple, see Michael Newton, *The Concept of Purity at Qumran and in the Letters of Paul* (SNTSMS 53; Cambridge: Cambridge University Press, 1995), 14-15, 53-60; Gärtner, *Temple*, 16-44. Heinz-Wolfgang Kuhn notes that, in the literature of the period of the second temple, the idea that a group constitutes God's temple is found only in Christian literature and the Qumran writings ("The Impact of Selected Qumran Texts on the Understanding of Pauline Theology," in *The Bible and the Dead Sea Scrolls: The Second Princeton Symposium on Judaism and Christian Origins*; ed. James H. Charlesworth; Waco, TX: Baylor University Press, 2006, 1:162).

passages point back to Ps. 118:22: "The stone that the builders rejected has become the chief cornerstone." In 1 Cor. 3:10-15, Paul refers to Jesus as the foundation of a construction, yet also affirms that he himself laid a foundation "as a skilled master builder" (cf. Rom. 15:20). This occurs immediately before he tells the Corinthians that they are God's temple (1 Cor. 3:16-17).

The idea that believers constitute a new temple raises the same type of difficulties noted above with regard to the covenant and the people of Israel. For Paul, how did the temple he identifies with believers relate to the Jerusalem temple, which was still standing when Paul wrote 1 and 2 Corinthians and Romans? Was the new temple thought to have replaced the temple at Jerusalem? Did the Jerusalem temple perhaps prefigure the temple composed of believers, just as the people of Israel who passed through the Red Sea prefigured those who would come to faith in Christ and the Passover celebration pointed forward to the new reality that would come through Christ (1 Cor. 5:7; 10:1-10)? Although after the destruction of the temple in 70 CE the community of believers would be seen as replacing the temple at Jerusalem, it seems unlikely that such an idea would be common among Jesus' followers before then. Friedrich Horn, for example, has argued that, in spite of Paul's allusions to the community of believers as a new temple, he did not see the community as a substitution or replacement for the Herodian temple, nor did he criticize the worship carried out at the temple.[53] Similarly, after looking at John's view of Jesus as the new temple, Beate Kowalski argues that Jesus has become "the true 'location' of God's presence and worshipping him," yet claims: "This is not meant in form of a substitution."[54] Jonathan Klawans observes that the common Jewish belief in the existence of a heavenly temple did not necessarily imply a negative view of the Jerusalem temple.[55] And Jane Lancaster Patterson insists that "the metaphorizing of sacrifice by early followers of Jesus need not mean that they no longer perceived the Jewish cult as valid."[56] She also points out that "Paul was using metaphors of sacrifice at the same time that he participated in the cult itself. Neither metaphor nor actual practice took precedence over the other. Rather, the metaphors drew meaning, legitimation, and power from the ongoing cult."[57] Even the view that the Jerusalem temple was temporal or transitional to the eschatological

---

53. Friedrich Wilhelm Horn, "Paulus und der Herodianische Tempel," *NTS* 53 (2007): 184-203. In contrast, Richard B. Hays simply assumes that, in 1 Cor. 3:16-17, Paul asserts "that the church has replaced the temple" (*First Corinthians*; Interpretation; Louisville, KY: John Knox, 1997, 57). Similarly, Martin Hengel claims that Paul thought that Jesus' death "had made the Temple obsolete" and that the interpretation his first followers gave to his death "necessarily led to a break with the sacrificial cult in the Temple," yet he cites no evidence to support that claim (*The Atonement: The Origins of the Doctrine in the New Testament*; Philadelphia: Fortress, 1981, 44, 47).

54. Beate Kowalski, "Anticipations of Jesus' Death in the Gospel of John," in *The Death of Jesus in the Fourth Gospel* (ed. Gilbert Van Belle; BETL 200; Leuven: Peeters, 2007), 608; see 603-8.

55. Jonathan Klawans, *Purity, Sacrifice, and the Temple: Symbolism and Supersessionism in the Study of Ancient Judaism* (Oxford: Oxford University Press, 2006), 129.

56. Jane Lancaster Patterson, *Keeping the Feast: Metaphors of Sacrifice in 1 Corinthians and Philippians* (ECL; Atlanta: SBL, 2015), 4, 48.

57. Ibid., 48.

temple to come, reflected in the book of Tobit, need not be understood as a rejection of the Jerusalem temple.[58] Similarly, among Jesus' first followers, the relation between the two temples would probably be regarded as similar to the relationship between physical and spiritual circumcision. Just as the spiritual circumcision of believers and other aspects of faith and life in Christ were seen as fulfilling realities originally associated with the covenant made with Abraham and Moses, so also the new temple constituted by believers represented the fulfillment of the temple God had ordained to be built in Jerusalem. The ongoing existence of that temple before 70 CE could therefore be seen as the visible sign of a new invisible reality that had come into existence through Christ.

A Holy People

The idea that believers are now God's people and constitute God's temple is closely related to the claim that they are now holy and have been sanctified. Throughout the New Testament, the most common term used for believers is "saints" or "holy ones."[59] The fact that in Acts and Paul's epistles this term is used repeatedly to refer not only to believers in general but those in Jerusalem and Judea in particular suggests that its usage goes back to Jesus' first Jewish followers. When applied to non-Jewish believers, however, it would take on new meaning. This was because in Judaism the language of holiness had commonly been used to set Israel apart from other nations as a people distinct from all others due to their unique relationship with YHWH, the one true God. For Jesus' followers now to speak of gentile believers as holy in the same way that faithful Jews had been considered holy was therefore a novelty that must have sounded strange and extraordinary to many Jews who were not accustomed to such a usage. The language of holiness applied to gentile believers would constantly serve to remind both Jews and non-Jews of the radical change that had taken place in the lives of those believers, especially those who had previously worshiped other gods and practiced idolatry.

It is not surprising, therefore, that the allusions to believers having been sanctified or made holy appear most frequently in passages that speak of the incorporation of gentiles into the *ekklēsia* or that contrast the new life of believers with their previous life, or with the life of gentiles who are not followers of Christ. In Acts, Paul is presented as referring twice to the inclusion of gentiles among "those who have been sanctified" (Acts 20:32; 26:18). Other passages from the New Testament letters speak of the sanctification or holiness of gentile believers in terms of their being "called" (Rom. 1:6-7; 1 Cor. 1:2; 1 Thess. 4:3-7; 5:23-24; 2 Thess. 2:13-14; 2 Tim. 1:9; 1 Pet. 1:15-16; 2:9). In Rom. 6:19, 22 Paul speaks of sanctification when contrasting the

---

58. See Michael E. Fuller, *The Restoration of Israel: Israel's Re-gathering and the Fate of the Nations in Early Jewish Literature and Luke-Acts* (BZNW 138; Berlin: Walter de Gruyter, 2006), 130.

59. On this and other self-designations among Jesus' first followers, see Meeks, *First Urban Christians*, 84-94.

former impure ways of the Roman believers and their slavery to sin with their present freedom and life of righteousness. As noted above, after reminding the Corinthian believers of what they "used to be" when they practiced all sorts of sinful behavior as gentiles, Paul tells them: "But you were washed, you were sanctified, you were justified in the name of the Lord Jesus Christ and in the Spirit of our God" (1 Cor. 6:11). The author of Colossians contrasts the present holiness of believers with their former life, in which they "were once estranged and hostile in mind, doing evil deeds" (Col. 1:22) and then, like the author of Ephesians, tells them that they are now "holy" to the extent that they have put off their old self in order to be clothed with a new self (Eph. 4:22-24; Col. 3:5-12). In several passages, the letter to the Hebrews refers to believers as "those who are (being) sanctified" (Heb. 2:11; 10:10, 14).

A few of the passages just cited relate explicitly the sanctification of believers to the presence and activity of the Holy Spirit in them (1 Cor. 6:11; 1 Thess. 4:3-8; 1 Pet. 1:2). In Rom. 15:15-16, Paul speaks of the grace given to him by God "to be a minister of Christ Jesus to the Gentiles in the priestly service of the gospel of God, so that the offering of the Gentiles may be acceptable, sanctified by the Holy Spirit." The author of 2 Thessalonians tells his readers: "God chose you as the first fruits for salvation through sanctification by the Spirit and through belief in the truth." In fact, the adjective "holy" that is consistently used as a modifier to refer to God's Spirit serves to stress repeatedly that all those who receive that Spirit are thereby sanctified or made holy, not only in the sight of God, but in their thinking and conduct as well.

According to the story of Peter and Cornelius in Acts 10:1—11:18, what convinced Peter and the other Jewish believers to accept gentiles as full members of the community of Jesus' followers was the pouring out of the Holy Spirit on Cornelius and the other gentiles gathered at his home. Their reception of the Spirit is said to have moved them to speak in tongues and extol God. When Peter had arrived to Cornelius's home and had begun to preach there, evidently his intention had been that, even if some of the gentiles believed his message, they would nevertheless not be fully incorporated into the community of Jesus' followers through baptism, but would instead remain at the margins of that community in some way. Just as God-fearing non-Jews could attend the activities of the Jewish community at places such as the synagogue without actually becoming full members of that community through circumcision and the observance of the law, so Peter seems to have imagined that any of the gentiles who believed his message concerning Jesus would still not be candidates for baptism and full inclusion into the community of believers. The words attributed to him at the beginning of his speech imply that, even though they would not become full members of the community of believers through baptism, they would still be accepted by God: "I truly understand that God shows no partiality, but in every nation anyone who fears him and does what is right is acceptable to him" (Acts 10:34-35). According to the Acts account, however, when he sees that Cornelius and other gentiles have received the Holy Spirit, Peter asks, "Can anyone withhold the water for baptizing these people who have received the Holy Spirit just as we have?" (Acts 10:47; cf. 11:15-18; 15:8). The conclusion of the story is that gentile believers must be fully incorporated into the community of Jesus' followers through baptism, the same rite of initiation that Jewish believers underwent, because the Holy Spirit has in effect already made them full members of that community by descending upon them.

While many scholars would question the historicity of this account from Acts, Paul's letters provide further evidence that the experience of the reception of the Holy Spirit by gentile believers was an important factor in their incorporation into the community of believers. In Gal. 3:2-5, Paul writes: "The only thing I want to learn from you is this: Did you receive the Spirit as a result of works of the law or as a result of hearing with faith? Are you so foolish? Having started with the Spirit, are you now ending with the flesh?... Does God supply you with the Spirit and work wonders among you as a result of works of the law or as a result of hearing with faith?" Here Paul apparently points to visible manifestations of the Holy Spirit among uncircumcised believers. Similar manifestations of the Holy Spirit are mentioned in 1 Corinthians 12 and 14, where Paul seems to be addressing primarily believers of non-Jewish origin, and Rom. 15:16-19. In this latter passage, after referring to the "offering of the Gentiles" who are "sanctified by the Holy Spirit," Paul continues: "For I will not venture to speak of anything except what Christ has accomplished through me to win obedience from the Gentiles, by word and deed, by the power of signs and wonders, by the power of the Spirit of God." These passages reflect experiences that appear to be similar to that described by Luke in Acts 10.

What is not clear from these passages, however, is whether it was expected that all gentiles who came to faith would manifest some visible sign of the Holy Spirit's presence. This seems unlikely.[60] The fact that in 1 Corinthians 12 and 14 Paul argues that believers receive different gifts and abilities from the Holy Spirit, many of which do not involve any type of miraculous manifestation, seems to indicate that not all believers underwent the same type of experience. In fact, the problem at Corinth was that some were claiming to be superior to others on the basis of the spiritual gifts they had received, which implies that other believers had *not* received such spiritual gifts. If all were expected to manifest visibly the presence of the Holy Spirit, no doubt many of the problems characteristic of many charismatic Christian communities

---

60. Philip F. Esler, for example, simply assumes that the "initial reception of the Spirit" in baptism involved "an explosion of charismatic phenomena" and "dramatic experiential aspects" that included "a variety of ecstatic states ('altered states of consciousness') and phenomena, including trances, visions, auditions, prophecy, and glossolalia, that often produced feelings of peace and even euphoria" (*Conflict and Identity in Romans: The Social Setting of Paul's Letter*, Minneapolis: Fortress, 2003, 197-98, 206-7). Nevertheless, he presents no firm evidence in support of such claims, outside of pointing to 1 Corinthians 12-14 and Heb. 6:4-5. Neither of these passages mentions explicitly most of the phenomena to which Esler refers, such as altered ecstatic states and feelings of euphoria, nor do they suggest that all believers underwent such experiences or began to prophesy, speak in tongues, or manifest visibly their reception of the Holy Spirit when baptized.

today would have arisen. Not only would there be divisions in the community over these gifts, but those who did not receive them would be considered inferior and perhaps even be prevented from joining the community until they manifested such gifts. This would lead to the practice of exclusion and marginalization in the communities, similar to what was occurring in those places in which some were claiming that gentile believers needed to be circumcised and observe the law. Many of those who had come to faith in Christ might even feel pressured to pretend to have received some visible sign of the Holy Spirit's presence so that they might not be discriminated against. Furthermore, when entire families came to be incorporated into the *ekklēsia*, it would be unlikely that each individual member of the family would give evidence of having received some such spiritual gift. It seems doubtful, therefore, that miraculous visible manifestations of the Holy Spirit's presence were seen as the norm among gentile believers.

What was expected of all believers, however, was that they manifest the Holy Spirit's presence in their lives through their conduct. In the passage from Romans just mentioned, Paul points not only to signs and wonders but to the obedience that the Holy Spirit has brought about in gentile believers (Rom. 15:18). Similarly, in his discussion of the gifts and activity of the Holy Spirit in believers in 1 Corinthians 12–14, he repeatedly stresses the centrality of love and the need for believers to act in ways that contribute to the edification of others. The gifts that the Spirit gives all are given "for the common good" so that members "may have the same care for one another" (1 Cor. 12:7, 25); those gifts are to be used "for building up the church" (1 Cor. 14:12). While God may have brought about different kinds of signs and wonders in the Galatian believers through the Holy Spirit, in his letter to them, Paul dedicates much more attention to the "fruit" that the Spirit brings about in them and the love and righteousness that characterize the lives of believers as a result of their reception of the Spirit (Gal. 5:5—6:10). There, as in Romans 8, Paul contrasts the life of the Spirit with life in the flesh. Elsewhere, Paul repeatedly associates the Holy Spirit with things such as love, communion, compassion, righteousness, and a life of holiness (Rom. 5:5; 8:3-14; 14:17; 15:30; 1 Cor. 6:9-20; 2 Cor. 12:13; Phil. 2:1; 1 Thess. 4:7-9; 5:13). The same ideas are associated with the presence and activity of the Holy Spirit throughout the rest of the New Testament. The Holy Spirit produces love, unity, sanctification, obedience, and a renewal of life in believers, strengthens believers in their inner being, and distributes gifts among them (Eph. 3:16-17; 4:3; Col. 1:8; Tit. 3:5-6; Heb. 2:4; 1 Pet. 1:2; 1 John 3:23; 4:12-13; Jude 20-21). Many of these passages stress once more the contrast between the new life of gentile believers and their former conduct, or the conduct of gentiles who have not come to faith.

Neither Paul nor the other authors of the New Testament writings ever offer any explanation as to precisely how the Holy Spirit was thought to bring about the new life of love and obedience in believers. The passages that do describe the Holy Spirit's activity, however, focus on the Spirit's influence on the understanding and thinking of believers. The Holy Spirit instructs them as to what they are to say and gives them the wisdom and the words they need to edify others or speak on behalf of God (Mark 13:11; Acts 6:3, 10; 1 Cor. 12:8). In the Fourth Gospel, the disciples are told:

> "[T]he Advocate, the Holy Spirit, whom the Father will send in my name, will teach you everything, and remind you of all that I have said to you.... When the Spirit of truth comes, he will guide you into all the truth; for he will not speak on his own, but will speak whatever he hears, and he will declare to you the things that are to come. He will glorify me, because he will take what is mine and declare it to you. All that the Father has is mine. For this reason I said that he will take what is mine and declare it to you" (John 14:26; 16:13-15).

The passage in which Paul discusses in greatest detail the Spirit's working in believers is 1 Cor. 2:9-16, where he writes:

> But, as it is written, "What no eye has seen, nor ear heard, nor the human heart conceived, what God has prepared for those who love him"—these things God has revealed to us through the Spirit; for the Spirit searches everything, even the depths of God. For what human being knows what is truly human except the human spirit that is within? So also no one comprehends what is truly God's except the Spirit of God. Now we have received not the spirit of the world, but the Spirit that is from God, so that we may understand the gifts bestowed on us by God. And we speak of these things in words not taught by human wisdom but taught by the Spirit, interpreting spiritual things to those who are spiritual. Those who are unspiritual do not receive the gifts of God's Spirit, for they are foolishness to them, and they are unable to understand them because they are spiritually discerned. Those who are spiritual discern all things, and they are themselves subject to no one else's scrutiny. "For who has known the mind of the Lord so as to instruct him?" But we have the mind of Christ.

Although these passages do not explain how the Holy Spirit works in believers, they do seem to indicate that the Spirit's influence was seen in terms of affecting the thought processes of believers, that is, the way they understood and interpreted God's will in light of their faith, their reading of Scriptures, and the teaching they received in their communities. The Spirit instructs, guides, reminds, declares, reveals, and enables believers to discern, interpret, and comprehend. This means that the Holy Spirit was not believed to bring about some type of magical or ontological change in believers. There thus seems to be no basis for reading such ideas back into passages such as Rom. 5:5, for example, where Paul affirms that "God's love has been poured into our hearts through the Holy Spirit that has been given to us." In light of passages such as the one just cited from 1 Corinthians 2, Paul's words in Rom. 5:5 should not be understood in the sense that God's love is some type of mysterious substance infused into the hearts of believers that automatically produces a change in their conduct. The same observations should be made with regard to Gal. 5:22-23, which describes the fruit of the Spirit. Paul's idea there is that this fruit is brought about as believers "live by the Spirit" and are "guided by the Spirit" (Gal. 5:25). The same understanding of the Spirit's work is reflected in Rom. 8:3-17, where Paul speaks of believers walking in the Spirit, setting their minds on the Spirit, being led by the Spirit, and putting to death the deeds of the body through the Spirit. These affirmations and others (Rom. 8:26-27; 1 Cor. 12:3; Gal. 4:6; 1 Thess. 5:19) describe a process in which believers are active in a type of dialogue with the Spirit, rather than the outworking of some ontological change mysteriously effected in them with which they must now cooperate.

As we have noted previously, the idea that God's Spirit would some day be poured out on God's people in order to enable them to live according to God's will is found both in the Hebrew Scriptures and in other ancient Jewish writings.[61] In Acts 2, this promise is said to come to fulfillment on the Day of Pentecost, although the idea there seems to be that the promise of the gift of the Holy Spirit would be fulfilled not only on that day but from that moment on. For this reason, Paul also speaks of gentile believers receiving through faith the promise of the Holy Spirit in Gal. 3:14 (cf. Eph. 1:13). God has given them the Holy Spirit as a pledge or deposit (*arrabōn*, 2 Cor. 1:22; 5:5; Eph. 1:14), since the Spirit's presence in them anticipates the full reception of the Spirit in the age to come as well as the perfect righteousness that will one day be theirs (Gal. 5:5).

The idea that believers receive as a gift the obedience and new life God desires and requires also appears throughout the New Testament. In Acts 5:31 and 11:18, God is said to "give repentance" to those who believe. As in Jewish thought, repentance here should be taken as referring not merely to remorse over past sins, but to a change in the way believers think and behave. In addition to 1 Corinthians 12, several other passages speak of God giving gifts to believers in order to enable them to serve others (Rom. 12:6-8; Eph. 4:7-16; Heb. 2:4; 1 Pet. 4:10). In Rom. 5:16 and 10:4-9, the gift given is that of righteousness, which should be understood not merely as a righteous status before God but a new way of life in conformity with God's will (cf. Phil. 3:8-9). These passages can be seen as affirming the same basic idea Paul mentions in Rom. 5:5. The Spirit pours love into the hearts of believers by giving them gifts and enabling them to practice justice or righteousness so as to live in harmony with one another (Rom. 15:5). Paul also speaks of God being at work in believers in Phil. 1:6 and 2:13, while in 1 Thess. 2:13 it is God's *word* that is at work in them.

The affirmation that believers are strengthened by God, Christ, or the Holy Spirit is found over a dozen times in the New Testament letters (Rom. 12:25; 1 Cor. 1:8; 2 Cor. 12:7-10; Eph. 3:16; 6:10; Phil. 4:13; Col. 1:11-12;

---

61. W. D. Davies points to numerous texts in the Hebrew Scriptures and second-temple Jewish literature that reflect the idea that the messianic age "was expected to be a period when the rebelliousness of 'Israel' would be undone and righteousness enthroned...." According to Davies, "in most, if not in all cases, this righteousness would differ from that which was demanded by the Torah," which "would be better studied and better observed than ever before, even by Gentiles" (*Torah in the Messianic Age and/or the Age to Come*; JBLMS 7; Philadelphia: SBL, 1952, 47-48, 84).

1 Thess. 3:13; 2 Thess. 1:11-12; 2:16-17; 3:3; 1 Pet. 4:11; 5:10). A similar idea appears in Eph. 3:20, where the author alludes to "the power at work in us," as well as 2 Pet. 1:3, which affirms that God's "divine power has given us everything needed for life and godliness." The writer of Colossians also associates this power with the "energy" of Christ (Col. 1:29). On the basis of Luke's use of the word "power" in his Gospel and the book of Acts, it might even be argued that the allusion in these passages is to the Holy Spirit (see Luke 24:49; Acts 1:8; 26:17-20). When Paul writes that the Roman believers have become "obedient from the heart" to the teaching they received (Rom. 6:17; cf. 1 Tim. 1:5), he may once again have in mind the passages from Ezek. 11:19-20 and 36:26-27 that speak of God putting a new heart in his people so that they may obey him, or the allusion to God writing his law in the people's hearts in Jer. 31:33. This latter passage is seen as being fulfilled in believers in Heb. 10:16.

These passages and others, therefore, clearly communicate the idea that the obedience that characterizes the life of believers is brought about in them by God as a gracious gift. Undoubtedly, many passages also speak of the need for believers to respond to this gift and thus imply that the obedience of believers is something they enact willingly. Curiously, in fact, immediately before telling the Philippians that "it is God who is at work in you, enabling you both to will and to work for his good pleasure," he exhorts them: "work out your own salvation with fear and trembling" (Phil. 2:12-13). This makes it clear that for Paul the new obedience is not something that God brings about automatically or magically in believers. For this reason, Paul saw no contradiction between affirming that the new life of believers is the work of God and at the same time is the work of believers themselves.[62]

It would be a mistake, however, to regard this divine activity in believers as something God was thought to bring about only *directly* through the presence of Christ or the Holy Spirit in their hearts and minds. Rather, in New Testament thought, God is also seen as acting *through the community of believers* to accomplish his purposes of strengthening, empowering, encouraging, exhorting, admonishing, and directing those who form part of that community. The passages we have noted that speak of God giving believers gifts to build one another up and respond to their various needs point to this fact: through each believer, God is active in the lives of others in order to accomplish his purposes. Running throughout the New Testament is also the idea that God has placed certain people in positions of leadership in the church so that they can attend to the needs of the members, provide them with the strength and guidance they need, enable them to practice love, compassion, and justice in their dealings with others inside and outside of the community,

---

62. On this aspect of Paul's thought and his conviction that it is God who brings about the new life of obedience in believers through Christ and the Holy Spirit, see especially Kyle B. Wells, *Grace and Agency in Paul and Second Temple Judaism: Interpreting the Transformation of the Heart* (NovTSup 157; Leiden: Brill, 2015), 209-23, 253-311.

and equip them to carry out the particular activities of ministry to which they have been called.

This is the activity attributed to the apostles and other leaders in Acts. Paul, Barnabas, Silas, and Timothy make themselves present in the different churches to encourage the believers and strengthen them in their faith (Acts 14:22; 15:32, 41; 16:4-5, 40; 18:23; 20:1-2). Paul tells the Romans that this is the purpose of the visit he hopes to make there: "I am longing to see you so that I may share with you some spiritual gift to strengthen you—or rather so that we may be mutually encouraged by each other's faith, both yours and mine" (Rom. 1:11-12). Here Paul not only gives encouragement, but also receives it from the Roman believers. In 1 Thessalonians, Paul tells those to whom he writes that he is sending Timothy to strengthen them, yet he also exhorts them to encourage and build one another up (1 Thess. 3:2; 4:18; 5:11-14). The idea that the community's leaders are to strengthen and guide others is combined with the exhortation for believers to build one another up in Eph. 4:7-16 as well. There the author says that God has given the community different types of leaders to "equip the holy ones for ministry" and then describes how the community's members grow up together in truth into Christ as a body "building itself up in love." A few verses later, he also exhorts them to speak "what is useful for building up, as there is need, so that your words may give grace to those who hear" (Eph. 4:29). Elsewhere he tells the Galatian believers to bear one another's burdens (Gal. 6:2) and instructs the Philippian believers to look out for the interests of one another (Phil. 2:1-4). In Colossians, the believers are told to "teach and admonish one another" (Col. 3:16). The author of Hebrews calls on believers to "exhort one another every day" and "to provoke one another to love and good deeds" by "encouraging one another" (Heb. 3:13; 10:24-25). Examples of these kinds of affirmations in the New Testament could be multiplied, yet they all point to the same idea: the community is itself a means by which God strengthens, transforms, and builds up believers and brings about in them the life of obedience, love, and justice that he desires to see in all. It might be said, therefore, that the community is a "means of grace" in relation to each believer, though at the same time each believer is also a "means of grace" in relation to the community.

More than anything else, it was the commitment to practice love, compassion, and justice in obedience to Christ and in the manner defined by him that was thought to make of Jesus' followers a type of alternative community that stood in contrast to the rest of society and the world. The New Testament writings stress this idea in a variety of ways. The solidarity among all believers is like that of a family, in which all are brothers and sisters. Believers are to be the salt of the earth and the light of the world (Matt. 5:13-16). The contrast between light and darkness is used frequently elsewhere to stress that believers are to live differently than the world, putting away evil and injustice in all its forms in order to walk in the truth and live openly according to God's will, seeking to give witness to others of all that they have received through their faith in Christ (Luke 16:8; John 3:19-21; 8:12; 11:9-10; 12:46; Acts 26:17-18; 2 Cor. 6:14—7:1; Col. 1:13; 1 Thess. 5:5; 1 John 2:9-11). Believers are repeatedly told that their conduct is to set them apart from others outside of the community. They are not to live as if they still belonged to the world (Col. 2:20), since "friendship with the world is enmity with God" (James 4:4). For Paul, however, this does not mean withdrawing from the world, but simply not tolerating the persistent and willful practice of evil and injustice, particularly within the community itself (1 Cor. 6:9-13).

This same attitude is reflected in the use of the word *world* in the Johannine writings. On the one hand, believers do not belong to the world, which hates them, and are not to love the world (John 15:18-19; 17:14-16; 1 John 2:15-17; 3:13; 4:5-6). On the other hand, however, believers are to love the world in the way that God does and seek its salvation rather than its condemnation (John 3:16-17; 6:33, 51; 12:46-47; 17:21-23; 1 John 4:9, 14). They are to serve others inside and outside of the community and even give their life for that cause, as Jesus did (Mark 10:41-45; Luke 22:25-27; 1 John 3:16). In short, what God expects from believers is expressed in Paul's words to the Philippians, a passage already cited above: "Do all things without murmuring and arguing, so that you may be blameless and innocent, children of God without blemish in the midst of a crooked and perverse generation, in which you shine like stars in the world" (Phil. 2:14-15).

The Forgiveness of Sins under the New Covenant

As has been noted briefly above, in the Hebrew Scriptures and ancient Jewish thought, the promise of divine forgiveness was closely associated with the covenant. There, while God promised to punish and discipline Israel for its sins in order to bring the people into conformity with his will, he also promised to forgive them their sins. The promise of forgiveness is also associated with the *new* covenant in Jer. 31:34, where God says: "I will forgive their iniquity and remember their sin no more." In a passage already cited, Paul relates the covenant with the forgiveness of sins in Rom. 11:27: "This will be my covenant with them, when I take away their sins." Throughout the Hebrew Scriptures and ancient Jewish literature, however, divine forgiveness is consistently said to be dependent upon Israel's repentance and obedience to God. At the same time, God promises to bring about in the people the obedience he desires to see.

In the present age, of course, God's forgiveness was always provisional and temporary. There were times in Israel's history when God was thought to have forgiven Israel once it had turned back to him in order to live in conformity with his will. Individuals might also enjoy God's forgiveness when they repented so as to live as God desired once again. Both the nation and the individuals belonging to it, however, always remained sinful and therefore were always in need of God's forgiveness. For this reason, it was necessary for

God to tolerate his people's sins in the present age until he acted to make the new age a reality.

According to the proclamation of Jesus' first followers, God had now designated Jesus as the one who would bring about in God's people the obedience God desired. As we saw in Chapter 6, for that reason, Jesus was also seen as the one through whom God granted forgiveness, both in this world and in the world to come. This belief led Jesus' followers to proclaim that, while God had overlooked the sins of Israel in the past, prior to Jesus' coming, all were now to repent in the sense of coming to live according to God's will as defined by Jesus (Acts 2:38-39; 3:19; 5:31; 20:21). This involved living under the covenant of which Jesus had spoken at the Last Supper as members of the community of those who called him Lord.

Yet because non-Jews could also come to live under that covenant as members of Jesus' community without submitting to the provisions of the Mosaic law, the apostolic proclamation called on people from all nations to repent by coming to live as Jesus' followers (Acts 11:18; 20:21; 26:20). Through Jesus, repentance was now open to all. This proclamation included the affirmation that God would no longer take into account the past sins of those who turned to Jesus in faith. The clearest expression of this idea is in Paul's sermon at the Areopagus in Athens in Acts 17:22-31. There, after affirming that all are the offspring of the one true God who created all the nations, Paul proclaims: "While God has overlooked the times of human ignorance, now he commands all people everywhere to repent, because he has fixed a day on which he will have the world judged in righteousness by a man whom he has appointed, and of this he has given assurance to all by raising him from the dead" (vv. 30-31). Here the idea is that, now that God has revealed to all peoples his plan aimed at the salvation of all through Jesus, he is willing to overlook the sin and evil that people from among the nations have committed in the past, leaving those nations unpunished, as long as they now look to Jesus as Lord.

This same idea is hinted at several chapters earlier in Acts, when the inhabitants of Lystra take Paul and Barnabas to be Hermes and Zeus (14:8-13). Paul responds to them, "We are mortals just like you, and we bring you good news, that you should turn from these worthless things to the living God, who made the heaven and the earth and the sea and all that is in them. In past generations he allowed all the nations to follow their own ways; yet he has not left himself without a witness in doing good—giving you rains from heaven and fruitful seasons, and filling you with food and your hearts with joy" (14:15-17). Here, although Paul is not able to finish his discourse, we find once more the idea that God had simply allowed all the nations to go their own ways until the salvation he intended for all would be revealed. Like Paul's speech in Athens, this speech emphasizes God's goodness and God's desire to relate to people from all nations.

A couple of passages from Paul's letters seem to allude to the same idea. In 2 Cor. 5:18-20, Paul writes. "All this is from God, who reconciled us to himself through Christ, and has given us the ministry of reconciliation; that is, in Christ God was reconciling the world to himself, not counting their trespasses against them, and entrusting the message of reconciliation to us. So we are ambassadors for Christ, since God is making his appeal through us; we entreat you on behalf of Christ, be reconciled to God." As in the passage from Acts 17, the idea is that God simply overlooks and leaves unpunished the sins of the past, as long as people now turn to him in order to be reconciled with him through Christ.

Paul's affirmation in Rom. 3:25 should also be understood in this sense. After mentioning that God put forward Christ as a *hilastērion* so that all can be justified by grace through him or his blood, Paul continues: "He did this to show his righteousness, because in his divine forbearance he had passed over the sins previously committed." These words seem to reflect the ideas we have just seen: God tolerantly let the nations go their ways and practice sin in the past in view of the salvation that he would some day come to offer them in Christ.[63] Had God punished those nations by destroying them for their sins, they would not have had an opportunity to turn to God through Christ and thereby attain righteousness, as they do now. These ideas may also be behind the allusion to "the cleansing of past sins" found in 2 Pet. 1:9.

These passages from Acts and Paul's letters speak of what we would today call a "general amnesty": God declares his willingness to forgive all the sins of the past as long as people now come to faith in Christ so as to be transformed by him. Up until the time of the gospel's proclamation throughout the world, God had tolerated the sins of the nations, knowing that they had still not received what was necessary for them to turn to him in obedience. For that reason, he did not punish or destroy them for their sins. Through Christ, however, he had now provided them with what they needed.[64] Of course, the same was true with regard to Israel: now that God had sent Jesus in order to fulfill the promises he had made to Israel, he was willing to overlook the sins that his people had committed in the past, as long as they turned to Jesus in faith in order to live under his lordship in the covenant God had established or renewed through him.

This idea of overlooking past sins is therefore similar to that which appears in the parable of the unforgiving servant in Matt. 18:23-35. In that parable, the king, who seems to represent God, simply forgives the debt accumulated by the servant out of pure grace and mercy. Once this forgiveness has been offered, however, the king expects that the servant will treat others with the same kindness and compassion. When the servant does not do so, the king revokes his forgiveness of the servant's debt. In the same way, in the passages

---

63. See Jewett, *Romans*, 291.
64. I would agree, however, with Neil Elliott that if Rom. 3:25 is understood in terms of a "general amnesty," this amnesty should be understood as a temporary and provisional one, since in Paul's thought "[t]he ultimate accountability of all to God's judgment—sounded from the beginning of the letter—remains firmly in place; it has not been cancelled or absolved by a doctrine of vicarious atonement" ("Paul's Political Christology: Samples from Romans," in *Reading Paul*, ed. Ehrensperger and Tucker, 48).

just considered, out of pure grace and mercy, God in essence wipes the slate clean in order that Jews and non-Jews may now come to faith in Jesus. Because God's goal is the regeneration of both Israel and the nations, he is willing to overlook the past as long as that regeneration begins to take place in the present through faith in Christ.

The same idea is associated with the rite of baptism in the New Testament. Both John's baptism as well as baptism in the name of Christ involve a washing away of past sins and a new beginning. After Paul encounters the risen Jesus on the road to Damascus, Ananias tells him: "Get up, be baptized, and have your sins washed away, calling on his name" (Acts 22:16). On the Day of Pentecost, Peter tells the crowds in Jerusalem who have been convicted of the sin they committed in crucifying Jesus, "Repent, and be baptized every one of you in the name of Jesus Christ so that your sins may be forgiven; and you will receive the gift of the Holy Spirit" (Acts 2:38). The language in these passages is similar to that of Paul in 1 Cor. 6:11: "But you were washed, you were sanctified, you were justified in the name of the Lord Jesus Christ and in the Spirit of our God" (cf. Eph. 5:25-27). If Paul has in mind here the baptism of the Corinthian believers, as seems likely, he is referring to the way in which God has overlooked their past sins and made them holy, not only by forgiving them what they had done previously, but by conferring the Holy Spirit upon them so as to enable them to live in obedience in the present. The Pauline language of dying and being buried with Christ in baptism and putting off one's old self in order to put on a new self also seems to convey the same idea (Rom. 6:3-11; Eph. 4:22-24; Col. 2:12; 3:9-10).

According to passages such as these, baptism symbolized one's break with the past and one's turning to God in order to live a new life out of faith. The logic is that God overlooks the sins of one's former life now that one has submitted to Christ in order to live under him as Lord. As Christiansen has stressed, this involves a *change of identity*.[65] The idea that those baptized receive the Holy Spirit, however, should not be understood in the sense that the Holy Spirit is mysteriously communicated to the person baptized by means of the water used in the rite. In New Testament thought, the Holy Spirit is poured out first and foremost on believers collectively (John 20:22; Acts 2:33; 4:31; 8:17; 10:44-47; 13:52; 19:6; Rom. 5:5; 1 Cor. 12:13; Gal. 4:6). Those who are baptized into Christ to live under his lordship with the rest of believers therefore enter into the realm where the Holy Spirit is active in a unique manner, and in this way come to live under the Spirit's influence in the community, together with other believers. All are to live in "humility and gentleness, with patience, bearing with one another in love, making every effort to maintain the unity of the Spirit in the bond of peace," since "there is one body and one Spirit, just as you were called to the one hope of your calling" (Eph. 4:2-4). As we have seen above, through the Spirit and the community of believers, Christ brings about in them the new life of obedience God desires to see. This

---

65. Christiansen, *Covenant*, 291-318.

new life of obedience therefore constitutes the *basis* upon which God forgives them. Once again, although this forgiveness is free and is not given on the basis of any works or merit on the part of those baptized, in New Testament thought it is offered on the condition that, from the moment they come to faith and are baptized, they will live under Christ's lordship in faith so that Christ and the Spirit may be at work in them through the community to bring about in them graciously the new way of life necessary in order for God to declare them righteous.

This same logic is behind the New Testament affirmations that the forgiveness of sins is granted by God in Jesus' name, just as believers are baptized in Jesus' name (Acts 2:38; 8:16; 10:48; 19:5; cf. 1 Cor. 1:14-18; 6:11). In Acts 10:43, Peter proclaims that "everyone who believes in him receives forgiveness of sins through his name." Paul repeats the same claim in Acts 13:38-39: "through this man forgiveness of sins is proclaimed to you; by this Jesus everyone who believes is set free from all those sins from which you could not be freed by the law of Moses." As just noted above, Paul himself is told by Ananias: "Get up, be baptized, and have your sins washed away, calling on his name" (Acts 22:16). The author of 1 John similarly tells his readers: "your sins are forgiven on account of his name" (1 John 2:12).

While God offers forgiveness to all, therefore, that forgiveness is conditional upon people turning away from their sinful ways in order to turn to God in Christ. As 1 John indicates, this also requires that all acknowledge their sins so as to renounce them: "If we say that we have no sin, we deceive ourselves, and the truth is not in us. If we confess our sins, he who is faithful and just will forgive us our sins and cleanse us from all unrighteousness" (1 John 1:8-9). Jesus' name does not constitute some type of magical formula given by God through which people can automatically obtain forgiveness or other blessings they ask of him. Rather, to invoke God's forgiveness and blessings in Jesus' name is to indicate that the basis upon which one is approaching God and asking for that forgiveness and those blessings is that one is committed to doing God's will as defined by Jesus, living under his lordship in faith so as to form part of his community of followers, the "new temple."[66] On that basis, God receives the petitions presented to him favorably, knowing that those who follow Jesus are being transformed in the way he desires. Because of this, God can rest assured that the forgiveness and blessings he will grant will contribute to that transformation, rather than having the opposite effect of leading those who approach him to fall further into sin by responding to that forgiveness and those blessings by living in a way that is harmful and thus contrary to God's will.

Undoubtedly, there are passages in the New Testament in which no conditions are attached to divine forgiveness. Generally, however, fulfillment of

---

66. In this regard, Paul M. Hoskins argues that, in the Fourth Gospel, because "praying in Jesus' name acknowledges that Jesus is the means by which those who pray have access to God," it is "possible that prayer in Jesus' name is meant to fulfill and replace prayer in or toward the Temple" (*Jesus as the Fulfillment of the Temple in the Gospel of John*; PBM; Milton Keynes: Paternoster, 2006, 174).

those conditions seems to be implicit. Jesus freely forgives the sinful woman who washes his feet at the home of Simon the Pharisee in Luke 7:36-50. However, the fact that she is weeping should be seen as indicating a spirit of repentance, while her act of washing his feet represents an act of devotion to him as Lord. When Jesus forgives the sins of the paralytic who is lowered through the roof in a home in Capernaum, there is no mention of any type of repentance on the part of the paralytic and, after the healing, the paralytic simply departs (Mark 2:1-13). It may be significant, however, that the people gathered at the home were there to hear Jesus' *teaching*, which implies that all those present were considering following Jesus. This would therefore have been true of the paralytic and those who brought him to the house as well. In any case, in this account and others, the forgiveness of sins is related to Jesus' work of healing and is a response to the common belief that, when people suffered illnesses and physical ailments, it was because God was punishing them for their sins or those of someone close to them. In a similar account in the Fourth Gospel, after healing a paralytic who then carries his mat on a Sabbath, Jesus tells him: "Do not sin any more, so that nothing worse happens to you" (John 5:14). Thus, even when Jesus forgives sin freely, the expectation is that the one forgiven will at some point come to live in the way Jesus teaches.

Of course, in New Testament thought, God can also use free forgiveness as a means to bring people to faith in Jesus so that their lives may be changed by him. Jesus himself was remembered as one who openly received people regarded as sinners without demanding that they first repent. Nevertheless, his hope was that, for their own well-being and wholeness, they might be brought to follow him and thereby live according to the will of the God he proclaimed and called "Father." At the same time, those who persistently refused to live according to God's will and instead insisted on practicing evil and injustice were the object of Jesus' condemnation. Ultimately, then, even when the God of Jesus was thought to grant forgiveness freely, the condition upon which people continued to receive that forgiveness and acceptance was that they be committed to refraining from behavior that harmed themselves and others. This gracious forgiveness and acceptance was offered to them with the hope that they might be brought to live in conformity with God's will through faith in Christ.

Throughout most of the New Testament, divine forgiveness is said to be granted independently of any allusion to Jesus' death or any type of sacrificial offering. This presents a problem for much traditional Protestant theology, which has claimed that forgiveness is always dependent upon the death of Jesus or that of a sacrificial victim. Obviously, such an idea is a theological presupposition that is read back into the texts. Undoubtedly, there are a number of passages in the New Testament that affirm that Jesus' death was "for sins" and relate it to the justification of believers. Only a few passages, however, explicitly use the phrase "forgiveness of sins" in connection with Jesus' death or blood.[67] Matthew's version of Jesus' words over the cup at the Last Supper relate forgiveness both to Jesus' blood and the covenant established or ratified through him: "This is my blood of the covenant, which is poured out for many for the forgiveness of sins" (Matt. 26:28). The idea reflected in this passage, however, is not that believers are forgiven by virtue of Jesus' death or blood. Rather, as we saw in Chapter 7, the basis upon which believers are forgiven and justified is the new life of righteousness that God brings about in them through Christ, the Holy Spirit, and their brothers and sisters in the faith. For Matthew, as for the authors of the other New Testament writings, the purpose of Jesus' life and death was the formation of a community in which people might receive both the obedience God desires as well as the forgiveness of their sins. In other words, the idea behind Matt. 26:28 is *not that believers obtain forgiveness simply because Jesus died or shed his blood, but rather that by means of his death or blood he has established a new covenant and a new covenant community in which all may now obtain the forgiveness of sins through him.*

It can also be said, therefore, that Jesus lived and died in order to constitute a new basis upon which people are to relate to God and one another. The covenant established or renewed through Jesus must be understood in these terms: God now relates to human beings through Jesus, whom he raised and exalted in response to his faithfulness unto death to the task God had given to him. At the same time, believers now relate to God and one another through Jesus as members of his community of followers. This makes the covenant established or ratified through Jesus distinct from the covenant with Israel, since in the latter covenant, those relationships were defined by the Mosaic law. In the new covenant, the blessings of salvation and the forgiveness of sins are promised to those who live under Jesus' lordship with their sisters and brothers in the faith rather than being tied to obedience to the law per se.

JESUS' DEATH AND THE NEW COVENANT

What we have seen in this chapter and the previous two provides us with the background necessary to consider in greater detail the meaning that Jesus' first followers ascribed to his death. In order to respond to the questions of why Jesus had died and what his death signified, they would have looked to the new historical reality that had resulted from his life, ministry, death, and resurrection, as well as the aims and objectives that they ascribed to Jesus and the God he called "Father." In their mind, the primary objective of Jesus had been to form around himself a people who would live according to God's will as it had been redefined through Jesus. That objective could be accomplished only by Jesus giving up his life in love for others when his efforts to define God's will more fully and bring others into conformity with that will had met with opposition and had led to the possibility of a violent death. More than anything else that he had done, Jesus' willingness to give up his life and

---

[67]. Those passages, including Rom. 3:25, 4:25, 5:9, 18, 1 Cor. 15:3, 2 Cor. 5:21, Gal. 1:4, Col. 2:13-14, and Heb. 10:16-19, will be examined further on in this study.

die such a death out of love for others defined what it meant to live as God desired, loving God with one's whole heart, soul, mind, and strength, and loving others as oneself. As we have seen, if Jesus and the God he called "Father" truly wished to establish a community of people who would live in such love and solidarity with one another and also with others outside the community, when Jesus' activity had led to the threat of the cross, it was necessary for Jesus to offer up his life to God rather than seeking to save his life.

Jesus' death would also have been seen as accomplishing other purposes intimately related to that primary objective. The fact that Jesus had trusted fully in God to the very end without wavering and that God had responded to the trust and love for others that Jesus had shown by raising him and exalting him as Lord enabled Jesus' followers to trust in God in the same way and to be willing to love others as Jesus had done, in spite of the consequences. Because of the way Jesus had died, they could live in faith and love boldly, rather than living in fear and being enslaved by those who sought to dominate them by power and intimidation. God's response to Jesus' faithfulness to death to the task given him also validated everything that Jesus had said and taught about the God of unconditional love he had called "Father." Due to their relationship with Jesus and the concept of God that he had communicated to them, they could now approach God confidently, knowing that through Jesus God would receive them and their prayers favorably and forgive them any sins they had committed. Thanks to the way Jesus had related to God in his life and death, the vision of God that his followers had was transformed. They came to see God as their loving Father or *Abba*, a God who cared so deeply for them and all people that he had been willing to send his Son into the world and hand him over to death on a cross in order that they might come to know him more fully and live as his children. In this way, they came to know themselves as persons who were loved unconditionally, not only by God and his Son Jesus, but by their sisters and brothers in the community that Jesus had established through his death. The experience of such love also led them to offer up their lives to God as Jesus had done and dedicate themselves to seeking the well-being of others in joyful obedience to Jesus their Lord, savior, and brother.

By reaching out to Israel and the nations and giving his Son over to death before raising him as Lord, God had therefore made it possible for all people to receive as a gift the new life of repentance and obedience he desired to see for the good of all. This new life became a reality as people lived under Jesus' lordship, guided by the Holy Spirit and strengthened by their brothers and sisters in the faith, who shared the same commitment to the values and way of being for which Jesus had given up his life. The proclamation of the gospel regarding Jesus and the God whose love he had embodied enabled those who had lived in sin and injustice, following their passions and selfish desires and serving oppressive idols, to leave behind their destructive behavior. By coming to faith in Jesus and being baptized in his name, they could wash away their transgressions and become slaves of God and of justice for their own well-being and happiness, rather than living as slaves of sin, fear, and the vices that characterized the life of those who did not know God. Ironically, by offering up their lives to the God of Jesus so as to belong to him rather than belonging to themselves, they became truly free. They left behind the darkness so as to come into the light and live sanctified, holy lives by practicing the love, compassion, and commitment to justice that had characterized the life of their Lord, who had died for them. In this way, they fulfilled God's law and the "law of Christ."

Following Jesus, believers thus adopted a new way of life. They came to delight in doing God's will, obeying him not out of fear of punishment or in an attempt to gain his favor, but out of love and gratitude for all he had done for them. Rather than seeking power, prestige, or wealth for themselves in this world, as followers of the crucified one they came to denounce greed, injustice, and the lust for domination boldly and prophetically, as Jesus had done. Their community thus represented an alternative to the oppressive political, economic, and social system represented by Rome and its allies, whose power they resisted by living their lives rooted in Christ as their Lord.[68] By practicing love and solidarity and caring for one another's needs, they created a system of mutual support and interdependency. By means of the resources and gifts they graciously received from God through his Spirit, they came to constitute a body composed of many parts, of which Christ was the head. Each member of that body came to be a gift to the others and a means by which all were built up in their faith and love. Their submission to Jesus as their Lord and shepherd enabled him to guide, strengthen, comfort, nourish, and embolden them so that they might serve as God's instruments for accomplishing the same objectives among their sisters and brothers in the new family God had given them through Jesus' death and resurrection. They thus provided each other with mutual support, forgiving one another as God had forgiven them, and finding healing, encouragement, consolation, fellowship, joy, and peace in one another's company.

The values embodied in this community also served to strengthen family and kinship bonds among its members. Distinctions and divisions based on gender, class, and ethnicity were challenged and to some extent overcome. Women and men, old and young, masters and slaves, Jews and non-Jews came together in a spirit of reconciliation and solidarity. The hatred, jealousy, rivalry, and enmity that had characterized relationships between people of different

---

68. Michael Wolter rightly notes that the first believers' acclamation of a crucified man as God's Son and Lord over all inevitably led to a view of the world that was vastly different than the predominant view in antiquity: "the 'word of the cross' separates the Christian understanding of reality from *all other* understandings of reality" and "establishes a *Christian* identity that stands alone, which is dominant over all other ascriptions of identity.... The fact that Christians ascribe their salvation to a death on a cross or that they confess one who died on the cross as their Lord therefore indicates in fact a 'fundamental difference' between a Christian and a non-Christian understanding of reality" (*Paul: An Outline of His Theology*, trans. Robert L. Brawley; Waco, TX: Baylor University Press, 2015, 120, 123).

groups were no longer to have any place among those who followed Jesus as their crucified Lord. They sought to reconcile Jews and non-Jews to one another and to reconcile people in general to one another, so that all might live in peace. Together they experienced not only the gifts and blessings of God in the present, but the hope of new life in the world to come, which would be established when Jesus returned in glory and power to deliver them from the present evil age. This hope gave them the strength necessary to endure the sufferings and hardships that characterized their life in Christ in this world.

While the formation of such a community had constituted the primary objective of God and Jesus, it was not only an end in itself, but also a means for God to reach out to the world in general in order to accomplish his loving purposes. Jesus' followers were to be committed to caring for the poor, the sick, and the suffering, and sharing generously with those in need, not only within their own midst, but outside of their communities as well. They were to love their enemies and pray for those who persecuted them, seeking the same peace and reconciliation that they had found among their brothers and sisters in the faith. Their desire was that all people might come to experience the new reality that had become theirs as they lived under Jesus their Lord.

This summary of the ideas we have seen in this chapter and the previous ones brings us back to the question of Jesus' death. In the minds of his first followers, *all of this was what Jesus had not only lived for, but above all what he had died for.* This new reality had come to pass only because he had been willing to give up his life when his efforts to create such a community had met with resistance, opposition, and the threat of a violent death. When his followers spoke of the new covenant that had been established through his death or blood, *they had in mind all of the realities just mentioned.* The promises of salvation that Jesus had sought to see fulfilled involved not only the life of the age to come, but a life in community such as that described in the preceding paragraphs.[69] Such a life had constituted the objective not only of Jesus in his life and death, but the objective of his Father as well, who had sent him and had given him up to death before raising and exalting him as Lord. Through Jesus, God had established a *new basis* upon which all might relate to him, to one another, and to the world around them. According to Jesus' first followers, this new basis or new covenant had become a reality only because Jesus had been willing to give up his life to bring it about, and because God had sent his Son and handed him over to death, rather than sparing him the suffering of the cross. Jesus' ministry of healing, teaching, and preparing disciples, as well as the death that resulted from that ministry, had laid the foundation for this new reality. The objective had never been that Jesus die, as if something might be accomplished by his death itself, but that through him and his death this new covenant might come into existence and spread throughout the world.

---

69. As Luke Timothy Johnson stresses, the idea that salvation involves forming part of a community in the present is central to the thought of both Luke and Paul (*Contested Issues in Christian Origins and the New Testament: Collected Essays*, NovTSup 146; Leiden: Brill, 2015, 183-204).

The same points must also be stressed when considering the New Testament passages that relate Jesus' death or blood to the forgiveness of sins. In the mind of Jesus' first followers, *the condition upon which people are forgiven and accepted by God is not Jesus' death or blood per se, but their commitment to living according to God's will as defined by Jesus.* Nevertheless, the reason why forgiveness is often related to Jesus' death is that he went to his death seeking, not only that God enable others to be brought into conformity with his will through him as God's instrument, but also that God accept and forgive all who would live under his lordship in faith once he had been raised and exalted. The task that Jesus' Father had given him was not that of obtaining divine forgiveness for their sins, but that of constituting a new people who would live as God desired for their own well-being and that of others. Jesus' faithfulness to that task to the very end, however, not only made it possible for such a community of people to exist, but also resulted in God's accepting and forgiving all those who would live in that community, in spite of their past and present sinfulness. The reason why the New Testament often relates Jesus' death or blood to the forgiveness of sins is to stress that, more than anything else, it was Jesus' love for others and his total commitment to the task of forming a people who would be pleasing and acceptable to God that led to his death, to the existence of such a people, and to God's gracious acceptance of that people.

Jesus' Death and the New Temple

According to a number of passages from the New Testament, Jesus' death served to establish not only a new covenant, but a new temple. We have already examined above the idea that believers themselves constitute a temple or new temple. Several passages from the Gospels, however, associate Jesus himself with a new temple. When Jesus affirms that "something greater than the temple is here" in Matt. 12:6 (cf. 12:42), the allusion seems to be to Jesus personally or to his activity as mediator. In John 2:19-21, after driving out the vendors and money changers at the temple and overturning their tables, Jesus tells "the Jews": "Destroy this temple, and in three days I will raise it up." After they ask how he can build the temple in three days, the author of the Fourth Gospel comments that Jesus "was speaking of the temple of his body." Here the new temple is identified with Jesus' body or Jesus himself.[70]

Passages such as the account of the adoration of the magi, who come from afar to bring precious gifts to the infant Jesus, also seem to imply that Jesus is in some way the fulfillment of the temple in Jerusalem (Matt. 2:1-11). In

---

70. As Kåre Fuglseth has stressed, similar to what we noted above with regard to the Pauline idea that believers constitute the temple of God, to speak of Jesus or his body as a new temple does not necessarily imply a rejection of the Jerusalem temple or its replacement by Jesus (*Johannine Sectarianism in Perspective: A Sociological, Historical, and Comparative Analysis of Temple and Social Relationships in the Gospel of John, Philo, and Qumran*; NovTSup 119; Leiden: Brill, 2005, 136-76). If we speak of the replacement of the Jerusalem temple by Jesus, therefore, this need not be taken in the sense that Jesus' followers believed that, after his death and resurrection, the Jerusalem temple no longer was of any value or fulfilled any purpose.

this case, the magi represent the gentiles who were expected to flock to the Jerusalem temple some day to worship Israel's God there with their gifts.[71] Several passages from the Fourth Gospel and Colossians appear to speak of Jesus as a new temple in which God dwells.[72] In Rev. 21:22, both Jesus and God together constitute the heavenly temple.

As in John 2:13-22, the construction of a new temple is associated explicitly with Jesus' death in the passion narratives of Matthew and Mark. There Jesus is accused of having said that he would tear down the temple and rebuild it or build another one in three days (Matt. 26:61; 27:40; Mark 14:58; 15:29). Scholars such as Donald Juel and Timothy Gray have drawn attention to the centrality of the Jerusalem temple in Mark's Gospel, and especially in his passion narrative.[73] Mark also stresses that this new temple is "not made with hands" (14:58).[74] While the construction of a new temple in Matthew and Mark is obviously an allusion to Jesus' resurrection, it is not clear whether the temple to be built or rebuilt is to be identified with Jesus himself, with his community of followers, or perhaps even with an eschatological temple.[75] The idea that some type of spiritual or eschatological temple exists in heaven and will be revealed at Jesus' coming seems to be present in 2 Cor. 5:1-10, where Paul writes that "we have a building from God, a house not made with hands, eternal in the heavens" (v. 1). Because heaven is the place from where the risen Jesus will come and the hope of believers is to attain the same type of resurrection body that Christ now has in heaven (see Phil. 3:20-21), it is at least possible that in the thought of Matthew or Mark, the temple that Jesus would build in three days is one that believers now await from heaven.

---

71. See Charles Scobie, "Israel and the Nations," *TynB* 43 (1992): 302. Fuller Dow also points to other passages in Matthew that present Jesus as the fulfillment of the Jerusalem temple, as well as "the true Israel and the true Zion, the one of whom Zion of old was a foreshadowing" (*Images of Zion*, 146; see 140-46).

72. Christopher A. Beetham claims that the affirmation that "all the fullness of God" dwells in Christ in Col. 1:19 (cf. 2:9) should be understood in the sense that "the temple presence of God has taken up residence in Jesus Christ," and on that basis concludes, "Christ is here depicted as a 'temple'" (*Echoes of Scripture in the Letter of Paul to the Colossians*; BibInt 96; Leiden: Brill, 2008, 152-55). Alan R. Kerr has argued that the idea that Jesus constitutes the new temple or sanctuary is found not only in John 2:13-22, but also in John 1:18, which contrasts Moses' meeting with God in the tabernacle to the manner in which God's word came to dwell in human flesh (*The Temple of Jesus' Body: The Temple Theme in the Gospel of John*; JSNTS 220; London: Sheffield Academic Press, 2002, 112). Similarly, Andreas J. Köstenberger notes that the idea of Jesus as the new temple may also be present in other passages of John, including the allusion to the new tabernacle (1:14), the place where angels descend and ascend (1:51), and the "true vine" (15:1) ("The Destruction of the Second Temple and the Composition of the Fourth Gospel," in *Challenging Perspectives on the Gospel of John*; ed. John Lierman; WUNT 2/219; Tübingen: Mohr Siebeck, 2006, 97-108).

73. See Donald Juel, *Messiah and Temple: The Trial of Jesus in the Gospel of Mark* (SBLDS 31; Missoula, MT: SBL, 1977), 56-58; Timothy C. Gray, *The Temple in the Gospel of Mark: A Study in its Narrative Role* (WUNT 2/44; Tübingen: Mohr Siebeck, 2008).

74. On the significance of Mark's use of the word *acheiropoiētos* here, see especially Gray, *Temple*, 174-75. On the basis of the observation that, in the fourteen passages in which *cheiropoiētos* is used in the Septuagint, it describes idols, Gray concludes there that Mark's use of that adjective to describe the Jerusalem temple implies that the temple has become an idol.

75. Juel considers it likely that the temple "not made with hands" refers to the community of believers, yet allows for the possibility that Mark intended the phrase to be understood in some other way (*Messiah and Temple*, 144-57).

Whether the new temple is associated with Jesus himself, the community of believers, or an eschatological temple, for our purposes here, it is important to note that it is especially through Jesus' death and resurrection that the new temple comes into being. If the new temple is identified with Jesus himself or his body, then it is through Jesus' faithfulness unto death and God's response to that faithfulness that he becomes the place in which all people can have access to God and God's blessings, including that of forgiveness. Such an understanding would emphasize Jesus' role as mediator. If the new temple is associated with the community of believers in the way that Paul does, the logic is that, through his death and resurrection, Jesus has laid the foundation for a new community to exist in which God's Spirit dwells and in which all are sanctified. The members of that community now offer up to God their spiritual sacrifices as well. Jesus may also be said to have died and risen so that, as exalted Lord, he might fulfill the eschatological promises God had made. This will take place at his return.

Any of these ideas may be behind the affirmations in Matthew and Mark's Gospels that Jesus would destroy the temple and raise up a new one in three days. These words are ascribed to Jesus by his adversaries, so that it is not clear whether Matthew and Mark regard this as a saying of Jesus himself. In fact, Mark states that these words were attributed to Jesus by false witnesses (Mark 14:57). If so, then the allusion may be to God, the Romans, or even the Jews who rose up against Rome as the ones who would destroy the Jerusalem temple. In John's Gospel, in fact, Jesus explicitly refers to his Jewish adversaries as the ones who will destroy the temple, which can be understood either as the Jerusalem temple or Jesus' own body (John 2:19). Of course, by the time Matthew, John, and possibly Mark were written, the Jerusalem temple had already been destroyed. The emphasis in all three of these Gospels, however, seems to be more on the raising up of a new temple. This idea must be seen as intimately related to that of a new covenant: through Jesus and his death, God and his people will relate to each other in a new way and on a new basis.

The conclusion of the parable of the wicked tenants in the Synoptics also points to the idea that a new temple or construction will come into existence through Jesus' death. In all three Synoptics, after affirming that as a result of the killing of the son by the tenants God will destroy them, Jesus quotes Ps. 118:22: "The stone that the builders rejected has become the cornerstone." Although the temple is not explicitly mentioned, the idea of a cornerstone implies some sort of building. The fact that elsewhere Jesus is seen as the cornerstone of the new temple seems to suggest that the allusion is indeed to the temple.[76] At the very least, some type of new construction must be

---

76. Gray, for example, argues that by "quoting Psalm 118 in the temple, therefore, the Markan Jesus is claiming to be the new cornerstone of the eschatological temple" (*Temple*, 76; see 68-77). An allusion to Jesus' resurrection may also be present in the passage, since the rejected stone *becomes* the cornerstone, as Rikk Watts has argued ("The Psalms in Mark's Gospel," in *The Psalms in the New Testament*; ed. Steve Moyise and Maarten J. J. Menken; NTSI; London: T & T Clark, 2004, 35).

involved.⁷⁷ Even if the *lithos* is understood as a copestone rather than a cornerstone, as Joachim Jeremias argued, the basic idea would still be essentially the same: that of Jesus "consummating all previous building activity and standing supreme over the whole structure."⁷⁸ In that case, however, the imagined construction would be built on top of the old one rather than being rebuilt from the bottom up. This would imply continuity between the old temple and the new temple of the community of believers, rather than the destruction of the former and its replacement by the latter. In either case, however, the parable implies some type of divine rejection, either of the chief priests or of Jerusalem and its temple.⁷⁹

Among Jesus' first followers, this parable would therefore have been interpreted in the sense that Jesus' death was salvific in that it had led to the construction of a new reality. Whether or not Jesus had actually pronounced the parable as it appears in the Synoptics, his followers would have seen in it the idea that, by remaining faithful to his mission of forming around himself a new, obedient people in the face of the opposition of the Jewish authorities—against whom the parable was supposedly told—Jesus had made it possible for that people to be brought into existence. This new people is identified with a new temple, of which Jesus is the cornerstone or copestone. The rejection of Jesus by Israel's leaders thus ironically led to the construction of a new temple, since God responded to Jesus' faithfulness by exalting him to a position of supreme power as Lord. When God raised Jesus, in essence he raised up as well the new temple, that is, Jesus himself and the new community of those who live according to God's will under Jesus' lordship.

It is not entirely clear how Jesus' followers would have understood the affirmation that the vineyard would be given to others (Mark 12:9; Luke 20:16), or according to Matthew's version, to "a people that produces the fruits of the kingdom" (Matt. 20:41, 43). The allusion to the fruits of the vineyard that the tenants were to give the owner should probably be understood as the works of justice and obedience that God desired from Israel.⁸⁰ If so, then the idea behind the parable is that God's original objective in establishing leaders over

---

77. The editors of *Jesus' Last Week* note in the "Appendix: Critical Notes on the VTS" that the allusion to the cornerstone in Ps. 118:22 would be understood as referring "to an appointment of honor" and that, in later Jewish literature, Psalm 118 was understood as messianic (*Jesus' Last Week*, Vol. 1 of *Jerusalem Studies in the Synoptic Gospels*; ed. R. Steven Notley, Marc Turnage, and Brian Becker; JCPS 11; Leiden: Brill, 2006, 300).

78. On this discussion, see Richard N. Longenecker, *The Christology of Early Jewish Christianity* (SBT 2/17; London: SCM, 1970), 50-53.

79. As Blake R. Grandgaard notes, even if one sees an allusion to the destruction of Jerusalem in the parable, "its primary reference is to the destruction of the religious leaders, the tenants of the vineyard" (*Conflict and Authority in Luke 19:47 to 21:4*; StBL 8; New York: Peter Lang, 1999, 89). George J. Brooke instead argues that the vineyard is Jerusalem, yet still sees the parable as "about how the leaders of Judaism have abused their privileged role in Jerusalem and its temple" (*The Dead Sea Scrolls and the New Testament*; Minneapolis: Fortress, 2005, 253; see 251-53). Craig Evans rightly stresses that the issue in the parable "is not what the vineyard is but who will care for the vineyard" (*Mark 8:27—16:20*; WBC 34B; Nashville: Thomas Nelson, 2001, 222).

80. John S. Kloppenborg notes that elsewhere Matthew uses *karpoi* for good works or righteousness, and that the Septuagint version of Isa. 5:7 interprets the fruit of the vineyard as justice and righteousness (*Tenants in the Vineyard: Ideology, Economics, and Agrarian Conflict in Jewish Palestine*; WUNT 195; Tübingen: Mohr Siebeck, 2006, 180-81).

Israel, represented by the tenants of the vineyard, was that they bring about an obedient people.[81] When this did not happen, God sent prophets, yet the authorities had mistreated them, sent them away, and even killed them.[82] In response, God sent his Son with the objective that he bring about in the people the works or fruits of obedience that God originally desired, but the tenants killed him as well. Although it is not clear who the "others" are to whom the vineyard is given, the parable presupposes that once this happens, the works of obedience God originally desired will come about. This would relate to the idea of the new temple, the community brought about as a result of Jesus' death in which God's will is done. These same ideas may be behind other passages in the New Testament that use similar imagery. Craig Evans sees a possible allusion to the parable in 1 Cor. 3:9, where Paul speaks of the Corinthian believers as God's field and God's building.[83] George Brooke also notes a relation between the parable and Heb. 13:6-16, as well as 1 Pet. 2:4-10, which also contains allusions to Ps. 118:22.[84]

The Synoptics' affirmation that the temple veil was torn in two when Jesus died also seems to convey the idea that, through his death, Jesus obtained access to God's presence, not only for himself but also for others, who can now approach God through him. Jesus therefore fulfills a role that the temple did previously (Matt. 27:51; Mark 15:38; Luke 23:45). Naturally, this access only became a reality with his exaltation to heaven, yet because Jesus' exaltation was God's response to Jesus' willingness to give up his life due to his total commitment to the task God had given him, his death would be seen as the means by which believers would obtain access to God in a new way.

Of course, each of the Synoptic evangelists may have understood the tearing of the temple veil in other ways as well. A wide variety of scholarly proposals exists on this question.[85] Rivka Nir notes that in several works from the patristic period, the tearing of the temple veil is interpreted in terms of God's abandoning the temple.[86] According to George Nickelsburg, it "may well be

---

81. N. T. Wright sees the purpose of the vineyard in terms of Israel being called to reach those "beyond her own borders" (*New Testament*, 75). He also argues that the "new tenants," at least in Mark's version of the story, cannot "be Gentiles *per se*, but must be a new group of Jews through whom the purpose will be fulfilled" (76).

82. Claudia Setzer has noted that the killing of the prophets is "a standard motif in early Jewish literature" (*Jewish Responses to Early Christians: History and Polemics, 30-150 C.E.*; Minneapolis: Fortress, 1994, 21).

83. Craig A. Evans, "Are the Wicked Tenant Farmers Peasants? Jesus' Parable and Lease Agreements in Antiquity," in *Jesus in Context: Temple, Purity, and Restoration* (Bruce Chilton and Evans; AGJU 39; Leiden: Brill, 1997), 250.

84. Brooke, *Dead Sea Scrolls*, 251-53. Although the author of Hebrews does not allude explicitly to Ps. 118:22, the fact that he cites the Septuagint version of Ps. 118:6 (LXX 117:6) in Heb. 13:6 suggests he may have had Ps. 118:22 in the back of his mind. On the important role that Psalm 118 as a whole plays in the Synoptics and the Fourth Gospel, see Andrew C. Brunson, *Psalm 118 in the Gospel of John: An Intertextual Study on the New Exodus Pattern in the Theology of John* (WUNT 2/158; Tübingen: Mohr Siebeck, 2003), 102-377.

85. For a survey of views, both ancient and modern, see especially Daniel M. Gurtner, *The Torn Veil: Matthew's Exposition of the Death of Jesus* (SNTSMS 139; Cambridge: Cambridge University Press, 2007), 1-28.

86. Rivka Nir, *The Destruction of Jerusalem and the Idea of Redemption in the Syriac Apocalypse of Baruch* (EJL 20; Atlanta: SBL, 2003), 81. Hans-Ruedi Weber observes that the interpretation of the tearing of the temple veil would depend on which of the two veils is meant; if it is the innermost veil, "the sign must indicate that

intended as a proleptic fulfillment of Jesus' prophecy in [Mk] 13:1-2" regarding the destruction of the temple.[87] Donald Senior notes that the meaning of the tearing of the temple veil in Luke may be different than that found in Matthew and Mark, since in Luke it precedes Jesus' death rather than following it. According to Senior, this suggests that for Luke it involves "a moment of revelation" for Jesus in that he has "a vision of God through the now separated curtain that had shrouded the inner sanctuary."[88] Ernest Best suggests that the rending of the veil in Mark "symbolizes that the gospel applies to Gentiles," who thereby are given access to God.[89]

Other scholars, such as Raymond Brown, have seen the rending of the veil in Mark as representing an expression of God's anger at the chief priests and Sanhedrin for their unjust treatment and condemnation of Jesus. Just as the high priest tore his robe before the Sanhedrin in demanding Jesus' death (Mark 14:63), so God now tears the veil.[90] According to Brown, Luke may have understood the tearing of the veil as a sign of God's wrath as well.[91] Clearly, some type of symbolism is involved, yet we cannot assume that each of the Synoptics understood that symbolism in the same way.

Even if the tearing of the veil is seen negatively as foreshadowing the destruction of the Jerusalem temple or God's abandonment of that temple, however, this would probably not be seen as an end in itself. In the thought of the Synoptics, if the temple is to be destroyed, it is because something else is to take its place. The idea that Jesus in some way assumes the previous role of the priests and the sanctuary also seems to be present in the Synoptic accounts. This echoes what we find in Hebrews, where the author employs the image of Jesus entering into the Holy of holies behind the veil in order to gain access on behalf of believers (6:19; 10:19-20). The second of these passages relates this access to Jesus' blood, implying that his death had the objective of enabling others to draw near to God through him. This reflects ideas in Eph.

---

the holiest of holies is now there for all to see," while if it is the veil at the temple entrance, "the sign would mean the end to the exclusion of non-priests and non-Jews from the place where God is present, and thus indicate the end of Jewish temple services altogether." The sign might also symbolize "the threatened or actual destruction of the temple itself" (*The Cross: Tradition and Interpretation of the Crucifixion of Jesus in the World of the New Testament*, trans. Elke Jessett; Grand Rapids: Eerdmans, 1978, 49).

87. George W. E. Nickelsburg, "The Genre and Function of the Markan Passion Narrative," *HTR* 73 (1980): 181.

88. Donald Senior, *The Passion of Jesus in the Gospel of Luke* (Pass 3; Wilmington, DE: Michael Glazier, 1989), 139-42. There Senior also relates the tearing of the veil with the darkness to see the event as a sign of the impending destruction of the temple. Gurtner argues that Matthew associated the tearing of the veil with the idea of God's deliverance of the people from the captivity and exile of their sins by removing the "cultic barriers" between God and humanity and pointing to the "turning of the era inaugurated by the death of Jesus" (*Torn Veil*, 197-98, 200-201). For Gray, in Mark, the tearing of the veil points to the destruction of the temple and is related to the tearing of the heavens at Jesus' baptism; the basic idea is that of the turning of the ages between the old and new creation (*Temple*, 185-94).

89. Best, *Essays on Ephesians*, 111.

90. Raymond E. Brown, *The Death of the Messiah: From Gethsemane to the Grave. A Commentary on the Passion Narratives in the Four Gospels* (ABRL; New York: Doubleday, 1994), 2:1100-1101. Brown also looks at the possible meaning of the event for Matthew and especially Luke and relates this to the mention of the veil in Hebrews (2:1102-9).

91. Ibid., 2:1106.

2:11-22, already considered above. The basic idea behind all of these passages, then, is that Jesus gave up his life in order that through him others might attain divine forgiveness and acceptance, as well as access to God.

The idea of a new temple must also be seen as intimately related to *the inclusion of the gentiles among God's people*. As Eph. 2:11-22 stresses, those who previously had no access to God because they lived outside of the covenant and the law could now have access to God through Jesus. Those who previously were not allowed to draw near to God's presence in the temple could now draw near to God as members of a new temple through Jesus as their high priest. Gentiles who could not fully obtain God's forgiveness, favor, and blessings under the covenant with Israel could now obtain these things thanks to what Jesus had done. In the minds of his first followers, as Jesus had gone to his death, his objective had been precisely to obtain all of these things for the "many" (Matt. 20:28; 26:28; Mk 10:45; 14:24). This group included not only those who lived under the covenant with Israel, but also those who had been excluded from that covenant, and therefore did not have access to God and were unable to live in the way God had commanded in the law. Jesus was therefore thought to have died for the "many," including the gentiles, in the sense that his death would lead to the establishment of a new system or new covenant in which people might relate to God in a new way through him. It was this that he had accomplished through his death, and that God had accomplished through that death as well.

* * *

Whether or not the *language* of a new covenant was common among Jesus' first followers, on the basis of what we have seen here, there can be little doubt that the *concept* of a new covenant was of great importance for them. Associated with this concept were a series of ideas related to the new realities they came to experience, the new way of life that became theirs, and the new basis they had for relating to God and to others. Thanks to Jesus' faithfulness unto death in seeking that this new reality come to pass, believers now had a new basis for relating to God, to one another, and to the world in general.

CHAPTER 9

THE FULFILLMENT OF THE SCRIPTURES AND THE DIVINE PLAN

The idea that the Hebrew Scriptures find their fulfillment in Jesus and the new reality brought into being through him is a constant theme throughout the New Testament writings. The origin of this idea remains uncertain. It is possible that Jesus saw certain events related to his coming, ministry, sufferings, and eventual death as fulfilling the Hebrew Scriptures in some sense, as the Gospels all report.[1] Many scholars, however, would question this possibility. Even if Jesus did not apply specific passages of the Scriptures to himself, he may have seen himself as some type of new Moses or new Joshua, as Scot McKnight has suggested.[2] Jesus may also have identified himself with some awaited figure such as the Messiah or the Son of Man, or simply have had some general idea that what had been promised of old was being fulfilled through him and his ministry.[3] Although the Gospels attribute to Jesus the repeated use of Scripture to describe himself and his ministry, it is not clear how much of this material can be considered historical. Once more, one's views on these questions will depend primarily on the presuppositions with which one approaches them.

What is clear, however, is that by Paul's time the notion that the Scriptures had been fulfilled through Jesus and the community he founded had been firmly established. Paul's letters provide strong evidence not only that he read Scriptures in this way, but that this interpretation of Scripture had been handed down to him.[4] The clearest indication of this is in 1 Cor. 15:3-4, where

---

1. N. T. Wright, for example, argues that Jesus regarded key passages from Isaiah 40-55, the Psalms, Zechariah 9-14, and Daniel 7 as programmatic for his ministry (*Jesus and the Victory of God*, Vol. 2 of *Christian Origins and the Question of God*; Minneapolis: Fortress, 1996, 597-604). Like Wright, Craig Evans claims that Jesus interpreted his ministry and death on the basis of passages from the Hebrew Scriptures, though Evans also recognizes that the early community of believers embellished Jesus' interpretations of Scripture and developed them further, especially by proof-texting ("'Have you not Read...?' Jesus' Subversive Interpretation of Scripture," in *Jesus Research: An International Perspective. The First Princeton-Prague Symposium on Jesus Research, Prague 2005*; ed. James H. Charlesworth and Peter Pokorný; Grand Rapids: Eerdmans 2009, 182-98).
2. Scot McKnight, "Jesus' New Vision within Judaism," in *Who Was Jesus? A Jewish-Christian Dialogue* (ed. Paul Copan and Craig A. Evans; Louisville: Westminster John Knox, 2001), 82-84.
3. See, for example, Bruce Chilton and Craig A. Evans, "Jesus and Israel's Scriptures," in *Studying the Historical Jesus: Evaluation of the State of Current Research* (ed. Chilton and Evans; NTTS 19; Leiden: Brill, 1994), 310-13.
4. On this question and the characteristics of Paul's use of the Hebrew Scriptures in general, see Brevard S. Childs, *Biblical Theology of the Old and New Testaments: Theological Reflection on the Christian Bible* (Minneapolis: Fortress, 1993), 237-43; Hans Hübner, "New Testament Interpretation of the Old Testament," in *Hebrew*

Paul writes: "For I handed on to you as of first importance what I in turn had received: that Christ died for our sins in accordance with the scriptures, and that he was buried, and that he was raised on the third day in accordance with the scriptures." Here Paul seems to be alluding not simply to a few particular passages from the Hebrew Scriptures, but to a collection of passages that were thought to have found fulfillment when Jesus died and was raised. What was therefore handed down to him was a way of interpreting these passages, as well as Scripture as a whole.

THE FULFILLMENT OF THE SCRIPTURES IN JESUS' DEATH AND RESURRECTION

When we examine the New Testament writings, the number of quotations from and allusions to the Hebrew Scriptures is astounding. According to the *Nestle-Aland Greek New Testament*, there are over three hundred direct quotations from the Hebrew Scriptures in the New Testament, and allusions to the Hebrew Scriptures there number in the thousands.[5] This amounts to an average of over ten allusions to the Hebrew Scriptures per chapter of the New Testament. Many of the New Testament citations, of course, come from the Septuagint rather than being translated directly from the Hebrew Scriptures.[6]

According to Luke's account of the church's beginnings in Acts, from the very start those proclaiming the message about Jesus quoted numerous Scripture passages so as to claim that these had been fulfilled through Jesus. These include passages that point to Judas's betrayal (Acts 1:16-20), the pouring out of the Holy Spirit (2:16-21), Jesus' not being abandoned to Hades (2:25-31), and his exaltation to God's right hand (2:34-36). Above all, Jesus' betrayal and crucifixion are said to have taken place "according to the definite plan and foreknowledge of God" (2:23).

Throughout the rest of Acts, the apostles are repeatedly presented as seeking to convince their hearers that what had taken place through Jesus had been foretold in the Hebrew Scriptures. Above all, they use the Scriptures extensively to attempt to demonstrate that Jesus is the Christ.[7] In Acts 17:2-3,

---

Bible/Old Testament: The History of its Interpretation, Vol. 1: *From the Beginnings to the Middle Ages* (*Until 1300*) (ed. Magne Sæbø; Göttingen: Vandenhoeck & Ruprecht, 1996), 340-47; James D. G. Dunn, *The Theology of Paul the Apostle* (Grand Rapids: Eerdmans, 1998), 169-73; Timothy H. Lim, *Holy Scripture in the Qumran Commentaries and Pauline Letters* (Oxford: Oxford University Press, 1997), 140-76. As Lim observes, "Paul lived at a time when the biblical text remained fluid" (160). John P. Meier has suggested that Paul's messianic and eschatological reading of the Hebrew Scriptures had its origin in his Pharisaic background (*A Marginal Jew: Rethinking the Historical Jesus*, Vol. 3: *Companions and Competitors*; New York: Doubleday, 2001, 325). Christopher D. Stanley questions many of the assumptions we make regarding Paul's use of the Hebrew Scriptures and their reception by his audience, who may not have understood him clearly ("Pearls before Swine: Did Paul's Audiences Understand His Biblical Quotations?," *NovT* 42 [1999]: 124-44).

5. See *Nestle-Aland Novum Testamentum Graece*, 28th rev. ed. (ed. Barbara and Kurt Aland et al.; Stuttgart: Deutsch Bibelgesellschaft, 2012), 836-69.

6. On the different ways in which the Septuagint is used in the New Testament, see Hübner, "New Testament Interpretation," 334-39.

7. Donald Juel questions Barnabas Lindars's "conviction that the speeches in Acts represent an early stage in exegetical tradition," and argues that "Acts represents a rather developed stage of sophisticated scriptural

for example, Luke says that Paul went into the synagogue in Thessalonica, "as was his custom, and on three sabbath days argued with them from the scriptures, explaining and proving that it was necessary for the Messiah to suffer and to rise from the dead, and saying, 'This is the Messiah, Jesus whom I am proclaiming to you.'" Later on in Ephesus, Apollos is said to have "powerfully refuted the Jews in public, showing by the scriptures that the Messiah is Jesus" (Acts 18:28). When Paul appears before Felix after his arrest in Jerusalem, he tells him, "I worship the God of our ancestors, believing everything laid down according to the law or written in the prophets" (24:14). Further on he tells Agrippa, "To this day I have had help from God, and so I stand here, testifying to both small and great, saying nothing but what the prophets and Moses said would take place: that the Messiah must suffer, and that, by being the first to rise from the dead, he would proclaim light both to our people and to the Gentiles" (26:22-23). The book of Acts ends with Paul surrounded by other Jews in Rome, where "from morning until evening he explained the matter to them, testifying to the kingdom of God and trying to convince them about Jesus both from the law of Moses and from the prophets" (28:23). In fact, Luke's affirmation that, from the time he became a believer, Paul or Saul "confounded the Jews who lived in Damascus by proving Jesus to be the Messiah" (9:22) should be understood in the sense that, from the start, Paul was using the Scriptures to claim that they pointed to Jesus and what was to take place through him.

Of course, in addition to these general claims about the way in which all of the Scriptures pointed to everything that was to happen through Jesus, the book of Acts points to many specific passages from those Scriptures. In Acts 2, these include passages from the Psalms regarding the fate of Judas and the resurrection and exaltation of Jesus, as well as the prophecy from Joel regarding the pouring out of the Holy Spirit, just mentioned above. In particular, the Hebrew Scriptures foretold Jesus' suffering and death. In Acts 3, Peter proclaims that when the people in Jerusalem had Jesus put to death, "God fulfilled what he had foretold through all the prophets, that his Messiah would suffer" (3:18). Peter then continues by claiming that, now that Jesus has been raised, he

> must remain in heaven until the time of universal restoration that God announced long ago through his holy prophets. Moses said, "The Lord your God will raise up for you from your own people a prophet like me. You must listen to whatever he tells you. And it will be that everyone who does not listen to that prophet will be utterly rooted out of the people." And all the prophets, as many as have spoken, from Samuel and those after him, also predicted these days. You are the descendants of the prophets and of the covenant that God gave to your ancestors, saying to Abraham, "And in your descendants all the families of the earth shall be blessed" (Acts 3:20-24).

---

argumentation" (*Messianic Exegesis: Christological Interpretation of the Old Testament in Early Christianity*; Philadelphia: Fortress, 1988, 140). Even if the content of the speeches in Acts represents later developments, however, the practice of arguing from Scripture in order to demonstrate Jesus to be the Messiah seems to have begun in the years immediately following Jesus' death, if not during Jesus' own lifetime.

Here Peter proclaims not only the fulfillment of what was prophesied from Samuel's time forward, but also Moses' promise that God would raise up another prophet like him, as well as God's promise to Abraham to bless all the nations of the earth through him. In Acts 4:11, Peter points to Ps. 118:22 to claim that David there foretold Jesus' rejection, as well as his becoming the cornerstone of a new construction. Shortly thereafter, when Peter is released by the Jewish authorities, the believers rejoice and pray to God on the basis of Psalm 2, "it is you who said by the Holy Spirit through our ancestor David, your servant: 'Why did the Gentiles rage, and the peoples imagine vain things? The kings of the earth took their stand, and the rulers have gathered together against the Lord and against his Messiah.' For in this city, in fact, both Herod and Pontius Pilate, with the Gentiles and the peoples of Israel, gathered together against your holy servant Jesus, whom you anointed, to do whatever your hand and your plan had predestined to take place" (Acts 4:25-28). Here again, all that happened to Jesus in his last days in Jerusalem is seen as being foretold in the Scriptures.

In Acts 7:52, Stephen alludes to the prophets who "foretold the coming of the righteous one," while further on Philip begins with Isaiah 53 and then continues discussing other passages in order to proclaim the gospel to the Ethiopian eunuch (Acts 8:27-35). In his proclamation regarding Jesus at Cornelius's house, Peter claims that "all the prophets testify about him" (Acts 10:43). In the only extensive sermon of Paul that Luke presents in Acts 13, Paul argues that, because those who had sentenced Jesus to the cross "did not recognize him or understand the words of the prophets that are read every sabbath, they fulfilled those words by condemning him" (Acts 13:27). At the gathering of the apostles and elders in Jerusalem, James proclaims that the incorporation of the gentiles into the church "agrees with the words of the prophets, as it is written, 'After this I will return, and I will rebuild the dwelling of David, which has fallen; from its ruins I will rebuild it, and I will set it up, so that all other peoples may seek the Lord—even all the Gentiles over whom my name has been called. Thus says the Lord, who has been making these things known from long ago'" (Acts 15:58; see Amos 9:11-12; Isa. 45:21).

These same themes appear at the end of Luke's Gospel. On the road to Emmaus, Jesus tells the disciples with whom he is walking, "Oh, how foolish you are, and how slow of heart to believe all that the prophets have declared! Was it not necessary that the Messiah should suffer these things and then enter into his glory?" Luke immediately continues: "Then beginning with Moses and all the prophets, he interpreted to them the things about himself in all the scriptures" (Luke 24:25-27).[8] When Jesus disappears from their sight, the disciples say to one another: "Were not our hearts burning within

---

8. As I. Howard Marshall observes, the affirmation that Jesus began with Moses and the prophets in order to interpret all of the Scriptures in Luke 24:27 "may be construed in two ways: 1. It may mean that the speaker started from the law and the prophets in finding things written about himself. 2. More probably it means that he searched in *all* the Scriptures, but starting from (i.e. principally from) the law and the prophets...." (*The Gospel of Luke: A Commentary on the Greek Text*, NIGTC; Grand Rapids: Eerdmans, 1978, 897). If Luke's

us while he was talking to us on the road, while he was opening the scriptures to us?" (24:32). Later on in the same day, Luke recounts Jesus' appearance to the disciples gathered in Jerusalem: "Then he said to them, 'These are my words that I spoke to you while I was still with you—that everything written about me in the law of Moses, the prophets, and the psalms must be fulfilled.' Then he opened their minds to understand the scriptures, and he said to them, 'Thus it is written, that the Messiah is to suffer and to rise from the dead on the third day, and that repentance and forgiveness of sins is to be proclaimed in his name to all nations, beginning from Jerusalem'" (24:44-47). Here again it is not only Jesus' death and resurrection that are said to be foretold in the Scriptures, but the proclamation of the gospel to all the nations as well. At the beginning of his Gospel, Luke also points to the fulfillment of the promises God had made in the Hebrew Scriptures to raise up a savior (1:54-55, 68-79).

Similar ideas are reflected elsewhere in the Synoptics. Matthew points to the fulfillment of numerous passages from the Hebrew Scriptures in his account of Jesus' birth and Jesus' ministry (Matt. 1:22-23; 2:1-6, 13-23; 3:1-4; 4:1-4, 13-15; 5:17; 11:2-5, 12-14; 12:38-42; 13:13-16, 34-35; 15:7-9; 17:9-13; 21:1-5, 42-44; 22:41-45). Matthew also quotes Isaiah twice to summarize Jesus' ministry as a whole in terms of bearing the infirmities of many and bringing justice after God's Spirit had been poured out on him (Isa. 53:4; Matt. 8:16-17; Isa. 42:1-4, 9; Matt. 12:15-21). Luke has Jesus define his ministry from its very beginning on the basis of Isa. 61:1-2, where God is said to anoint his chosen one with his Spirit so that he may proclaim good news to the poor and oppressed (Luke 4:16-21; cf. Isa. 58:6). Both Matthew and Mark look to Isa. 6:9-10 and 29:13 LXX to claim that the rejection of Jesus and his message was prefigured or foretold in the story of Israel; the former passage is cited in Acts as well (Matt. 13:1-15; 15:8-9; Mark 4:12; 7:6-7; Acts 28:26-27). At the beginning of John's Gospel, Philip tells Nathanael, "We have found him about whom Moses in the law and also the prophets wrote, Jesus son of Joseph from Nazareth" (John 1:45).

In particular, however, the four Gospels all point to the fulfillment of Scriptures with regard to Jesus' last days and hours in Jerusalem. In several passages, this fulfillment is described in broad terms. The "necessity" to which Jesus' predictions regarding his passion and death in Jerusalem refer is simply the necessity that the Scriptures in general be fulfilled (Matt. 16:21; Mark 8:31; Luke 9:22; 18:31-33; 22:37). In the arrest scene in Matthew's Gospel, Jesus says, "Do you think that I cannot appeal to my Father, and he will at once send me more than twelve legions of angels? But how then would the scriptures be fulfilled, which say it must happen in this way?... All this has taken place, so that the scriptures of the prophets may be fulfilled" (Matt. 26:53-54, 56). Mark repeats the same basic ideas in his version of the arrest scene (Mark 14:21, 49). Luke makes use of the Greek verb *dei* at numerous

---

affirmation is interpreted in the second of these two ways, the idea is that it refers to the Hebrew Scriptures as a whole.

points throughout his Gospel to point to the need for Jesus to suffer, die, and be raised (Luke 13:31-35; 17:25; 24:7, 26, 44).[9]

However, the Gospels all point as well to specific events as fulfilling particular passages from the Hebrew Scriptures. All four Gospels see Jesus' entry into Jerusalem as an event foretold in the Scriptures (Matt. 21:1-11; Mark 11:1-11; Luke 19:28-40; John 12:12-16). They also look to passages from the Hebrew Scriptures to interpret his action in the temple (Matt. 21:13; Mark 11:17; Luke 19:46; John 2:17). Throughout John's account of Jesus' passion and crucifixion, the evangelist repeatedly affirms that certain things took place "so that the scripture might be fulfilled." This includes Jesus' betrayal by one who ate bread with him (John 13:18), Jesus' being hated for no reason (15:24-25), the scattering of the disciples (16:32), the loss of one of his disciples in Judas (17:12), the dividing of his garments among those who crucified him (19:23-24), Jesus' thirst (19:28), and his bones being left unbroken (19:33-37). The Synoptics also point to many details surrounding Jesus' last hours that were foretold in the Scriptures, including most of those just mentioned, as well as his drinking of vinegar and gall, his being reckoned among evildoers, and his burial at the hands of Joseph of Arimathea (Matt. 26:20-25, 31; 27:3-10, 29-31, 34-35, 40-44, 57-60; Mark 14:18-21; 15:20-24, 27, 29-32, 43-46; Luke 22:21-22; 23:11, 33, 35-37). Like Luke, in his account of the day of Jesus' resurrection, John claims that the disciples "did not understand scripture that he should arise from the dead" (John 20:9; cf. Luke 24:25-26).

The Development of Beliefs regarding the Fulfillment of Scripture in Jesus

While it is not entirely clear when and how this use of Scripture to support the claims regarding Jesus made by his first followers originated, on the basis of the book of Acts, the Gospels, and other New Testament writings, we can reconstruct in broad terms the way in which this development probably took place. Whether or not Jesus had affirmed that the Scriptures spoke of him, the fact that his followers proclaimed him as the Messiah or Christ means that from the start they must have applied to Jesus passages from the Hebrew Scriptures that were thought to foretell the coming of a messianic figure.[10] This would include passages such as 2 Sam. 7:12-16, where YHWH promises David that his descendants would continue on the throne perpetually (Luke 2:32-33; Acts 3:22-23; Heb. 1:5), Psalm 2, which refers to the Lord's anointed (*Christos*) as God's Son (Acts 4:25-26; 13:33; Heb. 1:5), Isa. 11:1-10, which speaks of the root of Jesse bringing justice and peace to the earth (Matt. 3:16; Rom. 15:12; 2 Thess. 2:8), as well as numerous other

---

9. On the wide range of meanings of the verb *dei* in Luke's work, see Charles H. Cosgrove, "The Divine *Dei* in Luke-Acts: Investigations into the Lukan Understanding of God's Providence," *NovT* 26 (1984): 168-90.

10. Juel suggests that the texts of the Hebrew Scriptures commonly understood as messianic may have been the first applied to Jesus by his followers, followed by other texts not traditionally considered messianic (*Messianic Exegesis*, 172).

passages that speak of David's descendants and God's anointed, especially from the Psalms and Isaiah (Luke 1:68-79; 4:18-19; Acts 13:34; Rom. 11:26; 15:21). Psalm 72 may also have influenced the way Jesus' messiahship was understood.[11] In this regard, it is important to note that, because David was believed to be the author of all the Psalms that bore his name, it was not just the Psalms in general that were said to have foretold what was to happen to Jesus, but David himself.[12]

Once Jesus' followers came to believe that he had risen from the dead, they also looked to other passages from the Hebrew Scriptures to claim that not only Jesus' resurrection but also his exaltation to heaven to a place of power and authority alongside God had been foretold. As Donald Juel notes, this included "adopting as messianic passages that had previously not been understood in that sense."[13] The first passage applied to Jesus in Acts is Ps. 16:8-11, where David the Psalmist tells God, "you do not give me up to Sheol, or let your faithful one see the pit" (Acts 2:24-31).[14] Paul is later presented as using this same passage, along with Ps. 2:7 and Isa. 55:3 (LXX), to claim that, after those who crucified Jesus "had carried out everything that was written about him," God raised Jesus from the dead as his Son so that he might never see corruption (Acts 13:29-37). Psalm 2, which was also understood as a royal Psalm written by David, is applied to Jesus elsewhere in the New Testament as well (see, for example, Acts 4:25-26; Heb. 1:5; Rev. 19:15).[15] However, the passage from the Psalms used most frequently throughout the New Testament to give meaning to Jesus' resurrection and glorification is Ps. 110:1, a Psalm of David, which begins: "The Lord says to my lord, 'Sit at my right hand until I make your enemies your footstool.'" According to the Synoptics, Jesus himself cited this Psalm to support the claim that the Messiah was greater than David as David's Lord (Matt. 20:23; Mark 12:36; Luke 20:42-43). The same verse is cited or alluded to repeatedly throughout the New Testament (Acts 2:34-35; Rom. 8:34; 1 Cor. 15:25; Eph. 1:20; Col. 3:1; Heb. 1:13).[16] The earliest evidence of the claim that Jesus' resurrection took place according to the Scriptures is in 1 Cor. 15:4, already cited above. It is not clear exactly to

---

11. See Craig C. Broyles, "The Redeeming King: Psalm 72's Contribution to the Messianic Ideal," in *Eschatology, Messianism, and the Dead Sea Scrolls* (ed. Craig A. Evans and Peter W. Flint; SDSSRL 1; Grand Rapids: Eerdmans, 1997), 23-40.

12. On the beliefs regarding Davidic authorship of the Psalms in second-temple Judaism, see Margaret Daly-Denton, *David in the Fourth Gospel: The Johannine Reception of the Psalms* (AGJU 47; Leiden: Brill, 2000), 59-113. On the centrality of David in Mark's Gospel, see Stephen P. Ahearne-Kroll, *The Psalms of Lament in Mark's Passion: Jesus' Davidic Suffering* (SNTSMS 142; Cambridge: Cambridge University Press, 2007), 51-58, 137-67. Juel points to the centrality of the Psalms in the passion accounts of the Gospels in general (*Messianic Exegesis*, 89-117).

13. Juel, *Messianic Exegesis*, 173.

14. On this passage, see Serge Ruzer, *Mapping the New Testament: Early Christian Writings as a Witness for Jewish Biblical Exegesis* (JCPS 13; Leiden: Brill, 2007), 117-18.

15. See Broyles, "Redeeming King," 25.

16. On the important role that Ps. 110 plays in the New Testament, see W. R. G. Loader, "Christ at the Right Hand: Ps. cx.1 in the New Testament," *NTS* 24 (1978): 199-217; David M. Hay, *Glory at the Right Hand: Psalm 110 in Early Christianity* (SBLMS 18; Nashville: Abingdon, 1973).

what texts from the Hebrew Scriptures Paul was referring in that passage, but it is likely that he had in mind a cluster of passages, including the ones just mentioned.[17] Matthew and Luke suggest that the story of Jonah spending three days and nights in the belly of the great fish was among those passages thought to foreshadow Jesus' resurrection after three days (Matt. 12:38-42; 16:4; Luke 11:29-32).[18]

When Jesus' first followers began to proclaim him as risen Christ and Lord, however, the most difficult question they had to answer was why God had allowed Jesus to die in the way he had. As Paul notes in 1 Cor. 1:23, the proclamation that he who was the Messiah had died by being executed on a Roman cross seemed outrageous to many, "a stumbling block to Jews and foolishness to Gentiles." The extensive allusions to the Hebrew Scriptures noted above in the account of Jesus' passion and death were a response to this difficulty. Most scholars would agree that it was probably the need to explain and justify Jesus' passion and death that initially led his first followers to turn to the Scriptures to defend their claim that, in spite of the fact that he had been crucified, he was nevertheless the Messiah.[19] The practice of citing Scripture also enabled Jesus' followers to argue that there was a divine purpose behind his suffering and death.[20]

It is not difficult to imagine the way in which many passages from the Hebrew Scriptures came to be seen as foretelling the events surrounding Jesus' passion and death. Even if Jesus had not foreseen many of the details that took place during his last hours, some of the things that happened to him seem clearly to have reflected ideas found in the Hebrew Scriptures. The historicity of a number of these events seems fairly certain. For example, it is likely that Jesus was mocked by at least some of the bystanders during the process against him or while he was on the cross. This would have reminded Jesus' followers of passages such as Ps. 22:6-8 and 109:25, both Psalms of

---

17. The passage most often cited in this regard is Hosea 6:2; see for example, Petr Pokorný, *The Genesis of Christology: Foundations for a Theology of the New Testament*, trans. Marcus Lefébvre (Edinburgh: T & T Clark, 1987), 144. While I disagree with N. T. Wright's emphasis on the idea of redemption as a return from the exile, I believe he is correct in affirming that in this passage Paul is referring to Israel's scriptures *as a whole* rather than to isolated proof-texts (*New Testament*, 400-401). On the question of the passages from the Hebrew Scriptures to which Paul is referring in 1 Cor. 15:4, see also Peder Borgen, "'In Accordance with the Scriptures,'" in *Early Christian Thought in its Jewish Context* (ed. John Barclay and John Sweet; Cambridge: Cambridge University Press, 1996), 198-200.

18. As Jonathan L. Reed observes, while Jonah would be seen as prefiguring Jesus due to the three days he spent inside of the great fish, Jesus may also have been seen as fulfilling Jonah's role as a prophet of repentance ("The Sign of Jonah [Q 11:29-32] and Other Epic Traditions in Q," in *Reimagining Christian Origins: A Colloquium Honoring Burton L. Mack*; ed. Elizabeth A. Castelli and Hal Taussig; Valley Forge, PA: Trinity Press International, 1996, 130-43). Simon Chow has suggested that, in Rom. 10:6-7, Paul was also following a tradition according to which Jonah prefigured Jesus typologically (*The Sign of Jonah Reconsidered: A Study of Its Meaning in the Gospel Tradition*; CBNTS 27; Stockholm: Almqvist & Wiksell International, 1995, 37-38).

19. See Paul van Buren, *According to the Scriptures: The Origins of the Gospel and of the Church's Old Testament* (Grand Rapids: Eerdmans, 1998), 33.

20. As John T. Squires argues, the use of Scripture to speak of a divine purpose or plan was therefore primarily apologetic in purpose (*The Plan of God in Luke-Acts*; SNTSMS 76; Cambridge: Cambridge University Press, 1993, 192-94).

David, which describe him being mocked and scorned.[21] The way in which Jesus had been mistreated would bring to mind Isa. 50:6: "I gave my back to those who struck me, and my cheeks to those who pulled out the beard; I did not hide my face from insult and spitting" (Matt. 26:67-68; 27:26-31, 39-44; Mark 14:65; 15:15-20; Luke 22:63-65; 23:11; John 19:1-3). The fact that Jesus was crucified as a criminal together with others condemned as criminals would evoke the image of the righteous one being reckoned with the transgressors (Luke 22:37; Isa. 53:12).[22] Judas's betrayal of Jesus would remind Jesus' followers of Ps. 41:10, another Davidic Psalm: "Even my bosom friend in whom I trusted, who ate of my bread, has lifted the heel against me" (Mark 14:18; John 13:18; Acts 1:16). The fact that Jesus' disciples had abandoned him after his arrest led some of his followers to find a similar idea in Zech. 13:7: "Strike the shepherd, that the sheep may be scattered" (Matt. 26:31; Mark 14:27; cf. John 16:32). If Jesus was actually given something to drink while on the cross, when his followers looked back on Psalm 69, which also describes the suffering of the righteous one, they would have noticed v. 21, which speaks of the Psalmist receiving gall and vinegar (Matt. 27:34, 48; Mark 15:23, 36; Luke 23:36; John 19:28-30). The way in which Jesus' hands and feet were pierced as he was crucified would have reminded his followers of Ps. 22:16, where the hands and feet of David the Psalmist are also said to be pierced. Mark particularly seems to emphasize the fulfillment of the Psalms in his passion account.[23]

In some cases, of course, the use of the Psalms and other passages from the Hebrew Scriptures may have led Jesus' followers to claim that certain ideas present there were fulfilled in Jesus' last days and hours, even when this had not necessarily been the case. Matthew, for example, is the only evangelist who mentions Judas receiving thirty pieces of silver for betraying Jesus and then returning it to the priests, who bought a field with it (Matt. 26:15; 27:3-10). This reflects closely what is described in Zech. 11:12-14 (cf. Jer. 9:2-3). To what extent this involves reading ideas from the Hebrew Scriptures back into the actual events is not clear. Luke, for example, gives a different account of Judas's death in Acts 1:15-20, suggesting that in his own account of Judas's death, Matthew may have embellished the material from his sources in certain ways to strengthen the argument that Scripture was being fulfilled in all

---

21. On this point, see especially Paul Winter, *On the Trial of Jesus*, 2nd ed. (StJud 1; Berlin: Walter de Gruyter, 1974), 144-52. With regard to Psalm 22, Hans-Ruedi Weber writes: "It is to be assumed that details contained in the psalm were 'history-creating' as soon as the psalm had become a 'key text' for the interpretation of the crucifixion. But it would be wrong to maintain that the *entire* pre-canonic crucifixion narrative had its origins in the reflection on quotations of key-texts contained therein" (*The Cross: Tradition and Interpretation of the Crucifixion of Jesus in the World of the New Testament*, trans. Elke Jessett; Grand Rapids: Eerdmans, 1978, 40).

22. According to Donald Senior, the "transgressors" to whom Luke was referring when he quoted Isa. 53:12 may have been not only the criminals who were crucified alongside of him, but also those who put him to death, and perhaps even the sinners with whom he had fellowship during his ministry (*The Passion of Jesus in the Gospel of Luke*; Pass 3; Wilmington, DE: Michael Glazier, 1989, 81).

23. For references, see Rikk Watts, "The Psalms in Mark's Gospel," in *The Psalms in the New Testament* (ed. Steve Moyise and Maarten J. J. Menken; NTSI; London: T & T Clark, 2004), 42-43; Ahearne-Kroll, *Psalms of Lament*, 40-136, 168-226.

that took place in connection with Jesus' death and resurrection. Similarly, the fact that all four Gospels mention the soldiers casting lots over Jesus' clothes suggests that this was historical, yet it is possible that this tradition arose under the influence of Ps. 22:19 when the story of Jesus' passion was first told (Matt. 27:35; Mark 15:24; Luke 23:34; John 19:24).

We can therefore imagine Jesus' first followers combing meticulously through the Scriptures, actively looking for further parallels between the events surrounding Jesus' death and events or prophecies that appear in the Hebrew Scriptures, especially in the Septuagint version. In some cases, their reading of part of a Psalm as referring to Jesus could lead them to look for other things within the same Psalm that could be applied to him.[24] When they read Psalm 2, for example, the first verses, which speak of the kings of the earth rising up against God's anointed or "Christ," would lead them to think of Herod and the Roman authorities (Ps. 2:1-3; Acts 4:25-26).[25] They also apparently saw Ps. 2:7, "You are my son; today I have begotten you," as an allusion to what took place in Jesus' baptism. The application of Ps. 110:1 to Jesus eventually led the author of Hebrews to apply v. 4 of the same Psalm to Jesus to develop the idea that Jesus is a "priest forever according to the order of Melchizedek." If Jesus cried out something similar to the words of Psalm 22:1 on the cross, asking God why he had forsaken him, this may have led his followers to apply other passages from that Psalm to Jesus. Or the reverse could have happened: the belief that other things mentioned in the Psalm had taken place at Jesus' crucifixion, such as the mocking and the casting of lots over his clothes, could have led his followers to claim that he cried out to God asking why he had been forsaken. The same thing must have happened with other key passages from Scripture. As Joel Marcus notes, in some cases, Jesus' followers may even have found more than one passage from the Hebrew Scriptures that could be seen as pointing to a particular occurrence during Jesus' passion and crucifixion. Jesus' words over the cup with regard to the "blood of the covenant" could have been seen as an allusion to both Exod. 24:8 and Zech. 9:11. Similarly, John's claim that Jesus' bones were left unbroken following his death seemed to fulfill Exod. 12:46 and Num. 9:12, which speak of the bones of the Passover lamb, as well as Ps. 34:20.[26]

In addition to citing isolated verses from various parts of the Scriptures and looking to entire Psalms to interpret the events of Jesus' ministry and death, Jesus' followers also came to see lengthier passages from the Scriptures as referring to Jesus. John Nolland, for example, has shown how Zechariah 9-14 seems to have played an important role in Matthew's passion account.[27]

---

24. See Weber, *Cross*, 39-40.

25. See Gerard S. Sloyan, *Jesus on Trial: A Study of the Gospels*, 2nd ed. (Minneapolis: Fortress, 2006), 72-73.

26. Joel Marcus, "The Old Testament and the Death of Jesus: The Role of Scripture in the Gospel Passion Narratives," in *The Death of Jesus in Early Christianity* (John T. Carroll and Joel B. Green; Peabody, MA: Hendrickson, 1995), 225.

27. See John Nolland, "The King as Shepherd: The Role of Deutero-Zechariah in Matthew," in *Biblical Interpretation in Early Christian Gospels*, Vol. 2: *The Gospel of Matthew* (ed. Thomas R. Hatina; LNTS 304;

The most important of these passages, however, seems to have been Isaiah 53. As we noted in Chapter 4 of this study, scholars have debated how important this passage was for early interpretations of Jesus' death among his followers. Following Morna Hooker, many have argued that Isaiah 53 did not play any great part in the thinking of the authors of the New Testament writings.[28] Serge Ruzer has made a similar argument with regard to the passages from Isaiah 53 that speak of the servant dying for the sins of others. According to Ruzer, "even Luke does not use Isaiah 53 as a proof text for either expiatory death or resurrection—the biblical passage is referred to exclusively in connection with the circumstances of Jesus' passion and his bearing under suffering."[29] Marinus de Jonge notes that the consensus opinion today seems to be that "the importance of the suffering servant [of Isaiah 53] for early Christianity has been greatly overrated."[30]

Other scholars, however, have argued that evidence for the use of Isaiah 53 among Jesus' first followers is fairly strong. Joel Marcus, for example, points to repeated allusions to Isaiah 53 in the passion accounts of all four Gospels.[31] Undoubtedly, the same process noted above with regard to the use of the Psalms took place among Jesus' first followers when they read Isaiah 53. Several of the verses of that chapter seemed to anticipate precisely what had happened when Jesus was arrested, tried, sentenced, and executed. He had been mocked, disfigured, despised, rejected, wounded, crushed, bruised, stricken, afflicted, and oppressed (Isa. 52:14; 53:2-5, 7, 10). After justice had been perverted, he was killed (53:8-9, 12). During this process, he had remained silent before his accusers (53:7). In his death, he had offered himself up to God and prayed for others, even though he was counted among the transgressors (53:10, 12). After he had been buried with the rich, he had then been vindicated and exalted (52:13; 53:9, 11-12). As Otfried Hofius notes, when Isaiah 53 was applied to Christ, it was at times interpreted in ways that did not represent its original sense. For this reason, according to Hofius, among the first believers, Christ "is not merely and not primarily explained by Isaiah 53: Isaiah 53 is rather explained by *him*."[32]

This way of reading Scripture eventually led Jesus' followers to apply numerous other passages to what they believed to have taken place in accordance with the Scriptures both before and after Jesus' passion and death. The

---

London: T & T Clark, 2008), 139-46. Marcus contains a list of apparent allusions to passages from Zechariah 9-14 in the passion narratives of the four Gospels ("Old Testament," 218-21).

28. Morna D. Hooker, *Jesus and the Servant: The Influence of the Servant Concept of Deutero-Isaiah in the New Testament* (London: SPCK, 1959), 127, 154-59.

29. Ruzer, *Mapping the New Testament*, 208.

30. Marinus de Jonge, *God's Final Envoy: Early Christology and Jesus' Own View of His Mission* (SHJ; Grand Rapids: Eerdmans, 1998), 31; see 30-33.

31. Marcus, "Old Testament," 214-18.

32. Otfried Hofius, "The Fourth Servant Song in the New Testament Letters," in *The Suffering Servant: Isaiah 53 in Jewish and Christian Sources*, trans. Daniel P. Bailey (ed. Bernd Janowski and Peter Stuhlmacher; Grand Rapids: Eerdmans, 2004), 188. In Chapter 10 of this work, we will look more closely at the use of Isaiah 53 among Jesus' first followers, including especially the verses that speak of the servant suffering and dying for the sins of others.

affirmation that the figure mentioned in Ps. 110:1 was subjecting his enemies under his feet led Jesus' followers to make the same claim regarding him, even though they apparently did not believe that Jesus was gradually subjecting one by one the rulers of this age.[33] Jesus' pouring out of the Holy Spirit and other charismatic gifts, for example, seems to have led them to apply Ps. 68:18 to him: "When he ascended on high he made captivity itself a captive; he gave gifts to his people" (Eph. 4:8).[34] The idea that the stone rejected had become the cornerstone in Ps. 118:22 was interpreted in the sense that Jesus' rejection by the Jewish authorities led to his becoming the foundation for a new temple or new construction, understood primarily as the *ekklēsia*.[35] In addition to Isaiah 53, other passages from the Scriptures also came to be seen as fulfilled in Jesus' ministry of healing and teaching, including Isaiah 35, 42, and 61. It is not clear, for example, to what extent Matthew's account of Jesus' birth and ministry is constructed from traditions that had been passed down regarding those events, or alternatively from passages from the Hebrew Scriptures that Matthew wished to claim had been fulfilled in Jesus.

It seems fairly certain, therefore, that in order to interpret the significance of Jesus' passion and death, his first followers took as a starting-point not the Scriptures, but those events themselves as they were seen in light of the ministry that preceded them. Their claims that the Scriptures foretold those events followed afterwards.[36] Juel observes that it is "unlikely that Jesus' story was ever told as a recitation of facts," since from the start it was told with the help of Scriptural texts, particularly from the Psalms.[37] This does not necessarily mean, however, that we are justified in going to the extreme of maintaining, as John Crossan does, that the passion accounts and other events related in connection with Jesus' birth, ministry, and resurrection have little if any historical grounding, and instead were invented by looking to the Hebrew Scriptures.[38] Much more likely is the thesis put forward by Christopher Bryan:

---

33. Psalm 110:1 may have been combined with Ps. 8:7 in the early interpretations of Jesus' resurrection; see Marc Turnage, "Jesus and Caiaphas: An Intertextual-Literary Evaluation," in *Jesus' Last Week*, Vol. 1 of *Jerusalem Studies in the Synoptic Gospels* (ed. R. Steven Notley, Marc Turnage, and Brian Becker; JCPS 11; Leiden: Brill, 2006), 150. Loader offers a list of passages that relate Ps. 110:1 to Jesus' present rule from heaven, noting that it is not clear "when this subjection begins, whether at the parousia or already in part at the exaltation itself" ("Christ at the Right Hand," 208-10).

34. Turnage notes that, in rabbinic tradition, Ps. 68:18 was interpreted as relating to Moses' heavenly ascent up Sinai ("Jesus and Caiaphas," 152). If this idea is in the thought of the author of Ephesians, this passage provides us with an example of a text that was interpreted both prophetically, as a prediction of what would take place some day through Jesus, and typologically, in that Jesus fulfilled what was prefigured in Moses' day.

35. While the Fourth Gospel does not include the parable of the wicked tenants, Andrew C. Brunson has argued that Psalm 118 plays an important role throughout the Gospel as a whole (*Psalm 118 in the Gospel of John: An Intertextual Study on the New Exodus Pattern in the Theology of John*; WUNT 2/158; Tübingen: Mohr Siebeck, 2003).

36. See Weber, *Cross*, 32, 56-57. Juel sees the confession of Jesus as the crucified and risen King of the Jews as the starting point of the interpretation of Scripture by Jesus' first followers (*Messianic Exegesis*, 89, 171).

37. Juel, *Messianic Exegesis*, 113.

38. John Dominic Crossan, *The Historical Jesus: The Life of a Mediterranean Jewish Peasant* (San Francisco: HarperSanFrancisco, 1991), 375-76.

We are not to imagine that the community originally had a, so to speak, "pure" historical memory of Jesus, and then imported Scripture so as to explain, refine, or defend that memory. We can, I believe, make no such artificial separation. Rather, the community's memory of Jesus *always and essentially* involved articulation in the motifs, narrative patterns, and diction of Israel's story. This way of remembering was inevitable because Jesus' life and death were, in the eyes of Jesus' first followers, things that happened as a continuing and crucial part of that story.[39]

The Typological Interpretation of Scripture

As is evident to us today, of course, many of the passages said to be fulfilled through Jesus in the New Testament were not prophecies per se, but were believed to allude to events that took place in the times of David, Isaiah, and other figures of Israel's past. This process of combing through the Scriptures to find passages that could be seen as applying to what had taken place through Jesus led his first followers to claim that many passages that had never been read as referring to a messianic figure had also found fulfillment through Jesus.[40] This includes even passages such as Isaiah 53 and 61, which speak of God's servant only in the past tense, rather than some type of messianic figure, in spite of the use of the verb "anointed" in Isa. 61:1.[41]

This way of interpreting Scripture also seems to have led to the kind of typological interpretations we find throughout the New Testament.[42] Most of the sufferings that David was describing in the Psalms that bore his name, for example, were believed to have actually taken place during his own lifetime. Strictly speaking, therefore, they were not prophecies regarding a future messianic figure. However, because the Messiah was David's descendant, it could be claimed that the things that David had suffered prefigured or were repeated in what Jesus would later suffer as the "son of David" or Messiah. David would then be seen as a "type" of Jesus, that is, someone whose experiences anticipated or foreshadowed what would come to take place in Jesus. Such readings of Scripture would eventually lead to the idea that God had brought about certain events described in the Hebrew Scriptures for the purpose of pointing forward to what he intended to accomplish many centuries later through Jesus.

---

39. Christopher Bryan, *Render to Caesar: Jesus, the Early Church, and the Roman Superpower* (Oxford: Oxford University Press, 2005), 65-67. Bryan questions Crossan's affirmation that "early Christianity knew nothing about the passion beyond the fact itself" (66).

40. For a summary of the allusions to the Hebrew Scriptures in the passion narratives, see Marcus, "Old Testament," 207-9. Marcus affirms that most of these allusions "are embedded rather than explicit" and would have been familiar to the earliest readers (209).

41. See Lidija Novakovic, "Matthew's Atomistic Use of Scripture: Messianic Interpretation of Isaiah 53:4 in Matthew 8:17," in *Biblical Interpretation*, ed. Hatina, 2:182-83, 188-89.

42. Richard Davidson offers a helpful summary of the history and discussion of typology among New Testament scholars since the publication of Leonhard Goppelt's groundbreaking book on the subject in 1939 (*Typology in Scripture: A Study of Hermeneutical Typos Structures*; AUSDDS 2; Berrien Springs, MI: Andrews University Press, 1981, 1-190). The German original of Goppelt's book is *Typos: Die typologische Deutung des Alten Testaments im Neuen* (Gütersloh: Bertesmann, 1939). The book was subsequently translated into English as *Typos: The Typological Interpretation of the Old Testament in the New*, trans. Donald Madvig (Grand Rapids: Eerdmans, 1982).

This kind of typology, therefore, was different from the allegorical approach to Scripture employed by Philo and others in antiquity. As Larry Hurtado notes:

> We should not confuse the typological approach to the Old Testament with allegorizing exegesis, which became more and more dominant in Christian circles in the third century and on into the medieval period. The aim in allegorizing exegesis is to show that the Scriptures encode timeless truths that are already known and accepted, which can be found in a text by treating as symbolic the characters, events, and statements in it. In this approach the biblical characters and events are purely the literary veil beneath which lies the body of philosophical, religious, and moral truths; the actuality of the characters and events is irrelevant. But in the typological approach practiced in earliest Christianity, it is essential that the biblical characters and events be treated as *real*, for the fundamental point is to show that God's prior actions and statements prepared for and foreshadowed the final redemptive events now proclaimed in the gospel. Moreover, the religious truths asserted in typological exegesis derived entirely from what were proclaimed as further real events in which God had now signaled the fulfillment of the redemptive promises, most importantly, Jesus' appearance, death, resurrection and heavenly exaltation.[43]

The narratives of the Hebrew Scriptures therefore lent themselves to this type of reading. We find this already in Paul's letters.[44] As noted in Chapter 7 of this study, in 1 Cor. 5:7 Paul identifies Jesus with the Passover lamb. This probably means that Paul believed that, when God instituted the Passover celebration at the time of Israel's exodus from Egypt, God was also thinking ahead to what would take place in Jesus, instituting types or antitypes

---

43. Larry W. Hurtado, *Lord Jesus Christ: Devotion to Jesus in Earliest Christianity* (Grand Rapids: Eerdmans, 2003), 571-72. On the characteristics of typological interpretation, see also William Horbury, "Old Testament Interpretation in the Writings of the Church Fathers," in *Mikra: Text, Translation, Reading, and Interpretation of the Hebrew Bible in Ancient Judaism and Early Christianity*, CRINT Section 2: *Literature of the Jewish People in the Period of the Second Temple and the Talmud* 1 (ed. Martin J. Mulder; exec. ed. Harry Sysling; Philadelphia: Fortress, 1988, 766-68); Jacques Schlosser, "Déluge et typologie dans 1 P 3,19-21," in *Typologie Biblique: De Quelques Figures Vives* (ed. Raymond Kuntzmann; LecDiv; Paris: Éditions du Cerf, 2002), 177-79. Citing the work of Anthony C. Thiselton, Donald A. Carson argues that typology is grounded in history and presupposes corresponding events, while allegory "depends on an extra-textual grid, some extra-textual key, to warrant the explanation" ("Mystery and Fulfillment: Toward a More Comprehensive Paradigm of Paul's Understanding of the Old and the New," in *Justification and Variegated Nomism*, Vol. 2: *The Paradoxes of Paul*; ed. Carson, Peter T. O'Brien, and Mark A. Seifrid; WUNT 2/181; Tübingen: Mohr Siebeck, 2004, 404). Davidson notes that the older view of typology "in terms of divinely pre-ordained and predictive *prefigurations*" has been replaced by a more recent consensus describing typology "in terms of historical *correspondences* retrospectively recognized within the consistent redemptive activity of God," and that "Barr and others contend that one cannot really distinguish between allegory and typology...." (*Typology*, 94-96; see also his discussion on 1-14, 93-104). According to Stephen Finlan, typology "posits an earlier event as a *prefiguration* or 'stamp' (*typos*) of a later event, while allegory involves a spatial or ontological correlation, seeing a 'higher' level of reality reflected in the 'lower.' In my analysis, typology correlates temporal levels, while allegory relates spatial or ontological levels.... The typologist sees evidence of the activity of the divine in time, in *events*; the allegorist believes the divine exists at a higher ontological level of reality; the divine is in the higher *level*" (*The Background and Content of Paul's Cultic Atonement Metaphors*; AcBib 19; Atlanta: SBL, 2004, 68-70). On this distinction, see also Robert Hamerton-Kelly, "Allegory, Typology, and Sacred Violence: Sacrificial Representation and the Unity of the Bible in Paul and Philo," *SPhA* 3 (1991): 53-70. It is important to stress that, for the most part, these distinctions did not exist in the first century CE, but are the creation of modern scholarship.

44. On Paul's use of typology, see especially Carson, "Mystery and Fulfillment," 404-10.

(*antitupa*, Heb. 9:24; 1 Pet. 3:21) that would be fulfilled centuries later.⁴⁵ Of course, it is also possible that Paul thought that God had led Jesus to go up to Jerusalem and had acted to bring about certain things once Jesus was there so that what had originally taken place when the first Passover was celebrated might be replicated in some way. In this case, when God instituted the Passover celebration, he was not necessarily contemplating what would some day happen to Jesus in Jerusalem. Rather, it was only in Jesus' time that God had decided to influence the events that took place in Jerusalem in order to remind others of the Passover celebration and give new meaning to that celebration. In 1 Cor. 10:1-11, Paul also claims that Israel's passing through the Red Sea, the miraculous feeding of the Israelites with manna, and the provision of water from the rock that Moses struck foreshadowed what would come to pass through Christ.⁴⁶ When Paul affirms that these things "were written down to instruct us" (v. 11), he seems to be claiming that from of old God contemplated not only what would happen to Jesus himself, but the fact that he would bring into existence a new community of people through Jesus. For this reason, God had the writers of the Scriptures allude to those events long ahead of time, so that centuries later this new people might learn from them.

In Gal. 4:21-31, Paul argues that Sarah and Hagar represent two covenants that correspond to "the present Jerusalem" and "the Jerusalem above." Although he uses the Greek word *allēgoroumena* in v. 24, according to the distinctions in use today, this interpretation of the Genesis story involves typology rather than allegory.⁴⁷ Again, we cannot be sure whether Paul believed that, when the events associated with Sarah and Hagar originally occurred, God already contemplated what would later come to pass through Jesus. In any case, Paul's typological interpretation of this story, together with 1 Cor. 5:7-8 and 10:1-11, strongly suggests that this type of reading of Scripture had already developed at least to some extent even before Paul wrote his letters, rather than originating with Paul himself.

We find other examples of this reading of the Hebrew Scriptures throughout the rest of the New Testament. When Jesus' first followers read the story of the bronze serpent in Numbers 21, it was natural for them to see this as foreshadowing the way in which Jesus would be lifted up on a cross in order to bring salvation to others (John 3:14; cf. 8:28; 12:32). The fact that in 1

---

45. On the distinction between type and antitype in the New Testament and modern biblical scholarship, see especially Karl-Heinrich Ostmeyer, "Typologie und Typos: Analyse eines schwierigen Verhältnisses," *NTS* 46 (2000): 112-31; Paul M. Hoskins, *Jesus as Fulfillment of the Temple in the Gospel of John* (PBM; Milton Keynes: Paternoster, 2006), 18-36.

46. Davidson contains an extensive discussion of Paul's typology in 1 Cor. 10:1-13, which he regards as possibly the earliest of the hermeneutical *typos* passages (*Typology*, 191-277). On the same passage, see also Carson, "Mystery and Fulfillment," 408-9.

47. On Paul's use of the verb *allēgorein* in Gal. 4:24 to refer to typological rather than allegorical interpretation of the Hebrew Scriptures, see especially Daniel Gerber, "Ga 4,21-31 ou l'indéfinissable méthode?," in *Typologie Biblique*, ed. Kuntzmann, 173-76; Steven Di Mattei, "Paul's Allegory of the Two Covenants (Gal. 4.21-31) in Light of First-Century Hellenistic Rhetoric and Jewish Hermeneutics," *NTS* 52 (2006): 102-22.

Cor. 10:8-9 Paul refers to the death of twenty-three thousand Israelites in the wilderness and recalls how the Israelites were bitten by serpents indicates that he may have been acquainted with this typological interpretation of Numbers 21.[48] If so, Paul himself was reading the book of Numbers in a similar way.[49]

The affirmation that Jesus had to be in the heart of the earth for three days and three nights like Jonah was in the belly of the fish also represents a typological reading of the Hebrew Scriptures (Matt. 12:38-41; cf. 16:4; Luke 12:29-32). Though it seems doubtful that this affirmation dates back to Jesus, the fact that the "sign of Jonah" apparently formed part of Q makes it reasonable to conclude that, even outside of Pauline circles, the Hebrew Scriptures were being interpreted typologically only a few years after Jesus' death. In fact, this kind of typological reading of the Hebrew Scriptures is already suggested by the ministry of John the Baptist. Not only was he seen as a prophet prefigured by Elijah, but he seems also to have intended his baptizing activity in the Jordan River to evoke images of Israel's exodus from Egypt through the Red Sea and the people's entrance into the promised land.[50] As William Horbury has pointed out, this kind of typology is present already in the Hebrew Scriptures themselves, as well as other Jewish writings in antiquity and even classical Greek literature.[51] It is therefore certainly not out of the question that Jesus himself taught his disciples to read the Scriptures in typological fashion.[52]

While we do not yet find in the New Testament the degree of development of the typological reading of Scripture that appears in Justin Martyr's *Dialogue with Trypho* (c. 150), it can hardly be doubted that this type of reading gradually became more and more common over the course of the following decades among Jesus' first followers. Oskar Skarsaune notes that Justin did not consider himself to be an innovator, but "was convinced that his way of expounding the Old Testament had been handed over to the church by the apostles, and that the apostles had learned it from the risen Christ."[53] In

---

48. Although Paul does not mention the bronze serpent explicitly in 1 Cor. 10:8-9, the fact that he alludes to the story from Numbers 21 there suggests that this story may already have been interpreted typologically by his time (see Davidson, *Typology*, 260). For a comparison between how that story was read in ancient Judaism and in early Christianity, see Turnage, "Old Testament," 71-88.

49. The allusion in 1 Cor. 10:8 seems to be to Num. 25:1-9, although the number there is 24,000 rather than 23,000; the latter number appears in Num. 26:62. Ellen Bradshaw Aitken argues that, in 1 Cor. 10:5-10, Paul has in mind primarily the incident with the golden calf (*Jesus' Death in Early Christian Memory: The Poetics of the Passion*; NTOA/SUNT 53; Göttingen: Vandenhoeck & Ruprecht, 2004, 37-40).

50. See Scot McKnight, "Jesus' New Vision within Judaism," in *Who Was Jesus?* ed. Copan and Evans, 80-81; Craig A. Evans, "The Baptism of John in a Typological Context," in *Dimensions of Baptism: Biblical and Theological Studies* (ed. Stanley E. Porter and Anthony R. Cross; JSNTSup 234; London: Sheffield Academic Press, 2002), 46-59.

51. Horbury, "Old Testament Interpretation," 766. On the different kinds of typology used in the New Testament and the influence of Jewish interpretation of the Scriptures on New Testament typology, see especially E. Earle Ellis, "Biblical Interpretation in the New Testament Church," in *Mikra*, ed. Mulder, 691-725. On Philo's use of allegory, see Hamerton-Kelly, "Allegory," 53-70; Borgen, "'In Accordance,'" 233-64.

52. So argues Ben F. Meyer, "Appointed Deed, Appointed Doer: Jesus and the Scriptures," in *Authenticating the Activities of Jesus* (ed. Bruce Chilton and Craig A. Evans; NTTS 28/2; Leiden: Brill, 1999), 157-58.

53. Oskar Skarsaune, *In the Shadow of the Temple: Jewish Influences on Early Christianity* (Downers Grove, IL: InterVarsity, 2002), 267; see also 265-66.

fact, certain key biblical texts were cited by a variety of authors in the first two centuries. This suggests that those texts played a significant role in the thought of Jesus' followers at a very early stage.[54] As they reread the Scriptures closely, looking for any ideas that could be seen as pointing to Jesus, certain passages seem to have lent themselves naturally to a typological reading. Like Jesus, Joshua—who in Hebrew and Greek shared the same name with Jesus (*Yeshua, Iēsous*)—had been a kind of "second Moses" who had led the people of Israel into the promised land.[55] Like Solomon, Jesus could also be seen as the son of David who had built a "new temple" to the Lord. Stories involving salvation that had to do with water, such as the passage through the Red Sea (1 Cor. 10:1-2) and the flood in Noah's day, when "eight persons were saved through water" (1 Pet. 3:20-21; cf. Luke 17:26-27), would be read as allusions to baptism.[56] Likewise, stories in which wood and trees played a part, such as the account of Adam and Eve in the Garden of Eden (see Rev. 2:7), would easily be seen as pointing forward to Jesus' crucifixion on a wooden beam.[57] The sacrificial animals mentioned in the Hebrew Scriptures, especially the lambs who went passively to their deaths, might be seen as foreshadowing Jesus' death (John 1:29; 1 Pet. 1:19). The "bread from heaven" or manna God gave in Moses' day could be interpreted as prefiguring either Jesus or the bread used in the eucharistic celebration (John 6:32; cf. Rev. 2:17). As Paul's letters show, Adam could also be seen as a "type of the one who was to come" (Rom. 5:14; cf. 1 Cor. 15:45-49).[58]

However, not only the biblical narratives but also the commandments God had given in the law of Moses could be interpreted typologically. Similar to the way in which Jesus' followers regarded themselves as fulfilling the original meaning and purpose of the Mosaic commandments in their conduct,

---

54. See Oskar Skarsaune, "The Development of Scriptural Interpretation in the Second and Third Centuries—Except Clement and Origen," in *Hebrew Bible/Old Testament*, ed. Sæbø, 1:376, 396. On the relation between the early reading of the Hebrew Scriptures and that of the second and third centuries, see 372-437, where Skarsaune notes that the fullest collection of prooftexts from the Hebrew Scriptures is found in Novatian's *De Trinitate* and Cyprian's *Testimonies (Ad Quirinum)*, both of which were written in the third century.

55. Some New Testament scholars, such as Armand Puig i Tàrrech, see the account of Jesus' transfiguration in the Synoptics as presenting Jesus as a new or second Moses ("The Glory on the Mountain: The Episode of the Transfiguration of Jesus," *NTS* 58 [2012]: 151-72).

56. On Paul's idea that the crossing of the Red Sea by the Israelites prefigured baptism in Christ in 1 Cor. 10:1-2, see Davidson, *Typology*, 213-23. For a detailed consideration of the typology in 1 Pet. 3:20-21, see Schlosser, "Déluge," 177-201.

57. David Rokeah provides a summary of the passages from Justin's *Dialogue with Trypho* in which Justin claims that Jesus' crucifixion or cross was prefigured in the Hebrew Scriptures, especially in passages that mentioned wood or trees (*Justin Martyr and the Jews*; JCPS 5; Leiden: Brill, 2002, 36-41). Rivka Nir notes that the story of Adam and Eve combined the imagery of wood with water, since the waters of baptism were identified with the rivers in paradise (*The Destruction of Jerusalem and the Idea of Redemption in the Syriac Apocalypse of Baruch*; EJL 20; Atlanta: SBL, 2002, 168-69). The same combination of elements is found in the story of Noah, which speaks not only of the waters of the deluge but also of the wood of which the ark was constructed.

58. As Ryan S. Schellenberg has argued, strictly speaking, the idea of Paul in Rom. 5:18-19 is not that Adam prefigured Christ typologically, but rather that Adam's sin prefigured the righteous act of Christ ("Does Paul Call Adam a 'Type' of Christ?," *ZNW* 105 [2014]: 54-63).

observing those commandments "in spirit" rather than solely "in letter," so also they could interpret typologically many of the commandments in order to argue that they pointed to the new reality that was to come about through Christ.[59] In this case, the distinction between allegory and typology would not always be clear. For example, the commandment regarding circumcision could be seen not only as foreshadowing the "circumcision of the heart" that would take place among believers in Christ (Rom. 2:25-29), but as a type that prefigured Christian baptism. This understanding of baptism as a "spiritual circumcision" is mentioned explicitly in Col. 2:11-12 and is hinted at in other Pauline passages.[60]

Similarly, as the letter to the Hebrews demonstrates, the Mosaic commandments regarding sacrifice, the priesthood, the tabernacle, and the Day of Atonement rites could be seen as "types," "symbols," "shadows," and "figures" (*tupa, hupodeigmata, skia, antitupa*) of what would take place through Christ (Heb. 8:5; 9:23-24; 10:1).[61] Paul's letter to the Colossians also speaks of "matters of food and drink or of observing festivals, new moons, or sabbaths" as "only a shadow (*skia*)" of what was to come and claims that "the substance (*sōma*) belongs to Christ" (Col. 2:16-17). For the authors of Hebrews and Colossians, then, the laws and rites originally prescribed pointed to Christ, giving meaning to what he had done and what he continued to do from heaven.[62] Similarly, one might see the mercy seat of the ark of the covenant as a type of Christ, who through his death or blood had become the place in which God now made himself present in order to grant forgiveness of sins (Rom. 3:25).[63] Just as the temple or house built by Solomon prefigured the "spiritual house" that would come into existence through Christ, so also the stones used in its construction could be seen as prefiguring the way in which believers would constitute "living stones" in the new temple (1 Pet. 2:2, 5; cf. Eph. 2:20-22).[64]

---

59. On the relation between the spiritualization of the Hebrew Scriptures and their typological interpretation, see William Horbury, "Land, Sanctuary and Worship," in *Early Christian Thought*, ed. Barclay and Sweet, 214-16; Davidson, *Typology*, 225-48.

60. Géza Vermès, for example, argues that "the whole structure of the Pauline theology of baptism is strictly related to the contemporary Jewish doctrine of circumcision" ("Baptism and Jewish Exegesis: New Light from Ancient Sources," *NTS* 4 [1958]: 319; see 308-19).

61. On Hebrews' use of typology, particularly with regard to the "heavenly tent," see Lincoln D. Hurst, "Eschatology and Platonism in the Epistle to the Hebrews," *SBLSP* 23 (1984): 46-74. On the meaning of *hupodeigma* and *antitupos* in Hebrews, see Hurst, "How 'Platonic' are Heb. viii.5 and iv.23f?," *JTS* 34 (1983): 156-68.

62. Graham Hughes distinguishes among three different classes of citations from the Hebrew Scriptures in the letter to the Hebrews: "those used in a 'messianic' or eschatological way...," "those which, in their original context, were addressed to Yahweh but are now taken as addressed to Jesus; and those which are placed on the lips of Jesus" (*Hebrews and Hermeneutics: The Epistle to the Hebrews as a New Testament Example of Biblical Interpretation*; SNTSMS 36; Cambridge: Cambridge University Press, 1979, 57).

63. Of course, not all scholars agree that, in Rom. 3:25, the word *hilastērion* refers to the mercy seat of the ark of the covenant, as we shall see further on in this study.

64. Bertil E. Gärtner, *The Temple and the Community in Qumran and the New Testament: A Comparative Study in the Temple Symbolism of the Qumran Texts and the New Testament* (SNTSMS 1; Cambridge: Cambridge University Press, 1965), 73, n1. Gärtner also discusses the idea of "living stones" in this context, where even the term *living* may be seen as synonymous with "spiritual" and *logikos*. On the extensive use of stone imagery

THE DIVINE PLAN

Today, of course, the typological reading of Scripture we find in the New Testament is considered highly problematic. This is not only because the idea that concrete events taking place in Jesus' day were prophesied centuries beforehand runs counter to our modern worldview, but also because we have been taught that the true meaning of a biblical passage is to be identified with the author's original intention.[65] This rules out the possibility of typological and allegorical interpretations of Scripture in our contemporary contexts, and even makes such interpretations appear strange and irrational. Obviously, however, this was not how the ancients read Scripture.[66]

Nevertheless, it is important to stress that this way of reading Scripture did not merely involve proof-texting or claiming that isolated events had been foretold by the biblical authors in antiquity. Rather, these passages were thought to relate to one another in the context of a whole. Above all, this reading of Scripture pointed to a *divine plan* that supposedly existed prior to the world's creation. The notion of a pre-ordained divine plan seems to have already existed in some Jewish circles by the first century CE, where it was thought that God had intended and foreseen the giving of the Torah, the election of Abraham and Israel, the sending of the Messiah, and other events in human history long before they happened and perhaps even before creation. In fact, these realities might even be identified with the *purpose* for which the world had been created.[67] Similarly, Jesus' first followers came to see all that had taken place through Jesus as prefigured and foretold in the Scriptures. This was true with regard not only to Jesus' birth, life, death, resurrection, and exaltation, but also the apostolic mission, the church, the new covenant, the rejection of the message concerning Jesus by many Jews, and the inclusion of gentiles as members of God's people. The divine plan contemplated *all* of these things.[68]

---

in the typology of early Christianity, see Ken Derry, "One Stone on Another: Towards an Understanding of Symbolism in the *Epistle of Barnabas*," *JECS* 4 (1996): 515-28.

65. On this basis, modern scholars have been highly critical of Paul's use of the Hebrew Scriptures, yet this has often involved imposing on Paul "a set of modern categories in regard to what constitutes correct exegesis," as Childs has pointed out (*Biblical Theology*, 239-41). According to van Buren, today we have been trained to look at what is *behind* a text, whereas first-century Jews "saw reality lying directly in the text itself" (*According to the Scriptures*, 30; on these differences, see 30-33). Van Buren also comments on the difficulties that typological and allegorical readings present for modern thought (96).

66. On the characteristics of the "pre-critical realistic reading of the biblical narrative" that was prevalent before the rise of biblical scholarship, see Edward W. Klink III, *The Sheep of the Fold: The Audience and Origin of the Gospel of John* (SNTSMS 141; Cambridge: Cambridge University Press, 2007), 121-27.

67. On these ideas, see Friedrich Avemarie, *Tora und Leben: Untersuchungen zur Heilsbedeutung der Tora in der frühen rabbinischen Literatur* (TSAJ 55; Tübingen: J. C. B. Mohr, 1995), 50-60; Werner Förster, *Palestinian Judaism in New Testament Times*, trans. Gordon E. Harris (Edinburgh: Oliver & Boyd, 1964), 184-86.

68. Of course, as Alexander J. M. Wedderburn points out, it is one thing to affirm that Jesus' first followers came to believe in the existence of a pre-conceived divine plan centered on Jesus on the basis of their assumptions and convictions, and another thing altogether to affirm that Christians today should believe that such a divine plan existed from eternity (*The Death of Jesus: Some Reflections on Jesus-Traditions and Paul*; WUNT 299; Tübingen: Mohr Siebeck, 2013, 183-86).

The Divine Plan in the Pauline Epistles and Other New Testament Writings

The letters attributed to Paul in the New Testament provide ample evidence that, when he and other believers of his time looked to the stories of Abraham, Sarah, and Hagar, as well as the exodus of Israel from Egypt, its time in the wilderness, and the giving of the law through Moses (Rom. 4:1-25; 1 Cor. 10:1-11; Gal. 3:1—4:31), they saw these as part of an overarching story that had come to its fulfillment in Jesus and the new community he had founded. The narratives regarding Adam and the patriarchs, the departure of the Israelites from Egypt, their passage into the promised land under Moses and Joshua, and the consolidation of the monarchy under David and Solomon pointed forward to what would take place in the days of Jesus and Paul and also into the future. If the Scriptures foresaw that God would justify the gentiles or nations by faith when it told of Abraham's faith being reckoned to him as righteousness, and if it spoke of Christ as Abraham's "seed," as Paul affirms in Gal. 3:16, then clearly at the time of Abraham God had already intended to bless the nations through Christ.[69]

The letters to the Ephesians and Colossians even claim that this plan went back to a time before the world was created. The author of Ephesians begins by affirming that believers were chosen in Christ "before the foundation of the world to be holy and blameless before him in love," and then speaks of "a plan for the fullness of time, to gather up all things in him, things in heaven and things on earth" (Eph. 1:4, 10). The "mystery of his will" consists of believers "having been destined according to the purpose of him who accomplishes all things according to his counsel and will" (1:9, 11). Later on in the letter, the author develops these ideas even further, alluding to "the mystery that was made known to me by revelation" (3:3) and defining his ministry in terms of bringing to light "the mystery of the gospel" (6:19). In Eph. 3:5-12, he writes:

> In former generations this mystery was not made known to humankind, as it has now been revealed to his holy apostles and prophets by the Spirit: that is, the Gentiles have become fellow heirs, members of the same body, and sharers in the promise in Christ Jesus through the gospel. Of this gospel I have become a servant according to the gift of God's grace that was given me by the working of his power. Although I am the very least of all the saints, this grace was given to me to bring to the Gentiles the news of the boundless riches of Christ, and to make everyone see what is the plan of the mystery hidden for ages in God who created all things; so that through the church the wisdom of God in its rich variety might now be made known to the rulers and authorities in the heavenly places. This was in accordance with the eternal purpose that he has carried out in Christ Jesus our Lord, in whom we have access to God in boldness and confidence through faith in him.

Here the plan or mystery involves, not merely the coming of Christ, but above all the inclusion of gentiles as members of God's people. Before

---

69. Juel notes that, in second-temple Jewish thought, the term *seed* may have been used as a designation for the Messiah (*Messianic Exegesis*, 82).

creation, God had determined that people from among the nations would some day have access to him through faith in Christ.[70] This was God's eternal purpose or plan, hidden for ages, that he had now accomplished through Christ. According to this passage, however, an important part of this plan was to send out apostles such as Paul to bear the good news to the nations.

The letter to the Colossians looks back all the way to the creation of the world, when "all things in heaven and on earth," both "visible and invisible," were created through and for God's Son as "the image of the invisible God" and "the firstborn of all creation" (Col. 1:15-16). There Paul has come to serve the church "according to God's commission" that was given to him "to make the word of God fully known, the mystery that has been hidden throughout the ages and generations but has now been revealed to his saints" (1:25-26). While here the mystery is defined in terms of Christ being in believers, it also embraces the inclusion of the gentiles in God's people, as well as their growth and maturation (1:27-28). God's mystery is additionally identified here with "Christ himself, in whom are hidden all the treasures of wisdom and knowledge" (2:2-3). This is the mystery declared by Christ, for which Paul is in prison (4:3).

Paul's language in Romans echoes some of the same ideas. There he affirms that his proclamation of Christ and the gospel involves "the revelation of the mystery that was kept secret for long ages but is now disclosed, and through the prophetic writings is made known to all the Gentiles, according to the command of the eternal God, to bring about the obedience of faith" (Rom. 16:25-26). Here we find the same stress on Paul's role in the revelation of this mystery, the fulfillment of the prophetic writings, and the inclusion of gentiles through faith and obedience.[71] Earlier in Romans, expressing ideas similar to those we find in Ephesians and Colossians, Paul presents God's plan in terms of his eternal purpose to bring people to reflect God's image in the way Christ does: "those whom he foreknew he also predestined to be conformed to the image of his Son, in order that he might be the firstborn within a large family" (Rom. 8:29). Paul also speaks of the grace given him by God to "be a minister of Christ Jesus to the Gentiles in the priestly service of the gospel of God" and stresses what Christ has accomplished through him "to win obedience from the Gentiles" (Rom. 15:15-19). Significantly, Paul sees this as the fulfillment of Isa. 52:15 LXX, "Those who have never been told of him shall see, and those who have never heard of him shall understand" (Rom. 15:21).

Similar ideas are reflected in the opening verses of Romans: "Paul, a servant of Jesus Christ, called to be an apostle, set apart for the gospel of God, which he promised beforehand through his prophets in the holy scriptures,

---

70. On the concept of mystery in the Hebrew Scriptures, see Sigurd Grindheim, "What the OT Prophets Did Not Know: The Mystery of the Church in Eph. 3, 2-13," *Biblica* 84 (2003): 533-34.

71. On Paul's use of the concept of *mustērion*, see Carson, "Mystery and Fulfillment," 412-25. For a comparison between Paul's understanding of the term *mystery* and that reflected in the writings of Qumran, see Joseph Coppens, "'Mystery' in the Theology of St. Paul and its Parallels at Qumran," in *Paul and Qumran: Studies in New Testament Exegesis* (ed. Jerome Murphy-O'Connor; London: Geoffrey Chapman, 1968), 132-58.

the gospel concerning his Son, who was descended from David according to the flesh. For whatever was written in former days was written for our instruction, so that by steadfastness and by the encouragement of the scriptures we might have hope" (Rom. 1:1-4). Here Paul sees the Scriptures as contemplating beforehand Jesus' descent from David, the content and proclamation of the gospel, Paul's apostolic calling, and the instruction and encouragement of those who would some day believe in Jesus as the Messiah.

In his Corinthian correspondence, Paul also points to his own ministry and that of others as something that was foretold in the Scriptures and formed part of God's plan. This idea is central to 1 Cor. 1:17—2:16, where Paul claims that he was sent by Christ to proclaim the message of the gospel, which appears to the world as foolishness, but in reality represents God's eternal wisdom. There he cites Isa. 29:14: "For it is written, 'I will destroy the wisdom of the wise, and the discernment of the discerning I will thwart'" (1 Cor. 1:19). In his wisdom, through the foolishness of the proclamation of Paul and others, God had decided to save those who would believe (1:21). After mentioning "the mystery of God" that he proclaimed to the Corinthians, Paul claims that he speaks "God's wisdom, secret and hidden, which God decreed before the ages for our glory" (2:1, 7). According to Paul, had the rulers of this age understood these things, they would not have crucified Christ (2:6-8). This is a clear allusion to the idea that God conceived of Christ's suffering and death far ahead of time and foretold what was to happen in the Scriptures. Here again, Paul cites Scripture: "But, as it is written, 'What no eye has seen, nor ear heard, nor the human heart conceived, what God has prepared for those who love him'—these things God has revealed to us through the Spirit" (2:9-10). He also points to the revelation of these things through God's Spirit, who "searches everything, even the depths of God," as well as the "mind of the Lord," which can be grasped only through the Spirit (2:10-16). While much of Paul's language here is slightly different from that which appears in Romans, Ephesians, and Colossians, Paul is once more pointing to a formerly hidden divine plan foretold in the Scriptures that is now revealed to the world through him and others as God's agents. This is how Paul defines his own task and that of his co-workers; they are "servants of Christ and stewards of God's mysteries" (1 Cor. 4:1).

Similar ideas appear in 2 Cor. 3:4-18, where Paul writes: "our competence is from God, who has made us competent to be ministers of a new covenant, not of letter but of spirit" (vv. 5-6). He contrasts the ministry of death and condemnation carried out through Moses with the glory of his own ministry of the Spirit and justification (vv. 7-11). At the same time, he claims that the minds of others are "hardened" so that, when they read Moses and the old covenant, they do not understand (vv. 12-14). His allusion to Moses' veil can also be understood as a typological interpretation of the Exodus account: Moses had "put a veil over his face to keep the people of Israel from gazing at the end of the glory that was being set aside"; today, that veil is still there, lying "over their minds" so as to conceal from them the truths concerning Christ contained in the Scriptures (v. 15). Only when one turns to Christ as Lord is that veil removed (v. 16). The idea that believers are transformed into the image of Christ as Lord also appears here (vv. 17-18), echoing Rom. 8:29.[72]

For Paul, the hardening of Israel so that the gentiles might come in also constituted an intrinsic part of this divine plan previously hidden from human sight, but now revealed. Paul alludes briefly to the hardening of the minds of God's people Israel in 1 Cor. 2:1. In Romans 9–11, however, he develops this idea extensively. He begins this passage arguing that the promise made to Abraham regarding his descendants is fulfilled in those who have come to believe (Rom. 9:6-8). Paul's argument regarding election should be understood according to the ideas we have already seen: he has in mind, not the election or predestination of particular individuals, as Protestant theology has generally taught, but the election of gentiles as members of God's people. It is significant that nowhere in Paul's letters does he cite the Hebrew Scriptures as extensively as he does in these three chapters.[73] Those Scriptures reveal that what God had "prepared beforehand" was the calling of people "not from the Jews only but also from the Gentiles" (Rom. 9:24). In this regard, he cites Hosea 2:23 and 1:10: "Those who were not my people I will call 'my people,' and her who was not beloved I will call 'beloved.' And in the very place where it was said to them, 'You are not my people,' there they shall be called children of the living God" (Rom. 9:25-26). What the Scriptures foretold was that people both from among the Jews and from among the gentile nations would attain the "righteousness of faith" that would be given through Christ (Rom. 9:30—10:13). The proclamation of the gospel throughout the world by God's messengers such as Paul was foretold by both Isaiah and David (Rom. 10:14-18; see Isa. 52:7; 53:1; Ps. 19:4).

The Scriptures also foretold the hardening of many members of God's people Israel.[74] Similar to the way in which God hardened Pharoah's heart, he has now hardened the hearts of many within Israel, who mistakenly seek righteousness through the law and have stumbled over Christ, the stumbling stone (Rom. 9:11-33).[75] This has made it possible for the gospel to go out to the nations. Paul develops these ideas at the end of Romans 10:

---

72. Grindheim points out a number of parallels between Eph. 3:2-13 and 2 Cor. 3:5—4:1, even though the latter passage does not use the terminology of mystery ("OT Prophets," 546-47).

73. B. J. Oropeza has observed that most of Paul's citations from the Hebrew Scriptures are found in Romans, and of these, most appear in chapters 9-11 of the epistle ("Paul and Theodicy: Intertextual Thoughts on God's Justice and Faithfulness to Israel in Romans 9–11," *NTS* 53 [2007]: 58).

74. Referring to the use of Isaiah 6 by Jesus and several of the New Testament writers, Craig A. Evans writes: "For them this text explained the mystery of the rejection of Jesus and the apostolic witness to him. The Gospel has been rejected, not simply because its hearers were dull, but because it was and continues to be God's will.... But this affirmation of faith also carried with it the belief that ultimately good would come out of it" (*To See and Not Perceive: Isaiah 6.9-10 in Early Jewish and Christian Interpretation*; JSOTSup 64; Sheffield: JSOT, 1989, 165). On the use of Isaiah 6 in Paul's letters, the Synoptics, Acts, and John, see 81-136.

75. Ira Brent Driggers rightly observes that the hardening of Jesus' disciples is a central idea in Mark's Gospel (*Following God through Mark: Theological Tension in the Second Gospel*; Louisville, KY: Westminster

But not all have obeyed the good news; for Isaiah says, "Lord, who has believed our message?" So faith comes from what is heard, and what is heard comes through the word of Christ. But I ask, have they not heard? Indeed they have; for "Their voice has gone out to all the earth, and their words to the ends of the world." Again I ask, did Israel not understand? First Moses says, "I will make you jealous of those who are not a nation; with a foolish nation I will make you angry." Then Isaiah is so bold as to say, "I have been found by those who did not seek me; I have shown myself to those who did not ask for me." But of Israel he says, "All day long I have held out my hands to a disobedient and contrary people" (10:16-21).

For Paul, however, this rejection is only temporary. While in the present God has hardened Israel's heart so the gospel may go out to the gentiles, he has by no means rejected Israel. Instead, he has conserved a remnant (Rom. 11:1-10). While the people of Israel have "stumbled" so that the gospel may go out to the gentiles, they have not fallen entirely: "So I ask, have they stumbled so as to fall? By no means! But through their stumbling salvation has come to the Gentiles, so as to make Israel jealous. Now if their stumbling means riches for the world, and if their defeat means riches for Gentiles, how much more will their full inclusion mean!" (11:11-12). Through the gentiles, God is provoking the people of Israel to jealousy so that they may be saved (11:14). While God has broken off some branches of the olive tree to graft gentiles into that tree like wild branches, many of those from among Israel who have been broken off will be grafted into the tree once again, so that "all Israel" may be saved (11:17-26).[76] The gentiles, who were once disobedient to God, have now received mercy and obedience through the disobedience of many Jews, yet in this way those now disobedient will be shown mercy and return obediently to God (11:30-32). In the end, Paul can only marvel at the wisdom and inscrutability of this divine plan (11:33-36). As his extensive citations of Scripture throughout these chapters demonstrate, all of this is something that God conceived of long ago and revealed ahead of time to those who wrote the Hebrew Scriptures.

The idea of a divine plan foretold in the Scriptures appears repeatedly, not only in the letters attributed to Paul, but in most of the other writings of the New Testament as well. The Synoptics and Acts use the verb *dei* to speak not only of Jesus' suffering and death as necessary, but also other events. Elijah, identified with John the Baptist, needed to come before the suffering of the Messiah and the restoration of all things (Matt. 17:10-13; Mark 9:11-13). Luke speaks of the necessity of Jesus proclaiming the gospel throughout the villages and towns of Galilee and Judea (Luke 4:43-44). In Acts, Luke says that it was necessary for the Scripture regarding Judas to be fulfilled and for someone to take his place (Acts 1:16-26), as well as for Paul to carry out his ministry, suffer opposition, and later appear before the Caesar in Rome

---

John Knox, 2007, 51-57). This temporary hardening of the disciples can therefore be seen as paralleling the temporary hardening of Israel in Romans 9-11.

76. Grindheim rightly stresses that, for Paul, the hardening of Israel so that the gentiles may enter in is not an end in itself, but is aimed at the eventual salvation of Israel ("OT Prophets," 550).

(Acts 9:6, 16; 19:21; 23:11; 27:24; cf. 14:22; 25:10). The eschatological events to come are also seen as a necessity in the Synoptics: before the end, there must be wars and rumors of wars, and the gospel must be proclaimed first to all the nations (Matt. 24:6, 14; Mark 13:7, 10; Luke 21:9).[77] According to Acts, Jesus "must remain in heaven until the time of universal restoration that God announced long ago through his holy prophets" (Acts 3:21). These passages imply once more that the divine plan foretold in the Scriptures not only stretches back to a period before creation but, from the start, contemplated the consummation of all things.

The idea of a divine plan lies behind other passages in the Synoptic Gospels and Acts as well. Allusions to the fulfillment of the Scriptures in the work of John the Baptist and the betrayal of Judas indicate that this plan contemplated what would take place through both of them (Luke 3:3-6; Mark 14:18-20; John 13:18-26; 17:12; cf. 18:9). In Acts 1:7, the risen Jesus points forward to the "times and periods that the Father has set by his own authority," while Paul tells the church leaders gathered at Ephesus that he has proclaimed to them the whole purpose or plan of God (*boulē*, Acts 20:27).

More importantly, however, we find in these writings the theme that the rejection of Israel and the subsequent incorporation of gentiles into God's people was foretold throughout the Hebrew Scriptures. This idea is particularly stressed in the Gospel of Matthew. Already in the opening verses, the inclusion of gentiles is contemplated. Many have noted that three of the four women mentioned in Jesus' genealogy are of foreign origin (Matt. 1:1-17). Those who first recognize and worship Jesus as the messianic king are the gentile magi (Matt. 2:1-23). They stand in contrast to Herod, who as "king of the Jews" rejects Jesus. The ability of the gentile magi to understand what was foretold in the Hebrew Scriptures contrasts with the inability of the Jewish experts in the Scriptures whom Herod consults to interpret those Scriptures. Matthew has Jesus begin his ministry "in the territory of Zebulun and Naphtali, so that what had been spoken through the prophet Isaiah might be fulfilled: 'Land of Zebulun, land of Naphtali, on the road by the sea, across the Jordan, Galilee of the Gentiles—the people who sat in darkness have seen a great light, and for those who sat in the region and shadow of death light has dawned'" (Matt. 4:13-16; cf. Isa. 9:1-2). In Matt. 12:14-21, after noting how the Pharisees conspired to kill Jesus for having healed on the Sabbath, Matthew mentions Jesus' healing ministry and then continues, "This was to fulfill what had been spoken through the prophet Isaiah: 'Here is my servant, whom I have chosen, my beloved, with whom my soul is well pleased. I will put my Spirit upon him, and he will proclaim justice to the Gentiles. He will not wrangle or cry aloud, nor will anyone hear his voice in the streets. He will not break a bruised reed or quench a smoldering wick until he brings justice to victory. And in his name the Gentiles will hope'" (Isa. 42:1-4).

---

77. On Mark's use of the verb *dei* to speak of the necessity for the divine plan centered upon Jesus and the gospel to be carried out, see especially Alexander Weihs, *Die Deutung des Todes Jesu im Markusevangelium: Eine exegetische Studie zu den Leidens- und Auferstehungsansagen* (FB 99; Würzburg: Echter, 2003), 207-13, 284-90.

Immediately after this, Jesus begins to teach in parables. When asked why he speaks in parables, he responds by alluding to Isa. 6:9-13: "The reason I speak to them in parables is that 'seeing they do not perceive, and hearing they do not listen, nor do they understand.' With them indeed is fulfilled the prophecy of Isaiah that says: 'You will indeed listen, but never understand, and you will indeed look, but never perceive. For this people's heart has grown dull, and their ears are hard of hearing, and they have shut their eyes; so that they might not look with their eyes, and listen with their ears, and understand with their heart and turn—and I would heal them'" (Matt. 13:13-15). After narrating other parables of Jesus, Matthew adds: "Jesus told the crowds all these things in parables; without a parable he told them nothing. This was to fulfill what had been spoken through the prophet: 'I will open my mouth to speak in parables; I will proclaim what has been hidden from the foundation of the world'" (Matt. 13:34-35). Both of these passages occur in the context of the parable of the sower, which describes how some will listen and believe, while others will either fail to believe or begin to believe but then fall away. In these passages, therefore, we find the idea that it had been prophesied that many among Israel would reject Jesus' message. While the word *mystery* does not appear here, what Jesus reveals is something that up until then had been "hidden from the foundation of the world."

Other parables also communicate the idea that many among Israel were destined to reject Jesus' message. These include the parables of the weeds of the field (Matt. 13:24-30), the wedding banquet (22:3-14), the two sons (21:28-32), and the wicked tenants (21:33-46). Jesus also alludes repeatedly to the rejection and violence that both he and his followers will endure at the hands of the Jewish authorities (Matt. 5:10-12, 44; 10:16-39; 16:21-25; 23:34-39; 24:9). The scribes and Pharisees, for example, must "fill up the measure" of the sins of their ancestors who killed the prophets (Matt. 23:32).[78]

At the same time, Jesus tells the Canaanite woman that he has been sent only to the lost sheep of Israel, and also instructs his disciples to go out only among those who belong to Israel (Matt. 10:5-6; 15:24). This stands in contrast to Matt. 24:14, where Jesus says that the gospel will be proclaimed in all the world, and especially to Matt. 28:19-20, where the risen Jesus sends his disciples out to make disciples of all the nations or gentiles. However, the logic clearly seems to be that the gospel must first be proclaimed to Israel. Only when that has happened, and those belonging to Israel have had the opportunity to accept or reject that gospel, is it to be proclaimed to the gentiles or nations.[79]

---

78. The idea behind this verse is that, while Israel had acted disobediently throughout its history, "with the killing of God's final envoy, Jesus... *now* the measure of sins was full" (de Jonge, *God's Final Envoy*, 16).

79. According to Wesley G. Olmstead, the ending of Matthew's Gospel makes it clear to the reader that Jesus' prohibition to the disciples against going to the gentiles or Samaritans "was temporary and has now been explicitly rescinded" (*Matthew's Trilogy of Parables*; SNTSMS 127; Cambridge: Cambridge University Press, 2003, 78-79). On Matthew's understanding of the role of the nations in the divine plan, see 71-97.

In addition to the passages noted above in which Luke uses the word *dei* to speak of the necessity of certain events, several other passages from his Gospel and Acts stress the same idea. At the very start of his ministry, Jesus reads from the scroll of Isaiah and proclaims that the prophecy concerning the one who will bring good news, redemption, liberation, and justice is fulfilled in him (Luke 4:16-21). After those present initially react favorably to Jesus' words, he then mentions that, even though there were many widows in Israel in Elijah's time, he was sent only to a gentile widow in Sidon; and even though there were many lepers in Israel in Elisha's time, the only one cleansed was Naaman the Syrian. Immediately, the crowd turns against him and seeks to kill him (4:16-30). Like Matthew, Luke also presents Jesus as proclaiming that the "queen of the South" and the "people of Niniveh" will rise up at the judgment and condemn the "people of this generation," evidently referring to the large number of Israelites who refused to believe in him (Luke 11:30-32; Matt. 12:41-42). These passages, therefore, stress not only Israel's rejection of Jesus, but also the salvation of many who do not belong to Israel, as well as the exclusion of many within Israel from God's reign.

From the beginning of Acts, Luke has the risen Jesus tell the disciples that they will be his witnesses not only in Jerusalem, Judea, and Samaria but "to the ends of the earth" (Acts 1:8). This continues the theme mentioned at the end of his Gospel, where the risen Jesus tells the disciples that they are to be his witnesses and proclaim repentance and forgiveness of sins in his name "to all nations, beginning from Jerusalem" (Luke 24:47-48). It is important to note, however, that in this latter passage Jesus speaks of this proclamation to the nations as something that had been foretold in the Scriptures as following upon his death and resurrection. In other words, for Jesus' first followers, *the proclamation to the nations was just as much a part of the divine plan as Jesus' death and resurrection.* This idea is repeated later on in Acts as well, where Paul tells Agrippa that he affirms "nothing but what the prophets and Moses said would take place: that the Messiah must suffer, and that, by being the first to rise from the dead, he would proclaim light both to our people and to the Gentiles" (Acts 26:22-23).

The rejection of Jesus and the apostolic proclamation by many Jews, along with the positive reception of that proclamation by many gentiles, is one of the primary themes in Acts. The first chapters present an initially positive reception by many Jews to the apostles' message, yet gradually this reception grows cold, and Luke begins to stress the way in which many Jews not only reject the gospel but actively fight against it. This leads to its proclamation among the other nations. The stoning of Stephen results in an outbreak of a persecution against Jesus' followers, who are "scattered throughout the countryside of Judea and Samaria" (Acts 8:1). Yet this scattering leads to the proclamation of the gospel and its acceptance in Samaria, Caesarea, Phoenicia, Cyprus, and Antioch, as well as to Philip's encounter with the Ethiopian eunuch (8:4-31; 11:19). In Acts 9, immediately after Saul accepts the gospel, he is persecuted by Jews and departs to Tarsus, from where he would be called in order to begin his mission work around the empire (9:19-30; 11:25). When he refers to his Damascus experience elsewhere in Acts, he claims that from the start he was sent to the gentiles, an idea that enrages his Jewish audience and is met with rejection (22:21-22; 26:17-24).

At the end of the only lengthy synagogue sermon ascribed to Paul in Acts, he warns his hearers: "Beware, therefore, that what the prophets said does not happen to you: 'Look, you scoffers! Be amazed and perish, for in your days I am doing a work, a work that you will never believe, even if someone tells you'" (Acts 13:40-41; see Hab. 1:5). A short time later, after some Jews and Gentiles accept his message, other Jews become jealous and begin to attack Paul verbally. In his response, Paul once again points to the fulfillment of the Scriptures, saying: "It was necessary that the word of God should be spoken first to you. Since you reject it and judge yourselves to be unworthy of eternal life, we are now turning to the Gentiles. For so the Lord has commanded us, saying, 'I have set you to be a light for the Gentiles, so that you may bring salvation to the ends of the earth'" (Acts 13:46-47). Luke then continues: "When the Gentiles heard this, they were glad and praised the word of the Lord; and as many as had been destined for eternal life became believers" (13:48). Here again we find the idea of a divine plan in which the rejection of many Jews and the acceptance of the gospel by many gentiles is predestined.

From that point on in Acts, this pattern is repeated frequently: many Jews reject the gospel and turn violently against Paul, yet among the gentiles, many accept it (Acts 13–14). After the Jews in Corinth oppose and revile him, for example, he tells them in protest: "Your blood be on your own heads! I am innocent. From now on I will go to the Gentiles" (18:5-6; cf. 14:1-7; 17:1-10; 19:8-9). This rejection constantly forces Paul to go elsewhere with his message, thereby ironically contributing to its spread. In fact, the rejection of the Jews in Jerusalem and their attempt to kill Paul eventually leads to his arrival in Rome, where he was destined to "stand before the emperor" to proclaim Christ (27:24).

The book ends with the same theme. When Paul proclaims the gospel among the Jews in Rome, according to Luke,

> they disagreed with each other; and as they were leaving, Paul made one further statement: "The Holy Spirit was right in saying to your ancestors through the prophet Isaiah, 'Go to this people and say, You will indeed listen, but never understand, and you will indeed look, but never perceive. For this people's heart has grown dull, and their ears are hard of hearing, and they have shut their eyes; so that they might not look with their eyes, and listen with their ears, and understand with their heart and turn—and I would heal them.' Let it be known to you then that this salvation of God has been sent to the Gentiles; they will listen" (Acts 28:25-28).

Here Paul quotes Isa. 6:9-10, the same passage cited elsewhere in the Gospels (Matt. 13:14-15; Mark 4:12; Luke 8:10; John 12:40). Paul himself appears to allude to it as well in Rom. 11:7-8, where he looks to Isa. 29:10 to claim that the elect obtained what Israel was seeking, but "the rest were hardened": "God gave them a sluggish spirit, eyes that would not see and ears that would not hear, down to this very day."

The words of Isa. 6:9-10 were therefore seen as foretelling the rejection of the gospel concerning Jesus by many from among Israel, but also as affirming that God intentionally hardened them further so that he might carry out his plan of reaching out to the gentiles.[80] The meaning of Isa. 6:9-10 in its original context is that God wishes to justify the destruction of many within Israel in order to purify an obedient remnant. Because of the people's persistent sinfulness, he does not want them to turn back to him, since this return to him would be short-lived, as it had always been, leading to the need for God to punish them once more after he had forgiven them. Therefore, rather than continuing to repeat endlessly the cycle of sin, punishment, repentance, and forgiveness, God prefers to act in definitive fashion by destroying a large part of the people in order to purify a remnant that will finally be holy and obedient. At the same time, however, God needs to proclaim his plan to the sinful people in order that they may know what his plan is. Such is the logic behind the Isaiah passage. This idea changes somewhat in the New Testament, where God sends his messengers to proclaim the gospel to Israel, yet at the same time hardens his people's hearts. Although the people's hearts are already hard, by hardening them further so that they not only reject the gospel but do so violently and aggressively, God enables that gospel to go out to the nations. Had Israel accepted the gospel halfheartedly or merely reacted apathetically to it, the apostles would have continued their efforts to win more believers from among God's people rather than being forced to go out to the gentiles.

The motive of blindness mentioned in Isa. 6:10 also appears elsewhere in the New Testament. In Rom. 11:7-10, after citing the passages from Isa. 6:10 and 29:10, Paul looks to Ps. 69:22-23 (LXX 68:23) in order to affirm: "And David says, 'Let their table become a snare and a trap, a stumbling block and a retribution for them; let their eyes be darkened so that they cannot see, and keep their backs forever bent.'" In John 9, after the Jewish leaders reject Jesus for having healed a blind man on the Sabbath, Jesus tells them: "I came into this world for judgment so that those who do not see may see, and those who do see may become blind" (John 9:41). Other passages in the Synoptics in which Jesus heals the blind may also be seen as referring symbolically to the way in which some fail to understand the truth regarding Jesus. In Matthew in particular, the Jewish leaders are called blind (Matt. 23:16-19, 24, 26). As noted in Chapter 8, the metaphor of having one's sight restored and turning from darkness to light is used regarding gentiles as well (Eph. 1:18; Rev. 3:18; cf. Matt. 4:15-16; Luke 1:78-79; Rom. 1:21; 2:19; Eph. 4:17-18; 1 Pet. 2:9). In fact, the temporary blindness Paul experiences after his encounter with Jesus before his sight is restored to him may have symbolic significance for

---

80. On the use and interpretation of Isa. 6:9-10 in the Hebrew tradition, second-temple Judaism, and the New Testament, see especially Evans, *To See and Not Perceive*.

Luke (Acts 9:8-19; 22:9-16). It is precisely as Paul recounts his encounter with the risen Jesus on the road to Damascus that he refers both to the light from heaven that shone on him at that moment and to the opening of the eyes of many gentiles so they might turn from darkness to light, as well as Jesus' proclamation of "light both to our people and to the Gentiles" (Acts 26:12-23).

At the gathering of the apostles and elders in Jerusalem in Acts 15, James is presented as affirming that the incorporation of the gentiles was part of a divine plan conceived "from long ago":

> "My brothers, listen to me. Simeon has related how God first looked favorably on the Gentiles, to take from among them a people for his name. This agrees with the words of the prophets, as it is written, 'After this I will return, and I will rebuild the dwelling of David, which has fallen; from its ruins I will rebuild it, and I will set it up, so that all other peoples may seek the Lord—even all the Gentiles over whom my name has been called. Thus says the Lord, who has been making these things known from long ago'" (Acts 15:13-18).

Although Mark does not present these ideas as strongly or explicitly as Matthew and Luke, he may have them in mind in his accounts of Jesus' parable of the wicked tenants (Mark 12:1-12), his cursing of the fig tree (11:12-14, 20), the accusation that Jesus said he would tear down the temple in order to build a new one (14:58; 15:29), and the tearing of the temple veil at Jesus' death (15:38). After the Jews act to have Jesus crucified, it is the Roman centurion who confesses his faith in Jesus, exclaiming, "Truly this man was God's Son!" (Mark 15:39). Mark almost certainly sees the centurion as prefiguring the way in which other gentiles would come to faith in Christ so as to attain access to God through Jesus.

Jesus' Death as Part of the Divine Plan

All of this is extremely important for understanding the way in which Jesus' death was interpreted by his first followers. When the Gospels present Jesus as foretelling his own death before he arrives at Jerusalem and repeatedly affirm that the events surrounding his suffering and death were foretold in the Scriptures, *the idea is not that there was simply some type of destiny or fate that Jesus had to fulfill.*[81] Nor is it the concern of the Gospels to provide support for the claim that Jesus was divine, since he knew ahead of time what was going to take place. Instead, the idea of the evangelists is that *Jesus' death formed part of a divine plan that contemplated not only his betrayal, suffering, rejection, death, resurrection, and exaltation to God's right hand, but also the proclamation of the gospel to all nations from around the world.* The plan or purpose that God had

---

81. Squires, for example, repeatedly uses the word *fate* to speak of Luke's understanding of the necessity of Jesus' death and the accomplishment of the divine plan, and compares Luke's language of necessity with that of the Hellenistic thinkers who spoke of fate (*Plan of God*, 155-85). From my perspective, this misrepresents Luke's thought, since the language of fate does not imply any type of purpose in the event to take place. In contrast, the New Testament writings definitely see a purpose in Jesus' passion and death, and thus speak of a *plan*.

conceived before creation and the mystery revealed to Moses and the Hebrew prophets that had now been brought to light through Paul and the other apostles contemplated Jesus' death as *one of a whole series of events that God intended to bring about in history*. The claim of Jesus' first followers that Jesus' death took place according to God's will and that Jesus had been handed over to death by God must be seen in the context of their belief regarding this divine plan: it was not only Jesus' suffering and death that had to take place, but all that *preceded* those events, as well as all that would come about *following* that death and *as a consequence* of that death. This included not only his resurrection and exaltation, but the sending out of apostles, the (temporary) rejection of the gospel among many from within Israel, the apostolic mission to the nations, their incorporation into God's people, and ultimately the eventual subjection of all things and all people to Christ.

The idea that Jesus' death was *necessary* must also be understood on the basis of this idea of a divine plan. For centuries, this idea has been understood on the basis of later atonement theologies that have followed Anselm in claiming that God's justice made it impossible for God to forgive sin freely without Jesus' death. In contrast, the idea appearing throughout the New Testament is that *Jesus' death was necessary because it formed part of the divine plan foretold in the Scriptures that aimed at the salvation of people of many nations throughout the world*. For this reason, in the Synoptics Jesus repeatedly foretells not only his suffering and death at the hands of the authorities, but his resurrection as well (Matt. 16:21; 17:22-23; 20:18-19; Mark 8:31; 9:12; 10:33-34; Luke 9:22; 17:25; 18:31-33; 24:6-7, 25-27, 44-47). What was necessary was *not only that Jesus die, but that the entire plan foretold in the Scriptures come to pass*. Jesus' death was *no more* and *no less* necessary than everything else that took place before and after his death.

All of the other New Testament passages mentioned above that speak of the necessity of the events surrounding Jesus' death must also be understood against the background of these same ideas. Furthermore, those passages point to the idea that Jesus' death was necessary, not only because it formed part of a divine plan, but also because *his death would enable the community of his followers to take the form and shape he and his Father had desired*. In other words, the divine plan contemplated not only Jesus' death and resurrection, but also the establishment of the *ekklēsia*, that is, a community of followers who would share Jesus' same dedication to serving others in love.

Thus, for example, when the author of John's Gospel affirms that it was necessary for Jesus to be "lifted up" like the serpent in the wilderness (John 3:14-15), he does not have in mind some type of destiny, blind fate, or mere fulfillment of prophecy. Nor does he see Jesus' death as necessary in order for the demands of divine justice to be satisfied. Rather, Jesus' lifting up on the cross will make it possible for "whoever believes in him" to "have eternal life" in that it will lead to his being glorified at God's side in order that he might be the kind of Lord mentioned in John 13:13-15: one who dedicates his existence to serving and saving others, symbolized by his act of washing his disciples' feet. According to John 8:28-29, Jesus would be lifted up so that all might know that he did nothing on his own, but spoke as the Father had instructed him, and did what was pleasing to the Father. In other words, his obedience unto death would define not only the type of Lord he would be, but also the type of community over which he would exercise his lordship. Similarly, in John 12:31-33, Jesus says that he will be lifted up so that he might draw all people to himself and drive out the ruler of this age. For John, the ruler of this age would be driven out, not because Jesus would overpower him with his divinity in some type of violent struggle, but because others would see that Jesus always does as the Father commands and loves the Father; that knowledge would lead his followers to do the same (John 14:30-31).

A number of passages from the Synoptics reflect the same understanding of the need for Jesus to give up his life in obedience to the Father in fulfillment of the divine plan. In Matthew and Luke, when Satan tempts Jesus at the beginning of his ministry, what he offers Jesus is the possibility of attaining his lordship over all *without going through the toil, hardships, and suffering that he would endure both in his ministry and in his death* (Matt. 4:1-11; Luke 4:1-13). For this reason, in the Gospels of Matthew and Mark, when Jesus announces his imminent passion and death, and Peter attempts to dissuade him from this path, Jesus rebukes him by calling him Satan and tells Peter to "get behind" him, since Peter is setting his mind on human things rather than divine things (Matt. 16:21-23; Mark 8:31-33). Immediately after that, Jesus tells his disciples that they and others must also deny themselves, take up their cross, and follow him, since only by losing their life will they gain it (Matt. 16:24-26; Mark 8:34-35; cf. Luke 9:23-26; 14:27). The ideas here are clear: *the reason why Jesus had to be rejected, suffer, die, and rise was not simply because those events had been prophesied or predestined to take place, but because only in that way could Jesus bring about a community of followers fully committed to doing God's will in the same way that he had been, serving others by serving the God of Jesus and the gospel.*

Several passages from Paul's letters hint at the same ideas. In Rom. 5:6, Paul writes: "For while we were still weak, at the right time Christ died for the ungodly." These words indicate that, in Paul's mind, God had chosen a specific time in human history in which he would send Jesus and hand him over to his death. Jesus' death would therefore lead to many being reconciled to God through him as they came to live as part of the community he had lived and died to establish (Rom. 5:9-11). In fact, just as Paul sees Jesus' death resulting in the reconciliation of others to God here, so also in Rom. 11:15 Paul sees the rejection of Jesus by many from Israel as leading to that reconciliation: "their rejection is the reconciliation of the world." For Paul, therefore, the result of both Jesus' death *and* the rejection of Jesus' messiahship among many Jews is that many throughout the world from among the nations are becoming reconciled to God, since those events formed part of the divine plan aimed at the reconciliation of the world. In fact, in 2 Cor. 5:14-21, Paul also points to his own ministry as something entrusted to him by God in order to reconcile the world to himself. As has been noted above, in Paul's thought, it was not only Jesus' death and Israel's rejection that formed part of the divine plan, but also the sending of apostles such as Paul throughout the world in order to proclaim the message about Christ. Furthermore, what was necessary was not simply that these things take place at a certain point in time, but that the conditions favorable to the spread of the gospel among all nations be brought about through God's activity in the world. In fact, Paul believed that he himself had been "set apart" to proclaim God's Son to the nations prior to his birth (though not necessarily prior to creation; Gal. 1:15-16).

In Gal. 4:4-5, Paul also claims that God had intended to send Jesus at a specific moment of human history in order to accomplish his plan: "But when the fullness of time had come, God sent his Son, born of a woman, born under the law, in order to redeem those who were under the law, so that we might receive adoption as children." In the verses immediately preceding this affirmation, Paul affirms that God had given the law to Israel to serve as a "custodian" until the time in which Christ would come (Gal. 3:24-26). Just as heirs need to wait to take possession of what is theirs "until the date set by the father," so also both Jews and gentiles needed to wait until the law's role in God's plan might be fulfilled. This would make it possible for God to adopt people from among the nations as his children by bringing them to faith in Christ (Gal. 4:1-7).

Similarly, in 1 Cor. 1:23—2:16, Paul speaks of the way in which God made known his wisdom through Christ's death and the constitution of the *ekklēsia*, which is composed of those who are foolish, weak, low, and despised. The wisdom revealed through Christ and decreed before the ages has made it possible for many to be brought to glory by receiving God's revelation through the Spirit (1 Cor. 2:6-10). This passage communicates not only the idea that Christ's death and the constitution of the church formed part of an eternal divine plan revealed in the Scriptures, but also that *Christ's death is the means by which God has brought into existence the type of community he desired from the start*: a community in which God shows his wisdom and love in ways that contrast with the wisdom of this world and the manner in which the rulers of this age exercise power.

The author of 1 Peter reflects similar ideas. After telling his readers that they have been "chosen and destined" by God and reminding them that they have "an inheritance that is imperishable, undefiled, and unfading, kept in heaven" for them, he exhorts them to be patient in the time of trials they are suffering (1 Pet. 1:1-9). He then continues:

> Concerning this salvation, the prophets who prophesied of the grace that was to be yours made careful search and inquiry, inquiring about the person or time that the Spirit of Christ within them indicated when it testified in advance to the sufferings destined for Christ and the subsequent glory. It was revealed to them that

they were serving not themselves but you, in regard to the things that have now been announced to you through those who brought you good news by the Holy Spirit sent from heaven—things into which angels long to look! (1 Pet. 1:9-11).

Here we find the same ideas: God had foreseen the time in which his Son would suffer and be glorified, just as he foresaw what would happen after Jesus' suffering, death, and glorification.

For the author of 1 Peter, however, Jesus suffered what he did, not because he had to fulfill some type of destiny or fate, but so that believers might be redeemed from their futile ways inherited from their ancestors "with the precious blood of Christ, like that of a lamb without defect or blemish. He was destined before the foundation of the world, but was revealed at the end of the ages for your sake" (1 Pet. 1:19-20). It is significant that this letter is written to non-Jews, since as we have seen elsewhere, what God wished to accomplish was the inclusion of gentiles as part of his new, obedient people. Yet, as this last passage indicates, it is precisely through Jesus' death that God has made it possible for such a people to exist. Christ's sufferings and death enable them to "live for righteousness" in that they indicate to believers how they are to conduct themselves (1 Pet. 2:21-25). What Christ "suffered in the flesh" makes it possible for them to live "with the same intention," led "no longer by human desires but by the will of God" (1 Pet. 4:1-2). It is in this sense that Christ's death redeemed them, not from death or the devil per se, but from the futile ways they inherited from the past as gentiles. All of this makes it clear that for the author of 1 Peter, like the other New Testament writers, Jesus' death formed an integral part of the divine plan in that it made it possible for the type of community that God had always desired to come into being.

The language in Hebrews 9 regarding the necessity of Jesus' death must also be understood in terms of the need for a divine plan foretold in Scriptures to be fulfilled, rather than in the sense that, due to God's strict justice, it was impossible for God to forgive human sins or save human beings without Jesus' death. In Heb. 9:15-21, the author argues that a *diathēkē* goes into effect only when the person establishing it dies. It is impossible to grasp the author's argument here without recalling that, in his mind and that of his Greek-speaking audience, a *covenant* (*diathēkē*) was the same as a *testament* or *last will*. Therefore, even the first *diathēkē* made through Moses had to be established through the shedding of blood in death—not because God's justice required blood or a death in order for God to forgive, but simply because, by definition, a last will or testament requires the death of the one establishing it in order to go into effect. For this reason, Jesus also had to die or shed his blood in order to establish a new covenant. When the author continues: "under the law almost everything is purified with blood, and without the shedding of blood there is no forgiveness of sins" (Heb. 9:22), he is not claiming that it is impossible for God to forgive sins unless blood is shed. Rather, he is making an observation about how forgiveness is obtained by means of the rites prescribed in the Mosaic law: generally—but *not always* (*"almost* everything")—a sacrificial death is necessary for the rite to be carried out properly and for forgiveness to be obtained. According to this idea, Jesus' death was necessary *only because what the law prefigured in the commandments prescribing sacrifice had to be fulfilled through Jesus*. In other words, the idea is once more that *the plan foretold in the Scriptures needed to be fulfilled*.

This is evident from the way in which the author of Hebrews continues: "Thus it was necessary for the sketches of the heavenly things to be purified with these rites, but the heavenly things themselves need better sacrifices than these. For Christ did not enter a sanctuary made by human hands, a mere copy of the true one, but he entered into heaven itself, now to appear in the presence of God on our behalf" (Heb. 9:23-24). The necessity of which the author speaks is that, just as the earthly things, which were mere sketches or copies (*hupodeigmata*) of the heavenly things, had to be purified by the earthly rites prescribed under the law of Moses, so also the heavenly things to which the earthly things pointed needed to be purified by Jesus and his blood or death. The sanctuary into which Jesus entered was not the earthly sanctuary, which was merely a type (*antitupon*) of the heavenly one, but the true sanctuary in heaven. In other words, what was necessary was that the reality prefigured typologically in the Mosaic law find its fulfillment in Christ.

At the same time, however, for the author of Hebrews, in bringing the new covenant into existence, Jesus had to suffer and die not merely so that an antitype might find its fulfillment, but so that the kind of community or people God had intended to create from of old might come into being. In Heb. 9:14, the blood of Christ "sprinkled" on believers serves to "purify our conscience from dead works to worship the living God." A better sacrifice was needed, that is, one capable of taking away the sinfulness of God's people in a way that the Mosaic sacrifices never could (Heb. 9:23-28). Jesus' death enables believers to approach God "with a true heart in full assurance of faith, with our hearts sprinkled clean from an evil conscience" (Heb. 10:19-22). In other words, in the thought of Hebrews, the necessity of Jesus' death had to do not only with the fulfillment of the Scriptures, but with the bringing into existence of a new covenant people who would live in the way God desired, cleansed in their interior through faith so that they might do the works that please him. According to the divine plan prefigured in the Mosaic law and the Scriptures, *it is this that Jesus' death was intended to bring about*; and it has served to accomplish this objective by laying the foundation for a community that is sanctified through its commitment to doing God's will in the same way that Jesus was sanctified (Heb. 10:5-10).

In New Testament thought in general, then, Jesus' death was necessary *not merely because it formed part of a divine plan conceived before the world's creation and foretold in the Scriptures, but because only through Jesus' absolute obedience to God could a community of people be created that would be committed to the same kind of obedience to God*. This occurs *by faith*, as believers acknowledge Jesus as their Lord. The fact that the one they trust in and follow as Lord was fully committed to loving and serving others in the way his Father desired means that they cannot truly form part of his community of followers unless they share that same commitment. As a result of the unbounded love for all that he demonstrated in life and death, those who call him "Lord" cannot but dedicate their lives to doing with joyful and thankful hearts what both he and his Father desire out of love for them and what they themselves desire above all else, namely, to follow him as members of his community of disciples, taking up their cross so as to reach out to others with the same love they have found and experienced in him. *It was this that constituted the objective of God's eternal plan.*

Election and the Divine Plan

The ideas just considered provide the background necessary to understand more clearly the New Testament language regarding the predestination or election of believers. When this language is used, its purpose is not to claim that God foresaw the life and fate of each human being who would live on earth and elected some individuals for eternal salvation, while failing to elect others. Rather, the idea is that, from before the world's creation, God intended to bring about an obedient people who would be "conformed to the image of his Son, in order that he might be *the firstborn within a large family*" (Rom. 8:29). When the author of Ephesians affirms that God "chose us in Christ before the foundation of the world to be holy and blameless before him in love" (Eph. 1:4), he means that from eternity God planned to bring into existence through Christ a people who would live in love in the way he desired.

These passages particularly focus on the election *of gentiles* and serve to counter any Jewish claim that, prior to the creation of the world, God had chosen Israel alone to be his people or children. Rather, from the start God intended to form a people composed of *both Jews and gentiles* who would live according to his will. In New Testament thought, God's election of Israel was *not an end in itself*, but served a greater purpose, namely, to serve as the means by which God would accomplish what he has now accomplished through Christ among peoples from around the world. Ironically, not only Israel's election but also Israel's rejection of Jesus as the Messiah formed part of this plan, and has served to make it possible for it to come about.

Of course, from a theological standpoint, the ideas of election and a divine plan are extremely problematic. In particular, they raise the question of how it can be affirmed that everything that took place through Christ was planned by God from before creation, while at the same time maintaining that human beings act out of free will. It would appear that certain details of human history, including the precise manner in which Jesus would be betrayed, the concrete actions of particular persons such as Judas Iscariot and Pilate, and the exact time and date of Jesus' death were not only determined by God before creation, but revealed to figures who lived many centuries prior to Jesus. In addition, today it seems fairly certain that most of the writings of the Hebrew Scriptures traditionally ascribed to figures such as Moses, David, Isaiah, and other figures from Israel's history were actually composed and revised by others who lived in later centuries. For this reason, we can hardly affirm that, in the Hebrew Scriptures, those figures foretold all that would some day take place in Jesus' day.

The New Testament writings never attempt to explain logically how the events they narrate could have been foreseen in detail many centuries before they happened. The first Christian writer to address this problem explicitly was Justin Martyr, who claimed that God had only seen ahead of time what would happen, but had not *foreordained* or *determined* those events.[82] In this way, Justin sought to avoid the notion that God had *caused* persons such as Judas, Pilate, or the Jews who rejected Jesus and persecuted the church to act in the way that they did. Such a distinction, however, is impossible to maintain once it is recognized that only what has been fully determined ahead of time can be foreseen. This means that the type of solution to the problem offered by Justin does not really resolve the difficulties involved.

What must be stressed, however, is that Jesus' first followers elaborated these arguments *in retrospect* as they sought to make sense of his death. They became convinced that the new reality they experienced had not merely come about by chance, but rather was something God had intended to bring about from the start. This was not to affirm, however, that God himself had forced figures such as Judas, Pontius Pilate, and the Jewish leaders to do the things they had done, contrary to their will. The New Testament consistently holds these figures responsible for their own actions. If God was thought to have hardened human hearts, for example, this involved merely hardening further hearts that were already hard. At the same time, Satan is repeatedly seen as having influenced those who acted against Jesus to behave in the way that they did (Luke 22:3-4, 51-53; John 8:44; 13:2, 27; 14:30; 1 Cor. 2:6-8).[83] Nevertheless, the writers of the books that came to make up the New Testament apparently saw no need to reconcile the idea that God and figures such as Abraham, Moses, David, and Israel's prophets had foreseen many centuries previously what was to take place in Jesus' day with the belief that those responsible for the persecution of Jesus and his followers acted of their own free will. God had merely influenced those who freely committed those wrongs to commit them in a certain way so that the things foretold might come to pass. Thus, for example, even though it was the decision of the Jewish

---

82. For references and a discussion of this idea in Justin Martyr's writings, see Squires, *Plan of God*, 178-79. In his *Peri Pascha*, written around 160-170 CE, Melito of Sardis tells Israel that while it had been necessary for Christ to suffer and be crucified, these things did not have to be done through Israel, but could have been carried out by some other nation or people (74-76)

83. As Timothy B. Savage observes, Paul affirms that Israel's blindness is the product both of divine hardening and the work of Satan, without apparently seeing any conflict between the two affirmations (*Power through Weakness: Paul's Understanding of the Christian Ministry in 2 Corinthians*; SNTSMS 86; Cambridge: Cambridge University Press, 1996, 134-35). The idea may therefore be that "God sometimes accomplishes his work through the activity of Satan (cf. 2 Corinthians 12.7; 1 Corinthians 5.5)" (135).

and Roman authorities to have Jesus put to death, God could be thought to have led them to carry out that act by means of crucifixion rather than by some other means, such as stoning.

It is not surprising that many in antiquity, such as Trypho in Justin's *Dialogue with Trypho*, found the arguments of Jesus' followers regarding a divine plan foretold in the Scriptures problematic. Yet it is equally unsurprising that many found the Christian arguments to be very powerful and convincing. The vast and impressive array of passages from the Hebrew Scriptures cited by Jesus' followers in order to claim that what had taken place through Jesus was foreseen in those Scriptures could easily lead many to the conviction that this correspondence between what was written of old and what had now taken place through Jesus was no mere coincidence. In fact, this manner of interpreting Scripture would contribute even further to a hardening of positions between many Jews and Jesus' first followers. The latter would consider the biblical evidence in support of their arguments so convincing and overwhelming that they could only conclude that the hearts and minds of those who rejected their arguments had been hardened either by Satan or by God himself. As noted above, this is precisely what Paul claims in 2 Cor. 3:14-16, where he speaks of the minds of those reading the old covenant being hardened and veiled, and 2 Cor. 4:4, where he claims that "the god of this world has blinded the minds of the unbelievers, to keep them from seeing the light of the gospel of the glory of Christ." Those Jews who did accept the arguments of Jesus' followers would need to alter radically not only their manner of interpreting Scripture, but also their core convictions regarding realities such as Israel, the covenant, and the Mosaic law.

The way in which Jesus' first followers used Scripture played a vital role in enabling them to gain credibility for their claims, particularly in Jewish circles. Interpretations of Scripture such as those we have considered in this chapter made it possible for them to respond with weighty and convincing arguments to the question of why God had allowed his Son the Messiah to die the humiliating death of a slave on a cross. Nevertheless, to many Jews those interpretations seemed to represent a grave misuse and misreading of Scripture.

Ultimately, however, it seems that the decisive factor that led some to believe in Jesus and others to reject him was not so much the reading of Scripture that developed among Jesus' first followers, but the personal experience of those who heard the proclamation concerning Jesus. On the one hand, many Jews would be so convinced that the traditional Jewish beliefs and the traditional ways of reading the Hebrew Scriptures in their communities were correct that they would find the beliefs and interpretations of Jesus' followers incredible and even ludicrous. On the other hand, those whose experiences in relation to Jesus and his followers were positive would not only regard the claims made about Jesus as credible, but would also become extremely passionate in their convictions. The commitment to love, compassion, equity, and solidarity that they would encounter in the context of the communities of believers in Christ, as well as the fact that people from very different backgrounds were being brought together in a new type of family that transcended and overcame traditional distinctions among human beings, would convince them beyond any doubt that the proclamation regarding Jesus was true. The fact that the two groups eventually become polarized between themselves is therefore not at all surprising.

Of course, in the years immediately following Jesus' death, the most convincing argument that Jesus' followers could present in favor of the claims they made about him was that his first disciples and others such as Paul had actually seen and spoken with Jesus after his resurrection (1 Cor. 15:3-9). Over time, however, as the first generation of Jesus' followers died out and their testimonies regarding the risen Jesus became second- and third-hand, this argument would lose much of its force. For this reason, in addition to pointing to the positive experiences that those who formed part of the communities of Jesus' followers enjoyed, those proclaiming the gospel continued to look primarily to the Hebrew Scriptures to develop and strengthen their arguments in favor of the claims they made regarding Jesus.

The argument on the basis of Scripture also allowed Jesus' followers to respond to another objection to their beliefs raised both by Jews and by non-Jews, namely, that the faith they practiced could not be true because it had arisen only recently. In antiquity, it was commonly believed that for any system of beliefs regarding God or the gods to be true, it had to have existed from time immemorial, since truth was something eternal and unchangeable. The interpretations that Jesus' followers developed on the basis of the Hebrew Scriptures, which were generally recognized both by Jews and non-Jews as ancient documents that dated back many centuries, allowed them to counter the claim that their belief system was new and recent and instead maintain that what had recently taken place in Jesus was planned even before creation and foretold many centuries earlier.[84]

In the end, what developed was a "battle for Scripture" between Jesus' followers and those Jews who rejected their claims concerning Jesus.[85] As Irenaeus later argued, the non-Jewish believers in Christ argued that they were not usurpers but the legitimate heirs of the promises made to Israel, and hence of the Scriptures as well.[86] Just as the author of the *Epistle of Barnabas*

---

84. As David Peterson has noted, the way in which Jesus' followers used Scripture served as a "legitimation device" in Hellenistic circles, since it enabled Jesus' followers to "appeal to an argument from antiquity" ("The Motif of Fulfilment and the Purpose of Luke-Acts," in *The Book of Acts in Its Ancient Literary Setting*; ed. Bruce W. Winter and Andrew D. Clarke; BAFCS 1; Grand Rapids: Eerdmans, 1993, 103).

85. Claudia Setzer argues that competition for gentile converts between Jesus' first followers and other Jews may also have been a motive for the polemics over the interpretation of Scripture (*Jewish Responses to Early Christians: History and Polemics, 30-150 C.E.*; Minneapolis: Fortress, 1994, 184). Jaime Clark-Soles presents an enlightening comparison of the ways in which the Qumran, Branch Davidian, and Johannine communities sought to "wrest Scripture away from their opponents" (*Scripture Cannot Be Broken: The Social Function of the Use of Scripture in the Fourth Gospel*; Leiden: Brill, 2003, 318; see 316-36).

86. On this point, see Dennis Minns, "Truth and Tradition: Irenaeus," in *The Cambridge History of Christianity*, Vol. 1: *Origins to Constantine* (ed. Frances M. Young and Margaret M. Mitchell; Cambridge; Cambridge University Press, 2006), 264.

claimed that the covenant belonged to believers in Christ rather than to the Israelites (*Barn.* 13:1; 14:4), so also from the time shortly after Jesus' death believers would have begun to affirm that the Scriptures belonged to them, rather than to those Jews who did not believe in Christ. In no way would Jesus' first followers have thought that they were "reading someone else's mail."[87] The fact that Jesus himself was remembered as having engaged in polemics with other Jews over the interpretation of Scriptures was also significant for his followers, since they could argue that Jesus himself had claimed the Scriptures as his own and had a special authority over those Scriptures.[88] While both sides seem to have agreed in general as to which books had been written under divine inspiration,[89] the fact that it was not long before most of those belonging to the communities of Jesus' followers had no knowledge of Hebrew meant that the use of the Septuagint became increasingly important. The traditional story of the miraculous manner in which the Septuagint version had been composed could be used by Jesus' followers to argue that not only the Hebrew Scriptures but the Greek translation of those Scriptures had been inspired by God.[90] Naturally, this led many Jews to reject the Septuagint, particularly because some of the passages to which Jesus' followers pointed in support of their claims seemed to be at variance with the Hebrew original. What is particularly remarkable is that, soon after Jesus' death, many believers of non-Jewish origin also became extremely fluent in the Scriptures, including those who had previously had no contact with Judaism. This is evident from the fact that Paul can quote those Scriptures extensively when writing to non-Jewish believers and expect that they will have no difficulty in understanding his allusions to the passages to which he refers.

Even after the church came to be composed almost entirely of believers of non-Jewish origin, the type of interpretation of the Scriptures found among Jesus' earliest followers continued to be seen as important. Petr Pokorný notes that "the fact that the proof from the Scriptures retained its importance even in the non-Jewish world shows that its deepest function was the demonstration of the true pre-history of the emergent Christ Church" through its relation with Israel.[91] Over time, however, it became more difficult for believers of non-Jewish origin to grasp some of the arguments from Scripture found in the New Testament and early Christian teaching, or to use the Scriptures in this way themselves.[92]

---

87. So Paul van Buren, "On Reading Someone Else's Mail: The Church and Israel's Scriptures," in *Die Hebräische Bibel und ihre zweifache Nachgeschichte: Festschrift für Rolf Rendttorff zum 65. Geburtstag* (ed. Erhard Blum, Christian Macholz, and Ekkehard W. Stegemann; Neukirchen-Vluyn: Neukirchener, 1990), 595-606.

88. See, for example, Warren Carter, "Love as Societal Vision and Counter-Imperial Practice in Matthew 22:34-40," in *Biblical Interpretation*, ed. Hatina, 2:39-40.

89. On this point, see E. Earle Ellis, "The Old Testament Canon in the Early Church," in *Mikra*, ed. Mulder, 655.

90. On the ancient Jewish beliefs regarding the miraculous origin of the Septuagint, see Sidney Jellicoe, *The Septuagint and Modern Study* (Oxford: Clarendon, 1968), 35-41.

91. Pokorný, *Genesis of Christology*, 191.

92. See Judith M. Lieu, "Self-Definition vis-a-vis the Jewish Matrix," in *Cambridge History*, ed. Young and Mitchell, 1:219.

THE DIVINE PLAN AND THE DEVELOPMENT OF CHRISTOLOGY

In the space of a few short years after his death, Jesus' followers came to speak of him in highly elevated terms. They referred to Jesus not only as Lord and Messiah or Christ, but also as Son of God and perhaps even God (Rom. 9:5). How and why this development took place is a very complex question. While I will not attempt to address that question in detail here, a number of general observations are in order that are important for the overall argument of the present work.

It seems quite certain that shortly after Jesus' death, his disciples and first followers became convinced that he had been raised from among the dead. The empty tomb probably influenced them in this regard, yet it seems doubtful that this alone led them to believe in his resurrection. Instead, it is likely that at least some of his disciples reported having some sort of experience or vision of the risen Jesus, as Paul claims in 1 Cor. 15:3-8. It is difficult to believe that Jesus' followers would simply make up stories about having seen Jesus alive again. If they had, they would probably not have acted with the boldness and the conviction that seems to have characterized their conduct.

Several possibilities exist as to what led Jesus' first followers to claim that he had not only risen, but had also been exalted to heaven to a position of power and authority. This belief would probably not have derived entirely from faith in his resurrection, since one might be raised from among the dead without necessarily being exalted as Lord over all. Hurtado has suggested that, in addition to experiences or visions of the risen Jesus, his first followers may also have had "visions of the exalted Jesus in heavenly glory, being reverenced in cultic actions by the transcendent beings traditionally identified as charged with fulfilling the heavenly liturgy (e.g., angels, the 'living creatures,' and so on)."[93] This possibility cannot be ruled out, although there is no clear evidence in the New Testament to support it. While Stephen is said to have had a vision of this type in Acts 7:55-56, this is described as taking place *after* Jesus' disciples had begun to proclaim him as exalted Lord.

There are a couple of other plausible explanations as to how Jesus' first followers came to maintain that he had been exalted to God's right hand. If during his lifetime Jesus claimed to have some type of special or unique divine authority, his resurrection would then be understood as God's confirmation of that authority. As Hurtado notes, even before his death Jesus seems to have been a highly controversial figure. The most likely explanation for this is that either he or others around him made strong claims concerning his divine authority, which required that others either accept those claims or reject them: "[T]he *effect* of his public activity was very much to polarize a good many of his contemporaries over the questions of how to regard him, whether to take

---

93. Larry W. Hurtado, *How on Earth did Jesus Become a God?: Historical Questions about Earliest Devotion to Jesus* (Grand Rapids: Eerdmans, 2005), 203.

a negative or positive stance about him. It is, I think, a reasonable inference that there was likely something in Jesus' own actions and statements that generated, or at least contributed to, this polarization."[94] In this case, once it was claimed that he had risen from the dead, those who had taken a positive stance toward Jesus might argue that his resurrection demonstrated that he did indeed possess the divine authority that had been attributed to him.

Another possibility is that it was the use of biblical passages such as Ps. 2:7 and Ps. 110:1 that led Jesus' first followers to the conclusion that Jesus had been exalted to God's right hand and enthroned as God's Son. In this case, once Jesus was proclaimed as the Davidic Messiah or Son of David, his followers began to interpret certain Davidic Psalms as referring to Jesus. As noted above, this may have been because, in his passion and death, Jesus was thought to have suffered some of the same things described in the Psalms attributed to David. Once they were convinced that he had risen from among the dead, it would also be natural for them to apply to him Davidic Psalms such as Ps. 16:8-11, as Acts 2:25-32 indicates, so as to argue that David had foreseen Jesus' resurrection. Sooner or later, they would also apply Ps. 110:1 to Jesus and interpret it in the sense that Jesus was greater than David because David had called him Lord and because God had seated Jesus at his right hand.[95] If Jesus himself had applied either this Psalm or others to himself, as the Synoptic Gospels affirm, it is even more likely that his first followers would have been led to interpret his resurrection as his exaltation to God's right hand. This is particularly evident with regard to the idea of Jesus as a priest of the order of Melchizedek found in Hebrews 7.[96] Apparently, they did not start with the belief that a Melchizedek figure needed to come because it had been prophesied in that Psalm, or because they held beliefs like those reflected in the Qumran writings. Rather, as suggested above, it seems to have been their application of Ps. 110:1 to Jesus that led them to apply the rest of the Psalm to him as well.

Whether it was visions of Jesus enthroned in heaven, the unique claims made regarding Jesus during his lifetime, or the application of Davidic Psalms to Jesus after his death, belief in Jesus' resurrection soon became inseparable from belief in his exaltation to God's right hand. In fact, more than one of these things may have played a role in the development of this belief. From

---

94. Hurtado, *Lord Jesus Christ*, 55.

95. See Loader, "Christ at the Right Hand," 199-217; Aquila H. I. Lee, *From Messiah to Preexistent Son: Jesus' Self-Consciousness and Early Christian Exegesis of Messianic Psalms* (WUNT 2/192; Tübingen: Mohr Siebeck, 2005), 210-23.

96. On Jewish beliefs regarding Melchizedek in the second-Temple period and the allusions to Melchizedek in Hebrews 7, see Paul J. Kobelski, *Melchizedek and Melchireša* (CBQMS 10; Washington, DC: Catholic Biblical Association of America, 1981), 115-29; Richard N. Longenecker, "The Melchizedek Argument of Hebrews: A Study in the Development and Circumstantial Expression of New Testament Thought," in *Unity and Diversity in New Testament Theology: Essays in Honor of George E. Ladd* (ed. Robert A. Guelich; Grand Rapids: Eerdmans, 1978), 161-82. As Longenecker observes elsewhere, the association of Melchizedek with Jesus may also have been a reaction to the Hasmonean rulers who had attempted "to legitimize their reign by declaring themselves priest-kings 'forever after the order of Melchizedek', as is said in Ps. 110.4" (*The Christology of Early Jewish Christianity*; SBT 2/17; London: SCM, 1970, 117; see 116-18).

what we have seen in the first part of the present chapter, however, it seems clear that, in the years following his death, for Jesus' first followers the interpretation of Scripture became increasingly important in defining who Jesus was. Once they came to the conclusion that the Hebrew Scriptures pointed to Jesus and all that had come to take place through him, they inevitably began to apply to Jesus passages from those Scriptures that had not previously been understood as pointing to a messianic figure.

Although the conviction that Jesus was the Messiah or Christ constituted a starting-point for Jesus' first followers, their beliefs regarding Jesus' unique authority and their reading of the Scriptures soon led them to develop that idea in ways that went beyond whatever other Jews believed regarding a Messiah. For this reason, it is relatively unimportant whether many or most Jews in Jesus' day believed that God had promised to send a Messiah to Israel. When we look at the New Testament, we do not find Jesus' followers first attempting to convince others that a Messiah had been promised, in order then to argue that Jesus had fulfilled the traditional messianic expectations and subsequently conclude that he was indeed the Messiah. Rather, they began by pointing to Jesus and to his resurrection and exaltation, and only then argued that he was the Messiah announced in the Scriptures. For some Jews who heard this message, the novelty may have been not only that Jesus was the promised Messiah, but also that God had promised to send a Messiah in the first place. What mattered to Jesus' followers, however, was not so much that others believe that Jesus was the promised Messiah, but that they believe in Jesus as one who had unique authority from God.

This also means that precisely what many Jews believed regarding a Messiah is of little importance for understanding the proclamation of Jesus' first followers. Whether or not other Jews believed in a priestly Messiah or a kingly Messiah who would wage war on the gentiles, for Jesus' followers it was not previous conceptions regarding the Messiah that defined Jesus, but rather Jesus who defined the term *Messiah*. Undoubtedly, previous conceptions regarding a Messiah must have played some role in their understanding of Jesus; yet, whatever those conceptions were, they were redefined around Jesus. If other Jews believed in a priestly Messiah, Jesus' followers would proclaim Jesus as the fulfillment of those expectations as the high priest appointed by God. Among those Jews who expected a kingly warrior figure as Messiah, Jesus' followers would present Jesus as the one who would some day defeat all of Israel's enemies as Israel's king. Even this, however, would be redefined in light of Jesus' command to love one's enemies, as well as the eventual inclusion of non-Jews among Jesus' followers. They would understand Israel's "enemies" not so much in political terms, but as referring to those who actively opposed the divine plan of salvation that had come to light through Jesus and was now being carried out throughout the world.

Similar observations must be made with regard to other titles used of Jesus in the New Testament, such as Lord, Son of Man, and Son of God. In whatever ways Jews in antiquity may have understood titles such as these, for Jesus' first followers, once those titles had been applied to Jesus, it was no longer the titles that defined Jesus, but Jesus who defined the titles. Undoubtedly, they incorporated into their proclamation whatever previous beliefs existed regarding these titles or figures and adapted those beliefs to correspond to what they believed concerning Jesus. While this process led them to think of Jesus in new ways and perhaps make new claims about him, their proclamation regarding Jesus ultimately did not depend on what Jews had previously believed about such figures, but rather their own experiences regarding Jesus, the traditions that were passed on from his first disciples, and the interpretations of the Hebrew Scriptures that became common in the communities of believers.

Christology and the Eternal Divine Plan

For reasons we have seen above, beliefs concerning a divine plan that had been conceived of by God even before creation and foretold in the Scriptures would also have led Jesus' first followers to affirm that Jesus had in some sense existed prior to creation. At the very least, this would have involved what James Dunn has referred to as an "ideal pre-existence," according to which God had conceived of Jesus' existence and what would take place through him long before Jesus was born. Thus, for example, while Dunn regards Hebrews as "the first of the NT writings to have embraced the specific thought of a pre-existent divine sonship," he argues that the author of this epistle had in mind "an ideal pre-existence, the existence of an idea in the mind of God, his divine intention for the last days...."[97] For Dunn, this means that when we read passages such as 1 Cor. 10:1-11, which speaks of Christ as the rock from which water flowed in the wilderness, we should not assume that these passages reflect the idea that Christ existed and was active in a real or literal sense during Israel's history: "There is no evidence that any NT writers thought of Jesus as actually present in Israel's past, either as the angel of the Lord, or as 'the Lord' himself."[98] Instead, such a belief regarding Jesus would be similar to what we find elsewhere in ancient Judaism, where realities such as the Torah, the Messiah, the world to come, and Abraham were said to have existed in God's mind prior to creation.[99]

According to Jesus' first followers, if many passages from the Hebrew Scriptures pointed forward to Jesus as their fulfillment, it followed logically that from antiquity Jesus' coming, as well as his life, death, resurrection, and

---

97. James D. G. Dunn, *Christology in the Making: A New Testament Inquiry into the Origins of the Doctrine of the Incarnation* (London: SCM, 1980), 54-55 (emphasis removed).
98. Ibid., 158 (emphasis removed); see also 183-84.
99. See Förster, *Palestinian Judaism*, 185-86. The question of whether there was any concept of a preexistent Messiah among Jews in Jesus' day has also been debated among scholars; see the discussion in Lee, *From Messiah to Preexistent Son*, 99-116. In any case, I would argue once more that if such a concept did exist, it would have been applied to Jesus *after* his followers became convinced that he was God's Messiah, rather than influencing them to come to the conclusion that he was the Messiah.

exaltation, had been contemplated. As Dunn notes, this would be understood not "in the sense that Jesus just happened to be the one who fitted the divine specifications, but in the sense that Christ was the one who from the beginning had been pre-ordained for this role."[100] Similarly, both Jesus and the divine plan revolving around him would be seen as having existed at least in the mind of God from the beginning of human history once it was maintained that Adam was a type of Jesus (Rom. 5:14), that the stories about Abraham, Sarah, and Hagar anticipated what would take place through Jesus (Gal. 3:16; 4:21-31), and that the events surrounding the flood in Noah's day prefigured Christian baptism (1 Pet. 3:20-21).

A number of scholars have argued against Dunn's claim that in the undisputed Pauline letters we find only the idea of an ideal preexistence on Jesus' part as God's Son, and that the idea of some type of real or actual preexistence is not yet present there.[101] Contrary to what Dunn maintains, for example, Paul's affirmation in 1 Cor. 8:6 that all things were created through Christ should probably be seen as implying some type of actual preexistence on the part of Christ. The reason for this is that, if Paul had in mind only an ideal preexistence, he would have understood Christ as a created being who had come into existence in a real sense only when God acted to create everything else in the world. If Paul thought that Christ as God's Son had actually been created by God, then he would have seen Christ as *forming part* of the created order. This would run contrary to the claim that Christ was *above* the created order; yet it is difficult to conceive of Christ being *above* the created order if he was not also regarded as *superior* to it and as having existed *prior* to it. Thus to say that all things had been created *through* Christ by definition seems to distinguish Christ from the created order itself. Of course, God might be said to have created his Son first and then acted through that Son to create everything else, as Arius later came to affirm, yet in that case Christ as God's Son would be preexistent in relation to the rest of the created order. This would therefore involve an *actual* preexistence and not just an *ideal* one.

Whether or not one sides with Dunn or with his critics regarding his claim that Paul conceived only of an ideal preexistence on the part of Christ, there are a couple of points on which almost all seem to agree. First, as both Dunn and others recognize, the New Testament writings seem to indicate that, almost from the start, Jesus' followers had a very "high" Christology, conceiving of Jesus in lofty and even divine terms. For a long time it was common for New Testament scholars to argue that Jesus' first followers started with a "low" Christology, initially believing in Jesus merely as a prophet or human envoy sent by God, and then gradually developed the high Christology reflected in passages such as Col. 1:15-20, Heb. 1:3, and the Johannine prologue. Today,

---

100. Dunn, *Christology*, 235.
101. John F. Balchin, for example, writes: "If something exists because it is in the mind of God, everything could be described as pre-existent.... Ideal pre-existence is really a misnomer. It is not really pre-existence at all, but predestination couched in terms of pre-existence" ("Paul, Wisdom and Christ," in *Christ the Lord: Studies in Christology Presented to Donald Guthrie*; ed. Harold H. Rowdon; Downers Grove, IL: InterVarsity, 1982, 209).

however, many scholars have argued convincingly that Paul's writings give evidence that a high Christology existed already in Paul's day. In fact, in some of the Pauline passages that seem to allude to Jesus' preexistence, most notably 1 Cor. 8:6, 2 Cor. 8:9, and Phil. 2:5-11, Paul may have been drawing on traditional or older hymnic material that was not originally his own and therefore would have been passed on to him by others.[102] It seems clear that we should no longer conceive of the development of Christology in first-century Christian thought in terms of a direct linear progression. Nils Dahl notes, for example, that it would be "misleading to conceive of the historical development as a trajectory that led from a 'low' to a 'high' Christology.... The Christology of Paul is higher than that of Luke/Acts, and the Christology of the Pastoral Epistles appears to be lower than that of Colossians and Ephesians."[103]

A second point on which most New Testament scholars seem to agree is that Jewish beliefs regarding the wisdom of God played an important role in the development of Christology among Jesus' first followers.[104] Both Prov. 8:22-31 and Sir. 24:3-34 speak of God's wisdom as existing before creation and as the instrument through which God created all things. These passages also personify that wisdom, describing it as if it had the ability to act independently of God in some way, though precisely how this was understood is not clear. In Jewish thought, this wisdom came to be associated with the Mosaic law, which was regarded as the definitive expression of God's wisdom. This led to the idea that the law itself existed before creation and was the means by which God created the world. This idea is most clearly expressed in the rabbinic writings, some of which affirm that "the universe conforms to the Torah" and that "nature itself is after the pattern of the Torah."[105] *Genesis Rabbah* claims that the world was made not only *by means of* the law but *for the sake of* the law (1:4; 8:2).[106] This also implies that the law existed in heaven before it

---

102. Thomas H. Tobin points out that the Christology of Phil. 2:6-11 can even be considered as more developed than that found in John, Colossians, and Hebrews in that, unlike the preexisting figure in those writings, "the pre-existing figure of Christ in Philippians thinks and makes decisions" by emptying himself and taking the form of a servant ("The World of Thought in the Philippians Hymn [Philippians 2:6-11]," in *The New Testament and Early Christian Literature in Greco-Roman Context: Studies in Honor of David E. Aune*, ed. John Fotopoulos; NovTSup 122; Leiden: Brill, 2006, 94).

103. Nils Astrup Dahl, *Jesus the Christ: The Historical Origins of Christological Doctrine* (Minneapolis: Fortress, 1991), 130.

104. Among the few scholars to reject this idea is Gordon D. Fee, who claims that "Paul neither knew nor articulated anything that might resemble a Wisdom Christology.... On no occasion does Paul say, or hint at the possibility, that Wisdom was involved in God's creation of the world. On this matter, he does not even echo the wisdom texts that speak of creation reflecting God's *attribute* of wisdom.... What Paul says, rather, is that all things that God created came into being through the agency of Christ, either as the Lord or as the divine Son.... In light of the evidence, therefore, both in Paul's letters and in the Wisdom literature, we must conclude that Wisdom Christology is *not* found in Paul's letters and thus has no role in the reconstruction of Paul's Christology" (*Pauline Christology: An Exegetical-Theological Study*; Peabody, MA: Hendrickson, 2007, 619-20). From my perspective, however, Paul's idea is not so much that *Christ himself* was wisdom personified, but that Christ *fulfilled a role* that in Jewish thought had traditionally been ascribed to God's wisdom.

105. W. D. Davies, *Torah in the Messianic Age and/or the Age to Come* (JBLMS 7; Philadelphia: SBL, 1952), 170, 174 (commenting on rabbinic and Midrashic thought).

106. As George Foot Moore noted, *Genesis Rabbah* is attributed to Rabbi Hosha'ya, who was a contemporary of Origen (*Judaism in the First Centuries of the Christian Era, the Age of the Tannaim*; New

was revealed on earth.[107] Influenced by Platonic thought, Philo believed that God had made a heavenly model of the cosmos, comparable to Plato's world of ideas, prior to creating the material world. While Philo does not explicitly relate this to the Mosaic law, the idea is clearly similar.[108] The law is also called "eternal" in several Jewish writings dating back to the second-temple period, though this does not necessarily mean that it existed from eternity.[109]

Once Jesus' first followers began to identify God's will with Jesus rather than the Mosaic law and to claim that the law had been displaced from its central role by Jesus as Lord, it would have been natural for them to apply to him any beliefs regarding the preexistence of divine wisdom and the Mosaic law. If God's wisdom had been present when God created the world and had served as God's instrument for that purpose, then for Jesus' followers that wisdom was to be identified with Jesus himself rather than the law. Rather than affirming that all things had been created by means of the law and for the sake of the law, Jesus' followers would claim that all things had been created through *Jesus* and for *him*, as Col. 1:16 states.[110] The heavenly image or model on the basis of which God had created humankind and the world would also be associated with Jesus, as Col. 1:15-20 demonstrates. Rather than pointing to the law as reflecting perfectly God's glory, the ultimate expression of his will, and the means by which God sustains the universe, Jesus' followers would see Jesus himself as "the reflection of God's glory and the exact imprint of God's very being," and affirm that "he sustains all things by his powerful word," as Heb. 1:2 does.

These affirmations by Jesus' first followers, of course, would eventually lead to intense debates with Jews who rejected the notion that Jesus was above the law and had displaced it as the ultimate expression of God's will. In the context of these debates, it is likely that those on each side would be led to assume even more extreme positions in order to respond to the claims of their opponents. For this reason, we cannot be sure whether the rabbinic thought regarding the Torah's preexistence and its instrumentality in the world's creation already existed in Jesus' day, or if instead it developed as a response to Christian arguments regarding Jesus. Conversely, the affirmation in Col. 1:16 that all things were created *through* Christ and *for* Christ either could have been a counterargument to Jewish claims regarding the law or instead could have led to the development of the Jewish claims. Similarly, the saying

---

York: Schocken, 1971, 1:268). For further references on the idea that the world was made for the sake of the law, see 1:267-269. On this point, see also Jacob Neusner, *Torah: From Scroll to Symbol* (Philadelphia: Fortress, 1985), 118-19; Bruce Chilton and Jacob Neusner, *Judaism in the New Testament: Practices and Beliefs* (London: Routledge, 1995), 133; Davies, *Torah*, 50-52, 170-74; Martin McNamara, "Some Targum Themes," in *Justification and Variegated Nomism*, Vol. 1: *The Complexities of Second Temple Judaism* (ed. D. A. Carson, Peter T. O'Brien, and Mark A. Seifrid; WUNT 2/140; Tübingen: Mohr Siebeck, 2001), 311-12.

107. See Dahl, *Jesus*, 129.
108. See Moore, *Judaism*, 1:267.
109. For references, see Moore, *Judaism*, 1:269.
110. Even if Colossians is not a Pauline letter and was written after Paul's death, if Col. 1:15-20 formed part of a hymn, as many scholars believe, then the ideas in this passage are older than the letter itself.

ascribed to Jesus in Matthew's Gospel, according to which wherever two or three are gathered he is in the midst of them (Matt. 18:20), may have been a response to Jewish beliefs regarding the presence of God wherever several gather to study the Torah.[111] It is also possible, however, that the Jewish affirmation arose as a result of the saying attributed to Jesus. Jesus' words in Matt. 11:28-30 also reflect Jewish ideas regarding the law: "Come to me, all you that are weary and are carrying heavy burdens, and I will give you rest. Take my yoke upon you, and learn from me; for I am gentle and humble in heart, and you will find rest for your souls. For my yoke is easy, and my burden is light." These words appear in the context of Jesus' thanking God for hiding certain truths from the wise in order to reveal them to infants and claiming that only those who know the Son know the Father. These statements stand in contrast to Jewish thought, which identified the revelation of God's wisdom with the law and spoke of the need to take upon oneself the yoke of the law.

This association of Jesus with God's wisdom and the Torah would also lead Jesus' followers to identify Jesus with God's word. In biblical and Jewish thought, like God's wisdom, God's word was considered the means by which God had created all things. The personification of God's word in certain passages from the Hebrew Scriptures would also contribute to the identification of that word with Jesus (Ps. 147:15; Isa. 45:23; 55:11).

At some point, the notion that Jesus was God's Son also became associated with these concepts and the belief in Jesus' preexistence. We cannot be sure if Jesus spoke of himself as God's Son during his own lifetime or whether others ascribed this title to him. Even if Jesus was considered God's Son prior to his death, this phrase could have been understood in many different ways, and would probably not have been thought to imply the notion of preexistence in and of itself. The phrase might have been understood merely as a messianic title: Jesus was God's son in the same way that the kings of Israel, including David, were considered God's sons. However, after Jesus' followers became convinced not only that he had been raised and exalted to God's right hand but also that he had existed with God before creation in some sense, they would have understood Jesus' divine sonship in a more exalted and unique fashion.

Jesus' Relation to God

Precisely how Paul and the other followers of Jesus in his day conceived of the relation of Jesus to God is, of course, not entirely clear from the New Testament writings. This lack of clarity is exactly what we would expect, however, if the beliefs regarding Jesus' divinity and preexistence developed out of the manner in which Jesus' first followers applied to him texts and ideas taken from the Hebrew Scriptures, as well as from debates with other Jews over the centrality of Jesus vis-à-vis the Mosaic law.

---

111. For references to this idea in Jewish thought, see Michael Newton, *The Concept of Purity at Qumran and in the Letters of Paul* (SNTSMS 53; Cambridge: Cambridge University Press, 1985), 37.

In a sense, the logical sequence of ideas was the reverse of that which is common in Christian systematic theology today. Rather than beginning with the idea that Jesus as God's Son was divine and on that basis arguing in favor of his centrality both for the life of human beings and the created order in general, they seem to have started with their convictions regarding his centrality, and on that basis came to believe in his divinity, however that was understood. This means that their Christology *developed as a result* of their new interpretations of the Scriptures and the discussions they had with other Jews over questions related to the Messiah, the wisdom of God, and the Torah. They did not take those interpretations or Jewish ideas as a *starting-point* for their Christology, but instead adopted and adapted those interpretations and Jewish ideas to the basic convictions they had previously had about Jesus.

This view of the way in which Jesus' first followers developed their Christology is also important for understanding how Jesus came to be identified so closely with Israel's God YHWH. No doubt, the Septuagint translation of YHWH as *kurios* played at least some role in this process, since the title of "Lord" was ascribed to Jesus probably even before his death. Nevertheless, once his followers became convinced that he had been exalted to heaven as Lord, they inevitably applied the term *kurios* to Jesus in new ways that stressed his unique divine power and authority. Their application of Scripture passages that used the word *kurios* to speak of Jesus also must have contributed at least in part to their close identification of Jesus with God.[112]

Yet it is highly unlikely that the use of the Septuagint or the Hebrew Scriptures alone led Jesus' first followers to identify Jesus so closely with Israel's God. Instead, this must be regarded in large part as the result of their belief that God had revealed himself fully in Jesus and that Jesus now constituted the most perfect expression of God's will. Jesus' followers had come to identify God's revelation, God's wisdom, and God's will *with a person* rather than with a written law in the way that other Jews had traditionally done. This meant that it was now no longer a question of the relation of an impersonal reality such as the law to a personal God. Instead, what was involved was the relation of *one person to another*. These two persons were now so closely identified with one another that they came to be regarded as inseparable from one another. Once God's will, God's activity, and God's being were fully identified with Jesus, the distinction between God and Jesus would become blurred and unclear.

In this regard, it is important to note the observations of Richard Bauckham, who has argued that, rather than attributing to Jesus some preexistent "divine essence or nature," Jesus' first followers conceived of Jesus in terms of possessing the same "divine identity" as the God of Israel, and therefore exercising

---

112. This is the argument of Richard Bauckham, *Jesus and the God of Israel: God Crucified and Other Studies on the New Testament's Christology of Divine Identity* (Grand Rapids: Eerdmans, 2008), 186-232. There Bauckham cites the relevant New Testament texts.

the same divine functions that "are intrinsic to who God is."[113] This means that they did not start with some abstract or ontological conception of "divinity" in order then to ask in what sense Jesus was himself "divine." Because neither Jews in general nor Jesus' first followers conceived of God in terms of some divine essence or nature, it was not a matter of explaining how Jesus as God's eternal Son might share in the same essence or nature as the one God who created heaven and earth. Such questions would arise only later as a result of the influence of Hellenistic thought. Rather, what led Jesus' followers to identify him with God was their belief that Jesus constituted the ultimate and definitive expression of God's will and that God had been present and active through Jesus in a way that he had never been present and active in any other human being. In fact, because they had come to regard Jesus' words and actions as the words and actions of God himself, for them Jesus and God became in some sense indistinguishable from one another.

This also means that it was not some previously-conceived notion of who God was that defined Jesus and his divinity. Rather, for Jesus' first followers it was Jesus who had defined, or *redefined*, who God was. Just as they redefined God's will on the basis of their experiences and beliefs regarding Jesus, so also they redefined the way they understood God's relation to the world and the way that God was active in it on the basis of those experiences and beliefs.

In other words, Jesus' followers did not simply begin with a certain concept of God and on that basis develop an understanding of who Jesus was. While they undoubtedly retained the basic features of God as God had been conceived of in the Hebrew Scriptures and the Jewish tradition, they instead came to understand God in light of Jesus. Their belief in Jesus' resurrection led them to embrace a new concept of God that included not only what Jesus had said and done, but the way in which he had given up his life, dying on a Roman cross. To identify God with one who had died by being crucified required them to rethink God's identity and seek new answers to the question of who God is. They therefore looked to Jesus to define who God was, rather than merely looking to Israel's God as traditionally understood in order to define who Jesus was.

This would lead Jesus' followers to the conviction that the God they proclaimed was *not* the God in whom those Jews who rejected Jesus believed in. The God of Jesus' followers had sent Jesus and raised him; the God of those who rejected Jesus had not only *not* sent and raised Jesus, but also willed that faithful Jews reject the claims Jesus' followers were making about him. The God of Jesus' followers had from before the world's creation conceived of a plan revolving around Jesus as God's Son and had foretold this plan in the Hebrew Scriptures, while the God of those Jews who rejected Jesus had neither planned to send Jesus nor foretold anything about him in the Scriptures. Instead, that God had rejected and even cursed Jesus by allowing him to be put to death on a cross.

---

113. Ibid., x.

Each of these two Gods willed that the Scriptures be read in different ways. Only for Jesus' followers did those Scriptures anticipate his coming and what would take place in him. The God proclaimed by Jesus' followers had given the Mosaic law as a tentative measure in preparation for what he would come to do through Jesus and no longer demanded literal obedience to that law in the same way that he had previously. In contrast, the God of other Jews had given the law for all generations of Israelites and expected them to fulfill all of its prescriptions literally to the best of their abilities. The God of Jesus' followers had sent them out to proclaim a message that others were to accept, in contrast to the God of those who rejected Jesus, who willed that others refuse to believe in that message, since it was false. In short, we can say that the God of Jesus' followers identified himself fully with who Jesus was and all that he stood for, while the God of those Jews who refused to believe in Jesus instead rejected Jesus and many of the things that he stood for. This means that Jesus' followers *believed in a God who was in some ways different than the God of other Jews*. While the God Jesus called "*Abba*" was undoubtedly the God of Israel of whom the Hebrew Scriptures spoke, in a sense he was not the same God of Israel in whom the Jews who rejected the messianic claims concerning Jesus believed.

God's Love and Jesus' Death

To say that the God whom Jesus called "*Abba*" was different from the God of other Jews is not to say, of course, that the God proclaimed by Jesus' followers was a God of love and grace, while the God of other Jews was not. In fact, as we have seen in Chapter 2 of this study, the God revealed in the Hebrew Scriptures is also a God of grace and unconditional love. In each case, however, this grace would be understood as *taking different forms and expressing itself in different ways*. In the Hebrew Scriptures, the God of Israel had manifested his love, grace, and mercy by electing Israel as his people, giving them the law, and demanding that they obey it for their own good. Out of love, he had promised to bless them when they obeyed it and to take measures to correct them when they disobeyed it. He had also sought to use Israel as a light to the nations so that others might be drawn through his people to seek him out. While these things were still believed to be true among Jesus' first followers, according to them, the definitive and most complete expression of God's love, mercy, and grace was the sending of Jesus and the establishment of the community of his followers by means of Jesus' ministry, death, and resurrection, as well as the outpouring of the Holy Spirit. This means that, while Jesus' first followers were not alone in believing in a God of unconditional love and grace, they associated that unconditional love and grace *with Jesus* in a way that other Jews did not.

As we can see in the New Testament, for Jesus' first followers, what defined both God and God's unconditional love and grace more than anything else was Jesus' death on the cross. This was not because Jesus' death had fulfilled some requirement of divine justice that could be met in no other way, thereby making it possible for God to forgive human sins. Rather, Jesus' death was seen as demonstrating the *total commitment of God to bringing about in human beings the way of life he wished to see for their own good*. God's willingness to give Jesus over to his death once he had sent him to accomplish the task of forming a community in which people might be transformed through him and the love he demonstrated in life and death was for Jesus' followers evidence that God was fully committed to doing whatever was necessary for that transformation to take place. When Jesus had given up his life, he had done so *out of obedience to his Father*. This meant that Jesus' death was an act of love on the part of God.

At the same time, of course, Jesus' willingness to die on a cross was evidence of his own commitment to that same objective and therefore the supreme expression of his own love for human beings. And once Jesus' death was seen as part of a divine plan aimed from the start at bringing about a new people committed to doing God's will as defined through Jesus, not only Jesus' death but also his coming into the world would be seen as evidence of that same commitment and his love for others throughout the world. This way of thinking led Paul to write to the Corinthians, "For you know the grace of our Lord Jesus Christ, that though he was rich, yet for your sakes he became poor, so that by his poverty you might become rich" (2 Cor. 8:9). The same idea also seems to be behind his words in Phil. 2:5-8: "Let the same mind be in you that was in Christ Jesus, who, though he was in the form of God, did not regard equality with God as something to be exploited, but emptied himself, taking the form of a slave, being born in human likeness. And being found in human form, he humbled himself and became obedient to the point of death—even death on a cross."

In passages such as these, the unconditional love and grace of both God and Jesus as God's Son involve not merely giving human beings something external to themselves, such as a list of commandments, or communicating some type of knowledge, truth, or guidance to them, but rather *giving of one's very self to and for others*. The New Testament repeatedly conveys an image of God that is extremely intimate. The belief that God sent his only beloved Son and out of love gave him up to death on a cross due to his commitment to establishing a community that would reflect that same love represents God in a way that is unprecedented in the Hebrew Scriptures. While the God of the Hebrew Scriptures gives of himself in many ways to his people, he never actually gives of his own self to the world by giving up his own Son, as he is said to do in the New Testament.

This understanding of the manner in which God had given himself to and for the world through Jesus would suggest that the identification of Jesus with God among Jesus' first followers was not simply the result of reflection on the Scriptures, their experiences of him as risen, or their association of Jesus with God's wisdom, will, or word. Rather, the belief that Jesus was God's Son and perhaps in some sense even God must have been the logical consequence of their convictions regarding the love of God. If the God who had sent Jesus had willed that Jesus give of himself entirely and fully in order to bring about in others the transformation of life that God desired to see in them for their own good, then that God could only be understood as one who had also given of himself entirely and fully in Jesus. This meant identifying Jesus with God's own self, rather than seeing him merely as some prophet or Messiah figure through whom God had spoken. From the perspective of Jesus' followers, if Jesus had been sent by God to carry out a divine plan that involved Jesus' giving of himself fully in the name of a God who through Jesus also gave himself fully, then in some sense Jesus must have been God. If Jesus died due to his total dedication and commitment to the well-being of others, the God whom he had proclaimed and in whose name he had died must also have been totally dedicated and committed to the well-being of all in and through Jesus. This conviction would also lead to a community of people who would understand love for God and commitment to God's will in a way that distinguished them from other Jews.

No New Testament passage states these ideas more clearly than Rom. 8:31-39. After speaking of the redemption of creation that believers anxiously await, the intercession of God's Spirit on their behalf, and God's plan to bring many to be justified and glorified by being "conformed to the image of his Son so that he might be the firstborn within a large family" (Rom. 8:18-30), Paul continues:

> What then are we to say about these things? If God is for us, who is against us? He who did not withhold his own Son, but gave him up for all of us, will he not with him also give us everything else? Who will bring any charge against God's elect? It is God who justifies. Who is to condemn? It is Christ Jesus, who died, yes, who was raised, who is at the right hand of God, who indeed intercedes for us. Who will separate us from the love of Christ? Will hardship, or distress, or persecution, or famine, or nakedness, or peril, or sword? As it is written, "For your sake we are being killed all day long; we are accounted as sheep to be slaughtered." No, in all these things we are more than conquerors through him who loved us. For I am convinced that neither death, nor life, nor angels, nor rulers, nor things present, nor things to come, nor powers, nor height, nor depth, nor anything else in all creation, will be able to separate us from the love of God in Christ Jesus our Lord (Rom. 8:31-39).

While the Hebrew Scriptures and Jewish literature from antiquity undoubtedly conceive of God as a God of love and grace, it is impossible to find there any passage that speaks of God in the same way that this passage does. The immense love of God is manifested supremely in the immense love of Christ, and particularly in Christ's willingness to give up his life for others and God's willingness to hand his Son over to death before raising him as Lord over all. This is a God who has given what is most precious to him, his own Son, to and for human beings. More than anything else, then, what led Jesus' first followers to their belief in Jesus' divinity and his preexistence was their conviction that, out of God's deep love for humanity, in and through Jesus God had given of his very own self in order that human beings everywhere might receive God's Spirit so as to live as his beloved children and cry out to him, "*Abba*, Father!" (Rom. 8:14-17).

While the New Testament writings, of course, never use the word *Trinity* to speak of this God, they undoubtedly conceive of the God of Jesus as one who is love in his very being and essence, precisely because of the love between Jesus as God's Son and the God he affectionately called "*Abba*." The New Testament repeatedly speaks of the love between Jesus and his Father, both explicitly and implicitly, and also associates the Holy Spirit with that same love. The Fourth Gospel particularly stresses the love between the Father and his Son (John 3:35; 5:20; 10:17; 15:9). In New Testament thought, God is love in his own essence precisely because of the relationship of God to Jesus his Son and the Holy Spirit. God's giving of Jesus and the Spirit is God's giving of his own self in love.

Non-Jewish Influences on the Christology of the New Testament

Although the Christology of Jesus' first followers seems to have developed primarily in dialogue with Jewish thought, the possibility of influences from non-Jewish sources must also be considered. Jesus may have been compared and contrasted with deities worshiped in non-Jewish contexts or other significant figures of antiquity. As noted previously, passages from the Gospels contrast Jesus with the gentile rulers and their "great ones" (Matt. 20:25; Mark 10:42), as well as gentile kings and those called "benefactors" (Luke 22:25). In 1 Cor. 8:5-6, Paul also contrasts the many so-called gods and lords with the one God and the one Lord, Jesus Christ.

Of course, in the context of the Roman Empire, the primary figure with whom Jesus would be compared would be that of the Roman emperor. Jesus' followers would counter claims regarding the power, divine authority, or lordship of Caesar with similar and even greater claims regarding Jesus. Rather than speaking of the need to submit to Caesar as Lord, they would call on others to submit to Jesus' lordship. They would also contrast Jesus' commitment to serving others and truly seeking their well-being with the way in which Caesar sought to impose his will on others by force, pursuing his own interests, as well as the imperial ideology that falsely touted Caesar as the benefactor of all.[114] The fact that Jesus had died on a Roman cross would also be seen as ironic, and would serve to contrast the way that Rome imposed its power with the way in which Jesus' divine power had been manifested. Thus many of the claims made regarding Jesus in the New Testament should probably be understood as reactions to rival claims regarding the Roman emperor.

---

114. On the practice and ideology of benefaction among the Roman imperial authorities, see Brigitte Kahl, *Galatians Re-Imagined: Reading with the Eyes of the Vanquished* (PCC; Minneapolis: Fortress), 193-201. On this point, see also Adam Winn, "Tyrant or Servant? Roman Political Ideology and Mark 10.42-45," *JSNT* 36 (2014): 325-52.

The fact that the emperor was accorded some type of divine status may also have led Jesus' followers to stress Jesus' divinity in those contexts. Once more, however, the God of Jesus would be seen as a God who was fundamentally different from the god or gods associated with Caesar and the Roman Empire. Paul's affirmation in Phil. 2:10 that every knee will bow before Jesus must have been seen as counter-imperial in some sense, since among those who would bow their knees some day would be all of the Roman emperors and every other ruling figure throughout the empire and human history. If Jesus' followers continued to show respect for Caesar and did not openly question his imperial authority, as appears to be the case, their reason for doing so must have been that they believed that at the present time it was God's will to maintain the Roman emperor and authorities in place in order to accomplish his purposes in connection to the proclamation of the gospel throughout the world.

Sooner or later, then, the lofty claims Jesus' followers made regarding Jesus would have generated opposition from the Roman authorities. Even if the authorities did not take those claims seriously, they would interpret them as a lack of respect for Caesar, in spite of the efforts of Jesus' followers to demonstrate the contrary. Their beliefs regarding Jesus would also have generated opposition from certain sectors of the general populace who were supportive of Caesar and his claims. It is not clear to what extent non-Jews were expected to participate in activities worshiping Caesar's divinity or to sacrifice to his genius.[115] No doubt, this varied from one context to another. However, the refusal of Jesus' followers to take part in those activities and other public celebrations and rituals honoring the Greek and Roman deities would have been understood as an implicit rejection and condemnation of the beliefs and practices of the majority.

Many Jews would have reacted negatively to the claims made about Jesus by his first followers out of the same concern for their social and political status within the empire. As scholars such as Paula Fredriksen and Brigitte Kahl have argued, most Jews both in Palestine and in the diaspora were convinced that it was in their own best interest to maintain good relationships with the authorities established by Rome. Therefore, they also would have wanted to distance themselves from any Jews who made claims regarding Jesus that called into question Rome's authority.[116] Thus it is likely that many Jews cooperated with the Roman authorities in seeking out and at times persecuting Jesus' followers. When non-Jews were incorporated into the community of Jesus' followers, they would also have faced opposition and even persecution

---

115. On the subject of sacrifices made to the emperor's genius and the expectation that those under Rome's rule participate in those sacrifices, see especially Lily Ross Taylor, *The Divinity of the Roman Emperor* (Middletown, PA: American Philological Association, 1931), 183-204.

116. Paula Fredriksen, discussing why Paul persecuted the church and later endured persecution himself, writes: "The open dissemination of a messianic message... put the entire Jewish community at risk" ("Judaism, the Circumcision of Gentiles, and Apocalyptic Hope: Another Look at Galatians 1 and 2," *JTS* 42 [1991]: 556). On this point, see also Kahl, *Galatians Re-Imagined*, 220-29.

from those Jews who rejected the claims they made regarding Jesus, especially if those non-Jews were now identifying themselves as "Jewish" or "Israel" in some sense.

The fact that the one whom Jesus' first followers proclaimed as risen and exalted Lord over all other lords, powers, and authorities had been executed by crucifixion must also have played a role in these tensions and conflicts. It is unclear whether Jews in general would have regarded Jesus as accursed by God. As Hyam Maccoby notes, "Many Jews died by crucifixion and were regarded as heroes and martyrs, not as under a curse."[117] Brad Young makes a similar observation: "During the Second Temple period, Jews were crucified for being loyal to Torah and observing their faith traditions. Moreover, Jewish writers who witnessed these acts of persecution wrote about faithful Jews who suffered a martyr's death upon a cross."[118] The difference, however, was that other Jews who had been crucified had not been understood as claiming to be the Messiah and savior of Israel and had not been tried and condemned by the highest Jewish authorities, those who made up the Sanhedrin. While other Jews had been condemned for their *faithfulness* to the Torah and the worship of Israel's God at the temple, in the minds of many Jews, Jesus had been condemned for calling the Torah and the temple into question. Obviously, Jesus' condemnation and crucifixion under the orders of the Roman proconsul Pontius Pilate would have led those Jews and non-Jews who sympathized with Rome to regard Jesus as an enemy of Rome. The claims made by Jesus' followers regarding his lordship and authority over all, including the Roman emperor and those who ruled under him, must therefore have been seen as scandalous and foolish by non-believers in light of Jesus' crucifixion.

---

117. Hyam Maccoby, *Paul and Hellenism* (London: SCM, 1991), 75.
118. Brad H. Young, "A Fresh Examination of the Cross, Jesus and the Jewish People," in *Jesus' Last Week*, Vol. 1 of *Jerusalem Studies in the Synoptic Gospels* (ed. R. Steven Notley, Marc Turnage, and Brian Becker; JCPS 11; Leiden: Brill, 2006), 200.

CHAPTER 10

JESUS' DEATH FOR OTHERS: THE STORY AND THE FORMULAS

On the basis of what we have seen in Chapters 2–9 of this work, we may now return to the question with which we began Chapter 1, namely, the meaning that Jesus' first followers ascribed to the brief, formulaic phrases that they used to speak of the salvific significance of his death. Before addressing this question, however, it is important to understand clearly in broad terms the story centered on Jesus that his first followers told. The reason for this is that, in order to make sense of the formulas used throughout the New Testament to allude to Jesus' death, some type of underlying narrative is required. Because in this chapter we will be reviewing and summarizing material that has already been examined in detail in the previous chapters, references and notes here will be relatively sparse.

JESUS' DEATH IN THE CONTEXT OF THE STORY TOLD BY HIS FIRST FOLLOWERS

Like other stories regarding the election and redemption of Israel that existed among Jews in Jesus' day, the story of salvation that Jesus' first followers told began even before creation. In whatever way the origin of Jesus as God's Son was understood, from beginning to end that story revolved around him. Through him, God had created the world and had intended to bring about an obedient people who would do God's will and share in God's glory. Although the people of Israel played a vital role in this story, from the start God's plan had contemplated the inclusion of people from all nations and tongues as members of his people. In Paul's words, God's intention from the start was to establish a worldwide family of sisters and brothers who would be "conformed to the image of his Son," Jesus Christ (Rom. 8:29).

It is not clear if Jesus' first followers believed that God had anticipated from the start the sin of Adam and human death. While neither the Hebrew Scriptures nor the New Testament writings speak explicitly of a "fall" into sin, Paul seems to attribute the origin of death to Adam's sin in Rom. 5:12-21, although it is not entirely clear in what sense he uses the language of death and dying there and elsewhere. If God foresaw human sin even before creation, then evidently God's eternal plan also contemplated the sending of God's Son into the world to redeem human beings from their sin. It is also possible that the first believers would have said that it was only after the first human beings had sinned that God determined to send God's Son into the world. In later centuries, theologians came to debate whether God's Son would have become human had Adam and Eve not fallen into sin,[1] yet it is unclear how Jesus' first followers would have responded to this question.

In any case, the fundamental problem to which Jesus' followers pointed was human sinfulness. This understanding of the human plight was in continuity with Jewish thought. In particular, the gentile nations were thought to be irremediably immersed in sin, due in large part to their polytheism and their idolatrous practices. They were considered to be far from the true God and to live in ways that God strongly condemned. However, like other Jews, Jesus' first followers also pointed to the sinfulness of Israel. While this sinfulness was defined in different ways according to the diverse interpretations of the law that existed among Jews, ultimately it was understood in terms of a failure to live according to God's will. Many Jews no doubt interpreted the fact that the land of Israel as well as Jews around the world continued to be subject to Rome and other powers on the basis of the idea running throughout the Hebrew Scriptures, according to which disobedience merited divine chastisement and obedience merited blessings and redemption. In that case, if Israel had not yet been redeemed but instead continued to be chastised, it was because the people had not yet become sufficiently obedient or an insufficient number of Jews were practicing the obedience God demanded.[2] Nevertheless, not all Jews understood their situation in these terms, since eschatological hopes varied greatly, and many Jews apparently did not have any clear eschatological hopes at all.

Numerous texts from the New Testament speak not only of sin but of death as the plight from which human beings needed to be saved (Matt. 4:16; Luke 1:79; John 5:24; 8:52; Rom. 5:12-21; 6:16-23; 7:5, 24; 1 Cor. 15:26, 51-56; Eph. 2:1-2; Col. 2:13; Heb. 2:14-15; 1 John 3:14; Rev. 20:12-15). Precisely how the relationship between sin and death was understood in ancient Judaism and among Jesus' first followers is not entirely clear. Death could be regarded in physical terms or as referring to some type of spiritual reality both in this world and the world to come.[3] In either case, because death was the result of human sin, the real problem was not believed to be death itself but human sinfulness. If God had imposed death because of sin, whatever

---

1. As Georges Florovsky has shown, the debate over whether God would have sent his Son into the world had human beings not sinned took place primarily in the twelfth and thirteenth centuries among Western theologians, though Florovsky argues that this debate was already anticipated by St. Maximus the Confessor in the sixth century (*Creation and Redemption*; Belmont, MA: Nordland, 1976, 163-70). On this question, see also Alister E. McGrath, *Christian Theology: An Introduction*, 5th ed. (Malden, MA: Wiley-Blackwell, 2011), 282.

2. See N. T. Wright, *The New Testament and the People of God*, Vol. 1 of *Christian Origins and the Question of God* (Minneapolis: Fortress, 1992), 270-73.

3. Ernest Best points to numerous passages from second-temple Jewish literature that present physical or biological death as the result of human sin, yet also observes that many texts speak of spiritual death in the present world as the consequence of sin (*Essays on Ephesians*; Edinburgh: T & T Clark, 1997, 78-82, commenting on Eph. 2:1).

his purpose was in doing so, the only thing that could lead God to do away with death was that people renounce sin and distance themselves from their sinful ways. Death was therefore not an end in itself, as if God accomplished his purposes or satisfied his justice merely by punishing sinners with death; nor did God's imposition of death on human beings involve any type of solution to the problem of human sin. The view that death was the intrinsic and natural consequence of human sin rather than a divinely-instituted punishment would also lead to the conclusion that the real problem that needed to be resolved was not death itself, but the sin that led to death.

In the thought of Jesus' first followers, therefore, the plight from which human beings needed to be saved was not *divine condemnation itself*, but rather *the sinful way of life that had divine condemnation as its consequence*. This understanding of humanity's plight runs contrary to that associated with penal substitution views, which define Jesus' saving work in terms of delivering human beings from death as the divine punishment to which they were subject on account of their sins. From the perspective of Jesus' followers, however, if human beings lay under God's condemnation, it was because their persistent sinfulness would not allow them to be brought to the fullness of life that depended upon their living in conformity to God's will.

For Jesus' first followers, the law alone was incapable of addressing the problem of the sinfulness of Israel and the nations. In the latter case, it was obvious to all that large numbers of non-Jews were never going to become law-observant Jews. Even if that were possible, however, Jesus' followers maintained that the Mosaic law had never been able to bring God's people Israel into conformity with God's will, nor could it ever do so. This was partly because the law itself did not give one the power to observe it, but also because Jesus' followers did not identify God's will fully with the law. Therefore, even if one was able to live in accordance with its commandments, it did not follow that one was thereby living fully in conformity with God's will. Because of their convictions regarding Jesus, his first followers defined God's will by looking to Jesus and the way he had lived and died. For them, the law had fulfilled a temporary purpose in placing a wall around Israel to preserve it as a people, holding sin in check and preparing the way for the coming of Christ.

According to the story told by Jesus' first followers, the law had also had the purpose of prefiguring what God intended to accomplish through his Son. This was true of the rest of the Hebrew Scriptures as well, including the narratives, the prophetic writings, and the Psalms. The idea that events associated with Adam and Noah foreshadowed typologically what would take place through Jesus suggests that Jesus' first followers believed that the divine plan being realized in their day had been devised at least from the time in which human history had begun, if not earlier. The events that had taken place in the days of figures such as Abraham, Isaac, Jacob, Moses, Joshua, and David played a role in this plan in several ways. Historically, those events represented different stages in the realization of the divine plan and laid the foundation for what was to follow. Everything that had taken place in the centuries prior to Jesus' coming paved the way for what would take place through Jesus, the apostles, and the *ekklēsia* that was to result from their work. Those events also served as figures or types of what would come to take place through Jesus and in the period following his death and resurrection. God had revealed to Israel's prophets and other figures such as David what would some day come to pass through Jesus and had led them to put into writing what they had foreseen.

Jesus' Death and Resurrection as the Consequence of his Ministry

In the thought of Jesus' first followers, the heart of the divine plan began to be fulfilled with Jesus' coming. As a descendant of David, he was the messianic king God had promised to Israel. Nevertheless, the people of Israel had not understood this plan nor conceived of Jesus' kingship in the proper terms, since they had not expected a lowly king who would serve others humbly in love and attempt to bring others to do the same. God had sent John the Baptist to prepare the way for Jesus' ministry by beginning to proclaim the coming of God's reign and calling others to repentance through the baptism he offered.

According to the story told by Jesus' first followers, Jesus' ministry had included a number of different aspects, all of which were aimed at the wholeness or *shalom* of others. He had dedicated himself to healing others physically and casting out evil spirits from those oppressed by those spirits. Jesus' teaching, however, had also been aimed at bringing about the wholeness of others in several ways. He proclaimed God as a fatherly figure who was fully committed to the wholeness of all, and thus called on people to believe in and trust fully in that God and in Jesus himself as his unique representative and spokesperson. Due to his desire for the wholeness of all, the God of Jesus also demanded that people assume that same commitment in the way they dealt with others. As God's Son, Jesus had instructed others how to live in this manner both through his words and his actions. He called on others to follow him as their Lord by dedicating themselves to seeking the well-being of all together with him and under his guidance and direction.

An integral part of Jesus' teaching had been the rejection and denunciation of beliefs and practices that ran contrary to his own vision of God and God's will. In particular, he had stood in opposition to those who spoke of a God who was *not* unconditionally committed to the wholeness of all out of love for all. This involved speaking out not only against the conduct of those who sought things such as power, honor, and wealth at the expense of others, but also against interpretations of the Mosaic law that he regarded as oppressive and unjust in that they gave priority to something other than the well-being of all or did not contribute to that well-being. When the law was interpreted in that way, it was no longer fulfilling its purpose, but had become an end in itself rather than a means to promote human wholeness. Jesus had especially lashed out against those who justified the oppression of others in the name of Israel's God and the law, especially when they claimed to be speaking and acting as God's representatives. Among such people were not only many of the Jewish teachers of the law, but also those belonging to the high-priestly elite in Jerusalem.

According to Jesus' first followers, when Jesus spoke of God's reign, he continually contrasted it with many of the the values, attitudes, and practices that were widespread in his day, both among Jews and non-Jews. He also questioned the dominant political, economic, social, and religious system, as well as the foundational beliefs on which it was based. This meant rejecting many of the common conceptions of God promulgated among both Jews and non-Jews in order to proclaim a different God. It also involved reaching out especially to those who had been marginalized, excluded, and hurt by the beliefs regarding God that he rejected and by the systems and people who upheld and propagated those beliefs.

Jesus was also said to have anticipated the coming of God's reign in its fullness, that is, a new situation in which the present system would be overthrown and replaced by a new order characterized by justice and wholeness for all. Those who stubbornly persisted in injustice would be excluded from that new order, while those who were committed to the values proclaimed by Jesus would participate in it. Even the faithful who had passed away would be able to participate in that reign, since they would be raised in order to share in the blessings of the age to come. Jesus had told his disciples that he was the one through whom that reign would be established, often referring to himself as the Son of Man. In this way, Jesus had identified himself as the Messiah or Christ, as well as the Son of God.

While in one sense all were to follow Jesus, in another sense Jesus had called only a few disciples in particular to follow him wherever he went in his itinerant ministry. Jesus' purpose in calling disciples had been to prepare those whom he would later send out as apostles to carry out a ministry of the same type to which he had dedicated himself.

According to the story told by Jesus' first followers, these various aspects of Jesus' ministry had generated a great deal of controversy and conflict, leading many who opposed Jesus to seek to have him put to death. Fully aware of this reality, Jesus had gone up to Jerusalem with his disciples at the time of the Jewish Passover. There he had taught and carried out a prophetic act at the temple. In response, the Jewish authorities had made plans to arrest Jesus in secret in order to have him executed at the hands of the Romans. Knowing what was to happen, Jesus had celebrated a final meal with his disciples and several hours later had been arrested, tried by the Jewish and Roman authorities, and finally put to death on a Roman cross. At no point, however, had Jesus sought to escape death or attempted to save his life. Rather, he had gone to his death trusting fully in God and asking that all that he had sought for others might soon become a reality through him. God's response to all that Jesus had done had been to raise him from the dead on the third day following his crucifixion and then exalt him into heaven.

Although God had exalted Jesus to a position of full power and authority at God's right hand, it was necessary for some time to pass before Jesus would return in glory to establish God's reign definitively. When that day came, all would be raised from the dead and judged by God together with Jesus. Prior to Jesus' return, however, it was necessary for the good news regarding the salvation God promised to bring through Jesus to be proclaimed throughout the world. This would be the task primarily of the disciples or apostles Jesus had prepared during his ministry, as well as other apostles called by Jesus and those who worked with or under those apostles. During this time, a worldwide community of believers in Jesus known as the *ekklēsia* or "church" would be formed. Those forming part of this community would live according to the values taught and embodied by Jesus, rather than submitting to the oppressive system and its rulers, and could have assurance that they would participate in the reign he was to bring. They could thus be confident that God forgave them their sins and accepted them as righteous. As they confessed their faith in Jesus as Lord and were baptized in order to live under Jesus' lordship, they were incorporated into the community of believers.

Jesus' rejection at the hands of many of the Jewish leaders and many of the Jewish people had also foreshadowed the way in which Jesus' disciples and followers would be rejected by many after he had died and been raised. Just as many Jews had persecuted Jesus due to the claims he had made regarding his authority, as well as his teaching and practices, so also those who followed him and proclaimed the gospel would face rejection and persecution as they sought to share the gospel and live it out in their daily lives. Ironically, however, this persecution would lead to the proclamation and acceptance of the gospel among the gentile nations throughout the world. All of this formed part of the plan that had been foretold long ahead of time in the Hebrew Scriptures.

In general terms, this is the story about Jesus and salvation that his first followers told. Undoubtedly, many parts of this story are found only in some of the New Testament writings. Only in the Pauline letters, for example, do we find explicitly the idea of a divine plan or mystery existing from before the ages and read about the sin of Adam and its consequences for human beings. Alternatively, the Pauline letters have little to say regarding the ministry Jesus carried out and the circumstances surrounding his death. We can hardly doubt, however, that Paul and the authors of the other letters found in the New Testament were acquainted with the story of Jesus' ministry, death, and resurrection, at least in broad terms. In fact, as a number of scholars have argued, a close look at the letters of Paul and the authors of the other New Testament letters reveals that they do indeed seem to have been acquainted with much of the material found in the canonical Gospels and Acts, even though those letters allude explicitly only to very little of that material.[4]

---

4. On Paul's knowledge of the material that appears in the Gospels and Acts, see especially David Wenham, *Paul: Follower of Jesus or Founder of Christianity?* (Grand Rapids: Eerdmans, 1995); James D. G.

THE DEVELOPMENT OF BELIEFS REGARDING THE SALVIFIC SIGNIFICANCE OF JESUS' DEATH

As I argued in Chapter 5, precisely how Jesus conceived of his death is not entirely clear. In general terms, we can be fairly certain that he believed that the giving up of his life would contribute in some way to the salvation of others, yet beyond this it is difficult to say. Even if one accepts as historical the *lutron anti pollōn* saying attributed to Jesus in Mark 10:45 and some version of the words attributed to Jesus over the bread and wine at the Last Supper, these brief formulas are open to so many different interpretations that we cannot be entirely sure what he meant by them. For this reason, just as we cannot take such brief formulaic sayings as a starting-point to understand what Jesus thought of his death, so also must we begin elsewhere in order to address the question of how his first followers interpreted his death. The best starting-point is the overarching story told by Jesus' first followers that we have just seen, as well as the different aspects of that story that we have examined in Chapters 6–9 of this work.

Initially the greatest challenge Jesus' first followers faced was that of explaining why God had allowed Jesus to die the humiliating and scandalous death of the cross if he was indeed the Messiah and God's Son. Jerry Sumney notes that "anyone who would continue to value [Jesus'] life and teaching to such an extent that they formed their group identity around them had to develop responses to outsiders who interpreted the death of Jesus by giving crucifixion one of its usual meanings.... [T]he Jerusalem church would have had to reject explicitly those meanings (e.g., that Jesus was a criminal or a false messiah) and provide alternative meanings. Any kind of adherence to Jesus after his crucifixion would have entailed the same demand."[5] As Michael Wolter stresses, it was virtually unthinkable to ascribe some type of salvific significance to death by crucifixion:

> Josephus called it "the most miserable death" (*B.J.* 7.203), and for Cicero it is the "most despicable and revolting execution" (*Verr.* 2.5.165).... This evaluation has its basis in the fact that crucifixion was not only a decisively gruesome but also a degrading means of execution. It was regarded typically as punishment for slaves, as *servile supplicium*, with which in New Testament times mainly bandits and insurrectionists in Roman provinces as well as other violent criminals were executed.... [W]e can plainly see where the provocative and shocking element in the Christian interpretation of Jesus' death as salvific must have lain in the eyes of the majority of the non-Christian society in light of this constellation—it lay in the claim that a salvific effect came from a dishonorable death on a cross, that it thus was not a heroic death, a "voluntary" and "glorious" death, to which a salvific

---

Dunn, *The Theology of Paul the Apostle* (Grand Rapids: Eerdmans, 1998), 183-95. Passages from New Testament letters other than those of Paul, such as 1 Tim. 6:13, Heb. 5:7-10, 7:14, 13:12-13, 1 Pet. 2:21-23, 2 Pet. 1:17-18, and Rev. 1:7, 11:8 also seem clearly to presuppose a knowledge of the events narrated in the Gospels on the part of the readers.

5. Jerry L. Sumney, "'Christ Died For Us': Interpretation of Jesus' Death as a Central Element of the Identity of the Earliest Church," in *Reading Paul in Context: Explorations in Identity Formation. Essays in Honour of William Campbell* (ed. Kathy Ehrensperger and J. Brian Tucker; London: T & T Clark, 2010), 171.

effect for others was ascribed, but an imposed and horrible, even disgraceful and ignominious death.[6]

In spite of these difficulties, apparently it was not long after Jesus' crucifixion that his first followers began ascribing some positive and salvific meaning to his death. Undoubtedly, they did so as a result of their reflection upon all that Jesus had said and done, both throughout his ministry and in his last hours.[7] Nevertheless, as Cilliers Breytenbach has noted, there seems to have been little in their Jewish tradition that would have assisted them in the process of finding meaning in what had happened to Jesus: "Seen from Jewish tradition, the question of the possible beneficiary purpose of the death of the crucified 'King of the Jews' was a *novum*. There was no exact model into which Jewish Christians could fit in the crucifixion of Jesus. Being confronted with this crucifixion as being that of the 'King of the Jews' they had to assign meaning to it."[8]

More than anything else, what seems to have influenced Jesus' first followers to begin to ascribe salvific significance to his death was their conviction that God had raised Jesus up from the realm of the dead. If God had the power to raise and exalt his Son *after* he had died, then obviously God could have intervened *prior* to Jesus' death to save him from the suffering and humiliation associated with the cross. The fact that God had chosen not to do so could only mean that God had had some purpose or reason for allowing his Son to be crucified. Their task was therefore to discern that purpose or reason. If God had allowed Jesus to suffer and die, it must have been because his suffering and death contributed to the salvation of others in some way, making possible something that would not have been possible if God had spared his Son the cross. As I have argued in the previous chapters, from their perspective, the reason Jesus' death had been necessary was not because there was no other way for God to forgive sins, deliver human beings from the forces of evil, reveal to them the extent of God's love, provide them with the example they needed to live in love, or enable them to participate in a death to sin and a resurrection to new life. Rather, Jesus' suffering and death had been necessary because, as the consequence of all that he had lived for, it was the only way in which Jesus might be established as the type of Lord he had now become, and at the same time establish the type of community God had desired to create. In other words, it had been necessary for Jesus to suffer and die in order to accomplish what he had sought to accomplish through his ministry, and what God had sought to accomplish through him: a new people

---

6. Michael Wolter, *Paul: An Outline of his Theology*, trans. Robert L. Brawley (Waco, TX: Baylor University Press, 2015), 115-16.

7. In principle, of course, it is possible that the risen Jesus interpreted his own death to his disciples following his resurrection, as Luke reports, though most historians would consider this highly unlikely (see Luke 24:25-27, 44-47; Acts 1:3).

8. Cilliers Breytenbach, "The 'For Us' Phrases in Pauline Soteriology: Considering their Background and Use," in *Salvation in the New Testament: Perspectives on Soteriology* (ed. Jan G. van der Watt; NovTSup 121; Leiden: Brill, 2005), 166.

who would dedicate themselves fully to living in love and solidarity with God, with Jesus, and above all, with one another and with humanity as a whole.

As I argued in Chapter 6, the conviction that Jesus had risen from among the dead led his first followers to the conclusion that he must have gone to his death asking God that he might be raised and exalted as Lord so that he might consummate the salvation of others that he had sought in life and death. Just as he had *lived* for others, seeking the salvation of all, so also he had *died* for others, and had asked God to be *raised and exalted* for others.[9] And the way he would be "for others" and save them was by exercising his lordship in order to bring all to live for God and others like him.

On the basis of their belief in his resurrection and exaltation, Jesus' first followers must have concluded that what had made it possible for this new community of followers to exist and to live in the way Jesus had taught and embodied was not only what Jesus had done *prior* to his death, but also what he continued to do from heaven. They came to believe that Jesus had poured out the Holy Spirit to guide and strengthen them, and that he would some day return in glory to save them and others. At the present time, he also interceded on their behalf as mediator, thereby giving them assurance of God's forgiveness and acceptance. From their perspective, Jesus had been exalted by God not only on account of what he had done in his life and death, but also on account of what he would do in the future. In effect, the way Jesus had lived and died for others ensured that, once he had been raised, he would continue to consecrate himself entirely to the salvation of others. On this basis, God had exalted him to his right hand of power.

In Chapter 6 of this study, we noted that it was natural for Jesus' followers to begin to interpret Jesus' death in sacrificial terms. In his death, Jesus had offered himself up to God on behalf of others, interceding to God for them. The content of this intercession was not only that God forgive them their sins, but also that God continue to act to strengthen them in their faith and commitment and to enable them to reach out to others so that their community might grow and expand. As we saw in Chapter 8, Jesus was believed to have died not only so that his followers might live in a new community under him, but also so that this community might be fully committed to living in love in the same way that he had. Through his faithfulness unto death to that task, he had established a new basis upon which God related to all those who followed him, as well as a new basis upon which his followers related to God and one another. Whether or not Jesus had spoken of a new covenant, this new basis for relating to God and one another, independently of the Mosaic law, would eventually lead his followers to understand themselves to be living under a

---

9. Bernd Janowski rightly notes that the language of giving one's life for others used in the New Testament has to do just as much with Jesus' *life and ministry* as it does with his *death*: "Der Begriff der „Lebenshingabe" meint die *Gesamtexistens* Jesu, d. h. das Leben, das Jesus in liebender Hingabe an die anderen gelebt hat, *und* den Tod, der die Konsequenz—und nicht das Ziel (Finalsinn)—dieses Lebens war" ("Das Leben für andere hingeben: Alttestamentliche Voraussetzungen für die Deutung des Todes Jesu," in *Deutungen des Todes Jesu im Neuen Testament*, ed. Jörg Frey and Jens Schröter; WUNT 181; Tübingen: Mohr Siebeck, 2005, 116; see 97-118).

covenant that was distinct from that which God had established with Israel many centuries earlier.

The convictions of Jesus' first followers regarding Jesus' identity as risen and exalted Lord and Son of God also led them to develop the interpretations of Scripture we examined in Chapter 9. Those interpretations enabled them to convince others of their own convictions and to defend those convictions against those who questioned and criticized them. Their use of Scripture allowed them to argue that, rather than demonstrating that Jesus was not who they believed him to be, Jesus' crucifixion had defined more than anything else the extent of his love for all people, as well as the love of the God whom he had called "Father" or "*Abba*." Jesus' willingness to die on a cross, and his Father's willingness to hand him over to such a death, had shown that the love, solidarity, and self-giving of God and Jesus knew no limits or bounds. That same love was to define the identity of his community of followers, who could only truly call Jesus "Lord" if they loved God and others in the same way Jesus had done.

The narratives regarding Jesus' passion that quickly developed among his followers served to stress all of these same points.[10] Jesus' death had been a miscarriage of justice, perpetrated by sinful men opposed not only to Jesus, but to God himself. Nevertheless, all that had taken place had been God's will in the sense that God had intended to bring the greatest good out of the greatest evil ever perpetrated by human beings. Neither sinful human beings nor the evil powers of the present age had been able to prevail over the love of God and of his Son Jesus for all people.

Jesus' Death as the Death of a Prophet

New Testament scholars have often argued that initially Jesus' first followers understood his death as similar to the violent deaths that Israel's prophets and other righteous individuals from Israel's history had endured. This idea is in fact well-attested in the New Testament (Matt. 21:11, 46; 23:29-39; Luke 11:46-51; 13:33-34; 24:19-20; Acts 3:14, 22-23; 7:52; 1 Thess. 2:14-15). Frequently, however, the same scholars also affirm that those who viewed Jesus' death along the lines of the death of a prophet or righteous leader would have ascribed no real salvific significance to it.[11] Obviously, this involves

---

10. On the development of the pre-Marcan passion narratives, see especially Raymond E. Brown, *The Death of the Messiah: From Gethsemane to the Grave. A Commentary on the Passion Narratives in the Four Gospels* (ABRL; New York: Doubleday, 1994), 1:53-106. John T. Carroll and Joel B. Green rightly question Martin Kähler's affirmation that the Gospels were in essence passion narratives with extended introductions and note that the "form-critical consensus on the ancient, autonomous existence of the passion narrative" has gradually been disappearing (*The Death of Jesus in Early Christianity*; Peabody, MA: Hendrickson, 1995, 5-6). Ellen Bradshaw Aitken is probably right to affirm that "the account of formation of a story of Jesus' suffering and death" was rooted in ritual practice: "stories were told, songs were sung, and rituals were performed in such a way that Jesus' death became the central point in the reenactment of the cultic life of the community.... To tell a story about Jesus' death was also to tell a story about the identity of the community" (*Jesus' Death in Early Christian Memory: The Poetics of the Passion*; NTOA/SUNT 53; Göttingen: Vandenhoeck & Ruprecht, 2004, 16).

11. James Dunn, for example, writes: "An important corollary to the Acts sermons' concentration on the resurrection is the absence of any theology of *the death of Jesus*. His death is mentioned, but only as a bare fact (usually highlighting Jewish responsibility). The historical fact is not interpreted (2.23, 36; 3.13-15; 4.10; 5.30;

equating salvation with the forgiveness of sins. Since the death of a prophet was not thought to make atonement for the sins of others, supposedly those who regarded Jesus' death as similar to that of a prophet would not have believed that anyone had been saved by his death.

While scholars are undoubtedly correct in maintaining that in ancient Jewish thought the death of a prophetic figure did not make atonement for the sins of others, the reason for this is that, as I argued in Chapter 4, Jews in antiquity did not believe that suffering and death in themselves atoned for sin. In Chapter 5, however, we saw that the deaths of leaders or prophetic figures who are violently and unjustly put to death, such as Martin Luther King Jr. and Archbishop Oscar Arnulfo Romero, can indeed serve to bring about the liberation and transformation of others. This occurs when those who identify with the cause or principles for which those leaders stood and for which they gave up their life become so incensed and outraged that they lose their fear and instead stand up against those who are oppressing them.

One of the ways in which the deaths of prophetic figures affect others is that they tend to polarize the members of the community or society of which they form part by forcing all to take sides either for or against the person who was killed or executed. Some justify the death of the prophetic figure by affirming either that he or she deserved to die, or else that he or she was to blame for acting in ways that provoked others to anger, including those responsible for the killing. Others, however, consider the figure's death to be a grave injustice and take the side of that figure over against those who carried out or justify the killing, viewing them as oppressive, immoral, or unjust.

Among those who identify with a leader or prophetic figure who is killed or put to death, two very different reactions can be observed. Some respond with fear and seek to avoid a similar fate by hiding, fleeing, or disassociating themselves from the person killed. Some may simply become discouraged and on that basis abandon whatever cause or movement the prophetic figure had been leading. This is generally what those responsible for the leader's death hope will happen. It is likely that this was the reason why those who arrested Jesus and put him to death left his disciples and followers alone. They believed that, once Jesus had been put to death, his followers would be overcome with fear or simply become discouraged and disband, since Jesus would no longer be present to direct and inspire them. In this way, any threat that Jesus or his followers posed would come to an end.

However, the violent death of a leader or prophetic figure can also lead those who identify with him or her to respond very differently. They may not

---

7.52; 10.39; 13.27f). It is never said, for example, that 'Jesus died on our behalf' or 'for our sins'; there are no suggestions that Jesus' death was a sacrifice" (*Unity and Diversity in the New Testament: An Inquiry into the Character of Earliest Christianity*, 2nd ed.; London: SCM, 1990, 17). Similarly, Marinus de Jonge affirms: "It is generally accepted that a very early stage [sic] *Jesus' death was seen as that of an envoy of God rejected by Israel*.... No positive meaning is attached to his death as such" ("Jesus' Death for Others and the Death of the Maccabean Martyrs," in *Text and Testimony: Essays on New Testament and Apocryphal Literature in Honour of A.F.J. Klijn*; ed. T. Baarda et al.; Kampen: Kok, 1988, 143).

only lose all fear and turn against those responsible for that death, but also take some action against those they regard as responsible for that death. This action may involve physical or verbal attacks or simply some type of prophetic denunciation. Rather than disbanding or disassociating themselves from the prophetic figure, they may come to identify even more strongly with that figure and rally around the cause that they associate with him or her. In this way, the effect of the death of the prophetic figure or leader is the opposite of what those responsible for that death desired.

According to the Gospels, initially the disciples reacted precisely as those who had Jesus put to death hoped they would. They fled when Jesus was arrested, denied him, abandoned him to die alone, hid behind closed doors out of fear, and perhaps went back to the life they had lived prior to knowing Jesus. At some point not long after his death, however, at least some of Jesus' first followers lost their fear and began to proclaim boldly their message with regard to Jesus. They became willing to suffer persecution and even die for what they believed concerning Jesus and the reign of God he had proclaimed. As noted above, it is likely that their boldness was due to experiences that led them to the conviction that Jesus had risen from among the dead.

It is not clear, however, to what extent Jesus' first followers actively opposed the authorities whom they considered responsible for his death. The Gospels and the book of Acts contain numerous passages that castigate the Jewish authorities and leaders for putting Jesus to death and persecuting his followers as well. Nevertheless, both those writings as well as others in the New Testament indicate that Jesus' followers tended to obey both the Jewish and Roman authorities in general terms and opted for non-violent resistance rather than open rebellion.

While Jesus' death may not have led his first followers to resort to physical violence against those whom they considered responsible for having Jesus killed, at some point it does seem to have moved them to identify more strongly with Jesus and the ideas they associated with him. From their perspective, the fact that he had died in the same way that other prophetic figures and leaders had died contributed to the salvation of others by leading many to grow even stronger in their commitment to Jesus and everything he stood for. This does not mean, however, that Jesus' followers initially saw Jesus' death simply as a model or example to be imitated.[12] Rather, their conviction that God had raised and exalted Jesus after he had offered up his life for others led them to identify with Jesus personally as their crucified and living Lord, rather than merely identifying with the past event of his death or the love he had shown by going to the cross. That love was not merely something that they were called to reproduce on their own. What moved them to commit

---

12. Undoubtedly, the idea that in his death Jesus provided his followers with a model or example of love that they are to imitate runs throughout the New Testament texts (see especially Michael Wolter, "Die Heilstod Jesu als theologisches Argument," in *Deutungen*, ed. Frey and Schröter, 305-8). Nevertheless, the salvific significance of Jesus' death in New Testament thought can in no way be reduced to this idea, as we shall see further on.

themselves to practicing the same love Jesus had shown in his death was not his death per se, but their faith in him and in the God whom he had proclaimed. In other words, it was not so much what Jesus *had done* that transformed them, but the way in which *they continued to relate* to him, to the God he had called "Father," and to one another through him. It was belief in Jesus' resurrection that distinguished Jesus from the other great prophetic figures of history, many of whom had died exemplary deaths as Jesus had.

The conviction that Jesus had risen from the dead would also enable the first believers to overcome their fear of the authorities and others who sought to persecute them for following Jesus. Although they might still suffer a great deal, they could be confident that in the end God would raise them as he had raised Jesus. They would also be led to conclude that if they denied Jesus or refused to stand up for him as they should, some day they would meet with the disapproval of both God and Jesus himself, and perhaps even be condemned by God and Jesus. Faith in Jesus' resurrection would thus strengthen their resolve to follow and proclaim him as Lord. In this case, however, this resolve would be the result of their belief in Jesus' resurrection, rather than any effect that his death had on them.

If Jesus' first followers initially saw his death as akin to that of the prophets who had preceded him, therefore, that would have been enough for them to begin to affirm that he had died for them and their sins. In this case, they would have meant that Jesus had given up his life instead of seeking to preserve it in order that his community of followers might be emboldened to turn away from their sinful ways and instead dedicate their lives to serving God and others in love as he had, thereby experiencing salvation both in the present age and the age to come. Jesus had been free to live for others and dedicate himself to doing God's will because he had trusted that, even if he was put to death, God would raise him from among the dead. In the same way, their faith in Jesus' resurrection provided them with assurance that they too could serve God and others without fear, since no matter what happened to them, some day Jesus would return to bring about their salvation. Their love and service of others, however, was not to be motivated by a selfish concern for their own salvation. In that case, rather than loving others, they would be using them as a means to another end, serving them not because they truly cared for them, but because they wanted to gain something for themselves. In contrast, to love in the way Jesus and God himself had loved was to see the well-being of others as an end in itself and to care deeply for others. By definition, only those who loved in that way could truly attain the salvation God had promised through Jesus.

At the same time, it was natural for Jesus' first followers to begin speaking, not only of Jesus suffering and dying *for them*, but of their suffering and dying *for Jesus and for others as well*. Just as many Jews in antiquity had suffered and died for the Mosaic law in the sense that they were willing to endure hardships and death so that others might continue to value and obey the law, so also Jesus' followers were willing to suffer and die for him in the sense that they valued serving him out of love for others above all else, even their own life. Through this service and dedication to the well-being of others, they also sought to serve as Jesus' instruments to bring others to faith in him so that they too might find life in him. Thus, just as Jesus had suffered and died for believers, believers were also to be willing to suffer and die for Jesus, which meant giving their lives for others continually as he had.

These same ideas would lead Jesus' first followers to speak of suffering and dying *with* Jesus as well. Their dedication to Jesus and to God's will as it had been redefined through Jesus would bring them to endure the same type of persecution that Jesus himself had endured. At some point, some of them would even be killed or put to death as Jesus had. They would therefore not only identify with Jesus as their Lord, but also with his sufferings and death. To follow him meant to suffer both *for* him and *with* him and, in some cases, to *die* for him and with him as well.

For these reasons, even if initially Jesus' first followers primarily saw his death as comparable to the deaths of other prophets, leaders, and righteous persons, it is incorrect to maintain that they would not have ascribed any salvific significance to his death. As they viewed Jesus' death in light of the ministry that had preceded and occasioned it and the resurrection and exaltation that had followed upon it, Jesus' followers would come to the conclusion that, through his death, Jesus had accomplished the salvation of others in the sense that he had made it possible for others to live under God's will as members of the community he had lived and died to establish. As they dedicated themselves to serving God and others in the way Jesus had alongside of their sisters and brothers in the faith, they looked back on Jesus' willingness to suffer and die as the decisive moment that had made this new reality possible.

Did Jesus' First Followers Believe He Had Undergone the Messianic Tribulation?

In Chapter 5 of this study, I have argued against the proposal of scholars such as Albert Schweitzer, Dale Allison, and N. T. Wright that Jesus believed that in his death he would undergo the messianic tribulation that many Jews expected to take place before the consummation of all things. In principle, even if Jesus did not view his death in that way, it is possible that his first followers came to ascribe such a meaning to his death. However, when we look closely at the New Testament writings, we find not only little if any evidence in support of such a possibility, but also good reasons to reject it.[13]

---

13. Richard Horsley goes so far as to affirm, "The scholarly impression that a 'great tribulation' would be a principal event in the supposed 'apocalyptic scenario' may be the result of tricks that their own translation and literal reading played on the scholars. There is no reference to a special time of tribulation or suffering in any of the second-temple apocalyptic texts, except for the brief statement in Daniel 12:1b.... [T]he 'sufferings' mentioned in Mark 13:19, 24a (also) referred to the effects of Roman military attacks or acts of repression and persecution by Roman client rulers, i.e., to historical-political conflict and distress. In both Daniel 12:1b and Mark 13, on the basis of recent experience, the political repression was expected to become more severe

The New Testament passages that speak of a period of intense sufferings and tribulations before the end consistently refer to that period as something that is to take place *in the future, following* Jesus' death and resurrection (Matt. 24:3-51; Mark 13:3-25; Luke 21:7-36; Rom. 2:5-9, 16; 1 Thess. 4:13—5:3; 2 Thess. 1:6-10). Nowhere does one find the idea that this time of tribulation was believed to have taken place already during Jesus' own lifetime or when he died. When Jesus describes this tribulation in the Gospels, he regards it as something that his disciples and others will experience, but he never affirms that he himself or the Son of Man will endure it. On the contrary, the Son of Man will come from heaven to put an end to that tribulation. Neither Jesus' followers nor others are ever said to be delivered from having to endure that tribulation as a result of Jesus' death. Furthermore, as we noted in Chapter 5, for Jesus to endure that tribulation in the place of others would defeat entirely its purpose, which was to test all people to see who would be truly faithful and to purge sin and evil from among God's people and the world in general before the new age might be brought in.

Undoubtedly, numerous New Testament texts allude to Jesus' own suffering and his crucifixion by using some of the same imagery associated with the time of tribulation to come. Prior to his death, Jesus experiences intense anxiety and affirms that his heart is troubled (Matt. 26:37-38; Mark 14:33; Luke 22:44; John 12:27). During his crucifixion and immediately afterwards, the earth becomes dark, the ground quakes, and some of the dead arise (Matt. 27:45, 51-54; Mark 15:33; Luke 23:44-45). Yet there is no good reason to equate Jesus' personal anguish and these other phenomena with the tribulation expected to take place at the end of the present age. They may be similar, but they are not the same.

All of this suggests that Jesus' followers regarded Jesus' death as salvific, not because he had endured the expected tribulation himself in the place of others, but because his death had made it possible for there to be a period of time in which more people could be brought to faith and incorporated into his community of followers in order to attain salvation through him (Matt. 24:14; Mark 13:10). Had God or Jesus acted during Jesus' lifetime prior to his death to bring to pass the events associated with the establishment of God's reign, including the resurrection of the dead and the final judgment, the number of those saved would have been relatively small. Nevertheless, because Jesus' proclamation of that reign was generating such conflict that the authorities would not tolerate Jesus' ministry for much longer before seeking to put him to death, the only way for there to be more time for the gospel to be announced throughout the world was for Jesus to accept death. His death would therefore be regarded as "for others" or "for the many" in the sense that it made it possible for there to be a period during which many more people

---

before the people were delivered. In neither case, however, does it seem to refer to a special period of time in an eschatological scenario" (*The Prophet Jesus and the Renewal of Israel: Moving beyond a Diversionary Debate*; Grand Rapids: Eerdmans, 2012, 45-46).

from all over the world might come to hear and believe the gospel through the apostolic proclamation, and thereby attain salvation.

While no passages in the New Testament state this idea explicitly, it is implied in a number of passages. The Synoptics and Acts as well as several of the New Testament epistles consider the time between Jesus' resurrection and his second coming as a time of opportunity for more people to repent and dedicate themselves to living in a way pleasing to God, as Jesus taught.[14] As we have seen in Chapter 9, Jesus' death and resurrection are also viewed as part of a divine plan aimed at the proclamation of the gospel throughout the world. The way in which this divine plan is presented in the New Testament also suggests that it was necessary for Jesus' disciples and first followers to go through the experience of seeing Jesus suffer and die and then contemplating him in his risen, glorified condition. Only in that way would they become fully convinced of Jesus' lordship and divine authority and be emboldened and empowered to endure hardships and persecution as they went out into the world to proclaim the gospel.

A related question that Jesus' first followers may have felt the need to address is why God could not simply have exalted Jesus to a position of glory and power for the whole world to see in order to usher in the kingdom immediately following his death and resurrection. In this way, all people could be brought to believe in Jesus and become convinced of his lordship. Some may have asked why, if God wanted all people to come to faith, the risen Jesus had shown himself only to a small number of his own followers. Jesus' followers may have responded to this question by affirming that, had God acted in that way, people would have come to faith in Jesus and acknowledged his lordship, not out of conviction, but solely out of fear or self-interest, desiring merely to escape condemnation. They would therefore not have become truly committed to the values and way of life taught and embodied by Jesus. For people to be fit for God's reign, they needed first to be transformed in their way of thinking and learn to give of themselves in love to and for others as Jesus had done in his life and death. This could only take place as they identified not only with the risen, glorified Jesus, but also with the love for God and others that he had shown in his suffering and his death on the cross.

What many Jews found unique and strange about the proclamation of Jesus' first followers was that in effect they proclaimed *two different comings* of the Messiah. For the most part, those Jews who expected a Messiah seem to have believed that the messianic age would become a reality as soon as that Messiah was made manifest. A number of New Testament passages contrast two different comings of Jesus as the Messiah. In John's Gospel, Jesus assures his disciples that, even though he is going away in his death, he will return once more for them (John 14:2-3, 18, 28; 16:16-22). The book of Acts also affirms that it is necessary for Jesus to come *again* in order to bring about

---

14. See, for example, Matt. 24:42-51; Mark 13:31-37; Luke 21:34-36; 24:46-47; Acts 2:38-40; 3:19-21; 5:31; 17:30-31; 26:20; 1 Thess. 3:12-13; 5:1-10; 2 Thess. 2:1-2; 1 Tim. 6:11-15; James 5:7-8; 2 Pet. 3:1-18.

the new age of salvation that many Jews associated with the Messiah's first and only coming (Acts 1:11; 3:19-21). According to Heb. 9:27-28, Jesus' first coming was to "deal with sin," while his second coming will be to save those who hope in him. This implies that Jesus' first coming was necessary in order to bring about in God's people the moral transformation necessary in order for them to be saved at his second coming.

Jesus' Death and Isaiah 53

As we noted in Chapter 9, the manner in which Jesus' first followers interpreted the salvific significance of his death was also greatly influenced by their reading of the Scriptures of Israel. While they came to believe that a number of passages from the Psalms had been fulfilled in Jesus' sufferings and death, sooner or later they also came to interpret Isaiah 53 in that same sense. Because several verses of Isaiah 53 allude to the servant's suffering for the sins of others and bringing about their healing and justification in some way, New Testament scholars have almost universally agreed that this passage played a vital role in leading Jesus' first followers to see his death as an atonement for sins.

The New Testament writings do seem to indicate, however, that when Jesus' first followers looked to Isaiah 53, their initial focus was not on the verses that speak of the servant's suffering and death for others or for their sins, but other aspects of the chapter. Sam Williams has noted that all of the six explicit quotations from Isaiah 53 in the New Testament allude either to Jesus' ministry, to the manner in which Jesus was persecuted and put to death, or to the proclamation of the gospel, but do not reflect any idea of expiation for sins.[15] Matthew, for example, sees Jesus' healing activity as fulfilling Isaiah's words about God's servant taking away infirmities and diseases (Matt. 8:17).[16] In his epistles, Paul cites Isaiah 53 only twice: to support his affirmation that "not all believed the gospel" in Rom. 10:16-17 (see Isa. 53:1) and to argue that his work of proclaiming the gospel where it has not been heard previously is guided by the principle articulated in Isaiah 52:15: "Those who have never been told of him shall see, and those who have never heard of him shall understand" (see Rom. 15:20-21).[17] As noted in Chapter 9, certain parts of Isaiah 53 would have been seen merely as pointing forward to what Jesus would suffer and the way he would die. In fact, the only New Testament

---

15. Sam K. Williams, *Jesus' Death as Saving Event: The Background and Origin of a Concept* (HDR 2; Missoula, MT: Scholars Press, 1975), 222-24.

16. As Lidija Novakovic has argued, this is the sense of the Hebrew original, in contrast to the Septuagint, which speaks of the servant carrying the sins of others and emphasizes his suffering on behalf of others ("Matthew's Atomistic Use of Scripture: Messianic Interpretation of Isaiah 53:4 in Matthew 8:17," in *Biblical Interpretation in Early Christian Gospels*, Vol. 2: *The Gospel of Matthew*; ed. Thomas R. Hatina; LNTS 304; London: T & T Clark, 2006, 155-59).

17. See Francis Watson, *Paul and the Hermeneutics of Faith*, 2nd ed. (London: Bloomsbury T & T Clark, 2016), 505-6. While the belief that what was prophesied in Isaiah 53 has been fulfilled in Christ may be embedded within the "substructure of Paul's thought," as Watson argues, Paul's epistles provide no basis for claiming that he found in Isaiah 53 any answers to the question of precisely how Christ's death benefits others, as Watson himself must recognize (503-16).

passage that explicitly relates Jesus' sufferings and death with the verses from Isaiah 53 that refer to the vicarious nature of the servant's death is 1 Pet. 2:22-24.[18] Nevertheless, we may still explore in general terms the question of how Jesus' first followers would have come to see Jesus as having fulfilled the verses from Isaiah 53 that speak of the servant suffering and dying for others and for their sins.[19]

In verses 5 and 8 of the Hebrew version of Isaiah 53, as well as verses 5 and 12 of the Septuagint, we find the affirmation that the servant suffered and died *because of* the people's sins and transgressions (MT *mippesha'*; LXX *dia tas hamartias/anomias*). This involves positing some causal relationship between the people's sins and the servant's sufferings. Some New Testament scholars have claimed that Jesus' disciples and earliest followers considered that Jesus had died on account of their sins in the sense that he had been put to death as a result of their own shortcomings and failures in his last days and hours, rather than for any personal sins he had committed himself.[20] This seems unlikely, however, since the sins that were thought to have led to Jesus' death would have been not only those of his closest disciples, but those of other human beings as well, including especially the Jewish and Roman authorities. What had led to Jesus' crucifixion was not anything his followers had done, but the active opposition to sinful practices and structures that had characterized his entire ministry, as well as his activity on behalf of an alternative community and system. On the basis of what we have seen so far in this work, we must also rule out the possibility that Jesus' first followers interpreted these verses from Isaiah 53 in the sense that the sins of humanity had made it necessary for Jesus to die as humanity's substitute in order to deliver human beings from the punishment their sins deserved.

According to Jesus' first followers, what was necessary was not that human sin be punished, but that the members of God's people turn back to him in love and obedience in order to live in accordance with his will. This was the purpose for which God had sent Jesus. The affirmation that Jesus had suffered and died on account of the people's sins would be understood in the sense that the persistent sinfulness of the people had made it necessary for Jesus to come and carry out a ministry designed to bring about in others the life of righteousness God desired to see. His dedication to this ministry of saving people from their sinful ways had led to conflict and ultimately the cross. Therefore, because Jesus' suffering and death had been the consequence of Jesus' coming and his faithfulness to the task given him, he could be said to have suffered and died *because of* the people's sins.

---

18. On the New Testament passages that show the influence of Isaiah 53, see especially Hans-Ruedi Weber, *The Cross: Tradition and Interpretation of the Crucifixion of Jesus in the World of the New Testament*, trans. Elke Jessett (Grand Rapids: Eerdmans, 1979), 53-58.

19. For the discussion that follows, the reader may wish to refer to the table that appears in Chapter 4 on page 207.

20. See, for example, Jacob Kremer, *Der erste Brief an die Korinther* (RNT; Regensburg: Pustet, 1997), 322-23.

In any case, Jesus' first followers would not have seen his sufferings and death in themselves as bringing about in others the change of life God desired to see. Rather, his sufferings and death formed part of an overarching divine plan aimed at establishing a community of people who would leave behind their sinful ways in order to live in conformity with God's will as defined through Jesus. This community had now been established not only as a result of what Jesus had done in life and death, but also as a result of all that had taken place and would continue to take place following his resurrection, including Jesus' ongoing activity through the Holy Spirit, as well as his heavenly intercession on behalf of believers. Everything that God had done through Jesus had made it possible for believers to be delivered from their sins and transgressions by living in a new way and on that basis receive divine forgiveness, not only for the sins of the past, but also for the sins they would inevitably continue to commit after coming to faith. Jesus had suffered and died in order that all of these things might become a reality.

The divine plan to save people from their sins, therefore, had required that Jesus die. As mentioned in Chapter 9, however, this was not because of some blind fate or merely the necessity that the Scriptures be fulfilled, but because *only by giving up his life could Jesus establish a community in which all would be fully committed to doing God's will in the way defined by him through his life, sufferings, and death*. Only if he himself had been fully committed to that will to the end could he expect to bring into existence a community of followers who would share the same commitment and serve as his instrument for bringing one another and others outside of the community into accordance with that will. Furthermore, for such a community to exist, it was necessary that it be under a Lord who had dedicated his life to the salvation of others. The only way that Jesus could be such a Lord was by offering up his life to God when his work on behalf of others had led to the threat of the cross.

According to this understanding of Jesus' sufferings and death, it would not matter whether phrases such as "our sins" and "our transgressions" in Isaiah 53 would be seen as alluding only to the sins of Israel or to those of the nations as well. Even if Jesus' first followers believed Isaiah had had in mind only the sins of Israel when he spoke of the servant suffering on account of the sins of others and bearing those sins, they would nevertheless eventually come to maintain that people of all other nations needed to be saved from their persistent sinfulness just as much as the people of Israel did. The fact that, from the perspective of the first believers, Jesus had died seeking to establish a community of followers composed of people from all the nations meant that Jesus could also be viewed as having died, not only for the sins of believers, but for the sins of all people, even though many would not ultimately be saved.

Jesus might also be thought to have died for the sins and transgressions of people from past generations. This was because in some way their sin had contributed to the ongoing sinfulness of their descendants. It is likely that Jesus' first followers believed that those who had lived prior to Jesus' coming might also come to be saved from their sins through Jesus when he returned to judge all people. If Jesus was believed to have preached the gospel to the dead during the time he had passed in the realm of the dead, as 1 Pet. 3:18-20 and 4:6 affirm, the purpose of his proclamation must have been seen as that of sharing with at least some of the dead the good news regarding the fulfillment of God's promises of salvation through him so that they too might attain salvation by coming to live under his lordship some day.

The other affirmations of Isaiah 53 could also be understood on the basis of these same basic ideas. The phrase in Isa. 53:6, "the Lord has delivered him up for our sins" (*kurios paredōken auton tais hamartias hēmōn*), could be read in the sense that the people's sins had been the cause of the servant's being given over to death in three ways. First, it was the persistent sinfulness of God's people and their resistance to God's previous efforts to deliver them from that sinfulness that had made it necessary for Jesus to come and carry out a ministry aimed at bringing them to change their ways—a ministry that would result in his violent death. Second, the people's sinfulness had led them to reject Jesus and have him killed. While of course only a small number of persons had actually been responsible for having Jesus put to death, their sin might be seen as paradigmatic of the sin of all and as an expression of the sinfulness of God's people or human beings as a whole. In that case, because all people had consistently rejected God's efforts to bring them to abandon their sinful ways, the sin of those who had acted to have Jesus crucified was simply one more instance of the sinfulness of all people. And third, it had been Jesus' efforts to establish a people who would no longer live in sin that had led to his death. The same interpretations could be given to the Septuagint version of Isa. 53:8, which states that "because of the lawless deeds (*apo tōn anomiōn*) of my people he was led to death."

In Isa. 53:5, both the Masoretic text and the Septuagint affirm that through the servant's wounds the people were healed. This could simply be understood to mean that, as a result of Jesus' willingness to endure physical abuse at the hands of those who mistreated him and put him to death, many had found salvation. This was true both in the sense that they now lived in conformity with God's will and in the sense that they had attained wholeness to some extent in the present age, and could be certain that they would be made fully whole in the age to come. Similarly, the affirmation that "the chastisement of our peace was upon him" in Isa. 53:5 could be read as referring to the notion that Jesus' willingness to endure suffering and death in accordance with God's will had made it possible for many to come to experience the *shalom* God desired for all. As we observed in Chapter 4, both the Hebrew *musar* and the Greek *paideia* used in this verse refer to chastisement that has *a corrective purpose*. In this case, in order to bring others into conformity with his will so that they might have peace—including both peace with God and peace in a general sense in the present world and the world to come—, God had willed that Jesus endure the type of suffering that sinners deserved for their sins.

Nevertheless, Jesus' sufferings and death had not been an end in themselves, as if they had been necessary for a perfectly holy and just God to forgive sins or grant peace, but rather had been the consequence of his efforts to establish the *ekklēsia* or church, the community of those who would practice the righteousness God desired. Jesus' willingness to endure this "chastisement" on behalf of others had made it possible for this new reality to come to pass and for them now to participate in it.

In the last two verses of Isaiah 53, both the Masoretic text and the Septuagint affirm that the servant bore the people's sins in some sense (vv. 11-12). Similarly, in the Hebrew text, v. 6 speaks of God having laid the iniquity of the people on the servant, while v. 4 states that the servant bore the blows or wounds of the people. This last phrase could be read either in the sense that it was the people themselves who struck the servant or in the sense that the servant bore blows that were intended by some for others, whether justly or injustly. No matter how Jesus' first followers read these words, they would not have understood them in the sense that it had been necessary for God to inflict suffering and death on Jesus in order to forgive human beings. Nor did they conceive of human sins as some type of actual metaphysical entity or substance that could be transferred to Jesus. N. T. Wright's notion that the sins of humankind had to be "concentrated" and "piled up in one great obvious heap" in order to be condemned by being placed on Christ in his death would have been entirely foreign to their thought.[21] Jews in antiquity did not believe that sins were actual entities or substances that could be "concentrated" or "piled up in a heap," and much less transferred to another person, such as Jesus. Even if Jesus' followers had conceived of sin in this way, they would not have thought that there was some reason why it was impossible for God to deliver human beings from that sin simply by overlooking it or destroying it by *fiat*, without Jesus having to suffer and die.

Undoubtedly, Jesus' followers might affirm that, because of their sins and Jesus' innocence, it was they rather than Jesus who deserved to suffer the type of things that Jesus had suffered. However, their logic would not be that God's strict and inflexible justice required that all sin receive its proper retribution but rather that, if they were the ones whom God was attempting to correct and bring into conformity with his will, it was they rather than Jesus who should have suffered and endured chastisement. Even if they believed that Jesus had suffered what they deserved to suffer, they would not have concluded that he had endured their suffering in their place as their substitute. Rather, he had suffered what their sins deserved in order to save them and others from their persistent sinfulness and the divine condemnation that resulted from that sinfulness. However, it was not his sufferings in themselves

---

21. N. T. Wright, *The Climax of the Covenant: Christ and the Law in Pauline Theology* (Edinburgh: T & T Clark, 1991), 196, 198. Characterizing the thought of Paul in Rom. 8:3, Wright speaks of "the strange plan of God to deal with sin by collecting it in one place and condemning it there," and affirms that "only so can sin be properly dealt with" (198).

that saved them and others from their sinfulness, but all that he had taught and embodied in life and death, as well as everything that God had continued to do through Jesus, the Holy Spirit, and the community of believers following Jesus' resurrection and exaltation.

According to what we saw in Chapter 4 of this study, the allusion to the servant having borne the sins of others would probably not have been understood in the sense that Jesus bore the *punishment* that others deserved for their sins in order to bring them back to God. Rather, what he had borne was the responsibility of bringing others to leave behind their sinful ways or the consequences of his commitment to that task, in spite of the suffering that this entailed for him. Jesus might also be said to have borne the sins of others in the sense that he had been willing to suffer and die in order for others to be delivered from their persistent sinfulness and the divine condemnation that resulted from that sinfulness. This deliverance would take place as a result of their incorporation into the community of followers that would be brought into existence through Jesus' faithfulness unto death to the task given him.

Because it was God who had sent Jesus to carry out the ministry he did and handed him over to death when that ministry had led to conflict, in a sense God could also be seen as the one who had been responsible for Jesus' sufferings and death. In reality, of course, it was the sins of the people that were ultimately responsible for Jesus' death, since had they not been mired in sins, it would not have been necessary for God to send Jesus and have him carry out a task that would lead to his death. Jesus' followers would therefore interpret Isaiah's affirmation that God had laid upon his servant the iniquity of all to mean that God had laid on Jesus' shoulders the task and responsibility of doing what was necessary to deliver the people from their persistent sinfulness and, when that task had led to the threat of death, God had willed that Jesus remain faithful to that task to the very end. Only in that way could that task be fully accomplished.

Jesus' followers would have understood the allusion to the servant's interceding for the transgressors in the Hebrew version of Isa. 53:12 as referring either to Jesus' petition that God forgive those who crucified him (Luke 23:34) or to the implicit petition on behalf of the salvation of others that he was believed to have made as he faced death. This does not necessarily mean that Jesus' first followers believed that Jesus had actually prayed to God asking him to save and forgive others in his last hours and minutes. As we saw in Chapter 6, the fact that Jesus was offering his life up to God due to his commitment to seeking the salvation of sinners, as he had throughout his ministry, would lead his followers to see Jesus' death as an implicit petition for God to grant forgiveness and salvation to all those who would come to live under his lordship. Because Jesus' followers believed that he had been fully conscious of the divine plan of which his death formed part, they would also have interpreted his death as an implicit petition that people from all over the world be brought to form part of the church or community of followers that would be established through his death. In that case, the transgressors on whose behalf Jesus had interceded would be thought to have included all people.

The manner in which Jesus had offered up his life to God as a result of his dedication to bringing others into conformity with God's will would provide Jesus' followers with the basis necessary to apply to Jesus the affirmation that many would be made or declared righteous as a result of the servant giving up his life (Isa. 53:11 MT). From their perspective, Jesus' faithfulness unto death in seeking to form around himself a people committed to practicing righteousness had not only accomplished that objective, but had provided a basis upon which God might declare righteous the members of that people. The justification of many and the bearing of their sins mentioned in Isa. 53:11-12 would also be seen in relation to Jesus' intercession. He could be said to have borne them and their sins on his heart as he went to his death in that his ultimate objective was that through him they might find healing and salvation from their persistent sinfulness and be accepted by God as righteous, in spite of their sins.

Although Jesus' first followers must have interpreted Isaiah 53 on the basis of what had taken place in Jesus' final days and hours in Jerusalem, their reading of Isaiah 53 undoubtedly affected the way they interpreted Jesus' death as well. This does not necessarily mean that they made up certain events in order to make the narrative they told regarding Jesus' passion and death conform to Isaiah 53. They apparently did, however, emphasize in that narrative certain ideas mentioned in Isaiah 53 that could be seen as having been fulfilled in what had happened to Jesus, such as his being rejected, beaten, counted among the transgressors, and finally killed, even though he had not done anything deserving of such a fate. It is less certain whether Jesus actually remained silent before his accusers or was buried in the tomb of a wealthy person (Isa. 53:7, 9).

More importantly, the fact that Isaiah 53 affirms that the servant suffered and died for others and for their sins and transgressions may have led Jesus' first followers to use the same type of formulas to allude to the salvific significance of his death. If so, *it was not their understanding of Jesus' death that led them to use such formulas, but rather the existence of such formulas in Isaiah 53 that led them to speak of Jesus' death in new ways*. In that case, they came to employ language that was not their own in order to refer to the manner in which Jesus' suffering and death had contributed to the salvation of others. In other words, they adapted their understanding of Jesus' death to fit the formulas found in Isaiah 53, rather than simply realizing that the formulas articulated ideas and interpretations of Jesus' death that had already arisen among them. Therefore, even though Isaiah 53 was not a starting-point for their interpretation of Jesus' death, it served as a catalyst for their reflection and brought them to speak and conceive of the salvific significance of Jesus' death in new ways.

The Influence of 2 and 4 Maccabees on the Early Interpretations of Jesus' Death

There seems to be little evidence that passages from the Hebrew Scriptures other than Isaiah 53 led Jesus' first followers to begin to affirm that Jesus had died for others or for their sins. As we noted in Chapter 4, outside of Isaiah 53, the idea of vicarious death is virtually absent from the Hebrew Scriptures. Nevertheless, as we also saw in Chapter 4, the books of 2 and 4 Maccabees provide evidence that by the first century CE some Jews could speak of certain persons suffering and dying for others and for the law. On this basis, a number of scholars have argued that some of Jesus' first followers looked to the "martyr-theology" that is found in 2 and 4 Maccabees to define the manner in which Jesus' death was salvific.[22]

Of course, nothing in the New Testament indicates that these two writings had any direct influence on the way Jesus' first followers came to interpret his death. Because Jesus was neither attempting to uphold the law when he died nor being persecuted by the Romans for having remained faithful to the law, it is doubtful that Jesus' first followers would have seen any direct parallel between him and figures such as Eleazar, the seven brothers, and the mother who had died for the law. The notion of dying for the law, however, could have influenced Jesus' followers to speak of Jesus dying on behalf of something else, such as the truth of what he had taught, the salvation of others, or the church. In that case, just as those persecuted and tortured in 2 Maccabees were said to have died because of their commitment to the law and in order to strengthen others in that same commitment (2 Macc. 6:27-28; 7:9, 11; cf. 4 Macc. 7:9; 18:4), so Jesus could be said to have died due to his commitment to bringing others into conformity with God's will and seeking the salvation and transformation of others. For reasons we have seen previously, the faithfulness that he had shown in his death would strengthen others in their own commitment to living in the way Jesus had taught and embodied, thus leading to the formation of a community of followers dedicated to practicing justice and righteousness in the way God desired.

Some New Testament scholars have argued that Jesus' first followers would have seen the Mosaic law as the agent or instrument through which Jesus was condemned and, on that basis, come to regard the law as a power

---

22. See, for example, Jarvis J. Williams, *Maccabean Martyr Traditions in Paul's Theology of Atonement: Did Martyr Theology Shape Paul's Conception of Jesus' Death?* (Eugene, OR: Wipf & Stock, 2010), 85-119. Whereas in this work Williams argued that "martyr theology *primarily* or *exclusively* shaped Paul's conception of Jesus' death," he now has softened his claim so as to affirm that "it is more plausible to argue that martyr theology was one tradition (among other traditions) that influenced both Paul's *conception of* and *presentation* of Jesus' death and the benefits of his death for others...." (*Christ Died for Our Sins: Representation and Substitution in Romans and Their Jewish Martyrological Background*; Eugene, OR: Wipf & Stock, 2015, viii-xi). While Williams looks to the accounts of the Jewish martyrs in 2 and 4 Maccabees to argue for a penal substitution understanding of Christ's death, David Seeley argues that those same passages instead led Paul to a "mimetic" interpretation of Jesus' passion and death (*The Noble Death: Graeco-Roman Martyrology and Paul's Concept of Salvation*; JSNTSup 28; Sheffield: JSOT, 1990, 84-99, 145-49).

hostile to Jesus.[23] This manner of thinking would set Jesus and the law at odds with one another and could even lead to the conclusion that, since Jesus was innocent of any wrongdoing, the law had been shown to be contrary to God's will and therefore might even be abolished. It is doubtful, however, that Jesus' first followers thought in these terms. The Gospel passion accounts and other New Testament passages stress both Jesus' innocence and the injustice of the authorities in condemning Jesus to death. Those authorities were not acting in *conformity* with the law, but *contrary* to it. The process against Jesus in the four Gospels is presented as highly irregular. The authorities arrest and judge Jesus surreptitiously at night rather than trying him publicly, make use of false witnesses, and end up condemning Jesus without having demonstrated that he has in fact done anything illegal and deserving of death, as even Pilate is forced to recognize. They incite the mobs and end up pressuring Pilate to sentence an innocent man to death. The process leading to Jesus' condemnation is a sham and a travesty of justice.

In the New Testament, therefore, it is not the law but sinful human beings who act to have Jesus put to death. The fact that the authorities acted contrary to the law in condemning Jesus is stressed in several passages from Acts, as well as in 1 Pet. 2:19-23. In Acts 2:22-23, Peter explicitly mentions that Jesus was "crucified and killed by the hands of those outside the law," while Stephen accuses the Jewish leaders of betraying and murdering Jesus as the righteous one, and immediately claims that those leaders have not kept the law (Acts 7:52-53). Similarly, Luke presents Paul as stressing that the people and leaders acted contrary to the law in condemning Jesus to death: "Even though they found no cause for a sentence of death, they asked Pilate to have him killed" (Acts 13:28). The author of 1 Peter speaks of "suffering unjustly" for doing what is right and applies Isa. 53:9 to Jesus in the context of allusions to what he endured in the process against him: "He committed no sin, and no deceit was found in his mouth" (1 Pet. 2:19-23). For all of these reasons, it seems doubtful that Jesus' first followers saw the Mosaic law as responsible for Jesus' death.

The notion that the law was condemned and brought to an end when it sentenced Jesus to death, therefore, would have been foreign to the thought of Jesus' first followers. Even though Jesus was supposedly condemned for

---

23. Heikki Räisänen, for example, writes that "Paul's encounter with the risen Christ revealed to him that the law had come to an end, for God's vindication of Jesus simultaneously signalled his judgment over the very law that had condemned Jesus, put him under a curse and brought him to the cross" (*Paul and the Law*, 2nd ed.; WUNT 29; Tübingen: J. C. B. Mohr, 1987, 249). Morna D. Hooker claims that, for Paul, "the inadequacy of the Law is seen in the fact that one who was *condemned by the Law* has been *pronounced righteous by God*. Christ has been declared righteous, not only *apart from the Law*, but *in spite of the Law*. In the resurrection, the Law's verdict has been overthrown" ("Paul and Covenantal Nomism," in *Paul and Paulinism: Essays in Honour of C. K. Barrett*; ed. Hooker and S. G. Wilson; London: SPCK, 1982, 55). Similarly, Johan Christiaan Beker affirms that, for Paul, "Christ had died not only to forgive the sins, which were committed under the law, but also to break the power of the law itself, because the law had cursed him whom God had vindicated. Paul's interpretation of Christ's death and resurrection never wavers. It means above all the end of the dominion of the law and our transfer to a new lordship that saves us from the law's condemnation and grants us new life in Christ" (*Paul the Apostle: The Triumph of God in Life and Thought*; Philadelphia: Fortress, 1980, 261).

blasphemy due to his claim to be God's Son, from the perspective of Jesus' followers, Jesus had not in fact committed blasphemy, since he had told the truth. Therefore, the commandment that sentenced to death those who blasphemed did not apply to him (Lev. 24:16). In fact, Jesus' followers would almost certainly have claimed that Jesus was the one on the side of the law. Because he had taught the true meaning and proper interpretation of the law, which pointed to him as its fulfillment, in reality he was the one defending the law against those who interpreted and used it improperly to justify their oppressive and unjust actions.

For this reason, Jesus' first followers might have agreed in principle with the notion that Jesus had died for the law in the way that Eleazar, the seven brothers, and their mother had done, according to 2 and 4 Maccabees. However, because they believed that Jesus was greater than the law and had sought to bring others to obey and follow him rather than merely obeying and following the law, they apparently did not affirm that Jesus had died on behalf of the law. Instead, he had given up his life for something that went beyond the law.

Another significant difference between Jesus' death and the deaths of Eleazar, the seven brothers, and their mother is that the latter were said to have suffered on account of their sins (2 Macc. 7:18, 32). As we have seen in Chapter 4, the idea behind such an affirmation is that God was chastising the people through Antiochus for having disregarded the Mosaic law and attempting to bring them back into a life of conformity with his will as expressed in the law. Because Jesus' followers regarded Jesus as innocent of any sinful behavior, they would not have made the same type of statement regarding Jesus. It is possible, however, that they intended to contrast Jesus with figures such as those mentioned in 2 Maccabees by affirming that Jesus had suffered and died, not for his own sins, but for the sins of others. This would be understood in the sense that God's purpose in subjecting his Son to sufferings and death was to bring back into conformity with his will, not *Jesus*, but *others through Jesus*. The idea would be the same as that just noted with regard to Isaiah 53, where God has the innocent servant suffer so that the sinful people may be brought back to repentance and obedience.

Both the sufferings of Eleazar, the brothers, and their mother in 2 and 4 Maccabees and the sufferings of the servant of Isaiah 53 are said to bring about in God's people a recommitment to a life of obedience to God by means of the effect that those sufferings have on those who observe them. The sinful people realize that it is their own sins that are the cause of the sufferings of the figures in 2 and 4 Maccabees and Isaiah 53, since the purpose for which God is inflicting suffering is to bring the people as a whole to repentance. Nevertheless, in these passages, those suffering on account of the guilty majority are relatively righteous or innocent in comparison to the majority. In contrast, in the New Testament, Jesus is not said to have endured any type of suffering that by right should have been inflicted upon the people as a whole for their sins.

Nevertheless, an important point of similarity between Jesus' death and the deaths of the figures in 2 and 4 Maccabees as well as the servant of Isaiah 53 is that Jesus' death also convicts others of their sins and reveals to them the depths into which they have fallen and their need for repentance. This is especially clear in Peter's Pentecost sermon, where, after he tells the crowd that they have crucified and killed the Messiah whom God sent to them, they are "cut to the heart" (Acts 2:22-23, 36-37). In a general sense, both Jews and non-Jews could see their own sin as responsible for Jesus' death in that it was their sinfulness that had made it necessary for Jesus to come and carry out a ministry aimed at bringing them back to God—a ministry that had resulted in Jesus' death. Some might even have compared themselves with those who unjustly condemned Jesus and have seen their own sinfulness reflected and expressed in the unjust acts of those who had acted to have Jesus put to death. On the basis of these ideas, it might be said that Jesus had died for the sins of others in the sense that he had died to make evident to all the sinfulness of their ways. He had also died for their sins in the sense that their sins had led God to send his Son into the world to attempt to bring all to repent of their sins and turn back to God through him. The inevitable consequence of his coming and his efforts to accomplish these objectives in the midst of a sinful people had been his death.

It seems probable that 4 Maccabees was written some time after Jesus' death, in which case it could not have influenced directly the way in which Jesus' first followers interpreted his death.[24] It is possible, however, that some of the ideas regarding vicarious suffering and death expressed in 4 Maccabees already existed in some form among Jews in the time of Jesus. If the book is dated toward the end of the first century CE, the interpretations Jesus' first followers were giving to his death may even have exerted some direct or indirect influence on the author of 4 Maccabees. While of course we cannot draw any firm conclusions regarding these possibilities, even if Jesus' followers drew on ideas such as those found in 4 Maccabees in order to give meaning to Jesus' death, they would have understood those ideas against the background of the interpretations of Jesus' death that we have seen in this chapter and the previous ones.

Thus, for example, just as in 4 Macc. 6:28 Eleazar is presented as praying to God, "Make my blood their purification," Jesus may have been seen as going to his death asking that what he was suffering result in the purification of others from their sins. This purification, however, would not be the direct consequence of his death, as if in itself his death would purify others forensically by making it possible for God to forgive them. Rather, the idea would be that Jesus was asking God that his death serve as a means by which what he had been seeking throughout his ministry might become a reality, namely, that others come to live a life of purity in conformity with God's will. This

---

24. As was noted in Chapter 4, most scholars consider that 4 Maccabees was written toward the end of the first century CE.

would take place once Jesus had risen and the community of followers he had sought to establish had become a reality. His blood—understood as his faithfulness unto death to the task given him—would lead to the purification of others in that it would define forever the community of followers who lived under his lordship as a community of persons fully committed to serving God and others in love as Jesus had. By practicing love, compassion, justice, and righteousness in solidarity with Jesus, who by virtue of his willingness to die for others had been exalted as Lord, not only would they be purified in their way of life, but they would also be accepted by God as pure.

Although the New Testament never presents Jesus as praying to God, "Receive my soul as their *antipsuchon*," as Eleazar does in 4 Macc. 6:28, or affirms that Jesus "became an *antipsuchon* for the sin of our nation" (4 Macc. 17:21), the basic ideas reflected in these phrases might nevertheless be applied to what Jesus had done. Jesus could be said to have offered himself up to God as an *antipsuchon* for others or for their sins in the sense that he had sought to obtain something for others from God in exchange for giving up his life, namely, salvation and the forgiveness of sins. In effect, Jesus had asked God to respond to the sacrifice of his life by receiving favorably all those who would identify with Jesus and with his death by living under his lordship as his followers and by dedicating their lives to others as he had. Likewise, Jesus had offered himself up to God for others asking that God respond by granting forgiveness to all those who would form part of his community of followers. Once more, however, the *basis* both for Jesus' petition and for God's favorable response to that petition would be the new life of righteousness and obedience that would be brought about in those who lived as Jesus' followers. The idea would therefore be similar to that of 4 Maccabees, where God accepts the death of Eleazar and others who die out of faithfulness to the law as an *antipsuchon* for others and for their sins on the basis of the renewed obedience to the law that would be brought about among the members of God's people, thanks to the willingness of Eleazar and others to give up their lives for the law. Just as Eleazar, the seven brothers, and the mother had died seeking to remain obedient to the law, not only for their own sake, but in order that others might be strengthened in their obedience, so Jesus had gone to his death seeking to bring about in others the obedience to God that God desired to see.

In the minds of Jesus' first followers, what distinguished Jesus from those like Eleazar who had died for the law, however, was that Jesus had risen from among the dead and had been exalted as Lord following his death. Seen in connection with his resurrection, the idea that Jesus had died seeking salvation and forgiveness for others would therefore also be understood in the sense that, once risen, he would continue to carry out his efforts to bring others into conformity with God's will by means of the Holy Spirit and the community of followers itself.

If Jesus' followers did come to speak of Jesus offering up his life *in exchange* for others or for their sins, they would not have seen this in terms of some type of negotiation between Jesus and God or as a kind of *do ut des* transaction. In his justice and love, what God desired was not that someone die so that human sin might be punished, but that all be brought into conformity with his will. Because this would be possible only through Jesus' own dedication to doing God's will until the very end of his life, God could be said to have responded to Jesus' death by granting the salvation that not only Jesus but God himself wanted all people to receive. Therefore, what Jesus had been seeking for others in exchange for giving up his life was not something that God was refusing to grant unless he received a "payment" or "ransom" from Jesus. Rather, God promised to grant forgiveness and salvation to Jesus' followers in exchange for Jesus' death because that death was the means by which God would obtain the righteous, obedient people he had always desired to have.

To some extent, Paul's affirmation in Rom. 3:25 that God put Christ forward as a *hilastērion* through his blood (*en tō haimati autou*) seems to echo 4 Macc. 17:22, which asserts that "through the blood of these devout ones and the *hilastērion* of their death, divine providence preserved Israel" (4 Macc. 17:22). Although we will examine Rom. 3:25 more closely in Chapter 12, here we may briefly note that if Jesus' followers came to think of Jesus or his death as a *hilastērion* in the same sense that 4 Maccabees does, they would have understood this in the sense that God put away his wrath against the people for their sins on account of Jesus' self-offering on their behalf. However, what would be seen as appeasing God's wrath was not Jesus' death or blood in itself, as if God and his justice were satisfied by Jesus' bloody death on the cross, but Jesus' faithfulness unto death to his God-given task of bringing into existence a people who would live in accordance with God's will under Jesus' lordship. Only because Jesus had remained faithful to that task all the way to his death was it now possible for that people to exist and live as God desired, since had Jesus himself not been fully obedient to God up to the end, he could not have been established as Lord over a people who would also be committed to the same type of obedience. Here again, the idea of Jesus' followers would have been similar to that of 4 Maccabees, where those who give up their life and shed their blood for the law put away God's wrath by bringing others to assume their same commitment to living in accordance with the law. Ultimately, it was not blood or death that put away God's wrath, but the unbending commitment to doing his will. The death of the faithful was at times the consequence and ultimate expression of that commitment, yet it might also serve to bring about in others that same commitment.

Jesus' Death and the Akedah, the Bronze Serpent, and the Passover Lamb

Another passage from the Hebrew Scriptures that many scholars believe exerted a strong influence on the way in which Jesus' first followers came to interpret Jesus' death is the story of the binding of Isaac or *Akedah* in Genesis 22. As we saw in Chapter 4, it is important to avoid reading back into that passage any ideas of penal substitution, which are entirely foreign to ancient Jewish thought as well as the thought of Jesus' first followers.

At first glance, it would seem that this passage did not lend itself to being applied to Jesus' death, for several reasons. First, what was thought to have moved God to ask Abraham to sacrifice Isaac was not the sin of Abraham, Isaac, or anyone else, but merely God's desire to test Abraham to see whether he would be fully obedient to God's will, no matter what God asked of him. Second, in contrast to Jesus, Isaac was not actually sacrificed, and thus did not actually die. Third, and most importantly, there does not seem to be any point of comparison between Jesus and either Isaac or Abraham in the story. In principle, Jesus would not be compared to Isaac, because Isaac was not the one offering himself up. Rather, it was Abraham who was to offer up Isaac. The words "your only son, whom you love" that God addresses to Abraham with regard to Isaac in Gen. 22:2 seem to echo the New Testament allusions to Jesus as God's only-begotten and beloved Son. In Genesis 22, however, Isaac is the only beloved son, not of God, but of Abraham. The fact that God is not the one being asked to offer up his only Son, but the one who asks Abraham to offer up his son and the one to whom Isaac is to be offered up in sacrifice, seems to rule out any comparisons between the God of Jesus and Abraham. For the same reason, Jesus would not be compared to Abraham since, in contrast to Jesus, Abraham was the father of the only beloved son, rather than the son himself. Furthermore, whereas Jesus had offered himself up to God as God's Son, Abraham had not. Abraham had instead been at the point of putting his son to death, whereas in the thought of Jesus' first followers it was not God who had put his Son to death but evildoers. God had merely allowed those evildoers to crucify his Son.

It therefore seems unlikely that Jesus' first followers looked to the story of the *Akedah* to interpret Jesus' death. Nevertheless, that possibility cannot be ruled out entirely. A comparison might be drawn between the way in which Abraham had been willing to give up his only beloved son and the way in which God had also been willing to hand his only Son over to death. The story of the *Akedah* could be seen as illustrating the truth that it was more difficult and painful to offer up the life of one's only son than to offer up one's own life. Thus God's willingness to give up the life of the Son he loved would be regarded as the greatest expression imaginable of God's love. It is worth noting, however, that none of the New Testament writings allude explicitly to the story of the binding of Isaac as prefiguring typologically what would take place in Jesus.

As we noted in Chapter 4, in later Jewish thought the willingness of Isaac to offer up his own life to God came to be stressed. The story thus came to be seen as an expression not only of Abraham's total obedience to God, but that of Isaac as well. Those Jews who identified with Isaac in offering their lives up to God as he had and presented their sacrificial offerings to God with the same spirit that Isaac had shown could be assured of God's acceptance.

If Jesus' first followers applied these ideas to Jesus, then they would have compared the way Isaac offered up his own life to God with the way Jesus had done so. This would reinforce the idea that Jesus' death had been sacrificial. If as Jews they believed that, when Isaac offered up his life, he was conscious of the fact that future generations would invoke his sacrifice and that their sacrifices would be accepted by God on the basis of his own, then Jesus' followers might believe that Jesus was also offering up his life thinking of those who would come to believe in him and identify with his sacrifice. In this way, Jesus' sacrifice would serve as a basis for the self-offering of believers, which would be acceptable to God by virtue of their identification with Jesus. Nevertheless, just as it was not Isaac's sacrifice itself that moved God to accept the sacrifices of later generations, but rather their *identification* with Isaac's sacrifice and the fact that they offered themselves and their gifts to God in the same spirit as Isaac, so also Jesus' first followers would not see Jesus' sacrificial death in itself as moving God to accept believers in spite of their sins. Rather, what would lead to God's acceptance and forgiveness was the identification of believers with Jesus' sacrifice and with the same spirit of dedication to God that Jesus had manifested when he offered up his own life on behalf of others.

While it is doubtful that Jesus' first followers looked to the story of the binding of Isaac to interpret the significance of Jesus' death, it seems clear from the New Testament that they believed that the story of the lifting up of the bronze serpent and the sacrifice of the Passover lamb prefigured the manner in which Jesus would be lifted up on the cross and offer up his life or blood on behalf of others, as we saw in Chapter 9. The fact that both the story of the bronze serpent and the story of the first Passover celebration in Egypt pointed back to moments when God had acted to save Israel meant that both stories could be seen as anticipating typologically the way in which God would act through Jesus to bring salvation to those who would live as members of his chosen people.

When they looked to the first of these two stories, Jesus' followers could claim that, just as the Israelites in the desert were delivered from the sufferings God had inflicted on them on account of their sin when they looked up at the bronze serpent erected by Moses, so now all people could be saved by looking up in a spiritual or metaphorical sense at Jesus, once hung upon the cross but now risen and exalted. Nevertheless, the story of the bronze serpent did not lend itself to further comparisons with what had taken place in Jesus' death. The bronze serpent had been neither a sacrificial offering nor a living being who had endured death voluntarily in obedience to God's will. Although the Israelites had been delivered from divine punishment by means of the serpent, in reality God had granted them this means of deliverance out of compassion for them only when they had acknowledged their sin and asked Moses to intercede to God for them (Num. 21:6-9). Thus, even if through Jesus and his death God had now provided a means by which sinful people might be saved, it was still necessary for them to repent as the Israelites had done. This means that it was not Jesus' death per se that was thought to save others.

Both Paul and the Fourth Gospel seem to see the death of the Passover lamb as prefiguring what would take place in Jesus. Many scholars have claimed that, when Jesus' first followers read the story of the first Passover in Exodus 12, they would have seen it as alluding to the ideas of substitutionary death and the power of the blood of a sacrificial lamb to avert God's wrath or death itself. Just as the blood smeared on the doorposts averted the angel of death, so also the blood of Jesus averted the death penalty.

There are several problems with this interpretation, however. First, in the original text, there is no hint of the idea that God sent the angel of death as a punishment for the sins of Israel or even those of the Egyptians in general. Instead, it would have been clear to Jesus' followers that God had slain the firstborn sons of the Egyptians in response to Pharaoh's stubbornness in refusing to release the Israelites from their bondage, and in order to demonstrate to the Israelites his power so that they might believe in him. The blood of the Passover lamb was therefore not tied to the forgiveness of sins.[25]

Second, Jesus' followers would not have seen the blood of the lamb as having some type of mysterious or quasi-magical power to save the Israelites. Rather, it was simply a means by which the Israelites had identified which homes were theirs so that the angel of death might pass over those homes. For the same reason, even if Jesus was identified with the Passover lamb, his blood would not be seen as possessing any type of power to effect the salvation and forgiveness of others, much less to place God under obligation to save and forgive anyone.

Third, the slaughtering of the Passover lambs was not seen as an end in itself, nor was its primary purpose that of obtaining the lamb's blood so as to use it as some type of talisman against the angel of death. Rather, the Israelites slaughtered the lambs primarily to eat them in a ritual meal. Although when the first Passover was celebrated in Egypt the Israelites had used the blood of the lambs to identify their homes, from that time on, as far as we know, no type of ritual was performed with the blood of the lambs sacrificed at the tabernacle or temple on the festival of Passover, other than returning that blood to YHWH or offering it to him. Thus neither the original sacrifice of the Passover lambs nor the annual reenactments of that sacrifice were thought to have the purpose of saving those who participated in them from God's wrath or even from death itself.

---

25. This point is rightly emphasized by Jane Lancaster Patterson, who observes that the Passover feast involved joyful celebration of Israel's deliverance from slavery in Egypt (*Keeping the Feast: Metaphors of Sacrifice in 1 Corinthians and Philippians*; ECL; Atlanta: SBL, 2015, 54-62). In particular, the fact that those participating in the meal ate "reclining, as free people, not sitting, as was the custom for servants," reminded the people of their liberation (60; cf. 134). She adds that the theme of God's forgiveness was not a principal part of the Passover celebration, but was simply "*assumed*": "the death of the lamb is an act of obedience that initiates God's deliverance of the people from oppression, not forgiveness of past sins" (133, 135).

Once again, then, Jesus' first followers would interpret typologically the story regarding the Passover lamb without drawing further comparisons between the sacrificial death of the lamb and the sacrificial death of Jesus. Neither Paul nor the Fourth Evangelist appear to relate the blood of Jesus to the blood of the Passover lamb. Nor do they ascribe any salvific or atoning power to Jesus' death or blood in the passages in which they compare Jesus to the Passover lamb. While the celebration of the Eucharist would have brought to mind the Passover meal and the consumption of the meat of the Passover lamb, particularly given the fact that Jesus' Last Supper with his disciples was remembered by many as having been a Passover meal, in itself the comparison of Jesus with the Passover lamb would not lead them to speak of Jesus' death or blood as producing some salvific effect for others.

The Use of Sacrificial Language to Speak of Jesus' Death

As we have seen in Chapter 6, at some point Jesus' followers came to look to the prescriptions regarding sacrificial offerings in the Hebrew Scriptures and the sacrificial practices at the Jerusalem temple in order to interpret the significance of Jesus' death. The analogies, however, would not be as readily evident as one might imagine. Strictly speaking, Jesus' death had not been a sacrificial offering. Obviously, he had not been ritually slaughtered in the way sacrificial victims were, nor had he been offered up to God on an altar. Undoubtedly, the Jewish high priests had been involved in having him put to death, yet neither they nor anyone else understood their condemnation of Jesus in terms of having offered Jesus up to God as a sacrifice. Rather, they had merely judged Jesus to be a wrongdoer deserving of death.

In addition, as we saw in Chapter 3, it is a mistake to suppose that the biblical prescriptions regarding sacrifice or the worship activities carried out in the Jerusalem temple were thought to revolve around the death of sacrificial victims. There were many types of sacrificial offerings made at the temple that did not involve the death of animals, just as there were many acts of worship and piety that took place there in which no type of sacrifice was offered. The temple was primarily a place of prayer. Those who presented sacrifices were in essence offering up to God prayers together with offerings that embodied the desires and sentiments behind those prayers. Furthermore, most of the sacrifices offered to God were not for sins, but instead were expressions of thanksgiving and devotion to God, as well as petitions for God's blessings.

Of course, the animals sacrificed at the temple were also not thought to be offering themselves up to God voluntarily or expressing their own devotion or dedication to God. Although the animal victims undoubtedly suffered, efforts were made to make their death as painless as possible. An important part of most of the animal sacrifices was also the consumption of the animal's flesh. Other parts of the animal's carcass, such as the hide, the breast, and the limbs, were given to the priests or to the offerers to be used for a variety of purposes.

The use of the blood was especially important, since it needed to be offered or returned to God or else disposed of properly.[26]

For these reasons, it is probable that Jesus' first followers would not immediately have associated Jesus' death with the death of sacrificial animals. They had not taken Jesus to the temple and offered him up sacrificially there or consented to his death in the way that those involved in the sacrificial rites consented to the death of animal victims. If God's acceptance of a sacrifice for sin depended on the repentance and commitment to obedience of those offering it, then Jesus' followers would have continued to see their own repentance and commitment to God's will as a necessary condition for obtaining forgiveness. Although Jesus had no doubt bled during his ordeal, none of the Gospel passion accounts stress this point. The only bleeding of Jesus mentioned explicitly takes place when he prays at Gethsemane and when his body is pierced after his death (Luke 22:44; John 19:31-36).[27] Jesus had suffered a great deal, in contrast to the sacrificial animals whose suffering was limited. There were very few analogies between what went on at the temple and what had taken place in Jesus' death.

Initially, if Jesus' first followers looked at Jesus' death in light of sacrificial practices, they would probably have drawn comparisons between Jesus and the priests rather than between Jesus and the sacrificial victims put to death. It was the priests who actually offered up sacrifices on behalf of others and communicated to God in words and actions the sentiments and petitions of which the offerings were an expression. As we see in the letter to the Hebrews, if Jesus' followers spoke of Jesus as a sacrificial victim, they would do so only after they had come to see him as fulfilling the role of a priest, since it would then be said that the offering he had made was not an animal, but himself.

As we saw in Chapter 6, because the primary task of the priests was not to put animals to death but to offer up petitions to God together with the sacrifices, Jesus' death would be seen as a petition on behalf of others. The emphasis would therefore be, not on Jesus' suffering and death per se, as if these were salvific in some way, but on the implicit petition he had made on behalf of others as he went to his death. It was this petition embodied in the offering of himself that had led God to grant acceptance and forgiveness to those on whose behalf Jesus had offered himself, namely, all those who would repent of their sins and commit themselves to living according to God's will as defined through Jesus. Ultimately, it was not the sacrificial death of Jesus itself that

---

26. On the use of the blood and other parts of the animals sacrificed at the Jerusalem temple, see Roland de Vaux, *Ancient Israel: Its Life and Institutions*, Vol. 2: *Religious Institutions*, trans. John McHugh (New York: McGraw-Hill, 1965), 415-21.

27. Of course, there are doubts as to whether Luke 22:44 formed part of the original Gospel of Luke and, strictly speaking, the passage does not speak of Jesus bleeding, but only of his sweat becoming like drops of blood. On the problem of the authorship of this verse and of the interpretation of Luke's allusion to Jesus' sweat falling as drops of blood, see Brown, *Death of the Messiah*, 1:180-86. With regard to John 19:31-36, it is significant that the shedding of Jesus' blood there takes place *after* Jesus had died.

pleased God and obtained God's forgiveness for others, but the fact that the love that Jesus had shown in offering his life up to God would be reproduced among those who identified themselves with Jesus and his sacrifice. Jesus' self-offering on behalf of others was pleasing to God because it would lead to the existence of a people who would approach God through Jesus in the same spirit, making Jesus' self-offering their own.

A number of passages from the New Testament indicate that at some point Jesus' followers came to speak of Jesus' blood as salvific in some sense. Of course, the word "blood" could be used in many different ways and could mean many different things. To speak of blood was not always to speak of *sacrificial* blood, since blood could also refer to things such as kinship, human corporality ("flesh and blood"), violent death, or simply the substance that runs through the veins of animals and human beings. When Matthew presents Pilate as washing his hands of Jesus' blood, for example, and has the crowd exclaim, "His blood be upon us and our children" (Matt. 27:24-25), the word *blood* is not being used in a sacrificial sense. In this and many other passages from the New Testament, blood merely refers to a violent death. In itself, of course, a violent death would not be considered as salvific for anyone. Only when such a death served to put an end to the oppressive ways of certain individuals or groups or provoked others to protest and take action against those who had acted unjustly could it be seen as benefitting others.

As we saw in Chapters 3 and 4, among Greeks, Romans, and other peoples in antiquity, the offering of sacrificial blood in itself could be thought to please the gods and appease their wrath. However, this was due to concepts of the divinity that were very different from the Jewish view of Israel's God YHWH. What caused YHWH's wrath was not the failure of his people to offer sacrifices to him, as if he needed or desired the sacrificial offerings in themselves, but the people's persistent sin and injustice, particularly when they were unrepentant of their sinfulness. There is no reason, therefore, to think that Jesus' first followers would have believed that the shedding or offering up of Jesus' blood in itself had pleased God or appeased his wrath at human sins. Like other Jews, they would have believed that only the repentance and return to God of those who had sinned could bring God to forgive them and accept them again.

Jesus' followers could have related Jesus' blood to the salvation or redemption of others without necessarily understanding his blood in a sacrificial sense. However, this would have required focusing not only on the violent nature of his death, but on the fact that he had remained faithful to the task for which God had sent him in spite of and in the midst of the violence directed at him. Once again, it would not be his death per se that led to the salvation of others, but his total commitment to seeking the salvation of others in life and death. His faithfulness to that objective had led God to raise him as Lord and had made it possible for others to attain salvation by living under him in faith and loving obedience.

When Jesus' first followers began to speak of Jesus' blood in a sacrificial sense, they must have done so because they associated his blood with the offering of himself that he had made in his last days and hours. They would have had in mind not so much the actual, physical blood that Jesus had shed in his passion and death, but the fact that he willingly endured a violent death out of dedication to God and love for others. Although Jesus' death had been a violent one, his disciples were aware that he had not merely been a passive victim of the violent aggressions of others, but to some extent had brought that violence upon himself. Jesus had gone up to Jerusalem of his own volition, in obedience to the work his Father had given him to do, fully conscious of what awaited him there. He had not only taught openly and undauntedly at the temple in ways that angered the authorities, but he had also carried out a provocative act at the temple, violently turning over tables and driving out those doing business there. Undoubtedly, he had been aware of what the consequences of his actions would be. His followers believed that Jesus had also gone to pray in the Garden of Gethsemane knowing that he would be arrested and subsequently mistreated, mocked, beaten, humiliated, and crucified. Whether or not they knew much about what had taken place during his process before the Jewish leaders and Pilate, they believed that he had to a large extent remained silent, and that he had not resisted the authorities, implored them to spare his life, or tried to defend himself against the injustices being perpetrated on him.[28]

Therefore, even though they saw Jesus' death as a violent and unjust act committed against him, they also saw it as something that he had endured and embraced willingly. This made it possible to speak of Jesus as having offered himself up to God and to associate his blood not only with the violent death he had suffered but with the sacrifice of his life. Furthermore, because everything Jesus had done had been motivated by his love for others rather than any type of self-interest, when his first followers associated sacrificial ideas with his blood, they would have seen that blood as symbolizing and representing not only Jesus' offering of himself up to God, but also the fact that he had offered himself up to God *on behalf of others*, whose salvation he had been seeking and had continued to seek up until his last breath.

When Jesus' followers spoke of Jesus' blood in a sacrificial sense, the most important image that would come to mind for them would be that of the priests sprinkling blood in the holy place or presenting that blood to God by

---

28. Citing the work of scholars such as Clifford Geertz, Sallie McFague, John Aston, and George Lakoff, Patterson argues that "sacrifice has become so embedded in Christian thought (particularly in relation to the crucifixion of Christ) that it has almost lost its metaphorical sense and become, to a certain extent, literalized, or what some would call a 'dead' metaphor" (*Keeping the Feast*, 27). She quotes McFague's observation, "The greatest danger [for a powerful metaphor] is assimilation—the shocking, powerful metaphor becomes trite and accepted...." (27; see McFague, *Metaphorical Theology: Models of God in Religious Language*; Philadelphia: Fortress, 1982, 41). According to Patterson, the result of the extensive use of metaphorical images related to sacrifice in association with Jesus' death on the cross resulted in the minimization or loss of the political significance of the crucifixion, particularly the culpability of the Roman authorities in Jesus' execution and the resistance to Rome's rule that led to his crucifixion (23, 27).

means of the other rites prescribed in the Mosaic law. They would especially recall the Day of Atonement rites, in which the high priest went into the Holy of holies to sprinkle blood before YHWH on the mercy seat during the days of the tabernacle and first temple. Because in their day the Holy of holies no longer contained the ark of the covenant and the mercy seat, they may have simply thought of Jesus entering into God's presence to offer him his own blood or life. Just as the priests who approached God with sacrificial blood offered up prayers to God together with that blood, so Jesus would also have been thought to have been offering up to God prayers on behalf of others together with his blood or life as he died, seeking the salvation of others. God's act of raising Jesus from the dead would be understood as his favorable response, not only to Jesus' sacrificial offering of himself to God, but also to the petition he had made on behalf of the salvation of those who would identify themselves with his sacrifice by living as members of the community on whose behalf he had offered up his life.[29]

In ancient Hebrew and Jewish thought, sacrificial blood was also said to cleanse. While it could cleanse sacred places and objects, it was also thought to cleanse the people themselves. Nevertheless, as we saw in Chapter 3, this was not because they came into contact with the blood or because it was applied to them in some way. According to Lev. 16:30, not only the sacred places and objects were cleansed through the Day of Atonement rites but the people themselves, even though the people never come into contact with sacrificial blood during those rites. Thus it was not the blood itself that was thought to cleanse the people, but the confession of their sins, as well as the fact that they "denied" or "humbled" themselves before God (Lev. 16:21, 29, 31). They were cleansed from their sins in the sense that, by virtue of the repentance and recommitment to God that they expressed by means of their participation in the rite, they could be assured that God accepted them and had put away from his consideration the sins they had committed. Of course, those who participated in the sacrificial rites in this way could also experience a sensation of having been cleansed in their interior and their heart. In Jewish thought, it was in this sense that the rites with blood served to purify the people from their sins.

When Jesus' first followers said that they had been cleansed through Jesus' blood, therefore, they would have understood this affirmation on the basis of these same ideas. They identified themselves as those on whose behalf Jesus had offered up to God his life or blood and identified as well with the spirit of love and self-sacrifice of which Jesus' death on their behalf had been the ultimate expression. Through their faith and repentance, they counted themselves

---

29. Patterson rightly notes that the metaphorical interpretation that Jesus' followers began to give to his death resulted in their appropriation of "a web of related ideas involving (among many other things) atonement, priesthood, holiness, oath-making, eating, community, thanksgiving, death, life, cleanliness, men's work and women's work" (*Keeping the Feast*, 24). Of course, among the most important metaphorical images they came to use in order to stress the sacrificial aspect of Jesus' death were those that were related to the shedding and use of sacrificial blood.

among those on whose behalf Jesus had interceded in his death in the same way that those Jews who participated in the Day of Atonement rites counted themselves among those on whose behalf the priest approached God with blood, pleading for mercy and forgiveness. By participating in those rites, of course, it was presupposed that the people had repented of their sins and were committing themselves to living according to the covenant. In the same way, by definition, to approach God now through Jesus' blood implied a commitment to leaving behind one's sinful ways and living under the covenant that had been established or ratified through Jesus. While in Moses' day God had prescribed that the members of his people who had repented of their sins draw near to him through the blood of sacrificial animals to ask for and receive his forgiveness so as to be purified, now God had come to prescribe that all people repent and approach him in the same spirit through the blood of Jesus. Because God had accepted Jesus' self-offering on behalf of all who would draw near to him through Jesus, those who now did so could be confident of their acceptance by God in spite of their sinfulness. In this way, then, they would see themselves as having been cleansed through Jesus' blood.

Jesus' first followers also related his blood to the establishment of the covenant, or new covenant, that God had brought into existence through him. In the Hebrew Scriptures, the only account in which sacrificial blood is said to have been sprinkled on the people is Exod. 24:1-8, where Moses is said to have taken the blood of oxen that had been sacrificed to God and, after sprinkling half of it on the altar, to have sprinkled the rest of it on the people. There is no evidence that in ancient Judaism this contact with blood was thought to have actually purified the people physically or to have obtained their forgiveness. In fact, in the Exodus account, the people had consecrated themselves to God prior to the rite Moses performed, and thus were already in a state of purification (Exod. 19:11-15). The sprinkling with blood would therefore be understood as symbolizing the way in which YHWH and the Israelites were being bound together as a result of God's giving them the law and their expression of their commitment to live according to that law. After listening to the commandments Moses had given them, as well as hearing of God's intention to make them his special people, they had responded, "All that the Lord has spoken we will do, and we will be obedient" (Exod. 24:7; cf. v. 3). On the basis of this response, Moses sprinkled the blood on them and told them, "See the blood of the covenant that the Lord has made with you in accordance with all these words" (Exod. 24:8).[30]

Among Jesus' first followers, this passage would obviously have brought to mind what Jesus was remembered to have said and done at the Last Supper over the bread and wine. Jesus' words over the bread, "This is my body," would

---

30. Zechariah 9:11 also uses the phrase "blood of the covenant" in the context of allusions to the arrival of Israel's king riding on a donkey and the establishment of his dominion from sea to sea (see 9:9-10), yet it is not clear whether this verse influenced Jesus' followers to ascribe salvific significance to Jesus' blood or played any role in their interpretation of the words attributed to Jesus over the cup at the Last Supper.

have been understood in a sacrificial sense, especially when the phrase "given for you" was added to those words. Jesus had offered up his life to God, handing his body over to death, on their behalf—not because God would accept that offering in their stead, but because Jesus was consecrating himself entirely to their salvation as their Lord and asking that God bring about for them that salvation through him. While his first followers apparently remembered Jesus' words over the wine in different ways, whether they spoke of the cup as his blood of the covenant poured out for many (Matt. 26:27-28; Mark 14:24) or as the new covenant in his blood (Luke 22:20; 1 Cor. 11:25), the idea seems to have been that, by offering up his life, Jesus was establishing a covenant with them and all others who would become his followers. The love for others shown by Jesus in his death or by means of his blood would also be seen as defining the *nature* of the new covenant established through him. Whereas in the covenant sealed with sacrificial blood under Moses, the people had committed themselves to living according to the prescriptions of the Mosaic law, in the covenant established through Jesus' blood, those following Jesus committed themselves to living under Jesus' lordship according to God's will as it had been defined through Jesus, especially in his death.

When Jesus' followers used and heard the words "blood of the covenant" or "new covenant in my blood" in connection with Jesus and his death, then, multiple ideas would come to mind. Participating in the eucharistic celebration by eating of the bread as Jesus' body and drinking of the cup as Jesus' blood of the covenant would be understood in terms of identifying with Jesus' sacrificial death, both in the sense of including oneself among those for whom Jesus had died and in the sense of committing oneself to giving of oneself as Jesus had done, living under his lordship in the new covenant established through his death. In relating the forgiveness of sins with Jesus' death or blood, they would have these same ideas in mind. Through his death or blood, Jesus had established a new covenant in which they could obtain God's forgiveness as they lived under Jesus as their Lord. At the same time, of course, the one establishing this covenant had been God himself, who had sent Jesus, handed him over to death, and subsequently raised him as Lord.

Once all of this is understood, there is no reason to maintain that when Jesus' first followers spoke of partaking in Jesus' body and blood (1 Cor. 10:16-17), they believed that they received Jesus' body and blood in a real or ontological sense, as if these constituted some type of actual substance that was mysteriously communicated to them through the bread and wine. Nor is there any evidence that when they spoke of Jesus' blood in a sacrificial sense, they thought that it had some type of power to atone for human sins or obtain God's favor and forgiveness, and much less that God forgave them their sins simply because Jesus had shed his blood. Nowhere in the New Testament is Jesus spoken of as interceding to God with his blood in heaven. If his first followers did conceive of such an idea, perhaps by recalling images of the Jewish priests interceding before God with sacrificial blood, they would have understood this not in the sense that Jesus' spilled blood now put God under obligation to forgive their sins but rather in the sense that, through his death, Jesus had obtained God's acceptance and forgiveness for all who would live under his lordship. Thanks to their relation with Jesus and their inclusion among those who lived under the new covenant established through his death and his exaltation to God's right hand, from where Jesus interceded on their behalf, they could have assurance that God forgave and accepted them.

One sacrificial image that appears nowhere in the New Testament is that of the goat for Azazel or scapegoat mentioned in Lev. 16:20-26. In spite of this, due to the influence of penal substitution ideas, scholars have repeatedly claimed that Jesus' first followers believed that the loading of sins on the scapegoat and its subsequent death prefigured the way in which the sins of the world would be laid upon Jesus, who would die for those sins on the cross.

In reality, however, there is no evidence that Jesus' first followers applied scapegoat imagery to Jesus or his death in that sense. Even Hebrews, which stresses so strongly the Day of Atonement rites prescribed in Leviticus 16, never alludes to the scapegoat ritual. The first explicit comparisons between Jesus and the scapegoat appear in the second century in the *Epistle of Barnabas* and Justin's *Dialogue with Trypho*. While Barnabas sees the cursing of the scapegoat as comparable to the way in which Christ was cursed, he sees not God but the Jewish leaders as the ones who pronounced that curse (*Barn.* 7:6-11). Justin also sees the scapegoat as a type of Christ in the sense that the priests and elders laid hands on Christ and sent him off to die (*Dial.* 40:4). For Justin, the two goats symbolize the two comings of Christ, the first of which involved suffering, humiliation, and death. Neither *Barnabas* nor Justin make any mention, however, of the idea that the sins of God's people are taken away by the goat for Azazel.

There is no reason, therefore, to think that Jesus' first followers associated Jesus' death with the death of the scapegoat on the Day of Atonement rites. While they associated the forgiveness of sins with Jesus' death, which they considered sacrificial, they believed that no one's sins were taken away without repentance and a commitment to living according to God's will. Nothing would lead them to think that their sins had been laid on Jesus when he died and in that way had disappeared from God's sight. As we have seen, sacrifice was never understood in that sense in the Hebrew Scriptures or ancient Judaism. Even if at some point Jesus' followers did come to view Jesus' death in relation to the way sin was said to be loaded on the scapegoat and removed from God's sight, they would have understood this in symbolic fashion, just as the Jews in antiquity understood that rite. Unlike the scapegoat, however, Jesus had ascended to God's presence to be at his side in glory forever rather than being left out in the wilderness to die and decay.

Jesus' Death and the Christus Victor *Idea*

As we saw in Chapter 1, in recent decades many New Testament scholars have claimed that Jesus' first followers drew on ideas derived from apocalyptic thought to make sense of his death. According to these scholars, Jesus' followers considered his death to be some type of "cosmic event" that had put an end to the world as it had been previously and had ushered in a new age.[31] Some have affirmed that Jesus was thought to have engaged and defeated apocalyptic powers of sin and evil.[32] In particular, Jesus' followers supposedly believed that Jesus had taken on Satan and overcome him. In this way, even though evil in the world had not yet been done away with definitively, Jesus had achieved the decisive victory over the evil powers, thereby assuring their ultimate defeat. All that was left was a "mopping-up" operation.

Undoubtedly, there are several New Testament passages that speak of Jesus achieving a victory over Satan and the forces of evil (John 12:31; Col. 2:15; Heb. 2:14). There is no reason, however, to read these in ontological terms, as if some actual cosmic, apocalyptic victory had been fought and won by Jesus in some invisible or other-worldly sphere. Undoubtedly, in the New Testament writings, Satan and the forces of evil are presented as being active during Jesus' last days and hours through figures such as Judas and the human authorities who had Jesus put to death, as we noted in Chapter 9. Seen in the context of the story we have seen previously, what those forces of evil were thought to have sought was not so much to destroy Jesus, but to dissuade him from being faithful to his mission. This is what Satan was thought to have been doing in the stories concerning Jesus' temptation at the outset of the Synoptics and through Peter when he rejected the notion that Jesus might suffer and die in Jerusalem (Matt. 4:1-11; 16:22-23; Mark 1:13; 8:32-33; Luke 4:1-13).

The sense in which Jesus would be thought to have defeated Satan and these other forces of evil, therefore, was simply that he had not allowed them to dissuade him from his commitment to doing God's will, in spite of the consequences. Undoubtedly, those powers could be said to have accomplished some type of victory over Jesus by having him put to death. In the end, however, Jesus' faithfulness unto death had made it possible for God's plan of bringing about a new, obedient people through Jesus to continue and eventually reach its consummation some day. When that day came, evil would come to an end, together with all those who unrepentantly persisted in practicing evil.

---

31. Such an idea is especially associated with Rudolf Bultmann, who spoke of Christ's death as a "cosmic event" and maintained that, for Paul, Christ's death and resurrection are "cosmic occurrences" that ushered in the new age and the new humankind (*Theology of the New Testament*, trans. Kendrick Grobel; New York: Scribner, 1951, 1:296, 299-300).

32. See, for example, Beker, *Paul*, 182-208; Beverly Roberts Gaventa, "Interpreting the Death of Jesus Apocalyptically: Reconsidering Romans 8:32," in *Jesus and Paul Reconnected: Fresh Pathways into an Old Debate* (ed. Todd D. Still; Grand Rapids: Eerdmans, 2007), 125-45.

While it could therefore be said that Jesus had been victorious over the forces of evil, this would not be understood in the sense that he had physically overpowered those forces by virtue of his divinity, as many of the church fathers later came to claim. In the thought of Jesus' disciples, God had always been capable of overpowering Satan and the forces of evil physically, even without Jesus or his death. To the extent that Jesus was believed to be God's Son, the same was thought to be true of Jesus as well. As God's Son, Jesus had not had to become man, die on a cross, and then rise from the dead in order to defeat Satan and the demonic powers. Nothing in the New Testament suggests that Jesus was thought to have defeated those powers by actively engaging them in combat in some invisible sphere. Nor were those powers thought to now exist in a weakened state or to have been bound in some way so that they were no longer free to act in the way they had prior to Jesus' death. Among Jesus' first followers, the defeat of those powers would take place at the *eschaton*, when Jesus would return to establish God's reign in its fullness. In the meantime, they remained just as active as they had been previously. Similarly, their ultimate defeat was no more certain after Jesus' death than it had been before he died, since in Jewish apocalyptic thought God had always intended to do away with them when the time came. What Jesus had done did not alter this in any way. The one thing that had changed was that, thanks to what God had done through Jesus in his ministry, death, and resurrection, many people were being brought into conformity with God's will and thus were no longer living subject to the power of Satan. If anything, the powers of evil were thought to have responded to this new reality by becoming even more hostile and aggressive toward Jesus' followers.

Jesus' Death and Greco-Roman Beliefs regarding Vicarious Death

Although Jesus' first followers seem to have looked primarily to ideas from their Jewish background to develop their understanding of the salvific significance of Jesus' death, due to the Greek and Roman presence in Palestine during the three centuries prior to Jesus' birth, in principle we cannot rule out the possibility that they were influenced by Hellenistic thought and culture. This means that, as they reflected on Jesus' death, they may have looked to ideas such as those we saw in Chapter 4 with regard to vicarious death and atonement in ancient Greco-Roman literature. While there would be no apparent parallels between the way certain figures had died in the midst of armed conflicts and the way in which Jesus had died, Jesus' first followers might compare his death to that of someone like Socrates, who had died for the truth he had taught. The words attributed to Jesus about drinking from the cup given him by the Father may have been derived directly or indirectly from the tradition regarding Socrates (Matt. 20:22-23; 26:39; Mark 10:38-39; 14:36; Luke 22:42; John 18:11). Of course, there were important differences between the death of Socrates and that of Jesus. Yet both had chosen to die rather than to deny what they regarded as the truth, just as Eleazar, the seven brothers, and the mother had chosen death over disobedience to the law.[33]

Undoubtedly, Jesus' first followers saw his willingness to die if necessary as an expression of the firmness of his convictions about what he had taught and done. What distinguished Jesus from Socrates and the figures mentioned in 2 Maccabees, however, was that in the eyes of Jesus' followers, he had not merely defended and died for some truth, principle, or law independent of himself, but for the claims he had made regarding his divine identity and authority. His resurrection had also provided divine confirmation of the truth of those claims.

For the most part, however, it does not appear that Jesus' followers looked to Greco-Roman accounts regarding figures who had died for their country or law in order to develop their own understanding of the salvific significance of his death.[34] To do so would have involved identifying God with the enemies who attacked the people on behalf of whom the heroic figure had died, and thus to affirm that Jesus had to die to save people from God himself. Nor did Jesus' followers derive their interpretations of Jesus' death from Greco-Roman ideas regarding the manner in which the death or blood of an individual could appease the wrath of the gods, since the God Jesus had proclaimed was very different from the gods of the nations, whose wrath was aroused not by sin and injustice but by the failure of human beings to give them the sacrifices and offerings that they needed or desired.

THE COMMON, SHARED FORMULAS USED TO REFER TO JESUS' DEATH

On the basis of everything we have seen in our study up to this point, we can now finally turn to the question of how Jesus' first followers understood the type of formulaic allusions to his death mentioned at the outset of Chapter 1 of this work. As I have argued there, the fact that the same kinds of formula appear scattered throughout the various writings that make up the New

---

33. On the comparison between the death of Socrates and that of Jesus, as well as the possible influence—whether direct or indirect—that the story of Socrates's death had on the thought of Jesus' followers, see especially Wenhua Shi, *Paul's Message of the Cross as Body Language* (WUNT 2/254; Tübingen: Mohr Siebeck, 2008), 53-66, 78-80. Greg Sterling has argued convincingly that Luke made use of the traditions regarding Socrates in composing his passion narrative ("*Mors philosophi*: The Death of Jesus in Luke," *HTR* 94 [2001]: 383-402).

34. In fact, Jeffrey B. Gibson has argued that, when the first believers affirmed that Jesus had died for the sins of others, they wished to contrast the death of Jesus with that of other figures who were said to have died for others in Greco-Roman literature: "I would suggest that in using this 'dying formula' Paul was engaged in a profound polemic against the prevailing values of his day with respect to what ordinarily was thought to create personal and public 'salvation' (*sōtēria*). The one whose death Paul proclaims as salvific is the very antithesis of those who in the secular instances of the 'dying formula' are known, proclaimed, and honored as having brought about peace and security through their deaths. Instead of seeking or grasping *doxa*, he shuns it (Phil. 2:6-8). Instead of engaging in or embracing war when he dies, he embraces defenselessness. Instead of dying for his own, he dies for his enemies" ("Paul's 'Dying Formula': Prolegomena to an Understanding of Its Import and Significance," in *Celebrating Romans, Template for Pauline Theology: Essays in Honor of Robert Jewett*; ed. Sheila E. McGinn; Grand Rapids: Eerdmans, 2004, 39; see 22-39).

Testament suggests that, by the time those writings were composed, those formulas had already been in widespread use for some time and formed part of a tradition shared by communities of Jesus' followers in many different places. Sumney, for example, has argued that, because in Paul's letters there is no evidence of disagreements with others over the meaning of Jesus' death and its centrality, and because Paul repeatedly uses traditional formulas to refer to Jesus' death without bothering to explain how those formulas should be understood, there can be little doubt that he believed that throughout all of the communities of believers, there was a common understanding of the significance of Jesus' death.[35] We might say that a kind of "shorthand" or encoded language had arisen within those communities that enabled Jesus' followers to summarize or encapsulate in a short phrase the wide variety of ideas that they associated with Jesus' death and the meaning that his death had for them. The use of such formulaic phrases made it possible for them to allude quickly and easily to an entire constellation of shared beliefs regarding Jesus and what he had done without having to mention all of those beliefs explicitly or explain exactly what they meant each time they wished to refer to the way in which they had been saved by means of Jesus' death.[36]

While the New Testament writings use a variety of formulas to allude to the salvific significance of Jesus' death, for our purposes here we can categorize them under five different groupings: 1) those that speak of Jesus suffering or dying for or on behalf of others; 2) those that affirm that he obtained some salvific benefit for others through his death or blood; 3) those that use the language of redemption or acquisition; 4) those that relate his death to the sins or transgressions of others; and 5) those that refer to believers suffering and dying together with Jesus.

Undoubtedly, to categorize in this way the different formulas used in the New Testament to allude to Jesus' death involves including under each grouping a variety of different phrases that were not necessarily interchangeable or entirely synonymous with one another. This means that we must exercise caution when attempting to reconstruct what the different phrases may have meant and avoid assuming that phrases that are similar to others convey the exact same ideas. We must also not assume that a certain phrase would mean the same thing in different contexts. Nevertheless, we must not overlook the fact that those who composed the New Testament writings used the same types of formula in addressing readers with whom they were often not personally acquainted. They thus presupposed that their readers would be able to understand the formulaic phrases they used without difficulty. Even if they could not be sure that the readers were familiar with the exact phrase they used, they could expect that the readers would understand that phrase on the

---

35. See Sumney, "Christ Died For Us'," 164-70.

36. Wolter agrees that many of the "soteriological formulas" that appear in Paul's letters were taken over from older Christian communities, yet he also notes that, among New Testament scholars today, "the possibility of identifying or indeed of reconstructing such 'formulas' is assessed with skepticism, for good reasons" (*Paul*, 95). Precisely for that reason, I will not enter into such a discussion in the present work.

basis of their acquaintance with similar phrases that communicated the same basic ideas.

There are, of course, a number of formulas used in the New Testament to speak of the salvific significance of Jesus' death that do not fit under any of the five headings just listed. Nevertheless, because those formulas appear only in the writings of a single author, such as Paul, or are relatively infrequent in the New Testament writings, we cannot assume that they were as widely known and used as the phrases to be considered here under the five headings mentioned.

Because the purpose of this section is to discern the way in which the formulaic phrases most frequently used in the New Testament to speak of Jesus' death would have been understood by his first followers collectively in the different communities of which they formed part, here we will not analyze the particular passages in which those phrases appear. The question of what those formulas meant in general terms must be distinguished from the question of what those formulas meant in each of the contexts in which they were used. Once we have explored the ways in which Jesus' first followers collectively would have understood the different formulas, we can then analyze each occurrence of those formulas in the New Testament texts to ask why the author of a certain writing chose to use a particular formula in the context of his argument or narrative. In other words, in this section we will look at the most common formulas that the authors of the New Testament writings had at their disposal to refer to the salvific significance of Jesus' death, while in Chapters 11–16 we will examine the ways in which they used those formulas to articulate the ideas that they wanted to communicate to those to whom they wrote.

Jesus' Death "For Us"

The most common and briefest of the formulas found in the New Testament to refer to the salvific significance of Jesus' death are those that speak of him dying "for" others. Usually the preposition *huper* is employed in these formulas, although in several passages *peri* appears instead. In one instance, the *lutron* saying of Mark 10:45 and Matt. 20:28, we find the preposition *anti*, which implies some type of exchange.

Generally, these phrases leave open the question of the persons or group to whom they refer. Jesus is said simply to die or give his life up "for us," "for you," or "for the many." The phrase "for all" is found in a number of passages, yet that phrase does not necessarily refer to all human beings universally. "All" may mean all believers or Jews and gentiles together, rather than just one of the two groups, without necessarily implying that every member of both groups is included. It can also be understood as referring to all of the members of a particular group or to the author together with the readers, as in the phrase "all of us." On one occasion, Paul even affirms that Jesus gave himself "for me" (Gal. 2:20). Obviously, he does not mean to exclude others with the use of this phrase. On the contrary, its use seems to invite others to make the same type of affirmation regarding themselves.

When the phrase "for you" is used, it generally seems to refer not only to the listeners or readers, but to others as well. Thus, for example, as we noted in Chapter 5, when Luke and Paul present Jesus telling the disciples at the Last Supper, "This is my body (given) for you" (Luke 22:19; 1 Cor. 11:24), they seem to understand Jesus' words as referring not only to those who were present with him at that moment, but also to others who would come to faith and share in future celebrations of the meal he had instituted.

Particularly ambiguous is the phrase "for us." When used in these kinds of formulas, it generally seems to refer to the church or community of believers. In theory, however, it could also refer to human beings in general. Therefore, its meaning must be determined by its context, although at times even when viewed in context it remains ambiguous. In some New Testament passages, in fact, the ambiguity may be intentional.

In considering this phrase, however, it is important to remember that the authors of the New Testament writings were not contemplating that what they wrote would be read some twenty centuries later by people around the world of many different cultures and languages. It is common for Christian interpreters, including many biblical scholars, to read New Testament passages as if they referred directly to believers today. Commenting on Paul's language in Romans 6, for example, Brice Martin writes that "the Christian has been set free from sin by Christ's death," and that "[b]y participation in Christ's death and resurrection we have died to sin (6:1-23).... We are no longer under the rule of sin but of grace."[37] However, when Paul spoke in these terms, whether or not he was referring to all people generally or only believers, he had in mind those living in his day rather than ours. It is of course likely that he believed that in the years and even decades to follow, the world would continue to exist and many more people would be incorporated into the church Jesus had founded. Nevertheless, we cannot and must not simply assume that he had future generations in mind when he used such language, since he was addressing his letters only to a particular group of people in his own day. As was mentioned in the Introduction to this work, while Christians today certainly identify themselves with those to whom the New Testament writings were addressed, to see those writings as referring to people of our own time interferes with the task of reconstructing their original meaning in their own historical context.

Due to the influence of penal substitution ideas in New Testament scholarship, the preposition *huper* has often been understood in the sense that Jesus did something in the place of others rather than on their behalf. In fact, for a long time it has been so commonplace to claim that *huper* is synonymous with *anti* that scholars feel no need to argue in favor of such a claim. While undoubtedly the meaning of prepositions is always extremely variable, there is

---

37. Martin, *Christ*, 109.

no reason to read ideas of substitution or exchange back into the texts that use *huper* in relation to Jesus' suffering and death. The normal meaning of *huper* is simply "on behalf of" or "in favor of." Throughout the New Testament, *huper* is used particularly when referring to prayer on behalf of someone else.[38]

When Jesus' first followers spoke of Jesus having suffered, died, or given up his life on behalf of others, they probably had in mind a combination of ideas rather than a single meaning. On the basis of the story they told, above all they would have meant that Jesus had died seeking the salvation of others, including of course not only those who were his followers at the time of his death, but also those who would come to believe in and follow him after his death and resurrection.

Since the time of the Reformation, Protestant theologians have debated over the question of whether Jesus died for all people or only for believers. This debate is based on the mistaken assumption that Jesus' death was believed to fulfill some necessary condition in order for human beings to be forgiven and saved. According to penal substitution views, this condition was that he undergo the penalty to which others were subject on account of their sins. The question then becomes whether in his death Jesus fulfilled the necessary condition for *all* people to be forgiven and saved or only for *believers*.

This understanding of Jesus' death was entirely foreign to the thought of Jesus' first followers. For them, Jesus' death in itself did not fulfill some condition that made it possible for God to forgive and save human beings. As we have seen, in ancient Jewish thought and the thought of Jesus' first followers, the condition for people to be forgiven and saved was that they repent of their sins and commit themselves to living in accordance with God's will. In the mind of his first followers, Jesus had gone to his death hoping that, as a result of his death, people from all over the world would be brought to repent and live as God desired by being incorporated into his community of followers. In that sense, he had offered up his life for *all people*. When they spoke of Jesus dying for all people, however, Jesus' first followers had in mind only the people of their day and perhaps future generations who would hear the gospel. The only sense in which Jesus could be said to have died for people of previous generations or people from faraway places who would never hear the gospel was that, through his death, he had sought to be exalted to a position of power and authority as Lord so that he might some day raise the dead and bring about the salvation of people who had lived in diverse times and places. As I argued at the end of Chapter 7, in New Testament thought, those who had been committed to practicing righteousness and justice on the basis of the knowledge of God and God's will that they had received would be saved, even if they did not know of Christ.

While the salvation Jesus had sought for others in life and death undoubtedly had to do with the well-being of people in the present age, in the minds

---

38. See, for example, Matt. 5:44; Acts 8:24; Rom. 8:27, 34; 10:1; 15:30; 2 Cor. 1:11; 9:14; Eph. 1:16; 5:20; 6:19; Phil. 1:4; Col. 1:9; 4:12.

of his first followers, what he had ultimately sought in life and death was the coming of God's reign. At that time all would be able to experience God's blessings in definitive fashion. Because his followers were convinced that Jesus himself was the one who would serve as God's instrument to establish that reign and usher in the awaited new age, they must have thought that Jesus had died asking that God make that reign a reality through him. At the same time, it was obvious to Jesus' followers that neither God's reign nor the new age they longed for had been established yet. Instead, what had happened was that, following his death, Jesus had been exalted to God's side, from where he would come again in glory and power in order to bring to pass what God had promised.

From the perspective of his followers, then, Jesus had attained the salvation of others in a proleptic sense. By remaining faithful to his Father's will up until his last breath, he had obtained from the Father the response he desired, since he had now received the power and authority to bring about the salvation of others at his second coming. Of course, the reason God had raised and exalted Jesus was that, through his faithfulness unto death, he had shown himself to be worthy and capable of being God's instrument to bring about the salvation of others. Just as Jesus had been seeking power, not for his own sake, but for the sake of others, so also God had raised Jesus, not only for his own sake, but so that he might accomplish the salvation of others that God desired to bring to pass through Jesus. It is a mistake, therefore, to claim that God's primary purpose in raising Jesus was merely to vindicate him or correct the injustice committed against him.[39] While Jesus' first followers probably conceived of Jesus' resurrection in these terms, they were also convinced that God had raised and exalted Jesus for *their* sake. Just as God had sent Jesus for their sake—not for the sake of God himself or Jesus—and had handed him over to death for their sake, so also God had raised Jesus for their sake.

Because it was necessary for people to repent of their sins and live according to God's will in order to be saved, Jesus' followers no doubt came to believe that Jesus had also given up his life in order to make it possible for this condition to be fulfilled in those who would come to believe in him. As he faced death, he had desired and asked God to be raised, not only so that he might return some day to bring in God's reign, but also so that he might continue to be active in the world from God's side in the present by pouring out the Holy Spirit on others, by illuminating and guiding them through that Spirit, by presiding over the community of those who would live under him as Lord, and by working through his followers to bring others to faith in him. In other words, Jesus' followers believed that as he went to Jerusalem and then to his death, Jesus had had in mind not only the definitive establishment of God's

---

39. Marinus de Jonge, for example, is typical in seeing Jesus' resurrection as "his personal vindication" ("Jesus' Rôle in the Final Breakthrough of God's Kingdom," in *Geschichte–Tradition–Reflexion: Festschrift für Martin Hengel zum 70. Geburtstag*, Band III: *Frühes Christentum*; ed. Hermann Lichtenberger; Tübingen: J. C. B. Mohr, 1996, 285).

reign, but also all that he would do in the time between his resurrection and his second coming to bring others into communion with God through himself so that they might participate in that reign.

Of course, it was not only what Jesus would do after he had risen that made it possible for believers to live in a new way, but all that he had done during his ministry and the way he had faced his death when that ministry led to conflict. Therefore, he could also be said to have died for others in the sense that he had willingly endured the consequences of his dedication to bring about in others a life of conformity to God's will through everything he had taught and embodied in his life and death. Thanks to Jesus' willingness to give his life for them both during his ministry and in his last days and hours, by denying themselves, taking up their cross, and following Jesus, believers could now experience God's salvation in the present age as well as the age to come.

The belief that the glorified Jesus continued to intercede for others from God's side in heaven would also lead Jesus' first followers to conclude that, as he went to his death, he had sought not only that he might remain active in and among his followers once he had risen, but also that he might carry out that ministry of intercession on their behalf. He had also died for them in that sense. The basis for his intercession was the new way of living that was being brought about in his followers by his past, present and future ministry on their behalf. His past ministry had provided others with the understanding necessary to do God's will. In various ways, that ministry had also laid the foundation for the community of followers of which they now formed part to exist and to take the shape it did. His present ministry from heaven involved pouring out the Holy Spirit to strengthen and guide the members of his community in the way that they should live in order that they might form part of God's reign. That heavenly ministry included petitioning God to provide them with all that they needed so that they might remain constant and faithful. The community of followers Jesus had prepared and established during his lifetime also served as a means by which he continued to be active both among believers and in the world at large. In addition, Jesus' future activity of returning to raise the dead and establish God's reign definitively transformed his followers in the present, since it gave them hope and thereby strengthened them in their faith and commitment to follow him. Thus Jesus could be said to have died for others in the sense that he had given up his life so that all that he had done for others in the past and all that he would continue to do for others in the present and future might bear fruit and enable people from around the world to attain the salvation he had sought for them by living under his lordship.

Jesus' death had also served the purpose of bringing about in others the same total commitment to God's will that he had manifested throughout his life, and particularly in his last days and hours. Only by assuming that commitment himself could he hope to see it in others. Assuming that commitment, however, meant assuming its consequences as well, and therefore dying on behalf of others in order to bring about in them that same commitment for their own sake. As we have noted previously, this did not mean that Jesus had died simply to provide an example for others to follow. While he did wish for others to offer up their lives for others as he had done and was continuing to do as he went to his death, this was not something that they would simply do on their own independently of him by attempting to imitate what he had done for its own sake. The example they were to follow was *not that of suffering and dying, but rather being willing to endure all things in order to live for God and others like Jesus.* By giving up his life for them, what Jesus sought was not the suffering and death of his followers, but their dedication to sharing with others the love, compassion, and justice he had taught and embodied, thereby giving witness to his lordship of service. What Jesus had wanted was not that others *imitate* him, but that they *follow* him as their Lord.

Another sense in which Jesus could be said to have died for others is that, through his death and the ministry that had led to his death, Jesus had come to define God's will for them. In order to attain the promises associated with God's reign, people needed to be committed to living according to God's will. However, they could only live according to God's will if they understood what that will consisted of. While Jesus' teaching and ministry had led them to grasp more clearly what God's will entailed, it was his death more than anything else that came to define God's will as a life of total trust in God and an absolute dependence on God's goodness, grace, and mercy, as well as a willingness to love others unconditionally and dedicate oneself to the well-being of all, as Jesus had done. Jesus' death had thus been for others in that it had enabled them both to know what God's will consisted of and to live in accordance with that will. What motivated his followers to strive to live according to that will was not only their conviction that true life, peace, and happiness could be attained only by living in the way that Jesus had lived, but also their belief that, if they followed the same path that Jesus himself had followed, they would be raised to the life of the new age as he had been.

Jesus' death would also be understood as being for others in the sense that it was the ultimate and supreme expression of everything he had stood for and attempted to accomplish in others. In fact, Jesus' followers would have believed that when he had taught his disciples and others who had heard him, he had been thinking not only of them, but also of others who would come to hear his words through them. Jesus could be said to have *died* for others not merely because of what he had done in his last days and hours, but because his death was the consequence of *all* that he had done for others throughout his ministry, which had generated conflict with the authorities and had ultimately led them to have him crucified. Under those circumstances, Jesus had embraced death so that his followers would be able to stand for everything he had stood for and also help to lead even more people to do the same so that they might attain life not only for themselves but for others.

As already noted above, according to numerous passages in the New Testament, Jesus' followers believed that Jesus had taught his disciples that a period of time would pass between his resurrection and his second coming. During this time, the gospel would be proclaimed to both the Jews and the nations, enabling many to come to faith in Jesus so as to take part in God's reign. Jesus would therefore be seen as having died for others in the sense that his death had opened up a window that made it possible for many others to be saved through the proclamation of the gospel around the world. Not only did Jesus' death create more time for the expansion of the gospel and the church, but it also served to prepare, strengthen, and embolden his apostles and disciples to go out into the world to share the gospel with others. By seeing how Jesus had died and how God had responded to his death, they received assurance that if they followed him in sharing with others the gospel of God's reign, they had no reason to fear what might happen to them, since one way or another, God would take care of them as he had taken care of Jesus.

According to this logic, Jesus could even be said to have died for particular individuals, such as Paul or the brothers and sisters for whom he had died in Corinth and Rome (Gal. 2:20; 1 Cor. 8:11; Rom. 14:15). This was not because either God or Jesus had contemplated the salvation of those individuals ahead of time, but rather because, from even before creation, God had intended to bring into existence through his Son an obedient people composed of persons from all the nations of the world. In fulfillment of this intention, Christ had died so that all persons, whether Jew or gentile, might come to form part of this people. Therefore, whoever came to belong to the community for which Christ had given up his life could affirm that Christ had died *for him or for her*, that is, so that he or she might come to form part of this new people under Christ's lordship. In the same way, each believer could say that she or he had been chosen by God before creation, not because God had foreseen the future existence of that believer and had chosen her or him personally by name, but because that believer had been incorporated into the community of people that God had foreseen and elected before creation. As Wolter observes with regard to Rom. 14:15 and 1 Cor. 8:11, "each person who belongs to the Christian community becomes one 'for whom Christ died'."[40]

On this basis, then, we can see that when Jesus' first followers affirmed that Jesus had suffered, died, or given up his life for others, they had a wide array of distinct but inseparably connected ideas in mind. It also becomes evident, however, that there is no need or reason to read back into these texts the notion that Jesus had died in the stead of others. In his death, Jesus had not undergone something that others would no longer have to undergo now that he had done so. He had not suffered instead of others, since his followers would still suffer as he did. He had not died instead of others, since all but those who would be alive when he returned in glory would still die. He had not saved them from eternal condemnation by enduring eternal condemnation in

---

40. Wolter, *Paul*, 109-10.

their stead, since neither his death on the cross nor his descent into Hades to preach the gospel there involved suffering eternal condemnation. He had not saved others from God's judgment by enduring that judgment in their place, since all would still be judged by him and by God through him. The assurance believers had that they would be judged favorably in the end rested, not on Jesus' death or blood per se, but on the new life of love and obedience that God had now graciously brought about in them through their faith in Christ, their crucified Lord. Thus it is important to avoid reading back into the texts that speak of Jesus' suffering and death being for others ideas that arose in later Christian theology and continue to be affirmed by interpreters today.

Jesus' Death or Blood as the Means of Salvation

Throughout the New Testament, we find formulaic sayings that affirm that believers have been redeemed, purchased, justified, sanctified, cleansed, brought near, and reconciled to God *through* Jesus' blood or death. Three types of phrases are used in Greek to express this idea: the preposition *dia* with the genitive (Acts 20:28; Rom. 5:10; Eph. 1:7; Col. 1:20-22; Heb. 13:12), the dative of means (1 Pet. 1:18-19), and *en* with the dative (Rom. 5:9; Eph. 2:13; Heb. 10:19; Rev. 1:5; 5:9; 7:14; cf. Rom. 3:25). In each case, the Greek phrase refers to the *means* by which something is accomplished.

The influence of penal substitution thought in New Testament scholarship has repeatedly led scholars to interpret these passages in the sense that Jesus' death or blood fulfilled some condition that made it possible for God to declare unrighteous, sinful believers righteous in a forensic sense so that they might be saved. This involves attributing some type of atoning power to Jesus' death or blood, which is said to *effect* redemption, justification, cleansing from sin, and reconciliation with God.

This understanding of Jesus' death or blood can be attributed at least in part to the influence of the English, German, French, and Spanish translations of the New Testament that have been used by Western interpreters. In all of these languages, the preposition that expresses the *means* by which something is accomplished is also used to refer to the *agent* of constructions with a passive voice. In English this is *by*, in German *durch*, in French *par*, and in Spanish *por*. The result of this is that, even though scholars acquainted with the Greek original of these diverse formulas are aware that they refer to the means by which something is accomplished rather than the agent or instrument accomplishing it, when they and others have read the relevant texts in their own language, they tend to read the latter idea back into those texts. In Greek, this would be equivalent to replacing the prepositions *dia* or *en* with *hupo* plus the genitive case of the noun in many of the formulas found in the New Testament. For example, in Rom. 5:9-10, Paul uses the Greek phrases *dikaiōthentes en tō haimati autou*, "justified by means of his blood," and *katēllagēmen tō theō dia tou thanatou autou*, "we were reconciled to God through [Jesus'] death." The meaning of these phrases changes considerably if we substitute the prepositions *en* and *dia* with *hupo* so as to affirm that believers are justified *by* his blood, *dikaiōthentes hupo tou haimatos autou*, and were reconciled to God *by* his death, *katēllagēmen tō theō hupo tou thanatou autou*. This is equivalent to affirming that Jesus' blood in itself has justified believers and that his death in itself reconciled them to God.

If we look at Rom. 5:9-10 in the versions of the Bible that have been most widely used and thus most highly influential among Christians and biblical interpreters over the past four centuries, we can see that they translate the passage in ways that imply that the Greek preposition used is *hupo* rather than *dia* or *en*:

> Much more then, being now justified *by his blood*, we shall be saved from wrath through him. For if, when we were enemies, we were reconciled to God *by the death of his Son*, much more, being reconciled, we shall be saved by his life (KJV).

> Since, therefore, we are now justified *by his blood*, much more shall we be saved by him from the wrath of God. For if while we were enemies we were reconciled to God *by the death of his Son*, much more, now that we are reconciled, shall we be saved by his life (RSV).

> So werden wir ja viel mehr durch ihn bewahrt werden vor dem Zorn, nachdem wir *durch sein Blut* gerecht geworden sind. Denn so wir Gott versöhnt sind *durch den Tod seines Sohnes*, da wir noch Feinde waren, viel mehr werden wir selig werden durch sein Leben, so wir nun versöhnt sind (Luther Bibel 1545).

> A plus forte raison donc, maintenant que nous sommes justifiés *par son sang*, serons-nous sauvés par lui de la colère. Car si, lorsque nous étions ennemis, nous avons été réconciliés avec Dieu *par la mort de son Fils*, à plus forte raison, étant réconciliés, serons-nous sauvés par sa vie (Louis Segond 1910).[41]

> Luego mucho más ahora, justificados *en su sangre*, por él seremos salvos de la ira. Porque si siendo enemigos, fuimos reconciliado con Dios *por la muerte de su Hijo*, mucho más, estando reconciliados, seremos salvos por su vida (Reina-Valera antigua)

All of these translations lend themselves to ambiguity. They can give the impression that justification and reconciliation with God are the *effect of* Jesus' death or blood. When read in this way, they lend support for the traditional views of atonement, which claim that Jesus' death or blood in itself satisfied God's justice and thus effected the justification of believers and their reconciliation with God.

The way in which the New Testament formulas are understood changes significantly when the idea of means is stressed in the translation used. In English, this would be: "Much more surely then, now that we have been justified *by means of* his blood, will we be saved through him from the wrath of God. For if while we were enemies, we were reconciled to God *by means of* the death of his Son, much more surely, having been reconciled, will we be saved

---

41. The *Bible de Théodore de Bèze 1588* translates these verses: "Beaucoup plustost donc, estans maintenant iustifiés *en son sang*, serons-nous sauvés de l'ire par lui. Car si lors que nous estions ennemis, nous avons esté reconciliés à Dieu *par la mort de son Fils*; beaucoup plustost, estans desia reconciliés, serons-nous sauvés par la vie d'icelui" (Rom. 5:9-10).

by means of his life" (Rom. 5:9-10). Such a translation not only preserves the meaning of the original Greek text, but also precludes the idea that Jesus' death *in itself* justifies believers or reconciles them to God.

If the affirmations that believers have been redeemed, purchased, justified, sanctified, cleansed, brought near, and reconciled to God through Jesus' blood or death are understood on the basis of the story told by Jesus' first followers as we have reconstructed it in this chapter and the previous ones, the meaning of those affirmations is relatively simple and straightforward. Both Jesus' blood and his death would be understood as referring to his faithfulness unto death in seeking the salvation of others, as well as the manner in which he offered his life up to God on behalf of others with the same objective. By giving up his life in accordance with his Father's will, he had brought into existence a community of people committed to obeying God and living in love in the way Jesus himself had done. Those who form part of that community have become God's possession, practice justice and righteousness, and live a holy and pure life. They are redeemed and cleansed from their former way of living so as to be reconciled to God. On that basis, they are accepted by God as righteous, holy, and pure and can approach God confidently through Jesus, in spite of the fact that they are not without sin. All of these things are now possible, however, because Jesus was willing to give up his life so that they might become a reality. His blood or death was therefore the *means* by which God accomplished his salvific purposes, creating a community of people who now live as God's own under the lordship of the crucified and risen Jesus.

For Jesus' first followers, therefore, it was not Jesus' death in itself that was salvific, but the life and ministry that had preceded it, the manner in which he had given up his life rather than seeking to save it, and all that God had done and would continue to do through Jesus after he had given Jesus over to death and then raised him. Nevertheless, because Jesus' death represented the ultimate and supreme expression of the love of God and Jesus himself and constituted the basis for all that followed upon that death, including Jesus' exaltation as Lord over all and the existence of a community of people committed to living in the way God had always desired, the authors of the New Testament repeatedly point to Jesus' blood or death in particular as the *means* by which the new reality believers now experience has been brought about.

Redemption and Acquisition through Jesus' Death

The language of redemption was used in various ways in antiquity in both Jewish and Greco-Roman literature. In general, it had to to with the purchase or acquisition of either goods or people.[42] The idea of restoring someone or

---

42. On the background and usage of the language of liberation, acquisition, and redemption in Greek and Hebrew writings in antiquity, see especially Stanislas Lyonnet, "The Terminology of Redemption," in *Sin, Redemption and Sacrifice: A Biblical and Patristic Study* (Lyonnet and Léopold Sabourin; AnBib 48; Rome: Biblical Institute, 1970), 79-119. For a survey of research on the metaphors of redemption in New Testament scholarship, see D. Francois Tolmie, "Salvation as Redemption: The Use of 'Redemption' Metaphors in Pauline Literature," in *Salvation in the New Testament*, ed. van der Watt, 247-51.

something to a previous state or a state in which that person or thing originally or naturally belonged was also associated with the language of redemption. Thus, one might redeem some object or property that one had previously owned from the one who had come to possess it either by right or through some act of injustice. If one had given some object in pledge to another in exchange for a loan, for example, one redeemed that object by means of a payment. If a person had been sold into slavery or forcibly enslaved as a result of violence or war, that person might be redeemed through some type of ransom payment or exchange. Slaves might also redeem themselves in the sense of purchasing their freedom from their master. This would restore them to a condition of liberty.

Throughout the Hebrew Scriptures, the verbs *padah* and *ga'al* are used to speak of redeeming goods, property, and persons. The basic idea was that of acquiring or reacquiring something or someone that was previously or rightfully one's own through some type of payment or act. As we saw in Chapter 3, in the case of both persons and animals, the first-born were considered to belong to God, yet they might be bought back from God through a sacrificial gift so as to be reincorporated into their family or, in the case of animals, into their flock. It is important to stress, however, that these payments or offerings were not seen as penalties or punishments. Rather, they were merely means by which one acquired or reacquired something one desired.

The language of redemption could thus be used in a wide variety of ways and in many different senses. Such language particularly lent itself to metaphorical usage. Even today, we use the language of redemption metaphorically: one is said to "redeem oneself," for example, by doing something to make up for a wrong or an error one has committed. Obviously, when used in a metaphorical sense, redemption does not involve any type of actual monetary exchange or transaction.

The Hebrew Scriptures frequently use the language of redemption metaphorically. In particular, God is said to have redeemed Israel from Egypt or from bondage or captivity to other peoples.[43] In this case, the idea is that the people originally and by right belonged to YHWH as his possession. They needed to be redeemed, however, when they came to be held captive by another people or ruler, either because this other people or ruler had unjustly enslaved them, as in the case of Pharoah and the Egyptians, or because God had chastised the people by subjecting them to a foreign power in order to correct or discipline them. Some scholars have argued that, by definition, redemption always involved the payment of a price. Supposedly, even when God himself redeemed his people, he inevitably paid a price, namely, that of expending some effort or energy in order to rescue or liberate his people.[44]

---

43. See, for example, Exod. 6:6; 15:13; Ps. 25:22; 107:2-3; Isa. 35:10; Jer. 31:11.

44. Leon Morris, for example, argues that the word *lutron* "necessarily involves thought of a ransom price, a substitute, this being demanded by every occurrence of the term," and that in the Septuagint, "redemption consistently signifies deliverance by payment of a price" (*The Apostolic Preaching of the Cross*, 3rd ed.; Grand Rapids: Eerdmans, 1965, 26-27; cf. 19). Morris also claims that, in biblical thought, the redemption God

Such claims, however, involve forcing the metaphor in a way that goes beyond its original intent or meaning. It seems doubtful that the ancient Hebrews or Jews conceived of God in that way. Just as God had created the world simply with his word, as the all-powerful and sovereign Lord of all, he could accomplish anything he proposed simply by desiring it to be so.

It thus seems likely that when the ancient Hebrews and Jews spoke of God redeeming his people, they did not associate the idea of a payment with God's liberating activity. Rather, the reason that they used the language of redemption was that they wished to stress the idea of God making the people *his own* once more after they had passed into the possession of some other power. Thus, for God to redeem his people went beyond merely rescuing them or liberating them from bondage or oppression. It involved *bringing them back into a relationship* in which they might once more live as his "treasured possession out of all the peoples" (Exod. 19:5; cf. Deut. 26:18). Obviously, God desired this not merely for *his* sake but *for theirs*, due to his love for them. Only by living obediently as his people could they experience the *shalom* that God wanted them to possess.

A variety of terms are used in ancient Greek literature, including the Septuagint and the New Testament, to convey these same basic ideas. The most common of these are words derived from the noun *lutron*, such as the verb *lutroun* and the nouns *lutrōsis* and *apolutrōsis*. At times the Septuagint uses the verbs *ruesthai* and *sōzein* to translate *padah* and *ga'al*, thereby stressing the idea of deliverance, rescue, or salvation, without alluding to any type of payment.[45]

In the New Testament, Luke uses the language of redemption to refer simply to God's act of liberating Israel from its present condition of bondage or subjection to foreign powers. Mary, Anna, and the disciples on the road to Emmaus on the day of Jesus' resurrection are said to have looked forward to the redemption of Israel or Jerusalem (Luke 1:68; 2:38; 24:21; cf. 21:28). Other passages from the New Testament also use the language of redemption simply to speak of the salvation of believers (Rom. 3:24; 8:23-24; 1 Cor. 1:30; Gal. 3:13; 4:6; Eph. 4:30; Tit. 2:14; Heb. 9:12; Rev. 14:3-4). The idea of any type of payment, exchange, or ransom is absent from these passages. In Rom. 8:19–22, Paul speaks of the creation itself being redeemed some day. The idea there is that by right and by nature, creation belongs to God as the maker of all, yet at present it has been "subjected to bondage." Its redemption therefore involves an act of liberation, though once again no type of actual payment is involved. God does not need to "exert some effort" at a cost to himself to deliver creation from its bondage.

---

effects "is not regarded as something he performs with effortless ease.... This stress on Yahweh's effort seems to be the reason for applying the redemption terminology to his dealings. The effort is regarded as the 'price' which gives point to the metaphor. Yahweh's action is at cost to himself" (21-22). Further on, he adds that, "though the idea of price may fade when God is the subject, it never disappears.... [T]he Old Testament writers were not unmindful of the meaning of the words they were applying to God's dealings with his people, for they think of him as delivering at some cost" (27, 29).

45. See, for example, Job 5:20; 6:23; 33:28; Ps. 69:18; Isa. 1:27; 48:20; 54:5, 8; Hosea 13:14.

This general background enables us to understand the way in which the New Testament writings use redemption language in connection with Jesus' death or blood. Such language conveys three basic ideas. First, there is some type of bondage or plight from which sinful human beings must be delivered. This condition of bondage may be attributed to evil powers, the sinful way of life of those enslaved or held captive by their sin, their ignorance or faulty ways of thinking, or their subjection to other people (Mark 10:45; Luke 1:68, 74; Rom. 8:19-24; Gal. 1:4; 3:13; Tit. 2:14; 1 Pet. 1:18; 2 Pet. 2:1).

Second, in addition to being delivered from their condition of bondage, those redeemed are brought into a new condition in which they are not only free, but also have become the possession of God or of Jesus (1 Cor. 6:19-20; 7:23; Eph. 6:6, 9; 1 Pet. 2:9-10; 2 Pet. 2:1). As in biblical and Jewish thought, of course, in a sense this involves a contradiction, since if one becomes the possession of God or of Jesus, it would appear that one is not actually free, but has only passed from one master or owner to another. However, because in the New Testament both God and Jesus are conceived of as being concerned only with the well-being of those who belong to them and wish to be served by them, not out of selfishness, but only so that those serving them may experience the *shalom* that results from that service, those who become the property of God or Jesus and live as the slaves (*douloi*) of God or Jesus are paradoxically seen as being free. In his letter to the Romans, for example, Paul refers to believers both as the slaves of God and as the children of God (Rom. 6:22; 8:14-17; cf. Gal. 4:1-7).

In principle, the redemption of believers could be understood in various ways. As in Jewish thought, redemption could be understood in an eschatological sense as referring to the final condition of salvation that believers will some day attain. It could also be regarded as referring to some type of spiritual or emotional liberation from something that was oppressing them. This might be related to the eschatological redemption in the sense that believers were thought to have obtained peace, joy, and hope due to the certainty they now possessed regarding their future salvation. However, believers could also be said to have been redeemed from a life of sin. In that case, sin would be viewed not as a form of freedom or liberty, as many non-believers undoubtedly thought, but as a type of slavery or oppression. Those who were redeemed from their sinful ways were enabled to leave behind their destructive conduct of the past, which led only to suffering and death, and to live in ways that contributed to their own well-being and that of others.

There is no reason to think that Jesus' first followers believed that their redemption involved some type of mysterious or magical ontological transformation that took place in them. Rather, it was seen simply as a result of following Christ and receiving through him the knowledge, inspiration, and capacity to live according to God's will in the way he had taught and exemplified. The ability to leave behind sin and lead a different life in conformity with God's will is also understood in the New Testament as the fruit of the work of the Holy Spirit, who is said to transform the hearts and minds of believers so that they can follow Christ.

Of course, when believers were said to be redeemed from their former sinful way of life, they were at the same time redeemed from the divine condemnation that resulted from that way of life. A life lived in fear of death or condemnation represents a type of slavery, since one is held captive by one's fears. If the devil is seen as the one through whom God acts in order to impose death or condemnation on those who are sinful and unrepentant, then redemption from death and condemnation is equivalent to redemption from the devil's power (see Heb. 2:14-15).

The third idea that appears repeatedly in the New Testament in relation to the language of redemption is that the sacrificial death or blood of Jesus is the means by which believers are redeemed from their former condition of bondage and accepted into a new condition in which they belong to God and Christ (Matt. 20:28; Mark 10:45; Acts 20:28; Rom. 3:24-25; Gal. 1:4; Eph. 1:17; 1 Tim. 2:5-6; Tit. 2:14; Heb. 9:12; 1 Pet. 1:18-19). Once again, this redemption through Jesus' sacrificial death or blood should be understood on the basis of the same ideas we have seen previously. God had sent Jesus to form around himself a people who would live as God desired. Throughout his ministry, Jesus had dedicated himself to the task of laying the foundation for the existence of that people through his teaching and example, the works he performed, and the formation of disciples who would be prepared to lead and guide others and proclaim the gospel among the nations. Jesus' faithfulness to that task all the way to his death and God's willingness to hand his Son over to death had made it possible for this new, obedient people to come into existence.

In this way, then, believers had been redeemed through Jesus' blood. However, because Jesus was now alive at God's side in heaven, from where he continued to be active on behalf of believers and from where he would return to establish God's reign, the present and future redemption of believers could also be ascribed to Jesus' blood or death. This redemption involved delivering believers from their sinful way of life, but also from the condemnation that resulted from that life. From heaven Jesus continued to work to transform them and on that basis interceded to God asking that God strengthen them and forgive them their sins. At the final judgment, Jesus would also redeem them from God's wrath at sin and injustice. All of this was the result of his having been faithful unto death to the task given him by God.

In a sense, of course, both God and his Son Jesus had paid a high price to bring about this new reality. The price Jesus had paid to redeem others was that of his life, as well as the suffering he had endured throughout his ministry and especially in his last hours. The price his Father had paid was that of seeing his Son suffer at the hands of evildoers and die a cruel death on a Roman cross. There is no indication, however, that Jesus' first followers believed that either Jesus or God had paid a price *to* someone. Jesus was not believed to have effected some type of exchange or transaction with God, as if God had demanded a ransom payment in order to set human beings free from the condemnation to which they were subject. Much less was God thought to have paid a price to himself or to his justice. The idea that God's strict justice made it impossible for him to forgive and accept sinners without receiving the life or blood of an innocent victim was entirely foreign to the thought of Jesus' first followers. Equally foreign to their thought was the idea that Jesus' death constituted a payment made to the devil in order that he might release those who had fallen under his power.

As we saw in Chapters 4 and 5, for this reason it is inappropriate to translate the Greek words *lutron* and *antilutron* as "ransom" when they refer to God liberating his people and making them his own possession. In the minds of his first followers, Jesus' death or blood had not been any type of ransom payment made to God, the devil, or anyone else.[46] Jesus' life (*psuchē*), death, or blood could, however, be seen as a redemption price, even though no type of ransom payment was involved. Just as today we speak of people paying a high price to achieve some goal or objective without implying that they actually make a payment to someone, so also both God and Jesus could be said to have paid a high price to liberate those who would live under Jesus' lordship from their bondage to sin and evil, and thereby to make those people their own treasured possession. Just as people often attain objectives at a great cost to themselves, so God and Christ had established the community of believers or *ekklēsia* at a great cost to themselves.

Even if Jesus' death was not understood as some type of ransom payment made to God or the devil, the language of exchange could properly be used to describe what Jesus had done. If Satan was seen as the one who desired Jesus' death and had acted through figures such as Judas, the high priests, the mob who clamored for Jesus' death, and Pontius Pilate to have Jesus put to death, then by giving himself over to death, Jesus could be said to have given Satan what he wanted. Furthermore, in exchange for doing so, Jesus had obtained the redemption of all who would live under his own lordship, contrary to what Satan had desired. Ironically, then, by acting to have Jesus put to death, Satan and the forces of evil had brought about their own defeat in the sense that what they had done inadvertently led to Jesus' resurrection and exaltation and the existence of a people committed to doing God's will. To think in these terms, however, was by no means to imply or suggest that some type of transaction or agreement between Jesus and Satan had taken place.

---

46. On the basis of two ancient Greek "confessional inscriptions" that speak of persons offering a *lutron* to a god in order to expiate their offenses, Adela Yarbro Collins argues that the phrase *lutron anti pollōn* in Mark 10:45 should be understood as a ransom payment made to God as an act of substitutionary expiation for others (*Mark: A Commentary*; Hermeneia; Minneapolis: Fortress, 2007, 502-3). In reality, however, the inscriptions she cites have to do with offerings made to gods in which people sought forgiveness from those gods for offenses they had committed, and at the same time rededicated themselves to the service of those gods by means of a gift. There is therefore no reason to read back into these inscriptions the notion of substitution or that of a ransom payment made to the gods.

God could also be said to have desired Jesus' death in the sense that he had willed that Jesus give up his life instead of attempting to save it. This was because only in that way would the new, obedient people God desired to see be brought into existence. Of course, Jesus himself also desired that this people come to exist. On this basis, it was possible to affirm that, in exchange for giving up his life, Jesus had obtained or acquired this people both for himself and for God when God raised him. This was not merely because by raising Jesus God had granted Jesus what he desired, namely, that this people be brought into existence under his lordship, but also because the fact that Jesus had been obedient to God's will all the way to his death meant that the lives of all who considered him their Lord would also be characterized by the same type of obedience. In fact, it could even be said that God himself had obtained or acquired this new, obedient people in exchange for the life of his Son. Once again, this was not because God had made some type of payment to someone, but because his willingness to hand his Son over to death had led to the existence of the obedient people he had always longed and intended to have.

By now it should be clear that this understanding of the manner in which Jesus redeemed others through his death or blood is fundamentally different from the interpretations of Jesus' death that we examined in Chapter 1 of this study. For the authors of the New Testament writings, Jesus' death was redemptive, not because of any effect that it had had on God, human beings, or Satan, but because of everything that had preceded it and would follow upon it. Jesus' death was both the *consequence* of God's activity through Jesus to bring a new, obedient people into existence and also the *means* by which that objective had been accomplished.

It is also important to stress that when Jesus' first followers affirmed that they had been or would be redeemed through Jesus' death or blood, in no way were they rejecting the idea that a commitment to living according to God's will as defined through Jesus was necessary in order to participate in the redemption that Jesus would bring one day. This does not mean that they believed that they redeemed or saved themselves through their own obedience or works. Rather, it was God alone through Jesus who had redeemed them. While it was necessary for them to live a new life, that new life was not something that they brought about on their own, but rather something that God graciously brought about *in them* through Jesus and his faithfulness unto death to the task given him by God, as well as through their own faith in God and Jesus.

This also means that Jesus' first followers did not maintain that through Jesus' death *all people* had been redeemed objectively or "in principle." Certainly, Jesus was believed to have died seeking the redemption of all. His objective had been that all people might be delivered from their sinful ways of life and come to live in conformity with God's will under his lordship. Yet while he had died for this purpose, his death itself had not achieved the redemption of anyone. Rather, as we have seen, it was his faithfulness unto death that had led to the formation of a new community of people who understood themselves as belonging to God and to Jesus, since they lived under the lordship of Jesus, whom God had sent. When redemption was spoken of in the *past* tense, what was meant was that those who had come to submit to his lordship had now become God's own possession and no longer dedicated themselves to serving sin or Satan as their lord, as they had previously. It could also be said that they had already been redeemed in the sense that they now had certainty of their coming redemption, as long as they continued to live under Jesus' lordship. Strictly speaking, however, their redemption still lay in the future. Only when Jesus returned in glory would they be fully and definitively redeemed.

"For Our Sins"

A number of New Testament passages speak of Jesus' death or blood being "for sins" in some sense, yet the phrases employed vary greatly. Paul uses the phrase *huper tōn hamartiōn hēmōn* twice: in 1 Cor. 15:3, "Christ died for our sins in accordance with the scriptures," and in Gal. 1:4, where he says that the Lord Jesus Christ "gave himself for our sins to set us free from the present evil age, according to the will of our God and Father." The first of these two passages is particularly significant because Paul affirms that this formula was handed down to him. He also relates Jesus' death to the sins of others in Rom. 4:25, where he writes that Jesus "was handed over to death for our trespasses and was raised for our justification." Here the Greek phrase is different: *dia ta paraptōmata hēmōn*. Many New Testament scholars believe that here also Paul is employing a traditional formula handed down to him. It has been common to see an allusion to Jesus' death in Rom. 8:3 as well, where Paul affirms that by sending his Son "in the likeness of sinful flesh, and for sin (*peri hamartias*)," God "condemned sin in the flesh." Here the word *sin* appears in the singular. In contrast to the Pauline passages just cited, Eph. 1:7 mentions explicitly the forgiveness of sins through Christ: "In him we have redemption through his blood, the forgiveness of our trespasses."

The epistle to the Hebrews makes extensive use of the imagery of Christ as a high priest. Christ is said to have "made purification for sins" (*katharismon tōn hamartiōn*, Heb. 1:3) and to have "offered for all time a single sacrifice for sins" (*huper hamartiōn*, 10:12). In both of these passages, the author continues by alluding immediately to the idea that Christ sat down at God's right hand. Jesus' sacrificial death is also mentioned in the context of his second coming in Heb. 9:27-28: "And just as it is appointed for mortals to die once, and after that the judgment, so Christ, having been offered once to bear the sins of many, will appear a second time, not to deal with sin, but to save those who are eagerly waiting for him." Earlier in the same chapter, after referring to those who have been called to live under a new covenant, the author affirms that "a death has occurred that redeems them from the transgressions under the first covenant" (9:15). Other passages in Hebrews mention the way in which the priests are said to offer sacrifices for sin in order to relate this to what Jesus was to do (5:1; 9:7; 10:11).

In 1 John, the readers are told that if they walk in the light of God, "the blood of Jesus his Son cleanses us from all sin" (1:7). Here, as in Rom. 8:3, the word *sin* is used in the singular. Two other passages from the same letter speak of Jesus as the "expiation for our sins" (*peri tōn hamartiōn hēmōn*, 1 John 2:2; 4:10). In the Fourth Gospel, John the Baptist refers to Jesus as the "lamb of God who takes away the sin of the world" (John 1:29). Even though Jesus' death or blood is not mentioned explicitly in this verse, most would agree that it is implied or assumed. In the introductory verses of Revelation, Jesus is said to have "freed us from our sins by his blood" (*ek tōn hamartiōn*, Rev. 1:5). Citing Isa. 53:4, 12, the author of 1 Peter writes that Christ "bore our sins in his body on the cross" (1 Pet. 2:24), and further on in the epistle tells the readers, "Christ also suffered for sins once for all, the righteous for the unrighteous, in order to bring you to God" (*peri hamartiōn*, 1 Pet. 3:18). As we have seen previously, in Matthew's Last Supper scene, Jesus refers to the cup as "my blood of the covenant, which is poured out for many for the forgiveness of sins" (Matt. 26:28).

Outside of the phrase *huper tōn hamartiōn hēmōn* in 1 Cor. 15:3 and Gal. 1:4 and possibly *dia ta paraptōmata* in Rom. 4:25, it is not clear that any of these phrases actually represent formulas that were in common use in New Testament times. They do provide evidence, however, that Jesus' death or blood was related in some way to the forgiveness of sins and that a variety of formulas could be used to express this idea.

It has been common for scholars to claim that many of the passages just cited derive their language from Isaiah 53. While at least in some cases this appears to be true, it should be noted that, for the most part, the phrases used in the Septuagint version of Isaiah 53 to speak of the servant's suffering and being put to death for the sins of others do not appear verbatim in the New Testament.[47] The exceptions are the allusions to Christ bearing the sins of others in Heb. 9:28 and 1 Pet. 2:24 and the phrase *peri hamartias*, which appears in Rom. 8:3. In Isa. 53:10 LXX, however, this latter phrase refers to a sin-offering to be made by the readers rather than by the servant figure. It is possible, of course, that phrases such as *huper tōn hamartiōn hēmōn* and *dia ta paraptōmata hēmōn* originated in the earliest circles of Jesus' followers, where it may have been common to use free translations from the Hebrew original of Isaiah 53 rather than drawing on the Septuagint. Even if certain verses of Isaiah 53 are behind many of the formulaic phrases used in the New Testament to speak of Jesus' death, of course, we must still discern in what sense those phrases were used and understood.[48]

---

47. The phrases used in the Septuagint version of Isaiah 53 are *dia tas anomias hēmōn, dia tas hamartias hēmōn,* and *apo tōn anomiōn*, as well as the dative *tais hamartiais hēmōn* (vv. 5-6, 8, 10, 12). Wolter also notes that the phrases that use the prepositions *huper, peri,* and *dia* to speak of dying for the sins of others found in New Testament passages such as Rom. 4:25, 8:3, 1 Cor. 15:3, Gal. 1:4, 1 Pet. 3:18, and 1 John 2:2, 4:10 are found neither in the Greek version of the Hebrew Scriptures nor in extra-canonical Jewish texts in antiquity ("Die Heilstod Jesu," 303).

48. Simon Gathercole points to several passages from the Hebrew Scriptures in which the Septuagint version uses the same phrases that Paul uses to speak of Christ dying for the sins of others in order to claim

As I have argued above, Jesus' first followers would not have interpreted Isaiah 53 on the basis of ideas related to the penal substitution interpretations of Jesus' death that arose many centuries later. Instead, they would have seen Jesus' sufferings and death as being "for sins" in the sense that the sins of God's people and perhaps human beings in general made it necessary for God to send his Son into the world to bring into existence a new people who would be empowered to leave behind their sinful ways in order to live in conformity with God's will. Jesus' dedication to this task would ultimately lead to conflict and the cross. Thus, as in the parable of the wicked tenants, the consequence of Jesus' coming into the world to save others from their sinful ways would be his death. The sins of others would thus be seen as the cause of Jesus' death in two different ways. First, those sins made it necessary for God to send his Son into a context in which his work to bring about in others a new life of righteousness would result in his being put to death; and second, the sinfulness of many would lead them to reject Jesus and have him killed.

Because the penal substitution interpretation of Jesus' death has been so deeply ingrained in the thought of biblical scholars, including even those who find such an interpretation theologically problematic, the New Testament affirmations that Jesus suffered and died for the sins of others and bore their sins have almost invariably been understood in the sense that Jesus died *so that God might forgive human sins*. Of course, this implies that without Jesus' death, it was not possible for God to forgive sins. On this basis, the human plight is defined in terms of the need to be saved from divine punishment for sins.

As we have seen throughout this study, however, in the Hebrew Scriptures and among Jews in antiquity, including Jesus' first followers, the plight of God's people and human beings in general was defined in terms of the inability to live according to God's will. It was therefore *this problem*, rather than any "problem of forgiveness," that needed to be addressed. The forgiveness of sins would follow upon the transformation of the hearts and minds of all who would form part of God's people and the new life of righteousness that would result from that transformation. Undoubtedly, because righteousness was not synonymous with absolute perfection, even those transformed would continue to sin at times and still be in need of forgiveness. Yet, as in Jewish thought in general, the basis upon which they would be forgiven was their repentance and their commitment to living in conformity with God's will.

---

that these passages "lend weight to the view that *the language that Paul uses* should be understood as referring to vicarious death" (*Defending Substitution: An Essay on Atonement in Paul*; ASBT; Grand Rapids: Baker Academic, 2015, 71; see 70-73). The passages to which he alludes are 1 Kgs. 16:18-19, Num. 27:3, and Josh. 22:20. None of these passages, however, has anything to do with vicarious death. In each case, the persons involved die as divine punishment for their own sins or as a result of the sins of an individual with whom they were associated. Their deaths, however, are not viewed as atoning for their sins, and much less for the sins of others; they do not offer up their lives voluntarily in order to procure some benefit for others. Furthermore, none of these passages can be used as a basis to claim that in biblical thought every human being dies as punishment for his or her own sins—especially in the sense of being condemned to eternal damnation—, since in these passages the punishment is that of dying a premature, violent death or having to die in the wilderness.

This is precisely the view that we find running throughout the New Testament. As we saw in Chapters 7 and 8, the basis upon which people consistently are said to obtain forgiveness is their repentance and their commitment to live according to God's will. Yet because God's will is defined in terms of following Jesus in faith and living in the way he taught and embodied, forgiveness is also tied to faith in Jesus as the one who represents and speaks for God. People are forgiven *through* Jesus or *in his name*, that is, as they submit to Jesus as their Lord and live under him. Strictly speaking, then, they are not forgiven on the basis of Jesus' death. However, because what Jesus was seeking as he went to his death—and what God was seeking through Jesus—was that this new reality in which people would live in righteousness under Jesus' lordship so as to be acceptable to God might come to pass, the forgiveness of sins is associated with Jesus' death or blood.

Behind some of these formulaic allusions to Jesus' suffering and death for sins is undoubtedly the idea that, as he went to the cross, Jesus had made intercession for those who would come to live in faith under him, seeking that God accept them and forgive them their sins. In that sense, Jesus' death had been a sacrifice for sins, since it had involved an implicit petition for forgiveness on behalf of others. Believers could also be said to have been justified, purified, washed, or redeemed from their sins through Jesus' death for the same reason: Jesus had offered his life up to God seeking that God justify, purify, wash, and redeem those who would come to follow him from their sins. Once again, however, the reason that these things were associated particularly with his death or blood is that his death had been the ultimate expression of everything he had lived for and had sought for others. It had been the consequence of his commitment to bringing about in others the way of life God desired to see in them, and had also been the means by which God would be able to create a people fully committed to living according to his will.[49] This was because, from that point on, to identify with Jesus as Lord and live as his follower would by definition mean to identify with the same type of total dedication to God's will and self-giving for others that had characterized Jesus in his death. It was precisely the fact that Jesus' death would serve as the means to create a people totally committed to God's will that had led God to raise Jesus as Lord and grant forgiveness and salvation to all those who would live under Jesus' lordship. Of course, while it was only those who would live under Jesus in faith who could be said to have been justified, purified, washed, and redeemed from their sins through his death or blood, the fact that Jesus had sought that people from all the nations might come to live under him once he had been exalted as Lord meant that it could rightly be said that he had died *for the sins of all people*, seeking their salvation and forgiveness.

---

[49]. On the basis of his analysis of similar formula in ancient Greek literature, Wolter argues that in passages such as 1 Cor. 15:3 and Rom. 4:25, the phrase "for sins" should consistently be translated "as a consequence of sins" ("infolge der Sünde"), *Paul*, 102-5. Nevertheless, even this phrase could be understood in a variety of senses.

When Jesus' first followers affirmed that Jesus had suffered and died for their sins, then, they had in mind the idea that he had died as a result of his commitment to bringing them to abandon their sinful ways and live according to God's will as members of his community of followers. For this reason, to avoid the idea that Jesus had died simply so that God might forgive people their sins, it may be preferable to translate the phrase *Christos apethanen huper tōn hamartiōn hēmōn* in 1 Cor. 15:3, "Christ died for our sinful actions," that is, to deliver "us" from living in sins, as well as from the consequences of such a life. To speak in these terms is not to deny that Jesus' first followers believed that through his death he had obtained from God the forgiveness of sins for all who would live as members of the community under him. The basis upon which God had granted believers forgiveness of sins, however, was that through Jesus' death a new covenant and new community would be established in which all would be committed to living in accordance with God's will under Jesus' lordship.

It is also possible that when Jesus' first followers spoke of Jesus dying for their sins, they had in mind the heavenly intercession he carried out on their behalf. As noted above, a number of the allusions to Jesus' death for the sins of others occur in passages that refer to his resurrection and exaltation as well. Because Jesus had gone to his death seeking to be raised for others as their Lord, savior, and mediator, he had died for the sins of others in the sense that, as he went to his death, he asked God to raise and exalt him so that he might remain active from heaven to continue and consummate his work of bringing about the transformation of those living under his lordship and obtaining God's forgiveness for them on the basis of the new life they lived as a result of their faith.

A number of scholars have argued that the affirmation that Jesus died "for our sins" may have been intended as a response to the notion that Jesus had died on account of *his own* sins.[50] According to this idea, it would have been natural for both Jews and non-Jews to consider that, if Jesus had been sentenced to crucifixion by the Jewish and Roman authorities and God had not intervened to save Jesus from the cross, it was because he was guilty of wrongdoing and therefore deserved such a death. For this reason, Jesus' first followers may have stressed that it was not Jesus' own sins that had led to his death, but the persistent sinfulness of Israel, as well as the sinfulness of the Romans and people from the other nations as well. Jesus had died *as a result* of that sinfulness or due to his efforts to bring that persistent sinfulness to an end.

---

50. Commenting on 1 Cor. 15:3, for example, Peder Borgen claims that "the words 'died for our sins in accordance with the scriptures' presupposes that an opposite view was held by those who executed him. They maintained that he, in accordance with the laws, died for his own sins, his own crimes." According to Borgen, this was Paul's view prior to his conversion, but he "then changed his understanding and identified himself with the traditions transmitted in Christian communities: Christ was *crucified for our crimes*" ("Crucified for His Own Sins—Crucified for Our Sins: Observations on a Pauline Perspective," in *The New Testament and Early Christian Literature in Greco-Roman Context: Studies in Honor of David E. Aune*, ed. John Fotopoulos; NovTSup 122; Leiden: Brill, 2006, 18, 35; see 17-36).

It is worth noting that the two passages in which Paul uses the phrase *huper tōn hamartiōn hēmōn*, 1 Cor. 15:3 and Gal. 1:4, are found in letters addressed primarily to non-Jewish believers. This indicates that, although Paul undoubtedly had in mind the sinfulness of Israel when he used that phrase, he also believed that Christ had died so that people from the nations might be saved from their sinful ways and obtain divine forgiveness. The use of this formula and others that are similar may therefore have constituted an allusion to the entire divine plan designed to save both the people of Israel as well as the nations from their sins. Jesus' death "for sins" had taken place "according to the Scriptures" (1 Cor. 15:3) in the sense that it formed an integral and vital part of this divine plan. As we have seen previously, God would overlook the sins of the past as people now turned to him through faith in Christ. Naturally, this involved God's putting away his wrath at the sins of Israel and the nations as well. Nevertheless, it was not Jesus' death in itself that had put away that wrath but the fact that, thanks to his death for others and for their sins, it was now possible for people from all nations to repent and live obediently as God's children under Jesus. By means of faith and baptism, people could "wash away their sins" and be incorporated into God's people as full members. This was the new reality that Jesus had brought about through his death. In that sense, he had died for the sins of all people.

Suffering and Dying with or for Christ

Among New Testament scholars, the idea that believers suffer and die together with Christ has generally been considered almost exclusively a Pauline doctrine. While there are several reasons for this, the most important of these seems to be that suffering and dying with Christ has commonly been understood as something that happens *to* believers rather than something that believers themselves do actively. As we saw in Chapter 1, because the Pauline epistles use the past tense so as to affirm that believers died with Christ *in the past* and in several passages relate this dying with Christ to baptism, many New Testament scholars have maintained that either believers or all people in general were thought to have died with Christ in some mysterious manner either when they came to faith and were baptized or when Christ himself died. Even though the Pauline epistles never speak of people "participating" in Christ or his death, most New Testament scholars today seem to agree that the idea of participation is faithful to Paul's thought. Many even regard it as central for Paul's understanding of salvation.

While we will consider Paul's thought on this subject in greater detail in Chapter 11, several observations are in order here in the present chapter. The supposition that Paul's doctrine of "participation in Christ" is very different from anything we find in the Jesus tradition or the Synoptic Gospels has led scholars to either ignore the presence of similar language in the Synoptics or to claim that the idea there is fundamentally different from that which we find in the Pauline writings. All three Synoptics, however, repeat the idea that Jesus' followers must take up their cross and follow him and be willing to give up their life for him and for the gospel (Matt. 10:38-39; 16:24-25; Mark 8:34-35; Luke 9:23-24; 14:27). To take upon oneself Jesus' yoke also seems to be roughly equivalent to taking up the cross (Matt. 11:28-30). In Matthew and Mark, Jesus tells James and John that they will "drink the same cup" as he will (Matt. 20:22-23; Mark 10:38-39; cf. Acts 12:1-2). In the passion narratives, Peter and the other disciples also tell Jesus that they are willing to die with him and give up their lives for his sake (Matt. 26:35; Mark 14:31). Jesus himself tells his disciples that they will suffer the same things he will suffer, being persecuted, hated, and even put to death on his account (Matt. 5:10-12). In Acts, Luke presents Paul as affirming that he does not count his life of any value to himself (Acts 20:24), and indicating his willingness "not only to be bound but even to die in Jerusalem for the name of the Lord Jesus" (Acts 21:13).

These ideas are also found in the Fourth Gospel, where Thomas exhorts the other disciples to go to die with Jesus (John 11:16). Peter tells Jesus, "I will lay down my life for you" (13:37). After affirming that a grain of wheat cannot bear fruit unless it falls into the ground and dies, Jesus adds that "those who love their life will lose it" (12:24-25). During the Last Supper, Jesus tells his disciples, "No one has greater love than this, to lay down one's life for one's friends" (15:13), and then foretells the persecution his disciples will face at the hands of those who will put them out of the synagogues and even put them to death (16:2). The world will hate Jesus' disciples in the same way it first hated him (15:18-19).

The meaning of these affirmations that we find in the Gospels is relatively simple and straightforward. Those who are committed to following Jesus can expect to face opposition, persecution, and violence as he did and perhaps even be threatened with a violent death. While none of the disciples actually died with Jesus when he did, according to the New Testament and early Christian tradition, after they became convinced that he had been raised by God and exalted to God's right hand, at least some of the disciples became willing to suffer and die as a result of their commitment to Jesus and the work that he was thought to have assigned to them on behalf of others.

To die "for" Jesus, of course, would be understood as being willing to give up one's life, not in order that Jesus might himself be benefited personally in some way, but so that the same objective that he had sought in life and death might be attained—namely, that others obtain God's blessings and salvation through him. Although, of course, only a handful of Jesus' first followers were actually put to death for their faith, all believers could be said to die for and with Jesus in a metaphorical sense: they dedicated themselves to following him, leaving behind their former way of life and the values and conduct associated with it. In many cases, they encountered the rejection of their family and former friends, thereby dying metaphorically to their former relationships and life. Because they did this due to their faith in Christ, they could be said to die for and with Christ. However, while the present tense could be used to speak of them dying for and with Christ every day, they could also be said to have died with Christ in the past when they came to faith and were baptized, since that was the moment in which they had committed themselves to putting away their old way of life in order to live as Christ's servants or slaves.

Of course, because what Christ had lived, suffered, and died for was the well-being and salvation of others both in the present age and the age to come, to suffer and die for and with Christ was inseparable from suffering and dying for and with others. This idea is reflected in 1 John 3:16: "We know love by this, that he laid down his life for us—and we ought to lay down our lives for one another." While this passage does not speak of believers dying with or for Christ, the idea is that they are to be willing to lay down their lives for others both literally and metaphorically, seeking the well-being and salvation of others just as Jesus did.

As we shall see in Chapter 11, there is no reason not to take Paul's language of dying with Christ in the same way. In fact, the idea of being willing to endure hardships and persecution as a result of one's commitment to following Christ clearly seems to be behind the language of suffering with Christ found in Rom. 8:17, where Paul affirms that believers are "heirs of God and joint heirs with Christ—if, in fact, we suffer with him so that we may also be glorified with him" (cf. 2 Tim. 2:11-13). When Paul speaks of believers having died with Christ (Rom. 6:8; Gal. 2:19), this should be understood in the sense just mentioned above: they have put away their former way of living and have committed themselves to living according to God's will as defined through Christ. For Paul, this involves identifying with Christ's death and everything which that death represented and stood for.

Christ's Death "For Us": Some Analogies

In order to understand more clearly the formulas that Jesus' first followers used to refer to his death on their behalf, it would be helpful to consider several analogies from the context of the waging of war. When a country sends out its soldiers to fight against the enemy, it can be said that it sends them out *to die*. Obviously, the country does not want its soldiers to die. However, it knows that the death of many of its soldiers will be the *result* of sending them out to fight against the enemy. In the case of those who do die, it will be said that they died *for others*, that is, for their fellow citizens and compatriots, since the objective of the soldiers had been to preserve, defend, and protect the liberty, safety, and well-being of their country. In the same way, in the minds of Jesus' first followers, it could be said that God had sent his Son *to die*. This did not mean that God desired his Son's death, but that God knew that the mission that his Son would carry out would lead to his death. Furthermore, Jesus' followers could affirm that Jesus had died *for them and others*. This meant that he had died as a result of his faithfulness to the mission he had been given to make it possible for them and others to live in freedom and enjoy the blessings God desired for them in the context of the community of faith that Jesus had worked to establish, as well as the blessings that would be theirs in the life to come. In that sense, he had died *on their behalf*.

When soldiers are sent out to war and some subsequently die as a result, prior to dying, they do many other things aimed at making it possible for their country to enjoy peace, well-being, and security. First of all, they leave behind their former life and activities as well as their loved ones in order to join the armed forces. This in itself constitutes a great *sacrifice* on their part. They then spend endless hours training and preparing themselves for battle. When they are sent out to the places in which they will need to confront the enemy, they endure many hardships, such as hunger, thirst, sleeplessness, mental anguish, physical sufferings, many dangers, and harsh weather. When they become involved in battle, they may also be wounded or experience a great deal of pain before they ultimately die at the hands of the enemy.

Nevertheless, when those on behalf of whom they were fighting are asked what those soldiers did for them, they will sum up everything that those soldiers did by saying that *they died or gave up their life for their country*. When they say that, they have in mind *all the things that those soldiers did from the time they left their homes to join the armed forces until the moment when they were killed*. Nevertheless, they may affirm only that the soldiers died or gave up their life for their country not only because in that way they are able to sum up quickly and efficiently all that those soldiers did, but because *nothing else that those soldiers did prior to dying demonstrates as clearly their dedication and love for their country as the fact that they died as a result of having put their lives at risk for the good of the country*.

In the same way, Jesus' first disciples—including Paul—were undoubtedly well aware of all the things Jesus had done prior to his death in order to make it possible for them to come to experience true life, freedom, joy, and peace as part of a community in which all were dedicated to the well-being of one another, as well as to the well-being of all those outside of that community. They knew that he had left behind everything in order to carry out his ministry and dedicate his life to establishing such a community. He had spent endless hours teaching and preparing his disciples and others, helping those in need, and traveling from one place to another in order to reach as many people as possible. Like the soldiers just mentioned, he had endured great hardships, including hunger, thirst, weariness, sleepless nights, and harsh weather. He had often had no place to rest his head or get some respite from the constant onslaught of many who sought his attention or help. He had also had to deal with those who opposed him and sought to silence or harm him. In the end, he had denounced through his words and his action at the temple the corruption and injustices of the religious authorities, yet he nevertheless had continued to teach undauntedly on the temple grounds, all the time well aware of what the result of these actions on behalf of others would be. Finally, when he had been arrested, he had continued to stand firm for all that he had lived and worked for rather than cowering in fear before those judging him, and had opted to endure great physical abuse and even a violent death rather than renounce his activity on behalf of others or recant what he had said and taught.

Yet, as in the analogy of the soldiers who had given up their lives for their country, when Jesus' first followers spoke of what he had done for them, rather than going into detail regarding all of the different aspects of the activity that he had carried out for them and others from the start of his ministry to the end of his life, they could merely say, "He gave up his life for us." Undoubtedly, when they said this, they had in mind not merely his death on the cross, but *everything he had done for others throughout his ministry up to his final hours, all of which had led to his being put to death on the cross.* However, by saying that Jesus had died for them and others, his followers could not only sum up in a few words all that Jesus had done on their behalf, but at the same time point to his death as *the ultimate and supreme manifestation and expression of his dedication to his mission of making a new life possible for them and others*. Nothing else that he had done could ever communicate as powerfully his love for others as his death on the cross. At the same time, in order to stress these points even further, rather than merely saying that he had *died* for them and others, they could say that he had *given his life* for them, *offered up his life* for them, or even that he had *sacrificed his life* for them. Seen in the light of these ideas, it is not at all difficult to understand why Jesus' followers began to employ sacrificial language and imagery to refer to his death. He had shed his blood for others, just as soldiers shed their blood and sacrifice their lives on the battlefield for their country. He had offered up his life to God on behalf of others, seeking from God for them all that he had sought for them throughout his life and ministry. He had endured the cross for others and poured out his soul unto death for them. Yet *it cannot be stressed strongly enough that, when Jesus' first followers said that he had died for them, given himself up for them, or sacrificed his life for them by offering it up to God, they were not merely referring to his death but also had in mind everything Jesus had done that had led to his death on the cross.* Thus it was *not Jesus' death in itself* that had led to life and salvation for others, but *the absolute dedication to a ministry aimed at giving life and salvation to others of which his death had been the result*.

These observations make it possible as well to understand the problem with the idea that Jesus died in order to provide others with an example of love to imitate and to kindle greater love in them—the idea that is commonly associated with Peter Abelard. Above all, when soldiers are engaging the enemy in battle, while they may hope that their courage and bravery will also inspire others to be courageous and brave under those circumstances, this is not their primary purpose. The objective they seek to accomplish is not to provide an example for others to imitate, but to save their people from becoming subjected to the enemy. In fact, that is why they wish others to be courageous and brave as well, so that together they may accomplish that objective.

Furthermore, if in the midst of battle, for no reason at all, a soldier suddenly jumps out of a trench in which he was protecting himself and runs toward the enemy only in order to be shot and killed needlessly, such an action is in no way considered an act of love for others. Rather than affirming that the soldier had sacrificed his life for his country out of love for his compatriots, his fellow soldiers would say that he had committed an act of suicide and had even done harm to the cause of the country by depriving it of a soldier that it needed to fight on its behalf. If other soldiers took his act as an example to imitate, the country would merely continue to lose needlessly the soldiers it needed to defeat the enemy.

In the same way, Jesus' mission or intention had not been to suffer, to die, or to have himself killed. That is not what God his Father desired nor the reason for which God had sent Jesus. Had Jesus sought to be put to death on the cross for no good reason, but simply as an end in itself, his death would have been seen, not as an act of love for others, but as a senseless suicide that benefited no one and only deprived those whom he had served of the ministry he had been carrying out on their behalf. Such a death would not have been regarded as an example for others to imitate. For the same reasons, rather than kindling greater love in his followers, Jesus would have been kindling bewilderment and disillusion. Undoubtedly, of course, Jesus had wanted others to be inspired to stand up to evil and injustice with bravery and courage as he had. Yet this was not his primary objective. Rather, what he had sought in life and death was to establish a community in which people might be saved from sin and evil by living in harmony, love, justice, and solidarity with one another so as thereby to experience true life in both this world and the world to come.

To continue the analogies, if the country sending out its soldiers to war was seeking to liberate itself from the oppression and domination of a foreign power, once the country had been freed from that power, it would be said that those soldiers who had died had liberated others *through their death or blood*. This would be seen as an act of supreme love and sacrifice on their part on behalf of others. It could also be said that they had saved, delivered, or freed their country *at the cost of their life* or that they had *paid the ultimate price* to attain the liberation of their country. Essentially, this is the language of *redemption*, which involves paying a price in order to obtain something else in exchange.

Following this same logic, Jesus' first followers would affirm the same things regarding what he had done for them and others. He had liberated them from their bondage to sin, selfishness, fear, hopelessness, and other evils and had attained new life for them *by means of his death or blood*. He had *paid the ultimate price* to obtain the freedom and salvation they now enjoyed as members of his community, *the price of his life*, which would be regarded as the *cost* of their deliverance. By dedicating his ministry to their liberation and then giving up his life so that their liberation might become a reality through him, he had *redeemed* them or attained their *redemption* through his life or blood. In their case, the "enemy" could be defined in a number of ways: as the human and demonic forces of evil and the power of sin that enslaved them, as the fear of suffering and death that paralyzed and terrorized them, or as other oppressive powers that sought to impose themselves on them. Military terms such as *victory*, *triumph*, and *defeat of enemies* such as sin and evil could also be used to refer to that which Jesus had accomplished on their behalf. Nevertheless, when they used these terms, Jesus' followers would not have in mind any type of hand-to-hand combat that Jesus had waged against the devil in Hades or against some cosmic power in some invisible realm. Rather, they would merely be affirming that his dedication in life and death to the objective of freeing others from the powers that had oppressed them had accomplished that objective. And by liberating them from those powers, he had *saved* them by giving them a new life that would ultimately lead to an eternal life in the age to come.

When an army of soldiers defeats the enemy that holds their country in fear and bondage, the way in which they have given of themselves to overcome the enemy brings rejoicing to their compatriots and also brings about a greater unity among them. All the members of that society put aside any differences or conflicts they have previously had with one another in order to come together in solidarity as one. The dedication and love for country that the soldiers have manifested by putting their lives at risk in order to fight for their country, and in many instances by dying for their country, will also inevitably inspire the same type of love for one another in their compatriots, as well as a willingness to make sacrifices for the good of others. Once again, it would be said that this new reality of harmony, peace, unity, and sacrificial self-giving on behalf of others *cost the lives* of many who by dying had *paid the price* of bringing that new reality to pass. They had attained that objective by means of their death or blood. If the president, prime minister, or commander-in-chief had demonstrated great courage and boldness and had devised and implemented an excellent strategy that had led to the victory, that figure would no doubt be honored and thanked. To a great extent, the victory would be attributed not only to the soldiers who had fought but also to the leader who had overseen and directed the war effort. Both the leader and the armed forces would be said to have inspired the victory and to have instilled in others bravery and dedication through their own courage and steadfastness.

In a similar way, as Jesus' first followers gathered together in the alternative communities that he had sought to establish and for which he had sacrificed his life, they would ascribe the new reality they were experiencing to his death or blood. The manner in which he had loved others to the point of giving up his life would bring his followers to be dedicated to practicing the same type of love. In fact, that same love for others both within and outside of their community would define that community and be expected of each member. All would also be expected to put aside any differences or conflicts they had with others in the community, forgiving one another and sharing their lives and themselves with one another. Thus it could be said that they had been *reconciled to one another through the death or blood of Jesus*. He had died or given up his life for them in the sense that he had died precisely so that this new reality might be brought about. For reasons we have just seen, when his followers would affirm that Jesus had reconciled them to one another through his death or blood, they would be attributing that reconciliation, not to Jesus' death per se—which in itself had accomplished nothing—, but to the love, dedication, and commitment to others he had shown throughout his life up until its end, that is, the love for others of which his death had been both the result and the supreme manifestation.

At the same time, because it had been God who had sent Jesus for the purpose of bringing about this new reality and who had accompanied, empowered, and directed Jesus from the beginning of his ministry all the way to the cross, Jesus' followers would attribute their reconciliation to one another not only *to Jesus* but also *to God*. God had made that reconciliation a reality by sending his Son and giving him over to death, just as he had made their redemption a reality through Jesus. Jesus' followers would naturally respond to what God had done through Jesus by honoring and thanking God and dedicating their lives to him. Thus they would see in God the origin and cause of their love for one another and their new life in the community established through Jesus' life and death. Once again, that same type of love would be expected of all of the members of the community—not because it was *demanded* of them, but because it was recognized that once they had grasped and understood all that God had done for them through Jesus, that same type of love would arise *spontaneously* in their hearts. Any who were not committed to such love would therefore not be scolded, reprimanded, or condemned. Rather, it would be clear that the reason that they had not come to love others in the way they should was that they either had not understood or had not experienced the love of God and of Jesus as they should have through the other members of the community. What was necessary, therefore, was for the members of the community to show even greater love toward those who were not living in love as they should and communicate to them more clearly the love of God and of Christ. Nothing but that could bring them to live in love as well.

What God had done for the members of Jesus' community through Jesus would also lead them to speak of *God having reconciled them to himself through Jesus and his death or blood*. Whatever their relationship with God had been previously, as a result of what God had done through Jesus, that relationship would now be characterized by an even greater love for God and a sincere desire and commitment to put out of their lives anything that was an obstacle to that relationship or ran contrary to God's love for all people. The tremendous love that God had shown for them by sending his Son to carry out a ministry aimed at bringing all to live in justice and solidarity and then handing him over to death when that ministry led to conflict would also leave no doubt in their minds that God accepted them fully and forgave them any wrongdoing that they had committed. God would scarcely have sacrificed so much to bring into being the community of which they now formed part only now to reject or condemn those who came to live in that community. The fact that the love God had shown for them through Jesus' life and death would arouse in them the same type of love together with an earnest desire to live as God desired for their own good would also lead them to say that they had been *justified by means of Jesus' death or blood*. Because they would come to understand clearly that the righteousness or justice God desired to see in them consisted of the same love that God and Jesus had shown for them, and because their having been the objects of that love would have spontaneously produced the same type of love in them, they could be assured that God accepted them as righteous. In other words, as faith in the God of Jesus and in Jesus himself came to constitute the core of their being, they would inevitably live righteously, and on that basis they would be declared righteous or justified. Once again, however, all of this would be attributed to Jesus' death or blood, that is, his willingness to sacrifice or give up his life for them.

Finally, if the members of a certain country had lived in a way that had made it possible for an enemy to subdue and oppress them, it could be said that they were suffering and being oppressed on account of their own errors, misdeeds, or cowardice. Those errors or misdeeds and that cowardice had destroyed the fabric of the country and had weakened it, making it possible for the country's enemy to gain power over the country. If the enemy was much stronger than the people of that country, in order for them to be delivered from their enemy, the people would need assistance from a foreign power stronger than their enemy that would be capable of driving that enemy out of the land in order to deliver the people from their suffering. In itself, however, this would not be sufficient, since the people might continue to commit the same errors and misdeeds that had weakened them previously and had made it possible for the enemy to overpower them in the first place. Therefore, the people would also need to identify and acknowledge their errors and misdeeds, recognize that their faulty behavior was responsible for their suffering and oppression, and subsequently strive to leave behind those errors and misdeeds by living differently. If the foreign army liberating the people assisted them by pointing out to them their errors and misdeeds and instructing them as to how they might avoid falling back into the behavior that had previously weakened them and had enabled the enemy to gain power over them, that foreign army could be said to have liberated the country, not only by defeating the enemy, but also by making it possible for those people to live in such a way that they would be strong enough to resist their enemy in the future. However, what would have liberated the previously oppressed people from their bondage would have been not only the guidance, orientation, and instruction given them by the members of the foreign army, but also the courage and bravery that the soldiers of that army had displayed in their fight against the enemy. By observing the way in which those soldiers had fought and died for them, the liberated people would be brought to grow in courage and bravery and in their willingness to stand up boldly against their enemies in the future.

For these reasons, it could then be said that the foreign power had saved the people from their errors, misdeeds, and cowardice. However, because many of the foreign soldiers had died as a result of their efforts to save the people of the country from their enemy, those soldiers could also be said to have died for the errors, misdeeds, and cowardice of the people of that country. This would mean that they had died *because of* those errors and misdeeds and that cowardice in two senses. First, had the people not been in a weakened state due to their living in error, misdeeds, and cowardice, it would not have been necessary for the foreign army to come to their aid, since the people would not originally have fallen prey to their enemy. In that case, none of the soldiers of that army would have died fighting to liberate that country. Second, however, those soldiers would also have given their lives for the people of that country in the sense that they had died so that their fellow soldiers might be able to work with the members of that country in order to enable them to leave behind the errors and misdeeds that had characterized their life. In addition, the bravery and courage that the soldiers had shown when giving up their lives would also have enabled the people to overcome their cowardice and thereby put away the fear that led them to act in ways that made it possible for the enemy to subjugate them. The foreign soldiers could then be said to have died for the people's cowardly actions in the sense that their courage made it possible for the people to stop acting out of cowardice and fear.

This last analogy makes it possible to understand more clearly what Jesus' first followers meant when they said that Jesus had died or given up his life *for their sins*. This could be understood in several senses. The fact that God's people had fallen into bondage under forces stronger than them and for that reason were living sinful lives had made it necessary for Jesus to come into the world to free them from those forces. As a result of his faithfulness to his efforts to accomplish that goal, however, he had been put to death. It could therefore be said that he had *died for their sins* in the sense that he had died as a result of his efforts to free the people from the forces that held them in bondage, causing them to sin.

Throughout his ministry, out of love for others, Jesus had dedicated himself to the task of pointing out to others their sins and indicating to them how those sins were harming and destroying their lives. He had also called on them to repent of those sins and put them out of their life for their own good and that of others. For various reasons, this activity had angered many who refused to acknowledge their sins and instead sought to silence him. Because Jesus nevertheless continued to point out to others their sins and call them to repentance in spite of the anger his activity was generating among many, he was put to death. In that sense, he had *died for the sins of others*. At the same time, the love, instruction, and guidance that Jesus had offered others during his ministry had made it possible for many to leave behind their sinful ways in order to live differently. However, when that work led many of the oppressed to see and understand the causes of their oppression, they abandoned their loyalty and allegiance to the political and religious leaders who were oppressing them. Those leaders therefore sought to put Jesus to death. Because Jesus' unswerving commitment to his work of saving people from their sins through his love, instruction, and guidance eventually led to his death at the hands of those authorities, it would be said once again that he had *died for the people's sins*.

Similarly, because Jesus had stood up firmly against those authorities, denouncing openly their unjust and oppressive ways and seeking to free people from their control, those authorities had responded by having him crucified. Jesus, however, had trusted in God and had proclaimed to others that there was no need to live in fear because it was God rather than those authorities who ultimately had power over life and death. Jesus' boldness in this regard had led to his death, but it had also had the effect of instilling his same boldness in others. The boldness, hope, and trust in God that Jesus' faithfulness to death to his God-given task had brought about in them enabled Jesus' followers to overcome their fear and thus to stop living in sinful ways as a result of that fear. In this way as well, Jesus had *saved others from their sins* by giving up his life rather than seeking to save it.

Furthermore, by paying the price of his life in order to enable and empower people to leave behind their sinful life, Jesus had obtained God's forgiveness and acceptance for those people and had delivered them from God's wrath at their sin and injustice, since through faith in Jesus and their incorporation into his community of followers, they would now be able to leave behind the sinful and unjust way of life that had occasioned God's wrath. This was another sense in which he had *died for their sins*. Finally, Jesus had gone to his death asking God to raise and exalt him so that he might continue to be active from heaven to enable people to abandon their sinful lifestyle so as to practice God's righteousness or justice. Once raised and exalted, he would also continually intercede to God on behalf of those people, asking God to strengthen them in their faith and forgive them their sins on the basis of his activity to transform them into new people. Because he had offered up his life with the implicit petition that he be raised and exalted for others so as to bring about their transformation and salvation, once more he could be said to have *died for their sins*. When Jesus' first followers said that he had died or given himself up for their sins, therefore, they undoubtedly had *all of these ideas in mind*.